BIRTH OF BANGLADESH AS CANADA WALKS A DIPLOMATIC TIGHTROPE

MUSTAFA CHOWDHURY

Copyright © 2024 by Mustafa Chowdhury.

Library of Congress Control Number:		2024919225
ISBN:	Hardcover	979-8-3694-2920-4
	Softcover	979-8-3694-2919-8
	eBook	979-8-3694-2918-1

All rights reserved. No part of this book may be reproduced or transmitted in any form or by any means, electronic or mechanical, including photocopying, recording, or by any information storage and retrieval system, without permission in writing from the copyright owner.

Cover photo credit: Methila Mallick

Any people depicted in stock imagery provided by Getty Images are models, and such images are being used for illustrative purposes only.
Certain stock imagery © Getty Images.

Print information available on the last page.

Rev. date: 11/07/2024

To order additional copies of this book, contact:
Xlibris
844-714-8691
www.Xlibris.com
Orders@Xlibris.com
723410

To all those Bengalis who were killed or maimed
by the Pakistani military personnel who wanted to
perpetuate military power in East Pakistan.

To all those who fought for and sacrificed their
lives for the liberation of Bangladesh.

To all Canadians of diverse backgrounds who condemned the
military reprisals and lobbied for the establishment of democracy.

CONTENTS

Foreword ix
Preface.. xiii
Acknowledgments.. xxi
Introduction... xxv
A Brief Note on Research Methodology and Sources xxxvii

Chapter 1   1971: Looking Back.. 1
Chapter 2   Surreptitious Military Attack and Canada's
            Immediate Reaction 77
Chapter 3   Canada's Media Onside with the Freedom Fighters
            of Bangladesh 125
Chapter 4   Vox Populi: Canadians Speak Out 196
Chapter 5   NGOs and Religious and Business Organizations:
            Get Behind Bangladesh.. 302
Chapter 6   Parliament Debates Canada's Role in Bangladesh
            Struggle 395
Chapter 7   Canada's Initiatives Feature Her Trademark of Tact
            and Fairness 463
Chapter 8   Canada Faces Dilemma: A Chronology of Quiet
            Diplomacy 539
Chapter 9   Canada Finally Gets It "Right": Bangladesh
            Recognized and a Friendship Restored 609
Chapter 10 Grand Finale: Bangladesh Takes its Rightful Place
            on the Global Stage..677

Select Bibliography 713
Appendix A: Glossary of Terms 727
Appendix B: Chronology of Events from November 1970 to
             December 1972 737
Appendix C: Abbreviations 749

Appendix D: Archival Records 751
Appendix E: Canadian Parliamentarians whose names
              frequently appear in the House of Commons and
              Senate 841
Appendix F: Canadian parliamentarians who raised the East
              Pakistan issue in the House of Commons and Senate ... 845
Appendix G: Canadian news reporters, media personalities,
              intellectuals, NGO workers, diplomats and
              members of the public 853
Appendix H: East Pakistani Bengali Canadians who demanded
              recognition of Bangladesh 859
Appendix I: Canadian religious missionaries in East Pakistan,
              India, and Canada who did not abandon their
              missionary work. They assisted the refugees and
              displaced people by doing whatever they could
              within their limited capability..867
Appendix J: The provisional Government of the People's
              Republic of Bangladesh was formed on April 10,
              1971, and sworn in on April 17, 1971. 873
Appendix K: Bengali Political Leaders who fled to India and
              supported the liberation movement under the
              leadership of the Awami League 877
Appendix L: Members of the Bangladesh Mission in
              Washinton who lobbied the government of
              Canada for Bangladesh... 879
Appendix M: First Bangladeshi and Canadian High
              Commissioners and Diplomats 881
Appendix N: Canada-Bangladesh Friendship since 1972 883
Index 887

FOREWORD

We were so happy to hear that our good friend Mustafa Chowdhury had written another book about the birth of Bangladesh. In this book, Mustafa Chowdhury has covered the period from March 1971 to December 1971, from the time of the military crackdown in East Pakistan to the liberation of Bangladesh in December, as well as, in parallel, the same timeframe in Canadian political history and the role of the government of Canada, the media, the public, and the NGOs about the Pakistan-Bangladesh conflict. Chowdhury describes in detail new information on Pakistan's conflict surrounding the transfer of power to the elected Bengali leader of East Pakistan, Sheikh Mujibur Rahman, betrayal by the West Pakistani military regime; the Bengali rebels fight for the liberation of their native land, and covert and overt involvement of India to dismantle Pakistan and liberate East Pakistan that became Bangladesh. Although Canada leveraged influence through multilateral organizations, advancing ideas and interests while respecting differences and building consensus to achieve common goals, Canada could persuade neither President Yahya Khan nor Prime Minister Indira Gandhi. With corroborative detail, Chowdhury skillfully fitted all these pieces into a driving narrative to pull a reader along the book.

Chowdhury's research is of extraordinary importance since it is the first comprehensive book on Canada's tightrope diplomatic walk during the Liberation War of Bangladesh in 1971. In other words, unlike other works on the Liberation War of Bangladesh, it is the first book we know of that deals with Canada's role in the Bengalis' struggle for independence. It is based on various primary sources, including interviews conducted by Chowdhury. It is an exhaustive study of Canada's political dichotomy in 1971 concerning the Bengalis' struggle for independence. In his analysis of the part played by the Pierre Trudeau administration in resolving the conflict between the military regime, represented by President Yahya Khan, and Sheikh Mujibur Rahman, leader of the majority party in East Pakistan, Chowdhury delves into the matter having alluded to the superpowers' game plan. He scrupulously outlines the political landscape of Canada back in 1971. Canada had a lot on her plate—foreign affairs, domestic affairs, government reorganization, approach to spending control, new economic order, Western alienation, and, most importantly, Canada's national unity, since the 1970 October Crisis was only five months old.

Chowdhury uses primary sources excellently by referring to explanations and evaluations to clarify their meaning for his central thesis. With indefatigable meticulousness and ingenuity, Chowdhury documents Canada's reactions and actions at a time when Canada was constrained by her own foreign policy options. Chowdhury painstakingly examined thousands of telexes and memos sent to Ottawa officials by Canada's High Commissioners to Pakistan and India. Foreign affairs cognoscenti in Ottawa interpreted them to take a public position. Chowdhury tries to stay within the evidence—governmental and non-governmental records housed in the Library and Archives Canada.

One of the most significant characteristics of this book is that Chowdhury has been able to refer to the House of Commons and Senate debates and use originals, such as records of the Department of External Affairs and many Canadian NGOs. In addition, Chowdhury examined pertinent documents emanating from the governments of Canada, Pakistan, India, and the provisional government of Bangladesh. He used classified telexes and Situational Reports (SITREPS) of Canadian High Commissioners to India and Pakistan and the ministerial briefing notes in the Library and Archives Canada, available through Canada's Freedom of Information and Protection of Privacy Act. At the same time, Chowdhury used secondary sources that represented essential points of view to broaden and develop his thoughts. Having spent twenty-five long years doing the research, Chowdhury has mastered the materials and carefully inferred the relationship between facts, precision, and clarity of his words.

In this well-researched book, Chowdhury engages his readers absorbingly from the beginning, as the book is vivid, compelling, and authentic. What did Canada, a "helpful fixer" and a "brigade builder," do during the entire nine long months of the war of liberation? Chowdhury attempts to find answers using primary and secondary sources and writes his narrative with clarity and intelligence. Having interviewed scores of

Members of Parliament (MPs) and many politicians of the day, Chowdhury crystalizes his information into this intelligent and objective book for the first time, outlining Canada's position on the Pakistan-Bangladesh Conflict that was variously referred to as Bangladesh's War of Independence, Liberation War of Bangladesh and the Bengalis' Struggle for Independence. It was launched on March 26, 1971, and East Pakistan emerged as an independent state on December 16, 1971, as Bangladesh after a nine-month civil war with West Pakistan following India's direct military intervention.

Chowdhury has an unerring eye for the hidden facts buried in heaps of Islamabad and New Delhi telexes. As one browses through the pages, one would notice his narrative based on the documentary evidence of how Canada reacted to the imposition of martial law and the ongoing reprisals by the Yahya regime. A combination of historical knowledge of Canada and the Indian subcontinent, analytical insight, and literary flair marks his narratives. Chowdhury has shaped his materials and thoughts into a coherent and well-argued book by revealing his central thesis and conclusion. His technique involves a narrative consisting of a series of exact, detailed discussions that arrest readers' attention and make them curious to continue reading until the end of the book.

Finally, it's a gripping narrative and a fascinating case study in realpolitik. It demonstrates a genuine historical truth regarding Canada's diplomatic challenges in 1971.

Fred Cappuccino, CM
Bonnie Cappuccino, CM
19014 Concession 7, Maxville, Ontario, Canada
K0C 1T0
E-mail: fred@childhaven.ca
May 4, 2024

PREFACE

It has been almost thirty years since I started researching the emergence of Bangladesh vis-à-vis Canada's dichotomy in endorsing the movement when my professional work as a federal public servant in Canada required me to travel across the country. This allowed me to meet with many key players. When I started my project, I did not know that I was in for it for the long haul. I was working on my manuscript at my own pace—there was no rush. I was comfortably writing it as I had gotten used to my pace. With the sudden passing of my two childhood cronies, Shahidul Mithu and Rahat Chaudhuri, I was devastated. Having moved at a snail's pace, I realized I had neither a plan nor a roadmap. Seeing how so many of my buddies have left for their eternal journey, my mind returned to John Donne's famous lines—For whom the bell tolls, it tolls for thee. Feeling haplessly unaccomplished, I also realized that I had not come up with my manuscript yet, which had been long overdue as far as the publisher was concerned.

As doubts and uncertainties racked my disturbed mind, I kept reminding myself of one of life's inescapable blows. I recalled Robert Frost's *Stopping by Woods on a Snowy Evening,* which I read years ago while at university. Every line I found bears a message for me – "But I have promises to keep, and miles to go before I sleep, and miles to go before I sleep." Instantly, not only did I feel rejuvenated, but I also experienced a passionate feeling from inside that determined me to move forward with no dilly-dallying. Having burned the midnight candle at both ends, I quickly learned the rope through a Sisyphean task. I felt like racing against the clock, biting off more than I could chew. With COVID-19, when I was in a lockdown situation, I hit the ground running, being busy as a beaver. I worked my fingers to the bone. I never looked back until I dashed off the manuscript to the publisher. Might I say, though it was a labor of Hercules, more importantly, it was a labor of love?

In substantive terms, the book offers a penetrating analysis of Canada's diplomatic challenges in dealing with an issue that was mindboggling for Canada. It advances the view that Canada, having no strong ties of strategic interests in Pakistan or India, attempted to gain a sympathetic understanding of the two main parties involved—the military regime, represented by President Yahya Khan, and the provisional government of the People's Republic of Bangladesh. Relying on both pro-Pakistani and pro-Bangladeshi sources of information, the cumulative effect of the information gathered from overseas allowed Canada to appreciate the psychological and emotional dimension of the conflict stemming from economic disparity and political discrimination in Pakistan. Canada saw how the two key concepts—freedom and future—had remained in the minds of Pakistan's military administrators and politicians. With quite a bit of discomfort, Ottawa opted to follow the drama ever since it started to play with the destiny of the Bengalis. Ottawa watched how the Bengali Canadians of East Pakistani origin took to the streets across Canada as soon as they heard about the sudden and surreptitious military crackdown.

My objective is to document Canada's role in the War of Liberation by examining government and non-government documents available in Canadian depositories. I have included their references in a brief note on sources and research methodology. I have tried to view the subject and sequence of events from a Canadian perspective through research based on the primary sources. I have attempted to present the most detailed assemblage of evidence. The historical narrative includes some broad observations based on my examination of Canada's role throughout the period the Bengalis were fighting for independence. It reiterates Canada's friendship with the newborn country. It ends with the 2016 and 2018 visits of then Prime Minister of Bangladesh, Sheikh Hasina, who hand-delivered a plaque to Prime Minister Justin Trudeau for Canada's support for democracy and friendship with the people of Bangladesh dating back to the time of Pierre Elliott Trudeau. At the same time, the historical narrative also includes the story of the duplicity of the Yahya regime, its clandestine attack on Bengali civilians, their determined resistance, declaration of independence, fight for the liberation of Bangladesh, and Canada's role in the conflict between the two wings of Pakistan until the surrender of the Pakistani army, the birth of Bangladesh as an independent country, and instances of friendship between Bangladesh and Canada to date.

As one browses through various chapters, one would find how Canada's support for aiding the victims of the military crackdown and her mediatory role became Canada's priority. Along the line, readers would also recognize Canada's position regarding the conflict, which eventually involved the military government of President Yahya, the provisional government of the People's Republic of Bangladesh, and the government of India. Canada was inextricably bound up with her own collective historical experiences. The initial reaction of the Canadian government, it shall be seen, is difficult to characterize in any specific terms. Unlike the Nixon administration, which was openly in favor of the military government of Pakistan, the government headed by Pierre Elliott Trudeau procrastinated in assessing the situation, considering Canada's constraints and limited foreign policy options.

Throughout the narrative, I have incorporated quotations from Canadian government officials and details from various sources to allow me to make final observations regarding Canada's view of what was happening and what should have been Canada's response. Canada was placed between a rock and a hard stone, especially when she saw how the debates around the world were continuing immediately following the departure of millions of Bengalis to India within a span of a few months. Whether or not the conflict in Pakistan remained an "internal affair" of Pakistan appeared as a tricky question for the Trudeau administration to address. Canada was convinced that the expanding dimension of the human tragedy was much more profound than it had appeared. When looking at the issue from a humanitarian perspective, the Trudeau administration believed that any intervention under the circumstances would perhaps have been considered legitimate.

As the continued military reprisals resulted in the exodus of millions of Bengalis, the people of Canada began to pressure the government to express its position in more precise terms. With assistance from the Canadian high commissioners to Pakistan and India, John Small and James George, respectively, Mitchell Sharp, Secretary of State for External Affairs, and his team members began to focus on the events as they were unfolding in the Indian subcontinent. More and more members of Parliament (MP) began to challenge the government, demanding that it be more transparent in its public position and represent Canadians' wishes. In the House of Commons, the government was barraged with the following questions: Was the military take-over and crackdown a violation of the democratic rights of the people of Pakistan? Should the process of democracy be upheld under all circumstances? Should President Yahya Khan continue his military reprisals in East Pakistan since the integrity of Pakistan was at stake? Should power be transferred to the elected leader of East Pakistan regardless of what the military government thought of the majority party's leader? There were no clear answers to these questions since the declaration of independence for Bangladesh by the provisional government of the People's Republic of Bangladesh had already created yet another new twist in the complex issue of power transfer to the leader of East Pakistan. Amid the domestic crisis, Ottawa asked, "What was India's role? Was India dragged into the situation due to the influx of refugees? What role should Canada play as a senior member of the Commonwealth for the two commonwealth sisters who had been at war since the partition of India back in 1947?"

Such questions were raised when the Trudeau government tried to cope with one of its crucial problems in Canada's backyard—*le crise d'octobre* (October Crisis) in 1970. The government was attempting to assess the impact of the proclamation of the *War Measures Act* following the *FLQ* (*Front de libération du Québec)* crisis of 1970. As a result, the government, being doubly careful, could not unequivocally condemn Pakistan's central government's intervention in its internal affairs. Naturally, External officials were faced with many behind-the-scenes questions that had no apparent answers for the Ottawa mandarins, such as the following: How long could the government maintain its notion of neutrality? At what point does a domestic affair become an "international affair"? How many millions of Bengalis must flee their homeland to take refuge in India so that the international community may get their act together? These were difficult questions for the Trudeau administration throughout the liberation war. It was thus natural for Ottawa to remain cautious from the beginning of the conflict. However, at a later stage, Canada found ways to express disappointment, but not condemnation, of the military government.

Unfortunately, Canada's non-condemnation of the war of aggression, its conflictual situation due to her foreign policy constraints, and her assistance to the victims of military oppression have neither been well-documented in the form of researched monographs nor studied by any historian or scholar that I am aware of except for a few well-researched scholarly articles. Specifically, while there are some materials concerning Canada and India-Pakistan, mainly through Canada's link with the

Commonwealth, nothing has been written on or about Canada's role in the emergence of Bangladesh back in 1971. I was encouraged by Professor Habiba Zaman of Simon Fraser University, who organized a conference titled Canada 150 Conference Proceedings: Migration of Bengalis (2017). The key objective was documenting Bengalis' history and settlement patterns in Canada. I was privileged to be a participant in that conference.

Three critical players, Prime Minister Pierre Trudeau, his close foreign policy adviser, Ivan Head, and Mitchell Sharp, Secretary of State for External Affairs, did not include in any detail the East Pakistan crisis of 1971 in their respective writings, which are Trudeau's *Memoires* (1993), Trudeau and Head's *The Canadian Way* (1995), and Sharp's *Which Reminds Me* (1994). Arnold Smith's *Stitches in Time: The Commonwealth in World Politics* is the only monograph that contains several pages with a narrative of his efforts to negotiate a political solution to the conflict with the help of Canadian high commissioners to India and Pakistan.

Abul Mal Muhit's book titled *American Response to Bangladesh Liberation War* (1995) encouraged me to delve into the response of the people and the government of Canada. I then found a few more well-researched articles in the following chronological order. They are the work of Peter Dobell (1995) and John Small (1996), followed by a few other scholars, such as Zaglul Haider (2005), Rayan Touhey (2007), and Richard Pilkington (2011). Peter Dobell's much-talked-about scholarly article in *Canada in World Affairs, Vol. XVII, 1971–1973* is the first detailed analysis of Canada's conflict in dealing with the East Pakistan crisis. Dobell mainly focused on the provision of aid rather than on the policy of the decision-making process, given Canada's limited options, mainly due to Canada's foreign policy of neutrality and nonintervention. John Small, Canadian high commissioner to Pakistan during the crisis, described the exceedingly difficult situation Canada was in due to Canada's position of neutrality and Canada's fear of provoking President Yahya's conniption. He outlined the challenges he had to overcome in working with the military regime without being political and remaining neutral. He continued to communicate Canada's grave concerns to the military regime without straining Canada's friendly relationship with Pakistan.

My conversation with Dr. Zaglul Haider on Canada's role in 1971 and Canada-Bangladesh trade and friendship was most rewarding as I broadened my understanding after reading his two significant write-ups. They are "Unfolding Canada-Bangladesh Relations," published in *Asian*

Survey, Vol.XL5, No. 2, March/April 2005. pp. 323–341; "Canadian Policy Towards Bangladesh: Does the North Look at the South" published in *African and Asian Studies* 10 (2011) pp. 281–305. These two articles fill a serious gap in the trade between Canada and Bangladesh and the Canada-Bangladesh friendship.

In his 2006 PhD dissertation, Rayan Toohey focused on Indo-Canadian relations between 1941 and 1976. Unfortunately, many found Touhey's work on Indo-Canadian relations inadequate in explaining the East Pakistan crisis since he deals with it only in two short paragraphs. However, Richard Pilkington's article titled, *In the National Interest? The Canada and East Pakistan crisis of 1971* is perhaps the most comprehensive analysis that I have read thus far. Using archival documents and having done investigative research on Canada's conflict, Pilkington carefully outlined with evidence Canada's challenges in formulating a response to the satisfaction of India and Pakistan. He showed how Canada had no choice but to adhere to her policy of neutrality and yet protect Canada's relationship with Pakistan and India, two sisters of the Commonwealth. This single argument succinctly outlines Canada's most significant challenge in 1971 and her failure to adjust her policy of non-interference in Pakistan's internal affairs.

To understand the actions of the three protagonists, Bongobondhu (Sheikh Mujibur Rahman), leader of the Awami League (AL), Zulfiqar Ali Bhutto, leader of the Pakistan People's Party (PPP), and President Yahya Khan, in this historical drama, one must go beyond what happened and ask, How did the actors perceive the facts and how did they relate to them as a matter of critical analysis? While assessing the situation, Canada came to recognize that the Pakistan-Bangladesh conflict that challenged the territorial integrity of Pakistan and the inevitability of the emergence of Bangladesh had posed substantial threats to international peace and human life, and superpowers, other governments, and global organizations were called upon to influence, intervene, or broker an acceptable solution to it. Canada undertook a few initiatives throughout the nine long months of Bangladesh's struggle for independence. There were occasions when Canada's action, or lack thereof, could not be explained linearly as one tries to find answers to various related questions to understand Canadian perspectives vis-à-vis the Pakistan-Bangladesh conflict. Nevertheless, many of Canada's initiatives may be seen as favoring Bangladesh despite Canada's neutral stand; indeed, they did not favor Pakistan. Seeing the tragic situation of the Bengalis as a gripping story of human suffering and a story of denial of the democratic rights of the people of Pakistan, Canada chose to be a player to the extent possible to do her best, having, at the same time, adhered to her foreign policy of non-intervention.

I was impressed to see the vastness of the information, which seemed like a gold mine. I wrote this book in the hope that my research in this area will go beyond merely satisfying historical interest and curiosity through its narrative that brings out the unknown and unforeseen dimensions of historical insight as they relate to the birth of Bangladesh vis-à-vis Canada's performance on the world stage as a middle power with no axe to grind. More importantly, given that no comprehensive book has been written on this subject matter highlighting Canada's diplomatic tightrope walk, I hope this book may fill an existing lacuna in the historiography of the War of Liberation of Bangladesh and Canadian diplomacy about the birth of Bangladesh.

The larger objective of my book is not simply to present a historical narrative of the liberation of Bangladesh and Canada's diplomatic challenges but to begin a historiography of the liberation of Bangladesh and Canada-Bangladesh Friendship since 1972. My research may also trigger interest among students in sociology, history, political science, ethnic studies, international relations, Canadian studies, and international development studies in Canada and Bangladesh. In that sense, I believe my work may be of interest to researchers and groves of Academe. I am hopeful that, over the years, a body of historical literature will grow for future students and researchers. It is also my hope that this book will serve to stimulate more informed public discussion and debate in Bangladesh and Canada regarding Canada's role in 1971 regarding the birth of Bangladesh. In that case, my purpose will have been served.

ACKNOWLEDGMENTS

In my research for this book, I have received much valuable advice, assistance, and inspiration from several people. I treasure the memories of aid and cooperation I received from Canada's archivists, historians, and librarians. Their support of my work was a pillar of strength during my frustration. I am particularly grateful to Ted Kelly, resident archivist at the Department of External Affairs, who went through hundreds of records, some of which were already at the Library and Archives Canada while some were still at the departmental record office for classification and review before being transferred to the archives. His assistance and his personal touch allowed me to get a clearer understanding of the nature of the records, their relevance, and the proper use and citation in the text.

Many Canadian players, such as Members of Parliament, senators, NGO workers, diplomats, former high commissioners, and media personnel who were involved in various capacities in Canada, India, and Pakistan, have provided me with the base on which I have attempted to write and present my findings and their analysis in this book. I am grateful to Mitchel Sharp, Secretary of State for External Affairs (1969–1974), Senator Heath Macquarrie (former Conservative MP), and John Small (Canada's high commissioner to Pakistan in 1971). I met them on several occasions. They were generous not only with their time but also in recounting many of the challenges they confronted in 1971 concerning the Pakistan issue. I will always remain grateful for their unwavering support, observations, and openness. Many Canadian Jesuit and Holy Cross Order members have helped with my endless questions. To thank them all, I wish to mention Holy Cross Father R. W. Timm, Brother Raymond Cournoyer, and the Jesuit Father William German for their particular assistance and encouragement. I was blessed with many touching and informative letters and emails from many NGO personnel. Every time I went to their office premises, their faces would expand in a smile of welcome that would raise my comfort level.

I would also like to thank the following who read parts of the manuscript and made helpful comments and suggestions: Terry O'Donnell and Robert Mercier, my friends and former colleagues in the Department of Human Resources and Development Canada. O'Donnell looked at the manuscript constructively appraisingly and brought to my attention any incongruity he noticed. He also suggested several titles for the book, including the present one. Again, when I found chapters 7 and 9 particularly difficult, I toiled on it for months. I struggled with ordering the chapters—whether the arrangement should be topical or chronological. I debated for weeks whether I should exhaust the topic first and then jump to the next or keep the narrative in a tightly coherent manner in the story depicting Canada's initiative or lack thereof in taking any action during the Bengalis' struggle for independence. I was not sure. I felt dispirited. It was not until O'Donnell came to my rescue that I felt relieved. He assisted me in showing how to combine it all regarding their chronology, topical unity, and coherence. Again, in addition to doing French/English translation, now and then, Bob Mercier provided a lucid articulation of an often confused and misunderstood phenomenon—the Canada-Québec relations - until all assumptions and interpretations were clarified and honed. I have incorporated his comments from a critical reading of various drafts of the manuscript and valuable suggestions into the book. I owe particular gratitude to Selina Ali, who contributed uniquely and invaluably. Her critical comments have been beneficial. She stood by me through the several phases of my work, donating hours of editing and proofreading and always offering the best professional help, support, and friendship while working on this book.

I am also grateful to Kazi Nur Bangali, Dr. Q. M. Zaman, and Dr. Syed Sajjad Rahman for their cogent and incisive comments and suggestions, which led me to rewrite some of my narratives. They gave me their valuable advice, encouragement, and guidance, that had given me the greatest joy of my professional life. I give them my warmest thanks. I am grateful to Syed Zulfiquer Sadeque, a history buff with an ongoing fascination for everything historical. His work with the Department of Foreign Affairs took him to several postings outside of Canada. With insider knowledge and experience, he helped me learn a lot about the corporate milieu of the Department of Foreign Affairs, the classification system of its records, the information control and retrieval system, and the process of obtaining departmental records through ATIP (Access to Information and Privacy) Online Request. Again, insofar as this book is concerned, I owe an enormous debt of gratitude to Diane Parsonage, a friend, confidant, and invaluable associate.

I am grateful to many individuals and institutions in Canada, where I live, and Bangladesh, where I traveled, for their cooperation and assistance throughout my research. I am indebted to many people who have contributed to making it possible for me to write the book. They provided unceasing moral support during my 20-year-long research, having contributed invaluable insights. Over the years, I have also contacted many people with whom I corresponded with specific questions. Upon receipt of their written responses, I contacted them again for clarification with many follow-up questions. All of them cooperated. I am indebted to High Commissioners/Ambassadors Dr. Nazrul Islam, Yakub Ali, Mohammed Masud, and Dr. Khalilur Rahman. All four helped me when looking for specific information that I failed to gather. I remain ever grateful to all of them. I would have been unable to develop the narrative without their cooperation and contribution. Their names appear in the text appropriately. I am grateful to Ranazit Mazumder and Farzana Naz Shampa.

A few wanted their names to remain off the record. I have respected their request to remain anonymous. I am thankful to Ashfaque Rahman, Nehar Ahmed, and Rameen Biswas for all kinds of computer assistance and for helping me with pictures, annexes, and other related work throughout the years. They have assisted me in various capacities—whether about a photo or a piece of information. I am grateful to all of them for their help, encouragement, and natural cheerfulness. Ashfaque Rahman deserves special thanks for his assistance in formatting the text. I am also indebted to Aneela Rahman for frequently accessing Ottawa and Carleton University library facilities. I am grateful to Jaseem Chowdhury for printing my drafts every few months and for providing regular reprography service as needed.

Another set of thanks is also due to colleagues and friends who gave me the unique and invaluable encouragement necessary to complete the book. They frequently bounced off ideas throughout my research, while others, such as Jerome D'Costa, Amin Islam, Habia Zaman, Abdur Rahman Choudhury, Mizan Rahman, Zamil Zaman, Hasanat Murtaza, Luthful Kabir, Luthfur Rahman Chowdhury, Alimur Hydari, Imam Uddin, Sohel Khan, Nowsher Ali, Sadera Sujon, Salim Juberi, Professor Fazle

Baki, Rummana Chowdhury. Julian Francis and Abdullahel Hadi had instinctively encouraged at just the right time. Again, many people read the draft manuscript, each offering a particular perspective on Canada during the liberation war of Bangladesh.

I am thankful to the Bloomington-based Xlibris, publisher of this book. Working with Xlibris, a publisher who has supported my present and previous books, has been a pleasure. Xlibris' staff members have spent hours with me on the phone, saving me from countless significant and minor errors I had overlooked in my manuscript. They made innumerable wise suggestions and an invaluable editorial contribution. Xlibris prepared the index. I want to acknowledge the valuable advice and assistance I have received from everyone, including Xlibris. I want to thank them for their enthusiastic support in helping me refine my findings and observations and bring them to completion. While I have significantly benefited from everyone's advice and encouragement, I take responsibility for any errors, omissions, or shortcomings in this book. I stand on the firing line, for I lay no claim to comprehensiveness as the subject continues to challenge me.

Above all, thanks are due to my wife, Afroza Chowdhury, for her patience and forbearance with my frequent absences both in mind and body during the time of absorption in writing this book. Frankly, I owe my wife more than I could ever repay for her continued encouragement, patience, understanding, and sensitivity throughout my research. As well, I recall with gratitude our children, Tarik (and Mahareen, his wife), Seema (and her husband Asef), and Jaseem (and his wife Emma) for their unconditional support for my work and for supplying me with cups of tea. Without their love and support, it would have been impossible for me to complete the journey, which had been one of my life's most satisfying and enjoyable experiences. Publishing the book is a great pith and moment.

Finally, a few wanted their names to remain off the record. I have respected their request to remain anonymous.

Mustafa Chowdhury
E-mail: Mustafa.chowdhury49@gmail.com
448 Rougemount Crescent
Ottawa, Ontario, Canada, K4A 2Y8

INTRODUCTION

This book attempts to focus on three areas. Firstly, an enlarged understanding of the dichotomy in Pakistan's polity and the nature of the conflict surrounding democratization in Pakistan from a Canadian perspective. At the same time, it recognizes that as a middle power, Canada had no strategic interest in the Indian subcontinent. Canada took a close look at the claims of President Yahya Khan, the military dictator, to resolve the conflict to the extent possible. Secondly, it looks at the demands of Sheikh Mujibur Rahman (Bongobondhu), elected leader of Pakistan, and the covert and overt role of the government of India under the leadership of Prime Minister Indira Gandhi. Thirdly, it tries to see how Canada reacted to the conflict and what, if any, Canada's role was in the emergence of Bangladesh. Relying on both pro-Pakistani and pro-Bangladeshi sources of information, the cumulative effect of the factual information gathered from overseas allowed Canada to appreciate the psychological and emotional dimension of the conflict stemming from economic disparity and political discrimination in Pakistan.

As a middle power, Canada recognized that the sheer size and scale of the tragedy and the involvement of the superpowers had made it difficult to play a substantive role due to her foreign policy constraints. Foreign affairs cognoscenti in Ottawa quickly brought Mitchel Sharp, Secretary of State for External Affairs, up to speed. They recognized the regime's game plan, that once the Bengalis were brought to submission, then it would be a whole new ball game. Ironically, for the Yahya administration, Canada saw how, despite continuing efforts to suppress the Bengalis' aspirations for sharing more power with the central government, the military regime found the Bengalis more revitalized by intensifying the politico-military system they challenged and pledged to change. Following the declaration of independence, the Bengali rebels saw the imposition of martial law as the "virtual colonial serfdom" of the military regime in what they called "Occupied Bangladesh" by the "Occupation army" of Pakistan.

Canada closely saw how the two concepts—freedom and future—remained on the minds of Pakistan's military administrators and politicians. The crux of the issue, as Canada understood, was the power-sharing between the two wings of Pakistan—East and West. This was to take place following the power transfer to the elected Bengali leader of East Pakistan. Instead, on March 25, 1971, Pakistani military personnel secretly let loose a massive burst of violence on unarmed and defenceless Bengalis of East Pakistan while *negotiations* among the three leaders - President Yahya Khan, Bongobondhu, the Awami League (AL) leader of the majority party; and Zulfiqar Ali Bhutto, leader of the Pakistan People's Party (PPP)—were going on. Sources obtained by John Small and James George, Canadian high commissioners to Pakistan and India, respectively, through diplomatic channels, indicated that President Yahya Khan was perfidious. It was in that, while officially talking about the transfer of power to the AL leader, he was secretly bringing in his troops from West Pakistan.

The Trudeau administration later learned that the entire Yahya-Bongobondhu-Bhutto parley might be seen as a Trojan horse, a deceptive means to buy the extra time the regime needed. The news was shocking enough for Ottawa officials to make their hair curl. They were appalled by the harrowing accounts of mass killings being perpetrated against the Bengali people of East Pakistan. Canadians raised their voices in anguish to express their sense of outrage at the crimes committed by an increasingly unpopular military regime against the defenceless Bengalis. To the Bengalis, as Canadians viewed the situation, it was their struggle for emancipation. Canada chose not to officially condemn the actions of the Yahya regime in an unequivocal term. Though condemnable, Canada regarded Yahya's actions as an "internal affair" of Pakistan. Nevertheless, despite many constraints, Canada became involved to the extent possible without being overtly political. Throughout the crisis period, Canada neither remained silent nor indifferent to the "man-made" tragedy in East Pakistan. Canada worked around these issues in her own ways, using the foreign policy options she had to adhere to.

Ottawa spent much time conducting a comprehensive analysis of the situation. While doing the analysis, Ottawa focused its energies toward a political solution within the framework of a united Pakistan. With quite a bit of discomfort and anxiety, Ottawa followed the drama ever since it started to play with the destiny of the Bengalis. Sharp was constantly briefed about the reactions of the people of Canada. Within days, it was clear to see the responses of the Canadian public; the mainstream and Canadians of East and West Pakistani origin reacted differently. Sharp learned that by and large, Canadians of all stripes were appalled to see the brutal attack on civilians in East Pakistan. Sharp was also informed how the surreptitious military crackdown on Bengali civilians had instantly divided the people along the lines of Canadians of Bengali and non-Bengali origin.

The feelings among the outraged Bengali Canadians were running so high that, to them, the attack was a cruel blow, doubly cruel and ironic because it came clandestinely from the government that was responsible for protecting the lives of its people. They immediately brought out demonstrations in several cities condemning the military action. Having disassociated with Pakistan, they demanded Canada's recognition of Bangladesh. Whereas the non-Bengali West Pakistanis, having been supportive of the military regime, welcomed the imposition of martial law and military intervention to save Pakistan from Indian conspiracy. Within weeks, the news media tried to raise awareness about the issue to secure the public's support in favor of an independent Bangladesh. In Chapter 4, we shall see in detail how the great bulk of the Canadian public, who were outraged, condemned the military regime. They also believed that the ball was in Yahya's court and that efforts should be made to establish democracy in Pakistan. The Trudeau administration remained conflicted as it had to adhere to its policy of non-intervention in the "internal affairs" of another country. Yet, it wanted to support democracy in Pakistan.

A doubly cautious Trudeau administration categorized the issue as the Indo-Pakistan Issue. This was so, even though, as a middle power, Canada recognized that the phenomenon of Bangladesh was a game changer in the subcontinental body politic. The East Pakistan Issue, as Canada termed it later, was to be resolved through corrective measures, and Canada argued to the extent she could put forward her take on the conflict. Having ignored the appeal from the Bengali Canadians for Canada's prompt action, Ottawa officials remained focused on finding a way to transfer power to the majority party's leader. Throughout the nine long months of struggle for the independence of Bangladesh, Canada continued to maintain its neutrality. However, there were occasions when Canada became involved both actively and passively. Again, there were occasions when Canada's actions, or lack thereof, could not be explained linearly, as one needs to find answers to various related questions to understand Canada's position. Canada thought long and hard but never changed her strategy—her game plan. As readers flip through multiple chapters, they shall see that the potential reality of an independent Bangladesh was not on Canada's radar screen during the entire War of Liberation period. All of Canada's efforts through her game plan were directed at finding a solution within the framework of a united democratic Pakistan.

This book has the following ten interrelated chapters that cover the alpha and omega, the story of the imposition of martial law, and the surrender of the Pakistani army vis-à-vis Canada's role during the Bengali's struggle for independence:

Chapter 1: 1971: Looking Back outlines the political landscapes of Canada and Pakistan. It describes how Canada emerged as a nation that broke out of its isolation in the 1930s. It also refers to Prime Minister Pierre Trudeau's rejection of the day's foreign policy, which underwent an intense review. The review proposed the most fundamental departure from Canada since the Second World War (1939–1945), shifting from the pre-war policy of isolationism to post-war internationalism. It briefly describes Canada's concerns with the "Quebec question"—demands for a separate nation by the FLQ *(Front de libération du Québec)*. It touches on the North Atlantic Treaty Organization (NATO) vis-à-vis Canada's role and membership. It also talks about Canada's role in the Commonwealth and its relationship with the two sister countries – India and Pakistan. It also describes the presence of Canadian missionaries in India and Pakistan from the early 1900s, along with trade and business.

In outlining Pakistan's political landscape since its creation in 1947, it describes how, from the beginning, the people of East Pakistan (Bengalis) were discriminated against by the West Pakistani (non-Bengali) rulers, as well as East Pakistanis' cumulative grievances that they were falling through the cracks since the central government did not have an equal representation in the government. Under the leadership of the Awami League (AL) Chief Sheikh Mujibur Rahman (Bongobondhu), the Bengalis came up with the Six-Point Program, which envisioned laying a solid foundation of prosperity on which a socialist edifice could be subsequently erected in a democratic Pakistan. It points out how Zulfiqar Ali Bhutto, leader of the Pakistan People's Party (PPP), played a devious political game, taking advantage of his friendship with the military hawks. Unable to withstand the paralyzing pressure and being influenced by Bhutto, President Yahya suddenly postponed the National Assembly session just a few days before the scheduled date. In protest, the AL leader began a non-cooperation movement, demanding the immediate withdrawal of the military and transfer of power to the elected representative to form a democratically elected government in Pakistan. It touches on the Yahya-Mujib-Bhutto parley that failed and how the military regime secretly cracked down on innocent Bengali civilians to suppress the Bengalis' movement for greater autonomy.

Chapter 2: Surreptitious Military Attack and Canada's Immediate Reaction describes how, instead of lifting martial law and returning to barrack, the military regime, with the declaration of martial law, imposed a massive clampdown on East Pakistani Bengalis having outlawed the AL, the bona fide party of the majority Pakistanis. The West Pakistani troops, the Pathan, the Baluchi, and the Punjabi soldiers remained convinced that their mission was a crusade against the Bengalis as "mutineers" who had defied the law and order of the very government it was charged with running. Initially, since the news from overseas was sketchy and somewhat conflicted, it had been challenging to find the truth from the welter of reports originating from the subcontinent that reached Ottawa from Canadian high commissioners to Pakistan and India. The difficulty of obtaining authentic information due to the imposition of censorship in Pakistan has been highlighted regarding many questions and the chronology of the events immediately following the furtive military crackdown—a problem fundamental to all historical writing.

Upon review of incoming materials, Ottawa officials realized that the Yahya regime's claim that it was a "cleansing operation" was nothing but a euphemism for killings. Canada viewed the killing of the Bengalis that began on March 25 as an attempt by the Pakistani army to crush the resistance movement. The Trudeau administration also believed that any quick reaction, one way or another, on Canada's part, would be "politically incorrect." Canada's excellent relationship with Pakistan made Ottawa analysts counsel Sharp along the vein that Canada must not even appear to sympathize with the Bengali rebels who were committed to leaving Pakistan to liberate their native land. In her reaction to the events, Canada gave priority to the provision of humanitarian relief assistance as her immediate goal, thus assisting the Bengali victims in India and displaced persons in East Pakistan to the extent possible.

Chapter 3: Canadian Media Onside with the Freedom Fighters of Bangladesh describes how Canadian journalists, reporters, editorial writers, columnists, commentators, analysts, and "initiators" of news worked in close collaboration in both selecting and analyzing the heart-rending and cataclysmic chain of events involving the governments of Pakistan and India and the provisional government of Bangladesh. Because of censorship, the media found the military to interfere with their ability to report the events with penetrative analysis. The news media went to the bottom of the Pakistani mindset rooted in the psyche of the military rulers by asking the following: *What is at stake for the military regime? What is at stake for the majority of Bengalis?* The media coverage, whether print or non-print media, was not a mere summary of wire reports backed by film of press conferences; instead, Canadian news reporters and commentators decried the military regime's autocratic stance. Considering the events in the subcontinent as a grim human tragedy, the news media successfully generated discussions among the Canadian public. The media expected prompt and vigorous actions on the part of the Trudeau administration, although it was aware of the government's limitations.

There were many detailed narratives of how the military personnel was beating the Bengali prisoners, performing vivisection, and decapitating them, as well as emasculating them and nailing them to trees and wantonly using them for bayonet practice and burning or burying them alive. The media never agreed on the cynicism and perfidy of the Yahya regime. Instead, the media strongly suspected Yahya's motive—that he must have been an elaborate ruse. While it is never possible to determine how the gory details of the war that the reporters presented had influenced the course of politics in Canada, it is possible to get a sense of its immense impact on shaping public opinion and political perceptions in Canada. As the champions of truth and openness, the reporters worked with scrupulous attention to detail and accuracy. Readers shall see the role of a visionary crusading media whose comprehensive news coverage contributed to the Canadian public's more precise understanding of the notion of the actual conflict from the Bengalis' point of view as opposed to the military regime's narrative.

Chapter 4: Vox Populi: Canadians Speak Out describes the position of the three segments of the Canadian public, such as the Bengali Canadians of East Pakistani origin, non-Bengali Canadians of West Pakistani backgrounds, and the mainstream Canadian public of diverse backgrounds. The first group, comprised of Bengali East Pakistani origin Canadians, supported the liberation of Bangladesh. Having condemned the sudden and covert attack on Bengali civilians and ongoing military reprisals, this group lobbied for the recognition of Bangladesh and the release of Bongobondhu. The pro-Pakistani Canadians, consisting of non-Bengali West Pakistanis, however, counter-argued, stating that the demand for greater autonomy, if realized, could lead the way for the dismemberment of Pakistan with India's covert support.

Again, most of the mainstream Canadians experienced the Pakistan-Bangladesh conflict not as participants or stakeholders but as spectators who were observing the stark tragedy as it was unfolding. The public argued that if the deep-rooted grievances of the Bengalis were allowed to fester, mounting tensions between India and Pakistan could explode into a war that might quickly involve one or more of the superpowers. Having condemned the Yahya regime's military move and repression, they demanded Bongobondhu's release as they found the regime's arguments preposterously at odds. The greater public demanded that the superpowers, other governments, and international organizations be called upon to influence, intervene, or broker a solution to the conflict. They insisted that, as a middle power, in the face of this significant divergence among the great powers, Canada should direct her energy to steer the management of the conflict to the UN. Except for the Bengali Canadians, most of the public favored a solution that would keep Pakistan as one country in a re-engineered and democratic Pakistan instead of a split into two nations.

Chapter 5: NGOs, Religious and Business Organizations: Get Behind Bangladesh outlines the activities undertaken by Canadian NGOs during the crisis period, having worked closely with international, national, and local organizations in Canada, India, and Pakistan. Facilitated by the momentum of the coalition-building process, Canadian NGOs demonstrated an extraordinary example of cooperative multi-tasking during a crisis. They worked on the premise that, as the events would continue to unfold in the Indian subcontinent, the need for immediate action on their part would become urgent regardless of the lens through which one viewed the crisis. Canadian NGOs' work remains a treasured and inspiring reminder of how to forge partnerships to take advantage of the synergies of the diverse groups in the field.

Notwithstanding a growing sign of financial overstretch when they had no access to capital, political connections, and a reliable private donor base with its attendant pressures to choose between competing priorities, the NGO communities undertook greater responsibilities in providing urgently needed humanitarian assistance. They created a new relationship by pulling their strengths, weaknesses, and styles—a new way of being, a paradigm in which each organization knew what to expect from the other. They knew best to complete the tasks, even under the most exigent circumstances, through collaboration and not confrontation. Their engagement demonstrates a magnificent example of complementary work. In carrying out their public awareness programs, the relief and NGO workers faced the challenges with courage, tact, and diplomacy by remaining calm in the face of insults, provocations, and accusations. It shall be seen how tactfully the NGOs had to stay demonstrably apolitical regardless of the individual member's views.

Chapter 6: Parliament Debates Canada's Role in Bangladesh Struggle in the House of Commons and Senate provides an account of the issues raised by Members of Parliament (MPs) and Senators throughout the period under discussion. Themes, such as preservation of democracy, transfer of power to the democratically elected representatives, the secession of the repressive measures, resolution by constitutional means, humanitarian assistance, etc., had continued to dominate the discussion throughout the period the military was in power reveal how deeply the Canadian Parliament was disturbed by what was happening in East Pakistan. The government was faced with a barrage of questions at a time when it genuinely feared that Canadians could quickly find a nexus to the problem at home about Québec's quest for independence and the Bengalis' fight for the liberation of their native land.

There was unanimity on significant issues surrounding the Pakistan crisis once the MPs and senators were brought up to speed, having recognized the nature of the conflict—that this was only the tip of the iceberg in the Pakistan-Bangladesh conflict involving the military regime and Bongobondhu. Canadians stood behind Mitchell Sharp, Secretary of State for External Affairs, and a responsible squeaky-clean politician.

Taking advantage of the collective wisdom of the politicians of all parties, Sharp responded to the questions raised by his colleagues and the news media to the best of his ability. Canada was more interested in seeing how best she could help resolve the conflict and achieve democracy in Pakistan. Canada's emphasis was on assisting the victims of military repression in East Pakistan and refugees in India, as well as to see a genuinely democratic Pakistan that would be representative of its people. This approach resonated with Canadian parliamentarians of all political stripes and the mainstream public.

Chapter 7: Canada's Initiatives Feature Her Trademark of Tact and Fairness deals with various initiatives, actions, and advocacy activities following the military operation in East Pakistan. Canada had to remain doubly careful amid all the kerfuffle while the Liberation War of Bangladesh was going on since Canada had a "hands-off" policy even when the Trudeau administration became aware of the dreadful facts that were being confirmed. Canada explored several ways having addressed the issue individually by counseling the national leaders of India and Pakistan to exercise restraint and collectively by pressuring the United Nations, providing funds to the national and international NGOs, lobbying for the release of Bongobondhu, who was to take charge of the country.

By the time readers come to the end of the chapter, they will appreciate the practicality of the various initiatives and their success or lack thereof. Since Canada could not come out with its official position paper in an unequivocal term, an attempt has been made to characterize the various government undertakings to see whether they favor Bangladesh or Pakistan. Seeing how Pakistan was departing from the rank of the civilized nations of the world, Canada endeavored to save the Bengalis from the terror of the Yahya regime's countless acts of burning, intimidation, and sadism. Although Canada preferred procrastination, Ottawa officials moved forward quietly and worked discretely behind the scenes. It was a case of hoping against hope that there might be a breakthrough resulting in the transfer of power to Bongobondhu, the democratically elected leader of Pakistan. This chapter sheds some light on the following recurring question: What did the government do or did not do to support or oppose the positions of the conflicting parties during the Bengalis' fight for independence? Readers shall find some answers in chapters 7 and 9.

Chapter 8: Canada Faces Dilemma: A Chronology of Quiet Diplomacy outlines the extraordinary caution with which Canada interacted with the parties involved. Canada could not develop a declaratory position paper under the rapidly changing circumstances. Despite her reputation for outreach and important inspirational commitment to internal problem-solving, Canada was unsuccessful in bringing the two parties face-to-face. As a middle power, Canada formulated her game plan with no political agenda other than that of the superpowers. The Trudeau administration was shocked at the fragility of the democratic process manipulated by the regime entrusted with that responsibility. Canada was outraged to see how Bongobondhu became the fall guy despite being the leader of the majority party in Pakistan. Although the Opposition MPs recognized Canada's vulnerability and unwillingness to discuss the issue of separation and self-determination in Pakistan, they still expected to hear its official position from the government. Canada's actions, inactions, and position of wait and watch were based on a broader context of non-intervention in the internal affairs of another country.

Canada helplessly noted how the top military man, Yahya, was being inexcusably callous and self-indulgent in managing the fate of millions of Pakistanis. The Trudeau administration was disturbed to see how the military regime had steered a challenging course between firebrands (adhering to Pakistan's integrity) and extremist diehard Mujibites (supporters of Mujib/pro-liberationists). It was also distressing to see the consequences of the ongoing military reprisals; Canada remained convinced that the government must not remain indifferent to the dreadful tragedy that was being enacted in East Pakistan. Canada saw how the rebel forces, with covert assistance from the Gandhi administration, had been making substantial progress toward achieving their goal - the liberation of Bangladesh. Nevertheless, Canada never considered the importance of the game changer—Bangladesh's phenomenon in the subcontinental conflict. Canada directed all her efforts towards a political settlement between East and West Pakistan within the framework of a united Pakistan. An independent Bangladesh out of Pakistan was never on Canada's radar screen.

Chapter 9: Canada Finally Gets It All Right: Bangladesh Recognized, and a Friendship Reinforced gives an account of how the Trudeau administration had to turn a deaf ear to the request of the provisional government of Bangladesh for recognition—something that was out of the question during the War of Liberation. As soon as Bangladesh became independent, Canada tried to embrace the newborn country by recognition as she was under no constraint. Ottawa worked behind the scenes to expedite the process for Canada's formal recognition of newborn Bangladesh. Readers shall appreciate Canada's greatest challenge: that diplomacy demanded that she re-align her position considering the latest situation in the subcontinent vis-à-vis the political positions of major powers regarding the timing of recognition of Bangladesh.

Seeing the presence of the Indian army, however, Ottawa was faced with a paradox as it believed premature withdrawal of the Indian military would threaten to return Bangladesh to chaos, the outcome of which would more than likely be further bloody revenge on each other's part. While seeking answers to such grave questions, Canada quickly began to move forward with no procrastination that readers had noted in the preceding chapters. Canada's behind-the-scenes work involved a diplomatic campaign to provide further salience to social justice and good governance in the newly independent country. Canada managed to persuade the Commonwealth countries to move forward as quickly as possible by recognizing the reality of Bangladesh. Ottawa handled the matter with tact and diplomacy, yet with a sense of urgency in order not to cause any further delay. Canada also lobbied and succeeded in securing Bangladesh's UN membership.

Chapter 10: Conclusion: Grand Finale: Bangladesh Takes its Rightful Place on the Global Stage reminds readers of what they have read in various chapters—a middle power Canada's inability to intervene in the internal affairs of Pakistan due to her foreign policy constraints. It was impossible to play a significant mediatory role when the Bengalis were fighting for independence. As a senior member of the Commonwealth, Canada neither wanted to antagonize Pakistan and India nor wanted to see the two Commonwealth sisters on a collision course. And yet, despite all kinds of limitations, in the case of the *Padma,* Canada charted an increasingly independent course, much to the profound anger of the Nixon administration that expected Canada to toe the United States. Canada's high-profile action demonstrates that Canada is not an automatic ally of any partner or cause but a fully independent nation capable of making decisions for herself based on her *raison d'être* when possible.

Canada made an independent decision completely devoid of US influence. Canada championed the idea that Canada should remain cautious and pragmatic in her deeds and rhetoric and shy away from overly divisive or belligerent actions that could compromise Canada's reputation as a calm, conciliatory, friendly nation. In typical Trudeauvean style, he maintained that the world needs to be managed cooperatively and diplomatically. During the War of Liberation, Canada watched anxiously President Yahya's aggressive solution to the political problem in a classic example of hubris and nemeses of force. However, following the birth of Bangladesh, when Canada was under no constraint, Canada turned out to be a "friend in need is a friend indeed." As noted, Canada immediately began lobbying for Bangladesh's entry into the Commonwealth and the UN and succeeded quickly. As well, Canada became directly involved in rebuilding the war-ravaged Bangladesh.

A BRIEF NOTE ON RESEARCH METHODOLOGY AND SOURCES

In 1972, when I left Bangladesh for Canada as a twenty-three-year-old, my ideas were still taking shape. I was then becoming aware of the conflict and the complex political history of the subcontinent with exhilarating and depressing episodes. For me, it was a matter of finding Canada's take on the conflict as embedded in her official records. Throughout my research, I was aware of how the work of the historian divides itself into the following two stages: first, the writer must ascertain the facts, and second, to interpret them. In other words, the first stage was mainly a matter of evidence that I had to scrutinize and compare the available sources of information and judge from them as to the alleged facts. At that stage, some were classed as "doubtful" since the information related to the military government that was committing the crime of killing and suppression. In the second stage, I no longer required the judicial faculty only. Still, insight and imagination suggest why the military government had continued its repression, the motives that swayed the chief military protagonist, the actors in events, and how it all happened in front of the world. Between these initial and final stages, I found myself in a state of creative historical thinking, which demanded the fullest commitment of my intellectual ability and emotional energy. In the process, through strenuous efforts, I was fortunate to be able to exercise the "historian's craft." I was lucky to put it all together with a synthesis of Canada's diplomatic tightrope walk to the actions of the superpowers as they relate to the Bengalis' struggle for independence back in 1971 when Canada was still dealing with the fallout of the October Crisis.

The great bulk of the present research is based on primary sources, such as records of the Departments of External Affairs (now Global Affairs

Canada), Manpower and Immigration (now Immigration, Refugees and Citizenship Canada), Library and Archives Canada, Canadian International Development Agency (now a part of the Global Affairs Canada) and the Privy Council. I have accessed their records through Canada's *Freedom of Information and Protection of Privacy Act*, which enabled me to review the declassified information made available to researchers upon request. The plethora of materials constitutes a rich and wide-ranging source of primary materials for researchers. Before I even began sifting through, I was mindful of the information found in historical sources designated by terms like fact, inference, and opinion.

All primary sources I have examined fall under manuscript group (MG) series MG 28 and 32 and record group (RG) housed in the Library and Archives Canada and the Department of External Affairs called E-Pak-1-4; 47-9 India-Pak; 38-11-1 Bangla; 38-11-1Pak; Bangla; 20-Bangla-1-4. The documents dated between 1970 and 1972 consisted of daily telegrams, air grams, telexes, dispatches, demarches, memos, confidential briefing notes, statistical information, factual references, and situational reports (SITREPS) from Canada's high commissioners to India and Pakistan. The documentary evidence consisting of telexes, memos, and emissaries housed in the Canadian archives reflects the complex nature of the stream. Indeed, the quotes from the original telegrams from New Delhi and Islamabad were so mammoth and extensive that I was stuck with the proverbial task of finding the needle in the haystack. Thousands and thousands of daily telegrams cluttered up my mind. I quickly learned to read and interpret the often abbreviated diplomatic telexes and messages. I have tried my best in persuasive detail to see that the narrative flows well and carries the reader backward and forward easily without distracting his or her attention.

In a sense, both high commissioners to Pakistan and India, John Small and James George, worked as though they were diplomatic historians while gathering the diplomatic history of the time. Soon, I became familiar with their knowledge of the Indo-Pak polity. Having engaged themselves in information gathering, they delved into what historian G. J. Renier observed, the "lives and idiosyncrasies of individuals" (Reiner, G. J. *History: Its Purpose and Method.* Harper & Row, Publishers, New York, 1950. p. 63.). Frequent references to the actions of the superpowers in their memos and messages made it clear that while providing information, they, like a diplomatic historian, made sure to "keep an eye upon the world at large." While examining and analyzing the records, I reminded myself of Reiner's cautionary remark, "Any narrative, every narrative, implies explanation, a reference to causes, motives, effects, and results. To say that a narrative of experience is needed implies that there will also be an explanation." Without wandering in the land of speculation, I have also reviewed the telexes of Canada's high commissioners to other Commonwealth countries as the Ottawa team in charge of briefing the Minister needed to examine the reports of Canadian high commissioners to Pakistan and India, but also to other Commonwealth countries. I have reconstructed my narrative based on my understanding of Canada's reaction, or lack thereof, to the events related to the liberation of Bangladesh.

Under primary sources are also the papers of a few federal Members of Parliament (MPs) and senators in the Library and Archives Canada. I have looked at the personal papers of Prime Minister Pierre Trudeau; Mitchell Sharp, Minister of External Affairs; Heath Macquarrie, Conservative MP as well as Canadian delegate to East Pakistan; NDP MP Andrew Brewin, also Canadian delegate to East Pakistan; NDP MP Les Benjamin; and Arnold Smith, Secretary-General, Commonwealth. All my interviews with parliamentarians were free-flowing conversations rather than structured interviews—whether it was Mitchell Sharp, John Small, a Canadian high commissioner to Pakistan, Senator Heath Macquarrie, or MP Les Benjamin. All of them received me with warmth and friendliness, which I will never forget.

In addition, I have examined many unpublished records of non-governmental Organisations (NGOs), such as Oxfam of Canada, Care Canada, Mennonite Central Committee, World Vision Canada (WVC), Archives of the Canadian Catholic Conference (CCC), and a few others available in the Library and Archives Canada or the individual NGO's archives. I have waded through the massive materials contained in thousands of files. There were also numerous records of the Ottawa-based Indian High Commission, which was involved in a campaign program involving the Canadian public for which the Gandhi administration had encouraged the high commissioner in charge. The records created in Ottawa consisted of a Memoranda of Conversations with heads of governments, foreign ministers, and essential world leaders, briefing notes for the Minister, and records sent by the Commonwealth Secretariat in London, UK. Also, some records were of the Commonwealth countries that had worked together in several areas while taking a particular position to brief the Minister.

Among other primary sources that fall under official publications, I have examined the following: (1) the debates of the House of Commons, (2) the debates of the Senate, (3) the report of the Standing Committee on External Affairs and National Defence, and (4) several briefs to the Commons Committee, which may be found in the bibliography.

The secondary sources that I have examined include various reports and submissions. I have also reviewed the major Canadian newspapers for three consecutive years (1970–1972) housed in the Library and Archives Canada. I had to visit the city's municipal library, provincial library, or archives for some newspapers. For the activities of the provinces or provincial governments, I had to use the provincial archives that maintain such records. Having traveled from St. John's, Newfoundland to Victoria, British Columbia, to identify Canadian politicians, parliamentarians, social workers, and former government officials who were involved in various capacities, I have interviewed several distinguished Canadian Members of Parliament (MPs), Senators, foreign service personnel, and many Canadians who had been to Pakistan and India during the period under study. I was agreeably surprised by the readiness of most parliamentarians to talk to me frankly about their involvement and trust in my discretion and historical craftsmanship. I have interviewed and corresponded with numerous Bengali Canadians in Canada during the period under study in various capacities. Their names appear throughout the text. My research work was thus complemented by interviews with many Bengali Canadian (then known as East Pakistanis) members of the public and NGO officials who worked with local, national, and international NGOs. Frankly, it was a "feel-good" exercise for me. To my utter satisfaction, I was lucky to have a burgeoning rapport between myself and the interviewees.

Upon receipt of their responses, I called back and clarified, when necessary, specific points that I could not interpret. Although I had a standardized interview questionnaire, I had to customize particular questions depending on their responses for elaboration. I allowed them to recall the events of 1971 and their involvement in whatever capacity they could think about. The format was flexible enough to allow me to increase the interviewees' comfort level in that it helped them recall their participation. It permitted me to directly solicit information from them about their participation, whether it was a case of fundraising or awareness-raising. Depending on the response and the level of enthusiasm, or lack thereof, I had to paraphrase my questions continually. There were open-ended and specific questions to allow the interviewees to speak their minds as they wished.

During the second round of interviews, my follow-up questions often triggered their memories, and as a result, they remained enthusiastic and cooperative. In some instances, I had to abandon many of the questions I had intended to ask. Though unstructured in format, I guided myself by an extensive and topical but flexible outline to suit everyone's sense and sensibility. Fortunately, the interviewees trusted me and were friendly and forthcoming in approaching my inquisitive questions. Amazingly enough, though not all, for some interviewees, 1971 had been etched in their minds. Some recalled in photographic details, while some had to take time to remember. As it turned out, it was more like an information exchange with the interviewees who were in Canada at that time and reacted to the news of the massacre and military reprisals in East Pakistan. My free and frank conversation with them helped me cross-check the media report of the day and determine the integrity of the events or reactions to such events and their consequences. My in-depth interviews led me to various sources I would have missed otherwise.

The progress of the interview guided the use of each specific question. In some cases, I interviewed simply through correspondence with general questionnaires. It also helped me deepen my understanding of Canada's dichotomous situation while the events unfolded in the Indian subcontinent. For me, examination and analysis of the available relevant files and documents, whether at the External Affairs' Departmental Records Office or the Library and Archives Canada, had been a monumental task. I treated them not as belonging to just "one sort" of materials but a diverse conglomeration of materials helpful in examining the Trudeau administration's interpretation of the events.

As I proceeded, using primary or secondary sources, I needed to grasp the general distinction between statements of facts, statements of opinion, and statements that are inferences. I did not have to give extraordinary effort in determining the date, place, source, or author of a particular document from the Canadian high commissioners to Pakistan and India, as they were clear, straightforward telexes.

My challenges were, therefore, not so much regarding the authenticity of the sources but selecting the documents that seemed more pertinent to my work at hand—having made a judgment about the comparative importance of the vast material housed in the Department of External

Affairs before they were sent off to the Library and Archives Canada. With due diligence, I comprehensively analyzed the information obtained by Ottawa officials responsible for formulating Canada's official position regarding the Pakistan-Bangladesh conflict. My effort was focused on developing a clear picture of events in the Indian subcontinent as seen through Canadian eyes. Throughout my research, I read primary and secondary sources extensively, sometimes even exhaustively. I had to be on my mettle just so that I could prove my worth. My research took twenty years on the spadework before I could write. This way, I could reconstruct a narrative to achieve a thoughtful account.

All other reports and studies, together with a host of information that I have used and found useful, are to be found in the bibliography I have put together at the end of the book.

CHAPTER 1

1971: Looking Back

This chapter summarizes Canada and Pakistan's political landscape of the 1960s and early 1971—the year martial law was re-imposed in Pakistan, followed by a sudden and secret military clampdown. It highlights Canada's national and international accomplishments as a nation that has emerged from isolationism to internationalism—how, through the Commonwealth, Canada became involved in underdeveloped and developing countries. It also refers to Canada's aid program that grew substantially under the Colombo Plan, providing food aid, project financing, and technical assistance to Pakistan and India. It describes Canada's relationships with India and Pakistan that were enhanced through Canada's Commonwealth link with the Indian subcontinent, as well as the involvement of Canadian missionaries long before the partition of India and the participation of Canadian NGOs in Pakistan. It touches on some issues affecting Canada in 1971, such as the separation of Québec.

It also outlines Pakistan's political landscape, creation, constitutional crisis, military rule, and grievances of the people of East Pakistan. It highlights the demand of the Bengalis for greater autonomy in East Pakistan, Pakistan's first-ever National Elections held in 1970, and the failure or unwillingness of the military regime to transfer power to the elected leader of the majority. It describes Pakistan's relationship with India since the creation of Pakistan as a sovereign and separate state in 1947. It refers to 1970, a tumultuous year in both the Indo-Pak subcontinent and Canada.

The political landscapes of Canada and Pakistan bring readers up to speed, enabling them to recognize the context of the subcontinental polity as they easily leaf through the chapter.

Canada's Political Landscape

It was not until after the Second World War (1939–1945) that Canada emerged as a nation broken out of its isolationism of the 1930s. Between 1950 and 1953, Canadian troops had already been to North Korea. While working closely with the international peacekeeping operations, when due to the Anglo-French military venture, the Suez crisis of 1956 nearly wrecked the Commonwealth, Canadian diplomat Lester B. Pearson played a pivotal role that brought Canada to the international limelight. Pearson was at once a Canadian scholar, statesman, soldier, diplomat, and, of course, a Nobel Prize winner who became the prime minister of Canada in 1963. He collaborated with the secretary general, Dag Hammarskjold, to enable the UN to launch the first peacekeeping force that provided a face-saving formula for withdrawing British and French troops. From the late 1950s, Pearsonean internationalism surfaced with an emphasis on building solid international institutions as a forum for managing conflict between states, replaced by isolationism as the dominant theme in Canadian foreign policy. By then, Canada's new international stance forced Canada to be aligned with the US and Western Europe against the USSR, and the communist bloc became more entrenched.

All through the 1950s and 1960s, Canada also played a crucial role in working closely with African and Asian members of the Commonwealth. Having opposed South Africa's official policy of apartheid, at the March 1961 Prime Ministers' Meeting, John Diefenbaker, Canadian Conservative prime minister who returned to power in 1957, wholeheartedly supported Nigeria and India. They demanded that South Africa's official communiqué affirm racial equality at the heart of the Commonwealth. Canada forced South Africa to withdraw its application as a catalyst, allowing the Commonwealth to evolve as a multiracial association based on mutual respect. Canada was engaged in reducing tension throughout the globe, buttressing international cooperation, and strengthening the possible continuity of an ongoing *détente*.

Internal Political Dynamism

Throughout his leadership from 1957 to 1963, John Diefenbaker relentlessly argued for "unhyphenated Canadianism" or the "two nations" concept of Canada. Since 1963, the Liberal Party remained in power until 1979 despite prime ministerial changes. The 1960s were marked by change and charisma in the Canadian political arena, both at the federal and provincial levels, especially in Québec. The "three wise men," Gérard Pelletier, Jean Marchand, and Pierre Trudeau, who came to the federal government from Québec in 1965, played a significant role in the federal-provincial relations in the areas of accommodation and devolution, which had been slowly emerging in Canadian politics. Following the defeat of Diefenbaker, Robert Stanfield, Member of Parliament (MP) for Halifax, Nova Scotia, became the leader of the Conservatives in 1967. Having reviewed the changing political dynamism in Québec, he sought more significant participation of all Canadians. He took a new approach to deal with the 1968 election platform - the "two nations" concept and its more excellent accommodation with the Canadian federation.

Again, all through the 1960s, the federal government was under a lot of pressure from the government of Québec during the administrations of both the Liberal Premier Jean Lesage (1960–1966) and the Union Nationale Premier Daniel Johnson (1966–1968) to make more extraordinary provisions for Québec. By then, the federal government had already established the famous Royal Commission of Bilingualism and Biculturalism (B&B) to accommodate the political realities of Canada along the lines of an equal partnership between the two founding people of Canada. By 1967, Canada was already a jubilant country that had just celebrated its 100th birthday. Over 50 million people came to Montreal's extravaganza of Man and His World, the World Fair EXPO '67.

In April 1968, Pierre Elliott Trudeau, then justice minister, was elected leader of the Liberal Party of Canada, representing a high point in the Canadian political scene. Canadians were dazzled by Trudeau's charm and good looks, and a large fan base was established throughout the country. At that time, Trudeau's popularity was at his zenith. Canada was swept away by a wave of Trudeaumania, an eponym derived from Trudeau's name given in early 1968 before he entered into the leadership of the Liberal Party of Canada. His celebrity-esque position differentiated him from politicians of all other stripes.

Having won a majority government, when Pearson resigned, Trudeau became the fifteenth prime minister on April 22, 1968. Immediately, Trudeau began a period in his office that would last longer than any prime minister before him, except Mackenzie King and Sir John A. Macdonald. It was not until the next election in late 1972 that his popularity declined to a certain extent. The Trudeau administration brought a new vision of Canada—that of a bilingual country that predominated as a solution to the problems of French-English relations in Canada. With Trudeau was Mitchell Sharp, one of the most veteran politicians of the day, as Secretary of State for External Affairs.[1]

Federally, Canada committed to middle-power diplomacy as a member of the Western alliance and to a Canada that would be a fair-minded peace monger and generous aid donor. In the meantime, the Pearsonean internationalism—honest broker, helpful fixer, and Boy Scouts to the world—found its way through international relations.

Politically, in 1971, the two major parties, the Liberal Party of Canada (Liberal) and the Progressive Conservative Party of Canada (PC) dominated national politics with others, e.g., the National Democratic Party (NDP), which grew out of the Co-operative Commonwealth Federation (CCF) in 1961, having only minor political strength. The Liberals were often considered center-left and the Conservative center-right, while the NDP was on the moderate left of the political spectrum. Apart from the Liberal and PC parties, the NDP had a marginal role in federal politics, especially respecting Québec, under the leadership of Tommy Douglas. He called for a federal system in which Québec's relations with Ottawa differed from those of other provinces, in effect, for limited de facto special status. In April 1971, David Lewis became the national NDP Leader. Other minor political parties in the federal scene were the Socialist Credit Party (Socred), more of a regional party from the West, and the Ralliement créditiste du Québec, which had only a few representatives in the House of Commons. The official opposition leader during the period under study (1971) was Conservative Robert Stanfield.

Although by the 1960s, Canada had already earned the prestige of becoming a peacemaker and a conciliator for making impressive strides in the world, a dynamic Trudeau also recognized the importance of adaptation in Canada's foreign policy regarding her geopolitical strategy. The pillars of Canada's foreign policy were (1) sovereignty, (2) independence, (3) collective security, (4) national unity, (5) democracy, (6) human rights, and (7) international aid. By then, more and more Canadians came to see their foreign policy as one that should be humanitarian and donor-oriented. Trudeau demanded a complete reassessment of Canada's shift in foreign policy and its continuing relevance in the fast-changing post-war decades. To this day, this remains an example of Canada's middlepowerism and mediation. This was outlined in the first *White Paper on Foreign Policy,* tabled on June 30, 1970, by Mitchell Sharp, Secretary of State for External Affairs. A review of NATO resulted in overwhelming majority support for NATO, favoring Canada's continued membership.

The new *Foreign Policy for Canadians* underscored two areas: (1) repudiation of the policy of internationalism of former Prime Minister Pearson with a reduction of commitment abroad and placement of greater emphasis on the trade component of foreign policy; and (2) foreign policy shift articulated in the white paper—that there could be no lasting peace in the world without China's cooperation. Considering the juxtaposition of world powers and the importance of ending Peking's (now Beijing) isolation, Canada sought diplomatic relations with the communist regime to "contribute to bringing China into a more constructive relationship with the world community."[2] Canadian recognition of the People's Republic of China in 1970 was heralded as an extraordinary diplomatic achievement, partly because it was done ahead of the Americans even though the Nixon administration opposed it. Under Trudeau, Canada moved from biculturalism to multiculturalism. Trudeau promised Canadians a "just society" with equality for all within a pluralistic society.

Commonwealth of Nations and Its Activities

The Commonwealth of Nations, formerly the British Commonwealth of Nations (1931–1949), is a voluntary association of sovereign equal states comprising the UK and several of its former dependencies. In 1965, the Commonwealth Secretariat was established in London to coordinate Commonwealth activities. By 1970, it was an international body of service for about thirty-three member countries committed to promoting consultation services, conferences, information dissemination, and coordination of various activities.

The entrance of Pakistan, the world's most significant Muslim power of the time, into the Commonwealth was welcomed by Canada. It was believed that the Commonwealth could play a more substantial role in voicing the

Islamic point of view through Pakistan. Canada and Pakistan established bilateral relations shortly after the creation of Pakistan in 1947. Canada also participated in the UN peacekeeping in the volatile region of Kashmir back in 1949. Again, India was considered the greatest non-Communist nation in Asia and was to remain an example of the most extensive freedom trained in the ways of Western democracy. The opening of Canadian diplomatic missions in Asian and African countries increased contacts with the new Commonwealth countries and "educated" Canadians, who, in turn, influenced and shaped the development of Canadian thinking. Briefly, 1945 to 1957 may be considered the golden age of Canadian diplomacy.

Canada paid severe attention to two events, both of which erupted in 1965—the Rhodesian crisis with the white regime's illegal and unilateral declaration of independence (UDI) and the Indo-Pakistan war over Kashmir. Seeing the bitter relationship between India and Pakistan, Canadian politicians were concerned about the long-term future relationship between the two sister countries. "It is hoped that the peoples of India and Pakistan, like the people of Canada, will continue to find the Commonwealth a worthwhile club to which to belong." Thus, Louis St. Laurent, then Secretary of State for External Affairs, observed in 1948, shortly after the 1947 partition of India concerning the two Commonwealth sisters.[3] Again, state visits of Pakistan's Prime Minister Liakat Ali Khan to Canada in 1950 and Prime Minister Louis St. Laurent to Pakistan strengthened their friendship. Donald Masters, one of the renowned historians of Canada, wrote: "St. Laurent's visit to India, Pakistan, and Ceylon [now Sri Lanka] in February 1954, as part of his world tour, helped to make more cordial Canada's relations with the governments of these Asian countries."[4] Again, in 1970, Canada's friendly relationship with Pakistan was reinforced when Dr. Golam W. Chowdhury, then Pakistan's Minister of Communications, visited Canada as a government guest and discussed with Eric Kierans and Jean-Luc Pepin, Minister of Communications and Minister of Industry, Trade, and Commerce, respectively.

During the period under consideration, there were, however, two irritants. The first one was Canada's deliberate avoidance of taking sides with the Kashmir issue, much to the displeasure of Pakistan; second, Canada's nuclear power assistance to India, which Pakistan saw as contributing to India's nuclear weapons capability, and, therefore, to India's overall military potential.[5] Canada's relationship with Pakistan, however, grew stronger with time. As far as India and Pakistan were concerned regarding Canada's relationship, Canada pursued the notion of *mutatis mutandis*, that is, parallel policies toward the two Commonwealth sisters. One might call it an unofficial doctrine of parallelism, although India and Pakistan never improved their relationships with each other.

Establishing the Commonwealth Fund for Technical Cooperation in 1971 was the most important step the Commonwealth took. India and Pakistan were to receive a large part of the Commonwealth Assistance to raise their farming standards, health, education, and scholarship in technical cooperation. Again, in 1971, John Small, Canada's high commissioner to Pakistan, laid the cornerstone of the satellite station built by the Royal Canadian Airforce and funded by a Canadian soft loan.[6] Following the agreement between Pakistan and the International Atomic Energy Agency (IAEA) on the issue of nuclear safeguards, the completed project was officially inaugurated in January 1971.

Colombo Plan

Colombo Plan for Co-operative Economic Development in South and Southeast Asia was established following a January 1950 meeting of foreign ministers in Colombo, Ceylon (now Sri Lanka), with a framework for international cooperation with the following objectives: (1) to attack the poverty upon which communist political movements in Asia were thought to feed; (2) to promote technical cooperation and assist in the transfer of technology among member countries; as well as (3) to keep under review relevant information on technical cooperation between the member governments, multilateral and other agencies to accelerate development.

Canada's strong desire to extend assistance is evident in the 1951 *Speech from the Throne* debate. Initially confined to the Commonwealth countries of India, Pakistan, Sri Lanka, Australia, New Zealand, the UK, and Canada, its membership soon widened to include most other South and Southeast Asian countries and the US as the largest donor. In 1955, the *Globe and Mail* wrote: "The Colombo Plan by its very nature is not dramatic or subject to sensational headlines, but it can show a record of steady and gratifying progress in promoting human goodwill."[7] Briefly, Canada's positive economic assistance to India and Pakistan made the two sister countries of the Commonwealth grateful to Canada. India showed her gratitude by naming the Canada-funded dam the *"Canada Dam."* In contrast, Pakistan's gratitude was evident in naming the Canada-funded dam at Warsak as the *"Maple Leaf Dam."*

Trade with Pakistan and Joint Projects

Historically, Canadian representation in Pakistan began with the opening of a trade commissioner's office in Karachi in 1947, when Pakistan was born. The first high commissioner was appointed in 1950. Canadian aid to Pakistan started in 1950 and has been sizable ever since. By 1970, Canadian trade with Pakistan amounted to approximately $65.7 million.[8] Imports came to $9.9 million, of which about $5 million came from East Pakistan. The imports consist almost exclusively of raw and processed jute products, representing 70 percent of Canadian imports. Exports amounted to $55.8 million, of which about $20 million went to East Pakistan[9].

Earlier, the natural disaster of East Pakistan in November 1970 also brought the Canadian government and its agencies together since both groups appealed for help. The Canadian food aid allocation of $4 million in 1970-71 was increased to $7.5 million because of the cyclone in East Pakistan, and another $7 million in loans supported the purchase of equipment for tube-healthy irrigation schemes.[10] Again, by 1970, in West Pakistan, the Kanupp Nuclear Generating Plant near Karachi, a $52 million project that started in 1965, had been financed jointly by the Export Development Corporation (EDC) and Canadian International Development Agency (CIDA). The project was soon operational, completing the Warsak Dam and the Sukkur Thermal Plant in a trio of electricity-generating stations spaced down West Pakistan. In January 1971, Prime Minister Trudeau officially opened a Canada Deuterium Uranium (CANDU) nuclear power reactor in Pakistan.

Paul Gérin-Lajoie, CIDA's president, remained busy traveling across Canada to raise awareness among Canadians about the gap in the third world between the poorest and the wealthiest countries. He saw 1971 as a year "marked by disaster and human suffering on a great scale."[11] As early as January 1971, Canada had already shipped 3,000 tons of relief supplies to Chittagong, East Pakistan, to help an estimated 22,000 cyclone and tidal wave victims.[12] In March 1971, Canada's development assistance to Pakistan, which commenced in 1951, had totaled $359 million.[13]

Religious Missionaries in the Indian Subcontinent and Canadian Expatriates in Pakistan

Canada's linkage with the subcontinent dates back to the early 1900s through the religious missionaries who went to India as representatives of the Holy Cross Brothers and Sisters and the Jesuits. The earliest trace of the Canadian Holy Cross Order in the Indian subcontinent, including the state of Bengal, dates to the 1920s. The missionaries remained busy assisting the locals in dispensaries, orphanages, schools, crèches, hospitals, refugees, widows, and abandoned mothers. Canadian Holy Cross Sisters, in particular, had provided young girls training as nurses' aides and some as midwives in dealing with different health issues and raising awareness of illiterate villagers. To help stop mortal epidemics, especially cholera and smallpox, the Holy Cross Sisters also gave classes on hygiene, nutrition, sanitation, cleanliness, etc.

There were no Canadian Jesuits in Pakistan in 1971, nor are there any at present. Nevertheless, they were and still are in the mountainous Buddhist kingdom of Bhutan, Nepal, and the northern Indian city of Darjeeling, only 15 kilometers away from East Pakistan. In Chapter 5, we shall see how the Canadian religious missionaries of the Holy Cross Order and Canadian Jesuits of the Darjeeling District of West Bengal, India, instantly came forward to aid the Bengali refugees.

The work of the Canadian missionaries, whether in India or Pakistan, was primarily in the service of faith and promotion of justice. It also involved indigenizing the local church by supporting specific pastoral work and projects, primarily on sustainable religious and community development through education.

In addition to Canadian missionaries, there were approximately 200 Canadians who lived in East Pakistan during the beginning of 1971 employed mainly by Acres International of Niagara Falls, W. P. London Construction of Niagara Falls, and Pelletier Engineering of Montreal as engineers, hydrologists, and technicians who worked on transmission lines. There were also a few employees of CIDA assigned to train Pakistanis on how to operate power lines built with Canadian aid.

Relationship between Canada and Québec

French Canada's struggle regarding identity had begun long before the British conquest of 1759. By then, the people of New France had already started to consider them a distinct national group. Despite the centralized policy of the French monarchy and the absolutism of French state institutions imposed on New France, the concept of a distinctive *Canadien* nation had been growing over the years. The British policies of assimilation introduced by the conquerors mainly to serve their own "national" interests did not seem to work. Instead, the spirit of a "distinct" national identity that remained at work led to the idea of an independent French-speaking state in North America has emerged as a clear and influential political objective.[14]

French-Canada's dream of "une nation Canadienne," a sovereign French-speaking state in North America, and the political realities of sharing power with the federal government goes as far back as the time of Confederation (1867) and the years following it. Leaders like Louis Riel (1844–1885, founder of the province of Manitoba and a political leader of the Métis people of the Canadian prairies), Louis-Joseph Papineau (1786–1871, leader of the reformist Patriote Movement before the Lower Canada Rebellion of 1837–1838), Honoré Mercier (1840–1894; ninth Premier of Québec, 1887–1891, as the leader of the Parti Nationale or Québec Liberal Party), Henri Bourassa (1868–1952, outspoken French Canadian political leader), Lionel Groulx (1878–1967; Canadian Roman Catholic priest, historian, and Québec nationalist), and René Lévesque (1922–1987, a reporter, a minister of the government of Québec, 1960–1966, founder of the Parti Québecois political party and Premier of Québec, from 1976 to 1985) had persistently raised the issue of French realities in Canada; their choices and options ran from equal sharing of power to decision-making. The demand for equality and greater participation had been a familiar theme in Canada.

Since the 1960s, the winds of change became noticeable everywhere in Québec—a change to take more direct control over health care and education, which had previously been in the hands of the Roman Catholic Church. When, following the death of Union Nationale party leader Conservative Premier Maurice Duplessis (1936–1939; 1944–1959), Jean Lesage (1960–1966) immediately became the premier of Québec, the thrust of Canadian politics manifested a spirit of independence and self-assertiveness. Lesage moved forward quickly with his nationalistic agenda, preaching a belief deeply embedded in the subconscious minds of French Canadians since the days of Riel and Honoré. It also meant expanded public service, massive investments in the public education system, and a more robust provincial infrastructure with a new middle class battling for greater control over Québec's economic resources.

Lesage openly talked about his strategies to end what he called "economic colonialism" in Québec, having begun to cherish the notion that the government of Québec was the national government of French Canadians—something that led them to refer to themselves as *Québecois*. At the same time, Québec was the fatherland of French Canadians. The Tremblay Commission's four-volume report (1956)[15] supported the view that the federal government was a creation of the provinces and that the role of the political regime of 1867 was to establish a framework within which English and French communities could live in a federal state. It called for greater provincial autonomy, proposing that social programs be under provincial jurisdiction, implying Canada be a country of two people, which had been the wish and aim of the Fathers of Confederation.

Lesage expanded and resurrected the Tremblay Commission, calling it *Un Québec dort dans une nouvelle Confédération* (A strong Québec in a new Confederation) that highlighted two key concepts: (1) French Canadians could not accept greater centralization as this would result in the reduction of the amount of self-government that the community had. It was feared that a continuation of this would put the fate of French Canadians more and more in the hands of a government that would express the sentiments of English Canadians; (2) the task of developing the French-Canadian nation required not only the retention of such powers as had been granted to Québec in 1867 but the enlargement of that self-government. The Lesage government demanded a special status for Québec. A confident Lesage was surrounded by the most critical and influential cabinet ministers of the day. They were Eric Kierans, René Lévesque, Pierre Laporte, Georges-Emile Laplame, and Paul-Gérin Lajoie. Provincially, the Liberals came out with a catchy nationalistic slogan, such as *"Maîtres-chez-nous"* (Masters in our own house), and drew the undivided attention of the Québecois under Lesage's charismatic leadership.

The Lesage years (1960–1966) coincided with what came to be called the *Révolution tranquille* (Quiet Revolution) in Québec's history. The story of the Quiet Revolution of Québec, which was a period of unbridled economic and social development in Québec, soon began to appear in the day-to-day conversation of the people of Québec. Lesage became so popular in Québec that even though Lesage's predecessor, Premier Duplessis, had made tremendous progress from the late 1940s to the time of Lesage's assumption of power in 1960, his legacy became questionable. Despite many accomplishments, Duplessis's reign was criticized as La Grande Noirceur (The Great Darkness). During the later years of Lesage's reign, Québec experienced rapid modernization and the rise of new French nationalism that crystallized in the formation of *Le Partie Québecois* in 1968, two years after the end of Lesage's years.

In the meantime, federally, the Pearson government (1963–1968) made many attempts to accommodate the demands of the Québec governments. Since it was always a minority government, its strength and political position depended largely on solid (Liberal) support from Québec. It was a period of intense socio-political and socio-cultural change, primarily in the province of Québec, characterized by the effective secularization of society, the creation of a welfare state, and the alignment of politics between Québec and the federal government. Major Liberal initiatives of the 1960s fell under the Pearson administration (1963–1968) and the Trudeau administration (1968–1979; 1980–1984). In 1967 alone, two grand celebrations, the Expo 1967 and the celebration of Canada's centenary in 1967, that we have alluded to already, generated euphoria and a feeling of self-assertiveness among both the English Canadians across Canada as well as the French Canadians in Québec.

Again, around this time, the Union Nationale Chief, Daniel Johnson (1966–1968), also came up with a much-talked-about book titled *Égalité ou Indépendance* (*Equality or Independence*), which was a product of his vision of a future Québec. His argument was so strong that he warned that if the federal government did not respond with positive measures, the independence of Québec would be inevitable. In no uncertain terms, without using the word "separatism," Johnson argued that the choice for the federal government was between "equality within Canada" and "independence." Despite every effort by the federal government, the relationships between the governments of Canada and Québec remained strained during the 1960s as the Québec leaders continued to push the envelope for autonomy and separation if need be. Having refused federal initiatives in provincial matters, the Lesage and Johnson governments implemented their programs.

In the late 1960s, Canada also began to experience challenges as many francophone countries started to deal directly with the government of Québec, having ignored the federal government, as though Québec was an independent country. In March 1971, an enraged Ottawa was pushed to the hilt when the tiny African Republic of Gabon government invited Québec to a conference of ministers of education of French-speaking states mainly in Africa, except that France was included in the invitation. Gabon did not even bother to discuss the matter with Canada's federal government. Instead, Gabon dealt directly with the provincial government. For the federal government, all the previous worries were replaced by a dominant and disturbing crisis: the thought of a separate Québec outside the fabric of the Canadian Confederation. Ottawa officials, being infuriated, were bent out of shape to learn that the initial conference was held in Libreville, Gabon, in February 1968. This led to the suspension of Canada's diplomatic relations with Gabon. When the same meeting was resumed in Paris two months later in April, much to Canada's conniption, Canada was unsuccessful even though she solicited an invitation informally. Unsurprisingly, therefore, Canada's relationship with France became imponderable. A courageous Trudeau, having disregarded the usual diplomatic niceties, gave France a stern warning: "If France were ever to do that, invite a Province to sit at a conference as an independent state, in such a case, we would have to treat France as we treated Gabon."[16]

Similar situations also arose on two other occasions when President Mobutu Sese Seko Kuku Ng bendu wa Za Banga of the Democratic Republic of Congo (later named Zaire in 1971) invited Canada to the Kinsha conference without inviting Québec at the same time. This was, however, handled by the Québec veterans, such as Marc Lalonde and Claude Morin, who decided with the Québec delegation to represent what they called the "Québec-Canada" team. Again, when President Hamani Diori of the Republic of Niger, evidently under the influence of France, invited Québec but not Canada to Niamey, Ottawa had to find ways to deal with such sensitive issues.

The federal government, however, did not wish to relinquish some of its fiscal powers without opposing strong resistance since not all Canadians were on the same page with the concept of Québec as the homeland of all French Canadians. At that time, many English Canadians were opposed to the idea that Québec was the home of French Canadians, and they argued that, to have a strong and united Canada, ideally, all of Canada should be the home of French Canadians. There were accusations and counteraccusations among federalists and separatists who found themselves at loggerheads. Premier Johnson confronted then Justice Minister Pierre Trudeau, whom he accused of being "backward" and having "retrograde attitudes"[17] toward French Canada.

A straightforward Trudeau, who plunged onto a roller-coaster ride of great peaks of popularity, firmly stated that the federal government would not condone or accept Premier Johnson's attempt to redefine Canada. He characterized Johnson as a politician "more interested in power for himself than rights for French Canadians."[18] Despite the federal Liberal's focus on issues identified by Québec to become equal partners in the Confederation, Québecers remained frustrated. They looked upon federal initiatives with a grain of salt. A strong federalist, Trudeau remained firm in his determination to ensure that Québec stayed in Canada. He demonstrated how the French-speaking ministers played a significant role in the federal scene, having various portfolios. Such thinking led to developing and enacting the *Official Languages Act (1969),* a central feature of Trudeau's new federation.

Amid uncertainties, frustrations, and pessimism, in the Québec election of 1970, Robert Bourassa got elected to be the premier of Québec with a commitment to achieving a place for Québec in a federal Canada, giving Ottawa the confidence necessary for a new approach. Bourassa's victory in Québec in 1970 created a new way of looking at Québec separatism, which caused the people of Canada anxiety and goosebumps. Nevertheless, with Bourassa in charge of Québec, there was also a sigh of relief across the country, at least for some time.

At that time, the term "state of Québec" became fashionable among Québec politicians, historians, and social scientists when they talked about Québec's "particular status" within the Canadian Confederation. Also, terms like "associate state," "two nations theory," "sovereignty-association," etc. surfaced as catchphrases along with the appearance of many provincial nationalist parties. They were Rassemblent pour l'independance nationale; Raillement Nationale; Front de libération du Québec (FLQ); l'Armee revolutionnaire du Québec; l'Armee de libération du Québec; Partie Republicain du Québec (which later became Front Republicain pour l'independance); and Partie Québecois (being founded by René Levésque with the avowed purpose of taking Québec out of Confederation) that made demands on their respective aspirations. Again, stories of mailbox bombing and Québec guerillas being trained in Cuba, Algeria, and various other Arab countries were a source of concern to Ottawa.

The rise of nationalism in Québec among Québecois was triggered more intensely since the French Republic's President Charles de Gaulle's infamous visit to Québec on July 24, 1967, when he uttered the words from the balcony of Montreal City Hall, "Vive le Québec libre [Long live free Québec]." It was as though he instantly seemed to have hit the rallying cry of the Québec separatists. Being unprepared to hear such a provocative call, Ottawa officials became highly uncomfortable with the event. The French president was immediately advised that he was not welcome to Ottawa as his speeches were not at all acceptable to the government of Canada. Prime Minister Pearson rebuked de Gaulle with an official statement on national television: "The people of Canada are free. Every province in Canada is free. Canadians don't need to be liberated."[19] De Gaulle returned to France without meeting federal representatives. Canada's relationship with France began to strain. Indeed, from that time on, President de Gaulle was known to have waged a verbal war on Canada.

In the post–De–Gaulle era, when Georges Pompidou was France's president, Canada became interested in rebuilding Franco-Canadian relations to what had existed before that incident. Ottawa suspected that Gaullist forces in the Pompidou administration were still sympathetic to the cause of the Québec independence movement. Canada's relationship began to get strained again when she became aware that the French government had been encouraging the government of Québec to seek international standing, particularly in the field of culture and education. Since the French government was involved in dealing with the government of Québec without following the diplomatic protocols, Canada's relationship with France began to get even worse. Trudeau observed unequally: "There is one way to keep Canada united, and that is to make sure Canada speaks with one voice in the world…The federal government will not attempt to carve out an interpretive role without ensuring the federal government's consent."[20]

In 1971, Trudeau was also occupied with one of the most significant challenges of his time - the Conference of First Ministers, held in June 1971 in Victoria, British Columbia, on the 100th anniversary of British Columbia's entry into Confederation (1867). Although the prime minister and the provincial premiers agreed to negotiate the conditions for the "patriation" of Canada's Constitution, the British North American Act (BNA) from Westminster in Britain, Trudeau's efforts brought no fruition. Having made amendments to the Constitution, the provincial premiers who drew up the Victoria Charter, Constitutional Reform, and Québec in 1971 seemed promising to build and strengthen capacity. Down the road, it was rejected by the Québec Cabinet—something that remains to this day as a reminder of Canada's ongoing issues with Québec.

Therefore, Québec's role in the Canadian Confederation had been demanding. French Québec's theory that Canada is composed of two equal "founding peoples," "English and French," had complicated the matter. Among other things, their demand that the Constitution recognize the duality of this phenomenon and make it real and functional became a challenge. The dramatic changes in the notion of self-identity that had also occurred within Québec, which both underlie and fuel support for sovereignty, were very aggravating for the federal government. Over the years, the Francophone Québecers' sense of self-identity had also gradually shifted. From being "Canadiens (Canadian)" until the end of the First World War to "Canadiens-Français (French Canadians)," then, until the mid-1960s, the French-speaking Canadians saw the English Canadians (*les Anglais*) as distinct from them (French Canadians). Again, from the late 1960s, Québec Francophones also began to identify themselves as "Québecois (the people of Québec.)" It was as though the word "province" disappeared from the vocabulary of the Québecois who began to refer to their province as "L'Etat du Québec" (the State of Québec).

Other than the separation of Québec, there were also a few more immediate issues, such as constitutional reform, Western alienation, or free trade with the US, that were deemed urgent public issues. There was also another issue—the demands by the natives in Canada for their land, greater autonomy, and even self-government. They argue that they had been there from the beginning of Canada's life. In reality, although the federal government was aware of the concerns of the native people that had been a source of discontent, this was still on the back burner. The issue regarding Aboriginal rights had never been high on the government's political agenda until recently. The demands of natives for land began to receive much attention from the federal government only around 1971.

FLQ (Front de libération du Québec) Crisis of 1970/October Crisis

The FLQ, a separatist/terrorist and paramilitary group in Québec, was founded in 1963. With its goal to achieve the independence of Québec by resorting to terrorism, if necessary, the FLQ rapidly developed into the most severe terrorist group that carried out its activities on Canadian soil. Also known as the October Crisis, the movement was financed mainly by bank robberies. Those involved usually threatened the public through their official communication organ, *La Cognée*. Between 1963 and 1970, the FLQ conducted several attacks, which totaled over 160 violent incidents and killed eight people and injured many more. Specifically, it was a series of events triggered by two terrorist kidnappings within a week of James Cross, the British trade commissioner in Montreal, and Pierre Laporte, Québec's minister of immigration and labour, by members of the said Québec nationalist terrorist group. It began on October 5, 1970.

Canadians watched with alarm how rapidly the situation had been deteriorating. And yet, amid a frightening environment, on October 15, 1970, three thousand people gathered at Paul Sauvé Arena in Montreal to show their passionate support for the FLQ's agenda for separation triggered by the FLQ's lawyer, Robert Lemieux, known for his fiery speeches on nationalism. Canadians recalled the activities of the FLQ and other terrorist groups that had been successfully spreading fear from the time of international events, such as the royal visit of 1964 and Charles de Gaulle's tour of Canada in 1967.

However, by the time the military takeover took place in East Pakistan, five months had already passed since the FLQ crisis. The federal government had no strategy in place even at that time. Ottawa was also aware that the two Québec provincial governments, the Liberal Party of Jean Lesage (1960–1966) and the Union Nationale of Daniel Johnson (1966–1968), had discarded the idea of a separate sovereign Québec. Nevertheless, the federal government remained deeply concerned despite its knowledge that, historically speaking, there was a lack of effective leadership with the separation movement in Québec, as pointed out by Meherunnisa Ali.[21] Even René Lévesque, leader of Le Partie Québecois, maintained that his party was not on the same page about language and violence back in 1968.

In any event, the tempestuous events surrounding the FLQ crisis and its fallout kept haunting Ottawa officials, partly due to the protracted trial of the defiant Paul Rose, a Québécois nationalist who admitted responsibility for the kidnapping but not for the murder of Québec's minister of immigration and labour, Pierre Laporte. The trepidation on Ottawa's part was so intense that Ottawa was inclined to believe that, with Québec's secession, the glue of federalism would be gone. Ottawa officials were so worried that they could not even imagine what would happen if the rich provinces, such as British Columbia, Alberta, and Ontario, decided to subsidize no longer the poorer provinces, such as Newfoundland, Nova Scotia, and Manitoba. The Cabinet was resolute in downplaying all hints of the danger of disunity. A courageous Trudeau urgently needed to suppress the separatists for good.

The War Measures Act (WMA)

On October 16, 1970, the Governor-General in Council approved the proclamation of the War Measures Act (WMA) "concerning a state of apprehended insurrection."[22] Under the increased powers of arrest granted by the WMA, ordinary liberties were suspended, and arrests and detentions were authorized and prolonged without any charge or the right to see a lawyer. The FLQ was outlawed, making its membership a criminal act. The military deployment and control by the government of Québec gave every appearance that martial law had been imposed. Within hours, over 450 persons were detained in Québec, most of whom were eventually released without the laying or hearing of charges. The troops in the Québec bases and elsewhere in the country were dispatched under the direction of the Sûreté du Québec (Québec's provincial police force) to guard vulnerable points as well as prominent individuals at risk. It was the first time in Canadian history that an act of such nature was used during peacetime.

Just two days following the invocation of the WMA, Québec Immigration and Labour Minister Pierre Laporte was strangled to death. His body was found dead on October 18, 1970. It was the first political assassination in Canada since the murder of Thomas D'Arcy McGee (1825–1868), a member of Parliament, a Catholic spokesman, a journalist, a poet, and a Father of the Canadian Confederation. Upon hearing the savage execution of his colleague Laporte, and in a desperate bid to keep his people calm, Premier Bourassa stated that Laporte was a victim of "a hatred, a criminal hatred" and continued to appeal for solidarity among Québecers to overcome "this crisis."[23] Federally, Trudeau reassured fellow Canadians: "Canada remains one of the most wholesome and humane lands on this earth. If we stand firm, this current situation will soon pass. We will be able to say proudly, as we have for decades, that within Canada, there is ample room for opposition and dissent, but none for intimidation and terror."[24] For Trudeau, a lifelong champion of individual rights, it was a defining moment.

Telegrams began arriving at the prime minister's office at that time, giving him strong support for the government's decision to invoke the act. Yet, the WMA also raised the ire of many civil rights activists. Québec nationalists and civil libertarians criticized Trudeau as excessive. The WMA repealed and replaced the more limited Emergencies Act in 1988.

However, the Opinion Polls later showed overwhelming support in Québec for the WMA. Now, years later, supporters of the respondents claim that the disappearance of terrorism in Québec is evidence of its success. At the same time, it is also maintained that the disappearance might be equally attributed to the public distaste for political terror and the steady growth of the democratic separatist movement in the 1970s, which led to the election victory of a Parti Québecois (PQ) government five years later, in 1976.

To sum up, in 1971, Canada's three most important challenges were (1) modernizing the nation, (2) thwarting the threat of Québec separation, and (3) distinguishing Canada from the United States. Trudeau was considered a transformative leader who was expected to rejuvenate the nation and keep up with the idealistic hopes and aspirations of the people of Canada at the time.

Pakistan's Political Landscape

Geography, Language, and Earlier Political Development

From 1857 until 1947, the countries now known as Pakistan, Myanmar (previously Burma), India, and Sri Lanka (previously Ceylon) were all part of the British Empire known as British India. The formal independence came to four Asian states when the British Parliament passed three independence acts, titled the *India Independence Act* (1947), which set up the separate dominions of India and Pakistan; the *Ceylon Independence Act* (1947); and the *Burma Independence Act* (1947). Specifically, Pakistan, as a sovereign state, received its independence on August 14, 1947.

The two wings of Pakistan, East and West, were separated by 2,208 kilometers (1,372 miles) of Indian territory and sea. There was no direct route between East and West Pakistan. There were two indirect routes—the sea route via Colombo (Sri Lanka) and the air corridor over India. It used to take 2.45 hours to arrive from one wing of Pakistan to another. East and West Pakistan were united under a single political authority when the partition of India was agreed upon following a sudden outburst of communal riot. Comprising a total area of 365,529 square miles, Pakistan was thus made up of two unequal regions comprising two wings and five provinces. Physically speaking, Pakistan was unique in its geographical dimension.

East Pakistan sat astride the delta region formed by the mighty rivers Ganges and Brahmaputra. It is primarily low-lying flat land, a mass of islands and waterways near the sea. It consisted of the eastern half of Bengal Province, a portion of Assam, and the tribal areas of the Chittagong Hill Tracts being separated from West Pakistan by 2,208 kilometers of India and sea. From the beginning of its creation, West Pakistan's composition had been problematic—it included Sind, Northwest Frontier, Baluchistan Agency, Punjab, and the small princely states of Amb, Bahawalpur, Chitral, Dir, Kahan, Las Bela, Markan, and Swat. Certain Pathan tribes also swore allegiance to the new government. The central government was in Karachi. Eventually, however, all these areas, except for Chitral and Swat, were merged into four provinces: Baluchistan, North-West Frontier, Sind, and Punjab. Based on the various ethnic and linguistic identities of the Provinces, Pakistan became a multi-ethnic nation.

While Pakistan was born in 1947 as the Dominion of Pakistan, on March 23, 1956, Pakistan's first constitutions were promulgated, and the Dominion of Pakistan became the Islamic Republic of Pakistan. Again, on October 27, 1958, the country was taken over by General Muhammed Ayub Khan. He promulgated Pakistan's constitution on March 1, 1962, as the Constitution of the Republic of Pakistan survived for twenty-four years as a separate country consisting of East and West Pakistan. For convenience, the twenty-four years' life of a united Pakistan, following its independence in August 1947, may roughly be divided into three periods: (1) the parliamentary period (1947–1958); (2) the Ayub Khan era (1958–1969); and (3) the Yahya Khan period (1969–1971).

In terms of its size, the eastern wing consisted of the Province of East Pakistan (55,126 square miles), which was only one-sixth of the size of the entire West Pakistan, while the western wing, or West Pakistan (310,403 square miles), consisted of the above-mentioned four provinces.

According to the 1961 Census, the latest available at that time, the population density per square mile in 1971 was about 143 persons in West Pakistan and about 933 in East Pakistan. In West Pakistan, the people belonged to several ethnic and linguistic groups whose major languages were Urdu, Punjabi, Baluchi, Sindhi, and Pushto. At the same time, in East Pakistan, the vast majority, almost 95 percent, spoke one language - *Bangla* (Bengali). Here is a short breakdown of the languages spoken in Pakistan in 1971:

Bengali ----------------54.6 percent
Punjabi ----------------28.4 percent
Urdu ------------------7.2 percent
Sindhi ----------------5.8 percent
Pushto-----------------7.1 percent
English----------------1.8 percent[25]

Although West Pakistan had 80 percent of Pakistan's total area, East Pakistan's 75 million people constituted 56 percent of the people of Pakistan. In addition, 56 percent of the people of Pakistan who lived in East Pakistan were culturally and linguistically different from the 44 percent of Pakistanis who lived in the four provinces of West Pakistan. In Canadian terms, back in 1971, East Pakistan was slightly larger than Newfoundland and had a population of approximately 75 million; West Pakistan was smaller than British Columbia and had a population of roughly 44 percent. Pakistan's geographic and linguistic absurdities were often seen as impediments to national integration since the linguistic cleavage reinforced the geographic split of Pakistan.

Back in 1947, it was argued that Pakistan was founded as a refuge for the Muslims of British India. It did not turn out to be the "dream country" where parliamentary democracy with guaranteed consolidated rights was envisioned to prevail. A military dictatorship replaced the democratic means, which brought Pakistan into being. The non-Bengalis in East Pakistan, too, felt increasingly threatened and less hospitable in a country (or the province) they chose to opt for.

With no clear explanation to the people of Pakistan, the central government arbitrarily declared Urdu as the state language of Pakistan when Urdu was spoken by only 3.4 percent of the country's total population, or, in other words, 7.1 percent of the West Pakistani population. At that time,

Bengali was spoken by 64.6 percent of the total population of Pakistan and Urdu by only 7.2 percent. From the beginning, the Bengali-speaking East Pakistanis suspected the central government's Urdu-controlled bureaucracy was trying to impose Urdu, having ignored Bengali, the language of the numerical majority in Pakistan. Therefore, the issue of Pakistan's national language triggered a widespread linguistic-nationalistic movement in East Pakistan. This was led by students, intellectuals, and professionals supported by the masses.

In early 1952, the Bengalis of all spheres of life started to protest vehemently with all their might, even though the government had outlawed public meetings and rallies. Having defied the law, the students at Dhaka University, affiliated colleges, and other political activists organized mass demonstrations on February 21, 1952. While the demonstration was on, the police on duty killed several student demonstrators. This single incident provoked widespread civil unrest and discontent across East Pakistan.[26] Within days, the East Pakistani Bengalis immediately constructed the *Shaheed Minar*[27] monument in the heart of Dhaka near the Medical College in memory of the movement and its victims.

While the Urdu-Bengali controversy remained, the Bengali nationalists continued raising their voices in protest demonstrations, still demanding recognition of Bangla as the state language. To the Bengalis, their language became a leading symbol of Bengali nationalism and emancipation. They continued to oppose the imposition of Urdu as the state language of Pakistan, claiming that a different language was being "rammed down people's throats" by the insensitive central government at the cost of their mother tongue. Despite the rumblings of discontent of the Bengalis, the Muslim League, which had both non-Bengali and Bengali membership, was committed to guarding its position that Urdu ought to be the lingua franca of the new Muslim nation, Pakistan, as opposed to Bangla.

The central government failed to appreciate that, to the Bengalis, their language, *Bangla*, is the *sine qua non* of their national identity. Having ignored the legitimate demand of the Bengalis, the central government tried to come up with initiatives, such as the one that was characterized by the Islamization of East Pakistani culture and the Arabicization of the Bengali language. Taking just the opposite view, the Bengalis made it clear that they would never lose their fundamental language rights. A determined central government, however, continued to use Urdu as the state language, which it argued is distinctive for Muslims. The All-Parties Action Committee, comprising representatives of the opposition, such as the Awami League, Tamaddun Majlis, Islamic Brotherhood, Youth League, student bodies of Dhaka University, and various affiliated colleges, however, continued to demand Bangla in state affairs.

By the time the Bengalis geared up for the 1954 elections, they had nothing but bitterness against the central government for its anti-Bengali position. They were resolved to see the end of the Muslim League rule. The 1954 provincial election in East Pakistan resulted in a crushing defeat of the Muslim League by the United Front, principally led by the *Krishak Sramik* (Worker and Peasant) Party of Sher-e-Bangla (Tiger of Bengal), Abul Kashem Fazlul Huq, the former premier of Bengal.[28] Interestingly, while India took two and a half years to devise a fundamental law, Pakistan was ruled for nine long years under Britain's colonial law for its inability to agree on a constitutional document. The Constitution of 1954 was never put into effect by Governor-General Ghulam Muhammad, who dissolved the first constituent assembly to be held on essentially the same indirect basis as those of July 1946 in pre-partitioned India. A constitutional order was never established in Pakistan.

In the meantime, four years later, following the 1952 language movement, the central government relented and granted official status to the Bangla (Bengali) language in 1956, making it one of the state languages of Pakistan. Urdu and Bangla thus became Pakistan's official languages.[29] Nevertheless, looking back, undoubtedly, the central government's denial of Bengali as one of the country's official languages remained in the minds of the Bengalis as a sort of "original sin."

Pakistan's first constitution, adopted in 1956, divided Pakistan into East and West Pakistan (the two parts were popularly referred to as the eastern and western "wing" of Pakistan). The three provinces of West Pakistan were constituted as "One Unit"[30] for representation in the National Assembly; Baluchistan, also a part of West Pakistan, was later made a fourth province, becoming part of the One Unit. The 1956 Constitution lasted only for two years.

During 1956–1957, the Awami League (AL) leader Huseyn Shaheed Suhrawardy also served as the prime minister of Pakistan in the Awami-Republican cabinet of the central government. By this time, the AL, however, had demonstrated its success in politicizing the masses. The history of Pakistan reveals that democracy was never allowed to function. Regrettably, the creator of Pakistan, Muhammad Ali Jinnah, died unattended and uncared for. Liaquat Ali Khan, the first prime minister of Pakistan, was assassinated in a public meeting in Rawalpindi. Within a year, on October 7, 1958, President Iskandar Mirza suddenly dismissed Feroz Khan Noon, then prime minister, having dissolved the Parliament. He immediately proclaimed martial law with General Ayub Khan as chief martial law administrator.

In quick succession, General Ayub ousted Mirza within three weeks and began to assume greater power. It is important to note that the Ayub Era (1958–1969) started and ended with martial law. Immediately upon the assumption of power, Ayub proscribed political activities and the movement of prominent politicians of the country with the Elective Bodies Disqualification Ordinance (EBDO) until January 1, 1967.

Within a year, Ayub introduced his brand of democracy (electoral activity), which he named Basic Democracy. Under the system, local representatives called the Basic Democrats had to be chosen by direct election. This was roughly at the rate of 80,000 in all of Pakistan, 40,000 from each wing. The Basic Democrats were responsible for local administration under Union Councils in rural areas and Union Committees in urban areas. Meanwhile, martial law had continued. Ayub declared his opposition to regionalism and his readiness to enforce his view.

Following the passage of the *Political Parties Act* in 1962, Ayub seized control of the Muslim League, then in disarray, and perpetuated his rule. The 1958 coup by General Ayub served to consolidate a West Pakistani coalition of military, bureaucracy, and economic oligarchy in the interests of West Pakistan and foreign capital based upon the appropriation of resources from East Pakistan. Specifically, Ayub formed a new party out of Muhammed Ali Jinnah's Muslim League and named the party the Pakistan Muslim League (Convention), generally called the PML(C). The remainder of the Muslim League was named the Council Muslim League (CML) under Mian Mumtaz Khan Daulatana, former defense minister of Punjab and chief minister of Punjab. Another faction of the Muslim League that grew out of the CML(Convention) and PML(C) was known as the Pakistan Muslim League (Qayyum) or, more commonly, the PML(Q) under the leadership of Khan Abdul Qayyum Khan, former chief minister of the Frontier Province and a central minister. The party favored a strong central government in Pakistan but less provincial autonomy than the other two Muslim leagues.

In 1964, new polling for Pakistan was held, followed by further presidential and assembly elections in 1965. The AL and other parties formed a coalition, the Combined Opposition Party (COP), to run against Ayub's Muslim League. The COP had no luck, as Ayub came out as the winner in the election. Meanwhile, political agitation started in both wings of Pakistan. Ayub remained resolved in his belief that regionalism in Pakistan was an issue raised only by a handful of self-serving politicians who were there to stir the masses for their gains. Despite Ayub's "Decade of Reforms (1958–1968)," most of the disparities in the studies indicated that the disbursement of resources for development purposes was going to West Pakistan. Simply put, Ayub's rule was characterized by an increasing dependency on East Pakistan for export revenue, although, ironically, East Pakistani Bengalis were excluded from political influence.

Major Grievances of the People of East Pakistan against the Central Government of Pakistan

From the mid-1960s, the Awami League (AL) better articulated the significant grievances. It remains a classic example of how a grassroots political organization was motivated by a deep sense of new "nationalism." Ideologically, Pakistan was promised to become an Islamic Democratic State. Still, the idea was ignored by the country's exclusively non-Bengali West Pakistani rulers, who were replaced by either a combination of engineered democracy or military dictatorship purely by military rulers. The East Pakistanis encountered a spiraling cycle of economic difficulties and political recriminations, leading to individual and collective distrust of the central government. Most Bengalis could not consider the government their own as it primarily consisted of West Pakistani non-Bengalis. In the late 1960s, the Bengalis accounted for only 15 percent of the central government services and less than 10 percent of the defense services. The representation of Bengalis was almost nonexistent in the army's upper echelons and civil services.

As the Trudeau administration came up to speed, it learned how the West had been dominating the East in what many economists call a colonial relationship. Over the years, West Pakistan has been using the foreign exchange earnings from jute to finance development projects in the West while allocating an insignificant amount to the East. Again, as Ottawa saw, the imposition and continuation of martial law was considered by the Bengalis as the institutionalization of the dominance of the West Pakistanis in the military state apparatus. The power was concentrated in the hands of a few military leaders of Pakistan, none of whom were Bengalis, argued the Bengalis.

Having experienced years of systemic discrimination and economic disparities, the Bengalis became mistrustful of the central government regarding their future in Pakistan. Many believed that they had no *locus standi* in the country's politics. That, with the condescending military rulers of West Pakistan, the Bengalis would be destined for further marginalization. Potentially, it was a case of politics of domination or politics of exclusion, argued the Bengalis. The policies adopted by the quasi-military regimes did not take into consideration the demands of the Bengalis, who had been feeling alienated in a united Pakistan. Consequently, the common Bengalis thought they had enough of the central government's hubris—a "we know what's best for you" type of condescending attitude. At that time, Sheikh Mujibur Rahman, leader of the Awami League (AL), appeared to lead his people in a new direction to empower them. The litany of the demands of the Sheikh was not so much about leadership. Still, it was about the whole ball of wax—conceitedness, disproportionate representation, exclusiveness, and the arrogance of the West Pakistani rulers.

The gist of the grievances, as the Bengalis understood, was that realistically, East Pakistan had been the prosperous breadbasket for the small coterie of West Pakistani non-Bengali families. The civil bureaucracy represented by non-Bengalis and the military establishment, again consisting of the West Pakistanis, had turned the more populous East Pakistan into a colonial state market.

Details of the Six-Point Program Platform

The Sheikh's Six-Point Program embodied the following six points:

- The Constitution should provide for a Federation of Pakistan in the true sense based on the Lahore Resolution and a parliamentary form of government based on the supremacy of a directly elected legislature based on universal adult franchise.

- The federal government shall deal with only two subjects: defense and foreign affairs. All residuary subjects will be vested in the federating states.
- There should be two separate, freely convertible currencies for the two wings or one currency with two separate reserve banks to prevent the inter-wing flight of capital.
- The power of taxation and revenue collection shall be vested in the federating units. The federal government will receive a share to meet its financial obligations.
- Economic disparities between the two wings shall disappear through economic, fiscal, and legal reforms.
- A militia or paramilitary force must be created in East Pakistan, which currently has no defense of its own.

Source: http://storyofpakistan.com/awami-leagues-six-point-program

Implicit in the equality-seeking Bengalis' demand was a clear warning to the supercilious central government not to aggravate the predicament. This was to be achieved based on equal and respectful partnership so that no province would remain at the bottom of the economic totem pole if decentralization were done to achieve equality.

Naturally, the Six-Point Program Platform immediately found resonance with the Bengalis. Feelings of deprivation and exploitation by the central government brought the Bengalis closer as a "nation." Having been frustrated with the military rulers, the Bengalis gravitated toward their leader, Mujib, who became a drawing card. He began to gain unprecedented popularity in his province. His followers tried to conjure nifty ideas about the economic future with a substantive measure that would change the bottom line.

Succinctly, the Six-Point Program recognized the value of equity and had a sense of having a stake in a joint enterprise within Pakistan. In the context of Pakistan, the joint enterprise was meant to have a "better life" in a "better society" in a united Pakistan. Political analysts and policy wonks in Pakistan examined the Six-Point Program. They noted how Mujib articulated a defiant political agenda in an attempt to reform the Pakistani polity by decentralizing the power held by the central government and making the provinces more equitable. Unsurprisingly, the Ayub regime quickly reacted negatively by putting Mujib and many of his party workers in jail almost immediately. The Bengalis, however, neither stopped their demands for Mujib's release nor greater autonomy. Between 1966 and 1968, the student movement continued demanding Mujib's release.

More Student Unrest and Agitation in Pakistan

In 1968, the AL leader and several co-workers were implicated in a case of conspiracy when they had already been in jail since the beginning of Mujib's full-fledged campaign for greater autonomy. It was called the *Agartala Conspiracy Case*. The regime maintained its allegation that a plot was hatched in the city of Agartala, in Tripura State in India, in 1967 to ignite an armed revolution against West Pakistan that would result in secession from East Pakistan through an armed uprising by "liberating" through the Indian army's covert support to create an independent Bangladesh. The Ayub government immediately initiated the case against Mujib and thirty-four other Bengali leaders, alleging high treason. Accordingly, a special tribunal was set up to try the alleged conspirators at the Dhaka Cantonment. However, the reality on the ground was very different since the tide was against the government with anti-Ayub agitation in the form of *hartal* (strike) and *gherao* (encirclement) across Pakistan. Though in jail, by then, Mujib had already reached a stage where no obstruction could turn the tide.

The student movement that started earlier soon engulfed the whole of East Pakistan—peasants, artisans, labourers, and all types of workers joined the movement *en masse*. In January 1969, leaders of the East Pakistan Students Union (EPSU, Menon Group), the East Pakistan Students League, the East Pakistan Students' Union (EPSU, Motia Group), and a section of the National Students' Federation (NSF) formed *Sarbadaliya Chatro Sangram Parishad* (All Parties Students Action Committee, SAC). They declared their 11-Point Program centered around students' demands and the demands relating to the workers' problems in East Pakistan.[31] Most importantly, the SAC endorsed the AL's Six-Point Program (greater provincial autonomy being the key demand) that Mujib floated three years ago.

In the meantime, the opposition's demand for the release of Mujib became so forceful that it immediately stirred up a particular type of "nationalist" passion hitherto unknown. The student community chafed at the heavy-handed rule of the military governments - Ayub himself pathetically watched the rise of the anti-Ayub movement. He tried to strike a deal with the political leaders, especially Mujib, who had become one of the most articulate leaders representing the Bengalis by then. The Round Table Conference (RTC) of leaders convened in February–March 1968 to resolve his government's political impasse failed. It made people aware that the Bengalis were unwilling to accede to any restructuring of power led by the West Pakistani leaders.

The tremendous pressure from the Student Action Committee (SAC) and the chaotic situation in both wings of Pakistan forced Ayub not only to withdraw the Agartala Conspiracy Case against Mujib and his co-defendants but also to step down within months. The public in both wings of Pakistan was overjoyed to see how the popular upsurge of workers, peasants, and students helped Pakistanis achieve not only Ayub's resignation but also the release of Mujib and most political prisoners. The political leaders quickly secured an opportunity to move forward with their respective demands and agendas. Mujib instantly became a hero and a savior. It was time for a celebration as far as the people of Pakistan were concerned. To the people of East Pakistan, hopefully, it was the end of what they believed was "Punjabi imperialism."

In the meantime, the warmth of Mujib's release and euphoria immediately began to reflect across the province. To celebrate the occasion of Mujib's release, the SAC held a reception on February 23, 1969, at the Race Course Maidan (now *Suhrawardy Uddan*) where, amid tens and thousands of assembled people and jubilant students, on behalf of the Bengalis of East Pakistan, Tofail Ahmed, then chairman of SAC, conferred the title of Bongobondhu (Friend of Bengal) to Sheikh Mujib as a mark of gratitude for the hardship and sufferings he had already endured in the struggle for political and economic emancipation of the Bengalis. To set the record straight, according to Dr. Selim Jahan, a renowned economist of Bangladesh, the title Bongobondhu was conceived by Rezaul Haque Chowdhury Mushtaque, then Dhaka College Student League leader. Mushtaque wrote an article in the college magazine proposing the title of Mujib back in 1968. As Tofail Ahmed made the announcement publicly, he is often regarded as the proposer of the title, but this was not the case. From now on, Mujib shall be referred to as Bongobondhu throughout the rest of the book.

On March 25, 1969, General Aga Muhammad Yahya Khan, then commander-in-chief of the armed forces, succeeded Ayub, who had assumed power as Pakistan's chief martial law administrator. Six days later, on April 1, 1969, according to the modus operandi of the government of Pakistan, Yahya began to wear four different hats simultaneously - he was at once (1) president, CMLA (Chief Martial Law Administrator); (2) executive head of the armed forces; (3) supreme commander of the armed forces; and (4) commander-in-chief of the army. Yahya quickly refurbished his public image with a promise of democracy in Pakistan. In his first national broadcast on November 28, 1969, Yahya acknowledged that East Pakistan had suffered from discrimination and that some degree of political and fiscal autonomy was a legitimate demand. Much to Yahya's credit, he made a series of announcements on his major decisions on some outstanding issues. Showing a marked difference from his predecessors, Yahya seemed to have recognized their necessity to the people of Pakistan.

Yahya did not ban any political party. Instead, he immediately promised the people that power would be transferred to the elected representatives following the first-ever National Elections, which would take place on October 5, 1970, to elect National Assembly Members who would then frame a constitution for the country. Martial law restrictions on political activities were relaxed, and political parties were allowed to propagate their views. The immediate reaction of the people of Pakistan was positive. For a while, Yahya's wooing of East Pakistan offered renewed hope that the nation could go on an equal footing.

As the winds of change began to sweep across the province, the Bengalis hoped to be at the leading edge of change in a re-engineered Pakistan. They happily accepted Yahya's speech to the nation, which included two significant changes. First, the "One-Unit" government of West Pakistan to be dissolved and divided into four provinces—Punjab, Sind, Baluchistan, and the Northwest Frontier. The government reverted to the situation before 1955; the new parliamentary body would be based on population and not on "parity" between the two wings—thereby giving East Pakistan a numerical majority of the seats. Second, Yahya also decreed that those elections would be direct and on universal suffrage, "one man, one vote" (i.e., in today's gender-neutral language, it meant "one person, one vote"), to allow the removal of artificial political imbalance between East and West Pakistan resulting in giving a permanent majority to the East Pakistanis in the National Assembly. The Bengalis interpreted Yahya's efforts, in general, as a sincere attempt to redress the wrongs of the past. Nevertheless, deep down, despite Yahya's stated intention to attempt to implement a policy of gradual political liberalization, many suspicious Bengalis saw his assumption to power perhaps as a continuation of the main policy lines of his predecessor, Ayub.

Relaunching of the Six-Point Program

Taking advantage of the release of Bongobondhu and lifting political restrictions, the AL immediately re-launched a vigorous campaign in East Pakistan for greater autonomy, as outlined in its election manifesto. In a burst of colloquially exuberant rhetoric, Bongobondhu continued to lambaste the regime's haughtiness in the treatment of the Bengalis. He traveled across the province and pointed out the central government's discriminatory treatment resulting from stereotyping of the Bengalis. In a typical Mujibean style, he argued that the characteristics of an individual Bengali were attributed to the characteristics of the Bengalis. Wherever he went, he was idolized as though he was in a political theater playing vividly to firsthand witness to the entire province via the television, the radio, and the press.[32]

The disproportionate representation in the armed forces and the fear of diminished status raised serious questions among the Bengalis about the concept of "inclusiveness" and the regime's disregard for instituting redress mechanisms. For Bongobondhu, this meant the endless search for equality or the lessening of inequalities between the two wings of Pakistan through economic development and social change by forging partnerships where the East and West would be co-equals. As a result of a new crusading ideology against the non-Bengali authorities of central Pakistan, Bongobondhu soon began to gain unprecedented popularity by becoming the centre of attraction. His grassroots movement promised to fulfill that long-awaited dream of participatory democracy and a significant shift away from the West Pakistan central government. It embodied a radical change or startling phenomenon in the Pakistani polity to the Bengalis. To put it briefly, the Six-Point Program opened the eyes of the Bengalis.

The demand for greater autonomy did not seem to threaten the military regime for the time being since such demands were neither sudden nor new in the history of Pakistan. The 1954 elections marked the first landmark in the move toward greater autonomy in East Pakistan with the victory of the United Front, which won 97 percent of seats, ultimately defeating the Muslim League that had not only fought for the partition of India but also formed the basis of the unitary Pakistan state. Leaders of various West Pakistan–based parties had raised the issue of autonomy throughout the 1960s. While campaigning for provincial autonomy, Ghulam Murtaza Syed, president of Sind United Front, reminded the central government about its stereotyping of the Sindhis.

Having cautioned the government, he even pointed out that when one speaks for his province, he does not stand in conflict with his country and that "a man must, in the very nature of things, have a special niche in his heart for the piece of land which has given him birth that does not mean that his heart should have no place for his country." [33] He went further: "A Scotchman is known for his love for Scotland, but that does not deter him from laying down his life in the cause of Great Britain."[34] Once Bongobondhu hit the campaign trail, his theme of economic exploitation instantly began to gain momentum, surprising the military authority. Nevertheless, the military authority did not react negatively.

Consumed with a romantic passion and euphoria in their picturesque minds, the Bengalis immediately created a legend out of Bongobondhu, who, they believed, was capable of sublime devotion. Instantly, Bongobondhu became a heroic figure of mythic proportions. It became fashionable to deride the Urdu language and argue along a Bengali renaissance encompassing the idea of a *Shonar Bangla* (Golden Bengal) that Bongobondhu had been discussing. The stress on nationalist iconography was particularly intense at that time. Sniffing the political winds in the province, the public realized that the AL was rightly heading under its super-star leader, who had already emerged as the most inspiring figure in their native land. Everyone was carried away by Bongobondhu's artful rhetoric and mesmerizing personal charm.

And yet, out of the same milieu, there also emerged, not inexplicably, but for historical reasons, a very small or insignificant group of determined Pakistani nationalists of Bengali origin who saw themselves as loyalists or pro-unity group. They were not swayed by Bongobondhu's brand of "nationalism." By not responding to Bongobondhu's call in the same manner and enthusiasm, this group (later called quislings) saw the Mujibites (supporters of Mujib) as being involved only in agitational politics. They considered themselves to be no less patriotic than the rest, having remained adherent to the concept and ideology of the founder of Pakistan, Muhammad Ali Jinnah, who expected the people of Pakistan to embrace the notion of unity, faith, and discipline. Without getting carried away, they found the idea of a breakup of Pakistan unacceptable. To them, the national integrity of Pakistan was the foremost important point in any discourse on democratization in Pakistan. Such opposing political beliefs intensified the ideological rift among the revolutionaries, revisionists, and reformists.

For Bongobondhu, it was a matter of gearing up to be competitive in a global economy to achieve greater social justice in Pakistan. Just as the Québecers were trying to redefine the role of francophone society in Canada, so did Bongobondhu, the future role of the Bengalis in a democratic and reformed Pakistan—democratic through the National Elections and reformed through the implementation of his Six-Point Program. Alternatively, Bongobondhu had another agenda for which he was prepared simultaneously. Like the Québec Premier Jean Lesage years (1969–1966), the thrust of East Pakistani politics under Bongobondhu's leadership manifested a spirit of independence and self-assertiveness. In fact, with the call of *Joy Bangla* (Victory to Bengal), a new state of mind with an enduring impression upon the life and outlook had already emerged among the Bengalis—the irredentists, the petit-bourgeois, intelligentsia, status-seeking business groups, nouveau riches, union leaders, and students alike. Like Lesage, Bongobondhu also moved forward with his nationalistic agenda.

Bongobondhu's passionate appeal to nationalist sentiments soon began to permeate the new Bengali plays, novels, short stories, other art forms, and most homemade music and films in East Pakistan. The Bengalis from all walks of life, such as journalists, influential playwrights, novelists, poets, composers, singers, filmmakers, actors, actresses, and comics, came to rally around under Bongobondhu. Their audiences grew significantly among the rapidly expanding college and university-educated people who, in turn, influenced the average person in the street. It was an emotion-laden call that evoked the spirit of the people of East Pakistan—creative and performing artists, humanities and social sciences intellectuals, media professionals, and provincial civil servants. Peculiarly, it was a noble feeling of "nationalism" that merged with romanticism.

Legal Framework Order (LFO)

The LFO formula was officially issued on March 30, 1970, while the election campaign was underway. As mentioned, it dissolved One Unit in West Pakistan, and the direct ballot replaced the principle of parity. It envisaged the formation of a National Assembly where seats would be allocated to provinces based on their population according to the latest 1961 Census. Accordingly, of 313 members, 169 would come from East Pakistan, 85 from Punjab, 28 from Sind, 19 from North-West Frontier Province, five from Baluchistan, and seven from centrally administered tribal areas. The Constituent Assembly was to stand dissolved if it could not frame the Constitution within 120 days. The LFO was to act as an interim Constitution, and the following five principles were deemed fundamental: (1) an Islamic ideology; (2) territorial integrity; (3) free elections and the independence of the judiciary; (4) a federal system ensuring autonomy to the provinces as well as adequate legislative, administrative, and financial powers for the central government; and (5) full opportunities to the people of all regions for participation in national affairs. The directive principles demanded an Islamic way of life, observance of Islamic moral standards, and teaching of the *Qur'an* and *Sunnah* to the Muslims.

The president was given the power to reject any Constitution framed by the Constituent Assembly if it did not fulfill the abovementioned criteria. It stipulated that if the president refused to authenticate the constitution, the National Assembly would stand dissolved, and the president would be the sole arbiter in interpreting the order. In that case, the president also had the power to amend the Constitution, and his decision could not be challenged in a court of law. The opposition leaders criticized the stipulation regarding the president's control of authentication as they saw this as the curtailment of the sovereignty of the National Assembly. They were, however, paying more attention to the election campaign at that time.

Election Campaign and the National Elections of 1970

Right at the outset of the election campaign, the central government admitted that the people of East Pakistan had been subject to discrimination and that there existed disparities between the two wings of Pakistan. The central government, though late, instituted redress mechanisms, such as Special Measures Programs, in its Fourth Five-Year Plan, which became effective in July 1970. It accelerated East Pakistan's development expenditures to reduce the disparities in per capita income between East and West Pakistan.

In West Pakistan, Zulfiqar Ali Bhutto, a former foreign minister who formed the Pakistan People's Party (PPP), successfully combined a nationalist appeal. He called for a strong central government, a strong army, a renewed attempt to liberate Kashmir, and "a thousand-year confrontation with India" based on the class war. The first appeal was attractive to the traditionalists, particularly in the army. To some extent, it neutralized the "Islam-pasand" (that is, parties that favored Islam as a guide for the country) parties. The PPP claimed to be pro-Chinese, anti-bourgeois, anti-capitalist, and anti-landlord when it was, in fact, financially supported by the middle class and the landlords. It was even backed by some of the "22" leading industrialists of West Pakistan.

A few saw these contradictions but were willing to skip them for the moment. Bhutto's mob oratory attracted an enormous crowd in the cities. The party's flags dominated city streets and towns throughout Punjab and Sind. His popularity was at its peak. In East Pakistan, however, the AL's election campaigns were based primarily on the issue of greater autonomy for East Pakistan under the leadership of Bongobondhu. The overwhelming political force was Bengali nationalism, enflamed by the Bengalis' grievance against what the AL claimed the west-wing domination. In a sense, even before the National Elections, both Bhutto and Bongobondhu emerged as charismatic leaders, successfully triggering an anti-Ayub movement throughout both wings of Pakistan that resulted in Ayub's downfall in 1969.

Only a month before the scheduled National Elections, while the campaigns were going on in both wings of Pakistan, on the night of November 12–13, 1970, a cyclone and tidal wave struck the Ganges River delta of East Pakistan, killing one-half-million people and leaving millions more homeless. The Bengalis believe the military government's relief efforts were ill-coordinated and poorly planned. Naturally, the Bengali politicians and civilians accused the military government of being indifferent to their urgent needs. This immediately intensified the spirit of Bengali nationalism even more, especially at a time when the Bengalis were already harbouring a kind of antipathy for West Pakistanis (non-Bengalis).

The government was forced to postpone the National Elections to December 7, 1970. The two National Awami Party (NAP) leaders, NAP Bhashani, headed by the octogenarian Maulana Abdul Hamid Khan Bhashani (pro-China), and the NAP headed by Professor Muzaffar Ahmad (pro-Soviet Union), having disagreed with the new date, demanded that the election be postponed further. The military regime did not agree to change the date again. The two political leaders angrily expressed dissatisfaction and announced they would boycott the National Elections. Having reminded himself that one should strike the iron when it is hot, Bongobondhu agreed to participate in the National Elections, taking full advantage of the national announcement to keep the momentum going in his favor. He neither wanted to take a chance nor trusted the military regime 100 percent lest it changed its mind.

Results of the 1970 National Elections

As many as twenty-two political parties and groups participated in the National Elections. About 55 million voters were in the polls, and 1,700 candidates were contested. The results of the first National Elections in Pakistan based on universal suffrage were clear-cut.

The Bengalis demonstrated their faith in the leadership of Bongobondhu, who had spent a decade in Pakistan's jail for his dissenting views in an unequivocal manner. The AL, to the right of the center, won as many as 167 out of 169 seats in the 300-member National Assembly, out of which thirteen seats were designated for women MPs. Having campaigned for the economic autonomy of East Pakistan but within the framework of *one* and *united* Pakistan, the AL gained 80 percent of the popular vote for his long-enunciated Six-Point program, Bongobondhu's appeal to the nostalgic notion of the ubiquitous slogan *Shonar Bangla* (Golden Bengal), a term that had already entered into the day-to-day vocabulary of the Bengalis, was held dear within the Bengali psyche.

In West Pakistan, Bhutto and his party, the PPP to the left of center, emerged as the most potent force, capturing 83 of 144 seats in the 313-seat assembly. Since the AL won all but 2 of the 169 seats allocated to East Pakistan, it was assured of an absolute majority in the assembly. At the national level, the AL also had an absolute majority, i.e., 75 percent of the votes out of 56 percent exercised votes.[35] Again, the AL received 98.8 percent of the votes at the provincial level. In that sense, the AL's victory was a landslide by any democratic yardstick.

In the meantime, both Bhutto and Bongobondhu, having demonstrated their popularity, became widely known as their respective provinces' charismatic leaders. Bhutto was described as the "left-leaning Zulfiqar Ali Bhutto,"[36] "the left-wing spellbinder,"[37] and the "socialist politician Z.A.

Bhutto."[38] Similarly, Bongobondhu was variously described by the print media such as the "the consummate politician and flamboyant orator,"[39] "the leader of the secessionist Awami League,"[40] the leader of the "Bengali nationalist movement in East Pakistan,"[41] the "unchallenged political leader,"[42] and "East Pakistan's secessionist leader."[43]

The gist of the world news media was somewhat like the following: the victory of Bongobondhu, who was seen as the Bengali nationalist firebrand, in the first-ever free National Elections of Pakistan had opened the door not only for the genuinely democratic government but also expanded trade with India, thus far opposed by Pakistan's central government. Surprised by the strength of their electoral victory, the AL and PPP needed time to adjust to the post-election situation. Commendably, with the productive completion of the 1970 National Elections, Pakistan successfully went through the first critical step in restoring electorally based civilian government. As an observer, Canada had no reason to worry about anything up to this time.

Activities Following the Election

Publicly, Yahya's attitude immediately following the elections seemed to have been one of satisfaction, although the military regime's strategists were caught off guard. On December 24, 1970, Yahya described Bongobondhu as "our future prime minister"[44] and had agreed that the constituent assembly would *sit in Dhaka*. Within weeks, on January 4, 1971, Bongobondhu publicly swore to himself and all the AL MPs that they would unconditionally adhere to the Six-Point Program, from which they would never deviate while framing the constitution for Pakistan. Having unanimously agreed, the MPs remained committed to crossing the t's and dotting the i's of the text of the Six-Point Program and treating it as sacrosanct.

In the meantime, having shown his full support for Bongobondhu, on January 9, 1971, Maulana Bhashani (the firebrand socialist leader of the National Awami Party, pro-China) called a conference of all those who favored independence. It was reported in the newspapers that Bhashani, Mashiur Rahman (general secretary of the East Pakistan National Awami Party), Ataur Rahman Khan (a distinguished politician), and Commander Moazzam Hussain (a leader of the Lahore Resolution Implementation Committee) met at Santosh in Tangail district to discuss the implementation of a five-point program which essentially vowed to accept no less than

Bangladesh, a separate country for the Bengalis. The five-point program envisaged the following: (1) The establishment of a sovereign East Pakistan based on the 1940 Lahore Resolution; (2) boycotting of imported goods, including those from the Western wing; (3) gradual socialization of the means of production; (4) adherence to the principles of anti-fascism; and (5) launching of a mass movement for pressing a referendum on these issues. The case for Bangladesh, with Bhashani's unequivocal demand, thus became even more robust with support from other major political parties.[45] In a sense, Bhashani was ahead of Bongobondhu in dreaming about a separate Bangladesh out of East Pakistan should the Pakistani government refuse to accept the demands of the Bengalis. We shall see in Chapter 2 that as early as 10 March 1971, Bhashani had already called for outright independence since the December 7 general election.

The second phase, from mid-January to mid-February 1971, marked the beginning of political skirmishing. Bhutto came to Dhaka on January 12 to meet with Bongobondhu. Since his meeting with Bongobondhu brought no positive result to his satisfaction, he immediately returned to West Pakistan unhappily. A dissatisfied Bhutto advised Yahya to delay the calling of the Assembly session to allow both parties to come up with options to break the impasse. In the meantime, Bongobondhu invited Yahya to visit his province (East Pakistan). By then, Yahya recognized that Bhutto and Bongobondhu were single-mindedly relentless in their stated positions. Frankly, Yahya faced two strong parties, one representing Bengali nationalism and the other West Pakistan Islamic socialism—poles apart. Seeing that neither of the political party leaders was making any progress, Yahya broke the ice in mid-January by visiting Bongobondhu and Bhutto separately.

With the passage of uncertain days, the Bengalis, who were exhilarated about the election results, began to have misgivings thinking about whether the Bengalis' landslide victory would be acceptable to both Yahya and Bhutto. Much to their downheartedness, the Bengalis realized that summoning the National Assembly without modifying the Six-Point Program was seen by the Yahya regime as a direct challenge. Given that there had been no success in moving forward, the AL began to suspect even more the actual motive of the military regime, which seemed resentful of Bongobondhu's unprecedented popularity and potential as a mover and shaker of Pakistan.

It would be learned later more clearly that, instead of moving forward, the regime secretly began to craft arguments to negate the results of the National Elections. Although Yahya went along with the Six-Point Program Platform during the election campaigns, soon after the election, he began to feel threatened by Bongobondhu's resounding success and substantial political support and legitimacy. A power-hungry Yahya could not come to terms with losing power and status. He found himself at direct loggerheads with Bongobondhu. The notion of separation and/or independence embodied in the Six-Point Program in the name of greater provincial autonomy in managing East Pakistan's economic, commercial, and financial affairs came to haunt the military regime. The regime started a new narrative by expressing the view that the AL's victory could not be considered 100 percent representative of Pakistan's population.

Even though the AL had emerged with an absolute majority and PPP as the second largest, neither party had captured a single seat in the other part of Pakistan, thus argued the regime implying that the results of the elections represented incongruity. Ottawa officials also noted that the PPP's strength was confined to West Pakistan while the AL's to East Pakistan. Continuing along the same vein, the military regime began to argue that, even though the AL claimed to be an All-Pakistan Party, it had been East Pakistan–based only. Bongobondhu's popularity among the Bengalis and support from India reinforced both Yahya and Bhutto's suspicion of Bongobondhu harboring a secessionist agenda even more. To the military regime, Bongobondhu's extraordinary popularity was a red flag.

In the meantime, feeling threatened, a mischievous Bhutto, who won a majority of the seats in West Pakistan, had two quick strategies to undermine Bongobondhu: first, to cast doubts over Bongobondhu's loyalty to Pakistan and influence a gullible Yahya along this line; and second, to mobilize political elements in West Pakistan against Bongobondhu's loyalty to Pakistan, and assert that he is the true patriotic leader of a *united Pakistan*. Soon, with Bhutto's manipulation, the military regime's abhorrence for Bongobondhu began to grow faster than ever before along the line that he was neither a national hero nor a warm-hearted leader. However, the Bengalis saw him as their savior.

Yahya and Bhutto began to look at Bongobondhu not as a national leader but as a rabble-rouser. Seeing that Bhutto's initial scheme worked, both Bhutto and Yahya treacherously started publicly saying that Bongobondhu's policy was acceptable to neither the Pakistani army nor Bhutto. They began to entertain a different kind of "truth" about Bongobondhu. Needless to mention, Yahya had earlier considered Bongobondhu a famous national hero, and declared him as the prime minister-designate. The military regime began to regard Bongobondhu as a pro-Indian *agent provocateur,* a troublemaker for Pakistan.

Taking advantage of an indecisive Yahya's state of mind, a deceitful Bhutto made a determined move to counter the seemingly impregnable advantage Bongobondhu held through his party's simple majority. By mid-February 1971, Bhutto informed the news media of his decision not to attend the National Assembly session scheduled for March 3 in Dhaka. This was an attempt to outmaneuver Bongobondhu, who ignored Bhutto's plans. Then came another critical step in this tragic progression with Bhutto's stern reminder to Yahya on February 28 of the consequences he would face if he ratified a constitution unacceptable to Punjab (and, by inference, to the middle ranks of the army). Another threat followed this: he would boycott the Assembly session if the AL leader did not realign his position by modifying the conflicting text outlined in his Six-Point Program.

An intractable Bhutto then openly launched another campaign of intimidation against all other parties in West Pakistan to prevent them from attending the session in Dhaka. In the meantime, a rumor also surfaced that a crafty Bhutto had cut a secret deal with an undecidable Yahya who had been in touch with Lieutenant General Ghulam Umar, chairman of the National Security Council. The Bengalis suspected that Yahya was already a party to Bhutto's evil scheme to beguile Bongobondhu into the belief that they were seriously negotiating when, in fact, the regime was gaining time to reinforce the troops it had in East Pakistan. So furious and agitated were the embittered Bengalis that they not only believed it but called it Yahya's deal with the devil, one giving a nudge and a wink to the other. A diabolic Bhutto went further ahead to warn party members that he would break their legs should they leave for Dhaka. Despite Bhutto's warning, some West Pakistani leaders had already begun to reach Dhaka, while many others had booked their seats in Dhaka by March 2.

Ironically for Bhutto, his constant threat made Bongobondhu see the events with an apocalyptic vision—something that made his team members perceptive and judicious, resulting in consolidation of the support from both the nationalists and moderates. The more Bhutto reacted, the more the Bengalis detested him, displaying their undivided solidarity. By the end of February, the Bengalis were convinced that Yahya must have yielded to the hawks among his military junta and that he had also surrendered to the wiles of Bhutto. In the meantime, Bongobondhu's support was growing daily, making him the focal point for a movement of emancipation for the entire Bengali populace. In a sense, this situation was reminiscent of the French Canadians' nationalistic slogan, *"Maîtres-chez-nous"* (Masters in our own house) that drew the undivided attention of the Québecois under the charismatic premiership of Jean Lesage (1960–1966) in Québec. As mentioned, just like the political situation of the Lesage years in Québec, East Pakistani politics also manifested the spirit of independence and self-assertiveness of the French Canadians of the 1960s.

The majority of West Pakistani politicians, other than Bhutto, however, came to show a wave of goodwill toward East Pakistanis. An uncompromising Bhutto, however, remained ever cantankerous in defense of what he believed to be the right thing to do for his country. He strongly argued that the Constitution based on the Six-Point Program could not provide a viable future for Pakistan. We shall see in Chapter 2 how the two crucial Canadian diplomats (John Small and James George), stationed in Islamabad and New Delhi, respectively, as Canada's high commissioners, briefed Ottawa in this regard along the vein that it was the refusal of Bhutto to sit down with Bongobondhu with his charter of autonomy concerning Pakistan's political system that resulted in a deadlock and precipitated the crisis. Neither of the two Canadian diplomats blamed Bongobondhu for the impasse in their report.

This cat-and-mouse game continued from mid-January to the end of February, leading an undecided Yahya nowhere. Unable to deal with the forces underlying the reality, Yahya himself became more rigid and stubborn and relied more on his mistrust of the democratic wisdom of the people of Pakistan. Personally, a credulous Yahya became more inclined to accept Bhutto's concocted story about the Bengalis' secret plan to disintegrate Pakistan through assistance from India. A dupable Yahya was so disturbed that he could not brook the situation, seeing how Bongobondhu's popularity in his province reached its zenith. Consequently, Yahya became so resentful of seeing how the Bengalis of all backgrounds looked upon Bongobondhu as their *savior* that in no time was he brainwashed by a villainous Bhutto. A politically inexperienced charlatan, Yahya found the entire issue mindboggling, being in a state of hemming and hawing. Looking through the military lens, Yahya became convinced that the Six-Point Program for

East Pakistan's autonomy, if written into the new constitution, would mean the end of Pakistan.

Postponement of the National Assembly and Non-cooperation Movement

By the first day of March, much to the military regime's umbrage, Bongobondhu threatened the country. The Six-Point Manifesto ought to be watered down to ensure the country's unity, argued Bhutto. The more Bongobondhu was viewed with passionate admiration by the Bengalis with the *"Joy Bangla"* slogan, the more inflamed Yahya became, only to abhor him more intensely. An ambitious Bhutto with a penchant for arbitrariness and manipulation was not ready to sit in the opposition at a time when Bongobondhu, leader of the majority party in the Assembly, was expecting to be asked to form a representative government.

Yahya turned to both Bongobondhu and Bhutto. He urged Bongobondhu to interpret the Six-Point Program flexibly and Bhutto to approach the situation with an open mind. Yahya resented that a rapacious Bhutto did not care about two straws. As Yahya saw, both were at daggers drawn. This was a frustrating experience for Yahya, who found both to be headstrong, unbending, and stiff-necked, being opposed to each other to the hilt with no intention of finding a solution based on flexibility and political wisdom. With no political sagacity, Yahya was placed between the devil and the deep blue sea as both recalcitrant leaders (Bhutto and Bongobondhu) further complicated the matter. With no knowledge of the complex subcontinental polity, the military dictator was surrounded by hawkish military personnel who failed to advise him in the right direction. Having found himself in stress and difficulty, Yahya desperately tried to confront the impasse. To a furious and disillusioned Yahya, the Bengali leader was possessed by a "national" ideal at the cost of a united Pakistan. Being on a hot seat, an unsuspecting Yahya succumbed to a hard-nosed Bhutto's pressure.

On March 1, 1971, Yahya abruptly announced the postponement of the opening session of the newly elected National Assembly *sine die* (until further notice) as an attempt to appease Bhutto. With the announcement of the postponement of the National Assembly, all hell broke loose. The Bengalis felt betrayed—a kick in the teeth[46]—to deny the Bengalis their aspirations for greater autonomy, which was a nonnegotiable demand.

On March 3, the president invited twelve leaders of Parliamentary Groups in the National Assembly to meet at Dhaka on March 10 to discuss how to solve the constitutional crisis. The same evening, Bongobondhu announced his rejection of the president's invitation. This resulted in a complete breakdown of trust between the Bengalis and the military regime, leading to riots and much bloodshed in Dhaka, the port city of Chittagong, and many other towns of the province. The Bengalis began pointing fingers at Bhutto, who became the Bengalis' *bête noir* and the gravedigger of Pakistan.

Calling themselves vigilantes, the militant students immediately started to go around the city, tearing down English and Urdu signs, looting the non-Bengali-owned stores, and burning motor vehicles in the presence of the supportive Bengali police who remained inactive as though the officers on duty were only a spectator to such unlawful actions. The world media records indicate that prejudice and violence rose along an exponential curve. The violence began to beget more violence. Regular services, including the Pakistan International Airline (PIA), were canceled. Seeing a rapid deterioration of mounting chaos, foreign diplomatic missions began to discuss arrangements to evacuate their nationals.

From March 2–6 onward, the daily rallies, protest demonstrations, nightly lootings, and burnings continued unabated while the major cities were on pins and needles. Earlier, Small from Islamabad also informed Ottawa that the timing of the National Assembly session's convening rested solely with the president. He should have made his position unambiguous as a mediator, argued Small, saying that Yahya could have picked a date instead of postponing *sine die*. This would have been probably more acceptable to all parties, wrote Small. He also observed that the postponement of the National Assembly was due to Bhutto's refusal to take his people to the session, which "provided the peg on which to hang continuation of martial law."[47] On March 3, Bongobondhu launched a nonviolent and noncooperation movement, having rejected a round table conference (RTC) proposed by Yahya.

Bongobondhu firmly declared that his party would consider the question of attending the session *only* if Yahya immediately (1) lifted the martial law, (2) withdrew troops, (3) restored civilian rule, and (4) ordered an inquiry into the recent killing in East Pakistan. Almost all the East Pakistanis strongly supported Bongobondhu's declaration. Even the West Pakistani leaders, except Bhutto and Abdul Qayyum Khan (Pakistan Muslim League, Qayyum group), considered all four just and reasonable conditions and advised the president to accept them. They were Mian

Mumtaz Daulatana (chief of Council Muslim League), Maulana Mufti Mahmud (leader of the Jamaitul-Ulema-i-Islam), Khan Abdul Wali Khan (chief of National Awami Party), Air Marshall (Retd.) Asghar Khan (chief of Tehrik-i-Ishtiqbal), Jamal Mohammad Korjea of Convention Muslim League, Abdul Ghafoor of Jamaat-i-Islam, along with a large number of independent MNAs, all of whom blamed Bhutto for the impasse. Their collective demand was that Bhutto "should not be allowed to disintegrate the country and suggested that powers should be transferred to the majority party, namely Shiekh Mujib's Awami League, to save the situation and the country."[48]

Fast forward to March 4, Bongobondhu again issued several directives to continue daily strikes, with exceptions for essential services, utilities, state and commercial banks, government offices, and the press. Reportedly, on the same day, three hundred people were killed in army action against the AL workers. The non-Bengalis, however, felt immeasurably vulnerable with the beginning of civil disobedience. A vicious circle emerged out of a maelstrom of ethnic violence, insecurity, and impunity. The Bengalis saw the regime's action as yet another nail in the coffin. The cheering crowd's slogan, *Bhuttor Mukhe Lathi Maro, Bangla Desh Shawdhin Koro* (Kick on Bhutto's Face; Make the Bengal Homeland Independent), went viral. Feeling disenfranchised, the Bengalis, in utter frustration, came to believe that under the military regime, the idea of equality was far from reality—they would have to wait until hell froze over. Across the province, tens of thousands of students joined the daily processions. Amid confusion, frustration, and anger, the entire East Pakistan was sitting on a volcano that could go off at any time.

On March 6, Yahya announced that the assembly would meet on March 25, but things had gone too far. Under the circumstances, Yahya vowed to maintain the country's political integrity by *force, if necessary.* The world media viewed how, with the postponement of the National Assembly, Yahya became the most detested man among the Bengalis; on the other hand, Bongobondhu appeared to be their *savior.* He plummeted to the height of popularity amid uncertainties. He genuinely believed he held all the aces, and while there was a sort of romantic fatalism about him, he gave the impression of a man who felt he had reached the summit. As far as the Bengalis were concerned, the time for intimidation was over. The common perception across the province swung from fear of military attack in the cities to a smug assumption that Bongobondhu would opt for UDI (Universal Declaration of Independence). Everyone awaited Bongobondhu's marching order through his speech to the "nation."

Bongobondhu's Historic March 7, 1971, Speech and Immediate Reaction

Amid joy, enthusiasm, and excitement, Bongobondhu appeared with his slightly graying hair, expressive black eyes, and a well-groomed upturned mustache, wearing a loose black vest over the billowing white cotton pantaloons (pajama) and a long-sleeved shirt. Generally, Bengalis call it Punjabi. When Bongobondhu was called to the microphone at the dais for his most powerful speech to the "nation" at Dhaka Ramna Race Course Field (now Suhrawardy Uddan), there came an electrifying dive with a great whoop of "Bongobondhu" from the audience that instantly burst into tumultuous cheers—on the dais, fluttered the newly unfurled flag of Bangla Desh, a gold outline of East Pakistan in a red circle on a green background.

His more than average height, tall, imposing figure, and deep, mellifluous voice, at once earnest and commanding, gave Bongobondhu a distinguished appearance. He delivered his now-immortal speech characterized by precise words and intonation that took the attention of millions who came to hear him. As soon as Bongobondhu delivered his speech, he proved himself to be a superb orator who could grip and rouse the masses. The first half of the speech was devoted to a defense of the Awami League's actions and an effort to rebut the president's charges concerning the league's intransigence and obstructionism toward the president's efforts to achieve a smooth transition of power to the elected representatives of the people. The second half of his speech threw out a direct challenge to the president's authority and martial law regime.

Bongobondhu laid down conditions for Awami League participation in the National Assembly, called for March 25, and outlined ten steps in the "nonviolent and noncooperation movement" on March 8. In an unequivocal term, he announced that he would attend the assembly provided the following four conditions were satisfied: (1) withdrawal of the troops to the barracks; (2) holding of a judicial inquiry into the killings by the military; (3) withdrawal of martial law; and (4) immediate transfer of power to the elected leader of the majority. By asking for a transfer of power before the National Assembly meets to debate the issue, Bongobondhu made the de facto granting of East Pakistan's autonomy necessary for his attendance.

Standing on the dais, Bongobondhu ordered a ten-point civil disobedience campaign to the central government to back his demands to end martial law and return to popular rule. His effortless aplomb and extraordinary oratorial quality instantly made him a winning personality.

The Bengalis of every occupation—the butcher, the baker, and the candlestick maker—supported their leader with *lathis* (heavy poles or sticks), iron bars, or sticks of one sort. Bongobondhu's dramatic performance immediately won him the role of a redeemer who would bring salvation, having shown extraordinary courage and confidence.[49] When Bongobondhu boldly roared with his "get tough" and "take action" appeal, his choice of words was pitch-perfect in tone and reflective of the mood and yarning of the people. Within hours following his fiery speech to the "nation," the pent-up fury of the crowd reached full force. His earth-shattering speech deeply affected the Bengalis across the province by its power and beauty—the power to drive them to action and beauty to move them to a visionary future. Everyone was so touched by his passionate appeal that it was as though one could see Bongobondhu's cry from the heart.

So forceful was the speech that, in a sudden blaze of illumination, the Bengalis visualized their dreamland, a country devoid of the West Pakistani military ruler. With greatness and dignity of his own and with a will of iron, a confident Bongobondhu called upon his people, students, and members of the public, who were roused to the hilt, to come forward with a new frame of mind by blowing the cobwebs. Like a latter-day Pied Piper of Hamelin, a flamboyant Bongobondhu mesmerized and lured millions of Bengalis to fight for their liberation. They did not think, even for a minute, the reality of an inevitable confrontation with the military already around them. Being carried away, they took up the cudgel. They sought to escape to a new realm of a *Swadhin Bangla Desh* (Independent Bangla Desh) with its mores, customs, and institutions. They believed they had already taken their destiny into their own hands to shape their future in their motherland. This was reminiscent of the Québec of the 1960s when, as noted, the word "province" almost disappeared from the vocabulary of the nationalist Québecois who began to refer to their province as "L'Etat du Québec" (the State of Québec).

Nevertheless, to those suspicious of the military regime, it appeared highly doubtful that President Yahya would want to transfer power to the elected Awami League without first doing all he could to preserve its central control. "The prospects of him being able to do so without bloodshed and prolonged civil strife appear extremely remote."[50] Thus, the acting minister was briefed.

Nevertheless, Bongobondhu's call to "get tough" come hell or high water also meant many things to many people because of the semantic subtlety in using certain words of appeal. To the extremists, Bongobondhu's appeal meant immediately organizing armed volunteers and vigilantes to secure the support of the Bengali soldiers and policemen to rebel against the West Pakistani officers for creating what Bongobondhu called "*Shonar Bangla*" out of East Pakistan. To the ordinary Bengalis, it was interpreted as a call for independence, though not an outright UDI; again, to some, it was a step in the direction with caution and vigilance. Except for a few loyalists, everyone supported Bongobondhu's demand - to rid the Bengalis of a regime that held them in serfdom. In that sense, Bongobondhu's appeal made the Bengalis feel like they were in a spirit reminiscent of the Age of Enlightenment.

Canadian news media analyzed Bongobondhu's March 7 speech to determine the movement's direction. "Even so, Mujib did not, as many felt he would declare unilateral independence."[51] Thus, wrote journalist John Walker. To keep his readers in the loop, he added further that Bongobondhu "had always tried to work within the present Pakistani system and when, on March 7, when he fully threw down the gauntlet to President Yahya in an impressive and forthright manner, he only went as far as asking for the withdrawal of martial law and the transfer of power to the elected representatives"[52] of the people in all of Pakistan.

Like the romanticists of the eighteenth century who stressed the role of feeling and imagination, the emotionally charged Bengalis' feelings were above reason, being attracted toward an unknown future. They despised the army and underestimated its power. With a sense of "national" pride bordering on indignation, they felt as though the eastern wing or their land belonged to them and them only. Many unsure of what was happening were alarmed and thought perhaps it was a folie de grandeur for the overexcited Bengalis. The take-home message for the average Bengalis was to prepare themselves for sacrifices and to resist any force against them, for the spirit of Bangladesh would not be extinguished. While dreaming of an independent Bangladesh, many drew inspiration from the liberation movements transforming Asia and Africa. At least three dozen states gained their independence between 1945 and 1960—specifically, seventeen

African nations, such as Nigeria and the Democratic Republic of Congo, and tiny nations like Togo and Burkina Faso, gained their independence in 1960 alone.

The Bengalis, in their naïvety, were carried away without any regard for the consequences of an army crackdown. Already fed up with the West Pakistanis' paternalistic attitude and their peculiarly defined Pakistani nationalism accompanied by an authoritarian government, they recognized how the regime regarded them as lesser breeds for whom it was divinely commissioned to be its brothers' keepers. In a sense, in Charles Dickens's terms, "it was the best of times, it was the worst of times." It was the best of times for those who uttered with profound anger, "To hell with Pakistan." It was the worst of times for those who were still dimly hoping for a united Pakistan with full autonomy for East Pakistan. The Bengalis' sullen and inextinguishable hatred for West Pakistanis and non-Bengalis (Biharis) turned into a kind of xenophobia amid the cry of *Joy Bangla* (Victory of Bengal). The non-Bengali Muslim Biharis, who were a minority in East Pakistan, came from the Indian province of Bihar, having migrated to East Pakistan following the creation of Pakistan in 1947. Aligned linguistically and culturally with the Urdu-speaking West Pakistanis, the Biharis in East Pakistan had always felt the repercussions of East-West tension. At that time, instant widespread political paralysis was evident. College and university campuses went through a paroxysm of disdain, rage, riot, and arson. In the day's parlance, Bongobondhu was a dazzling performer who knew how to perform on a political platform.

Immediately following his March 7 blaring call to the "nation," Bongobondhu asked East Pakistani officials to take orders from him, the details of which he outlined in the newly formed *Sangram Samities* (Liberation Committees) that began to issue decrees, having assumed the responsibility for the entire province. A charismatic Bongobondhu's demand for change and a new vision for the province continued to appeal to the people's passion. The notion of an independent Bangladesh carried the Bengalis away by a wave of *Mujibmania,* an explosive mix of love and admiration fueled by media and the Bengali renaissance—a nationalist fervor. His meteoric rise to leadership that generated extraordinary excitement and popularity reminded the Bengalis of the wave of Trudeaumania, a passionate quest for a new Canada that aspired to define the values of Canada, only less than three years ago. Trudeau appealed to all Canadians across the country, while Bongobondhu's appeal was only to the Bengalis in East Pakistan for Bangladesh with a nationalist ambition hitherto unknown.

The next day, by March 8, much to the profound vexation of the Yahya government, the entire civil administration openly pledged its loyalty to Bongobondhu's stewardship in quick succession by putting themselves under his orders. They renamed the administration from East Pakistan to Bangladesh administration under Bongobondhu. Again, with the issuance of thirty-five directives, Bongobondhu assumed control following the expressed wishes of the people of his native land. Having seized civil power in East Pakistan, the AL became a de facto government. While stopping just short of a UDI (unilateral declaration of independence), Bongobondhu laid down his conditions—only upon acceptance of the above-noted conditions would he attend the National Assembly called for March 25, 1971. Yahya viewed Bongobondhu's position as a roadblock to democratization, having maintained that he was strictly committed to following the LFO (Legal Framework Order). In the meantime, people took to the streets daily to register their frustrations in large processions. They chanted the *Joy Bangla* slogan with radiant faces, expressing their confidence in establishing a democratic government under a constitution of their own making.

The Bengalis became both resentful and euphoric - resentful because they felt betrayed by the military; euphoric because they cherished the idea that they were heading for an independent Bangladesh. Naturally, anti-state slogans, prejudicial to the national solidarity of Pakistan, became a common sight in Dhaka. It instantly galvanized the Bengalis as one "nation" against *them* - the West Pakistani armed forces. An overenthusiastic Bengalis were exposed to sudden and dramatic pitches, upturns, and unexpectedly abrupt curves since the events were moving with breathtaking speed like they were riding a giant roller-coaster train. The majority of the Bengalis, being emotionally charged, were ready to take responsibility for their native land.

Individually, a vainglorious but undecided president could not come to terms with losing power and status. Historically, the National Awami Party of Sind's slogan *"Jai Sind"* had been used long before Bongobondhu's *Joy Bangla* slogan. Earlier in Pakistan, the concept of a separate Pakhtunistan was already led by Khan Abdul Wali Khan of the National Awami Party in the North-West Frontier Province many years ago. Khan's declaration of "full determination to fight for the just cause of all the cultural and linguistic minorities in Pakistan, especially the Pakhtoons" [53] was propounded by

Major-General Ghulam Jilani. Wali Khan was not alone in his demand in Pakistan as politicians like Abdus Samad Khan, Prince Abdul Karim, and Sardar Bagte of Baluchistan had also been known to have openly endorsed their support for his demand for a separate Pakhtunistan. Over the years, there was a distinct revival of the Punjabi slogan "Punjab for Punjabis" in Pakistan.

And yet, Bongobondhu's demand for autonomy for East Pakistan began to cause a different kind of wave among the military strategists, especially following Bongobondhu's clarion call that showed how quickly Bongobondhu was visibly becoming the most popular leader in Pakistan whose followership was growing day by day. The military regime could not come to terms with the present reality. Although these concepts of provincial autonomy had been kicked around in Pakistan's politics for years, Yahya began to feel genuinely threatened by Bongobondhu's demands. In his self-righteous belief, the president and the conspiracy peddlers around him felt intensely resentful of Bongobondhu's move toward greater autonomy. Naïvely enough, they came to believe that they were on the right side of history as the true defenders of Pakistan. Having considered Bongobondhu, an anti-Pakistani Indian agent, the military regime found the AL leader's demand for greater autonomy incompatible and irreconcilable with the national integrity of Pakistan.

Although furious, Yahya and the martial law authorities made no move to confront Bongobondhu, who, the president believed, had already defied the country's laws (Pakistan). [54] Meanwhile, the Bengalis were so excited that they had no time to think about the consequences of defying the country's laws, which were still legally controlled by the military. Canadians followed the impasse and saw how Bongobondhu practically seized complete control of the eastern wing of Pakistan since the beginning of March through strikes, protest demonstrations, and administration. It is important to note that, at the commencement of his noncooperation movement, Bongobondhu took a principled stand against violence. Canadians read in Selig Harrison's write-up on the unfolding of the dramatic events in East Pakistan in which he asked: "Is Pakistan heading for an inevitable final breach between its eastern and western wings?" [55]

Again, Dan Coggin, foreign correspondent of the London-based *TIME* magazine, followed Bongobondhu's historic March 7 speech to the "nation." His knowledge and familiarity with the subcontinental polity made him concerned about the future of Pakistan. "Pakistan, as it stands today, is finished," and that "there is no longer any hope for a settlement."[56] Thus observed Coggin. A rookie in real politics and lamentably weak in the affairs of his country, Yahya was inflamed to see the gall Bongobondhu was displaying through his speech—he could not take the flak. A disturbed Yahya struggled in his mind when placed between a rock and a hard stone. On the one hand, the AL leader had asked for the transfer of power before the National Assembly meets to debate the issue; on the other hand, he had also made the *de facto* granting of East Pakistan's autonomy a necessary condition for his attendance. Despite being the supreme commander and head of Pakistan, an ineffective Yahya felt abandoned, passed over, ignored, and powerless.

Yahya-Bongobondhu-Bhutto Parley

Between January and March 1971, Bhutto and Yahya came to Dhaka and held in-camera meetings with Bongobondhu separately, for which no official version existed. Every day following the meeting, there used to be quick media interviews in which the leaders made general observations without giving the details of the progress or lack thereof. Bhutto came to Dhaka thrice: first on January 12, then on January 27, and then again on March 21. Following the first two meetings, which did not produce any results, Bhutto left Dhaka both times, infuriatingly blaming Bongobondhu for the impasse. Both leaders were reported to have remained bull-headed and unshakable in their demands for which they could not agree. Bhutto assumed the patriotic high ground that Bongobondhu's demand for reshaping Pakistan was tantamount to secession. Bongobondhu remained cool and maintained that he could not backtrack from the election pledge stipulated in the Six-Point Program, which the people of Pakistan had endorsed and on which the government held the election without any objection.

Yahya came to Dhaka twice, first on January 12 and then again on March 15. The first meeting—reportedly an in-depth three-hour discussion between Bongobondhu and Yahya—took place in Dhaka on January 12 to break the political impasse. The tense situation was cooled off a little bit by Yahya's gesture of flying to Dhaka to negotiate with Bongobondhu. The Bengali leader remained determined throughout the meeting, insisting that there was no room for amending the Six-Point Program, which his people mandated. The president, too, remained firm in his insistence that the unity of Pakistan is paramount without clearly explaining the various ramifications of the constitution as he saw it. The president also demanded that both the PPP and AL leaders come to an understanding and put aside their obduracies. It was reported later that, regrettably, they drifted apart, and Yahya flew back the same day.

Upon his return to Karachi, Yahya described his talks as satisfactory, although that was certainly not the case. He was so furious and dissatisfied that, reportedly, five days later, he traveled to Bhutto's baronial family estate in Larkana, Sindh, to meet with Bhutto accompanied by S. G. Pirzada, principal staff officer to the president and a number of the PPP leaders from the Punjab and Sindh. There was no media coverage regarding what transpired from the meeting that later came to be referred to as the Larkana Conspiracy. The media only reported that Yahya and other generals went to Bhutto's home on a duck-shooting trip at nearby Drigh Lake—something that reinforced the Bengalis' suspicion that this was a meeting of a bunch of conspiracy peddlers and that Yahya and Bhutto had already formed an *entente* against Bongobondhu.

After weeks of "he said," "she said," when all was said and done, a desperate Yahya came to Dhaka again of his own volition, although with a secret agenda that no one knew about at that time. The next round of discussions was held from March 15 to 25 between Yahya and Bongobondhu and their respective advisers. Before Yahya arrived in Dhaka, reportedly, he was alarmed to note that Bongobondhu's thirty-five directives were working perfectly well in the province in the face of martial law. The conflict turned into a fight between the Bengalis and non-Bengalis—the Bengalis identified with Bongobondhu, and the non-Bengalis identified with the Yahya regime. The military government was frightened to notice the news of *Bihariphobia* (harboring anti-Bihari sentiment) by the ultra-nationalist students and consequent killings of the Biharis by the Bengalis armed with *lathis* and lethal weapons in the non-Bengali neighborhood. As far as the Bengalis were concerned, they saw all non-Bengalis as spies or informers in the emotionally charged milieu.

When Yahya arrived in Dhaka on March 15, 1971, to meet with Bongobondhu, the *Joy Bangla* slogan had already gained unprecedented momentum, giving rise to a new kind of awareness embedded in the legends of resistance and self-immolation. Successful virtual self-rule had begun following the launching of thirty-five directives by Bongobondhu. Upon his arrival in Dhaka, Yahya immediately recognized that he was not genuinely welcome as the head of the country. Although he felt like a cuckoo in the nest, he ignored everything, having carefully buried his head in the sand. Despite everything, he continued as though it was business as usual, pretending it did not put a damper on him. By then, the noncooperation movement had already gained full endorsement from the Bengalis, so the military regime could not even find any High Court judge in East Pakistan to administer the oath for the new governor, Lieutenant General Tikka Khan.

So successful was Bongobondhu's call that the entire civilian administration, including the East Pakistani government officers (mostly Bengalis) of police and civil service, refused to attend the offices, businesspeople stopped supplying food to the army, and even the civilian employees of the defense establishment responded enthusiastically. The Indian radio stations continued to air the latest developments in East Pakistan with critical commentaries. Being overjoyed, the Bengalis talked about their national future with a great deal of zeal and passion. A steamed-up president, the supreme commander of Pakistan's armed forces, and the head of state found the situation disgustingly intolerable.

As an apostle of the Bengalis' solidarity, Bongobondhu's conviction was such that he believed that if fair is fair, greater autonomy for East Pakistan could be achieved given his overwhelming victory in the National Elections. He also thought that the Bengalis would soon be self-reliant in every sphere and take their rightful place in the community of nations. He was seen as an indomitable symbol of the Bengalis' self-respect, infusing fellow Bengalis with self-confidence. Bongobondhu is reported to have continually referred to East Pakistan as "Bangla Desh" and threatened secession but only as a last resort. A veteran politician in the subcontinent was evident in his utterance that his hope and dream of a *Shonar Bangla* was only an alternative to his demand for greater autonomy for East Pakistan since his people were enchanted with the same vision he had been cherishing. He knew such a dream was not a pie in the sky either.

He urged the president to accept a compromise formula giving the Bengalis full autonomy, which they had voted for, except for defense and foreign affairs, as stipulated in the Six-Point Program. Yahya argued that Pakistan would lack a constitution under the suggested arrangement since the Legal Framework Order prescribed power transfer to the center only after the National Assembly had formulated a constitution. Bongobondhu argued that some legislative device should implement the actual transfer immediately and that the National Assembly could subsequently sit as two separate committees representing the two wings of Pakistan to draw up two sets of proposals. The entire assembly would meet later and choose the one it would deem suitable. Not wanting to side with either Bongobondhu or Bhutto, a highbinder Yahya was betwixt and between even though he already had four rounds of discussion with Bongobondhu. An anti-Bengali Yahya, having remained convinced of the Bengalis' pro-Indian inclinations, was still unsatisfied. Being irresolute, Yahya could not decide without bringing Bhutto into the loop. He then summoned Bhutto to join them.

Bhutto, having accepted the offer, arrived in Dhaka on March 21. He immediately joined Yahya and Bongobondhu. His arrival brought the last hope among those still thinking that something could be worked out. Bongobondhu had the full support of the Bengalis. The historic parley consisted of three protagonists: Bongobondhu (leader of the AL), Zulfiqar Ali Bhutto (chairman of the PPP), and Yahya (the *de facto* chairman or umpire of the negotiation). With Bongobondhu, there were three critical leaders—Khondakar Mushtaq Ahmed, Tajuddin Ahmad, and Kamal Hussain. The stated purpose of the three leaders, at least outwardly, was to explore each other's overall position: to restate each leader's bottom line and to attempt to find a way out of the impasse to transfer power to the elected representatives. It was later learned that Bongobondhu noticed that both Bhutto and Yahya sang a different tune from a different hymn sheet. He could not fathom all the slings and arrows directed against him.

During the negotiation, Yahya had all the aces as the head of the country. Bhutto also had an ace up his sleeves since he was chummy with Yahya, who had already made a deal. In that sense, Bhutto's friendship with Yahya was like a suit of armor—a kind of protection for him. Being quick on the draw, Bhutto, a bare-knuckle fighter, threatened to torpedo the negotiation. Bhutto was showing his true colors, proving himself to be a snake in the grass, a hidden treacherous enemy. Unsurprisingly, therefore, Bongobondhu was at a disadvantage. His Achilles heel was that he was neither chummy with Yahya nor keen on conspiracy. He was not able to sail under false colors. He knew the Bengalis had given him *carte blanche* to speak for them.

Under the circumstances, Bongobondhu remained extra-cautious, knowing he was walking on eggshells and using every word since he knew he was surrounded by two players who had already ganged up against him and his people. In a sense, all three *dramatis personae* were on pins and needles. There were a lot of swings and roundabouts, but nothing concrete was developed. The long and short of it is that a conspiracy against Bongobondhu became evident later. At that point, a disturbed Yahya, feeling "enough is enough," decided to lance the boil with a feeling of "it's got to end." The objective was to bring Bongobondhu to his knees, but little did they know that a courageous Bongobondhu was not the man to surrender to, even though he was in a knife-edge situation. After quite a bit of huff and puff, Yahya's "take a hike" or "my way or the highway" kind of attitude became more noticeable. Bongobondhu quickly realized that Bhutto and Yahya were playing hardball politics in the name of national integrity and that the notion of give-and-take was markedly missing.

While the negotiation was going on in full gear, two more factors came into play. First, Abdul Qayyum Khan of the Qayyum Muslim League, who had his main strength in the northwest frontier region and nine members in the assembly, declared his support for Bhutto and provincial autonomy but opposed Bongobondhu's brand of independence that he believed would jeopardize the unity of Pakistan. In the meantime, in East Pakistan, Yahya's meeting with Bhutto at his Larkana residence around mid-January, in the presence of General Abdul Hamid Khan, something that has already been alluded to, came to haunt Bongobondhu's team. The alleged Larkana Conspiracy case began to come up in daily conversations among the Bengalis. Although there was no specific media coverage on the subject discussed by Yahya and Bhutto at that clandestine meeting, the Bengalis came to suspect that a conspiracy against the transfer of power had already been hatched. It was a case of Yahya's deal with the devil, claimed the Bengalis.

Since Bhutto was "the bastion of power," [57] he could not be bypassed by the AL leader, whose victory was confined *only* to East Pakistan, thus argued Bhutto preposterously. Negating Bongobondhu's position as the leader of the numerical majority, Bhutto saw himself as another protagonist representing the west wing of Pakistan. Unsurprisingly, Bhutto's lust for power forced him to argue against the Six-Point Program and insist on recognizing the "two majority groups" in Pakistan and not just one in East Pakistan[58] Naturally, during the last phase of the parley, Yahya's suspicion of Bhutto also grew more assertive. Bhutto was so determined that he went to the extent of demanding that he assume power in all of West Pakistan, even at the cost of one Pakistan.

An outraged Yahya was struck by Bhutto's doggedness for persistent demand for direct power-sharing with him. Moving forward, a rapacious Bhutto introduced his concept of two nations by denying Bongobondhu the right to speak on behalf of all Pakistanis. The news media also talked about two Pakistans broached by Bhutto,[59] who saw him as indispensable, having compared himself with the prince of Denmark, without whom no one could stage *Hamlet*. Yahya was forced to hold separate meetings with each leader to hear about one's bottom line. Discussions centered on Bongobondhu's new demand for immediate power transfer to the AL first; then, whatever party or group of parties could form a government in West Pakistan do that accordingly. Bhutto strongly opposed that. Yahya's attempts to bring Bhutto and Bongobondhu together were unsuccessful. While seething with rage, a profoundly dissatisfied Yahya continually tried to intimidate Bongobondhu by saying he was in charge. As was the case, both Bhutto and Yahya tried to twist Bongobondhu's arm. He realized it was a treacherous act, a betrayal by rapacious Bhutto and stubborn Yahya, who were trying to squeeze on him. But no arm twisting worked because Bongobondhu was made of sterner stuff.

Bongobondhu never wanted to be putty in Yahya's hands. Toward the end of the negotiation, Bongobondhu realized that his relationship with the two leaders and their representatives was freezing. Having shot his last arrow, Bongobondhu tried to persuade them but had no luck, as Bhutto and Yahya remained stiff, straight-backed, and unyielding. Seeing that Yahya and Bhutto had the cards stacked against him and that he was the head of the country, Bongobondhu realized that Yahya had the game in his hand.

In the meantime, an arrogant Yahya tried to make everyone around feel that he was carrying a lot of muscle. In the end, an infuriated Yahya personally became so resentful of the Bengalis' *Joy Bangla* slogan that seemed to have shaken the very existence of the military government that watched with alarm the situation under a transformative Bongobondhu's leadership. In other words, this kind of leadership provided an instructive demonstration of his standing firm on autonomy. At that time, the entire province was controlled by one man who was hailed as a hero by his fellow Bengalis. Being deeply upset and vehemently wrathful, Yahya questioned who was in charge of East Pakistan. The president was so inflamed that he felt umbrage at every action of Bongobondhu. Yahya intensely hated to see how the *Joy Bangla* slogan became the new rock-and-roll among the nationalists. His indignation for Bongobondhu reached a point where he could not bear Bongobondhu's preparedness and chutzpah.

Seeing that Bongobondhu had remained obdurately resolute in his position despite the two negotiators' insistence to modify the Six-Point Program to ensure the national integrity of Pakistan, the regime became even more corybantic. An embittered Yahya found absolutely no room for compromise. He fumed over the politics he believed Bhutto and Bongobondhu were playing. Being deeply distrustful of the pro-Indian Bengalis, Yahya seriously questioned Bongobondhu's steadfast faith in the national integrity of Pakistan. Although he felt bitter after experiencing Bhutto's stubbornness, there is no evidence that he ever suspected Bhutto of his loyalty to Pakistan. Ironically, Bongobondhu's reiteration of the necessity of the participation of the Bengalis in the decision-making process by the central government was neither clearly understood nor appreciated by a mistrustful military government.

Consequently, Bongobondhu's insistence was misconstrued by the regime that regarded his die-hardism as a declaration of his separatist intent. Yahya's obsession led him to test the Bengalis' loyalty to Pakistan through one's affiliation with the AL and the Bengalis' enthusiastic response to Bongobondhu's call for the noncooperation movement. He took that as a sign of being anti-Pakistani. So outraged was the president that he felt humiliated, degraded, and rebuffed. Seeing Bongobondhu's pigheadedness, an obsessed Yahya recognized that this was Bongobondhu's most vital characteristic, for which he built up a groundswell of support in no time. Instantly, he became a mesmerizing figure, a spellbinder. The entire regime came to see the dissent and noncooperation movement of the Bengalis as elements that Yahya equated with subversion and disloyalty.

In a sense, being surrounded by Bhutto and Bongobondhu, it was as though Yahya was caught in the battle of the giants. Although Yahya gave the impression that the parley was to be a fair crack of the whip, both Yahya and Bhutto had already been conspiring against Bongobondhu. Even when Yahya had the ball at his feet, he chose to side with Bhutto, his partner in crime. Canada's High Commissioner Small had an inkling of what was happening in Islamabad. He had evidence to believe that an ambitious Bhutto did not seem like a happy camper despite having Yahya's support. When the band began to play, Bhutto joined Yahya using bandy words and a note of warning. Although Bhutto and Bongobondhu were in cahoots with each other, Bhutto positioned himself well in advance since he had a card up his sleeves.

A myopic Yahya, with his intense antipathy for the Bengalis, failed to find an acceptable answer to the following question: "Does Bongobondhu want to give national integration a positive meaning?" Bongobondhu is known to have left the door open for the two leaders to work out the concept of greater autonomy within the framework of the Six-Point Program endorsed by the people of Pakistan. Bongobondhu was not the leader who could be in Yahya's hip pocket. Ottawa noted how Bongobondhu remained firm and insistent, but he was ignored. To the extent possible, Bongobondhu wanted to build bridges. At the same time, Bongobondhu warned Yahya of either *greater autonomy* or *independence*. In the face of Bongobondhu's persistent demand for greater autonomy, Yahya's dilemma was apparent. If he yielded to Bongobondhu, he would lose the power he then held under a martial law decree to veto a constitution granting too much autonomy to East Pakistan. Such obsessive thoughts reinforced the common belief that the Bengalis (except for a few die-hard Muslim Leaguers and Islam *pasand* parties) were working against the integrity of Pakistan.

Although a pretentious Yahya displayed certain flexibility initially, he dealt with the matter with an iron hand in a velvet glove, giving Bongobondhu an impression of cordiality. Yahya was as stiff as poker as he and Bhutto trumped up charges against Bongobondhu, challenging his loyalty to Pakistan. Having partnered with Bhutto, Yahya's name of the game was to keep Bongobondhu in the dark—the naked truth that became clear over time. Being outraged, Yahya went ballistic. As was the case, it was learned later that behind Bongobondhu's back, the two dramatis personae had already conspired to call it quits. Bongobondhu had no knowledge that, having turned their back on him, they had ended the negotiation and would not return to the drawing board again.

Under the circumstances, Bongobondhu was given Hobson's choice - no choice. One of the ironies of all this is that when the president was required to be politically sagacious, he demonstrated a lack of foresight in analyzing the situation. Faced with an outraged populace and warnings of imminent separation, Yahya reportedly reaffirmed his right to veto a constitution that he believed went too far in the direction of autonomy. A determined Bongobondhu, however, was not ready to play second fiddle, having known that his people stood four squares behind him. This was his source of strength and encouragement that never made him run out of steam.

In the meantime, the news media insinuated that a self-centered Bhutto was seen to have put his political career ahead of his people. From what little information was available during the last stage of the parley, the media gathered that an overambitious Bhutto had already begun to cast serious doubts over Bongobondhu's loyalty to Pakistan. He then successfully mobilized the political elements in West Pakistan against Bongobondhu and constructed a new narrative by claiming that he was the leader of Pakistan. Bhutto cast himself as a defender of Pakistan's integrity as a sovereign state, which made the already vulnerable Yahya believe that, at least for some time. To Bongobondhu, the entire matter was a cloak for the continuation of the dominance of the West Pakistani ruling clique. Yahya's premonition that Pakistan's integrity would undoubtedly be at stake made him lose control over his sense of judgment. Finding Bongobondhu despicable and uncompromising, Yahya flew off the handle.

The in-camera negotiations that had continued from mid-March until 25 used to give some news coverage that the negotiations were going well. In fact, at one point during the talks, the news media reported that the three leaders were within a whisker of working out a satisfactory negotiation. However, later, what came to be known was that Bongobondhu soon realized that Bhutto was a loose cannon who had already made a deal with the military regime. At that point, Bongobondhu could neither trust Bhutto nor Yahya. As part of his game plan, in a sense, Bongobondhu was hedging his bits by preparing his people for liberation and keeping the door open for negotiation. No one was aware of the latest development, or lack thereof, of the exact outcome of the talks. Some people, however, did believe that "certain progress" had been made toward a "political settlement." According to the local news media, Yahya had publicly stated that he had "agreed in principle" to the demands placed by Bongobondhu. Amid uncertainties, many were receptive to such news when rumors of a political settlement with Bongobondhu surfaced again. There was some glimmer of hope in the talk of further negotiation. Some people's expectations were such that all three parties were about to strike a deal successfully.

Having remained distrustful of the regime, most of the public, however, had a gut feeling that the meeting was not going well. Many suspected that Yahya had a game plan. They also sensed the regime's jiggery-pokery- that it was all smoke and mirrors. Even before hearing officially, they were inclined to conclude that Yahya's game was up. They were convinced there must have already been a deal with the devil—between Yahya and Bhutto. They regarded this as an instance of a hawkish Yahya's lack of judgment, his lust for power that forced him to disrespect the verdict of the people of Pakistan.

In the meantime, the vigilantes hit the ground running. Yet, never for a minute did most people think about the consequence of the failure of the negotiation. They heard many rumors, but no one ever believed that the regime was preparing for an alternative approach—a coercive theory of retaining power through the imposition of martial law. The Bengalis were so excited that they never entertained the idea that there could be a sudden and secret military crackdown on civilians, banning of the AL party, and arresting of its leaders.

Failure of the Yahya-Bongobondhu-Bhutto Parley

What exactly happened toward the end of the negotiation? Or how the negotiation came to an end? It's hard to answer these questions. While the parley was supposedly going on, a particular rumor was circulating among the diplomats in Islamabad and New Delhi along the line that General Abdul Hamid Khan, chief of staff of the Pakistan Army, with backing from the top, would likely assume power in the event of a constitutional deadlock. It was also rumored that a disillusioned Yahya was handling the situation in a very condescending manner. No one, not even his close associates, had a clue - all were in the dark. The media also remained vague, failing to give concrete information about the three leaders' bottom line.

We cannot reconstruct the questions raised at the negotiation table due to a lack of documentary evidence. Although talks were continuing, it became apparent that by March 23, they had reached a *cul-de-sac*. By then, the law-and-order situation had already broken down, the banks had been plundered of their deposits, and full-scale warfare had broken out at Chittagong following the mutinies there and elsewhere of the East Pakistan Rifles (EPR) and the East Bengal Regiment (EBR). What is known for a fact, and something for which there is documentary evidence, is that Bongobondhu wanted a broad new economic vision for a modern, united, democratic Pakistan. With no knowledge of the political phenomena, one must consider the military regime failed to understand the epitome of the Six-Point Program.

As the struggle to control the country's destiny ensued, the age-old bastion of nationalism appeared like a Greek chorus to intone warnings and admonitions. Discussions were deadlocked on March 23, when both Bhutto and Yahya saw Bongobondhu's proposal as tantamount to the constitutional separation of the two wings. An incredulous Yahya helplessly saw the success of Bongobondhu's effectively launched noncooperation movement in the following manner: that the AL had become a mass political party based on a radically expanded concept of autonomy under its leader and that, out of frustration and having harbored repugnance, a kind of poisoned atmosphere of intolerance had been developing against the Bengalis and non-Bengalis. Everyone was brimming with over-excitement, displaying their indignation against the non-Bengalis who were seen as anti-Bongobondhu. Each was looking upon the other with rancor and revengefulness. At this critical stage, Yahya, though an experienced military personnel, deplorably lacked tact, flexibility, and, more importantly, political *savoir-faire*. He failed to achieve compromise and stability. A gullible Yahya could not fathom the nature of the mischievous Bhutto's intrigues and political artfulness that made Yahya himself a part of Bhutto's conspiracy and pressure technique without his knowledge. Tragically, Yahya's dictatorial paranoia, doubtless, sowed the seeds of uncertainty in his mind against Bongobondhu.

Without the original transcripts of the March 15-25 in-camera meetings, Ottawa gathered from unconfirmed sources that several things had happened during the last four days following Yahya's desperate plea to both leaders to compromise. What is known is that, personally, Yahya was conflicted with the entire issue as he could not come to terms with the idea of the Six-Point Program implementation, especially when he saw that as the end of a united Pakistan. Although all three failed to reach a consensus, Yahya squarely blamed Bongobondhu. He accepted Bhutto's argument that the degree of provincial autonomy that Bongobondhu was demanding would amount to a virtual secession. No matter how Bongobondhu tried to present his arguments, an obsessed Yahya believed that the Bengali leader's demand embodied the quintessence of Bengali separatism, that it was Bongobondhu's dream to break away from Pakistan eventually. This was anathema in the military regime's eyes. Yahya, however, has not given up yet. He remained busy explaining to the two leaders the importance of agreeing.

In the meantime, again, the military regime was infuriated seeing how Pakistan's Republic Day, the national festival day observed on March 23 every year, was renamed by the militant students as "Resistance Day." The expectation was that Bongobondhu's declaration of the "Republic Day" as the "Resistance Day" or "Bangla Desh Day" throughout East Pakistan following the issuance of a "declaration of emancipation" meant that the birth of Bangla Desh was in the offing. At that time, Small, having learned from Werner Adam, the Islamabad correspondent of the *Neue Zurcher Zeitung* and the *Far Eastern Economic Review* who was there in Dhaka, informed Ottawa about Adam's report in the following manner: "The Bangla Desh flag was flying everywhere; only in the Cantonment and at the president's house were Pakistan national flags seen flying." [60]

Amid all the furor, Bongobondhu also attended a mass rally in Dhaka where the green-and-gold flag of "Bangla Desh" was again unfurled. Simultaneously, hoisting the new Bangladeshi flag at shops, schools, and public buildings instantly became an issue of grave concern to the president as the people were already "pledging" allegiance to the new state. Naturally, this happened much to the harassment and indignity of an outraged Yahya who found it upsetting being provoked to the hilt—the situation was like a red rag to a bull.

This seemed to be the climax or breaking point in the president's tolerance of the situation. The ultra-nationalist students and Awami League's para-military extremists, with their disdain for West Pakistanis (non-Bengalis), were carried away in their minds and hearts, especially when they heard Bongobondhu's pledge that sacrifices will still be made for achieving "Bangla Desh." As far as the president was concerned, it was unacceptable—an absolute no-no for the regime.

As the Bengalis saw the situation, the hoisting of a Bangladeshi flag at the home of Bongobondhu, especially in his presence, by the ultra-nationalist students dramatically brought a hysterical roar of approval from the crowd who had been thronging the streets since the beginning of March, as though they had already defeated the military dictator. The scenes of hoisting the Bangladeshi flag, the tearing up of the Pakistani flag, or trampling underfoot the universal symbol of Pakistan amid joy and cheers at several places by a bunch of overenthusiastic ultra-nationalist students made the regime's blood boil. Some from the motley crowd, having ripped the Pakistani flag, even burned it. To an enraged Yahya, desecrating the national flag meant repudiating one's allegiance to one's country.

To an exasperated Yahya, no one should have defiled the country's flag, which the Bengalis spat at having brought Pakistan's nationality into disrepute. In the eyes of a disturbed Yahya, the contemptuous ultra-nationalists, in their actions, had already crossed the Rubicon. He could not tolerate that Bongobondhu, with his ultra-nationalist followers, was in *de facto* control of the entire province. The central government's authority had already ceased to apply in the province. The winds of change had started to blow. There was no way to turn the tide. This got the regime's dander up—it was unacceptable to the president.

Having carried handmade Bangladeshi flags, the revolutionary extremist students joined the ongoing agitation movements on the streets. They also painted pro-independence graffiti on the walls of the buildings in Dhaka and other major cities of the province. Their emotion ran so high that it seemed like the Bengalis had just discovered a new identity for themselves and their native land. In their minds, it was as though they almost did away with the state of Pakistan out of resentment, anger, and frustration.

Being carried away with a new sense of ultra-nationalism, earlier, the Bengalis were asserting themselves as *"Bangali"* in a united Pakistan; and now, with the hoisting of a Bangladeshi flag under the changed circumstances, they instantly began to see themselves as *"Bangali"* of a free and sovereign Bangladesh— devoid of Pakistan. It was as though, as already noted, the passionate Bengalis were following the same path as the French Canadians who, in the 1960s, were demanding the government of Premier Jean Lesage (1960–1966) to declare Québec as a unilingual French state, that the fleur-de-lys provincial flag flies above all others in the buildings in the province. In that sense, the Bengalis' feelings of euphoria were reminiscent of the French Canadians' shifting of identity from being *"Canadiens* (Canadians)" to *"Canadien-Français* (French Canadian)" until the mid-1960s and then to "Québecois" (people of Québec).

The final act of defiance that triggered the military government's intense choler was the desecration of portraits of Quaid-i-Azam Muhammad Ali Jinnah (the maker of Pakistan), whose status in Pakistan is no less than Mahatma Gandhi's in India. When Yahya saw with his own eyes how the photograph of the nation's founder had been trampled underfoot, he was filled with profound anger, having lost his temper. The newspaper coverage indicated that having felt powerless, the president flipped out, being at the end of his tether. The country was heading toward an unpredictable future without a concrete outcome for the Yahya-Bongobondhu-Bhutto parley, which was supposedly still happening.

Seeing that the Bengalis stood four square and were proudly asserting to be a Bengali in an independent Bangladesh, a courageous Bongobondhu never hesitated to have an eyeball-to-eyeball confrontation with the military. Naturally, he did not want to see the subversion of the great institution of democratic free will. In a sense, the Bengalis, being connected viscerally with the Québeckers of the 1960s, were commanding the absolute loyalty of Bongobondhu. Again, their situation was like the reaction of the nationalist slogans of the Québecois, *"C'est le temp que ça change"* (It's time for a change). The Bengalis were unitedly moving forward under the national stewardship of Bongobondhu, who innately connected with the Bengalis across the province and those living in foreign countries, including Canada.

In the meantime, Yahya, once lost in his obsessive thoughts, was fully convinced that being under the influence of India, the anti-Pakistani Bengalis were committed to creating an independent Bangladesh out of East Pakistan. A helpless Yahya recognized that his game was up and that his recourse to hocus-pocus to bring the Bengalis to their knees did not work. He also realized that Bongobondhu, his adversary, was an indefatigable leader, a go-getter who was not a quitter. Deep down, Yahya became furious at the thought that his adversary (Bongobondhu) was firm in his demand for his people with their full support. Yahya came to believe that if Bongobondhu were left with Hobson's choice, then for sure, he would go for an independent Bangladesh devoid of Pakistan.

As a military man, Yahya's besetting sin was his rapacity for power. Having talked in riddles, finally seeing a bound and determined Bongobondhu, came Yahya's warning across the bows that he would take drastic action against anti-state pro-Indian elements. With that realization, he turned to his plan B - to move the army in secretly, as though waving a magic wand would do the job. Although a military veteran, Yahya was a new political kid on the block.

At this game stage, no one knew that Yahya was opting out of negotiation secretly and treacherously instead of handing over power to the elected representative. Naturally, he did all this without discussing it with any political leaders. It would be learned only later that the president had already decided it was time to crack the whip by then. He chose to flout the mandate of the people unmistakably expressed through the National Elections—a traitorous act indeed. Given the scarcity of materials, the Trudeau administration believed that the Yahya regime probably had already adopted a contingency plan to put down a popular uprising. When the law-and-order situation deteriorated, the actual decision to implement plan B was made while the negotiation was still going on, but it was not moving to Yahya's satisfaction. A constitutional solution was impossible. Along the line, at some point, the talks must have irretrievably broken down, informed Small.

We shall see later how the negotiation was replaced by a combination of political expediency and raw bigotry that played directly into the hands of Yahya as he set in motion his plan for the elimination of the ultra-Bengali nationalists. There was no media coverage of the exact chronology at that time. Based on the scattered information, under the circumstances, Ottawa officials came to see the entire Yahya-Bongobondhu-Bhutto parley as a Trojan horse—a deceptive means to buy the extra time the regime needed. To better understand the chronology of events, let us take a quick look at how the relationships of the two Commonwealth countries, Pakistan and India, were fast deteriorating before we move to the subsequent events, as pointed out by Small.

Pakistan's Relations with India and East Pakistan's Attitude toward India before the Crackdown

Pakistan's ongoing relationship with India, which had been rapidly deteriorating, directly contributed to Yahya's game plan for subjugating the Bengalis once and for all. We need to take a step back to see the historical animosity between Pakistan and India and the factors that prevented them from establishing a friendly relationship. As the partition of India was not willingly conceded by the Hindu Indians, Pakistanis innately harbored a firm conviction that India would do everything to "undo" Pakistan. The relationship between India and Pakistan had never been what may be termed as "normal" since the creation of Pakistan in 1947.

Only two months following the creation of Pakistan, India had sent its army to occupy Jammu and Kashmir - a Muslim-majority area in the subcontinent. This was often referred to as the "Kashmir issue" or the "Kashmir question," which became one of the most critical hot-button issues in India-Pakistan relations. All through the 1950s and 1960s,

Pakistan maintained that the Indian government's assurances that the occupation was temporary and that the people of Kashmir would be allowed to determine their future by a plebiscite did not take place. The government of Pakistan maintained that if self-determination was the governing principle for the partition of India, then the people of Kashmir should also be allowed to exercise such rights.

Also, although Bongobondhu and thirty-four other Bengali politicians and nonpoliticians were released, the Agartala Conspiracy Case brought by the government of Pakistan in 1968 strained the Bengalis' relationship with the military regime. Since the military regime did not trust the Bengalis, it made political sense to the government to remain on its guard against India—Pakistan's archenemy and its Bengali agents. From 1947 to 1970, several issues cropped up between Pakistan and India that forced the two governments to remain vigilant against each other. The East Pakistani Bengalis, however, did not look upon India as such like their West Pakistani compatriots.

Moving forward, the relationship between Pakistan and India came to its worst stage following the incidence of hijacking on January 30, 1971, of a Fokker Friendship aircraft of Indian Airlines in Lahore, West Pakistan. This caused a significant escalation of tension in the already-strained Indo-Pakistan relations. Two members of the Kashmiri Liberation Front forced the aircraft to fly to Lahore, Pakistan. They demanded the release of some thirty-six political detainees held by the Indian authorities in Kashmir. The passengers were returned to India by bus, but the aircraft was blown up since the Indian government refused to pay the ransom. This was done despite the effort by the Pakistani authorities to prevent this.

The apparent discomfiture of the Indian government over the Lahore incident embarrassed the Yahya government at its inability to control the situation. When the two hijackers were granted political asylum in Pakistan, the Indian government immediately accused Pakistan of complicity in the hijacking and of failing to prevent the destruction of the aircraft. It retaliated by banning all Pakistan overflights of Indian territory. Having denied any responsibility, Pakistan pointed its finger at Gandhi herself. It accused her of having precipitated the crisis through her decision in January to exile Sheik Muhammad Abdullah, who had been fighting for the rights of the Kashmir region. Earlier, the exiling of Abdullah and banning his Plebiscite Front Party had made Pakistan furious. Pakistan argued that the ban had forced all flights between East and West Pakistan to go around India via

Ceylon (now Sri Lanka), creating a significant burden on the Pakistanis. The Gandhi administration argued that Pakistan should pay compensation for the aircraft that was destroyed in Pakistan. India also believed that this would work as a solid deterrent to Pakistan in any future act of hijacking.

Both countries sought Canada's intervention because the relationship between India and Pakistan was rapidly weakening. We shall see in Chapter 2 how the Indian high commissioner to Canada immediately approached officials at External Affairs in Ottawa to intervene in an unofficial capacity for mediation. Canadian High Commissioner to Pakistan John Small too was asked by Pakistan's foreign ministry "for anything Canada could give to reduce tension" [61] and to "do anything to persuade India to lift its unilateral ban on overflights (which appears to be a contravention of the Chicago Convention as well as the bilateral Air Agreement between the two countries)."[62] Although both high commissioners became involved in "bringing the two countries together to work out a mutually acceptable resolution of the dispute," [63] Canada believed the parties themselves should resolve this type of dispute. Canada's effort underscored the necessity of taking urgent steps to prevent hijackings. Small alerted Ottawa by saying that the observers believed that the situation seemed increasingly likely to occur given the asylum granted to the two Kashmiris in Pakistan.

Domestically, the situation got even worse when the two leaders of East and West Pakistan adopted entirely contrary attitudes toward the hijacking incident, reflecting their widely different positions on the Kashmir issue. While Bongobondhu immediately condemned the hijacking as a "senseless act and deplored the destruction of the aircraft, Bhutto visited the airfield at Lahore and personally congratulated hijackers"[64] for their heroism. The opposing views of the two leaders of the same country left the citizens polarized, making the military government wonder about the kind of cooperation it would receive from the Bengali leader shortly.

In the meantime, Islamabad kept its eyes open and ears to the ground regarding the Indian National Elections held from February to March 1971. Pakistan speculated that, because of factionalism, Gandhi probably would not win a clear majority and that an uncertain coalition would probably emerge. When the National Elections gave Prime Minister Indira Gandhi, the Indian National Congress leader, a massive verdict that the people were gaining absolute control over India's newly elected Parliament, Pakistan was utterly taken aback. Naturally, a disappointed regime's fear and suspicion were reinforced even more strongly because of India's support for the Bengalis. Bongobondhu's stated pro-Indian position, "Friendship to all and malice to none," made the military regime vehemently frenetic. Yahya was so disheartened that he could neither tolerate the AL's position nor do anything about it. Being furious, the president went berserk at his inability to countenance the fact that the Gandhi administration was extending its full support to the anti-Pakistani nationalist Bengalis.

Feeling thwarted and outmaneuvered, a frustrated Yahya turned to do a reality check. He recognized how years of outright discrimination had resulted in a strained relationship between East and West Pakistanis and the Bengalis' feelings against the central government that had been allocating resources to defend Pakistan against India, even at the cost of East Pakistan. Upon further reflection, Yahya appreciated the *why* and the *how* of the grave concerns of the Bengalis, although, to the West Pakistani rulers, it was inconsequential. The regime's indignation toward India made it dissatisfied with Bongobondhu's way of looking at Pakistan's lifelong adversary. Despite the official "hands-off" policy, the Gandhi administration's promotion of the view that East Pakistan had not only suffered linguistic suppression and humiliation but had also been suffering colonial economic exploitation in the hands of a military dictator drove a hopping mad Yahya up the wall. He became so deluded that he was convinced that the majority of the Bengalis were secessionist and pro-Indians and, therefore, anti-Pakistani.

Pakistan on the Eve of Military Crackdown

In the meantime, while the negotiation was going on, the Bengalis learned through the grapevine that, at a closed-door meeting with General Abdul Hamid Khan, chief of staff of the Pakistan Army, Yahya had been discreetly discussing the military's desire to perpetuate power. It was learned only later that, reportedly, Yahya had called Lieutenant General Tikka Khan on the night of March 24, 1971, to share his frustration concerning the negotiation not proceeding to his total contentment. At that time, the replacement of Vice-Admiral Syed Mohammad Ahsan, a non-Bengali known for his sympathy toward the Bengalis, by Tikka Khan was noted with caution even by the news media. The Bengalis knew about the glaringly ill-famed Khan, who had earlier earned the sobriquet of the "Butcher of Baluchistan" for his bloody repression of a similar movement for autonomy in that province.

Being in the dark, no one could tell whether the negotiation that began on March 15 had broken down or what was going on militarily or politically. To the Bengalis, the appointment of Khan demonstrated Yahya's profound insensitivity, which gave the Bengalis an ominous sign. Naïvely, the Bengalis, however, were so overexcited with the idea of an independent Bangladesh that they never imagined that a possible brutal military suppression was in the offing. Early on the twenty-fifth evening, about twenty to thirty truckloads of armed "Red Caps" (followers of the extremist "Bangla Desh" peasant leader and chief of the National Awami Party, Maulana Abdul Hamid Khan Bhashani), were moving into Dhaka.[65] The National Awami Party (NAP) followers were visibly over-enthusiastic in responding to their leader's call. No one at that time knew that the dialogue between the three protagonists (Yahya, Bongobondhu, and Bhutto) and their associates had already broken down and that the regime had secretly put up the shutters.

It was learned later that Governor Tikka Khan was immediately brought up to speed. Yahya personally ordered him to remain prepared if called upon to act.[66] The same evening, on March 24, GOC 14 Division, Major General Khadim Hussain Raja, and the adviser to the governor, Major General Rao Farman Ali Khan, were summoned by Tikka to give them a heads-up. Yahya was so obsessed that he needed immediate advice from his close associates, but surrounded by a bunch of hawks, no one was around to reason. Sadly, although to everyone in the military, Yahya was well-known for his hedonistic life of drinking, sexual pleasure, and carefree entertainment, even when the country's integrity and stability were at stake, no one was there to advise or chide the president about his near insanity. Influenced by a mischievous Bhutto, the president ordered his people to plan for a possible emergency.[67] So secret was the president's game plan that no one knew anything about his behind-the-scenes work while the regime was cleverly pretending it was still engaged in negotiations. Following the clandestine clampdown, it was only later that the news media learned that the president had left secretly but kept the military powder dry, being ready, armed to the teeth for further action—implementing his policy through brute force.

With no knowledge of what was being planned, the Bengalis learned that, according to the regime, both Bongobondhu and Bhutto had floundered on the issue of autonomy vis-à-vis national integrity. The Bengalis did not know that Yahya and Bhutto had remained steadfast in sticking to their agendas only to stall the democratization process. Consequently, Bongobondhu found himself in a catch-22 situation. On the one hand, he argued that the Six-Point Program was the *only means* to remedy the wrongs of the past by ensuring equality for all Pakistanis—sharing power with those elected by the people, establishing democracy, and equal participation of all Pakistanis across the country. Conversely, the two headstrong leaders, Yahya and Bhutto, saw Bongobondhu's insistence on greater autonomy as a veil for secession with India's help. By then, Bongobondhu recognized Yahya as a tough nut to crack, and Bhutto was going off the rails.

Bongobondhu became convinced that Yahya, who held the card, had the power entirely in the hollow of his hands and that the regime would not offer greater autonomy on a silver platter. He also decided not to harp on the exact string. Again, seeing that throughout the parley, Bhutto was making a gesture of derision being cut up rough, Bongobondhu also had a gut feeling that Bhutto, having made a deal with Yahya, was playing hardball politics. A courageous Bongobondhu clarified that he would not put up with Bhutto's absurd demand nor Yahya's use of the "national integrity" card when he should have focused on transferring power. Unsurprisingly, therefore, with a sinking feeling, Bongobondhu remained both stubborn and persistent in his demand. Pretending that he was putting his best foot forward, Yahya continued to use the "song and dance" strategy while playing the same "national integrity" card. To Bongobondhu, this was Yahya's final turn of the askew to intimidate him. Bongobondhu concluded that the issue of integrity was a pretext to perpetuate military rule in Pakistan as the regime wanted to remain in the saddle, having ignored the unequal status quo.

With the availability of information later, Ottawa learned that the totalitarian-minded dictator Yahya had already been persuaded against Bongobondhu by a politically self-centered Bhutto while the negotiation was going on. Yahya refused to lay down the mantle of military leadership even though Bongobondhu was the prime minister-designate. Having ignored the democratic legitimacy to which Pakistan was committed, Bhutto and Yahya ganged up to knock the stuffing out of Bongobondhu. With a stout heart, Bongobondhu was made of sterner stuff who would not allow the regime to keep a tight rein on the Bengalis. Despite being under tremendous pressure, Bongobondhu is known to have remained cool and calm and yet hellbent on his demands. In the meantime, Yahya realized that his game was up and that he had met his Waterloo. A vainglorious Yahya's tomfoolery is that he immediately resorted to the military crackdown, which was his plan B, eliminating his challengers through Machiavellian means. A deluded and politically charlatan, Yahya merely took steps to fix a man he loved to hate intensely. Complete censorship of all news (print and nonprint) was imposed with the secret military clampdown.

Looking back, as Ottawa officials interpreted it, the parley was merely a scene of fruitless debate used as a Trojan horse to strategize the military regime's secret game plan. The action of *Operation Searchlight* was under wraps. It was not until after the crackdown of March 25, 1971, that the people learned about the final episode in the choreographed drama. Although the initial information was scarce and misty, through the world media, Ottawa later learned about the abrupt, mysterious, and clandestine departure of a weakling Yahya on the evening of March 25, when he was still officially engaged in a negotiation with Bongobondhu and Bhutto.

Having ended his brief dalliance with democracy, as he left, Yahya ordered his army "to crush the movement and restore the full authority of the government."[68] Most Bengalis were shell-shocked—stupefied. They were paralyzed with fear and confusion, not knowing what was happening. They also learned a few days later that Bhutto, escorted by Brigadier Jahanjeb Arbab, had left Dhaka the next day (March 26) for Karachi—all under wraps. Upon his arrival in Karachi, Bhutto is reported to have said to his chief escort: "Thank God, Pakistan has been saved." [69]

In re-imposing complete martial law, a determined military regime was under no illusion concerning its comprehensive plan to wipe out the nationalist movement, thinking that there would be no formidable difficulties in snuffing out the pro-Indian Bengali rebels once and for all. In his naïvety, the military leader did not realize he would be fighting a losing battle. When the Bengalis got wind of the army's intended military assault just a couple of hours before, the AL leaders, ultra-nationalists, and many members of the public, afraid for their lives, began to go into hiding. Many began to flee to India to seek asylum. It was later learned that Bongobondhu was arrested the same night from his house.

Evidence obtained after the fact suggests that the Yahya-Bongobondhu-Bhutto parley was stalled, only to give more time to the Chief of the Army Staff, General Abdul Hamid Khan, to enable him to reinforce the West Pakistani army already stationed there. We shall see later how Ottawa would also learn that, while the negotiation was going on with

Bongobondhu, more than 60,000 troops of the Punjab Baluch regiment had reached East Pakistan just before the planned clandestine military crackdown.

In the next chapter, we shall see how the Yahya regime went about its surreptitious clampdown on the Bengalis.

Notes and References

1. The author met Mitchel Sharp on several occasions when he was retired. He was, however, still working as then Prime Minister Jean Chretien's honorary adviser from 1993 to 2003. On September 10, 1995, in one of his informal meetings with the author, Sharp recalled many challenges he encountered when the Bengalis were fighting for their independence; he also described how he was placed between a rock and a hard stone. At that time, Sharp had ample time to talk to the author. He also narrated to the author how he sought advice from his colleagues. The author was impressed by Sharp's personality, the conviction of his arguments, and, more noticeably, how he engaged himself in an utterly frank conversation with the author.
2. *Canadian News Facts: Journal Magazine.* Marpep Pub. Toronto. 1970, p. 467.
3. Statement by the Secretary of State, *External Affairs Daily,* Louis S. St. Laurent (CHCD. April 29, 1948, pp. 341–2). Mentioned in R. A. Mackay, *Canadian Foreign Policy 1945–1954, Selected Speeches, and Documents.* McClelland and Stewart Limited, Toronto, 1971, p. 361.
4. Donald C. Masters, *Canada in World Affairs, 1953 to 1955.* Toronto, Oxford University Press, 1959, p. 122.
5. For details, see "From Pakistan to Bangladesh 1969–1972: Perspective of a Canadian envoy," by John Small in "Special Trust and Confidence," published in *Envoy Essays in Canadian Diplomacy,* edited by David Reece, Carleton University Press, 1996, pp. 209–237. Hereinafter referred to as *Envoy Essays in Canadian Diplomacy.* Canada's relationship with Pakistan, however, grew stronger with time.
6. For details, see "From Pakistan to Bangladesh 1969–1972: Perspective of a Canadian envoy." *Envoy Essays in Canadian Diplomacy. Op. cit.* p. 213.
7. *The Globe and Mail,* dated October 18, 1955.
8. Confidential Memorandum for the Minister titled Canadian Policy on Recognition of "Bangla Desh." Canada. Department of External Affairs, dated January 5, 1972. File # 20-Bangla-1-4. Hereinafter, all information used in this chapter from the Department of External Affairs' records shall be referred to as External Affairs.
9. *Ibid.*

10. Canada. Canadian International Development Agency. *Annual Report, 1971*, p. 24.
11. *Ibid.* p.5. As early as January 1971, Canada had already shipped 3,000 tons of relief supplies to Chittagong, East Pakistan, to help an estimated 22,000 cyclone and tidal wave victims.
12. Canada. Canadian International Development Agency. *Annual Report, 1972*, p. 47. In March 1971, Canada's development assistance to Pakistan, which commenced in 1951, had totaled $359 million.
13. Canada. Department of External Affairs. *Annual Report, 1971*, p. 14.
14. For detailed information on this subject, see Peter Hullett Desbarats, René: *A Canadian in Search of a Country*, McClelland and Stewart, Toronto, 1976, pp. 142v143.
15. https://www.thecanadianencyclopedia.ca/en/article/royal-commission-of-inquiry-on-constitutional-problems. The Royal Commission of Inquiry on Constitutional Problems (Tremblay Commission) was appointed by the Québec government under Chairman Justice Thomas Tremblay to study the distribution of taxes among the federal government, the provinces, the municipalities, and the school boards; the "encroachments" of the federal government into the field of direct taxation, especially its taxes on revenue, corporations, and inheritances; the consequences of these "encroachments" for the legislative and administrative system of Québec and the collective, family, and individual life of its population; and generally the constitutional problems of a fiscal character.
16. *Montreal Star*, dated March 7, 1968.
17. *Canadian News Facts: Journal Magazine.* Marpep Pub. Toronto. Vol. 2, no.7, April 19, 1968, p. 30.
18. *Ibid* p. 30.
19. https://en.wikipedia.org/wiki/Vive_le_Qu%C3%A9bec_libre
20. *Montreal Star*, dated May 9, 1968.
21. "The Problem of Québec." By Meherunnisa Ali in *Pakistan Horizon*, Third Quarter, 1971, Vol. 24, No. 3, pp. 20-31.
22. *Canadian News Fact*, 1971, p. 525. *Op. cit.*
23. *Ibid,* 1971, p. 528.
24. Notes for a national broadcast, dated October 16, 1971 – First Among Equals, p. 7.
25. Handel, Dan. *The Process of Priority Formulation: U.S. Foreign Policy in the Indo-Pakistani War of 1971.* Westview Press, Boulder, Colorado. 1978, p. 72.
26. We shall see later how the 1952 Language Movement catalyzed the assertion of Bengali national identity in East Pakistan and became a forerunner to Bengali nationalist movements, including the Six-Point Program and, subsequently, the Bangladesh Liberation War. From 1953, February 21

was the Language Movement Day, a national holiday in Bangladesh (then East Pakistan). Moving forward, in 1999, UNESCO declared February 21 as International Mother Language Day in tribute to the 1952 Language Movement and the ethnolinguistic rights of people worldwide. Today, February 21, is, like before, a national holiday. It is observed throughout the country with solemnity. The credit for this is attributed to two Canadians, Rafiqul Islam and Abdus Salam, of Bangladeshi origin, for their relentless efforts in realizing their dream through their work with UNESCO.

27. *The Shaheed Minar* is a national monument in Dhaka, Bangladesh, established to commemorate those killed during the Bengali Language Movement demonstrations of 1952 in what was then East Pakistan.
28. In 1955, the name of the organization was changed from East Pakistan Awami Muslim League (EPAML) to East Pakistan Awami League (EPAL) to reflect the secular nature of the organization) by Huseyn Shaheed Suhrawardy).
29. The central government's belated action, however, did irreparable damage to the pride and sentiments of the Bengalis. The tragic killings of 1952 never obliterated the wounds the Bengalis were subjected to for their demand for recognition of their vernacular language. In that sense, almost from the beginning of their lives in Pakistan, most of the East Pakistani Bengalis found non-Bengali West Pakistanis, including those in power, to be arrogant, patronizing, and condescending. They believed that the majority of West Pakistanis were indoctrinated with a negative stereotypical view of the Bengalis.
30. See *Glossary of Terms*
31. The author vividly recalls participating in the 1969 mass upsurge by attending most rallies and demonstrations organized by the Dhaka University Student Union. At that time, he was a third-year student at Dhaka University.
32. The author recalls his experience in one such public meeting of Bongobondhu in June 1966 when he addressed a large crowd in Sylhet Registry Field as part of his province-wide meetings. Seventeen-year-old author and his childhood crony Rahat Ahmed Chaudhuri, both of whom saw Bongobondhu face-to-face for the first time in their life, recall the question Bongobondhu asked them point-blank: "Are you young boys ready to go to jail if need be?" "Yes, we are ready for sure," was their instant answer.
33. *Pakistan Times,* dated November 20, 1969, Speech of G.M. Syed.
34. *Ibid.*
35. I. N. Tewary. *War of Independence of Bangla Desh: a documentary study with an introduction*, Varanasi, Navachetna Prakashan, 1971, p. 9.
36. *Newsweek,* dated August 2, 1971.
37. *Newsweek*, dated March 15, 1971.
38. *Kitchener-Waterloo Record*, dated May 3, 1971.
39. *Newsweek*, dated March 29, 1971.

40. *Kitchener-Waterloo Record*, dated April 12, 1971.
41. *Kitchener-Waterloo Record*, dated May 5, 1971.
42. *Newsweek*, dated March 29, 1971.
43. *Montreal Star*, dated March 29, 1971.
44. Peter Hazelhurst, "How Ali Bhutto's political moves led to catastrophe in Bengal" in *The Globe and Mail,* dated June 12, 1971.
45. Syed Abul Maksud. *Maulana Abdul Hamid Khan Bhashani.* Bangla Academy, Dhaka, 1994, pp. 367–368.
46. Postponement of the National Assembly reminded the Bengalis of the sudden dismissal by the central government within six weeks of the assumption of power of the United Front Ministry of the Awami League and the Krisak Sramik Party, which had won the 1954 election in East Pakistan. At that time, the central government's target was Sher-e-Bangla Fazlul Haque, the provincial Chief Minister who called for the establishment of full regional autonomy based on the Lahore Resolution on which India was partitioned in 1947. In the same way, this time around, the target was Bongobondhu; instantly, the Bengalis were so profoundly dismayed at the sudden, unexpected action that they saw this as a betrayal of election promises—yet another Punjabi maneuver.
47. Confidential telegram from John Small, high commissioner to Pakistan, to Ottawa. Telegram # 285, dated March 2, 1971. File # 20-India 1-2 Pak. External Affairs. *Op. cit.*
48. Hossain Ali, high commissioner for Bangladesh in India. "PAKISTAN-ITS BIRTH AND DEATH," published in *Bangladesher Shadhinota Juddho: Dolilpotro (History of Bangladesh War of Independence: Documents),* Volume 4, p. 437. Government of the People's Republic of Bangladesh. Ministry of Information. Dhaka, edited by Hasan Hafizur Rahman, 1982.
49. The author, 21 then, was present at the Dhaka Ramna Race Course Field on that day and heard the speech; he recalls his feelings of exuberance, excitement, and uncertainty.
50. Confidential Memorandum for the Acting Minister titled *Crisis in East Pakistan*, signed by A.F. Broadbridge, Bureau of Asia and Pacific Affairs. Dated, March 8, 1971. File # 20-Pak-1-4. External Affairs. *Op. cit.*
51. *The Ottawa Citizen,* dated March 29, 1971.
52. *Ibid.*
53. Akhtar, Jamna Das. *The Saga of Bangla Desh.* Oriental Publishers, Delhi, 1971. p. 250.
54. Years later, Yahya's intense abhorrence for Bongobondhu became known through the work of Major General Rao Farman Ali Khan, who wrote about what Yahya told him: "I am going to sort out that bastard." Major Gen (Retd) Rao Farman Ali Khan. *How Pakistan Got Divided.* Jang Publishers, Lahore, Pakistan, p. 55. 1992.

55. *Kitchener-Waterloo Record,* dated March 15, 1971.
56. *TIME* (The Time Magazine UK Ltd. London,) dated March 15, 1971, p. 31.
57. *Pakistan Times,* Lahore, dated February 16, 1971.
58. *Ibid.*
59. Major Gen (Retd) Rao Farman Ali Khan. *How Pakistan Got Divided.* Jang Publishers, Lahore, Pakistan, pp. 54–55. 1992
60. Confidential telegram from John Small, high commissioner to Pakistan, to A. E. Ritchie, Undersecretary of State for External Affairs. Telegram # 274, dated March 29, 1971, p. 2. File # 20-E-Pak-1-4. External Affairs. *Op. cit.*
61. Memo from Legal Operations Division to Pacific and South Asia Division, External Affairs, reference # Seabed Geneva telex # 515 March 15/71, dated March 19, 1971. File # 20-India-1-3-Pak. External Affairs. *Op. cit.*
62. *Ibid.*
63. *Ibid.*
64. Confidential Memorandum for the Minister, signed by A. E. Ritchie, Undersecretary, Secretary of State for External Affairs, dated February 16, 1971. File # 20-India-1-3 Pak. External Affairs. *Ibid. Op. cit.*
65. This was reported by John Small, high commissioner to Pakistan. He gathered this information from Werner Adam, the Islamabad-based correspondent of the *Neu Zurcher Zeitung* and the *Far Eastern Review,* who was present in Dhaka during that time and was ordered to leave Dhaka the next day following the imposition of martial law. This was made possible by the Islamabad-based Henning Heider, chargé d'affaires for Switzerland, who convened a small group to meet with Adam. CONFIDENTIAL telegram from John Small, high commissioner to Pakistan, to A. E. Ritchie, Undersecretary of State for External Affairs. Telegram # 274, dated March 29, 1971, p. 2. File # 20-E-Pak-1-4. External Affairs. *Op. cit.*
66. Fazal Muqeem Khan stated this in his book *Pakistan's Crisis in Leadership,* National Book Foundation, Islamabad, 1973, p. 66.
67. *Ibid.* p.66.
68. *Newsweek* (Newsweek Inc. New York, NY), Dated April 5, 1971, p. 31.
69. Salik Siddiq. *Witness to Surrender.* Oxford University Press, Karachi, Pakistan. 1977. p. 77.

CHAPTER 2

Surreptitious Military Attack and Canada's Immediate Reaction

*T**he Trudeau administration came to learn about the sudden secret military attack code-named Operation Searchlight on Bengali civilians in East Pakistan within hours. The military regime's plan for a clandestine assault, which commenced on March 25, 1971, in East Pakistan, was outlined on March 19, 1971, by Major General Khadim Hussain Raja GOC 14th infantry division and Rao Farman Ali in the GHQ of the Pakistani army in Dhaka, East Pakistan. President Yahya Khan secretly left Dhaka on the night of March 25, having instructed his army to "do their duty and fully restore the authority of the Government"*[1] *He did that perhaps without ever realizing that the military government had failed to seize the last opportunity of an acid test of his government's willingness to accept the reality of equal partnership in a fundamentally changed and re-structured Pakistan by the sharing of power with Zulfiqar Ali Bhutto, leader of the Pakistan People's Party (PPP) and other leaders in West Pakistan under the leadership of the Awami League (AL) Chief Sheikh Mujibur Rahman (Bongobondhu).*

On the night of March 25, 1971, the army surreptitiously launched a sudden but planned, brutal, and treacherous attack on the unarmed civilian population to crush the autonomy movement and enforce the military government's authority in all of Pakistan. Instead of moving forward toward democratization, it launched a campaign of massacre, genocide, and cultural suppression of the Bengalis. The chaos, systematic military repression, and decimation of the Bengalis in East Pakistan had continued unabated. The killing led to a re-invigoration of Bengali nationalism among the people of the land. The attack by the very people who are responsible for protecting the Bengalis instantly forced people to leave their native land and seek refuge in India. During the first few days, Ottawa officials examined the various sources of information and considered some sources apocryphal, unsubstantiated, doubtful, unauthentic, equivocal, and spurious. They relied on sources from Canadian high commissioners in Pakistan and India to determine Canada's reaction.

Canada's knowledge of the background information up to the crackdown of March 25, 1971

Within the Department of External Affairs, the Bureau of Asia and Pacific Affairs was entrusted with coordinating and managing Canada's relations with Asian and Pacific states. The South Asia Division was concerned with Canada's ties with India, Pakistan, Afghanistan, Ceylon (now Sri Lanka), Nepal, Bhutan, Sikkim, and the Maldives Islands. The bureau was responsible for gathering and analyzing all pertinent information from India and Pakistan to brief the minister. Canada had been keeping herself posted on the deteriorating circumstances in East Pakistan since the 1970 National Elections. The newspaper reports of the tumultuous weeks after last year's National Elections in Pakistan were a part of Ottawa's newsgathering strategy. Canadian Broadcasting Corporation's (CBC) journalist David Praag's write-ups on Pakistan's polity used to appear regularly in Canadian newspapers. Praag and a few of his colleagues, such as Selig Harrison, wondered if the military regime was politically competent to cross the finish line in its quest for democracy. Immediately after Bongobondhu's overwhelming victory, Praag brought to the attention of readers in Canada the extraordinary wave of patriotic hysteria of the Bengalis who were getting ready to give more blood to have their rights accepted by quoting Bongobondhu: "If it [that is, to give blood for greater autonomy] is needed, I'll call for revolution."[2] The report implied that it would test the wisdom of the military government and West Pakistani leaders on how they chose to react to a hitherto unrivaled expression of the Bengalis' right to self-determination.

Around mid-February, Zulfiqar Ali Bhutto, leader of the Pakistan People's Party (PPP), insisted that the Six-Point Program must be modified, while Sheikh Mujibur Rahman (Bongobondhu), chief of the Awami League (AL), who won the majority of seats, had been strictly maintaining that the said program was not subject to revision. John Small, Canada's high commissioner to Pakistan, worried about India's potential involvement, the impasse, and its impact on the future direction in which Pakistan was heading. A concerned Small immediately outlined the grim future of Pakistan that he could see, given the demonstrated doggedness of the two leaders. He warned Ottawa: "If both sides remain adamant, there will be no constitution, with all the dangers that such a situation would engender. If the Six-Point Program is accepted as the basis of the constitution, there will be two Paks in effect. In either case, the result may not be very different."[3] He further noted that though the Yahya regime was resentfully surprised to see Bongobondhu's popularity, the results of the National Elections of 1970 had exposed with greater clarity the strength of democracy and the rise of Bengali nationalism.

Although Bongobondhu was at the zenith of his popularity with his Six-Point platform on which he won the National Elections, the full support of Maulana Abdul Hamid Khan Bhashani, leader of the National Awami Party, was deemed to be crucial for national solidarity. This was particularly relevant to maintaining Bongobondhu's influence in the villages and among leftist groups across the province. Fortunately for Bongobondhu, unconditional support instantly came from the Bhashani group, which did not skip the notice of the Canadian media. As early as 10 March, the *Globe and Mail* wrote that Bhashani had already "called for outright independence ever since the December 7 general election."[4]

The "main political forces represented by Mujib and Bhutto seem irreconcilable. The military can no longer ensure unity by force,"[5] thus wrote a disturbed Small. It was a critical time in East Pakistan since any substantial watering down of Bongobondhu's Six-Point Program was unlikely to be accepted by the Bengalis, argued Small. As he viewed the situation, there was no room for compromise between the two leaders. According to Small, if Bhutto were more of a statesman than he had given evidence of being to date, there might be a hope of salvaging the country. But he was not sure of saying anything anymore. "How much were the West Pakistanis, the Punjabis in particular, willing to pay for a united

Pakistan?"[6] Thus, Small begged Ottawa the same question he had been asking himself.

By mid-February, Ottawa gathered that Bhutto was not prepared to play by democratic rules for which the Bengalis were ready to go their way. Small saw this as a red flag that "for any thoughtful and patriotic Paki political outlook for his country is anything but promising."[7] There was a sour, querulous, and resentful expression by most of the Bengalis in social gatherings and shindigs, observed Small, whose curt but cautionary note was that "Pak is headed for separation."[8] Small also noted the rising bitterness on both sides, pushing Yahya and Bongobondhu into a potentially uncontrollable challenge and response cycle. Daily street demonstrations by ultra-nationalist students who were openly demanding an independent Bangladesh made Small believe that "parting of ways is not far off."[9] To Ottawa observers, there were too many contradictions and uncertainties surrounding the power transfer.

The day after the sudden postponement of the National Assembly *sine die*, Small informed Ottawa how most of the Pakistani newspapers of March 2 quoted Bongobondhu, who was outraged to see Yahya's arbitrary flouting of the democratic process. Within hours, Ottawa also learned from Small about Bongobondhu's immediate launching of a powerful noncooperation movement. Ottawa did not fail to note how quickly, under Bongobondhu's leadership, the Awami League (AL) became a mass political party based on a radically expanded concept of autonomy. An apprehensive Small, however, saw only grim and uncertain days ahead of the country. He alerted Ottawa by saying how the president had been attributing to the "hard attitudes of the two leaders" and to the "general situation of tension created by India" that had "further complicated [the] whole position."[10]

Given the deplorable situation, a sharp-eyed Small suspected that Yahya was looking for a scapegoat for the impasse. He warned Ottawa of Yahya's attempt to shift the blame without taking responsibility. In a prophetic note about his observations within forty-eight hours of Yahya's announcement, Small wrote: "Bengalis are impatient to seize reins of their destiny, and if Pak wishes to ride with them, they are welcome but strictly on EastPak [East Pakistan's] terms."[11] He feared that Bongobondhu and his followers would, for sure, "take to the streets and demand independence for East Bengal,"[12] and that "any chances of East and West Pak remaining united as a country in my view have all but certainly disappeared."[13] Any attempt on West Pakistan's part to nudge East Pakistan aside, or even to share driving at this stage, would not be tolerated by the Bengalis. Thus was the high commissioner's message from Islamabad.

Following Bongobondhu's appeal for the noncooperation movement, the reactions of both groups were reported daily by the news correspondents stationed in the subcontinent. The foreign affairs cognoscenti responsible for the Pakistan file quickly recognized the ominous nature of the news that was being reported. They noted Praag's cautionary note that "in the long run, a determined people cannot be held down."[14] The next day, he also wrote: "How long can such a non-violent, non-cooperation movement stay non-violent with the hatred presence of that symbol of East Pakistan's exploitation, the army, on every street corner?"[15] Ottawa made a note of Bongobondhu's earlier appeal to Pakistan radio and television not to blackout the news of what was going on in Dhaka since the imposition of strict censorship on the news by the regime had made it a prison offense to report anything prejudicial to the nation's interest. Ottawa was disturbed by the growing intense contempt and bitterness between the Bengalis and non-Bengalis.

In the meantime, many interpreted Bongobondhu's historic 7 March speech to the "nation" as his call for the independence of Bangladesh. Having followed the events closely and being suspicious of what was happening, Small expressed his concerns that it appeared highly doubtful that Yahya would want to transfer power to the elected AL leader without first doing all he could to preserve Pakistan's unity and central control. As noted in Chapter 1, according to Small, a disturbed Yahya's dilemma must have stemmed from seeing Bongobondhu's charismatic leadership and blind followership. A vulnerable military dictator, Yahya could not ensure the complete and absolute integrity of Pakistan anymore, wrote Small. According to Small, "the prospects of him [Yahya] being able to do so without bloodshed and prolonged civil strife appear extremely remote."[16]

In the meantime, Small traveled to Dhaka to learn as much as possible. He shared his personal views on the events with government officials and politicians, all in an informal way. Ottawa again made a particular note of the outcome of Small's discreet meeting with Bongobondhu, which took place in Dhaka on March 8, the day after Bongobondhu's acclaimed speech, "to discuss the constitutional crisis" then "threatening the dissolution of the country."[17] To Small, it already seemed like two countries where the leaders mistrust each other. He explored with Ottawa to see *if* and *how* Canada could be discreetly involved in bringing the two parties to an agreed settlement since Small had no direct communication with Bongobondhu in Dhaka from Islamabad. Small wrote to Ottawa underscoring the consequence of a communication breakdown between Dhaka and Islamabad: "Should the Pakistan government be interested in our initiative to convey information from East Pakistan elected leader, it is extremely doubtful, given our lack of communications with Dacca [sic], if we could play a continuing role as messenger."[18]

Ottawa held the view that it would not be prudent to intercede in what was an overly sensitive "internal" political question. Mitchell Sharp, Secretary of State for External Affairs, was thus briefed along the line that there had been no communication between the two leaders, Bongobondhu and Yahya, and that, due to Canada's policy of "nonintervention," it would be advisable to "watch" and gather more information to see how things were panning out. Information from the field came only in dribs and drabs through telexes, news releases, and Situational Reports (SITREPS). Ottawa's advice to the high commissioner in Pakistan was that the government would instead prefer to keep up a certain distance from the conflict, at least momentarily. Two weeks later, however, during the Yahya-Bongobondhu-Bhutto parley, Ottawa remained keen on receiving daily updates from Pakistan. Small continued to keep Ottawa *au courant*.

In the meantime, James George, Canadian high commissioner to India, also joined Small, who provided information from Islamabad to complement Ottawa with additional information from New Delhi. Together, both Small and George began to assist Ottawa as much as possible to help Ottawa wake up to its perils. While the noncooperation movement continued, Ottawa expounded on the rapidly deteriorating situation in East Pakistan and predicted more uncertainties. Like the Canadian diplomats, Ottawa officials were also concerned about the future direction of the impasse. Within a matter of a few days, there was more disconcerting news. "A volatile mixture of economic despair and political frustration, East Pakistan sits perennially on the edge of revolutionary violence,"[19] thus wrote Craig Harrison, a Canadian reporter. Having noted the warnings of the impending tragedy and the precariously explosive situation, Ottawa continued to gather more information from every possible source.

Ottawa was informed that the resumption of the Yahya-Bongobondhu-Bhutto parley, which started on March 15, was going well initially. When Bhutto joined the parley after a few days, Canada became even more hopeful, thinking that the three leaders would find some solution to the political crisis that had threatened to tear the country apart. The media, however, did not fail to notice Yahya's attitude toward Bongobondhu, whom he regarded as the "militant" AL leader, much to his profound resentment. The Bengali leader's astronomical political power in the province made the regime detest Bongobondhu's chutzpah. On March 24, the Canadian news media reported that "plans to form an interim civilian government for the whole of Pakistan has virtually collapsed."[20] The Canadian public was not surprised. Coincidentally, on the same day, Canadians also read excerpts of the newly published book, *The October Crisis,* written by Gerald Pelletier, then Secretary of State, who defended the *War Measures Act* of 1970. This added a distressing emotion among Canadians who had witnessed the October Crisis only five months ago. Pelletier stated that the fear of Québec and Ottawa was real even though what was happening in Pakistan was contextually different from the situation in Québec. [21]

Learning about the news of crackdowns, rebellions, massacres, and reprisals

Sharp's team members in Ottawa also remained busy sifting through hundreds of telexes from India and Pakistan. They tried to reconstruct a narrative of what had happened until the night of March 25. The team came up with something like the following. With the National Assembly scheduled to meet in March, the military regime began a covert troop building, flying soldiers dressed in civilian clothes to East Pakistan at night. Then suddenly, being influenced by Bhutto, Yahya postponed the assembly session, stating that it could not be met until he could decide precisely how much power and autonomy the Bengali leader wanted for East Pakistan that would be acceptable to him. Even though the Bengali leader had not espoused complete independence, the military government interpreted the situation as a loose confederation under which each wing would control its taxation, trade, and foreign aid. As Ottawa understood, the Bengali leader's demand was acceptable neither to Yahya nor the West Pakistani leader Bhutto. Ottawa expected to receive more information from Islamabad daily. Naturally, being confined to Islamabad, Small found himself placed in an awkward situation. He did due diligence with care, having continued to send every bit of information he could get his hands on since there was a complete news blackout immediately following the imposition of martial law.

Without communication links between Dhaka and Islamabad, Small could not send any messages confirming the last outcome of the Yahya-Bongobondhu-Bhutto parley. Strange as it may sound, due to an unknown incident, Canada's high commissioner from Islamabad was unable to communicate with Ottawa immediately following the outbreak of hostilities on March 25 in East Pakistan. "We had no telegraphic contact with our high commission during this period," thus wrote A. E. Ritchie, undersecretary of State for External Affairs, informing the minister.[22] Ottawa immediately took the matter with the high commissioner for Pakistan and was able to restore communications within days.

Again, with strict press censorship imposed throughout Pakistan, reports that were trekking through to Indian towns from across the border became the only source of information about the situation in East Pakistan. Earlier, only a day before the military takeover, Ottawa received two types of news from Islamabad. In one of his telegrams, Small noted that the "Awami League has been becoming more restive as negotiations dragged on, and extremists have undoubtedly been pressuring Mujib to maintain [a] hardline."[23] A concerned Small ended his telegram by stating, "I can see no hope of reconciliation without the sort of statesmanship that has never…existed to date in Pak [istan]."[24] Ottawa immediately sought further clarification from Islamabad.

At the same time, Ottawa was also given to understand that the leaders were about to break through the impasse. Under the heading "Yahya settles Pakistan crisis, parties report," it was briefly noted in a Canadian daily that the "Leaders of five minor groups in Pakistan's National Assembly said yesterday that President Yahya Khan and Sheikh Mujibur Rahman had reached complete agreement on constitutional questions that threatened a political split between East and West Pakistan."[25] The same paper quoted Mian Mumtaz Daulatana, president of the Council Muslim League, who said: "Pakistan has been saved from division, and its integrity has been maintained."[26] In the face of a complete reversal with a lack of information on the latest development and/or deterioration in their endeavor to reach an agreement, such positive information made the assessment almost impossible. Naturally, Ottawa had several questions: (1) Why was it necessary to expel the foreign correspondents immediately after the army action? (2) Why were their notes, TV films, etc., destroyed before they were obliged to leave Dhaka? Ottawa officials had no straight answer.

With the expulsion of the foreign correspondents from Dhaka on March 26, journalists began to file stories from safe places, away from the troubled area. The news, of course, was based on what the reporters were hearing, second-hand reports. During the initial period, the international disruption of communications between the two wings, the travel restrictions placed on resident diplomats in Dhaka, and the inability of foreign observers to fly from the west to the east wing contributed at large to the obscurity of the immediate past conditions in East Pakistan. While Ottawa was awaiting the situational reports from Canada's high commissioners to India and Pakistan, Ottawa regarded the news as a mixture of lies, half-truths, and juxtaposition of events.

Having kept in tune with the political grapevine, Small gathered more firsthand information that confirmed his suspicion: that the Pakistani army secretly launched a sudden large-scale operation designed to enforce the central government's authority in East Pakistan. "All signs commencing yesterday indicated [that] something had gone wrong in constitutional negotiations in Dacca [sic],"[27] observed Small. This information was obtained through a network involving the US ambassador consul general, Archer Blood, who was in Dhaka then. Small also confirmed that all political leaders, including Yahya, had returned to West Pakistan and that, according to the press, there were two versions of the shooting. "[The] Awami League's version being the cold-blooded army killing of unarmed civilians; official version alleging the use of the army to restore law and order."[28] "The whereabouts of East Pakistan's breakaway leader Sheik [h] Mujibur Rahman, remained a mystery today as fighting in Pakistani civil war entered its fourth day."[29]

It was not clear as to how exactly the crackdown started—whether the Yahya regime's clampdown came first or whether the ultra-nationalist Bengali rebels declared independence first. Reliable news from East Pakistan was unavailable since the military government enforced strict censorship. The bits and pieces of news were coming as a shock, simply because of the magnitude of the military action—that it was Yahya who called the shots. However, the events leading up to the attack had not been altogether unexpected. Ottawa recognized how a restive Small's cautionary remarks were coming palpably true.

With the availability of gory detail, Ottawa was horrified at the news that the West Pakistani soldiers, having stormed out of their barracks on the outskirts of cities, had killed thousands of unarmed Bengali men, women, and children. Small informed Ottawa that the troops opened fire with artillery on the town while tanks rumbled through the streets, gunning down people. He also reported that large-scale massacres and senseless killings, brutalities, and atrocities were being committed on a massive scale, along with widespread burning and destruction of property and the multitude of indignities that the Bengalis were being subjected to every day since the sudden crackdown. Based on the latest situation, Small outlined his message in the following manner: while the negotiation was going on, Yahya imposed martial law, and the Pakistani army, as planned, secretly started military actions on the unarmed civilians and against units of the EPR (East Pakistan Rifles), EBR (East Bengal Rifle) and the provincial police on the night of March 25, where the incidence of the casualty was beyond any estimation.

Small informed Ottawa that due to the massacre of the Bengali police forces in and around Dhaka on the night of March 25 by the West Pakistani army, the surviving members of the East Pakistan Regiment (EPR) and East Bengal Regiment (EBR), the Mujahids[30] and Ansars[31] also revolted and immediately broke their allegiance to Pakistan. Ottawa concurred with Small that the Bengalis were the victims of a planned, secret, and sudden crackdown. Personally, wrote Small, to the Bengalis, it was an attempt by the Pakistani army, a ruthless agent of the Yahya government consisting almost entirely of West Pakistanis (Punjabis, Baluchis, and Pathans), to crush the resistance movement. Small believed the Bengalis should not be judged by their reaction to the sudden attack.

In the meantime, following President Yahya's speech to the nation, one of the Canadian dailies reported that "Sheik[h] Mujibur Rahman today proclaimed East Pakistan the sovereign independent People's Republic of Bangladesh according to a clandestine radio report maintained near the East Pakistan border."[32] The reporter added that "the broadcast identified as the 'voice of independent Bangla Desh.' ...The Sheik [h] has declared the 75 million people of East Pakistan citizens of the sovereign independent Bangla Desh."[33] The next day, another Canadian daily wrote: "Radio Pakistan said Sheik [h] Mujibur, leader of the outlawed Awami League, was arrested several hours after he proclaimed independence."[34] The same paper added that "the rebel leader, Sheik [h] Mujibur Rahman, was reported to have called on his people to resist the army after it clamped a 24-hour curfew on Dhaka and other areas." In a clandestine broadcast,

Sheikh Mujib told East Pakistanis to "resist the enemy forces at any cost in every corner."[35]

Within hours, Ottawa also learned through its diplomatic channels about the same development—announcement by the Bengalis of the formation of Bangla Desh (as it was spelled by the news media in two syllables then) as a *sovereign* and *independent* state through a clandestine radio broadcast as early as the morning of March 26. This was when all foreign correspondents had been quarantined, and there was a complete news blackout throughout East Pakistan. Later, it was learned that this radio broadcast originated from a telegram from Bongobondhu himself, who sent it before his arrest. Mohammad Abdul Hannan of the Chattogram District Awami Party Secretary General read it. Ottawa was unable to verify this information at that time.

The next day, however, Ottawa also learned that on March 27, there were two more announcements in quick succession by Major Ziaur Rahman, Second in Command of the 8th East Bengal Regiment in Chattogram from Swadhin Bangla Betar Kendro. In the first announcement, having announced Bangladesh's independence, Zia was also declared to be the provisional head of the government; and in the second broadcast that followed immediately, Zia, on behalf of Bongobondhu Sheikh Mujibur Rahman, claimed that an independent Bangladesh had been established. Again, due to the strict censorship, Ottawa could not verify the exact timing and wording of these announcements. Amid chaos and confusion, at that critical moment, Small informed Ottawa with certainty that the Bengalis who fled to India had already formed the core *Mukti Bahini* (Liberation Forces) that began to operate as guerrilla units within the military-controlled areas of East Pakistan with the direct help of the Indian army personnel. Ottawa also learned that, instantly, the Bengalis, encouraged by Zia's bold announcement, had begun to refer to their native land as "Occupied Bangladesh" under the "Occupation army" instead of the Pakistani army all through the period the Bengalis were fighting for independence.

Ottawa found it ironic that, to Yahya, Bongobondhu manifested two extremes within less than two and half months. Ottawa recalled that Yahya said on January 15, 1971, "Sheikh Mujibur Rahman is going to be the country's future prime minister."[36] Shockingly enough, in his address to the nation on March 26, 1971, Yahya said just the opposite: "Sheikh Mujibur Rahman's action of starting his non-cooperation movement is an act of treason...He has attacked the solidarity and integrity of this country. This crime will not go unpunished."[37] Although the environment was murky and ominous, Ottawa had yet optimistically assumed that there might be an agreement among the three parties - the military regime, Bhutto, and Bongobondhu, prime minister-designate.

Being hard-pressed for reliable information, Ottawa lagged. Officials did not know that the Yahya-Bongobondhu-Bhutto parley had failed and that when Dhaka city was heaving with people, Yahya left Dhaka secretly, having instructed the military personnel "to do its job." Yahya branded the Bengali leader and many of his colleagues as the "enemy of Pakistan" and affirmed that they would be tried for their crimes. Contradictorily, he also claimed that he remained committed to transferring power to the people's elected representatives. Ottawa learned that the military regime considered the Urdu-speaking non-Bengali members in the Mujahid Bahini [38] who collaborated with the Pakistani army as patriotic Pakistanis.

In the meantime, Small also reported that the "EastPak [East Pakistan] rifles and police were disarmed, dispersed or rounded up, and in the process, many were killed and wounded." [39] He also informed that on the morning of March 26, the army seized the radio station at Dhaka, and after that, the radio station made fifteen new martial law regulations. The military regime proscribed the Awami League (AL) and banned all political gatherings and processions. The army ordered all government servants to return to work, civilians to surrender vehicles and arms, and schools and banks to remain closed. In addition, the army assumed powers of entry and search. On the same day, Yahya also addressed the people of Pakistan in a national radio broadcast and gave his version of the events regarding the Bengali leader of East Pakistan, who had referred to his obstinacy. Small cautioned Ottawa: "Dissension within military ranks could result in further changes...The drama is only just beginning to unfold."[40] Upon receipt of information from Canada's diplomats in India and Pakistan, Ottawa officials found Yahya's March 26 Speech to the Nation a hollow speech completely divorced from truth and reality.

Small pointed out to Ottawa Yahya's abhorrence for the rebellious Bengali elements and their leader, which was discernible in Yahya's speech. Ottawa quickly learned about the kind of resentment that existed in the minds of the military regime. As Ottawa understood, Bongobondhu's party, which had won a landslide victory on a platform that would have given East Pakistan virtual autonomy, was prevented from fulfilling its pledge to the voters. Ottawa also looked back and recognized how, until the military crackdown, there were reports of rampant violence and expression of hatred and antipathy between the Bengalis and the military regime. As officials came up to speed, they also learned that the plan for the attack by the largely Punjabi army of West Pakistan upon the Bengalis was entirely under wraps, having planned it meticulously to ensure its success.

Without any documentary evidence on the details of the Yahya-Bongobondhu-Bhutto parley, it was impossible to piece together all the bits and pieces of available information. Small kept Ottawa up-to-date to the extent possible and warned Ottawa officials that, faced with conflicting information and many unknowns and imponderables, any assessment under the circumstances would be speculative. Apart from Yahya's position on the issue, the difficulty observed by Small was further complicated and compounded due to Bongobondhu and Bhutto's uncompromising stand. When it came to the crunch, all three leaders, observed Small, became so adamant that they were reported to have failed to adhere to one of the basic principles of negotiation: that solutions come from a favorable compromise in which no one ultimately wins or loses—one must be ready to win some and to lose some even though the stake for each party is exceedingly high.

Again, being on the lookout, Small was quick to connect with several evacuees from Dhaka whose testimonies became a valuable source of information. He was distressed, having heard from the returning diplomats who had the misfortune of witnessing some brutal crimes committed by the Pakistani army. Among other sources was one from Werner Adam, a Swiss journalist who gave the actual account of the news of the massacre he had witnessed—the material evidence of killing, burning, looting, and destruction of property. On that fatal night, Adam was outside the Hotel Intercontinental, where there were about thirty-four other journalists, including three CBC TV team members. They were first quarantined and then, later on, forced out of East Pakistan on the early morning of March 27 (that is, the night of March 26). They testified to the vicious treatment meted out to unarmed Bengali civilians since the night of March 25, which the regime had continued to reinforce to crush the rebellion. All these journalists and reporters were thoroughly searched. They were relieved of any films, tapes, letters, or anything else the military personnel thought useful— something about which we shall read more in Chapter 3.

The daily dispatches of Small and George, along with the media coverage from various sources, assisted Ottawa officials in getting a picture of killings and burnings by the Pakistani army despite the regime's denial. As they sifted through telexes and newspaper clippings containing the eyewitness accounts of the evacuees, they were horrified to recognize the nature of the violence that was beyond any framework of moral comprehension. They also learned from the media coverage of the horrendous picture of the situation in East Pakistan, the indiscriminate killings of the non-Bengalis by the Bengali rebels during the early part of the days following the imposition of martial law with the beginning of the crackdown. Ottawa gathered from the two high commissioners that since the night of March 25, the demonic army, driven by irrational bloodlust, was alleged to have behaved mercilessly against the civilian Bengalis - killing in cold blood and reveling in their infernal work.

When the communication facility with Islamabad improved and became a bit easier for Small, he met with his diplomatic colleagues and many more recent foreign evacuees to hear their versions of the events from the horse's mouth. At that time, Small also learned about the secret plan of the military regime - that its objective was to trap and lure the political leadership into a dialogue, gain time, build up arms strength, and strike when the precise time arrived, that is, on March 25. Small also learned from the eyewitness accounts of foreigners who left East Pakistan how the gangs of gun-toting Pakistani soldiers had turned Dhaka city into a nightmare landscape of shattered streets and burning houses. Small immediately communicated to Ottawa by saying that Yahya's negotiations were merely a smokescreen to buy time until enough West Pakistani troops had been brought to launch the planned secret attack.

While gathering information, Ottawa officials remained dismayed, having found news bits about the ferocious ways in which the Bengalis' houses were blown up, how they were forced to observe the most rigorous curfews, and how people were beaten up and murdered. Countless women picked from the streets or their houses were apprehended and confined to the barracks. The overwhelming evidence of all incoming materials and testimonies of the evacuees suggested that it was the Pakistani army that had triggered the "reign of terror." Canada learned that the military regime had been using naked terror and brute force to crush the freedom fighters and suppress the rebellion.

It was essential to verify every bit of news, instant reporting, and commentary, as the Trudeau administration believed that if errors of fact recur persistently, such reported facts would often be repeated as accurate.

Ottawa's examination revealed the regime's trajectory of uncontrollable violence that continued in the regime's macabre operation. The gist of the high commissioner's message from Islamabad was that the army was allowed to terrorize the Bengalis who felt as though their province was struck by the specter of persecution—invoking their worst nightmare.

Despite strict censorship, Small's confidential messages from Islamabad did not contradict what was reported in the international news media. In that sense, Ottawa was glad that the telexes from Islamabad and New Delhi were consistent - one less thing to worry about. Given their rich backgrounds, Ottawa considered both George and Small as veteran diplomats who were thought to have not only the knowledge of the subcontinental body politic but also knowledge of human relations that was required for power relationships, whether between individuals or states, and that the most important thing to know was the power to do *what,* to *whom,* and *under what conditions.*[41] Being engaged in ritualized behavior in countries like India and Pakistan, where many utilize symbols in their diplomacy, Canadian diplomats knew to recognize the temperament and eccentricities of the behavior of the people in power and those around them. To help Ottawa understand the complex subcontinental body politic, both Small and George took it upon themselves to provide their knowledge of the subcontinent's history while interpreting and narrating the events. Ottawa became familiar with the manipulation of symbols and the use of metaphorical gestures common to subcontinental politicians. One may regard this as the transfer of knowledge by experienced diplomats regarding the subcontinental polities to Canadian analysts living in Ottawa.

The up-to-date information from the subcontinent enabled Ottawa to get a better sense of the mysterious inner world of the diplomats and recognize the pressures and constraints under which diplomats operate using their own experience at brinkmanship. With his expanded understanding of the perspective on what had been happening in the field as opposed to what the military regime had been propagating in the name of transfer of power, Small cautioned Ottawa about what *could* happen since the army's operation had been a planned attack to suppress the forces of democracy: "[The] Army can probably control the major cities of East Pakistan temporarily, but opposition exists, will grow, and ultimately is sure to triumph. We are witnessing a classic colonial display reminiscent of the final years of Brit raj in India."[42] While reviewing the events considering the subcontinent's history, Ottawa officials became aware of how, by then, the Bengalis had lost their faith in the country for which they fought in 1947 first for its independence and, again, in 1965, for its defense against Pakistan's archfoe India. High Commissioner Small did not hesitate to say what he saw regarding the West and East Pakistanis' antipathy toward each other.

Ottawa officials relied on their own "sources of information" from George and Small. In addition, in New Delhi, George successfully connected himself with the representatives of the Gandhi administration and the rebel forces at his initiative. As a result, George procured regular news dispatches from the rebels' radio station in India. This added a new dimension to the knowledge base when there was no official news on the freedom fighters' progress.

To assist Ottawa in briefing the minister, both George and Small immediately began to send detailed Situational Reports (SITREPS) that kept Ottawa abreast with the latest happenings in the field—news of killings and exodus of refugees and their implications, etc. Ottawa officials, however, had some reservations about the reported number of deaths. They believed the media was inflating the number but could not estimate it under specific circumstances. In any event, Ottawa received enough information to agree with the generally held view that the Pakistani army's military operations from the first day of its planned clampdown had been both brutal and ceaseless.

The messages from the veteran diplomats helped Ottawa officials deepen their understanding of the events— how the socio-geo-demographic factors (that is, population size, the linguistic composition of the population, and distance between the regions) had contributed to the strength of the nationalist movement that found its final expression in the declaration of independence of Bangladesh. Nevertheless, as officials began to analyze the incoming information from the field, specific questions cropped up: "How to sort the truth from propaganda in a world of conflicting accusations and counteraccusations?"

However, those in charge of analyzing information found that the events were seen from two different perspectives, making it difficult for them to find the truth from the welter of reports originating from the field. However, the availability of more information from New Delhi and Islamabad soon created another problem for Ottawa officials regarding consistency in interpreting what had been happening in Pakistan. Proactively, both Small and George found a way to facilitate the process of endorsing. Having made a *tour d'horizon* of the general situation to react, the two high commissioners worked together. They compared their take on each issue to clarify the contradictory nature of the news bits before sending them off to Ottawa to interpret them from a Canadian perspective. Despite efforts of the martial law authorities to control information on East Pakistan, the world media showed that the military takeover was not as smooth as it was claimed. Although the regime expected that the rest of the world would believe its narrative, in reality, its communication strategy did not work to serve its purpose. Questions about the chronology of events following the clandestine military clampdown had remained unanswered—a problem fundamental to all historical writing.

In the meantime, the discussion on the Indo-Pakistan conflict became a subject of daily ritual in Sharp's schedule. Ottawa analysts were teamed up to piece the information into a single narrative for Sharp. Although Undersecretary of State for External Affairs A. E. Ritchie's team oversaw writing the main briefing notes, Ritchie was under tremendous pressure to assess the latest situation in East Pakistan. The team was disturbed to learn about the killings in East Pakistan that were taking place daily and the frightened Bengalis' flight to India in thousands seeking refugee protection. The regime's choler and disdain for the Bengalis, who were supposed to have been protected and guarded against, became much too evident to many news correspondents who witnessed the "sacking of the premises of the Awami League paper, *The People* near [the] Intercontinental Hotel [on the] night of March 25... "[43]

The news, both official and unofficial, that reached Ottawa ascertained that President Yahya had categorized the Bengali leader of the majority (Bongobondhu) as "separatist," having offered his justification for military action. The more the team members reflected on the events with information at hand, the more they came to see how the Yahya regime's irreversible decision, the killing of innocent civilians at unawares, and every other conspiracy began to fall into place in the breathtakingly fast environment. Ottawa put together various fragmentary pieces of information from New Delhi and Islamabad to determine the veracity of the news. Richie's team was competent enough to coordinate the information quickly, efficiently, and effectively for the minister.

Canadians were reminded by their competent news reporter, John Walker, who quoted Bongobondhu's March 7 speech, delivered to thousands of enthusiastic Bengalis. In it, he alluded to the military regime's patronizing attitudes and condescending manner of governing the country: "The dark conspiratorial forces have always intervened in our country whenever the people were to take over power through the democratic process."[44]

Within a matter of five days, the team summed up all of Small's expressed misgivings in the first assessment report in the following manner: "At present, it appears that serious fighting continues, and it is generally agreed the government forces probably have gained the upper hand, at least in the major cities. In the long-term, our High Commissioner, in his latest report from Islamabad, has predicted that the Army can probably control the major cities of East Pakistan temporarily. Still, opposition exists, will grow, and eventually is sure to triumph."[45] On the sixth day of the military clampdown, while Ottawa officials were still receiving information from Islamabad and New Delhi, their assessment of the situation ran somewhat like the following: To the Bengalis, the sudden swift attack on the civilians seemed like valid evidence of a deep-seated hatred of the Bengalis by the murderous regime. The Bengalis' reaction to the indiscriminate killing also instantly began to beget hatred against each other—the Bengalis and non-Bengalis.

Ottawa officials also informed Sharp about the reaction of the government of India in the following manner: "Due to public sympathy in favor of East Pakistan's struggle for autonomy, both Indian Houses of Parliament passed a resolution calling on all governments to take urgent and constructive steps to prevail upon the Government of Pakistan to put an end to the systematic destruction of the people of East Pakistan."[46]

Analysis of Information by Ottawa Officials from April and May 1971

Ottawa found the information mindboggling as it continued to receive more disturbing information from the field. In any event, having gathered as much information as possible from a variety of sources, Ottawa officials, on the last day of March, briefed Sharp about Ottawa's attempt to obtain the latest reliable information from the field in the following manner: "News censorship and lack of communications make it particularly difficult to obtain an accurate assessment of the situation in East Pakistan. The problem is compounded by a breakdown in our telex link with Islamabad, which we suspect has occurred due to a directive from the Pakistan

Government, which is making every effort to maintain a news blackout and avoid unfavorable publicity on their handling of the crisis."[47]

Those in charge of analyzing the news from overseas were aware that news reporters often tend to be skilfully disingenuous. Many times, some aspects of news are consciously or unconsciously falsified through defects of observation, understanding, short memory span, or slanted according to the needs of the interested parties. Ottawa made special efforts to pay attention to such instances as people view news bits through different lenses of loyalty. Having gathered information from India and Pakistan, Ottawa officials evaluated its accuracy to determine how it fitted into the rest of the information.

In the meantime, Sharp was also brought up to speed regarding the position of the Gandhi administration in the following: "The Indian Government is under strong pressure to take some action over the situation in East Bengal and on April 1st Parliament unanimously adopted a resolution introduced by the Prime Minister Gandhi expressing "solidarity, sympathy, and support for the struggle of the people of East Bengal. Despite the reference to 'support,' the secretary of the Indian Cabinet denied any government intention to go beyond moral support at this time; our High Commissioner has heard reports, however, that the Indian Cabinet has been discussing further assistance and support that might be offered to Bangla Desh."[48]

Ottawa also made a note of how the Yahya regime was viewing the situation from a different angle. Canada was struck by the regime's blaming of India for everything that was happening in Pakistan. Despite the bland assurance of the military government that things were under control in East Pakistan, all evidence suggested the contrary. Receiving more information from the field, Ottawa learned that Yahya was firm in his decision to "restore law and order." As far as the regime was concerned, there were mass killings of non-Bengalis in an outburst of Bengali hatred. This was, therefore, followed by a sudden wholesale massacre of Bengalis, Muslim as well as Hindu, as the Pakistani army attempted to destroy both the leadership of the Bangladesh movement and its popular support. The regime's *raison d'être* was that the AL leaders had no mandate from the people of Pakistan to dismember the country. Ottawa was disturbed to see Yahya's abhorrence of Bongobondhu—so intense that he assigned guilt even before demonstrating Bongobondhu's guilt through the court system.

Ritchie's team began assessing every bit of information on the furtive military operation by conducting a week-by-week examination of the daily dispatches from India and Pakistan. To assist the Ottawa team, high commissioners to Pakistan and India focused on the following questions while speculating on the events unfolding in the subcontinent: (1) What could be expected to happen shortly? (2) What could President Yahya hope for and work toward, in the long run, to preserve the country? (3) After what had happened, would the Bengalis trust the military regime? An anxious Small reinforced his fear, having predicted that it would be difficult in the long term to keep Pakistan united after what had happened to the Bengalis.

While reviewing the incoming telexes, Ottawa wanted to learn more about how India was reviewing the situation since India had a direct stake in the matter. George had evidence that India had the full backing of its citizens. Based on this, he wrote to Ottawa: "We have mentioned in several telegrams the virtual unanimity of Indian opinion in favor of Sheikh Mujibur Rahman and his supporters in the current struggle with the martial law regime in East Pakistan. The unanimous resolution passed by the Indian Parliament on March 31 was the most striking example of this sentiment and remains the most authoritative statement of the official policy of the Government of India."[49] George also noted an apparent contradiction in India's position concerning self-rule or greater autonomy and shared with Ottawa his concerns. He was stuck by India's *raison d'être* for her intervention in support of Bongobondhu in East Pakistan "when it was denying recourse to democratic procedures in Kashmir to Sheikh Abdullah."[50]

Just about the same time, Ottawa was informed that "a purge of Bengalis and their supporters from the armed forces, foreign services, and key civil service posts have started in full swing" and that "all Pakistan Embassies and High Commissions have been placed under the direct control of the military attachés"[51] from whom the ambassadors and high commissioners were asked to take orders. It was further reported that the "Bengalis, particularly belonging to the diplomatic corps, have been put under strict surveillance and are under orders of immediate transfer to Islamabad."[52]

Ottawa approached the entire matter with caution in order not to be directly involved in the "internal matter" of another country. Using multiple sources, the team drafted three memoranda for the minister within two weeks—between March 31 and April 16. Ritchie's analysis helped Sharp understand that he would need additional time to articulate his government's position based on a consistent application of Canada's foreign policy options. Ritchie's memo to the minister, dated April 2, 1971, explained that "it is an internal problem of a member country" and that Islamabad had not yet received any "information to confirm published reports of mass killings." [53] Sharp was then advised succinctly: "We are watching the situation closely, but we were not convinced that declarations by outside governments were likely to be particularly helpful at this time."[54] In each note, Ritchie briefly highlighted the following questions: "What had happened in East Pakistan? What was the reaction of the Bengalis to the military takeover and reprisals? What is the extent of involvement of the government of India at each stage of the crisis? What will happen nationally within India and Pakistan and internationally involving the superpowers?"

For Ottawa officials, it was a quick learning curve - how the spirit of "Bengali nationalism" found its place among the discouraged Bengalis that originated historically in reaction to the ideological basis on which Pakistan was created back in 1947. They also learned about the political movements for greater autonomy and freedom that were triggered by the non-Bengali West Pakistani–dominated central government's imposition of a cultural, political, and economic hegemony upon East Pakistan. Ottawa recognized that neither Yahya Khan nor the military regime ever understood the depth of the commitment to the concept of Bengali nationalism by the disenchanted Bengali populace of East Pakistan. In the meantime, Small wrote what he believed would likely happen realistically: "With the countryside under the effective control of the Awami League and dissident Bengali army units, and it is unlikely that the Central Government will be able to pacify the province by military means alone."[55]

A comparison of the military regime's version with other primary sources, i.e., factual accounts giving firsthand reports of the situation by those who had witnessed the clandestine clampdown and ongoing reprisals, revealed many contradictory news items. Ottawa analysts had difficulty accepting the authenticity of any news coming out of Pakistan due to a credibility gap between the Yahya regime's claim and its actions. Ottawa found the regime's persistent claim that its actions were its appropriate measure against the "breakdown of law and order" situation in East Pakistan was, in fact, a euphemism for a military takeover.

Ottawa recognized how the entire province was dominated by the assertion of a particular kind of Bengali consciousness that united the Bengalis of all classes - peasants, workers, and petty bourgeoisie - under the latter's hegemony. Earlier, Small cautioned that the ultranationalists were discussing a separate and independent Bangladesh. With all such background information, Ottawa also gathered how Bhutto in West Pakistan had been advocating a strong central government and a *united Pakistan*, having fiercely resisted Bongobondhu's insistence on East Pakistan's autonomy.

In the meantime, the news from Islamabad and New Delhi reinforced that the army had stepped in to suppress the results of the electoral victory. The key point that emerged from the Canadian representatives' frank and straightforward messages was that the president was viewing the Bengalis as mutineers who had defied the law and order of the very government he was charged with running. As Ottawa officials delved more into the matter, they also recognized the military regime's perception of the Bengalis as headstrong "Hinduized" rabble that had already aroused derision in Yahya's mind.

Ottawa became convinced that Bongobondhu's overwhelming victory must have made Yahya believe that the AL leader had become a game changer, making him more demanding, single-minded, and uncompromising, having been influenced by India. Yahya found him a changed man since he won the election; the president believed that the people of East Pakistan voted for provincial autonomy and not for the country's disintegration, wrote Small, indicating the regime's view of the post-election situation. Small further elaborated his take on it by saying that, instead of settling the controversial and constitutional issues with mutual understanding in a spirit of giving and taking for the sake of national solidarity, all parties (Yahya, Bongobondhu, and Bhutto) became intransigent and defensive. This made Ottawa believe that the regime was not interested in transferring power but aimed to find ways to perpetuate power. A further review of several essential messages from Small helped Ottawa conclude that Yahya's game plan was to blame the Bengali leader, openly and forcefully, whom he saw as a "rabble-rouser." Unsurprisingly, Ottawa also noted how the military regime tried to brand Bongobondhu as "a CIA agent and a tool of Soviet revisionism." [56]

In any event, Ottawa then examined the regime's line of argument and found that, to the government, the Bengali leader chose a path of defiance, disruption, and secession. Much to Ottawa officials' astoundment, while still reviewing the information, they saw the military regime's deliberate differential treatment of the actions of Bhutto and Bongobondhu. Ottawa already knew about an obdurate Bhutto warning to the MPs about not attending the National Assembly session. Ottawa was dumbfounded to note the military regime's treatment of the Bengali leader with prejudice and repugnance since the regime found only Bongobondhu culpable of non-cooperation. There had been no pointing of fingers at Bhutto, who had evidently ganged up against Bongobondhu and had openly refused to attend the National Assembly session.

Following the first round of review of all incoming messages, dispatches, telexes, memos, and situational reports from New Delhi and Islamabad on the events starting with what the military regime called "restoration of law and order," Ottawa officials reencountered the same problem—determination of the integrity of many reports of atrocities, killings, and destruction. Ottawa officials became suspicious simply due to the contradictory nature of the information compared to the world news. Ottawa became convinced that the Yahya regime was stretching the truth to convey its narrative to the rest of the world. A distressed Small wrote to Ottawa: "Whatever the tragedy unfolding in EastPak - and it is both heartrending and immense - I think we must try to maintain an overall perspective and distinguish between rumors and emotions (however legitimate). On the one hand, facts and genuine Cdn (Canadian) interests; on the other, it is necessary to avoid the temptation to swallow whole ... and unsubstantiated info that feeds the former but distorts the latter. Pakis complain bitterly of Western press distortion of EastPak situation based largely on exaggerated reports from Indian sources, but they are themselves largely to blame for having expelled foreign correspondents from EastPak for enforcing rigid censorship and for issuing patently false accounts of their own."[57]

It was disturbing to hear from Small the reason for the mass exodus - that was both actual reprisals, the fear of continuous reprisals, and endless persecution that had already begun to drive the majority of Bengalis vehemently against the Yahya regime and non-Bengalis; hence, the killing of each other. In fact, so swift and so sudden was the catastrophe that Ottawa did not fail to notice the regime's use of the time-worn cliché, such as national integrity and restoration of power, to justify the regime's brutal action. Ottawa officials found strong and unshakable evidence of what was being alleged against the Yahya regime. Both the evacuees and news reporters maintained that the Awami League supporters and strongholds in Dhaka were being systematically hunted down and wiped out. Ottawa noted with alarm how the regime was moving ahead with absolute callousness and cruelty following the regime's secret game plan. Having blamed India, the regime maintained that the Indian radio was a vital accomplice in the dissemination of false and baseless reports and the perpetuation of a divisive myth that was encouraging the gullible Bengalis to seek asylum in India without realizing India's ultimate motive—the dismembering of Pakistan.

In the meantime, unlike before, the horror thus far revealed by the fragmentary evidence estimated that the actual killings would be far greater than all the facts that had come out by then. Ottawa officials, therefore, suspected even more destruction of lives and properties. As it turned out, Ottawa's suspicions were well-placed. Within a matter of days, the more Ottawa reviewed the telexes about the holocaust, the more convinced it became that West Pakistan's military bureaucrat landlord elite was willing to shed more blood to perpetuate power in Pakistan. Canada recognized that, in blaming Bongobondhu, the regime did not seem to consider why the Bengalis had been demanding greater autonomy, equal partnership, economic development, self-respect, etc. Instead, the government continued to propagate the myth that no one accepted as it was contrary to the evidence available at that time. Canada concluded that there was enough evidence that the events taking place in East Pakistan could be described only as a carefully coordinated premeditated attack on a defenseless population to crush a movement whose main tactics had been nonviolent and noncooperation. Nevertheless, despite the mounting evidence of an overall plan for mass murder, the Trudeau administration still wanted additional information before it would be able to react officially.

By the end of the second week of April, upon completing the second review of a multitude of information emanating from different sources, Ottawa became aware that the situation in East Pakistan was beyond West Pakistan's control. Ottawa recognized that in the regime's scheme of things, there were wheels within wheels - a complicated process as more news of massacre and rebellion from a variety of sources were surfacing continually. Due to its denials and paradoxical statements, the regime's credibility took a nosedive. The emergence of a rebellion was met with the "brutality and cruelty with which the president's order to the army to reestablish central government's authority in East Pakistan is being executed. Known Awami League supporters and strongholds in Dacca (sic) are being systematically hunted down and wiped out," wrote Small.[58]

Ottawa did not like how the military regime was going ahead with its covert game plan. Instead, Ottawa accepted the high commissioner's version of what happened all of a sudden and his envisioning of the future of the Bengalis' struggle for independence: "The Pakistan of Quaid-I-Azam Mohammad Ali Jinnah is dead."[59] Upon receipt of this telex from Small, Ottawa became gravely concerned. Still, it did not yet seem ready to formulate its formal reaction to the military clampdown and its consequences since the phenomenon of Bangladesh was not yet on Ottawa's radar screen. It was disquieting for Ottawa officials. Since Canada was already involved in assisting the victims of the 1970 natural disaster, she recognized this to be a man-made catastrophe at a time when many homeless Bengalis were still suffering from hunger caused by the tidal waves. Canada was distressed to see another man-made or manufactured political disaster.

Sharp was updated daily with bits and pieces of information on how the Bengalis situated themselves regarding the conflict, having referred to the ultimate objectives of the freedom fighters. While briefing the minister, Ottawa officials frequently referred to the predictions made by the Canadian diplomats stationed in the capital cities of India and Pakistan, with the advantage of watching the events right from the start. Sharp was advised along the following vein by quoting Small, who was utterly frank without being a prophet of doom: "In my view, the ultimate end is clear—whether it takes one year or ten—and that is the final defeat and withdrawal of central government military forces and establishment of an independent Bengal. This I see as a realistic picture of the situation as it exists today and as it will be in the future."[60] Regardless of how Canada wished to view the events, Ritchie felt that it was imperative to keep Sharp in the loop about the diplomats' take on the events as they unfolded.

In the meantime, Yahya's pointing fingers at India prompted Ottawa to gather more information to verify whether that was the case. Although earlier, George alluded to Indian support of the rebels, on April 13, he formally wrote about the virtual unanimity of Indian opinion in favor of Bongobondhu and his supporters in the current struggle with the martial law regime in East Pakistan: "The unanimous resolution passed by the Indian parliament on March 31 was the most striking example of this sentiment and remains the most authoritative statement of the official policy of the government of India."[61]

George's telexes convinced Ottawa officials that the Gandhi administration's actions and declared the position were somewhat antithetical. At the same time, there also came a blow—the news about Hussain Ali, a Bengali, then Pakistan's deputy high commissioner based in Kolkata, West Bengal, India. Following a carefully staged proclamation of the Bangladesh Republic on April 17, 1971, Ali and most of his staff hit the international news by hoisting the Bangladesh flag over his mission, having taken the precaution of withdrawing all mission funds from the bank the previous day. Through George's dispatches, Ottawa learned that Ali had pledged to continue to work in the Bangladesh mission. He then immediately charged the government of Pakistan with instituting a "planned attempt to subdue and crush the entire Bengali nation."[62]

Ottawa also learned a bit more about establishing the provisional government of Bangladesh through George's reports and the determination of the Bengali rebel forces to liberate their native land. As early as April 18, 1971, George shared with Ottawa a critical statement of Tajuddin Ahmed, acting prime minister of the provisional government of Bangladesh: "Pakistan was now dead and buried under a mountain of corpses."[63] The same source said, "No power on earth can unmake this new nation, and sooner or later, both big and small powers will have to accept it into the world fraternity."[64]

Seeing that the provisional government of Bangladesh was established within Indian territory, Ottawa asked George to explore the Gandhi administration's probable future involvement and assistance. George's immediate answer was that, without Indian sanctuary and help, the Bengalis could not have organized the inaugural meeting of a high magnitude. Earlier, George checked with one of the cabinet secretaries who assured him that there was no "intention whatever of GOI (Government of India) support for Bangladesh beyond moral support."[65] George was unconvinced of the Gandhi administration's claim that it would not go "beyond moral support." George was also not confident of "India's claim that she would neither recognize Bangladesh nor make things difficult[66] for "the provisional government of Bangladesh formed on 17th April 1971 in Mujibnagar, half a mile beyond the Indian border, east of Krishnanagar, in a mango grove near the village of Baidyanathala in Kushtia district.[67]

As was the case, George became even more suspicious of India's ongoing active role and her continued and direct intervention since the stakes were highly high for India. By then, Ottawa found it a tad disturbing as there had already been many instances of direct material support for the Bengali rebels by the Gandhi administration. Under these circumstances, Canada saw the Kolkata-based new Bangladesh mission of the provisional government of Bangladesh as an instance of the Gandhi administration's complete support for the Bengalis in their fight to liberate their native land. This was even though the Gandhi administration had been denying its secret involvement. True, India had not recognized Bangladesh yet. Nevertheless, Canada viewed this arrangement as having the same quasi-diplomatic mission, somewhat like the unofficial status accorded to the League of Arab States in New Delhi.

Again, seeing far too many contradictions in India's actions, her apparent position, and covert assistance to the rebel forces, both George and Small spent some time together to determine the government of India's secret game plan, the extent of its unofficial and clandestine role in the conflict, and the events that were unfolding as a result of its surreptitious support and intervention. To help Ottawa comprehend the situation, Small echoed the same sentiment expressed by Yahya earlier - that there had already been clandestine Indian involvement. Small also brought to Ottawa's attention several new press releases by the government of Pakistan that stated that there had been an armed infiltration in East Pakistan by Indian elements and that India had been involved secretly from the beginning. Gorge and Small successfully provided documentary evidence to Ottawa officials in that regard.

Having established the Gandhi administration's covert role, George believed India would recognize Bangladesh sooner rather than later, regardless of what it was saying. After probing into anticipated recognition of Bangladesh by India, George stated in one of his confidential memos to Ottawa that it was made clear to him that the provisional government "must first meet innatl (international) norms of being in effective control of the most territory of East Bengal."[68] On the same note, George also informed Ottawa that one source had indicated that "recognition was imminent and would be followed by covert assistance through unofficial West Bengal volunteers joining Mujib's forces."[69] George also brought to Ottawa's attention a vital part of the discussion that took place in the Cabinet meeting: how far the government of India would "afford to go in support of Sheikh Mujib when it was denying recourse to democratic procedures to Sheikh Abdullah (in Kashmir)?"[70] George then commented that because of different approaches, the decision at the cabinet level might not necessarily correspond to the recommendations of the Indian bureaucracy.

In the meantime, Ottawa also noted that both houses of the Indian parliament, on March 31, passed a resolution in support of the Bengali secessionists. The assemblies of other Indian states also followed suit in support of Bangladesh. Ottawa did not miss to recognize Gandhi's position regarding the military regime's ongoing action and the world reaction - how she rose in Parliament to accuse the world powers of "dragging their feet in reacting to the situation in East Pakistan... "[71] Ottawa also noted Gandhi's warning: "I have pleaded with all countries to recognize this threat to peace in the subcontinent," and that "if the world does not take heed, we shall be constrained to take all such measures as may be necessary."[72]

Examination of the Reaction of the Superpowers

In the meantime, Ottawa examined the world's reaction, especially the responses of the United Nations (UN), the People's Republic of China, the UK, the USSR, and the USA, to the news of military crackdown and ongoing repression. Ottawa remained extra cautious in its reaction due to the nonchalant reaction of the UN itself. Though the response of Secretary-General U Thant was not indifferent, Ottawa initially saw it as less proactive. Canada was not surprised to see how strongly China came out in support of Yahya's effort to preserve the unity of Pakistan, having warned India of any aggression against Pakistan. As an ally of Pakistan for a long time, China saw the events in Pakistan as a case of a "civil disorder" with a conflict between her practical and ideological goals. In the meantime, Ottawa also learned about the position of the British government through its foreign secretary, Sir Alex Douglas Hume. He made it clear that "it is the people of Pakistan themselves who must decide their destinies" and that "intervention of outside will only complicate a very different and distressing situation."[73]

About the USSR, Canada knew initially, within days, that Nikolai Viktorovich Podgorny, the president of the USSR Supreme Soviet, had sent a message to Yahya which contained a strong appeal "to take the most urgent measures to cease the bloodshed, their repressions against the population in East Pakistan, and to go over to the methods of a peaceful political settlement."[74] As for the USA, it was within Ottawa's knowledge that traditionally, the Nixon administration supported Pakistan's military-bureaucratic relationship with each other. Having supported Pakistan, the US was downplaying the potential of the rebel forces with an emphasis on Pakistan's territorial integrity. Ottawa saw the Nixon administration's reaction to the military takeover and the events following the crackdown as demonstrably pro-Pakistani and anti-Indian. Ottawa was also aware that Archer Blood, the US counsel-general in East Pakistan, had sought the Nixon administration's support in condemning the Pakistan government for its military reprisals on its citizens but had no luck. Again, Kenneth Keating, the US ambassador to India, was also known to have attached a higher priority to maintaining good relations with India since Nixon's Indo-Pakistan scheme, which, by then, had generated suspicion among the government and the people of India.

With knowledge of such a backdrop, Ottawa concluded that, as a middle power, and due to Canada's foreign policy constraints, it would be prudent to wait and see before articulating Canada's official reaction. Under the circumstances, seeing the inaction of the UN and the opposing positions of the superpowers, Ottawa followed Canada's "go slow" policy while still reviewing further implications of the reactions of significant countries. At the same time, Ottawa also recognized that, with no direct stake in the subcontinent, Canada's response would be vastly different - much unlike the reaction of the superpower countries of the world.

In the meantime, a resourceful Small continued to seek information from every possible source, such as the British and American missions in Dhaka and Islamabad and foreigners who were being evacuated from East Pakistan immediately following the military takeover. It was only a group of "infiltrators, miscreants, and anti-state elements" and Bengali personnel of East Bengal Rifles and East Pakistan Rifles who "were misled by anti-state elements in the border districts (that) had been sealed off."[75] Thus, it claimed the military regime. Having noted the contradictory nature of the military regime's claim, Small pointed out that Yahya's wrath against the Bengali leader was so deep that he wanted to do away with the Bengalis' demand for its totalitarian solution - through decimation.

While Canada's sympathies were with the victims, she still needed more authentic information to analyze to its satisfaction as the military government's strategy was one of continual "denial" of its repressive measures, starting with its secret crackdown on the Bengali civilians. Small cautioned Ottawa by pointing out that the military regime's "denial" might give only "an appearance of (a) communal issue rather than a political issue."[76] Whatever might have been the military regime's game plan, its "claims of complete army control and return to normality put out by martial law authorities seemed "equally ridiculous and reprehensible,"[77] wrote an observant Small. According to him, the regime was constantly bending the truth. Despite all kinds of disinformation, Ottawa could pick up the main thread to judge Yahya's motive - that having failed to work out a formula, Yahya was head over heels in hate with Bongobondhu.

To move forward with a strong strategy, Ottawa needed to examine the following two items better to understand the game plans of both India and Pakistan: (1) the Yahya regime's secret agenda and (2) the extent of the Gandhi administration's covert assistance to the freedom fighters and its future role. In the meantime, Ottawa also learned about India's inability to "resist the temptation to interfere openly."[78] Small, a bit timorous, thought that "matters could become even more complicated" because "in such an event, Chinese involvement would seem likely."[79] Naturally, messages and dispatches along such veins made Ottawa slightly edgy and disquieted about the dangers ahead. In his analysis of future scenarios, Ottawa concluded that Small was most probably referring to an armed struggle of more expansive proportions that had already existed at that time, with fear of the international repercussions that could ensue from such action. Ottawa needed more time to determine the next steps.

Regardless of what the military regime was saying, Canada found every bit of news consistent in reinforcing the story of ongoing military repression throughout East Pakistan. There was no dispute about whether the reported news from the field came through Canada's diplomatic channels or the world media. Naturally, Ottawa was disturbed. By then, Zulfiqar Ali Bhutto, leader of the Pakistan People's Party (PPP), had already "branded Mujib a calculating secessionist bent on the destruction of a united Pakistan, charging that Mujib had been struggling for the separation of the East Wing since 1966."[80] Ottawa was also disconcerted to note Bhutto's blame game, his absurd stand having welcomed the imposition of martial law. Unsurprisingly, Bhutto had his blessings for Yahya's decisive action to weed out what he called the "secessionists" in East Pakistan. At this stage, Bhutto called for the backhanding of Yahya's actions by all patriotic Pakistanis. To expose the Yahya regime's denial of its brutal activities, Small quickly compiled a roundup of press releases for Ottawa that the military government was putting out. It naïvely thought that putting out frequent press releases stating India's covert supply of arms would be a valuable technique to convince the rest of the world of India's involvement in the "internal affairs" of Pakistan and make people overlook its repressive measures upon the Bengalis. As it turned out, the military regime could convince neither Canada nor the rest of the world.

Within four weeks, Small flew to Dhaka, where he met with Lieutenant General Tikka Khan, governor of East Pakistan, on April 30, 1971. During the appraisal of the situation in East Pakistan, Khan indicated that there were still pockets of resistance. Small raised the question of the security of Canadians, especially members of the Holy Cross Order, some of whom had remained in East Pakistan. Upon Small's request, Khan provided him with a helicopter to meet his fellow Canadian missionaries in a designated spot during his brief visit. During the helicopter tour of the Barisal-Padrishibpur-Noakhali areas, Small also saw the extent of damage to houses and surrounding villages with his own eyes. Small did not have to rely on the testimonies of the evacuees as he saw the devastating situation. Small was flown to the Oriental Institute in Barisal to chat over tea. He met about forty Canadian priests who were still there living in the vicinity. They discussed the general situation concerning transportation and communication problems and what was happening. Small was horrified to hear from them how the invading soldiers went on a rampage in the old city of Dhaka, a particular stronghold of the Bengali leader, breaking down doors, dragging people into the streets, and shooting them instantly.

The missionaries also talked about Canada's continuing interest in the development assistance program in the absence of many Canadian experts who had left East Pakistan. Small learned that several Canadian Holy Cross brothers and sisters had reportedly chosen not to go but to stay in the remote areas of the province. Upon his return to Islamabad, Small reported to Ottawa what he saw firsthand during his visit to various premises in East Pakistan. Small remarked on how the president's vicious recourse to brutal military actions had triggered intense hatred between the Bengalis and non-Bengalis and how both groups were harboring such hatred. Ottawa found Small's special report on his on-site visit to East Pakistan adequate to recognize what the military regime was up to. Ottawa officials also noted that the actions and reactions of both the Pakistani army and rebel Bengali forces were dangerous as they were seen as precedent-setting examples for the unknown future.

In the meantime, George from New Delhi also reinforced his point that because the killings were going on, the terrified unarmed Bengalis were running away every day from the province for their lives, being panicky about their uncertain future. Ottawa was distressed to see the dreadful nature of the military reprisals on the unarmed civilians. This was a time when the ruthless army people desperately looked for what they called the "Indian agents" to finish them off.

From the beginning of the military crackdown on March 25, 1971, to the end of April 1971, Ottawa spent five weeks analyzing the information it received from India and Pakistan and a few other sources from the world media. Ottawa tried to interpret them to determine their political implications by conducting more reviews of the daily incoming materials to remain engaged in a mediatory role. Ottawa regarded this to be a never-ending task as more information was forthcoming. With the release of the official statement on the East Pakistan Situation during the first week of May by the government of Pakistan, Ottawa came to learn that "the small hours of March 26 had been set as the zero hour for an armed uprising and the formal launching of the 'independent Republic of Bangladesh'... (and that) the Armed Forces made a series of preemptive strikes around midnight of March 26, seized the initiative and saved the country."[81] Small further alarmed Ottawa: "We do not accept this explanation of events, but it is now part of the folklore in East Pakistan."[82] Foreign affairs cognoscenti in Ottawa concurred with Small.

Canada's Official Reaction and Provision of Immediate Relief (March-May 1971)

Canada's immediate reaction to the secret military crackdown and the subsequent events following the military takeover depended mainly on her diplomatic channels that we have just looked at through their representatives in Pakistan and India. From the beginning, the Trudeau administration wanted to see a genuine effort on Yahya's part to place the nation on a democratic path through the transfer of power to Bongobondhu. Naturally, Ottawa needed to interpret all incoming news items to bring the minister up to speed through the prism of Canada's official position about the internal affairs of another country to formulate Canada's official reaction/response regarding the reported killings, ongoing reprisals, and the resultant exodus of the Bengali refugees from their homeland. Ottawa needed to weigh its relevance to Canada's position in world politics and its foreign policy options to make a meaningful contribution to resolving the conflict. Therefore, those in charge of analyzing the news reports in Ottawa concluded that additional time would be required to cautiously examine all the incoming dispatches for information and action.

The first challenge in articulating Ottawa's reaction was respecting Canada's friendly relationship with India and Pakistan. Since, over the years, Canada had been enjoying an excellent relationship with both Pakistan and India, she needed to be sure of the facts before formally expressing her immediate reaction to the events surrounding the killings without kindling the wrath of either country. It was a mind-boggling exercise to analyze in minute detail every bit of incoming information about the ongoing military repression and the consequent flight of the terror-stricken Bengalis. While culling facts from exaggeration and assessing their implications considering much-unconfirmed news, analysts found themselves in a difficult position about the stark tragedy unfolding. Ottawa recognized that the Yahya government was primarily to blame for having expelled the foreign correspondents from Dhaka by enforcing rigid censorship and issuing patently false accounts of its own.

The Undersecretary of State for External Affairs, A. E. Ritchie, conducted another round of assessment of the worsening situation to brief the minister. What helped Ottawa was that reports from Islamabad were based not only on what was happening in East Pakistan but also on commentaries about *why* such events occurred there. Naturally, Ottawa relied on Small's situational reports from the time of the postponement of the National Assembly through Yahya's meeting with Bongobondhu and Bhutto during the last week of March until the secret military clampdown. His dispatches from Islamabad pointed out two minimum requirements for Bongobondhu: establishing a provisional government headed by the elected representatives and withdrawing martial law. Again, upon reviewing George's messages from India, Ottawa also recognized that his messages were particularly important since part of the drama following the mass exodus took place in India.

While verifying and cross-checking the authenticity of certain pieces of news, Ottawa began to face a new kind of problem with diplomatic relations and protocols. As the relationships between India and Pakistan hit rough patches, Ottawa officials were flooded with unsolicited correspondences from the high commissions of India and Pakistan addressed to Sharp. They insisted on meeting with Sharp or the undersecretary to deliver the messages of their respective governments—messages that contained each government's version of what had happened and what was likely to occur. Every time Mir Muhammad S. Shaikh, Pakistan's high commissioner to Canada, expressed his government's apprehension of Indian intervention in the "internal affairs" of Pakistan, Ottawa officials' typical bureaucratic response was along the line that the matter was still under review. The high commissioners never stopped sending notes. Ottawa officials began to experience quite a bit of discomfort in their interaction with the representatives of the high commissions of India and Pakistan for their insistence on having a face-to-face meeting with Sharp. This was in addition to receiving volumes of unsolicited propaganda materials. On each occasion, Ottawa officials, however, remained calm in referring to Canada's policy of nonintervention in the internal affairs of another country; they repeated the same response - that the matter is still under review. Sharp prevaricated to the extent possible without more concrete, verified, and authenticated information to Ottawa officials' satisfaction and being desirous of not acting precipitously.

While following Canada's neutrality and "wait and see" strategy, a heedful Sharp used a standard curt media line for his responses—that his office was still waiting to ascertain the facts. He remained wary as his team was still reviewing the dispatches and did not want to make, to use today's vocabulary, a politically incorrect gesture to either party. Despite pressure from the opposition MPs in the House, Sharp's team remained extra forethoughtful regarding Canada's immediate reaction as it was a case of dêja vu. Ottawa worried that any uncalled-for help might invite more criticism than goodwill. Sharp's most significant challenge at that time was to learn how to ensure that his procrastination in taking immediate action was not interpreted as a kind of acquiescence to Yahya's actions by Canada. Although Ottawa officials felt badgered, they continued the review of the situation without officially reacting to Yahya's military action in East Pakistan. Official records, such as internal memos and briefing notes, reveal that departmental senior officials strictly discussed Ottawa's immediate reaction within the room's four walls. The consensus was that Canada should refrain from intervening. There was also a mutual understanding among officials that sharing the decision with anyone was unnecessary and that there was no need to publicize Ottawa's decision to go slow, either. This was done to buy more time while continually reviewing the rapidly changing situation.

In the meantime, in New Delhi, George found a new channel through which he began to receive the latest information, gossip, and innuendoes. He was in an advantageous situation since he knew Bali Ram Bhagat, former foreign trade and supply minister, who later became the senior unofficial government of India liaison with Bangladeshi leaders in Kolkata, West Bengal. This enabled George to be privy to important information from top sources that Bhagat used to pass on to him, something that generally would have been impossible to hear about. Through Bhagat and his network of friends and colleagues, George began receiving highly confidential information from several sources, such as the US Consul General, the British Deputy High Commissioner, and foreign press members. Being on the lookout and having maintained close liaison with many of his diplomatic colleagues in New Delhi, George frequently snooped around the refugee camps to learn about their knowledge of what had been happening in their homeland. When Ottawa officials heard about how George was hunting for information, he was admonished that his way of gathering information might be seen as inappropriate and politically incorrect for a Canadian diplomat.

At that time, Ottawa also noted the Canadian public's reaction to the military regime's abandonment of its responsibility to protect its citizens—sadly, how it had lapsed into barbarism. The public was shaken up by the ongoing repression and savagery with which the regime was treating its citizens. Many Canadians were crestfallen and dissatisfied, seeing that the government was not ready to condemn the military regime. The public did not know anything about the behind-the-scene, proactive mediatory efforts of Prime Minister Trudeau and his correspondence with Yahya and Gandhi, something that readers shall see in Chapter 7.

Once the Trudeau administration became convinced of the reports of indiscriminate killing, arrest, detention, and repression of the Bengalis, it found the regime's claim unacceptable regarding the transgression of human rights. Although the military regime insisted that this was an "internal affair" of Pakistan, the world observers saw this as far beyond being a domestic issue. Canada, however, did not wish to be involved in any debate regarding whether the conflict had ceased to be an "internal affair" of Pakistan even when three distinct parties (Pakistan, the provisional government of Bangladesh, and India) were directly involved. Ottawa disagreed with the regime's narrative of what was happening but chose not to be seen as meddling in Pakistan's "internal affairs." Given Canada's foreign policy toward India and Pakistan, the two sister members of the Commonwealth, Ottawa officials needed to do more thinking. They did not wish to ruffle anyone's feather.

While reviewing the situation, another critical factor contributed to circumspect measures by the Trudeau government, which was already preoccupied with the issue of the separation of Québec. This sensitive issue has already been described in Chapter 1, and we shall reread more about this issue in Chapters 6 and 7. The press in Québec, particularly *Le Devoir*, was quick to allude to the secessionist movement of Québec by having drawn a parallel between the demands of the Bengalis in East Pakistan and the needs of the French Canadians in Québec. Officials at External were sensitive to the fact that many Ontario dailies had already published letters to the editor on this susceptible topic. Discussions in some of the published letters centered on the question of separation and/or secession of Québec and its parallel to the situation in East Pakistan. The level of angst was such that none of the analysts attempted to see whether there were parallel situations. Ottawa dreaded the appearance of a parallel; that is, if Ottawa was seen to be supporting the Bengali rebels, this might be interpreted as supporting the cause of the Bengali separatists in East Pakistan. The undersecretary advised Sharp, "It would be equally unwise, in my view, for Canada to appear to be supporting, even indirectly, a secessionist movement against a friendly government."[83]

An oversensitive Trudeau administration believed it was unnecessary to clarify the issue as it was too delicate. This nervousness weighed heavily on the government throughout the crisis until Bangladesh's final liberation was achieved. Besides Canada's obsessive fear of the Québec question, another inhibiting factor slowed down the exercise. Canada's constant fear was that any interference would strain Canada's congenial relationship with India and Pakistan. Although the public expected Canada to react quickly, Canada remained jittery and worried about the chances of straining its ties with India and Pakistan, more so than finding a quick expression of condemnation based on facts.

When Ottawa came up to speed, it recognized how the events were constituting a grim witness to the colossal dimension of the East Pakistan tragedy. Ottawa realized that it could not continue to stall its exercise. It must make its position public. Naturally, Ottawa tried to precisely determine Canada's actual position regarding the conflict. Recognizing that this enormous humanitarian problem that the refugee situation had spawned deserved immediate and dramatic attention, Canada quickly developed a strategy to deal with the urgent issues relating to relief and rehabilitation. Ottawa, however, could not formally pronounce her immediate reaction. Given the urgency of the situation and the idea of coming up with Canada's immediate response to the events in Pakistan, which would then have to be expanded to Canada's formal position on the conflict, Canada found herself in a challenging situation.

Strict adherence to Canada's foreign policy constraints did not allow her even to appear to tilt toward one country against another since both were members of the Commonwealth. Having recognized that there was no silver bullet to turn things around, Ottawa asked, "How can Canada maintain its traditionally cordial relationship with India and Pakistan?" This was perhaps the most challenging question that Ottawa struggled with for weeks without finding a satisfactory answer, maintained Sharp.[84]

In the meantime, even though Canada was aware of India's covert plan, including the provision of financial help to the freedom fighters and training facilities by the Indian armed forces, she still needed to assess India's continuing secret role in the political affairs of Pakistan. Ottawa recalled Small's earlier situational reports that talked about India's keen interest in East Pakistan for a long time. Again, Ottawa officials were also aware through George that, although Gandhi was under tremendous pressure to recognize the provisional government of Bangladesh, she was not yet ready to do that.

By then, Ottawa officials also received additional information from George that they took into consideration. Ottawa noted how the Swatantra Party (Independent Party) of India had already expressed admiration for the socialist program of Bongobondhu. Atal Bihari Vajpayee, leader of the Bharatiya Jana Sangh, an Indian right-wing political party that existed since 1951, was openly supporting Bongobondhu's secular policy. Having argued that the people of East Pakistan were their brothers, it campaigned for immediate recognition of Bangladesh. It actively planned for a twelve-day demonstration in New Delhi in early August, which was to be capped by a massive *satyagraha* (holding firmly to the truth). Simultaneously, Ottawa officials also learned that West Bengal's deputy chief minister, Bijay Singh Nahar, spoke on behalf of the people of West Bengal in the following way: "That we in West Bengal recognize Bangladesh although the Central Government has not done so yet."[85]

Moving forward, Small further expanded his point by stating that, provided that India continued her support, guerrilla forces could no longer be controlled by Mujib even if he were to try. He then prophesied, "Initiative and drive have already passed to other hands that were unlikely to be attracted to a settlement, which left East Pak within Pak federation; however, liberal terms of association might be. As long as secessionists are backed by India, chances of peaceful settlement are remote."[86] Canada's view of a peaceful settlement did not consider the phenomenon of Bangladesh as an independent country devoid of Pakistan. Ottawa was uncomfortable in her reaction to the conflict with the discontented body politic in Pakistan about the following in particular: (1) slaughtering of the non-Bengalis by the Bengali militants (during the time of rebellion), (2) continuous reprisals by the military, and (3) supply of arms to the rebels by India. The first news item (killing of the non-Bengalis by the Bengalis), though very disturbing, was from the past weeks, dating back to the reaction of the Bengalis to the postponement of the National Assembly before the imposition of martial law when the Bengalis had the upper hand. Upon reexamination, it was, however, no longer an issue since such killings by the Bengalis took place before the crackdown, and that continued until the rebels were driven out of East Pakistan. Ottawa thus remained concerned about two directly related news items—the Yahya regime's ongoing reprisals and India's covert assistance.

Ottawa was convinced that the Gandhi administration had the full blessings and support to establish the Bangladesh government on Indian territory. This made Ottawa rethink two more related items of significance: (1) Yahya's ultimate intention (which Ottawa believed to be the perpetuation of military rule) and (2) India's denial of her covert assistance to the freedom fighters and her expected role in the conflict according to India's secret game plan.

Having gathered enough information from the two high commissioners, Ottawa focused on the following questions: What has happened in Pakistan since martial law's imposition? What happened to the process of democratization in East Pakistan that started a year ago? Those in charge of drafting the position paper must carefully reinterpret the events, considering Canada's policy of non-interference in the "internal affairs" of another country. Ottawa felt that there was a need to examine with more clarity India's clandestine plan, including the provision of financial help to the freedom fighters and training facilities by the Indian armed forces. Practically speaking, this meant further delay since Ottawa officials found the situation even more complex, with the receipt of additional information every day contributing to further consternation.

The drafters relied heavily on one of Small's telegrams in which he shared his "emotions of horror and abhorrence at what (had) occurred."[87] According to Small, Canada could only act from two motivations: (1) humanitarian and (2) Canadian interests.[88] Small advised Canada to articulate Canada's immediate reaction to the army crackdown through the provision of relief work in India and, with extra attention, should also craft a letter of Canada's condemnation of the military regime's sudden and secret attack and ongoing repression. Nevertheless, given the gravity of the situation, Ottawa officials needed more time to reflect on these issues. This was particularly so because of new information along the line that the Gandhi administration was directly involved in every step of the way. This meant, for Ottawa, more analysis of the situation - ongoing reprisals and the Bengalis' pledge to liberate their homeland with the help of India[89] before formally expressing Canada's position.

Despite the mounting pressure, the Trudeau administration chose neither to condemn the military regime openly nor to broach the matter publicly. Ottawa was mindful of the Nigerian/Biafran experience (1967–1970) that taught Canada a vital lesson - that there would always be much resentment at any attempt at moralizing or interfering. Sharp's firmly held view was that any such effort might be counterproductive and that the trouble was far more significant in its depth and intensity than that which involved Nigeria and Biafra. This could even be far greater than what involved Vietnam, maintained by Sharp's team. Under the circumstances, Ottawa preferred to procrastinate by putting aside Canada's mediatory role momentarily and working in two phases. In the first phase, officials recognized that, while they were reviewing the situation, Canada should try to ease the crisis by fulfilling her role as the *leading humanitarian nation* of the world community by bringing international aid and relief to the millions of refugees in India and displaced persons in East Pakistan. In the second phase, which began simultaneously, Ottawa decided to continue its position paper, which should be transparent to the public. It was also to be used for Canada's strategic involvement nationally and internationally in resolving the conflict.

Nevertheless, even at this stage, though foreign affairs cognoscenti narrowed down the areas about what should Canada's immediate reaction be, they still needed to deepen their understanding in the following four key areas to come up with an acceptable position paper from a Canadian perspective concerning the conflict: (1) the true nature of the conflict between the two wings of Pakistan and barriers to democratization, (2) the Gandhi administration's involvement in assisting refugees and its motives in sheltering them by opening India's door from the very first day, (3) whether there will be an acceptable situation in East Pakistan for as long as the military remained in force, and (4) explore the democratic aspirations of the Bengalis to free the native land they had named Bangladesh.

In the meantime, Ottawa felt a twinge of embarrassment at the expressed diplomatic displeasure of Yahya. Ottawa, however, remained concerned as it became more aware of the growing strains within the military hierarchy. Small's message was that in recent months, observers have not been able to help but notice the increasing strains in their previously harmonious relationship amid rumors that General Abdul Hamid Khan was a potential candidate to replace Yahya, with support from senior Punjabi officers. Another rumor was that Bhutto had ordered the establishment of revolutionary committees throughout West Pakistan that might attempt to seize power. Ottawa was also quite disturbed to see the Yahya regime's constant slogans and posters on the walls saying, *"Hate India," "Crush India,"* and *"Conquer India."* It sounded ludicrous to Ottawa observers, who saw it as mere sound and fury signifying nothing.

After weeks of reviewing a whole surfeit of information, Ottawa came up with Canada's reaction for their use only as they related to the events in East Pakistan. Fortunately for the Trudeau administration, there was complete consensus among the Cabinet members and MPs of all stripes regarding the immediate needs of the refugees. It was agreed that Canada should provide relief assistance to the refugees in West Bengal, India, keeping in line with her tradition of humanitarian assistance to the victims of natural and political calamities. Expressly, officials agreed that Canada should focus on the following three areas: (1) humanitarian assistance and lobbying the governments of Pakistan and India and international organizations for a political resolution of the conflict, (2) no imposition of economic sanction, and (3) demand that there should be no repressive measures during the continuation of martial law.

Sharp was then briefed to take a position along the line that Canada's priority should be to give the urgently needed humanitarian assistance to the victims of military repression - the Bengali refugees in India and displaced persons in East Pakistan and promote the well-being of the people of Pakistan to decrease their sufferings. The immediate aspects of the refugee matters were considered urgent and grave, and every possible effort at alleviation must be made. This was to be conducted with a deep sense of mission. Canada had no foreign policy constraints for the priority item since it fell under the humanitarian assistance program. Canada was comfortable interacting with national and international organizations in this regard. Canada's second priority was to provide Pakistan's developmental assistance to promote stability, economic growth, a higher standard of living, and the general well-being of the people. Ottawa paid attention to the advice of Small and George, both of whom strongly urged Ottawa that there be no cut-off of aid to Pakistan - something with which Ottawa officials had already agreed. We shall see the details of this in Chapter 7. Sharp was also advised that the international community, over a period, should use its leverage with the Pakistan government to persuade them to cut their losses and ease out military domination of East Pakistan "as soon and as gracefully as possible."[90]

While reviewing the news, Ottawa recognized the print media's power to influence the process of a nationalist revolution, which culminated in the demand for an independent Bangladesh. The media's repeated emphasis on two historical facts did not skip Ottawa's attention: (1) that the Bengalis were living in the smaller of the two territories, (2) but they were the larger population (75 million as opposed to 55 million) being the underdog in terms of actual power even though they carried the economic load for the whole of Pakistan.

Those in charge of drafting Ottawa's reaction understood the true nature of the conflict that mainly arose from the deprivation of the people of East Pakistan, whose pain and anger spilled onto the streets with their demand for a fair share of the economic pie. In a sense, it was not difficult for Ottawa officials to relate to the problems in Canada. This is because they could specifically recall a situation similar to the Canadian Confederation regarding deprivation. Seeing the disparity between the two wings of Pakistan, Ottawa officials reminded themselves of how, to the French Canadians, the confederation had established, once and for all, political and economic inequality between the French and English Canadians.

As Ottawa officials began to see more about the real issues, they also began to appreciate Bongobondhu's fundamental argument. It became clear to them that the Bengalis were being discriminated against and that through the Six-Point Program, Bongobondhu was proposing to right the wrongs of the past. Nevertheless, it did not take long for Ottawa officials to be convinced that the regime was not interested in transferring power to the elected leader. Having considered various implications of the subcontinental events, Ottawa also came to believe that sudden military withdrawal from there would be almost as disastrous as the present policy, argued Canada. If that happened, Ottawa feared that under the circumstances, East Pakistan would be left virtually without civil or military authorities. Ottawa thus concluded that the military should remain in East Pakistan but that it must stop its repressive measures. Canada's greatest challenge was to continue to struggle hard in her attempt to assist the victims. At the same time, she did not want to ruffle Yahya's feathers. Due to the extremely sensitive nature of the issue, Ottawa recognized that it must not encourage any conversation in this regard that could ignite a firestorm in Canada. Given the context of Ottawa's augury, avoiding any reference to secession and/or separation is understandable.

Under the circumstances, and given the need for more time for reflection, Sharp was advised in the following manners not to take a public position: "Canadian public opinion in favour of government action to help alleviate human suffering has grown as reports of atrocities have emerged. The issues will increasingly present two options: condemn Pakistan or ignore the situation. Complete silence is not a realistic option. Nevertheless, humanitarian objectives in Pakistan will best be served by declining to adopt a public position against the military government."[91]

Ottawa felt somewhat justified in its dilatory action with no deadline for its official position paper on the conflict. Like before, Ottawa officials worked on the premise that there would be no immediate response even though the public demanded the government announce its declaratory position. Canada resorted to her "wait and see" policy, believing she was on the right track and had no desire to be in a race against time. To Ottawa officials, Canada's silence seemed like a better option that would make more political sense.

Canada, therefore, chose not to come up with a statement of condemnation or any formal statement on Pakistan's "internal affairs" despite being under pressure. Canada temporarily placed the condemnation matter on the back burner. This was the immediate official reaction only for official use strictly within the department. In other words, Canada took a strong position to react differently by conforming to Canada's foreign policy requirements regarding the internal affairs of another country. This was not to be shared with the public or the news media. Sharp's team decided there should be no announcement about Canada's immediate reaction - it should be avoided to the greatest extent. It was thought to be prudent to maintain a low-keyed response while working behind the scenes with those who could help resolve the current stalemate to allow the military authority to begin to rebuild the nation being torn apart.

Consequently, Canada never announced its reaction to the conflict but paid more attention to providing humanitarian assistance. The general public, who had no clue about what was happening inside the Trudeau administration, demanded that Canada continue to pressure the military regime to stop its repressive measures and make an effort to place the nation on a democratic track, as promised earlier.

Having reflected for some time, Ottawa concluded that the violent military clampdown on the part of the Pakistani army could be seen as blitzkrieg, a kind of German notion that the Yahya regime resorted to believing that the military campaign would result in a swift victory by bringing the Bengalis to their knees. As far as Ottawa was concerned, the army build-up, the three leaders' conversation, the clampdown, the whole shebang, must have been Yahya's resort to ruthless Machiavellian means - the elimination of his challenger.

In a nutshell, Canada's immediate official reaction was to *refrain from public condemnation* of the events and follow the tradition of quiet diplomacy. This was even though the Yahya regime followed its blood and iron policy through brute force. Canada's priority was to exert pressure for a political and humane solution. In the following few chapters, we shall learn more about how Canada reacted to the actions of the governments of Pakistan and India from the beginning to the end of the conflict to bring an end to the conflict. More particularly, in Chapter 7, we shall see Canada's persistent efforts without ever taking a back seat in reinforcing her appeal to the international conscience that she believed must be roused to restore democracy in Pakistan.

In Chapter 8, we shall see how Canada was conflicted as a middle power.

Notes and References

1. Government of Pakistan, Press Information Department Handout titled, *Official Statement on East Pakistan Situation,* dated May 6, 1971. E. No. 961-R. p. 1. This handout is attached to a Restricted memo from John Small, high commissioner to Pakistan, to A. E. Ritchie, Undersecretary of State for External Affairs. Telegram No. 424, dated May 5, 1971. Canada. Department of External Affairs. Hereinafter, all telegrams and other information used in this chapter from the Department of External Affairs shall be referred to as External Affairs.
2. *The Globe and Mail,* dated January 7, 1971. At that time, Van Praag was reporting from Rawalpindi, Pakistan.
3. Telegram from John Small, high commissioner to Pakistan, to Ottawa. Telegram #310, dated February 11, 1971. File #20-E-Pak-1-4. Canada. Department of External Affairs. Hereinafter, all records used in this chapter shall be referred to as External Affairs.
4. *The Globe and Mail,* dated March 10, 1971.
5. See footnote #3.
6. *Ibid.*
7. Confidential telegram from John Small, high commissioner to Pakistan, to Ottawa. Telegram #133, dated February 15, 1971. File # E -Pak-20- 1-4. External Affairs. *Op. cit.*
8. *Iid.*
9. *Ibid.*
10. *Ibid.*
11. *Ibid.*
12. Confidential telegram from John Small, high commissioner to Pakistan, to Ottawa. Telegram #179, dated March 2, 1971. File #20-E -Pak-20-1-4. External Affairs. *Op. cit.*
13. *Ibid.* p. 3.
14. *The Ottawa Citizen,* dated March 4, 1971.
15. *The Ottawa Citizen,* dated March 5, 1971.
16. Memorandum for the Minister, dated March 9, 1971. File #20-E -Pak-1-4. External Affairs. *Opt. cit.*
17. Confidential memorandum, titled *Crisis in East Pakistan*, from the Bureau of Asia Pacific Affairs, p. 2. Dated March 12, 1971. File #20-E-Pak-1-4. External Affairs. *Op. cit.*
18. *Ibid.* File #20-Pak-1-4, p.1. External Affairs. *Op. cit.*
19. *Kitchener-Waterloo Record*, dated March 15, 1971.
20. *The Globe and Mail,* dated March 24, 1971.

21. *The Ottawa Citizen,* dated March 24, 1971, titled *"The October Crisis,"* Pelletier's book defends the *War Measures Act* decision.
22. Memorandum for the Minister, from A. E. Ritchie, Undersecretary of State for External Affairs, to Mitchell Sharp, Secretary of State for External Affairs. Dated April 29, 1971, p. 1. File # 20-1-2-Pak. External Affairs. *Op. cit.*
23. Confidential telegram from John Small, high commissioner to Pakistan, to Ottawa. Telegram #264, March 23, 1971. p. 2. File #20-Pak-1-4. External Affairs. *Op. cit.*
24. *Ibid.*
25. *The Globe and Mail,* dated March 25, 1971.
26. *Ibid.*
27. Confidential telegram from John Small, high commissioner to Pakistan, to Ottawa. Telegram #264, dated March 26, 1971. File # 20-E-Pak 1-4. External Affairs. *Op. cit.*
28. *Ibid.*
29. *Toronto Daily Star,* dated March 29, 1971.
30. See *Glossary of Terms.*
31. *Ibid.*
32. *Toronto Daily Star,* dated March 26, 1971.
33. *Ibid.*
34. *Ottawa Journal,* dated March 27, 1971.
35. *Ibid.* dated March 26, 1971.
36. *Dawn* (Karachi), dated January 15, 1971.
37. This was in President Yahya's speech on March 26, 1971, included in the *White Paper on the Crisis in East Pakistan,* released on August 15, 1971, Appendix A, pp. 12–13. File # 20-E Pak-1-4. External Affairs. *Op. cit.*
38. See *Glossary of Terms.*
39. Confidential telegram from John Small, high commissioner to Pakistan, to Ottawa. Telegram #278, dated March 30, 1971. File # 20-E-Pak-1-4. External Affairs. *Op. cit.*
40. *Ibid.* p. 6.
41. James George lived in Sri Lanka as high commissioner of Canada between 1960 and 1964 and in India as high commissioner of Canada between 1969 and 1972, whereas John Small lived in Pakistan between 1963 and 1965 as a counselor in the Canadian High Commission in Karachi and between 1969 and 1972 in Islamabad as high commissioner and ambassador of Canada.
42. Confidential telegram from John Small, high commissioner to Pakistan, to Ottawa. Telegram #270, dated March 27, 1971. File #20-E-Pak 1-4. External Affairs. *Op. cit.*

43. Confidential telegram from John Small, high commissioner to Pakistan, to Ottawa. Telegram #278, dated March 30, 1971, p. 1–2. File #20-E-Pak 1-4. External Affairs. *Op. cit.*
44. *The Ottawa Citizen,* dated March 29, 1971.
45. Memo from A. E. Ritchie, undersecretary to Secretary of State for External Affairs. Dated March 31, 1971. File #20-E-Pak 1-4. External Affairs. *Op. cit.*
46. Memorandum for the Minister, from A. E. Ritchie, Undersecretary, to Secretary of State for External Affairs, titled *Situation in East Pakistan,* Dated March 31, 1971. File #20-Pak-1-4. External Affairs. *Op. cit.*
47. *Ibid.*
48. Secretary of State for External Affairs. Dated April 2, 1971. File # 38-11-Pak. External Affairs. *Op. cit.*
49. Restricted memo from James George, high commissioner to India, to A. E. Ritchie, undersecretary of State for External Affairs, titled *India and the Situation in East Pakistan.* Memo no J-98, dated April 13, 1971, p. 1. File #20-India-1-3-Pak. External Affairs. *Op. cit.*
50. Confidential telegram from James Goerge, high commissioner to India, to Ottawa. Telegram #1267, dated, April 1, 1971. File #20-India-1-3-Pak. External Affairs. *Op. cit.*
51. Under the caption Purge of Bengali Civil Servants, this was quoted in *Bangladesh – Campaign for Self-Rule of East Bengal,* No. 4, April 26, 1971 (International Section) published by Fareed S. Jafri, London, U. K., p. 2. This is contained in the Department of External Affairs folder. File #20- E- Pak-1-4. External Affairs. *Op. cit.*
52. *Ibid.*
53. Restricted Memo from A. E. Ritchie, Undersecretary to Secretary of State, External Affairs, dated April 2, 1971, p.2. File #20 - E- Pak-1-4. External Affairs. *Op. cit.*
54. *Ibid.*
55. Confidential Summary of an attached Memorandum titled *Situation in East Pakistan.* It is dated April 19, 1971. Fille #20 - E. Pak-1-4.
56. *The Globe and Mail,* dated April 5, 1971.
57. Confidential telegram from John Small, high commissioner to Pakistan, to Ottawa. Telegram #330, dated March 31, 1971. File #20-1-2- Pak. External Affairs. *Op. cit.*
58. Confidential telegram from John Small, high commissioner to Pakistan, to Ottawa. Telegram #291, dated April 6, 1971. File #20- E-Pak-1-4. External Affairs. *Op. cit.*
59. *Ibid. Op. cit.*
60. Restricted memo from A. E. Ritchie, Undersecretary, to Mitchell Sharp, Secretary of State for External Affairs. Dated April 16, 1971, p. 2. File #20-1-2- Pak. External Affairs. *Op. cit.*

61. Restricted letter from James George, high commissioner to India, to Undersecretary of State for External Affairs. Dated April 13, 1971. File #20-India-1-3-Pak. External Affairs. *Op. cit.*
62. Confidential telegram from James George, high commissioner to India, to Ottawa. Telegram #1472, dated April 19, 1971, p. 3. File #20-E-Pak-1-4. External Affairs. *Op. cit.*
63. *Times of India,* dated April 18, 1971.
64. *Ibid.*
65. Confidential telegram from James George, high commissioner to India, to Ottawa. Telegram #1267, dated April 1, 1971. File #20 - India 1-3 Pak. External Affairs. *Op. cit.*
66. Confidential telegram from James George, high commissioner to India, to Ottawa. Telegram #1473, dated April 19, 1971, p. 3. File #20- E-Pak-1-4. External Affairs. *Op. cit.*
67. *Ibid.* p. 2. External Affairs. *Op. cit.*
68. Confidential telegram from James George, high commissioner to India, to Ottawa. Telegram #1267, dated, April 1, 1971. File #20- India 1-3 Pak. External Affairs. *Op. cit.*
69. *Ibid.*
70. *Ibid.*
71. *Dawn* (Karachi), May 24, 1971.
72. *Ibid.*
73. *Weekly Guardian,* dated April 10, 1971.
74. Outlined in a document titled *Indian–Pakistani Conflict and Peeking's anti-Sovietism,* dated December 8, 1971 p. 2. File #20-India -1-2 Pak. External Affairs. *Op. cit.*
75. Confidential telegram from John Small, high commissioner to Pakistan, to Ottawa. Telegram #430, dated March 31, 1971. File #20- India -1-2 Pak. External Affairs. *Op. cit.*
76. Confidential telegram from John Small, high commissioner to Pakistan, to Ottawa. Telegram #315, dated April 1, 1971. File # 20- India-1-2 Pak. External Affairs. *Op. cit.*
77. Confidential telegram from John Small, high commissioner to Pakistan, to Ottawa. Telegram #330, dated April 13, 1971, p. 1. File #20-India-1-2 Pak. External Affairs, *Op. cit.*
78. Confidential telegram from John Small, high commissioner to Pakistan, to Ottawa. Telegram #451, dated April 3, 1971. File #20-India -1-2 Pak. External Affairs, *Op. cit.*
79. Confidential telegram from John Small, high commissioner to Pakistan, to Ottawa. Telegram #471, dated April 16, 1971. File #20-India -1-2 Pak. External Affairs, *Op. cit.*

80. Confidential telegram from John Small, high commissioner to Pakistan, to Ottawa. Telegram #207, dated April 27, 1971, p. 1. File #20-India -1-2- Pak. External Affairs, *Op. cit.*
81. Restricted memo from John Small, high commissioner to Pakistan, to A. E. Ritchie, Undersecretary of State for External Affairs. Memo #253, File #20-E-Pak-1-4. External Affairs. *Op. cit.*
82. *Ibid.*
83. Confidential memo from A. E. Ritchie, Undersecretary, to Mitchell Sharp, Secretary of State for External Affairs. Dated April 16, 1971, p. 2. File #20-India1-2-Pak. External Affairs. *Op. cit.*
84. Mitchell Sharp, Secretary of State for External Affairs in 1971 and, later, an honorary advisor to Jean Chretien, prime minister of Canada, expressed this to the author in one of his informal meetings with Sharp on September 10, 1995. In the late 1990s, Sharp gave the author free access to his office. The author's notes indicate that this was said to him in one of his informal meetings with Sharp.
85. *The Economist* (London). Volume 239 Number 6661, dated April 24, 1971, p. 8.
86. Confidential telegram from John Small, Canadian high commissioner to Pakistan, to Ottawa. Telegram #384, dated August 12, 1971. File #20-India-1-2 Pak. External Affairs. *Op. cit.*
87. Confidential telegram from John Small, high commissioner to Pakistan, to Ottawa. Telegram #330, dated April 13, 1971. File #20-India 1-2. External Affairs. *Op. cit.*
88. *Ibid.*
89. Confidential telegram from James George, high commissioner to India, to Ottawa. Telegram # 4176, dated November 4, 1971. File #20-India-1-3-Pak. External Affairs. *Opt. cit.*
90. Restricted memo from A. E. Ritchie, Undersecretary, to Mitchell Sharp, Secretary of State, External Affairs. Dated April 28, 1971, p. 2. File #20 India 1-3 Pak. External Affairs. *Op. cit.*
91. Memorandum for the Prime Minister titled *Prospects for Canadian Policy Toward Pakistan, Policy Considerations.* Dated May 4, 1971. File #20 -E-Pak-1-4.

CHAPTER 3

Canada's Media Onside with the Freedom Fighters of Bangladesh

This chapter summarizes the effects and impacts of the Canadian news media coverage of the East Pakistan conflict and its appeal to the general public and the Canadian government, thereby inciting response to provide humanitarian aid and financial support. The terms "news" and "media" are used to refer to editorials, opinion pieces (op-ed articles), letters to the editor, photographs, video footage, and unique articles on world politics. Nowadays, we use social media like Facebook, Instagram, TikTok, Snapchat, Zoom, and Twitter to post content, gauge opinion, and share information with others, including news articles, both domestic and international. Using the Internet and technological applications in social media with various means of communication, such as WhatsApp, Imo, Viber, Messenger, and e-mail, the news media is capable of leading news feed in today's world. Large broadcast networks like CNN (Cable News Network) use print and broadcast formats and social media to enable us to see the unfolding of events in real time, twenty-four hours a day, seven days a week. They provide an open door to receive public reaction and invite information custodians to debate on public television in digital broadcast so that the general public can understand issues more fully. In 1971, neither the more extensive broadcast networks nor social media existed. Therefore, this chapter will focus on traditional newspapers, television, and radio.

Canadians took advantage of acquiring knowledge and information through reading newspapers, watching television, or listening to radio programs. They considered the dailies to be a platform of public discussion and a vehicle for moulding public opinion. Within the context of the Pakistan-Bangladesh conflict, Canadian media fulfilled various roles: acting as a common carrier of information on international affairs from overseas and serving as a watchdog over government, including Canada's relationship with Pakistan and India. The quality and quantity of reporting on the liberation war remain an example of continuous coverage of the staying power of a foreign news theme. The underlying message was that years of discriminatory treatment of the Bengalis by the ruling West Pakistanis had widened the gap between the people of East and West Pakistan to what probably became unbridgeable, leaving politics and the democratic process in disarray. The news media successfully exposed President Yahya Khan for his flip-flop on major decisions, resulting from his antidemocratic and misguided impulses. It proved that Yahya's plan was illusory - merely a mare's nest. Canadian media, unlike the government of Canada, attempted to influence readers, listeners, and viewers in favor of an independent Bangladesh.

When radio and television emerged as alternative media sources, before the twenty-four-hour news cycles and all news networks, Canadian newspapers were still the foremost purveyor of information that had not begun their circulation declines. In 1971, a significant proportion of coverage touched upon foreign relations, economies, and crises such as civil wars, political upheavals, and natural disasters, as there was an appetite for international news. Canadian newspapers were still the dominant news source covering various information from Pakistan and India. The news media covered the Pakistan–Bangladesh conflict, which the government referred to as the East Pakistan Crisis, in two distinct ways: (1) What was the government of Canada doing regarding humanitarian assistance? and (2) What were the people of Canada doing about the events happening in Pakistan? We shall review two key questions: (1) How extensively and effectively did the media outlets in Canada cover the news related to the Pakistan-Bangladesh conflict? and (2) How and to what extent did the media influence its clients?

The news media successfully sustained the readers' interest by providing the most up-to-date news from the field and then analyzing the events surrounding the military actions and widespread and ruthless military assault on unarmed civilians. To understand the role of the media (both print and nonprint) during the period under discussion, the following fourteen headings have been used selectively: (1) Immediate Report Through Television, Radio, and Newspapers; (2) Coverage of the Eye-Witness Accounts and Analysis of Ongoing Repression; (3) Awareness and Education; (4) Pakistan's Geography and Polity; (5) Reprints of Articles Written by Distinguished Individuals; (6) Instant Allusion to the 1970 October Crisis; (7) Letters to the Editor Column; (8) Editorial Disquisitions; (9) Emotional Appeal and Medical Assistance for Cholera Epidemic; (10) Role of a Watchdog; (11) News on Defection by Bengali Envoys and the Progress Towards Liberation; (12) Community Newspapers and News Magazines; (13) Photojournalism; and (14) Regular Radio and Television News and Talk Shows.

Immediate Report Through Television, Radio, and Newspapers (March 25–mid-April 1971)

The summary of the initial report from various sources indicated the following: On the night of March 25, feeling betrayed and attacked by the Pakistani army personnel, the Bengali rebels reacted along with two more battalions of troops loyal to Bongobondhu: The East Bengal Regiment (EBR) and the East Pakistan Rifles (EPR). To the extent possible, the news reports also described when and how the West Pakistani troops tried to disarm the reserved forces and how the Bengalis were fleeing to India following the commencement of the military crackdown to take safe shelter.

Canadian Broadcasting Corporation (CBC)

The Ottawa-based Canadian Broadcasting Corporation (CBC) has been the largest newsgathering organization, with radio service since the 1930s and television since 1952. Being the center of Canadian broadcast journalism to date, CBC was the first Canadian news media that arrived within forty-eight hours of the military outbreak. Within hours, it broke the news of a military takeover in Pakistan. Though often unconfirmed and fragmentary, Canadians quickly learned about the military intervention that halted the Yahya government's political modernization process through power transfer. An initial news blackout, confinement, and expulsion of foreign correspondents from the region contributed to a scarcity of reliable information concerning the military actions and the resultant exodus. On the night of March 25, 1971, CBC had three Hong Kong-based journalists or CBC-TV crews in East Pakistan. They were Joe Schlesinger (CBC's Far East correspondent based in Hong Kong since 1966), Raymond Grenier, Bob Whyte, and thirty-five journalists from around the world.[1] They were quarantined for one night (March 25) in the Intercontinental Hotel when the Pakistani army moved into the city of Dhaka. Naturally, the media faced immediate challenges in gathering firsthand information about the secret military operation.

On the morning of March 26, CBC relayed Khadiza Naqvi's newscast from Dhaka Radio Pakistan news under the title *Radio Pakistan Announcing Emergency Measures*: "In East Pakistan, martial law administrator, zone B, has promulgated several martial law orders with immediate effect. In the interest of national security, no news can be published in the press or put out over the radio or television without prior censorship of the authorities."[2] This was followed by a quick assessment of the situation by Patrick Keatley of London, UK: "The only channel remaining is, of course, the confidential diplomatic service operated by Western embassies in Dacca (sic), the capital of East Pakistan. And through the censorship and news blackout, therefore, there are glimpses this morning of what looks like a full-scale civil war. Diplomats have heard that President Agha Muhammed Yahya Khan's troops tried to arrest hundreds of Bengali civilians last night and this morning in Dacca (sic), the capital, and in Chittagong, the second city, and the market town like Comilla."[3] Because of the news censorship, news items came in small bits that were insufficient to give Canadians an accurate picture of the fast-unfolding events.

On the night of March 26 (i.e., the early morning of March 27), all the foreign reporters were flown to Karachi via Colombo, Ceylon (now Sri Lanka). Although news reporters were strictly searched by the military authorities, both at the Dhaka and Karachi airports, where all their films, videos, and tapes were confiscated, some reporters could hide some films containing partial shots of military action.[4] Canadian reporters then flew from Karachi to Vancouver via Tokyo. The American Broadcasting Corporation's (ABC) chief diplomatic correspondent, Ted

Koppel, picked up the film Schlesinger hid from the military authority. Koppel then provided wider dissemination of it in the U.S.A. at a time when, following the expulsion of foreign correspondents, there was strict military censorship in Pakistan.

In Vancouver, Joe Schlesinger was taken straight to the CBC office where he was interviewed by a CBC reporter who flew in from Toronto. Schlesinger was the first Canadian journalist to provide firsthand information to Canadians. In that sense, for the first time, Schlesinger's film exposed the regime's secret actions against innocent Bengalis to suppress their democratic aspirations. Following the interview, he flew back to Hong Kong, where he continued covering the news for the rest of the year. He also shared some information with a Swiss reporter expelled from Rawalpindi.[5] Since all three Canadian reporters had been expelled from Dhaka on the morning of March 27, CBC had to rely on the reports of the BBC (British Broadcasting Corporation) and the National Broadcasting Corporation (NBC) during the first few weeks. CBC used to reproduce the news locally, quoting from the exact sources - a practice that continued for quite some time.

Two days following the actual military operation (that is, on the morning of March 27), CBC stated that the spark setting off the crisis was the arrival of six military vessels from West Pakistan loaded with arms and equipment and an airlift of troops which seemed to come by way of China since India had banned Pakistani plane from entering its air space. "This partial reinforcement, numbering perhaps as many as ten battalions, looked like treachery to Mujibur (Bongobondhu) and his Bengal supporters since they were still bargaining in good faith in political talks. Now, General Yahya Khan has abruptly departed for his capital in West Pakistan, and a long-dreaded military battle is underway. Mujibur, the civilian leader, won 95 percent of the vote in the abortive election… So, presumably, he has solid support now in the new contest that has begun."[6] Thus, Canadians were informed.

Bongobondhu's whereabouts remained unknown for some time. No one knew what had happened to him or, for that matter, how many people had been killed. The CBC's 1:00 pm broadcast included BBC's Mark Tulley's report titled *An Assessment of Pakistan Crisis* that ran in the following: "I think the fundamental fact that Yahya Khan has finally in his patience broken with Sheikh Mujib's noncooperation movement, he realizes that he could no longer go on calling himself president of Pakistan unless he brought this movement to a halt."⁷ It was emphasized that Yahya had the army behind him. However, there were specific forces whose loyalty was somewhat in doubt; Tulley added further, "One must remember that this East Pakistan is a very difficult terrain for any army to maneuver itself in, and also, he'll have to face the fact that he is considerably unpopular in East Pakistan."⁸

With no print coverage during the weekend, Canadians wondered what had happened and what would happen due to the military's move. The CBC quoted Yahya's March 26 address to the nation in which he warned that the "crime must not go unpunished" and that his government "will not allow playing with the destiny of millions."⁹ Listeners were shocked to hear Yahya's statement that he regretted that he "should have taken actions against Mujib a few weeks ago."¹⁰ Since, said the President, "Mujib had continued to flout the government," ¹¹ the law must deal with him. In an initial newscast, CBC then predicted that no arm and no living force could control the determined seventy-five million people of East Pakistan. There might be more bloodshed since the people were awakened, having been determined to achieve their goal, observed one news commentator. According to the reporter, it would be difficult to suppress the Bengalis. On the third day, BBC's Milner Preston commented that each leader pushed the other from behind by people who neither saw the difficulties nor a need to compromise; that is, all were unshakable and obdurate.

Again, on March 27, Canadian print media covered the news of the covert military crackdown and the immediate open rebellion by the ultranationalist Bengalis in East Pakistan. Canadians heard two essential news items: (1) the Yahya regime's positions when Radio Pakistan announced Bongobondhu's arrest at his residence in Dhaka and (2) that the president had flown back to "West Pakistan after the failure of his eleven-day negotiations with Mujib," having ordered the "armed forces to do their job and fully restore the authority of the government."¹² The sequence of events surrounding the surreptitious attack on civilians was described by Radio Pakistan in the following: "Soon after the breakdown Thursday of the president's talk with Sheikh Mujib, the martial law administrator for East Pakistan, Lt. Gen. Tikka Khan began issuing stringent orders to assert army control."¹³ President Yahya's formal position regarding the leader of the majority party in Pakistan was that since Sheikh Mujib had attacked the integrity of all Pakistan, his crime must not go unpunished. In addition to hearing about the arrest of Bongobondhu, Canadians most stunningly came to learn about the operation of a clandestine radio station broadcasting a proclamation of an independent people's republic.

Complete censorship and secrecy surrounding the military takeover, imposition of complete martial law in East Pakistan, and the expulsion of foreign correspondents made it impossible to gather information and verify conflicting news bits emanating from the field. The reports on the situation in East Pakistan ranged from the official government claims that it had been able to crush the secessionists who were getting direct help from India to Indian reports that the Bengali freedom fighters were in control of the more significant part of their native land. However, the distortion of the facts by both governments of Pakistan and India created a great deal of confusion. While the news regarding the flight and plight of the refugees, once they crossed the border, were available, reliable news of military repression and the condition of the displaced Bengalis within East Pakistan was unavailable. The news received was often deemed inadequate to provide an accurate perspective. It was impossible to broadcast the enormity of crimes being committed by the Pakistani army personnel. As far as the Canadian news media was concerned; initially, the news that came through the Press Trust of India had often been confusing, unconfirmed, and, at times, exaggerated and contradictory. Due to the urgency, reporters sent their reports as they received them without attempting to corroborate.

To bring readers up to speed, most of the significant newspapers outlined what was happening since the beginning of the political impasse to contextualize the events that were taking place. Due to the sudden secret attack on March 25 on unarmed Bengali civilians, the media reported how the East Bengal armed forces reacted by killing West Pakistani officers where possible, especially in the Chittagong area started by the Awami League extremists. Having dug up the chronology of events, the media also reported on the news regarding the slaughtering of the Biharis (non-Bengali Urdu-speaking Muslim minority in East Pakistan) by the Bengalis themselves following the postponement of the National Assembly almost three weeks before the army crackdown. The Biharis identified themselves with the non-Bengali West Pakistanis. They sided with the Pakistani military for a united Pakistan even though they were living in Bengali-speaking East Pakistan. Despite the lack of accurate information, using eyewitness accounts, most newspapers reported indiscriminate killing on both sides. That, however, lasted for a few weeks until the military drove the rebels out of East Pakistan and began to resume ongoing repression of the Bengalis.

Canadian dailies began by providing an overview of the origins of the conflict so that an average reader would understand the genesis of the problem in layperson's terms. This made readers feel as though they were having a face-to-face exchange with a refugee who had to flee from the scenes of crime. When the news reporters were told that several armed Indians had infiltrated into East Pakistan to bolster Mujibur's ragtag army of East Pakistan riflemen and home guards armed with spears, old cutlasses, and muzzle-loading guns,[14] it was reported without any comment. Some reporters avoided the Pakistani censors and began to file their dispatches from places such as Bangkok. David Van Praag, one of Canada's renowned journalists, was in India (New Delhi) until he was removed by the Indian government in 1969. Having been stationed in Penang, Malaysia, he regularly covered the news. Although Canadians did not know precisely what was happening, they could deduce the depth of the tragedy from the reports of looting and burning of human lives and properties.

The gist of all reports of the first few days convinced readers that it was a carefully planned military operation that was complex as the power of the army regime was being brutally employed in the repression of the Bengalis. Seeing that the army reprisals continued since March 25, the newspapers also wrote about human suffering and dislocation in Occupied Bangladesh, a term the media used for East Pakistan. Reportedly, by the end of March, Yahya's West Pakistani army (occupation army) was in control of the eastern wing of Pakistan, while the Bengali leader Bongobondhu was under arrest as a traitor.

Coverage of the Eyewitness Accounts and Analysis of Ongoing Repression

Since news reporters were still barred from entering Pakistan, as a practice, the print media continued to publish excerpts of the interviews and reports of those who had witnessed what was variously referred to as massacre, bloodshed, destruction, brutal invasion, army persecution, savage slaughter, pogrom, and premeditated extermination. Following their expulsion from Dhaka, news reporters gave immediate coverage with the highest attainable degree of accuracy, clearly distinguishing between confirmed fact and responsible conjecture and as much justification for the latter as possible. While the evacuees could not verify what the governments of Pakistan and India claimed, the eyewitness reports constructed a consistent and plausible account of what was reported to have been happening in the subcontinent. One of the crucial characteristics of the eyewitness accounts was that they were not only direct news from the field but also unique interpretations of the causes to expose the political chicanery of the military regime.

From a variety of sources, such as diplomats, expatriates, missionaries, and tourists who were in East Pakistan during the early days of the military attack and ongoing repression, the media seized every opportunity to gather the generally ghastly eye-witness reports of news that filtered out of East Pakistan, informing the world of the massacre of the Bengalis by the military regime. It shall be seen how, through the local print and nonprint news, the media affected a change in the public's attitude, whose support was essential to gain. Often referred to as conscientization, or in the original Portuguese word, awareness creation among the public was an excellent means to retain readers' attention continuously. They described the greatest massacre in Pakistan's history of military brutality that was critical in that when they appeared in newspapers and/or on television and radio, Canadians were still in utter disbelief and shock. The coverage of the eyewitness accounts brought about a new consciousness in the minds of the general public about the acts of brutality of the military regime.

Joe Schlesinger (Canadian Broadcasting Corporation)

As mentioned, the first eyewitness account in Canada came from Canadian journalist Schlesinger, who was quarantined during the night of March 25–26 and let go the next day. Schlesinger's interview with a CBC reporter in Vancouver supplied the facts and feelings to complete the image of the events about the story of the secret military attack and its aftermath. Following the media reports, Canadians recognized the fear that this could be the tip of the iceberg. Schlesinger was not known as a flag-waving Canadian journalist but a responsible journalist whose undertaking was marked by high professionalism.

The symbolic message component of the story at that time seemed increasingly natural and convincing to shell-shocked Canadians who were hanging in the dark until Schlesinger's public appearance on national television. Schlesinger spoke his mind and appealed to the government to come forward for assistance. Readers and viewers were mindful of what they read and heard earlier from the reporters only a few weeks before the imposition of martial law - how the pro-Bongobondhu Bengalis were getting ready to fight if their rights were denied. Seeing that Schlesinger was telling it like it is, his interviews began to shape the thoughts and actions of Canadians living thousands of kilometers away from where military reprisals were going on.

Michael Laurent (Associated Press Photographer)

Canadians were horrified to read the report of a shocked Laurent, who could hide on the hotel roof to evade the ban on a dreadful night. The following day, he sojourned around the devastated areas of the city before he was deported on March 27. "Tanks kill (ed) seven thousand in a surprise raid on Dacca."[15] This single statement may be considered as *prima facie* evidence of what was claimed to have been happening in the hands of the military regime about whom he wrote again: "Touring the still burning battle areas Saturday and Sunday, one found the burned bodies of some students still in their dormitory beds."[16] Quoting the original from Reuter, the same newspaper wrote: "Thousands dead - Pakistani massacre saw by an evacuee."[17] An engineer, who was evacuated but declined to give his name, said to a Canadian reporter what he witnessed before leaving East Pakistan's port city Chittagong: "There was a terrible massacre in the town... The Army men were rounding up people and machine-gunning them down."[18] Such accounts reinforced the story of the massacre and added to the credibility of the papers that cited examples of victimization through firsthand reports that internationalized the issue.

Simon Dring (*The Daily Telegraph*)

Dring also evaded the roundup by hiding on the hotel roof with his colleague Laurent. Like Laurent, he too managed to tour the burning city immediately following the military crackdown despite the curfew. Dring and other foreign journalists flew to West Pakistan and Bangkok early Monday the next day. As soon as he arrived in Bangkok, he dispatched the following: "Hundreds of police slain - Dacca [sic] residents flee crushed and frightened... " "Students dead in their beds, butchers in the markets killed behind their stalls, women and children burned to death in their houses, Pakistanis of Hindu religion shot *en masse,* bazaars and shopping areas razed by fire. By Sunday, the Pakistani flag flew over nearly every building."[19] Having secretly made their way out of their barracks during the wee hours of the morning, "the soldiers made the people come out of their houses. Then they shot them in groups,"[20] wrote Dring. "The operation apparently planned and led by Lt. Gen. Tikka Khan, the West Pakistani military governor of the East, has succeeded in driving every last drop of resistance out of the people of Bengal,"[21] Dring added.

His quick estimation was that, at the very least, the army must have three battalions for use in the attack on Dhaka - one armored, one artillery, and one infantry. "Tanks opened fire first, and then the troops moved in and leveled the men's sleeping quarters, firing incendiary rounds into buildings,"[22] wrote Dring with a note that an accurate estimate of civilian casualties was impossible. With the filtering of more news bits from outlying areas, including Chattogram, Cumilla, and Jashore, Dring put the figure, including Dhaka, "at about fifteen thousand dead,"[23] with a comment that, as the evacuation of the city continued over the weekend, it became increasingly apparent to him that the Pakistani army had achieved exactly what it had set out to do. This was about the first round of testimonies of international and Canadian reporters expelled from Occupied Bangladesh.

Peter Hazlehurst (*The Times*)

The "cities of Dacca and Chittagong" had been "the scenes of pitched battles between West Pakistani soldiers and the followers of Sheikh Mujibur Rahman's Awami League,"[24] wrote Hazlehurst about the death and destruction. "With the fire of nationalism flaming in East Pakistan, it seems doubtful that the army will be able to keep seventy-five million people permanently under control, even if the current harsh suppression succeeds."[25] Thus, prophesied a fearful Hazlehurst that the military action, which had already provoked new hatred, would only deepen the chasm preventing a lasting settlement.

Again, critical information was his secret rendezvous with Tajuddin Ahmed, then acting prime minister of the provisional government of Bangladesh, at an undisclosed location in Bangladesh. Canadian dailies reported the summary describing Ahmed's desperate appeal for moral support to recognize his government. Parts of Hazlehurst's interview of the acting prime minister highlighted the misrepresentation of truth by the military regime. "We are independent, but I must stress that this was not secession in the normal sense. We wanted to participate in the union of Pakistan, and as such, we fought in the elections. We won with an overwhelming majority of 167 of the 169 Bengali seats. With the declared support of several West Pakistan parties, we would have been able to frame a constitution for Pakistan with a two-thirds majority."[26] Ahmed's utterly frank statements persuaded Canadians to regard Ahmed as the man of the moment and recognize Yahya's mischievous hugger-mugger game plan - *"You ain't seen nothing yet."* The media successfully exposed the regime's antithetical position using smoke and mirrors when compared with its repeated statement that there was an armed rebellion first.

Louis Haran (Deputy Editor of The Times)

The following critical eye-witness account came through CBC's Patrick Keatley's news presentation sourced from Louis Haran, who originally obtained the testimony from someone evacuated from Dhaka immediately following the crackdown. Quoting an evacuee, CBC Radio observed that there was a typical sequence of killing and eradicating the civilians. CBC confirmed that "a systematic pattern of physical and psychological destruction became apparent during the first night of the fighting" and that "certain groups (were) selected to be victims of completely unrestrained brutality."[27] Unmistakably, the group was the Bengali nationalists who voted 95 percent in favor of Bongobondhu in the National Elections held three months ago. Their demand for greater autonomy roused Yahya's wrath to the hilt. The media quickly learned that, having abandoned the negotiation, Yahya left Dhaka secretly, giving his people specific instructions "to wipe out the key civilians who represented the separatist movement of Bengal." The Bengali nationalists were rounded up and shot at.

Alan Hart (British Broadcasting Corporation)

Consistent with the print media, both radio and television also provided information to their listeners and viewers alike on what the military crackdown was all about—the conniption of the military regime and its blueprint to perpetuate power. Having indicated that what "it adds up to is a comprehensive plan for the extermination of the intellectual leader of seventy-five million people in East Bengal," *Time* flatly branded the military action as genocide.[29] On April 2, Hart crossed the border to Jessore, forty kilometers into East Pakistan. He reported what he saw with his own eyes—convinced that the military regime was not telling the truth. "The fighting is still going on; a lot of innocent civilians have been killed, women and children. The army is not in control of the province - certainly not in control of the town in any way,"[30] wrote Hart. Even though Yahya moved with his brutal force to destroy the will and the morale of East Pakistanis, he failed. "Hundreds, thousands of peasants" who were then coming to Jessore joined forces with East Pakistan Rifles (EPR) - the sort of paramilitary police that had "actually driven the troops out of the town,"[31] observed Hart.

Michael Hornsby (The Times Daily)

In mid-April, Hornsby's eye-witness account appeared with additional information. Having visited the battlefield in East Pakistan and India, Hornsby initially followed the guerrilla war around the Kushtia district. The growing indignation for the West Pakistani rulers and non-Bengali East Pakistanis who quickly associated themselves with the military government seemed confident to Hornsby. "The conflict is a racial one, and the slender thread of Islam, the one bond in a country without a common language, race or culture, has been broken, probably for good,"[32] prophesied Hornsby. Sustained by the indestructible will and courage of seventy-five million, the Bengalis seemed more resolved to nurture the roots of a new sense of nationalism. "The seeds of hatred sown in the past few weeks will ensure that two parts of Pakistan can never be joined in any meaningful sense,"[33] was Hornsby's take on the future. The media reinforced the implicit message that an independent Bangladesh would surely be a reality despite the Yahya regime's attempt to crush the movement.

Sydney H. Schanberg (Southeast Asian Correspondent of The New York Times)

"It is difficult, after witnessing what is taking place in East Bengal, to imagine some justification for the Army's action. This is because the army, from all the available evidence, has set out to kill the leaders of East Bengal and to destroy the economic base of the region,"[34] commented Schanberg.

There were times when no one knew how many Bengali families the army had machine-gunned down or how many migrant settlers (Biharis) the Bengali secessionists had slashed to death. Schanberg's widely read article described the pitiful scenes of the teeming refugee camps. As the army regained control, the embittered non-Bengali civilians immediately took their revenge, adding more deaths to the toll. He concluded by saying what he believed to be a mammoth task: "Whoever is in charge will face an economy heading for collapse, with the occupation of the East a ruinous but unavoidable running."[35]

Senator Edward Kennedy (Chairman of the Subcommittee on Refugees)

When Senator Kennedy's report was made public throughout the U.S.A., its abridged version immediately appeared in Canadian newspapers, highlighting the pertinent areas to broaden readers' understanding of the conflict. It was noted that "the issue from the beginning in East Bengal had been self-determination and democratic principle. While the East Pakistani Bengalis were negotiating for democracy and autonomy, the West Pakistani army was preparing for systematic repression and organized terror."[36] Again, referring to countless thousands who were butchered during the days that followed March 25 and many millions more were dislocated within East Pakistan, Kennedy observed: "What I saw in India was the human debris from that night of terror and the subsequent weeks of violence."[37]

Again, when in an impassioned address to the National Press Club, Kennedy talked about his impression of the predicaments of the refugees in India, the North American public remained keen on hearing about Kennedy's observations. "We must demonstrate to the Generals of West Pakistan and the peoples of the world that the U. S. has a deep and abiding revulsion of the monumental slaughter that has ravaged East Pakistan."[38]

Readers were touched to read the excerpts of Kennedy's report on what he heard from many - how the refugees continued to trudge along unknown roads for days and weeks without food or shelter while their children died along the way. Having defied the torrential rain, Kennedy saw for himself how so many refugees walked thousands of miles during the monsoons and found them ravaged by raging cholera, which made him recognize the need for a coordinated international response.

Foreign Correspondents in East Pakistan with special permission (May 6–11, 1971)

In May, the military regime allowed six foreign news correspondents from foreign countries to enter East Pakistan following six weeks of a complete news blackout. Canada, like many countries, jumped at the offer. The foreign correspondents were placed in a batch of six, including Pakistani journalists, on a conducted tour between May 6-11, 1971. They were escorted by military personnel under strict supervision and carefully circumscribed conditions. Following their guided tour, the reporters made two critical observations: (1) some people were petrified to see the soldiers who used to gaze through the gun slits of their sandbagged bunkers, while some people used to run away from their sight like a frightened rabbit and (2) The extreme militarization created a climate of fear and disbelief. Major Canadian dailies published short write-ups on the personal observations of the reporters whose key message was that the exodus of the terror-stricken Bengalis to a haven (India) seemed a logical choice even though the military regime was claiming otherwise.

The explosion of hand grenades was alleged to have been used by anti-Pakistani elements that required the massive deployment of militias, the presence of military vehicles everywhere, and the searches for bombs and explosives in every public building. A contemptuous military regime deemed most Bengalis to be pro-Indians and, therefore, anti-Pakistani. "There was a lot of massacres, mainly directed against pro-Pakistani and pro-regime elements, and Bengalis against non-Bengalis,"[39] observed the martial law administrator, Lieutenant General Tikka Khan. Through newspaper reports, Canadians learned how the military regime contradicted the world media reports.

The foreign correspondents, however, saw for themselves how thousands of terrified and impoverished Bengalis were frantically attempting to flee to India, while office buildings, shops, homes, and everything else in every nook and corner of the country was reminiscent of military brutalities. "All over East Pakistan, decimated families pick among the blackened remains of their homes and businesses, wondering where to start again," commented the *Globe and Mail* on May 13, 1971. Ironically, the result was the opposite despite the Yahya regime's expectation of a favorable report. The reporters saw the naked truth: that the authoritarian Yahya regime was looked down upon by the Bengalis with suspicion and hatred for its engagement in a ruthless suppression of democracy - yet another nail in the coffin.

Dr. Robert McClure (Former Moderator of the United Church of Canada and Board Member of OXFAM Canada)

Immediately after his return from India and Pakistan in July, the major Canadian newspapers covered Dr. McClure's media interviews. Having seen the refugee camps and the ongoing repression that was resulting in a continuing exodus of the terrified Bengalis, both McClure and the reporters assigned to India and Pakistan returned with a sorrowful memory. "They have no choice but to become guerilla fighters. And fight, they will. There is always somebody around to supply the weapons,"[40] observed a distressed McClure with a note of caution. Seeing the aggressiveness of the regime, McClure predicted that the sheer number of refugees would grow for sure and that the situation would not only deteriorate rapidly but also epidemics of all sorts would spread like wildfire, resulting in the death of hundreds of thousands of refugees.

John Wieler (Associate Executive Director of the Mennonite Central Committee)

The eye-witness account of John Wieler, MCC's associate executive director, also touched the minds and hearts of Canadians, especially when he presented his findings to the House of Commons Standing Committee on External Affairs and National Defence. His narrative was not just a recitation of the burning, looting, and killing of civilians but also a description of the consequent displacement and exodus of millions of Bengalis who sought temporary asylum in India. Seeing the distressing conditions in which Wieler found the refugees suffering from congestion and the lack of adequate supplies at a time when many more were wandering toward an uncertain fate, Wieler reflected on the unknown future of the refugees: "The despair, the filth, and the general conditions here have gripped me as I have never yet experienced. The suffering of these people is immense. As I think about these refugees, I also think about my people back in Canada and the United States, wondering how I can convey the message of suffering here to them."[42] Thus, wrote an apprehensive Wieler.

"Her little home in East Pakistan had been destroyed by a marauding soldier. Her husband had disappeared, apparently killed in the bitter fighting between the Bengalis and Punjabis. She had gathered her children and a few possessions and fled to the border, hoping to find food and shelter somewhere in the Indian province of Bengal. But her expectations were short-lived. Her children vanished, her possessions were stolen, her clothing literally torn off her back. Nothing was left but to die."[43] Thus, Wieler wrote again about another refugee woman he followed from the beginning to the end. He then wrote how the unlucky woman finally perished, as anyone would have thought so. Again, those who stayed back in the country, wrote Wieler, were internally displaced, having been forced to flee to the countryside from one place to another in fear for their lives at a time when dodging tanks were firing at them at random.

Vernon Reimer (Mennonite Central Committee's Representative in India)

Through his narrative of the predicaments of the refugee children in the overcrowded camps, which were visited by many Canadian doctors, social workers, parliamentarians, and government and non-government officials, Vernon Reimer, MCC's representative in India, instantly drew the Canadians' sympathies. He drove home the vulnerability of children in particular—how hundreds and thousands of children were dying every day despite every effort to save their lives. His appeal emphasized the notion of the milk of human kindness that one should strive for in the tragic situation of the refugees in the squalid camps. "We continue to trust and pray that the leaders of nations will be able to agree that these suffering millions may again live in relative harmony."[43] Thus, Reimer reminded fellow Canadians, having kept his eyes open and ears to the ground while expressing his innermost feelings of angst.

Raymond Cournoyer (Canadian Holy Cross Brother)

Testimonies of Brother Cournoyer, Canadian Field Director for OXFAM Canada, directly carried a key message for Canadians: "To do more, much more, to relieve human suffering in Pakistan."[44] Cournoyer called for the assistance of the world community at large. News headings, such as "Pathetic Squatters" and "Settlements Without Sanitation," where Bengalis were swarming in to find a place in the refugee camps, were truly scary to the point that gave goosebumps to those who were following the news. While celebrating space exploration around this time in the world news, Canadian media also continued to narrate the pathetic plight of millions of refugees and displaced persons who were suffering from diseases, such as cholera and smallpox and were dying of starvation. These reminded readers of the agonizing tragedy of the Bengalis in the field.

Ernest Hillen (Weekend Magazine)

Around July, the Montreal-based *Weekend Magazine* sent Ernest Hillen to India to visit the refugee camps to obtain firsthand information on what constituted a "grim witness to the colossal dimension of the East Pakistan tragedy."[45] Hillen's two extraordinary articles titled "So Many Will Die" and "A Man in the Middle of Misery" in the *Weekend Magazine* of July 31, 1971, outlined the genesis of the problem to reach out to the average Canadian. To use Hillen's own words, having viewed the situation through a Canadian lens, he "felt an obligation - an obligation as human beings - to try to drive the fact of this tragedy into your (that is, readers') minds."[46] Why? Having asked this question, Hillen answered: "Because there are terrors in this world," and despite conscious efforts, there were "horrors that we refuse to contemplate."[47] A frank Hillen then wrote: "The blame for the catastrophe rightly enough belongs to the men who run the West Pakistan government, but that the shame belongs to all of us."[48] His thrust was to involve the rest of the world in condemning the action of the Yahya government and seeing the problem as a global responsibility: "It must be stopped now - by whatever manner or means. Our children will inherit enough shame."[49]

Apart from the refugees, Hillen also met with diplomats, missionaries, and expatriates who were on the scenes of army atrocity during the early days of the military attack and spoke about dreadful stories of looting, burning, and brutality of the Pakistani army and indiscriminate killings of the Bengalis by the same. The refugees' testimonies seemed like licensed mayhem that reeked with horror, which Hillen portrayed in his articles, depicting a sordid picture of the refugees who were crossing the border in search of a crammed-in make-shift arrangement, a haven in India. The refugees were running away only to escape inevitable death due to the regime's indiscriminate killings, resulting in a pogrom. Simple, straightforward description with accompanying picture of the grubby and overcrowded refugee camps with bodies seeking shelter from the blistering sun and the torrential rain with no exaggeration outraged readers in Canada.

Father Edgar Burns (Canadian Jesuit Mission)

To reinforce the message of Father Burns of the Jesuit Mission of India, the Toronto-based Canadian Jesuits Mission (CJM) sent Father Frank West from Toronto to the field to visit the refugee camps in India to assess the relief operation undertaken by the missionaries. Between July 9-14, 1971, West was in India and traveled extensively to the refugee camps, where he met with many people engaged in relief operations in the Darjeeling District and West Dinajpur of West Bengal. Upon his return to Canada, Father West recounted his observations, having complemented them by the writings of Father Burns in a widely circulated report titled, "Let My Children Live! An Eye-Witness Report."[50] Father West's presentation package also included a film titled *They Passed This Way,* approximately six hundred feet of movie pictures (16-millimeter color) showing the enormity of the refugee situation in India to illustrate the work of the Canadians in the grief-stricken refugee camps in India.

Father West traveled across Canada. He frequently used Senator Edward Kennedy's remark during his visits to the refugee camps: that the refugee crisis was perhaps one of the greatest tragedies in the history of humans seemed no exaggeration. Canadians were happy to hear the words of praise from Kennedy, who saw their efforts as "a worthy tribute to Canada for what it is doing in the field for the East Pakistani refugees."[51] "Thousands are hugging trees to protect themselves from the rain and cold nights—clothes, medicines, and foods are needed... We will construct temporary shelters of bamboo and straw with the refugees' help," [52] Father Burns appealed. He also displayed pictures of the refugee camps, miseries, and uncertainties using terse but powerful sentences like the present PowerPoint presentation. "Millions of human beings face starvation and live in hovels that are not fit for dogs,"[53] was Father West's key message. He believed that Canadians ought to view the predicament of the refugees living in the conditions of squalor, misery, and disease in the refugee camps as an inescapable challenge to the conscience and resourcefulness of the rest of the world.

John Drewery (Canadian Broadcasting Corporation)

Drewery, a longtime CBC reporter and foreign correspondent who was thoroughly professional and well-versed in the emerging genre of objective journalism, was concerned about expelling all foreign journalists. He maintained that the introduction of strict censorship did not stop journalists from sending photos and testimonies. Having gone to India and Pakistan as one of the CBC's reporters, Drewery wrote news stories and sent them from India for Canadian readers. His frequent eye-witness accounts opened the eyes of readers who did not fail to recognize the motives of the military regime behind the repression of the Bengalis. Reporting on the reactions of those who returned from the scene of military reprisals and violence, Drewery noted that many untold members of destitute victims remained unaccounted for and unattended in the rural areas of East Pakistan. According to Drewery, many evacuees had observed that learning about their whereabouts would require a Herculean effort. Comments from the eye-witness account reflected the pent-up but deep-seated hatred that the Bengalis and non-Bengalis were harbouring against each other, wrote Drewery.[54]

The eye-witness details of the long pieces, whether from Brother Cournoyer or journalist Hillen from the ground, provided historical perspectives with a careful explanation of what had been happening politically. They were consistent with the situational reports that Ottawa officials received from Canadian high commissioners to India and Pakistan. Though readers in Canada were far away from the troubled countries, the testimonies they heard and read did ring true to what they had been reading or hearing about. To use journalistic jargon, the helpless refugees in India and the displaced civilians in "Occupied Bangladesh" became readers' reflex of tears. The touchy rendition provided by the eyewitnesses became a tale within a tale - a firsthand account.

Regular News Coverage (Mid-April 1971 - December 1971) Under Selective Headings

By mid-April, as the flow of news increased, the media was able to describe in some detail how the army, under orders of the military regime, treacherously launched a ferocious armed attack against unarmed Bengali civilians. News reporters immediately conducted further research and gained additional accurate information down to the smallest detail to present the realities of what was happening in Pakistan. To mitigate that risk, they made it a practice to include astute analysis, interpretation, and objective reporting of facts either seen directly or obtained through firsthand eyewitness accounts. The major Canadian dailies thus placed the Pakistan–Bangladesh conflict within the context of Pakistan polity concerning the potential situation in East Pakistan.

Overall, complementing the stories of massacre and rebellion, the print media's narratives included a strong theme of a guerrilla movement, which had been born with renewed determination, having received direct encouragement and assistance from the Gandhi administration. According to the news analysts, the conditions in East Pakistan, with a population of seventy-five million, were perfect for a guerrilla war to encounter the West Pakistani army. They predicted that the guerrilla war would continue and East Pakistan would be independent.

Canadian reporters saw the establishment of the provisional government of Bangladesh within two weeks following its declaration of independence as a firm step taken by the Bengalis toward achieving their goals. This was done at a function at Mujibnagar, about 150 kilometers from Kolkata, West Bengal. The Trudeau administration, however, was not yet ready to react in any way. Many news analysts tried to see if the Declaration of Independence was, in fact, due to the armed rebellion or due to the planned attack on civilians: "The army went into action to stop a rebellion planned for three o'clock the next morning. They [i.e., official spokesmen] insisted that the army killed no one but those who fired at the soldiers,"[55] wrote a Canadian daily. Most reporters, however, thought that "the rebellion plot was only an assumption"[56] and that the army jumped the gun. "The army shelled towns and fired at anything that moved. The army action was far more brutal than anything seen in the Nigerian civil war."[57] Under the circumstances, reporters published all news items they thought would interest Canadians. "If there was a conspiracy, the Awami League played right into the hands of the conspirators,"[58] wrote one reporter.

Education and Awareness

From the beginning of the political impasse, the media's understanding was that it would have to play the role of an educator to *inform* its readers about the crisis by giving the proper context of the conflict so that readers may be "educated" and engaged in understanding the peculiar subcontinental body politic. The narrator took responsibility for narrating the news by alluding to the partition of India in 1947 and the relationship between Pakistan and India since then. This allowed readers to get up to speed by learning about the Indo-Pakistan political phenomena and remaining connected to know more about what was happening in the subcontinent. The media deemed this more necessary to readers in Canada than being the first on the scene. To provide an appropriate context, the print media started its educator's role by describing the 1970 National Elections campaigns and the preparation for the transfer of power to the elected representatives. Moving forward, the media resorted to a chronological account of what had happened since the 1970 National Elections and why the power had not been transferred to the majority party's leader. This became a helpful starting point for reportage as it enabled readers not only to self-educate themselves on the complex nature of the conflict but also encouraged them to be engaged in doing something for the victims of military reprisals once the root cause of the conflict became apparent.

The media's first challenge in educating readers was to familiarize them with the events within the context of Pakistan, a militarily ruled country from birth in the quest for democracy. Almost invariably, the media referred to the creation of Pakistan, its subsequent politico-military history, ongoing constitutional crisis, and the Bengali East Pakistanis' sense of deprivation and feeling of betrayal by the military rulers. Pakistan is "a country which from its birth amidst communal strife in 1947" had "never really had a full opportunity to exercise the democratic process,"[59] reported *The Ottawa Citizen*. The media also reported on accusations and counteraccusations between the military regime and the Awami League (AL) leader in East Pakistan and how tensions have been building up since the National Elections.

It would have been impossible for an average Canadian reader to comprehend the complex political game that was going on in the subcontinent without the knowledge of the background information and analysis. News analysts also looked at other political phenomena on the ground - the AL led by Bongobondhu as well as other emerging issues, such as the leadership of Professor Muzaffar Chowdhury and Maulana Abdul Khan Bhashani, leaders of the two National Awami Party (pro-Moscow) and (pro-Peking) respectively, as well as the role of the Naxalites, adherents of Chinese communism, who were believed to have denounced Bongobondhu as an agent of CIA and a tool of Soviet revisionism. Earlier, during the political impasse, the Canadian media had already made predictions for more significant political disturbances involving the West Pakistani-led military regime and civilian Bengalis in East Pakistan following the declaration of semi-independence and appeal by Bongobondhu to Bengalis to stop paying taxes. The media also noted that some political observers were still sanguine in believing President Yahya Khan might find ways to strike a deal with the Awami League. This did not happen, and the military regime refused to cooperate with the league. The news coverage of the ongoing political impasse and the rapid deterioration of the situation included commentaries on the next probable political turns in a country that, ideally, should have been moving forward smoothly in its quest for democracy.

The print media situated the news items within the context of power-sharing between the two wings of Pakistan, specifically the Bengalis' demand for greater autonomy and, later, their fight for an independent state. Extensive coverage along this vein helped readers learn quickly more about the how and the why of the political impasse and the sudden but planned military action, as well as how and under what circumstances the Bengali rebels declared the independence of Bangladesh. Most newspapers reported that the army clampdown was a carefully organized operation by the ruling military, including Yahya himself, who was "deeply involved in planning, supervising, or commanding the Dacca massacre which plunged this country into civil war two weeks ago."[60]

While providing background information and the political hegemony, all explanations and analyses included Pakistan's relationship with India to get readers up to speed. The media also touched on the role of the Gandhi administration and the historical animosity between India and Pakistan, each viewing the other as one's archfoe. To help Canadians appreciate Canada's awkward position, Canada's overall relationship with India and Pakistan as members of the Commonwealth was also included in the narrative.

By the end of April, the media predicted that the issue would involve superpowers, with the USA supporting Pakistan and the USSR supporting India and the Bengali freedom fighters. It is because, wrote the news media, the USSR, which had a deep stake in the Indian subcontinent, would lend its support to the Bengalis and stop bloodshed and repression against the people of East Pakistan.[61] The newspaper also warned its readers that, though the conflict in East Pakistan was purely local, there were signs that, in certain circumstances, apart from the U. S. involvement, others such as India, the People's Republic of China, and the USSR could become involved in a long and vicious guerrilla war.[62] Conflicting views indicated that the issue, if not resolved, could threaten world peace.

By the beginning of May, the coverage of the Pakistan-Bangladesh conflict increased, including more descriptions of military repression, the resultant ongoing exodus, and the miserable plight of the refugees in India. "The killing and devastation defy belief,"[63] filed Mort Rosenblum, whose story from Bangkok was beyond the reach of Pakistani censorship. Through his stories, Rosenblum brought back a picture of the death, destruction, and devastation of millions of Bengalis being driven into desperate exile across the border. The media described what the Bengalis called the War of Liberation and continued to file stories of events they found in every nook and cranny of occupied Bangladesh. With a two-pronged technique, readers were shown the horror of the indiscriminate killing of the Bengalis by non-Bengali army personnel. Soon, readers learned about the Bengalis' feelings of betrayal by those who were supposed to provide them security by becoming their greatest enemy. The reporters aroused a passionate sense of resentment toward the military authority in Pakistan, which was seen as malevolent and unjust. The media successfully conveyed to its readers in Canada its vital message that it was a cruel military regime ruthlessly engaged in a genocidal decimation of fellow East Pakistani Bengalis.

Again, continuing to "educate" the Canadian public, the print media expanded its strategy to explain India's present and future role in Pakistan's domestic affairs in more precise terms. Even though the Gandhi administration denied all along its link with the provisional government of Bangladesh and its covert support of the Bengali freedom fighters, the news media considered the Indian government's version as untrue. Canadian journalists who went to India and East Pakistan had a chance to see what was happening on the ground. The media noted India's welcoming signals of refugees from its supporters and sympathizers throughout India. The media pointed out the brutal actions of the Yahya regime and the potential role of India in the conflict to realize her hidden agenda - dismember Pakistan. "Doubtless, India will continue to supply the guerillas with arms and assist in their training. And so, the slaughter within East Pakistan will go on for many months."[64] Thus, it predicted a Canadian newspaper. Readers were quick to get a sense of what the respective governments of Pakistan and India were up to - strategizing their own but different respective game plans.

The news reporters also noted the use of words and terminologies having semantic subtleties to reinforce the message of ongoing military repression. Readers were alerted by showing how the regime chose to describe the Bengalis, who were always referred to as mobs, rioters, miscreants, rabble-rousers, and vicious antisocial elements. In contrast, the regime referred to the Pakistani army as the forces of law and order and Pakistan's disciplined troops. Once alerted, readers recognized the military regime's recasting of the Bengalis into the imagery of a small group of mutineers, Indian agents, ultranationalists, and anti-state elements engaged in disrupting the law-and-order situation in Pakistan. Such narratives and commentaries assisted readers in deepening their understanding of the nature of the conflict and the ulterior motive of the Yahya regime.

Whether it was the sheer stubbornness of the military regime or its naïvety, readers were frequently reminded of the military regime's fabricated storyline—that the vast majority of the Bengalis were in agreement with the economic system with its corrective measures for parity and equality, and that the political process heading toward democracy would be okay except for a few disturbances (not a civil war), which were due to the Machiavellianism of a few Indian agents. Through various examples, the media debunked such myths and pointed out the ultimate objective of the regime - how, having blamed the Bengali leader of the majority party, it planned to remain in power by being long on promise and short on substance.

Pakistan's Geography and Polity

The news media held the view that readers must have an enhanced understanding of the conflictual relations between Pakistan and India since the partition of India in 1947 and the present issue concerning the Bengalis' demand *vis-à-vis* the Indian government's direct stake in the issue. To assist readers in expanding their understanding of Pakistan's geography and polity, the media situated the conflict in the minds of the Canadian public within the context of a host of hot-button issues, such as fundamental human rights, the economic disparity between the two wings of Pakistan, restoration of democracy, end of military rule, good governance, political autonomy, self-government, separation and, finally, sovereignty and recognition of Bangladesh as an independent country.

Frequent write-ups on the historical context of the advancement of militarism and its embodiment from the outset in the political and economic fortunes of powerful West Pakistan helped readers be mindful of the true nature of the conflict between the people of the two wings of Pakistan. The news media successfully helped readers learn how the people of East Pakistan encountered unique economic, social, and political obstacles to Pakistan's unity, equality of participation, and cohesion. More particularly, the media tried to show how the Bengalis were disenchanted when the National Assembly session was postponed *sine die,* and then, within a matter of three weeks, how the military launched its sudden and secret but planned attack on the unarmed Bengali civilians who are supposed to be protected by the same army.

Tied to the historical and political backgrounds was a deliberate technique used by the print media to portray Pakistan as having congenital problems from its creation. The idea was to depict the very creation of Pakistan as a country that, as many political analysts worldwide maintained, was a geographical absurdity. At every opportunity, whether it was a news write-up, a commentary, or an editorial disquisition, Pakistan was described as a country that was physically divided into two separate wings stretching over India, her archenemy. In pointing out the difference between the people of East and West Pakistan, ethnicity, food habits, and lifestyle were also mentioned: "They are darker and eat rice in contrast to the wheat and lentils of westerns. Only the bond of Islam reinforced by a shared fear of Indian domination holds the two wings together."[65] No attempt was ever made to examine the Hindu–Muslim dichotomy in British India before the partition of India. "Separated by more than one thousand miles of Indian Territory, the Bengalis of East Pakistan are worlds apart linguistically and culturally from the Punjabis, Pathans, and Sindhis of the west," wrote the *Kitchener-Waterloo Record*.[66] This was a helpful technique for the news media to reinforce the message that aimed at restating every time East Pakistan was physically separated from West Pakistan, where the central government was located.

President Yahya's calling upon the armed forces to crush the movement for autonomy following the democratic process in East Pakistan was considered the beginning of the end of a united Pakistan, which was described as a geographically divided country.[67] The print media highlighted more dissimilarities than similarities between the two wings of Pakistan. "The union of East and West Pakistan has been a tenuous one from the beginning. East Pakistan's people are Bengalis, a short, dark-skinned race. They have ancestral ties to the Indians who live across the border in West Bengal and are culturally and linguistically distinct from the West Pakistanis. The Punjabis, the Sindhis, and the Afghans who inhibit West Pakistan are taller, lighter in skin color, and culturally closer to the Islamic nations of the Middle East."[68] Thus, the *Globe and Mail* reinforce its point - that the people of the two wings of Pakistan are culturally and linguistically different.

A particular question, though worded variously, was repeatedly asked by the news media: "Would Pakistan, after the military crackdown of March 25, ever remain one country?" Both Canadian high commissioners also raised this question to Pakistan and India. Readers did not fail to recognize how the hatred of the military regime and non-Bengali West Pakistanis against the Bengalis had already reached a point where there was no possibility for reconciliation. Many news analysts went to the extent of expressing their apprehension regarding the national integration of Pakistan, seeing the nature of the ongoing reprisals. Canadian print media supported the idea of a separate homeland for the Bengalis - Bangladesh. Statements like the "future of Pakistan as a nation looks as disjointed as its geography"[69] appeared time and again from the time the Bengalis declared the independence of Bangladesh until the ultimate surrender of the Pakistani army in December 1971. The media's narratives helped Canadians learn more about the discrimination the Bengalis had been subjected to since the birth of Pakistan.

Again, there was also some news coverage on those minuscule minority Bengalis and almost all non-Bengalis in East Pakistan who did not renounce the idea of Muhammed Ali Jinnah's Two Nations Theory: that India and Pakistan were two separate countries, something that had already been alluded to in Chapter 1. It was reported that the Pakistani loyalists, having ignored the military actions, supported the military regime despite its genocidal activities in East Pakistan. They remained firm in their belief in the unity of Pakistan at any cost. Naturally, they found themselves at ideological loggerheads with the majority, whom they called neo-nationalist Bengalis. They considered themselves to be patriots - Pakistani nationalists.

Another important noticeable strategy of the print media was to inform readers of the military regime's duplicity regarding its political moves. Time and again, the media pointed out how there existed many contradictions between what the military government was saying and purporting to be doing and its suspicion that the regime would not fulfill the verdict of the people of Pakistan expressed through the 1970 National Elections. The print media painstakingly explained in layperson's terms - that, as far as the military regime was concerned, those who took part in anti-state activities would be unqualified, and by-elections would fill their places. It was unclear as it seemed paradoxical to the majority of the public that demanded more clarification from the regime. It is because, in the same breath, Yahya also declared that all governments, meaning both central and provincial, would have the cover of martial law at their disposal for a period. Canadians were stunned by Yahya's web of lies. They did not take long to be convinced that Yahya was talking the talk - and that he would not walk the talk.

Canadians were reminded through daily newspapers, radio, and television news how the refugees were streaming across the Indian border to seek a safe haven. While describing the horrible situation resulting from ongoing military repression, the reporters used an interactive style that involved readers directly as they read: "Why are these refugees?" Putting the events within the context of the democratic rights of the Bengalis and the denial of their fundamental rights by the Yahya regime, the print media shot straight questions. Again, Yahya's tightly held view that any party confined to a specific region was not a national party for all practical purposes did not make sense to Canadians. This created confusion as the media noted how Yahya started to sing a different tune.

No one in the military cared to take the time to interpret his antithetical statements and assertions or Yahya's approaches to the division of power between the provincial and central governments at a time when martial law remained in force. The media argued that Yahya was also constructing a new narrative about the election results, shifting the political landscape to the post-election period with a mischievous intention to nullify the results. The journalists on the ground became convinced that (1) the military authority in Pakistan was resolved to crush the Bengalis' movement for greater autonomy and (2) the Bengalis were equally determined to kick the military personnel out of their homeland. Within a short period evidently, the news coverage made the Canadian public more aware of how a new sense of nationalism had already entered into the minds and vocabulary of the Bengalis for a collectively emotional and rational attachment to the native land they passionately named Bangla Desh (as it was spelled then).

Many Canadian dailies frequently published articles dealing with Yahya's particular brand of power sharing to ensure that readers understand the specific context, the military mindset, and the diametrically opposing views held by the governments of Pakistan and India, more particularly, the ulterior motives, strengths, and weaknesses *vis-à-vis* the steadfast resolve of the *Mukti Bahini* (Liberation Forces) to free their native land. To pursue the above point, one newspaper quoted a rebel commander, Captain Abdul Halim, at the Jashore headquarters of the East Pakistan Rifle: "We have all the men we want, but Yahya's men have all the weapons... All our people are taking part in the fight... There have been many casualties, but we shall fight until the end. The Pakistani army cannot defeat seventy-five million people. They cannot hold out forever in a hostile land. We shall starve them into surrender."[70] The implicit message reflected in the title, "Rebels Lack Arms: Pakistan Near Standoff," was that the determined Bengali rebels would not give up their fight, come what might. It was predicted that the guerrilla war would be predominantly urban, particularly vicious and destructive, and that the Bengalis would fight a guerrilla war that might go on for years until they achieved their goal.[71] Such analysis resonated with readers in Canada, who began to appreciate the Bengalis' cause for the liberation of their native land.

Reprints of Articles written by Distinguished Individuals

Major Canadian newspapers used an age-old technique of reprinting news articles and write-ups by distinguished individuals from Canada and around the world. This technique soon became a part of the news dissemination strategy, giving prominence to such reportage. Though written separately, words and phrases used by renowned authors had profound meanings. Below are a few reprints.

Anthony Mascarenhas (Assistant Editor of The Morning News of Karachi, Pakistan)

As mentioned, Anthony Mascarenhas, a Pakistani journalist of Goan origin and a Karachi correspondent of the *Sunday Times*, was one of the eight Pakistani journalists invited by the government to observe firsthand the situation in East Pakistan. His report in the *Sunday Times* of June 13, 1971, a shattering piece of an eyewitness account of the wanton killings of the Bengali civilians and the destruction of their properties, was immediately reprinted in many newspapers as the lead story on the front page. Using Mascarenhas' text extensively, Robert Duffy of the *Globe and Mail* described the ongoing army action throughout East Pakistan. "There is only one word for it: genocide. The Pakistan army is carrying out a government policy of systematically murdering and terrorizing the Hindu population of East Pakistan, as well as exterminating secessionist elements in the Moslem Bengali population."[72]

"While Moslem Bengalis are being hunted down and slaughtered for political reasons, the Hindus die or flee simply because they are Hindus."[73] Thus, Duffy quoted Mascarenhas to drive home the brutal actions of the military regime. Again, Mascarenhas also quoted Major General Shaukat Raza, commanding officer of the army's ninth division, about the government's policy: "We have undertaken a job. We are going to finish it, not hand it over half-done to the politicians so they can mess it up again. The army can't keep coming back like this every three or four years. It has a more important task. I assure you that when we have gotten through with what we are doing, there will never be a need again for such an operation."[74] The commanding officer's candid confession of the regime's current and future plan convinced Mascarenhas as to why the Bengalis were frightened of having to live with a sense of being under seizure.

Peter Hazlehurst (The Times)

Perhaps the most widely reprinted article in the Canadian dailies following Mascarenhas' write-up was Hazlehurst's writing on his meeting with the acting prime minister of Bangladesh. We have already seen this under the caption "Coverage of Eye-Witness Accounts and Analysis of Ongoing Repression." "Taking events to their logical conclusion, there is no doubt that the present holocaust was precipitated by President Yahya Khan when he postponed the Assembly without consulting the Bengalis, but even more so by Mr. Bhutto's deliberate decision to boycott the Assembly on March 3,"[75] wrote Hazlehurst. The characterization of the military's action as an intolerable denial of human and democratic rights allowed the Canadian public to look at the action as "an indiscriminate act or an act of genocide that would remain a witness to one of history's most massive examples of genocide.[76]

Chester Bowles (Former US Ambassador to India 1951–1953)

When Bowles warned the world community, Canadian newspapers reprinted his write-ups to give readers a sense of the grim future of Pakistan. The original July 15, 1971 article in the *New York Times* was cited in many Canadian dailies that warned readers that South Asia was in imminent danger of erupting into a tragic and needless war.[77] Bowles' articles reminded Canadians of the Nixon administration's continuous effort to sweep the situation under the rug: "What is happening in East Pakistan is immoral and humanitarian outrage which must be condemned and stopped. At the same time, India must be relieved of the responsibility for the care of the six million refugees." [78] Canadians read in fine print something they had been trying to say regarding the need for economic assistance to help India out of her financial burden. In a very subtle way, the newspapers also attempted to discredit the Nixon administration, which was hypocritical in expressing its position *vis-à-vis* the Pakistan-Bangladesh conflict.

Alvin Toffler (Author of Future Shock)

One of Toffler's widely published articles, "The Sorry U. S. Role in the Pakistan Refugee," was reprinted in several Canadian dailies depicting a strong sense of helplessness. This pattern helped reinforce the predicament in readers' minds. "A planetary catastrophe is taking place in Asia, a human disaster so massive that it could bathe the future in blood, not just for Asians, but for those of us in the West as well,"[79] remarked Toffler. His observations on the Nixon administration's apparent contradictions reiterated what Canadians had already noted regarding the US policy toward Pakistan, which had been murky. "On the one hand, the United States promises India $70 million in relief funds. On the other hand, it continues to supply arms to the same West Pakistani generals who launched the bloodbath so that they can terrorize even more of their subjects into fleeing across the Indian border,"[80] wrote Toffler. The reprint of Toffler's write-ups caused waves among readers as though it started another round of discussion on the lives of innocent civilians in East Pakistan and the lives of the refugees in India, giving rise to questions as to what could be done collectively.

John Kenneth Galbraith (Canadian-born economist and a Former U. S. Ambassador to India from 1963–1969)

The *Globe and Mail* reprinted Galbraith's write-up titled "East Pakistan: The Need for Autonomy to Guarantee Peace" along the line that greater autonomy should be given to East Pakistan. "Both the overwhelming vote for autonomy earlier this year and the events since make it certain that East Pakistan cum East Bengal will only be peaceful if full autonomy and self-government are accorded to it."[81] He elaborated on the issue by suggesting that the circumstances ought to be assessed and that complete autonomy would be the only way to resolve the governance issue. "No action of ours should encourage or seem to encourage military domination of the East by the West,"[82] wrote Galbraith, whose appeal resonated among Canadians.

Kenneth Keating (U. S. Ambassador to India, 1969–1972) and Others

When Keating, then the U. S. Ambassador to India, declared that the situation in East Pakistan could no longer be considered an internal affair, most international newspapers, including Canadian dailies, reprinted his observations on the conflict, which he speculated had the potential to shake the Indian subcontinent and South Asia.

There were also writings of General Jayanto Nath Chaudhuri (former commander in chief of the Indian army and former Indian high commissioner to Canada who was, at that time, with the Centre for Developing Areas Studies at McGill University), Claire Hollingworth of the *Sunday Telegraph*, and Murray Sayle, foreign correspondent of the *Sunday Times*. Many of their write-ups carried stories of the worst horrors of civil war and relentless military suppression of dissidents and reprisals on civilians. According to the news media, the military regime never made it clear why he undertook a secret military attack on the civilians while he was officially engaged in a negotiation with the political leaders of Pakistan. Canadian readers failed to appreciate President Yahya's *raison d'être* for the military operation as his jiggery-pokery dealings were beyond their comprehension. The media also saw it as a stab in the back.

Reprinting write-ups may be seen as an example of piggybacking on current stories published in international newspapers that allowed Canadians to read about something they might have missed. Many of these reprints dealt with topics like Pakistan's militarism, regionalism, India–Pakistan's hostility, and others, which provided additional interpretation for readers, many of whom were not expected to be satisfied having known about what happened. Frequent reprinting of pertinent articles allowed Canadian readers to read again and again the difference between what was happening and what was likely to occur in the future and, more precisely, how the military regime was proposing to resolve what the media called the Pakistan-Bangladesh conflict. Reprints of such write-ups helped readers develop an enlarged understanding of the how and the why of the military takeover and what might happen as a result of the reprisals by the army and the declaration of independence by the Bengali rebels. This, in turn, generated ongoing interest among Canadians who engaged themselves in public discourses.

The Allusion to the 1970 October Crisis/FLQ Crisis

From the outset, the media appreciated the government's fear of the secessionists at home - in Canada's backyard. Having recognized the Trudeau administration's reluctance for a declaratory position, the media had been both respectful and mindful of the situation in its analysis of the events as they were unfolding with the news coverage on the concepts of sovereignty, separation, and independence throughout the period the Bengalis were fighting for the liberation of their native land. Any news regarding separation and independence was sensitive and provocative to the government as it raised a fear that always lurked behind. Initially, for a while, there also existed a strong feeling of uncertainty among the Canadian public and parliamentarians who were shaky about this hot-button issue.

We need to step back and examine how the events following the 1970 National Elections under the Yahya regime were reported in the Canadian media. Some observers were cautious in thinking that there were "many a twixt between the lips and the cups of tea." The media emphasized that the Six-Point Program platform on which Bongobondhu ran and won the election was deemed legitimate by the Yahya regime, to which the result was acceptable. It was not seen as a manifestation of secession or independence.

When the disturbing news of the military takeover surfaced in the news media, Canadians were still grappling with the nature of the crisis *vis-à-vis* their fear of the Québec question.[83] The news coverage regarding the East Pakistan crisis reminded Canadians of what happened in Canada only less than six months ago. For many Canadians, the crisis, at least during its early period, also evoked the haunting memories of the Nigerian Civil War of 1966-1970 when the federal regime sought justification in the name of national unity and Biafrans in the name of self-determination.

With their determination to realize their rights, the Bengalis embraced Bongobondhu as someone who had been riding a tiger—his unleashed people, ever since the AL swept the nation's election in December 1970 with a call for autonomy for Pakistan. Canada noted how the Bengalis followed Bongobondhu blindly. Many Canadian newspapers wrote about Bongobondhu's clarion call to the Bengalis on March 7, 1971, speculating what was likely to happen. As soon as he seized control of the provincial government of East Pakistan in a move for autonomy from the central government, the *Globe and Mail* wrote: "What East Pakistanis desire ardently is to be able to govern themselves—complete autonomy, self-rule, home rule, Swaraj, call it what you may like, in association with West Pakistan if possible."[84] Without endorsing the course of action of the Bengali leader, it was pretty emphatic in predicting what was likely to occur: "Once assured that they are masters in their home, East Pakistanis, according to all indications, would be willing to take part in a federal government but with a fragile center devoid of the power of interfering with East Pakistan's affairs."[85]

Before the army crackdown, as and when the issue of separation and independence of Bangladesh was reported in the newspapers, many were exacerbated by the fact that Canada was preoccupied with a similar problem. Immediately following the military crackdown by the Pakistani army personnel and the declaration of independence by the Bengali rebels, the Trudeau administration was awaiting authentic information from the field. It was the media's understanding that Canada neither wished to be a sad spectacle nor endorse a separation movement in a sister Commonwealth country where the issue, it feared, had more tremendous implications for Canada. The media was also fully aware of a profound sense of uncertainty and a high level of discomfort among government officials and the people of Canada on the separation issue. Seeing how the very question of an independent Bangladesh or the dismantling of Pakistan was creating a problem for Canada from the beginning, the media took into cognizance the sensitivity and the Trudeau administration's uneasiness in discussing concepts like separation and secession. The press also recognized how Mitchell Sharp, Secretary of State for External Affairs, and his senior officials in his department had been gravely concerned over the Pakistan situation as a whole—the denial of the rights of the people of Pakistan, the plight of the Bengali refugees in India, and the certainty of the win of the sovereigntist.

As part of its strategy to deal with the Trudeau administration's fear of the Québec question, a circumspect news media prudently used the terms separation or independence while discussing what was happening in Pakistan. It ensured, first and foremost, that Canadian readers recognized the difference between the two scenarios. A doubly careful media referred to the Bengalis' fight for separation in such a manner that it did not ignite a debate in Canada on Canada's Québec question. Taking a strong position on the Pakistan–Bangladesh conflict, the media argued that, with the military takeover and ongoing military reprisals, the separation of East Pakistan, or the independence of Bangladesh, was inevitable. With that in mind, the media carefully raised the moot issue: "How did the demand for greater autonomy take the shape of a struggle for independence?" "East Pakistan and its leader had been moving closer and closer to separation in the past week, but if one retraces the past four weeks, one can hardly apportion all of the blame to the Sheik (h)."[86] The media's key message was that Canada should not forge any link with the Yahya regime, which was neither democratic nor representative of the people of Pakistan. According to the media, the military authority, having denied the results of the 1970 National Elections of a legitimate political party that won the majority votes, was engaged in suppressing the Bengalis. Instead of facilitating the transfer of power, it launched a clandestine and planned attack on civilians in the name of restoring law and order.

The media appreciated Canada's fear in expressing her opinion since Canada could be misconstrued as inclined to endorse a separation movement overseas, or Ottawa may be seen as sympathetic to the cause of the separatists abroad. To explain to Canadians what was considered secession and what was more appropriate to be seen as an independence movement, as the Bengalis called it, Canadian newspapers presented a series of selected articles to bring more clarity to the concept and the present situation of the Bengalis. The main idea behind this was to show

how different it was from the actual situation in Québec. The media carefully presented arguments and counterarguments of the analysts who justified the separation of East Pakistan or the creation of an independent Bangladesh. Through such news coverage, readers recognized the denial of the Bengalis' democratic rights. Canadians quickly came to learn how a planned covert attack by the military regime drove the Bengalis to declare independence. Most Canadian readers also recognized that the Bengalis' fight for freedom had no direct political nexus to the situation in Québec as was erroneously thought of by many.

Consequently, any reference to separation and independence worked as a quick learning curve for readers; many initially did not have an expanded understanding of these concepts related to the subcontinental polity. Having learned about the different historical contexts, many came to see the activities of the FLQ from a different angle. Accordingly, Canadians understood the fact that the FLQ supporters were engaged in promoting the violent overthrow of the Canadian democratic system and that the FLQ had been responsible for bombing over two hundred buildings, hitting such targets as McGill University, the Montreal Stock Exchange, and the house of the then-Montreal mayor, Jean Drapeau. For that matter, a group of self-styled revolutionaries of the 1970 October Crisis led to a movement of grave concern when violent and fanatical Québecers were attempting to destroy the unity and the freedom of Canada. Canadian readers were made to understand that this was certainly not the case with the Bengali rebels who were fighting for democracy in a military-ruled Pakistan. Though unprepared to engage in any discourse for fear of the unknown, Canadians soon became comfortable speaking their minds, having understood these concepts and their appropriate contexts. Canadians learned about the exact historical context between Bangladesh and Québec - the actual difference regarding the independence movement of Bangladesh and the demands of the Québec separatists. The media successfully educated Canadians by debunking the mythical fear surrounding the political situation in Québec and its nexus to the East Pakistan crisis.

Letters to the Editor Column

The Letters to the Editor columns were used for public discourse on intrinsically valuable local and world issues. This column was used as a journalistic tool to complement editorials and news items on the Bengalis' demand for greater autonomy at a time when some ultranationalists were firm in their demand for an independent Bangladesh. Having provided an exciting juxtaposition of views from both pro-Pakistani and pro-Bangladeshi Canadians, as well as the opinions of many others who did not necessarily endorse any side but condemned the Pakistani army's actions, there appeared divergent viewpoints reflecting how the public interpreted the conflict. By summer, the Letters to the Editor columns of many dailies became almost a centerpiece of the newspapers by creating a heated debate, especially on nonintervention and humanitarian assistance. In expressing their views on nationalism, ultranationalism, separation, independence, conspiracy, treason, national integrity, genocide, economic aid vs. sanctions, military repression, and democratization in Pakistan, the letter writers marshaled their arguments and counterarguments as to what role should or could the government of Canada play to find a political solution.

This column pandered to the diversity of views, using this as a forum to express each other's opinions, often opposed to the hilt. Canadians frequently expressed their views as if they were talking directly about overcoming the country's geographic boundaries. Those who opposed the sanction tried to drive home the point that a continuation of aid would be seen as Canada's support for the military regime. They claimed that the government was engaged in a civil war against its people. Continuation of assistance to the Yahya regime, they argued, would mean that Canada would be aligning with a military dictatorship pursuing policies opposed to which Canada claimed to remain committed. We shall see more in Chapter 4 about the Pakistan–Bangladesh conflict, which demonstrated the division of the two particular segments of the Canadian public consisting of Pakistani background. Being remarkably well-informed, they exchanged letters as though they were having a face-to-face conversation.

The political news from the Indian subcontinent for the Indo–Pakistani segment of the Canadian citizenry was essentially more centralized in their information-seeking behaviors, evident through their engagement in the public discourse of great magnitude. This may be referred to as what S. J. Ball-Rokeach and L. DeFleur call the dependency model of mass media effects. Media dependency is a notion that occurs because societal members need to maximize their effectiveness in goal attainment.[87] The tenor of the debate, due to the very nature of the associated issues and sub-issues, such as liberation, democratic rights, genocide, and others, generated a body of redefined knowledge that became important information that the Canadians needed to possess to form their individual opinions.

As was the case, such people are often torn between their country of origin and the country of adoption. The manifestation of vital attributes is common mainly among first-generation immigrant Canadians who embrace multiple identities, no matter what country they call home. Their timely input became a primary source of information for Canadians at large. In other words, Anthony J. Eksterowicz and Robert N. Robert referred to placing citizen input as the center of journalistic concern.[88]

One particularly discernible characteristic of these letters was the use of simple, straightforward language with no gobbledygook to allow both pro-Pakistani and pro-Bangladeshi groups to put forward their arguments from their perspectives to engage readers. One group argued in favor of the Yahya regime's stubborn denial of its ongoing repression and insisted that it was business as usual. The military government was bending the truth at a time when there was concrete evidence to the contrary. At the same time, the other group wrote about how the freedom fighters were making strides in their fight for the liberation of their homeland. Both parties were allowed to argue freely.

As a result, the Letters to the Editor columns provided a platform for a continued debate about who was right and who was wrong from their perspectives, allowing others to join the discussion. One can easily recognize the importance and popularity of this column in the dailies when one considers the fact that this had happened years before the use of the present-day Weblogs or blogs, Twitter, Instagram, and/or any other social media networks that have now opened up the discourse with the audience. It was like real-time citizen journalism at a time when there were no online social networks to e-mail stories and post comments. The Letters to the Editor column became a delivery platform for sharing ideas in 1971.

Editorial Disquisitions

The Canadian dailies adhered to the catchphrase, "give the readers what they want," as their policy, which stated that the public has a right to know. Historically speaking, Canadian journalism spawned a host of aphorisms, many of which derive from this well-grounded and right-sounding principle. Canadians viewed the newspaper as a comprehensive presentation of all the national and international events in the past twenty-four hours, just like today. Nevertheless, it would be remiss to say that resolutely populist sensational journalism did not exist then. Since there was a sizable reading public who demanded regular news updates concerning the tragic events in Pakistan, the media responded to the demands accordingly, though with caution. Once the sad story of the military repression of unarmed Bengali civilians moved on to the hands of the editors, those in charge recognized that the enlightened citizenry expected an analysis of the events going beyond existing beliefs, reconciling opposing viewpoints and assembling all new information *vis-à-vis* Canada's position of wait and see.

Initially, as a practice, the newspapers published only what was deemed newsworthy without demanding Ottawa's intervention except for humanitarian assistance. In the absence of a specific power-sharing plan for the democratization of Pakistan by the Yahya government, the news media became even more alert, recognizing the potential for further deterioration of the situation. This was the same position maintained by the Trudeau administration. The media, however, started to question its initial acceptance of the regime's argument that the transfer of power was an internal affair of Pakistan. After a while, many editorialists debated whether the destruction of human life and property in East Pakistan and the exodus of the refugees had remained an internal matter as claimed by the military regime.

The media argued that it was a case of a denial of fundamental rights under the UN Declaration of Human Rights. The press claimed that the continuing exodus could no longer be seen as an isolated foreign event in Pakistan but as an issue of great magnitude to the world's conscience. Editorialists saw in the unfolding of the tragedy a task requiring compassion to alleviate the sufferings of the victims of repression in both East Pakistan and India, where the refugees had been streaming in to escape military reprisals. Adherence to the government's official foreign policy line and its nonintervention policy meant that the Trudeau administration had no scope to intervene. The media recognized that the government could not even condemn military action but found it problematic.

To keep readers on the same wavelength, the media attempted to put the Bengalis' demand and the war of liberation strictly within the same historical context, showing how the ongoing military reprisals and the suppression of their demands drove them to seek independence. Given Canada's serious concerns about the Québec question and the Trudeau administration's strong reluctance to be seen to have anything to do with the separation or independence movement in the subcontinent, Canadian editors remained doubly cautious about this fact. The media, having recognized Canada's conflicted situation, remained sensitive to the particularly delicate position of the Trudeau administration. Many Canadians became convinced that the Bengalis would never accept Yahya's offer, no matter how it was worded, especially in the face of rising nationalism and ethnic fragmentation. With the rapid deterioration of the situation, clearly for the worse, the media, however, became convinced that Ottawa should neither procrastinate nor the people of Canada should be left in the dark about Canada's actual position.

The news editors, generally called gatekeepers, played an essential role in deciding what was newsworthy regarding the Pakistan–Bangladesh conflict and what aspects of the issue were to be presented to the public. In their choice of material in the context of the Pakistan–Bangladesh conflict, editors gave much thought to deciding what item would be used and what would be deleted. It was not surprising to see how the news media attempted to highlight the national identity of the Bengalis to allow the general readers to place the Bengalis' position within the context of the Pakistan–Bangladesh conflict that arose as a result of military intervention to a political problem. The effectiveness of the visceral and emotional impact of the news from the subcontinent may be judged because editorial disquisitions were frequently written to keep readers informed, educated, and engaged.

The media noted carefully how the Yahya regime was claiming that the Bengalis who were streaming into Indian territory were pro-Indian and labeled as voluntary cross-border migrants. Yahya expected the rest of the world to believe him—that he was dealing with the pro-Indian Bengali dissidents and ultranationalist mutineers. To the news media, the military regime's argument was ludicrous. To disprove this, the press showed how, due to repression, the horrified Bengalis were running away from the scene of the crime like a bunch of frightened rabbits. The military regime was beleaguering the entire population, argued the newspapers. The situation was deteriorating, with no sign of a political settlement with the interned leader of the majority party. Again, when an outbreak of cholera among the Bengali refugees in the West Bengal region threatened to take a significant toll, Canadian newspapers editorialized their concerns, expressing how the international contributions for the Bengali refugees had come only in dribs and drabs at a time when much more was needed. The inclusion of opinions, statements of choice, and the persuasion of readers to a specific course of action are some noticeable techniques in editorial writing.

Fortunately, with Canada's conflicted position, the media became doubly circumspect in guarding the press–government relationship that was not to be adversarial. At the same time, the press also believed that the Pakistan–Bangladesh conflict could not be put aside just because events were taking place overseas. Having provided both sides of the controversy in the various newspapers' pages under various columns, editorial disquisitions dealt with the pros and cons of the political and economic issues as Canadians saw them. Using powerful editorials, it was maintained that the problems were extraordinary, with a potential threat to world peace that demanded Canada's positive intervention to the extent the government's foreign policy options had allowed. Given Canada's international reputation and exceptional track record, Canada should play a critical mediatory role in resolving the Pakistan–Bangladesh conflict, argued the media. While conforming to Canada's policy of nonintervention, Canada could still exert its influence through the Commonwealth as its senior member, the press argued further. How could Canada intervene? Many editorialists repeatedly asked for this, and they maintained that Canada should continue her efforts through the UN.

With time, the media noticed severe public resentment in the minds of many simply because Canada had no *declaratory position* on the conflict. Many cynical public members were inclined to believe that, if Canada had a position, it was probably having tacit support for the Yahya administration interested in keeping the country undivided, having ignored the democratic process that had started a year ago. Canada's physical proximity to the U.S.A., in addition to being an ally of the Nixon administration, led many to believe that Canada was not outside the ambit of the foreign policy of the US superpower. A doubly careful media, appreciative of Canada's conflictual situation, intervened positively by honestly portraying the actual happenings. Without antagonizing the government, the media tried to convince both the Trudeau administration and the Canadian public to take an unequivocal stand against the Pakistani military dictator.

In doing that, the media followed the general rule of thumb, or the generally held adherence to journalistic ethics, by superbly addressing the issue within the constraints of space and time in the pre-Internet era. In its way, the media urged the government to react to the events. New and more analytical write-ups appeared frequently with the belief that if the political applecart were to be upset by investigatory journalism, so be it. Much to its credit, the media successfully ensured that the press-government relationship remained nonadversarial and complementary. Without placing the government in an awkward situation, the editorial writers successfully put forward their *raison d'être* to the educated Canadian citizenry, who, in turn, continued to pressure the government.

Emotional Appeal for Food and Medical Assistance for Cholera Epidemic

All major newspapers kept their readers informed about the fear of fast-deteriorating situations regarding food supply and the cholera epidemic both in the refugee camps in India and inside East Pakistan. Seeing that the Yahya regime was downplaying the plight of the refugees and the possibility of food shortage, the media challenged Pakistan's nondisclosure of facts. Readers were encouraged to consider what they could do under the circumstances to alleviate the conditions of the refugees in Indian refugee camps and displaced persons in Occupied Bangladesh. The ongoing news regarding the food shortage included a warning that there was a pressing need for vaccines, saline solutions, and mass-inoculation machines. For every dollar withheld by a particular government, there would be a delay on the part of a government's response, for which human lives would be lost, argued the media. The most urgent need, it urged again, was life-saving baby food, powdered milk, antibiotics, vaccines, and similar supplies, for which there was even greater demand from the refugee population. Canadian dailies soon began to alert their readers/viewers about the possibility of famine.

Internationally, two doctors, Jon Rhode and Lincoln Chen, then Harvard Medical School representatives, were the first to raise the issue of the cholera epidemic in the subcontinent while simultaneously talking about the imminent famine. This was a time when Canadians, in general, hardly knew about cholera, an acute diarrheal illness that could sometimes be severe and life-threatening. Many Canadians did not realize the potential cholera that could decimate the populace. To make Canadians understand the cholera epidemic, it was compared with concepts of objects with which readers in Canada were familiar in their environment. Under the title pathetic squatters' settlements without sanitation in swarming refugee camps hold seeds of disaster, the *Montreal Star* cited Brigadier Michael

Blackman, OXFAM UK's disaster operations officer. Blackman broached the danger of the cholera epidemic spreading across Kolkata, the nerve center of the relief operation in India's eastern states of West Bengal, Meghalaya, and Tripura.[89]

Canadian major dailies immediately referred to the tireless work of Brother Cournoyer, OXFAM Canada's field director stationed in Kolkata, West Bengal. Evidently, following the same vein, Brother Cournoyer also emphasized the same two dangers: famine and the incidence of cholera among the refugees. Having lived in India and Pakistan since the mid-1950s, Cournoyer was familiar with the cholera epidemic. "We know what cholera is... "C'est un feu de forêt (it's a forest fire, author's translation)...I think if cholera gets to Calcutta, (sic) God help us. It could be like the Great Plague of London."[90] Readers, who became more aware of the pathetic situation, were touched by Cournoyer's remarks about the cholera epidemic and the food shortage. The simultaneous appeals of Drs reinforced his appeal. Jon Rhode and Lincoln Chen insisted on focusing on immediate intervention to avoid one of the most severe famines in history. "The opportunity to prevent a major famine is rapidly slipping away. Responsible members of the world community concerned with human welfare must insist that strong action be taken now"[91] was their joint appeal.

At about the same time, CUSO volunteer Nany Gerein's short write-up in one of CUSO's flyers for dissemination made Canadians realize the miserable conditions of the refugees in India. "To have 800 people using a few small fields as their bathrooms and two wells for their drinking water is a certain road to an epidemic. We did have a small cholera epidemic in our camp, but in the large government camps all around us, which at one stage had a few workers and no medical care, the cholera quickly killed many people— 100 per day in a camp of 200,000."[92] Again, fearing the specter of famine, Professor Joseph O'Connell of St. Michael's College, who was very concerned, wrote directly to Pakistan's high commissioner, expressing his misgivings regarding the deteriorating situation. "It will be a greater tragedy still if by inadequate efforts at relief and rehabilitation, for whatever reasons, epidemic and famine are allowed to decimate the populace of East Pakistan in the months ahead and in the process to undermine the credibility of your government as the just and rightful sovereign of East Pakistan. I respectfully await your reply."[93]

Tied to the food shortage was the unavailability of transportation and distribution of food stocks and medical supplies, which were at a standstill, including the areas ravaged by the previous year's natural disaster. "Help is on the way from many governments and charities, but there are fears that it may be too little and too late,"[94] wrote a reporter who had just returned from India, having no illusion about the urgency. Again, following the publication of the Agency for International Development report, the Canadian print media carried excerpts of it to warn its readers that the outlook for the future of East Pakistan was bleak. Such fear was expressed for quite some time, reinforcing its points that there would be "an even bleaker situation over the next year with the vital rice crop expected to fall 19 percent below past estimates."[95] The media underscored its fear that the threat of starvation would drive many more to India unless immediate and long-range actions are taken urgently. Anticipating further deterioration, many dailies reprinted excerpts of news of this nature.

Having followed the same vein, James Pankratz, a Canadian researcher who was living in India, also emphasized the needs of the refugees who constituted the grim odyssey of millions and made a simple appeal to come forward to assist the refugees who were facing cholera and endemic plagues in any possible way they could. "Whether the East Bengalis are secessionist or freedom fighters is a matter which may be debated comfortably from miles away. But that debate is useless to the homeless and hungry refugees,"[96] was Pankratz's appeal. In another write-up, he observed: "We are to be ministers of reconciliation amid perpetual warfare. We are to be missionaries of hope where the situation appears hopeless."[97] Again, the *Fredericton Gleaner* alerted its readers by saying: "While the Indian government is doing an excellent job of feeding the refugees, food supplies are diminishing."[98]

The news regarding food shortage and the cholera epidemic received worldwide attention for the prediction that about three million tons of food grants would be needed to prevent the imminent famine directly affecting about twenty-five million people who are likely to face starvation. All through summer and fall, short but powerful write-ups appeared depicting how the hapless Bengalis had been displaced and uprooted, crops neglected, roads, railways, and communications cut off, and houses, shops, and villages looted and burned. Canadians picked up the key message: Although food production had fallen in successive years, the military government remained indifferent to such predictions. Such a warning was an eye-opener for Canadians since it sharply contrasted with what they had heard from the Yahya regime; neither acknowledged that a crisis was imminent nor did it do anything about it. Canadian readers learned about how the army crackdown had prevented rice planting. As the situation reminded readers of the intensely tragic and bloody war and the refugees who were facing the specter of widespread disease in the overcrowded refugee camps, Canadians remained disturbed for days. They were haunted by seeing in the dailies the depiction of the pitiable conditions of the victims of military repression. The media coverage touched readers' minds with intense emotion, the kind shared by all human beings regardless of geographical boundaries.

Role of a Watchdog

To the news media, the exodus of tens of thousands of Bengalis was not the end of the story. The media engaged the more comprehensive readers who consider themselves patrons of the oppressed and were always proud of Canada's egalitarian and democratic tradition. Although initially, the media was content with the Trudeau administration's work with other nations and international institutions to strengthen the collective capacity to prevent outbreaks of mass killings, later, it became convinced that the government was not sufficiently transparent. Several Canadian dailies wrote in unison and reported using long, illustrated coverings focusing on exhaustive descriptions and analyzing the news. At the same time, the media also appealed to the public to continue their demand for the government's intervention to the extent its foreign policy option permitted.

The news correspondents, news commentators, and reporters from the ground soon began to suspect the regime's secret agenda: total suppression (not merely the sullen submission) of the Bengalis' demand for greater autonomy. The media did not take long to recognize Yahya's duplicity—that his claim to establish a law-and-order situation in East Pakistan was, in fact, a cleansing operation, which was a euphemism for the massacre. The heedful reporters figured out the regime's frequent use of the two terms: miscreants and infiltrators. To the media, in a sense, this was a part of the charade enacted for the world community to misrepresent the truth.

The media wanted Canada to recognize how the West Pakistani army went far beyond what was needed to restore their control over what they called the militant Awami League. Since the news media had been closely monitoring the government's actions, reactions, and inactions, the press was ahead of the government in interpreting the events. It did not wish Canada to be on the verge of another Biafra, which was a case of a combination of rationalized inaction and moral insensitivity of the government that cost millions of lives. Using persuasive language, the media urged Ottawa to declare Canada's official position on the Pakistan-Bangladesh conflict without dragging her feet.

In particular, to wake up the people of Canada to the terrible happenings in East Pakistan to make them face their moral responsibility to do something about the refugees, the media urged: "The indifference of governments and people - including us in Canada—or the slowness of their token gestures in money and words, are hard to understand. It's beyond comprehension, standing in the rain in one of the human garbage dumps that dot the lush land around Calcutta (sic),"[99] Canadian writer/reporter Ernest Hillen wrote. Again, having known about Canada's inability to intervene politically or directly as a watchdog, he regretted that "no real effective political or economic activity had been taken to stop the Pakistan army's organized killing of which the millions of fearful runaways are living proof."[100] He also emphasized the need for more humanitarian assistance and the significant role Canada and the rest of the world should play. A concerned Hillen, having pointed fingers at the indifference and apathy of the world communities, observed: "The world communities' response to the disaster - for which there is no precedent - continues to be minimal."[101]

Like the rest of the newspapers of the world, Canadian newspapers also talked about the brutal military repression, reprisals, and mass killings of the Bengalis, having characterized the Pakistani army operation as a pogrom. As a watchdog, the media also provided meaningful legal contexts, being steadfast in its conviction that the secret military crackdown on unarmed Bengali civilians was of genocidal proportion. This was particularly so when the media saw how the gruesome horrors were being ceaselessly perpetrated by the Pakistani army personnel, who seemed almost depraved in their bloodlust. Canadian journalists also watched with dismay how the Bengali people, despite the military force's brutality, doggedly withstood the danger all around them. By and large, reporters risked their own lives to witness the events, the intensity, and the severity of the traumatic stressors they encountered in covering horrific events.

The news stories emanating from the field were woven with journalistic professionalism and presented straightforwardly, enhancing the news's quality and credibility. The media seized the first opportunity to remind its readers that Canadians were appreciative of the complex position of the government and that it was dealing with a thorny issue that, by all definitions, was political. The media also pointed out that Canadians were concerned "because there has not so far been any exterior political choosing of sides, public opinion is running to apathy."[102] The Yahya regime's game plan persuaded the public to regard its proposed measures as both preposterous and devoid of political reality compared to the tangible strides of the Bengali rebel forces in their fight for the independence of Bangladesh. With the news of every event, Canadians were going through growing pains in disgust. The media noted how Canadians had continued their demand that the government should come forward to condemn the Yahya regime.

Seeing the public reaction and the government's inaction, the media disappointed the Trudeau administration for sitting on the fence for too long. Naturally, the press became convinced that the government was moving at a snail's pace. Though sensitive to the government's position, the media did not hesitate to speak openly against Sharp's dilly-dallying on an international issue of grave magnitude unacceptable to the outraged Canadian public. However, it is also true that the news media was not necessarily aware of the behind-the-scenes activities, such as the discrete counseling of President Yahya Khan and Prime Minister Indira Gandhi by Prime Minister Trudeau himself from the beginning of the military aggression. The media expected Sharp to give at least a curt response regarding Canada's public position on the conflict. Unsurprisingly, the media pointed fingers at Sharp and his foreign policy cognoscenti to do something - the sooner, the better.

The media also watched the actions and reactions of Canadian NGOs in the field and noted their concerns regarding the rapidly deteriorating situation in the refugee camps. At the same time, it kept an eye on the supposedly apolitical NGOs to see if they were overstepping their charitable role by getting involved politically. Heartrending news items depicting the stark tragedy made readers respond positively not only to the needs of the refugees but also to the need for continuing dialogue between the parties involved in the conflict where, according to the media, Canada could potentially play a lead role.

Again, the media also raised the issue of immigration - an area in which it believed Canada could do something positively and promptly. Insisting that the government should expand immigration for the Bengalis, the media argued that immigration would make both economic and business sense for

Canada. It used a simple logic in favor of bringing the Bengali victims of repression based on Canada's immigration history: "If we do, someday the prairies may blossom with Bengali industry as they do today with the work of those who once were foreigners themselves."[103] The media argued that Canada could genuinely benefit by bringing in people from disaster areas in certain parts of Canada, where they would contribute if settlement were facilitated professionally by the government. OXFAM Canada's frequent on-the-air radio announcements regarding welcoming immigrants from East Pakistan, as we shall read in Chapter 5, is evidence of Canada's compassion for the suffering Bengalis and the news media's critical role.

In addition, the news media also modified its strategy appropriately to reinforce the need for the government's immediate and direct intervention when it was convinced that the Trudeau administration was not doing enough. Despite every intention to stay above the fray, now and then, the media became embroiled while performing its watchdog role. As was the case, through many television interviews of the refugees and other victims of military actions, Canadians heard about the "reign of terror" in East Pakistan. No one failed to notice the art of maneuvering and drilling by the news reporters. Actions and interactions of politicians, military administrators, and journalists show how one tried to discredit the other. More specifically, it shows how they played gotcha when Yahya, undaunted by public disdain, was still trying to create the grand illusion of political news. The media believed that having been guided by the idiom, "all's fair in love and war," the Yahya regime never felt accountable to anyone. Accordingly, the regime did not bother to provide any information on its roadmap. Canada should put more pressure on other countries to do more work internationally so that both the government and media could work toward the same goal, argued the media.

Impressively enough, although it worked as a watchdog, the media never placed itself in a hostile position vis-à-vis the Trudeau administration. The media's work with the government may be an example of non-adversary journalism even though the press, on sundry occasions, took a critical stance about the Trudeau administration's procrastination in taking a declaratory position. Without ever embarrassing the government, the media ensured that both remained respectful of each other and that no antagonism or adversarial relationship persisted through its appeals to the government. The news reporters remained cautious and exemplary in their close contact with government officials to save it from any discomfort for its dilatory response. Following such a technique, the media successfully addressed the public's demand to the extent possible. The press and politicians interacted together to work out the differences and examine the subtleties embodied in the issue, something they did quite successfully.

News on the Transfer of Allegiance (Defection) of Bengali Envoys and Progress Toward Liberation

Initially, due to the delicate position of the Trudeau administration, the news of the formation of the provisional government of Bangladesh in April 1971 in India was carefully reported without endorsing it in one way or another. Nevertheless, once the news media became convinced of the Yahya administration's secret game plan and hidden agenda, meaning it was not coming clean as to how it would transfer power to the elected leader of the majority party who was thrown in jail, it changed its reporting strategy.

The media soon began to simultaneously highlight the progress of the rebel forces and the activities of the provisional government of Bangladesh. It carefully followed the phenomenon of political defection by the Bengali foreign service personnel and the purging of Bengali officers from Pakistan's armed forces and foreign service. The media took it upon itself to highlight every defection (or, to use a more appropriate term, transfer of allegiance to the (provisional government of Bangladesh) by Bengali envoys from the government of Pakistan in the Bengalis' quest for independence. This was done to show readers the reality of the soon-to-be-born Bangladesh in the political landscape of the subcontinent. Whenever the news of defection by a Bengali diplomat appeared in the world news, Canadian media immediately used the same information as a piece of hot news item to keep its readers *au courant* about the strides the rebel forces had been making toward the independence of Bangladesh and simultaneous transfer of allegiance of the Bengali diplomats to the provisional government of Bangladesh.

It started with Hossain Ali, a Bengali-speaking East Pakistani deputy high commissioner of Pakistan, who was then stationed in India. Like most world newspapers, Canadian dailies covered the news of Ali's declaration of his allegiance to the breakaway republic of Bangladesh pictorially and comprehensively, having drawn tremendous public attention. Understandably, the coverage was done this way since Ali was the first diplomat to transfer allegiance to the provisional government of Bangladesh as early as April 1971. The news coverage described how the military government's request to India to evict the rebels from India was rejected by the Gandhi administration and the closure of the deputy high commissioner's office in Kolkata, West Bengal, India, by April 26, 1971. Detailed descriptions of the Bengali Pakistani envoy who hosted the green-red-and-gold flag of Bangla Desh above his three-floor missions in Kolkata, West Bengal, on April 19, 1971, and kept the issues alive. It reinforced the rebel forces' conviction that Bangladesh's reality was not far off. Also, news of such nature captured the attention of readers worldwide. This sensational story of the Bengali dissidents who took over the diplomatic mission in Kolkata later paved the way for many others to follow suit.

Throughout the year, the media regularly reported the incidence of defection by the Bengali foreign service officials, using careful terminologies and tangible examples, allowing readers to see how the provisional government of Bangladesh was gaining recognition. Readers in Canada learned how the Bengali-speaking career diplomats were being asked to take orders from their respective military attachés, most of whom were flown in from West Pakistan. The media argued that this was a part of the military regime's game plan. Readers quickly learned how the military authority was trying to strengthen its position in diplomatic missions by marginalizing the Bengali diplomats who were suspects of the regime. Soon, a brief memo filtered down from the top military brass with strict instructions for the Bengali diplomatic corps that they had been put under strict surveillance since the imposition of martial law on March 25 and that many Bengali officers were under orders of immediate transfer to Islamabad. The Bengali officers in various missions found themselves in a strained relationship with their non-Bengali colleagues as they were no longer trusting.

The news of defection in early August by Abul Mall Muhith, then diplomatic/economic adviser to the Pakistan embassy in Washington, D.C., and a former deputy secretary to the Pakistan Cabinet, received comprehensive coverage in Canadian media just like the first. Most of the major Canadian dailies quoted Muhith's underscoring of the message he had for the world community that Bangladesh was on its way to be born soon, something that made Pakistan look helpless, having lost all claim to legitimacy.[104] Again, when, within days, Muhit attended a conference in Toronto on the Bangladesh Crisis titled the Toronto Declaration of Concern held on August 19 - 21, 19171, many Canadian NGO officials and pro-Bangladeshi Canadians, who had been lobbying the Trudeau administration for support, embraced Muhith for his firmly held position on the sovereignty of Bangladesh as an independent country.

Similarly, when André Malraux, France's former cultural minister under General Charles de Gaulle, announced that, if called, he would fight for Bangladesh or that, if he could not fight due to his age, he would fight in a tank, Canadian news media grabbed the caption and highlighted it. The original news published in *The Statesman of Calcutta* was reprinted in several Canadian dailies focusing on the passion and wishes of Malraux - how the sixty-nine-year-old supported the Bengalis' fight for independence. The newspapers alluded to Malraux's heroic part in the French resistance during the Second World War and his active role in the Chinese Civil War in the 1920s, which earned him international fame. Commending Malraux for his expressed desire at old age, a Toronto-based magazine wrote, "It is truly one of the last noble causes."[105] The paper quoted Malraux, who reinforced his belief that there was a need to stand up to fight for one's freedom: "Since Vietnam, you cannot defend a cause without actual combat."[106] A brief caveat of Malraux endorsing the liberation of Bangladesh and the Bengalis' fight against Yahya's military regime appealed to readers' emotions.

It looked incongruous to many when contrasted with the news emanating from Pakistani sources that continued to claim that the conditions in East Pakistan were normal. Ironically enough, never for a minute did the military regime think that it was fighting a losing battle. Essentially, the description of the transfer of allegiance dispelled the military-asserted myth that everything was fine and hunky-dory as though it was business as usual in East Pakistan except for only a few saboteurs and anti-state elements who were working as Indian agents.

The Yahya regime's authoritarian actions, which provoked a profound reaction in the minds of the public, appeared as fodder for those who were outraged at its reign of terror. Its credibility was so low that it was openly challenged by journalists worldwide. Many Canadian dailies published news items that illustrated the apparent antithesis between what was happening and what was being said about the situation in Pakistan. The defected Bengali diplomats and their associates at foreign capitals worldwide were commended as leading protagonists, protectors, and promoters in their fight to liberate their native land. The public had complete trust in the news correspondents who they believed could conduct astute analysis of the politico-military situation in Pakistan. The media described the progress toward an independent Bangladesh by explicitly mentioning the names and positions of the diplomats, whether they were high commissioners, ambassadors, or individuals in charge of affairs. Hearing the voices of the defectors on the radio or watching on television of the diplomats who had just transferred their allegiance impacted the minds of readers and viewers.

Through a reality check, the news media had already predicted the future of Pakistan as a divided nation. Canadian readers and viewers did not fail to notice how rapidly the movement gained momentum, moving toward success within a much shorter time than the original estimated timeframe. The print media's strategy worked very well as the sensational news items evoked an immediate interest among the Canadian public, who followed the events from a clearer perspective. In a sense, the story of the Bengali diplomats' transfer of allegiance made Canadians think that the Bengalis were getting closer to the reality of Bangladesh. As far as the media was concerned, regardless of Canada's position, it ought to keep readers in Canada in the loop about the latest phenomenon of Bangladesh, a country whose birth was in the offing. The media balanced its reports without harboring an anti-establishment attitude and swinging the pendulum too far in journalistic zeal.

Community Newspapers and News Magazines

A cursory look at some of the well-known community newspapers shows how they, whether in a city or a rural town, provided their community with a localized expression in educational, religious, political, social, and economic life. Back in 1971, the community newspapers and/or neighborhood weeklies played an essential role in the community in their humble ways by bringing the events of the subcontinent to their daily lives through the selective depiction of pictures and write-ups despite having limited financial and human resources. In addition, international magazines, such as *Time Magazine* and *Maclean's*, and national magazines, such as *Canada and the World,* which already had an extensive distribution network in 1971, also played a significant role.

The media recognized that the military regime had dragged its feet to reposition itself to make a clandestine military attack on Bengali East

Pakistanis, pretending that it was busy negotiating with Bongobondhu and Bhutto. Like the mainstream media, the community newspapers argued that the conflict in Pakistan was not a Pakistan–India issue but instead a conflict between Pakistan's military authority and the Awami League leader Bongobondhu, centering around greater autonomy and the democratic right of the people of East Pakistan. "Pakistan, as it has existed for the past quarter-century, has a limited life expectancy."[107] Thus, it was predicted in *Canada and the World* as the media became firmer in its claim for the Bengalis' victory as soon as it noticed the progress of the freedom fighters. Naturally, during the last quarter of 1971, there was not much doubt left about Pakistan's future due to the freedom fighters' visible strides. "The guerrilla fighters of East Pakistan have much support among the local people. It is hard to believe that either the occupying West Pakistani Army or the military regime in Rawalpindi can long control the large and alienated population of East Pakistan."[108]

Again, the Winnipeg-based *Manitoba Brethren Herald,* one of the most widely read community newspapers serving the Mennonite community, published exciting articles several times. With the onslaught of mass killing, just like the Canadian public, the Mennonite community, too, was moved to tears. It was appealed that since Canada had a prestigious position in the world community, she must, without dragging her feet, recognize that it was time for Canada to take a leadership role either through the UN or the Commonwealth. "Surely, our government could also exert political influence to make the West Pakistanis feel the censure of other governments of the world for their brutal treatment of the East Bengalis,"[109] wrote Harold Jantz, the editor. He did not just stop there. Instead, he argued that Canada was well-placed to exercise her influence in assisting the victims of military repression. "Canada ought to do more given the gravity of the matter."[110] The paper reaffirmed the critical message: "Surely our government has an obligation to express some sense of outrage."[111] Canadians remained concerned throughout the crisis and wanted to do something to help the victims of military reprisals and political injustice. "The civil war that threatens to split the Pakistan union is, of course, not a religious war, but just another chapter in the age-old oppression of the poor and the powerless,"[112] the *Manitoba Brethren Herald* observed when Bangladesh had already become independent on December 16, 1971. The paper emphasized that Canada needed to be more proactive.

Again, the *Canada India Times* (CIT), which served the Indo–Canadian community across the country, published accounts of the actions and reactions of the governments of India and Pakistan and the flight and plight of Bengali refugees from Occupied Bangladesh into Indian territory. Like other immigrants, the subcontinental immigrants in Canada also remained interested in the affairs of the country they had left behind. It provided news for Indo–Canadians who needed to know what was happening in their country of origin. The news items covered by CIT interested them, whether the news was from Pakistan, India, or the provisional government of Bangladesh. The paper ran serialized stories about communities and events that were taking place in the Indian subcontinent. Seeing the continuous exodus of the terrified Bengalis, the paper warned its readers about the uncertain destiny of the dismayed Bengalis who were being victimized. Readers were warned that there were times when people felt that the entire East Pakistan was under the grip of a whimsical military regime that was continually victimizing civilians. "It's not really Mujibur Rahman who is on trial; it is the world's conscience that is on trial," wrote the tabloid."[113]

Though a small community newspaper, the *Pembina Triangle Progress* also analyzed Pakistan's political situation from the start of the conflict. Canadian Mennonites were in an advantageous position since Paul Kniss, a U. S. Mennonite, then a member of the Mennonite Central Committee (MCC) posted in India, kept the community up-to-date. Soon, Kniss became a contributor to many local newspapers in the Mennonite community. When Canadians were trying to look for the root cause of the conflict, Kniss was quick to inform them about his take on the tragedy. He did not hesitate to point fingers at the military rulers whose only desire, he believed, was to perpetuate their authority. "Their (that is, the Bengalis) only crime was voting for a man to whom the military rulers of Pakistan didn't want to turn over authority,"[114] wrote Kniss. He clearly stated that Bongobondhu, leader of the majority party in Pakistan, was not the Pakistani military ruler's choice, even though Bongobondhu was the prime minister-designate. Kniss's write-ups, first published in local newspapers and community news magazines in Canada and India, were also published in local newspapers and church bulletins in the USA down to the south of Canada's border during the liberation war.

Also, the *Canadian Mennonite Reporter* was vigilant, keeping its readers *au courant* by showing the firm determination of the Bengali freedom fighters. Though apolitical, the Mennonite community's position during the crisis period was that they, like all other observers, were convinced that, given the situation, the Bengalis were resolved to drive out the occupation army. They could neither be stifled nor could the spirit of the freedom fighters be extinguished. As pacifists, deep down, they also believed that journalists, through their cameras and reportage, should be able to depict the actual truth. "We continue to trust and pray that the leaders of nations will be able to reach an agreement that these suffering millions may again live in relative harmony," observed Vernon Reimer, MCC's director for Asia, stationed in Kolkata, West Bengal.[115] Information, such as military reprisals and guerrilla attacks by the *Mukti Bahini* forces, were gathered from various sources and cited under managerial editors' watchful eyes. The tragic story of death in utter degradation of the hapless Bengalis heightened readers' awareness of what had been happening to those who were leaving their homes to find a haven in India. Readers also learned that many of the frightened asylum seekers could not even arrive at the refugee camps as they perished on their way. Their stories were far too familiar that they could be repeated a thousand times.

All community newspapers served as a forum for discussing political issues and challenges in which Canadians of subcontinental backgrounds had an abiding interest. Briefly, the community newspapers thus worked on two fronts in pushing the envelope for the cause of the Bengalis: to depict the pathetic situation of the refugees and the strides of the freedom fighters while the military reprisals and the guerrilla war with India's covert assistance were continuing. Readers quickly noticed how the news of the success of the rebel forces' fight found places in their favorite newspapers with more extraordinary rapidity.

Using factual information, the community newspapers included write-ups that enhanced their stories for readers expected to run with them in an informed way. Their narratives, such as the plight of the refugees, the ongoing exodus from Occupied Bangladesh, and the progress of the freedom fighters, were described in detail by journalists, reporters, researchers, writers, and editors to keep their readers up-to-date.

Photojournalism

Photography, generally speaking, falls within the popular and is excluded from the realm of the serious press as it is rarely admitted as an element of journalism. Nevertheless, in covering the news from overseas, the print media showed exquisite use of photos relating to military repression and its fallout. Although the technology of 1971 was not yet developed like today, the most noticeable feature of the dailies was the increased picture content, which enhanced immediate visual appeal to readers. News items with pictures, whether on the front page or inside page, had always been an additional attraction for readers.

In describing the exodus of the frightened Bengali civilians and the predicaments of the refugees forced out of their homeland, news stories were woven with journalistic professionalism. The facial expressions of the refugees in an incomprehensively chaotic world allowed the reporters to actualize the reality and trauma of the situation the refugees were placed in during the time military repressions were carried on. Though far away from the field, Canadian readers were struck by the sordid tragedy. The timely interviews of those involved in the crisis were also judiciously used with befitting headlines and epigrammatic subtitles to make the case. Often, selection board members faced a grisly dilemma: whether to publish a ghastly photograph or not. Most reports contained relevant photos with due attention to factual correctness, balanced judgment, clarity, contextuality, and authentic reference to the news sources.

Naturally, all carefully arranged photographs and titles heightened the issues at hand - how, because of the ongoing military repression, the frightened Bengalis were fleeing to India to avoid persecution, leaving behind those who could not walk for being too old or frail. Having remained in severe jeopardy, the rest of the family members risked their lives as they could not go away like others. Readers could see for themselves how close-ups and juxtaposed photos conveyed the intense sufferings of the Bengalis, either as refugees in Indian camps or as objects of the regime's prey in Occupied Bangladesh. It was as though these extraordinary photos were emphasizing that, unless a well-thought-out relief program was quickly launched, countless poor civilians might die in the coming months.

Whether it is the *Globe and Mail*, the *Toronto Star*, *The Ottawa Citizen*, or, for that matter, any other Canadian newspaper, readers were touched by their depiction and use of accompanying photos with attractive captions. All associated images were incorporated to highlight the event's importance, which readers found especially useful. In that sense, the media's emphasis on photo selection, placement, and display went down in the audiences' consciousness as salient. They enhanced the credibility of the newspapers and their acceptability by readers in Canada.

Radio and Television News and Talk Shows (April 1971–December 1971)

Radio

In 1971, Canada was served by Canadian Broadcasting Corporation (CBC) radio stations across the country on both AM and FM bands. Due to the proliferation of radio stations, the emergence of networks, and the increasing affordability of mass-produced radio receiving sets, radio had already entered the vast majority of Canadian households by 1971. In fact, with many radio stations, radio's expanding reach was a remarkable phenomenon even in the 1960s. The radio stations across Canada thus played an important role by bringing the news from the ground to Canadian listeners right from the time of the political impasse in Pakistan in March 1971. Though CBC did not have any reporters stationed in Dhaka during the beginning of the political deadlock in 1971, it sent a team of three-man crew to convene the National Assembly, which had been postponed since early March. As mentioned, the reporters were Joe Schlesinger, Raymond Grenier, and Bob Whyte from CBC's Hong Kong-based office to Dhaka to cover the Yahya-Bongobondhu-Bhutto parley in mid-March. Since then, CBC has followed with interest and curiosity the ups and downs of Pakistan's political and constitutional deadlock and the demands of Bhutto and Bongobondhu.

The two most powerful aspects of the radio programs were the news, whether morning, afternoon, or evening, and the radio talk shows, usually with those involved in some capacity, either as eyewitnesses or workers in the field. Canadians became involved in various capacities in talk shows and phone-in programs. True, newsgathering under the unusual circumstances in Pakistan and India was a tedious, drawn-out process of probing, questioning, and digging. Nevertheless, having used simple and plain language and vocabulary, talk show hosts brought to life the authentic voices of ordinary Canadians from coast to coast to coast, its ubiquity, and its immediacy about the agonies of the suffering refugees in India and displaced persons in Occupied Bangladesh. Frequent radio talk shows with eyewitnesses or field workers from Pakistan and India generated great enthusiasm among the public. The radio phone-in, one of Canada's most time-honored traditional programs for as long as radio usage in Canada, became so popular that it caused waves in the public's minds.

Like the newspapers, Canadian radio also raised the immigration issue and appealed to the government for consideration. Specifically, while parliamentarians were debating the renewal of visas, extended work permits, political asylum, sponsorship, and immigration of East Pakistanis, radio stations reminded their listeners: "Canada needs a population. The Pakistani refugees need a home. Canada should give them that home."[116] Several radio stations referred to what the media called the tragedy of the century. Some other typical appeals on the air were: "Instead of sending aid, let's bring the victims to fill our empty land."[117] The media believed Canada could accommodate newcomers in large numbers: "We should settle not a token hundred but a significant one million Bengalis in a new city on the prairies. That number is big enough to create employment rather than unemployment."[118] Echoing the public sentiment, the news media believed immigration was the best answer under the circumstances: "The Economic Council (of Canada) warns that our only hope is developing a strong domestic market. In one word: more population."[119]

In between the news, listeners were reminded again and again how innocent Bengali civilians were subjected to military reprisals and how they were forced out of their homes and hearths. At every opportunity, the radio appealed to the government's attention, ending with a question with the potential for a prolonged debate: "How about Ottawa? Or, is the just society for WASPs only?"[120] This was probably targeted at those who had difficulty accepting that Canada was changing demographically from a bicultural Canada to a multicultural Canada, which the Trudeau government embraced through the enactment of Canada's Multiculturalism Policy in the same year.

To ensure that the public was engaged in a fruitful conversation on the tragic man-made disaster, several radio stations consistently offered a space for the representation of the Canadian public to phone in to voice their concerns. As a result, the CBC's radio talk show became a popular show that triggered conversation among Canadian readers and listeners with its continued coverage. Now and then, all through the liberation war, observers joined discussion groups to speak their minds and critique Canada's role in the Pakistan–Bangladesh conflict. CBC used to bring in individuals from the ground, which compelled listeners to absorb firsthand testimony and form a favorable position after thoughtful consideration. The presentation of the guests and their way of probing into the matter produced a kind of vivid immediacy that added a powerful dimension reaching overseas. The more provoked the public was, the more the CBC talk show reached wider groups of Canadians. They became more decisive in their government intervention and action demands. In that sense, such forums were indeed a venue for populist deliberation at a time when sympathetic Canadians had many questions with no answers.

In particular, the Toronto-based radio talk show titled *Nancy Edwards Reports,* a Berkeley studio production for interchurch radio with fifty-seven stations in fifty-five communities across Canada, was perhaps the most commonly known radio station. This interchurch radio included interviews with those who had visited the refugee camps in India and witnessed how the refugees were streaming in every day. Regular talk shows put across to their listeners the tragic predicaments of the refugees, having recognized that listeners were often in different stages of their knowledge and understanding of the Pakistan–Bangladesh conflict. When World Vision Canada's Dr. Helen Isabel Huston, an expert on cholera epidemics, returned from India, Nancy Edwards interviewed her. Dr. Huston referred to the postmilitary clampdown as a tragic story that touched the hearts of Canadians. So secret and so sudden was the military crackdown that it immediately resulted in a mass exodus that sent people to India to become refugees crammed in squalid camps amid the outbreaks of cholera, observed Huston.[121] She was accompanied by Rowen Repp and Paul Edwards of UNICEF, who also narrated what they witnessed while visiting the refugee camps in West Bengali, India.

The pitiful conditions of the refugees came to further light through Nancy Edwards's interviews of these dedicated people from whom the Canadian public came to hear more precisely about the heartbreaking situations in Pakistan and India. They also learned more about how this compounded into an actual horror situation by the recent outbreak of cholera in the refugee camps. Having categorized the events as the largest mass migration in modern times,[122] radio stations involved various people on the air to talk about what they saw there and what the public could do to help alleviate the situation. Huston's interview had a substantial impact on the minds of the Canadian public. She became a point of reference for many subsequent discussions as people began to cite Huston as an example of what they had heard about the dire needs of the refugees in India.

Again, interviews of many well-known Canadians were repeated (just like the reprints of critical articles in the print media) to reinforce the message that Canadians must come forward to assist the Bengali victims of military reprisals. During summer, the Geneva-based Dr. Alan Brash, a New Zealander who worked as head of the World Council of Churches, division on interchurch aid, refugee, and world service, spoke to Canadians. He tried to help Canadians understand the grave situations in Pakistan and India. His interview is cited as an instance of the radio's proactive role in raising awareness among Canadians who must come forward to do their bit to alleviate the pathetic situation of the Bengalis. Dr. Brash also talked about the work of the World Council of Churches and alluded to its effort to help the two governments resolve the issue through negotiation. Those hopeful that a political solution might still be found felt relieved to hear from Dr. Brash that efforts had continued to solve a problem of this magnitude. Even though the chances were slim, the fact that many were still seeking a political resolution gave Canadians some hope of seeing a democratic Pakistan with a sigh of relief. In the meantime, Canadians became so used to tuning in to *Nancy Edwards Reports* every day, Monday through Friday, that Nancy Edwards instantly became a household name among Canadian listeners, especially in the Toronto area.

Again, while in India in September 1971, CBC's John Drewery could sneak into East Pakistan's interior to see what was happening. He had opportunities to speak to guerilla leaders secretly and spend time with a few freedom fighters. He also had the chance to have several meetings with James George, the Canadian high commissioner to India. His close and frequent informal meetings with George helped him compare each other's notes, exchange official and unofficial information, and channel that information to the news media (CBC) for Canadians at home.[123] It was through Drewery's regular reports that Canadians were informed how the indomitably resolute freedom fighters were carrying a variety of weapons, including Chinese rifles, Sten guns, and machine guns.

Two more Canadians, Stanley Burke and Vernon Reimer, also brought their listeners closer to the subcontinental conflict. Burke's voice was already familiar to Canadians across the country. Back in April 1971, he provided a vivid description of the army brutality and exodus of millions of terror-stricken Bengalis just to set the stage for generating discussion by reminding his radio and TV clients of the cataclysmic predicament of Biafrans, the people of the Middle East, South America, and Vietnam with whom Canadians already had some familiarity. This time, he drew an analogy regarding the size of Bangladesh with New Brunswick so that the Canadian public could visualize a better picture of eight million Bengali refugees (in August 1971). Having created a new way of putting the crisis close to the real-life environment for Canadians, Burke asked: "If all the people in all of Canada's major cities are put into a major city, for example, in Southern Saskatchewan, one could ask Premier Allan Blakeney what he would need to feed and shelter all the people there. Even with the best intentions, one would be inclined to call it impossible,"[124] thus warned Burke, his listeners, and viewers. Without being overtly political, Burke's focus was to find a way to *political resolution* of the issue by ending military rule. "While you've got your pen and envelopes handy, blow yourself to another seven-cent stamp and write to your MP. Ask him to get our government to support an immediate return to civilian government in Bangla Desh,"[125] appealed Burke earnestly.

Again, the Mennonite Central Committee's Reimer's voice on the air became familiar to Canadians at home who used to have the opportunity to tune in to the program now and then. Although stationed in India, Canadians across the country became used to Reimer's frequent appearances on the air with a passionate appeal to help the hapless victims of atrocities.[126] Whether it was Burke or Reimer, their appeals aroused empathy and passion among listeners and viewers with a fear that, if the atrocities continued, Canadians would soon be in a state of passion fatigue.

Taken together, the most exciting aspect of CBC's radio talk show program was its presentation of the dramatic contrast between the good, represented by the Gandhi administration, and the evil, defined by the Yahya administration, through its wanton killing of Bengali civilians and their repression by the Yahya regime. The technique was to appeal to the listeners, who had obtained the latest news from the field and made the news items into a unified storyline. Having complimented the newspapers and television coverage on this issue, Canadian radio played a significant role in participatory programming where knowledgeable Canadians could make their firmly held opinions on the Pakistan–Bangladesh conflict heard by all.

Television News and Talk Shows

At a time when there was no Internet, no text messaging, no Instagram, and/or no Twitter, Canada saw the events of 1971 not through the delayed newsreel (or heard over the radio hours later) but on nightly television news broadcasts. Like today, even back in 1971, CBC operated English and French television networks. In fact, because of its sheer existence and the vital role it was committed to playing, television brought Canadian families face-to-face with live news from the ground. The average viewer saw how the capital city, Dhaka, was gripped by the highest military security imposed in the country's history—pictures of the long lines of refugees and hungry babies who were dying of cholera. One might legitimately ask: "When most Canadians generally look for infotainment, how much does foreign news interest Canadians?"[127] The quick answer is that many were interested in hearing and reading about what was under some of the following exciting headings: "Foreign Affairs," "News from Abroad," and/or "News from the Subcontinent." More specifically, they wanted to find out about the fallout of the ongoing military reprisals and sexual violence and the progress of the freedom fighters in their fight for the liberation of their native land.

Thanks to the technology that enabled television viewers even in 1971 to get an instant feeling of being there in East Pakistan vicariously to experience the traumas and agonies of the tragic and dismal happenings that no other communication could offer. The minute CBC began to show glimpses of the events unfolding in Pakistan and India on the television screen, it had, as though, already brought the issue for the Canadians into their homes. Television, with its electronic bells and whistles, gave Canadians up-to-date and on-the-scene news with the camera's uncompromising delivery of stark truth: burning and looting of properties and killing of unarmed Bengali civilians. Pictorial highlighting of what had been happening in East Pakistan was one of the unique features Canadians became used to. Many members of the public maintained that the gruesomeness of the news surrounding the Bangladesh Liberation War was reminiscent of what they had watched in the late 1960s when Vietnam burst into North American living rooms on the evening news.

With its apparent advantages over newspapers in immediacy, motion, and color, television media played a pivotal role in informing and keeping the Canadian public posted on the Pakistan-Bangladesh conflict. The news media was also aware that many Canadians, while seeing the news of the military crackdown in East Pakistan and the subsequent declaration of independence by the Bengali rebels, were mindful of the 1970 October Crisis, which was a national liberation movement founded in Québec in 1963 that called for the independence of Québec. The media, however, felt obliged to clarify the nonparallel situation about the Bengalis' declaration of independence. To do that, CBC brought in experts to talk firmly about dissimilarities instead of similarities surrounding the action of the FLQ, such as the abduction of British diplomat James Richard Cross and Provincial Immigration and Labor Minister Pierre Laporte by the FLQ members, the proclamation of the War Measures Act and the subsequent calling of the army. We have briefly touched on it in Chapter 1 and the present chapter under the subheading Instant Allusion to the 1970 October Crisis we have already looked at.

Much to the credit of the news media's dissemination techniques, readers and viewers in Canada recognized Yahya's constant lying, supply of disinformation, manipulation of information, political chicanery, and secrecy in the name of national security - all resulted in cover-ups and criminal actions creating a vast credibility gap. It was not an exotic curiosity for Canadians to be exposed to the vastly different struggles of life and politics on the other side of the world. Instead, it was the shock of stifling democracy and usurpation of power by a bunch of hawkish military brass in Pakistan that compelled Canadians to be concerned. The democratic-minded and peace-loving Canadian public felt sympathetic toward the suffering Bengalis whose political rights were suppressed to perpetuate military rule. As a gatekeeper, the media focuses on news values in selecting and prioritizing its stories. One might ask: "Why did information on the Pakistan-Bangladesh conflict get past the gate in such volumes while other details did not? What were the criteria for inclusion or exclusion?" Or, to put it differently: "How was it possible that the demand for news from Pakistan remained high from Canadians living so far away from the subcontinent?" The answer for the print media boils down to circulation figures, while for the broadcast news, it is the viewer ratings. The news on the Pakistan–Bangladesh conflict survived through what is usually called the selective elimination test for space and time.

One might ask: *"What impact did the media have on Canadians?"* While it may seem difficult to gauge the exact impact, given that the press provided Canadians their only window to the liberation war in faraway

Bangladesh, indicators to address the question were, in fact, present. Take the example of a few newspaper articles. First, it was evident by the volumes of letters that swarmed into the offices of OXFAM Canada, amongst other channels, that public opinion swayed considerably toward the Bengalis' fight for the autonomy of East Pakistan. Second, as shall be seen in Chapter 5, the number of monetary donations collected by OXFAM's Combined Appeal for Pakistan Relief (CAPR) initiative and other such organizations for refugee relief indicated Canadians were very sympathetic to the desperate plight of the Bengali refugees. Canadians recognized how the blameless Bengalis were being deceived, driven out, and left for dead. It was clear to Canadians that the Bengalis had no other course of action but to fight for their lives by declaring independence, which garnered the undivided attention and concern on the world stage.

Perhaps the most commendable point of the media (both print and nonprint) is that the press was not alleged to have published or aired apocryphal stories, nor was there any use of anonymous sources, which generally makes them appear untrustworthy to an increasingly skeptic public. This is an extraordinary achievement because many examples of news stories from foreign correspondents/stringers are often filled with inaccuracies and, in some cases, complete fabrications. This was especially so, given that it was much too evident that what the military regime told the world was untrue. Splashing lurid headlines across their front pages and without resorting to yellow journalism, most of the newspapers described fierce battles and bloody atrocities in East Pakistan with no exaggeration. In covering the news from the subcontinent, the reporters paid attention, first and foremost, to the newsworthiness of the military action. Amid the tumult, newspapers delivered to Canadians a reasonably complete and independent account of the reality of the Pakistan–Bangladesh conflict.

Whether it was a community newspaper or a regular newspaper, the print media repeatedly referenced questions like the following: "What had gone wrong? How had it gone bad? Who is to blame?" In analyzing the events in Pakistan, news analysts did not hesitate to call a spade a spade. They did not distort or exaggerate the actions of the vicious and murderous military regime. The military regime used naked terror and brute force to crush the freedom fighters and suppress the rebellion. The media worked on the premise that only when an informed public could they respond to the appeals for help more promptly and positively.

The news media's construction of the Pakistan–Bangladesh reality and broadcasting the news day and night through eye-witness reports was an effective way to give an appalling amount of evidence of reprisals. Frequent and widespread coverage of savage destruction, government lying, and dangerous expansion toward a war despite intense peace efforts gave Canadians at home a vicarious sharing of experiences of the refugees. Tales of personal experiences and observations enabled the media to dramatize the heartbreaking situation of the victims of reprisals and their haplessness, something that engendered more public sympathy for the victims. The media's narratives also instantly connected readers with the sheer tragedy unfolding while reading the narratives. Having provided a seamless communication web between Ottawa and the field, readers were made to communicate with the victims trapped in a faraway country. This instantly shifted the attitudes of readers and viewers from one of curiosity to one of commitment. Such news items triggered readers and viewers to reflect on and share their feelings of angst and horror against the military regime.

In a sense, one could say that although Canadians did not experience the military reprisals firsthand, it was as though they could see and feel the distressing situation of the victims. Canadian media, like the news media of the rest of the world, recognized the endless details of the circumstances of the ill-fated victims both in India and Occupied Bangladesh (East Pakistan) when viewed through their lenses. Undoubtedly, such a method of focusing was one of the effective journalistic techniques that enabled readers to recognize the sufferings of the victims that illustrated the intensity of the crime committed. This might be called what is usually referred to as the personalization of news, which is allied to the dramatization technique. The impact of such emotion-laden narratives also empowered Canadians to interpret the hickory-pokery deal between the East Pakistani leader Bhutto and President Yahya and the hidden agenda of the diabolic regime determined to hang on to power instead of transferring to the Bengali leader of the majority party (Bongobondhu).

Finally, perhaps the most noticeable feature of the Canadian media was that the newspapers stated that the Awami League won most seats in Pakistan's 1970 National Elections at every opportunity. Time and again, the media reminded its readers and viewers that when everyone was getting ready to join the National Assembly session, the military authority suddenly postponed it without ever discussing it with the majority leader.

The media consistently put across this message, with no exaggeration in the reporting or misrepresenting the truth. Despite many constraints, the media was focused on sensitizing its clients through awareness of the news from overseas. The subsequent engagement of the community members in fundraising campaigns that resulted from a successful awareness program was covered comprehensively. The media's role remains an example of how the press and government intersected by affecting public perception, thereby arousing a collective position and action to uphold democracy and human rights on the world stage.

In a sense, the role of the Canadian media may be cited as an example of advocacy journalism that promoted and championed a particular cause - the democratic rights of the Bengalis. In the end, increased media coverage, enhanced word of mouth, and greater awareness all came to build exponentially from the tragic turn of events in the hands of the military regime, which carried the story of repression by many legs.

Notes and References

1. Restricted telegram from John Small, high commissioner to Pakistan, to Ottawa. Telegram #781, dated March 29, 1971. File #20-E-Pak-1-4. Department of External Affairs. Hereinafter, all telegrams used in this chapter from the Department of External Affairs shall be referred to as Telegram. External Affairs.
2. Canadian Broadcasting Corporation radio news, March 26, 1971. *Morning News.* CBC, Toronto.
3. *Ibid.*
4. Restricted telegram from John Small, high commissioner to Pakistan, to Ottawa. Telegram #381, dated March 29, 1971. File #20-E-Pak-1-4. Telegram. External Affairs. *Op. cit.*
5. Records indicate that Schlesinger was supposed to meet with Bongobondhu on the night of March 24, an arrangement made through Sheikh Moni, a nephew of Bongobondhu. However, Schlesinger told the author on May 23, 1995, that he could not meet with Bongobondhu for his scheduled formal interview on the evening of March 25, 1971.
6. Canadian Broadcasting Corporation. *Radio News (Morning News, audio)* March 26, 1971. CBC Archives. Toronto.
7. *Ibid.*
8. *Ibid.*
9. *Ibid.*
10. *Ibid.*

11. *Ibid.*
12. *Ibid.*
13. *Ibid.* March 27, 1971.
14. *Toronto Daily Star*, dated April 1, 1971.
15. *Kitchener-Waterloo Record*, dated March 29, 1971.
16. *Ibid.*
17. *Ibid.*
18. *Ibid.*, dated April 10, 1971.
19. *Ibid.*, dated March 30, 1971.
20. *Ibid.*
21. *Ibid.*
22. *Ibid.*
23. *Ibid.*
24. *The Globe and Mail*, dated April 2, 1971.
25. *Ibid.*
26. *The Globe and Mail*, dated May 25, 1971.
27. Canadian Broadcasting Corporation. *Radio News* (*Morning News*, audio) March 26, 1971. CBC Archives. Toronto.
28. *Ibid.*
29. Canadian Broadcasting Corporation. *Radio News* (*Morning News*, audio) April 2, 1971. Morning News. CBC Archives, Toronto. CBC relayed the news from the British Broadcasting Corporation (BBC).
30. *Ibid.*
31. *Ibid.*
32. *Ibid.*
33. *Ibid.*
34. Sydney H. Schanberg, *The Scotsman*, dated April 18, 1971, reported from Agartala.
35. Sydney H. Schanberg, *The Scotsman*, dated April 19, 1971, reported from Agartala. Schanberg's message was originally published in the *New York Times* and reprinted in Canadian newspapers.
36. *The Indiagram.* Information Service of India, Office of the High Commissioner for India, Ottawa. No. 27/71, p. 3. MG 32, Volume 32, File: 32.3. Canada. Library and Archives Canada. Hereinafter, all information used in this chapter from the Library and Archives Canada records shall be referred to as Library and Archives Canada.
37. *Ibid.*
38. *Ibid.*
39. *The Globe and Mail*, dated May 7, 1971.
40. *Toronto Daily Star*, dated 31 July 31, 1971.
41. John Wieler, *Canadian Mennonite Reporter*, 3 August 1971, p. 5.
42. *Ibid.*

43. Vernon Reimer, *Canadian Mennonite Reporter,* October 18, 1971, p. 7.
44. *The Guardian,* Prince Edward Island, dated August 3, 1971.
45. *Weekend Magazine,* July 31, 1971, p. 3.
46. *Ibid.* p. 2.
47. *Ibid.*
48. *Ibid.*
49. *Ibid.*
50. *Canadian Jesuits Mission,* vol. 6, no. 5, September–October 1971, p. 10.
51. *Canadian Jesuits Mission,* vol. 6, no. 5, September–October 1971, p. 4.
52. *Ibid.*, vol. 6, no. 3, May-June 1971 p. 2.
53. *Ibid.*
54. The author interviewed John Drewery on June 20, 1999, when he was living in a small town near Ottawa, Ontario. Drewery confirmed his conversation with the author in a July 10, 1999 follow-up note.
55. *Kitchener-Waterloo Record,* dated May 12, 1971.
56. *Ibid.*
57. *Ibid.*
58. *The Ottawa Citizen*, September 17, 1971.
59. *The Ottawa Citizen,* March 28, 1971.
60. *Montreal Star*, dated April 21, 1971.
61. *The Globe and Mail,* dated April 5, 1971.
62. *Ibid.* Dated April 10, 1971.
63. *Kitchener–Waterloo Record,* dated May 12, 1971.
64. *The Ottawa Journal,* dated September 4, 1971.
65. *The Kitchener–Waterloo Record,* dated March 15, 1971
66. *Ibid.*
67. *The Ottawa Citizen,* dated March 28, 1971.
68. Richard Schroeder: "Pakistan holy war is feared" in *The Globe and Mail* of April 7, 1971.
69. *The Globe and Mail,* dated April 2, 1971.
70. *Kitchener–Waterloo Record,* dated April 3, 1971.
71. For further reading on this civil war aspect, please see John Gellner's article entitled, "How Civil War Can Lead to the International Crisis" in *The Globe and Mail, dated* April 10, 1971.
72. *The Globe and Mail,* dated June 14, 1971.
73. *Ibid.*
74. *Ibid.*
75. 76 *The Times,* dated 4 June 1971.
76. *Ibid.*
77. Cited in *Bangla Desh Documents.* The B. N. K. Press Private Ltd. Madras, India. Ministry of External Affairs. New Delhi, 1971. P. 460.

78. Chester Bowles's article titled "More Tragedy for South Asia?" *The Globe and Mail,* dated 7 July 7, 1971.
79. *The Globe and Mail,* dated August 16, 1971.
80. *Ibid.* Originally published in the *New York Times* on August 4, 1971, under the title *The Ravaged People of East Pakistan.*
81. *The Globe and Mail,* dated August 21, 1971.
82. *Ibid.*
83. 84 Québec question refers to Canada's fear of the separatists who want to separate from Canada.
84. *The Globe and Mail,* dated March 13, 1971.
85. *Ibid.*
86. *The Globe and Mail,* dated March 28, 1971.
87. For details, see S. J. Ball-Rokeach and M. L. DeFleur. 1976. A Dependency Model of Mass Media Effects. *Communication Research* 3:3-21 cited by Karen S. Johnston-Cartee *News Narratives and news framing, constructing political reality,* Rowman and Littlefield Pub. Inc. N.Y 2005, p. 6.
88. For details, see Anthony J. Eksterowicz and Robert N. Robert: Public *Journalism and Political Knowledge,* Rowman and Littlefield Public Inc. London, N. Y., 2000 p. X111.
89. *Montreal Star* described in detail the desperate plight of the Pakistani refugees, dated June 7, 1971.
90. *Report from Raymond Cournoyer.* Dated May 14, 1971, p. 11. Kolkata, West Bengal, India. MG 28 1 270, Volume 5. File: *Pakistan: Action* 71–72. This information is also available in the OXFAM Canada's File in the Library and Archives Canada. MG 32 C31, vol. 32. Library and Archives Canada. *Op. cit.*
91. *Famine and Civil War in East Pakistan* by John E. Rodhe and Lincoln C. Chen, Harvard Medical School. September 18, 1971, pl 10. File: OXFAM Canada. MG 28 I 270 Volume 18. Library and Archives Canada. *Op. cit.*
92. This is from a flyer that Nancy Gerein wrote when she returned to Canada in the summer to assist her colleague Jean Stilwell, who was involved in fundraising. This flyer was handed out to the members of the public. Gerein gave the author a copy of the flyer in her collection, along with other information and many short write-ups.
93. Letter from Professor Joseph O'Connell to M. Y. Shaikh, high commissioner of Pakistan, dated May 21, 1971. MG 28 I 270 Vol. 18, File: *Pak Relief General.* Library and Archives Canada. *Op. cit.*
94. *Kitchener Waterloo Record,* dated June 7, 1971.
95. *The Globe and Mail,* dated July 24, 1971.
96. Letter by James Pankratz, then a doctoral student at McGill conducting research in India, Toronto Daily Star, June 16, 1971.
97. *Manitoba Brethren Herald,* dated August 27, 1971.
98. *Fredericton Gleaner,* dated August 25, 197.1

99. *Weekend Magazine,* dated August 21, 1971, p. 5.
100. *Ibid.*
101. *Ibid.*
102. *The Globe and Mail*, dated July 31, 1971.
103. This and other references to frequent radio announcements and radio spots may be found in the Draft Memo to Public Service Director, CAPR, Churches & Agencies, re: Blanket Appeal, no date. MG 28 I 270, vol. 19. File: *CAPR.* Library and Archives Canada. *Op. cit.*
104. *The Globe and Mail,* dated August 1, 1971.
105. *Pro Tem, Special Supplement, The Student Weekly of Glendon College,* York University, dated October 6, 1971, p. S4.
106. *Ibid.*
107. *Canada and the World*, October 1971, p. 23.
108. *Ibid.*
109. *Manitoba Brethren Herald*, dated June 11, 1971.
110. *Ibid.*
111. *Ibid.*
112. *Ibid.,* dated December 31, 1971.
113. *The Canadian India Times,* dated September 2, 1971.
114. Paul G. Kniss, a Mennonite Central Committee member in India in *Pembina Triangle Progress*, dated September 1, 1971.
115. *Canadian Mennonite Reporter,* dated October 18, 1971.
116. 1050 CHUM, All the News: *And here is how things look to Dick Smyth this morning*, 1 December 1971. MG 28 1 270 Volume 19. File: CAPR. Library and Archives Canada. *Op. cit.*
117. *Ibid.*
118. *Ibid.*
119. *Ibid.*
120. By WASP meant the White Anglo-Saxon White Protestants.
121. *Nancy Edwards Reports*, For Press Release: Week before July 12, 1971. A Berkeley Studio Production for Inter-Church Radio, Toronto. The report is titled *Eyewitness Account of Pakistani Disaster,* p. 30. MG 28 1 270, Volume 5, File*: Combined Appeal for Pakistani Relief and other Agency press releases, statements, and material, 1971.*Library and Archives Canada. *Op. cit.*
122. *Ibid.*
123. Letter from John Drewery to Mustafa Chowdhury, dated July 10, 1999. Following that, the author interviewed Drewery, who narrated his experiences to the author.
124. *THE TESTIMONY OF SIXTY: On the Crisis in Bengal.* OXFAM U. K., London, October 21, 1971. No page.
125. *Ibid.*

126. For example, on July 30, 1971, Vancouver time at 5 p.m., Vernon Reimer, George Hoffman from the Evangelical Association for Relief from the U.K., and Bob Brow of World Vision Canada were on the air from Kolkata through a telephone line to CJOR, Vancouver, British Columbia. Letter from Vernon Reimer to John Wieler dated July 29, 1971. Source #2. Mennonite Heritage Centre. Archives. File: *Asia, Pakistan (January – July 1971)*. Volume. 2446; 71 E 0007.
127. Infotainment coordinates information with entertainment values such as drama, emotion, plot simplicity, personal morals, and character conflicts, often presented with theme music and visually appealing scenery.

CHAPTER 4

Vox Populi: Canadians Speak Out

*T*he Canadian public was distressed by the suffering and loss of life that accompanied the military action in East Pakistan—the infliction of hardship, the death of masses of innocent human beings, and the violent suspension of the democratic process by the military regime. An alert news media had already been sensitizing the public to the extent of the devastation of the reprisals of the Bengalis since the secret military crackdown of March 25, 1971. As a result, the average Canadian was not only aware of the discord unfolding in the Indian subcontinent but also developed a soft corner in their hearts that became evident in later months. The mainstream public's immediate take was that it was an act of betrayal on the part of the military regime, and the rebellious Bengalis were to pay for it in savage bloodshed. They raised a few questions for the government along the following lines: Has the government's policy adequately responded to the human emergency? How has Canada been responding to the systematic reign of terror, mockery of justice, and brutality that characterized Yahya's regime? By early summer, the news media and the Canadian public found no reason to trust the Yahya regime, whose repeated appeals and fresh promises did not dent the people's minds. It was as though it did not matter anymore—let the chips fall where they might.

Seeing the brutal attack on the Bengalis, the Canadian public, except for non-Bengali West Pakistani Canadians, condemned the military *regime and demanded Canada's humanitarian intervention in the political injustice. The non-Bengali West Pakistani segment stubbornly remained adherent to the military government. The Bengali segment of the Canadian public, anguished by the suffering and loss of life due to the clandestine military clampdown and ongoing military repression, immediately condemned the military regime and remained insistent on their demand for an independent Bangladesh. Most of the public, however, insisted on furthering the democratization process in a united but reformed Pakistan.*

The Canadian public had been following the news from Pakistan, especially since the National Elections of 1970 began the democratization process in Pakistan. The Bengalis were getting ready for the transfer of power to their leader, who demanded greater autonomy for East Pakistan. The first public demonstration reported in the media was the one that took place in Ottawa on March 8, 1971. It was reported that approximately seventeen Bengali East Pakistani demonstrators, mainly from Toronto, huddled against the cold weather at the Peace Tower on Parliament Hill base under the leadership of Schams Ahad, a young Bengali-speaking Canadian engineer of East Pakistani background. The protest was against the military dictator's arbitrary postponement of the National Assembly. The group carried placards that said *Purbo Pakistan Zindabad*—Long Live East Pakistan.[1] Having spent some time at the Parliament premises, the demonstrators headed to the Pakistan High Commission premises on 505 Wilbrod Street. There was other news concerning East Pakistanis and their fight for greater autonomy and the proper distribution of power and resources, but there had been no demonstration. Records indicate that this was the first demonstration by East Pakistani Bengalis before the imposition of martial law.

Following the imposition of martial law and sudden military crackdown, news from Pakistan and India surfaced but only in dribs and drabs. Below is an account of the public's instant reactions and actions and the year-long activities under a few headings selected arbitrarily.

Immediate Public Reactions and Demonstrations

The initial broadcast to the Canadian public was made on Saturday, March 27, 1971, covering the imposition of martial law through to the declaration of independence of Bangladesh. At that time, the media could not determine when independence was declared. The Canadians of East and

West Pakistani origin immediately took to the streets of the major cities, such as Ottawa, Toronto, Montreal, Calgary, Saskatoon, and Vancouver. A few East Pakistani Bengalis had already formed an association in the Ottawa area in March 1971. "It transpired that they are among the twenty-odd members of the East Pakistan Cultural Association in Ottawa, formed on March 14 with the mailing address c/o Dr. A. B. M. Lutful Kabir, 87 Woodmount Crescent, Ottawa."[2] Thus, Mitchell Sharp, Secretary of State for External Affairs, was briefed by John Harrington, Head of the Pacific and South Asia Division of the same department.

"Our immediate reaction was one of shock and disbelief, followed by a spontaneous decision that it was no longer possible to live with the Pakistanis as a single nation. It was as though the non-Bengali West Pakistanis turned anti-Bengali, and Bengalis, with a few exceptions, turned anti-Pakistani,"[3] Professor Mizan Rahman of Carleton University recalled his involvement. The first recorded protest demonstration following the imposition of martial law took place in Ottawa on March 27, 1971, organized by Professor Nasir Uddin Ahmed of the University of Ottawa. About thirty area demonstrators, mostly Bengali-speaking East Pakistanis, gathered in front of Parliament Hill before marching on to 505 Wilbrod Street in front of the premises of the Pakistan High Commission. Calling President Yahya Khan an "assassin" and a "traitor," the demonstrators carried a hurriedly made flag of Bangladesh and burned a Pakistani flag and a photo of Yahya. Using a battery-operated megaphone, they shouted, "Death to Yahya" and "Stop Genocide," and attracted several people despite the cold wintry weather.

Pakistan's Republic Day celebration, scheduled for March 27 in Toronto, included a message at the opening ceremony from William Davies, then Premier of Ontario, and a two-hour concert by a Pakistani band in the presence of Akram Zaki, Pakistan's high commissioner to Canada. Having boycotted the Republic Day celebration, the Bengali segment immediately organized a protest demonstration. "Many of us went to the venue [Ontario Teachers' Training College on Bloor Street W] with placards condemning Pakistan's brutal crackdown," observed Ahsanullah Mullick, a Torontonian at the time.[4] He was among about fifty dismayed East Pakistani Canadians of the Toronto area gathered in front of the Ontario College of Education on Bloor Street West. They tried to disrupt the program by "supporting a new state of Bangla Desh under the leadership of Sheikh Mujibur Rahman. The police showed up and separated us. We did our best, and the Pakistanis got a taste of our true feelings of hatred toward them,"[5] recalled Mullick forty-one years later of the scuffle and heated arguments and counterarguments between pro-Pakistani and pro-Bangladeshi Canadians.

About one hundred or so non-Bengali West Pakistanis continued the day's activities. Yakub Khan, then president of the Pakistan Student Association, University of Toronto, condemned the Awami League (AL) leader Bongobondhu as a separatist. The Pakistani forces "should kill more of the separatist element,"[6] observed an angry Khan who maintained that he was "sympathetic to the people being killed who are not separatist" and that "the army should not be killing them."[7] Khan also observed that he "would favor killing five hundred thousand people, if necessary, to wipe out the supporters of a separate state of Bangla Desh."[8]

Joe Schlesinger, one of the foremost reporters of the Canadian Broadcasting Corporation (CBC), flew back to Vancouver after being released from Dhaka on March 27. "Some of us went to see Joe personally to get a briefing on the actual situation in Dhaka. His recounting of events in Dhaka left no doubt about the grave tragedy that was being perpetrated on the defenseless people."[9] Thus, Dr. Lutfor Rahman, accompanied by Shahid Hussain, then a PhD student at the University of British Columbia (UBC) and the president of the Pakistan Students Association, recalled his meeting with Schlesinger. Subsequently, Shahid and Rahman updated the community members on Schlesinger's eyewitness account and developed an action plan to raise awareness among Vancouverites.

An example of instant public reaction is the emergence of an ad hoc committee headed by Dr. Saghir Ahmad, a Canadian of West Pakistani origin, at the Department of Politics, Sociology, and Anthropology at Simon Fraser University. With a handful of mainstream Canadians and Canadians of West Pakistani non-Bengali backgrounds, this ad-hoc committee condemned the actions of the military regime. It supported the 75 million East Pakistanis (Bengalis) in their struggle for self-determination. It stands out as a distinct group since most members were non-Bengalis. Yet they supported full autonomy for East Pakistan, having urged President Yahya Khan to restore democratic procedure and stop the murdering of the Bengalis. The committee stated on March 27, with a critical message for all Canadians, "Since the founding of Pakistan, both the natural and human resources of East Bengal have been exploited to benefit West Pakistani elites in particular and West Pakistan in general."[10] It is unclear if the said committee endorsed the liberation movement of Bangladesh. It must have fizzled out in a few weeks since no further information is available in this regard in the Simon Fraser University archives.

April 1971

On April 2, the Ottawa-based Bangladesh-Canada Association again brought out another procession of about fifty people. Like the demonstration of March 27, the same group of people burned the national flag of Pakistan, which, at first, would not work due to the damp weather, even though they tried with a cigarette lighter. After a few tries, the problem was solved "by dipping the flag into the gasoline tank of a nearby parked car,"[11] Professor Mizan Rahman recalled forty years later. Again, CBC's Ken Colby reported that the demonstrators condemned the military intervention. Two demonstrators in the front carried an effigy of Yahya, and several demonstrators carried a few banners saying, "Long Live Bangla Desh, my country Bangla Desh," and "Death to Yahya." A Canadian daily reported, "Climaxing the Parliament Hill demonstration was a mock trial in which an effigy of Pakistani President Yahya Khan was convicted of crimes against the people of Bangla Desh and hanged."[12] The demonstrators were also joined by a group from Toronto under the leadership of Schams Ahad to represent the newly formed Bangladesh Association of Canada (Toronto). The National Democratic Party (NDP) MP John Gilbert's appearance among the protesters encouraged them to believe that Gilbert supported their demand for an independent Bangladesh.

Amid the crowd, a news reporter suddenly flagged Maqsud Ali, who joined the Ottawa demonstrators to express his misgivings while awaiting admission to the University of Waterloo for the fall session. The reporter asked Ali, "Do you consider this genocide?" "Yes, it is,"[13] was Ali's curt but firm response. The demonstrators then left for the Pakistan High Commission premises. They headed to the embassies of the USSR, China, Ceylon (now Sri Lanka), and Burma (now Myanmar) in the National Capital Region. They demanded an end to the "Yahya Khan's war" of atrocity against the new state. To many Canadians, the slogans and placards were reminiscent of the Québec Premier Jean Lesage's era (1960–1966) when the French nationalist party, the Rassemblement pour l'indépendence (RIN), frequently carried placards with the same following type of slogans: "Death to the Traitor, We want Liberty and Save Our Right."[14]

On April 9, Canadians of West Pakistani origin in Toronto organized a brief rally at St. Mary's Parish Hall on Adelaide Street to protest what they called "Indian interference in the internal affairs of Pakistan." The group, carrying signs proclaiming Long Live United Pakistan, shouted, "Down with Indian imperialism," and "We are Pakistanis—Not Bengalis or Punjabis,"[15] and marched out of Nathan Phillips Square through downtown Toronto streets. There was no reported counterdemonstration on that day.

In Kingston, Ontario, Hafizur Rahman, Qazi Islam, Mohammad Rashid, and Sarwar Alam of Queen's University at Kingston, with a handful of Bengalis, gathered in early April for a rally and condemned the military regime for its actions on unarmed civilians. A CBC reporter interviewed Rahman and Alam about the secret army takeover. "We emphasized the reasons for the dissatisfaction of the Bengalis with the national government—most importantly, that the military was refusing to hand over power to a legitimately elected leader."[16] Thus, Rahman wrote to the author about the conflicting news they received. Since most of the news items they gathered used to come from two Pakistani colleagues whose primary source was the Ottawa-based office of the Pakistan High Commission, they were often one-sided. "Days and months of my time were consumed in reading newspapers, listening to the radio, and discussing the news with Dr. Tarik Siddiqui of the Pakistan Civil Service Academy, who was then on sabbatical replacement in the Department of Political Studies" at Queen's University in Kingston, Ontario,[17] wrote Dr. Rahman.

There was another small segment of the public that called itself the Indian Progressive Study Group and took an issue with the government of India's interference in the "internal affairs" of Pakistan. This study group used to show up now and then in front of Pakistan and India's Ottawa-based high commission premises. It consisted of "twelve to fifteen in number, non-violent and Caucasians, one or two West Indians or other blacks, with the balance Indians and/or Pakistanis."[18] Maoist in belief and ideology, this study group that did not see the conflict as a national liberation movement of the Bengalis observed, "Liberation of the people of East Pakistan and the whole of Pakistan is inseparably linked with the defeat of the feudalist force and bureaucratic capitalists because it is these forces which are most eager to sell out the independence and serve as lackeys of US imperialism."[19] The minister was briefed on the group's activities, but no one in the government took the group seriously.

Hakim Sikander, president of the Bangladesh Association of Alberta (Calgary chapter), recalled what they heard had been happening around mid-April. "There was a frustrating feeling that much of what seemed to be happening was very unpleasant, but we did not know what was happening on the ground.[20] Simply because of the nature of the conflict, the problems would be unending and performance inadequate. In those pre-Internet days, the group used to listen to the BBC and CBC news, pick up short-wave broadcasts, and gather as many newspapers as we could get our hands on to read the news from Kolkata, India, and Karachi, Pakistan,"[21] recalled Sikander.

With the passage of each uncertain day, there began to appear more information about the sinister nature of the military operation with analysis. "Evening and nightly news brought fresh news from India, Pakistan, and other world countries. We would watch the CBC nightly news with Lloyd Robertson at 11:00 p.m. before going to bed,"[22] recalled Dr. Haripad Dhar, a graduate student at Ottawa University. "Like others, I'm no exception to Bangladeshi Canadian families living in Ottawa, worried and terrified every moment, scared to hear what news we would get from home,"[23] Bilquis Kabir recalled those nightmarish days.

Again, Rabi Alam, then a city planner in the Toronto municipality, recalled the immediate reaction and a lack of unanimity even among the Bengali fellow compatriots, "Some were skeptical about the reality of the independence movement, the motives of Sheikh Mujibur Rahman and were unsure about the extent of reported massacres. A few students on scholarships wanted to be neutral. Some were openly sympathetic to Pakistan's solidarity. Some of us were committed to moving forward, and some wanted to stay in the background for the safety of their family back home and for fear of job security in Canada."[24] Echoing the same sentiment, Harun Rashid, then a graduate student at the University of Saskatchewan, Saskatoon, wrote the following: "Things were so confusing at that time because of the divided loyalty among many of us and India's involvement, that we could not keep up with the events."[25] Recently, Rashid again recalled his own experience of uncertainty almost fifty years ago, "Shocked by the trauma of the military crackdown, the Bengali citizens of East Pakistan living in different parts of Canada were split into at least three schools of thought. Most condemned the attack and supported the movement for an independent Bangladesh. A small group, however, clinging to the past Islamic state ideology opposed the movement for the breakup of Pakistan. Some of them had even joined the pro-Pakistani street demonstrations. A third group supported the concept of an independent East Bengal as a homeland for Muslim Bengalis."[26]

Again, having recalled his instant reaction to the imposition of martial law, Nurul Islam, then a graduate student at McGill, observed, "Uniting people from East and West Pakistan, more than one thousand miles apart by an unfriendly territory, was an absurd hypothesis. It was evident that the nation's fabric will ultimately collapse."[27] Thus, prophesied Islam, who later became a professor at Concordia University. He supported the Bengalis' pledge to fight to liberate their native land. Again, Professor Saber Saleuddin, a Torontonian, observed, "As much as I remember, we were all united in our efforts in that we condemned the action of the army. We fully supported the independence movement for a free Bangladesh."[28]

By the end of April, the Pakistani segment of the Canadian public took two opposing routes. The non-Bengali West Pakistani Canadians were in favor of the military regime. However, many were critical of the way the democratic processes were being suppressed, while almost all Bengali East Pakistani Canadians, with very few exceptions, were in favor of an independent Bangladesh. The mainstream public respected the territorial integrity of Pakistan and its sovereignty as a state. The news of indiscriminate killings, especially with the availability of gory details from the subcontinent, sparked outrage and condemnation on their part. Having recognized the growing trend toward democratization in the world, the public agreed with the Trudeau administration's take on the Pakistan issue - that if Pakistan were to develop a credible democracy to enjoy a peaceful future for both wings of the country, the military regime would have to be brought into the broader process of political change. They expected the Trudeau administration to work quickly, effectively, and quietly, as far as possible, to help end hostilities.

Formation of Associations, Ad Hoc Committees, and Working Groups

Appalled by the news of the massacre, the Pakistani segment of the Canadian public reacted by forming various groups and associations. In 1971, the total population of Canada was 21,568,310. Canadians of Indian background numbered 67,925, while Canadians of Pakistani backgrounds, such as East and West Pakistanis, numbered 52,100.[29]

Link to PDF of publication: https://archive.org/details/1971927231973engfra/page/n2

1971
Canada Census

Provinces/ Territories	Canada's Population	Population of Indian Background Male	Population of Indian Background Female	Indian Background Population	Population of Pakistani Background Male	Population of Pakistani Background Female	Pakistani Background Population
Newfoundland	522,100	240	220	460	185	125	310
Prince Edward Island	111,640	75	60	135	70	60	120
Nova Scotia	788,960	785	565	1,350	705	465	1,170
New Brunswick	634,555	245	220	465	190	150	340
Quebec	6,027,765	3,240	3,270	6,510	2,760	2,240	5,000
Ontario	7,703,105	15,895	15,030	30,925	12,590	9,850	22,440
Manitoba	988,250	1,535	1,670	3,205	1,085	775	1,860
Saskatchewan	926,245	835	790	1,625	660	590	1,250
Alberta	1,627,875	2,205	2,195	4,400	1,755	1,460	3,215
British Colombia	2,184,620	10,350	8,440	18,790	9,365	6,990	16,355
Yukon	18,385	10	5	15	5	5	10
North West Territories	34,805	25	25	50	15	10	25
Total	21,568,310	35,440	32,490	67,930	29,385	22,720	52,095

Source: http://publications.gc.ca/collections/collection_2017/statcan/CS92-723-1971.pdf

There may be a discrepancy in some instances due to the random rounding of census data to a multiple of five or ten, a practice meant to protect census respondents' confidentiality. For more information, contact statcan.infostats-infostats.statcan@canada.ca

In 1971, there was no separate East Pakistan Association consisting only of Bengali-speaking East Pakistanis. In the absence of their association and because of linguistic affinity, the Bengali-speaking Indians of West Bengal had often attracted some Bengali-speaking East Pakistanis. In 1970, the Bengali students of Carleton and Ottawa University formed a citizens' group for the devastated cyclone victims in East Pakistan mainly through the initiative of Faruque Sarkar, then a graduate student at the University of Ottawa and president of the Pakistan Student Association. "Are we a part of Pakistan or their serfs or market for their goods only? Is there equal treatment for the Bengalis?" asked an enraged Sarkar, seeing the total apathy of the West Pakistani rulers.[30] For days, he could not sleep or eat, fearing that all his family members had perished, as there was no trace of his family. "I heard nothing from my family until the end of April. The stubble grew and became a beard. So, in a way, my beard is historic,"[31] recalled Sarkar, who formed an informal coordination committee and exchanged information with the committee's members in Montreal and Toronto. For the Sarkars (Faruk and his wife Suzie), "it was a never-flagging effort to create a world without exploitation and domination."[32]

The Sarkars were insistent on naming the group as the Bangladesh Association. The senior members of the community, anticipating military reprisals, did not want to flare up Yahya's condescending temper, which they feared might result in further military persecution of their family members back home. They preferred to call it the East Pakistan Cultural Association. Azmat Ali, an IT specialist now living in Washington, DC, was its first president, while Dr. Luthful Kabir and Dr. Mohammad Ahsanullah were its vice president and secretary, respectively. Other active members included Drs. Ehsanes Saleh, Mizan Rahman, and Nasir Uddin Ahmed; Jalaluddin Ahmed, Abdur Rahim, Abdus Sattar, and their spouses; and Tipu Sultan, who lived in Cornwall and joined the Ottawa group. In addition to Faruque Sarkar, there were a few more active student members, like Haripad Dhar, Abdul Awal, and Mohammad Hanif. Under Sarkar's stewardship, the group then took up the provocative work of mounting protest demonstrations on the streets of Ottawa.

Earlier, following the National Elections of 1970, the Bengali students in Toronto formed an association of their own, separate from the Pakistan-Canada Association. "We formed our own association called East Pakistan Association of Canada to express our specific viewpoints,"[33] observed Matiur Rahman, a student at the University of Toronto. With the slogan of autonomy, some enthusiastic Bengali students felt a need to reinforce their differences in language and culture, even though it was one country (Pakistan) at that time, recalled Rahman. Immediately following the secret military crackdown, they changed the name to the Bangladesh Association of Canada (Toronto). Rahman became its general secretary.

Another group, titled the Saskatoon Committee for the Protection of Human Rights and Lives in East Pakistan, appeared instantly on March 27, 1971. Headed by Dr. Asit Sarkar of the University of Saskatchewan, the Committee immediately demanded an inquiry commission on the military crackdown on civilians. Within days, however, the Saskatoon Committee also changed its name to the Bangladesh Association of Saskatchewan (BAS).

Again, on March 27, with a handful of Bengalis, Dr. Farid Shariff of Winnipeg also formed the Bangladesh Association of Manitoba to help the people of Bangladesh.[34] In the meantime, within weeks, the Bengali

Canadians across Canada hurriedly began forming the Bangladesh-Canada Association in larger cities, starting their new journey by strengthening their political consolidation. Typically, promoting the cause of Bangladesh was echoed through various associations across Canada despite slight variations in their names.

At the other end of the spectrum, supporters of a united Pakistan under the present military regime also began to organize by forming committees and working groups under the banner of the existing Pakistan-Canada Association in various cities. Within days, a new group titled the Pakistan Solidarity Committee appeared in Toronto, which had endorsed its full support for President Yahya Khan. Consisting mainly of non-Bengalis and some Bengalis who remained adherents to the concept of a united Pakistan, the committee viewed the situation as an Indian conspiracy against the integrity of Pakistan. Just about the same time, there also emerged another group in Toronto, the East Pakistan Relief Committee, that pledged to "work for the unity"[35] of Pakistan with an emphasis on Pakistan's integrity and solidarity supported mainly by non-Bengali Pakistani Canadians and a few Bengali Canadians. Chaired by Dr. Zafar Quraishi of Toronto, it argued that India had been enticing the Mujibites (those in favor of Sheikh Mujibur Rahman) against true Pakistanis. "We want our Canadian friends to help us achieve this goal [unity] by reporting impartially the happenings in Pakistan and supporting the cause of a solidarity campaign to unite the peoples of the two wings of the country."[36] Thus, Dr. Quraishi made his appeal.

By the end of April, both pro-Bangladeshi and pro-Pakistani segments of the Canadian public began to get their acts together separately to secure the support of the greater public for their bloc. The two opposing Pakistani segments found themselves at loggerheads, each claiming to be legitimate. The West Pakistani Canadians maintained that Yahya needed to take drastic military actions against pro-Indian anti-Pakistanis to ensure that the integrity of Pakistan was not compromised, while the Bengali-speaking East Pakistani Canadians, having denounced the Yahya regime as repressive and undemocratic and, therefore, illegitimate, whole-heartedly supported the revolutionary Bangladesh government.

Public Demonstrations in Chronological Order (From May 1971 to December 1971)

May 1971

Demonstrations by pro-Bangladeshis and pro-Pakistanis on the streets of large cities, with frequent reports of scuffles, became a familiar spectacle. "The problem of East Pakistan seems likely to be with us for some time and will probably give rise to demonstrations and counterdemonstrations at the Indian and Pakistani missions in Ottawa. It will be interesting. Therefore, if you could obtain from the National Security authorities an up-to-date report on various Indian and Pakistan[i] groups likely to be involved in demonstrations and the preparation of manifestos."[37] Thus, Mitchell Sharp, Secretary of State for External Affairs, was briefed by the Pacific and South Asia Division of External Affairs Head.

When Dr. Rehman Sobhan, then economic adviser of Bongobondhu and emissary to the UK and the United States, visited Toronto and Ottawa in May to lobby for Bangladesh, the pro-Pakistanis demonstrated against his presence in both cities. They tried to discredit Sobhan as an Indian agent, although, by that time, many had already been familiar with his writings as a strong Mujibite. Sobhan spoke from his heart, giving his voice, face, and personality. Flyers containing the *raison d'être* for an independent Bangladesh were widely distributed before his meetings. Sobhan went right to the point, unlike many who get mired in worn-out, threadbare tactics that effectively hinder one's train of thought. Having walked the audience through his roadmap to Bangladesh, Sobhan created a visionary message for his audiences, who remained captive, being on the same wavelength. He cited the number of killings of Bengalis to be five hundred thousand at that time.[38] The public comfortably situated themselves about the issues and learned what had been happening in "Occupied Bangladesh" following the military takeover.

His appeal that "all aid should be internationally supervised"[39] resonated with the audiences, who viewed Sobhan as a champion telling a compelling story of Bangladesh. The pro-Pakistani demonstrators, however, gathered outside in Toronto and Ottawa, having remained hard-headed and unimpressed.

In Calgary, the Bengali Canadians of East Pakistan and West Bengal (India) origin gathered strength as soon as they heard the news of the military takeover in East Pakistan. Among the East Pakistani Bengalis were Kazi Islam, Zahid (Jack) Rashid, Samar Mazumdar, and Andy Haque and their spouses, who teamed up under the stewardship of Hakim Sikander, president of the Bangladesh Association of Alberta (Calgary chapter). Canadians of East Indian backgrounds from the other States of India also joined forces in their condemnation of the military regime's attack on Bengali civilians. They brought a rally during the first week of May from Riley Park to Seventh Avenue SW in front of the City Centre. Mazumdar gave an impassioned speech highlighting the instances of brutality on unarmed civilians.[40] At the start of the meeting, they also raised a hastily made flag of Bangladesh and, in a fit of patriotic hysteria for an independent Bangladesh, an overexcited and emotionally charged Jack Rashid burned a Pakistani flag. Having partnered with local organizations and divvied the work, the core members developed an Action Plan for immediate implementation.

June 1971

During the first week of June, when Mir Muhammad S. Shaikh, Pakistan's new high commissioner to Canada, went to Montreal, members of the Bengali community came out to the street. They staged a protest demonstration against the high commissioner's statement at Marianopolis College, justifying the military intervention and blaming Bongobondhu for his stubbornness. "We did not let anything divide us,"[41] wrote Professor Nurul Islam, then a student at McGill, having particularly emphasized their group solidarity.

Demonstration against the S. S. Padma

The most significant public demonstration was against the *S. S. Padma*, a Pakistani ship carrying the US spare parts, berthed at Shed No. 8 at the foot of Saint Lawrence Boulevard during the week of June 27, 1971.[42] The Canadian public quickly found out that the *Padma* was the third ship to be carrying arms to Pakistan from the United States since the ban on arms shipment. The other vessels were the Kaukahla and the Sunderban. Rabi Alam of Toronto and Sadat Kazi of Montreal, the demonstration organizer, were the two outspoken members of the Action Committee. The media interviewed them. They demanded that Canada secure total measures to ensure that "no Canadian arms will be added to the US while the ship is loading in Montreal."[43] Many members of the Confederation of National Trade Unions (CNTU), the Montreal-based Palestine Liberation Organization, the Vietnamese Patriotic Group, and several teenagers off the street joined the demonstrators earlier in a park for a pep talk before they marched on toward the US consulate building. Kazi raised his voice against the United States and presented a petition to the assistant counsel general condemning the US actions. He headed for the port, marching under heavy police escort through the streets of Montreal, chanting the slogan, "Long Live Bangla Desh."

The public was outraged to find that the Nixon administration had been secretly sending arms to the transgressor, pretending that it was "business as usual." This was even though the US State Department and Pentagon had assured Congress, the press, and the American public that there would be no further deliveries of the US military equipment until a political settlement had been reached. Although the shippers claimed that only cobalt and foodstuff would be loaded,[44] the watchful protesters were mindful of the former US ambassador Chester Bowles's earlier accusation of the Nixon administration of clandestinely supplying arms to Pakistan and its attempt to "sweep the whole situation under the rug." Having accepted the US claims only with a grain of salt, the protesters entered the ship. To their fury, they discovered forty-six of Sabre jet's spare parts, which the news media immediately brought to light.

Simultaneously in Toronto, echoing the same concern, Stanley Burke, former Canadian Broadcasting Corporation's anchorman, and Rabi Alam, spokesperson for the Bangladesh-Canada Association of Toronto, joined the crowd. Alam wanted "assurances from the federal government that no Canadian arms will be added to the US supply while the ship is loading in Montreal."[45] They pointed out that the continuation of secret assistance to Pakistan meant that the Nixon administration had been aligned with a military dictatorship pursuing policies opposed to those to which the US government claimed to have remained committed. When Alam and Burke brought the matter to the attention of Barney Danson, then parliamentary secretary to Prime Minister Trudeau, he immediately invited them to his residence in Ottawa. While at Danson's place on the same night, they cautioned him that the arms being sent to Pakistan could well be used to suppress and murder more Bengalis. Discretely, they expressed their concern that if the freighter the *Padma* went via Montreal port, in a sense,

Canada could unwittingly become a partner to genocidal acts inside East Pakistan. Danson advised them to meet with Mitchell Sharp, Secretary of State for External Affairs, and Robert Stanfield, the leader of opposition parties,[46] to discuss further recalled Alam.

The same day, a group of pro-Bangladeshi demonstrators from Toronto and Montreal joined the Ottawa group's demonstration in Ottawa's Parliament Hill. The demonstrators met with David Lewis, then leader of the National Democratic Party (NDP). An open and ardent supporter of the democratic rights of the Bengalis, Lewis raised the issue in Parliament the same evening. Cummer Chowdhury, a Torontonian who came to Ottawa to join the demonstrators, "had serious misgivings about trans-shipment of the US arms through the port of Montreal."[47] Chowdhury recalled his brief encounter with Conservative MP Robert Stanfield, then opposition leader, who came out of Parliament to talk to the demonstrators personally. "Why are you guys demonstrating in Canada when Canada has been sympathetic to the plight of the Bengalis?[48] Stanfield asked the crowd point-blank. "We are grateful to Canadians for everything that Canada has been doing," was Chowdhury's immediate response.[49] The protesters were glad to learn more about the actions of the Trudeau government that, since the 1965 India-Pakistan conflict, the sale or supply of major items of offensive military equipment to either India or Pakistan had remained strictly prohibited. They noted with satisfaction that Ottawa had already suspended the shipper's license, leaving the Padma with no choice but to head back to Baltimore without the jet parts. "The Nixon administration's lack of concern for the terror-stricken Bengalis, together with its continuation of secretly supplying more arms to the military authority in Pakistan, was morally repugnant to the Canadian public."[50] Thus, Naiyyum Chowdhury, then a student at McGill University and general secretary of the Bangla Desh Association of Québec, recalled his observations at the time. Chowdhury remained active throughout the period under consideration, often at the risk of his studies.

In the meantime, Canada noted Indian Foreign Minister Swaran Singh's position concerning arms shipment and concurred with his view. "The supply of arms by any country to Pak[istan] in the present context amounts to condonation of genocide in Bangla Desh and encouragement to the continuation of atrocities by the military rulers of Pakistan."[51] Fortunately for the Trudeau administration, the public saw its action demonstrating its independent position. One could be inclined to see it as Canada's "tilt" toward the Bengalis or disgust toward the military dictator of Pakistan.

Canadians were satisfied and had reasons to hold their heads high as they believed the government had dealt with the matter transparently, unlike the surreptitious way in which the Nixon administration handled the entire matter.

In a letter to the editor, K. A. Akbar Ali, publicity secretary of the Bangladesh Association of Canada (Toronto), thanked the government for "preventing the loading of military equipment on the Pakistani Ship S.S. Padma docked at Montreal. What sort of democracy exists in the United States in which the government can so easily slight the wishes of the elected representatives?"[52] He then went on, "I appeal to our brothers in Canada and the United States to put pressure on the US government to stop aiding the Pakistan government."[53] In a sense, Ali echoed the public's sentiment for the government's bold step, independent of the US influence, even though it was at the cost of provoking Nixon's conniption.

July 1971

Seeing that Rehman Sobhan's May visit to Canada created an evolving platform and a forum for discussion, the military regime also arranged a similar gathering to counter Sobhan's presentation to tell its side of the "story." On July 18, Mahmud Ali and Hamidul Haque Choudhury spoke about Pakistan's "internal affairs" at two meetings arranged by the Pakistan Solidarity Committee in Toronto and Ottawa. Ali was the former vice president of the Pakistan Democratic Party (PDP), while Choudhury was a politician and a distinguished publisher of three national dailies - *Pakistan Observer, Purbodesh,* and *Watan.* Interestingly, both were Bengali-speaking East Pakistanis who remained staunch supporters of a united Pakistan. Both pro-Pakistani and pro-Bangladeshi groups carried placard sticks. They shouted at each other just about when the speakers were about to enter the Ontario College of Education premises on Bloor Street, Toronto. While some members of the Pakistan Solidarity Committee were ready to welcome the guests, several pro-Bangladeshi placard-bearing and slogan-shouting protesters tried to stop them. Although no arrests were made, *The Globe and Mail*, under the caption Police called to end scuffle over Pakistan, reported that police had to be called to intervene when "several shoving and shouting marches"[54] between protesters. While about one hundred Bengali protestors were standing outside, the volunteers whisked the speakers away to the auditorium. There were no arrests.

Similarly, three days later, on July 21, a group of pro-Bangladeshi demonstrators carrying placards that stated "Long Live Bangla Desh," "Down with Traitors," and "Alli-Choudhury Go Back Home" protested outside the National Press Building in downtown Ottawa across the street from Parliament condemning the guests and their supporters.[55] Canadians were already familiar with this type of slogan they heard on television or read in the newspapers since the beginning of the liberation struggle when the protesters from the Young Socialists League carried and waved special placards saying, "Bangla Desh Libre—Québec Libre."[56] The protesters attracted a few bystanders while the Ottawa police had them all on strict watch as they chanted anti-Pakistani slogans. Inside, Choudhury emphatically denied that "there was a genocidal policy being conducted by the soldiers of Pakistan President Yahya Khan."[57]

A few news reporters challenged Ali on statements of facts and misrepresentation of truth, but he chose not to respond. Instead, right out of the blue, he claimed that the news regarding the recently published report of the Canadian Parliamentary delegates was flawed "in alleging that between five hundred thousand and one million people had died in civil disturbances and war."[58] Arguing that "about thirty thousand seemed reasonable,"[59] Ali further observed, "If a country's integrity was at stake, it is the duty of the army to uphold it... Whenever necessary, the army and the police will be used. The same is true in Canada."[60] The use of the terms army, police, and Canada was a deliberate reference to the kidnapping of the British Trade Commissioner James Cross and the murder of Québec Labor and Immigration Minister Pierre Laporte during the FLQ crisis of 1970 and the subsequent invocation of extraordinary powers of arrest and detention under Canada's *War Measures Act* of 1970, which made it a crime to belong to or support the FLQ. We noted this in Chapter 1.

Many in the audience expressed dissatisfaction with the guests' performance, which fell short of their expectations as the speakers failed to give a clear situational overview and a roadmap for the audience. This was much unlike Rehman Sobhan, who defended the case of Bangladesh. Having failed to start with a bang, neither Ali nor Choudhury was able to formulate any meaningful statement about the Yahya government's critical path. Both presenters steadfastly denied any military atrocities, although it was maintaining political control through murder, torture, and forced disappearance. Some news media representatives, being disappointed, left the premises as they were convinced that the military regime was irresponsive and unaccountable. They were shouted at by the pro-Bangladeshi demonstrators standing outside while heading out. Both pro-Bangladeshi and pro-Pakistani groups were active, having remained predisposed to doing their part at any cost - the pro-Pakistanis were there to make the meeting a success, while the pro-Bangladeshi group was there to disrupt the same meeting.

The next recorded demonstration during the liberation war of Bangladesh took place in Vancouver on July 30, against the Nixon administration's actions organized by pro-Bangladeshi students of the University of British Columbia (UBC). They gathered in front of the US Consulate on Hastings Street, chanting slogans condemning the continuing secret shipment of economic and military aid to Pakistan.[61] In concert with the Vancouver-based Bangladesh Association, the rally also attracted several anti-US groups mainly because the people were disconcerted with what they saw as the insensitivity of the US policy.

August 1971

In early August, a group of pro-Bangladeshis of the Montreal area arranged to have a booth at the Man and His World (the site of Expo 67) on the condition that no leaflet or brochure would be handed out. A Québec police officer on duty, however, caught Naiyyum Chowdhury and his team members red-handed as they were secretly distributing pro-Bangladeshi information packages.[62] He was let go after receiving a warning. Chowdhury, however, ran into trouble again within days when he was waiting for a group of protesters, including the Confederation of National Trade Union leader Michel Chartrand, to join a demonstration in Montreal. A Royal Canadian Mounted Police (RCMP) officer on duty picked him up again and took him to the RCMP office for interrogation. At that time, many of Québec's intellectuals, actors, artists, writers, and student activists were still under the government's watch as it was keeping an eye on the activities of the FLQ members, many of whom were being detained in jail on suspicion of supporting Québec's separation. Chowdhury was let go upon signing a document stating that he and his group would be responsible for any physical damage to the US property. Fearful, Chowdhury signed the document and left the premises quickly. It was a successful demonstration in which the FLQ members and many left-wingers participated.

The following demonstration occurred in St. John's, Newfoundland, before the Arts and Culture Centre on August 5, 1971. Taking a lead role, Dr. Moyeenul Islam gathered some of his Bengali friends with a few mainstream Canadians who were appalled to see the barbarity of the regime. The demonstrators condemned the Yahya regime's military assault and ongoing repression of the Bengalis in their native land, Bangladesh. They handed out flyers, press clippings, and information packages highlighting many contradictions between what the military administration was claiming and what it was doing, recalled Dr. Wali Khan, a Bengali Newfoundlander who participated in the same demonstration.[63] Dr. Mohammed Matlib, who also attended the demonstration, recalled carrying several hastily made placards and feeling energized when they shouted pro-Bangladeshi slogans.[64] Coincidentally, Prime Minister Pierre Trudeau and Don Jamieson, minister of Transport and MP for Burin-Burgeo, Newfoundland, visited St. John's the same day. Reportedly, the prime minister met with three sets of protesters, according to one of the local dailies, which reported, "As he [Trudeau] walked to a press conference at the Arts and Culture Centre, flanked by plain and security men, he was greeted by fish plant workers from Burgeo, striking electricians from St. John's, and members of Bangladesh International protesting on aid to East Pakistan."[65]

Again, back in Toronto, when on August 14, Shaikh, Pakistan's high commissioner, appeared at Jarvis Collegiate Institute as chief guest of the Pakistan-Canada Association of Toronto on the twenty-fourth anniversary of Pakistan's Independence Day, several furiously embittered Bengali demonstrators gathered outside. "We are all one nation—just Pakistanis. Geographical areas of Pakistan are identified by different names only for the sake of administrative convenience,"[66] observed Shaikh, having remained as diplomatic as his position demanded. Many Bengalis had run away "because of the atrocities committed by the extremists," and many others had "left out of sheer panic resulting from the tirades of vicious and persistent propaganda spread from across the border,"[67] Shaikh added further. Amid about 250 cheering attendees, Shaikh was welcomed by non-Bengali West Pakistanis and supporters of the military regime, including a few Bengalis. Naturally, there was no one to question the speaker on the veracity of his statement as everyone was supportive of the Yahya regime. The Bengali protesters remained outside and, now and then, shouted, "Shame on Yahya."

During the third week of August, the Bangladesh Association of British Columbia and the University of British Columbia Bangladesh Student Association organized a joint rally at the City Centre (West Georgia and Burrard Street) to raise awareness of the plight of the Bengalis. "Delegates from the local Indian Consulate highlighted the human tragedy of 10 million refugees in India,"[68] recalled Dr. Lutfor Rahman, who participated in the demonstration. "A few dissenting heckling voices, commensurate with the sizable Pakistani presence in the city, were heard and were mostly ignored,"[69] Rahman added further. "We kept on chanting against the Pakistan government that the military regime was killers of innocent Bengalis," observed Sudhir Saha, then a student on Commonwealth scholarship from Pakistan and treasurer of the Bangladesh Students Association, UBC.[70] "We picked the US Consulate because the Nixon administration was the biggest supporter of the Pakistani military regime,"[71] said Saha.

September 1971

In September, Mustafizur Rahman Siddiqi, a Bengali East Pakistani Member of the National Assembly who later became head of the Bangladesh Mission in Washington, DC, came to Canada to lobby the government in favor of Bangladesh. He was confronted by members of the Pakistan Solidarity Committee on the National Press Building premises in Ottawa. A staunch supporter of a united Pakistan, the Solidarity Committee was steadfast in its opposition to the presence of Siddiqi, who they claimed to be an Indian agent. A clear-sighted Siddiqi pointed out the *raison d'être* for an independent Bangladesh gradually gaining international momentum. By then, the world had already recognized the hawkish military's idiosyncratic argument and effort at political engineering.

The military authority had been foolhardy and disdainfully haughty in believing that it would succeed in suppressing the Bengalis, observed Siddiqi. In no uncertain terms, did Siddiqi claim that "the root cause must be removed" and that "the Bangla Desh government must be recognized?"[72] While the inside was packed to the brim, several pro-Pakistani demonstrators remained outside the building premises throughout the meeting. To draw the attention of the people on the street, they frequently shouted anti-Indian slogans. They blamed the Gandhi administration for the actions and consequences of military assaults in East Pakistan.

October 1971

From the beginning of October, Canadians began to recall the nightmarish days following the October Crisis of the previous year. Partnering with the Vietnam Mobilization Committee, the Bangladesh Association of Toronto organized a protest rally against the blasting of atom bombs at Amchitka, Alaska. The protesters carried banners and placards and shouted slogans to propagate their solidarity with the oppressed people worldwide. The pro-Bangladeshi demonstrators conveyed their message—that they wanted an independent country, Bangladesh.

Amid frequent slogans by the two opposing groups of the Canadian public, another group also appeared that called itself the Young Socialist League. Despite the Trudeau administration's determination to avoid making any analogy to Canada's situation in Québec, the League reportedly joined the pro-Bangladeshis, having carried and waved their placards. Though only a handful of demonstrators compared to other demonstrations, the sight of special placards said, "Bangla Desh Libre—Québec Libre" (meaning free Bangladesh and free Québec). It caught many Canadians off guard. Instantly, it reminded them of the days following the 1970 FLQ crisis. Fortunately, the media purposefully downplayed the news, which did not cause any wave among the public.

November 1971

The Pakistan Students' Association of Ottawa University brought out a procession condemning India for attacking Pakistan and directly accused the Gandhi administration of doing everything possible to dismantle Pakistan. India's covert assistance to the rebels and mobilization of opinion against Pakistan were seriously affecting the integrity of Pakistan, argued the association's president. The association then made a written representation to the Department of External Affairs stating that India had "violated the United Nations Charter as usual by attacking the International Border of the Eastern province of Pakistan, without any formal declaration of war."[73] Javed urged the government to intervene immediately. He said, "We want that the Canadian government and the Canadian people must use their influence on India to stop the naked aggression against peaceful, loving, and small neighbor, Pakistan."[74] By the end of November, it became evident to the public that Pakistan and India were heading for a confrontation.

December 1971

The Toronto-based Defence of Pakistan Committee organized a protest rally in Toronto as soon as India and Pakistan declared an all-out war on December 3. Members of the public who joined the procession in downtown Toronto were mainly non-Bengali Canadians of West Pakistani origin who were desperate to do whatever they could to convince the greater public of India's chicanery in the name of sheltering the Bengali refugees. They shouted at the top of their voice "to show [their] support for their homeland as its armies fought those of India."[75]

They chanted the "Crush India" slogan as they headed to Queen's Park via Yonge Street. By then, the demonstration scenes across large cities were a bedlam; people were screaming and yelling, some with an ugly snarl, some angrily growling with bare teeth. Some were all too confused, while others were unfettered and unabashed. A good number of the people who attended these demonstrations simply feared that killing would beget killing only and that violence would do permanent damage to the constitutional fabric of Pakistan. By and large, the public also understood Canada's delicate position and, as a middle power, her inability to articulate her stand more openly, especially when the war had already been declared.

Another interesting aspect of public protestation was gathering several Christian Canadians of Pakistani and Indian origin who emphasized their religious faith more than the mundane political differences. The group showed the solidarity gained after seeing the subcontinental events through a spiritual lens. Calling themselves Christians first, regardless of their place of origin, Canadians of Indian and East and West Pakistani descent prayed together for peace and harmony. All group members gathered under the stewardship of Patrick Joshua, a Christian Canadian of Pakistani origin and a former judge, who established this group four years ago. It was reported that "about 150 Indian and Pakistanis will gather in an Etobicoke church Sunday for the fourth annual Christmas carol service."[76] Joshua's critical message for Canadians was, "Whatever our politics may be, we feel we are one in Christ."[77]

Sensitization and Dissemination of Pertinent Information by Province from West to East

British Columbia

The Bangladesh Association of British Columbia developed a framework paper on the independence of Bangladesh by highlighting the incidence of massive human rights violations in East Pakistan. It kept the association's partners updated on its activities through its publication *Joy Bangla* (Victory to Bengal).. The key Bengali players in BC were Shahid Hussain (a PhD student and president of the Pakistan Student Association at UBC), Sudhir Saha (a student at UBC and treasurer of the Bangladesh Students Association), Ziaul Haque, Shahjahan Kabir (president of the Bangladesh Students Association), Abul Manzur Murshid, Abdul Matin, Zia Shams, and Drs. Shafiqul, Islam, Khan, Lutfor, Rahman, and others undertook joint and individual initiatives. In early June, when Dr. Khan arrived in Vancouver with firsthand knowledge of mass slaughter in "Occupied Bangladesh," he immediately contacted the MP for his constituency. "The US role completely contradicts her assumed role as a protector of the free world and democracy worldwide." Thus, Khan exposed the Nixon administration.[78]

"We contacted the local print and electronic media to try to dispel the one-sided lies and propaganda that were emanating from the Pakistani army, to cover up its ruthless crackdown and the butchery of the civilian population in the East,"[79] wrote Dr. Rahman who worked closely with Dr. Khan and lobbied the government while raising awareness of the military regime's actions in East Pakistan. He also arranged a series of media interviews with Khan, who had witnessed some of the brutalities with his own eyes in the form of church and town hall meetings for the residents of Vancouver. "Dr. Khan's interviews and presentations added a new dimension to our efforts to dispel the misinformation that the military regime was spreading about the Pakistan armed forces. I remember his appearances on local radio call-in shows, which often attracted acrimonious rebuttals from the local Pakistani listeners,"[80] observed Rahman. Again, he described the situation: "Political demagoguery, threats, and counterthreats were flying back and forth with a masterly show of brinkmanship on all sides of the polarized political divides."[81]

Again, with cooperation from the UBC's student community, a public meeting was held in the International House premises on June 16, 1971. The keynote speaker, Jayaprakash Narayan of the Gandhi Peace Foundation, talked about the prevailing situation in India. Among the panelists were Professors Barrie Morris (UBC) and Ralf Nicholas (University of Michigan) and an array of impressive speakers. The entire hall was packed with enthusiastic audiences who were on the same page when the speakers blamed Yahya for military repression. The following resolution was shared with the media: "We call upon the president to cease terrorizing the people in whose name he governs and to re-open negotiation with the surviving elected members of the National Assembly so that domestic and responsible government can be restored to East Pakistan."[82]

During the sensitization program at UBC's International House in the same month, Shahid Hussain, president of the Pakistan Students Association, UBC, gathered several students to discuss the latest situation in East Pakistan. Interestingly enough, Hussain has not resigned from his post yet but has continued campaigning for Bangladesh while he was still officially the president of the Pakistan Students Association. He spoke on the Pakistan-Bangladesh conflict and reinforced the political nature of the conflict and the military regime's disregard for the results of the 1970 National Elections. The participants asked many follow-up questions, which Hussain diligently dealt with to their satisfaction. "We, the Bengali students, played an active role in trying to 'educate' Canadians interested in knowing about the situation. They tried to find out why East Pakistan was trying to secede,"[83] recalled Hussain years later. Although Canadians were sympathetic toward the Bengali victims of the military regime, according to Hussain, "many were also somewhat cautious and did not wish to take the side of Bangladesh and promote directly or indirectly the movement in Québec."[84] With the availability of more detailed information from the field, Canadians came to see the difference between the Bengalis' struggle for independence and Canada's fear of the separation of Québec," observed Hussain further with a note that "they were outraged and became convinced of the hypocrisy of the Yahya regime."[85]

Another project, the Teach-in on Bangla Desh program, ran for several months at the Langara Campus of Vancouver City College. It was replicated from the same program initiative developed first in Saskatoon in the fall session. With no core funding, the program got off the ground through the participation of a group of enthusiastic volunteers despite many hurdles.

In a sense, the Vancouverites had an additional advantage as the members generally had the involvement of the Bengali communities from the State of Washington—something that gave them a chance to seek ideas from each other.

Again, by late fall, when signs on the wall were showing how both India and Pakistan were getting closer and closer to a confrontation, the student volunteers of UBC and SFU (Simon Fraser University) distributed many handouts titled "The Tragedy of Bangla Desh (East Pakistan)" that highlighted the regime's actions in the form of massacre, genocide, bloodbath, terror, and starvation. The ongoing media coverage of the plight of the refugees helped the public relate to these headings concerning the stark tragedy without difficulty.[86] There were also a few individual initiatives by people like Hari Sharma, professor of sociology at SFU, often called the champion of the oppressed. Like many enlightened Canadians of the 1960s who earlier plunged into the anti-Vietnam war movement in the United States and Canada, a left-wing intellectual, Sharma, was supportive of the Bengalis' democratic rights to be realized even at the cost of a united Pakistan. He gave lectures on many occasions. As well, there were Dr. Chinnmoy Banerjee, a professor of English at SFU, and Bob Gallagher, then a student, who raised their voices against the military repression in Pakistan.

Alberta

The Bengali segment of the public in Edmonton and Calgary was quite creative in raising their concerns and doing their bit in highlighting the plight of the Bengalis in "Occupied Bangladesh" and refugees in India. Siddique Hussain, then a teacher with the Edmonton School Board, took a lead role as the president of the Bangladesh Association of Alberta (Edmonton chapter). His wife, Shahana Hussain (also a teacher), N. C. Das, Ziauddin Ahmed, Abdul Mannan, Abdur Rahim, and a few other students were with him. Hussain collected a tape recorder from New Delhi, with a recorded voice of the Bangladesh national anthem from a pro-Bangladeshi group in Chicago that made its way to Edmonton. Each time before their frequently called formal and informal meetings, the Hussains played the national anthem to emphasize the group's passion and solidarity. "This was a great source of inspiration as we often used to get carried away,"[87] the Hussains recalled their involvement.

Though only a handful of Bengali families consisted of their spouses, the Siddiques spent hours thinking about how best to raise public awareness. Hossain's right-hand man was Abdul Mannan, then a PhD student passionately interested in participating but was afraid as he was on a student visa. It was pretty risky for the students on scholarship to organize or attend any meeting to condemn the government of Pakistan while carrying a Pakistani passport. At that time, there were strict restrictions for students concerning engagement in any political activity. "Mannan showed a lot of guts in expressing his strongly-held views."[88] Thus, Hussain recalled Mannan's courage and the ardent desire to "do" something in his capacity, having defied the risk. With Mannan's assistance, the committee sent protest letters to members of federal and provincial Parliaments (MPs and MPPs) to bring the matter to the attention of the respective governments. Mannan took a lead role in photocopying the appeal letters in bulk and ensuring they were mailed immediately.

On July 5, the International Federation of Business and Professional Women's Congress held its meeting in Edmonton and discussed the disturbing news from overseas. The Indian representative saw it as a flagrant violation of the democratic rights of the Bengalis who had been driven out of their homeland. Her two-pronged appeal to the delegates was that the "world powers must put pressures on the Pakistan military to return the power to the elected representatives of East Pakistan."[89] Salima Ahmed of Pakistan Defence Services described the issue somewhat defensively, having chosen not to talk about the failure of her government to transfer power to the majority party's leader. The participants recognized that there was no solution in the foreseeable future as the blame game was continuing.

They concurred that, while it was Pakistan's "internal matter" because of the massive outflow of the Bengalis upon the soil of another country (India), the issue did not remain an "internal matter." It involved two countries - Pakistan and India. Isabel Menzies, chairperson of the Federation's Relief Committee, concluded that "the organization is concerned and moved by the pleas of both countries."[90] Still, the committee did not see it as a value-added discourse that could be pursued further. It was evident to the participants that by July, the provisional government of Bangladesh had already gained international momentum.

In Calgary, Hakim Sikander, president of the Bangladesh-Canada Association of Alberta (Calgary chapter), had a group of core volunteers like Dr. Kazi Islam, Samir Mazumdar, Jack Rashid, and Andy Haque, along with their spouses. They networked with members of Provincial Parliaments (MPPs) as well as federal MP Andrew Brewin, who was widely known to be sympathetic to the cause of Bangladesh. Personally, Sikander distributed an important analytical document written by three distinguished Harvard University professors—namely, Edward Mason, Robert Dorfman, and Stephen Marglin—titled "Conflict in East Pakistan: Background and Prospects" (April 1971) that described the situation in East Pakistan from the point of view of the cultural, linguistic, social, economic, and political case for an independent Bangladesh with a prophetic note.

One of the campaign brochures they distributed stated, "The independence of East Bengal is inevitable. What started as a movement for economic autonomy within the framework of a united Pakistan has been irrevocably transformed by the wholesale slaughter of East Bengali civilians into a movement that sooner or later will produce an independent East Bengal. Bangladesh is a matter of time."[91] In addition to the above write-ups, Sikander's team distributed copies of several Bangladesh press releases occasionally and frequent announcements from *Swadhin Bangla Betar Kendro* (the radio station of Independent Bangladesh).

Like their partners in Vancouver and Saskatoon, Sikander's team was also engaged in Teach-in Sessions designed for Calgarians with different levels of awareness of the Pakistan-Bangladesh conflict, which the military regime persistently claimed to be an "internal affair" of Pakistan.

Saskatchewan

The people of Saskatchewan were aware of the tragedy from the beginning of the conflict as the National Democratic Party (NDP) government of the day, having been sympathetic toward the Bengali victims, had already contributed a large volume of rapeseed and wheat the same year. The NDP Premier Alan Blakeney's personal initiative and involvement in proclaiming September 5 to 11, 1971, as the "Pakistan Refugee Relief Week"[92] had also triggered extraordinary empathy for the victims of military repression. The two crucial persons who played a pivotal role are Dr. Asit Sarkar of the University of Saskatchewan, Saskatoon campus, also a member-at-large of the Regina-based Bangladesh Association of Saskatchewan (BAS), and Dr. Anwar Chowdhury of Regina, then president of the BAS.

Professor Sarkar's strategy was first to make the people aware of the tragedy and then seek their support. The response was phenomenal. Sarkar successfully engaged the university community with a different approach to complement the association's work in raising awareness and gaining acceptance for an independent Bangladesh. There were people not only from the University community but also from outside. As a faculty member, Sarkar had the advantage of hooking up with the University's Student Union, which favored an independent Bangladesh, through the cooperation of the student-run communication vehicle, *The Sheaf.* Many volunteers joined hands to voice their concerns.

Using the Saskatoon Public Library exhibition area, the volunteers, under Professor Sarkar's guidance, put together the latest photographs they obtained from the field for a display collectively referred to as An Exhibition on Bangladesh: What, Why, and How. Included in a fascinating collage of photographs were not only the scenes of looting, burning, and killing by the Pakistani soldiers but also the formidable resistance of the freedom fighters in the outlying areas, along with the pictures of captured areas of "Occupied Bangladesh." It was as though the viewers suddenly woke up and paid extra attention to the tragic events unfolding overseas. A conglomeration of the latest news and photos attracted many visitors and generated comments, conversations, and support among the people of Saskatoon.

To complement the photo exhibition, another awareness session was held in which both Sarkar and Monoj Das, a concerned Bengali Canadian, talked about the Yahya government's ruthless attempt to suppress democracy, the positioning of the superpowers, and the future direction of the independence movement. There were four speakers, all of whom spoke on the independence of Bangladesh. "Where does the independence struggle stand today? What can Canadians do to aid the people of Bangla Desh?"[93] An emotional Sarkar, the chairman of the meeting and a fellow member of the University community, asked. Again, in his paper titled "Role of International Political Opinion in Solving the Bangla Desh Crisis," Professor Satya Sharma said, "Till the fight is won, the freedom movement will be alive."[94] Professor Bernard Lall spoke directly about the Nixon administration's dubious role in the conflict and its collaboration, "It was sad for the people of Bangla Desh to be killed by the American arms when America propagates and cherishes the idea of democracy, freedom, etc."[95]

Again, in his paper titled "Role of U.N. in the Bangla Desh Freedom Struggle," Professor Colwyn Williams, also president of the United Nations Association of Canada, warned fellow Canadians that "the entire episode and the after-effects might lead to another catastrophe in that region and might provoke another World War unless peace and normalcy are maintained."[96] The participants were outraged at the Nixon administration's secret role in shipping illegal spare parts.

Perhaps the strongest statement came from the last speaker—the architect of the seminar—Professor Sarkar himself. In a typical interactive fashion, Sarkar asked, "Why did the Pakistan government do it? Why did Mao support the bloodbath? Why has the United States supported the butcher, Yahya Khan?"[97] Having waited for a response and generating an immediate interest, Sarkar gave his take on the military's actions. "Nobody can stop the freedom movement in Bengal, and we, the Bengalees, will win in the long run, however strong the military might be," said a strong-willed optimist Sarkar in a prophetic note.[98]

The association's photo exhibitions and Teach-in on Bangladesh program in Saskatoon were practical means of "educating" the public by raising awareness among many who were not entirely up-to-date on the extent of ongoing military repression and the progress the Bengali rebel forces were making toward the liberation of Bangladesh.

In Regina, the BAS President, Dr. Anwar Chowdhury's right-hand man, was the University of Saskatchewan's Regina campus, Professor Hari Narayan Gupta, a Bengali from West Bengal, India. Although Abdul Hafiz, a radiologist, chose to distance himself from the activities of the Association and its sub-committees, he lent his short-wave radio to the Association to listen to the news from the field. This was their primary source of up-to-date information that allowed them to hear the news even before it came out in the print media. Despite differences of opinion between a few, they worked closely to maintain the group's solidarity, as observed by Dr. Anwar Haque, another active community member who frequently disagreed with many on several issues.[99] Just like their colleagues in Saskatoon, they directed their awareness and sensitization activities in the following three areas: (1) Teach-in on Bangla Desh, (2) photo exhibition, and (3) panel discussions, followed by questions and answers.

The most talked-about work of the BAS in Regina was the distribution of a succinct one-pager titled "Weep, Muslims, Weep," highlighting

Yahya's unleashing of his army on East Pakistan to seek a military solution to what he claimed to be the age-old Hindu-Muslim rivalry. Attributed to M. al Mughaimish, Chowdhury and Gupta were the only two in the entire University who knew about the letter's origin since they, having crafted the letter, kept the matter under wraps. Chowdhury sent copies of the flyer to several Heads of Muslim countries in the Middle East, intending to catch their attention. Urging them to save another Muslim country, the flyer stated, "It is very disturbing to see the president of Pakistan making a pathetic appeal to the religious sentiments of his people at a time when his troops were doing everything to brutalize Islam in Pakistani Bengal."[100] "The world of Islam has not seen a worse band of Munafiqs [hypocrites] than that Islamabad brood of imposters around Yahya Khan," [101] Chowdhury wrote pseudonymously.

Manitoba

Awareness-raising in Manitoba was limited since the Bengali segment of the Canadian public was very small. In 1971, Canadians of Indian and Pakistani backgrounds numbered 3,205 and 1,860 out of 988,250 Manitobans. Within days, Dr. Farid Shariff formed the Bangladesh Association of Manitoba. The key players in Manitoba were Drs. Farid Shariff (president), Abu Zahirul Alam (general secretary), Amir Ahsan (treasurer) and Nirmalandu Pal (joint secretary). The association had a two-pronged strategy—to raise awareness of the military repression and the consequent exodus of the frightened Bengalis so that it could lobby the government in favor of Bangladesh and raise money for the refugees in India.

Dr. Alam, general secretary of the Bangladesh Association of Manitoba, wrote an open letter in which he was, as though, in an interactive conversation with fellow Manitobans. He stated, "By now, you are undoubtedly aware of the wholesale slaughter and genocide of unarmed Bengalees—men, women, and children—by the West Pakistani military forces. To give you an unbiased and clear picture of the situation in East Bengal, we are sending you a copy of a paper by three renowned professors at Harvard University. We urge you, in the name of justice and humanity, to spare a few minutes of your time to read this paper. We believe that the facts contained in this paper will convince you of the just cause of the people of Bangla Desh."[102] Having ensured that it was free of jargon and gobbledygook, Alam appealed in plain language, "We firmly believe that the Canadians believe in the principles of justice, humanity, and democracy. We, therefore, request you to help us in our efforts to help the suffering humanity in whatever form you can."[103] Alam worked closely with the local India-Canada Association and received full cooperation from its President, Dr. Birandra Sinha.

In a sense, Manitoba was ahead of many other provinces in terms of awareness raising, mainly due to the work of the government. As early as May, Premiere Edward Schreyer took the initiative in raising awareness of the military repression and the consequent exodus of the Bengali refugees by proclaiming Friday, June 18, 1971, as the Pakistan Refugee Day "to give recognition to the plight and urgent need of our fellow men from East Pakistan."[104] In doing so, Schreyer appealed to every citizen in the province for its sympathetic observance and support. Manitobans supported the government as they regarded the issue as important and urgent. In addition, according to Oxfam Canada records, the government of Manitoba had a 'grant of $25,000 for Pakistani relief to be sent to Oxfam of Canada for the purchase of drugs and medical supplies."[105] The Manitoba Premier's announcement undoubtedly created conversation among Canadians about what Canada could do concerning the persecuted Bengalis. Naturally, Schreyer's announcement immediately made the public more empathetic toward the refugees who were facing a double tragedy - the management of the tidal wave disaster since 1970 and the ongoing military reprisals of 1971.

Ontario

With a population of 30,925 Indian backgrounds and 22,440 Pakistani backgrounds out of 7,703,105 Ontarians, naturally, there were more activities in Ontario than in any other province. With the Indo-Pakistani communities, there were also members of the mainstream communities who remained concerned.

Organizational Activities

The most significant work in Ontario was the activities of the Ottawa-based Bangladesh Association of Canada, which used an exciting bulletin that originated in London, UK, and found its way to Canadian cities through several pro-Bangladeshi Canadians. It contained the Address Speech to the Nation of the first acting prime minister of *Swadhin Bangla Desh* (Independent Bangla Desh), Tajuddin Ahmed, who urged Bengalis worldwide to remain united to demonstrate their solidarity. "Out of the ashes, a new Bangladesh will rise committed to peace, democracy, and social justice resting on the secure foundation of creed, language, culture, and race and held together by the shared experience of a struggle which must take its place in the epic struggles of our time,"[106] declared Ahmed. Also, flyers with excerpts of the acting prime minister's prophetic messages designed to instill in readers' minds a new sense of nationalism and a spirit of cooperation were distributed through random mail delivery. The most frequently referred piece of information was the one in which the acting prime minister said, "Pakistan is now dead and buried under a mountain of corpses"[107] This single but profound statement Ahmed made at the Bangladesh independence ceremony on April 17, 1971, captured the minds and hearts of Canadians.

Earlier, Stanley Burke, active in Biafran relief work, had been in touch with Rabi Alam, the spokesperson for the Bangladesh-Canada Association of Toronto. Together, they became involved in raising awareness among the public.[108] "The most important role in advising and supporting the Bangladesh independence struggle must be Mr. Stanley Burke, the retired CBC News anchor,"[109] wrote Alam, recalling his ongoing network with Burke and the news media in raising awareness. Alam and Burke spent hours together digging deep into how to reach out to Canadians—connecting Canadians with the news media and opinion-makers in the government's higher echelons with a view to lobbying and raising awareness. Burke emotionally appealed to Canadians with a simple, straightforward question, "Should citizens step into the conflict in Pakistan?"[110] "In many respects, it's Biafra all over again,"[111] observed Burke, for whom the situation was a case of déjà vu. Since earlier, the UN had already invoked Article 39 to intervene in Kashmir, Cyprus, the Middle East, Congo, Rhodesia (now Zimbabwe), and South Africa because there were issues that constituted a threat to peace, it should immediately intervene in the present case also, argued Burke. "By what combination of imagination and logic can it be argued that Pakistan is qualitatively different?"[112] asked an enraged Burke.

Again, in May, Alam and Burke organized a meeting at the National Press Club for Professor Rehman Sobhan (whose activities have already been described in the preceding heading under Regular Protest Demonstrations) to present his case for an independent Bangladesh. Earlier, one of Burke's articles titled "Voice of the People," published in the *Toronto Daily Star* on April 25, 1971, highlighted the need to assemble a group of personalities of international standing, leading experts, including the Nobel laureates, to hear evidence and make recommendations to governments of most concerned countries.

The East Pakistan Relief Fund Committee led by M. Zafar Quraishi represented the pro-Pakistani segment of the public. Having remained busy making disparaging remarks, he blamed Bongobondhu for everything and branded Bongobondhu as an agent of India. "The military action taken in East Pakistan was the result of disruptive activities by Mujib and his party, who deliberately misled the common man. Nobody likes violence. Mujib could have done a great deal of constructive work for Pakistan if he had wanted to become the legitimate prime minister. Today, he has to bear the guilt for the bloodshed and destruction of innocent people."[113] Quraishi's statement was thus reported in the *Toronto Daily Star*. The Canadian public, however, was not on the same page in this regard.

There is also a reference to a particular group that called itself the Committee for an Independent Bangla Desh under the leadership of Janet Paglia of Toronto. No further information is available on this group that appeared in Toronto and claimed its intention to mount a significant publicity campaign and set up similar committees in other major cities. The only reference to the committee's existence and objective was reported in the *Toronto Daily Star*, where it was mentioned that a committee "was being organized to pressure the federal government to help set up an independent nation in East Pakistan."[114] The emphasis was on a "free" and "democratic" Bangladesh.

In Toronto, another small group grew out of student volunteers at Glendon College, York University, that disseminated "educative" information materials. Calling itself the Operation Life-Line of the South Asia Crisis Committee, the group was primarily involved in raising awareness among the students and the public and molding public opinion in favor of Bangladesh. Its tabloid, titled People to People Campaign, reprinted many widely read articles, such as *"The Testimony of Sixty: The Toronto Declaration,"* in addition to writing pro-Bangladeshi articles. Joyce Denyer, in charge of the publication, wrote an appeal letter in which she obtained the signatures of several celebrities. Readers were touched by the sordid details, such as "Bangladesh bleeds profusely, continues to be raped and looted, and is laid waste."[115] The same group also brought out an in-house publication, a special newsletter titled *Pro Tem*, and a supplement to *The Student Weekly* of Glendon College, York University, that used the names, endorsements, and pictures of distinguished individuals like Stanley Burke, Sydney Schanberg, Peter Hazelhurst, and Senator Edward Kennedy who condemned the military regime has been sympathetic toward the Bengalis. None of them, however, endorsed an independent Bangladesh. We noted this in Chapter 3.

Again, a symposium titled *The Case for Bangla Desh* organized by the Bangladesh Association of Canada (Toronto) in partnership with the Detroit-based Bangladeshi Association was held on July 7 at the Assumption College of the University of Windsor campus. It attracted people from the neighboring cities of Windsor and the state of Michigan (United States). Among the main presenters were Professors Ron Inden (University of Chicago), Ralf Nicholas (Michigan State University), Peter Bertocci (Oakland University), and Azizul Huq Khondoker of the Bangla Desh Defense League (United States).

In the meantime, the media interviews of the MPs who went to India and Pakistan as Canadian delegates on a fact-finding mission were covered in the newspapers. The summary of their interviews by journalists in India was already made public by the Ottawa-based office of the High Commission of India. Also, Burke, who had been busy interviewing many returning from the subcontinent, chaired another meeting of four Canadians on August 5, 1971. It was arranged by the Bangladesh Association of Canada (Toronto), which had already been to Pakistan and India to observe the actual conditions in the country. They were Andrew Brewin, MP (NDP), Frederick Nossal of the Toronto Telegram, Paul Ignatieff of UNICEF Canada, and Lesley Smith, representing Oxfam Canada. Brewin warned the military government, saying that the exclusion from the government of the members of the Awami League, which had swept the polls, was no solution and would have serious consequences.

This meeting caused waves among the hardcore pro-Pakistanis, especially the members of the Pakistan Solidarity Committee. Having vehemently opposed the meeting, it carried out an immediate demonstration in support of Yahya's action. With the non-Bengali Pakistanis who opposed the meeting, there were two pro-Pakistani Bengalis who were referred to as "quislings" by the public. They considered themselves as loyalists or members of the pro-unity group. The demonstrators soon became unruly, although, with the arrival of the police, all demonstrators were dispersed. The pro-Bangladeshis, however, went ahead with the meeting, which had about four hundred people inside.

A typical meeting place for the volunteers and activists in the Toronto area was the Royal Bengal Restaurant at College and Jarvis Street, owned and operated by Abdus Samad, a Bengali Canadian. An ardent supporter of an independent Bangladesh, Samad gave the organizers *carte blanch* to use his business premises for meetings, retreats, and get-togethers to develop action plans for lobbying Canadian officials. Because of its location, the venue was conducive to the Association members. Samad regularly handed out photocopies of flyers, write-ups, and editorials of many pro-Bangladeshi newsletters.[116]

The Indian Student Associations across Canada were also active in promoting the cause of Bangladesh and did everything to counter the members of the Pakistan Students Associations. In a sense, neither the governments of Pakistan nor India maintained the diplomatic protocol. The Ottawa-based high commissions of India and Pakistan, represented by A. Raichaudhuri, public relations officer, and Toukir Hussain, second secretary, respectively, were directly involved in presenting each country's case to the Canadian public through the news media. The Indian high commission's office had a comprehensive citizen engagement strategy for pro-Bangladeshi Canadians throughout the liberation movement. Members of the Canada-Bangladesh Association and India-Canada Association (ICA) of various cities took full advantage of the multiple services and resources offered by the office of the High Commission of India. It printed and distributed flyers and news releases on behalf of pro-Bangladeshi groups. "It was realistically easy to disseminate all desired information packages quickly and effectively at no expense of the public or pro-Bangladeshi Associations," recalled Professor Mizan Rahman.[117]

The Indian High Commission also showed two documentaries titled "Refugees 1971" (Refugees from East Bengal) and "Prime Minister's Visit to India" (1971) on major university campuses. The first one was a presentation of refugees living in the most unhygienic conditions in refugee camps, having remained vulnerable to disease and death. The second one highlighted Prime Minister Pierre Trudeau's visit to India in January (1971), which depicted Canada's friendly relationship with India. Kewal Krishnan, who was in the information services of the high commission of India, talked about the denial of the political rights of the Bengalis and their exodus. Given the seriousness with which the Indian high commission was engaged, the result was an instant success in raising not only awareness but also disgust and revulsion against the Pakistani military regime engaged in the continual repression of civilians.[118]

Again, on August 15, on the twenty-fourth anniversary of Indian Independence Day, Indian High Commissioner Ashok Bhadkamker was the chief guest at a function organized by the Indian Students Association in Ottawa. It included a cultural show and a formal discussion on the refugee situation. The same day, in conjunction with the celebration of the Independence Day of India, the Toronto-based India-Canada Association also organized a gathering in which the NDP Brewin was a guest speaker who gave a talk titled "Right to Live, Liberty and Human Dignity concerning Pakistan-Bangla Desh Conflict." Many heard from what they regarded as the "horse's mouth." Brewin had been to India and Pakistan and, on many occasions, had identified himself with incredible aplomb with the Bengalis and their aspirations for democracy. Canadians appreciated his sympathy for the helpless Bengalis in fighting for their political and fundamental rights. He was seen as a "champion" for the cause of democracy and the end of military dictatorship in Pakistan.[119] Nevertheless, one cannot tell whether a forthright Brewin formally endorsed an independent Bangladesh or the establishment of democracy in a reformed Pakistan. It was a tad unclear.

By the beginning of fall, there were even more sensational accounts of people who had been to the scenes of carnage in East Pakistan. One important and widely distributed write-up was titled "Bangla Desh For Real" by Jack G. Lakavitch, who was there when the military moved in on March 25 and stayed there until the first week of May.[120] He referred to the glaring realities of Bangladesh. He observed, "Bangla Desh is no phantom... Bangla Desh is genuine, it exists, it is desperately fighting for its life... Bangla Desh is no game of obscure guerrillas. It is a life and death struggle for dignity and freedom for the East Bengali people."[121] There were also powerful editorials in the Bangladesh Association of Canada (Toronto) newsletter titled *Bangladesh*, which stated, "Bangladesh means freedom from economic exploitation. It means democracy in the truest sense of the word—rule of the people. It means a secular state where there will be equality for all."[122] This write-up was widely distributed across Canada.

Pro-Bangladeshi Student Groups

A few small pro-Bangladeshi student groups in Ontario also actively solicited their support for an independent Bangladesh. The Bangladesh Association of Toronto, in cooperation with the Caribbean Student Organization, held a successful symposium on October 26 at McMaster University. Two Bangladeshi delegates to the UN, M.A. Sultan, and S. Ahmed, spoke about the latest situation on the ground. The next day, on October 27, the Political Science Association of McMaster University also held a meeting to honor the same guests from Bangladesh. Although to the regime, it was as though everything was fine, hunky-dory, that was not the case, maintained one of the speakers. The participants viewed and perceived their guests as trusted individuals with verifiable information.

Again, Pakistani students at the University of Waterloo also arranged a discussion on the conflict in October at the Campus Centre Building. Both Bengalis and non-Bengalis representing the two wings of Pakistan jointly participated in the meeting—something that was rare at that time as the two groups everywhere else were at loggerhead. A non-Bengali student "gave a conciliatory talk proposing a confederation instead of complete separation,"[123] observed Maqsud Ali, a Bengali East Pakistani who was then a graduate student. Incidentally, Ali was also at the first demonstration in Ottawa in March. "The Pakistani army was already losing the battle as the freedom struggle intensified. The East Pakistanis felt Canada supported the liberation movement instead of the United States under the Nixon administration,"[124] recalled Ali his emotional speech and his satisfaction with Canada's sympathetic stand on the Bengali issue. By then, Ali observed that no one would listen to Yahya's patronizing rigmarole, "we-care-for-you" type assurance. In fact, according to him, many were finding the Yahya regime obnoxiously repetitive and untruthful. The Bengalis, in unison, objected to Yahya's using "coup de force." Naturally, Yahya remained the object of the Bengalis' profound repugnance, observed Ali.[125]

On November 5, the University of Windsor again arranged a talk by Stanley Burke on the current situation in Bangla Desh, or East Pakistan. Although the government of Canada did not use the word Bangladesh in any of its references, the Canadian public and news media had already been referring to East Pakistan interchangeably as Bangla Desh from the beginning of the Declaration of Independence. This remains an example of a vigorous and productive public discourse among the people of Canada, to whom freedom is indivisible.

Individual Efforts

Rabi Alam and his wife, Madeline Alam, the most notable couple in Toronto, networked with several organizations and distinguished Canadians. They reached out to the average Canadians who were not necessarily on the same wavelength in terms of their knowledge regarding the political impasse in Pakistan. "Our biggest challenge was to make Canadians fully aware of the true nature of the East-West Pakistan conflict and its roots; the genocidal activities perpetrated by the Pakistani army inside East Pakistan; and, of course, the misinformation, lies, and propaganda from the Ottawa-based Pakistan high commission." [126] Their activities ranged from talking to friends and neighbors to organizing informal discussions.

Again, Rabi Alam and Stanley Burke also worked closely with Dr. Wahidul Haque, a professor of Statistics at the University of Toronto. Fortuitously, Professor Haque happened to be in Dhaka on that fateful night of March 25 and witnessed the military takeover, ceaseless reprisals, and the flight of the frightened Bengalis to the Indian territory to seek asylum to avoid indiscriminate killings. Haque, too, crossed the border and made it to Kolkata, West Bengal, where he sought direct help from Dr. Amartya Sen and others. They helped him meet with high officials of the provisional government of Bangladesh. Haque also had a chance to discuss with Indian senior officials the issue of military aggression and the Bengalis' pledge to continue their fight for the liberation of Bangladesh. Upon his return to Canada, Haque shared his observations with the news media and community members.[127]

Haque remained in touch with Toronto's Action Committee volunteers as a resource person and became directly involved in raising awareness among fellow Canadians about the unjust military involvement in East Pakistan. Both Alam and Haque frequently teamed up to assess their progress in sensitizing the issue among Canadians. The most important part played by Haque was his return to India in August 1971 to meet with Tajuddin Ahmed, acting prime minister of the provisional government of Bangladesh. Haque briefed Ahmed on the activities of the pro-Bangladeshis and pro-Pakistanis in Canada, reactions of the larger public as well as the Trudeau administration's struggle with its problem in Québec and its inability to declare Canada's official position on the issue. Haque also had an opportunity to meet with

Lieutenant Colonel Ataul Gani Osmani (commander-in-chief of Bangladesh Forces), who gave him an idea of the actual progress of the *Mukti Bahini* (Liberation Forces). Again, after returning to Canada, Haque reported to the Canadian public through media interviews.[128]

There were a few more untiring couples: Jalaluddin Ahmed and his wife Shakila Jalaluddin (Ottawa), Azmat Ali and his wife Jahanara Ali (Ottawa), Lutful Kabir and his wife Bilquis Kabir (Ottawa), and Professor Mir Maswood Ali and his wife Suraiya Ali (London, Ontario), all of whom remained active all through 1971 in sensitizing the issue. A senior bureaucrat with the Department of Agriculture and Rural Development, Jalaluddin Ahmed was well known to political leaders like David Lewis and many MPs and media personalities like Stanley Burke. In the early fall, he arranged a meeting of concerned citizens in the Party Hall of his apartment on Prince of Wales Drive. Among the attendees were the Indian high commissioner, Ashok Bhadkamkar, a group of MPs, University professors, senior government officials, and members of the Bengali community.[129]

Shakila Jalaluddin played a significant role in mobilizing public opinion in favor of an independent Bangladesh in Canada and West Bengal, India. Before arriving in Canada in the late 1960s, Shakila was an MLA attached to the Ministry of Refugee and Relief, the government of West Bengal, India. In late summer, Shakila visited several refugee camps in India. Upon her return to Ottawa, she briefed the community on the dire needs of the refugees. Again, when Abha Maity, former minister of refugee and relief, the government of West Bengal, visited Canada in August, Shakila chaperoned her around and arranged for a community meeting about the ongoing military reprisals in "Occupied Bangladesh."[130]

When the gruesome detail of military reprisals began to filter in, both Azmat Ali and Jahanara Ali of Ottawa remained busy knocking on the neighbors' doors to get a sense of what they were doing about the army brutality in "Occupied Bangladesh." The couple was convinced that the Bengalis' fight for independence had an emotional resonance with the people they had been talking to. Encouraged by their reaction, the couple expanded their network and began sending letters, telegrams, and couriers to local and national political and church leaders. In the ensuing days, the Alis (Azmat and Jahanara) brought along Professor Luthful Kabir and his wife, Bilquis Kabir, who also arranged several rounds of informal meetings with neighbors to raise awareness by encouraging the members to speak their minds and offer comments. Again, Professor Maswood Ali and his wife, Suraiya Ali of London, Ontario, made frequent trips to Toronto and assisted the Toronto-based Bangladesh-Canada Association in organizing meetings to inform Canadians about what had been happening in East Pakistan. They were accompanied by Momin Chowdhury, who often found ways to broach the matter with the people in the neighborhood.[131]

Individually, Aziz Chowdhury, then a resident of a small twin city of Kitchener-Waterloo, frequently appeared on Canadian Broadcasting Corporation's (CBC) radio talk shows. Throughout the liberation war period, Chowdhury raised awareness among the residents of the Waterloo-Kitchener twin city about what was going on in "Occupied Bangladesh." Within days, Chowdhury became a household name. Although, to the Yahya regime, it was as though everything was hunky-dory, Chowdhury persistently pointed out that, in reality, that was not the case. This was Chowdhury's key message to Canadians. Every time Chowdhury spoke, he seemingly forged a powerful relationship with those who heard his narrative depicting the excruciating circumstances of the Bengali refugees in Indian refugee camps and those who had remained in "Occupied Bangladesh." Chowdhury would frequently refer to the tragic plight of the Bengali refugees, whom he saw as the largest migration in recorded history. This reinforced his forebodings and premonitions.

By summer, when there began an unprecedented exodus and the displacement of the Bengalis within the country, Chowdhury made an emotional appeal to the general public for financial support of the refugees in India. The delivery of Chowdhury's carefully crafted narrative made his listeners believe he was speaking from his heart. Within weeks, Chowdhury shot into the glare of the media.[132] Listeners looked upon Chowdhury as a trusted individual who soon came to be known to the residents of the Kitchener-Waterloo area as a knowledgeable reference librarian who had at his fingertips the latest news from overseas. For months, every morning, he would access the most up-to-date news from the Indian subcontinent through Kessing's Contemporary Archives and share it with anxious residents through the news media.

Québec

The Bangladesh Association of Québec in Montreal was also active in disseminating information and raising awareness among the Canadian public throughout the liberation war and following Bangladesh's independence.

The leading players were Professors Syed Muazzam Hussain of Sherbrooke Uninversité, Sadat Kazi of Vanier College, and Nurul Islam and Naiyyum Chowdhury, both of whom were then graduate students at McGill University. In his media interviews, Hussain explained the issue from the viewpoint of the Bengalis, who were the direct victims of military repression—a fact about which there was no dispute. Hussain frequently reproduced booklets, excerpts of news articles, and write-ups such as "An Account of Three Days of Carnage At Dacca University" (April 1971) collected by the Bangla Desh Association of Canada; "An Eye-Witness Account of The Events In Dacca, East Bengal, in March And April 1971" (by an American citizen living in Dhaka at that time),[133] and Peter Hazelhurst's analysis of the beginning of the crisis that first appeared in the *Times* of June 4, 1971.

Under Professor Hussain's supervision, the volunteers took the necessary time to package important information on the nature of the conflict, the root cause, military repression, and the strides the freedom fighters were making toward achieving an independent Bangladesh. "By and large, the public was fairly quick in understanding the political nature of the conflict and the military regime's unwillingness to transfer power to the elected representative," observed Naiyyum Chowdhury.[134] Although the military regime conveyed its narrative of the events, no one was ready to accept its balderdash. "People simply saw the military's claim as political rhetoric of a repressive military regime which was insensitive to the terrible sufferings of the millions of Bengalis who were being forced to flee to India. Millions of Bengalis were being rendered homeless in their homeland for which the same regime was directly responsible."[135] This was the key message the Bengalis tried to convey to the public, observed Professor Nurul Islam.

Atlantic Provinces (New Brunswick, Prince Edward Island, Nova Scotia, and Newfoundland and Labrador)

New Brunswick

No record of any kind is available regarding awareness-raising by the people of New Brunswick. It is understandable when one looks at the total population of New Brunswick, which was 634,555, of which 465 were of Indian background, while 340 were of Pakistani background. There are, however, instances of donation by several New Brunswick-based business organizations. We shall see that in Chapter 5.

Prince Edward Island (PEI)

A relatively more minor province, PEI had a population of 111,640, of which 135 were of Indian background while 120 were of Pakistani background. There is, however, some information on the activities of the residents of PEI, which was represented by Heath Macquarrie, Conservative MP for Hillsborough, PEI, who was also the PC Caucus Spokesperson on External Affairs. Macquarrie himself is credited for persuading the PEI government to declare the week of 15 August 1971 as the Pakistani Relief Week to sensitize the issue across the province.[136] The PEI residents, like the residents of other provinces, were aware of Sharp's jitters and discomfort, which precluded Canada from taking a declared position.

Following his return from the subcontinent as a Canadian delegate, Macquarrie held a meeting at Charlottetown Rotary, where he briefed fellow Canadians on the latest situation. He "talked about the tragedy and heartbreak of the people of East Pakistan," intending to engage the people of Canada in pressuring the government for intervention.[137] "This is probably the greatest human tragedy of this century and one which will need massive amounts of food, clothing, and money if there is to be any hope of relieving the situation even slightly," observed Macquarrie.[138]

Nova Scotia

Out of 788,960 Canadians in Nova Scotia, there were 1,350 Canadians of Indian origin, while there were 1,170 Canadians of Pakistani origin. There is no record of the public's activity for the first few months. It was only after the arrival of the dynamic couple, the Alams (Rabi and Madeline) from Toronto to Halifax, Nova Scotia, that they successfully gathered a few Nova Scotians to raise awareness about the ongoing military reprisals in East Pakistan. Alam, who was then manager of regional planning in the Province of Nova Scotia, mobilized opinion and gathered several Canadians who were outraged by the atrocities perpetrated by the military regime. The couple recalled organizing an information session for the public. In August, there was a group session on the humanitarian crisis with the Pakistani and Bengali communities at Dalhousie University. The seminar title was "Inside East Pakistan," co-sponsored by Oxfam Canada. Among the participants were a representative on behalf of the Pakistan high commissioner to Canada, Mike Fitzsimmons from Oxfam Canada, and a few representatives of some local NGOs. Robert Stanfield, then Conservative leader of the opposition from Halifax, Nova Scotia, sent his wishes to the participants for his sympathy toward the suffering Bengalis. The discussion was led by Johanne Aucoin, who represented Dalhousie University's student council.

The keynote speaker, Jack Lakavitch, who had witnessed the army brutality in March 1971, read from his write-up titled "Bangla Desh For Real." It was distributed to all participants. We have already noted Lakavitch's name while discussing the awareness activities of Ontarians. Many in other Canadian provinces were already in possession of Lakavitch's much-talked-about write-up regarding military reprisals in "Occupied Bangladesh." Having blamed the international community and individual countries who could make a difference, Lakavitch pointed fingers at the world governments and the UN. "Everyone is afraid to embarrass the Pakistan Government! Why? Why is the bloody Pakistan government, a mere handful of power-hungry generals, more important than millions of innocent people only desiring freedom? Why? Why? The Pakistan Government and Army have broken every possible civilized canon of behavior, it has violated and broken all the human rights charters ever devised by civilized men, and it has acted in the vilest and inhuman manner imaginable against the 75 million Bengalees who are supposed to be Pakistani citizens, something no longer possible. Yet the governments of all the civilized countries of the world are afraid of embarrassing the Pakistan Government."[139] There was an agreement among the participants that all possible resources must be committed to relieving the humanitarian suffering and pushing the peace processes forward. It was a heated discussion involving arguments and counterarguments. It was so heated that some participants became very aggressive, and the moderator had to warn a few of them, recalled Alam.

While the pro-Pakistani groups condemned Oxfam Canada's initiatives, the pro-Bangladeshis viewed them as a step forward in their cause. This gave the pro-Bangladeshis hope to continue their work to persuade the public.

Newfoundland and Labrador

In 1971, out of 522,100 Canadians in Newfoundland and Labrador, 460 Canadians were of Indian origin, while 310 were of Pakistani background.

At that time, there was no formal association for Bengali-speaking Canadians in the province simply because there were only a handful of Bengalis. However, the Bengali-speaking Canadians of the St. John's area immediately formed an informal group under the leadership of Dr. Moyeenul Islam, who was then a resident of St. John's. Islam and his wife, Meherun Nissa, remained active. The Islams had four more players, Drs. Mohammed Abdul Matlib, his wife Mahbuba Matlib, Wali Khan, and his wife Cristeta Khan played an essential part in raising awareness. "Being a very small community, we did not form any committee, association, or organization, but most of us met regularly," intending to exchange information.[140] Thus, observed Islam. He made every effort to keep the people of St. John's up-to-date. Under Islam's supervision, the Bengalis of St. John's frequently distributed pro-Bangladeshi publications and handy-dandy hand-written write-ups on the Yahya regime's diabolical plans to subjugate the Bengalis. Even though the military regime talked about a political solution in Pakistan as late as the fall, the public never became enthused with the idea as they were suspicious of the perfidiousness of the military regime, recalled Matlib and his wife, Mahbuba Matlib.[141]

According to Matlib, having known about the vagueness with which the military regime demonstrated its commitment, the public did not take its declaration seriously.[142] It was as though the public was brought up to speed, having become convinced of Yahya's evil machination, recalled Matlib.[143] His observation was that the public looked upon the Bengalis with compassion as they were seen to be the sheer victims of military revenge and economic discrimination. To the public who followed the news trail very closely, "it was clear that Pakistan was on its way to being dismantled while Bangladesh was soon to be a reality."[144] Thus, Islam recalled those dreadful days and their efforts to raise awareness among the province's people. Islam added, "Although the reactions of the Canadian government toward Bangladesh were cool, aloof, and non-committal until the very end, I had found the local Canadian colleagues at my place of work sympathetic, and they had warm feelings toward me."[145]

Although years have passed, all three - Islam, Khan, and Matlib - remember what they believed Yahya was doing, stretching the truth and that he was not going to tell it like it was. They warned the people of St. John's to remember that Yahya's announcement of the "civilianization" program and the gesture of "amnesty" was nothing but window dressing, a part of a continuing plan to keep from the world the facts, some of which were already out to the world. Dr. Wali Khan observed that, since the information they provided included descriptions along with pictures of firing and mass graves, death, destruction, and execution of university professors, readers were outraged reading about the military reprisals of such magnitude. The distribution of pertinent documents assisted a great many Newfoundlanders in understanding the complex political history and the current situation in a convincing manner that persuaded them to look at the Bengalis' cause with a note of sympathy, observed Dr. Khan.[146]

Whether in British Columbia or Newfoundland, one of the value-added advantages of the frequent distribution of critical factual and analytical write-ups was the complementary nature of their contents. Interested readers cross-checked them against what they saw on the television or heard on the radio. Every time readers read a write-up, they could almost instantly conjure up images of the distressed refugees in dark, squalid, and muddy refugee camps. The sensitization activities contributed to national awareness of the obligation to help with a sense of joint responsibility. Canadians of Bengali origin remained persistent in their demand that it was time to act on the reality of Bangladesh.

Fundraising Activities in Various Provinces

Chapter 5 shows detailed fundraising activities undertaken by Canadian nongovernmental organizations (NGOs) from coast to coast. Below are instances of fundraising activities by members of the public through various community organizations in Canada by province.

British Columbia

In 1971, the population of BC was 2,184,620, out of which 18,790 were of Indian background, while 16,355 were of Pakistani origin. Given the size of the Indo-Pakistani Canadians in BC, there was quite a bit of activity. The first successful fundraising seminar in Vancouver, for which there is some documentary evidence, took place on October 8, 1971. Organized jointly by the Vancouver Peace Action League, the United Nations Associations, and the Vancouver Labour Council under the chairmanship of Reverend James Roberts, a Catholic priest in the Archdiocese of Vancouver, a seminar was held at the Christ Church Cathedral in Vancouver. The keynote speaker was Dr. Usha Mahajani, a professor of Political Science at Central

Washington University, who came from across the border. Her speech titled Pakistan, Bangla Desh, and the Future of Humanity generated mind-boggling questions among enthusiastic participants who inquired about civilianization and democratization in Pakistan. Having heard about the military regime's demonic actions on unarmed civilians, participants took umbrage at what they heard. While the seminar was going on, organizers collected contributions for the suffering refugees in India.[147] However, there is no record of how much money was raised.

The Bangladesh Association of BC organized the second event in collaboration with the Bangladesh Students Association of UBC. A dynamic Dr. Shafiqul Haque Khan, general secretary of the association, through cooperation from Dr. Philip White, Dean, Commerce, and Business Administration, UBC, organized a week-long activity during the week of November 15–19, 1971, as the "Bangladesh Week," which included a door-to-door campaign to collect money. Interestingly, unlike all other Associations and provincial governments that generally named their initiative something like "Pakistan Refugee Day," the BC organizers called it "Bangladesh Week." Dr. Lutfor Rahman and Sudhir Saha recalled the enthusiasm of the student volunteers and University community members who came forward to show their support for the victims of military reprisals. The UBC's "Bangladesh Week" is an example of a combined initiative that included fundraising and awareness-raising. The organizers, however, could not recall the money they raised fifty-two years ago.

The third example is British Columbia's Chilliwack East Pakistani Refugee Committee, which was struck to raise funds in the Chilliwack area. It worked closely with Sundar Rajan, then Oxfam Canada's Regional Director for British Columbia, to whom it handed over a cheque for $13,034.[148]

Again, the sale of Bangladeshi postage stamps as a historic souvenir was another additional attraction initiated by Dr. Khan himself in Vancouver. Through his contact with a few representatives of the provisional government of Bangladesh in India, Khan obtained copies of Bangladeshi postage stamps in late November, which became a hot sale. The stamp collectors and ordinary enthusiastic pro-Bangladeshis became interested in procuring these stamps. They did not necessarily purchase them simply for their philatelic value but for the sake of the history of Bangladesh that was in the making. Soon, there were demands for more from other associations as the souvenir stamps generated much interest among the people, who were fascinated by the idea of having them as keepsakes. While there is no record of how much money was raised following the campaign across BC, Khan recalled his correspondence with the London-based Medical Association of Bangladesh about the proceeds he sent to the Bengali refugee students in West Bengal, India.

Alberta

The population of Alberta was 1,627,875, out of which 4,440 were of Indian background, while 3,215 were of Pakistani origin. Fundraising in Alberta, for which there are some records, was confined to the province's two major cities, Edmonton and Calgary. In Edmonton, the fundraising was limited to a week-long collection drive to donate articles, such as winter clothing, canned and dry food, etc. A charity show of sitar recital by Pandit Ravi Shankar, the famous Sitar maestro, was a great success, recalled Samir Mazumdar. However, he does not remember how much money they raised forty years ago.[149] There were spontaneous donations mainly from the members of the University community who were sympathetic to the cause of the Bengalis.

Individually, Siddique Hussain, then a teacher with the Edmonton School Board and president of the Bangladesh Canada Association of Alberta, relied on Abdul Mannan, then a graduate student at the University of Alberta, who gave him a hand. Together, they went from door to door for donations in cash or kind. The pro-Bangladeshi community received financial support from the entire Indian community. Interestingly, a few Pakistani community members offered donations to the refugees. Professor Salim Qureshi of the Department of Political Science, University of Alberta, a Canadian of Pakistani origin, openly condemned the military aggression on unarmed Bengalis. He assisted the Bengali community in collecting donations. "There did not seem to be any problem in each other's interaction even with those who were pro-unity and opposed to the creation of an independent Bangladesh,"[150] recalled Hussain.

Again, under the leadership of Hakim Sikander, president of the Bangladesh Association of Alberta (Calgary chapter), a small team of dedicated volunteers successfully raised donations in cash or in-kind through various social activities in Calgary. "We met every evening after dinner and went from house to house in the Dalhousie and Brentwood neighborhood, explaining the purpose of collecting old clothes for the victims of the War of Liberation of Bangladesh to prevent death and exposure during the winter months."[151] Thus, Sikander recalled the overwhelming response to the clothing drive they undertook. All collected items were sent to Chicago, and Air India hoped to pick them up. Unfortunately, the boxes sat in storage for weeks (for paperwork regarding shipment) until Sikander was informed that he would have to pay for the boxes. It was then decided to give them away to some old clothing banks in the Chicago area for the poor. "In those years, there was no social media or other means of communication to connect with the larger body of supporters outside the city or country,"[152] wrote Danielle and Hakim Sikander.

According to Sikander, participation in the ethnic food fair at the Jubilee Auditorium in July, having a booth of its own, separate from the Pakistan-Canada Association's booth, was the most noteworthy achievement. At their initiative, the team members' spouses, Danielle Sikander, Masuma Anwar, Rowshan Kazi, and Anjali Samir, volunteered their time—they made snacks for sale. Again, a persistent Dr. Kazi Islam, having taken a lead role, was successful in hooking up with Pandit Ravi Shankar for a performance in Calgary for the Bangladesh Relief Fund (BRF). "It was a great success judging by the sale of tickets at the time,"[153] observed Sikander. An emotionally sympathetic Shankar was delighted to participate in the evening and donate the proceeds. Apart from the Bengali communities, many from other communities also came forward to raise money. Notable among the donors were many West Bengalis and other Indians, some Sikh medical specialists, university professors, European immigrants, and several mainstream Canadians. Although the proceeds were sent to the prime minister's National Relief Fund (India) to relieve East Pakistani refugees in India, the Sikanders could not recall the money they had raised. No record is available in this regard.

Saskatchewan

The population of Saskatchewan was 926,245, out of which 1,625 were of Indian background while 1,250 were of Pakistani origin. Though a relatively small community, the people of Saskatoon showed creative ways to tap into various sources to raise awareness and funds. By the time the appeal was made, the people of Saskatchewan had already been sensitized to some extent. As mentioned, the people of Saskatchewan generally appreciated Premier Allen Blackney's proclamation of September

5 to 11,1971, as the "Pakistan Refugee Relief Week."[154] As a result, they were moved by the pathetic situation of the Bengali victims of military repression.

Professor Asit Sarkar, as already noted, played a crucial role in pulling together the residents of Saskatoon and the University of Saskatchewan community members through the University's student union. "The Indians are not responsible for the situation and should not have to pay for it," and "Canada along with other nations should join hands."[155] Thus, Shushil Bhattacharjee appealed in the university's newsletter, *The Sheaf*. He then continued, "Any contribution from the young people of Canada, both students and teachers, will be welcomed by those working to achieve the goal of an independent Bangla Desh."[156] Arguing that "soon the refugees became a burden and a liability on India,"[157] Bhattacharjee underscored that, in the name of humanity, all freedom-loving Canadians should support India in cash or kind in the gigantic task of caring for the refugees in desperate need.

Again, in Regina, using his residence at 1220 Jubilee Avenue as the office of the BAS, its president, Dr. Anwar Chowdhury, and his team networked with Regina residents. Instantly, the volunteers began to raise funds for the refugees before launching a formal appeal. Under Chowdhury's guidance, the team became active in "doing" its bit for the victims of military reprisals. Chowdhury developed the Association's work plan and communication tools that included a flyer with a description of the plight of the refugees who were hurriedly leaving "Occupied Bangladesh" and heading for India to avoid military revenge. The volunteers held frequent meetings to determine their steps to approach the people of Regina and make a humble contribution to the best of their ability.

The fundraising team kept the local Oxfam Canada director, Donald Sheridon, in the loop so as not to duplicate their efforts. Together, the people of Regina collected donations in cash or in-kind from the people around for the refugees in India. One of the volunteers, Fazal Dar, a Canadian of Kashmiri origin and a friend of Tarek Ali, a leftist Pakistani student activist, managed to bring Pandit Ravi Shankar to a concert at Wascana Park in Regina. They received full cooperation from the local churches. No one recalled the amount of proceeds they collected. They only remember that the concert proceeds were sent to India's prime minister's National Relief Fund. However, before sending the money, there were some debates among the community members who argued and counterargued about how and where the donations should be sent. Having disagreed with the rest of the group, Dr. Anwar Haque stepped down from the position of treasurer but continued to work with the rest of the volunteers in other capacities.[158]

Like Dr. Khan of Vancouver, Dr. Haque added a new attraction to their fundraising drive by introducing the sale and display of Bangladeshi postage stamps as a historic souvenir. Through his contact with the representatives of the provisional government of Bangladesh in India, Haque obtained many of the first series of historic Bangladeshi postage stamps. Instantly, the souvenir stamps became one of the most fabulous mementos for stamp collectors and ordinary pro-Bangladeshis, who were delighted to purchase those memorable stamps for keepsakes. Dr. Haque recalled sending $1,500 to the Bangladesh Medical Association, London.[159]

Manitoba

Under the leadership of Dr. Farid Shariff, president of the Bangladesh Association of Manitoba, there was one single initiative, a cultural show, in the area of fundraising, for which there are some archival records. Though not a large group, Drs. Farid Shariff, Mohammed Tayaab, Amir Ahsan, Abdul Mannan, Birendra Sinha, Abu Zahirul Alam, Snehesh Kumar Sinha, along with his wife Rubena Sinha, and others, such as Ashim Roy, Rajat Mukherjee, Nirmal Pal, Samar Maitra, and Prabir Kumar Mitra, were actively involved.

In particular, Rubena Sinha, an active Bengali-speaking Canadian of West Bengali origin, was directly involved in the association's cultural programs. "Everyone who spoke Bengali became one, regardless of their boundaries. We felt we had to do something when we saw in the news and heard that so many people were in distress."[160] Thus, Sinha wrote about her participation and the group's solidarity. She was in charge of organizing and delivering a variety show called Bichitra. Her right-hand person was Hamida Akhtar Begum, then a PhD student at the University of Manitoba. Rubena worked closely with her husband Snehesh Sinha in bringing together several groups, such as Sarasomer Israeli dancers, sitarist Kalpana Mitra and Dr. Birandra Sinha, Indian classical dancers, and Madame Grandpierre to do a flamenco and ballet duet (where Rubena herself was the flamenco dancer) while Snehesh Sinha was on tabla.

Hamida Begum remained busy spreading the word around throughout the campus. She spent weeks preparing and distributing flyers to the campus community. They needed to create a budget in which they meticulously identified the details of the items that would be deemed as cost and items that would bring money. "Many people came, milled around, saw the show, and exchanged views," [161] observed Hamida. She also recalled that the auditorium at St. Mary's Academy, where the function took place on June 13, 1971, was packed to the brim. The number of attendees, the sign-up, and the pledge sheets for follow-up purposes gave the organizers a pretty good idea about the outcome of their initiative, which they considered a success.

At that time, each association was left responsible for disbursing the money as there was no standard channel for sending money. Some people sent their money through Mustafizur Rahman Siddiqi, head of the Bangla Desh Mission in Washington, and two of his active team members, Enayat Karim and Syed Muazzem Ali. In contrast, some sent money through the London-based medical association. Dr. Shariff, however, chose to send the money to the New Delhi-based Central Relief Committee for Refugees from East Pakistan. With a great deal of satisfaction and a sense of worthwhile achievement, yet with humility, he dashed off a few lines to his partners across the border to keep them in the loop regarding the variety show on June 13, 1971. "We are pleased to enclose a bank draft of $1,015.00 [one thousand and fifteen dollars, US]. We appreciate the work you are doing for the people of East Bengal. This is more of a token of our feelings, and we hope this amount, however small, could help alleviate part of the sufferings of the Bengali people."[162] In another letter, Dr. Shariff was even more specific about where exactly the money was supposed to be spent, stating, "We raised over $1,000 and forwarded an amount of $1,015 to the central relief committee for refugees from East Bengal on June 22, 1971, to contribute toward providing two ambulances for the refugees."[163]

Archival records in the Massachusetts-based Bangladesh Association of New England also indicate that, in addition to the above, the Bangladesh Association of Manitoba had sent another $2,000 to Bangladesh separately.

When, in the fall, the Washington Mission learned about the knowledge gaps of the pro-Bangladeshis in Canada about the channeling of money, Syed Muazzem Ali, then third secretary, immediately contacted Dr. Shariff on behalf of Siddiqi and explained the process relating to the deposit, collection, and disbursement of funds in the United States and Canada. He referred to the two types of accounts they had in place - the first one was called Bangladesh Mission A/C No 2, which was "meant for all contributions intended to assist the liberation struggle." In contrast, the second type of account was Bangladesh Mission-Relief, which was meant for relief.[164] Shariff immediately shared this helpful information with his counterparts in other provinces. From this time onward, Ali remained in touch with the presidents of all the Bangladeshi associations across Canada. He counseled them regarding fundraising, disbursement of the proceeds, and ongoing lobbying for Bangladesh. Ali played a crucial role in this regard as a liaison person between the United States and Canada.

Ontario

A fair amount of documentation exists concerning various organizational and individual fundraising drives, mainly in Ontario's two major cities, Toronto and Ottawa.

Organizational Activities

As a spokesperson of the Bangladesh-Canada Association (Toronto), a creative Rabi Alam remained active throughout the liberation period. He was instrumental in signing a memorandum of understanding (MOU) with A. Prakash, secretary of the India-Canada Association of Toronto, on July 23, 1971. The two agreed that a certain number of Indian movies would be shown at the Odeon Theatre in Toronto and that the proceeds would be sent to India for the Bengali refugees. Within weeks of signing the MOU, arrangements were made for several shows. The first showing of a widely acclaimed Satyajit Ray's 35 mm film titled *Dui Konna* (Two Daughters) with English subtitles at the Odeon Theatre at Danforth and Pape took place in Toronto on August 26, 1971. Though a Bengali movie, many from the mainstream came to watch the show mainly to express their solidarity with the suffering refugees. This remains an example of a successful partnership between the Bangladesh-Canada Association (Toronto) and the India-Canada Association. The audience of various backgrounds saw this as a way to make their humble contribution. Although it was a weekday (Thursday), the organizers arranged four shows from 2:00 p.m. to 9:30 p.m. to accommodate people with different schedules.

Volunteers from different communities collected donations and exchanged news and views between breaks. Among those present were Andrew Brewin, MP from Greenwood; Stanley Burke, a TV commentator and Oxfam Canada's executive committee member; Jack Grant, a millionaire businessman and philanthropist, and Murti Devata, chairman of the joint committee, the East Bengal Refugee Committee. Brewin "urged cooperation among Canadians for the cause" and said the "people should consider themselves privileged to be associated"[165] with an initiative of this kind. Encouraged by the Torontonians' enthusiastic response and seeing the first show's success, additional shows were arranged by some other groups.

The same paper also wrote about the upcoming show: "The Suman Kalyanpur soirée is scheduled to be this month's dollar earner."[166] The India-Canada Association referred to the week-long shows, stating that it had sent another $2,000 to the East Bengal Refugee Relief Fund of Oxfam Canada.[167] Those involved in fundraising became very creative, having found ways to involve new volunteers. "Their activities have ranged from door-to-door collections, fundraising at shopping plazas, and intensive drives for clothing. It is planned to have at least one major fundraising campaign a month."[168] Thus, the *Canadian India Times* of September 1971 issue reported the event.

In the meantime, fundraising activities of the South Asia Emergency Refugee Fund, mainly through the initiative of the community members of Glendon College, then an affiliate of York University in Toronto, got off the ground in late fall under the stewardship of Joyce Deneyer. This was a time when the Bengali refugees were still fleeing from the horrors of one of the bloodiest civil conflicts, reaching almost nine million in Indian camps.[169] The campaign focused on a holistic approach through "education." The foremost effort was to unite the college community, consisting of students, staff, and faculty members who joined under one single banner - People to People Campaign. With an impressive logo, Please Lend a Hand and Save a Life, it urged Canadians to demonstrate compassion and generosity. Deneyer emotionally appealed, "Consider that thirty-three cents a day feed a Bengali refugee. Thirty-three cents is not beyond the means of an average Canadian. This could then be applied on a family level to adopt an East Pakistani family. Actions such as these coordinated with a community effort could ensure the survival of many otherwise doomed people. Families, churches, groups, students, children, and PEOPLE can give up one meal for one day a week and be part of the People to People Campaign."[170]

Again, Larry Tubman, Oxfam Canada's assistant director, wrote to Professor Mizan Rahman, general secretary of the Ottawa-based Bangladesh

Association of Canada in the following: "Oxfam is most grateful to you and your fellow members of the Bangla Desh Association of Canada for your generous support of our efforts on behalf of the refugees for the East Pakistan crisis and looks forward to meriting your continued assistance."[171] Oxfam Canada's volunteer Leslie Smith, then a senior public servant at the Department of National Health and Welfare, also made personal sacrifices by giving his own time. Having volunteered and sacrificed his vacation, he went to India on behalf of Oxfam Canada and determined the refugees' drug and sanitation needs. He developed a list of essential pharmaceutical items for the refugees and coordinated an extensive collection of necessary items marked for donations from Canadian pharmaceutical companies.

Individual Activities

As mentioned, Abdus Samad, the owner of the Royal Bengal Restaurant, then the only Bengali (East Pakistani) restaurant in Toronto, was the first person in the restaurant business to offer his premises for meetings. "We used to come to the Restaurant all the time for our regular meetings to discuss how best we could raise awareness and funds for the refugees,"[172] recalled Ahsanullah Mullick. With Mullick was Chaitanya Keshavrao Kalevar, a non-Bengali Canadian of Indian origin and one of the most active members of the Canadian public involved in fundraising and awareness-raising. Keeping up the spirit of camaraderie that the media had already built up, Kalevar successfully involved the restaurant's workers and customers. Samad and his team were exemplary in taking a bold step by giving up a part of their income (daily tips). He asked the organizer, "Send me a signed reading, don't tip us, and donate to Pakistani relief."[173] No records show how much money was collected over the months. Mullick, active in 1971, recalled their efforts in inviting clients to visit Samad's restaurant and how their clients used to donate their last pennies but cannot recall the total amount of money they raised.

Again, Rabi and Madeline Alam, who remained active in the Toronto area, also sent out appeal letters to each chapter of the Bangladesh-Canada Association of various cities with reprints of analytical newsworthy articles related to the Bengalis' struggle for independence. They also sent recent write-ups describing the wanton destruction of human lives, the tragic situations on the ground, the context of democracy, and the violation of human rights. "Time and again," observed Alam, "the association presidents reiterated the same message that money was being sought because money was the means to an end."[174] There is also impressive evidence of volunteers who seemed to know the essential values and approaches that underpin good fundraising. When the students of Madeline Alam learned about the ongoing military reprisals and the plight of the refugees in India, they, too, raised money for the victims under her supervision.[175]

Mizan Rahman recalled how Ottawa's Bengali-speaking Canadians were committed to raising money for the freedom fighters as soon as they heard about the declaration of independence, "We decided to contribute 5 percent of our take-home income every month, which we did with no questions asked. There was no hesitation on the minds of any of us when the collection time used to come at the beginning of every month."[176]

Personally, Masuda Ahsanullah made a trip to India to hand over the money they raised in Ottawa. She recalled handing a cheque directly to Hussein Ali, the first-defected Bengali diplomat in Kolkata, West Bengal, but cannot recall how much they raised. However, she remembers the enthusiastic response from the community.[177] "It was as though the fundraising teams knew how the people of Canada looked upon donation at the time they were approached - giving whatever one could to help a refugee in dire need in India," recalled Azmat Ali and Jahanara Ali.[178]

The written materials they prepared for fundraising did not need to look slick and high-powered. Still, they needed to look pleasant and easily read, catching readers' immediate attention in the first second or two and blocking out the distractions. At its heart, it was one individual giving another, observed Ali.[179] They made every effort to combine words and pictures skillfully weaving into the story of military reprisals on unarmed civilians that would hold the Canadian public spellbound and inspired. "It was a challenge to remain consistent and yet engage the public at an emotional level to ensure that no one went overboard" and that "they all sang from the same song sheet," recalled Professor Lutful Kabir of Carleton University and his wife, Bilquis Kabir.[180]

There are also some records of another initiative by two distinguished members of the McMaster University faculty, Dr. Rajat Bhaduri and Dr. George J. Sorger. They raised funds under the name of Refugee and Fund for the Bengali victims in the Indian refugee camps. Through purely individual efforts, they launched a campaign throughout the Greater Hamilton area from June 10 to 23, 1971. The two men, accompanied by a group of young volunteers, went canvassing in the surrounding communities—Hamilton,

Burlington, Ancaster, Dundas, Stoney Creek, and Winona. On behalf of the committee, Hamilton Mayor Victor K. Copps presented a cheque for $1,300 to Mike Ryan, Oxfam Canada director for Ontario.[181] This may be seen as an example of cooperation among various groups and individual public members that worked horizontally with their local NGO chapters. As well, in the Kitchener-Waterloo area, there were Nathan Garber and Norma Sen Gupta, who spent an excessive amount of time organizing a free concert performed by Corry Bryant at Bandshell, Waterloo, Ontario, in aid of Oxfam's Pakistan Refugee Fund.[182]

Again, there was another way in which money was raised through the personal appeal of the Canadian Holy Cross Brother Raymond Cournoyer, Oxfam Canada's field director for Eastern India and East Pakistan. Many members of the Canadian public made instant contributions each time Brother Cournoyer made a national appeal through press conferences in Montreal and Toronto. His efforts have been detailed in Chapter 5 under Oxfam Canada. Whenever Cournoyer spoke, he immediately connected with the audience through life stories. His visits to Canada from the ground made him known to Canadians as an articulate advocate of refugees. The power of storytelling was one of Cournoyer's fortes - an approach that enabled him to get everyone on the same page.

Unsurprisingly, Brother Cournoyer caused waves in the news media. The people around were touched by a letter of appeal from a Kenora resident who broached the story of Brother Cournoyer's frequent appearance on television. *The Free Press Weekend* of Montreal also published a heart-rending story titled "A Man in the Middle of Miser," in which the writer expressed his gratitude, saying that it was reassuring to know that the people of Kenora, like Brother Cournoyer, were "very concerned with the condition of men" in India.[183]

The public was touched by the domino effect that Cournoyer created following his frequent appearances and appeals "to prevent a disaster of monumental proportions."[184] There was yet another exciting undertaking called the PEP (Pennies for East Pakistan) project initiated by a Kenora resident, Ellen Ronning, who arranged to sell cupcakes and donuts that she baked in a small town in Kenora, Ontario. Inspired by the stories circulated following Brother Cournoyer's media appearances, Ronning's PEP project instantly drew people's attention. As soon as she left the cupcakes for the staff members at the premises of the Miner News, the Woods Clinic, Eaton's, the Bank of Nova Scotia, and the Royal Bank of Canada, the word got around within the hour; many rushed to chip in for the cause. Encouraged by the astounding response, Ronning baked more cupcakes, resulting in a collection of $55.39 in two days.[185]

Québec

There is no documentary evidence of fundraising by the public, although some active members of the Bangladesh Association of Québec claim to have been involved informally in raising funds for the refugees. "The first thing we did was to raise some funds, whatever meager it was, to help our fellow citizens in the affected areas,"[186] recalled Nurul Islam. Sadat Kazi, who was active from the beginning, recalled assuming responsibility for organizing meetings to raise funds and awareness. He talked about using direct response marketing techniques, such as direct mail, telephone calls, and walk-a-thons, to cultivate donors. He also remembered how the volunteers found unique ways to approach the same pool of donors in the Montreal area with a new approach.[187] Unfortunately, Kazi did not remember the amount of money they raised.

Again, according to Naiyyum Chowdhury, then general secretary of the association, since some of the published reports carried many eyewitness accounts and testimonies, they helped Canadians see how the refugees were being exposed to cholera and typhoid.[188] This, according to Chowdhury, coupled with the repeated calls for contributions in cash or in-kind together by their favorite persona, the Holy Cross Brother Cournoyer, with the graphic picture of the refugees, touched the minds of the people of Canada.

New Brunswick

The only available documentary evidence from the province of New Brunswick is a letter written by Bob Hawkes of Mount Allison University, Sackville, NB, to the NDP federal office in which Hawkes talked about the university's intention to be involved in the "Pakistan-Bangla Desh Crisis," "Our aims are twofold—to provide relief aid for the refugees and to urge our government to seek a political solution to the problem. We are tentatively planning a 'teach-in' weekend in the third week of January as one step in our program."[189] A follow-up letter from Brewin, who responded to Hawkes, stated that the MPs would be interested in attending any such program to raise money and sensitize the university community depending on their time availability in January 1972. Unfortunately, no more information is available in the file in this regard. In any event, with the surrender of the Pakistani army to the Allied forces on December 16, 1971, Bangladesh became an independent country.

Prince Edward Island

There is some record of fundraising activities in Prince Edward Island (PEI). Earlier, Conservative MP Heath Macquarrie of PEI had invited Dr. Robert McClure, who was on the Oxfam Canada Board, to visit PEI when Dr. McClure traveled across Canada. Accordingly, during his visit to PEI, McClure made a unique appeal to the province's people and urged, "If every person in Canada were to give just one dollar, this country would contribute something worthwhile to the plight of the refugees."[190] Having described the tragedy in plain and straightforward language, the newspaper gave a positive spin to Dr. McClure's appeal and wrote, "We are sure that most readers will concern themselves with his appeal and will do whatever they can afford to do in the way of donation."[191] Unfortunately, there is no further information in this regard.

Nova Scotia

There is no documentary evidence of any fundraising activity in Nova Scotia.

Newfoundland and Labrador

There is some information on fundraising activities in St. John's, Newfoundland and Labrador. "Two percent of our salary was set aside monthly for the Bengali refugees," observed Dr. Matlib.[192] He also recalled the enthusiasm of Dr. Wali Khan, who came up with this idea first and convinced the rest of the group. Khan volunteered to pay more than 2 percent of his income to top up the monthly collection, recalled Matlib.[193] Initially, there was much discussion about where and to whom the money should be sent. Later, it was decided that the money would be sent to Justice Abu Sayeed Chowdhury, Bangladesh's London representative. There was no disagreement among the group members in this regard. They continued to send their contribution for some time, even following the liberation of Bangladesh, recalled Dr. Matlib. [194]

A Random Snapshot of the Public's Positive Response to the Appeals

- Colin Chisholm, president of the Students' Council at St. Mary's Junior High School in Medicine Hat, Alberta, collected sixty-three dollars through its "penny chain," which it created along with a homeroom contest held to aid the project.
- Under the initiatives of Miss Vera Baxter, Librarian at Essex Senior School (Toronto), a small group of students, she raised ten dollars for the victims of military assault.
- "After reading Ernest Hillen's article about the Pakistani refugees and the work done by our Canadian, Mr. R. Cournoyer, I feel I just had to send a little donation. My day's pay (thirty-five dollars), therefore. This year goes to the work of Oxfam among the Pakistan refugees. Miss E. M. Fellett, Toronto."
- William Dennison, then mayor of the City of Toronto, sent two cheques totaling $263.92, "which was contributed by the staff of the city hall to aid the plight of the Pakistani refugees flooding into India."
- "A little girl in Brampton sent us one dollar, which represented the entire proceeds of her freshie sale, and a woman in Morrisburg, Ontario, donated two dollars won at a horticultural show."[195]

These are only a few examples of how instantly the public responded to the appeal for donations with kindness, empathy, and concern for the helpless refugees. Given the grave situation and, on the ground of simple humanity, donations poured in throughout the entire period of the Bengalis' struggle for independence. One of the radio announcements thanked the members of the public for coming forward to assist the Bengali refugees in "some wonderfully ingenious ways."[196] Additionally, the government was impressed with the participation of the people of Canada. "While the Pakistan crisis has not become as contentious nor indeed as publicized or politicized as an issue as Biafra, it is interesting to note that the Canadian public has already contributed more to the Combined Appeal for Pakistani Relief than it did for the various Biafran appeals."[197] Thus, Sharp was briefed by Undersecretary A. E. Ritchie.

Use of the Letters to the Editor Column in the Canadian Dailies

Letters to the Editor column became a valuable tool for ongoing public discourse on the conflict, revealing the opposed opinions mainly of the two segments of the Canadian public - Pakistani Canadians consisting of non-Bengali West Pakistanis (pro-Pakistanis or pro-unity) and Bengali East Pakistanis (pro-Bangladeshis). The pro-Pakistanis argued that India was instigating the Bengalis, for which the military regime had no choice but to take necessary action against the rebels and Indian agents; the pro-Bangladeshis counterargued that, instead of transferring power to the elected leader, the military dictator was killing civilians in the name of restoration of law and order to bring the Bengalis into submission. The letter writers were like agents provocateurs who stirred up controversy to generate informed discussions surrounding humanitarian assistance, economic sanctions, nationalism, secession, and independence. The following are a few selective subject headings on which letters were written back and forth.

Condemnation of military assault and expression of shock

The first letter to the editor was published by the Montreal-based *Le Devoir*, dated March 27, 1971, written by Sadat Kazi, a Bengali Canadian of East Pakistani origin. Having expressed outrage about the sudden secret military move and the armed suppression of democracy, Kazi saw the secret army attack on civilians as the end of a united Pakistan. With a warning to the military authority that the "Bengalis *aujord'hui sont unis et plus résolus que jamais* (Bengalis are more united and committed than ever before, author's translation)."[198] Kazi ended his letter with a prophetic note on the appalling tragedy that was taking place, "*Rien ne poura les priver de leur liberté, de leur droit à l'autodétermination* (They will never be deprived of their freedom and their right to self-determination, author's translation)."[199]

The next letter, dated April 1, 1971, was written by Dr. Abdul Mannan, a Bengali Canadian physician from Hartney, Manitoba, in which he demanded the Canadian government's intervention, "We sincerely hope that the government of Canada will intervene officially to do its utmost in stopping that [military assault] in East Pakistan and in upholding democracy in the region."[200] Again, on April 8, another enraged Bengali Canadian who did not provide his name but indicated that they were Bengali wrote, "Whether good or bad, Pakistan is dead and an independent Bangla Desh has emerged... Canada must condemn Yahya Khan's mass slaughter and stop further aid to West Pakistan."[201]

Both letters reflected the mood and anxieties of all Canadians of Bengali origin in Canada. The next series of letters published in various newspapers across the country also echoed the same sense of awe and horror at the news of the massacre of civilians. The Canadian public became so involved in reading the news from the subcontinent that East Pakistan instantly became a metaphor for violence.

Whether the mass killings of the Bengalis were genocide or not, the people of Canada saw the killings as wanton, savage acts. "A pogrom has been going on. In this pogrom, the innocuous Hindu minority was savagely battered as a scapegoat by West Pakistanis who could not bring themselves to realize that it was they who had undermined and shattered the will of the Muslims of Bengal to live any longer in one Pakistan under West Pakistani rule."[202] Thus, Professor Joseph T. O'Connell of St. Michael College, University of Toronto, expressed his observation of what was happening.

There was also no shortage of just the opposite viewpoints on the crisis. Under the title "Indian hypocrisy," Linda R. Moore of Cornwall wrote, "The Indian sympathy for East Pakistan is nothing but hypocrisy. India became independent in August 1947, and within months, millions of Muslims were killed. In 1947, the Indian army marched into Junagadh and Hyderabad. The tortures inflicted on the Moslems must be without parallel. In 1962, the Indian army marched into Goa. In 1965, the Indian army marched into Pakistan without declaring war. India is happy about affairs in East Pakistan. Its dream of breaking up Pakistan will be shattered if this rebellion fails. The tears of the Indians are crocodile tears."[203] Again, along the same vein, Saidullah Khan of Cornwall wrote, "I have been one of those who fought for the establishment of Pakistan and settled in East Pakistan. I was a magistrate as well as an administrator over there... The present insurrection in East Pakistan is the result of the continuous propaganda that the Awami League leaders have been carrying on since 1951."[204]

Justification for Military Intervention and Blaming of Bongobondhu and the Gandhi Administration

"To preserve the solidarity and integrity of Pakistan is sacrosanct to every true Pakistani, and being a head of the state and the supreme commander of the armed forces, President Yahya could not preside over the liquidation of Pakistan,"[205] argued Syed Hassan, a Canadian of West Pakistani background, putting forward his justification for military intervention. He did not just stop there. He continued that the 1970 National Elections were not a referendum, "If people of East Pakistan want a separate state of their own, the issue should be decided by a referendum in that province."[206] Hassan further maintained that "Sheikh Mujibur Rahman's Awami League did not campaign for outright independence."[207] Another Canadian of West Pakistani origin, Iqbal Syed of Scarborough, blamed Bongobondhu for being responsible for the fallout, "From the beginning, Sheikh Mujibur Rahman was playing in the hands of enemies and anti-national elements inimical to the ideology and very existence of Pakistan."[208]

Then there followed another letter from Dr. M. Zafari Quaraishi, chairman of the East Pakistan Relief Committee, who also accused Bongobondhu, "The military action taken in East Pakistan was the result of disruptive activities by Mujib and his part who deliberately misled the common man. Nobody likes violence. Mujib could have done a great deal of constructive work for Pakistan if he had wanted to become the legitimate prime minister. Today, he has to bear the guilt for the bloodshed and destruction of innocent people."[209] He then went on to say, "Pakistanis, like Canadians, cherish their freedom and want their country to be united. We want our Canadian friends to help us achieve this goal by reporting impartially the happenings in Pakistan and by supporting the cause of a solidarity campaign to unite the peoples of the two wings of the country."[210] Having pointed his fingers at the Gandhi administration, he also observed that India was "making political hay out of the developments in Pakistan" and that he was hopeful that Pakistan would survive the "holocaust of anti-Pakistan propaganda."[211]

Again, the pro-Pakistani segment, having partnered with the Ottawa-based Pakistan high commission, tried to strengthen its arguments also by pointing out that there existed an element of bias against the government of Pakistan. "It is absolutely unfair to call the army's action in East Pakistan after March 26 a ruthless attempt to suppress the will of the elected representatives of the people of East Pakistan. Let me set the record straight. The elections were not fought by the Awami League on the platform of secession. The elections were contested by that party on the manifesto of autonomy for East Pakistan."[212] Thus, wrote Touquir Hussain, second secretary at the Pakistan High Commission. By the time the Pakistani spokesperson made his claim, many eyewitness accounts had already appeared in the Canadian dailies with detailed chronology since the 1970 National Elections. The public had already become relatively *au courant* about the succession of events in the subcontinent. They did not wish to be a prophet of doom but had enough evidence to challenge the regime's game plan.

The Geographical Absurdity of Pakistan and Systemic Discrimination against Bengalis

"The very existence as one state of that mysterious geographical entity called Pakistan for the last twenty-four years is a historical miracle. Pakistan was the result of political manipulation,"[213] written in the letter of a protestor who addressed themselves as a Bengali at the bottom of the letter without revealing the name in the newspaper. The same letter writer then went on, "Unfortunately, the altruist clique that led to the independence movement during the late 1940s deliberately twisted the contents and language of the 'Lahore Resolution' and managed to establish one state 'Pakistan' instead of *autonomous, sovereign states* for the Muslims of the subcontinent. As a result, the seeds of domination of one region by the other within that single and manipulated state of Pakistan were sown in 1947."[214]

Arguments along the vein that the West Pakistani rulers were discriminating against the East soon began to appear in many Canadian dailies, along with their responses from both pro-and anti-Pakistani groups for the benefit of the average Canadians. Syed Muazzam Hussain, president of the Bangladesh Association of Canada, Montreal, Québec, wrote, "If you would care to inquire about the present high commissioner, you will find that he is a West Pakistani, and so was his predecessor, and his predecessor, and so on."[215] He continued, "Historically, even though Bengalis form the majority, no head of state of Pakistan has been a Bengali, while frequently a French-Canadian has ruled Canada."[216] Showing the dissimilarity, he wrote, "Economically speaking, Québec has gained from the Canadian federal government, while West Pakistan has exploited Bangla Desh."[217]

Denial of Facts

A strong supporter of Bangladesh, Madeline Alam, about whose activities we already noted, played a lead role in organizing a media campaign to dispel various myths and stereotypes the regime was spreading. She challenged the supply of continued misinformation and lies by Toukir Hussain of the Ottawa-based Pakistan High Commission. She networked with Eileen Huq of Hamilton, and together, they remained active in raising awareness among the public through a regular letter-writing campaign using their English names. The idea was to convey to readers that the letter writers were not necessarily of Indo-Pakistani backgrounds. They were a part of the mainstream Canadians familiar with the subcontinental politics, about which many average Canadians did not know much. With this in mind, both Madeline and Eileen wrote ceaselessly.

They were furious to read Toukir's letter in which he wrote, "The Awami League and its leaders, carried away by the electoral victory, progressively refused to show any interest in maintaining the integrity of Pakistan."[218] Instead of telling the truth, he went on to downplay the news of military aggression in East Pakistan, having branded the students, professionals, and political leaders of the province as "miscreants," "Indian and foreign agents," or simply a group of "misguided individuals" who were out to break up the country. Madeline took it upon herself to expose the military regime's gargantuan lie regarding the statement of Touqir Hussain, who was representing the Pakistan High Commission. She was "dismayed by Pakistani propaganda of lies and degradation of Bengali leaders and masses fighting for survival."[219] She took serious objection to Hussain's statement that the Bengali refugees in Indian refugee camps are "mere rootless persons and misfits."[220] "With all due respect, I think Mr. Hussain, sitting in the cozy surroundings of his Ottawa enclave, has lost all touch with reality. The people of Bangla Desh don't need him to govern them,"[221] an enraged Alam wrote about her position.

Having asked Canadians how important Bengal is to us, she wrote, "Most of the reports from West Pakistan accuse the Bengalis of East Pakistan of being 'miscreants,' 'rebels,' 'traitors,' and the like. I find this impossible to believe as the Bengalis won an overwhelming majority in the recent National Elections, and the leader of the successful Awami League, Sheikh Mujibur Rahman, is, I have good reason to believe, a moderate, intelligent, dedicated politician, certainly no extremist."[222] She continued, "The West Pakistanis were stunned at the results. They had never expected their poor, exploited, neglected, distant compatriots to achieve such unity and direction. As the prize for winning this majority in a democratic, free election, the Bengalis are branded as traitors, and to ensure that it will not happen again in a hurry, the Bengali leaders, intelligentsia, and students are being methodically liquidated."[223]

Foreign and Economic Aid, Sanction and Separation of East Pakistan

Although, by and large, the public respected Canada's policy of neutrality and nonintervention in the internal affairs of another country, the issue of separation of East Pakistan frequently came up while talking about sanctions. The pro-Bangladeshis strongly argued that Canada should continue to provide relief assistance to the refugees who had been crossing over to the Indian territory to flee persecution at the hands of Yahya's barbaric soldiers. They argued that foreign aid must not be mixed with military assistance and that the military government's claim concerning its intention to establish the law and order situation in East Pakistan was simply a euphemism for suppression.

Many write-ups urged the government not to continue its economic aid under the circumstances. Sharp immediately made the following direct reference to the need for ongoing foreign and financial assistance to the Bengalis, regardless of the directions of the political movement: "In our decision about the aid program in general, we shall be guided by our understanding of the needs of the people of Pakistan, not by any desire to maintain the status quo of that country. I am sure that this holds for the other members of the consortium."[224] Having remained firm on the conflict, Sharp wrote, "If there is an obsession with our own separatists at work here, as your writer suggests, it is an obsession of *The Globe and Mail*, not the government of Canada."[225]

There were arguments and counterarguments among many Canadians, some of whom argued that the government should cut off all aid to Pakistan; some argued that the assistance should continue regardless. Seeing that there was confusion regarding Canada's position on the conflict due to the media's negative coverage vis-à-vis the Trudeau administration. There was still a lot of confusion. Sharp again responded to the editorial clarifying his government's position, "My statements were slanted to suggest that I was proposing the separation of East and West Pakistan."[226] The following day, in the House of Commons, Sharp further clarified his position, "I wanted to make it quite plain today as my own initiative that I had no intention of supporting separation in saying, as I did yesterday, that I supported the restoration of democratic government under the civilian rule in East Pakistan and preferably based on those who had been elected in the last election"[227]

Sharp's remark in Parliament and its coverage in the media, however, generated a lot of discussions among the Canadian public, some of whom agreed and some who disagreed. Taking an issue with such a statement, an angry Chaitanya Keshavrao Kalevar, who represented two organizations, the Canadian Committee for an Independent Bangla Desh and the World Federalist of Canada, claimed that the aid money was being used against civilians. Straightforwardly, Kalevar wrote again, "In my view, Mr. Sharp is not only failing the interests of secular democracy in supporting a Moslem military dictatorship by refusing to cut off economic aid but also has a distorted view of history, for there is little in the history of nations to suggest that a continuing support of an authoritative, inhuman and ruthless military dictatorship serves the interest of its common people."[228]

Following the same vein of argument, another Bangladeshi from Toronto also wrote, "By giving aid to the hands of rich dictators, any well-meaning country would only increase the suffering of the people."[229] Having taken an issue with Sharp's statement that "throwing a country into chaos" would not serve "the interests of its common people," the same letter writer posed a question directly to the minister, "May I ask, what more chaos can that country be in than what its own rulers have put it in? Do they include Bengalis? If so, then their interest will not be served under the present rules anyway."[230]

He then went on to say that the minister had "completely ignored the fact that, to the people of Bangladesh, there cannot be a united Pakistan again after what the military dictators have done to them."[231] Again, he argued further, "If Mr. Sharp is not obsessed with the separatists, as he so claims, then why does he consider it to be irresponsible to recommend the division of Pakistan - a country already separate, not only in its cultural, linguistic, and socio-economic dimensions but separated as a matter of geographical fact by 1,500 miles?"[232]

He claimed that Sharp's procrastination due to Canada's policy of "noninterference" might have led him to be "sitting on the fence" which he believed was showing the Trudeau administration's "sharp sense of diplomatic balance at the cost of human lives."[233] The letter writer furnished arguments by demonstrating differences between the situations in Québec and East Pakistan.

Unsurprisingly, Sharp's statement triggered a volley of letters on "separation" and "economic assistance." The following week, Sharp stated his speculated thought with no reservation. "It may be that this [independence of Bangladesh] will turn out to be the only solution; whether it would be the best solution is another matter."[234]

In fact, throughout July, the whole issue of economic aid became one of the most heated discussions. Critiquing Sharp's position on sanctions and the needs of the people of Pakistan, a dissatisfied Canadian joined hands against Sharp's arguments. It stated, "He [Sharp] seems to be suggesting here that from an economic point of view, Pakistan is better off as one country than as two. Yet there is little evidence to indicate that the people of East Pakistan, although poorer than those in the West, have been any better off under the present union than they would have been had East Pakistan been independent."[235] Thus, Professor G. Patrick Gough of the University of Guelph argued that the Bengalis would be better off without their West Pakistani brethren. "Despite Mr. Sharp's apparent doubts as to whether the division is the best solution, the vast majority of people in East Pakistan think that it is and did so even before the turmoil of the last few months."[236] Professor Gough argued further.

In early August, Kalevar, who had been writing regularly, wrote again, "Ottawa is obsessed with the separatists in Québec, but it does not realize the wide difference between the two situations."[237] He did not stop at that. As an ardent pro-Bangladeshi, he argued that the Bengalis were fighting for the independence of Bangladesh since they saw themselves as being different from West Pakistanis both geographically as well as culturally. "Geographically Bangla Desh is not an integral part of West Pakistan as Québec is of Canada,"[238] wrote Kalevar. "Electorally, the Awami League obtained 167 seats out of 169 in Bangla Desh, a convincing mandate by any standard,"[239] he argued further.

Again, alleging that the government seemed over-reactive about the issue of separation, he also urged the government to take a new look at the latest situation in East Pakistan, given the gravity of the matter. It was "a tawdry way of approaching a tragic humanitarian crisis,"[240] pro-Bangladeshi Kalevar wrote again. He then suggested that the government "should forget its obsession with its own separatists. It should call for the duly elected to govern East Pakistan and should punctuate the call by cutting aid to Pakistan."[241]

As solid and opinionated expressions found a place in individual letters of various dailies, Canadians were outraged. A pro-Pakistani immediately wrote back, lambasting Kalevar, whom he branded to be ignorant. He alluded to the Awami League's victory in the National Elections "not in the name of independence but of greater provincial autonomy."[242] He continued, "After the elections, Mujibur Rahman and some of his colleagues changed their stand from autonomy to separatism from Pakistan, presumably on Indian encouragement ... Bangla Desh cannot be independent in the subcontinent's political and geographical set-up. It can only be a protectorate of India and will share the same fate as Kashmir or the sixty million Indian Muslims who have been killed, looted. Their houses burned in over one thousand riots in so-called secular India."[243]

In the meantime, the Pakistan Solidarity Committee's President Masudul Alam Chowdhury, a Pakistani Canadian of Bengali origin, immediately accused the Trudeau administration of being "irresponsible toward East," having claimed that any "stoppage of economic aid to Pakistan would be detrimental to the economic health of East Pakistan whose economy is now balanced on a knife's edge as a result of the recent strife in the country."[244] The Solidarity Committee urged the government to provide more economic assistance since approximately $60 million had been "stolen away by the miscreants and anti-state elements to India from East Pakistan during the civil disorders, thus aggravating the economy of the private and public sectors in East Pakistan."[245] "To maintain the state of status quo in the subcontinent, the United States, Canada, France, and Great Britain will think it best to continue their arms pact with Pakistan... There is no reason why these arms will be used against the civilians in East Pakistan, for it is to be noted the situation in the country is quite normal,"[246] argued Chowdhury.

The word "strife" must have been purposeful since it undermined the situation. Typically, the pro-Pakistani segment never considered the Bengalis' fight for independence as a just cause. By referring to it as a kind of civil "strife," the letter writer tried to trivialize the National Liberation War of Bangladesh. It was an attempt to send a message through denial, ignoring the Bengali rebels' declaration of independence and their tangible progress toward liberation.

A close look at the next round of letters to the editor, editorials, and separate news items also reveals how, through their writings, the print media echoed the very stubbornly held mixed views of the two segments of the public - one supporting the military authority and its actions and justifications, while the other, condemning the actions of the military regime showing their disdain for the military dictators. This group found the Trudeau administration's position, or lack thereof, unacceptable. Sharp was both condemned and criticized. Many Canadians had serious questions for which there was no answer. They saw the government's procrastination as having no position at all, or, if the government had a position, it was thought to be so rigid that it did not seem like it was supportive of the Bengalis' demand for an independent Bangladesh. The range of emotions the letter writers displayed in writing is understandable when one considers the intersectionality of the identities of the originators of these letters.

The newspapers provided a continuous forum to argue and counterargue whatever one's point of view might have been. The public was aware that at every opportunity, the Trudeau government reiterated that it did not wish to be embroiled in a fiery debate on the separation or secession of East Pakistan, or, for that matter, the independence of Bangladesh. Most newspapers tried to maintain an evenness in the discourse on foreign and economic aid to Pakistan and the demand for the separation of East Pakistan. Often, readers were provoked to the hilt and, simultaneously, allowed to make the Column a site for empowerment for both pro- and anti-groups with polished and persuasive opinions. This was done through a balanced editorial disquisition, write-ups, and letters to the editor, highlighting arguments and counterarguments furnished by both pro-Bangladeshis and pro-military regimes.

We may look at the "Letter to the Editor" column as a sounding board for views on the Pakistan-Bangladesh conflict that provided a base as a reliable indicator of public opinion. Although, by and large, the pro-Bangladeshis were appreciative of Canada's discomfort in discussing separation, some Bengalis had a hard time accepting the Trudeau administration's overreaction to and nervousness about using the word separation. A cautious print media did not raise the matter to that extent because there existed an element of unease in the Trudeau administration to discuss the issue of separation and independence. At the same time, the media also believed that the general public must be allowed to read about both sides of the arguments expressed through "Letter to the Editor" columns.

Lobbying the Government (March 1971–February 1972)

By and large, Canadians were aware of Canada's foreign policy constraints and inability to intervene in Pakistan's internal affairs. Therefore, because of Canada's fame in the mediatory role, Canadians looked upon the government to address the issue through an international lens—the Commonwealth and UN lens in particular. The public remembered how the former prime minister, Lester B. Pearson (1963–1968), reacted to the Rhodesian unilateral and unconditional declaration of independence under white minority rule only six years ago in 1965. Being at the forefront, Pearson successfully argued that it was a Commonwealth issue rather than an internal matter of Pakistan only. Earlier, the Canadian government also won plaudits from the public, who took pride in the fact that, with Canada's effort, the Commonwealth members secured a Commonwealth Declaration of Racial Equality and prevented any member from withdrawing from the Commonwealth over the affair.

This time around, the same public, however, became a bit disillusioned seeing that there had been no progress even though Canada was, and still is, a signatory to the international instruments, such as the 1951 UN Conventions Relating to the Status of Refugees and its 1967 Protocol. The public was disappointed to see Canada's helplessness as a middle power as the issue remained explosive. It shall be seen that the public was still involved in lobbying the government both individually and organizationally in the following areas: (1) influencing the government to take a strong position against the military regime; (2) lobbying the government to impose economic sanctions and place embargo; (3) addressing the issue of immigration, extension of a student visa, etc. (4) demanding recognition of Bangladesh; and (5) making ongoing demand for the release of Bongobondhu.

Organizational Lobbying to Intervene

The Saskatoon Committee for the Protection of Human Rights and Lives in East Pakistan, which was formed instantly following the military crackdown, was the first organization to write to the Trudeau administration. Its members were appalled to learn that the military government in Pakistan used armored tanks and aerial bombing on unarmed civilians. On April 2, Dr. Asit Sarkar, the committee's convenor, wrote to Otto Lang, minister of Manpower and Immigration, and urged him "to use his good office to persuade the military government in Pakistan to take any possible action to put an immediate stop to these unfortunate events."[247] An essential observable difference between the Ottawa Group and the Saskatoon-based Committee is that the former instantly endorsed its full support for an independent Bangladesh, while the latter, having condemned the military regime for its clampdown on unarmed civilians but kept the name East Pakistan, the legal name of the eastern wing of Pakistan.

Soon, the Bengali segment of the Canadian public started thinking outside the box while continuing its lobbying efforts with a new strategy. Ottawa members of the Bangladesh-Canada Association crafted a letter for all MPs and senators in which they referred to the published news in *The Globe and Mail* that reported that, thus far, given the world opinion, the government of the United States had committed to giving "$80 million aid to Pakistan." Britain also earmarked "$45 million" while Japan "suspended $40 million."[248] Using straightforward language, the appeal letter urged the parliamentarians to "take necessary steps so that the government of Canada withholds any such aid and takes other possible measures to end the crisis in East Pakistan."[249]

Another critical part played by the Bengalis of Saskatoon and Regina was their success in stopping the visit of two Pakistani political leaders, Hamidul Haque Chowdhury and Mahmud Ali, who traveled to Ottawa and Toronto to tell their side of the story. This involved much lobbying by the Bengalis to persuade their Members of Parliament, Les Benjamin (Regina) and Alf Gleave (Saskatoon). A pro-Pakistani group in Regina, with the help of the Toronto-based Pakistan Solidarity Committee, invited the same speakers who were in Toronto and Ottawa in support of the military dictator, intending to mobilize their position among the Canadian public regarding the military regime's justification for its punitive measures. As soon as Dr. Asit Sarkar and Dr. Anwar Chowdhury of the Bangladesh Association of Saskatchewan (BAS) got wind of it, so they contacted their local MPs, Benjamin and Gleave, who were sympathetic to the cause of the Bengalis.

Sarkar and Chowdhury put enough pressure on the two MPs to intervene and discourage the speakers from coming to Saskatchewan. Benjamin and Gleave had enough clout to convey the message to the speakers through their political contact in Toronto. Their message was simple—the great majority of the people of Saskatchewan would neither encourage nor welcome even a brief conversation with the leaders at the provincial level, the supporters of a military regime engaged in reprisals and slaughter of the Bengalis. The MPs were firm in communicating the critical message that any attempt to provide the military regime's narrative of the events through the media would be vocally challenged by the people of Saskatchewan, who had empathized with the victims. The local MPs successfully discouraged the Pakistani leaders, who canceled their scheduled program for Saskatoon. Dr. Sarkar played a vital role in this matter.[250]

Individual Lobbying to Intervene

Individually, Dr. Anwarul Haque, a Bengali Canadian who was treasurer of the Bangladesh Association of Saskatchewan, wrote to Les Benjamin, MP for Lake Centre, Regina, in the following manner: "Aid given to Pakistan in any form other than a relief (under direct supervision) at this critical period will openly prolong the massacre of the people of East Bengal."[251] As far as the Bengalis were concerned, on the one hand, they saw foreign aid as an expression of humanity; on the other hand, an instrument of property that must not be mixed with military aid.

Dr. Haque also wrote a protest letter to Richard Nixon directly for his support of the Pakistani military regime. Dr. Haque wrote not as treasurer of the association but as a concerned Canadian. He recognized that Nixon received many unsolicited letters from outraged Americans and Canadians. Nevertheless, he felt very strongly that he ought to write, regardless. He found the attitude of the Nixon administration in engineering the famous tilt toward Pakistan through his spokesperson, Henry Kissinger, to be one of the most frustrating experiences.

In addition, three distinguished Canadians, Hugh Keenleyside, Robert McClure, and Stanley Burke, as Canadian citizens, jointly wrote an open letter to all MPs and senators. The following is a short excerpt of that letter: "The East Pakistan Tragedy has been called the greatest and most unnecessary facing mankind today. As citizens of the world, we cannot ignore it. As citizens of the Commonwealth, we have an obligation to act."[252] Continuing along the same vein, they asked, "Will you put the lives of the seventy-seven million people of East Bengal on your agenda?"[253] This was a time when Canadians were waking up to hear about how millions of people were waiting to die.

Again, being dissatisfied with the government's tardy reaction, Muriel Palen, a Torontonian, dashed off a letter to her MP with a copy to the prime minister in which she expressed her frustration, "It does seem to me that as Canadians, we should take a stand against this very obvious denial of the right of free elections and of the extreme suppression and brutality of the armies of West Pakistan."[254] Seeing that the government was not doing enough despite the immediate and open reaction of the people of Canada against the military repression in East Pakistan, Palen asked, "If the Government does not speak for the people whom it represents, then whom does it speak for? A country is not judged by its wealth but by what it ultimately stands for. In writing this letter, I believe I am expressing the feelings of our whole family and many other Canadians."[255]

Having recruited two active partners, Dr. Shafiul Haque and Momin Chowdhury, to give them a hand and do the leg work, Professor Mir Maswood Ali of the University of Western Ontario and his wife Suraiya Ali became active in voicing their misgivings. Using Ali's 480 Lawson Road residence as a meeting place, Ali mobilized public opinion and devised a communication plan for lobbying the Trudeau administration.[256] Accompanied by his wife, Suraiya Ali, and her brother, Momin Chowdhury, Ali frequently visited Toronto for group meetings with members of the Bangladesh-Canada Association of Toronto and shared each other's experiences. Dr. Ali established a network with other groups to remain *au courant*.

Under the stewardship of Momin Chowdhury, Ali's team did the following: (1) sent a telegram to Alexis Kosygin, prime minister of the Union of Soviet Socialist Republics (USSR), for his immediate intervention as the Londoners feared serious confrontation between superpowers; (2) wrote to Sirimavo Bandaranaike, prime minister of Ceylon (now Sri Lanka) urging her not to allow Pakistan to land Pakistani plane to refuel, an arrangement that the group believed was helping Pakistan; (3) wrote to Mitchell Sharp, Secretary of State for External Affairs, and (4) Lester Pearson, former prime minister of Canada, to put pressure on the Trudeau administration for intervention.[257]

When, by early summer, the movement of the refugees reached tidal proportions, Ali wrote to Sharp again asking a pointed question. "What forced people to leave their lands, homes, and property and seek sanctuary in the adjoining states of India?"[258] To fill Sharp with the background history and the proper context, having claimed his familiarity with the Pakistani polity, Ali pointed out that, even before the military assault, many Bengalis had severe misgivings about the genuineness of Yahya's negotiation with Bongobondhu and Bhutto. In his correspondence, Ali alluded to his experience in 1968 when he felt like a stranger while on sabbatical leave at Islamabad University, West Pakistan. Ali's firsthand experience of the condescending attitude of the West Pakistanis toward the Bengalis forced him to terminate his contract and return "home" (Canada) immediately.

Ali alerted Sharp by saying that he was one hundred percent sure that Yahya went to the bargaining table *mala fide*. Ali underscored the point that the world soon learned about the negotiations - how, while the parley was going on in Dhaka, the warship with the non-Bengali troops was sailing around the Indian Peninsula. A determined Ali again pointed out that it was a matter of common knowledge and suspicion of the Bengalis that the hawks in the military were the last ones to hand over power to the Bengali leader even though he was representing the majority. Ali also informed Sharp that, on behalf of the people of London, Ontario, he had already sent a similar note to Kosygin urging him for immediate intervention. Ali's message to Sharp was that Yahya was buying the time he needed to re-position himself against Mujibites, the Bengali nationalists. Ali urged Sharp to intervene immediately as "time was of the essence."[259] The response from the Department of External Affairs was the same as that from Dr. Shariff (Bangladesh Association of Manitoba Association), which has been cited above. To recap, Canada maintained a noninterference policy even as late as the fall of 1971.

The efforts of the London-based couple, Professor Maswood Ali and Suraiya Ali, remain an example of how a small group of people instantly connected with the people in the higher echelons of the government to convey the message of doom and gloom under the leadership of a military dictator in Pakistan.

Again, individually active among the Ottawa Bengalis was M. Abdur Rahim, who was outraged to see a caption he could not recall in which paper, "You have to be a Bengali to be shot at." He immediately dashed off the following telegram to Leonid Brezhnev, general secretary of the Central Committee (CC) of the Communist Party of the USSR: "Tell Yahya to stop the carnage."[260] The ongoing reports of the killing of the Bengalis evoked in Rahim's mind the haunting memories of the Nigerian Civil War of 1967–1970, recalled an enraged Rahim. He also immediately initiated a petition and collected many signatures. In September 1971, before moving to Hamilton, Rahim left a draft copy of his petition, which he had crafted after spending hours at the local downtown Public Library with Professor Nasir Uddin Ahmed, then president of the Bangladesh-Canada Association (Ottawa). Ahmed took over the unfinished work and, with help from a few volunteers, had the petition signed by several professors of both Carleton and Ottawa University and sent the petition to the UN secretary-general.

Organizational Lobbying Regarding Sanctions and Arms Embargo

Within hours of hearing about the military crackdown, four visibly distraught Bengali East Pakistani Ottawa residents showed up at the premises of External Affairs on March 29, 1971, for a meeting with Mitchell Sharp, Secretary of State for External Affairs, but had no luck. They met with J. M. Harrington, an experienced Mandarin Head of the Pacific and South Asia Division, External Affairs, with a hurriedly crafted document titled "Democratic Self Government of Bangla Desh." They informed Harrington that the people of Bangladesh wanted to restore democracy and achieve autonomy to ensure their economic future. As with many tricks in the devil's hands, mistrust, fear, and selfishness reigned the current Yahya regime, observed Azmat Ali, the team leader.[261] Ali urged the government to consider the following four steps outlined in the documents: (1) to recognize free Bangla Desh as an independent country; (2) to take necessary action to stop the invasion of the sovereign Bangla Desh by the troops of West Pakistan; (3) to withdraw recognition of the state of Pakistan as it does not represent the former geographical boundaries of the people thereof; and (4) to withhold all flow of foreign aid to the state formerly known as Pakistan, as such aid was being used against the people of Bangla Desh.[262]

Using typical bureaucratic language, a seasoned Harrington spoke in general terms and ended his conversation by frankly stating that "it was most unlikely that any of the requests would be met." However, the government "would follow the situation with sympathy" and that the government would "consider whether" anything "could be done to promote a return to more normal conditions."[263] Since it was only the second day following the military crackdown, Ali's team recognized that Sharp did not have adequate information. They were glad that they were able to flag the matter, having explained the gravity of the situation through a demonstration of their abiding hatred of the slaughter of the Bengalis.

Sharp was briefed on the same day along the line that the government "had been watching the situation with a great deal of sympathy and concern but, like observers everywhere, they were handicapped by the lack of precise information about what had been happening in the province during the last few days."[264] Harrington wrote, "Despite our sympathy, however, there could be no question of Canadian intervention in the internal affair of another country since despite the evident popular support for the Awami League, President Yahya Khan, and the Pakistan Government were the legal government of the province."[265]

In Manitoba, as president of the Bangladesh Association of Manitoba, Dr. Farid Shariff took it upon himself to pressure the federal government on economic sanction, relief work, and recognition of Bangladesh, having initiated correspondence with Sharp. Having partnered with the Washington-based Bangladesh Mission, he gradually mounted pressure. The correspondences of Shariff (president of Bangladesh Association of Manitoba), Sharp (Secretary of State for External Affairs), and Mustafizur Rahman Siddiqi (head of Bangladesh Mission, Washington, DC) reveal an interesting chain of conversation about sanctions and Canada's take on the Bangladesh issue. A persistent Shariff insisted upon the government by explaining its stand on economic sanctions and relief assistance to Canadians. Sharp clarified his government's take on the question of economic sanctions and intervention in Pakistan's "internal affairs" regarding Canada's foreign policy constraints, such as "nonintervention." He quickly responded by saying, "It is unlikely that suspension of all aid to Pakistan at present would bring a solution any nearer and certainly, to the extent that it means halting relief and rehabilitation assistance, it would add deprivations of the Pakistani people."[266]

Again, the British Columbia Bangladesh Association kept its members and supporters posted through its communication vehicle, *Bangla Desh*, regarding its efforts to persuade the Nixon administration not to supply arms to the military dictator. While lobbying the US government, however, it had the advantage of having proximity with Washingtonians who were also active in raising the issue with the Nixon administration. Though fragmented, there are some records of the BC Bangladesh Association's correspondence with two senators, Rupert Vance Hartke and John Goodwin Tower. The original letter from Dr. Shafiqul Islam Khan, general secretary of the association, to Senator Hartke is missing, but Hartke's response to Khan has survived. It may be gathered from the response that Dr. Khan must have expressed his misgivings regarding the Nixon administration's duplicity about the secret supply of arms.

Hartke, who was the leading player in cosponsoring Resolution 21 and Amendment 159 to the Foreign Assistance Act, was frank in expressing his forebodings and stated, "I fully share your horror and dismay at the recent bloody events in Pakistan, and I intend to support legislation to curtail arms aid... Here again, we have an example of the shocking misuse to which the United States arms aid is often put by its recipients. Weapons that we provide for the ostensible purpose of helping a friendly regime to defend itself against possible Communist aggression turn out to be used to crush internal disaffection or, as in the case of the India-Pakistan border war of a few years ago, are used for settling scores with hostile neighbors."[267]

Again, while no other correspondence in this thread has survived in Canada, Senator Tower's response to Khan fortuitously is also available. It ran in the following: "Contrary to many recent reports, the US Department of State asserts that we are currently operating no large program of military assistance to Pakistan. A limited number of supplies has been sent; however, the States Department has told me that no further equipment will be sent pending review of the current situation."[268] Tower's candid response indicates that even the Senators were lied to by the Nixon administration.

Though based in Washington, Muazzem Ali maintained an up-to-date list of Associations and volunteers in Canada. He worked closely with the Bangladesh-Canada Associations' executive committee members and encouraged them to carry on their federal and provincial efforts. Diplomatically speaking, Ali considered the enthusiastic pro-Bangladeshis Canadians as an informal army of ambassadors in their attempt to lobby the governments of Canada and the United States. As per his strategy of engagement, now and then, Ali would discuss with Siddiqi and write to his contacts in Canada. Typically, Ali would thank the volunteers for their relentless efforts in "propagating the cause of Bangladesh" in Canada.[269] This may be seen as an instance of the passionate desire of the pro-Bangladeshis, whether in Canada or the United States, who remained doggedly tenacious throughout the War of Liberation period.

Three well-known Canadians – Dr. Robert McClure, moderator of the United Church of Canada and part of the board of directors of Oxfam Canada, John Wieler of the Mennonite Central Committee, and Paul Ignatieff of UNICEF Canada – appeared before the House of Commons in the fall. They represented three different organizations and were also members of the Canadian public. The report was emphatic in its conviction that there was a "need for a political settlement"[270] between the two wings of Pakistan. McClure's appeal reinforced that Canada, an influential member of the Commonwealth, should be more proactive in taking initiatives to play a significant role as a go-between by "show[ing] more guts" in this area. Understandably, the report did not allude to the Bengalis' liberation movement. Instead, the emphasis was on finding a political solution between the two wings of Pakistan. As appeals for a resolution within a united Pakistan were all over the news media, the subject resonated with the public except for the following two segments of the Canadian public: Indo-Canadians and Bengali Canadians, who straightforwardly demanded an independent Bangladesh.

Just like the pro-Bangladeshi groups, the Pakistan Solidarity Committee also continued lobbying for ongoing economic assistance and military aid to Pakistan even though there was evidence that the military government was using weapons against its people. Nondelivery of "military aid from the Western nations will cause a major power rift... and at this hour of repeated threats and counterthreats of invasion between India and Pakistan, any false move on either side can plunge the entire globe into the holocaust of a world conflagration."[271] Thus, warned Masudul Alam Chowdhury, a concerned Bengali who favored a united Pakistan. He condemned the NGOs, especially Oxfam Canada, for their involvement in the "internal affairs" of Pakistan. He blamed the organization for hosting the conference in Bangladesh and maintained that Oxfam Canada went beyond its mandate and failed to "realize this humanitarian issue." By sponsoring the conference, Oxfam Canada had "behaved in a way which is not humanitarian, but political,"[272] maintained the letter writer.

Organizational and Individual Lobbying for Immigration Refugee Protection

The presidents of the various Bangladesh-Canada Associations across Canada made a concerted effort by writing to their local MPs to urge Otto Lang, minister of Manpower and Immigration, to permit the Bengali-speaking East Pakistani students in Canadian educational institutions to have their stay permits extended while the Liberation War of Bangladesh was still going on. Factually speaking, Canadians of all political stripes were on the same page regarding the immigration of the Bengali refugees. Given the intense scope of the problems, economic and political, only concerted action by Canada was likely to achieve the desired results, argued the public. Since the media coverage of the events in "Occupied Bangladesh" had already outraged Canadians, it was deemed high time to showcase the uncertainties of the students on study visas to receive an extension.

Dr. Anwar Haque of Regina, treasurer of the Bangladesh Canada Association of Saskatchewan (Regina chapter), about whose activities we noted in the present chapter, also actively lobbied the government for the Bengali students. Like before, he requested Les Benjamin, NDP MP for his riding, again, to broach the immigration matter for the Bengali students in the Commons. Dr. Haque said the public was satisfied with the government's leading review of the issue. It followed the principle it had adopted earlier in handling the foreign students from Nigeria during her recent internal disturbances. In Chapter 7, we shall see how Les Benjamin, NDP MP for Regina-Lake Centre, who worked closely with his constituents, played a key role by raising the issue of immigration in the forefront.

"The students from East Pakistan were given permission to stay and encouraged to apply for immigration and seek employment in Canada until the situation stabilized. Based on its revised policy, when the government of Canada allowed foreign students to apply for landed immigrant status from inside Canada, I was able to apply for Canadian immigration by visiting the immigration office in Saskatoon sometime in 1972,"[273] a now-retired Bangladeshi Canadian professor who was a graduate student wrote to the author. This might be an example of successful lobbying – a synergy among citizens, immigrants, students, and bureaucrats whose collective work demonstrates Canada's empathy for the suffering Bengalis.

There are also instances of ordinary Bengali students in Canada who became involved in lobbying for general asylum seekers for immigration for the East Pakistani Bengalis coming to Canada in various capacities. When, on August 17, 1971, three Bengali sailors deserted the Pakistani ship Sutlej in Montreal, members of the Bangladesh Association of Québec immediately came forward to shelter them and arranged for a press conference. With direct help from Dr. Muazzam Hussain, the deserters were accommodated by Bangladeshi students of the West Island of Montreal. They engaged Alex Miller, a Montreal Immigration lawyer, to represent them. They were able to obtain immigration down the road. Golam Rahman, one of the deserters, recalled how Omar Zanza, the Turkish Naval Captain, assisted them in getting off the ship.[274]

Demand for Bongobondhu's Release

The sudden public announcement of Bongobondhu's in-camera trial sent shockwaves across Canada among all except for pro-Pakistani Canadians who were accusing him of breaking Pakistan with Indian assistance. The proposed trial was deemed by most Canadians as "unwise" and "unfair" despite the military regime's explanation of its plan of action for the sake of the national integrity of Pakistan. Immediately, the government and the public appealed to the Yahya government for Bongobondhu's release. Canadians recalled how Yahya, in his speech to the Nation in March, having alleged Bongobondhu to have indulged in treasonous activities, wanted the people to know about Bongobondhu's culpability in waging war against Pakistan. All along, the pro-Bangladeshi Canadians maintained that without Bongobondhu (that is, if he is tried or made to disappear), there would be grave and perilous consequences in "Occupied Bangladesh."

Calling the proposed trial of Bongobondhu a "mockery of human rights for waging war against Pakistan," Sarwar Alam Khan, president of the Bangladesh Canada Association (Toronto), wrote, "We appeal to the people of Canada and Government of Canada to condemn this inhuman trial and do everything possible to save the precious life of the undisputed leader of seventy-five million people whose only crime is seeking freedom and self-determination."[275]

Three prominent members of the public who also represented three different organizations—Hugh Keenleyside, Robert McClure, and Stanley Burke - once again wrote an open letter to all MPs and senators insisting "on the unconditional release of the elected leader of the Bangladesh people, Sheikh Mujibur Rahman, as the first step toward a long-term political solution based on the will of the people."[276] In a sense, their letter represented the public sentiment of the time.

Again, Matiur Rahman, another active Bengali Canadian of East Pakistani origin, then a student at the University of Toronto and general secretary of the Bangladesh-Canada Association of Toronto, wrote open letters for the public, having been involved from the beginning. He said, "This was a time when emotion ran very high among those who believed that Bongobondhu's life ought to be saved as he was seen as indispensable for the victory of the Bengalis' struggle for independence."[277] Rahman observed that the Toronto chapter of the Bangladesh-Canada Association had sent more than one thousand copies of a petition titled Pakistan Justice Resolution to Canadians across Toronto City in the hope that it would expose the actual motive of the military regime. "The apparent denial of all traditional judicial procedures and safeguards can discredit the verdict. If the trial should end in the execution of Sheikh Mujibur Rahman, the inevitable result will be further bloodshed in a country that has already suffered so cruelly,"[278] Rahman appealed to the military government. He also appealed to fellow Canadians, "We feel that we must do whatever possible on our part to create a public opinion all around the world against this unjust trial."[279]

There are two more documentary records in the Library and Archives Canada of lobbying for the release of Bongobondhu by two Professors at Carleton University, Elliot Tepper and Mizan Rahman. "The crystallization of world opinion into public and private efforts to save Mujib may be the last chance that we have to affect the events on the sub-continent in a positive manner,"[280] wrote Professor Tepper to Andrew Brewin, MP for Greenwood, Ontario, who had just returned from India and Pakistan. Having joined the public, Professor Tepper raised his concerns, "I am writing to you to urge that you take effective steps to prevent the execution of Sheikh Mujibur Rahman. He is the only leader with the legitimacy and wisdom to lead Pakistan away from the present impasse. If he is eliminated rather than released, there may be no hope of a political solution to Pakistan's turmoil. The result, as you know, might be an exponential expansion of the present tragedy into a holocaust."[281]

Again, Professor Mizan Rahman, one of the vocal pro-Bangladeshi leaders, also personally wrote to Andrew Brewin and a few Ottawa

MPs urging for their intervention in seeking Bongobondhu's release the following message: "We appreciate your sympathetic approach to our problems and hope you and your learned colleagues will consider our case more deeply and act according to your conscience. I do not have to emphasize that the suffering humanity in Bangla Desh poses a test of conscience for the rest of the world."[282]

Following the same vein, Ellen Haq of Hamilton, who was active in raising awareness about the genocidal killings of Bengalis in East Pakistan, also wrote, "The combined efforts of Canada and all the other democratic nations of the world may not prove sufficient to sway Yahya from his vicious intent, but I think we must put pressure on him for the release of Mujibur Rahman. We should tell Yahya Khan that if Pakistan ever hopes for another cent of Canadian aid, he must cease the continuing genocide in Bengal, restore Mujib to freedom, and allow him and the other surviving elected representatives to assume power.[283]

Lobbying for Bongobondhu's release continued even at a tremendous pace after the birth of Bangladesh. For example, E. H. Johnson of the Toronto-based Presbyterian Church, who represented Canada at the Board of World Mission, took a different approach. He congratulated President Bhutto on the "firm beginning" of his "regime with magnanimous actions demonstrating concern for all" his people.[284] "As a friend of both Pakistan and India, I urge you to consider releasing Mujib [ur], Rahman, to facilitate a peaceful conclusion in East and peaceful relations with India and gain your respect and support as a statesman of major stature,"[285] wrote Johnson.

The news media also remained alert, keeping the issue of Bongobondhu's release alive until his release was announced in early January 1972. On January 8, 1972, the Bhutto government unconditionally released Bongobondhu from Pakistan. The Canadian public was relieved.

Demand for Recognition of Bangladesh

Throughout the Liberation War period, the Bengali segment of the Canadian public continued to lobby the Trudeau administration to recognize Bangladesh. The Trudeau administration was aware that the East Pakistani Bengalis, with assistance from the Gandhi administration, had already declared the independence of Bangladesh even though East Pakistan was still legally a part of a united Pakistan. Having remained transparent, a resolute Sharp stated his government's bottom line, "In conclusion, I should like to say that I am not convinced that anything positive would be achieved by confrontation with the present Government of Pakistan. On humanitarian grounds alone, I believe it is essential that relief and rehabilitation assistance be provided to East Pakistan, but new commitments of development aid will be conditional upon an agreed solution being found to the present political impasse."[286] Overall, the public appreciated the critical situation of the government.

And yet, despite having prior knowledge of Canada's position of "neutrality" and "nonintervention" in the "internal affairs" of Pakistan, the pro-Bangladeshis remained obdurately persistent in their steadfast appeal to the government. It was known to the Bengalis that the Trudeau administration did not wish even to be perceived as siding with the rebel forces. They tended to ignore this. Though stationed in Washington as head of the Bangladesh Mission, Canada was still a part of Siddiqi's new strategy. He left no stone unturned in urging pro-Bangladeshi Canadians to keep pushing the envelope for Bangladesh despite his knowledge about the over-sensitivity and limitations of the Trudeau administration in this matter. Siddiqi's two right-hand men in the Washington Mission were Third Secretary Syed Muazzem Ali and Enayat Karim, both of whom were aware of the knowledge of Canada's fear of the Québec hardliners who could easily find a nexus between the separation of Québec and the Bengalis fight for independence, something that could potentially cause waves.

While the pro-Bangladeshis demanded that Canada should recognize Bangladesh, the sooner, the better. The demand of the non-Bengali pro-Pakistani Canadians, who favored a united Pakistan, was that Canada should make a prompt intervention with an appeal to India to stop meddling in Pakistan's "internal affairs." The Trudeau administration was under pressure from both groups. They maintained that the government could do more since it was moving along at its own pace "diplomatically." The public, however, was encouraged to see the media's efforts to call a spade a spade. They appreciated the media's use of the terms for killings by the military regime as "massacre," "genocide," "pogrom," and "indiscriminate slaughter," which resulted in the declaration of the War of Liberation by the Bengalis to free their homeland as well as the news coverage by the media on the freedom fighters' bold role in liberating their homeland.

The majority of the public recognized the cautious approach of the Trudeau administration, which remained on its guard not to categorize the issue in the same manner. The public became more sensitive about it, seeing how a tight-lipped Sharp had remained doubly circumspect, not to use any such terminology. Sharp, they noted, was comfortable in referring to the brutal military actions as the "events in Pakistan," or "confrontation with the present government of Pakistan," or the "present political impasse," just so that the Trudeau government would be seen as "politically correct."

As part of their communication strategy, the pro-Bangladeshi public made sure that the "demand for recognition of Bangladesh" remains on their agenda as one of their top priorities. By instantly dissociating them from Pakistan and having endorsed their full support for an independent Bangladesh, members of the Bengali segment carried placards saying "Recognize Bangla Desh" at all public demonstrations and rallies. This had been an integral part of their strategy, whether lobbying the government or having street demonstrations.

Having condemned the slaughtering of unarmed civilians and the suppression of a democratically elected majority in Pakistan, the pro-Bangladeshis continued to express their misgivings. They urged the government to recognize Bangladesh even though they were aware of Canada's vulnerability to questions related to the "separation" or "independence" of Québec. We noted in Chapter 3 how the news media became convinced of the military regime's duplicity, the blame game, and sheer politics in the name of national integrity. Both the press and the pro-Bangladeshi public recognized that the Trudeau administration was caught between the devil and the deep blue sea for its problem with the members of the FLQ. They knew that, for the Trudeau administration, it was out of the question even to put the notion of an independent Bangladesh on its radar screen for discussion. But, despite it all, the pro-Bangladeshis never ceased lobbying the government for recognition of Bangladesh.

The pro-Bangladeshis even tried to find various ways to put pressure even though they knew that Canada was struggling with the idea of disintegration of Pakistan since Canada wanted to see the leader of the majority (Bongobondhu) in power in a democratic Pakistan ending the military rule. For example, as part of his game plan, Dr. Farid Shariff, president of the Bangladesh Association of Manitoba, ensured that two facts must be borne in mind - that those in favor of Bangladesh would also appreciate Canada's inability to take a lead role as a middle power regarding Bangladesh as well as Canada's particular difficulty in addressing the issue of separation or independence of Bangladesh. Shariff carefully explained to Mustafizur Rahman, head of the Bangladesh Mission in Washington, Canada's political vulnerability and innate fear, which is often referred to as Canada's "Québec question," to ensure that the pro-Bangladeshis do not interpret Canada's position negatively. "Canada finds it difficult to take a position at present as it has a similar and unique problem related to the Province of Québec."[287] Thus, Shariff wrote to Siddiqi hoping that the pro-Bangladeshis, whether in Canada or the USA, would recognize Canada's diplomatic limitations and consequent incapability to broach the matter.

A passionate Siddiqi was so committed to moving forward with the mission that he never took no for an answer. He engaged his right-hand man, Syed Muazzem Ali, to liaise with the pro-Bangladeshi groups in Canada. Although based in Washington, Ali actively pursued Canadian parliamentarians. Ali secured an appointment for Siddiqi with Minister Sharp and arranged for a reception for Siddiqi on the evening of September 21, 1971, with several senior officials along with a few liberal-minded MPs to join pro-Bangladeshi Canadians in Ottawa. Behind the scenes, however, Sharp was advised by Ottawa officials to maintain a certain distance from the Bangladesh Association of Canada, which had been pressuring the government to recognize Bangladesh. Undersecretary A. E. Ritchie's cautionary note ran in the following: "While there is undoubtedly a great deal of sympathy in Canada for the Bangla Desh cause, there is a danger that our relations with the government of Pakistan will suffer should it appear that 'Canadian government officials are patronizing Bangla Desh' functions."[288] Ritchie advised that the minister "may wish to raise the problem in Cabinet and point out that it is not in the government's interest to acknowledge or associate itself in any way with the Bangla Desh Association."[289] Not privy to Ritchie's cautionary remarks, both Siddiqi and A. B. Sattar (executive secretary of the Bangladesh-Canada Association) met with Sharp. They did not have the foggiest notion about how his advisers briefed Sharp.

It was good that the pro-Bangladeshis were in the dark about how Sharp was briefed. Naturally, they remained inexorably resolved not to give up since they were working on the premise that the historical and political contexts between the Bengalis' struggle for independence and the Québecer's demand for an independent Québec were different. Having compared their notes regarding the situation between Canada and East Pakistan, Sharif and Siddiqi agreed to have a new strategy to underscore the *differentness* of the political contexts. Siddiqi emphasized the following two points in his latest plan: (1) that all pro-Bangladeshis will "have to impress on them [Canadians at large] the basic difference between the Bengalis' struggle for independence and the demand for separation of Québec. I am sure you will be working on this line,"[290] and (2) they "should try and persuade Canada to be the pioneer in supporting an independent Bangladesh movement."[291] Siddiqi's argument that, politically, things were changing at a frenetic pace in East Pakistan made sense to Shariff, who agreed to continue his efforts. It was evident to interested parties that freedom fighters were making substantial strides toward liberating Bangladesh.

Under the leadership of Dr. Shariff, all association presidents worked tirelessly between mid-October and early December 1971 with government officials and parliamentarians to push the envelope for recognition as part of a new strategy. Shariff encouraged pro-Bangladeshis to be more creative in finding ways to broach the Bengalis' struggle for independence vis-à-vis the separation of Québec in their regular conversations with the public. To make the matter more convincing, the more politically astute part of the community highlighted the rapid progress the freedom fighters were making. While continuing their conversation, they asked, "How can we generate support among the elected officials who had the influence over policymaking within the executive and legislative bodies of the government?" Dr. Luthful Kabir recalled how they spent days together reflecting on how to draw attention to the atrocities that were being committed in "Occupied Bangladesh?"[292] They found no specific answer but did not get discouraged. They remained active in lobbying the government as an organized advocate for Bangladesh, to whom it was a matter of gathering strength and learning by experience. Ongoing questions regarding what else could be done to enhance their cause are evident in the works of the various associations, committees, and individuals.

In the meantime, on December 16, 1971, the Pakistani army surrendered to the joint Indian and Bangladeshi forces, paving the way for the birth of an independent Bangladesh. From then on, all efforts centered exclusively on Canada's recognition of the newborn country - this became the topmost priority for the pro-Bangladeshis in Canada. The Ottawa members of the Bangladesh Association of Canada quickly crafted a succinct appeal letter in which they thanked the government and people of Canada for their moral and financial support while the Bengalis were fighting for independence.

They pressed not only for immediate recognition of Bangladesh but also for establishing diplomatic relations with the newborn country. In their demands, they also emphasized obtaining permission for training opportunities for Bangladeshis in urgently needed technical, medical, paramedical, social sciences, and other subjects in Canada. The pressure for recognition of Bangladesh continued until Canada formally accorded recognition to Bangladesh on February 14, 1972.

Put differently, the pro-Bangladeshis wanted Bongobondhu to take charge of Bangladesh as a separate sovereign country that would no longer be a part of Pakistan. They immediately crafted an appeal letter free of all jargon to stimulate a meaningful conversation among Canadians. With their distinctive positioning message, they made sure that there was no room for compromise. Lobbying for Bangladesh was confined only to the Bengali East Pakistani segment of the Canadian public and Canadians of Indian origin who continued to vie for the government's attention.

The pro-Pakistanis, mainly consisting of the non-Bengali West Pakistanis, lobbied the government for a united Pakistan under the present military dictator, Yahya. They neither condemned the military regime nor demanded its removal. They commended the military regime for its prompt action against Indian agents. Having unwaveringly supported the military dictator, they did not consider Yahya a usurper of power. They lobbied the Trudeau administration to maintain the status quo, having claimed that it was "business as usual" in Pakistan other than some interference in destabilizing Pakistan's economy and infrastructure through the help of a bunch of pro-Indian misguided Bengali rebels.

They condemned the Gandhi administration for its direct interference in the "internal affairs" of Pakistan and insisted on the commencement of Bongobondhu's trial as early as possible. Within the pro-Pakistani segment, however, there was a bit of a nuanced difference between the two sub-groups. A handful of Bengali Canadians supported a united but reformed Pakistan. Again, many non-Bengali West Pakistani Canadians also demanded a united Pakistan based on the result of the 1970 National Elections. This means that, in a sense, the latter favored Bongobondhu to become the ruler but within the framework of a united Pakistan.

The pro-Pakistani Canadians, who openly favored the Yahya regime, remained so stubborn that even after the liberation of Bangladesh, they did not accept the political reality of an independent Bangladesh. They desperately lobbied the government for its support of the military regime even weeks following the formal surrender of the Pakistani army. They even tried to dissuade the Trudeau administration from recognizing Bangladesh. To them, the loss of East Pakistan - they did not see it as the birth of Bangladesh - was the result of an Indian conspiracy through the dismantling of Pakistan. It was as though the "Occupation army" had neither surrendered nor had the rebel forces won their victory even though Bangladesh had already become sovereign and independent since December 16, 1971.

The rest of the Canadian public, the mainstream Canadians, or the greater public, was neither with the pro-Bangladeshis nor pro-Pakistanis in the true sense. Like the pro-Bangladeshis, they were dismayed at seeing the stark tragedy. For them, it was time to flex the muscles of compassion for the victims of military reprisals. They were appalled by the military regime's barbarity, continuous repression, and fallout of the war. Like the pro-Bangladeshis, they also experienced the ineffectiveness of the UN. Most of the public was with the pro-Bangladeshis in that both demanded Bongobondhu's unconditional release throughout the troubled months. There is, however, a significant difference in their objectives and goals.

Again, the views of the pro-Bangladeshi Canadians were different and pronounced than the views of the mainstream public, even about the release of Bongobondhu. While the Bengalis were demanding Bongobondhu's release to become the leader of Bangladesh, which became an independent country out of Pakistan, the mainstream public joined hands with pro-Bangladeshis in their demand for Bongobondhu's release to become the head of a *reformed* but *united Pakistan*. Unlike the pro-Bangladeshis, the greater public took a strong position on democratization in Pakistan, where the elected leader, Bongobondhu, was supposed to form the government. Politically speaking, the greater public believed that, by adopting a neutral stance on the sovereignty dispute, Canada would reduce the risk of appearing helpful in fueling the notion of "nationalism" among the Bengalis at the cost of a united Pakistan. In expressing their concerns, the mainstream public demonstrated to the world their devotion to the sanctity of human life. Dr. Wali Khan of St. John's, who talked to many of his clients/patients, observed that Canadians were outraged at the incidences of death, destruction, looting, and incendiaries. They had mixed feelings; some were overenthusiastic, some neutral, while others had no particular view as to whether Pakistan should be dismantled or not.[293]

The point is that most of the mainstream public did not divide themselves as pro or anti. They condemned the military regime and demanded a political resolution for a *democratic Pakistan*. As noted, many members of the public showed unconditional sympathy for both the victims living in East Pakistan and the refugee camps in India - their focus was on providing support to the victims of military reprisals and, at the same time, preventing the tragedy of Pakistan's breakup. They hoped that, with a strong push for support for restoring democracy in Pakistan, efforts should be made to place Bongobondhu, the uncontested Bengali leader whose popularity had already reached epic proportions, in charge of a reformed and democratic Pakistan without dismantling the country.

As far as the mainstream public is concerned, the keyword was establishing democracy in Pakistan without breaking the country into two halves. How exactly that was to be approached when Bangladesh was seemingly becoming a political reality was a million-dollar question. Neither the Trudeau government nor the Canadian public could find an answer. The views of most Canadians also echoed the views of the Trudeau administration. We shall read more about Canada's position on the conflict in Chapter 8.

Notes and References

1. *The Ottawa Citizen*, dated March 9, 1971.
2. Restricted Letter from Head of Pacific South Asia Division from GPS to PDM. Dated March 29, 1971. File # 20-E-Pak-1-4. Subject: Call by East Pakistani Students. Canada. Department of External Affairs. Following the military clampdown, the organization changed its name to the Bangladesh Association of Canada. There is no record indicating the date the name was changed. However, Professors Lutful Kabir and Mizan Rahman, who were directly involved, recall that it must have occurred immediately after the military takeover. Again, following the independence of Bangladesh, the name Bangladesh Association of Canada was changed to the Bangladesh Canada Association of Ottawa Valley (BACAOV) to reflect the changing demographic of the Bengali Canadians in the National Capital Region (NCR). Hereinafter, all information used in this chapter from the Department of External Affairs' records shall be referred to as External Affairs.
3. Email from Professor Mizan Rahman to Mustafa Chowdhury, dated March 8, 2011. Dr. Rahman has lived in Ottawa throughout his career. The author

had numerous opportunities to discuss his involvement in various activities supporting Bangladesh with Professor Rahman.
4. Letter from Ahsanullah Mullick, then a Torontonian, to Mustafa Chowdhury, dated February 23, 2012. Mr. Mullick is currently living in Edmonton. The author met Mullick in Montreal numerous times, where he lived for several years. The author interviewed him formally in 2012.
5. *Ibid.*
6. *The Globe and Mail*, dated March 27, 1971.
7. *Ibid.*
8. *Ibid.*
9. Letter from Dr. Lutfor Rahman, a Vancouverite, to Mustafa Chowdhury, dated October 10, 2011. Before that, the author met Dr. Rahman in Vancouver in 2000 and had been in regular touch with him.
10. *Bangladesh: Campaign for Self-rule of East Bengal*, published by Fareed S. Jafri, London, U.K., No 4, 26 April 1971 (International edition) p. 1. This document is contained in File # 20-E-Pak-1-4 in the Department of External Affairs. *Op. cit.*
11. Email from Professor Mizan Rahman to Mustafa Chowdhury, *Op. cit.*
12. *Kitchener-Waterloo Record*, dated April 13, 1971.
13. Email from Dr. Mir Maqsud Ali, Professor Emeritus, the University of Illinois at Urbana-Champaign, to Mustafa Chowdhury, dated May 15, 2017. The author followed up with him and interviewed him three times in 2017. The author has known Ali since the 1960s.
14. *The Making of the October Crisis: Canada's Long Nightmare of Terrorism at the Hands of the FLQ*. Doubleday Canada. Montreal. 2018. p. 13.
15. *The Globe and Mail*, dated April 10, 1971.
16. E-mail from Professor Hafiz Rahman to Mustafa Chowdhury, dated July 19, 2011. The author has known Dr. Hafiz since the 1970s. Over the years, both have discussed the events on several occasions.
17. *Ibid.*
18. Confidential Memorandum, dated April 26, 1971, to PSI from J. M. Harrington, Head of the Pacific and South Asia Division. File # 20-E- Pak-1- 4. External Affairs. *Op. cit.*
19. This was in a leaflet entitled Statement of the Indian Progressive Study Group on the Recent Situation in East Pakistan and Opposing Interference by the Reactionary Indian Government in the Internal Affairs of Pakistan, dated April 3, 1971. The demonstrators distributed it to the public, who staged their first demonstration in front of the Indian High Commission in Ottawa on April 3, 1971. *Ibid.* External Affairs. *Op. cit.*
20. Email from Hakim Sikander, then President of the Bangladesh Association of Alberta (Calgary chapter), to Mustafa Chowdhury, dated February 18, 2011. The author then followed up with Dr. Sikander. Dr. Hakim Sikander

and Danielle Sikander visited the author in Ottawa in 2017 and discussed the couple's involvement in 1971.
21. *Ibid.*
22. Email from Dr. Haripad Dhar to Mustafa Chowdhury, dated June 3, 2012. Since then, the author has spoken over the telephone on several occasions.
23. Bilquis Kabir of Ottawa told the author in an interview on July 10, 2019. She followed up in a letter dated July 15, 2019. The author has known the Kabirs since the early 1970s.
24. *Recounting the birth of the nation of Bangladesh: A Canadian perspective*, by Rabiul Alam, who did a presentation at the 40th Anniversary of the independence of Bangladesh. The magazine sub-committee, Vancouver, published this on March 26, 2011, pp. 14–15. Also, the author has been in direct touch with the Alams since 2010. Chowdhury formally interviewed him on June 10, 2011, and has corresponded since then regarding his role in 1971. The author met him in Vancouver in 2017.
25. Letter from Dr. Harun Rashid, Professor, Lakehead University, to Mustafa Chowdhury, dated August 26, 1996. The author has known Dr. Rashid since the mid-1970s and has been in touch with him for years. The author followed up with him on many occasions regarding the public's role in 1971.
26. E-mail from Professor Harun Rashid to Mustafa Chowdhury, dated August 20, 2020.
27. E-mail from Professor Nurul Islam to Mustafa Chowdhury, dated May 1, 2012. The author has known Dr. Nurul Islam since the 1970s. He met Dr. Islam several times in Montreal and heard about his involvement in raising awareness in the Montreal area.
28. Letter from Professor Saber M. Saleuddin to Mustafa Chowdhury, dated May 20, 1996. The author then followed up with Dr. Saleuddin.
29. Statistics Canada. 1973. *Ethnic groups = Groupes ethniques.* Statistics Canada Catalogue no. 92-723. Ottawa.
30. E-mail from Faruk Sarkar to Mustafa Chowdhury, dated May 1, 2012. Sarkar was a graduate student at the University of Ottawa at the time. The author has known Sarkar and his wife, Suzie Sarkar, since the 1970s.
31. *Ibid.*
32. *Ibid.*
33. E-mail from Matiur Rahman, then a student at the University of Toronto, to Mustafa Chowdhury, dated January 10, 2011. The author then followed up with Rahman and is in touch with him.
34. Letter from Dr. Farid Shariff to Mustafa Chowdhury, dated October 11, 2001. The author met Dr. Shariff in Winnipeg several times and had been in touch with him until his passing in 2023.
35. *Toronto Daily Star*, dated April 1, 1971.
36. *Ibid.* Dated June 28, 1971.

37. Confidential Memo dated April 26, 1971, to PSI from J.M. Harrington, Head, Pacific, and South Asia Division. File # 20 -E- Pak-1- 4. External Affairs. *Op. cit.*
38. *Ottawa Press Conference*. Dated, May 25, 1971.
39. *The Globe and Mail*, dated May 26, 1971.
40. The author interviewed Dr. Samar Mazumdar on July 20, 2001. Unfortunately, he does not recall the exact date, although he remembers that it was around the first week of May. The author then followed up with him in writing.
41. E-mail from Professor Nurul Islam to Mustafa Chowdhury, dated April 10, 2010. The author has known Dr. Islam since the 1970s and has been in touch with him since then.
42. *Montreal Star*, dated June 29, 1971.
43. *Toronto Daily Star*, dated June 28, 1971.
44. *Montreal Star*, dated 29 June 1971.
45. *Toronto Daily Star*, dated June 28, 1971.
46. E-mail from Rabiul Alam to Mustafa Chowdhury, dated July 10, 2020. *Op. cit*
47. E-mail from Cummer Chowdhury to Mustafa Chowdhury, dated March 23, 2012. The author then followed up with Chowdhury.
48. *Ibid.*
49. *Ibid.*
50. This was stated by Naiyyum Chowdhury, General Secretary of the Bangla Desh Association of Québec cited in the book titled *Bangladesher Shadhinota Judho: dolilpotro (History of Bangladesh War of Independence: Documents)*, volume 3, p. 785. Ministry of Information, Government of the People's Republic of Bangladesh. Dhaka, 1982. Edited by Hassan Hafizur Rahman. Hereinafter referred to as the History of Bangladesh War of Independence. Chowdhury also narrated the same story to the author on July 12, 2009, when he met the author in Ottawa.
51. Confidential telegram from John Small, high commissioner to Pakistan, to Ottawa. Telegram # 2843, dated July 22, 1971, p. 3. File # 21-3-India-Pak-SITREP. External Affairs. *Op. cit.*
52. *Toronto Daily Star*, dated July 6, 1971.
53. *Ibid.*
54. *The Globe and Mail*, dated July 19, 1971.
55. *The Globe and Mail*, dated July 22, 1971.
56. *Ibid.*
57. *Ibid.*
58. *Ibid.*
59. *Ibid.*
60. *Ibid.*

61. *Sphulinga,* Bangladesh Association of Québec, dated August 1, 1971, mentioned in the History of Bangladesh War of Independence, vol. 4, p. 357. *Op. cit.* In addition, the author interviewed Dr. Sudhir Saha, then Treasurer of the Bangladesh Students Association, UBC. Dr. Saha later became a professor at the Memorial University of Newfoundland. Between 2011 and 2013, the author conducted several rounds of interviews with Dr. Saha. The author is in regular touch with Dr. Saha.
62. Naiyyum Chowdhury, then General Secretary of the Bangla Desh Association of Québec, stated this to the author. The author interviewed Chowdhury in Ottawa again on July 12, 2009, and had been in touch with Chowdhury until his passing in 2019.
63. The author interviewed Dr. Wali Khan in Saskatoon on July 15, 1998, where he lived during the interview. Since then, the author has met Dr. Khan several times in Saskatoon and discussed his role in raising awareness among the people of St. John's.
64. Dr. Mohammad Matlib narrated his experience to the author during the demonstration in which he participated and other awareness-raising activities throughout 1971. The author corresponded with him for several years. He formally interviewed Dr. Matlib on August 13, 2017.
65. *Evening Telegram*, dated August 5, 1971.
66. *The Globe and Mail*, dated August 16, 1971.
67. *Ibid.*
68. E-mail from Dr. Lutfor Rahman to Mustafa Chowdhury, dated May 5, 2011. The author first met Dr. Rahman in Vancouver in 2000. The author is in touch with Dr. Rahman and has followed up with him on many occasions regarding his testimonies.
69. *Ibid.*
70. E-mail from Dr. Sudhir Saha to Mustafa Chowdhury, dated 12 August 2011. *Op. cit.*
71. *Ibid.*
72. *The Globe and Mail*, dated September 17, 1971.
73. This letter was sent to Mitchell Sharp, Secretary of State for External Affairs, on a letterhead titled Pakistan Students' Association of Ottawa, dated November 24, 1971, and signed by the Association's Secretary, Asif Javed. File # 3; 20-India-1-3-Pak. External Affairs. *Op. cit.*
74. *Ibid.*
75. *The Globe and Mail,* dated December 6, 1971.
76. *Toronto Daily Star,* dated December 14, 1971.
77. *Ibid.*
78. Editorial note in *Joy Bangla*, Bangladesh Association of British Columbia, dated September 27, 1971, printed in the *History of Bangladesh War of Independence*, Volume 4, p. 364. *Op. cit.* The author also interviewed Dr.

Khan twice in 1999 and 2000. Over the years, the author has maintained contact with Dr. Khan.
79. E-mail from Dr. Lutfor Rahman to Mustafa Chowdhury, dated May 25, 2011. *Op. cit.*
80. *Ibid.*
81. *Ibid.*
82. Professors Barrie Morris of the University of British Columbia and Ralph W. Nicholas of Michigan State University forwarded the resolution. This is stated in the *History of Bangladesh War of Independence*, volume 3, p. 785. *Op. cit.*
83. E-mail from Dr. Shahid Hussain to Mustafa Chowdhury, dated 14 July 2011. Upon receipt of his input, the author formally interviewed Dr. Hussain on August 19, 2011. He then had another follow-up interview with Dr. Hussain. Later, the author corresponded with Hussain again on September 20, 2011. The author is in touch with him.
84. *Ibid.*
85. *Ibid.*
86. Editorial in *Joy Bangla*, dated November 15, 1971, Bangladesh Association of British Columbia, reprinted in the *History of Bangladesh War of Independence*, vol. 4, p. 374. *Op. cit.*
87. The author interviewed the couple, Siddique Hossain and Shahana Hossain, in Edmonton, Alberta, on September 7, 2007. Over the years, the author has discussed their role in 1971 on many occasions. The author is in touch with them and has recently verified some information.
88. *Ibid.*
89. *The Globe and Mail*, dated July 6, 1971.
90. *Ibid.*
91. *Bangladesh: Campaign for Self-rule of East Bengal*, published by Fareed S. Jafri, London, U.K., No 4, dated April 26, 1971 (International edition) p. 1. File name: Pakistan Background Reports, Statements, Clippings 1971 (July). File # 20-E-Pak-1-4; MG 32 C26 vol. 87. External Affairs. *Op. cit.* Also, a letter was addressed to MP Andrew Brewin from Hakim Sikander, President of the Bangladesh-Canada Association of Alberta. The letter is dated July 21, 1971. It is contained in Andrew Brewin's Papers in Library and Archives Canada. MG 32 C26, vol. 87. Hereinafter, all information used in this chapter from the Library and Archives Canada records shall be referred to as Library and Archives Canada.
92. File Name: Pakistan Government Communication re 1971. MG 28 1 270 Volume 5. Library and Archives Canada. *Op. cit.*
93. "Bangla Desh struggle: an overview" by Sushil Bhattacharjee in *The Sheaf*, University of Saskatchewan, Saskatoon, vol. 61, no. 7, dated October 5, 1971, p. 1. The meeting was in solidarity with the University's observance

of Bangladesh Day on Thursday, September 30, 1971, at the University of Saskatchewan, Saskatoon. This was when the independence movement gained a fair amount of respect in the Western world.
94. *Ibid.* Professor Satya Sharma's paper, "Role of International Political Opinion in Solving the Bangla Desh Crisis," was read at Teach-in on Bangla Desh. *Ibid.* p. 1.
95. *Ibid.* Professor Bernard Lall, Faculty of Education, University of Saskatchewan, Regina campus, was Secretary of the Bangla Desh Association of Saskatchewan. His paper Bangla Desh Liberation - pros and cons was read at the Teach-in on Bangladesh. *Ibid.* p. 3.
96. *Ibid, p. 2.* This is quoted from Professor Colwyn Williams' paper, "Role of U.N. in the Bangla Desh freedom struggle," read at the Teach-in on Bangladesh.
97. *Ibid.* p. 3.
98. *Ibid.* p. 3. Asit Sarkar's speech at the Teach-in on Bangladesh session. The meeting was held on September 30, 1971, at the University of Saskatchewan, Saskatoon.
99. This was observed by Dr. Anwar Haque, Treasurer of the Association, to the author when he was in Ottawa to visit the author on July 24, 2004. Dr. Haque discussed his disagreement with Dr. Anwar Chowdhury, then BAS' President.
100. This is contained in a flyer titled *Weep, Muslims Weep,* attributed to M. al Mughaimish, which has no date, although it was written following President Yahya's June 28 speech to the nation. This was drafted by Professor Hari Narayan Gupta of the University of Saskatchewan in collaboration with Dr. Anwar Chowdhury, President of the Bangladesh Association of Saskatchewan (BAS). This was hand-delivered to the University community members and selectively mailed to the local MPs, MPPs, and several heads of Muslim states during summer and early fall. Dr. Anwar Chowdhury gave the author a copy of the flyer from his collection.
101. *Ibid.*
102. An Open Letter of Appeal written on the Bangla Desh Association of Manitoba's letterhead, signed by Abu M. Zahirul Alam, General Secretary, dated April 28, 1971. This was sent to MPs, MPPs, and the general public. People were asked to send a cheque payable to "The Bangla Desh Relief Fund." Photocopies of the original documents were made available to the author by Dr. Farid Shariff, President of the Association, from his archival collection in 1997.
103. *Ibid.*
104. Government of Manitoba. Information Services Branch, Proclamation, Pakistan Refugee Day, June 17, 1971; Manitoba Will Aid Pakistan Refugees.

MG 28 1 270 Volume 5, File: Pakistan Re Manitoba. Library and Archives Canada. *Op. cit.*
105. *Oxfam of Canada Press Release*, July 12, 1971, p. 1. *Ibid.*
106. See footnote # 89.
107. This was one of the most powerful statements made by Acting Prime Minister Tajudduin Ahmed of the provisional government of the People's Republic of Bangladesh, which impacted the minds of Bengalis worldwide.
108. In a sense, Alam's involvement in Canada regarding the liberation of Bangladesh was a natural carryover from the early 1960s when he was on the front line of the students' movement in East Pakistan to repeal the infamous Education Policy introduced by the Pakistani government. During the entire liberation movement, Alam remained in touch with his friends in East Pakistan and India, with whom he was deeply involved during his student years.
109. E-mail from Rabiul Alam to Mustafa Chowdhury, dated July 10, 2020. Several video calls on WhatsApp followed this.
110. *Toronto Daily Star*, dated April 28, 1971.
111. *Ibid.*
112. *Ibid.*
113. *Ibid.*, dated June 28, 1971.
114. *Toronto Daily Star*, dated July 10, 1971.
115. The following people were asked to endorse: Jack Grant, Doug Creighton, Frederic Nossal, Bob Raguey, John Drewery, Reverend E. Johnson, Dr. Robert McClure, Georges Lachance, Andrew Brewin, Stanley Burke, Ernest Hillen, J. Lakavitch, Northrop Fry, and James Eayrs; PEOPLE TO PEOPLE CAMPAIGN Action, South Asia Emergency Refugee Fund, p.10. MG 28, I 270, vol. 5, File: Action Pakistan, 1971-1972. Library and Archives Canada. *Op. cit.*
116. The author frequently met the Samads in the 1970s through family connections. Specifically, the author interviewed Abdus Samad twice in 1998 and 1999 while living in Toronto. His memory was then a bit vague. But he recalled basically what is stated here.
117. See footnote # 2.
118. High Commission of India, Ottawa. *India News,* No. 33/71, dated August 17, 1971, pp. 9-10. The network was established among members of the India-Canada Association, the Indian Students Association, the Indian High Commission, and the Oxfam Canada personnel working in all activities. MG 28 1 270 Volume 5. File: Combined Appeal for Pakistani Relief and Other Agency Press Releases, Statements, and Material, 1971. Library and Archives Canada. *Op. cit.*
119. High Commission of India, Ottawa. *India News*, No. 30/71, July 27, 1971, pp. 9–10. *Ibid. Op. cit.*

120. Jack Lakavitch left Dhaka on May 6, 1971, and went on to Japan, from where he returned to Canada to work for the Student Christian Movement in Canada. Before returning to Canada, he spent about five weeks in Kolkata, West Bengal, to make himself "right up to date on the Bangla Desh situation" and make his "findings available to whoever cared to have them." p.1. MG 32, C31, vol. 32, File # 32-2. Library and Archives Canada. *Op. cit.*
121. *Ibid.* p. 5.
122. Editorial note in the newsletter titled Bangladesh, Bangladesh Association of Canada (Toronto), dated August 25, 1971, cited in the *History of Bangladesh War of Independence,* vol. 4, p.360. *Op. cit.*
123. E-mail from Dr. Mir Maqsud Ali, Professor Emeritus, the University of Illinois at Urbana-Champaign, to Mustafa Chowdhury, dated May 15, 2017. The author has regularly contacted Dr. Ali and followed up regarding his participation in the London and Waterloo, Ontario rallies.
124. *Ibid.*
125. *Ibid.*
126. E-mail from Rabi Alam to Mustafa Chowdhury, dated July 10, 2020. *Op. cit*
127. Letter from Dr. Wahidul Haque to Mustafa Chowdhury, dated April 10, 2000. The author formally interviewed him on May 12, 2000, and then followed up with him on several occasions until his passing in 2020.
128. *Ibid.*
129. Jalaluddin Ahmed stated this to the author during his August 14, 2005, interview in Ottawa. The author also interviewed Shakila Jalaluddin. Professor Lutful Kabir was also present with the author, who had known them for a long time. The author spoke with the Ahmeds on many occasions.
130. *Ibid.*
131. The author stayed at the residence of Professor Maswood Ali and his wife, Suraiya Ali, while pursuing graduate studies at the University of Western Ontario in the early 1970s. He discussed their role with them on numerous occasions back in 1971.
132. The author formally interviewed Aziz Chowdhury on February 10, 2000, and followed up with him in later years. Chowdhury also gave the author several newspaper cuttings from his archival collections.
133. The author of this report had asked to remain anonymous to not jeopardize the possibility of returning to East Pakistan and to protect the identity of the people who provided the information.
134. Naiyyum Chowdhury, then General Secretary of the Bangla Desh Association of Québec, stated this to the author. See also footnote # 50.
135. Professor Nurul Islam of Concordia University stated this to the author. See also footnote # 27.
136. MG 32 C26 Vol. 87 File # 87-12. Library and Archives Canada. *Op. cit.*

137. *The Evening Patriot*, Patriot Publishing Company Ltd. Charlottetown, PEI, dated August 12, 1971.
138. *Ibid.*
139. Lakavitch. P.9. *Op. cit.* See also footnote # 113.
140. Letter from Dr. Moyeenul Islam to Mustafa Chowdhury on June 29, 1996, while living in Ottawa. Following that, the two met several times and discussed the activities Islam and his group engaged in during the period under review.
141. This was first narrated to the author by Dr. Abdul Matlib on June 3, 2012. Over the years, the author has remained in touch with Dr. Matlib and has incorporated many of his statements and recollections to raise awareness about the ongoing military repression and fundraising for the refugees in India. Dr. Matlib also indicated that throughout the Bengalis' struggle for independence, his wife, Mahbuba Matlib, remained active like them. See also footnote # 63.
142. Dr. Abdul Matlib narrated this to the author on 3 June 2012. *Op. cit.*
143. *Ibid.*
144. Letter from Dr. Moyeenul Islam to Mustafa Chowdhury. *Op. cit.*
145. *Ibid.*
146. Dr. Wali Khan, who lived in St. John's in 1971, narrated this to the author. The author met him in Saskatoon in 1997, where he was living. Since then, the author remained in touch with Dr. Khan until his passing in 2003.
147. Pakistan-correspondence with news media, # 1, 1971. RG 28 1 270 Volume 6, Library and Archives. *Op. cit.*
148. *Inside Oxfam*, Fall Edition, No. 23, p.6. MG 28 1 270 Volume 5, File: Combined Appeal for Pakistani Relief and Other Agency Press Releases, Statements, and Material, 1971. Library and Archives Canada. *Op. cit.*
149. Letter from Samir Mazumdar to Mustafa Chowdhury, dated February 12, 2012. Before that, the author interviewed him in Calgary and followed up with him regarding his narrative.
150. Siddique Hossain and Shahana Hossain of Edmonton, Alberta, stated this in an interview with the author on September 7, 2007.
151. E-mail from Hakim Sikander to Mustafa Chowdhury, dated August 10, 2012. The author then followed up with him. Over the years, they talked at length. Sikander and his wife, Danielle, visited the author in Ottawa in the summer of 2017.
152. *Ibid.*
153. *Ibid.*
154. See footnote # 89.
155. "Bangla Desh: A movement for Independence" by Shushil Bhattacharjee in *The Sheaf*, University of Saskatchewan, Saskatoon, 28 September 1971, p. 3. *Op. cit.*

156. *Ibid.*
157. *Ibid.*
158. The author regularly corresponded with Dr. Anwar Haque from the 1990s to early 2000 when he lived in Regina, Saskatchewan. This was mentioned to the author when Dr. Haque visited the author in Ottawa on July 24, 2004.
159. Dr. Haque gave the author a few stamps he had treasured all these years.
160. E-mail from Mrs. Rubena Sinha to Mustafa Chowdhury, dated May 1, 2012; also, the author had several rounds of telephone interviews with Sinha following receipt of her e-mails
161. The author interviewed Dr. Hamida Begum, a retired professor of Psychology at Dhaka University. He learned from Begum about her role in 1971 as a PhD student at the University of Manitoba. The first interview was on January 14, 2014, and then again on March 3, 2020. Despite the passage of time, Begum comfortably recalled the uncertain time and her project regarding the cultural show.
162. Letter from Dr. Farid Shariff, President, Bangla Desh Association of Manitoba to Chief, Central Relief Committee for Refugees from East Bengal, New Delhi, India, dated June 22, 1971. Dr. Shariff has the original copy of this letter in his archives. He gave the author a photocopy copy of the letter.
163. *Ibid.*
164. There are two sources for this piece of information. (1) letter from Dr. Farid Shariff to Abdul Momin, high commissioner of Bangladesh to Canada. The letter is dated July 19, 1974, cited above. It is in the personal archival collection of Dr. Shariff, who gave the author a photocopy. (2) This was also written in a letter addressed to Bangabandhu Sheikh Mujibur Rahman, Prime Minister, People's Republic of Bangladesh, by Mahbub'ul Alam, President, Bangladesh Association of New England, dated December 14, 1972. Dr. Shariff also has a photocopy of this letter in his archives. Again, he gave the author a photocopy of this letter.
165. *Canadian India Times*, September 2, 1971, p. 11. This paper is kept in the Archives under MG 32 C26 Volume 84, File 84-20. Library and Archives Canada. *Op. cit.*
166. *Ibid.*
167. *Ibid.*
168. *Canadian India Times*, September 2, 1971, p. 11. This paper is kept in the Archives under MG 32 C26 Volume 84, File 84-20. Library and Archives Canada. *Op. cit.*
169. The People of Bangla Desh need your help, PEOPLE TO PEOPLE CAMPAIGN, South Asia Emergency Refugee Fund, 17 December 1971, p. 8; MG 32 C31, vol. 32, File: Bangla Desh 1971. Library and Archives *Op. cit.*
170. *Ibid.*

171. Letter from Larry R. Tubman, Assistant Director, Oxfam Canada, to Dr. M.M. Rahman, General Secretary, Bangladesh Association of Canada, dated November 12, 1971. MG 28 I 270 Volume 18 File: Pakistan Ref General. Library and Archives Canada. *Op. cit.*
172. The author interviewed Mr. Ahsanullah Mullick in 2011 and talked to him occasionally while living in Montreal. The conversation summary was outlined in a letter by Mr. Mullick to Mustafa Chowdhury, dated January 15, 2012. *Op. cit.* See also footnote # 3.
173. *Ibid.*
174. Rabiul Alam stated this to the author in an e-mail dated August 12, 2011. Over the years, the author discussed their role with the Alams in 1971 and obtained various information.
175. The author interviewed Madeline Alam, who lives in Vancouver, on May 30, 2011. She then outlined the interview summary in a letter addressed to Mustafa Chowdhury, dated June 10, 2011. The author is in regular touch with the Alams.
176. E-mail from Professor Mizan Rahman to Mustafa Chowdhury, March 8, 2011. *Op. cit.* See also footnote # 2.
177. The couple lived in Ottawa for several years and then moved to the States in the late 1980s. The author met them several times. Specifically, the author interviewed Dr. Mohammad Ahsanullah and his wife, Masuda Ahsanullah, on March 22, 2011. They confirmed the summary of their input in a letter to Mustafa Chowdhury dated May 6, 2011. The author then followed up over the telephone.
178. The author interviewed Azmat Ali and Jahanara Ali, who live in Washington, D.C., on January 11, 2008. The couple then confirmed the summary of the interview in an email to Mustafa Chowdhury dated March 10, 2008. Since then, the author has regularly contacted Azmat Ali and received more input, especially regarding awareness-raising in the Ottawa area.
179. *Ibid.*
180. Professor Lutful Kabir of Carleton University observed this in his interview with the author on May 12, 2005, in Ottawa. Since the author and the couple live in the same city, the author talked to the couple numerous times, both formally and informally, to gather as much information as possible. The Kabirs were active in 1971 from the very beginning of the military assault in Pakistan. Dr. Kabir confirmed the information he had provided over the years in a separate email to the author, dated July 10, 2011.
181. *Inside Oxfam,* Fall Edition, No. 23, p. 7. MG 28 1 270 Volume 5, File: Combined Appeal for Pakistani Relief and other agency press releases, statements, and material, 1971. Library and Archives Canada. *Op. cit.*
182. *Ibid.*

183. A Kenora resident's letter to the editor was printed in the *Kenora Daily Miner and News* on August 14, 1971. File: Pak Correspondence offers to help, thank yous, criticisms, political # 1. MG 28 I 270 Vol. 5. Library and Archives Canada. *Op. cit.*
184. *Inside Oxfam*, Fall Edition, No. 23, p.6. *Ibid. Op. cit.*
185. This information is available in Oxfam Canada's Library and Archives Canada file. MG 32 C31, vol. 32. Library and Archives Canada. *Op. cit.*
186. Email from Professor Nurul Islam to Mustafa Chowdhury dated July 10, 2011. *Op. cit.* See also footnote # 27.
187. The author interviewed Dr. Sadat Kazi on May 10, 2001, in Montreal and followed up regarding his role in arranging demonstrations in Montreal. Dr. Kazi spoke at length about the teamwork and the challenges they faced in raising awareness without making an analogy to the explosive situation in Québec's attempt to liberate the province from Canada.
188. See footnote # 61. *Op. cit.*
189. Letter from Bob Hawkes of Mount Allison University, Sackville, New Brunswick, to NDP federal office, Ottawa, dated November 23, 1971. This is contained in Andrew Brewin's file in the Archives under MG 32 C26, vol.87. Library and Archives Canada. *Op. cit.*
190. *The Evening Patriot*, Patriot Publishing Company Ltd. Charlottetown, PEI, August 12, 1971. The paper clipping is also available in the Archives under MG 32C26 Vol. 87 File # 87-12. Library and Archives Canada. *Op. cit.*
191. *Ibid.*
192. This was narrated to the author by Dr. Abdul Matlib on June 3, 2012. *Op. cit.* See also footnote # 139.
193. *Ibid.*
194. *Ibid.*
195. The above references are in the Oxfam of Canada file in the archives under MG 28, 1 270, vol. 5, File: Pak. Correspondence offers to help, Thank Yous, criticisms, political # 1. Library and Archives Canada. *Op. cit.*
196. Collection of radio announcements. MG 28, I 270, vol. 6, File: Pakistan, Human Interest. Library and Archives Canada. *Op. cit.*
197. Restricted Briefing Note from A. E. Ritchie, Undersecretary, to Mitchell Sharp, Secretary of State for External Affairs. Subject: International Contributions for Relief of Pakistan Refugees in India and Population of East Pakistan. Dated, October 22, 1971. File # 38 -11-1- Pakistan. External Affairs. *Op. cit.*
198. *Le Devoir Libre* Opinion under "La fin du Pakistan fedéral," mars 29,1971.
199. *Ibid.*
200. Letter to *The Globe and Mail*, dated April 1, 1971, by Dr. A. Mannan, Hartney, Manitoba. The author interviewed Dr. Mannan on two occasions

in the late 1990s. Dr. Mannan confirmed the discussion in a letter addressed to the author, dated February 11, 1999.
201. *The Ottawa Citizen*, dated April 8, 1971.
202. *Toronto Daily Star*, dated December 10, 1971.
203. *The Ottawa Citizen*, dated April 8, 1971.
204. *Ibid.*
205. Letter to the Editor, *The Globe and Mail*, dated April 1, 1971, by Syed Hassan of Clarkson, Ontario.
206. *Ibid.*
207. *Ibid.*
208. Letter to the Editor, *The Globe and Mail*, dated April 10, 1971, by Iqbal Syed of Scarborough, Ontario.
209. Letter to the Editor, by Dr. M. Zafari Quaraishi, the *Toronto Daily Star* of June 28, 1971. In the same letter, he indicated that he was from West Pakistan, his wife was from East Pakistan, and his 3-month-old daughter was Canadian. Dr. Quaraishi was the Chairman of the East Pakistan Relief Fund Committee Inc., Toronto.
210. *Ibid.*
211. *Ibid.*
212. Letter to the Editor by Touqir Hussain, Second Secretary, Pakistan High Commission, dated June 8, 1971, in the *Toronto Daily Star*.
213. Evening Telegram dated August 5, 1971.
214. *Ibid.*
215. Letter to the Editor, written by Syed Muazzam Hussain, in *The Globe and Mail*, dated May 14, 1971.
216. *Ibid.*
217. *Ibid.*
218. *The Ottawa Citizen*, dated June 2, 1971.
219. E-mail from Mrs. Madeline Alam and Mr. Rabiul Alam to Mustafa Chowdhury, dated April 26, 2012.
220. Letter to the Editor by Madeline Alam in the *Toronto Daily Star*, dated June 12, 1971.
221. *Ibid.*
222. *Ibid.*
223. *Ibid.*
224. Letter from Mitchell Sharp, Secretary of State for External Affairs, in *The Globe and Mail*, July 16, 1971, in response to the editorial comment of 7 July 1971.
225. *Ibid.*
226. *Ibid.*, dated July 10, 1971.
227. Canada. House of Commons. *Debates*, Queen's Printer, dated June 17, 1971, p. 6813.

228. Letter to the Editor by Chaitanya Keshavrao Kalevar, Publicity Director, the Canadian Committee for an Independent Bangla Desh, in *The Globe and Mail*, dated July 14, 1971.
229. Letter to the Editor by S.J. Ahmed of Toronto in *The Globe and Mail*, July 14, 1971.
230. *Ibid.*
231. *Ibid.*
232. *Ibid.*
233. *Ibid.*
234. Letter in *The Globe and Mail* of July 24, 1971, written by Mitchell Sharp, Secretary of State for External Affairs.
235. Letter to the Editor by G. Patrick Gough, University of Guelph, Department of Geography, in *The Globe and Mail*, dated July 14, 1971.
236. *Ibid.*
237. Letter to the Editor by Chaitanya Keshavrao Kalevar in *The Globe and Mail*, August 7, 1971.
238. *Ibid.*
239. *Ibid.*
240. *Ibid.*
241. *Ibid.*
242. M. I. Choudhury of Toronto, *The Globe and Mail*, dated August 13, 1971.
243. *Ibid.*
244. Letter to the Editor by Masudul Alam Chowdhury, President, Pakistan Solidarity Committee in the *Toronto Telegram*, dated September 1, 1971.
245. *Ibid.*
246. *Ibid.*
247. Ten individuals from the University of Saskatchewan signed the petition on March 3, 1971. The letter accompanying a petition addressed to Otto Lang, Minister of Manpower and Immigration, by A. K. Sarkar, Convener, Saskatoon Committee for the Protection of Human Rights and Lives in East Pakistan, dated April 2, 1971. File # 20-E. Pak-1-4. External Affairs. *Op. cit.*
248. Letter addressed to the Honourable Members of Parliament, by Bangla Desh Association of Canada (Ottawa chapter), dated April 22, 1971. MG 32 C26, Volume 87, File # 87-15. Library and Archives Canada. *Op. cit.*
249. *Ibid.*
250. E-mail from Dr. Asit Sarkar to Mustafa Chowdhury, dated October 20, 2021. The author then held two rounds of discussion with Dr. Sarkar immediately after receiving the e-mail
251. Letter from Dr. Anwarul Haque to Les Benjamin, MP for Lake Centre, Regina, dated May 26, 1971. MG 32 C26, Volume 87, File # 87-16. Library and Archives Canada. *Op. cit.*

252. There is no date for an Open Letter to all Canadian Parliament and Senate Members written by Hugh Keenleyside, Robert McClure, and Stanley Burke. This letter is in Andrew Brewin's file, Volume 27, File: Pak-Bang Reports August-September 1971 (87-12), p.2. MG C26. Library and Archives Canada. *Op. cit.*
253. *Ibid.*
254. Letter from Muriel B. Palen to Andrew Brewin, Member of Parliament for Greenwood, with a copy to Prime Minister Pierre Trudeau. The letter is dated December 5, 1971. This is contained in Andrew Brewin's file, Volume 27, File: Pak-Bang Reports August-September 1971 (87-13). MG C26. Library and Archives Canada. *Op. cit.*
255. *Ibid.*
256. The author gathered information from all four players: Dr. Maswood Ali, Suraiya Ali, Momin Chowdhury, and Dr. Shafiul Huq of London, Ontario. Over the years, in the 1970s and 1980s, the author talked to them on several occasions as follow-up discussions regarding their individual and group involvement in raising awareness among the Canadian public. Each occasion was rewarding as they recalled how, in 1971, they passed their days with apprehension and uncertainty, mainly because they were not getting the latest information from the field
257. *Ibid.* Dr. Ali shared with the author his correspondence with Canadian parliamentarians and foreign leaders and many newspaper clippings that he kept in his family archives.
258. *Ibid.* Specifically, Dr. Maswood Ali once again narrated this to the author on February 10, 2001, at his residence in London, Ontario, when the author requested Dr. Ali again recall his role in 1971.
259. *Ibid.*
260. This was narrated to the author by Abdur Rahim on July 5, 1997, in Ottawa. Following that, Rahim confirmed the same information in writing in a letter dated August 2, 1997. Since Rahim lived in Ottawa, the author had numerous opportunities to meet with him to discuss the unforgettable days of 1971 in Canada and Canada's awkward position regarding the conflict
261. The manifesto entitled *Democratic Self-Government of Bangla Desh* was written on behalf of the People of Bangla Desh. This was meant for submission to Mitchell Sharp, Secretary of State for External Affairs. In Sharp's absence, the manifesto was handed over to J. M. Harrington. File # 20- E. Pak-1-4. External Affairs. *Op. cit.*
262. *Ibid.*
263. *Ibid.* p. 2.
264. Restricted letter from J. M. Harrington, Head, Pacific and South Asia Division, to PDM, Department of External Affairs, dated March 29, 1971. The memo summarized the content of the Manifesto entitled Democratic

Self-Government of Bangla Desh, written on behalf of the People of Bangla Desh that was submitted to Harrington in the absence of Mitchell Sharp. File # 20-E-Pak-1-4. Subject: Call by East Pakistani Students. External Affairs. *Op. cit.*
265. *Ibid.*
266. Letter from Mitchell Sharp, Secretary of State for External Affairs, to Dr. Farid Shariff, President Bangladesh Association of Manitoba, dated July 7, 1971. File # 38-11-1-Pak. External Affairs. *Op. cit*
267. Letter addressed to Dr. Shafiqul Islam Khan, General Secretary, Bangladesh Canada Association of British Columbia, by Senator Rupert Vance Hartke, dated October 6, 1971. This was reprinted in the *History of Bangla Desh War of Independence,* vol. 4, pp. 365–366. *Op. cit.* Dr. Khan confirmed with the author the circumstances surrounding his initial correspondence and the support he received from the US senators.
268. Letter addressed to Dr. Shafiqul Islam Khan, General Secretary, Bangladesh Canada Association of British Columbia, by Senator John G. Tower, dated October 7, 1971. *Ibid.* vol. 4, p. 366. *Op. cit.*
269. Letter to Dr. Farid Shariff, President Bangladesh Association of Manitoba from S.M. Ali, Bangladesh Mission, Washington, dated October 29, 1971. ADMIN 1014/71. The original letter is in Dr. Shariff's archives. He made a photocopy for the author.
270. *Brief to the Commons Committee*, by Dr. Robert B. McClure; file: Re Les Smith. MG 28, I 270, vol.6. Library and Archives Canada. *Op. cit.*
271. *The Globe and Mail*, dated July 20, 1971.
272. Letter to the *Toronto Telegram*, dated September 1, 1971, by A.B.M. Masudul Alam Chowdhury, President, Pakistan Solidarity Committee.
273. *Ibid.*
274. A retired Bangladeshi Canadian Professor who wishes to remain anonymous told the author this. He was a graduate student in 1971 and applied for immigration following the announcement in late 1971. He received his immigration in early 1972.
275. The author interviewed Golam Rahman, who jumped off the boat. The interview took place on July 10, 2014. Their desertion is cited in the *History of Bangladesh War of Independence,* vol. 4, p. 362. *Op. cit.*
276. *The Globe and Mail,* dated August 12, 1971.
277. There is no date for an Open Letter to all Canadian Parliament and Senate Members written by Hugh Keenleyside, Robert McClure, and Stanley Burke. File: Pak-Bang Reports, August-September 1971 (87-12). MG C26 Volume 27. Library and Archives Canada. *Op. cit.*
278. *Ibid.* The author talked to Matiur Rahman, who is now living in Maui, Hawaii, on several occasions and has been in correspondence with him since 2001. They are also Facebook friends.

279. This is mentioned in the *History of Bangladesh War of Independence*, vol. 4, p. 358. *Op. cit.*
280. Letter addressed to the public by M. M. Rahman, General Secretary, Bangla Desh Association of Canada (Toronto), dated August 16, 1971. *Ibid. Op. cit.*
281. Letter from Professor Eliot Tepper, Department of Political Science, Carleton University, to Andrew Brewin, Member of Parliament, dated August 5, 1971. MG C26 Volume 27 File: Pak-Bang Reports August-September 1971 (87-12). Library and Archives Canada.
282. *Ibid.*
283. Letter from Professor Mizan Rahman to Andrew Brewin, Member of Parliament, dated May 31, 1971. MG 32 C26 Vol. 87 File # 87-15. Library and Archives Canada. *Op. cit.*
284. *The Globe and Mail*, dated July 29, 1971.
285. Telegram from E. H. Johnson, The Presbyterian Church in Canada, to the Board of World Mission, no date, placed in a confidential file in the Bangladesh High Commission, Ottawa, File: Pol/36, 73-V. Anwarul Alam, then acting high commissioner to Canada, granted the author full access during August 1996 to the high commission's confidential files.
286. *Ibid.*
287. Letter from Mitchell Sharp, Secretary of State for External Affairs, to Dr. Farid Shariff, President Bangladesh Association of Manitoba, dated July 7, 1971, p. 2. File # 38-11-1-Pak. External Affairs. *Op. cit.*
288. Letter from Dr. Farid Shariff, President, Manitoba Bangladesh Association, to Mustafizur Rahman Siddiqi, Head, Bangladesh Mission in Washington, dated September 28, 1971. This letter is in Dr. Shariff's archives. He gave the author a photocopy of the letter
289. Memorandum for the Minister from A. E. Ritchie, Undersecretary. Subject: Bangla Desh Association of Canada. Dated, September 21, 1971. File # 20-E. Pak-1-4. External Affairs. *Op. cit.*
290. *Ibid.*
291. Letter from M. R. Siddiqi, Head of Mission, Bangladesh Mission, Washington, to Dr. Farid Shariff, President, Bangladesh Association of Manitoba, dated October 12, 1971. ADMN/1009/71. This letter is in Dr. Shariff's archives. He gave the author a photocopy of the letter.
292. *Ibid.*
293. See footnote # 144.

CHAPTER 5

NGOs and Religious and Business Organizations: Get Behind Bangladesh

Canadian NGOs, along with religious and business organizations, played an essential role in assisting the victims of military reprisals in East Pakistan and refugees in India. The NGOs managed to act as catalytic agents, having coalesced with the diverse groups in addressing the needs of the refugees and demonstrating their capacity for public engagement in times of crisis. In 1971, despite the varying circumstances and having relied on the traditional values of innovation and dependency, Canadian NGOs were engaged in advocacy, lobbying, representation, and raising public awareness. In outlining their activities, the following two essential facts have been considered: (1) one needs to understand the very apolitical nature of NGOs and be mindful of the extent to which a particular organization could operate being subject to its strict policies and guidelines, and (2) that NGOs of 1971 were much, unlike the present-day NGOs that are powerful enough to make an impact on Canadian foreign policy options.

The Canadian NGOs immediately responded to the dire needs of the refugees, a daunting task considering their financial and human resources limitations. Having prioritized their tasks considering the crisis, they worked horizontally to meet their collective and individual goals. Through their guidance, the Voluntary Relief Agencies ensured no disconnect among international, national, or local NGOs. It was feared that if they embraced several mandates by articulating a broader policy framework, they would never know with whom to work and toward which goals to focus on determining a particular course of action. More importantly, the challenge was to have an agenda to ensure that it did not run roughshod over existing action plans. Together, they recognized the strengths of the network approach through parallel work, which was a potential cost-saving means. Though expected to be apolitical, they remained insistent on pointing out that the crisis would grow as long as the flow of refugees continued to be one-sided. Their work remains an example of how, despite being resource-poor, a group of dedicated volunteers adapted to changing circumstances. It worked collectively to maximize their efforts without being overtly political.

The Canadian NGOs, voluntary associations, humanitarian groups, public institutions, and foundations have long served as important channels of development assistance to South Asia. Specifically, Canadian voluntary development agencies had been active in the Indian subcontinent long before the government of Canada became involved there through its aid programs under the Colombo Plans in the early 1950s. By 1970, there were approximately six Canadian NGOs in Pakistan. When the military crackdown began on the night of March 25, 1971, in East Pakistan, Canadian NGOs were already providing relief following the devastating cyclone of November 1970. Though the NGO communities are expected to be nonpolitical by the very nature of their work, they were conscious of the critical issues that President Yahya Khan faced following the demand for greater autonomy by Sheikh Mujibur Rahman (Bongobondhu), the Bengali leader of East Pakistan.

The NGO community in the subcontinent noted with alarm the postponement of the National Assembly session, the noncooperation movement led by Bongobondhu, the impasse at the negotiation table, the Bengalis' constant demand for greater autonomy, and rumors about the unilateral declaration of independence (UDI) of Bangladesh (i.e., East Pakistan), to mention a few. Simply, it recognized that nothing went *"comme il fault."* They addressed the issue of military repression with a direct reference to Maurice Cardinal Roy, the Canadian representative at the ICVA (International Council of Voluntary Agencies), who referred to the Bengalis as the victims of both a "tragedy" and a "disaster." Their collective reaction, considering Cardinal's assessment of the situation, was to assist the hapless Bengalis who were seen as doubly victimized—first in 1970, as the victims of a natural disaster, and then in 1971, as the victims of a man-made disaster. Cardinal Roy's remark that "if we are able to bring about the change of heart that is more humane and just relationships in the world,"[1] many tragedies that could have been alleviated were widely disseminated to Canadians. The activities of the Canadian NGOs in Canada and their cooperative venture in the Indian subcontinent under the banner of Voluntary Relief Agencies in Kolkata in West Bengal, India, are described below in alphabetical order.

Canadian Hunger Foundation (CHF)

Although the newspapers of the day reveal occasional references to CHF's concerns about the food situation in the Indian subcontinent, the lack of archival records makes it impossible to review the full extent of its engagement. The CHF joined hands with other NGOs in raising awareness about the precarious conditions of the refugees and kept the Canadian public informed that despite the continuing delivery with considerable quantities still in the pipeline, the situation in the refugee camps, in particular, remained difficult because of the growing number of newcomers daily. Although war and civil disturbances in East Pakistan would not contribute to famine alone, other factors, such as drought, flood, and disruption of regular communication and supply routes, could easily lead to starvation in deficit areas, thus argued CHF.

Reportedly, there had been the destruction of grain stocks, particularly rice. As the army crackdown prevented rice planting in some areas, it was feared that millions of Bengalis would face starvation if outside food was not distributed. And yet, the regime maintained, "At the present moment, there is no shortage of essential supplies, such as foodstuff and medicines, in East Pakistan. The difficulty, however, is of movement of goods, because of the destruction of roads and bridges and channels of communication by infiltrators and other subversive elements."[2] In any typical year, East Pakistan imported between two to three million tons of food grains. Still, in 1971, the military authority did not allow any imports, argued CHF. Not only the 9.5 million refugees were likely to suffer, but approximately sixty-five million displaced Bengalis who had remained in East Pakistan would also be affected, it feared. Seeing that the refugees were "in urgent need of high protein foods, and skim milk powder,"[3] CHF sent Dave Eadie, a technical adviser with CHF, to investigate the possibility of setting up a plant to produce a high-protein food distribution system there. During his investigative trip to East Pakistan and India in late fall of 1971, Eadie met with various NGO representatives involved in food distribution among the refugees. He talked to them about CHF's increased involvement in cooperation with other agencies.

At the annual general meeting of the Christian Council of the National Capital Council in early December 1971, Eadie outlined his findings in India and Pakistan and shared his observations and concerns regarding the deteriorated situation with other members. CHF's message was the need for peace, feeding the hungry, tending to the sick, and sheltering the homeless Bengalis. However, within a few days of Eadie's meeting, Bangladesh became independent. Nevertheless, CHF continued its work by seeing how Bangladesh emerged from death and destruction. It was well on its way to "fly in a complete plant" so that "it could produce a high-protein food locally."[34] Unfortunately, the archives have insufficient information to know more about CHF's initiatives immediately after the liberation.

Canadian Religious Missionaries

Members of the Canadian Holy Cross Order and Canadian Jesuits played an important role in 1971. Starting with Brother Leon Brisson, the first Canadian Holy Cross Brother to work in what was then Bengal, where he served from 1912 to 1923, the number of members of the Holy Cross Order (fathers, brothers, and sisters) increased to approximately forty in 1971 only in East Pakistan. From the beginning of their presence in Bengal, throughout wars and turbulences, they remained attached to the people they served. Like all NGO officials, the missionaries of the Canadian Holy Cross Order in East Pakistan and Canadian Jesuits in India recognized the prevailing sentiment of the people of the land. The stark tragedy that followed as a result of the imposition of martial law, the sudden and secret military crackdown, and the grim sequence of events that unfolded there, resulting in the killing of civilians, remained a source of angst to the missionaries.

Canadian Holy Cross Order

There are no written official records of the activities of the members of the Holy Cross Order in East Pakistan during the war of independence (March 1971–December 1971). Understandably, because of the very nature of the conflict, deliberate attempts were made by the order's authority to dissociate from the hard-nosed view of the subcontinental political events that were taking place in East Pakistan. Some references to the Canadian missionaries in the government records and newspapers touch on some of their activities. Through granting interviews to individual journalists and having remained anonymous, Canadian missionaries informed the rest of the world regarding what had been happening within "Occupied Bangladesh." To them, this was a safe vehicle to communicate with the rest of the world about the tragedy. One of Sydney H. Schanberg's excerpts published in the *New York Times* on July 14, 1971, ran like the following: "Foreign missionaries who are posted even in the remotest parts of East Pakistan report new massacres almost daily. One missionary said that the army recently killed over one thousand Hindus in a day in a section of Barisal District in the south." Although the missionaries were not identified, it was well known that most Canadian missionaries at that time were in the Barisal area where the interviewee was residing.

The author obtained the primary source for the account below through personal interviews of the missionaries in Bangladesh and Canada, having spent excessive time doing follow-ups. As the missionaries saw the situation, life in "Occupied Bangladesh" was one of constant fear and agony until the liberation of Bangladesh had been achieved. Before the military crackdown, the missionaries silently witnessed a period of lawlessness, arson, looting, and wanton murder of non-Bengali supporters of the military regime in various cities of East Pakistan, especially at Saidpur, Chattogram, and Nilfamari by the nationalist Bengalis.[5] Although the missionaries knew it was not their job to be involved in the country's politics (Pakistan), where they lived, they did not remain a simple spectator. This was mainly so when they saw with their own eyes how the civil war was causing untold physical destruction and severe dislocation of the economies of both Pakistan and India. They chose to detach themselves from the political debates. Still, they felt duty-bound to respond to the needs of the people by doing whatever they could do very discretely within their limited ability.

Following the catastrophic cyclone of November 1970, the Holy Cross missionaries were already occupied with relief work headed by Joachim J. Rozario, Bishop of Chittagong, throughout the coastal areas of East Pakistan under the co-ordination and financing authority of CORR (Christian Organization for Relief and Rehabilitation). They chose to remain low-keyed without coming forward while characterizing the instances of brutality that appalled them—something consistent with their nonpartisan strategy. The military regime's high-handedness was evident to them, and yet, they did not wish to comment on the "internal affairs" of Pakistan. Publicly, they could neither take an open stand against the violence of the Pakistani army nor condemn the actions of the military regime. They generally expressed their views as irresponsible and a threat to the community.

Privately, they were outraged to see the persecution of both the Bengali Muslims and Hindus, who were terrorized and compelled to leave their homeland. As they saw the events, the military authority was treating the Muslim Bengalis as political enemies and the members of the Hindu community as religious enemies. Outwardly, the missionaries deliberately attempted to dissociate themselves from the political events, but they intervened surreptitiously despite the military authority's warnings. They changed how they used to work previously to a new modus operandi under the changed circumstances. Despite threats from the military rule and the risk of being on the military's list as "supporters" of Bangladesh or "pro-Indians," Canadian missionaries continued their work, having remained doubly careful in doing what they honestly believed to be the right thing to do.[6]

Due to the communication breakdown with East Pakistan, John Small, the Canadian high commissioner stationed in Islamabad, West Pakistan, did not know the Canadian missionaries' whereabouts following martial law's imposition. As early as the situation permitted, Small made a memorable trip to East Pakistan within four weeks to see the problem himself. Initially, he met with Lieutenant General Tikka Khan, commander of the Eastern Command and the newly-appointed governor-general of East Pakistan. Through his cooperation, he met with the Holy Cross Brothers and Sisters at the Oriental Institute in Barisal. Small's meeting with the Canadian missionaries gave them the first opportunity to speak about the brutality with which civilians were being suppressed following the military takeover. The missionaries put across the human dimensions of the displaced people within the country and frankly told Small how the fighting between the Pakistani army and Bengali rebels resulted in irreparable damage to the surrounding villages.

The Canadian priests confirmed that fighting went on right from the military crackdown until the military took over the towns on April 26. They also briefly discussed the need for sustained efforts to deal with the problems arising from the disaster. Small gathered that having maintained an apparent distance from the political turmoil, many members of the Holy Cross Order were still quietly assisting the victims of military atrocities by giving money or shelter in whatever humble ways they could. He also learned that most members of the Holy Cross Order had probably crossed the border and gone to India. At least a group of about twenty of their colleagues, instead of leaving for home (Canada), were still living in the remote areas of East Pakistan despite the imposition of martial law. In particular, Small was told that several sisters could not come to see him as they were away. They were the ones who "had helped at the hospital when casualties started to come in as all the doctors and nurses had vanished. They were joined by a Norwegian doctor and five Swedish/Norwegian nurses who had come from Bhola,"[7] wrote Small.

Upon his return to the Deputy Commissioner's house to fly back to Dhaka, an army officer came up to Small (high commissioner) and expressed his resentment with a threat that the Canadian priests were sympathetic toward the Bengalis, recalled Small. He did not forget the harsh tone and fury with which this particular army officer warned him by saying that if the Canadian missionaries were caught assisting the freedom fighters in any way, they would be severely dealt with.[8] Using his usual diplomatic demeanor, Small quickly responded by saying that he was a representative of the government of Canada in Islamabad. Then, he curtly pointed out that the members of the Canadian Holy Cross Order are independent citizens of Canada who chose to remain in East Pakistan to continue their missionary work. Small said he found it disturbing to hear how, on another occasion, in a visceral distrust of the actions of the missionaries, an angry lieutenant colonel is known to have spewed out a stream of insults threatening Father Paulin Demers, who was seen to have attended many wounded *Mukti Bahini*s (Liberation Forces).[9]

Tikka Khan told Small that the first secretary of the British Deputy High Commission in Dhaka, who looked after the Canadian interests, had failed to convince many Canadian priests to leave East Pakistan despite repeated attempts. According to Father Guy-Marie Tourangeau,, the military authority became furious when it heard that, despite its warning that there would be "rivers of blood,"[10] the missionaries, having defied the order/warning, remained in the province—something unacceptable to the military authority. Naturally, the army's mistrust of the priests grew even more. It suspected the missionaries to be involved in, among other things, the treatment of the wounded and the sheltering of the rebel forces. Since some missionaries were sharing a border with the Pakistani army that occupied the WAPDA (Water and Power Development Authority) building premises in Barisal, the military authority could watch their activities closely. They repeatedly warned the missionaries that they should not be involved in any capacity and that they should stay away from the "internal affairs" of Pakistan. Being convinced that the priests were secretly liaising with the rebels, the military branded the Canadian missionaries as "pros." However, the missionaries made every effort to keep a demonstrated distance between the "internal affairs" of Pakistan and the services of God for the needy people.

"We managed to remain in touch very discretely with the field staff of Oxfam Canada personnel stationed in India and worked on the following tasks: (1) treating the wounded, including both Bengalis and non-Bengalis and (2) feeding and sheltering the frightened Bengali civilians quietly by eluding the military authority's attention until they were able to escape to India on their own or through our cooperation,"[11] wrote Father Guy-Marie Tourangeau.

Again, Sister Eleanor Rose, who was also in East Pakistan during the Bengalis' struggle for independence, later moved to Montreal, where she lived in the 1990s, recalled the adventure of Father Charles Nadeau, who led a team of several missionaries in the Barisal area. They remained busy providing temporary/informal shelter to the displaced Bengalis. Father Nadeau spent an excessive amount of time in the Sadar Hospital in Barisal, giving daily services to the wounded since there were hardly any doctors or nurses, especially during the beginning of the secret military crackdown. Although Sister Rose downplayed her role, she often surreptitiously disguised Hindu women as "nuns" to hide their identity and assisted them in fleeing to India. The nature of help and assistance varied from providing temporary shelter to the homeless to giving "food and, at times, money, to those who were trying to leave for India, Muslims as well as Hindus."[12] The work of Sister Rose and her companion sisters, who took particular care of many displaced Hindu women with children who did not know where to go, is an illustration of the Holy Cross Sisters' direct response to the individual needs of the victims of military reprisals.

Similarly, Father Martial St. Pierre also provided shelter to many Hindu Bengalis who were later smuggled out of the country once the military authority challenged the priest. The sheltering of the Bengalis continued secretly until a mistrustful authority confronted Father St. Pierre. The minute he got wind of the military's arrival at his residence, he sought help from the people around. He successfully shipped the helpless bunch off to India before the army personnel checked out their premises.[13] Again, Sister Marie de Galillée around the Gaurnadi area also networked with the indigenous Sisters of the Little Handmaids of the Church and extended every possible assistance they could offer to those Bengalis in need of help, such as helping the wounded at the dispensary or crossing the border into the territory of India for a safe haven. Along with Sister Gaillée was Father Patrick D'Rozario, who helped a large number of Bengalis to escape from the Narikelbari area and then to the Faridpur district by directing them through the safest way to cross the border.[14]

Again, Father Paulin Demers worked closely with the Indigenous sisters at the dispensary, with the local people having taken a considerable risk in engineering the escape of many unprotected Bengalis into India to seek asylum to save themselves from indiscriminate killing at the hands of the brutal military officers. As soon as the *Mukti Bahini* (Liberation Forces) members heard the name of Father Demers, they began to contact him, seeking his help. He gave shelter to many freedom fighters under the strictest possible secrecy. However, it was short-lived. The minute the Pakistani army got the wind of it, Father Demers was warned to stay away from the anti-Pakistani elements. Although on the surface, Father Demers took the military authority's warning seriously, in fact, he was still assisting the Bengalis surreptitiously in fleeing to India, having found other ways and means to save the lives of these vulnerable people.[15]

In the Padrishibpur area, Father Germain de Grandmaison kept himself busy throughout the liberation war period despite the constant fear of being caught by the Pakistani army. When the military regime learned that he was taking a personal interest in sheltering members of the *Mukti Bahini*, naturally, it became furious. The risk was so grave that Father Grandmaison had to remain extra cautious about his hidden "activity." He noted an element of irony in that even though he was assisting many members of the *Mukti Bahini* in escaping to India by boat, those who kept vigilance on the missionaries did not know for sure if Father Grandmaison was siding with the army or *Mukti Bahini*. While the military authority had reason to suspect Father Grandmaison, who was seen with many Bengalis on several occasions, many freedom fighters were often unsure about some of the missionaries' positions. In that sense, some missionaries were a suspect to both parties. On the one hand, the *Mukti Bahini* members appreciated every assistance they were receiving from the missionaries; on the other hand, the missionaries' indiscriminate caring of the wounded non-Bengalis provoked resentment among the rebels and guerrilla fighters whose demands were that they should have no interaction with non-Bengalis and the military people representing Pakistan. As far as the missionaries were concerned, they were trying to help alleviate human suffering from what they saw as a man-made tragedy. They were caught in a conundrum.[16]

Again, in the district of Noakhali, Father Pierre Benoit worked with many support groups that had the misfortune of seeing the most significant number of dead bodies in one place. Having watched the enormity of murder and shelling, a heartrending spectacle, Father Benoit's team recognized how the already desperate situation was worsening day by day. The civilian hospitals were so severely damaged by shelling and bombing that they were practically rendered inoperative. Many dispensaries had to be closed. At the same time, a lack of basic medical supplies made the situation even worse.[17] The missionaries were deeply disappointed to see how the medical care in the country had been disrupted.

Individually, Father Laurent Lecavalier's efforts are commendable, especially when one recognizes the risks. He sheltered thirteen religious studies students in the Barisal district between May and October 1971. Throughout summer, he remained under constant threat as "they used to hear the sound of firing almost every night."[18] According to him, there were times when, functionally speaking, the communication system was nonexistent. "We were cut off from the rest of the world, and we only hoped that other nations would rescue East Pakistan,"[19] recalled Father Lecavalier. Father Lecavalier wanted to console the victims' families by referring to his faith to justify his involvement in such a matter. His conviction was strengthened by long periods of supplication and meditation, which made him do his best through prayer to Almighty God.

To avoid further threats from the unpredictable military personnel and to satisfy the military authority, the missionaries, under the leadership of Father St. Pierre, decided that they would teach a simple prayer and give the frightened Hindus an identification card printed with the Cross with a statement that the missionaries "consider them as Catechumens, that is, they have applied to become Christians."[20] Given the delicate situation, this approach was thought to be the best choice not to antagonize the military authority that was obdurate in its demand. "It would be for them to decide after the threat was over,"[21] observed Father Tourangeau, whether they would like to convert to any religion of their choice or retain their own religion. The vulnerable members of the community, upon hearing about the efforts of Father St. Pierre, who found a new way to save many Bengali Hindus through what came to be known as the "card system," immediately began to take advantage of the program. The story of temporary conversion also appears in the field reports of Bill Acworth of Oxfam UK.

Again, Father Edmund Goedert also provided shelter for about six thousand Hindus in "Occupied Bangladesh," who remained within the country. Father Goedert was an American priest of the Holy Cross Order who worked closely with the Canadian missionaries. Placed in utter helplessness, the ill-fated Bengalis sought help from the Canadian missionaries. According to Father Tourangeau, Father Godert managed to give shelter to "over six thousand Hindus, driven from their houses, not allowed to harvest their crops. He found it more dangerous to get supplies through for them and feels he and his flock may be overrun any day."[22] Defying the inherent risks involved, Father Goedert provided them with food and shelter as they were forced out of their homes. Naturally, they could not harvest their crops either. Speaking confidently to the Oxfam representative, Father Goedert reported that he found it extremely difficult to receive supplies for the displaced people for whom he had found shelter. Again, since they were Hindus, they were genuinely fearful of collecting a ration card for their use from the whimsically wayward local military authority. To solve the problem, Father Goedert made them honorary Christians—for the time being—by issuing them with Crosses, a means to avert military reprisals directed against Hindus.[23] This was just another area of military persecution. Canadian missionaries did their best to deal with the issue very discretely.

Although Fathers Goedert and Tourangeau's liaison with Oxfam was supposed to be confidential, the headquarters in London and Ottawa were already receiving Oxfam UK's situational reports sent by Acworth. In his reports, Acworth talked about their encounters with both parties when they used to take Father Goedert with the team on a riverboat ride at the risk of their lives. This was particularly risky around the coastal areas when fear and tension peaked since the sign of an all-out war loomed ahead. This was a time when both the members of the *Mukti Bahini* and Pakistani soldiers were actively seeking each other in the coastal areas, where each was engaged in destroying the other's foothold and making riverboats disappear without a trace.

Having ignored all insults and odds stacked against him, Father Goedert found work for the able-bodied, uprooted Bengalis in the field who needed monetary help on an urgent basis. Though expected to remain apolitical, in one of his comments, Father Godert is known to have observed that the situation of the refugees was still "tragic enough and that the urgency of finding a political solution increases for without that political solution, there is no hope of restoring the economy and the purchasing power of the masses."[24] He did everything with energetic effort, competence, and devotedness, demonstrating his high spirit and constant good humor. Today, fifty-two years later, people still remember Father Godert, a unique and unforgettably towering personality, with admiration.

Fortuitously, at that time, Canadian Holy Cross Father Benjamin Labbé, founder and Executive Director of the Christian Organization for Relief and Rehabilitation (CORR), undertook relief operations for the displaced people in "Occupied Bangladesh." Founded temporarily to take part in tornado relief following the disastrous cyclone of November 12, 1970, CORR was already involved in providing relief work to the victims of natural calamities. Having traveled across "Occupied Bangladesh," Father Labbé held meetings with representatives of international and national NGOs and several local voluntary organizations. He then initiated massive assistance programs for the hungry, homeless, and sick people who could not or did not go over to India. Father Labbé, like other members of the Holy Cross Order, also encountered threats and challenges from the military personnel who deemed him to be anti-Pakistani since all the missionaries were believed to be siding with the Bengalis.

As far as the army was concerned, CORR did not have any mandate to provide shelter to the victims of non-natural calamities. Naturally, the CORR personnel maintained a low key with no publicity, mainly because most of the people they were helping were Hindus whom the Yahya government labeled as the "enemies of the people"; therefore, the regime believed that it was a "fair game for oppression or extermination."[25] Simply put, the prevailing *raison d'être* of the military authority was that since they were regarded as enemies, it was OK to persecute or exterminate them to establish law and order.

Again, Brother Flavian Laplante of Saint Anne Québec is remembered as the apostle of the fishermen spread out in hundreds of villages on the seacoast of Bengal. The French-Canadian Province of the Holy Cross Congregation sent him to India (East Bengal) in 1933, where he worked in various places in the Chattogram diocese before arriving in Diang in 1945. He was gifted with brilliant intelligence and phenomenal memory, guided by a sure and practical judgment. Also known as a risk-taking adventurer, Brother Laplante remains etched on the minds of the Bangladeshis for his tireless work in the Chattogram area with the displaced persons in East Pakistan. His orphanage, Miriam Ashram (Miriam Orphanage) in Chattogram, was one of the first premises where the terrified civilians took shelter to hide from the Pakistani army immediately after the secret military attack. Within days, the school premises became overcrowded. Brother Laplante took an incredible amount of risk to shelter them secretly, along with the supply of food and necessities of life.

Earlier, much to the profound resentment of the Pakistani army, the military authority learned about Brother Laplante's offer of assistance to the area people and his work with the fishermen on the hills of Diang. Being strongly suspicious that the missionaries were siding with the Bengalis, a furious military authority began to monitor their movement even more closely. It was reported in a Canadian daily that the army was "threatening to destroy two Canadian Catholic mission stations, charging that the French-Canadian priests aided the guerillas. One of the missions is led by a priest who escorted [later] Prime Minister Pierre Trudeau on his visit to East Pakistan in 1948."[26] The reporter was referring to Brother Flavian Laplante. The regime's indignation for Brother Laplante's involvement with the fishermen was such that it was known that he had once been slapped in the face by a Pakistani soldier who accused him of assisting the Bengali rebels.[27] This outrageous act neither deterred Brother Laplante nor his colleagues from doing what they thought was the right thing to do for the victims of military repression. Believing that there was an obligation laid upon them to stand alongside the poor, the oppressed, and the repressed, Brother Laplante remained resolute in assisting the victims of a man-made tragedy.

Even though Oxfam Canada had no permission from the government of East Pakistan (GOEP) to enter its territory in 1971, Brother Laplante established secret communications with Brother Cournoyer while awaiting permission to enter East Pakistan as Oxfam Canada's representative. Interestingly, years ago, Brother Laplante worked with Brother Raymond Cournoyer in the Chattogram area following the cyclone of 1960 as chairman of the Emergency Relief Commission set up by the government of East Pakistan. They got along very well. In 1971, they had Bill Acworth liaise with Brother Laplante throughout the year. Cournoyer and Acworth used to sneak in and out of "Occupied Bangladesh" at every opportunity. With diplomacy, and despite the considerable risk, both Acworth and Cournoyer gave Brother Laplante a hand in his endeavors, all in a very discrete manner since the military authority in Pakistan was unwilling "to welcome private funds to operate in there."[28]

Brother Laplante also maintained correspondence with Prime Minister Pierre Trudeau, as they had known each other since the 1940s. The frequent exchange of information between the two, in a sense, indirectly assisted Ottawa officials in remaining *au courant*, especially about the activities of the missionaries. In one of Trudeau's letters to Brother Laplante, Trudeau mentioned how much he admired Laplante's "courage in bearing those misfortunes that continually afflict this country [Pakistan] where" Laplante had been working "for so many years with so much devotedness and magnanimity."[29] Despite being under direct military scrutiny, Brother Laplante took the risk and continued his relentless work with the displaced people. He never hesitated to express his personal views to the authorities on the civil war and let them know his own views on the turmoil, that it would be meaningless if appropriate measures were not taken to achieve an equitable distribution of the fruits of economic progress. Having known about Brother Laplante's courage and determination, no one around was surprised to see how he remained vigilant and continued his work, defying the risks.

Like Brother Laplante, all other missionaries also defied the risk and remained involved in the face of extreme danger—something that was possible due to their deep faith in Almighty God and their commitment to their work. "How we had been living with all these years? If we live with them peacefully, how could we abandon them when they are in severe difficulties? Were not their lives as valuable as ours were? And where could they go?"[30] Father Tourangeau asked as though he was speaking on behalf of all the missionaries assisting the freedom fighters. The missionaries' courage and faith were such that they never ceased their relief work even when their "fishing boat, used for relief, [was] being shot at by the freedom fighters, mistaking it for a Pakistan[i] army patrol boat."[31] The Pakistani army's frustration peaked when it became convinced that the sympathetic missionaries were, for sure, pro-Bangladeshis. Naturally, to the capricious military authority, this became a source of their profound rage and indignation, recalled Father Tourangeau.

The keywords "discrete" and "vigilant" may sum up the Canadian missionaries' efforts by offering prayers to the all-powerful creator. By providing shelter to the displaced people, helping them cross the border, and giving whatever money they could, coupled with intense prayer and meditation to the extent possible, the missionaries tried to save the victims of military reprisals within the country gripped by civil war. There were moments when they used to feel miserable, having no one to turn to. Such feelings often created a dilemma among them. On the one hand, they thought that they must not be involved in the "internal affairs" of the country they were living in; on the other hand, they felt that no response to help the needy (even though they were seen as the enemies of Pakistan by the military government in power) represented a cruel derogation of responsibility by the missionaries. Both Father Tourangeau and Sister Rose expressed their feelings of helplessness for their inability to respond to their complete satisfaction to the cry for help of endless neighbors whose family members were frequently taken away by the Pakistani army.[32]

Many years following the independence of Bangladesh, Brother Alberic (Robert) Houle spoke his mind, recalling the tragedy of 1971 and the Bengalis' indomitable resolution to free their native land. He said that "mad violence against a defenseless population had fuelled in the hearts of the Bengalis a fierce determination of resistance till they won their independence."[33] Brother Houle described the military crackdown and those caught in the crossfire as "a hellish night when the basest passions were given full rein!"[34] It is commendable that, even though the Canadian missionaries witnessed the brutal killing of a Catholic missionary in Jessore along with other native Christians by the Pakistani army, they neither abandoned their missionary work for the poor and helpless nor ceased their assistance to the needy.

Overall, in talking about the work of the missionaries in general, Reverend R. W. Timm observed in his memoir that "they lived heroic lives in faith, in solitude, and with zeal, deeply rooted in fidelity to their vocation."[35]

Canadian Jesuits in India

Canadian Jesuits, missions, and organizations are part of a larger international structure of the Society of Jesus, the Roman Catholic church's most significant all-male religious order. Back in 1971, there were no Canadian Jesuits in East Pakistan. Still, they had lived in the mountainous Buddhist kingdoms of Bhutan and Nepal and the District of Darjeeling in West Bengal, India, only 15 km away from East Pakistan, since the early 1940s. The Jesuits were engaged in pastoral duties within the communities where they lived and worked and in teaching on projects primarily on sustainable religious and community development through education and promoting justice without involvement in the country's political activities. During the furtive military clampdown of March 25, 1971, about thirty Canadian Jesuits lived in the Darjeeling District. The sheer brutality of the Pakistani army against unarmed civilians prompted the Canadian Jesuits to come to the rescue of the Bengali refugees.[36]

Initial Response

The *raison d'être* of the Darjeeling-based missionaries' involvement was based on a clear conviction that this was an essential work of mercy. In their initial response, the Jesuits held consultation meetings with the Red Cross, Oxfam, Catholic Relief Services, and Caritas. The Jesuits quickly developed a Joint Action Plan for relief operations that included two types of supporting activities to operationalize their own course of action to complement the ones already initiated by other NGOs. During the initial stage, there were two phases of relief operations under the supervision of Father Edgar Burns, Superior of the Darjeeling mission, who oversaw the camp operation in which the Jesuits generally played a supportive role.

The first phase was to provide immediate makeshift shelters and distribute food and milk to all the incoming refugees crossing into India at a rate of thirty thousand a day or one million a month. The initial tasks included setting up tents and supplying baby food, milk powder, medicine, firewood, kerosene oil, and shelters against wind and rain. It was more like a "crisis management,"[37] observed Father William M. German, then the students' counselor, who led the team during the first stages of the influx. They worked with the help of the school staff, local people, and the local Catholic Relief Service and Sisters of the Convent representatives. Having quickly recruited several young students, Father German devised a list of activities. Given the enormity of the situation, Father Henry Nun, the school principal, and the parents of the students immediately permitted them to engage Father German's "boys," as he used to call them affectionately.

The second phase consisted of a more structured approach, primarily in temporary or short-term relief assistance and medical support until the refugees were sheltered in designated camps. Using the slogan, "charity begins at home," Father German found a new approach to encourage not only his students but also school staff and the people around in the neighborhood to contribute to the pot in their humble way by working horizontally despite many constraints. Father German saw the community's prompt and collective responsibility as an example of a "wave of generosity."[38]

Out of some two thousand Bengalis who crossed over to the Darjeeling District alone within the first four weeks of the military crackdown, the Jesuits decided to shelter the refugees in two camps at Phansidewa and Bazarigach, near Choterhat from Kurseong, Gayaganga, Bhimbhar, and Hatighisa. Five educational institutions, students, and staff of St. Joseph's (school and college), St. Robert's School, St. Alphonsus School, St. Peter's School, and John XXIII Apostolic School, under the Canadian Jesuits participated in the relief work from the beginning of the influx of the refugees. Due to the sheer number of refugees, the line-ups were chaotic. Father German immediately appointed a group of young boys to supervise ration, medicine, and inoculation line-ups. It was a helpful service as the refugees used "to stand in line all day, every day, some would start lining up as early as 4:00 a.m. in the hope of getting a minimum of supplies to keep their families alive for one more day."[39] Affectionately calling them little "watchdogs," Father German recalled how they "did a magnificent job."[40] Father German was also involved in regular masses for Catholic refugees, although there was not a very high number of Christians compared to other faith groups.

Management of the Actual Refugee Camps by the Jesuits

By fall, about 210,000 refugees were welcomed with open arms under the supervision of the Superior of the Mission, Father Edgar Burns, all in the Darjeeling District. They were formally placed in the following four different camps, which continued to grow day by day: (1) the Kantibita

Refugee Camp, (2) the Darivitt Refugee Camp, (3) the Thakurbari Refugee Camp, and (4) the Maharaja Refugee Camp.[41]

The Kantibita Refugee Camp, situated near Kurseong, West Bengal, about 3.2 km from the East Pakistan border, sheltered approximately ten thousand refugees consisting primarily of tribals, namely aboriginals and nearly all Hindus, with a small minority of Christian Catholics. This was the smallest of the four camps under the Jesuits' supervision. Under the leadership of Father Burns, Father Charles Durt, a Flemish Jesuit on loan to the Canadian Jesuits, organized this camp with help from two more Canadian Jesuits, Fathers Michael Hawkins and William Bourke, and two Jesuits of Indian origin, Bishop Eric Benjamin of Darjeeling and Father Jacob, district coordinator of Caritas. Also, there were fourteen sisters of Indian origin engaged in medical work in the camps. The work of the daughters of the Cross, Franciscan Clarists, St. Joseph of Cluny, Sacred Heart, and Immaculate Heart of Mary was also recognized as an example of partnership. After he visited the refugee camps, Senator Edward Kennedy declared the Kantibita Refugee Camp "the best-managed refugee camp of all the camps" he visited.[42]

The Darivit Refugee Camp, about 3.2 km from the East Pakistan border, sheltered approximately fifty-five thousand refugees. The main organizers of this camp were Fathers Moe Stanford, Joe Brenan, Anthony Milledge, Gerard Van Wallegham, Michael Parent (a Jesuit Scholastic from Toronto), and Janet Perry, a volunteer teacher at a nondenominational school run by Canadian Jesuits of the Darjeeling District. About half of this camp's refugees were Rajbanshis, Santalis, and Oraons, three prominent Bengali tribes. By mid-July, volunteers at this camp in the Hatighisa area came to earn its name as one of the most successful camps with a hospital, a polythene structure 15" x 20" with eight bamboo beds.[43] Under Father Brenan's supervision, the hospital was used for emergency treatment. The team's work remains an example of synergy generated by volunteers called Brothers To All Men.

The Thakurbari Refugee Camp sheltered about forty thousand refugees under the supervision of two Jesuit Fathers, Gerard Van Walleghem and Joe Pappadil, along with several volunteers from the Social Service League of St. Joseph's College. The enormous influx of refugees at a rate beyond its capacity was its most significant challenge. By the sheer will of the Canadian Jesuits, together with their students with whatever know-how they had, they quickly erected shelters against wind and rain to provide dwellings for the incoming refugees.

The Maharaja Refugee Camp was the largest camp under the Canadian Jesuits. Although the name Maharaja (Great King) gave the impression of being majestic, in reality, the camp showed fast deteriorating conditions.[44] And yet, by November, the camp accommodated a refugee population of approximately fifty-five thousand with a mixed community of Hindus and Muslims and a small number of Christians. The primary workers in this camp were Father Gerard McDonough and Brother Carl Krull, along with Jesuit scholastics from St. Mary's, Kurseong, and a group of students from St. Robert's School.

Apart from the Jesuits, there were other Canadians, such as Barbara Wood of Port Credit, Ontario, who was a Canadian volunteer with the Jesuits involved in the relief work. Amid all sorts of squalors and miseries, she worked with whatever she had during the troubled months for all four refugee camps. "I hadn't had much experience with injections, but with so many people dying, there was no choice"[45] but to do something to alleviate the situation. Having no particular specialty, she saw herself as a generalist who had no specific duties but instead a member of what she called "empowered teams" whose duties ranged from "setting up tents," "digging ditches for latrines," "marking and distributing milk," "manning hospital tents usually full of cholera patients," "helping camp cook," to "visiting tents and offering encouragement"[46] to the refugees in all of the four designated camps.

Awareness Raising and Fundraising in India and Canada

The Jesuits' work also included two other types of activities - raising awareness and funds under the direction of Fathers Edgar Burns in India and Frank West in Canada and entertainment and cultural nights in the refugee camps. The dissemination of information was quite a challenge since it was not an easy task for a religious order to be involved in raising awareness and assisting the victims of military atrocities, especially when it was conscious of the political reality of the issue involved. The Jesuits brought out news releases, short write-ups, and flyers, collectively called their awareness package, urging the community members to donate.

The Toronto-based Canadian Jesuit Mission (CJM) sent Father Frank West to the field to meet with the Darjeeling-based Father Burns and visit the refugee camps in India to assess the relief operations. Father West was in India between July 9 and 14, 1971, and traveled extensively to the refugee camps in the Darjeeling District and West Dinajpur of West Bengal. Upon his return to Canada, Father West recounted his observations in a widely circulated report titled *Let My Children Live! An Eye-Witness Report*.[47] This report, along with write-ups of Father Burns, remains an example of firsthand information amid the denial of ongoing reprisals by the military regime of Pakistan. The report contained pictures of the refugee camps where the victims of military oppression took shelter. "Millions of human beings face starvation lives in hovels not fit for dogs,"[48] was the critical message of appeal. "Thousands are hugging trees to protect themselves from the rain and cold nights. Clothes, medicines, and food are needed. We will construct temporary shelters of bamboo and straw with the refugee's help,"[49] wrote Father Burns to reinforce the message characterized by negativity and a feeling of having no hope due to "civil strife," a term used by the Yahya regime's vocabulary.

Father Burns deliberately did not go into the root cause of the matter, although the missionaries were cognisant of the political nature of the conflict. Instead, he focused on the consequences of the exodus of millions of Bengalis from their homeland who were "faced with starvation, disease, and death."[50] So that readers in Canada do get a clear sense of the word "million," to which after a while many people became so used by seeing it on the printed page, Father West wrote, "To put the situation in terms of more readily understood, we have only to think of the chaos that would result if every man, woman, and child in both Montreal and Toronto were to arrive in Ottawa on foot, hungry and sick, in rags, and with no money."[51]

While traveling across Canada and distributing the information package for awareness, Father West spoke with Canadians about his observations in India. He frequently mentioned the name of Senator Edward Kennedy, who saw the Canadians' efforts as "a worthy tribute to Canada for what it is doing in the field for the East Pakistani refugees."[52] His awareness package also included a film titled *They Passed This Way*, which was approximately six hundred feet of movie pictures (16 mm color) showing the enormity of the refugee situation in India to illustrate the type of work the Canadians were involved in assisting the grief-stricken refugees in Indian camps. Father West and his team were optimistic and eager to continue their work despite many obstacles. "The plight of the refugees is truly appalling, and the reality is, in fact, far worse than any reports we get of conditions through the press and other media, but I do not think sufficient stress has been placed on the positive side of the problem—the amount of good work that can be done for the refugees with organization, effort, and generosity,"[53] Father West wrote to W. V. Harcourt of the Canadian Broadcasting Corporation.

There was also a display of pictures of the refugees in their camps and their miseries with succinct sentences like in a PowerPoint presentation: "What a heartbreaking reality. Why oh why! We can only do a little. I think that little is important. The government is doing its best, like other agencies. What a tragedy! Pure charity is in order, so we will do our utmost. Pray the trouble in Pakistan is soon settled."[54] "I must also say that the need grows greater each day. We must have your help to continue the work that we have begun,"[55] Father West stated, appealing to fellow Canadians -good Samaritans - to join forces.

Simultaneously, a few write-ups of Arnold Zeitlin, Bureau Chief of The Associated Press in Pakistan, 1969–1972, and Janet Perry, a young Canadian volunteer, also appeared in many Canadian newspapers and impacted Canadian readers' minds. "Dinajpur, once one of the most prosperous areas in the rice-growing province of more than seventy million people, you drive two miles without coming across a human being."[56] This uncensored dispatch from Darjeeling was sent by Zeitlin, who went inside Dinajpur (East Pakistan) to obtain firsthand information. The vivid description of Dinajpur, where the refugees were streaming into the Darjeeling District, enabled the Canadian public to recognize the gravity of the situation. Again, readers were touched by Janet Perry's description of a female refugee—"Her tattered sari does not conceal ribs painfully visible under an old woman's wrinkled, withered flesh. But beneath the glistening sweat, I see a darkly beautiful child's face. I shudder at her beauty. What suffering it must have brought her in these last few months! The atrocities of Pakistani soldiers are now a legend, and I feel the fear she must have felt."[57]

Music Therapy in the Refugee Camps

In addition to providing the basic emergency supplies in all four refugee camps, the Jesuits also paid attention to the social and cultural needs of the refugees by playing Bengali music tapes using two loudspeakers (megaphones). Volunteer students played guitar and harmonium and rendered their voices to entertain the refugees. Whether in the Darjeeling refugee camps or anywhere else under the *Bangladesh Mukti Shangrami Shilpi Shangstha* (Bangladesh Liberation Movement Artists' Organization), everyone around was attracted by the daily program, which provided a sense of relief. The refugees used to gather every evening to be away from the harsh reality of an uncertain life in the refugee camps, having come from "far and wide" to listen to the "musical entertainment in their own language to forget even for a short time, the grim existence of their lives."[58] Thus recalled Father German, their entertainment program, which "soon became a popular event for the refugees amidst their worries and anxieties."[59] Julian Francis, one of Oxfam UK personnel who worked in the field, recalled how ardently the refugees in various refugee camps enjoyed the music during their melancholy days. Such was their passion that they believed that "if each the refugee community were given a harmonium and a set of tablas, the overall health situation would improve,"[60] observed Francis.

Unsurprisingly, while the peripatetic Bangladesh Mukti Shangrami Shilpi Shangstha, under the leadership of Professor Samir Paul, was visiting refugee camps and singing for the depressed refugees. Father German's team in the Darjeeling refugee camps was also conducting its musical soirée to entertain the refugees for some relaxation when they did not know about the itinerant music groups in other refugee camps. It was purely fortuitous that the volunteers in the Darjeeling refugee camps replicated the entertainment programs across India's different refugee camps. However, the organizers of the Darjeeling area did not necessarily know anything about how and what the refugees in other camps were doing. Francis and Father German were miles away and did not know each other. Yet a common thread that united them was the power of the music—its intense emotion and feelings of ineffable joy and profound satisfaction.

The music played in the refugee camps had a tremendous impact on the minds and health of the vulnerable refugees. It was as though Professor Paul's conversation with Francis also echoed in the minds and sentiments of the performers in the Darjeeling camps. "We have nothing, and yet we have everything. We have our music, songs, dreams, and respect."[61] Thus, Father German observed the same sentiment that struck his passion regarding the nightly music/entertainment he supervised. Whether it was Francis in Kolkata or members of the Canadian Jesuits in Darjeeling, India, everyone was passionate about recalling the cultural/music nights at the refugee camps. Both underscored the importance of music therapy for distressed refugees. The nightly entertainment program and the "cultural hours" of the volunteers in the Darjeeling camps were a remarkably creative initiative of the young volunteers who undertook that independently without any assistance from anyone else. Father German's entertainment program continued for a few months, and then, at one point, his "boys" could not continue it anymore as the tapes disappeared from the storage.

Father Burns's key message to Canadian Jesuits was the following: "True, the problem of millions of refugees is one no single nation or group of individuals can solve, but it is also true that there is always something everyone can do, if he has the will and if he believes that he is his brother's keeper."[62] The work of the Jesuits in India may be seen as an example of teamwork between Canadian Jesuits and their multi-faith students, demonstrating an innovative way in which they addressed a crisis.

Canadian University Service Overseas (CUSO)

Founded in 1961 by Canadian universities and several national organizations as an agency to make plans to send Canadian graduates to developing countries, CUSO has been involved in Southeast Asia, including the Indian subcontinent, from its inception. Its involvement in the relief operation was limited since CUSO recalled its nurses and aid workers from India in March 1971. Yet when the exodus began, CUSO became involved almost instantly in India and Canada through a network of organizations.

Activities in India

The three CUSO nurses about to finish their work in India were Jean Stilwell, Pat Phillip, and Nancy Gerein. Instead of leaving India, all of them, having secured clearance from the CUSO headquarters, immediately became involved in relief work in India with the beginning of the influx of refugees. Stilwell, who was in India from 1969 to early 1971, was brought back to Ottawa to institute an awareness-raising program for Canadians regarding the military repression in East Pakistan and the untold sufferings of the Bengali refugees to fellow Canadians. Phillip worked as a field staff officer on a mobile family planning team in Bangalore, India. Gerein, teaching clinical nursing at Kurji Holy Family Hospital, Patna, Bihar, worked in the field until the late summer of 1971.

Although Gerein and Phillip were assigned to assist in the emergency services for the incoming refugees, they chose two separate routes—Gerein stayed in Rajibpur while Phillip went to New Delhi. Being convinced that the magnitude of the refugee problem was so staggering that the continuation of substantial humanitarian assistance to India and East Pakistan was crucial, Phillip sought creative ways to engage themselves gainfully under the changing circumstances. She explored the idea of providing a quick supply of goods available locally and identified the purchase and distribution of winter blankets for one of the border area refugee camps. She sought permission from the CUSO headquarters. David Catmur, then the CUSO's director of overseas operations, approved her request immediately for a small project of $6,000 to meet the immediate needs of the refugees,[63] giving Phillip *carte blanche* to undertake the proposed project.

Gerein, under the guidance of the Kurji sisters, worked in the Rajibpur area, a small village town on the India-Pakistan border. Headed by Sister Elinor Rose of Kurji Hospital, Gerein's first task was recruiting as many volunteers as possible to respond to emergencies. As early as mid-May 1971, Gerein had a small team of two doctors, one midwife, two nurses, a sister to cook, a driver, and six seminarians to act as a jack of all trades. "We were struck by the eerie silence of the camps—200,000 people made no noise!" and how "silently they put up their shelters, drew water at the wells and cooked, silently they lay down to nightmare-filled sleep."[64] Thus, Gerein noted her first impression that nothing could deter the team members from doing what they could do under the unusual circumstances. A make-shift arrangement out of a small complex of mud buildings they referred to as "hospital" and "dispensary" was the first thing on which Gerein's team worked. A burlap was hung in the middle to separate the hospital into what was referred to as the infectious disease section and the everything-else section. It was called a hospital or dispensary, even though sometimes there were no beds for the patients. They used straw on the floor that sufficed twelve beds under the difficult circumstances. Only in July did they get iron bedsteads, which relieved them of nursing the weak and dilapidated refugees on their knees.[65]

Gerein's team made every attempt to maintain a schedule, although the service hours of the "hospital" or "dispensary" were flexible. In the mornings, refugee patients would come to the dispensary to see the doctor on duty and obtain necessary medical treatment and advice. The two doctors, who saw approximately four hundred refugee patients every morning, had only one and a half minutes to question, examine, diagnose, and prescribe medicine for each patient. Typically, in the afternoons, one peripatetic team carrying its medical kit would move from one camp to another in the surrounding area of Rajibpur, especially to camps where no medical care was available. The fully empowered self-managed team soon adapted to the changing needs of the extraordinary circumstances and became "experts" and "practitioners" by devising ways and means with their limited resources. When the doctors were often out for their scheduled visits, the nurses on duty had to attend to patients, assuming increased coordination, initiation, and self-supervision responsibilities. "It was up to us, the nurses, to start the intravenous and give necessary drugs, usually cardiac stimulants, vasopressors, and antibiotics."[66] Thus, Gerein recalled how their work kept them busy.

Activities in Canada

CUSO did not join the Ottawa-based CAPR (Combined Appeal for Pakistan Relief, described below) for fundraising since CUSO's Ottawa office had already established a fund titled Pakistan Refugee Relief Fund before the formation of CAPR in June 1971. CUSO officials and volunteers worked directly with their clients and played a supportive role with CAPR partners in the Ottawa area. In early spring, Stilwell raised awareness among the Canadian public about the tragedy.

The information package for awareness-raising and fundraising included newspaper articles, appeal posters, and photographs from the field. One of Stilwell's write-ups, titled "The Full-time Business of Existing Bangladesh: The Background,"[67] outlined the plight of the millions of Bengali refugees crossing over to India and carrying heart-rending stories of agonies. "It is almost incomprehensible for us to understand how one would feed, clothe, shelter, and provide medical care to a population equal to all of Ontario,"[68] wrote Stilwell. With this simple and powerful message, she toured and met with Canadians from coast to coast. Having seen the tragedy herself, Stilwell spoke confidently that short-term aid and treatment of people suffering from widespread political upheaval could not be sustained over time. Stilwell often described her premonitions of other dangers that had been lurking ahead in India - the greater need for food, winter clothing, and shelter during the monsoon season, which by then had already forced many people to sit up all night instead of lying in the mud and human excrement. Gerein, who was still in India at that time, also produced a two-page fact sheet on the latest situation with pertinent information on the wretched conditions of the refugees, having curtly described the unbearable circumstances of the refugees.

In the fall, Gerein joined Stilwell in Ottawa and immediately took a lead role in the public education campaign initiative Stilwell had started in early summer. Written for *The Canadian Press* and first published in *The Ottawa Citizen*, Gerein brought the issue close to the Canadians' radar screen through reprints of some of her write-ups. Readers were touched by a particular article titled "Jai Bangla." Exuberance degenerates into a monotonous struggle to stay alive with the picture titled "Face of Despair," the haunting eyes of the refugee.[69] Having described the miserable situation of the refugees in the overcrowded camps, a disturbed Gerein asked, "What will eventually happen to them? Who knows? Does anyone care? Do you?"[70] The accompanying photo of a hapless refugee reflected the despair felt by three million East Pakistani refugees seeking survival in India, which was mind-boggling.

It was as though, in her initial emotional appeal, Gerein was in a conversational mode with readers having captured the minds and hearts of fellow Canadians. Readers were instantly reminded of the declaration by the government of India of a cholera epidemic on June 4, as well as of the government's priorities, such as shelter, medical supplies, transport, and food for the refugees. The same day, readers were again touched by another write-up titled "Ex-Ottawan Saw How Tragedy has Six Million Faces"[71] with Gerein's picture in the middle. It was a depiction of the overwhelming problems of the refugee camps in India and tales of slaughter in East Pakistan with an emotional appeal to its readers to come to the rescue of the Bengalis crammed in the refugee camps.

People were asked to dig their hands into their pockets to help the victims of military repression. The critical message to Canadians, including parliamentarians, was "an urgent need for a quick political solution to the problem so that the refugees could return to their homes."[72] Throughout summer and fall, CUSO's fundraising drive, which included distributing flyers and short write-ups, continued under Stilwell's stewardship.

The paucity of records does not allow us to determine how much money was raised in Canada, either in cash or in-kind, for the refugees. While it is difficult to assess the success of the CUSO representatives' tour without adequate data on donations, one must note that information regarding CUSO's activities was widely covered in the mainstream print media, including radio talk shows. One must not forget how and under what circumstances the CUSO nurses had volunteered at their initiatives without adequate financial support from the CUSO headquarters. This significant fact reminds us of how tenaciously the Canadian nurses hung on to their commitment and how spontaneously the people of Canada responded to their appeals.

Combined Appeal for Pakistani Relief (CAPR)

CAPR was formed as a coalition of nine major Canadian NGOs in Ottawa on June 16, 1971, to deal with the new challenges of a "man-made disaster" in the Indian subcontinent with a coordinated strategy. It was an emergency appeal and, as such, was scheduled to continue until August 31, 1971. The NGO community was mindful of the large, cumbersome, and ineffective structure of the Nigeria/Biafra Relief Fund of previous years (1967–1970). With guarded optimism, the NGO community quickly revisited the lessons it had learned from the Nigeria/Biafra debacle before forming the coalition. It consisted of the following nine member organizations: (1) Canadian Catholic Organisation for Development and Peace (CCODP); (2) Canadian Council of Churches and its eleven member churches; (3) Canadian Red Cross Society; (4) Canadian UNICEF Committee; (5) CANSAVE Children Fund; (6) Care of Canada; (7) Oxfam of Canada; (8) United Nations High Commissioner for Refugees (UNHCR) and (9) World Vision of Canada. The Canadian Jewish Congress, however, was an associate member.[73]

As national coordinator, Major General Arthur E. Wrinch of the Canadian Red Cross Society was appointed to oversee the functioning of the CAPR initiative throughout Canada at all three levels - national, provincial, and local. The CAPR team used the following three essential techniques for its fundraising campaign: (1) frequent press conferences with well-known Canadians; (2) interviews of Canadians who had just returned from the troubled areas to give an account of their observations on the latest situation; and (3) the use of their views in its campaign literature. Individual activities of each CAPR member are outlined below in alphabetical order.

The Canadian Catholic Conference (CCC)

Established in 1943, the Ottawa-based Canadian Catholic Conference (CCC) is also a part of the below-mentioned Canadian Catholic Organisation for Development and Peace (CCODP). CCC is the association of cardinals, archbishops, and bishops of Canada. The CCC was already involved in providing relief and rehabilitation services to East Pakistanis since the devastating cyclone of 1970. The CCC's activities were essentially confined to the following three areas of work: (1) awareness-raising among Canadians, (2) fundraising, and (3) lobbying the government without being noticeably political. The leading players in coordinating its activities in fund and awareness-raising were Fathers Everett MacNeil, William Power, Guy Croissant, and Sister Ella Zink, all of whom spent excessive time with their constituents - only a month before the military clampdown on the Bengalis, the archbishop of Ottawa and CCC's president, Joseph Aurèle Plourde, presented a cheque for $40,984.69 to Father Robert Riendeau, treasurer-general of Caritas Internationals on February 25, 1971,[74] for the cyclone victims from its Aid to Pakistan fund. The CCC's new initiative got off the ground almost right away. By calling it "a challenge to the conscience of Christians,"[75] Archbishop Plourde appealed to *"tous les Canadiens pour leur manifestation de solidarité à l'égard de frères humains victimes d'un des plus grands catalysmes du siècle* (all Canadians to show solidarity to their brothers who are the victims of one of the century's great tragedies [author's translation])."[76]

To raise public awareness of the military atrocities and the killings of unarmed Bengali civilians, CCC dedicated a day to remind the people of Canada of the tragic events that were taking place in East Pakistan by observing Sunday, April 25, 1971, as the "Right To Life." At the Plenary Assembly, Archbishop Plourde urged all Catholics in Canada to reflect "on the numerous ways in which this God-given and most basic human right" was "forcibly denied or threatened throughout the world."[77] In his letter to Mitchell Sharp, Archbishop Plourde highlighted the killings of fellow human beings in "Occupied Bangladesh" without directly making any reference to the political issues. The idea was to get the public to react to the military atrocities and tragic killings. He then urged thoughtful Catholics to "have in mind the deplorable loss of innocent lives and reported atrocities" that were "taking place in the Pakistani conflict."[78] Sharp responded within days by saying, "The government shares your deep concerns at loss of life and stands ready when requested to assist in any international program to provide relief to innocent victims, as was done last year following the tidal wave disaster."[79] Though too early to give his view on the issue, Sharp ended his note by saying, "I share your hope that there will be an early end to the fighting and a resumption of negotiations for a political solution acceptable to all people of Pakistan."[80]

In the meantime, within a short time, Archbishop Plourde made a country-wide appeal. Immediately, the CCC volunteers successfully coalesced both church groups and members of the public by bringing out a large procession of religious leaders of several denominations in the national capital region. Their appeal for donation struck a sympathetic chord among Canadians across the country. Many from across Canada began to send donations. Reverend Richard T. McGrath, Bishop of St. Georges, Newfoundland, for example, immediately sent a cheque for $500 to Archbishop Plourde but regretted in the following way: "Our only regret is that we are not in a position to contribute an amount more in keeping with the acute needs of these poor people in their present crisis."[81] The CCC officers/volunteers soon found their desks swarmed with letters, petitions, and inquiries from Canadians of divergent denominations. Archbishop Plourde also appealed to the government of Canada by saying, "While we recognize that there are limitations and difficulties which now make difficult positive mediation of this lamentable conflict, we urge the government of Canada to persist by every available means in offering good offices and humanitarian assistance, through the UN or otherwise, in the hope that continued human suffering and loss of innocent lives may soon come to an end in East Pakistan."[82]

Nationally, having made his appeal, Archbishop Plourde immediately expressed his "desire of collaboration with all those who endeavor to promote justice and peace in the world"[83] and followed a different strategy that combined both national and international efforts. He met with Sharp again to reinforce his concerns and the concerns of the people of Canada about the killings of innocent lives. He discreetly referred to a communal bloodbath because of military intervention instead of a successful negotiation with the leaders who emerged triumphant in the 1970 National Elections. Despite CCC's recognition that negotiations are vital instruments in the foreign policy kit, it chose not to speak about the "regime change" that was the day's demand. An astute Plourde refrained from pointing fingers at the Yahya-led military regime or even mentioning the actual nature of the conflict. He focussed on matters related to the much-needed relief assistance.

Internationally, Archbishop Plourde also attended the Synod in Rome during the last week of September and shared the concerns of his constituent churches with the participants of Catholic relief agencies of other countries. The media coverage of the Synod meeting in which Archbishop Plourde followed the pilgrims in St. Peter's Square on October 2 generated a lot of enthusiasm, creating momentum among the public. On the same day, the Holy Father, Pope Vl, launched an appeal declaring Sunday, October 10, 1971, as the "World Day of Prayer, Fasting, and Almsgiving for Pakistani Refugees and the Eight Hundred Thousand Children in Danger of Dying."[84] The Holy Father emphasized that Catholics and believers of all other religious faiths were also urged to unite to demonstrate their grave concerns. "Take whatever initiatives they judge most appropriate, at the diocesan level, to mark this World Day of Prayer, Fasting, and Almsgiving proclaimed by Pope Paul."[85] Thus, the frank and straightforward message from the Holy Father resonated with Canadians of diverse backgrounds. Following the Thanksgiving Day Observance, according to the wishes of Pope Paul's appeal, CCC became more involved internationally through the relief arms of the Catholic Relief Agencies of the world.

The Canadian Catholic Organisation for Development and Peace (CCODP)

The CCDOP played an essential role in making the Canadian public conscious of their obligations toward the victims of military reprisals. Internationally, through the work of a group of pan-Canadian enthusiasts, CCODP's collective work helped them eliminate the duplication of efforts and expand the scale and scope of the work. The CCODP continued its teamwork, believing that while it could not carry on the work of peace alone, it could, at least, carry on its work together to assist the victims. Without ever referring to the gritty reality of the Bengalis' demand for greater political autonomy, transfer of power to the elected leader of the majority party, the refusal or failure of the military government to respect the principles of democracy, the suppression of the Bengalis to realize their legitimate rights, CCODP remained resolute in its commitment to assisting the refugees in India and displaced people in East Pakistan.

The Canadian Council of Churches (CCC)

With its eleven-member churches, the Canadian Council of Churches (CCC) actively raised money from the Canadian public under the CAPR campaign initiative. They were the following: (1) the Anglican Church of Canada, (2) the Armenian Church of America, (3) the Baptist Federation of Canada, (4) the Christian Church (Disciple of Christ), (5) the Greek Orthodox Church, (6) Lutheran Church in America (Canada Section), (7) Presbyterian Church in Canada, (8) Reformed Church of America (Classis of Ontario), (9) Religious Society of Friends (Canada Yearly Meeting), (10) Salvation Army, and (11) United Church of Canada.[86]

Like all other organizations, a cautious CCC remained on guard to avoid being seen as political. Yet, it continued to meet the challenges of working around its public position on a political issue. The CCC carefully crafted all its appeal letters informing Canadians of the situation that had "reached a turn in the road where it was no longer possible to say that a situation was outside our concern because it was an internal conflict in the global village, we were all one human family."[87] This was expressed by Dr. Eoin S. MacKay, who represented the Canadian Council of Churches at a special meeting at the Canadian Council for International Co-operation (CCIC) premises. The Canadian member churches distributed write-ups for the general public to the broadest extent possible through reprints of the press releases of various international church organizations.

To emphasize the nature of the conflict, church leaders Reverends E. W. Scott, primate of the Anglican Church of Canada, A. B. Moore, moderator of the United Church of Canada, and J. A. Plourde, chairman of the Canadian Catholic Conference and archbishop of Ottawa met with Mitchell Sharp, Secretary of State for External Affairs. Although Archbishop Plourde had already had a personal meeting with Sharp, he still accompanied the group again to raise the refugee issue. The news media widely covered the story of the "procession of petitioners for East Pakistan[i] refugees and war victims."[88] Reportedly, Archbishop Plourde wondered why only the Vietnam War remained a cause for public opinion while fatigue set in regarding the conflict in Pakistan. He said, "Is it because there is no political implication?"[89] Following the same line of argument that the Canadian public was pushing for, the church leaders urged Sharp to focus on how the issue could be resolved - "to use the

United Nations to pressure to prevent killing"[90] of the Bengalis in their homeland.

Again, as part of the CCC, the Salvation Army, a Christian organization that gives hope and support to vulnerable people in communities across Canada and many countries worldwide, also came forward to do its bit. It created a platform under the title *Give to the Charity or Church of Your Choice* and raised money for the CAPR initiative. "The Salvation Army in Canada is already receiving donations toward Pakistani relief and will undoubtedly receive much more from this nationwide appeal... The Commissioner gives his endorsement to this national appeal and would ask that all Salvationists be advised from our platforms and through our institutions to support this campaign, keeping in mind the donations directed specifically to the Salvation Army will come to us and be forwarded to the Salvation Army teams already at work among the refugees from East Pakistan."[91] Dr. E. S. Mackay of the Canadian Council of Churches reported that the Salvation Army had donated $2,347.99 to the CAPR Initiative.[92]

Canadian Red Cross Society (CRCS)

Internationally, the CRCS worked with the League of Red Cross Societies (LORCS) and the International Committee of the Red Cross (ICRC), offering services to the politically affected Bengali refugees in the Indian subcontinent. As a member of LORCS, CRCS had the advantage of a head-start in providing emergency services to the refugees in India and displaced persons in East Pakistan from the beginning of the refugee crisis when no other organization had permission to be involved.

Activities in India

There were approximately thirty-eight voluntary agencies that Indian and foreign workers ran under the banner of the Indian Red Cross. The LORCS sent three Canadians to India, and they collaborated with several international organizations to identify the refugees' needs. Albert Batten, former Executive Director, Toronto Central Branch, CRCS, was the first Canadian representative to attend India in May 1971 as LORCS' delegate. He was stationed in New Delhi with the national headquarters of IRCS and subsequently became a member of the Central Coordinating Committee.

He acted as the "liaison officer" and kept in close touch with the UN agencies and the office of the Canadian High Commission.[93]

In the second month, Batten moved to Kolkata, West Bengal, to expand his understanding of the modus operandi of the Indian Red Cross. He became involved in Operation Lifeline, a child nutrition program for refugee children in West Bengal. He successfully negotiated the LIFE-LINE Project with the Director of Relief Operations and the Field Director of UNICEF in Kolkata.[94] Spearheaded by the Red Cross, it was a joint venture of twelve to fourteen NGOs under the coordination and leadership of the Red Cross with the assistance of UNICEF.[95] His three-month assignment exemplifies the maximization of volunteers' efficiency in partnership, negotiation, and project initiation in times of need. By August 15, 1971, 889 milk feeding centers were in operation, supplying milk and high-protein foods to over eight hundred thousand children and mothers.[96] Thus, wrote Batten.

The second and third Canadian delegates to LORCS in India were Colin Evans, assistant commissioner of British Columbia, Yukon Division, CRCS, and John Anderson, business administrator and area director of the Blood Transfusion Service at CRCS. Stationed in Kolkata, both Evans and Anderson were also responsible for the coordination and cooperation of relief operations of all voluntary agencies in India, with particular emphasis on those of the Bengal, having assumed the title of league liaison officer under the banner of the Indian Red Cross (IRC). Within days, Evans expressed his concerns to the headquarters: "I visited a Refugee camp—130,000 people. It is terrible, but then, so are the slums. The health department tells us that thirty thousand children will die in the next *three weeks* unless they have immediate medical care and high-protein feeding. There is a world shortage of milk powder, so God knows what will happen."[97] All three Canadian representatives shared their concerns and observations with their superiors in Canada and made them react accordingly. At the same time, the press releases helped Canadians remain abreast, informed, and "educated."

Activities in Pakistan

The CRCS' work in Pakistan became extraordinarily daunting as those responsible found the situation across the landscape in an atmosphere of incomprehension, doubt, suspicion, and outright fear. As the military operations continued, so did the consequent crossing over to India by the terrified Bengalis, only to escape persecution at the hands of the military regime. While many of the displaced people were still receiving aid from voluntary organizations, more in thousands were again being rendered homeless every day by the Pakistani military. Again, being unable to cross the border, tens of thousands of people were forced to move from one place to another within the province. Naturally, CRCS was alarmed to see how, following the army crackdown, the Pakistan Red Cross Society (PRCS) president was relieved of his duties and replaced by a new president. It also noted that the Bengali secretary of the East Pakistan Red Cross Society (EPRS) himself had fled to India and sought asylum there. Consequently, it faced the challenge of reengineering the organization to establish new priorities.

Providing emergency services to the displaced persons within the province was deemed to be its priority throughout the fast-deteriorating situation during the army occupation. The most critical projects the League undertook in East Pakistan during the military occupation and reprisals included the cyclone warning system, emergency relief distributions, child nutrition program, assistance to Holy Family Hospital in Dhaka, supplementary medical care, and tracing and inquiry service. The tracing and inquiry service was an essential, unique service that helped the displaced persons in East Pakistan and refugees scattered across thousands of refugee camps in India connect with their family members.

Activities in Canada

Having partnered with several Ottawa-based NGOs, CRCS developed an action plan for collecting and shipping goods under the supervision of Major L. B. Benson, director of operations of the Department of National Defence (DND). Major General A. E. Wrinch, CRCS' national commissioner, personally appealed to Canadians for their cooperation in raising funds for its programs and services. He worked closely with both CAPR members and representatives of the DND and Canadian International Development Agency (CIDA) and brought many others together in the CAPR initiative. The CRCS' activities in Canada mainly fell under the following three areas: (1) awareness-raising, (2) fundraising, and (3) collection of miscellaneous donation items through its women's working group.

CRCS went into full gear by coordinating the collection of blankets from Canadians nationwide. With more awareness of the tragic situation of the victims in India and East Pakistan, the Canadian public made generous donations with a strong desire to "do something" constructive. Almost all Canadian Forces Bases, except those in the Yukon and Northwest Territories, received blankets from individual church agencies following CRCS' appeal for the refugees in India. Again, as part of CRCS' sensitization and awareness-raising program, Wrinch frequently appeared on talk shows in Nancy Edwards Reports, a Toronto-based Berkeley studio production for inter-church radio. In one of his interviews, having cautioned his listeners, he observed that the monsoon season would "result in further misery and outbreaks of cholera."[98] Depiction of the helplessness of the refugees who "fled in terror [and were], crossing the border into India"[99] to save their lives touched the hearts of Canadians who spontaneously responded to CRCS' appeals.

Again, CRCS' Women's Working Committee was also involved in a variety of work, such as knitting, sewing, collecting blankets and canned food items made or collected while taking care of their children at home, and nurturing the attitudes of trust, self-confidence, tolerance, and hope for a better future. By mid-May, thirty cases of clothing made by Red Cross Women's Work Committee members had already been released from the Singapore warehouse. According to CRCS' press release dated May 3, 1971,[100] the value of the clothing was $4,700 in addition to the ten-thousand-dollar cash grant. Collecting, packaging, and labeling sundry items were the committee's way of doing its part for the refugees, a quintessentially Canadian example of voluntary work.

Perhaps the most significant fact regarding CRCS' contributions is that, unlike many other organizations, CRCS was one of the few organizations that worked in India and both wings of Pakistan during the critical months of the Pakistan-Bangladesh conflict. The DND's armed forces aircraft remained in service for delivery of items in India at the Canadian federal government's expense—an expense often overlooked while examining individual agencies. The coordination work of Major Benson in this regard also remains an example of strength, courage, and partnership, as well as Canada's prompt response to the emergency needs of the displaced people engaging the greater public.

Canadian Save the Children Fund (CANSAVE)

By the time the Toronto-based CANSAVE joined the CAPR initiative, Canadians were already familiar with the basic issues surrounding the conflict, military reprisals, and the resultant ongoing exodus of the Bengalis from their homeland. Kenric R. Marshall, who represented CANSAVE at the CAPR meetings, seized every opportunity to express his organization's concerns about the influx of refugees to India and the news of the outbreak of cholera among the refugees in India. Following a reality check, CANSAVE estimated that it would require a minimum of $50,000 "as CANSAVE's share of this International Save the Children Fund project."[101] A personal appeal of Princess Anne, then president of Save the Children Fund, following her recent visit to British Columbia, triggered a province-wide eagerness for the cause. The most commendable effort is the provincial Liberal leader Dr. Pat McGeer's appeal to BC Premier Bill Bennett for a contribution from the British Colombia Disaster Fund and matching dollar for dollar of the public funds contributed.

Having partnered with local NGOs in India, CANSAVE focused on helping disadvantaged children. In one of his interviews with the media around the late summer of 1971, Marshall outlined the various initiatives CANSAVE had undertaken, particularly with its parent organization in Great Britain. He talked about Bal Sevika, one of CANSAVE's significant projects supporting Lifeline Beta, a unique feeding and medical care program for severely malnourished children in the refugee camps. A contribution of $5,000 was collected by June to support CASNSAVE's medical team comprised of English doctors, nurses, and field administrators. Worldwide engagements enabled CANSAVE to highlight the excruciating circumstances of the Bengali refugees and the concerted efforts of the Save the Children Fund's (SCF) medical teams engaged in treating the refugees.

Canadian UNICEF Committee

During the military takeover in Pakistan, the Canadian UNICEF Committee (also referred to as UNICEF Canada), a part of the United Nations Children's Fund (UNICEF), was already operating in the Indian subcontinent, having been engaged in building relationships. With the exodus of tens of thousands of Bengalis out of their homeland, UNICEF

Canada redirected its services toward the immediate needs of the refugees in India as well as the displaced people in East Pakistan.

Activities in India

The UNICEF, which worked closely with representatives of the UNHCR, World Food Program (WFP), Food and Agriculture Organization (FAO), World Health Organization (WHO), Indian Red Cross Society (IRCS), United Nations East Pakistan Relief Operation (UNEPRO) and a few national and local organizations, played a significant role both in Canada and India. It coordinated a substantial part of the emergency requirements for children, who formed a large portion of the camp population in India. UNICEF Canada's most successful program in India was with the International Red Cross Society's Operation Lifeline, designed to prioritize supplementary feeding to over one thousand refugee camps.[102] The program had two parts, Alpha and Beta, which received international recognition for their work for children. While initially, they provided milk and high-protein food to all the children in the camps, they later offered a more specialized feeding service, which was required for seriously malnourished children.

Activities in Canada

UNICEF Canada's work in Canada consisted of (1) awareness-raising and individual and collective fundraising through the CAPR initiative and (2) individual airlifting and delivery of supplies from Canada to India. Paul Ignatieff, UNICEF Canada's executive director, visited India in early July and met with UNICEF staff and a host of representatives from FAO, WFP, WHO, and UNEPRO. He also met with other volunteer agency representatives in India and East Pakistan. Together, they visited many refugee camps and obtained firsthand information from the refugees and those assisting them. Following his meetings, while piggybacking on those already in the field, Ignatieff determined UNICEF Canada's priority - to save the lives of children who were the principal victims in the refugee camps.

In June, UNICEF Canada's president, Sybil M. Darnell, having warned the public of the continuing exodus of the Bengalis, observed that the refugees were "still crossing the border at the rate of one hundred thousand a day."[103] She then went on to say that the number by then had amounted to "five million Pakistani refugees, equal to a quarter of the population of Canada, have suddenly moved to an area which is not only unprepared but also lacks the basic resources to feed them."[104] In the meantime, Ignatieff's field report titled "Pakistani Refugee Camps in India" contained stories of the killing and degradation of human lives along with goods and services in the cities, towns, and villages which he had seen - widespread destruction of the transportation and communication networks, disruptions of the operation of schools, commercial activity, and the breakdown of the regular system of food distribution.

Using the technique of familiarity with the people of Canada and offering his readers in Canada a sense of what it was like, Ignatieff picked the jargon that is known to Canadians. "The number of refugees who have now moved from East Bengal into India is equivalent to the entire population of Ontario—over seven million. Only someone familiar with the logistics of supplying an army or a city the size of Toronto could easily understand the problems being posed to the government of India in providing adequate shelter, food, and medical services for this number of people."[105] Implicit in Ignatieff's description was his attempt to put across to the government and Canadians a clear message—that obviously, a problem of this magnitude would require "assistance on a world-wide scale" to cope with the situation.

In early fall, Grant Deachman, Member of Parliament for Vancouver Quadra, picked up the issue again and raised his concerns about the specter of malnutrition to prompt Canadians from all walks of life to respond to UNICEF Canada's appeals. He reminded his colleagues in the House of Ignatieff's description of the tragic plight of the flight of refugees that was "undoubtedly the largest migration in accurately recorded history"[106] Deachman also demanded further government interventions since "the magnitude of the refugee problem defies description.'[107] The frequent airing of a segment of an interview with Paul Edwards of the UNICEF New York with its grim account also echoed Ignatieff's observations of what he saw in the Indian subcontinent.

Again, in October, UNICEF Canada appeared before the House of Commons Committee on External Affairs and National Defence and formally shared its findings from the field with government officials. Paul Ignatieff, UNICEF Canada's executive director, highlighted that not only was the situation an "emergency within an emergency,"[108] but a particular situation that required the immediate attention of the rest of the world. To transport the UNICEF materials, such as polyethylene and tarpaulins, which were identified as priority items in India, UNICEF Canada was in regular touch with the Canadian International Development Agency (CIDA) and DND's flight crews from 437 T Squadron Air Transport Command wrote Ignatieff. He also indicated that as early as July, it was already estimated that airlift projects included over fifty thousand tarpaulins to provide shelter for approximately 750,000 refugees.[109] Ignatieff's presentation immediately triggered serious discussions among the Canadian parliamentarians and the public.

Appreciating the work of UNICEF Canada, the New York-based UNICEF profusely thanked CIDA for its "exceedingly generous gestures, more so in the light of the tremendously active role played by CIDA and the Canadian authorities in providing many airlifts without charge."[110] In his conclusion, he thanked the CIDA personnel again for their "personal intervention at all points" of their activities, which to them were "beyond praise."[111] UNICEF Canada's involvement in India during the war exemplifies extraordinary collaborative efforts.

Care of Canada

Unlike today, CARE Canada, a voluntary organization in international development founded in 1946, had no separate office in India or Pakistan in 1971. CARE Canada has already coordinated relief work in East Pakistan through CARE USA since the massive tidal wave of November 1970. Following the military crackdown, when there began an unprecedented exodus and the displacement of the Bengalis within the province, CARE Canada's strategy was to (1) channel funds and (2) use volunteers in Canada, India, and Pakistan.

Activities in India and Pakistan

CARE Canada's activities in India and East Pakistan were providing emergency humanitarian relief assistance to the Bengali refugees, particularly in West Bengal, and continuing its housing project inside East Pakistan's cyclone-affected areas that had started earlier. This also meant that there had to be a shift in its focus on what was regarded as more urgent for those who stayed within the province but had left their homes in fear of persecution only to join the rank of the homeless. To meet the needs, an extra six thousand tarpaulins were obtained. At the same time, other projects in the province were undertaken throughout the liberation war period by CARE USA's Partnership Housing Programs and UNICEF's Child Feeding Program.[112]

To do all that, John Wise, Chief of Operations, reoriented his team members to the newly identified direction and re-channeled their activities in India for the refugees and for the displaced persons who, having risked their lives, had remained in "Occupied Bangladesh." CARE Canada, being directly involved in various phases of the relief operations, successfully provided both human and financial resources for these large projects.

Activities in Canada

CARE Canada personnel in Ottawa developed the following two-pronged strategy: (1) to strengthen its regular fundraising component, the Miles for Millions Committee, in various cities, which is a part of CARE Canada's committee to find ways to increase participation of Canadians in its walkathon programs throughout the country, and (2) having joined the CAPR initiative, to continue its joint appeal to the Canadians for immediate contributions. Throughout summer and fall, the Miles for Millions Committee toured Canada as part of CARE Canada's regular fundraising activities. The Committee members from different cities found the Canadian public receptive, having been already sensitized to the tragic predicament of the refugees.

In Chapter 3, we noted the media's description of the excruciating circumstances and CARE Canada's appeal to the general public for financial support to meet the desperate needs of the refugees. The media coverage struck a deep emotional cord in the minds of the public that still remembered the needs of the victims of a devastating hurricane in the Bay of Bengal, which took place less than a year ago. The public instantly responded to the appeal by contributing to the relief funds organized through the CAPR initiative. The work of CARE Canada teams demonstrates a sense of altruism—a characteristic of human nature that emanates from within.

Oxfam of Canada

Since the 1960s, Oxfam's operation in the Indian subcontinent consisted of Oxfam UK and Oxfam Canada personnel who worked jointly to further the implementation of the Oxfam projects there. In fact, Oxfam Canada was the first Canadian NGO to respond to the emergency needs of refugees in India.

Activities in India

The appointment of Brother Raymond Cournoyer, a native of Magog, Québec, a member of the Canadian Holy Cross Order, as field officer for East India and East Pakistan on February 1, 1971, is of profound importance. Stationed in Ranchi, Bihar, Brother Cournoyer began his relief work with a fund of $10,000.[113]

Cournoyer was well-liked by the people he went to serve. Throughout the crisis, he proved himself to be of incalculable value to the Bengali refugees familiar with his name since 1955 when he first went to East Pakistan. Under Cournoyer's leadership was Alan Leather, an Oxfam field director from the North of India, who liaised with the Gandhi Peace Foundation; Adrian Marshall was in charge of servicing and maintaining the vehicles. There was a local recruit, popularly known as Vikash Bhai, who, through the Gandhi Peace Foundation, solicited the volunteer services of many young Indian doctors, nurses, and social workers. Perhaps the most noteworthy was Julian Francis, from Oxfam's project in Bihar, in charge of clearing goods through customs and trucking them to depots, who worked closely with Brother Cournoyer.

Oxfam's focus was (1) recruitment of volunteers and (2) transportation and supply of medicine and equipment for the refugees. Having differentiated the types of skills needed to undertake different levels of work, Cournoyer broadened the human capital and volunteer base to accommodate a wide variety of interested volunteers with diverse skills and abilities. Julian Francis kept the Canadians posted by his frequent reports to Oxfam officials detailing how "the five areas where Oxfam-supported teams were working in Agartala, Bongaon, Barasat, Balurghat, and Jalpaiguri."[114] Overall, the activities in India ranged from networking to awareness-raising to actual relief operations through horizontal work with Christian Aid, Catholic Relief Services, War on Want, Bharat Sevashram Sangh, Indian Red Cross

Society, Gandhi Peace Foundation, Ram Krishna Mission, Gujarat Relief Society, and Bangla Desh Assistance Group in Kolkata, West Bengal. The close collaboration enabled Oxfam Canada to avoid duplication of efforts and streamline its relief work.

The Testimony of Sixty: On the Crisis in Bengal

Oxfam's most significant and far-reaching effort, through the initiative of Leslie Kirkley, director of Oxfam UK, published a remarkable account titled *The Testimony of Sixty: On the Crisis in Bengal*. Included in the testimony were observations of the journalists, writers, politicians, and social justice advocates of the heartbreaking situations the refugees were facing—something they had seen with their own eyes having visited the refugee camps. Notable among them were Mother Teresa (Missionaries of Charity), Edward Kennedy (a US senator), Bruce Douglas Mann (British MP), John Stonehouse (British MP), Nicholas Tomalin (*The Sunday Times*), Anthony Mascarenhas (*The Morning News*), David Loshak (*The Daily Telegraph*), Alex Hendry (*Financial Times*), and Brother Cournoyer (Oxfam Canada) who successfully brought together five well-known Canadians—Stanley Burke (Canadian Broadcasting Corporation), Frederick Nossal (*Toronto Telegram*), John Drewery (Canadian Broadcasting Corporation), Dr. Robert McClure (ex-moderator at the United Church of Canada and part of the board of director of Oxfam Canada), and Ernest Hillen (*Weekend Magazine*).

Having found the situation regrettable, Stanley Burke referred to the military reprisals of the Yahya regime as a "man-made disaster of almost unimaginable proportions... And yet, the world stands by, almost indifferent. Why?"[115] It was frustrating to him that the UN was crippled by the attitudes of its member governments and by the existing code of international conduct, which made it impossible to find a resolution to the conflict. Arguing that a mere protest was not enough and that the world community had a responsibility at a time when the world seemed indifferent to a tragedy affecting millions of Bengalis, Burke raised his voice, "Are there limits to the right of a government to use force against people it claims as its own to perpetuate a political system? The question cries out for attention."[116]

Frederick Nossal of the *Toronto Telegram* visited several refugee camps near Kolkata in June 1971. He described how "young children and old people were dying by the score from cholera, malnutrition, and diseases connected with food deficiencies."[117] His message to the rest of the world was that "since June [1971], conditions had worsened in many camps" and that "unless a concerted global effort is mounted, thousands more will die."[118]

The tragedy of the Bengali refugees in cramped refugee camps and the horrors reminded CBC reporter John Drewery of the harrowing scenes he had witnessed earlier while covering the wars in Korea, the Congo, Egypt, Vietnam, and Biafra. "It is simply that the magnitude of the tragedy is so immense, so overwhelming, [that] it overshadows all other things. The cry for help coming out of India and East Pakistan is echoing all around the world. If we ignore it, we are our future, too."[119] Thus, Drewery wrote about the brutalization of the Bengalis, which he believed was worse than what had happened to countless others throughout history. Again, in the tragically squalid circumstances, Ernest Hillen of the *Weekend Magazine* focused on the indifference of the governments of various countries, with no exception to the government of his own country, Canada. "The blame for catastrophe rightly enough belongs to the men who run the West Pakistani government, but that shame belongs to all of us,"[120] argued a distraught Hillen.

Again, Dr. Robert McClure, who represented Oxfam Canada and traveled to India, as well as all major cities of Canada, talked about the miserable conditions of the Bengali refugees. He immediately caught the attention of the world community through his description of the sick and dying refugees in the dilapidated camps under one of the most calamitous situations. Having examined a confused woman petrified for days, a mother of four boys suffering from typhoid, he wrote and talked about how the unarmed Bengali civilians were terrified by the brutality of the Pakistani soldiers.[121] Having appealed for more vigorous and extended Canadian participation in the East Pakistan crisis, Reverend McClure urged Canadians to demonstrate their support and concern for the hapless refugees by "flexing the muscles of compassion."[122] Given Canada's constraints and reservations, he was utterly frank in his appeal to the people of Canada, saying, "It is the duty and obligation of the voluntary agencies to cultivate the international interest and global awareness of the ordinary Canadian citizen. The government has great difficulty performing such functions because of the suspicion of partisan political sentiments in the Canadian social atmosphere."[123] He said, "The education, information, and motivation of Canadians to make them sensitive to injustice, political or economic oppression and famine and hunger is recognized as being the role of the voluntary agencies and church groups throughout Canada."[124]

On-site visit of Lesley Smith and others

Oxfam Canada received the voluntary services of Lesley Smith, then assistant superintendent of the Department of National Health and Welfare, who went to India to assess the pharmaceutical needs and acquire drugs from Canadian companies. "He came over to establish what medicines were required for Oxfam's program, which might be contributed from Canada as commercial gifts or at best prices. His experience was put to immediate use when discussing with the Indian medics who form the team's nucleus that Oxfam is now putting out in the field,"[125] wrote Phillip Jackson in his report regarding Lesley Smith.

Accompanied by Brother Cournoyer, the Canadian pharmaceutical expert held several rounds of meetings with Dr. Hiralal Shaha, Director of Health Services, West Bengal. Together with members of the Oxfam Committee, Indian doctors, and other pharmaceutical experts, Smith formed the nucleus of the team that identified the needs of the refugees in four areas as crucial—(a) sanitation, (b) clothing, (c) shelter, and (d) transportation. He then outlined his observations of the refugees' pitiable plight in the refugee camps. He alerted his colleagues and social workers about what he thought would be needed—millions of dollars to provide adequate relief for the refugees living under insufferable conditions. Smith also developed a list of medicines required for Oxfam's program, which might be contributed from Canada. From then on, Smith worked closely with the Ottawa-based Oxfam personnel and assisted them in their work.

Oxfam Canada's Secret Liaison with Bangladeshi Supporters Within East Pakistan

Oxfam Canada personnel had no permission from the government of East Pakistan to enter its territory. While Brother Cournoyer was awaiting permission to enter East Pakistan, he used to sneak in and out of East Pakistan frequently, having maintained close liaison with the Chattogram-based Brother Flavian Laplante, as mentioned at the beginning of the present chapter under the caption Canadian Religious Missionaries. He played an essential role in raising awareness of ongoing military reprisals. He also pushed the envelope for the liberation of Bangladesh. He witnessed what he called "the greatest tragedy of the century."[126] Brother Cournoyer saw the political nature of the issue entailing Pakistan and India as settling old scores. With his feet on the ground, a practical Brother Cournoyer wrote to his superior, "In a time of emergency, a lot of things have to be played by year, without any prejudice to planning and efficiency, and I would like Oxfam to understand this."[127]

Despite the political restrictions of the missionaries, Brother Cournoyer turned out to be an exception. His wrath toward the repressive regime and passion for an independent Bangladesh became known to both the NGO workers and the people of India and East Pakistan at large. Using his knowledge of the Bangla language and an appreciation of the sense and sensitivities of the Bengali people of East Pakistan, where he had been working since 1955, Cournoyer, with his bubbling effervescence and enthusiasm, won the hearts of the Bengalis. With tact and diplomacy, and despite the considerable risk, Brother Cournoyer and other missionaries assisted those in need and worked doggedly to alleviate their sufferings.

Activities in Canada

In Canada, Oxfam Canada directed its energies in the following three crucial areas: (1) lobbying the government to seek a resolution, (2) raising awareness among Canadians about the latest refugee situation in India, and (3) fundraising for the victims of military repression. Although the Bengalis' struggle for independence was often referred to as a "disaster," Oxfam Canada reminded its clients that this "disaster," in no way, resembled the "natural" disaster (cyclone and tidal wave) of November 12 - 13 of the previous year. "It is the result of political calculations (or miscalculations). The consequent responsibility of the leaders of both the nation involved and other nations of the world is much more serious simply because of its political nature,"[128] wrote Derek Hayes, chairman of the board of Oxfam Canada, having clearly stated the difference between "natural" and "man-made" disasters. This is perhaps the most courageous action that Oxfam Canada took through an open letter to the *Toronto Telegram* demanding that Canada should immediately "press for a much-expanded UN aid program to include UN negotiations with the authorities of Pakistan and Bangla Desh [as it was spelled then in two syllables] for the safe conduct of food and relief supplies, as well as the appointment for senior UN personnel to operate the program."[129]

For the record, Oxfam Canada was the first NGO in Canada to use the word "Bangla Desh" instead of East Pakistan in an open letter. Until now, Oxfam Canada, like all other Canadian organizations, has always used the name East Pakistan since no country has recognized Bangla Desh yet. Brother Cournoyer, well-known as an ardent separatist Québecois, is the only Canadian NGO worker who had been consistently referring to East Pakistan as Bangla Desh from the beginning. For the record, while he is the first Canadian NGO worker to do that, Oxfam Canada is also the first Canadian NGO to openly refer to East Pakistan as Bangla Desh in the news media. This is an example of the grave risk Oxfam Canada took as a nonpolitical organization. This is very significant in recognizing the Canadian perspective of the conflict.

Oxfam Canada worked on the premise that a broad base of public support for the issue would be needed to involve the Canadian government in any specific action. In a carefully crafted letter, it asked the government of Canada to (1) appeal to the government of Pakistan to end military operations immediately and admit neutral observers to East Pakistan; (2) urge conciliation by members of the Commonwealth; and (3) request an emergency session of the Security Council of the United Nations.[130] Specifically urging that Canada's government initiate immediate placement of the Pakistan situation on the agenda of the UN General Assembly, Hayes wrote on behalf of Oxfam Canada, "This is not an 'internal matter.' It's a matter which must actively involve the entire world community. It will be to our everlasting shame if we turn our back."[131]

In addition, Oxfam Canada also wrote two personal letters to Prime Minister Pierre Trudeau and Secretary of State for External Affairs Mitchell Sharp. In its letter to Trudeau, Oxfam Canada underlined the need for the prime minister's intervention. It pointed out that there was "no time for a debate" at a time when the people of Canada as "world citizens" were "faced with the responsibility for the possible deaths of four million human beings."[132] Again, stating that the "continued inactivity is intolerable,"[133] Oxfam vice-chairman reminded Mitchell Sharp of the context of the killing of unarmed civilians vis-à-vis Ottawa's position that was not yet fully known to Canadians.

Oxfam Canada also sought the endorsement of federal political party leaders, provincial premiers, leaders, and heads of provincial political parties individually. Urging the premiers to support Oxfam's "campaign with dollars," it asked them to appeal to their "citizens" and "communities" in their respective provinces "to donate generously for humanitarian reasons"[134] to the cause of the Bengali refugees. In the same letter, it strongly urged the premiers to proclaim Friday, June 18, 1971, as the "Pakistan Refugee Day" in their respective provinces so that such a gesture on their part "would help immeasurably" with Oxfam's campaign for the victims of military repression.

The federal opposition leader, Robert Stanfield, immediately wrote back, expressing his solidarity with all those concerned Canadians engaged in raising funds for the Bengali victims, "I sincerely urge all Canadians to give any assistance they can to the Combined Appeal to provide funds for food, temporary shelter, and many other actions necessary to alleviate the severe suffering."[135]

Additionally, Oxfam Quebec's enthusiastic team, having followed the national strategy, secured the endorsement of the following heads of Québec's four political parties: Premier Robert Bourassa (Liberal), René Lévesque (Parti Québecois), Camille Sanson (Creditiste Rally of Québec), and Jean-Jacques Bertrand (Union Nationale). Using excerpts of remarks from political leaders in their Fact Sheets and campaign literature, the team distributed them throughout Québec. The fact sheets used the cautionary comments of René Lévesque, then president of the executive council of the Partie Québecois—that it was a case of "inhuman repression of all the people of East Pakistan;" and that "unless the freedom of East Pakistan is accomplished morally, it will not become a political reality."[136]

The South Asia Conference/The Toronto Declaration of Concern

The South Asia Conference, also more frequently referred to as the Toronto Declaration of Concern, a high-profile three-day conference, took place from August 19–21, 1971, at St. Michael's College, University of Toronto, under the chairmanship of Dr. Hugh Keenleyside, former director-general of the UN Technical Assistance and former Canadian ambassador to Indonesia. It brought together thirty distinguished parliamentarians, churchmen, social workers, and other professionals from various countries to discuss the latest situation in East Pakistan under President Yahya's military dictatorship. It was an open forum where several Pakistani officials were invited to present their viewpoints. There was no Canadian government representative, but Canada discretely tried to bring both parties face-to-face in the hope that a conference of this magnitude would give Pakistan a chance to present her case since most of those involved in the project favored an independent Bangladesh.

When Ottawa officials failed to persuade the Pakistani high commissioner to participate in the conference, they suggested Small (Canada's high commissioner to Pakistan) inquire whether the government of Pakistan would be interested in such a conference to present Pakistan's perspectives. Small immediately delved into the matter and wrote to Ottawa with his findings, "Political circles here say that it is unthinkable that any patriotic Paki will agree to sit with rebels and secessionists or to allow discussions of internal affairs of Pak at a foreign forum dominated by well-known anti-Pak elements." [137] Naturally, there was no participant from Pakistan, except for Mr. J. Z. Jafrey, a Canadian of Pakistani origin and president of the Toronto-based Pakistan-Canada Association, who attended it.

The Toronto Declaration of Concern urged the governments to (1) terminate all military deliveries, (2) suspend all economic aid to Pakistan, (3) channel all possible resources into a massive emergency program for famine relief in East Pakistan, direct and administer by the United Nations, (4) make firm continuing commitments to share pretty the economic burden of supporting the refugees in India, (5) intervene to save the life of Sheikh Mujibur Rahman.[138] All participants agreed that Bongobondhu, the elected Bengali leader of East Pakistan, was crucially important because he alone had the authority required to persuade local officials of the province to cooperate with the central government. "If Mujib [Bongobondhu] were executed, all hope of a political solution would be lost, and guerrilla warfare would continue indefinitely with the possibility of war between Pakistan and India."[139] Thus, observed Mustafizur Rahman Siddiqi, Head of Bangladesh Mission in Washington, having challenged Yahya's allegation that Bongobondhu was guilty of a planned revolt. He declared that his government's struggle "was fought with ballots, not bullets."[140]

Ottawa purposefully stayed away from the conference, maintaining a visible distance. However, the NDP MP, Andrew Brewin, attended it as a private citizen and recounted his meeting with Yahya a month ago in Pakistan during his visit to Pakistan as a Canadian delegate. Expressing his moral condemnation for the brutal actions of the regime, he observed, "A political solution must be found to replace the military authority in Pakistan."[141] Having maintained that, since no compromise seemed "insight," Brewin said that one might have "to deal with the military."[142] The thrust of the conference was to ask all concerned to prevail upon their governments with utmost urgency to push for both "humanitarian" and "political" actions while there was still time.[143] It was resolved that this could "be achieved only in the context of a political settlement."[144]

In terms of impact, the Toronto Declaration of Concern caused waves in the minds of the citizens of various world countries. In the US Senate, for example, Senator Frank Church mentioned the resolutions that transpired out of the Toronto Declaration and obtained unanimous permission to print the entire declaration of the South Asia Conference in the Congressional Record of the Ninety-Second Congress.[145] Many major national and international newspapers carried the conference news, highlighting the apparent contradictions between the Yahya government's statements and actions.[146] It is important to note that the Canadian government has already taken positive action in all areas mentioned in the declaration, except for the cutting off economic aid to Pakistan. Time and again, Sharp mentioned in the House that he did not believe that the suspension of financial assistance to Pakistan could achieve any positive results but rather would increase the suffering and deprivation of the Pakistani people. Sharp's views resonated with the views of most Canadians. We noted this in Chapter 4.

South Asia Crisis Committee

Out of the Toronto Declaration of Concern/The South Asia Conference grew the South Asia Crisis Committee, which was mandated to implement the ideas that transpired from the three-day conference. This was a time when many concerned Canadians and people around the world felt frustrated seeing the UN's inability to deal with the situation in Pakistan effectively. Taking the pulse of the public perspectives, CBC's Stanley Burke noted that "in a world in which cultural strife has become the major cause of killing," it was evident "that some new means must be evolved to cope with the situation."[147]

Burke drafted a proposal to create a high-level nongovernmental group to investigate, hear evidence, and make recommendations. Referring to it as the Proposal for Pakistan Tribunal, Burke summed up the general concern in the form of the following two fundamental questions: (1) Do governments have the right to kill people claimed as their own citizens to maintain a particular political form? (2) [What are the] means to end the conflict?[148] Burke envisaged the proposed tribunal composed of men and women of the highest international reputation and unquestioned integrity. Still, his idea must have fizzled out as nothing more is available on this proposal in the Library and Archives Canada.

Brother Raymond Cournoyer's Work in India and Visits to Ottawa, Toronto, Montreal, and Europe

In India, "Brother Cournoyer recruited eighty Indian and Bengali doctors, nurses, and medical volunteers to head up medical teams to serve the needs of five hundred thousand people in Barasat, Agartala, Cooch Bihar, Balurghat and Tripura. The costs of the six-hundred-thousand-dollar program are being shared equally by Oxfam of Canada and Oxfam UK with the help of a $150,000 grant for the Canadian International Development Agency."[149] Thus, Oxfam Canada's Ottawa office was informed. Again, in addition to his day-to-day work in India, Brother Cournoyer drafted (1) briefing materials for Senator Kennedy, then chairman of the US Senate Subcommittee on Refugees, and (2) assisted his right-hand man, Alan Leather, in preparing his testimony before the Senate Subcommittee during the second week of August 1971. Cournoyer's team faced the challenges boldly—on the one hand, he could not be overtly political, while on the other hand, he wanted to point out the political reasons why the tragedy was taking place in the first place. In his testimony before the Senate Subcommittee, Leather characterized the situation as "a human catastrophe of unprecedented magnitude"[150] and re-iterated the dire need for massive assistance for the many starving and diseased Bengali refugees.

During each visit to Canada, Brother Cournoyer gave media interviews and held conferences. He appeared on phone forum shows in Montreal and Toronto as one of Canada's favorite men of self-confidence. He seemed like a walking encyclopedia commanding vast areas of knowledge on what was happening and what the people of Canada could do to alleviate the desperate situation. The news media found Brother Cournoyer's use of a chart of the weekly influx of refugees and corresponding food rations in the refugee camps handy. In his press conference of June 7, 1971, in Montreal, in an emotional appeal, Brother Cournoyer described how the Bengalis formed a human chain along the Indian border to escape death, destruction, looting, and incendiaries of the Pakistani army. Canadians were touched by his appeals, which reflected his passionate indignation about crimes against humanity. Much to the credit of Oxfam Canada's public relations officer, Betty Scott, who liaised closely with Canadian journalists nationwide.

Brother Cournoyer's meetings and interviews were immediately picked up by most major newspapers that used to run stories on Cournoyer's appeals that were simple and clear—that the needs of the refugees were "desperate" and that by "sparing a dollar," Canadians could "save a life." One of his persistent appeals, "For God's sake, send help now," for the victims of the "greatest tragedy of the century,"[151] was a frequent reference in Canadian newspapers. Frankly, although he was expected to be "apolitical," Brother Cournoyer did not hide his feelings of disgust and indignation while referring to the military as a "repressive" regime. A distressed Cournoyer urged fellow Canadians to be benevolent and bounteous in donating. The public responded generously to such emotionally charged appeals.

With time, Cournoyer's role began to expand to Europe. In June, while returning to India from Canada, he stopped in Rome to meet with two distinguished people to carry on his mission. Cardinal Roy, archbishop of Québec and chairman of the Justice and Peace Commission of the Vatican, arranged a private meeting of Brother Cournoyer with Pope Paul V1 in Rome. This was an extraordinary meeting as the occasion allowed him to apprise Pope Paul of the pathetically deteriorating conditions he had witnessed. He also discussed the possibilities of finding a way to use the Pope's appeal to draw public opinion against the ceaseless atrocities of the Pakistani army.[152] Brother Cournoyer then proceeded to Geneva, where he also met with Dr. Eugene Carson Blake, secretary-general of the World Council of Churches, with whom he discussed international cooperation in providing relief assistance to the Bengali victims of military reprisals. Soon, Brother Cournoyer's work and personality earned him heroic status in India. The news media and the Canadian public regarded Brother Cournoyer as a quintessential Canadian—knowledgeable, open, warm, and down to earth with pertinent information about the subcontinent and its people. Canadians came to see Cournoyer as an apotheosis - an articulate advocate of the Bengali refugees.[153]

Campaign for the Release of Bongobondhu (Mujib)

By far, this sensitive topic offered the most significant challenge to Oxfam Canada personnel, who knew from the get-go that the release of Bongobondhu was critical to any negotiation for a political resolution of the Pakistan-Bangladesh conflict. Although the Toronto Declaration demanded an immediate release of Bongobondhu to start any form of negotiation for a political resolution, Oxfam personnel were mindful of its mandate's limited and nonpolitical nature. Oxfam Canada also recognized that its involvement in any such matter could be seen as political interference by an NGO. Unsurprisingly, it remained involved in many behind-the-scenes activities, lobbying national and international organizations for Bongobondhu's release without being overtly public in their demand.

Oxfam Canada wrote two critical letters to the International Congress of Jurists and Amnesty International that may be regarded as Oxfam Canada's direct effort to go beyond its mandate in lobbying for the release of Bongobondhu. Arguing that Bongobondhu was innocent, Oxfam Canada made a direct and straightforward appeal to the International Congress of Jurists: "As an international organization dedicated to the relief of suffering in the case of a disaster, such as that in existence in East Pakistan, [we] are extremely concerned that Sheik[h] will be put on trial any day now, probably 'in-camera,' and we are turning to you as the one international legal body, which we feel can make its voice heard with the Pakistan authorities, on behalf of Sheik[h] Mujib."[154] Again, expressing its concern for a long-term solution to the problem and recognizing the part played by Amnesty International in putting pressure on the appropriate people and the government concerned, Oxfam Canada asked, "What steps, if any," had Amnesty International "made" or been "making toward securing the release of Sheik[h] Mujibur Rahman from jail in West Pakistan?"[155]

Fundraising Activities

The Sari Appeal

The Sari Appeal was launched in October 1971 under the distinguished patronage of Her Excellency Mrs. Ronald Michener, wife of the governor-general of Canada and the honorary patron for the appeal. It was common knowledge that many women had crossed the border with only a single sari she had worn. The same sari had to be worn even when wet after washing it, as there was no other cloth. Continued use of the same sari was reduced to rags after some time. Naturally, Her Excellency was "concerned and sad about all the misery and suffering of the millions of East Pakistani refugees in India."[156] Having visited the refugee camps several times, Oxfam's field team members recommended sari for the refugees to be of foremost importance, mainly when monsoon season was ending and the cold weather was about to begin. "They have nothing to put on when the monsoon rains soak them, so they are perpetually wet, always cold. Saris are needed for the women, pants for the men, and T-shirts and shorts for the children."[157] Thus was the appeal by Oxfam for proper clothing.

A press release titled "An Open Letter to the Women of Canada" was distributed in the far-flung parts of the country with the following explicit appeal: "One additional sari would allow a woman to change and bathe, a basic need in their desperate condition."[158] The appeal was for a dollar per sari - a nominal amount of money, but with an important implication for a mere dollar. By the time the Canadian public read the open letter, they were already familiar with the nature of the problems and the dire needs of the refugees through the general media coverage and various press releases that were being distributed to the public occasionally. Unfortunately, there is no record in the Library and Archives Canada regarding the money raised through the Sari Appeal.

The Tag Days

The Tag Days initiative was Oxfam's other cooperative venture with members of local groups and associations regarding fundraising. They gathered around shopping malls in the Metro Toronto Area to help shop owners tag their merchandise. The Tag Days' activities continued for five consecutive days with the help of enthusiastic volunteers of different age groups. Seeing their work, many more expressed interest in continuing such activities in close cooperation with the India-Canada Association and Bangla Desh Society. Archival records, however, indicate that the consecutive five-day Tag Days event at shopping malls only occurred in the Metropolitan Toronto Area and raised funds that went directly to Oxfam Canada's pool.

Although there is no complete account of the money raised in Ontario, there is some information regarding the Calgary CAPR Committee that raised $500 during the Tag Days event.[159] The money was to be spent according to Oxfam Canada's established priorities in India.

Blanket Blitz/Blanket Appeal

The Blanket Blitz, also referred to as the Blanket Appeal was an initiative of John Shea, Oxfam Canada's Executive Director, who came up with this idea following his visit to the refugee camps in India. One of Oxfam Canada's joint ventures brought together a host of partners within Canadian churches and relief agencies to work closely with the Canadian Red Cross Society to ensure that there would not be any duplication of efforts. Its initial commitment was to collect one million blankets from Canadians nationwide. Its appeal appeared regularly in Oxfam Canada's newsletters and press releases, the excerpts of which were also published in the general print media.

Again, many celebrity personalities spoke from their hearts during their speaking engagements, having ad-libbed their way through various talk shows. Their direct appeal to Canadians was to start a blanket drive in their neighborhood first. Being under-resourced and having faced a situation that had begun to deteriorate rapidly in the field, predicting the possibility of an all-out war, Major General Arthur E. Wrinch proposed to defer the formal mounting of the proposed Blanket Blitz until at least mid-February 1972 even though CIDA had already committed to giving $650.000 in support of the blanket blitz. The program, however, was not wholly abandoned.

Again, an exceptional nine-act benefit performance to aid the Oxfam Pakistan Relief Fund was held in Vancouver at the Queen Elizabeth Theatre through the office of the Mayor of Vancouver on December 13. The variety Show featured such bands as The Brotherhood, Pacific Salt, and Night Train Revue. Oxfam was presented with a five-hundred-dollar cheque from the West Vancouver Lions Club.[160]

The blankets collected by the CCODP and its member churches were shipped to India for delivery by December 1971. In the meantime, a working group representing the Canadian Red Cross Society, Canadian Council of Churches, Oxfam Canada, UNICEF Canada, and World Vision Canada was formed under the chairmanship of Larry Tubman of Oxfam Canada to determine the terms of reference for a comprehensive Blanket Blitz campaign for the next year, 1972. Unfortunately, there is no record to indicate what happened from this time on while blankets were being collected or exactly how or when the blankets, already collected, were shipped to India following the liberation of Bangladesh.

Radio Program

There are references to frequent radio announcements and radio spots - ten, twenty, thirty, and sixty seconds - announced by numerous CBC stations nationwide. Toronto's radio station, 1050 Chum's *All the News* program, under the title "And Here's How Things Look to Dick Smyth This Morning," carried frequent announcements daily morning. Again, also worth mentioning is Nancy Edwards of Berkeley Studio, who frequently appealed to Canadian listeners in various ways to move them to do their bit for the tragic victims of military reprisals. The *Nancy Edwards Show* also taped interviews with Alan Brash and Major General Arthur Wrinch, used on about sixty-two private stations during July.[161]

Below are some examples of short and frequent on-the-air radio announcements of appeals directed at the public for donations and the government for immigration.

- "How would you feel if a child of yours had to sleep in six inches of water? If you had to give him contaminated water to drink, to wash in? This is the plight of Pakistani parents in the refugee camps in India. Help now. Give to the Combined Appeal for Pakistani Relief, Box 1000, Station F, Toronto."
- Canadians apathetic? Not on your life.
- "Turn off your furnace and go to bed tonight without a blanket! Then you'll know how it feels to lie down to sleep in a refugee camp in India! The Pakistani Refugees in India are enduring freezing temperatures *without blankets*. Please help. Today, drop off a blanket—clean and in good condition—at the church nearest you."
- "Canada needs a population. The Pakistani refugees need a home."
- "We should settle not a token hundred but a significant one million Bengalis in a new city on the prairies. That number is big enough that it would create employment rather than add to unemployment."
- If we do, someday the prairies may blossom with Bengali industry as they do today with the work of those who once were foreigners themselves."
- "A gentleman who informs us that he is the 'oldest Miles for Millions Walker' came with a donation, and the list goes on and on and on—a list

- that symbolizes the kindness, generosity, and concern of the Canadian people."
- "The Christmas lights are winking on in homes bulging with rich food and expensive gifts."
- "Oxfam's magnificent efforts are like rag absorbing an ocean—an ocean of terror and cataclysm."[162]
- Canada should give them [Bengali refugees] that home." "If we do, someday the prairies may blossom with Bengali industry as they do today to with the work of those who once were foreigners themselves [referring to the earlier immigrants]."[163]

The key message of the radio program for the fundraising drive was that more funds were urgently needed to provide food, clothing, temporary shelter, and medicine to help alleviate the suffering of the refugees. By September 3, 1971, the CAPR volunteers raised $1,115,860 through its appeal to the broadcast media.[164]

Cultural Show

The Toronto-based Bangla Desh Association of Canada and the India-Canada Association joined forces in raising funds for Oxfam Canada through cultural programs. This was possible mainly, as mentioned in Chapter 4, due to the work of Rabi Alam, one of the key players in the Bengali community who was instrumental in signing an MOU with the India-Canada Association for a showing of movies in Toronto. For example, at the Odeon Theatre at Pape and Danforth in August 1971, the NDP MP Andrew Brewin, who had just returned from the subcontinent in July, was a guest speaker in one of the fundraising events. This was an opportunity for many Canadians to hear from Brewin directly about the situation in India and Pakistan, where he went as a Canadian delegate. This is a unique example of a cultural function with a small component that enabled the guest speaker to talk briefly about an issue of international magnitude. At the same time, the organizers had an opportunity to raise funds from the audience while the public was being updated on the situation in the field.

Among the volunteers who sold the tickets for a show at $2.50 were personnel of the Rochdale Records, the Royal Bengal Restaurant, and the International Students Centre of the University of Toronto. The success of the cultural show was evident. Within three weeks following the first set of benefit presentations, the India-Canada Association organized another series of presentations of the celebrated Indian playback singer Suman Kalyanpur and her entourage in September 1971 at Toronto's Eaton Auditorium, all proceeds of which were also sent to Oxfam Canada's pool.[165] Another additional attraction of Oxfam Canada's fundraising event, as already indicated in chapter 4, was the participation of renowned Canadian singer of the day, Corry Bryant, whose performance at the Bandshell Park, Waterloo, touched all those who attended the program having reminded them of the stark tragedies of the Bengalis.

United Nations High Commissioner for Refugees (UNHCR)

UNHCR, a part of the UN system, had already been in the field as the focal point upon the request of the government of India and the secretary-general of the UN before joining the CAPR initiative. In that sense, UNHCR was in an advantageous position to keep the East Pakistan crisis at the forefront. UNHCR also chaired the standing inter-agency consultation unit responsible for planning activities at the UN headquarters in Geneva. Canada was fortunate in that J. Lanctôt, a Canadian representative in UNHCR, had already been engaged in the field from early on. Naturally, he raised his concerns regarding the crisis, which, according to him, was of international magnitude.

Lanctôt re-assessed the situation vis-à-vis UNCHR's expected role in the network and the extent to which any new initiative would affect UNHCR's strategic plans. Lanctôt frequently visited Montreal, Ottawa, and Toronto, where he held press conferences and updated Canadians on the field situation. Excerpts of his media interviews and follow-up press releases were widely disseminated throughout Canada. Lanctôt's impassioned pleas to the Canadians were both direct and pronounced. Only through the cooperation of those involved can UNHCR "best perform its role of international coordinator and, in turn, by supporting the Combined Appeal for Pakistani Relief."[166] Thus, a fervid Lanctôt appealed to the fellow Canadian public to see how "best [to] help UNHCR perform its role as coordinator of relief activities among the Pakistani refugees."[167]

World Vision of Canada (WVC)

World Vision Canada (WVC) has served the Indian subcontinent in childcare, relief, and evangelism since 1951. Following the military crackdown of March 1971 and the flight of thousands of people from their homes into the already crowded areas of India, the situation rapidly deteriorated, and WVC immediately turned to other organizations in the Toronto area. Working closely with members of the United Church of Canada and its member churches, WVC joined the CAPR initiative within days.

Activities in India

From its own experience in the West Bengal area, known as the poverty-stricken part of Bengal, WVC personnel in the field recognized at the outset the seriousness of the problems of poverty, disease, malnutrition, early death, and the gigantic task of house, shelter and feed the vast number of refugees. Dr. Helen Huston of the Anglican Church of Canada and Bob Brow and Trula Cronk, the missionary wife, both United Church of Canada, went to India as World Vision International's representatives to set up projects and work with the refugees. They, along with the local WVC staff, partnered with other local organizations, such as Evangelical Fellowship of India, Northern Evangelical Lutheran, Indian Inter-varsity Christian Fellowship, and the Indian Government Relief Agency, as well as the Baptist, Lutheran, and Free Church missionaries from Norway, Denmark, Holland, Great Britain, and the USA. Having developed a new modus operandi, WVC worked horizontally with its partners on the following ten projects, for which there is very little documentation other than what is outlined below.

- The Edith Mulvaney Home of Kolkata (West Bengal), WVC's first project, aimed to alleviate the refugee childcare problem. The project accommodated many children with nowhere to go by taking in sponsored children.
- The Rajadighi Christian Hospital of Malda, WVC's second project, received financial assistance from the World Vision of Australia. The hospital was well-known for its specialized saline solution under the care of foreign-trained doctors.
- The Cooch Behar Refugee Service, WVC's third project, looked after ten refugee camps that had approximately two hundred thousand refugees who were provided tarpaulins and saline solutions under the directorship of Dr. Olab Hodne, a Norwegian missionary. Since there was no shortage of volunteers to assist in relief work, fortunately, WVC found this to be a big morale booster to take the hapless refugees under its care.

- The Kishanganj Refugee Relief Committee, WVC's fourth project, was established by Robert Brow of the United Church of Canada in conjunction with members of the Free Will Baptists and the local director of operation mobilization. Following her visits to the refugee camps in India during the beginning of a cholera epidemic in the summer of 1971, Dr. Helen Huston of Red Deer, Alberta, quickly set up an emergency hospital for cholera patients. Though no one died of starvation, Dr. Huston was distressed to see how the refugees were facing epidemics of cholera, smallpox, malaria, and dysentery, spread by the breakdown of sanitation. She was, however, glad to receive different types of transport equipment and medical supplies required for the project's completion—all through Brow's special initiatives. Being impressed with Dr. Huston's relentless work, many began to refer to the hospital as "Dr. Helen's hospital." Having found the work of the volunteers commendable, Brow considered it the most impressive life-saving operation of all time and joyously called the volunteers the "stars on earth."[168]
- Project in Sesengpara, WVC's fifth project in the State of Meghalaya, assisted approximately forty-three thousand Christian refugees in cooperation with the Evangelical Fellowship of India. The WVC underwrote the salary of a team of medical experts and part of transportation (a jeep pick-up) since several volunteers assisted in distributing blankets and clothing to the refugees. When the project still required additional resources as the refugee situation became disturbingly agonizing, almost beyond description, Brow successfully persuaded WVC to commit $10,000 more in addition to the $10,000 it had already spent.
- The Padhar Hospital in the Betul district of central India, USC's sixth project, assisted the refugees under Dr. Clement Moss's leadership. For this project, WVC had a budget of $3,000 for incoming refugees, for whom it developed a program of adjustment after long periods of malnutrition.
- Student Refugee Relief Committee, WVC's seventh project, was designed to be an outreach program mainly consisting of student workers from the Kolkata area, West Bengal. With a budget of $3,000 and under the leadership of Professor Rodrigues from a college near Kolkata, the project got off the ground amid the enthusiasm and support of the community. The WVC was determined to meet its key targets, which included recruiting Bengali volunteers from the various refugee camps so that they could assist in the relief operation. It successfully met its target with the help of many volunteers and young, able-bodied Bengali refugees who undertook increased

- responsibilities with full knowledge that they had a tremendous job ahead of them.
- Bangla Desh Christian Relief Committee, WVC's eighth project, grew out of a need to assist in setting up Christian refugees who were rendered homeless. The project had a budget of $2,000, which was spent on developing an outreach program.
- The WVC's ninth project, Model School at Sapgachi, Kolkata, West Bengal, initially designed by Zenon Zielinski, a Canadian architect, could not get off the ground due to the shortage of funds. With a budget of $3,000, it sought the cooperation of the Bengal Service Committee, which started the work earlier to look after the street children of Kolkata long before the influx of refugees. As the refugees began to stream in, the project, though not wholly funded, did what it could to provide relief services to the area refugees.
- Assam Refugee Relief was WVC's tenth project with years of experience dealing with emergencies. The idea was to assist the people of the Christian faith in gathering "together in several camps for worship and witness services" with a reminder to the refugees of the "World Vision's willingness to help in the name of Christ."[169] While there are no records regarding the project's budget or the number of refugees it served, the project is known to have reached people even in remote, inaccessible areas.

Activities in Canada

To keep the Canadian public *au courant* with the latest happenings in the subcontinent, WVC regularly exchanged information between Ottawa officials and those in the field to enable each party to be privy to important sensitive information. Brief snapshots of the frequent on-site visits of WVC's representatives were also a source of information on the consequences of the ongoing military reprisals. Upon returning to Canada, Dr. Huston and Bob Brow described what they witnessed in India in expressive detail. In narrating the extraordinary episodes that threatened the prevailing miserable conditions of the refugees in makeshift arrangements, WVC referred to the exodus as "the greatest human flood in all of history."[170] They portrayed the wretched conditions of the refugees—what it was like to be a refugee.

All CAPR members worked collaboratively not to duplicate their efforts and continue to be involved in every activity collectively and individually. Its most remarkable work was an on-air appeal to the public blitzes conducted throughout the summer of 1971. It turned out to be the most successful CAPR initiative in which all members were involved in one way or another. It was a matter of "seeing is believing." Father Guy Poisson of the Canadian Catholic Conference (CCC) and CCODP's André Tremblay and Tom Johnston, who organized a simultaneous conference in Toronto and Montreal, became household names to the public. Among some well-known Canadians whose appearances on radio and television made a difference were Archbishop J. A. Plourde of CCC, J. B. Lanctôt of the UNHCR, T. Kines (CARE Canada), Reverend Desmond McCalmont and Peter Flemington of Religious Television Associates, and Jack Dunlop (Canadian Broadcasting Corporation).

Another critical point to acknowledge is that, for all CAPR members, the government of Canada was their greatest supporter whose "readiness to cooperate"[171] had been evident from the beginning of the campaign. Whether it was Prime Minister Trudeau or the opposition leader, Robert Stanfield, all were genuinely interested in assisting the victims of atrocity and finding a political settlement of the conflict. "As I share the deeply held concern of the Combined Appeal for Pakistani Relief that all Canadians must do what they can to contribute to support disaster relief operations, I sincerely urge all Canadians to give any assistance they can to the Combined Appeal to provide funds for food, temporary shelter, and many other actions necessary to alleviate the severe suffering,"[172] Stanfield appealed.

Although the campaign's official closing date was August 31, 1971, it continued for some time beyond that date.

Below is a snapshot of the outcome of the seven-month CAPR and other non-CAPR initiatives by various voluntary agencies in Canada.

Combined Appeal for Pakistani Relief as of November 23, 1971	
Canadian Catholic Organization for Development & Peace (CCODP)	$ 257, 101.51
CCC	N/A
Canadian Red Cross Society	$ 41,770.25
Canadian UNICEF Committee	$ 42, 056.00
CARE of Canada	$75, 890.46
Canadian Save the Children Fund	$11, 295.72
OXFAM of Canada	$553, 049.67
UNHCR	$680.00
World Vision	$84, 475.00
Canadian Council of Churches	
Council	$7, 030 93
Anglican	$55, 000.00
Baptist	$19 ,000.00
Lutheran	$25, 000.00
Presbyterian	$33, 494.18
Salvation Army	$5, 341.40
United Church of Canada	$229, 175.65
Donation to CAPR Central Fund	$410, 072.04
CAPR Grand Total	**$1, 832, 628.34**

Other Voluntary Agencies Not Part of CAPR	
Mennonite Central Committee (MCC)	$120, 000.00
Unitarian Service Committee (USC)	$117, 418.00
Total Canadian Voluntary Agencies	**$1, 606, 438.12**

(The above figures do not include federal government donations to CAPR, its members, or other voluntary agencies)

Donations collected by Organizations and Associations in cooperation with the office of the Indian High Commission in Canada (Ottawa)
India Students' Association, Dept. of Chemical Engineering, University of Ottawa
India-Canada Association, Ottawa
Students and Friends of India Association, University of Toronto, Toronto
Cultural Association of India, Montreal
India-Canada Society of Calgary, Calgary
India Students' Association, University of Alberta
India Association of Winnipeg, International Centre, Winnipeg
East Bengal Refugee Aid Committee, Sudbury
India Students' Association, University of Manitoba, Winnipeg

Source: *The Indiagram*, Information Service of India, Office of the High Commissioner for India, Ottawa. No. 26/71, June 29, 1971.

Non-CAPR Organizations, Including Canadian Business Companies

McCain Foods Limited, Day and Ross, Mead Johnson, Thomas J. Lipton, Maislin Transport, and Continental Can Company of Canada

Canadian business organizations and companies also became involved in raising awareness by contributing either cash or in-kind, having supplied goods for the victims of military reprisals. Of the two New Brunswick companies, McCain Foods Limited of Florenceville and the Day and Ross of Hartland, the first is Canada's largest processor of potato products, and the second is the largest road transportation company in the Maritimes. The McCain Foods Limited donated one hundred thousand pounds of potato flakes and underwrote part of the sea shipping costs. At the same time, the Day and Ross of Hartland carried the shipment free of charge from Florenceville to Montreal, the ship's loading port. "The shipment, valued at $27,000, was equivalent to eight hundred thousand pounds of fresh potatoes and will provide three million meals for the refugees."[173] There was also a gift of $103,000 from reinforced plastic sheeting made in

Toronto by Canadian Tarpoly Company Ltd. and Bardel Universal Corp. Ltd.[174] for monsoon rains.

Again, the archival records indicate that the largest donor of goods by the late summer of 1971 was Mead Johnson and Company of Belleville, Ontario, which had already contributed about $15,000 in baby foods and nutritional supplements.[175] Another source indicates that other Canadian companies like Thomas J. Lipton, Maislin Transport, and Continental Can Company of Canada, though "half a world away, these soundly established firms are engaged in a precarious, incredibly high-risk venture—saving the lives of East Pakistan refugees."[176] It then pointed out, "The need is vast. The misery, hunger, and fear are incomprehensively deep and dehumanizing. Mercifully, the change is being met. Many Canadian companies, working quietly and eluding publicity, have done much to alleviate the situation, pouring thousands into a project whose returns are tallied in millions—not of dollars but of human lives."[177]

Canadian Friends Service Committee (CFSC)

A committee of the Religious Society of Friends (Quakers) in Canada, CFSC members had been to the refugee camps in India. They reported back on the unfortunate situations of the refugees from time to time. Toward the end of 1971, CFSC raised $4,100 and worked with Quakers. John and Erica Linton, on behalf of the CFSC, took a lead role and cooperated with Quakers intending to help refugees help themselves. It worked in the provision of blankets for children enrolled in schools, the organization of homeopathic clinics, services to girls pregnant through rape, and the organization of a Quaker sewing center.[178] As soon as Bangladesh was born, CFSC also lobbied the government to recognize Bangladesh as quickly as possible.

Mennonite Central Committee (MCC)

The establishment of the Mennonite Central Committee (MCC), an agency of Mennonite and Brethren in Christ churches in the USA and Canada, dates to 1920. By the late 1960s, the total number of MCC workers in the five Asian countries—India, Ceylon (now Sri Lanka), Nepal, Pakistan, and Afghanistan—with a population of approximately seven hundred million increased from eighteen to twenty under the directorship of Vernon Reimer. A native of Niverville, Manitoba, Reimer was the first Canadian MCC Director for Asia stationed in Kolkata, West Bengal, India, in 1962. Following the natural calamities in the coastal areas since 1963, Reimer became involved in relief work in East Pakistan. From the beginning, MCC personnel had been on loan to the East Pakistan Christian Council (EPCC) to assist in emergencies such as floods, droughts, etc. The MCC did not join the CAPR initiative as it had already been involved in the field long before the CAPR fundraising initiative got off the ground.

Activities in India

Reimer met with local representatives of the Indian Red Cross, Sisters of Charity, Catholic Relief Service, Caritas-India, and many foreign voluntary agencies, such as Oxfam Canada, Oxfam UK, CARE, Save the Children Fund, UNICEF, the Salvation Army, and United Relief Service. He also met with the representatives of the central government, the Refugee and Rehabilitation minister of the government of West Bengal, and the representatives of the Evangelical Fellowship of India (EFI), Southern Baptist, and Christian Agency for Social Action (CASA), the relief arm of National Christian Council (NCC). To determine MCC's service needs and the levels of synergy for cooperation, Reimer negotiated with Southern Baptist Mission in Richmond, Virginia (USA) regarding the services of Paul Kniss, a Canadian missionary with the Mennonite Board of Missions and Charities, to work on the refugee relief project under Reimer's overall supervision. Kniss alternated his work schedule between Ranchi and Kolkata.

With a budget of $350,000 for emergency measures, Reimer decided not to set up another relief project but to play a supportive role that was more realistic given the financial resources at his disposal. "The problem is so staggering that whatever we do will only be a small drop in the bucket. I continue to keep in touch with other agencies to provide whatever assistance we can,"[179] Reimer wrote to the MCC Pennsylvania, USA. Operationally, playing a supportive role meant assumption of a few responsibilities in the following three separate areas: (1) projects that would result in the self-reliance of the refugees so that they, in turn, could help themselves; (2) recruitment of volunteers for MCC through its outreach programs; (3) collection of donations and contributions from individuals and organizations by raising awareness of the tragedy.

The MCC also oversaw two projects in addition to developing small projects as add-ons to the existing projects under CASA in West Bengal and Assam. The first project was distributing clothes, blankets, and essential food items, such as dry food, through local agencies. The food distribution project also had a component of the Milk Distribution Network at the Sahara camp near Dum Dum Airport, Kolkata, that operated successfully. Interestingly, the milk served to the refugees was produced in Canada. The milk-feeding program included children, as is usually thought of, and a sizeable number of nursing and expectant mothers. The second project was in Assam, where MCC undertook emergency services throughout the contiguous border areas. Reimer also received cooperation from George Hoffman of the Evangelical Association for Relief (UK) and Bob Brow of World Vision Canada. In continuing his network with other service agencies, Reimer networked with the Christian Youth Council (Baptist) in the Dinajpur district of East Pakistan, a location closer to the needs of those who could not escape the army atrocities.

Reimer also implemented a self-help project for refugees who weaved mats for shelter material and floor covering. An essential aspect of this project was that it was designed in a way to order, purchase, receive, and distribute relief goods, such as rice, molasses, and blankets, locally, which helped not just the refugees in the camps or patients in the field hospital but also those around the area to boost the local businesses. This proactive project helped the refugees in the camps to weave and sell mats for the newly arrived refugees, for whom the immediate priority was providing shelter, food, and medicine. An important dimension of the self-help project was that a percentage of the earnings was set aside to be used later for educational purposes.[180] At a time when MCC personnel were under strict directives to concentrate only on the immediate needs of the refugees, a project that included some aspects of future activities toward making the refugees self-dependent is commendable, no doubt.

In addition to all of the above activities in India, Reimer's other task was to facilitate the visits of Canadians, whether it was the visit of representatives of CIDA and external affairs or other government officials and representatives of NGOs. His job with the Canadian visitors was one of "show" and "tell" so they could have a clear sense of urgency and priority for action. Immediately upon their return to Canada, the said visitors, too, would, in turn, do the same "show" and "tell" through a detailed display of photographs and various documentary evidence gathered from the field.

Activities in East Pakistan (Dhaka)

Activities of the MCC personnel in Dhaka were limited as its work had to be endorsed by the Pakistani military authority. Earlier, the Indian government rejected Reimer's request for a quick visit to Dhaka. Determined to open a three-tier communication network through the headquarters with MCC, Reimer brought Maynard Shelly and his wife, Griselda Shelly, both of Newton, Kansas, USA, to Dhaka. By the time the Shellys arrived in Dhaka, the relationship between India and Pakistan had already turned hostile and combative, each ready to attack the other. Immediately following their arrival in Dhaka, the Shellys kept their superiors posted by writing to them every few days. The Shellys promptly informed their superiors in the following manner: "The situation is tense here. Yesterday, we saw the smoke of a bomb that was set off within a half mile of our hotel balcony window, and we felt the concussion. We have noticed increased military presence in the two weeks we are here. We had a practice blackout last week, and today, instructions were issued for trenches to be dug at public buildings and private homes."[181]

The Shellys did not get discouraged. Despite the rapidly worsening situation, the couple immediately connected with a few key EPCC personnel who welcomed them with open arms. The Shellys reached out to four important players—Jim McKinley of Southern Baptist, Dr. Muherman Harun, an Indonesian who had been on loan from East Asia Christian Conference to EPCC, Henry Selz of CARE, and Father Benjamin Labbé, a member of Canadian Holy Cross Order. They had the following three primary tasks in Dhaka: (1) to meet and liaise with the NGO community to determine priorities, (2) to verify the food situation, and (3) to streamline the overall services among various partners to continue its supportive role. The couple received the cooperation of Samson Chowdhury of EPCC, a renowned businessman and philanthropist who made himself available during their stay in Dhaka. The couple was very appreciative of Chowdhury's hospitality.

It did not take long for the couple to identify the root cause of the conflict, "The civil war that threatens to split the Pakistan union is, of course, not a religious war, but just another chapter in the age-old oppression of the poor and powerless,"[182] wrote Maynard Shelly. The Shellys became convinced that the Pakistani military regime and the Bengali rebels were determined to stick to their gun. The army was resolved to "eliminate the secessionists," while the rebel forces were just as committed to freeing their homeland. "Everybody seems to be engaged in a holding operation with the anticipation that opportunity to serve and needs to be met will soon multiply. How can we establish our own holding operation without anything to hold? It seems to be the riddle for MCC just now."[183] asked the Shellys.

Within days, however, the situation deteriorated so rapidly that, by the first week of December, all voluntary agencies were warned to stay away from the border areas due to threats and counter threats from Pakistan and India for an all-out war. Everything came to a standstill with the service agencies' temporary withdrawal from the field at the advice of the Indian government, which could not guarantee their safety and security. The Shellys quickly returned to the United States.

Activities in Canada

As mentioned, by the time the CAPR initiative was launched in June 1971, MCC Canada was strategically well-placed in the field, having already raised $65,000 from its five-hundred-member churches across Canada. MCC's activities during the Bengali's struggle for independence mainly centered on the following three areas of work: (1) raising awareness of the urgent needs of the refugees in Indian camps and of those who had remained in East Pakistan through sensitization of the military reprisals; (2) launching of a vigorous appeal for funds to allow MCC personnel to continue all current projects in India against an unpredictable future; and (3) lobbying government officials simultaneously for a direct intervention through the mechanism of the Commonwealth or an indirect intervention through a financial consortium for sanctions against the government of Pakistan.

Sensitization

Reimer developed a two-pronged communication strategy to share with Mennonite and Brethren in Christ congregation in Canada—(1) publication and dissemination of news items of interest and (2) appearance on the news media, radio, and television. John Wieler, associate executive secretary of MCC, frequently appeared on local radio talk shows and TV to respond to the questions of listeners and viewers on the latest happenings in the field. This was a valuable vehicle to sensitize the public. While in India, from June 24 to July 17, 1971, Wieler and Reimer held several meetings with representatives of foreign and local agencies, such as the British Consortium, consisting of Christian Aid, UNHCR, Oxfam, CARE, and War on Want. Among the locals were the CASA, Southern Baptist Board, Bengal Christian Council, EPCC, and members of the Canadian High Commission in India. Reimer also held clandestine meetings in East Pakistan with members of EPCC who were desperate to meet with him to describe the potential risks they were taking every day. Following their tour in both countries, Wieler prepared a report based on his "conversation with those individuals" and his "personal impressions and observations right on the field."[184]

Wieler's observations were also published separately to underscore the gravity of the situation. He generated questions among readers regarding the legitimacy of the Yahya government's claim to hold on to East Pakistan when the Bengali rebels, with India's assistance, had already declared independence from their native land. Subtly but surely, Wieler referred to "murder," "rape," and "plundering" of the Bengalis by the military personnel without ever referring to the government's refusal to transfer power to the leader of the elected party who, instead, was locked up in a jail in a remote place in West Pakistan. "Another young fellow tells me how he managed to get away. The village was plundered. The family fled into the jungle. His fifteen-year-old sister was kept back by the soldiers,"[185] wrote Wieler.

Interestingly, nowhere in Wieler's writing was there any reference to eliminating the secessionist movement, as Yahya called it, or the Bengalis' fight for an independent Bangladesh as claimed by the *Mukti Bahini* (Liberation Forces). And yet, Weiler successfully conveyed the reason for the conflict to the Canadian public by deftly describing the events as they were taking place - how the killing, burning, and looting were driving the helplessly frightened Bengalis to head for India for a safe haven. "A younger child sitting nearby stares at us with uncertain eyes. He is a typical picture of the ravages of hunger,"[186] Weiler wrote again in the same article distributed among MCC constituent members nationwide. The uncertain look of a woman with a crying boy under her arm, with the boy's mouth wide open, was agonizing for readers to behold. It highlighted the message that the world had been witnessing—"one of the darkest moments in world history."[187] It is because "everywhere, of course, are the sick people, enduring the suffering and carrying the germs of diarrhea, tuberculosis, pneumonia, and many other diseases."[188] Thus, wrote Wieler.

Again, seeing the continuing influx of the refugees, Wieler cautioned everyone around, "Meanwhile, the refugees are flooding into India, hungry, naked, diseased, and imprisoned in their helpless situation."[189] This alerted the MCC personnel, who cautioned their readers that "by the end of the year, over ten million of its people will have been made refugees by civil strife and natural calamities."[190] Continuing his message, Wieler argued, "We are the rich, at least compared with the people of these refugee camps. We say the Lord has blessed us. What for? Let us not forget what Jesus said to his followers."[191] Being respectful of his organizational mandate, Wieler found a creative way to generate conversation among readers. Reiteration of Wieler's forebodings and premonitions clarified many conflicting reports Canadians were receiving, resulting in confusion and disbelief.

Similarly, American scholar and MCC leader John A. Lapp also wrote, "We are to be peacemakers in the context of seemingly endless conflict. We are to be ministers of reconciliation amid seemingly perpetual welfare. We are to feed, heal, and clothe. We are to be missionaries of hope where the situation appears hopeless."[192] Again, to complement what the MCC personnel had been talking about, MCC brought Reverend P. J. Malagar, Pastor and Bishop of Mennonite Church at Dhamatari, India, and director of Mennonite Christian Service Fellowship of India, as its guest to Canada and the USA in August. In his speech at the Steinbach E. M. Church, Reverend Malagar described the deplorable situation of the refugees, their heartache and sufferings, "They come with amputated arms, bleeding wounds; with babies dead, sick and dying and with hardly any clothes on their bodies."[193] By this time, of course, the Canadian public had already become familiar with the context of the conflict and the generally argued reasons for Yahya's reprisals against Mujibites (supporters of Sheikh Mujibur Rahman). Canadians found the MCC's short fact sheets and the published articles on news bulletins and church newsletters informative.

Fundraising

Immediately following the influx of refugees, MCC made an earnest appeal to its constituents to enable it to work for them in relief and temporary settlement for which money was needed. The MCC members from across the country responded positively to the appeal to help the victims of military attacks. As contributions began to pour in from various constituents, the local *Winnipeg Tribune* reported that by early fall, it had already raised "more than $19,000... so far from Mennonites in Manitoba in aid of the East Pakistan disaster."[194] Earlier, Arthur Driedger, executive director of the Manitoba branch of the Central Committee, expressed his appreciation of the response from 140-member churches in the province. He proudly assured that he "is confident [that] the Manitoba portion of the budget for the appeal will be met."[195] In reality, the response was so positive that by the end of September 1971, MCC could raise sufficiently to meet the $200,000 appeal it had aimed for. MCC was well ahead of most Canadian NGOs in raising funds for the victims of military reprisals.

The MCC leaders, however, did not remain complacent. Instead, while continuing their work, they asked the community members to show compassion and concern for the suffering people of East Pakistan. Vernon Reimer, though stationed in India, frequently made appeals to his people in Canada to show examples of love and care for the hapless Bengali refugees who were being subjected to "terror and destruction."[196] Being sympathetic, Canadians were carried away seeing the pitiful predicaments of the refugees and hearing about the tales of horror. Vernon's appeals worked. For example, the Saskatoon ladies' branch of MCC and its auxiliary remained busy raising funds through two successive drives, first in October at a rummage sale at the Pensioners and Pioneers Hall. Then again, in November, it also held a successful bazaar in Saskatoon for the Bengali victims of military reprisals. It netted $223.50 for the refugees in India.[197] Again, as the Thanksgiving and Christmas season approached, community members were asked to think of the refugees in India and displaced persons in East Pakistan and send an extra gift to the Mennonite Central Committee through their church treasury. The Mennonite community members demonstrated their Christian concern by helping MCC to give aid to millions of Bengali refugees and impoverished families.

While talking to the author, Wieler took great pride in recalling MCC's activities during its fundraising drives. "Our sensitization work in conveying the message of doom and gloom through its reports, photos, and the ability to implement an immediate response to this overwhelming tragedy had energized the constituency back at home,"[198] wrote Wieler. He then went on to say that the authenticity and immediacy of the action were also constructive when it came to involvement with the Canadian government.

Lobbying

Throughout the liberation war, MCC made conscious efforts to stay away from directly referring to the root causes of the killings of the Bengalis by the Pakistani army and non-Bengalis by the freedom fighters. Yet, it looked for every opportunity to broach the subject. As a witness to the House of Commons Committee on Defence and External Affairs, John Wieler, MCC's associate executive secretary, was accompanied by representatives from the Canadian Red Cross Society, Oxfam of Canada, and the Canadian UNICEF Committee. Wieler cautiously but surely joined the other agencies "urging the Canadian Government to work toward a political solution to the conflict in East Pakistan"[199] Though NGOs are supposed to be apolitical, Wieler said, "a political settlement is a prerequisite to providing effective help in East Pakistan."[200] In this way, MCC continued to lobby the government to the extent possible despite the strict mandate of the organization. It was not just MCC. Other NGOs also carefully lobbied the government, intending to influence its course of action.

While it is true that, by and large, Canadians were aware of the government's limitations, it is also true that they still expected the government to "do more" than what it was doing. "Surely our government could also exert political influence to make the West Pakistanis feel the censure of other governments of the world for their brutal treatment of the East Bengalis. Surely our government must express some outrage,"[201] wrote Harold Jantz, a member of the Mennonite community.

As part of its strategy, while addressing the members and representatives of the constituent churches, MCC personnel referred to Wieler's report to caution both the government and its constituents, "We alert our constituent members to the fact that despite valiant efforts on the part of the government of India, aid from foreign governments, as well as various social and church agencies, the magnitude of the refugee problem is such that the only real solution is a political one. We encourage our constituency to carry this concern to persons and places that have the power to influence policy, which is done quietly and positively, not in a condemning manner, in order not to jeopardize the plight of the affected people further and in a way that this does not cause unnecessary embarrassment to the authorities responsible."[202] At a time when political statements were, and still are, anathema for NGOs, statements of such magnitude sum up the courage and passion with which MCC saw the events.

All MCC personnel, whether in Canada or India, had to be careful not to flare up a whimsical Yahya. On a personal level, Reimer became involved in East Pakistan long before his official duties during the military repression of 1971. Through his frequent visits to Dhaka during the late 1960s, Reimer knew several prominent Bengalis, many of whom had crossed the border following the military clampdown. One of them, Samar Sen of the clandestine Bangla Desh Radio in Kolkata, wrote the music for the national anthem and was a friend of Reimer. Sen and Reimer used to talk about the latest happenings and instances of genocidal killings in East Pakistan. Out of sheer interest and feelings for the Bengalis, Reimer remained involved in receiving encouraging news from his network with the supporters of Bangladesh, which he used to share with Ottawa. To this day, Reimer treasures copies of the first Bangladeshi stamps depicting the killings in Bangladesh that he received as a present from Sen.[203]

Student Christian Movement of Canada (SCM)

SCM, a youth-led ecumenical social justice movement founded in 1921, also joined hands in expressing its consternation and pointed fingers at the military dictator so that Canadians would deepen their understanding of what was going on in Pakistan under the military regime. The SMC was active in raising awareness and writing to Prime Minister Pierre Trudeau with two specific demands on which it remained focused, like other NGOs and Bangladeshi associations. On behalf of the board of directors of the Student Christian Movement, it demanded that the government should "stop immediately sending any kind of aid or giving any kind of support to the Government of Pakistan because this will assist it to continue prosecuting the war in East Pakistan."[204] It also requested the government to "immediately increase substantially aid to the Government of India, to assist it in its relief work with refugees from East Bengal."[205] Unfortunately, there is not enough information on SCM in the archives.

Unitarian Service Committee (USC) of Canada

The Unitarian Service Committee (USC) of Canada has been in India since the 1950s, with its headquarters in Ranchi, Bihar, India, and shared its financial and administrative responsibilities with Ram Krishna Mission (RKM) in Bangalore, Bihar, and Kolkata. When the news of the sudden military takeover and its furtive attack on Bengali civilians reached Canada, USC instantly reacted like the rest of the country with a feeling of disbelief and shock. USC chose not to join the CAPR initiative since it had already been involved in fundraising activities long before the CAPR initiative got off the ground. The USC, however, attended the special CAPR meetings for partners and nonpartners to seek greater collaboration and clarification of roles and responsibilities.

Activities in Canada

The USC's most important activity in Canada was its fundraising campaigns throughout March–December of 1971 and then again in 1972 following the liberation of Bangladesh. At that time, many other organizations were also engaged in fundraising activities individually and collectively for the exact cause—supporting the victims of military reprisals. Naturally, USC faced the challenge of finding creative ways to approach the same donors uniquely in order not to allow the Canadian public to experience any donation fatigue. The USC's fundraising team also carefully designed its campaign strategy not to overburden its constituents. It began the campaign by setting its example, instantly approving $120,000 for the refugees in India. However, it was convinced that more resources would be required to look after the incoming refugees.[206]

The USC was also challenged to position itself thoughtfully due to the very nature of the conflict, which made it doubly circumspect in crafting its statements on a sensitive and political issue. Its message to its constituents was simple—due to the military atrocities, there was an urgent need to assist the large number of refugees who were taking shelter in India to flee the ongoing persecution. It also urged Canadians to do "anything possible" in their humble way under unusual circumstances. Pamela MacRae, an information officer who represented the USC Committee at the CAPR meeting as a non-CAPR member, vigorously maintained that "the voluntary agencies should form a lobby to pressure the government into taking action either politically to ensure a cease-fire or on humanitarian grounds to provide relief supplies."[207]

Activities in India

In India, Swami Yuktanda, USC's key person in charge of relief operations, supervised the USC personnel and promptly plugged in with the lead groups to offer services to the immediate needs of the arriving refugees. There were two primary sources for the USC's human resources—the Ranchi Rural Development and Training in Agriculture for Tribal Youth and the All-India Women's Conference (AIWC). It financed its relief work mainly for the homeless and needy through two local institutions—Swadesh Basu Hospital for Women and Children and a regional health center that received towels, bandages, soaps, baby food, Canadian skim milk powder, and many children's clothing. With the influx of refugees, USC entrusted the Kolkata office with supplementary feeding, medical, and social programs for 175,000 refugees in sixteen refugee camps and the border areas.

Dr. Lotta Hitschmanova, the USC's executive director stationed in Ottawa, maintained close liaison with Yuktanda and other officials in India and reassured the RKM office in Kolkata of the timely delivery of commodities on which the lives of the refugees depended. However, there was a constant revenue shortage to run the existing programs and take new initiatives. To address this, the representatives of the Ranchi RKM, USC, and CIDA officials in Ottawa agreed to underwrite the salaries of one additional doctor and a pharmacist who served on the USC's mobile van in the villages.[208]

As the work continued, Yuktanda and Hitschmanova, the key players, remained in touch with each other. They kept the headquarters *au courant* on every significant incident and the possible future political developments regarding the exodus of the refugees from East Pakistan. In July, the Canadian delegates who visited Pakistan and India noted Yuktanda's work with foreign NGO workers, government delegates, and media personnel worldwide. Upon his return from India and Pakistan, Heath Macquarrie, one of the Canadian delegates who met Yuktanda in the summer of 1971, commended the work of USC. Macquarrie saw Yuktanda as a "saint" for all the work he had been doing for the refugees through the work of volunteers of extraordinary courage and altruism, many of whom risked their lives in the festering make-shift refugee camps.

World University Service of Canada (WUSC)

Practically speaking, although WUSC came into the picture pretty late, it had been watching the political development in Pakistan from the beginning of the impasse. Members of the Canadian University community had been watching the situation with alarm. The WUSC did not fail to notice how some rapid changes were taking place for the worse, even before the military crackdown. It saw the influx of Bengali refugees in India following the clandestine army crackdown as a crisis that was creating problems in the area of housing, feeding, and the medical needs of the families.

The only available archival records indicate that it was only in the fall of 1971, following the formation of a new WUSC National Committee with Professor James D. Brasch of McMaster University, that WUSC articulated its strong desire to help the refugees. Its severe misgivings about the grave situation of the refugees in India are reflected in the minutes of the WUSC's November meeting. Though arriving late, the International Program Commission of WUSC Annual National Assembly recommended that "an appeal be launched for help the Camp School Project for Bangla Desh[i] refugees in India."[209]

All members approved the recommendations. The identical source records also indicate that all pertinent information was sent to the Student Council and local WUSC Committees to operationalize the recommendations approved by the plenary session of the November 19–21, 1971 meeting. The paucity of specific written information, however, makes it difficult to determine the extent of WUSC's activities in assisting the Bengali refugees in India immediately following the imposition of martial law and consequent military repression.

In assessing the engagement and activities of the Canadian NGOs during the Bengalis' struggle for independence, we must remember their greatest collective challenge—how to remain apolitical while continuing to work together at the same time, exerting pressure simultaneously. The NGO leaders, whether dealing with other organizations in the field or with the governments of India and Canada, demonstrated remarkable skills in establishing a harmonious working relationship. They successfully liaised at two levels. For example, their initial liaison with James George, Canada's high commissioner to India, reveals how they kept the New Delhi office of the government of Canada posted about their work in the field. At another level, they also kept the government in Ottawa, provincial governments, and various church groups of numerous denominations across Canada in concerted efforts. They did their best to give the passionate field workers more latitude to innovate, to be more creative, and to take risks, all in the hope that the refugees would receive the basic needs to survive safely. This was done through continuous alignment and realignment of operations with priority results, about which the Trudeau administration was always kept up-to-date. In doing that, the NGO workers became adept at serving the interest of the refugees and getting bang for the buck.

As was the case, all levels of government were au courant concerning the individual and collective work of the NGOs in the field. Such a strategy enabled the NGOs to secure greater government cooperation and avoid typical bureaucratic delays. Since the Trudeau government could not be involved directly, it depended on the work of the NGOs that successfully secured the support of the public through their ongoing donations. Frequent, up-to-date information from the field encouraged officials in Canada to cooperate enthusiastically. This helped remove the usual roadblocks, such as relationship breakdowns, intra-conflict, and lack of cohesion on the part of NGOs. The positive media coverage of the activities of the NGOs in the field also increased awareness of the tangible work of the NGOs in the field.

"I would like to take this opportunity to express our appreciation of the efforts made by the Anglican Church on behalf of the refugees. Relief actions by governments alone are not enough. The immediate and generous response of the churches and other groups of donors ensure that Canada will do its part in alleviating the human suffering created by this great tragedy."[210] Thus, Sharp wrote to Reverend E. W. Scott, commending the work of the NGOs and church groups concerning their assistance to the refugees in India. One may cite this as recognition of the work of Canadian NGOs—how many Canadian nonprofit voluntary organizations banded together in the field into a single cooperative consortium, which eliminated both competition amongst them for funds and a desire to upstage the government to attract public support for their particular point of view. This was a challenge for the NGOs.

Since voluntary organizations, by definition, are not partisan or political and ought to remain nonpolitical, any assessment of their involvement and contribution must be examined by considering their respective limited mandates and resource constraints. The political reality of the situation and the nonpartisan nature of his organization did not allow the MCC's Vernon Reimer to be involved in the political affairs of Pakistan. Throughout the crisis, Reimer was conscious of the need to maintain a political distance; consequently, the NGOs' discomfort remained evident. In this context, we may recall Reimer's reference to the potential problems inherent in the work of the NGOs. "To me, it seems the West was not going to permit the political strength to shift to the West, which should have happened according to the election results. They were not about to let their poorer brethren in the East be on an open footing with them. This, they felt, was unacceptable to them and even considered to be disastrous."[211] Thus, wrote Reimer. In another letter to his colleague in the States about the same subject, Reimer also wrote about how he had to be doubly cautious, "The whole situation is so tense that we cannot engage in anything that smacks of any political involvement. In fact, I don't use the term 'Bangla Desh' but prefer to use 'East Pakistan.' The Indian government has not yet recognized 'Bangla Desh' and, therefore, I am a bit cautious about using that term."[212]

MCC was not alone. All NGOs went through the same sense of disquiet and caution in their interactions with everyone. They had to demonstrate their nonpolitical stand when the entire issue was political. In that sense, it is safe to observe that it was as though Reimer was speaking on behalf of all the NGOs working in the Indian subcontinent during the crisis period. From this angle, ideally speaking, the NGOs' success must be attributed to two key concepts, conscientization, and partage, that they followed from the beginning. Conscientization, in the original Portuguese word, means "awareness creating." In contrast, the French word partage bespeaks cross-cultural cooperation in a spirit of human solidarity to engage the talents and wisdom of people in sharing with partners. One could say that the Canadian NGOs demonstrated their adherence to these concepts by being in a state of need on both sides of the partage/exchange. No doubt, their readiness to welcome each partner to assist the refugees was impressive and exemplary.

To appreciate Canadian NGOs' participation during Bangladesh's liberation war, we must also remember that NGOs of 1971 were much unlike the influential present-day NGOs. The role of today's environmental

NGOs on acid rain, ozone depletion, hazardous wastes, and climate change, or the involvement of peace and anti-nuclear groups in the campaign against NATO's immediate nuclear force acquisition in the 1980s, for example, is demonstrably different than the NGOs of 1971. The perspectives have changed since the 1970s, and they have become more globalized, network-oriented, and, therefore, more demanding. In 1971, the Canadian NGOs carefully positioned themselves to strategize in a way that could influence not only Canada, a middle power, but also other countries in making a concerted effort to press the Yahya government to "stop killing" innocent Bengali civilians.

Finally, to conclude, one could say that, instead of being the silent service providers, Canadian NGOs in the field set their agenda against the backdrop of the political debates and played their role as significant amplifiers of the diversity of voices among the population in the subcontinent. Concerned with poverty alleviation, education, and the environment to foster good governance and healthy living, Canadian NGOs played an important role in assisting the refugees and raising awareness among people around the world. Despite being resource-poor, they managed their limited resources in an environment of rapidly deteriorating changes, which called for increased creative engagement and horizontal initiatives. Functioning as *avant-garde,* the Canadian NGOs embraced the concept of new and challenging ways to network with officials of various levels of government for their deliverables. They showed their extraordinary ability to face the challenges without being overtly political.

Notes and References

1. International Council of Voluntary Agencies. General Conference, *Press Release*, Geneva, 1971, p. 1.
2. Memo from the high commissioner for Pakistan to the Department of External Affairs, dated June 8, 1971. Letter No. P/12/7/70. Canada. Department of External Affairs, File # 38-11-1-Pak. Hereinafter, all information used in this chapter from the Department of External Affairs' records shall be referred to as External Affairs.
3. Letter from Ernie Regehr to Daniel Zehr, Executive-Secretary, Mennonite Central Committee (Canada), dated December 14, 1971. Mennonite Heritage Centre. Archives. File: Asia, Pakistan (August-December 1971) Volume. 2446; 71 E 0008.
4. *Ibid.*

5. Father Guy-Marie Tourangeau, CSC, expressed this. He was then regional director for the Southern districts stationed in Barisal. He remained in East Pakistan throughout the liberation struggle. He wrote to the author on October 14, 1996, while he was in Montreal briefly. Following that, the author interviewed Father Tourangeau in Dhaka on two occasions at Notre Dame College on January 14 and 17, 2000. The author also corresponded with him and received copies of some of his essential papers dating back to 1971. Hereinafter, all citations regarding Father Guy-Marie Tourangeau shall be referred to as Father Guy-Marie Tourangeau.
6. Father Guy-Marie Tourangeau. *Op. cit.*
7. Memorandum for Files (Ottawa), from John Small, High Commissioner to Pakistan, titled Call on Governor-Lt. General Tikka Khan. Dated May 17, 1971, p. 3. File # 20-E-Pak-1-4. External Affairs. *Op. cit.*
8. John Small, High Commissioner to Pakistan, narrated this incident to the author in an interview on July 18, 1995, at his residence in Ottawa. Since then, the author has remained in touch with Small until his passing in 2006.
9. *Ibid.*
10. Father Guy-Marie Tourangeau. *Op. cit.*
11. *Ibid.*
12. Letter from Sister Eleanor Rose to Mustafa Chowdhury, dated January 12, 1997. In 1971, Sister Rose lived in the district of Barisal. When she wrote to the author, she was residing in Montreal. Following receipt of the letter, the author interviewed Sister Rose on January 19, 1997, and then followed up with her on several occasions.
13. This was narrated to the author by Father Guy-Marie Tourangeau in writing. *Op. cit.*
14. *Ibid.* Again, this was also narrated to the author by Father Guy-Marie Tourangeau in writing. *Op. cit.*
15. *Ibid.*
16. Letter from Father Germain de Grandmaison to Mustafa Chowdhury, dated February 1, 1997. At that time, Father Grandmaison was living in Montreal. The author was in touch with him for some years.
17. This was also narrated to the author by Father Guy-Marie Tourangeau in writing and during the face-to-face interviews on January 17, 2000. *Op. cit*
18. The author interviewed Father Laurent Lecavalier, who then lived in Montreal, on September 9, 1997. Father Lecavalier confirmed his narrative with the author in a September 17, 1997 letter. The author followed up with him a few times in the same year. Interestingly, following his return to Canada, Father Lecavalier continued his work with the Bangladeshi communities in Montreal.
19. *Ibid.*

20. This was also narrated to the author by Father Guy-Marie Tourangeau in writing and supplemented by a face-to-face interview on January 14, 2000. *Op. cit.* See also footnote 4.
21. *Ibid.*
22. *Ibid.*
23. *Ibid.*
24. This is from a field report titled *East Pakistan*, p. 1, submitted on November 13, 1971, by G. W. Acworth following his visit to India and East Pakistan; MG 28 I 270, vol. 7, File: Pakistan Refugees-Correspondence 1971–1972. Canada. Library and Archives Canada. Hereinafter, all information used in this chapter from the Library and Archives Canada shall be referred to as Library and Archives Canada.
25. Christian Organization for Relief and Rehabilitation. Dhaka, Bangladesh. Circular Letter No. 5, 6 January 1972, p. 1. Placed in the folder: MG 28 I 270, Volume 19, File: Pakistan, C2. Library and Archives Canada. *Op. cit.*
26. *Toronto Daily Star*, dated September 21, 1971
27. For details, see Brother Alberic Houle's *The Great Flavian.* The Skylab Printers & Packages Ltd., Bangladesh, 1991. P. 81
28. Excerpts of Reports, re Pakistan Refugee Situation, April 26, 1971, p. 2. These are under MG 28 I 270, vol. 7, File: Pakistan Refugees-Correspondence 1971–1972. Library and Archives Canada. *Op. cit.*
29. Personal letter from Prime Minister Pierre Elliott Trudeau to Brother Flavian Laplante, dated July 15, 1971. Cited in Brother Alberic (Robert) Houle's *The Great Flavian. Dhaka,* The Skylab Printers & Packages Ltd., 1991, p. 81.
30. Father Guy-Marie Tourangeau wrote to Mustafa Chowdhury and explained their situation. *Op. cit.*
31. *Ibid.*
32. *Ibid.*
33. Cited in Brother Alberic (Robert) Houle's *The Great Flavian*, Dhaka, The Skylab Printers & Packages Ltd., 1991, p. 80.
34. *Ibid.*
35. *Years of Holy Cross in East Bengal Mission*, Ed. by Reverend R.W. Timm, Congregation of Holy Cross, Dhaka, 2003, p. 203.
36. The names of Fathers Edgar Burns (Superior of the Darjeeling Mission), William M. German, Michael Hawkins, Anthony Milledge, Maurice Stanford, Gerard van Walleghem, James McCabe, Murray Abraham, Leo Forestall, Vincent Curmi, William German, Gerard McDonough, Joe Brennan, Edward McGuire, Brother Carl Krull, and two scholastics, Michael Parent and John Duggan, frequently appeared in the Canadian Jesuits Missions (CJM) records regarding relief work for the Bengali refugees in India. Together with the Canadian Jesuits, there were Belgian Jesuit Fathers Charles Durt and John Hendricks, two Indian Jesuit Fathers, Thomas

Paikeday and Joe Pappadil, and the diocesan priests Fathers James and Jacob, along with several local priests and volunteers who worked together.

37. The author interviewed Father William German on September 24, 1996, in Toronto at Jesuits House. Later, on October 5, 1996, Father German wrote to the author in detail, giving a complete interview narrative. Father German was available for further follow-up meetings in Toronto.
38. *Ibid.*
39. *Ibid.*
40. *Ibid.*
41. An Eyewitness Report on the East Pakistani Refugee Camps under the care of the Canadian Jesuits by Frank G. West, September 10, 1971, pp. 4 - 10. MG 28 I 270, Volume 19, File: Pakistan, C2. Library and Archives Canada. *Op. cit.*
42. *Canadian Jesuits Mission,* vol. 6, no. 5, September–October 1971, p.4.
43. Letter from Father Joe Brenan, Catholic Church, Hatighisha, Darjeeling District, to Father Frank West in Toronto, dated July 19, 1971. MG 28 I 270, Volume 19, File: Pakistan, C2. Library and Archives Canada. *Op. cit.*
44. *Ibid.* p. 6.
45. Interview of Barbara Wood, titled "More than You Give," published in *Canadian Jesuits Mission*, vol. 7. no. 3, May-June 1972, p. 2.
46. *Ibid.*
47. *Canadian Jesuits Mission*, vol. 6, no. 5, September–October 1971, p. 2.
48. *Ibid.* p. 2.
49. *Canadian Jesuits Missions*, vol. 6, no. 3, May–June 1971 p. 2.
50. *Ibid.*
51. *Ibid.*
52. *Ibid.* vol. 6, no. 5, September–October, 1971, p. 4.
53. Letter by Father Frank West to W. V. Harcourt, Canadian Broadcasting Corporation. Dated August 6, 1971, asking them to use his pictures. MG 28 I 270, Volume 19, File: Pakistan, C2. Library and Archives Canada. *Op. cit.*
54. Collection of excerpts of reports of individual Fathers and Brothers titled "Refugees from East Pakistan," p. 2. Published in 1971in the *Canadian Jesuits Mission*, September–October 1971, p. 6. MG 28 I 270, Volume 19, File: Pakistan, C2. Library and Archives Canada. *Op. cit.*
55. *Ibid.* p. 6.
56. *Kitchener-Waterloo Record*, dated July 12, 1971.
57. Janet Perry published it in the *Winnipeg Free Press*, dated October 8, 1971. Janet Perry is the sister of Father John Perry. After she graduated from the University of Calgary, she went to India in 1969.
58. Letter from Father William German to Mustafa Chowdhury. *Op. cit.* See footnote 34.
59. *Ibid.*

60. E-mail from Julian Francis to Mustafa Chowdhury. The author met Francis first in Canada in 1996 and then many times in Bangladesh, where Francis lives. The author is in regular touch with Francis. https://opinion.bdnews24.com/2013/07/07/songs-and-music-of-1971/
61. Letter from Father William German to Mustafa Chowdhury, dated February 1, 1997. *Op. cit.* See also footnote 37.
62. "An Eyewitness Report on the East Pakistani Refugee Camps Under the Care of the Canadian Jesuits" by Frank G. West, dated September 10, 1971, p. 6. MG 28 I 270, Vol. 19, File: Pakistan, C2. Library and Archives Canada. *Op. cit.*
63. In a letter to the author, Patsy Phillip wrote that she submitted the proposal to David Catmure, Director of Overseas Operations, at CUSO Headquarters. He immediately approved the suggested amount. The letter is dated October 10, 1995.
64. This is from a flyer that Nancy Gerein wrote when she returned to Canada in the summer to assist her colleague Jean Stilwell, who was involved in fundraising. This flyer was handed out to the members of the public. Gerein gave the author a photocopy of the flyer from her collection and other information, such as newspaper clippings and many short write-ups. The flyer was accompanied by a personal letter from Nancy Gerein to Mustafa Chowdhury, dated July 21, 1995. At that time, Gerein taught at Queen's University in Kingston, Ontario. Over the years, the author has remained in touch with Gerein, who lives overseas.
65. *Ibid.*
66. *Ibid.*
67. *CUSO Bulletin*, Number 3/71, pp. 1 - 5. Canadian University Service Overseas, Ottawa.
68. *Ibid.* p. 5.
69. *Ottawa Journal*, dated August 4, 1971.
70. *Ibid.*
71. Staff writer Eleanor Dunn wrote the article in *The Ottawa Citizen*, dated August 4, 1971.
72. Letter from Jean Stilwell to Mustafa Chowdhury, dated May 13, 1997. The author then interviewed Stilwell the following week.
73. A General Letter from A. E. Wrinch, Chairman CAPR, addressed to all, dated June 25, 1971. MG 28 1 270 Volume 5, File: Combined Appeal for Pakistani Relief and other agency press releases, statements, material, 1971. Library and Archives Canada. *Op. cit.*
74. *Communique-Press Release*, Reference # 45, dated February 25, 1971. General Secretariat of the Canadian Episcopate, Ottawa. Canadian Conference of Catholic Bishops Archives, Ottawa.
75. *L'église Canadienne*, avril 1971, p. 124. Editions, Fides. Montreal.

76. *Ibid.*
77. *Communique-Press Release* titled "Pakistani Conflict." Dated April 28, 1971, Reference # 58. General Secretariat of the Canadian Episcopate, Ottawa. Canadian Conference of Catholic Bishops Archives.
78. Letter from Archbishop J.A. Plourde, President, Canadian Catholic Conference, to Mitchell Sharp, Secretary of State for External Affairs, dated April 23, 1971. Proposed Statement re. West-East Pakistani Conflict, Reference: Plenary Meeting, Item 5-F, dated April 22, 1971. Canadian Conference of Catholic Bishops Archives, Ottawa.
79. Telegram from Mitchell Sharp, Secretary of State for External Affairs, to Archbishop J.A. Plourde, President of the Canadian Catholic Conference. Telegram # 79, dated April 30, 1971. Proposed Statement re. West-East Pakistani Conflict, Reference: Plenary Meeting, Item 5-F, dated April 22, 1971. Canadian Conference of Catholic Bishops Archives, Ottawa.
80. *Ibid.*
81. Letter from Reverend Richard T. McGrath, Bishop of St. Georges, Newfoundland, to Archbishop J. A. Plourde, dated June 19, 1971. Canadian Conference of Catholic Bishops Archives, Ottawa.
82. Presentation of Archbishop J.A. Plourde, President of the Canadian Catholic Conference, at a News Conference in Montreal, dated June 16, 1971. Canadian Conference of Catholic Bishops Archives, Ottawa.
83. *Ibid.*
84. Memo from Everett MacNeill, General Secretary, for information to Reverend G. Del Mestri, Apostolic Pro-Nuncio, Apostolic Nunciature. Re: Prot. N. 16333, October 4, 1971. MG 28 1 270 Volume 5, File: Combined Appeal for Pakistani Relief and Other Agency Press Releases, Statements, Material, 1971. Library and Archives Canada. *Op. cit.*
85. *Ibid.*
86. Canadian Council of Churches. Combined Appeal for Pakistani Relief, June 16, 1971. MG 28 I 270 Volume 5, File: Combined Appeal for Pakistani Relief and Other Agency Press Releases, Statements, Material, 1971. Library and Archives Canada. *Op. cit.*
87. Minutes of May 6, 1971, of a Special Meeting, convened at the invitation of Mr. Jack Shea, Executive Director of Oxfam of Canada, p.2. This special meeting was convened to discuss with partners and nonpartners of the Combined Appeal for Pakistani Relief; MG 28, I 270, vol. 5. File: Pakistan, Board of Directors Memoranda, 1971. Library and Archives Canada. *Op. cit.*
88. The meeting occurred on July 30, 1971, and was reported in *The Globe and Mail* on July 31, 1971.
89. *Ibid.*
90. *Ibid.*

91. Letter from Leonard Knight, Lieutenant Colonel, Information Services and Special Efforts Secretary to Provincial Commander, Divisional Commanders, Regional Commander, and Departmental Heads, dated June 15, 1971, sent to Dr. Floyd Honey, Canadian Council of Churches on June 18, 1971. MG 28 I 327 Volume 165, File # 5. Library and Archives Canada. *Op. cit.*
92. Minutes of the Fifteenth Meeting of Representatives of National Organizations in the Combined Appeal for Pakistani Relief, held at 2 pm on Monday, November 29, 1971at National Headquarters, Canadian Red Cross, Toronto, p. 33. MG 28 1 270 Volume 5; File: Combined Appeal for Pakistani Relief and Other Agency Press Releases, Statements, and Materials. 1971. Library and Archives Canada. *Op. cit.*
93. *Pakistani Refugees in India* by Albert Batten, Delegate, League of Red Cross Society, May 25 to August 25, 1971. The Report, p. 2. File # 38-11-1-Pak. External Affairs. *Op. cit.*
94. UNICEF and other agency Press Releases, Statements, and material, 1971. Library and Archives Canada. *Op. cit.*
95. CAPR meeting, September 15, 1971, p. 6. *Op. cit.*
96. See footnote # 92. Report by Albert Batten, former Executive Director, Toronto-Central Barnch, the Canadian Red Cross Society, on his Tour of Duty on the East Pakistani Refugee Operation in India as a delegate of the League of Red Cross Societies from May 28 to August 25, 1971. MG I 270, Volume 6, File: File # 47–49. Pakistan Refugees: Correspondence with News Media, Press Releases, and Clippings. Library and Archives Canada. *Op. cit.*
97. *News Release.* The Canadian Red Cross Society, British Columbia, Yukon Division, dated August 18, 1971. MG I 270, Volume 6, File: Pakistan Refugees: Correspondence with News Media, Press Releases, and Clippings. Library and Archives Canada. *Op. cit*
98. *Nancy Edward Reports*, *Press Release.* Titled "Eyewitness Account of Pakistani Disaster," p. 30. The week before July 12. A Berkeley Studio Production for Inter-Church Radio, Toronto. MG 28 1 270 Volume 5; File: Combined Appeal for Pakistani Relief and Other Agency Press Releases, Statements, and Materials. 1971. Library and Archives Canada. *Op. cit.*
99. *Pakistani Refugees in India* by Albert Batten. *Op. cit.* p. 10.
100. MG 28 1 270 Volume 5; File: Combined Appeal for Pakistani Relief and Other Agency Press Releases, Statements, and Materials. Press Release, dated May 3, 1971. Library and Archives Canada. *Op. cit.*
101. *News from CANSAVE.* Dated June 16, 1971. MG 28 1 270 Volume 5; File: Combined Appeal for Pakistani Relief and Other Agency Press Releases, Statements, and Materials. 1971. Library and Archives Canada. *Op. cit.*
102. *Pakistani Refugee Camps in India* by Paul Ignatieff, Executive Director, Canadian UNICEF Committee, July 7–27, 1971, p. 14. File name: Canada Caucus Committee on External Affairs. Re- statements, reports, clippings,

correspondences. MG 28 1 270 Volume 5. Library and Archives Canada. *Op. cit.*
103. *Toronto Telegram*, dated June 15, 1971.
104. *Ibid.* UNICEF Canada. *News Releases*, June 8, 1971, p.1. MG 28 1 270 Volume 5; File: Combined Appeal for Pakistani Relief and Other Agency Press Releases, Statements, and Materials. 1971. Library and Archives Canada. *Op. cit.*
105. *Ibid.*
106. Canada. House of Commons. *Debates*. Queen's Printer, September 10, 1971, p. 7732. Hereinafter, all information used in this chapter from the Debates shall be referred to as the *Debates.*
107. *Ibid.*
108. UNICEF Canada. *News Releases*, June 8, 1971, p.1. MG 28 1 270 Volume 5. Library and Archives Canada. *Op. cit.*
109. *Ibid.*
110. Letter from E. Henry, Chief, Operations Services, NY, to F.B.M. Smith, Planning Division, Canadian International Development Agency. Dated July 27, 1971, p.2 (file # NYH/910/SO). MG 28 1 270 Volume 5. Library and Archives Canada. *Op. cit.*
111. *Ibid.* p. 2.
112. *News Release.* CARE Canada, June 16, 1971. MG 28 1 270 Volume 5; File: Combined Appeal for Pakistani Relief and Other Agency Press Releases, Statements, and Materials. 1971. Library and Archives Canada. *Op. cit.*
113. An appeal letter was sent by Derek Wynne, Chairman of the Business and Industry Committee, to Oxfam Canada clients and patrons. MG 28 1 270 Volume 5; File: Combined Appeal for Pakistani Relief and Other Agency Press Releases, Statements, and Materials. 1971. Library and Archives Canada. *Op. cit.*
114. Pakistan: *Oxfam UK Bulletins*, 1971–1972; Julian Francis wrote this report titled Relief for Refugees from East Bengal, Bulletin No. 32, (August 13, 1971) p. 1. MG. 28 I 270, Vol. 5. Library and Archives Canada. *Op. cit.* Julian Francis' passion for Bangladesh is such that he ended up settling in Bangladesh following the liberation of Bangladesh. The government of Bangladesh awarded Francis the "Friends of Liberation War Honour" in recognition of his work among the refugees in India in 1971 and 2018 honored him with full Bangladeshi citizenship. In 2022, he also received the *Bangabandhu-Edward Heath Friendship Award* handed over jointly by State Minister of Foreign Affairs Shahriar Alam and Lord Ahmad, minister of State for the Middle East, North Africa, South Asia, and United Nations at the Foreign, Commonwealth, and Development Office.
115. *"The Testimony of Sixty: On the Crisis in Bengal."* Oxfam UK, London, October 21, 1971. No page.

116. *Ibid.*
117. *History of Bangladesh War of Independence: Documents. Bangladesher Shadhinota Juddho: Dolilpotro, 1982–1985.* Volume 13, p. 182. Published by Hasan Hafizur Rahman on behalf of the Ministry of Information. Government of Bangladesh.
118. *Ibid.* p 183.
119. *Ibid.* p. 193.
120. *Ibid.* p. 192.
121. *Ibid.* p. 184.
122. *Brief to the House of Commons.* by Robert B. McClure. MG 28 I 270 Volume 6, File: Pakistan: McClure's Brief to the Commons, 1971. Library and Archives Canada. *Op. cit.*
123. *Ibid.*
124. *Ibid.*
125. MG 28 1 270 Volume 6 File: Phillip Jackson Report 1971 titled *Report on Visit to West Bengal, June 20-22, 1971,* p. 5. Library and Archives Canada. *Op. cit.*
126. *Inside Oxfam*, Fall edition, number 23, p.1, 1971. MG 28 1 270, Volume 5. File: Pakistan: Action 71-72. Library and Archives Canada. *Op. cit.*
127. Report from Raymond Cournoyer. Dated May 14, 1971, p. 11. Calcutta, India. MG 28 1 270, Volume 5. File: Pakistan: Action 71-72. Library and Archives Canada. *Op. cit.*
128. Letter to the editor of the *Toronto Telegram* sent by Derek Hayes, Chairman, Board of Directors, Oxfam of Canada. The letter was published on June 10, 1971.
129. *Ibid.*
130. "Oxfam of Canada, Participating Member of Combined Appeal for Pakistan Relief," Oxfam in Action, Oxfam of Canada, June 16, 1971, p.1. File: Combined Appeal for Pakistani Relief and Other Agency, Press Releases, Statements, and Material, 1971. MG 28 I 270 Volume 5. Library and Archives Canada. *Op. cit.*
131. *Ibid.*
132. Letter from Derek Hayes, Chairman, Oxfam of Canada Board of Directors, to Prime Minister Pierre Trudeau. Dated June 7, 1971. File: Combined Appeal for Pakistani Relief and Other Agency, Press Releases, Statements, and Material, 1971. MG 28 I 270 Volume 5. Library and Archives Canada. *Op. cit.*
133. Letter from D. Wynne, Vice-Chairman, Oxfam of Canada Board of Directors, to Mitchell Sharp, Secretary of State for External Affairs, dated April 20, 1971. *Ibid. Op. cit.*

134. File: Combined Appeal for Pakistani Relief and Other Agency, Press Releases, Statements, and Material, 1971. MG 28 1 270 Volume 5. Library and Archives Canada. *Op. cit.*
135. Letter from Robert L. Stanfield, Leader of the Opposition to the Combined Appeal for Pakistani Relief. Dated, June 28, 1971. *Ibid.* Library and Archives Canada. *Op. cit.*
136. File: Combined Appeal for Pakistani Relief and Other Agency, Press Releases, Statements, and Material, 1971. MG 28 1 270 Volume 5. Library and Archives Canada. *Op. cit.*
137. Confidential telegram from John Small, high commissioner to Pakistan, to Ottawa head office. Telegram # Isabad 869, dated August 18, 1971. File # 20- Pak-E-1-4. External Affairs. *Op. cit.*
138. Confidential Memorandum for the Minister from UnderSecretary A. E. Ritchie. Subject: Pakistan: The Toronto Declaration of Concern. Dated September 15, 1971. File # 20- Pak- E-1-4. External Affairs. *Op. cit.*
139. *Ibid.*
140. *Ibid.*
141. *Ibid.*
142. *Ibid.*
143. *Ibid.*
144. *Ibid.*
145. United States of America. *Congressional Record Proceedings and Debates of the 92nd Congress.* First Session, vol. 117, no. 132, dated September 14, 1971.
146. There is no date for an Open Letter to All Canadian Parliament and Senate Members written by Hugh Keenleyside, Robert McClure, and Stanley Burke. MG C26 Volume 27 File: Pak-Bang Reports August–September 1971 (87–12). Library and Archives Canada. *Op. cit.*
147. *PRO TEM, Special Supplement to The Student Weekly of Glendon College,* York University, Canada. Toronto. January-December, 1971.
148. *Ibid.*
149. CAPR. *Oxfam of Canada Release,* July 9, 1971, p. 1. MG C26 Volume 27 File: Pak-Bang Reports August-September 1971 (87-12). Library and Archives Canada. *Op. cit.*
150. Statement on East Bengal Refugee Situation in India: U.S. Senate Sub-Committee on Refugees by Alan Leather, Oxfam field representative, p. 2; MG 28 I 270, vol. 5, File: Pakistan- Oxfam. Library and Archives Canada. *Op. cit.*
151. *Inside Oxfam,* fall edition, 1971, Number 23, p.1. MG 28 I 270, Vol. 5. Combined Appeal for Pakistani Relief and Other Agency, Press Releases, Statements, and Material, 1971. Library and Archives Canada. *Op. cit.*
152. *Montreal Star,* dated June 9, 1971.

153. Raymond Cournoyer, Oxfam Field Director for East India and East Pakistan, was given The Oxfam Award for Outstanding Service to the people of the Third World and the cause of international development. *Inside Oxfam*, fall edition, 1971, Number 23, p.6. MG 28 I 270, vol. 5. Library and Archives Canada. *Op. cit.*
154. Letter from Derek C. Hayes, Chairman, Board of Directors, Oxfam Canada, to the Honorable Mr. Justice J. T. Thornson, President, International Congress of Jurists. Dated July 30, 1971; MG, I 270 vol. 18, File: Pakistan Relief, General. Library and Archives Canada. *Op. cit.*
155. Letter from Mr. Derek C. Hayes, Chairman, Board of Directors, Oxfam Canada, to Amnesty International. Dated November 3, 1971; MG 28, I 270 vol. 18, File: Pakistan Relief, General. Library and Archives Canada. *Op. cit.*
156. Combined Appeal for Pakistani Relief. Sari Appeal. MG 28 1 270 Volume 19. Library and Archives Canada. *Op. cit.*
157. *Press Release*, Oxfam of Canada. Dated July 9, 1971, p. 3. Contained in the MG 28 1 270, Vol. 19 folder, File: Combined Appeal for Pakistani Relief. Sari Appeal. Library and Archives Canada. *Op. cit.*
158. Oxfam of Canada, *Sari Appeal.* An Open Letter to the Women of Canada, no date. Contained in the MG 28 1 270 Volume 5 folder, File: Pakistan-Ontario Regional Office, 1971. Library and Archives Canada. *Ibid. Op. cit.*
159. Minutes of the Fifteenth Meeting of Representatives of national organizations in the CAPR held at 2 pm on Monday, dated November 29, 1971, at national headquarters, Canadian Red Cross, Toronto, p. 3. CAPR File. MG 28 1 270 Volume 19. Library and Archives Canada. *Op. cit.*
160. *Oxfam Canada News*, January Edition, 1972, Number 2. File: Oxfam-Canada News, 1971. MG 28 1 270 Volume 10. Library and Archives Canada. *Op. cit.*
161. Summary of the Second Meeting of the Public Relations Working Committee of the CAPR Meeting held on June 21, 1971. MG 28 I 270, vol. 19. File: CAPR. Library and Archives Canada. *Op. cit.*
162. The above bullets are in the Draft Memo to Public Service Director, CAPR, Churches & Agencies, re: Blanket Appeal, no date. MG 28 I 270, vol. 19. File: CAPR. Library and Archives Canada. *Op. cit.*
163. Radio Spot. This became possible through the combined efforts of Oxfam of Canada and Reverend Desmond McCalmont of the Religious Television Associates, who had excellent working relationships with radio and television networks in the country. Ruth Tillman of the Canadian Council of Churches maintained close contact with members of the religious media. *Ibid. Op. cit.*
164. Letter addressed to all AM/FM radio stations and television stations' program managers, signed by Major General Arthur Wrinch, dated September 3, 1971. Combined Appeal for Pakistani Relief and Other Agency, Press Releases, Statements, and Material, 1971. MG 28 I 270 Volume 5. Library and Archives Canada. *Op. cit.*

165. *Inside Oxfam,* fall edition, 1971, Number 23, p.1. MG 28 I 270, Vol. 5. Combined Appeal for Pakistani Relief and Other Agency, Press Releases, Statements, and Material, 1971. Library and Archives Canada. *Op. cit.*
166. *Press Conference*, dated June 16, 1971. Combined Appeal for Pakistani Relief and Other Agency, Press Releases, Statements, and Material, 1971. MG 28 I 270 Volume 5. Library and Archives Canada. *Op. cit.*
167. *Ibid.*
168. "PAKISTAN- Rebuilding Broken Lives Through Christ." In the *Heartline To the World.* World Vision of Canada. September–October, 1971, pp. 1 - 5.
169. *Ibid.* P. 5.
170. *Ibid.* P. 3.
171. CAPR meeting of September 15, 1971. This was expressed in a letter by Lewis Perinbam, Director, Non-Governmental Organizations Division, Canadian International Development Agency (CIDA) to the CAPR National Co-ordinator Major General A. E. Wrinch is evident in its contribution of $1,000.00 through CIDA and the work of James George, Canadian high commissioner to India. MG 28 I 270, vol. 19. File: CAPR. Library and Archives Canada. *Op. cit.*
172. Letter of support from Robert L. Stanfield, Leader of the Opposition, to The Combined Appeal for Pakistani Relief, dated June 28, 1971. MG 28 I 270, Vol. 5, File: Pakistan Government, Communications Re: 1971. Library and Archives Canada. *Op. cit.*
173. *Information Release*, titled New Brunswick Aid for Pakistani Refugees from Al. King, Information Services Manager, McCain Foods Limited, Florenceville, New Brunswick, Release No. 35-71, p. 30. MG 28 I 270 Vol. 5. File: Pak McCain Foods, 1971. Library and Archives Canada. *Op. cit.*
174. *The Globe and Mail*, dated July 20, 1971.
175. CAPR, Report of the Contributions for November 10 to November 23, 1971. MG 28 I 270, Volume 5, Combined Appeal for Pakistani Relief, 1971. Library and Archives Canada. *Op. cit.*
176. *Board of Trade Journal*, September, 1971, p. 7.
177. *Ibid.*
178. Canadian Friends Service Committee. *Annual Appeal: Bangla Desh*, Volume 1, No. 10, April 1972, p. 1.
179. Letter from Vernon Reimer, Director for Asia, to Paul Longacre, Director for Asia, Mennonite Central Committee, Akron, Pennsylvania, USA, dated May 11, 1971. Mennonite Heritage Centre. Archives. File: Asia, Pakistan (January-July 1971), Volume. 2446; 71 E 0007.
180. *Confidential Report on India and East Pakistan Visit: June 21 - July 20, 1971,* by John Wieler, Associate Executive Secretary of MCC. Mennonite Heritage Centre. Archives. File: Asia, Pakistan (January–July 1971). Volume. 2446; 71 E 0007, p. 5.

181. Letter from Maynard and Griselda Shelly to Robert W. Miller, Mennonite Central Committee, Akron, Pennsylvania, dated November 12, 1971. The Shellys went to Dhaka in November 1971 on behalf of MCC to observe the situation and report back to MCC. Mennonite Heritage Centre. Archives. File: Asia, Pakistan (August–December 1971). Volume. 2446; 71 E 0008.
182. Maynard Shelly made this observation in his write-up under the title, Only a few were willing to take the risk published in the Mennonite Brethren Herald, December 31, 1971, p. 10.
183. Letter from Maynard and Griselda Shelly to Robert W. Miller, Mennonite Central Committee, Akron, Pennsylvania, dated November 5, 1971. Mennonite Heritage Centre. Archives. File: Asia, Pakistan (August-December 1971). Volume. 2446; 71 E 0008.
184. The author interviewed John Wieler, Associate Executive Secretary of MCC, on May 10, 1996, in Winnipeg, Manitoba. Before that, the author corresponded with Wieler and received several published records that Wieler had kept in his collection about his work with the Mennonite Central Committee. In 2020, the author reconnected with Wieler and received more documents and photographs.
185. "The Immense Agony of the East Pakistani Refugees" contained one of John Wieler's profound observations, published in the *News Service*, Mennonite Central Committee (Canada), dated July 20, 1971, pp. 1-2.
186. *Ibid.*
187. *Ibid.*
188. *Ibid.*
189. Letter from John Wieler, Associate Executive Secretary of MCC, to Don Ziegler, Information Service, MCC, Akron, Pennsylvania. Wieler wrote this letter while he was in India for an on-site visit. Mennonite Heritage Centre. Archives. File: Asia, Pakistan (August-December 1971). Volume. 2446; 71 E 0008.
190. "Pakistan refugees suffer immense agony," published in *Canadian Mennonite Reporter*, an Ana Baptist Periodical of News & Interpretation, August 3, 1971, pp. 1–2. There is a slight variation in the title cited above in footnote 185.
191. *Ibid.*
192. By John A. Lapp under the title "Stop the Killing in East Pakistan," published in the *Mennonite Brethren Herald*, August 27, 1971, p. 13.
193. *Carillon News*, August 11, 1971.
194. *Winnipeg Tribune*, dated September 17, 1971.
195. *Ibid.*
196. *Ibid.*
197. *Canadian Mennonite Reporter*, November 1, 1971, p. 3.
198. On August 10, 2020, John Wieler wrote to Mustafa Chowdhury and attached a short write-up on his recollection of his visit to India and Pakistan in

July 1971. The write-up is titled "Bangladesh: Refection on Events Half a Century Ago."
199. *Canadian Mennonite Reporter*, November 29, 1971, p. 4.
200. *Ibid.*
201. By Harold Jantz under the title "Aid to East Bengalis" in the *Mennonite Brethren Herald*, June 11, 1971, p. 7.
202. *Confidential Report on India and East Pakistan Visit: June 21–July 20, 1971,* by John Wieler, Associate Executive Secretary of MCC. Mennonite Heritage Centre. Archives. File: Asia, Pakistan (January-July 1971). Volume. 2446; 71 E 0007, p. 10.
203. Letter from Vernon Reimer to Mustafa Chowdhury, dated August 9, 1996. At that time, Reimer was living in Clearbrook, British Columbia, Canada, having retired from work. The author interviewed him on January 5, 1998, and May 7, 1999. During both interviews, Reimer recalled his take on the entire subject and talked about the constraints under which he had to work as a representative of an NGO. Since then, the author corresponded with Reimer and received copies of some of Reimer's carefully guarded personal documents about his work at MCC.
204. Letter from Beth Hutchison, Student President, Reverend Vince Goring, General Secretary, Student Christian Movement of Canada, to Prime Minister Pierre Trudeau. Dated October 18, 1971. MG 32 C26 Volume 87 File: 87-13. Library and Archives Canada. *Op. cit.*
205. *Ibid.*
206. Smith, Arnold and Sanger, Clyde. *Stitches in Time: the Commonwealth in World Politics.* General Publishing Co. Limited, Don Mills, Ontario. 1981, p. 203.
207. Minutes of May 6, 1971, of a Special Meeting at the invitation of Mr. Jack Shea, Executive Director of Oxfam of Canada, p. 2. This special meeting was convened to discuss the Combined Appeal for Pakistani Relief with both partners and non-partners; MG 28 I 270, vol. 5. File: Pakistan, Board of Directors Memoranda, 1971. Library and Archives Canada. *Op. cit.*
208. Facts and Figures on USC Aid to Pakistan Refugees in India by Unitarian Service Committee of Canada. October 26, 1971 p. 1; MG 28 I 270, vol. 18, File: Bangladesh Rehabilitation. Library and Archives Canada. *Op. cit.*
209. World University Services of Canada, *Press Release*, Document No. 71-11-590, November 29, 1971 p.1; MG 28, I 270, vol. 28, File: Pakistan Relief, General. Library and Archives Canada. *Op. cit.*
210. Letter from Mitchell Sharp, Secretary of State for External Affairs, to Reverend E. W. Scott, Primate, The Anglican Church of Canada. Dated, June 25, 1971. File # 38-11-1-Pak. External Affairs. *Op. cit.*
211. Letter from Vernon Reimer to Mustafa Chowdhury, dated August 9, 1996. *Op. cit.*

212. Letter from Vernon Reimer, Director for Asia, to Paul Longacre, Director for Asia, Mennonite Central Committee, Akron, Pennsylvania, USA, dated June 17, 1971. Mennonite Heritage Centre. Archives. File: Asia, Pakistan (January - July 1971). Volume. 2446, 71 E 0007.
213. CAPR, *Report of the Contributions for the period November 10–23, 1971.* MG 28 I 270, Volume 5, Combined Appeal for Pakistani Relief, 1971. Library and Archives Canada. *Op. cit.*

CHAPTER 6

Parliament Debates Canada's Role in Bangladesh Struggle

*I*n this chapter, we shall see how Canada looked at Pakistan's conflict within the context of a country's breakup. Canada was conflicted mainly due to her policy of "neutrality" and "nonintervention" in the "internal affairs" of another country. The debates reveal Canada's strong desire to assist the victims of military repression as a senior member of the Commonwealth without straining her cordial relationships with the two Commonwealth sisters, India and Pakistan, and use her skills in persuading the military regime of Pakistan to follow the process of democratization that began a year ago. The debates contain details about how several factors contributed to Canada's somewhat ambivalent position. Canada viewed the Indo-Pakistan conflict as more significant in depth and intensity than Nigeria and Biafra. It feared it could be far greater than that which involved Vietnam.*

Themes, such as the preservation of democracy, cessation of repressive measures, and resolution by constitutional means, dominated the discussion throughout the period covering the Bengalis' struggle for independence. Being doubly careful that she must not provoke the wrath of President Yahya Khan and Prime Minister Indira Gandhi, neither the Trudeau administration nor Members of Parliament (MPs) ever confronted the government of Pakistan or India by pointing fingers. The issue of "separation" and "secession," and all other related topics arising from debates, were dealt with extra caution in order not to find a nexus to the issue of separation of Québec. Some of the nagging questions were: How Canada might help alleviate the miserable situation of the refugees in India and displaced persons in East Pakistan? How could Canada work through the institution of the Commonwealth to apply pressure? How could Canada be involved through the UN in the political process to transfer power to Sheikh Mujibur Rahman (Bongobondhu), the elected leader of Pakistan? The debates also reveal Canada's diplomatic challenges in undertaking her activities based on her strategic considerations and independent thinking, which are devoid of US influence despite being a middle power. Whether it was an MP or a senator, the thrust of the discussion centered around finding a political solution within the framework of a united Pakistan.

The debates discussed below include the period covering the War of Liberation of Bangladesh (March 26, 1971 to December 16, 1971) with the surrender of the Pakistani army. The debates fall under the Third Session, Twenty-Eighth Parliament, 20 Elizabeth 11. The most crucial item discussed just before the secret military crackdown was "Assistance to Cyclone and Flood Victims" following the devastating cyclone of November 1970. The overall issues covered were *inter alia,* National Security, the *War Measures Act,* Canada-US Relations, Wage and Price Control, Cost of Living Insurance, Youth, Federal-Provincial Relations, Amchitka Nuclear Test, and the proposed Trans-Alaska Pipeline System, etc. On top of the government's agenda, however, was the question of *national unity.*

With the surreptitious military clampdown and takeover and the beginning of ongoing reprisals, Canadians expressed their concerns about the actual position of fear for their fellow Canadians who were stranded in Pakistan. Overall, the following items dominated the discussions under the broad heading: *External Affairs–Pakistan-East Pakistan-India.* The subjects discussed directly fell under some of the following topics: safety and security of Canadians in East Pakistan, direct emergency relief and action, emergency food supply, liaison with the UN, alleged shipment of arms, sanctions, the urgent need for a political settlement, restoration of democracy, political asylum, sponsorship, immigration of refugees, presentation of reports by nongovernmental organizations (NGOs) and the Canadian International Development Agency (CIDA) to the Standing Committee on External Affairs and National Defence. However, Canadian citizens' welfare, safety, and security had been very much in their minds.

In East Pakistan, there were approximately 200 Canadians, whereas in West Pakistan, 270 Canadians were registered with the Canadian High Commissioner's Office.[1] Below is a short account of the House of Commons and Senate debates under some common overlapping themes selected arbitrarily.

Initial Reaction while awaiting authentic information

When the MPs returned to the House on March 29, 1971, there existed an atmosphere of anguish as the stories of the gruesome massacre had already been on the news over the weekend of March 27. Upon hearing the news of the clandestine March 25 crackdown, officials at the External Affairs made serious efforts to obtain reliable information. Canada initially saw the military crackdown as "civil war" or "civil unrest" in East Pakistan, one of Pakistan's five provinces, and regarded this as Pakistan's "internal affairs." While the Canadians were conversing about what was happening in East Pakistan, Ottawa gathered more information about the *scope* and *nature* of the actual situation in Pakistan to the extent possible through Canada's high commissioners to India and Pakistan, James George and John Small, respectively. They referred to the Bengalis' demand for greater autonomy, the furtive attack by the military regime, its ruthless suppression of the Bengalis by denying their fundamental rights, and the declaration of independence by the followers of Bongobondhu (Sheikh Mujibur Rahman) by renaming the land as "Bangla Desh" (as it was spelled then in two syllables).

They also informed Ottawa that President Yahya had categorized Bongobondhu as a "separatist" and had offered this as his justification for military action. With the filtering of information, Ottawa officials learned more about the fast-changing circumstances—how the continuing struggle between the overwhelming majority of politically united but poorly equipped Bengalis and four or five divisions of the modern West Pakistani army turned out to be a War of Liberation with the beginning of the planned but secret military clampdown. In the meantime, the Trudeau administration noted a growing public concern among Canadians, who had already expressed horror, disgust, and the utmost indignation.

Tommy C. Douglas, the New Democratic Party (NDP) leader and MP for Nanaimo-Cowichan-The Islands, was the first of the three representatives who raised the issue of the military takeover, killing of civilians, and the "denial of the democratic rights of the people of Pakistan."[2] Referring to the reported "mass killings of civilians" along with repressive measures being adopted by the military government of Pakistan, he described them as a "disturbing situation in East Pakistan"[3] where the "democratically elected representatives have been refused the right to take office and have been outlawed."[4] Seeing the military action as a step toward extending military power, as opposed to moving forward with the government's promise to transfer power to the elected representatives, Douglas inquired with Mitchell Sharp, Secretary of State for External Affairs, whether or not "the Canadian government has made any representations to the government of Pakistan, particularly intending to preserve democratic government in that fellow member of the Commonwealth?"[5]

With no up-to-date information on hand, Sharp indicated that Canada's immediate priority was to promote the well-being of the people of Pakistan and not to increase their suffering. He did not wish to commit to the political ideologies of one group against another. It shall be seen that the Canadian parliamentarians deliberately avoided questions about the "separation" or "independence" of East Pakistan, whether the movement was an armed uprising aimed at materializing the results of the 1970 National Elections or a movement that was thrust upon the Bengalis.

The only time the question of *separation* came up was in response to Douglas's question regarding resolving the conflict by "constitutional means." Having cautioned his colleagues that one must not "oversimplify the situation," a cautious Sharp expressed his concerns: "If he were to ask me whether I think East Pakistan should separate, I would hesitate before making a definite reply."[6] Nobody further discussed whether the Yahya government had the right, expressly or by implication, to abandon the results of the 1970 National Elections in which the majority voted freely for establishing a constitutional regime based on the Six-Point program (discussed in Chapter 1). Besides Douglas, there was the NDP Andrew Brewin for Greenwood, who also raised a few questions regarding Canada's position. He was the first MP to raise the question of liaison with other organizations - whether or not the government had been in touch with the "interested governments to offer international humanitarian assistance to the victims in East Pakistan?"[7] Sharp's curt response was that his officials had "made it clear" that until the government had all the facts, they believed that any "intervention would not serve very much purpose."[8]

Viewed from this perspective, it is understandable *why* Canada was reticent in its condemnation of military actions in what she came to refer to as the East Pakistan Crisis. Evidently, amid the confusion of fighting and the exodus of refugees across the Indian border, there had been a striking absence of hard facts on which Canada could make a judgment, something that we discussed in Chapter 2. In the Commons, the issue of *military repression* and the need for *humanitarian intervention* was regularly raised during the next few days by the MPs of all the major political parties of Canada. The government believed that any interference from one country to another country's "internal affairs" could only lead to provocation. Ottawa initially believed that problems between countries should be settled through *negotiation* and *not war*. As Ottawa saw the situation, Canada's congenial relations that had evolved over the years between Pakistan and India must be guarded carefully, and it would make "political sense" not to provoke the choler of President Yahya Khan and Prime Minister Indira Gandhi, given Canada's friendship with the two Commonwealth sisters. The Trudeau administration's reaction was that Canada must react *cautiously*.

Although millions of battered and homeless Bengalis were being forced to abandon their homeland to seek shelter in cramped refugee camps in a foreign country (India), most of the opposition MPs were extra prudent to avoid any serious debate on whether the issue had remained an "internal affair" of Pakistan. While Ottawa officials remained on guard in choosing the appropriate words to describe the army's action, the MPs sought an answer to the following question: What could or should be done under the circumstances to help the refugees in India and displaced Bengalis in East Pakistan? Unsurprisingly, throughout the debates, there was also no mention of the words "freedom fighter," "guerrilla war," "war of liberation," "war of independence," or "freedom movement." This was even though the news media had already termed the military crackdown and reprisals as "mass murder" and "genocide" being perpetrated by the military regime in the Bengalis' struggle for an independent Bangladesh.

The issue of massacres in East Pakistan, however, continued to be raised. In one of his most emotional appeals, Health Macquarrie, the Conservative MP for Hillsborough, Prince Edward Island, as well as PC caucus spokesperson on external affairs, reminded the government that there were "widespread reports in respectable and responsible journals concerning the alleged bloodshed in East Pakistan which is said to have reached the proportions of genocide against intellectuals and young people."[9] Macquarrie himself did not characterize the event as genocide but simply indicated what the news media was consistently reporting, having variously described the killings as "genocide," "pogrom," and "systemic decimation of the Bengalis." There were no follow-up questions or debates as to whether it was genocide or, as the news media reported, Yahya's "licensed mayhem." Instead, both the government and Canadian parliamentarians resorted to careful use of phraseology to not give anyone a chance that their position could be interpreted as pro-regime or pro-Bangladeshi. They were very cautious in choosing words as it was essential to avoid further discussion. Unsurprisingly, therefore, Canadian parliamentarians were consistent in referring to the killings as a "disturbing situation,"[10] "a gripping story of fearful human suffering,"[11] "one of the most tragic circumstances that the world has ever witnessed,"[12] "killings and repressive military measures,"[13] "regrettable and deplorable incidents,"[14] "the greatest human tragedy in modern time,"[15] "civil war," "civil strife,"[16] "civil disorder," and, more descriptively, "agonizing situation."[17] The use of softer words by the MPs to refer to the killings of the unarmed people reinforces their *cautionary reactions* to what they initially saw as a civil war of a catastrophe beyond comprehension.

Placed in a challenge in the face of numerous conflicting reports, Sharp navigated with extreme difficulty through a raging tempest to avoid the slightest appearance of partiality. As a Good Samaritan state, Canada was placed in an awkward situation as it could not react. The consensus was that there ought to be a complete, speedy international inquiry into the events following the imposition of martial law. With a brooding apprehension of the trouble lurking in their minds, many MPs also began to raise specific questions about what the government had been doing regarding the humanitarian assistance program. Sharp assured the House that "the government is ready to help constructively in the humanitarian effort that may be launched."[18] He reminded his colleagues: "I should add, however, that bitter experience should have taught us the dangers of attempting to intervene in civil conflicts of this kind. We have had some examples where intervention would not have helped those who were thought to be the victims."[19] Sharp was probably referring to the 1967-1970 Nigerian–Biafran issue in which Canada did not get involved, and both sides saw Canada's noninvolvement negatively.

A doubly cautious Sharp cannily articulated his condemnation of the killings of civilians in a guarded speech: "This is something which I am sure we all deplore."[20] Canada's genuine fear of an *unequivocal condemnation* of Yahya had already been known to many world leaders. Canada's deploring of the event did not have the same degree of condemnation as the British Parliamentary reactions following their on-site visit to the premises. For example, one of the British Parliamentary delegates, Reginald Prentice, was much more outspoken in expressing their views. Having expressed their moral and humanitarian outrage, they were outspoken in condemning Pakistan's policy of genocide. Unlike the Canadian delegates, Prentice courageously observed what they gathered through interviews with the common Bengalis. Referring to the delegates' confidential interviews of the ordinary people regarding the precarious situation, Prentice observed: "They all added up to the same conclusion: not only had the army committed widespread killing and violence in the March/April period, but it continued. Murder, torture, rape, and the burning of homes were still going on. It was a story that would be powerfully reinforced by the accounts given to us by the refugees in India a few days later."[21] While debating, Canadian parliamentarians had been obsessively careful in reviewing the latest situation and expressing their feelings of shock and dismay. Canada was not yet ready to come out with a note of direct condemnation. Canadian delegates remained evasive in their condemnation.

Lack of Adequate Information from Diplomatic Sources

Discussions among the MPs took the form of questions and inquiries along the following lines: How and what might Canada provide as immediate assistance to the victims? What would be the best way to ensure the safety of Canadian nationals in East Pakistan? Specifically, Doug Roland, NDP MP for Selkirk, inquired, "What action the government of Canada is taking to ensure the well-being of Canadian nationals in East Pakistan."[22] Sharp immediately responded, "All Canadians in Dacca [sic] are safe and well. We have no information about the situation in Chittagong or other areas."[23] Sharp added, "There are still approximately 150 Canadians in East Pakistan and, following arrangements entered beforehand, the deputy British high commissioner will include them in arrangements made for protection and withdrawal to haven should this appear necessary."[24]

Again, Réal Caouette, the Ralliement des créditistes du Canada MP for Témiscamingue, Québec, raised his concern about the crisis by asking, "What is Canada doing about the conflict in Pakistan and what representations has it made to the government of Pakistan?"[25] Sharp responded, "Our problem is that we do not yet have facts. I believe it is important, before we take any action, for us to know what is going on and not to have to depend, as sometimes happens, upon newspaper reports which may or may not have substance."[26] Since as late as the first week of April, the government still did not have all the facts surrounding the events. Sharp's responses cautioned that the government needed *reliable information* from its sources. On every occasion, a determined Sharp referred to the government's *wait-and-see* policy.

Earlier, Heath Macquarrie, Conservative MP for Hillsborough, PEI, also raised his concerns that they needed to know whether Canada was "holding discussions on this serious question with representatives of Pakistan, India, or the United Nations to avert an even wider conflict."[27] For a while, typically, Sharp's curt reply used to be something like the following: that the "High Commissioner of Pakistan was recently in touch with the government" and that the Yahya government had urged the government of Canada to "prevail upon other countries not to intervene in this situation."[28] Again, when Conservative Robert Stanford, leader of the opposition, inquired about the "reports of mass killings and shortage of food and medical supplies"[29] in East Pakistan, Sharp's reply was negative, alluding to what he had already indicated—that his team had not yet received detailed information from either the UN or its diplomatic sources. By this time, the reports of indiscriminate genocidal killings had already hardened the conscience of the Canadian public and politicians alike. "The question before the Canadian government is how best it might be able to help, and I do not think pious declarations against violence are going to achieve anything. We are searching for some means by which we can be constructive, by supplying relief or something of that kind,"[30] thus stated an anxious Sharp.

By mid-April 1971, however, there appeared quite a bit of information on Yahya's secret military operations, which were characterized by duplicity, brutality, and repression. While many of his colleagues agreed with Sharp, whose office was busy verifying the information, some MPs, like the public, became vocal seeing the dreadful situation—how the Yahya government had been engaged in killing unarmed Bengali civilians to suppress the Bengali rebels. Though appreciative of the government's conflicted position, some MPs representing the East Pakistani Bengali Canadians were pressured by their constituents to raise the issue again. The Bengali Canadians of East Pakistani origin became convinced that the military regime was engaged in crushing the dissidents peremptorily and forcefully with no thought to the consequence of its action.

Sharp maintained that his team needed to ascertain first *what had been happening in Pakistan and India since the imposition of martial law*. "The Canadian High Commissioner had been for some days now in East Pakistan and he will be submitting a report shortly,"[31] Thus, was Sharp's curt response that visibly disturbed the opposition colleagues. Typically, it was something along the line that the government had "no direct communications," which would have enabled Ottawa to "decide the extent of bloodshed going on in East Pakistan."[32] A terse response along this line was considered a safe strategy throughout the period Ottawa awaited the report. The opposition MPs did not challenge Sharp. At that time, Ottawa regarded many news media reports as either exaggerated or unverified simply because, during the first few weeks, foreign journalists were expelled from East Pakistan. On numerous occasions, information was withheld, and occasionally, there were further embargoes on information or restrictions on access to any information. The reporters maintained that the news items collected from various sources were not authenticated. Sharp's focus group tried "to obtain a balanced assessment of the situation quickly"[33] out of the stories of slaughter, mutiny, arrest, detention, and continuing reprisals. However, Ottawa officials deemed the reports of Canadians who had just returned from East Pakistan via Penang, Malaysia, reliable.

Nevertheless, with his feet on the ground, a determined Sharp remained laconic in his remarks that he needed to hear from his diplomatic sources (high commissioners to Pakistan and India) first; otherwise, it would be impossible for him to make an informed decision. This left a few of his colleagues and the members of the public with the impression that the government was dragging its feet. But it was the opposite—the government had already started to work behind the scenes simultaneously with whatever information it possessed. Simply put, a strong-willed Sharp believed it would be premature to react instantly. He remained resolved and took the time required to review the situation. By and large, the MPs agreed with Sharp that it was important for Ottawa to gather all the facts first about the reported massacre of the Bengalis and to wait for official reports from Pakistan and India.

Immediate Relief Assistance on Humanitarian Grounds

The issue of military repression, its consequences, and the need for humanitarian intervention was continually raised throughout the crisis period as some opposition MPs were running out of patience even though they agreed with the government's assertion that it must gather authentic information first. In the meantime, the news media around the world, including Canada, had already been covering the horrific stories of killings and brutalities. In the face of constant pressure for humanitarian assistance, Sharp tried to appease his colleagues by repeating the same type of stock responses he had been giving—that once his office *could* ascertain the fact, he would "consider whether any useful purpose would be served by making representations."[34] The government had been "ready to help in a constructive way in the humanitarian effort that may be launched"[35] to mitigate the sufferings of the victims, observed Sharp additionally.

Again, when the NDP MP for Broadview, John Gilbert, inquired whether Ottawa "officials [had] been in touch with the Red Cross agencies to provide aid and assistance to the people in this area,"[36] Sharp's immediate response was positive. A concerned Sharp, appreciative of political expediency, reflected greatly on his priorities by examining the diplomatic ramifications of the tragic events. Though breviloquent in his responses, Sharp's key message was that Canada was "ready to help if they can find some way of assisting the people of East Pakistan."[37]

To assess the government's reaction, we need to put the government's response given by Sharp in a proper perspective at that critical time. Being concerned about the deteriorating situation, Conservative Heath Macquarrie directed his question to Sharp: "Can he [Sharp] advise if the government is contemplating any steps to ameliorate the terrible suffering of the people of East Pakistan? Can he also advise if, in concert with other Commonwealth states, the government is taking any initiative toward diminishing the fighting and the possibility of its broadening into a conflict between two of our Commonwealth members?"[38] Sharp, who seemed ready, responded, "The Canadian government has made it plain that we are prepared to join other countries in measures to assist in the relief of the people of East Pakistan. We are also urging, of course, that there should be a political settlement of the question and not one that involves so much bloodshed."[39]

Again, when Andrew Brewin asked "whether the government's general intention to assist in the relief of the people of East Pakistan ... has been discussed with the International Red Cross,[40] Trudeau quickly responded. Having mentioned that the Canadian high commissioner had been in East Pakistan to review the situation, he observed that Canada's representative was "to report to the government on the possibility of moving large supplies of foodstuffs and other supplies to East Pakistan and when the government requests them of that country."[41]

Liberal Pierre De Bané, member of Parliament for Matapédia-Matane, also asked Sharp the following question: "Is he in a position to tell the House whether the Canadian government has made known to the government of Pakistan its vigorous and unequivocal censure of the atrocities perpetrated in East Pakistan?"[42] Sharp immediately responded, "We have made it known that we favour a political settlement of this situation and not bloodshed, some of which unfortunately has already taken place."[43] Earlier, Canada was disappointed to learn that Yahya had refused to accept relief from the UN when the International Committee of the Red Cross (ICRC) planeload of relief goods arrived in Karachi (West Pakistan) without the consent of the military authority.

Macquarrie wanted to know more specifically whether the government had any "conversation with representatives of the governments of India and Pakistan and can he advise about the situation in East Pakistan, particularly concerning the acceptance by the authorities then of relief supplies."[44] Sharp's response was the following: "The Canadian government is trying to obtain a balanced assessment of the situation quickly," was Sharp's curt response. A concerned Macquarrie, however, continued by asking, "If the Pakistani authorities are now accepting the aid of the relief agencies and allowing them into East Pakistan?"[45] Sharp quickly replied in the following manner: "Mr. Speaker, we have had no requests whatsoever from the Pakistan government as such. The announcement that I was making was about the relief of refugees from Pakistan who are now in India."[46]

The point Sharp tried to put across was that Canada did not wish to be accused of "interfering" in the "internal affairs" of Pakistan but, like all Canadians, remained anxiously interested in "doing anything" it could in the area of *humanitarian assistance*. Having recognized the pulse in the House, a disquieted Sharp reassured his colleagues that the government had been ready to support the provision of relief. Nevertheless, under the circumstances, any insistence by Canada would be counterproductive, argued Sharp.

To appreciate Sharp's predicament, one must recognize the tremendous pressure he had been under to be more proactive when the government was still gathering as much information as possible from the field. To help his colleagues understand his government's position, Sharp underlined that he had been advising both the governments of Pakistan and India to do everything they could to "avoid an escalation of this conflict."[47] "The problem, however, is severe, and we recognize it as such. For the time being, at least, we feel that the most effective thing we can do is to provide aid to the refugees who are there,"[48] Sharp added further. Again, echoing the sentiments of the people of Canada, Macquarrie, the most vocal MP in the House, also began to prod the government to act more quickly. However, he respected Canada's "hands-off" policy: "There is a very serious situation in Pakistan, and while that country may well assert that the political aspects are not the subject of international scrutiny or concern, the humanitarian aspect should prompt the government of Pakistan to welcome the good intentions and efforts of people from many parts of the world."[49] Nevertheless, fortunately for Sharp, the general feeling in the House existed along the line that the government intended to be engaged in humanitarian efforts. Still, it had been tardy in its reaction and action since Sharp wanted to provide relief assistance without being involved in the *political nature of the conflict.*

Although Canada was expected to adhere to its "nonintervention" policy, Robert Stanfield, member of Parliament for Halifax and leader of the opposition, asked, "whether the government of Canada believes it should become involved in pressure of this sort, or on the other hand, does it feel it should remain aloof as far as Pakistan is concerned."[50] Sharp immediately responded, "I think that most countries of the world are operating carefully. I certainly do not want to cause additional hardship to any of the people of Pakistan in the East or West by denying projects that can be of immediate assistance. Nevertheless, it is recognized that the aid must be seen to be going toward helping the people on both sides."[51]

A non-interventionist, Sharp maintained that his government did not want to "get political matters mixed up with humanitarianism."[52] He repeatedly attempted with steadfastness to convey to his colleagues that his government had no intention of interfering in Pakistan's "internal affairs."

Without wishing to compromise his conviction and responsibility, Sharp remained vigilant by demonstrating his belief in the difference between *humanitarian help* and *interference.* Sharp confronted the challenge commendably with prudence and foresight. Sharp knew foreign policy ideas and strategies have a relatively short shelf life. Still, he was not yet ready to be dragged into a debate at a time when his *priority* was to search for *creativity* and *flexibility* in maintaining stable international relations. A veteran, Sharp remained on guard and handled the discussion with discreteness and forethought - that he must continue Canada's relief work in India and East Pakistan.

International Liaison and Action through the UN

Tied to immediate relief measures was the notion of international liaison through the UN to explore its formal provision of humanitarian assistance to the victims of military repression. Being on the hot seat, Sharp raised the East Pakistan issue with the UN but maintained that the conflict ought to be resolved by constitutional means or by "urging a cessation" through the intervention of the UN. Canadian parliamentarians were disappointed that it was impossible due to matters related to the existing UN protocol. By the first week of April 1971, however, Ottawa successfully initiated discussions regarding providing food grains and medical supplies to the refugees in India and displaced persons in East Pakistan. This was one of *Canada's high priorities,* observed Sharp immediately upon his return from Europe by the end of April.

Canada was disturbed by the Yahya government's claim that it was "business as usual" in East Pakistan, which was certainly not the case. Canada saw Yahya's responses as a misrepresentation of the truth, having resorted to lying. Despite the tragic situation of the displaced people within East Pakistan, not to speak of the frightened civilians who had been fleeing to India, Sharp had no choice but to remind his colleagues in the House that Canada had never been, nor ever was an *interventionist.* Sharp believed that any intervention from outside would only complicate the matter. Sharp's advice to his team was to remain firm in adhering to Canada's view and not to yield to any pressure to take an issue with Pakistan's government regarding human rights violations or democratic processes.

It was not until May 3, 1971, after tremendous pressure from Western countries, that the Yahya government agreed to accept official relief assistance from selected foreign countries and international organizations. On May 22, Ottawa was advised that Agha Shahi, Permanent Representative of the UNHCR (United Nations High Commissioner for Refugees) at the UN, had made a formal request to the member countries. Being on the ball, Ottawa immediately consulted with the International Council of Red Cross (ICRC) and the Canadian Red Cross Society (CRCS) and jumped at the offer to join forces to provide humanitarian assistance to the victims of military reprisals. The opposition MPs, too, were overjoyed. "The world cannot allow another large group of refugees to be cast adrift for years. Surely, the experience of the Palestinian refugees should jolt us out of complacency and stir us into action. Something must be done. I ask the government not to hesitate in giving leadership. It is for such leadership that I call once more."[53] Thus, Macquarrie observed after immediately welcoming Canada's decision to join forces.

Nevertheless, there still existed a sense of dissatisfaction and anger among the MPs who noted that the military regime had continued its repressive measures, killing civilian Bengalis indiscriminately as though it was engaged in decimating the Bengalis. A shocked James A. McGrath, Conservative member of Parliament for St. John's East, asked a straightforward question: "Has the government of Canada requested permission from the government of Pakistan to send observers into East Pakistan to determine whether or not the charges of genocide against the Hindus, especially, have any foundation in fact?[54] Sharp immediately responded in the following manner: "A complaint has been made to the Secretary-General of the United Nations that genocide was involved, and the Secretary-General has not considered it necessary to have the inquiries made. It should think that it would be incumbent upon the Secretary-General if he felt there was justification to have such an inquiry made."[55]

Nevertheless, throughout the crisis period, the UN proved useless as far as the Canadians were concerned. "The Security Council, having met hour after hour, seems to end with the use of the veto and in futility. Whether it will be necessary to move from the Security Council to the General Assembly through the technique of the 'uniting for peace resolution,' as it was once called, we do not know,"[56] thus, observed a disturbed Macquarrie. Again, while the war was going on, Macquarrie, on behalf of his colleagues, observed in one voice, "I can assure him [Sharp] that all my colleagues and, I am sure, all Canadians of decent outlook and concern for the peace of the world, will support the Canadian government in any measure which it can take to help roll back the frontiers of hatred and bring about as quickly as possible that which surely is of the essence today, the cessation of hostilities through a ceasefire."[57]

Approach through the Commonwealth

On the first day in the Commons following the military crackdown, the NDP MP Tommy Douglas asked whether the Canadian "government had made any representations to the government of Pakistan, particularly intending to preserve the democratic government in that fellow member of the Commonwealth?"[58] A concerned Douglas then continued: "Will the government of Canada consider making representations urging a cessation of the repressive military measures which are being pursued and an attempt to settle this matter by constitutional means?"[59] He did not receive any response to his satisfaction since the government was still awaiting two separate official reports from Islamabad and New Delhi. In the meantime, the MPs were outraged upon hearing the news that the bloodshed and destruction had been on a scale best described as a "pogrom."

The Trudeau government wanted to take a shot at it but did not wish to risk its traditional relationship of *respec*t and *cordiality* with the Commonwealth sister countries by even appearing to favour one country against another. Although behind the scenes, the Trudeau administration was engaged in pursuing the governments of India and Pakistan, the MPs were not necessarily up-to-date on the government's latest initiatives by the government. Seeing that Canada had not yet taken any initiative, Macquarrie, who had an in-depth knowledge of the Commonwealth, also echoed Douglas by asking whether the government was "taking any initiatives towards diminishing the fighting and the possibility of its broadening into a conflict between two of our Commonwealth members, India and Pakistan?"[60] He further maintained that the government of Pakistan should be implored "to do everything possible to open the situation to international scrutiny because it is not at all pleasing that one of our Commonwealth fellow members should have such a very poor image, as seems to be the case throughout the world."[61] This was followed by appeals from a few anxious MPs who considered forging a new form of partnership with the Commonwealth countries to address the problem as a *collective* Commonwealth problem.

There was complete unanimity in the House regarding Canada's use of the Commonwealth connection. Sharp, however, remained unmoved, having clung to his view that any quick reaction by Canada could be easily misconstrued. He believed it would be counterproductive. His preferred strategy was to work *discretely* and *quietly* by following Canada's *wait-and-see* policy before making a firm decision. In the meantime, behind the scenes, Ottawa officials also proactively reached out to Arnold Smith, a distinguished Canadian diplomat who, at that time, was secretary-general of the Commonwealth. Ottawa sought his advice regarding the timing of Canada's intervention. We shall see in Chapter 7 Canada's dilemma and her efforts through the Commonwealth connection. For a while, by and large, the MPs were okay with the government's dilatory approach. However, many MPs still expressed their misgivings, claiming that time was of the essence.

When the MPs did learn about Sharp's initiative with the Commonwealth secretary-general, they were happy to note that things had begun to move a tad faster. At about the same time, the idea of a fact-finding mission or the dispatch of "independent observers" from Parliament "to the scene as other countries of the Commonwealth have done"[62] also surfaced in the House following the visit of the US and British government delegations. Thomas M. Bell, NDP MP from Lancaster, immediately broached the subject of a Canadian delegation at the first opportunity. The government did not respond to the proposal immediately.

Fortuitously, within days, the government of India invited the government of Pakistan to visit the subcontinent, which the government of India subsequently echoed. The government immediately formed a three-member Standing Committee on External Affairs and National Defence, representing three major political parties of Canada (Liberal, Conservative, and NDP). By the first week of July 1971, the said Committee left for India and Pakistan to obtain firsthand information. We shall see the complete committee report in Chapter 7.

A policy of "neutrality" and "non-intervention"

Canada's unwillingness to intervene must be carefully considered in the context of the FLQ crisis 970. (This has been discussed below under the subheading Ideological Constraints and the Fear of the Québec Question to appreciate her unique predicament at the time.) Sharp's cautionary remark that "the situation is still not very clear"[63] may be seen as his way of using the extra time he needed to stall his immediate official response. "Surely, the House would expect that before we intervened in such a delicate situation, we should ascertain whether our intervention would be useful."[64] Thus, Sharp maintained in the face of continued pressure. As early as March 30, Sharp warned that it would be dangerous for Canada to interfere in the civil war. Sharp made it clear at every opportunity that his team had been trying to obtain a balanced assessment of the situation. Upon further inquiry, Sharp elaborated on his position. "We have been advising both the Indian and Pakistani governments to do everything they can to avoid an escalation of this conflict. The problem, however, is extremely serious, and we recognize it as such. For the time being at least, we feel that the most effective thing we can do is provide some aid to the refugees who are there."[65]

In the meantime, Ottawa remained mindful of Small's earlier advice that Pakistan's military leadership had been extremely sensitive to outside criticism. However, it probably had been divided over the wisdom of its decision to use force. We touched on this in Chapter 2. Since the military clampdown, the Yahya government had complained bitterly of distortion of the situation in East Pakistan by the Western press, mainly based on what he called exaggerated reports from Indian sources, informed Small. Ottawa remained firm in its conviction that it would be "politically incorrect" to take a position without examining the actual events that were taking place at a frenetic pace.

Robert Stanfield, leader of the opposition, asked a pointed question just about the same time: "Is it the policy of the government to continue simply to watch the situation, in which event the government of Pakistan might just disintegrate, or does the government of Canada propose to participate in the taking of some decisions? In other words, is it the policy of the Minister to let nature take its course in the hope that somehow the thing will work out, or has he a policy?"[66] Sharp immediately responded, "No one else in the world seems to have an easy solution. We are all doing our best to meet two problems: that of the refugees in India and the condition of Pakistan itself and the conflicts that now separate the two parts. This is one of the most serious international issues the world has been faced with; we are doing our best in an attempt to arrive at reasonable solutions, and that is the best we can do."[67] Canada's dilemma was that a committed Sharp did not want to cross the diplomatic Rubicon even by appearing to be disrespectful of Canada's policy of "neutrality" and "noninterference" in the case of the Pakistan issue.

While responding to the questions asked by his colleagues in the Commons, Sharp was mindful of George's cautionary notes. He remembered what George recommended, "a low profile for Cda [Canada] on this [recognition] issue at least until we can see more clearly than we can at present whether or not Bangla Desh liberation forces are going to win enough control to be candidates for eventual recognition as a separate state. Against that contingency, we should consider our relationships with GOI [government of India] and GOP [government of Pakistan] and one day with Bangla Desh. Meantime, the safest ground is a humanitarian concern, a plea for restraint and peaceful (i.e., political) settlement."[68] Sharp concurred with his advisers and reacted accordingly.

Sharp's curt responses concerning Canada's policy of non-interference in the internal affairs of another country are understandable when one recalls Canada's own experience in the Nigeria–Biafra conflict (1967-1970) only a few years ago, alluded to in Chapter 8. Canada's nonintervention in Nigeria, despite all the best of intentions, was not only disappointing but also an embarrassing experience. Sharp's determination not to intervene and its potential usefulness is understandable once put in the context of the previous ignominious experience. Naturally, Canada was mindful of the Nigerian government's ultimate accusation of foreign agencies of grave violation of their humanitarian charter, or for that matter, of gunrunning to Biafra during the civil war in Nigeria to further complicate the situation, making Canada doubly cautious. Unsurprisingly, therefore, even Prime Minister Trudeau did not hesitate to remind his colleagues of the fallout of the Nigerian-Biafran crisis only sixteen months earlier: "Canadians possess no secret formula for concluding wars; they are not gifted with any divine guidance into the rights and wrongs of the arguments of strangers. However, Canadians believe political quarrels cannot be successfully concluded on the battlefield."[69]

Although Canada did not feel the need for a significant pronouncement on the Pakistan issue, at least initially, when more news of massacre and rebellion began to become public, the debates and discussions on the East Pakistan Crisis, however, began to be more specific. The MPs did their homework to learn more about the sociopolitical history of the subcontinent, especially since the partition of India in 1947. They appreciated the sadness with which an extra cautious Sharp expressed Canada's concerns about the tragic happenings. As Sharp saw the situation, the American involvement in Vietnam had given the principle of "non-intervention" in the affairs of another country a cachet. Sharp was faced with a barrage of questions as to *what steps Canada was ready to take* considering the fast-changing deteriorating situation in East Pakistan from where thousands of Bengalis were pouring into the Indian States of West Bengal, Tripura, Bihar, Meghalaya, Madhya Pradesh, and Uttar Pradesh. A determined Sharp put forward the government's *raison d'être* for noninterference—that it would be *inappropriate* to be involved in the internal affairs of Pakistan. Canada remained wary enough not to be seen to be "interfering." Trudeau himself never hesitated to seek advice from his colleagues.

In the meantime, David Lewis, who became the NDP leader in April 1971, took some time to have an expanded understanding of the subcontinental polity from a Canadian perspective. Lewis then initiated a new round of debate armed with the argument that the issue ought to be looked at from the point of view of *military domination vs. stifling of the democratic processes.* He courageously argued that it was understandable and natural that the House was reluctant to hold any discussions on the internal affairs of Pakistan. Therefore, there was no pointing of fingers at anyone. Suddenly, Lewis began to question Canada's position, seeing that the military repression had been continuing, resulting in an ongoing exodus of the Bengalis. However, thus far, he had adhered to the government's neutrality policy and noninterference. Seeing that the situation had passed the stage of diplomatic niceties and that it was time to stand up and be counted in opposing the repressive forces of Yahya, Lewis observed, "We ought not always to remain neutral in these obvious situations of evil doing by military colonels and the like. I suggest that Canada ought now to terminate all military deliveries to Pakistan as well as the economic aid that now goes to that country." [70]

Lewis's emotionally charged speech caused a bit of a wave in the House. He immediately took full advantage of the momentum and urged the government to *condemn the Yahya government* and act regarding (1) economic aid and (2) military supply. He then went on to say, "When we continue to give military and economic aid, what we are enabling the present government of Pakistan to do is to use the foreign currency it might need to purchase things in the world to add to its military strength to continue to oppress not only the people of East Pakistan but of West Pakistan as well."[71] The MPs calmly heard Lewis's overly dramatic oratory without interruption as he went on in hyperbolic terms. It turned out that the momentum Lewis created at the beginning did not last long. Lewis's histrionic pitch fell flat, creating a lull in the House.

In the meantime, seeing the ongoing military reprisals, many MPs became frustrated as they found the sheer number of killings and ceaseless military brutalities in East Pakistan very disturbing. They wondered how that could be characterized as an "internal affair" in Pakistan. The MPs recalled that this question was also raised by the Gandhi administration, which asserted around the same time to all the heads of state that India could no longer accept the position that the situation in East Pakistan was an internal affair of Pakistan. Canadian parliamentarians were placed in an awkward situation as they recognized that India's claim resonated with the Canadian public. On the one hand, they felt that they must raise the matter regarding Canada's involvement; on the other hand, they also realized that there might be danger in any discussion along these lines. They became more conscious of the sensitivities of the Yahya regime. All through the crisis period, Sharp, therefore, remained extremely uncomfortable being mindful of Trudeau's earlier remark in the "internal affairs" of a country: "To intervene when not asked, however, would not be an act of courage; it would be seen as an act of stupidity."[72]

Ideological Constraints and the Fear of the Québec Question

The much-used term, Canada's fear of the "Québec question," in the present case, meant Canada's fear of the Québec's rising sense of *nationalism* and *demand for independence*. Since the Trudeau administration was still dealing with the fallout of the 1970 FLQ (Front de libération du Québec) crisis, it feared the seriousness of the issue in Canada in general and Québec in particular. Throughout the period covering the Liberation War of Bangladesh, the Trudeau administration was still seeking to find the right approach for Canada to the problem of Québec's place in the Confederation and the world. It favored the pan-Canadian vision of Canada, in which the francophones were French-speaking Canadians rather than people identified with a distinctive society and culture that would flourish in Québec.

To appreciate Canada's taciturnity in discussing the issues of separation and/or independence during the Bengalis' fight for an independent homeland of their own, one needs to have a good understanding of the historical forces that inhibited Canadian parliamentarians. On the first day of the session, following the imposition of martial law in East Pakistan, the term "separation" came up only once. This was in response to NDP Douglas's question regarding resolving the conflict by "constitutional means."[73] One must not "oversimplify the situation" was Sharp's immediate cautionary remark. This was the extent of discussion on the separation of East Pakistan on that day until the NDP Brewin brought up the topic again after eight long months in November 1971.

Fortunately for the Trudeau administration, due to Canada's policy constraints, Canadians became heedful enough to recognize the potential trouble that Canada *could be in* with the demands of the Québec separatists. Such thoughts prompted most MPs to understand that what was going on in Pakistan was still regarded as her "internal affairs" and that no one should reference the separation movement at home in Québec. Unsurprisingly, the debates demonstrate a high level of cooperation between the government and the opposition MPs in addressing what they called the East Pakistan Crisis from various perspectives, respecting Canada's mediatory role. Within weeks, however, Ottawa officials were already in close contact with the government of Pakistan and other countries that were interested in reaching a solution. "It is our view that through close collaboration with other countries, we can contribute most effectively to creating conditions in which a political settlement will be possible. The ultimate responsibility for reaching that political settlement rests with the contending parties."[74] Thus, Barnett Danson, parliamentary secretary to the prime minister, observed.

Again, it is also essential to look at what was happening nationally at the New Democratic Party (NDP) convention held only three weeks following the March 25 military crackdown in East Pakistan. Fortuitously, one of the complicating factors in the Canada-Québec relationship was the reports on the contentious debates that dominated the NDP leadership race. Internationally, by this time, of course, Yahya had unequivocally blamed the first elected leader of Pakistan, Bongobondhu, calling him an "enemy of Pakistan" whom he alleged to have been involved in a secessionist movement with the help of India. Yahya's much-quoted statement that he had asked the military to "do its job" had been on the news for days as he tried to defend his ruthless actions. With the commencement of the NDP national convention, some issues became a source of concern for all Canadians, including the government. Nationally, everyone in Canada came to know *how* and under *what* circumstances the delegates to the

NDP convention rejected the contentious version of self-determination championed by the Waffle movement[75] and the party's small Québec wing—a concept often considered a cloak for separatist tendencies. In Chapter 8, we shall see the Trudeau administration's awkwardness in even broaching the subject for a public debate.

The federalists feared that such news items would only help whip up ultranationalism among the separatists at the cost of Canadian unity that had constantly been threatened by ethnic heterogeneity, provincial autonomy, and the existence of widely separated regions, each with close informal ties to adjacent areas, in the US, etc. Historically, the NDP's call in 1968 - 1969 for a federal system in which Québec's relations with Ottawa had differed from those of other provinces in certain spheres, in effect, had limited *de-facto* status. The NDP MP Edward Broadbent, for Oshawa-Whitby, then a leadership contender and NDP's social-democratic politician, argued along the same vein that "a positive resolution should be adopted by the party," having reinforced his view by stating that "the unequivocal right to independence must reside in the people of Quebec."[76] Fortunately for the government, no questions were generated in the House or Senate since Canadian parliamentarians were unprepared to discuss the separation issue.

The retiring party leader, NDP Douglas, also made no direct reference to the radical Waffle wing of the party. Instead, in his farewell speech, he made a strong plea to the delegates for *Canadian unity* and the *prevention of Canada's disintegration* from within when there was much discussion in the news on *national unity* and the need for the *integration of Pakistan*. It was disturbing to the Trudeau government during the leadership convention debate to see how the contentious Québec issue had persistently remained on the public's mind. Naturally, the NDP delegates, as well as the MPs in the House, being suspicious about it, purposefully did not allude to the case of the Pakistan-Bangladesh conflict - Bongobondhu's call for an independent Bangladesh or to the formation of the provisional government of Bangladesh in India.

Since the news of the Pakistan-Bangladesh conflict, which the government consistently referred to as the East Pakistan issue, appeared every day in the news, the government feared that the natural reaction of the Canadians would be to instantly draw a parallel between the Québec separatists and the Bengali freedom fighters without thoroughly examining the actual dissimilarities of the situation in Canada. Unsurprisingly, after the April 1971 NDP convention, serious discussions began nationwide on *the people of Québec's right to self-determination.* Having continued his argument along the same vein, NDP's Broadbent observed, "Recognition of the right to self-determination implies that, in the event of a democratic decision in Québec in favour of breaking the federal tie, people would seek to negotiate the conditions of an honest separation rather than try to defeat the popular verdict by force."[77]

In their discussions, the MPs used the term "civil war" consistently and very carefully avoided asking any questions regarding whether the voters in East Pakistan thought they were voting for complete "autonomy" in that there would be two separate nations - East Pakistan and West Pakistan; or whether they were only voting for a separate province as part of a federal system within the framework of *one Pakistan.* There existed a note of warning among politicians of all-party backgrounds who remained on guard by avoiding questions regarding the "separation" and/or "independence" of East Pakistan. Canadian parliamentarians were fearful that the Québec separatists might very quickly, perhaps erroneously, find a nexus, even remotely, to the events in East Pakistan. The government remained determined to avoid discussing "secession" or an "independence movement."

The debate, therefore, reveals that Canada neither knowingly nor openly promoted the breakup of Pakistan, nor did Canada endorse the Bengalis' support for a movement that would break the country (Pakistan). The Trudeau administration remained vigilant. Despite having questions, the MPs did not wish to cause any wave in the House. The sensitivity surrounding the topic was such that the MPs purposefully did not want to discuss whether the separation movement had been thrust upon the Bengalis or whether the said movement was an armed uprising aimed at materializing the results of the 1970 National Elections. They also did not wish to discuss whether such a movement for the disintegration of Pakistan should be condoned or suppressed, or, for that matter, whether the Bengalis' claim for independence was legally and morally incontestable or not.

The debates also reveal that, within a reasonably short time, Canadian parliamentarians identified the *real issue* between the two wings of Pakistan, the west represented by the military regime (Yahya government), and the east by the rebel forces under Bongobondhu's leadership. According to the Trudeau administration, the conflict should not be categorized as an Indo-Pakistan issue since the conflict was about power sharing through the granting of greater autonomy and the regime's undeclared plan not to transfer power to the leader (Bongobondhu) despite his electoral victory. Canadian parliamentarians of all political stripes were on the same page, recognizing the root reason. Therefore, most MPs broached the subject carefully by referring to the need to establish democracy and political stability by respecting the results of the previous year's National Elections. They also emphasized the *immediate humanitarian needs of the refugees,* which was the Trudeau administration's top priority.

However, the overriding fear of the Québec question kept creeping into Canadian politicians' minds while debating in the Commons and Senate. Deep down, they knew that it was only *a perceived fear* because Canadian parliamentarians had already picked up enough knowledge to recognize the fact that the very context between the Bengalis' demand for independence and the demand of the people of Québec were different and that the FLQ crisis could not be compared to the Bengali *Mukti Bahini* (Liberation Forces). On the one hand, at one point, the Trudeau administration was relieved to see how the Canadian public also came up to speed to recognize the difference between the two scenarios. On the other hand, at another time, it worried about the possibility of a renewed sense of Québec nationalism at the cost of Canadian unity.

Naturally, the angst on the part of the Trudeau administration was such that neither the government nor Canadian parliamentarians wanted to take a chance. However, with increased familiarity with the *differentness* in the context, personally, Trudeau began to feel a bit better that the knowledge gap among the Canadian public was being filled. When Trudeau referred to the FLQ members' movement as "an armed revolutionary movement that is bent on destroying the basis of our [Canada's] freedom,"[78] Canadians, in general, did not look for a nexus between the Québec sovereigntists and the Bengali freedom fighters who were fighting the despotic military regime for freedom - the liberation of their native land.

Unfortunately, the Trudeau administration's sense of relief was short-lived. Soon, the government came to realize that although the public became aware of the different context between the objective of the Bengali freedom fighters and FLQ members, for many MPs and senators, the idea of separation of Québec was still unacceptable for which it became a perturbing issue to them. What was even more scary was that the Trudeau administration was aware that the Canadian forces in Québec already had several separatists, and more were applying to join the Canadian forces.[79]

While the Pakistan-Bangladesh conflict was not mentioned, the issue of the separation of East Pakistan remained in the sentiments of some like-minded MPs and senators. Not surprisingly, whether or not Québec should ban the right to secede had been a distressingly shocking topic that was on the minds of these parliamentarians even though they did not wish to be engaged in a formal discussion on it.

The notion of "separation," thus, remained a nagging question for many parliamentarians. Senators Paul Desruisseaux and Jacques Flynn, the opposition leaders, for example, did not hesitate to speak their minds. Himself a federalist Québecer, Desruisseaux, having expressed his shock, surprise, and discomfort, alluded to the report of a recent gallop poll which revealed the Canadians' views on separation. "The question put was this: Should Québec have the right to separate from Confederation?"[80] He said that "nationally, 40 percent said that they thought Québec should be allowed to separate; both in the Maritimes and Ontario, 41 percent thought Québec should be allowed to separate; and in the West, 40 percent thought so. In Québec, the controversial province in the eyes of so many, 30 percent thought that Québec should be allowed to separate."[81]

Similarly, a Québecer, Senator Flynn argued that he was "entirely and definitely in favour of Québec remaining within Canada." However, he was "in favour of self-determination where conditions exist as outlined in the Charter of United Nations."[82] "If a definite majority of Québec should decide to secede, the rest of Canada could not oppose it. This does not mean that I support separation. That is entirely different,"[83] thus, argued Flynn. As the debates continued, Flynn elaborated again, "I am quite sure that if there is one province in Canada with the nature of a distinct entity, it is Québec. Whether you like it or not, that is the case. There is a majority of French-speaking Canadians in Québec; there are borders that delimit Québec, even if you could extend these borders into New Brunswick or the northern part of Ontario. So, from the standpoint of both geography and demography, Québec can form an entity. Those are the principles of the basis of self-determination. You have to comply with these basic principles or basic conditions, and I suggest that you have them in Québec."[84] Although Flynn spoke forcefully, giving his view regarding the right of self-determination, he did not wish to continue further discussion.

In a sense, the issue of separation and/or national unity of Pakistan remained very much in the background that preoccupied many Canadian parliamentarians, even though no reference was made to the case of the

Bengalis' struggle for independence. Senator Paul Martin also claimed that he had lived practically all his life in the context of problems relating to the demands of the people of Québec. "It was the problem that faced Laurier when he became Prime Minister in 1896. That same problem faced him in his confrontation with Henri Bourassa in 1911. The dimensions may have differed, but the issue was the same." [85]

Perhaps one of the reasons why Canadian parliamentarians broached the issue of separation so frequently was that just about the same time, several informed responses to a pollster became publicly available. As it turned out, the publication of the results of a few polls on the *right of Québec to separate* outraged many Canadians, including parliamentarians. Naturally, this became a source of apprehension to the government, to whom the responses conflicted with both the *concept of the Canadian Confederation* and the Canadians' *idea of national unity*. It was both annoyingly alarming and intensely mind-boggling for the government since the results of these gallop polls had appeared for days in several newspapers nationwide. Naturally, news of this nature dominated the domestic politics of Canada for some time.

While it is difficult to say to what extent the Canadians, in general, were quivery about Canada's national disintegration, many Canadians across the country remained inhibited by the fear of Québec separation during the Liberation War of Bangladesh. We saw this aspect of public sentiment in Chapter 4. Sharp remained disturbed due to his obsessive thoughts regarding the Québec question. The government's consternation is reflected in how Sharp went around in the House while responding to the frequently asked questions on the East Pakistan Crisis. On every occasion, a disturbed Sharp's strategy was to impress upon the Yahya regime, especially about the dreadful consequences of failure to reconcile with the majority party's leader, Bongobondhu. He also informed the House that he had been continually seeking opportunities to raise his foreboding with the Pakistani authorities and with members of the Commonwealth. Following consultation with Canada's high commissioners to Pakistan and India, Ottawa concluded that accusations and counteraccusations in martial languages would continue, and so would Yahya's accusation that the separatist Bengalis were receiving assistance from India to dismember Pakistan.

At that time, an alternative soft term, "self-determination," also appeared in certain MPs' vocabulary. The Trudeau administration, however, remained uptight by the very thought that broadening the discussion along the line of self-determination, whether it concerned Ukraine in the USSR, the Bengalis in East Pakistan, or Québecois in Québec, could instantly open a can of worms. Ottawa's fear was reinforced in the summer when the Québec separatists were seen carrying placards in Parliament Hill in support of the independence of Bangladesh. Ottawa officials did not want to take a chance as they believed the Québec nationalists could perhaps identify themselves with the Bengali nationalists even though the scenario was different. Such angst and anxiety made the government think it would create many legal questions about Québec and Canada. Ottawa noted that by the end of May 1971, the movement for an independent Bangladesh had already gained respectability by generating a profound commitment to an independent country of its own among the repressed Bengalis. As a middle power with no direct stake in the subcontinent, Canada chose not to consider the Bangladesh phenomenon as Canada did not yet have a strategic game plan.

Naturally, the MPs and senators remained extremely circumspect in ensuring they did not invite any questions regarding the vulnerable situation in East Pakistan. Since Canada favored democracy, she fully supported the Bengalis' fight for democracy. Canada has always supported freedom and democracy at any cost, everywhere in the world. As the Canadian parliamentarians saw it, it was not a question of whether the military regime attacked the Bengali civilians first or the rebel forces attacked the army. Regardless of who did it first, the fact of the matter is that, for their defense, the Bengalis jumped the gun, *having declared the independence of East Pakistan out of a united Pakistan.* Consequently, by then, the conflict had manifested another dimension. Both government officials and Canadian parliamentarians genuinely feared that once the topic was broached in Parliament or the news media, it would undoubtedly generate disturbing debates that might involve the aspirations of the people of Québec. They had *bona fide* reasons to be afraid that the emotionally charged separatists in Québec would be inclined to view the events of East Pakistan against the backdrop of Quebec's demand for separation regardless of politically dissimilar circumstances.

Again, there appeared to be another factor that inhibited the debates in the House. This had to do with Trudeau's statement during his visit to the Soviet Union between May 17 and 28, where he held discussions on world peace and security. Ironically enough, when the two government representatives discussed renunciation of the use of force or the threat of force *vis-à-vis* the settlement of disputes by peaceful means and noninterference in the internal affairs of a country, the Ukrainians under the Soviet Union were still fighting for a separate homeland of their own. Upon his return, and much to the tension of the politicians, Trudeau found himself embroiled in a debate regarding one of his remarks about Ukrainians. The MPs noted with alarm how journalists and, more importantly, the Ukrainian Canadian Committee, which represented about thirty organizations reflecting the voices of over a million Canadian citizens of Ukrainian descent in Canada, were outraged by Trudeau's alleged comparison of the Ukrainians' fight for freedom with the motives of the FLQ members. Many national newspapers, such as the *Toronto Star*, *The Globe and Mail*, *Winnipeg Free Press*, and *Windsor Star*, immediately denounced the comparison as unjust and urged the prime minister to retract his statement and other aspersions.

The Ukrainian Canadian Committee immediately presented a strongly worded memorandum to the prime minister urging them to correct the unfortunate impression he had about the legitimate aspirations of the Ukrainian people. The next day, it was widely reported that the prime minister had said he was sorry that their feelings had been hurt. Immediately taking an issue with Trudeau, Senator Paul Yuzyk paraphrased Trudeau's statement in the Senate: "I was rather sure that their feelings had been hurt by people who misrepresented what I said rather than what I said in fact."[86] Yuzyk argued that the Ukrainians were legally struggling for their just rights and freedom and that they "were sentenced illegally and unconstitutionally in secret trials, on the same basis with the subversive and revolutionary FLQ."[87] Yuzyk argued that there could be no comparison between the Ukrainian freedom fighters and the supporters of the FLQ.

Whether it was Senator Yuzyk or Prime Minister Trudeau, all were doubly careful in ensuring that the Pakistan-Bangladesh issue was not to be mentioned even though the same problem was appearing in the news now and then. Senator Yuzyk eloquently articulated Canada's wish to uphold *freedom* and *democracy*, which past generations had won. Being more emphatic in expressing his views, he warned his fellow Canadians to remain vigilant to preserve the Canadian way of life. As far as Trudeau was concerned, there was no attempt on his part to put the FLQ on a parallel with the Ukrainian nationalists: "My position in the Soviet Union or Canada is that anyone who breaks the law to assert his nationalism does not get too much from me."[88] A frustrated Yuzyk said, "The defense of freedom, democracy, justice, and peace must always be the cornerstone of the Canadian foreign policy." [89]

In a sense, as noted, Ottawa's foreign affairs cognoscenti believed that any discussion on topics such as "separation" and/or "independence" of Bangladesh might encourage Québecers to look for a nexus between the *East Pakistan crisis* and *the separation of Québec,* regardless of the different political context. Naturally, they also saw direct endorsement as a two-edged sword likely to cause more harm than good at home and abroad. They remained extraordinarily cautious in their official reaction to the events. Simply put, the entire issue seemed too delicate to the Canadian parliamentarians, who seemed unprepared to initiate any debate on East Pakistan's political situation.

Around that time, Canadians of Ukrainian origin were preparing to celebrate the eightieth anniversary of their settlement in Canada. Their representatives held an informal meeting with Mitchell Sharp. When the news of Sharp's meeting with the Ukrainian Canadians came to the attention of Boris Miroshnichenko, the Soviet ambassador to Canada, he was so furious that he called Sharp immediately. Sharp recalled the telephone call from the Soviet ambassador, who was unhappy to hear about the meeting. Expressing his profound dissatisfaction and deep anger, an enraged ambassador warned Sharp that he would, for sure, immediately instigate the Québec separatists to stand up for their right to separate from Canada - that it would ignite a firestorm in Québec. Sharp recalled this single phone call that prompted him to broach the matter with Prime Minister Trudeau, who, upon hearing the matter, said, "That's your shop. You're the Foreign Affairs minister. You deal with it." [90]

Despite their knowledge of the *political situation differences,* the government and parliamentarians feared that this would open a Pandora's Box. Being doubly alert, they did not wish to broach the Pakistan-Bangladesh conflict under any circumstances. In that sense, one could say that there was an unwritten understanding among Ottawa officials and parliamentarians that an open endorsement of the nationalist cause of the Bengalis might provoke the Québec nationalists at home. In addition, Canadians had also been desperately attempting to find a broadly acceptable definition of *national unity* within Canada, though with no success. It was within their memory to recall how, in the 1960s, the independence of several underdeveloped nations, one after another, encouraged French Canadian separatists to make their demands more vigorously. Despite the dissimilarities, the government felt haunted by the memories of the kidnapping and subsequent murdering of Québec's labour minister Pierre Laporte by the FLQ members during last year's October crisis.

The Legitimacy of the Yahya Regime

Canada's cordial relationship with Pakistan and certain ideological constraints did not encourage Canadian politicians to talk about the *constitutional legitimacy* of the military government openly either. Canadian public and their political representatives viewed the East Pakistan Issue in a broader context, more along the lines of violating human rights, civil liberties, political rights, or negating democratic rights. The question of legitimacy, however, came up a few times during the debates. It was not until ten weeks of military repression had passed that the Conservative MP Robert N. Thompson for Red Deer, Alberta, raised a straightforward question concerning the legitimacy of the Yahya government. "Is it the position of the government that the present military government of Pakistan is the legitimate government of Pakistan?" [91]

A direct question such as the present one, the kind of which had so far been carefully avoided by the MPs, must have unsettled the Speaker himself, who immediately intervened in the following manner: "It seems to me that the question asked is an invitation to express an opinion or to make a statement of policy. I appreciate that it is a little difficult to draw the line." [92] The Speaker, however, continued in the same breath: "On reflection, it would seem that the question asked by the honorable member is acceptable." [93] Trudeau, who was present in the House, responded quickly, "We recognize no other government than the government of Pakistan." [94]

Nobody went further to discuss whether Yahya did have the right, expressly or by implication, to abandon the results of the 1970 National Elections in which the majority voted freely for the establishment of a constitutional regime based on the Six-Point Program, nor did anyone ask whether the Yahya government did have the lawful authority to overturn the electoral verdict in favor of greater autonomy. There was no debate on the legitimacy of the Yahya regime in East Pakistan. A sigh of relief was noticeable as the discussions centered around other issues of importance to Canadians domestically.

Continuing Economic Aid to Avert Famine

Canada's palpable foreboding about the food situation and commitment to alleviate the conditions of the refugees were reflected in how the MPs pleaded for ongoing assistance to the victims of atrocities and the development of a comprehensive plan to avert famine. A concerned NDP MP, Douglas, having wondered if the allocated resources by his government were adequate at a time of rapid deterioration of the situation, asked the minister, "Whether or not the Canadian government intends to increase the amount of money which it prepared to make available for refugee work in that area?"[95] While discussion regarding food shortage was going on, an undercover report of a recent rendezvous of the London-based *The Times'* Peter Hazelhurst with Tajuddin Ahmed, acting prime minister of the provisional government of the People's Republic of Bangladesh, was widely published in world newspapers, including many Canadian dailies. The public was touched by Ahmed's appeal to major powers to discontinue all aid to West Pakistan. Again, seeing that the situation had rapidly been fast-deteriorating due to continuing military reprisals, the NDP David Lewis raised his concern about what he considered as *inadequate humanitarian assistance* regarding the adequacy of food supplies.

Earlier, Canadians had read in *The Globe and Mail*'s Letters to the Editor column arguments put forward by a few concerned Canadian public regarding economic aid to Pakistan: "Any aid to West Pakistan will be used indirectly to kill my people. If aid is to be sent to Bangla Desh, it should be distributed by international agencies there and not by the Pakistani junta,"[96] a Canadian wrote in the paper. As far as Lewis was concerned, he was echoing a few apprehensions and fears voiced by many, including those who had raised the same concerns immediately following the imposition of martial law. Like Lewis, the NDP Andrew Brewin was also concerned about the use or, more appropriately, abuse of Canadian aid by the military regime. He, too, inquired whether "an effort [was] being made to assure that Canadian aid is not used to bolster the military repression of East Pakistan?"[97]

In one of his most moving and eloquent appeals, Macquarrie again urged the government to continue its efforts in aiding the Bengali victims: "Surely we have reached a stage of civilization where the victims of a war, which is not an international conflict but is designated as a civil war, should not be insulated from the kind of humanitarian help which people outside the country seek to provide."[98] In a sense, Macquarrie's appeal reflected the concerns of the Canadians in the face of the ongoing military repression and the resultant flight of the frightened Bengali civilians to India.

The Trudeau government was both conscious and appreciative of the fact that India had been placed in a difficult situation, having to shelter and feed the millions of Bengalis who were continually escaping to India. "The government accepts without hesitation that the financial burden of providing relief cannot be borne by India alone. To help meet the urgent needs in West Bengal and other border states, the government is providing $2 million in relief supplies, including foodstuffs, medicines, and medical supplies and cash contributions."[99] Thus, having quickly acknowledged his colleagues' concerns, Sharp informed them further of Canada's commitment: "This $2 million is a supplementary contribution to the international emergency relief appropriation and will not affect the bilateral development assistance program for India."[100] Two days later, on May 31, 1971, Sharp again pointed out that this was in addition to the earlier contribution of $50,000 to the Canadian Red Cross, supplementing its gift of $10,000 to the Indian Red Cross for relief to refugees.

Macquarrie was pleased to welcome the government's approval of it. Nevertheless, he indicated that he could not "judge as to the adequacy of the amount of $2 million" and how it related "to the magnitude of the problem."[101] Stanley Knowles, NDP MP for Winnipeg North Centre, also welcomed the contribution and stated that he would "trust that if events prove that an even larger contribution from Canada is required, the government will give favourable consideration to it."[102] Canada, a Good Samaritan country, did not remain a spectator, being gravely concerned about what Macquarrie called "the ominous portents of famine in East Pakistan."[103] The Trudeau administration's prompt action in this regard reflects the public's demand as well as Canada's willingness to assist the Bengali victims of military persecution.

Throughout the question period, Sharp tried to remain calm even though he was under constant pressure while explaining the government's general policy. He informed his colleagues that no donor country would enter any new commitment with the government of Pakistan but would continue to carry on with those commitments made before the military takeover. There was unanimity among the politicians of all parties to the government's conscious decision to abide by existing commitments rather than withdrawing the already approved aid. A strong-willed Sharp remained decisive when faced with a hard choice. To help his colleagues appreciate the situation, Sharp put forward his government's raison d'être: "As far as aid is concerned, it is an exceedingly difficult question of judgment how far to go in providing aid under these circumstances ... We certainly do not want to cause additional hardship to any of the people of Pakistan, in the east or west, by denying projects that can be of immediate assistance. Nevertheless, it is recognized that the aid must be seen as going toward helping the people on both sides." [104]

Sharp emphasized the importance of understanding the conditions under which sanctions might have desirable effects, as well as how they might also turn out to be counterproductive despite having the best of intentions. Sanctions tend to cause the most harm to the most vulnerable segments of the population, and as such, concerning the case of East Pakistan, it would be the Bengalis who would be the first victims of the sanctions, argued Sharp. He also underscored that perhaps not everyone in East Pakistan would suffer equally or in the same way, but most of the Bengalis would suffer. Sharp was not convinced that, being what it was, it would be practically impossible for Canada alone to craft a package of sanctions that would be forceful enough to cause the Yahya regime to reverse its course of action. Based on his years of experience, Sharp believed that in many circumstances, once imposed, sanctions tend to make regimes more recalcitrant. Since there were no follow-up questions following Sharp's explanation, one may see it as a tacit support of what he suggested.

By the beginning of June 1971, the MPs were back again to revisit the adequacy of the Canadian allocation of $2 million. In the face of immense tragedy and dire needs, Macquarrie's appeal was that "it is time to look at the question again to seek new avenues for translating the concern of the Canadian people into action by their government."[105] On June 22, he asked again, "If the government is considering the East Pakistan[i] refugee, which now works out at about 30 cents for the suffering people?"[106] Sharp quickly responded, "The government is considering the whole question of further help to the refugees and also looking at the question of whether there can be some humanitarian relief in East Pakistan itself. I would remind the honorable member that proportionately, Canada is one of the most generous contributors in this field."[107]

Again, concerning a question from Conservative MP for Wellington-Grey, William Marvin Howe, about the possibility of supplying mobile hospital units in cooperation with the Department of Health and Welfare Canada, Sharp was very prompt. He informed the member, "We have been trying to respond to the priorities established in India. As I think I reported to the House, we did provide some planes, and they took some ambulances provided by the government of Ontario. However, we will look at this suggestion in light of the priorities established on the spot."[108]

Tied to the debate was the report of the three MPs who went to Pakistan and India (described in detail in Chapter 7). The delegates' visit to India and Pakistan gave them a chance to hear from the actual victims as well as the representatives of the military authority. In addition to uncovering new dimensions of the various political cultures of Pakistan under military rule, the report summed up the dire need for aid money for the refugees in India and displaced persons within East Pakistan. Canadian delegates became more appreciative of their government's decision to continue economic assistance to both wings of Pakistan, although a few in the House had certain reservations about it. Even though the Canadian delegates characterized the events in Pakistan as a "grim and gripping human tragedy,"[109] Canadian parliamentarians did not want to debate the matter in the House.

The debates, however, continued slowly but cautiously. The opposition colleagues supported Sharp's reaction and believed it was the right thing to do - *not impose sanctions*. We may recall that when the question of Canadian aid was raised earlier in the spring, Sharp assured the House that the government would provide assistance *only to help economically* and that it was not going to *enter any new commitments* but would carry on with those that had already been made before the military takeover. However, the Bengali-speaking segment of the Canadian public was demanding full sanction. By then, a conscientious Sharp also reminded his colleagues that Canada, as a member of the Aid to Pakistan Consortium, had explored with the International Bank of Reconstruction and Development (IBRD) and the International Monetary Fund (IMF) and learned that they would be seeking appropriate arrangements regarding aid development. Sharp also informed his colleagues that there was a consensus among the consortium members *that aid for development programs should be continued*. Sharp was happy to share these few "feel good" news bits with his colleagues in the House, who supported him.

Again, at the beginning of the fall session, amid stress and tension, Sharp was pleased to announce that Canada, through her involvement with the UN, had provided "a grant of $500,000" in response to the "appeal to assist with the administrative costs being incurred by the United Nations." [110] Sharp also informed the House that it was hoped that the cash donation would help finance approximately 180 technical and relief experts that the UN was sending to East Pakistan to identify relief priorities and enhance the efficiency of relief distribution in the affected areas. As time passed, and being on the qui vive, a resilient Sharp found ways to withstand the pressure and respond satisfactorily to the queries regarding economic assistance for the ongoing relief operations in India.

In the meantime, Macquarrie made more inquiries regarding sending some dried potatoes to supplement the food aid program in India. "In light of the serious marketing difficulties of the potato growers of eastern Canada and considering the terrible food shortage among Pakistani refugees in India, is the minister considering taking some initiative in assisting in a crash program to provide vast quantities of dried instant potatoes to the people in dire need in India as requested by Oxfam of Canada?"[111] Marcel Lessard, parliamentary secretary to the minister of Agriculture, immediately responded positively in the absence of his superior by saying, "We will be pleased to comply with his request since there seems to be a surplus on the market at this time." [112]

On November 17, 1971, in one of his most celebrated speeches in the Commons, Sharp outlined his government's contribution to economic aid for relief and rehabilitation: "To date, the Canadian contributions from governmental and nongovernmental sources for refugees in India amounted to $6.6 million. Of this sum, $4.3 million was provided by the federal government, $370.000 by the provinces, and 1.9 million by voluntary agencies and the Combined Appeal for Pakistan Relief (CAPR). The government intends to supplement these contributions by an amount of $1.8 million, seeking the authority and funds from Parliament. This will bring the Canadian government's total contribution for the relief of refugees in India to $22 million, coincidentally representing approximately one dollar for every Canadian. ... In addition to the funds provided for refugees in India, Canada has contributed $7 million in food aid through the World Food Program for the relief of suffering in East Pakistan and provided to the UN $500,000 to help defray the cost of UN relief operations there." [113]

Like all other Canadian parliamentarians, Macquarrie was happy to have recognized India's economic burden. Nevertheless, he reminded the government of the need to continue to assist India to the extent possible. "The world must know that the Indian burden is immense and must be taxing the capacity of that country, and thus, we cannot overlook any avenue of assistance." [114] This was in line with Sharp's thinking, which, on sundry occasions, stated this. Fortunately for the Trudeau administration, the MPs were mindful of Sharp's remark that "one of the purposes of the Canadian government" had always been "to try to keep politics out of humanitarian endeavors." [115] Overall, the MPs, who represented the Canadian public through their constituencies, were satisfied with Sharp's position and believed that the resources should be used appropriately. There were no further discussions on this subject until the liberation of Bangladesh had been achieved.

Suspension of Military Supplies

All through the debates, Sharp remained firm in his position regarding "no supply of arms to Pakistan" and demonstrated Canada's "neutrality" without taking any "sides." Canadian parliamentarians, both the MPs and senators, supported the government's stand on the *non-shipment of spare parts to Pakistan*. It was their collective suspicion that the Yahya regime was likely to use arms against its people in East Pakistan. Canada's firm position to suspend military supplies, however, stood in contrast to President Richard Nixon's position - a far more one-sided position about the shipment of arms since the outbreak of the armed struggle in East Pakistan. Having known about the US double standard in this matter, Canadian politicians and the public alike remained vigilant to find out *when* and *how* the US was secretly shipping cargoes of military equipment to Pakistan. However, a few MPs in the House remained a bit *confused* and apprehensive regarding Canada's stand. They demanded Canada's *unequivocal position* on the Indo-Pakistan conflict based on Canada's actions thus far. Since the government had not announced a declaratory position, they claimed they needed to be sure about Canada's indisputable stand regarding *economic aid* and *suspension of military supplies*. The opposition MPs kept Sharp under pressure.

Continuing along the same vein, Réal Caouette, Social Credit Party MP for Témiscamingue and leader of the Ralliement des créditistes du Canada asked Sharp point-blank, "Has he received from the Bangla Desh Association of Canada a telegram containing the following allegation: '*We* suspect Canadian arms are also going to be shipped to Pakistan.' Is he able to assure the House that no Canadian arms will be shipped to Pakistan?"[116] Sharp's immediate response was in the affirmative, stating that he had received such a telegram. He then went on to assure his colleagues that "no export permits for arms have been issued for some time now because of the situation in that part of the world and, so far as I am aware, there will be no arms shipments from Canada on that ship." [117]

The next day, on June 29, having heard about the secret shipment of arms to Pakistan by the Nixon administration, Caouette raised the issue again, given that there were all kinds of rumors. He said he just wished to be sure about the latest situation about Canada's position. He wanted to know again whether the secretary of State had any update. He asked whether there was "any new information today on this subject. Is he in a position to affirm that no Canadian arms have been shipped or loaded on the *Padma*?" [118] Sharp's instant response was, "Instructions have been issued that no militarily sensitive items are to be loaded aboard the *Padma*." [119] Canadian parliamentarians felt reassured that steps were being taken to ensure that Canada was sending no arms and that Canada's noninterference policy was strictly adhered to. At that time, Macquarrie, who had been very keen on this subject, directed another question concerning armed shipment by others—whether Maritime Aircraft and Repair Limited was granted an export permit. Sharp patiently explained the process, saying that sometimes permits are given in advance when an application is made but are always subject to suspension or cancellation. He said, "In this instance, the export permit has been suspended." [120]

In the meantime, the news of Pakistan's reaction to the suspension of military aid to Pakistan hit the Canadian press within hours. Canada's decision not to supply spare parts to Pakistan was received positively by the news media in Canada and in major countries except Pakistan, where it was reported negatively. The decision of the governments of Canada and Great Britain in favor of a suspension of military aid was seen by the military regime as an *anti-Pakistani* gesture. In a fit of anger, the government of Pakistan immediately announced that it would leave the Commonwealth for its inability to help Pakistan and uttered a threat to the UK and Canada that Pakistan would take reprisals against both countries. Canada was taken aback when the news media reported that, because of Canada's decision not to supply military spare parts to Pakistan, "the military government in West Pakistan" was "considering the provision of aid to the separatist movement in Québec in retaliation for the suspension of Canadian aid." [121]

Ottawa officials were shocked at the news since they had been trying hard not to provoke an outcry by making a whimsical Yahya rancorous for Canada's decision against Pakistan. They were downbeat, alarmed to see the capricious nature of the furious military regime. When the Bengalis fought for independence, the Trudeau administration never wanted to provoke Yahya's ire. Yet Yahya became convinced negatively of Canada's decision to suspend new economic aid to Pakistan and, later, to withdraw the export license for spare parts for Pakistani aircraft. Pakistan regarded this as a favor to the *Bengali freedom fighters* by Canada. Similarly, despite Sharp's effort to maintain Canada's "neutrality," the provisional government of Bangladesh in exile cherished the illusion that *Canada supported* the liberation movement. It felt encouraged to hear Sharp's announcement in the Commons that no Canadian arms would be loaded in the *S. S. Padma* carrying US arms to Pakistan via Montreal, Québec.

In fact, at that time, the MPs of all political affiliations remained united—not to toe the Nixon administration's line even though Canada enjoyed a strong and mutually advantageous relationship with her neighbor, the mighty USA. Though a US ally and only a middle power, Canada refused to rubber-stamp Nixon's policy about the crisis. We saw this in Chapter 4 under the heading Suspension of the *S.S. Padma*. Ironically, although the Trudeau administration tried hard not to up the ante by staying away from being dragged into subcontinental politics, it failed to demonstrate Canada's neutral position to the military regime. Canada was disturbed to see how the Yahya and the provisional government of Bangladesh misconstrued Canada. Yahya believed that Canada's stand was in *favor of Bangladesh and that, for sure, Canada was against Pakistan*. At the same time, the provisional government of Bangladesh interpreted Canada's actions against the shipment of illegal arms as having a *pro-Bangladeshi stand*, even though Canada tried to demonstrate to both parties her position of neutrality.

In his responses to the concerns of his colleagues, Sharp remained *unequivocal* in stating his objective, which was to ensure that Canada did not provide any *economic* and *military* assistance to the Yahya regime engaged in an aggressive assault against its people. He clearly outlined to his colleagues his *raison d'être* for *financial aid* to the people of East Pakistan and *absolutely no supply of military spare parts* to Pakistan—something

Canadians were fully satisfied with. Sharp was convinced there was no silver bullet to resolve the age-old conflict in which Canada, only a middle power, had no direct stake. Sticking to his gun, Sharp faced the news media, believing he was not in a popularity contest to appease his constituents when he knew he had to remain committed to adhering to Canada's foreign policy options.

Oddly enough, for some strange reason, the NDP Lewis again brought up the issue of *economic sanctions* and *military equipment* as unresolved in the fall. The MPs instantly recalled that it was a done deal and that there was no need for anyone to raise any concerns again. Naturally, though melodramatic, Lewis's demand neither ignited a renewed debate for condemnation nor resonated with the MPs. There was no follow-up question at all. By then, both parliamentarians and the greater public had already accepted Canada's inability to come out with an *unequivocal condemnation* note to be "politically correct." In Chapter 4, we noted the Canadian public's contentment with Canada's handling of the issue of spare parts, unlike the covert action of the Nixon administration. The MPs trusted their government and had no reason to suspect otherwise. It is not clear *why* a shrewd Lewis brought up the issues again. Perhaps he got carried away and did not recall that his fellow NDP colleagues and the rest of the MPs in the House were already satisfied with how the government proactively dealt with these two items in late summer. In any event, the debate covering other issues continued for a while, and naturally, Lewis's specific demand for cutting off aid to Pakistan fell by the wayside.

Over the months, there were endless discussions on *whether and how Canada could craft a response* voicing Canada's genuine concern. Everyone, including the opposition members, knew how the military regime, not being pleased to see Canada's reaction, instantly came to consider Canada as *anti-Pakistani* about her position vis-à-vis that of the government of Pakistan. The public was on the same page with the government that tightly held the view that, without a *satisfactory political solution*, long-term aid to Pakistan would mean subsidizing a discredited military regime. Sharp was happy to recognize the public's support for his tough stand and that within Canada, public reaction had shifted with the mounting clamor for stricter action against Pakistan.

Political Asylum and Immigration

In Chapter 7, we shall see the government's proactive action regarding the immigration of potential applicants recruited from East Pakistan as late as November 1971. In the area of immigration, the NDP MP for Regina Centre, Les Benjamin, played a pivotal role throughout the period under discussion. There were also a few other well-known MPs, such as the Conservative MP for Hillsborough Heath Macquarrie, Robert Thompson, Conservative MP for Red Deer, and the NDP Andrew Brewin MP for Greensborough, who pushed the envelope for immigration. Macquarrie's precise question to the prime minister expressing his concerns about the Bengali refugees in India was, "Is it the view of the government that India should permanently sustain millions of refugees from another country, even with financial assistance from other lands, and, if not, can the right honourable gentleman advise what steps the government is taking to promote a long-range solution to this grave international problem?"[122] Prime Minister Pierre Trudeau, who had been candid all along in seeking ideas from his colleagues in the House, immediately observed, "I would not exaggerate the extent to which the Canadian government can settle this problem of refugees over the heads of the governments of India and Pakistan, but I would gladly entertain constructive suggestions from the opposition as to what might be done."[123] Trudeau's response in the House reveals his government's *readiness* to assist in matters relating to the refugees in India as well as the Bengalis' emigration from Pakistan and other countries.

Until the beginning of June, there is no record of Canada's plan to accept the Bengali refugees in Canada, although the MPs floated the idea back in April. The issue was triggered in mid-summer when many MPs began to receive letters, cables, and phone calls from anxious Bengalis living in their constituencies. The detailed newspaper accounts of the West Pakistani military atrocities against the Bengali civilian population also made the MPs disturbingly aware of the gravity of the situation. Conservative Thompson's straightforward question to the Prime Minister was: "Will the Canadian government consider accepting the refugees from East Pakistan as political refugees?[124] An utterly frank Trudeau responded to similar questions a week ago and reminded his colleagues: "The question has not been considered, Mr. Speaker."[125] Both the Canadian parliamentarians and the public had a great deal of empathy for the Bengali refugees in India and displaced persons within the province (East Pakistan) who had remained in their homeland but were in constant fear for their lives. Both the government and MPs were of the view that providing a haven in Canada would at least mean a new opportunity to save the lives of some of the unfortunate victims of repression. Since the idea resonated with the public, no one in the House objected to having East Pakistani (Bengali) refugees in Canada.

In the meantime, Benjamin and Brewin took it upon themselves to do their best by keeping the subject up for discussion. "May I also ask whether medical examination structures and other regulations will be eased to remove these people from the situation in that part of the world?" [126] thus asked a concerned Benjamin. The minister of Manpower and Immigration, Otto Lang, immediately responded in the affirmative: "We would always be glad to take a very lenient view to expedite the movement of people who may come here. In the interest of all concerned, I have some doubts about the wisdom of easing such requirements as medical examinations in the circumstances."[127] A persistent Benjamin then appealed, "Because probably no one from that particular area of the world who might otherwise qualify would be able to pass the medical examination, is the Minister making any provision for those who may apply to come to Canada to be placed in isolation either in Canada or in India until they are in good enough health to come?" [128] "That is an interesting suggestion, Mr. Speaker, that deserves to be looked into," [129] was the Minister's curt but positive response.

Apart from bringing Bengali refugees from outside of Canada, Benjamin also raised in the House the issue of asylum for those Bengali East Pakistanis living in Canada in various capacities. The MPs heard Benjamin with undivided attention as he used to speak with passion. The Immigration minister was also under pressure from the public to extend visas and work permits to those East Pakistanis living in Canada and to consider a special measure program for refugees and asylum seekers. Echoing Benjamin, the NDP Brewin also had a specific question for the Immigration minister for the East Pakistani Bengali students in Canada: "Will the government soon announce its policy regarding students and others now in Canada who come from East Pakistan; and will the government allow them to stay under permit until the situation in that country has cleared up?"[130] "Mr. Speaker, our usual policy in cases where there are difficulties or disturbances in the world is to make it easier for people from such areas who are in Canada, temporarily or otherwise, to stay until the situation has clarified itself, and that would apply in this case as well,"[131] thus was Lang's immediate response. There were no further questions for clarification, as Lang's response was clear-cut. Not only that, throughout the period, questions on students and refugees raised in the House were responded to by both Lang (minister of Manpower and Immigration) and Sharp (secretary of State for External Affairs) very positively. Their sincere responses show the government's sympathetic attitude toward the victims of military vengeance.

Following a review of the process, the government did not feel the need to address the issue of political asylum or ease immigration procedures to speed up the immigration regulations for those affected East Pakistanis already in Canada. According to the government, there was no need for a particular measure program for the Bengali refugees, unlike, for example, the Tibetan Refugee Program, which started in the late 1960s and continued during the period under review. Those in charge of immigration maintained that the current immigration regulations were not at all stringent in causing any delay in the case of the refugees in Canada, nor was there any need to change the current *modus operandi* for the Bengali refugees, argued the government. Since all MPs agreed with the government's view on the refugee and the immigration determination process to be followed, there was no counterargument from them either. The debates centered not on *whether* but on *how* and *how fast* the government could assist East Pakistani Bengalis in need of help concerning seeking political asylum, sponsorship, an extension of visa, etc.

Seeking a Political Resolution/Separation

Over the months, several MPs raised the idea of a *political resolution* under different subjects but always with the same concerns upon suspending the democratic processes that had started earlier with the 1970 National Elections. Despite their awareness of Prime Minister Trudeau's appeal to President Yahya Khan and Prime Minister Indira Gandhi immediately following the imposition of martial law in East Pakistan, they remained anxious. Neither the opposition nor liberal MPs elaborated on the meaning of the terms *political resolution* and/or *settlement*. They were used interchangeably. However, many MPs expressed their views supporting a political solution to achieve their goal. However, Canada's challenge in helping Pakistan achieve a political resolution is reflected in how Sharp advised his colleagues to remain watchful. "The ultimate responsibility for creating that political settlement necessarily rests with the contending parties." [132] Thus, Sharp observed that interference in Pakistan's internal affairs *would do no good*. He then went on to say that it is the government and people of Pakistan that would have to resolve the conflict by *democratic means* between the Awami League leaders and the Yahya regime and not between Pakistan and India. Canadian parliamentarians of all political stripes were on the same page with Sharp.

Within a short time, Barnett Danson, the North York Liberal MP and parliamentary secretary to the prime minister, explained the conflict to the House as the government saw it. "As we all know, the origins of this problem lie not in India itself but in East Pakistan and the breakdown of discussions between the government of Pakistan and the Awami League. In common with other governments, Canada has urged the government of Pakistan the need to resume the search for a political solution and to establish conditions which will permit refugees from East Pakistan to return to their homes." [133] As far as the Trudeau government was concerned, it had numerous reasons not to intervene in political matters. A straightforward Danson observed with chariness, "We have also offered relief assistance to East Pakistan. Beyond that, Mr. Speaker, there is little that outside governments, no matter how well disposed, can do in a situation where the contending parties would be understandably sensitive to any attempt to prescribe, much less impose, a solution."[134] Thus, although the MPs recognized the importance of Canada's role as an intermediary in promoting the spirit of a political resolution, Danson held the view that neither Pakistan nor India would appreciate the fact of Canada's intervention.

Again, emphasizing the need for a political resolution of the conflict, Macquarrie also observed, "While the immediate need is humanitarian, a long-range political solution must not be pushed so low in priority that the countries of the world will see another displaced band of refugees living forever in someone else's domain."[135] Echoing the same sentiment, Brewin too regarded the events in East Pakistan as "one of the most tragic circumstances that the world has ever witnessed."[136] Within two days, Conservative MP from Fundy-Royal, Gordon Fairweather, expressed his concern regarding the situation in the subcontinent. A watchful Sharp prudently responded with a note of warning, "Mr. Speaker, all of us are pressing for a political solution. It is the only possible way of dealing with the present situation. Unless there is a political settlement in Pakistan, the refugees are going to remain in India and will continue to be a thorn in the side of peace, if I may put it that way. Therefore, we are all working with everything at our command and using every possible means of impressing on the Pakistan government the need for a settlement, one that is democratic and made under civilian control."[137]

Seeking further clarification regarding a political settlement that Sharp was referring to, Halifax-East Hants Conservative MP Robert McCleave asked another straightforward question: "What type of political solution is being sought to this problem?"[138] Sharp, known for his nimble mind, quickly responded by saying, "Mr. Speaker, if you will permit a short answer, the preferred settlement, of course, would be one in which those individuals who have been elected under the recent election in Pakistan should be given the responsibility of governing Pakistan, particularly East Pakistan."[139] As most of the observers became aware of the *nature* of the political conflict through detailed media reports, they, too, began to pressure the government to network with influential countries and organizations to initiate a new round of negotiation.

Unfortunately, despite Sharp's careful articulation of his idea of a political resolution, his statements were misconstrued by many Canadians, especially pro-Bangladeshis as well as the Yahya regime: that Pakistan, particularly East Pakistan, should be returned to civilian rule and his use of the word "democratic government." It is important to note that even in June 1971, the Trudeau administration still maintained that intervention of any kind by the government would be seen as inappropriate, uncalled for, and, most importantly, "politically incorrect." Canada did not wish to provoke Yahya's wrath even when there was adequate media coverage of the mass killings of Bengalis. When James A. McGrath, Conservative MP for Saint-John's East, wanted to know if the government had raised the question "respecting the very serious charges of genocide made by a Pakistani journalist who very recently fled that country,[140] Sharp was utterly frank: "I have not made representations directly to the High Commissioner here nor to the government of Pakistan. The High Commission and the government of Pakistan have, of course, denied the charges." [141]

The Conservative McGrath, as part of his follow-up exercise, asked again: "Has the government of Canada requested permission from the government of Pakistan to send observers into East Pakistan to determine whether or not the charges of genocide against the Hindus especially have any foundation in fact?" [142] Sharp responded quickly, "A complaint has been made to the Secretary-General of the United Nations that genocide was involved, and the Secretary-General has not considered it necessary to have inquiries made." [143] Sharp left it to the UN to determine the fact of genocide. Taking issue with the government's stand on it, a few MPs, however, remained dissatisfied and voiced their concerns. They believed the Pakistan central government had a secret plan to perpetuate power even by Machiavellian means, if necessary.

The next day, the Liberal Marcel Prud'homme, MP for Saint-Denis, Québec, directed toward Sharp another sensitive question: "Could he tell us if the Canadian government supports or would be ready to support the separation of East Pakistan from the Republic of Pakistan?" [144] The Speaker immediately intervened, saying, "I still doubt that such a question is acceptable. However, if the Minister wants to reply to it, I do not see any objection."[145] Sharp's instant response was both terse and emphatic: he "would like to make it clear that the government of Canada is not supporting any movement for the separation of East Pakistan from Pakistan." [146]

Again, when David MacDonald, Liberal MP for Egmont, Ontario, asked for further clarification regarding Sharp's position on East Pakistan, Sharp quickly responded, "Yesterday my remarks were apparently misconstrued, and it was for this reason I wanted to make it quite plain today on my own initiative that I had no intention of supporting separation in saying as I did yesterday that I supported the restoration of democratic government under the civilian rule in East Pakistan and preferably based on those who had been elected in the last election."[147] There was no further discussion as to whether such a movement or the breakup of Pakistan was permissible in international law or whether, legally speaking, the Yahya regime had the *carte blanche* to suppress the will of the majority. There was also no further inquiry regarding Canada's exact position concerning the provisional government of Bangladesh or the government headed by Yahya. Sharp believes the best solution would be a duly elected, democratic government in Pakistan. He strongly felt that it would be irresponsible to recommend the division of Pakistan, a country already in dire straits, into two separate and weaker states.

By the end of June, many MPs had already found the Yahya government's statements contradictory and inexplicable. They could not interpret Yahya's June 28 address to the nation since opposing views were expressed in the same speech. Yahya talked about the transfer of power to civilian rule in Pakistan. Yet he reiterated his decision to neither hold a fresh election nor remove the ban on the Awami League as a political party with the most seats in the 1970 National Elections. Initially, Ottawa accepted the view that each province would be allowed to develop along the right line without detracting from the center's strength and the integrity of Pakistan. Soon, Ottawa recognized the actual meaning of the Yahya government's argument or a new narrative: that because the Awami League did not win a single seat in the provinces of West Pakistan, it could not be called a *party of national unity.*

An argument of such nature by the Yahya regime struck Canada as absurd. Ottawa officials found the regime's new narrative so bizarre that they became convinced that Yahya was resorting to rhetoric, talking the talk. Ottawa rejected Yahya's theory that any party confined to a specific region was not a national party in the practical sense of the term. Having found no rationale in such an argument, Ottawa considered the regime's new narrative ridiculous and nonsensical. Ironically enough, despite Canada's efforts to demonstrate her "neutrality," the military government began to state openly that Canada was not on Pakistan's side. Despite Sharp's frank explanation of Canada's position, some Canadians believed Canada was not doing enough.

In the meantime, having seen no sign of a political solution and after much reflection on the actions of the government and politicians alike, a frustrated Macquarrie observed that politicians of all affiliations had been myopic. Thinking along the lines of a united Pakistan that Canada had been working toward, Macquarrie observed that, to save the country, the initiative ought to have come from the Yahya government. "This will require some attitudes and adjustments from the Pakistan Government, which have not yet, so far as we know, been apparent."[148] As a middle power, Canada was doing its best. Still, the military repression should have been stopped first with a demonstration of a genuine desire to seek a political solution in consultation with the Bengali leaders, argued Macquarrie. In the same way, Brewin, who had been an ardent supporter in the public domain of the Bengalis' fight for democracy, reinforced his fear that Pakistan was about to be dismembered and that there was "no solution without a political solution."[149]

As uncertainties complicated understanding future events, Canadian parliamentarians could not focus on the exact demand with a prescribed road map. Because of Pakistan's dependence on Canada, it was proposed that perhaps an informal discussion with Pakistan, in the form of a positive intervention, could be initiated by Canada and other countries. Again, seeing India's covert role in the conflict from the beginning, Canadian parliamentarians became convinced of India's direct stake in the rivalry. Canada could not move forward with a specific proposal for a political solution since each of the three parties, Pakistan, India, and Bengali rebels (with direct assistance from India), was interpreting the events very differently from one's own angle. Although the MPs used to clamor for intervention, an analysis of the debates shows that they focused more on assisting the victims of military reprisals.

Canadian parliamentarians and the public were frustrated seeing how the despotic Yahya regime, instead of transferring power, developed a diabolical plan to suppress the verdict of the majority. A concerned Lewis observed, "It is possible for a military faction in a country to upset the decision of the people of that country and to oust those who were democratically elected by the people to represent them in the Parliament of that country, or to substitute for the democratic process a military dictatorship, which is in fact what we have in Pakistan now, and get away with it, even though millions of people are ejected from that country as a result of the circumstances created by the military dictatorship."[150] In a sense, Canadian parliamentarians interpreted the military takeover and its ongoing reprisals as the regime's way to subjugate most of the citizenry through the constant threat of terror—a Machiavellian means in its efforts to perpetuate power. The government realized that both the public and parliamentarians were focused on highlighting the fundamental point in their demand that Canada exert more pressure on the military regime to seek a political solution instead of a military one. Sharp's foreign affairs cognoscenti also recognized that having abandoned the negotiations without notice, the military government had desperately sought a *military solution* to perpetuate power.

Again, seeing that there was no development in any concrete form or shape while the evil military regime's genocidal acts were going on back and forth, some frustrated MPs continued to raise the issue to address it head-on. For example, the Abitibi Créditiste MP Gérard Laprise demanded the government to look for the root cause - that historically speaking, no one had to look too far. "The problem facing that area today did not just spring up but has been around for a long time, and I admit that we should hasten the solution of that crisis through political means, for it is, above all, a political question."[151] "The assistance Canada intends to give should be used by India, not to make investments and enslave part of Pakistan, but to help the Pakistani refugees who fled before the hatred born of political differences,"[152] Laprise observed further.

The implication was that the Gandhi administration must refrain from taking advantage of the situation. Being on the same page, regardless of individual politicians' views, Canadian parliamentarians were appreciative of Sharp's predicament - *how to respond to the pressure in a way that would be "politically correct" for Canada, a middle power?* They recognized not only Sharp's dichotomy but also his reasons for being at variance - how he had been making every effort to mitigate the distressing misgivings of his colleagues by explaining the complex nature of the subcontinental polity. Sharp elaborated on what he meant: "A political solution must be found which will allow the refugees to return to a secure and democratic society in East Pakistan. I regret, Mr. Speaker, that at the moment, I see little hope of an early resolution of the problem in urging upon the governments of India and Pakistan restraint and forbearance in the face of difficulties that must be overcome before a lasting settlement can be achieved."[153] Under the circumstances, the MPs still used the name East Pakistan as they did not wish to embarrass the government by uttering the name Bangladesh, which no country had recognized.

In the meantime, suddenly, an impassioned NDP leader, Lewis, began to argue again with renewed vigor—that it is imperative to understand the background of the conflict in question and determine *what* kind of a "political solution" to seek. It is important to note that although Lewis was the first MP in the House who openly referred to the Yahya regime as a *military dictatorship,* calling a spade a spade, there was no reactive response from the MPs. A gutsy Lewis remained forceful in his argument, having purposefully ignored the demonstrated silence of his colleagues. He retook the floor and spoke on behalf of Canadians' feelings for the Bengali victims of military reprisals and their aspirations for establishing a *free* and *independent* country of their own. Like the Liberal Gérard Laprise, who earlier talked about going to the root cause of the conflict, *Lewis argued that* the problem needed to be tackled at its root: *the restoration of democracy.* Having highlighted the need for international cooperation, an audacious Lewis openly stated that the Yahya government was solely responsible for the macabre tragedy—something no other MP ever dared to point the finger at like Lewis. An emotionally charged Lewis most poignantly repeated the need to *establish a popular government under the leadership of the Awami League leader Bongobondhu.* Again, it was implied that Pakistan would remain united but should be ruled by the leader of the majority (Bongobondhu).

Reactions to the Indo-Pakistan War

With time, frustration with the UN was already running very high among the MPs as their earlier hopes for resolving the conflict were dashed. The MPs immediately reacted to mount collective pressure for immediate UN intervention. However, the news media had already covered at length the inability of the UN and its members to act about an imminent war between Pakistan and India. The Calgary Center Conservative MP Douglas Harkness, having expressed his serious apprehension about what he called "a reported invasion of East Pakistan by Indian troops," wanted to know whether Canada had "taken any initiative in the United Nations in an attempt to bring the present outbreak of hostilities to an end and prevent it spreading more widely?"[154] A distressed Sharp immediately responded by referring to the usual denials and accusations of the parties involved. It confirmed that "there are hostilities going on in border areas between India and Pakistan" and that "the Indian government has denied this."[155] At a time when the UN System was seen to have been without any teeth in the face of the two countries' respective positions for a showdown, the reaction of the MPs was one of brooding silence with awe since no attempt at the UN had produced any tangible result in addressing the issue. And yet, despite recognizing the UN's ineffectualness, Canada remained persistent in still using the UN system.

The prevailing feeling was that the tragedy would widen and broaden to a dreadful dimension. The MPs maintained that the *Security Council should go beyond a simple call* for a ceasefire and address itself simultaneously to the root cause of the conflict—the repression in East Pakistan, which had placed intolerable strains on the economic, social, and political fabric of neighboring India. At this stage, Sharp was barraged with endless questions concerning the latest situation at the UN vis-à-vis the Indo-Pakistan war. He used his parliamentary skills to listen to all sides with patience. He reminded his colleagues of the emergency session of the UN Security Council that was called for on December 4, 1971, following the declaration of war, that it was an initiative of nine of its members to consider the rapidly deteriorating situation. All observers under the circumstances recognized how impossible it was for the Security Council to solve the problem of a war that seemed dangerous to the world's future peace. Canadian politicians, seeing the futility of the Security Council due to the use of the veto, quickly lost any hope they might have had.

While the debate was going on, the war broke out within days. Canada had reasons to worry about the future of the two countries whose armies were originally British-trained. Both countries were spending "a large part of their national budgets on military readiness: India, about a third of its national budget, and Pakistan, about half of its total budget."[156] In the meantime, the Trudeau administration was shocked to see the unanimous support of the familiar people of India and Pakistan for a confrontation. Canada was disturbed to see that there was no political divide, even in India, regarding attacking Pakistan. No one failed to see the media report on how cars on the streets in larger Indian cities were showing off bumper stickers proclaiming "Liberate Bangla Desh," "Punish Yahya," and "Finish Pakistan."[157] The political spectrum from the rightist Jana Sang Party to the Communist Party of India (Marxist) was committed to standing with the ruling Congress Party. Seeing that the two Commonwealth countries were at war, a frustrated Macquarrie regretted the international community's inaction to the restoration of democracy.

On December 6, 1971, Sharp informed the House with profound shock and dismay that an "open war has broken out on the subcontinent of India,"[158] following nine months of accusations and counteraccusation of each other. Macquarrie, in return, made the following statement with a firm conviction: "While neither a pacifist nor a dove, I can never believe that a warlike solution today is, in fact, a solution to problems of this kind."[159] All MPs thought about a political solution even at the last minute. This was despite the media report that the independence of Bangladesh seemed inevitable.

Seeing the destructive nature of the war, several MPs expressed their concerns about the Canadians living in the subcontinent, in particular in East Pakistan. In Sharp's absence, Trudeau answered their questions and assured them that a Canadian Boeing 707 was being sent and arrangements were made with the British High Commission regarding evacuating Canadians stranded in East Pakistan. Sharp also informed the House of two critical items about India's move for their knowledge in the following manner: "It seems fairly clear that neither side has committed its forces on the western front; in and around East Pakistan, however, Indian forces are exerting considerable efforts to gain territory. India has recognized the provisional government of Bangla Desh."[160] It was as though, instantly, the MPs' worst fear became more real just as they realized the painful dimension of the horrendous situations of the two countries and the imminent danger, hanging like a sword of Damocles, a catastrophic threat.

Given the hatred of Pakistan and India against each other, the MPs also recognized that it would never be easy to bury the hatchet. Although concerned about the consequences of an *all-out war* between Pakistan and India, Sharp was not yet ready to press the panic button. He wanted to review the situation again. He successfully answered all questions directed for his immediate attention. Sharp also informed the House that, at the request of the secretary-general of the UN, a Canadian armed forces c-130 had been diverted to Dhaka to help evacuate UN personnel; the UN had also arranged a local ceasefire with the Pakistani army. It was hoped that the Indian and *Mukti Bahini* forces would have permitted the aircraft to land in Dhaka, but the Pakistani troops attacked it before it could land. The airport was attacked at precisely the hour the plane was to begin its approach to the area. An anxious Sharp informed the House that the aircraft had returned to Bangkok safely.

Having found the situation deplorable, he observed, "Perhaps the world has not taken sufficient note of the dimension of the problem. Perhaps the international community should have moved more quickly. Now it is too late to pass judgment on the past."[161] Though supportive of the UN, Canada became hopelessly disappointed with the entire UN system amid pessimism and uncertainty about the future. There was no consensus on *how* to proceed. The same day, when the fighting between India and Pakistan started, one of the Canadian dailies wrote: "It would be closer to the truth to say that she [Indira Gandhi] calculatedly made up her mind to attack Pakistan when she concluded that China would probably not intervene on Pakistan's side and that Russia would continue arming and aiding India." [162]

Again, Bob Stanfield, Conservative leader of the opposition, also promptly made the same inquiry Lewis made: whether Canada had "taken any tentative position as to when the matter should be raised in the General Assembly of the United Nations?"[163] Fortunately, Sharp had just returned from Washington, where he had discussions with the US Secretary of State William Rogers on the same subject only two days earlier. Referring to his own experience, Sharp stated that he had grave misgivings and reservations about the process of hastening the matter at the UN. He advised the House that both he and his US counterpart were of the "view that what was important," at that time, was "a ceasefire" [164] under the circumstances. Given his years of experience and familiarity with the process in the UN and its complex modus operandi, a discouraged Sharp had no hesitancy in expressing his anger and apprehension. His frank and prudent remark was that the General Assembly was "not likely to produce results" to help "settling the dispute." [165]

When confronted with a series of follow-up questions by his colleagues, Sharp quickly responded that, as a last resort, the "Security Council should be seized of the matter as long as there is some hope that they can reach an agreed solution."[166] Sharp's responses to various questions at this stage were in the form of cautionary remarks to his colleagues that a "discussion in the United Nations General Assembly is not the same as getting an agreed resolution in the Security Council."[167] Sharp remained relaxed and informative in his responses, having assured the House that his government "shall do everything that is reasonable - even, indeed, things which may appear to be unreasonable - if it appears that anything can be done to help bring these hostilities to an end."[168] The debate continued for a while with no concrete result.

At a time when the MPs were fearful of the enormity of the situation, having recognized the powerlessness of the UN, whether it was the Security Council or the General Assembly, an embittered Lewis did not seem to give up his efforts altogether. Despite everything, he expressed his hope that through international intervention, there might be a "temporary ceasefire to be followed by a political solution that will recognize the rights and the freedom of the people of East Pakistan and, indeed, of West Pakistan, as well."[169] Having openly shown his support to the Bengalis in public, Lewis expressed his views in the following manner: "The military junta, to use a South American term for an Asiatic government, that now seeks to control all Pakistan will be disposed of its power by the free democratic process of the Pakistani people."[170] An exasperated Lewis urged that the people of Canada "should not fail to remember what Yahya has done to the democratic process in Pakistan and the people of East Pakistan and no step should be taken at the expense of the freedom and the future of the people of East Pakistan."[171] This was the second time in the House that the MPs heard, loud and clear, Lewis's fiery speech—accusation of the Yahya regime.

Again, in a desperate attempt, John Diefenbaker, former prime minister and Conservative MP for Prince Albert, argued that, since for "all intents and purposes, the Security Council appears to have become emasculated as a result of the division of opinion,"[172] perhaps Canada should take a different approach in her attempt to resolve the hostilities. He suggested that another round of talk with the representatives of India and Pakistan could perhaps be a better approach because of "Canada's peculiarly favourable position as a nation highly regarded in both India and Pakistan."[173] Most MPs immediately concurred with his thinking as they recognized what the veteran Conservative was referring to. Diefenbaker's appeal reminded his colleagues of the approach the US President Teddy Roosevelt took at the time of the Russo-Japanese War in 1905.[174] The point to note is that Diefenbaker's effort, even at that stage, was to find a "political resolution" to the conflict and to "resolve hostilities" between Pakistan and India to end the war. Like other Canadian parliamentarians, the independence of Bangladesh was not in Diefenbaker's equation either.

Meanwhile, the MPs of all political stripes remained uncertain as to what Canada *could* or *should* do under the circumstances. They heard Sharp's remark with utter seriousness: "From the beginning, Canada has been in touch with the governments of India and Pakistan at the highest levels. To the government of India, we have urged patience and restraint in a situation of great difficulty. To the government of Pakistan, we have stressed the urgent necessity of speeding up of a return to civilian and representative government, particularly in East Pakistan."[175] Seeing that the war had already started, Brewin wondered how would that affect the distribution of food to the refugees. His question to Sharp was "whether he [Sharp] would make it explicit that aid to the innocent victims will not be diminished by political events as long as it is possible to make sure that they are the actual recipients of the aid."[176] Sharp immediately responded, "I can confirm that position and add that it is one of the purposes of the Canadian government to keep politics out of humanitarian endeavours." [177]

The people of Canada, like the parliamentarians, were also aware of a few critical items on the national agenda. One significant event was Trudeau's meeting in Washington with President Richard Nixon on December 6, 1971. This was of profound significance as far as the Canada-US relationship was concerned. Readers must remember that this was a time when Canada-US relations were one of Canada's top priorities. Naturally, Trudeau was barraged with questions regarding his meeting with Nixon on December 5 regarding Canada's economic and political independence or dependency.

Even though India recognized Bangladesh on December 6, 1971, the Trudeau administration was not yet thinking along such lines. "Canada viewed the Pakistan-India situation with profound regret."[178] Thus, Sharp observed in an interview when he acted as prime minister while Trudeau was visiting President Nixon in Washington. Sharp continued, "Canada had no intention of recognizing the state of Bangla Desh as India had done."[179] Sharp went further to point out that Canada's position was that the people of East Pakistan should have their democratic rights restored and the East Pakistani refugees should be guaranteed a safe return to their homes. Even at this stage, Canada's recognition of Bangladesh was out of the question.

In the meantime, Sharp's colleagues had repeatedly asked him the same questions regarding a political settlement, perhaps in a different shape and form. At that time, many MPs had their hearts in the cause of the Bengalis, who they believed were fighting for their safety and security in their native land so they could live independently with dignity and honor. Yet, unsurprisingly, Canadian parliamentarians were still thinking along the lines of a *political solution within a united Pakistan*. They emphasized that both parties, the military regime, and the AL leaders/rebel forces, should strive to establish *democracy in Pakistan*. Put differently, the phenomenon of Bangladesh was not a part of Canada's equation even at that stage when the liberation of Bangladesh was in the offing.

In describing the extreme polarity of the situation, a discontented Lewis suggested following another route as a last resort. Since the Security Council had not been successful, the matter "should be taken to the General Assembly where the veto does not exist."[180] Though under excessive pressure to inform his colleagues of the latest development in the UN, Sharp's responses at that time were prompt and terse - that the matter was before the General Assembly and that he could not elaborate on the resolution's wording. There was no reaction on the part of his colleagues in the House, as by the beginning of December, all MPs were disenchanted with what was going on in Pakistan.

Finally, all sound and fury made in the Commons eventually came to signify nothing as neither the government party MPs nor opposition MPs made any comments. Upon hearing from Sharp, Trudeau's frequent consultation and overtures had only been "met with sympathetic understanding" and had "not produced the kind of initiative"[181] desired by all; the MPs were down in the dumps. Both groups, being profoundly disappointed, remained quiescent, making no gesture. A distressed Sharp observed: "At the moment, I do not think either side is disposed to do anything but continue the hostilities that unfortunately have begun."[182] One fails to understand *why* the MPs remained interested in creating a *political resolution* when the freedom fighters' progress was demonstrably tangible.

Upon hearing the news of India's recognition of Bangladesh and reflecting on the fallout of the war, MPs of all political stripes recognized that the same conflict would create a new dimension in the complex subcontinental polity. The idea of a political settlement was not raised anymore, although all demanded UN intervention. It would be learned later that the decision by the Gandhi administration to recognize Bangladesh pushed Pakistan into the abyss at a time when an obsessed Yahya began his steady descent into madness.

Having seen the signs of doom and gloom, political representatives of all backgrounds began to focus on two areas: first, to strike an immediate ceasefire successfully, and second, efforts should be continued for a political solution for which pressure would have to be mounted to persuade the governments of Pakistan and India through *moral suasion* to be undertaken by a majority of countries, including Canada. When, on December 7, Trudeau described the substance of his meeting with Nixon, everyone knew that it was critical to Canada given the context of the "North American neighborhood" and how to "profit from" Canada's "relations with the United States, while at the same time, remaining Canadian to the degree and extent"[183] possible. The MPs at that time also remained focused on the events that were taking place in the subcontinent. They were disquieted and jittery to hear more about Trudeau's discussion with Nixon on the subcontinental conflict, which was not the focus of Trudeau's discussion then.

During the beginning of the second week of December, the questions regarding Canada's role became more focused in the House, especially when the British government proposed a compromise formula in the Security Council, which called for a ceasefire in the Indo-Pakistan War. Sharp saw the resolution as an essential means for Canada to determine her position but was soon frustrated seeing no substantial progress. All the efforts to reach an agreement among the members of the Security Council had already failed. Since there was a split between the USSR and

Communist China, there was no consensus. Unsurprisingly, a feeling of dejection existed in the Commons, reminding the desperate MPs that time was running out. Whether it was due to the way the UN interpreted the nature of the conflict or it was a *game plan* of the superpowers, it still begs the question: *Was Canada realistic in pursuing through the UN system?* Canada was disturbed by the Security Council's seeming incapacity to act. One may wonder, *Why did Canada continue to believe that the involvement of the UN might help to create conditions for more rapid progress toward a "political settlement?"*

A veteran Sharp believed quick, concise, and wary responses would be safe for all, given Canada's vulnerability to the Québec question that is bound to come up the minute the issue regarding the independence of Bangladesh is broached. Being tight-lipped, Sharp preferred to give information-based responses *only when needed*. Canadian parliamentarians sadly experienced Canada's international limitations as a middle power despite her excellent track record in peacemaking. They found the reactions by the secret military regime waffled and prevaricated but remained united in Canada's unshakable belief in the *principle of democracy*.

It remains enigmatic, somewhat inexplicable, as to why the two vocal MPs, Brewin and Lewis, who remained active in voicing their concerns and suggesting solutions, never clarified what political solution they envisage. On December 15, seeing the certainty of the independence of Bangladesh, Brewin raised another straightforward question: "Does the Secretary of State for External Affairs go so far as to agree with the resolution that the people of East Pakistan should have the right to choose independence if they so desire?"[184] It is hard to understand *why* Brewin, known for supporting the Bengalis' fight for democracy and himself a civil libertarian, never expressed his views unequivocally in the House on the Pakistan-Bangladesh conflict. Instead, Brewin skirted around the issue subtly and chose not to articulate his stand. With no pretension of any kind, Sharp's cautionary remark was in the following manner: "The problem between self-determination and the principle of non-interference in the internal affairs of other states is an unsettled question." [185]

His inquiries centered on whether the resolution "realistically recognized the fact that the people of East Pakistan should have the right to choose independence if they so desire and that the withdrawal of Indian forces from East Pakistan is dependent on this recognition."[186] Even at the last stage, despite being privy to information regarding the tremendous success of the freedom fighters and the Gandhi administration's effective game plan, Brewin naïvely emphasized the need for a *political settlement,* leaving his colleagues with the impression that he would *prefer a political settlement* and/or *establishment of democracy* in a *united Pakistan.* His questions and inquiries remained unclear since, even a day before Bangladesh's independence; one could not tell whether Brewin favored a *separate* and *independent Bangladesh* or a *united Pakistan* where the Bengali leader Bongobondhu would be in charge. Similarly, Lewis's speech also makes it unclear whether he advocated for a separate country, Bangladesh, or a *united Pakistan* to be governed by the elected Bengali leader.

Time and again, Sharp told his colleagues that Canada had never been an interventionist. He responded quickly: "The problem between self-determination and the principle of non-interference in the internal affairs of other states is an unsettled problem."[187] Keeping his feet firmly on the ground in the Commons, a courageous Sharp never yielded to the pressure from his opposition colleagues. His handling of the questions remains an example of his solid diplomatic understanding reflected in his responses, which occasionally alleviated serious concerns of his colleagues in the House. Although the government's stringent precautionary statements were used to make some members of the public suspicious of the government's actual position, in the end, they recognized Sharp's vulnerability regarding Canada's official response. They became appreciative of Sharp when, after prolonged consultations with his Cabinet colleagues, they saw how Sharp demonstrated his strength and courage, having handled the questions with assured competence and remembering what was "politically correct" to say. Sharp's exceptional diplomatic finesse was such that, though curt, his responses did not generate any discussion on the subject of "self-determination" and/or "fight for independence." Everyone in the House knew that the liberation of Bangladesh was inevitable. On December 16, 1971, the Pakistani army was forced to surrender to the Allied Forces, making Bangladesh an independent country.

Coincidentally, Sharp, on the day East Pakistan became Bangla Desh, used the term Bangla Desh (as it was spelled then) for the first time instead of East Pakistan, which he had been using in the House, in response to a question concerning the refugees in India by Macquarrie.[188] Again, within four days following the liberation of Bangladesh, for the first time, the name Bangla Desh was printed in the official Hansard

(Debate) under the title/subject *Bangla Desh—protests against alleged atrocities* on December 20, 1971, for debate and discussion. Conservative Thompson was the first MP to use the name Bangla Desh in the House that day.[189] Then, the MPs comfortably used both names, East Pakistan and Bangladesh, interchangeably, perhaps because Canada had not yet recognized Bangladesh.

What is significant is that as soon as Bangladesh became independent, the MPs started to inquire about Canada's resource allocation to the war-ravaged country. In response to questions by Macquarrie and Thompson on Canada's aid program regarding the millions of suffering Bengalis, Sharp succinctly outlined his government's already thought-out plan: "Although the situation remains fluid, because of the formal cessation of hostility, it is now possible to proceed to distribute some of the $18 million which I assured would be available for the relief of Pakistan[i] refugees in India."[190] Sharp then elaborated on his plan. "To help meet these needs for relief and rehabilitation while they are in India and for a limited period after repatriating, a first tranche of $5 million had been decided upon. Two million dollars will be distributed to the UNHCR in his capacity as the international focal point for refugees, and $3 million will be channeled through Canadian voluntary agencies which are supplying relief programs in India and East Pakistan." [191]

Recognition of Bangladesh

Chapter 9 deals exclusively with the recognition of Bangladesh with an account of how the Trudeau administration went about the entire process of early recognition. Readers shall recall, during the first day of the debate immediately following the imposition of martial law, that the issue of recognition of Bangladesh came up briefly. Since there was not enough authentic information to discuss the matter, there were only a few questions along the lines of clarification regarding the government's position when the situation in Pakistan was fast deteriorating. The parliamentarians knew that any discussion on recognizing Bangladesh was out of the question for Canada due to her policy of "non-interference." From that point of view, it may be observed that both the MPs and senators had an expanded understanding of Canada's dichotomous position. On every occasion, through his serious demeanour, Sharp stated his government's efforts to *distance itself from* the complex political turmoil, which eventually turned into a full-fledged war between India and Pakistan, to make Bangladesh an independent country.

Canadian parliamentarians did not broach the subject until Sharp announced in the Commons of India's recognition of Bangladesh as an independent country on December 6, 1971. At that critical time, Conservative Thompson, who had thus far avoided the topic, raised a question regarding the recognition of Bangladesh by Canada: "In view of the fact that India this morning declared its intention to officially recognize the new state of Bangla Desh, and in light of reports that both India and Russia are attempting to persuade friendly states to extend similar recognition, may I ask whether the government of Canada is considering its own position in this regard?"[192] "We have not been formally requested to give recognition to Bangla Desh, but in any event, it is not our intention to do so,"[193] was Sharp's quick response. Despite his curt response, he was relieved that no one raised any follow-up questions or pursued the matter with any commentary. The debate on other issues relating to the war between Pakistan and India continued for the next ten days. It was only after the surrender of the Pakistani army on December 16, 1971, when Bangladesh became a *fait accompli,* the question of recognition resurfaced in the House. Canadian MPs then began to raise a plethora of issues more freely and forcefully regarding how Canada *could* or *should* accord recognition to Bangladesh and assist the newly liberated country.

A review of the debates during the question period points to two primary obstacles that Canadian parliamentarians had to overcome in their efforts to both uncover and grasp the significance of the claims by the parties involved in the conflict: The first difficulty was to gain a deeper understanding of the levels of problems that the politicians had in discussing the events taking place overseas; and the second point to note is to be aware that the news of East Pakistan was blacked out pretty well throughout the period under discussion. Amid the confusion of fighting and the exodus of the refugees across the Indian border, there had been a striking absence of hard facts. Canada could not make a judgment, at least during the initial weeks when neither the news media nor the government was privy to reliable information due to complete censorship. It is also essential to keep in mind how, in the last half-century, and particularly since the late 1970s, there have been dramatic changes in how information is gathered, collected, synthesized, analyzed, stored, and communicated.

In its totality, the debates reveal Ottawa's heartfelt efforts in persuading Pakistan to move forward with an inspired leadership—not the kind demonstrated by the military regime. The debates remind us how, given Canada's precarious situation in her backyard, the separation of Québec remained one of Canada's dilemmas since the abortive rebellion of 1837-1838 against Canada. Readers don't fail to note Canada's discomfort in discussing specific sensitive topics, such as "secession" and/or "separation," for fear of igniting a new round of debate on the Québec question. Despite the frequent upheaval in the House, a resolute Sharp remained adherent to the foreign policy requirements. At the same time, it also shows how Canada was able to deal with the two archfoes, Pakistan and India, through a network of national and international organizations and do her bit, which often went in favor of Bangladesh even though *Canada did not support the breakup of Pakistan.*

The fact that the Trudeau administration did not commit itself to the political ideologies of one group against another is an instance of *political astuteness* on its part. Although the frustration of some MPs was growing increasingly intense, deep down, they seemed to know that behind Sharp's unfailing charm and good humor, a man of immense determination was a cutting-edge intellect honed by years of experience. Toward the end of the question period, Sharp used to take the risk of being tautological. His colleagues did not forget Sharp's cautionary remark that he made earlier: "The problem between self-determination and the principle of non-interference in the internal affairs of other states is an unsettled problem."[194] Despite everything, Canada believed that, with all its imperfections, the UN is still the indispensable body for world politics. This was even though many Canadians were utterly frustrated and did not agree with the government.

The debates also reveal how the Canadian parliamentarians were disturbed to see the military regime's actions against the Bengalis. To them, Yahya's misguided impulses were anti-democratic, for which he showed little affinity for ideals long espoused by Pakistanis. It did not take long for the Trudeau administration to recognize the fundamental Indian political objective, which it believed was to establish an independent Bangladesh *by peace or by military force.* In August, Canadian parliamentarians noted with alarm how India secured the support of the USSR through the signing of the *Indo-Soviet Treaty of Friendship and Cooperation.* Canada felt discouraged to see how Yahya continued to shift the blame from himself to India, which did not fly well with Canadians.

As far as the Trudeau administration was concerned, the National Assembly in Pakistan was expected to frame a new constitution and end martial law by returning to democracy and a federal system of government in Pakistan, which is something very positive. What stands out is that, though, under political pressure and public grilling, a heedful Sharp courageously remained adherent to Canada's policy of nonintervention all along. Headstrong as he was, a committed Sharp was sticking to his gun, despite having recognized the whole range of outrageous Machiavellian manoeuvres by the Yahya regime. One might ask: *How practical was it to seek a resolution of the issue when both India and Pakistan had already been at war for more than ten days?* Sharp faced even more questions, with no satisfactory answers that he could furnish.

It is evident that each parliamentarian, whether an MP or a senator, was aware that Canada, as a middle power, could not do anything directly since her position was based on the premise that problems between countries should be settled *through negotiation*. In other words, the issue should be solved not *militarily* but *politically,* and any interference from different countries in one country's "internal affairs" could only lead to chaos. Nevertheless, there was no discussion in the Commons on modifying the government's game plan or considering the reality of the implications of the formation, existence, and support of the provisional government of Bangladesh, backed by the Gandhi administration right from the outset. There was no discussion, even though they saw Canada as a "helpful fixer" or a "brigade builder." Their collective belief was that what was required was a constant exercise of forethought, tact, and diplomacy. Even though the Canadian parliamentarians recognized that the birth of Bangladesh was inevitable, they did not wish to hold any discussion on sensitive issues like cessation, separation, or the independence of Bangladesh.

Again, despite the knowledge of killing, murder, torture, and savagery of the Pakistani army with its hidden agenda to perpetuate power, Canadian parliamentarians stubbornly remained focused on persuading the military regime to find a political solution. Canada naïvely continued her search for ways and means to bring India and Pakistan, the two arch enemies, face-to-face for a last-minute attempt at resolving the matter *politically,* even when the political reality of the liberation of Bangladesh was only a matter of days. The debates show Canada remained stuck to her position of *moral suasion*, which did not work in the beginning or the end. Looking back, one might be inclined to say, perhaps rightly, that Canada's ignorance of the two crucial subcontinental phenomena was flawed. They were the strides and commitments of the freedom fighters assisted by India and the direct stake of the Indian government in cutting Pakistan to size. Canadian parliamentarians did not discuss such issues, even for a brief discussion.

Finally, one could say that the debates reflect Canada's hope against the hope that Pakistan would become democratic and truly representative of its people. However, there was plenty of evidence to the contrary. This is an instance of Canada's efforts to play her *traditional mediatory role* in saving Pakistan through a political settlement between the parties involved in the conflict despite the sour and surly melancholy of discontent. Although it may sound tautological, it must be stated clearly in layperson's terms so that there will be no confusion regarding Canada's notion of a political settlement - that the solution must be found within the framework of *one* Pakistan. Guilelessly enough, Canada remained sanguine despite concrete evidence that the liberation of Bangladesh was imminent. Canadian parliamentarians continued to urge the Trudeau administration to pressure Pakistan for a political settlement even after Bangladesh was recognized by India, which covertly engineered the dismemberment of Pakistan from the beginning.

Looking back, one would be inclined to say that, much to Canada's profound dissatisfaction, her efforts in negotiation were replaced by a combination of political expediency and raw bigotry that played into the hands of Yahya as he set in motion his *secret plan* for the elimination of the ultra-Bengali nationalists. Canadian parliamentarians did not pay attention to the military regime's *hidden agenda*. One could observe that the Trudeau administration's efforts in this regard were utterly surreal, devoid of reality on the ground. The Trudeau administration's persistent effort to work out a deal with the military dictator proved to be an unending series of misjudgments. Put differently, our understanding of Canada's actions and reactions through an examination of the debates points out two important aspects of Canada's strategy: (1) her deep concerns for the hapless Bengalis who were subjected to excessive ongoing military reprisals and her substantial work toward relieving the humanitarian aspect of the crisis; and (2) her persistent efforts that were directed toward building a united Pakistani castle in the air even at the last minute.

In the following two chapters, Chapters 7 and 8, we will examine various activities undertaken by Canada and her attempt to determine its position on the conflict.

Notes and References

1. Canada. House of Commons. *Debates.* Queen's Printer, dated December 6, 1971, p.10155. Hereinafter, referred to as *Debates.*
2. *Ibid. Dated* March 29, 1971, p.4685. *Op. cit.*
3. *Ibid.*
4. *Ibid.*
5. *Ibid.*
6. *Ibid.*
7. *Ibid.* p. 4685.
8. *Ibid.* Dated April 5, 1971, p. 4899.
9. *Ibid.* Dated April 2, 1971, pp 4852-4853.
10. *Ibid.* Dated March 29, 1971, p. 4685.
11. *Ibid.* Dated May 31, 1971, p.6240.
12. *Ibid,* Dated June 24, 1971, p.6651.
13. *Ibid.*
14. *Ibid.* Dated December 7, 1971.
15. *Ibid.* Dated November 17, 1971, p.9636.
16. *Ibid.* Dated June 14, 1971, p.6651.
17. *Ibid.* Dated June 16, 1971, p. 6775.
18. *Ibid.* Dated April 2, 1971, p. 4853.
19. *Ibid.* Dated April 2, 1971, p. 4853.
20. *Ibid.* Dated April 7, 1971, p.4993.
21. India. Ministry of External Affairs. *BANGLA DESH Documents.* B.N.K. Press Private Ltd. Madras, India, 1971, p. 569.
22. *Debates.* Dated March 29, 1971, p. 4685. *Op. cit.*
23. *Ibid.*
24. *Ibid.*
25. *Ibid.* Dated April 2, 1971, p.4853.
26. *Ibid.*
27. *Ibid.* Dated April 5, 1971, p. 4899.
28. *Ibid.*
29. *Ibid.* Dated April 7, 1971, p. 4993.
30. *Ibid.*
31. *Ibid.* Dated May 4, 1971. P. 5474.
32. *Ibid.*
33. *Ibid.*

34. *Ibid.* Dated March 29, 1971, p. 4685.
35. *Ibid.*
36. *Ibid.* Dated April 5, 1971, p. 4899.
37. *Ibid.*
38. *Ibid.* Dated April 29, 1971, p. 5345.
39. *Ibid.*
40. *Ibid.* Dated April 30, 1971, p. 5388.
41. *Ibid.* Dated April 30, 1971, p. 5388.
42. *Ibid.* Dated May 4, 1971, p. 5475.
43. *Ibid.*
44. *Ibid.* Dated May 4, 1971, p. 5474.
45. *Ibid.*
46. *Ibid.*
47. *Ibid.* Dated May 25, 1971, p. 6070.
48. *Ibid.*
49. *Ibid.* Dated May 31, 1971, p. 6240.
50. *Ibid.* Dated May 25, 1971, p.6070.
51. *Ibid.*
52. *Ibid.* Dated October 28, 1971, p. 9116.
53. *Ibid.* Dated June 7, 1971, p. 6458.
54. *Ibid.* Dated June 17, 1971, p. 6813.
55. *Ibid.*
56. *Ibid.* Dated December 6, 1971, p. 10156.
57. *Ibid.*
58. *Ibid.* Dated March 29, 1971, p. 4685.
59. *Ibid.*
60. *Ibid.* Dated April 29, 1971, p. 5345.
61. *Ibid.* Dated May 28, 1971, p. 6155.
62. *Ibid.* Dated May 4, 1971, p. 5475.
63. *Ibid.* Dated March 29, 1971, p. 4685.
64. *Ibid.*
65. *Ibid.* Dated May 25, 1971, p. 6070.
66. *Ibid.* Dated May 25, 1971, pp. 6074-6075.
67. *Ibid.*
68. Confidential telegram from James George, high commissioner to India, to Ottawa. Telegram # 1387, dated April 10, 1971. File # 20-E-Pak-1-4. External Affairs. *Op. cit.*
69. *Debates.* Dated November 27, 1969, pp. 1318-1319. *Op. cit.*
70. *Ibid.* Dated November 17, 1971, p. 9637.
71. *Ibid.*
72. *Ibid.* Dated November 27, 1969, p. 1319.
73. *Ibid.* Dated March 29, 1971, p.4685.

74. *Ibid.* Dated June 7, 1971, pp. 6458-6459.
75. The Waffle, also known as the Movement for an Independent Socialist Canada, was a radical wing of Canada's New Democratic Party (NDP) in the late 1960s. The 1971 NDP leadership convention was a battleground between the party establishment and the Waffle. About 2,000 people, out of the NDP's approximately 90,000 memberships, were members of the Waffle in 1971.
76. *The Globe and Mail,* dated April 22, 1971.
77. *Ibid.*
78. See chapter 1, FLQ *(Front de libération du Québec),* p. 12.
79. *Debates,* dated September 29, 1971, 8217. *Op. cit.*
80. Canada. Senate. *Debates.* Queen's Printer, Dated May 19, 1971, p. 1004. Hereinafter, referred to as *Debates (Senate).*
81. *Ibid. Op. cit.*
82. *Ibid.*
83. *Ibid. Op. cit.*
84. *Ibid.* p.1005. *Op. cit.*
85. *Ibid.*
86. *Debates* (Senate) Dated 28 June, 1971, p. 1225. *Op. cit.*
87. *Ibid.* Dated June 28, 1971, p. 1224. *Op. cit.*
88. Trudeau's statement was re-stated by Senator Yuzyk in the Senate. *Debates (Senate). Op. cit.* Volume 2, 20 April 1971 to 16 February 1972. Dated 28 June 1971, p. 1226.
89. *Ibid.* p. 1227.
90. Mitchell Sharp narrated this to the author in an interview on June 3, 1996, while Sharp was an honorary adviser to Prime Minister Jean Chretien.
91. *Debates.* Dated June 10, 1971, p. 6561. *Op. cit.*
92. *Ibid.*
93. *Ibid.*
94. *Ibid.*
95. *Ibid.* Dated May 17, 1971, p. 5853.
96. *The Globe and Mail,* dated May 25, 1971.
97. *Debates.* Dated May 25, 1971, p. 6070. *Op. cit.*
98. *Ibid.* Dated May 28, 1971, p. 5853. *Op. cit.*
99. *Ibid.* Dated May 28, 1971, p.6154. *Op. cit.*
100. *Ibid.*
101. *Ibid.*
102. *Ibid.* p. 6155.
103. *Ibid.* Dated September 13, 1971, p. 7749.
104. *Ibid.* Dated May 25, 1971, p.6070.
105. *Ibid.* Dated June 7, 1971, p. 6458.
106. *Ibid.* Dated December 22, 1971, p. 7215.
107. *Ibid.*

108. *Ibid.*
109. Canada. House of Commons. Minutes of Proceedings and Evidence of the Standing Committee on External Affairs and National Defence. Third Session, Twenty-eighth Parliament, 1970-71. Issue No 32, October 5, 1971, pp.32-38.
110. *Debates.* Dated September 16, 1971, p. 7868. *Op. cit.*
111. *Ibid.* Dated November 9, 1971, p. 9475.
112. *Ibid.*
113. *Ibid.* Dated November 17, 1971, p 9635.
114. *Ibid.* Dated November 22, 1971, p. 9796.
115. *Ibid.* Dated December 7, 1971, p, 10218.
116. *Ibid.* Dated June 28, 1971, p. 7373.
117. *Ibid.*
118. *Ibid.* Dated June 29, 1971, p. 7437.
119. *Ibid.*
120. *Ibid.*
121. *The Globe and Mail,* dated July 16, 1971.
122. *Debates.* Dated June 2, 1971.p. 6296. *Op. cit.*
123. *Ibid.*
124. *Ibid.* Dated June 10, 1971, p. 6561.
125. *Ibid*
126. *Ibid.* Dated June 28, 1971, p. 7379.
127. *Ibid.*
128. *Ibid.*
129. *Ibid.*
130. *Ibid.* Dated June 28, 1971, p. 7379.
131. *Ibid.*
132. *Ibid.* Dated June 7, 1971, pp. 6458–6459.
133. *Ibid.* Dated 7 June 1971, p. 6458.
134. *Ibid.*
135. *Ibid.* Dated June 14, 1971, p. 6650.
136. *Ibid.* p. 6651.
137. *Ibid.* Dated June 16, 1971, p. 6775.
138. *Ibid.*
139. *Ibid.*
140. *Ibid.* Dated June 16, 1971, p. 6774. *Op. cit.*
141. *Ibid.*
142. *Ibid.* Dated June 17, 1971, p. 6813.
143. *Ibid.*
144. *Ibid.* Dated June 17, 1971, p. 6813.
145. *Ibid.*
146. *Ibid.*

147. *Ibid.*
148. *Ibid.* Dated June 7, 1971, p. 6458.
149. *Ibid.* Dated June 14, 1971, p. 6651.
150. *Ibid.* Dated November 17, 1971, pp. 9636–9637.
151. *Ibid.* Dated November 17, 1971, p. 9637.
152. *Ibid.*
153. *Ibid.* Dated 17 November 1971, p.9636.
154. *Ibid.* Dated November 25, 1971, p. 9873.
155. *Ibid.*
156. *Toronto Daily Star,* dated December 4, 1971.
157. *Ibid.*
158. *Debates,* Dated, December 6, 1971, p.10155. *Op. cit.*
159. *Ibid.* p.10156. *Op. cit.*
160. *Ibid.* p.10156. *Op. cit.*
161. *Ibid.* December 6, 1971, p.10156. *Op. cit.*
162. *Toronto Daily Star,* dated December 6, 1971.
163. *Ibid. Debates,* Dated December 6, 1971, p.10157. *Op. cit.*
164. *Ibid.*
165. *Ibid.* Dated December 6, 1971, p.10162.
166. *Ibid.*
167. *Ibid.*
168. *Debates.* Dated December 6, 1971, p. 10157. *Op. cit.*
169. *Ibid.*
170. *Ibid.* Dated December 6, 1971, pp. 10155–10156.
171. *Ibid.* Dated December 6, 1971, p. 10162.
172. *Ibid.*
173. *Ibid.*
174. *Ibid.* Dated December 6, 1971, p.10155.
175. *Ibid.* Dated December 7, 1971, p.10218.
176. *Ibid.*
177. *Toronto Daily Star,* dated December 7, 1971.
178. *Ibid.*
179. *Ibid.* Dated December 6, 1971, p.10156.
180. *Ibid.* Dated December 6, 1971, p.10162.
181. *Ibid.*, p. 10162.
182. *Debates.* Dated December 6, 1971, p. 10205. *Op. cit.*
183. *Ibid.* Dated December 15, 1971, p.10486.
184. *Ibid.*
185. *Ibid.*
186. *Ibid.*
187. *Ibid.* Dated December 16, 1971, p.10526.
188. *Ibid.* Dated December 20, 1971, p. 10614.

189. *Ibid.* Dated December 22, 1971, p. 10704.
190. *Ibid.*
191. *Ibid.* Dated December 6, 1971, p. 10163.
192. *Ibid.*
193. *Ibid.* Dated December 15, 1971, p.10486.

CHAPTER 7

Canada's Initiatives Feature Her Trademark of Tact and Fairness

*T*hroughout the liberation war of Bangladesh, the Trudeau administration reacted to events with extreme caution since Canada was placed in an awkward position. On the one hand, Canada was firm in her adherence to the principles of the UN charter, including the principles of sovereign equality and territorial integrity of each State. On the other hand, she was conscious of the duty not to intervene in the "internal affairs" of another country. For diplomatic "correctness," Canada based her premise on a strategy allowing her to pursue a "neutral" policy that would preserve Canada's interests abroad. It would also enable her to contribute toward relieving the humanitarian aspects of the crisis resulting from the planned military reprisals in East Pakistan. Constrained by her own policies of "neutrality" and "nonintervention" in the face of public pressure to be more transparent, Canada undertook several initiatives during the Bengalis' fight for independence.

Following the Canadian tradition of "quiet diplomacy" of peace and "policy of moderation," Canada's initiatives during the crisis, initially referred to as the Pakistan Issue and later as the Indo-Pakistan issue, are commendable. Although Canada could not demonstrate her overt support for an independent Bangladesh, some of Canada's actions and reactions reveal how Canada, as a middle power, situated herself diplomatically.

Several of Canada's undertakings may be deemed to be activist programs with various organizations to promote and reinforce the democratic institutions in Pakistan. Some of Canada's initiatives remain significant examples of her positive attitudes toward the cause of the Bengalis, who were seen as the actual victims of their demand for autonomy and greater participation in the country's affairs. Specifically, Canada focused on humanitarian assistance to the victims of military reprisals and establishing democracy in Pakistan under the leadership of Bongobondhu.

It shall be seen that Canada regarded the conflict as a *political* issue. Despite everything, she undertook several initiatives to diffuse the conflict and find a solution to the impasse between the two wings of Pakistan at a time when India also became involved. The Trudeau administration noted how the Gandhi administration was exploiting the displaced persons issue to promote the cause of Bangladesh; at the same time, Canada also recognized how the military regime was continuing its ongoing reprisals on unarmed Bengali civilians who were fleeing to India to seek asylum. As a middle power, Canada adopted a four-pronged approach to what she called the Pakistan crisis: (1) to maintain a neutral public position; (2) to urge both Pakistan and India to exercise restraint; (3) to provide humanitarian relief to East Pakistani victims; and (4) encourage the military regime to move toward a *political solution* instead of a *military solution.* Tied to this also was Canada's strategy to continue persuading Pakistan to come to an understanding with the leader of the majority parties in East and West Pakistan and, simultaneously, urge India and Pakistan to exercise restraint and begin a new round of meaningful dialogue. From its position of neutrality and nonintervention, Canada pursued other diplomatic avenues.

Canada's initiatives reveal her political dichotomy and limitations regarding her position on the conflict and the constraints under which she operated while trying to remain "politically correct" in her mediatory role. Canada's initiatives are outlined below in chronological order based on the availability of archival records.

Trudeau's Personal Intervention and Counseling Pakistan and India (April 1971–December 1971)

Having obtained firsthand information from James George and John Small, Canadian high commissioners to India and Pakistan, respectively, Ottawa officials briefed Prime Minister Pierre Trudeau along the following line: that Sheikh Mujibur Rahman's (Bongobondhu) Awami League (AL) swept the polls on a program demanding greater control over the state affairs in East Pakistan *within the union of Pakistan*. The league's Six-Point Program (discussed in Chapter 1) was not a manifesto for secession or independence. The actual declaration of independence came only in the wake of the bloodbath, which began clandestinely on March 25, 1971. Prime Minister Pierre Trudeau had serious misgivings due to the potential threat resulting from ongoing military reprisals. Fortuitously, just as Trudeau's team began to draft a letter for both President Yahya Khan and Prime Minister Indira Gandhi to advise them to exercise restraint, Trudeau received a letter from President Yahya.

In his letter to Trudeau, Yahya explained Pakistan's side of the story—that it had been his "constant endeavour to lead the country toward the restoration of democratic processes through elected reps of the people," but "unfortunately, however, the political leadership in East Pakistan and especially Sheikh Mujibur Rahman took a progressively rigid stand which made such an agreement impossible."[1] He then continued: "Murder, arson, and widespread disorder in defiance of the govtl [sic] authorities were let loose in the province;" [2] and that he (Yahya) was convinced that Bongobondhu and his followers "were not prepared for any compromise"[3] during the last round of talks. In addition, he wrote that the Bengali leader and his supporters had "no intentions of accepting any constitutional formula which would ensure the integrity and unity of the country."[4]

The AL's final proposal virtually amounted to the dismemberment of the country since the AL "had no such mandate from the people, and as the unity of the country was at stake, firm action had to be taken to assert government's authority and to safeguard the integrity of Pakistan."[5] Thus, Yahya claimed that the destructive actions of the Bengalis constituted a direct threat to Pakistan's security. Continuing, and while seeking Canada's support of his government's military solid action upon Bengalis to establish *peace* and *security* in the subcontinent, Yahya appealed, "In view of your Excellency's dedication to the cause of international peace and security and to the principle of 'non-interference' in the 'internal affairs' of other states, I hope your Excellency would consider the desirability of expressing your support to the forces of peace and stability in this region and of impressing upon the Indian leaders the paramount need of refraining from any action which may aggravate the situation and lead to irretrievable consequences."[6]

The gist of Yahya's letter, as Ottawa understood, was to blame Bongobondhu for the failure of the talks as well as to blame the government of India. Having come up to speed on the latest development and/or deterioration of the situation in East Pakistan through personal communication channels from Canada's high commissioners to Pakistan and India, Ottawa found Yahya's letter of appeal *contrary to what Ottawa officials had already received* from the field. To Ottawa's foreign affairs cognoscenti team, Yahya's narrative appeared instead as a defense for his military actions, whereby he sought Ottawa's endorsement without explaining how the three-pronged negotiation broke down. Ottawa did not fail to note how carefully Yahya avoided referencing Zulfiqar Ali Bhutto, the Pakistan People's Party (PPP) leader. However, Bongobondhu and Bhutto openly opposed each other regarding *how* the power would be shared. Bhutto's name was neither mentioned nor indicated what Bhutto's position was at the negotiating table. Ottawa was aware of Bhutto's preposterous demand that, if necessary, there would be "two Pakistans" so that he could assume power in the western wing of the country.

Ottawa also noted Yahya's expressed concerns regarding the government of India's deployment of its artillery regiments and parachute brigades to the border areas but disagreed with Yahya's finger-pointing at India, stating that the issue was between Pakistan and India. Ottawa interpreted the actual issue as the transfer of power to the democratically elected leader of Pakistan and Bhutto's objection to transferring power to Bongobondhu, the prime minister-designate. The secret military action in East Pakistan left Trudeau with unanswered questions about Yahya's fundamental objective.

Canada's high commissioner to Pakistan, John Small, immediately advised Ottawa along the following line about what should Trudeau's reply contain: that in Canada, "we do not subscribe to secession or … interference in our domestic affairs. I should think the Prime Minister's reply could be wholehearted in condemning such concepts … Although there is much truth in the President's explanation of events in EastPak, … it is not the whole story. Para four is something less than honest since life remains anything but normal. … The Indian interference may be argued with respect to a degree but not as to the fact of Indian meddling."[7] Trudeau responded by indicating that he "was particularly concerned when… [he] learned of the breakdown of negotiations which [Yahya] had been conducting with the representatives of the Awami League, and of the events which followed.[8]

To Ottawa, Yahya's allegations were essentially *political* and were subject to a process of a continuing evolution in the tempestuous political activities of Pakistan. "My colleague and I naturally recognize that the search for a political solution to current problems is the responsibility of the government and people of Pakistan and not of Canada,"[9] thus wrote a frank and forthright Trudeau. "I trust that you will understand my motives and recognize my sincerity; therefore, when I express the hope as a friend of Pakistan that it will soon be possible to resume the search for an agreed solution to your current difficulties."[10] Putting the onus on Yahya himself, Trudeau argued that the solution to Pakistan's conflict ought to be found by following the *democratic electoral process* if Pakistan were to restore confidence and persuade the refugees in India to return to their native land through an "agreed solution." Trudeau ended his letter by offering help. "I wish to assure you that we are prepared if requested to join other members of the international community in providing emergency relief assistance for those who have suffered hardship during this difficult time."[11]

The "Indian government is determined to exploit the presence of displaced persons in India to aggravate the tense situation and justify military intervention in East Pakistan."[12] Thus, a desperate Yahya claimed again in June, drawing Trudeau's attention to the deterioration of relations between Pakistan and India, which he feared could lead to hostilities between the two countries. He then continued, "It is in this serious situation and in the interest of preserving peace that I would request you to use your influence with India to persuade her to desist from actions which could lead not only to a breach of peace but, as a result of that, to unforeseen consequences which could affect the world community."[13]

In the meantime, the Trudeau administration was disappointed to see that, although under international pressure, President Yahya reiterated in his national statement on June 28, 1971, his intention to transfer power, in reality, he showed no demonstrated inclination toward restoring democracy. The events in Pakistan were reminiscent of the Nigerian/Biafran situation of the late 1960s when Canada did not want to be involved in what it deemed to be an "internal affair" of Nigeria. Trudeau made a deliberate attempt not to use words like "mass killing" or "genocide," etc. However, by then, the Canadian media had already been reporting of mass murder of innocent civilians, looting, burning, raping, etc., by the Pakistani military personnel.

In keeping with Canada's tradition of *mediatory role,* Ottawa purposefully chose to continue its intervention *personally* to counsel Pakistan *quietly* to bring Yahya to his "senses;" and India to a fuller appreciation of the grave situation without even showing intervention. Unlike the USA, whose "relations with India had achieved a state of exasperatedly strained cordiality,"[14] Canada had an excellent relationship with India and Pakistan and wanted to keep it that way. Canada remained concerned about *not straining its friendly ties with Pakistan and India by sticking to its* policy of *entente cordiale.* The Trudeau administration, therefore, chose to work primarily through *quiet diplomacy.*

Ottawa's straightforward take on the conflict remained the same—that the issue was between the two wings of Pakistan regarding greater autonomy for East Pakistan and not between India and Pakistan, even though Yahya had been trying to drive home a different narrative. To Ottawa, it was preposterous on Yahya's part to point fingers at India and shift the blame from himself to India. Having failed to understand Yahya's motives and logic, Ottawa found no justification for *not transferring power to the elected representatives of Pakistan.* Understandably, for diplomatic reasons, Ottawa did not wish to accuse the government of Pakistan directly in any manner. For the same reason, Ottawa neither challenged Yahya on his *undemocratic stand* and *secret military operations* nor accepted Yahya's version of the events.

With the availability of more information, however, Ottawa officials recognized that there was an element of truth in Yahya's blaming of India. Such realization complicated the matter even more as Canada needed to be circumspect. In his correspondence, Trudeau cautiously and discretely followed Canada's policy of non-interference in Pakistan's internal affairs. From the beginning, Small's advice from Islamabad was to keep a substantive relationship with India and Pakistan to counsel restraint and encourage a political solution effectively. Ottawa worked on the understood premise that Canada should neither *interfere* nor *condone* one's interference in another country's internal affairs. Canada's challenge was *how to become involved very discretely by playing her traditional peacemaker role in resolving the conflict in favor of democracy while remaining friendly with a military dictator.* Ottawa advised the Canadian high commissioners to Pakistan and India to compare their notes and consistently interpret the events before dispatching them to Ottawa to facilitate Ottawa officials' understanding of the problems.

In his correspondence to Yahya and Gandhi, Trudeau emphasized two key concepts: (1) the return of the refugees and (2) the resumption of negotiation to transfer power to the elected leader of Pakistan. Through his admonitory notes, Trudeau cautioned both heads of Pakistan and India, urging them to exercise restraint under all circumstances—that the "explosive situation must be kept under control and every effort made to reduce the present dangerous level of tension."[15]

"It is quite clear to me, Mr. President, that the flight of refugees from East Pakistan must be brought to an end and indeed reversed if the present threatening trend of events in South Asia is to be arrested. It is equally clear that further steps must be taken both internationally and within Pakistan to facilitate the return home of the millions of these displaced persons now in India.";[16] thus, a concerned Trudeau had written to Yahya, underscoring expediency.

Trudeau said, "I would not presume to offer advice to you personally or to the Government of Pakistan on the best way to create a more normal situation in the East Wing. This is a question to be decided among Pakistanis themselves. It is evident; however, those ways must be found to achieve a realistic political settlement and a climate of confidence in East Pakistan if the Bengali refugees are to be persuaded to return from India."[17] As a friend of Pakistan, Trudeau wrote that to be fully effective in his attempt, Yahya's initiatives must be "accompanied by political measures" on his side "to restore, a climate of confidence among Bengali—Muslim and Hindu alike."[18]

Simultaneously, a concerned Trudeau remained in touch with Prime Minister Indira Gandhi and wrote to her frankly. "The political problem in East Pakistan is, of course, at the root of the present crisis, and while it would be inappropriate for me to attempt to offer detailed prescriptions for solving it, I have, in a recent letter to President Yahya, urged on him the need to resume the search for a political solution. In my view, it is essential that any solution in East Pakistan be based on the will of the people and the democratic electoral process if it is to restore confidence and persuade the refugees in India to return to their own country.

I am aware that in answering your letter in this way, I am not providing answers to the agonizing problems which your Government is facing as a result of recent tragic developments. I admit that I see no obvious solution to these problems, but am sure that a first requisite for solving them is the establishment of a degree of confidence between the various groups in East and West Pakistan and between the governments of India, and Pakistan. I can assure you that if it appears that there is anything that we for our part can usefully do to help in this latter connection, my colleagues and I will give it the most careful consideration."[19]

Trudeau remained emphatic in putting across Canada's understanding of India's situation. "My colleagues and I are very conscious of the forbearance shown by India in the face of the refugee problem. We recognize that this gigantic influx has imposed serious strains not only on the Indian economy but on the whole social and political fabric of India, and those ways must be found urgently for the refugees to return in safety to their homes."[20] He further went on to say he saw "no other way of halting the present trend and making a start toward a peaceful solution."[21]

Having stressed the dangers ahead unless Yahya's proposed changes were accompanied by increased local participation in the government, Trudeau wrote, "It is widely understood that this will not come about. Indeed, there will not be an end to the continuing influx without a realistic political settlement in East Pakistan sufficient to restore Bengali confidence."[22] A concerned Trudeau did not stop there. He said, "I think the Government of Pakistan is increasingly coming to recognize the need to adjust its policies but while this evolution is in progress, I hope India will continue to avoid taking any positions which might serve to increase tension. I am concerned for example that any move to extend recognition to an independent government in East Pakistan could lead to overt military action which would be fraught with the gravest consequences, and could alienate the considerable sympathy India now enjoys."[23]

An unabashed federalist, Trudeau went to the extent of candidly urging Gandhi not to accord recognition to the newly formed provisional government of Bangladesh but to seek ways to find a *realistic political settlement* that would be a *solution within a united Pakistan*. It may be worthwhile to note that the same position was also taken by the people of Canada apart from the Bengali and Indian segments of the Canadian public. All the major political parties in Canada, both federal and provincial, also favored a united Pakistan under Bongobondhu. We shall see more about it in Chapter 8.

While corresponding with India and Pakistan, Trudeau remained extra careful in ensuring that Ottawa's actions or reactions did not provoke either country and that Ottawa would take up the matter only when it became an *issue of humanitarian concern*. Ottawa, however, was outraged seeing Yahya's machination by branding the prime minister-elect as the "enemy of Pakistan." And yet, Ottawa chose not to express its reaction in one way or another. True, a tight-lipped Trudeau did not wish to interfere. Still, behind the scenes, however, he found ways to exert pressure on the government of Pakistan to move as quickly as possible to take steps to begin the process of power transfer to the elected majority according to the result of the National Elections 1970. In doing all that, his challenge was to write a carefully crafted letter to ensure that he neither appeared to be interfering nor sounded like he was accusing India or Pakistan. The critical message for President Yahya was clear: wake up, smell the coffee.

Looking back, while insisting on moving along the path of a *united Pakistan,* Canada ignored two critical phenomena: (1) she did neither consider the Gandhi administration's *game plan* nor its *strategy of dismantling* Pakistan; (2) she did not consider the potential power of the rebel forces whose pledge was to *liberate their native land*—nothing short of it. When, in early fall, the Trudeau administration was looking forward to the Yahya regime's civilianization program through the appointment of Dr. Abdul Malik, a Bengali, as the governor of East Pakistan, it was cautioned by the Indian high commissioner who sent several notes dealing with various aspects of the situation regarding President Yahya's so-called initiatives. The Indian high commissioner in Ottawa reminded Sharp by citing an excerpt of a statement of Acting Prime Minister Tajuddin Ahmad: "Our enemy is not only barbarous but also covert and insidious. From time to time, he would float treacherous compromise formulae, the purpose of which could only be to mislead our people and to weaken our resolve to achieve independence. If the enemy seeks a compromise, it must be because he is weak or wants to lay a trap to which we must be on our guard."[24]

Because Canada had a different perspective on the issue throughout the crisis period, her proposed suggestion was a solution within Pakistan as *one country*. The ministerial correspondence reveals that Canada was much too naïve in directing her efforts in encouraging Yahya to bring the AL on board to reconvene negotiation when it was clear that neither the Bengalis agreed to any such proposal nor the Gandhi administration allowed that to happen. Though patently illusory, Canada tried to save the lives of the refugees and the lives of a *united* and *democratic Pakistan*.

Provision of Economic and Humanitarian Assistance (April 1971—December 1971)

Earlier, Ivan Head, special assistant to the prime minister, advised Sharp about the need for ongoing pressure while simultaneously providing economic and humanitarian assistance. "Our aim must be to exert whatever pressure we can on the government of Pakistan to attract the refugees back. My formula is designed to influence them in that fashion and thus avoid the establishment of a Palestine situation in West Bengal and, hopefully, avoid a complete economic breakdown of the entire country. I am quite certain that there will be increasing pressure within Canada to bring some political pressure to bear on the Government of Pakistan, and we must show that we have done something of this sort."[25] Head's point was that "it would be wrong for Canada to discontinue all its economic assistance to Pakistan at this time but that it would be equally wrong to continue to commit funds as if no crisis existed."[26]

Sharp noted it before meeting with the June 21, 1971, heads of the Aid to Pakistan Consortia delegation meeting. Consistent with its "neutrality" policy, Canadian participants naturally took a thoughtful position. Canada recognized that she was viewing her obligations as *economic assistance* to a problem, the nature of which was very much *political*. Canada's reaction to the military crackdown and its aftermath was reminiscent of Conservative Prime Minister John Diefenbaker's reaction toward South Africa's apartheid policy in the late 1950s, which maintained that any approach to resolving the apartheid problem in South Africa ought not to be actuated by alienating or withdrawing a spirit of goodwill toward South Africa, regardless of its government measures. At this time, Canada was also prepared to provide emergency relief assistance by believing that the resumption of developmental aid would have to be contingent upon establishing social, economic, and political conditions within East Pakistan, which would make developmental assistance effective.

In taking a firm *humanitarian stand* toward the suffering Bengalis, Ottawa officials' first challenge was to clearly distinguish between requests for *relief assistance* and *development work* that were being undertaken in Pakistan. Canada worked on the following three areas to resume a practical economic life: (a) that the regional allocation of $33 million for development assistance for Pakistan would stand for the fiscal year 1971/1972, but that the specific program of expenditures would be recast in light of the needs for relief and rehabilitation; (b) that the allocation would not be announced in Canada at present; and (c) that the government of Pakistan would not be informed of the allocation until a suitable climate for assistance had been achieved.[27]

Moving forward, Trudeau recognized that his misgivings were the same as all donor countries - that any substantial relief assistance for East Pakistan might serve to indirectly support the present military government, which was engaged in the suppression of East Pakistan. Ottawa prioritized Canada's plan of action to (1) outline the various actions up to the present stage; (2) provide short-term relief assistance, etc.; (3) provide direct refugee relief; (4) provide aid to the Indian economy; and (5) design plans for rehabilitation and development for Pakistan.

In the meantime, Small's carefully drafted situational reports from Islamabad disappointed Canada. It was unclear whether the military and security situation in East Pakistan had returned to the point where reconstruction activities could effectively be carried out. Inordinate delays in crossing the t's and dotting the i's made it impossible for Ottawa to understand the approach it should take clearly. Information regarding the aid requirements was also not readily available even though a UN mission had already been established in Dhaka under the direction of Mr. Bahgat A. El Twail, who was expected to have completed the assessment of immediate needs within East Pakistan but could not do that. It will be seen later that when a drama of human survival was enacted in the refugee camps in India, Canada, however, was not idle.

Mediating through the Commonwealth (May 1971—December 1971)

Though not a major power, Canada was not without influence; it was vestigial. From the beginning of the military repression, the Canadian public had been demanding a more significant leadership role for Canada on the world stage—to "do something." The Trudeau administration also agreed that *Canada must play an important role*. Fortuitously, Arnold Smith, then the Commonwealth secretary-general since 1965 and a distinguished Canadian diplomat, was keen on working out a political settlement. In early 1971, he visited both wings of Pakistan and held discussions with Yahya, who, Smith believed, was genuinely interested in transferring power to Bongobondhu, the elected leader of Pakistan. Again, in January 1971, only two months before the military takeover in Pakistan, Prime Minister Trudeau also visited both Pakistan and India. Upon his return, he, too, talked about his positive impression of Yahya. Following the policy of "quiet diplomacy," Sharp approached the Commonwealth to negotiate a lasting political settlement in Pakistan regarding the transfer of power to the democratically elected representatives.

Smith's first challenge was to ensure that all Commonwealth countries would act consistently. With this view in mind, by the end of June 1971, and with encouragement from Ottawa, Smith completed the first round of discussions with several Commonwealth heads of countries on the nature of the problems between India and Pakistan. Smith's peace initiative was immediately taken up by Sirimavo R. D. Bandaranaike, prime minister of Ceylon (now Sri Lanka), who planned for Smith to travel back and forth to India and Pakistan to teach the idea of exercising restraint to strive for reconciliation. Yahya did not respond to Smith's offer many times even though "several envoys came with messages from different sides"[28] to meet with Smith. The Gandhi administration formally rejected the offer and argued that "the Commonwealth initiative appeared to equate the situations in India and Pakistan" and that "this was a false equation since Pakistan's actions alone had created the vast exodus of refugees from which India now suffered."[29] Without disputing the accusation, Smith pointed out that the Commonwealth team was not equating the positions of the governments of India and Pakistan. He clarified both points by stating that he planned to hold talks with the AL leaders in exile in Kolkata, West Bengal so that they could develop a broader perspective on the crisis.

Though disappointed, Ottawa continued encouraging Smith not to give up his shuttle diplomacy efforts as the Commonwealth's spokesperson. Coincidentally, Smith met with Justice Abu Sayed Chowdhury, then spokesperson for Bangladesh in London. Chowdhury briefed Smith further on the nature of the grievances of the Bengalis, the destiny of their elected leader, and the atrocities of the Yahya regime. He requested Smith to urge "a suspension of Western aid to persuade the Pakistani government to release Sheikh Mujib and resume negotiations."[30] On May 2, 1971, Smith also met with his former colleague Arshad Hussain, a special envoy of Yahya, who came for talks with Alexi Kosygin, chairman of the Council of Members of the USSR, Georges Pompidou, president of the French Republic, and Edward Heath, prime minister of Great Britain. Smith also held meetings with a few Indian leaders, the most important of whom was

Jayprakash Narayan of the Gandhi Peace Foundation, who argued that Pakistan's unity was no longer possible and that India should recognize the provisional government of Bangladesh.

By fall, however, Smith realized this was an arduous task requiring the genuine cooperation of Yahya and Gandhi, who had their own secret agendas and game plans. Regardless, Smith offered them the services of the good office of the secretary-general for any potential mediatory role it could play. Sharp was then briefed along the line that, apart from the opposing position of the governments of India and Pakistan, the provisional government of Bangladesh and the rebel forces had made it clear that there could be no agreement with the Occupation Army. In the meantime, although Canada and Smith chose to ignore the achievement of the liberation forces, they did not fail to note how, by late fall, most of the news media had already concluded that the *emergence of Bangladesh was inevitable.*

At that time, a reality check also dampened their spirits, forcing them to realize that their efforts to persuade Yahya to transfer power to the prime minister-designate were an illusion. With no realistic prospects of success, Smith, after consulting with Canada, temporarily abandoned his quixotic proposal to find a political solution.

Canada at the United Nations (May 1971–December 1971)

Canada could not do anything at the UN because of Pakistan's claim that the crisis was an "internal affair of Pakistan" beyond the jurisdiction of the UN. Canada was aware of the efforts of the secretary-general, who had, since the beginning of the crisis, been continuously in touch with the governments of India and Pakistan through their permanent representatives at the UN and through other means as well, that is by sending *aide mémoires* and notes to the president of the Security Council, but had no luck. When, on May 25, U Thant, secretary-general of the UN, launched an appeal for emergency assistance for refugees, Heath Macquarrie (Conservative MP for Hillsborough, PEI) welcomed the action and suggested that Canada should focus on programs that would be considered *humanitarian* rather than *political.*

Canada came forward to play her part in both (1) emergency relief measures for East Pakistani refugees in India and (2) the promotion of their voluntary repatriation to Pakistan. Within weeks, however, Canada became frustrated seeing how *humanitarian* and *economic* issues were interwoven with political problems. India argued that any discussion on the East Pakistan issue, which she continually referred to as the "Bangladesh issue," in the UN should go into *the root cause of the conflict* and discuss the situation in East Pakistan along with the issues of relief, rehabilitation, and repatriation of the Bengali refugees then sheltered in India. Having vehemently opposed India's argument, Pakistan counterargued that the matter was an "internal affair" of Pakistan. Again, when Pakistan agreed to raise the issue in the Security Council, claiming that the situation had already appeared to threaten peace, India unsurprisingly objected, having claimed that the issue was not an "Indo-Pakistan issue." The situation fundamentally concerned a political reconciliation between the already-elected leader, Bongobondhu, and the military government of Pakistan, argued India. On seeing the accusation and counteraccusation of each other, Canada was disheartened that the governments of India and Pakistan were at complete loggerheads. This prompted Canada to question the effectiveness and relevancy of the UN at a time when neither India nor Pakistan agreed with each other.

Canada was among the thirty-seven nations that participated in the General Debate at the twenty-sixth session of the General Assembly in September 1971. When Adam Malik, president of the same session, ruled out the possibility of a debate on the East Pakistan situation in the General Assembly on the ground that, since it was an internal affair of Pakistan, it could not be discussed in the world forum; neither Canada nor the UN was in a position to address the *root cause* of the conflict. While some member country representatives made speeches at the UN, Canada chose to keep it low-key and remained silent. She maintained that she was a *promoter and facilitator of voluntary repatriation of refugees and displaced persons,* the details of which are outlined below in the present chapter under the caption United Nations High Commissioner for Refugees (UNHCR) initiative. Again, when Indian Foreign Minister Sardar Swaran Singh and Pakistan's chief delegate to the General Assembly Mahmud Ali accused and counteraccused each other, Canada, like most of the member countries, felt hapless.

During his four-day stay in New York, a watchful Sharp, who thought carefully before he spoke, heard with profound sympathy arguments from both sides. His discussion with Andrei Gromyko, minister of Foreign Affairs, Union of Soviet Socialist Republics (USSR), Sir Alec Douglas

Hume, British member of Parliament, and Sardar Swaran Singh, Indian foreign minister, to assess *what role Canada could play as a middle power,* deepened his understanding of the many facets of the conflict. Although Canada maintained that she would not be involved in the internal affairs of Pakistan, Sharp still expressed his concerns about the true meaning and implication of the term "internal affairs" as he understood: "At what point does an internal conflict affect so many nations to such an extent that it can no longer properly be accepted."[31]

A cautious Sharp observed, "I sense a growing concern that tragedies are unfolding and that nothing is being done about them by the world community as represented by the United Nations. The capacity of this Organization [UN] to resolve conflicts, whether domestic or international, is limited by two realities: the terms of the Charter and the will of the Member nations."[32] He went on further to say, "The United Nations does not constitute a supernational organization. Canada does not believe that the world is ready for such authority, for any kind of world. ... Today, most nations of the world, older and newer equally, are occupied with internal problems. Certainly, Canada is no exception. Canadians are facing internal problems of both an economic and a political nature. Canada believes that domestic problems are best dealt with by domestic solutions, and others feel the same way. The question is: how can the international community best assist in a situation where an internal problem has gone beyond the capacity of the Government concerned? The mere fact that the nations are preoccupied with internal problems and questions of sovereignty in the foreseeable future does not excuse us from making the best possible use of the instrument of the United Nations."[33] As Sharp feared a backlash in Canada, he did not encourage further discussion on the nature of the conflict.

Back in Canada, Sharp remained frustrated the following week following his return from New York. This is evident in Sharp's statement made at the meeting of the Standing Committee for External Affairs and National Defence: "We can see very little to be gained by having a debate in the United Nations where one side or the other would be trying to pin the blame for the present situation. We should now concentrate our efforts on solving the problem, not deciding who was to blame initially. This is the general position I would take as the representative of Canada at the United Nations."[34]

The following month, the same level of frustration persisted. On November 18, Paul Gérin-Lajoie, president of the Canadian International Development Agency (CIDA), represented Canada concerning human rights at the Third Committee, UN General Assembly. Having maintained that nothing constructive could result from procedural or political wrangling in the Third Committee, Gérin-Lajoie stressed Canada's continued support for relief efforts of the East Pakistan Relief Operation (UNEPRO) and sought the cooperation of the government of Pakistan. Canada's priority was to provide ongoing humanitarian assistance, and the second priority was to find a political solution, argued Gérin-Lajoie. In the same vein, Senator Paul Desruisseaux, who also attended the Twenty-Sixth Meeting of the UN General Assembly in November as an observer and guest of Yvon Beauline, permanent representative of Canada, saw Canada's participation at the UN as evidence of the highest *humanitarian objectives*. "We have a right to be proud of Canadian participation, even though it is not possible in all cases to give justice to the worldwide dimensions we believe it should have."[35] Thus, Desruisseaux encapsulated Canada's position.

As the issue ricocheted between the General Assembly and Security Council, Canada tried in vain with several fruitless attempts toward a potential *political solution* to the conflict. A consensus was urgently required, at least a passive acceptance among the superpowers with its current pro-and anti-Bangladesh positions. Canada felt helpless, finding no way to move forward as there was no agreed-upon consensus. Sharp was aware that the longer an attempt at a peaceful solution is delayed, the more will East Pakistan suffer - something that would make them increasingly reluctant to accept a solution agreeable to both wings of Pakistan should an early solution not be found. Canada welcomed the UN's decision to send a special envoy, Ismat Kittani, to Pakistan to develop an action plan. However, in reality, by December 3, both India and Pakistan found themselves in an all-out war. A disconcerted Canada immediately began to treat both India and Pakistan as belligerents. It considered the UN's inaction as a denial of fundamental human rights under the UN Declaration of Human Rights. Meanwhile, on December 6, the Gandhi administration recognized Bangladesh as a sovereign country, paving the way for a new ball game among the superpowers.

The next day, at the General Assembly meeting of December 7, Canadian delegates favored direct UN supervision of a ceasefire and the formation of a commission of inquiry when a resolution was passed for an immediate ceasefire and withdrawal of armed forces from each other's territory. Fifty-eight member countries presented statements during the debate. The voting was 104 in favour, 11 against, and 10 abstentions. In the end, however, India opposed the resolutions because they were not based on the *political realities of the situation* in the subcontinent. Canada also saw Yahya's initiative as impractical and impossible to implement since there were no mechanisms. On December 13, when the US moved a ceasefire resolution in the Security Council, it was immediately defeated by a Soviet veto. In other words, at the UN, both China and Russia did speak up but only as partisans, not as mediators. China branded India as the aggressor; Russia defended India. Canada feared that if the war was not terminated swiftly, Russia and China might fight each other. As Canada saw the situation, the dire threat indicated that the immediate *priority* should be an Indo-Pak ceasefire.

Nevertheless, Sharp imperturbably listened to impassioned arguments and counterarguments from the permanent representatives of Pakistan and India, Agha Shahi and Samar Sen, and, later, from Sardar Swaran Singh and Zulfiqar Ali Bhutto, foreign ministers of India and Pakistan, respectively. Canada argued in vain that the Security Council and its member states had both the right and the responsibility to do all in their power to forestall mounting tensions between Pakistan and India. While still pursuing all possible avenues, Canada felt stonewalled as she was experiencing firsthand the UN system's filibuster.

The member States recognized the UN's inability to exercise meaningful power in world affairs. It may sound ludicrous now, but it is very accurate that Canada still gullibly believed in the possibility of a political solution through a tad more *moral suasion.* Though frustrated, Canada was not yet ready to give up totally. While it is true that the UN was vulnerable to the charge that it should have done more, it is also true that the UN could do only what its members wanted done. In other words, the UN is no more robust than the collective will of its members. The evidence in the case of the Pakistan crisis showed that the will was pathetically weak as the influential members had their *own secret agendas.*

Unsurprisingly, therefore, seeing the future of East Pakistanis still unresolved, many concerned Canadians found the UN in disarray – like the "fall guy" for a mess that continued to grow with no prospect for a resolution. The UN seemed like an institution that had outlived its usefulness to them. Much to their displeasure, the Canadian public saw their government's intervention as too weak to impact.

United Nations High Commissioner for Refugees (UNHCR) (May 1971–December 1971)

The designation of the high commissioner, Prince Sadruddin Aga Khan, to act as a focal point for the coordination of the relief action provided by the members of the UN was welcomed by Canada, whose enthusiastic response remains an example of the proactive role she wanted to play in *humanitarian relief*. Having worked nationally within the country through its Ottawa-based office and internationally through the UNHCR's Geneva-based office, Canada was the first nation in the UN to demonstrate her commitment to assisting the Bengali refugees. Readers may recall reading about UNHCR's awareness activities in Canada in Chapter 5 under the Combined Appeal for Pakistan Relief (CAPR) caption. The following are details of Canada's international involvement in coordinating its activities with the New York-based UNHCR.

Canada made every attempt to separate the political aspect of the issue and see it as a humanitarian issue to assist the refugees. G. Ignatieff, the Canadian representative in the Permanent Mission of Canada to the Office of the UN in Geneva, kept Ottawa abreast all through summer and fall. Sharp was also mindful of the observations of both George and Small that a "visible UN presence would have stabilizing influence on EastPak generally and should act as a restraint on Army."[36] It was a frustrating experience for all. Having reached the peak of his disappointment, Sadruddin himself felt that "the situation remained extremely grave because the independence movement of Bangla Desh was now difficult to reverse, and a state of civil war existed."[37] On October 25, Canadian officials had an opportunity to meet with Sadruddin in person at an interdepartmental meeting in Ottawa, where he was the guest speaker. Sadruddin "stressed the importance of achieving a political solution" and informed the audience that the major donor countries "were promoting a political accommodation."[38]

Canada endorsed the UNHCR's proposed position, which was to undertake the following three steps to alleviate the precarious situation in Pakistan: (1) India should refrain from encouraging guerilla tactics; (2) Pakistan should arrive at some understanding with the Awami League; and (3) there should be a gradual withdrawal of the army.[39] The point to note is that implicit in the proposal was an understanding that any undertaking with the Awami League or other political body must be achieved *within the framework of present Pakistan* and *not a separate country* (Bangladesh) out of Pakistan.

Canada was among the thirty-one member countries that participated in the debate of the Third Committee of the UN General Assembly, Concerned with Human Rights, held on November 18–19, to debate the UNHCR's "focal point" activities (*humanitarian assistance*) in India and Pakistan. Sharp's discussion with the UNHCR team occurred so late that its plan was regarded as futile. In the meantime, out of sheer frustration, many recipients and donor countries were already directing criticisms at the UN and UNHCR. Canadian representatives, who experienced the same frustration, also found the entire operations of the UN System, including the UNHCR, to be dysfunctional.

Although the government of Pakistan approved the stationing of a UNHCR representative in East Pakistan, where reception centers were to be set up to facilitate the return of the refugees, the government of India objected to the idea. As the UNHCR saw, on the one hand, India was preventing refugees from going back to their homes; on the other hand, her propaganda for and support of the *Mukti Bahini* (Liberation Forces) virtually guaranteed that the refugees would stay in the Indian refugee camps. A frustrated Sadruddin, thus, shared his own experiences with member countries and the apparent contradiction between what the Gandhi administration was *claiming* and what *it was doing*. The Trudeau administration was also aware of the media coverage regarding India's position stated by Gandhi herself in the Parliament: "We have no intention of rehabilitating them [refugees] here. But we have no intention of letting them go back to be butchered."[40]

Just about the same time, the foreign affairs cognoscenti team in Ottawa reminded Sharp that the *"Joy Bangla"* slogan had already become widely popular among the Bengalis both in the refugee camps and in East Pakistan where everyone had been referring to the province as "Occupied Bangladesh." There was, however, no change in the UNHCR's modus operandi even when it became convinced of the Gandhi administration's diabolic game plan. Technically speaking, it was out of the question for UNHCR to bring the provisional government of Bangladesh on board since not a single country had yet recognized Bangladesh. Sympathetic to the plight of the refugees and displaced people in the province, Canada tagged along with UNHCR, having remained active in her illusory search for mediation with the AL leaders for a solution *within the framework of a united Pakistan* despite the evident success of the freedom fighters and India's direct military assistance to the rebel forces.

To appreciate the role of UNHCR and that of Canada during the Liberation War of Bangladesh, one must not lose sight of the enormity of the task and the very significant complexities devolving upon the UNHCR in the discharge of its role and also, UNHCR's official mandate derived from the convention relating to the 1951 Status of Refugees that was subsequently widened in scope by the 1967 Protocol. Canada was, and remains, a signatory. Every member country reminded each other of the need to strictly observe the *humanitarian, social,* and *nonpolitical* character of the UNHCR's tasks, as laid down in Article 2 of the Statute.

One could say both Canada and UNHCR remained engaged in an impossible, unrealistic, and unachievable mission. Naturally, in the end, neither UNHCR nor Canada was able to persuade Yahya to adopt a democratic shift to *realign* Pakistan. Canada's hope was against hope for a *reformed* Pakistan. This was utterly impossible to achieve since, by then, the freedom fighters had already made tremendous progress under the Indian army's direct supervision - something that Canada never took into consideration in her strategic plans.

Activities through the Senate (March 1971–December 1971)

In Chapter 6, we examined the arguments the MPs and senators put forward to recognize the moot point of the conflict. During his visit to the Soviet Union between May 17 and 28, Prime Minister Trudeau freely discussed the subcontinental issue and expressed his grave misgivings while discussing the matter with Leonid I. Brezhnev (secretary-general of the Central Committee of the Communist Party of the Soviet Union), Nicolai V. Podgorny (chairman of the Presidium of the Supreme Soviet of the USSR), and Alexei Kosygin (chairman of the Council of Ministers of the USSR). The discussion focused on Canada-Soviet relations, peace, security, and major international problems of common concern. Having considered the Indo-Pakistan crisis as an issue of significance, both Canada and the Soviet Union confirmed early in June their desire "to continue efforts to strengthen universal peace and reduce international tension."[41]

Canadians were happy that both leaders recognized the need for vigorous diplomatic intervention. Initially, the Trudeau administration was glad to note that the Soviet Union's role was more along the lines of finding a way to settle the Indo-Pakistan crisis in consultation with the leader of the majority (that is, Bongobondhu) and the military government of Pakistan.

Ottawa officials, however, noticed a drastic change in their interactions with the USSR within a few months when Kosygin was in Ottawa between October 17 and 26. Both heads of government "reaffirmed the attachment of Canada and the Soviet Union to peace and security and the development of international cooperation."[42] Ottawa officials were intrigued by the evident shift in Kosygin's attitude, which they found bizarre. Strangely enough, in his address to peace and security issues, the Soviet leader did not even bother to mention the conflict in the Indian subcontinent. Ottawa suspected the careful avoidance by Kosygin might be because the USSR had already signed the Indo-Soviet Treaty of Peace, Friendship, and Cooperation with India by then. Ottawa interpreted this as the loss of the Soviet "neutrality" vis-à-vis the subcontinental conflict. Naturally, as a middle power with no axe to grind, Ottawa officials became more careful about another dimension of the Indo-Pakistan crisis - the possibility of direct Soviet intervention.

Under the circumstances, when the news of killings and brutalities from the field was coming every day, Canadian parliamentarians could not determine precisely what role Canada, as a middle power, *could* or *should* play. This was particularly so since there was a delicate political divide among the superpowers. Canadian parliamentarians had reason to remain worried since "the presence of many million Pakistani refugees in India and the resulting tension in that area" had "continued to be a source of concern."[43] Cognizant of Canada's limited capability, Canadian parliamentarians sadly realized Canada's foreign policy constraints that could be summarized as follows from the Senate debate: "It was agreed that to maintain peace and to prevent further deterioration of the situation in that region, it was necessary to achieve an urgent political settlement in East Pakistan that would consider the legitimate rights and interests of its population and would facilitate a speedy and secure return of refugees. This would be facilitated if the interested parties exercised restraint."[44]

The Trudeau administration was not on the same wavelength as the provisional governments of Bangladesh, India, and the Soviet Union. In

Chapter 8, we shall explore Canada's declaratory position regarding the conflict.

Canadian International Development Agency's Team (March 1971–December 1971)

All through summer, CIDA consulted with several federal departments and agencies informally about the needs of the refugees in India and displaced people in East Pakistan and sent many of its representatives to Pakistan on several occasions between March and November while the liberation war was going on. Under the leadership of Paul Gérin-Lajoie, CIDA's president, a seven-member team went to India and Pakistan and stayed there from October 24 to November 4. The team concentrated on (1) the number of refugees, (2) the location of refugees, (3) the continuous flow of refugees, and (4) considerations of the governments of Pakistan and India regarding the conflict. In Dhaka, Gérin-Lajoie and his entourage met with a few military officials. They noted how, by resorting to force against the overwhelmingly popular Awami League (AL) and Bengali nationalists, the regime was inflicting savage wounds.

The team also noted how the army had virtually destroyed the province, having killed, imprisoned, and driven underground, or out of the country, both the Bengali politicians and civilians alike from the villages, resulting in total disruption of East Pakistan's infrastructure. Canada feared that the destruction of roads and bridges by the *Mukti Bahini* and the disruptions of marketing facilities would jeopardize the harvest of produce. The team also found that tea production, East Pakistan's second-largest export, was endangered. Worst of all, there was the possibility of famine within months. The potential consequence of increasing militancy of the freedom fighters, the accelerated pace of arms acquisition from India and the Soviet Union, and the likelihood of a violent flare-up all posed dangerous possibilities.

The team also obtained firsthand information from Mohammed Ali, a Bengali-speaking East Pakistan relief commissioner, with whom the team had a frank discussion on relief supplies and guerrilla activities within East Pakistan. A visibly angry commissioner sharply pointed out that the economy was already in a shaky state and that withholding aid would hasten the downfall of the Yahya regime. He appealed to Canada by saying that Canada should give no economic assistance to Pakistan. Perhaps because of Gérin-Lajoie's evident empathy and the relief commissioner's cordial relationship with the Canadian high commissioner in Islamabad, a candid Ali spoke his mind *discretely* in *confidence*. Canada, however, did not see the situation in the same light as sanctions.

To keep his colleagues posted, Mitchell Sharp, Secretary of State for External Affairs, informed them in the Commons: "To date, the Canadian contribution from governmental and nongovernmental sources for refugees in India amounts to $6.6 million. Of this sum, $4.3 million has been provided by three federal governments, $370 by the provinces, 1.9 million by voluntary agencies, and the combined appeal for Pakistani relief. It is the government's intention to supplement these contributions by an amount of $18 million, seeking the authority and funds from Parliament. This will bring the Canadian government's total contribution for the relief of refugees in India to $22 million, coincidentally representing approximately one dollar for every Canadian."[45]

In the meantime, upon returning to Canada, the CIDA team conducted a series of consultations with representatives from other departments and agencies, many of whom had also visited the two countries earlier during the year. They worked closely with the India-Pakistan Task Force, which was established to make new recommendations. As December loomed, everything came to a halt.

Socialist International Council's Conference in Helsinki (May 25, 1971)

Canada also participated in the Socialist International Council's Conference in Helsinki on May 25, 1971. At the said conference, Canada, along with the USA, Germany, Israel, Sweden, Norway, and several other countries, expressed profound concern about the tragic situation in Pakistan. "East Pakistan is another example, where the military junta blatantly flouted the people's clear mandate to Sheikh Mujibur Rahman,"[46] thus observed Lim Kit Siang, secretary-general of the Democratic Action Party, at the said conference in his inaugural speech. The participants called for an immediate ceasefire and for the commencement of negotiations that would achieve a settlement, taking into account the views of the people of both East and West Pakistan, as freely expressed in the National Elections of Pakistan in 1970.

It is important to note that while participants discussed political solutions to the issue, no one mentioned Bangladesh as a separate country.

Activities of the Department of National Defence (DND) (May 1971–December 1971)

The Canadian Armed Forces provided transportation facilities for Canadian and United Nations relief supplies throughout the crisis. In June, in response to a question from one of his colleagues, Sharp observed that "The Minister of National Defence has offered two Hercules planes for the immediate transport of supplies, including some of the ambulances donated by the Ontario government. These Hercules planes will be leaving tomorrow morning directly for Pakistan."[47] DND had several opportunities throughout the liberation war period to provide appropriate material and technical assistance, thanks to its involvement with many national and international organizations.

The DND's activities also entailed routine work, including rescue operations in the field. Before the actual war between Pakistan and India broke out in December, two DND C-130s and three transit transport flights made by Canadian Armed Forces Boeing 707 jet types of transport were already in use. DND was scheduled to take four more flights to Kolkata, West Bengal, India, as part of an emergency relief program for East Pakistani refugees. Again, under DND's emergency airlift operations program, Canadian Air Transport Command flew six ambulances and 300 tons of medical supplies, food, blankets, clothing, and material for shelter to the flood victims and refugees in the Kolkata-Dhaka region during the crisis period from March to December 1971.[48] In fact, for the record, as early as the end of June 1971, Canadian planes had already left the airbase at Trenton, Ontario.

Airlifting of foreign civilians was another area in which DND provided exceptional services. In December, a Canadian C-130 Hercules transport plane was sent to the war zone by the UN to aid in the removal of UN personnel, Canadians, and citizens of Commonwealth countries and other countries in East Pakistan. It was, however, attacked during the full-blown war, which had already started on December 3. The airport runway was strafed just as the plane unsuccessfully attempted to land.[49] Having tried several times, the Hercules finally returned safely to Bangkok. Fortunately, none of the Canadian forces' personnel, three pilots, five ground crews, and nine observers, was injured.[50] Similarly, another eleven-seater Canadian Forces Otter aircraft on loan to a UN observer team was strafed and destroyed on the fourth day of the war as it sat at the Islamabad International Airport in Pakistan.

In addition, working closely with the NGOs, DND made free warehouse space available in Toronto and Montreal throughout the crisis. Records indicate that Air Canada and Air India were flying supplies to Kolkata for OXFAM Canada on a space-available basis.[51] This remains an example of a concerted effort by government and non-governmental organizations.

Again, DND, under the stewardship of Robert Christie, head of the Special Pakistan-India Task Force (described below under a separate entry), also played an essential part in coordinating Canada's response through consultation with other departmental representatives.

Overall, the DND's involvement in the 1971 crisis is a remarkable example of the Canadian tradition of participating in a wide range of international humanitarian missions aimed at relieving the suffering inflicted by military repression on innocent civilians in East Pakistan. Canada was commended for the work of DND. The Canadian Armed Forces airlift in transporting relief supplies to Kolkata for the Bengali refugees "have been singled out as examples for other nations to emulate by such organizations as the United Nations High Commissioner for Refugees, the Red Cross, and the entire group of the co-operating United Nations Agencies."[52] Thus, Mitchell Sharp wrote to DND colleagues expressing his gratitude.

An important point to note is that while Canada's participation contributed to world peace and security, these efforts did not signal Canada's political support for Pakistan or Bangladesh.

Suspension of the *S. S. Padma* (June 1971)

Canadians had been hearing about a report by US Senator Edward Kennedy, which revealed that certain US tanks and F-86 fighters' arms were secretly destined for Pakistan. This was even though the Nixon administration maintained that no arms were being sent. On June 23, an article in the *New York Times* by Tad Szulc reported that the Pakistani freighter *Sunderbans* had already reached Karachi, Pakistan, clandestinely carrying munitions and other military equipment and that the Pakistani firefighter, the *S.S. Padma*, was on its way to Pakistan via Montreal. Canada's policy at that time did not allow the sale of arms to a military government if it were suspected that such weapons could be used to suppress the people of its own country. Canada was already disturbed to note that Pakistan had been secretly receiving military equipment from the USA and openly from several other suppliers, including China, the USSR, and France.

Ottawa officials immediately briefed Sharp, alerting him that the continuation of the US practice (clandestine shipment of military arms), in the eyes of Canada, amounted to approving Yahya's use of military force as a *political weapon*—the death of democracy. In the House of Commons, Réal Caouette, Conservative MP for Témiscamingue, asked Sharp whether "he received from the Bangla Desh Association of Canada a telegram containing the following allegation: *We suspect Canadian arms are also going to be shipped to Pakistan.* Is he able to answer the House that no Canadian arms will be shipped to Pakistan?[53] Sharp immediately responded that he had received such a telegram and had made inquiries. He added, "No export permits for arms have been issued for some time now because of the situation in that part of the world, and so far, as I am aware, there will be no arms shipments from Canada on that ship."[54]

Despite Canada's unequivocal stand, however, some confusion arose because of misinformation spread by the news media in India, where it was reported that Canada had "canceled" instead of suspending export permits on arms. The Canadian delegates, then in India, immediately articulated Canada's unambiguous position vis-à-vis shipment of arms to areas of internal or international tension. It was also reported in India that several *Canadian-made Sabre jets* operated closely with the Pakistan Air Force during the Indo-Pakistani War of 1965. The world media dug further and found that, back in 1957, the planes, which were part of a 225-plane order built under license for the Luftwaffe by Canadair Limited of Montreal, had changed hands from West Germany and that, subsequently, Germany sold ninety of the fighters to Iran, with Canadian approval. An uproar ensued after disclosing that the F-86 Sabres had been transferred from Iran to Pakistan. This caused quite a bit of embarrassment to Ottawa officials, who were befuddled by the news. They delved deep into the matter and discovered that, in fact, back in 1966, a year after the Indo-Pakistan War, the parts of a 225-plane order were shipped from Iran to Pakistan, which Canada had nothing to do with having already transferred the ownership.

Naturally, there was a bit of a disconnect between *what was happening* and *what was being reported*. The discomfiture for many arose because it was impossible to distinguish between Canadian-built Sabres and the

US-built Sabres being flown by Pakistan. A disturbed Sharp immediately confirmed that a certain number of planes had been returned to Iran and that, long ago, Canada stopped the sale of warplane parts to Pakistan in 1966, having been concerned from the beginning of the subcontinental trouble in 1965. Nevertheless, there was still a nagging feeling in Canada that Canadian-supplied military equipment was being used in East Pakistan against unarmed Bengalis, *which was certainly not the case.*

Since the Trudeau administration had yet to produce its position paper on the Pakistan conflict, some public members were suspicious of the government. They were inclined to interpret Canada's *silence as her tacit approval* of the military action by the Pakistani army. Canada was aware that, for several years, the USA, along with many other countries, had been flooding the authoritarian government of Pakistan with weapons to build up its military capacity. In any case, the Trudeau administration remained firm in its position—that there would be no supplying of arms. However, there were serious doubts about the long-term effectiveness of grounding the *Padma*.

Canada's stand was welcomed by most Canadians who were impressed with how the Trudeau administration handled the matter. "The decisiveness with which the Canadian government has blocked the shipment of aircraft spare parts to Pakistanis an encouraging contrast with the dubious position of the American administration has created for itself in this same area."[55] Thus, Canadian journalist W.A. Wilson wrote in the *Montreal Star*.

In the meantime, Canada's stand on the covert supply of arms by the Nixon administration had impressed the American public and politicians alike, even though the Nixon administration continued its secret supply of arms to the Yahya government, having ignored the vehement protests of the American public. Soon, people from other countries became aware of the hypocrisy of the Nixon administration at a time when Canada came to the fore, thanks to her strong stand on this issue. Although President Richard Nixon and his team remained stubborn in their support for the military dictator, the American public and parliamentarians, such as Senators William Saxbe (Republican) and Frank Church (Democratic), held the opposite views. They were impressed with Canada's reaction to the secret supply of arms by the USA.

To the majority of Americans, Canada's stand was very clear-cut: any aid at all to the Pakistani military dictator was unjustified. Senator Saxbe, having referred to "the Yahya regime's reign of terror," called it "the most brutal and deliberate genocide since Adolph Hitler."[56] He deeply regretted the role of his government as the surreptitious shipment of US arms, ammunition, and spare parts became blatantly apparent. He publicly commended the actions of the Trudeau administration and cited Canada's proactive measures of blocking the transportation of 46 crates of F-86 Sabre jet airplane parts as an example to follow. "Even if we have provided by license or other means arms for Pakistan which have not left the United States, why cannot we prohibit their shipment? No principle in law says that we must continue. For example, we could follow Canada's lead by asserting that our public policy overrides all contract law. A license is always subject to being withdrawn when it is contrary to public policy, for example, the license to practice law and the license to practice medicine."[57]

In the meantime, interestingly, the provisional government of the People's Republic of Bangladesh interpreted Canada's suspension of the export permit for arms supply to Pakistan as a *sign of Canada's support for the cause of Bangladesh.* Referring to the forty-six crates of F-86 Sabre jet parts that had been placed under embargo at Montreal before they could be loaded aboard the *Padma,* Khondakar Moshtaque Ahmed, then Foreign minister, thanked the government of Canada. He wrote, "The government and the people of Bangladesh have noted with a deep sense of gratitude this welcome consistency between the action and the policy which government of Canada had decided upon for banning all arms shipments to Pakistan since the end of March this year proves the greatness of the people of Canada."[58] Regarding Canada's support of Bangladesh, Ahmed continued, "It is our fervent hope that with stronger actions from all other freedom-loving countries on the lines taken by your esteemed government, the people of Bangladesh shall soon be able to breathe the air of freedom."[59] As far as the Trudeau administration was concerned, Canada had not yet recognized Bangladesh and had not taken a formal position. Under the circumstances, Ottawa was comfortable ignoring such kudos and, diplomatically speaking, maintaining a low profile.

However, the suspension of the *Padma* immediately provoked Yahya's asperity as it also represented a decisive blow to the over-sensitive Yahya regime. A furious Yahya swiftly began to consider Canada, though not an outright enemy, *indeed not an ally of Pakistan.* Up to this time, Canada was sensitive toward Pakistan, believing that Canada's relationship with Pakistan must not be strained. When it came to the crunch, Canada had no choice but to adhere to its foreign policy and take a strong stand against the covert supply of illegal arms. Though a US ally, Canada did not wish to be a part of this. Trudeau knew he was taking a considerable risk that would arouse the wrath of both presidents—Nixon and Yahya. Canadians across the country were satisfied with their government's prompt and proactive action that was seen to favor the Bengalis, who were fighting for a nation of their own.

The Nixon administration, naturally, was furious with Trudeau, usually a close ally of Canada, for his audacious step to stop the shipment from the US. Many Americans and their representatives, however, found Trudeau's stand laudable at a time when, according to Republican Senator Frank Church, "an estimated $35 million worth of military equipment was still in the 'pipeline' for delivery to Pakistan," and "President Nixon refused to stop the flow."[60] Frank Church and his Republican colleague Senator William Saxbe worked together on this issue. Both Church and Saxbe began to lobby their government to take a similar stand to Canada. Senator Church, for example, wondered why the Nixon administration was engaged in befriending the Yahya regime at a time when a continuing reign of terror existed in East Pakistan. He argued that the US should have taken measures to dissuade the government from military repression. Senator Church, having found it relevant to cite Canada's example, observed: "The most embarrassing commentary is that while the United States takes no action to stop its intervention on the oligarchy's side in Pakistan, the Canadian government stepped in, over the weekend to try to do what it could to prevent further arms from being loaded aboard the *Padma*, one of the ships loaded in New York harbor with American arms, ammunition, and spare parts"[61]

The Canadian protesters in Montreal followed the same pattern as the US protesters in Maryland's Baltimore harbor. Earlier, they had gathered to block the docking of the *Padma*, demonstrating with signs of "NO Arms to Pakistan."[62] The blocking of the shipment of weapons to Pakistan by Canada was emboldened by ordinary Canadians' abhorrence of Pakistan's military government. Canada took a calculated political risk in strongly opposing this dubiously legal arms shipment, much to the consternation of the military regime and the Nixon administration. Canada took a lead position by demonstrating that public policy should triumph over contract law. In doing so, Ottawa officials resigned themselves to the inevitable negative response by saying, if the Nixon administration becomes furious,

"So be it." Canada courageously moved ahead against the wishes of the Nixon administration.

Commendably, Canada was uniquely firm and transparent about her position on the conflict in this area. This position demonstrates Canada's opposition to the Pakistani military regime's use of arms against the Bengalis. Canada's determined position and prompt action, which we read about in Chapter 4, remain an example of her utmost desire to weaken the military regime engaged in military reprisals.

Canada did not believe that it was within the sovereign right of the Yahya government to use military force to preserve internal security in the name of restoration of "law and order." Canada saw the USA's arms dealing with Pakistan as a violation of its laws. To Canada, the suppression of citizens was *anti-democratic* and *authoritarian,* but she still viewed the events in East Pakistan as an internal affair of Pakistan. As far as Canada was concerned, her refusal to permit replacement spares to be shipped on the *Padma* was in no way intended to be an unfriendly gesture toward Pakistan.

Canada's policy of not shipping armaments into areas of conflict, whether international or internal, was clear and straightforward. "Our refusal to permit replacement spares from being shipped on the *'Padma'* was in no way intended as an unfriendly gesture toward Pakistan but was in keeping with our conviction that a political rather than military settlement must be achieved in Pakistan."[63]

Fifty-two years later, in retrospect, this initiative may be considered a "living example" of sanctions in the form of the arms embargo, foreign assistance reductions, cutbacks, etc., by Canada against the military regime that was engaged in denying the democratic rights of the Bengalis. One could also observe that Canada's reaction was unique because Canada is "next door" to the wealthiest and most powerful country in the world. This country overtly supported a military regime.

Canada's Position on Political Asylum and Immigration (June 1971–December 1971)

Canada's positive approach to political asylum and immigration is evident in the *Debates* and the records of the Department of Manpower and Immigration, which we have briefly looked at in Chapter 4. As the weeks passed, many MPs began receiving letters, cables, and phone calls from anxious Bengali East Pakistanis living in Canada. They broached the issue in the House, raised by their Bengali constituents of East Pakistani origin. From their accounts of the West Pakistani military clampdown on the civilian population, the MPs learned more about the military action that was causing immediate loss of life estimated to be in the hundreds of thousands. The most vocal among the politicians about immigration was Leslie Gordon Benjamin of the New Democratic Party (NDP) MP for Regina-Lake Center, who received numerous letters from Bengalis in and outside of Canada. He expressed his serious misgivings about those East Pakistanis in Canada whose immediate family members were "still residing either in East Pakistan or in refugee camps in West Bengal."[64] Benjamin brought the issue forward to the government's attention. Throughout the summer, reports of continued killings of Bengalis poured in, to the dismay of Canadians and politicians alike.

Describing his "feeling of endless insecurity and a savage massacre" in East Pakistan, a stranded Bengali who took temporary refuge in the UK wrote to Benjamin, having identified himself as Syed Mesbauddin Faruque in the following manner: "Doctors, lawyers, and other members of the Bengali educated class had been especially singled out and shot"[65] by the military regime. An outraged Benjamin immediately brought Faruque's letter to Otto Lang, then minister of Manpower and Immigration, for his prompt action. "Unlike the millions who took shelter in India, my wife and I could manage to arrive in England after surviving the genocide in East Bengal. We have been given transit shelter by one of our friends in Birmingham and are holding the necessary air tickets for our intended destination in Montreal";[66] thus, Faruque described the tales of terror and destruction. The helplessness of the tragic situation moved both Benjamin and Lang. Though succinct, this letter impacted the minds of the MPs who learned about Faruque's miserable plight, his subsequent flight with his expectant wife, and their safe arrival in the UK - all through Benjamin. The MPs who heard Faruque's testimony considered it as firsthand information from someone fortunate to escape an area of crime and destruction where civilians were being killed indiscriminately by the military regime. Faruque's letter, with its graphic eyewitness account, reinforced the gravity of the army assault and its fallout: death, destruction, looting, and incendiaries. It triggered a more extensive debate on political asylum in Canada.

Traditionally, Canada had been known for her special measure programs for immigration instituted in favor of such diverse groups, such as white Russians in Hong Kong, Chinese refugees from Hong Kong, Armenians in Greece, North African and Romanian Jews, and Belgians from the Congo. Canadian foreign policy, especially since the exodus resulting from the Hungarian Uprising of 1956, demonstrates a consistent commitment to the multilateral assistance and protection of refugees. The internal briefing notes of the immigration department, however, reveal the following arrangements regarding the Bengalis: "This department, in consultation with the department of external affairs, is considering what assistance may be extended to persons who may wish to come to Canada from Bangladesh. In the event of recognition, we will have to decide how best to facilitate the processing of applications. Until the political situation has stabilized and recognition has been extended, there is little we can do."[67]

Coincidentally, when the case of East Pakistani refugees was raised, the government's Special Measure Program for Tibetan Refugees for permanent settlement in Canada ended. Under the Tibetan Refugee Program instituted during the fiscal year 1970–1971, the government's commitment was to bring 240 Tibetan refugees to Canada. That program ended just as the military crackdown in East Pakistan was beginning. Regarding the Bengali refugees, the government did not feel the need to address the issue of *political asylum* or *ease immigration procedures* to speed up the process. Further examination of the departmental internal records regarding Bengalis states explicitly the following arrangements: "During the early stages of the Indo-Pakistani war, it was decided that we would deal with East Pakistani students in the same manner as was adopted in handling students from Nigeria during that country's internal disturbances. This meant that we would not ordinarily deport or otherwise require such persons to return to East Pakistan and would allow them to accept employment in Canada until the situation in East Pakistan had been stabilized."[68]

The Department of Manpower and Immigration's proactive steps are evident in its collaboration with the Canadian International Development Agency (CIDA). It quickly developed a particular *modus operandi* regarding the treatment of students from East Pakistan, having recognized that there was already adequate flexibility to address the issue. "If students indicate they do not wish to return to Pakistan and request an extension of their stay in Canada, this will be granted," and "Students applying for an extension would not be given any special status, such as refugees or asylum, but would merely have their permits to stay in Canada extended."[69] The MPs of all political stripes reacted with compassion. Someone familiar with the immigration processes may well appreciate the inherent complications in going through the whole shebang, which would include the time lag between the initiation of an independent application or sponsorship, assessment of the application, the formalities of undertaking the required medical examination through designated physicians located only in certain cities, and the final issuance of a visa to the successful candidate.

Concerning the Bengali refugees, whether from East Pakistan, India, or elsewhere (such as refugee Faruque, who fled from East Pakistan right after the imposition of martial law and military clampdown and came to Great Britain, cited above, where he and his wife took a temporary shelter), Ottawa dealt with each case on a *one-on-one basis.* It did so by doing everything possible to facilitate the prospective applicants' early passage to Canada. An examination of letters exchanged between various MPs and asylum seekers and/or applicants for immigration and Canadian immigration officials stationed in Canadian high commissions/embassies show their "remarkable compassion" for those Bengalis for whom time was of the essence. Canadian daily newspapers also covered many compelling stories of refugee claimants in Canada. Canadian NGOs, especially OXFAM Canada, ran radio announcements to influence the government in favour of a speedy immigration process for Bengali refugees. We noted this in Chapter 5.

In the absence of special measure programs, such as those instituted before and after 1971 for various affected groups, it is difficult to accurately estimate the extent of barriers encountered by those who applied. There is no reference to the unusual bureaucratic delays faced by those East Pakistanis who wrote to Canadian officials. As mentioned, the immigration records and correspondences with prospective immigrants show prompt action by immigration officials for processing the necessary immigration papers. A Bengali retired university professor, who was a graduate student at the University of Saskatchewan, Saskatoon, at that time and who wishes to remain anonymous, noted that he had the potential qualifications for immigration. He was asked to go outside of Canada to apply for immigration back in 1970. It was a bit cumbersome since he had not yet finished his thesis. While wondering what to do, he found a news article about the government's stated position in 1971. He then went to the local immigration office and soon received his immigration papers. The government's flexible position was reinforced by not a single MP opposing the idea of providing immigration/political asylum to those who applied for immigration in Canada throughout the crisis period. The MPs (such as Les Benjamin, who personally pleaded for the Faruque family and triggered a comprehensive discussion) intervened only to reduce red tape and bureaucratic delays to speed up the process.

Perhaps the most positive aspect of Canada's immigration policy in 1971 is that, although Canada did not institute any special measure program for the East Pakistani victims, she did not halt Canada's yearly recruitment of immigrants from Pakistan (both East and West) even during the time of the Liberation War. J. M. Gibson, immigration attaché, went to Dhaka to interview prospective immigrants from November 22 to 27, 1971, and reportedly interviewed forty-six Bengali East Pakistanis at Hotel Intercontinental. This was when the situation in East Pakistan was agitated and uncertain since Pakistan and India were preparing for a showdown. Gibson found the "caliber of immigrants interviewed was good, generally better than the run-of-the-mill prospective immigrant interviewed in West Pakistan."[70] The immigration officer's notes, now available in the Library and Archives Canada, indicate how "the people [he] interviewed seemed to be controlling their feelings on the 'war' with difficulty" and that "they were reluctant to speak freely about their political opinions, but there was a feeling of quiet desperation with many of them."[71] During the interview, Gibson learned how the Bengalis were "having great difficulty in obtaining passports" as the Pakistani officers were "deliberately being obtrusive."[72] Of the forty-six applicants, only one application was refused, and the remaining forty-five candidates were granted immigration.[73]

The point to note is that this immigration officer was touched by the pathetic situation in Dhaka, where he spent a few days confined mainly to his hotel. Gibson's compassionate consideration of the qualified candidates exemplifies how Canada chooses competent immigrants who demonstrate the potential to contribute to Canada. In this instance, Gibson's selection of qualified applicants reflects the positive feelings of the immigration officer who did his due diligence in picking the knowledgeable and competent candidates who were also victims of military repression.

The paucity of pertinent records, however, does not allow us to determine the entry of the exact number of Bengali refugees or immigrants of East Pakistani and/or Bengali origin in Canada. Examining the actual immigration data records of those who landed in Canada between 1970 and

1973 and those East Pakistanis who were already in Canada in 1971 under various capacities and received immigration may shed some light on the government's initiatives in this area.

Country of Last Permanent Residence and Destination of Immigrants for the Year 1971

Country of last Permanent Residence	Destination of Immigrants										
	Canada	Nfld.	P.E.I.	N.S.	N.B.	Que.	Ont.	Man.	Sask	Atla	B.C.	N.W.T. Yukon
India	5,313	37	0	92	48	464	2,284	206	101	298	1,780	3
Pakistan	968	0	1	14	5	156	633	32	19	70	38	0

Country of Last Permanent Residence and Destination of Immigrants for the Year 1972

Country of last Permanent Residence	Destination of Immigrants										
	Canada	Nfld.	P.E.I.	N.S.	N.B.	Que.	Ont.	Man.	Sask.	Atla	B.C.	N.W.T. Yukon
India	5,049	18	6	78	22	419	2,134	216	79	274	1,796	7
Pakistan	1,190	3	2	20	7	214	761	22	22	60	79	0

Country of Last Permanent Residence and Destination of Immigrants for the Year 1973

Country of last Permanent Residence	Destination of Immigrants										
	Canada	Nfld.	P.E.I.	N.S.	N.B.	Que.	Ont.	Man.	Sask.	Atla.	B.C.	N.W.T. Yukon
Bangladesh	151	5	0	0	8	53	70	4	2	8	1	0
India	9,203	45	4	95	54	766	4,662	332	74	376	2,786	9
Pakistan	2,285	5	5	6	13	389	1,511	60	23	138	133	2

Non-immigrants in Canada granted landed immigrant status during the calendar year 1971 is the following:

Country of Former Residence	Total
India	2,285
Pakistan	199

Source:
Canada. Department of Manpower and Immigration. Canada Immigration Division. Immigration Statistics. 1970, p. 5.
Canada. Department of Manpower and Immigration. Canada Immigration Division. Immigration Statistics. 1971–1972, p. 25.
Canada. Department of Manpower and Immigration. Canada immigration Division. Immigration Statistics. 1972–1973, p.31.

For the first time, the Annual Report of the Department of Manpower and Immigration for 1973 records the immigration data from Bangladesh, while, as shown above, there is no separate data for the Bengali Pakistani immigrants who emigrated to Canada in the years 1971 and 1972. Since they fall under *immigrants from Pakistan* for the same years, there is no mechanism to capture the data to determine how many Pakistani immigrants would be Bengali. As provincial or regional jurisdictions did not record the immigration data, the same applied to the linguistic background of the applicants. One could observe that the immigration records do not indicate the immigrants' language affinity, whether a particular immigrant's mother tongue is Bengali, Urdu, Punjabi, or any other language.

The same holds for those already in Canada and received landed immigrant status in 1971 and/or 1972. They were counted as immigrants and/or refugees of *Pakistani origin* who had used their Pakistani passports since they had applied as Pakistanis when Bangladesh had yet to be born. Those who applied after the birth of Bangladesh still held a Pakistani passport. This also includes the Bengali-speaking East Pakistanis who crossed over to India or were living in West Pakistan and were given immigration visas to Canada as Pakistanis.

Interestingly, the Trudeau administration's response to the 1971 East Pakistan crisis differed considerably from its response just a year later in 1972 to the situation of the Ugandan refugees. When President Idi Amin of Uganda announced his decision to expel tens of thousands of Ugandans of East Indian descent by November 8, 1972, the government's reaction to the announcement was both prompt and helpful. Canada's generous stand and her adherence to the United Nations Convention Relating to the Status of Refugees are all too consistent with how she has always responded in times of need.

Canada's initiative in addressing its immigration measures differently concerning the Bengalis might be explained by the fact that Canada's immigration policy was seen as adequate to deal with the Bengali refugees, who were only a few compared to other groups. A few instances of the immigration officers' remarks that we have already noted demonstrate Canada's empathy for the helpless victims of military reprisals. The media's frequent spot announcements regarding the need to welcome Pakistani (Bengali) refugees in Canada, which we have read about in Chapters 3 and

5, are, no doubt, praiseworthy. They also reflect the welcoming sentiments of the public and the government of the day, which we noted in Chapter 4.

International Monetary Fund (IMF) and the World Bank (WB) (June 1971–December 1971)

In 1971, Canada was a modest power in the global political community and one of eleven countries constituting the World Bank's Aid-to-Pakistan Consortium. Canada's development aid contribution to Pakistan was routed through the World Bank then. In reaction to the covert actions of the military regime against unarmed civilians, Canada's instant reaction was to *do something* about it to help the people of Pakistan. Canada immediately halted its assistance for new development projects in Pakistan— dams, railways, pulp mills, and shipments of fertilizers, among others. Commendably, Canada made its independent decision *before* the first scheduled Paris meeting of the World Bank. On its initiative, the Trudeau administration aimed to encourage other donor countries to adopt similar measures. Canada agreed with the USA and UK to head an international effort to shore up the precarious financial position of the government of Pakistan, and it was essential to hold discussions with the World Bank, the Aid Consortium, and other bilateral donors. This was mainly against a severe economic crisis in East Pakistan following the military takeover.

It shall be seen how Canada took special initiatives intending to weaken the government, which was seen to have been engaged in taking punitive military actions against unarmed Bengalis whose primary demand was for greater autonomy for their province. Canada remained an integral part of the World Bank, and the IMF team went to Pakistan in June to restore vital international assistance. In preparation for the World Bank meeting of June 11, 1971, in Paris, Canadian representatives mobilized opinion among the member countries to achieve a consensus honoring their commitments to supply aid for specific development projects in Pakistan; the countries resolved to make no further commitments for the present time.

The IMF and World Bank representatives concluded that foreign aid should be contingent on measures by Pakistan's central government to seek *political accommodation* with East Pakistani leaders. Canada additionally argued that assistance to Pakistan should be withheld to force Yahya to shift his focus from a *military solution* to a *consensual* and *political solution* involving both East and West Pakistanis. Taking a lead role, Canada argued for the minimum remedial measures. "In setting the goals for normalization, the first objective must be to avoid a catastrophe, large-scale hunger and starvation within Pakistan, and further massive movement of people out of the province."[74] Canada ensured the recommendations were implemented immediately since the situation quickly deteriorated.

In the meantime, the Canadian public became more vocal in demanding further action, which initially caused Ottawa to experience some discomfort and unease due to the public pressure for a drastic cutback on all aids. Fortunately, Sharp's appeal and justification, the idea of isolating the *provision of humanitarian relief* under proper UN supervision, resonated with the public. The greater public went along with Canada's endeavour to address the needs of the people of Pakistan, *not the needs of the military*. Individually, however, Canada was one of the few countries that continued to supply *emergency aid* to the victims of rebellion and military reprisals in East Pakistan since March 1971 by placing a moratorium on government-to-government assistance to Pakistan. Here again, although the majority of the Canadians agreed with the government's position, the pro-Bangladeshis, consisting primarily of Canadians of Bengali and Indian origin, expressed their disagreement in this regard.

Interestingly, once again, the provisional government of Bangladesh in India perceived Canada's initiative in the area of emergency relief to the victims of military repression as a *gesture in favor of Bangladesh*. Like before, this time also, Khandaker Moshtaque Ahmed, then minister for Foreign Affairs of the provisional government of Bangladesh, profusely thanked his Canadian counterpart for what he considered Canada's *pro-Bangladeshi* position. "We feel that so monstrous a crime has been committed in Bangladesh that no measure is too drastic to be used if it offers hope of undoing the evil swiftly. We are proud to enlist the help of every nation in this struggle for justice and humanity."[75]

There is no further documentation in the Library and Archives Canada about what happened following the receipt of Ahmed's letter. Without any record, it may be assumed that Ottawa did not feel compelled to acknowledge or respond to Ahmed's letter. In any event, the point to note is that as an individual country and as part of the IMF and World Bank team, Canada played a significant role in setting goals for normalizing the situation to avoid the country's division.

Special Pakistan-India Task Force (June 1971–December 1971)

The Special Pakistan-India Task Force consisted of staff from External Affairs, Agriculture Canada, National Defence, Health and Welfare departments, and the Canadian International Development Agency (CIDA). Its main objective was to have a central source of information to serve as a depository of information regarding the India-Pakistan conflict and encourage horizontal activities of various government departments and agencies on a need-to-know basis, especially in the absence of a clearly stated position of the Trudeau government on the conflict. The task force followed Canada's policy that stipulated the notion of *staying the course*, that is, to "wait" and "see" regarding two broad but interrelated aspects: (1) the internal situation in East Pakistan–*how it should be governed? What steps should be taken to introduce stability? How can we avoid the worst political consequences of continued instability?* and (2) *an* examination of the possibility of an all-out war between India and Pakistan. [76]

The task force was disappointed on two accounts: (1) Yahya's Address to the Nation in late June did not include his *action plans* regarding the transfer of power, and (2) the regime's plan to resolve the conflict *militarily*. Ottawa learned from George that "the war games intelligentsia"[77] in India had already calculated *that it might be cheaper to solve the problem by war*. The task force members wondered if they were "barking up the wrong tree." They also noted that Henry Kissinger, President Nixon's special security advisor, had secured an invitation from Premier Chou en Lai for Nixon's visit to China in the spring of 1972. While it was a diplomatic breakthrough for the US at the beginning of what came to be referred to as *detente* between the USA and China, there were causes for concern as the Soviet reaction to the story of the Sino-American deal was on the news for some time.

Canada believed the bitter Sino-Soviet relations would worsen, and the Soviet Union would naturally feel closer to India. It asked: *Will the political steps announced by the government of Pakistan create a sufficient atmosphere of confidence in their personal safety and the possibility of gaining a livelihood in East Pakistan to encourage the refugees now in India to return to their homes?*[78] The Task Force's concerns were again reinforced following George's warning that Gandhi and Swaran Singh (Foreign Minister) would likely be unable to counter the continuing pressure of many of the Prime Minister's Cabinet colleagues, members of her party, and opposition MPs. Having recognized that India and Pakistan might receive potential help from the superpower countries, the Task Force asked: *Will India, therefore, take more active steps than at present to help establish the state of Bangla Desh in all or part of East Pakistan?* [79]

Since Canada was constrained by her "hands-off" policy, which posed a barrier, the task force could not develop an *effective dynamic strategy* due to its limitations in exploring any option other than following Canada's "staying the course" policy. Naturally, this precluded its members from thinking "outside the box." Ottawa concurred with George's apprehension that, since the predominantly Hindu refugees were in the strongholds of the right-wing Jana-Sangh Party, increased pressure would be brought to bear upon the government to expel Indian Muslims to Pakistan or to "liberate East Pakistan."[80] As head of the task force, Christie seriously questioned the government's staying-the-course strategy that ignored the reality of the provisional government of Bangladesh. Moving forward, Christie also examined the situation from a practical point of view. Having looked at the problem, he came to believe that, realistically, the team must move beyond.

Much unlike Ottawa officials in the Trudeau administration, the task force recognized the strength of the freedom fighters growing daily. "If the Chinese do not help Pakistan and barring a complete bungling of the job by the Indian military, I fail to see how the Pakistan Army could keep control of East Pakistan,"[81] thus, observed Christie. Accordingly, he argued that since the task force was convinced that the government's attempts to discount the strides of the freedom fighters were wrong, *it was time to modify the strategy*. The task force, therefore, turned its attention to the conflict from a *realistic and political perspective* and considered the possibility of a Canadian initiative in the form of a *peacekeeping mission*. This was like the placement of the UN observers along the lines of the UNEF (United Nations Emergency Force) operation in the Middle East, which prevented the Arab-Israeli war until the enforced withdrawal. The team also examined the possible implications of the recently signed Indo-Soviet Treaty of Peace, Friendship, and Co-operation.

In the meantime, the task force members found out that lobbying for recognition of Bangladesh was so strong that, internationally, it was gaining greater credence at an accelerated rate. Christie became convinced that Sharp's team members must be brought up to speed immediately. He took a bold step after ignoring the Yahya regime's insistence that everything was "fine and dandy" in East Pakistan. He insisted on a *reality check* to assess the strength of the freedom fighters whose success was gaining momentum daily. Given the *latest political situation,* an astute Christie also recognized the need to think ahead of the Ottawa mandarins, that the Task Force had no choice but to look upon the *Mukti Bahini* as a "third uncontrollable faction" which "would put the U.N. forces in an untenable position since neither the Indians nor Pakistanis could guarantee their safety."[82]

The tangible progress of the *Mukti Bahini, coupled with India's overt support of the guerilla war,* forced Christie to put his foot down courageously. He did not take long to recognize that finding a solution to the conflict within the *framework of one Pakistan* was a remote possibility; in fact, it was far from reality. By early fall, Ottawa was already receiving George's prophetic notes from New Delhi that were more reflective of the rapid political changes. Christie also came to believe that any attempt to "send a UN peacekeeping contingent to act as a stabilizing influence between India and Pakistan" was "not feasible" since India had not yet "agreed to the establishment of a UN force in the area."[83]

The task force, thus, leaped forward, having set aside the restrictive guidelines and ventured far in thinking "outside the box." Naturally, when the task force began to examine the possibilities of a peacekeeping force in the border areas, it was disappointed to see the ominous signs. It noted with alarm how the respective armed forces of India and Pakistan and the third force, the *Mukti Bahini,* were improving each force's readiness for possible hostilities. In a sense, an astute Christie was disappointed to note how the Trudeau administration deliberately ignored the entire phenomenon of Bangladesh from the beginning. Having reflected on the current situation from a practical point of view following the review of the up-to-date information from the high commissioner to India, the task force briefed Sharp in the following manner: "The fighting in East Pakistan will continue until the independence of Bangla Desh becomes an established fact."[84]

Undoubtedly, the task force took a bold step by calling "a spade a spade." It was as though the task force finally moved *from illusion to reality, showing no hesitation* in referring to the issue in its official documentation as the "Bangla Desh issue." Until then, Ottawa officials referred to it as the "Pakistan issue"; later, they described it as the "Indo-Pakistan Crisis." Commendably, the task force members, under the leadership of Christie, did what they thought *they ought to do.*

To Christie's way of thinking, the *Mukti Bahini* had become a powerful force that should be reckoned with. As such, for the first time, having made an exception, Christie interpreted the situation from the point of view of the governments of India, Pakistan, and Bangladesh. Putting aside all policy constraints, the task force developed an interim framework paper on the proposed UN Observer Force for India and Pakistan. It was then presented to Sharp, but he was not ready to respond immediately. However, simultaneous cautionary notes from Small and George prompted the task force not to explore the possibility of mounting a peacekeeping operation. Even though traditionally, peacekeeping had been a standard Canadian commitment in the international arena, the task force decided to abandon the idea, being convinced that any such proposal would encounter monumental technical and political difficulties domestically and internationally. As a result, no formal proposal was submitted to the minister of defence.

The most tangible outcome of the task force's activities was its direct communication with Sharp's think-tank members, who also became convinced that Ottawa's "staying the course" strategy was not the best under the rapidly changing circumstances. It successfully persuaded the Trudeau administration to consider the *political reality* of the soon-to-be-born Bangladesh and that it would be counterproductive *not to recognize* the goal of the Bengalis: the liberation of Bangladesh with a hundred percent support from the government of India.

In a sense, Ottawa officials had no choice but to accept the task force's findings, predictions, and conclusions. Unfortunately, it was too late for the Trudeau administration to undertake any new initiative. In any event, the task force's activities illustrate a slow shift in gears in having recognized the *actual nature* of the conflict from a more pragmatic perspective.

Initiatives on the Political Front (July 1971–December 1971)

As a middle power, Canada knew well that she could not solve the world's problems. Nevertheless, since the Trudeau administration wanted to play a substantive role in ending the political crisis by establishing democracy in Pakistan, it proactively looked for opportunities for any initiative in the political arena whenever possible. Ottawa was particularly keen on hearing the views of Canadian high commissioners and ambassadors from all major countries worldwide, not only about their views on the issue but *how best* and *through whom* Canada could initiate *mediation activity*. External affairs personnel also met with the Ottawa-based high commissioners and ambassadors of various countries to hear their individual take on the issue. This was made possible through the face-to-face meetings of Ottawa officials with the representatives of sovereign individual countries.

Initially, Sharp and Boris Miroshnichenko, then Soviet ambassador to Canada, met a few times. He was perceived as neutral, particularly when the situation in East Pakistan appeared as one of the most serious threats to peace. Sharp felt encouraged upon hearing from the ambassador that there was "no civil war in Pakistan, but simply one-sided suppression."[85] Ottawa agreed with the Soviet ambassador after seeing evidence of wanton killings of Bengali civilians. The expressed view of the department was that "in the present circumstances, Canada would go on doing what it could for the refugees"[86] and seek the cooperation of other countries. At a time when Canada was attempting to preserve and redefine her federation, Sharp remained prudent and doubly circumspect so as not to encroach into the internal affairs of Pakistan. Nevertheless, once the Indo-Soviet Treaty of Friendship and Cooperation between India and the USSR was signed, Canada did not wish to initiate any public discussion on this with the USSR. Canada believed that the USSR had already lost its "neutrality."

Again, during the crisis, Sharp met with several representatives of Canadian nongovernmental organizations (NGOs) and urged them to come forward to assist the Bengali refugees in India in the face of the steadily worsening situation. It was evident that the Trudeau administration remained willing to support the fundraising and other initiatives of the NGOs, whether it was the Combined Appeal for Pakistani Refugees (CAPR), Mennonite Central Committee (MCC), or other organizations engaged in assisting the Bengali victims discussed in Chapter 5. It is worth noting that *even* when many of these NGOs exceeded their mandates, the government overlooked their involvement.

Ottawa officials, however, were upset with the direction in which the Indo-Pak conflict was proceeding while working closely with the UN and other international voluntary agencies. In all her efforts with the UN and individual countries, Canada's concern was to ensure that the process toward democracy, already underway with the 1970 National Elections, should be continued under all circumstances. Unfortunately, that was not happening in Canada's way of thinking.

Mediation through High-Profile Individuals and Politicians (July 1971–December 1971)

However, Canada's failure to mediate through membership in the Commonwealth did not deter Canada from her determined search for a political solution to the grave situation in the subcontinent. The *raison d'être* for Canada's diplomatic intervention through shuttle diplomacy was to assist Pakistan in her critical path toward democratization, which Canada passionately believed in. Canada remained interested without giving up the idea, although she recognized it would require a monumental effort for its "soft power" (art of persuasion) diplomacy. Ottawa officials vigilantly sought out distinguished individuals who *could act* as mediators. Intending to work out a *politically consensual settlement,* Ottawa officials proceeded "quietly" as a part of Canada's behind-the-scenes action, though with no luck. Seeing that a conflict as intense and long-standing would not end without a concerted effort of individuals who could make a difference, Ottawa continued to search for celebrities and/or illustrated personalities, especially individuals who would be regarded with high esteem in Pakistan and could make a strenuous effort.

Among other possibilities, Ottawa seriously considered using the good offices of Sir Mohammed Zafrulla Khan, a distinguished world figure and a highly credible Pakistani national. Well-known for his political wisdom and sagacity, Khan stood above the confrontation between the military government of Pakistan and the demands of most East Pakistani Bengalis. Ottawa instructed the Canadian mission in The Hague, where he was stationed then, to explore the possibility of a meeting between Khan and former prime minister of Canada Lester B. Pearson, then a professor and chancellor of Carleton University.

Pearson agreed to act on behalf of the Canadian government and meet with Khan to inquire about his interest in the role of a conciliator. Since Pearson decided to meet with Khan in late August 1971, Sharp alerted the Geneva office to determine whether, in fact, "there is any prospect of approach along these lines" that could be "fruitful" and whether "some positive results"[87] would come out of a discussion between the two parties. Unfortunately, no record or anecdotal information on this potential initiative is available in the Department of External Affairs records office or the Library and Archives Canada to indicate if the matter was pursued further. Had there been more information on this initiative, regardless of its outcome, this would have been an example of Canada's *quiet diplomacy*.

Standing Committee on External Affairs and National Defence (July 1971–October 1971)

On July 2, a three-member Commons Committee on External Affairs and National Defence left for India to study the situation in East Pakistan. They were Liberal Georges C. Lachance (vice chairman, Standing Committee on External Affairs and National Defence), Conservative Heath Nelson Macquarrie (PC caucus spokesperson on External Affairs), and Andrew Brewin (NDP caucus spokesperson on External Affairs). They also accepted President Yahya's invitation to visit East and West Pakistan. The primary objective of the "fact-finding" tour was "to see at first hand the plight of East Pakistan [i] refugees who have been moving in such vast numbers across the border into India."[88] The team first flew to India, then Pakistan (both East and West Pakistan), and then returned to India before flying back to Canada.

In India, the team met with Prime Minister Indira Gandhi, Rehabilitation Minister Raghunath Keshav Khadilkar, and Foreign Minister Sardar Swaran Singh. In addition, the delegates met several senior officials in the central government who were associated with relief work. They had a long meeting at *Lok Sabha* (Parliament) on July 6, with approximately seventy MPs in the presence of Deputy Speaker George Gilbert Swell and Raj Bahadur, minister for Parliamentary Affairs. Discussions were in the form of questions and answers focussing mainly on (1) the need for the refugees to return to East Pakistan, (2) the desirability to create conditions whereby the refugees might return to East Pakistan, and (3) the possibility of a dialogue between Indians and Pakistanis.

The Gandhi administration argued that the only way the refugees would return to East Pakistan was to create proper conditions, thereby forming a government headed by Bongobondhu, the famous leader of the now-defunct Awami League (AL). Canadian delegates indicated that they were in favor of this condition. Again, when the delegates were asked whether an independent East Pakistan was the only solution and if Canada would support such a move, the team members quickly referred to Canada's official position of "non-interference."

In West Pakistan, the team held meetings with President Yahya Khan, Mirza Muzaffar Ahmed, the President's economic adviser, and a group of senior officials who addressed a wide range of subjects, such as (1) Canadian suspension of export permits for military shipments to Pakistan; (2) continuing turmoil on East Pakistan's borders; and (3) reasons for the exodus of refugees and restoration of democratic rule in Pakistan. The delegates firmly indicated that they were not persuaded by the regime's argument that the planned rebellion of East Pakistani forces necessitated army action to save the country.

Though difficult to broach, the delegates cautiously inquired about the status of Bongobondhu and the regime's proposed course of action. The president adamantly refused to respond by saying he did not wish others to be involved in matters "internal" to his country. Just about the same time, the delegates were caught off guard when they heard Pakistan radio's airing of commentaries on the similarities between the Bengali separatists and Québec secessionists. A doubly careful Brewin handled the media interviews diplomatically by reiterating Canada's policy of nonintervention and expressing the team's concerns over the absence of dialogue between leaders of two major members of the Commonwealth.

In East Pakistan, the delegates visited Dhaka and Chattogram, where they saw with their own eyes how so many villages were systematically destroyed and depopulated and how the special army groups were deployed to prevent anyone from leaving or entering the cities without authorization by the established checkpoints. They could relate to Yahya's forces that were frequently resorting to terror, bloodshed, and murder in the name of establishing law and order. One alarming encounter was the testimony of a group of non-Bengali East Pakistanis whose account was in the form of a memorandum from Anjuman-e-Mohajreen Mashriqui Pakistan titled "Massacre of Non-Bengalis in East Pakistan by Awami Leaguers and Indian Infiltrators: A Short Story of Their Tears and Blood" Dacca [sic], East Pakistan, 1971.[89]

This report was submitted to the Canadian Parliamentary Delegation on July 14, 1971. It stated that "inevitably, the central figure" of the tragedy was the "Bihari" (non-Bengali)[90] people, many of whom were brutally slaughtered during the early days of March and April. The delegates also saw the selective ruination of properties by the *Mukti Bahini* and the indiscriminate destruction of the Bengali-owned properties by the Pakistani army. They heard Pakistan's argument that India was primarily responsible for the continuing unrest in East Pakistan, that by supporting the guerrillas and through exaggerated radio broadcasts, India had been successfully frightening the villagers into leaving their homes. India had been pursuing her unaltered objective to destroy Pakistan and claim the military authority.

Upon their return to India, and before leaving for Canada, the delegates in India also visited the refugee camps. Firsthand accounts of the refugees and evacuees moved the public, seeing their helplessness and ordeals. At the same time, they also listened to India's argument that she was an innocent victim of Pakistan's ruthless attempt to preserve her *political unity by force*. The delegates also conveyed President Yahya's message to Prime Minister Gandhi that he had agreed "to talk at any time or any place with the Prime Minister of India."[91] The delegates recognized how India and Pakistan saw each other as one's *arch enemy*. They were disturbed by the mutual *distrust* and *hatred* that had been souring the relationship between the two countries. The delegates also noted the military regime's characterization of the followers of the AL as *Indian agents*.

Given the peculiar situation, the delegates believed that it was important to discuss this with the now-defunct Awami League leader (Bongobondhu) and India since India was encouraging and keeping the refugees in her territory. Having expressed their concern that there was no dialogue between the governments of India and Pakistan, the delegates "expressed [their] concern over the absence of dialogue between leaders of two major members of Comwel [Commonwealth] and claimed that consultation is preferable to confrontation.[92]

As far as India was concerned, she had always appreciated Canada's work. The Gandhi administration said: "In discharging its international responsibility, Canada has already made a generous start, and we truly applaud the sentiments of universal involvement and humanitarian purpose that have prompted the Government and the people of Canada to such action."[93] India's reply, in this instance, was curt and straightforward: "The essential dialogue was not between the heads of government in Pakistan and India but between President Khan and the leader of the Awami League Sheikh Mujib [Bongobondhu]."[94] Thus was India's instant counterargument.

In their interaction with the representatives of India and Pakistan and the media interviews, the delegates remained tight-lipped. They expressed their "fear that in its anxiety to look after the seven million refugees from

Bangla Desh, the international community might only be perpetuating another Palestinian crisis and on a much larger scale."[95] The delegates returned to Ottawa during the third week of July, having deepened their understanding of the complex nature of the conflict. Calling the situation "a grim human tragedy,"[96] the committee made the following four recommendations, all of which were accepted by the government:

- that Canada's commitment to the "relief of refugees" be increased immediately from two million to five million dollars;
- that the government set aside substantial funds to provide needed supplies of food grains, edible oil, and transportation facilities to prevent famine in East Pakistan;
- that the government should bring the question to the attention of the United Nations as a question of conscience, stressing (a) the right of humanitarian intervention on behalf of the world community and (b) the willingness of the United Nations to make available observers to supervise and encourage the return of refugees from West Bengal to East Pakistan; and
- that the government should urge upon the parties concerned, namely, the government of Pakistan and representatives of East Pakistan, that a political settlement is reached reflecting the clear expression of opinion demonstrated in the election of last December for greater autonomy and a role in their affairs.[97]

Having avoided making any direct comment regarding either a loose federation or complete independence of Bangladesh, the Committee unanimously recommended a *long-range solution to the political problem* based on the results of the 1970 National Elections. Implicit in the last recommendation was that Yahya needed to work out a *political settlement* with the *leader of the majority party* and *not India*. Unsurprisingly, therefore, even following the submission of the Committee report, the need to discuss it with Bongobondhu remained at the top of Canada's agenda. There is a "need to talk to Sheikh Mujibur Rahman and Awami League as a means of stabilizing the situation and relaunching political activity," thus insisted Small.[98]

The pro-Bangladeshi Canadians, however, were expecting a more straightforward recommendation. Since they were not necessarily privy to Canada's behind-the-scene diplomatic work, they were inclined to believe that Canada had been maintaining continued silence on the issue.

A discouraged Chaitanya Keshavrao Kalevar, publicity director of the Canadian Committee for an Independent Bangla Desh, immediately wrote to Brewin expressing his disappointment that there was no recommendation for recognizing Bangladesh. Admitting that the delegates had to work under *foreign policy constraints*, Brewin wrote in utter frankness, "Had I personally felt at liberty to express my opinions, they would have been much closer to those expressed by yourself, but we were actually in a representative capacity."[99]

Brewin also reiterated that the committee's "recommendations included the urging of a political settlement reflecting the clear expression of opinion in the election of last December, a greater autonomy and a role in their affairs."[100] At the risk of being tautological, Brewin made his bid plain and clear: "The answer must be a political one. The refugees must be allowed to go home. They cannot go without a political settlement. A political settlement involves allowing the people elected from the Awami League by a majority in the 1970 elections to control the government."[101]

The committee's four recommendations were based on Canada's strict adherence to her policy of noninterference by remaining *apolitical*. Nevertheless, the delegates could express their diverse viewpoints as free Canadian citizens. At public forums, all three delegates representing three different political parties in Canada were noticeably more relaxed and less prescriptive in their comments on the conflict relative to their observations and findings. The delegates' speeches at public forums allowed them to raise awareness not only among the people of Canada but also among conscientious citizens of the world through their interviews with international news media. The delegates were convinced that the Bangladeshi forces that were being pushed back to the frontier would reappear, and border clashes would continue until the liberation of Bangladesh had been achieved. And yet, they chose not to mention any such point in their official report.

No matter how one dissects the official recommendations and the speeches of the Canadian delegates given at various public forums following their return to Canada, it is clear that the delegates recommended a political solution *within* the framework of a *united Pakistan* in which Bongobondhu, the undisputed leader of the Bengalis, would be in charge. Although the delegates were comfortable expressing their opinion *differently*, substantively, they remained on the same page with the government's recommendations in which there was no reference to the creation of an independent Bangladesh out of East Pakistan. As well, there was *no condemnation* of the military regime for its ongoing genocidal act.

En passant, one notable impact of the committee report was the immediate reaction of Mir Muhammad S. Shaik, Pakistan's high commissioner to Canada. He met with Sharp on July 20 to express his dissatisfaction with Canada. He warned Sharp that the committee's report "would cause indignation" in Islamabad and could seriously strain Canada-Pakistan relations. Blaming India, the high commissioner observed that India had been providing misinformation about the crisis. Sharp is reported to have remained extraordinarily calm. He firmly indicated that the recommendations were based on a series of exhaustive interviews conducted by the delegates in India and Pakistan. As far as Ottawa was concerned, the recommendations for supporting the "elected representatives" were pretty much the same position that Sharp took in the Commons in mid-June. The thrust of the arguments was *humanitarian* - it was done so by downplaying the *political side of the conflict.* Sharp did not hesitate to defend the findings of his parliamentary colleagues in his follow-up media interviews.

This is much unlike the report of the British delegates and their reaction to the army repression of the Bengalis. Although both the British and Canadian delegates were heartbroken the same way, all four British delegates, Arthur Bottomley, a former minister of Overseas Development; Reginal Prentice, Labour MP; Toby Jessel, Conservative MP, and James Ramsden, also Conservative MP and former Secretary of State for War, *openly condemned* the Pakistani army action in East Pakistan since the secret military clampdown. Substantively, the British delegates' findings led them "to put the blame for the current disruption in East Pakistan squarely on the Pakistani army."[102] Prentice, for example, was utterly frank in stating, "There could be no Government without the Awami League, which had won the majority of seats in the elections. The President [Yahya] should be talking to them."[103] Bottomley, who also headed the delegation, warned President Yahya against the dangers of "another Vietnam" in East Pakistan.[104]

The critical difference in the reaction of the British and Canadian governments is that while the British government *openly condemned* the Yahya regime, the Trudeau administration dealt with the issue using Canada's mediatory skills. Thus, even though Ottawa was aware of the details of resorting to extreme measures, causing bloodshed and repression by the Pakistani army, and the Indian government's secret supply of arms to the *Mukti Fauj* and covert accompaniment of the Indian regulars deep into Pakistani territory, as was reported by Claire Hollingworth of the *Daily Telegraph* (July 19, 1971), Canada had a different strategy to deal with the issues. Ottawa was typical in choosing to exert diplomatic, political, and economic pressure on Pakistan and India simultaneously - all in a very *discrete manner* on a one-on-one basis *without condemning* the regime's military reprisals and the Gandhi administration's assistance to the rebel forces.

However, the committee's decision to reiterate the need for a consensual political settlement remains an example of how important it was to a "neutral" Canada to be "politically correct" in making official recommendations.

Lobbying for the release of Sheikh Mujibur Rahman (Bongobondhu) (August 1971–January 1972)

During the initial months, Small tried to find out as much information as possible on the imprisoned leader but had no luck since the military government kept everyone in the dark regarding the whereabouts of Bongobondhu. Later, Ottawa learned that Bongobondhu was alive and that he was interned somewhere in a jail in the textile town of Lyallpur, ninety kilometers south of Rawalpindi, West Pakistan, under military authority. Although the Yahya regime did its utmost to discredit him, the Trudeau administration respected Bongobondhu as the democratically elected leader of most Pakistanis. The military regime's distorted perceptions appeared particularly ironic to Ottawa officials when they recalled that Canada was at the forefront of an effort to find common ground.

Despite Yahya's patent obduracy, Ottawa officials and Canadian representatives in Pakistan remained firm in their "quiet" diplomatic efforts. Maintaining their composure, Ottawa officials looked for ways to exert pressure, reminding them that Canada was only a "helpful fixer" and that she must not take any side.

Fortuitously, while drafting a letter of appeal to Yahya, Ottawa also received a letter from Justice Abu Sayeed Chowdhury, then London-based special representative of the provisional government of Bangla Desh. Claiming that he was writing "with great anguish and deep regret" about the news that he "heard of the decision of the Army Junta of Yahya Khan to put Sheikh Mujibur Rahman, the accredited leader of 75 million Bengalis, on trial on 11th August 1971,"[105] Chowdhury appealed to the government of Canada to do all in its power by an immediate intervention "to stop this insanity before it is too late."[106] He appealed by saying, "To put Sheikh Mujibur Rahman [Bongobondhu] on trial is to put a Nation on trial."[107] Practically speaking, it was out of the question for Canada to respond to the letter of the special representative of a country that had neither been recognized by Canada nor by any other country in the world.

In the meantime, Small left no stone unturned in his effort to learn about the latest situation about Bongobondhu. Whether through Sultan Khan, foreign secretary, or Mufti Abbas, director general for the Americas, Small tried to gather as much information concerning the interned leader as possible from these two essential persons. He had no luck when he suggested that they should be talking to Bongobondhu. The answer was: "The Pak leaders are convinced Mujib and his extreme supporters tried to break Pak [istan], and because a united country is the foundation of Govt. policy, they must be tried as traitors and excluded from national life."[108]

The interview of President Yahya by Charles Wassermann of CBC-TV is the first and most reliable source of information on Yahya's own views on what had been happening regarding Bongobondhu. In fact, if it were not for the media's continued coverage of Bongobondhu, his name would have fallen into political oblivion, something that the Yahya regime would have loved to see. When Yahya was asked upfront about the fate of Bongobondhu, Yahya observed, "Sheikh Mujibur Rahman [has] deviated from his aim of the electoral campaign in which he demanded autonomy for East Pakistan."[109] Since he had "committed acts of treason, acts of open rebellion, inciting armed rebellion against the State, and being a citizen of Pakistan, he should be dealt with according to the law of Pakistan,"[110] thus argued Yahya.

Ottawa officials disagreed with Yahya's position that Bongobondhu alone was to blame for the eleven-day aborted negotiation. Ottawa's position concerning Bongobondhu was that he must be freed, first and foremost, and that the military regime must engage Bongobondhu in negotiating the future course of action based on the result of the 1970 National Elections. The sooner Bongobondhu, prime minister-elect, is released, the better it would be for Pakistan to *restore democracy*, argued Ottawa. Ottawa maintained that only through Bongobondhu could Yahya come to a permanent political resolution.

As soon as the news of Bongobondhu's trial came out, Small wrote to Ottawa the following: "Charges are said to include conspiring with India to secure secession of EastPak, staging a revolt against lawful authority by running parallel govt from Mar [ch] 1-25, creating commotion in section of armed forces, and organizing large scale murder, rape, looting and arson against section of population of EastPak which was opposed to his secessionist plot."[111] Small tried to draw Ottawa's attention to the uncertain fate of Bongobondhu, still confined in a jail in Pakistan. In an alarming dispatch to Ottawa, Small stated that if Bongobondhu were tried, no doubt, "he would then become a martyr and symbol"[112] something that would unite the Bengalis even more. Small added, "As long as secessionists are backed by India, chances of peaceful settlement are remote.'[113]

In fact, throughout the crisis period, both George and Small maintained that it was imperative to engage Bongobondhu if the military regime was genuinely interested in resolving the conflict. George, for example, argued that "unless there can be a political settlement with Mujib,"[114] there was no chance of a genuine settlement. George firmly believed that "if Sheikh Mujib were to be released and negotiations were to be resumed, the tension would lessen rapidly."[115] Ottawa officials noted how both high commissioners were disappointed with the military regime.

Set to commence on August 11, 1971, the trial was held *in camera* - with proceedings kept under wrap. Bongobondhu was formally charged with waging war against Pakistan after a civil war broke out in East Pakistan. Yahya's version of Bongobondhu's "deviation" was neither acceptable to the people of Canada nor Ottawa officials since both saw this as preposterous and vindictive, aimed to vilify Bongobondhu by declaring him a "traitor" first and then deciding to "try" him in a special military court. The Canadian public viewed the entire drama as a mockery of justice. This was against all principles of national and international law as far as the Trudeau administration was concerned. Keeping Bongobondhu in jail was an obvious negation of the democratic principle of majority rule, argued Canada. From Canada's perspective, it was not just Bongobondhu but the future prime minister of Pakistan who was being tried. Simply, to the Trudeau administration, it was democracy that was being tried by a military.

Ottawa was already drafting a letter to Yahya when rumors of Bongobondhu's imminent trial circulated in early August. In the meantime, Ottawa received a letter from Prime Minister Gandhi. Having stated that the "so-called trial will be used only as a cover to execute Sheikh Mujibur Rahman," she expressed her grave anxiety. She directly appealed to Prime Minister Trudeau "to exercise your influence with President Yahya Khan to take a realistic view in the larger interest of the peace and stability of the region."[116] Gandhi's appeal arrived when Trudeau had decided to intervene *discreetly* so as not to "ruffle Yahya's feathers."

As Ottawa tried to gather more information from Sultan Muhammad Khan, Pakistan's foreign secretary, Small learned more about Yahya and his close military associates' strong feelings against Bongobondhu. The "decision to put him [*Bongobondhu*] on trial had not been taken hastily but after four and one-half months of mature consideration,"[117] wrote the high commissioner, implying that it was not the result of mere whims or caprices on the part of the regime.

Telexes between Ottawa and Islamabad also reveal Small's keen observations on Yahya's temperament, impatience, and strange behavior patterns; despite his apparent relaxed manner and bantering tone, he looked "extremely tired" [118] and impervious to alien influence. To Small, Yahya seemed like a man with no clear vision of the country he oversaw. Yahya himself did not even pretend to disguise his feelings toward Canada, observed Small. The Trudeau administration found it ironic that the more it tried to remain friendly with Canada, the more she became a suspect to the military authority as being against Pakistan and/or pro-Bangladeshi.

Individually, many MPs and general public members, like the government, also wrote to Yahya expressing their concerns in their appeals for Bongobondhu's release. Heath Macquarrie, for example, sent a telegram to Sharp that read that the government of Canada has a major role to play "as any miscarriage of justice at the hands of Pakistan Government might well lead to the type of catastrophe in that region that all civilized men must act to prevent. No action should be spared in this regard."[119] In a sense, it was as though Heath was speaking on behalf of Canadians who believed that Bongobondhu ought to be freed first if Yahya sincerely wanted a political solution to the crisis. Whether it was the Canadian public or the Trudeau administration, their letters regarding Bongobondhu intended to urgently implore Yahya to resolve the matter *politically* and *not militarily*. Cumulatively, the demands from Canada's highest officials and ordinary citizens underline Canada's deep-rooted belief in democracy.

By this time, Ottawa recognized the true motives of the governments of Pakistan and India with an appreciation of the *issue* between East and

West Pakistan – the perpetuation of power by the military regime by force having ignored the result of the 1970 National Elections. Ottawa also learned from George that Parmeeshwar Narayan Haskar, Gandhi's Principal Secretary, had heard that even Pakistan's Foreign Secretary had denied knowledge of any such trial. Ottawa interpreted this as confirmation of its suspicion of Yahya's stubborn move with no discussion even with his team regarding *Bongobondhu,* who had already been declared a "traitor" in his speech to the Nation. At the same time, Small also referred to Yahya's inordinate cynicism and indifference, that he believed that nobody, not even the foreign intervention, would prevent the trial or conviction of Bongobondhu.

Again, having discussed this *discretely* with his colleagues in the diplomatic circles, Small also learned that the handling of Bongobondhu was the direct responsibility of the President, who was determined to proceed with the case. Ottawa officials were disturbed by the apparent contradictions between Yahya's *statement of intention* and the *continuing military assaults* by his army. Small cherished the notion that Bongobondhu should be freed before any proposal was made. Ottawa agreed with Small and insisted on the urgency of Bongobondhu's release, which could assist in replacing the present confrontation against the "renegade province" with peaceful exchanges and dialogues.

Not being thoroughly convinced, the Trudeau administration was getting ready to write to Yahya again. Just about that time, there came a few disquieting news bits again. The first one was that the military regime was going ahead with the trial for sure at a time when Yahya was reported to have been "making more and more of his own decisions in contrast to his former practice of consulting his close associates, such as Gen [eral] [Abdul] Hamid [Khan], and LtGen [Lieutenant General] [S. G. M.] Peerzada."[120] It was as though Yahya had suddenly mysteriously changed his *modus operandi*—withdrawing from his colleagues and showing signs of severe strains.

Trudeau again personally appealed to Yahya exclusively on Bongobondhu's release when the world media focused on his imminent trial. By then, Ottawa also came to know about Yahya's anger and dissatisfaction with Canada for quite some time—a fact that was reconfirmed by Small in mid-August when he, on behalf of Trudeau, met with Yahya to plea for the release of Bongobondhu. "Cdns [Canadians] were giving him trouble these days," wrote Small about Yahya's remark to the director-general, Ministry of Foreign Affairs in Small's presence at a reception on August 18, 1971.[121]

By the beginning of the third week of August, Small learned about another twist in the military regime's decision vis-à-vis Bongobondhu's fate through Sultan Khan, Pakistan's foreign secretary. "We believe Mujib will be tried, convicted, condemned to death (or life imprisonment) and reprieved, though he will still be jailed."[122] Small was both happy and disappointed. He was relieved that whatever Bongobondhu's punishment might be, he would later be reprieved even though he would be condemned. He was unhappy because he could not trust the military regime. Nevertheless, Ottawa took that piece of information with a grain of salt as, to Ottawa, Yahya seemed unpredictable.

In the meantime, the in-camera trial that commenced on August 11, 1971, naturally did minimal reporting. Suddenly, on August 24, about two weeks into proceedings, there was an announcement that the court would be in recess. Since Bongobondhu was the democratically elected leader of the majority party in Pakistan, Canada strongly believed that efforts must be continued for Bongobondhu's unconditional release. Ottawa remained looking for opportunities to carry on its endeavours *quietly* and *diplomatically*. For Trudeau, punishing those who won the previous year's National Elections was out of the question. In that sense, his keen interest in the release of Bongobondhu had much to do with his hatred of military rule, which his cabinet colleagues shared.

In a typical Trudeauvean style, Trudeau raised the question of Bongobondhu's release by stating the "importance of Mujib as a symbol of Pak intentions."[123]

However, there was insufficient information even though the military government postponed the trial. The regime provided no information about *the trial's stage* or *when* it might resume. The world remained in the dark regarding the future of Bongobondhu, whose fate was in Yahya's hands. When Sultan Khan (Pakistan's foreign secretary) met with both Sharp and Trudeau in Ottawa during the time the court was in recess, they inquired about Yahya's special measures regarding the future of the imprisoned Bengali leader. Khan stated that opposition forces were against the release of Bongobondhu and that "hostile public opinion in Pak would make Mujib's release extremely difficult."[124] It was also mentioned that Khan did not "confirm any of recent rumours about consultations between Yahya Khan (or his rep) and prisoner of Lyallpur [Bongobondhu]." [125]

A persistent Trudeau continued his second round of appeal letters to Yahya despite being privy to detailed information to the contrary. This time, Ottawa officials worked closely with Amnesty International's chairman, Sean Macbride, whose letter to Yahya was available to Ottawa officials to compare to ensure that the key message was the same: "A Military Tribunal should try no civilian." It was argued that justice could "never be seen to have been done" in a secret trial.[126] It also stressed the same critical point: keeping Bongobondhu in jail negated the democratic principle of majority rule.

In the meantime, the demand for Bongobondhu's release continued in full swing from three different groups. The first group was the pro-Bangladeshi Canadians; the second was the Canadian public and the NGOs; and the third group was the government of Canada. The pro-Bangladeshi Canadians demanded Bongobondhu's release to take charge of Bangladesh, independent of Pakistan. They did not want to have anything to do with Pakistan anymore. Most of the Canadian public, the NGOs, and the Trudeau administration, while sympathetic to the plight of the Bengalis, saw the matters differently. Both groups appealed for Bongobondhu's release in the hope that *a political solution* could be found within the framework of a *single* and *united* Pakistan. Bongobondhu would form the government without breaking Pakistan into two halves in their vision.

Amid doubt and distrust, however, certain confidential but now-declassified records in the Department of External Affairs reveal some startling information regarding the fate of Bongobondhu. While lobbying for the release of Bongobondhu was continuing, on November 16, Ottawa was stunned to receive some positive information about the fate of Bongobondhu. As soon as Ottawa learned about it, Sharp was briefed on Bongobondhu's status in the following manner: "We understand that his trial is over and that he was condemned to death by hanging (CEO). His sentence is currently before the president for confirmation or commutation. In an interview with the correspondent of *Newsweek* (published on November 8), Yahya Khan is reported to have said that although many people might not believe him, he thought that if Mujib went back to East Pakistan, he would be killed by his people who hold him responsible for their suffering. He added that, in any case, it was an academic discussion."[127] Trudeau and Sharp were relieved to hear this highly confidential information.

To Ottawa's utter surprise, it also learned that although the Nixon administration had been openly anti-Bangladeshi, there was some astonishing information regarding a deal between Yahya and Nixon as far as the life of the imprisoned Bongobondhu was concerned. "We understand that the Americans have for some time had Yahya's assurance that whatever the outcome of the trial and whatever the sentence, he was open to a plea for mercy. Additionally, he had given them the definite assurance that Mujib would not be executed. According to another report we have received, President Yahya said he had given much thought to using Mujib to assist in the restoration of normal conditions in East Pakistan. Still, he could not see what could be done: he was open to suggestions."[128] Thus, Sharp was briefed.

Although the Trudeau administration believed it and felt relieved, it could not share this information with its partners that Bongobondhu would not be executed. Since the Canadian public and the NGOs did not have the foggiest notion of the highly confidential assurance by the military regime, they never stopped demanding Bongobondhu's release.

Fifty-Ninth Inter-Parliamentary Conference (September 2–10, 1971)

Canada participated in the Fifty-Ninth Inter-Parliamentary Conference held in Paris from September 2 to 10, 1971. It expressed concerns at the unfortunate events and disastrous situation in East Pakistan, which the secretary-general of the United Nations had described as a terrible blot on the page of human history.

The conference adopted four resolutions to seek international cooperation in favor of the populations and refugees of East Pakistan. Canada agreed with all four recommendations. Briefly, they were: (1) that the fate of the refugees in India is a source of preoccupation and that all countries should fully share this sentiment; (2) that all member countries should welcome the international efforts and urge the governments and other public or private agencies to contribute generously to the refugee relief efforts in East Pakistan Relief Program; (3) that the member countries should urge the government of Pakistan to continue to offer every facility to the UN and the International Committee of the Red Cross for the development of the action they were undertaking; and (4) that all national groups and their governments should encourage the steps required to create the political, economic, and social conditions for the safe return of the refugees.[129]

They were purely humanitarian and related to the refugees. For example, Sharp had publicly deplored the situation from the beginning, having expressed concern for the growing hostilities. Since the resolutions centered around the needs of the refugees and their safe return to their native land, Canada had no difficulty incorporating them into her various undertakings in the subcontinent. Earlier in the summer, Sharp commended the appeals launched by the Combined Appeal for Pakistani Relief (CAPR) and encouraged Canadians to contribute. Again, all Canadian funds were channeled through the UN and voluntary agencies. During the crisis, Canada maintained that only a *political settlement* would achieve a lasting and peaceful solution in the subcontinent. As noted already, Prime Minister Trudeau remained busy corresponding with both India and Pakistan to exercise restraint and seek a solution acceptable to the leader of the majority (Bongobondhu). Canada implemented all of the four recommendations mentioned above.

Commonwealth Conference in Kuala Lumpur (September 13–17, 1971)

One of the most important international forums on the Indo-Pak crisis was the Seventeenth Commonwealth Parliamentary Conference held in Kuala Lumpur, Malaysia, from September 13 to 17, 1971. The week-long conference was attended by 152 delegates, twenty-three secretaries to delegations, and eight observers. The Canadian team consisted of seventeen delegates, of which eight represented the federal government, and the rest represented nine provinces of Canada (less Alberta, which was holding its provincial election at that time). The Canadian delegation was headed by George J. McIlgraith, a longtime member of the Cabinet with considerable experience in dealing with international crises.

The conference covered various topics, including Challenges to Parliamentary Democracy, the Freedom of individuals, Human Rights, Economic Development, and Problems of the Environment. Dr. Gurdial Sing Dhillon, speaker of the Indian *Lok Sabha* (lower house), attempted to include the case of East Pakistan as a separate item on the agenda for discussion but was unable to do so as there were *no procedural means* to introduce a new resolution. It was, however, possible to introduce the subject under the topic The Commonwealth and Problems of World Security.

Arthur Bottomley, representing the government of the UK, personally appealed to the delegates by reading a message from President Yahya Khan in its first session. He believed Yahya to be genuine when he appealed to Bottomley, saying, "Anything you can do, Bottomley, to bring about a transfer from military to civil rule would be welcome."[130] Although impressed, Bottomley regarded Yahya as an *army man*, not *a politician*. To Bottomley, the nature of the crisis was very much *political*. "The only way in which peace and security can be restored in that part of the world is by the president of Pakistan recognizing that the democratically elected leader of East Pakistan, Sheik[h] Mujib, is the one who should speak for the people";[131] thus, argued Bottomley. Delegates from countries such as Australia, New Zealand, and Sri Lanka were vocal in *condemning* the Yahya regime and urging other countries to pressure Yahya to uphold democracy and resolve the crisis by involving Commonwealth countries. There was a visible reluctance from the Canadian delegates to take a definite position.

Again, when Gerald Regan, premier of Nova Scotia, spoke about the Sharpville massacre of 1960, the world's response to it, and the continuation of economic sanctions against South Africa, he did not allude to what was happening in East Pakistan. Strange as it may sound, though he was deeply concerned about the events in East Pakistan while he was in Canada, he chose not to speak out against the military reprisals in East Pakistan. His closest remark was an allusion to the August 1971 signing of the Treaty of Peace, Friendship, and Co-operation by the USSR and India. Interestingly, Tommy Douglas, the first MP in Canada to raise the issue in the Commons on the opening day of Parliament on March 29, 1971, remained silent even when he had the floor at the Commonwealth Forum.

Apart from Douglas, four other delegates, such as Jimmy Walker, Joe Guay, Romuald Rodrigue, and Robert Coates, all of whom had been participating in the debates regarding what role Canada should *play* as an influential member of the Commonwealth, also refrained from exchanging their views with other delegates. Ironically, when the opportunity presented to Canadian delegates to cooperate with their "Commonwealth equals," Canada went silent. Similarly, although Senator Allister Grossart, as chairman of the federal branch of the Commonwealth Parliamentary Association, was placed in a position to influence his Commonwealth colleagues and steer the discussion, he remained silent on the subcontinental issue. It was apparent that Canada intentionally eschewed any "leadership" role in the subcontinental conflict.

While participants brainstormed to find a way out of the impasse, Canadian delegates remained calm, unemotional, and detached even though they were expected to actively participate and lead the discussion. Evidently, and sadly, both Canadian MPs and senators, having followed the same pattern of *excessive caution* and *direct avoidance* in the Commonwealth conference, neither broached the issue nor mobilized the sentiments of the people of Canada. Canadian parliamentarians chose not to convey the expressed views of Canadians to "do anything" possible to intervene using the Commonwealth connection. This "no show" clashed with Canada's usual vigilance on human rights and democracy as Canada remained *inactive* and had no worthwhile input at the conference. This was even though the Canadian delegates saw the military reprisals as an unfortunate case of human suffering and degradation—a renunciation of all the rules of public morality and international justice. Although the Canadian MPs and senators represented the people of Canada, they did not care to convey the gravity, significance, and urgency with which the people of Canada were demanding Canada's involvement.

As it turned out, none of the delegates expressed the true sentiments of the people of Canada on the Pakistan-Bangladesh conflict, where *continuous repression* and *indiscriminate killings* were going on. In a sense, it may be observed that, unfortunately, the Canadian delegates, who represented both the Senate and Commons, *misrepresented* the demands of the Canadian public. One is intrigued by Canada's nonparticipation in the discussion, which remains an example of a *standoffish* role in actual discourse and exchange of ideas and concerns. Many countries worldwide openly condemned the military regime; Canada did not wish to be dragged into a fiery debate over the subcontinental conflict at any given time.

Why did Canada choose to cave in and not stand up and be counted? It is inexplicable why Canada remained silent and nonchalant throughout the meeting. There is no clear answer. Canada's total avoidance of the subject at the Conference, which brought together delegates representing over 700 million people, seems to highlight her rigid position of "nonintervention" in the "internal affairs" of another country. Canada did not have to resort to diplomatic doublespeak by going on radio silence. There was, however, no pretension on the Trudeau administration's part since Canada remained sincere—albeit highly awkward - in her position at the conference.

As a senior member of the Commonwealth and with no adversarial relationship with any country worldwide, Canada always believed that she could carve out a globally influential role by cooperating closely with its Commonwealth partners. Canada had no luck. The delegates' reticence, especially when the gathering offered a unique opportunity to share each other's views on the Indo-Pakistan crisis, raised an important question about *Canada's role in the conference.*

International Conference on Bangladesh (September 1971)

The Gandhi Peace Foundation organized the three-day international conference on Bangladesh titled *World Meet on Bangladesh,* held in New Delhi, India, between September 18 and 20, 1971. It was an opportunity for pro-Bangladeshi governments worldwide to meet and greet. Its objectives were to emphasize the (1) case for Bangladesh, (2) support for Bangladesh, and (3) obligations of the international community. It attracted more than 150 delegates representing all continents and twenty-four countries. Since it was held unofficially, the representatives attended the conference in their capacities as individuals, statespersons, pacifists, social rights activists, social workers, lawyers, journalists, and NGO workers. Jayaprakash Narayan, a distinguished member of the *Sarva Seva Sangh* and the Gandhi Peace Foundation, was the chair of the Conference Preparatory Committee. Canada was also aware of the role of the leader of Bharatiya *Jana Sangh,* Atal Bihari Vajpayee. It strongly expressed the views of Krishnaswamy Subrahmanyam, director of the New Delhi-based Institute for Defence Studies and Analyses, who had been making bellicose statements against the unity of Pakistan over the last few months.

As a middle power with no geopolitical stake in the Indian subcontinent, Canada noted the new dimension in the conflict. By early September 1971, Ottawa was already in receipt of an aide mémoire from the office of the Pakistan High Commission that claimed that the Indian government was bearing the entire expenditure of the conference and that the conference would "discuss the so-called issue of 'Bangla Desh'" to enlist the support of its participants for India's blatant interference in Pakistan's internal affairs.[132] It warned that Pakistan would view the presence of representatives from friendly countries in the proposed conference with concern. It appealed to

Sharp that Pakistan "would be grateful if the government of Canada could use its influence to advise its nationals against participation." [133]

Narayan personally invited Canada's former Prime Minister Lester Pearson (1963–1968). Still, Pearson sent a carefully worded message of regret since Canada did not wish to participate in an entirely nongovernmental conference on such a thorny issue. Pakistan's representative in Ottawa frequently requested Ottawa officials to discourage Canadian nationals. The Trudeau administration, however, purposefully did not dissuade Canadians from attending. Among unofficial Canadian representatives who participated in the Conference were Murray Thompson, a CUSO (Canadian University Services Overseas) representative stationed in Bangkok, Stanley Burke of INTER-PAX, Glendon College, and Jack Grant, secretary of the board of OXFAM Canada. This is an instance of Canada's *openness* and *flexibility*.

The conference ended with the approval of three broad resolutions, some of which contained several sub-areas on the Bangladesh liberation movement: (1) The first resolution was the wholehearted support of the "struggle of the people of Bangla Desh against West Pakistani dominance," with a declaration that the international community should view the "political struggle of the people of Bangla Desh as a national struggle for freedom";[134] (2) establishment of an international committee of friends of Bangla Desh to disseminate information based on authoritative sources to peoples, governments, and nongovernmental agencies and to take other effective measures to foster public support for the liberation movement in Bangla Desh; and (3) adoption of the following five resolutions addressing: (a) the release of Sheikh Mujibur Rahman (Bongobondhu), (b) violation of human rights, (c) an appreciation of the commendable work by the government of India in giving relief to refugees from Bangla Desh, (d) immediate initiative to be taken by the International Committee of the Red Cross, and (e) many humanitarian activities that individuals and organizations might be able to undertake.[135]

In a sense, the significant resolutions reflected the Canadian position regarding the conflict, with two exceptions that are also a matter of interpretation and articulation. The first exception to the resolutions was directed toward recognizing *Bangladesh as a sovereign nation*—that Bangladesh has all the characteristics of a sovereign nation and that the government of Bangladesh should play a predominant role in the affairs of East Pakistan. True, Canada was not even close to recognizing the provisional government of Bangladesh, but her persistent insistence was on negotiation that had to be between Bongobondhu and the military regime. The absence of official representation by the Canadian government in no way undermined Canada's position that it was a *better strategy* than being embroiled in an endless debate as to whether or not the issue was an internal affair of Pakistan. Since neither Canada nor any country in the world had yet recognized Bangladesh at that time, all parties remained committed to mounting persistent efforts for a peaceful resolution.

The second *exceptional* resolution, not supported by Canada, was the establishment of an international committee of friends of Bangla Desh to disseminate information. While the Trudeau administration did not promote this or any such initiative, many Canadians have disseminated positive pro-Bangladeshi information throughout the country since April 1971. In Chapter 4, we noted the public's activities in this regard, reminding us of the numerous groups that sprang up across Canadian cities. The Bengali Canadians had been vigorously disseminating information on and/ or about the liberation of Bangladesh from the beginning.

Besides these two significant resolutions, Canada was on the same page regarding all other resolutions adopted at the conference. Both the government and the people of Canada were unanimous in expressing their profound sorrow and concern for the Bengali civilians—widely seen as victims of gratuitous repression. Again, Canada's persistent demand for the unconditional release of Bongobondhu to achieve a settlement with the people of East Pakistan has been well documented. Canada agreed with the world views that the government of India alone should not bear all the costs. Gandhi, too, was appreciative of Canada's firm stance that the Indian government should receive international assistance in sheltering and caring for the millions of refugees flooding into India for asylum.

Again, the Trudeau administration also encouraged national and international NGOs to get involved in relief operations, having provided adequate resources to Canadian NGOs, considering this to be an effective way to address the issue through an *indirect route*. Since the NGOs had the respect and support of the international community, Canada believed that they could perhaps *mobilize public opinion* against the military regime while providing relief even though they were supposed to be apolitical. Canada also thought such a strategy would enable the NGOs to exert indirect pressure on the Yahya regime to seek a *political solution*.

Regarding the last resolution related to the formation of several ongoing ad hoc committees to attempt to foster public support for the liberation movement in Bangla Desh, both the people of Canada and Canadian NGOs played a positive role even though the Trudeau administration did not, in any way, wish to be involved directly. Archival records indicate that Jack Grant of OXFAM Canada had signed on behalf of a small group mandated to work out the details of sanctuaries inside Bangla Desh for children and the supply of food aid for relief activities.

Unfortunately, we know very little about what happened from then on. The only information we have on file is that Grant's persistent efforts and success in organizing the work on behalf of OXFAM Canada in the Toronto area received widespread publicity nationwide. However, there are no records documenting the results of this initiative. Such initiatives by Canadian NGOs are commendable examples of their support for the victims of military reprisals.

Working with the Nixon Administration (September 1971–December 1971)

On two different occasions, Canada thought about working closely with the Nixon administration even though Nixon had a different agenda. The first occasion came from James George, Canada's high commissioner to India. Seeing that none of the UN initiatives came to fruition, George came up with an initiative in early fall that was not entirely novel. He suggested that "a worsening situation could be avoided if Yahya was prepared, in return for a kind of Tet truce on the part of the *Mukti Bahini* [Liberation Forces]."[136] A la George, Yahya would be asked "to release Mujib [Bongobondhu], permit him to have contacts with his people in East Pakistan and Calcutta [sic], and then try to conclude some sort of a deal whereby power would be turned over to the Awami League in East Pakistan [not an independent Bangla Desh]." [137]

This seemed like a good idea since George's proposal appeared immediately after Trudeau failed to persuade Yahya to release Bongobondhu. This proposal was also presented at a time when, coincidentally, the Commonwealth Secretary-General Arnold Smith had also just acknowledged his failure to obtain mediation through the prime minister of Ceylon (now Sri Lanka). Seeing that Yahya had delayed a final verdict on Bongobondhu, Ottawa officials felt encouraged to give "one more shot" as a moral suasion. Thus, George's proposal was well received by Ottawa officials who desperately hoped it might still be possible to bring Yahya to his "senses." Unfortunately, no archival records are in the relevant folders documenting whether Canada undertook any such initiative.

The second occasion for Ottawa was to lobby the US through Marcel Cadieux, Canada's ambassador in Washington. Naïvely, despite everything, Canada remained hopeful that a climate of confidence might still be achieved in East Pakistan and that the Bengali refugees, the *casus belli* [138] in the India-Pakistan confrontation, might be persuaded to return to their own country. As soon as Ottawa officials heard from Cadieux that there was an interest within the Nixon administration, they jumped at the idea to proceed even though they were aware of some antithetical statements from the Nixon camp regarding Canada's policies and practices. President Nixon's sudden change and interest in assessing the situation along Canada's line of thinking to resolve the conflict made Ottawa officials a bit hopeful.

Ottawa's immediate instruction to Cadieux was, therefore, to closely liaise with the Nixon administration on this matter—all in the hope that the Nixon administration would perhaps raise the issue with Prime Minister Gandhi, who was scheduled to meet with Nixon during her upcoming visit to the States in October. Within days, however, Cadieux formally advised Ottawa against any such move as he anticipated certain risks in discussing truce possibilities with the State Department. Cadieux indicated that at the outset, Canada would be required to know the costs of her expected contribution to persuade the two countries' leaders to make such an effort. In the end, the idea was dropped.

An examination of various Canadian initiatives, or lack thereof, demonstrates that Canada did not remain a spectator despite Canada's inability to be involved *directly*. As a middle power with no direct stake in the Indian subcontinent, Canada saw her role as a *conciliator* rather than a *confrontationist*. Looking at Canada from such an angle, one can appreciate why Canada's reactions differed from those of other countries, including the UK. Unlike the British delegates who openly blamed the Yahya regime, Canadian delegates considered the events "a gripping story of fearful human suffering"[139] but carefully refrained from "pointing fingers." This was Canada's way of reacting as a middle power while conforming to her foreign policy constraints.

Canada's actions, reactions, and inactions reveal how constantly the Trudeau administration had to pay attention to ensure that she antagonized neither India nor Pakistan, although conscious of the tangled story of Indo-Pakistan relations. In her letter of November 26, 1971, Prime Minister Gandhi, having regretted that she could not travel to Canada when she came to the States in late fall, wrote to Prime Minister Trudeau that she had "always valued and attached particular importance to Indo-Canadian friendship and cooperation."[140] She then observed, "This, and our admiration for you, prompt me to write and share some thoughts about my recent tour and the situation in our sub-continent."[141] Having referred to President Yahya's preposterous arguments and actions, Gandhi continued, "Islamabad's policy of farcical and 'unanimous' by-elections to fill up the seats of those alleged to be 'traitors,' attempts to install a quisling civilian government and a bland repudiation of the fact of continuing refugee influx into India are, in our view, a dangerous exercise in self-delusion."[142] No record in the archives indicates whether Trudeau sent any response.

The minister was briefed that the delegates "called for increased Canadian economic assistance for humanitarian relief to both India and Pakistan and the creation of a climate psychologically conducive to stimulating both parties to enter into negotiations."[143] That being the case, naturally, providing immediate economic and humanitarian assistance remained Canada's top priority. This was when Canada also recognized that critical refugee problems could not be treated in isolation from the political, social, and economic events that gave rise to them in the first place.

Until the last minute, Canada continued to look for ways and means to persuade Pakistan to respect the results of the 1970 National Elections without considering the role of the Gandhi administration in achieving her goal of seizing Pakistan. Canada had no luck with the regime, which showed little inclination to negotiate a political settlement with the elected leaders of the AL, which was then a defunct political party. Canadian officials recognized the display of realpolitik that contributed to Canada's essential dilemma with a thorny question: *How not to intervene and yet do her best in dealing with the UN and the Nixon administration?* Canada recognized that having made ill-considered decisions, Yahya, with incurable obsession, believed he was putting the *country first;* in fact, he put *himself* and *his ego* ahead of the will of the people of Pakistan, as expressed through the National Elections 1970.

Canada's genuine support for the Bengalis and her intense dislike for the military rulers is evident in how Canada risked her relations with the US by occasionally taking independent and unpopular positions. Canada's strong position about foiling surreptitious arms shipments through the *Padma* (documented in Chapter 4) contrasted starkly with Nixonian foreign policy. Sensing the right opportunity, Canada "upped the ante" against her mighty "next-door" neighbor, the world's wealthiest and most powerful country. In a unique and stunning display of diplomatic force, Canada successfully opposed her usual ally at a time when President Nixon expected that, as an ally, Canada would "toe the line"—as she usually does. That was not the case in this instance, much to Nixon's profound wrath.

Time and again, Canada maintained that when a nation's leadership becomes paralyzed by possession, prejudice, irrationality, and a simple determination to remain in power by Machiavellian means, that nation cannot longer survive unless the leaders are reformed, replaced, or circumvented.

In the next chapter, we shall examine Canada's dichotomy.

Notes and References

1. Letter from President Yahya Khan to Prime Minister Pierre Trudeau, dated April 6, 1971, delivered by Pakistan's high commissioner in Ottawa. File # 20-E-Pak-1-4. Canada. Department of External Affairs. Hereinafter, all government records emanating from the same Department shall be referred to as External Affairs.
2. *Ibid.* p.2.
3. *Ibid.* p.3.
4. *Ibid.* p.2.
5. *Ibid.* p.2.
6. *Ibid.* p.3.
7. Confidential telegram from John Small, high commissioner to Pakistan, to Ottawa. Telegram # 307, dated April 8, 1971. File # 20-E-Pak-1-4. External Affairs. *Op. cit.*
8. Letter from Prime Minister Pierre Trudeau to President Yahya Khan, dated April 27, 1971. File # 20-E-Pak-1-4. External Affairs. *Op. cit.*
9. *Ibid.*
10. *Ibid.*
11. *Ibid.*
12. Letter from President Yahya Khan to Prime Minister Pierre Trudeau, dated June 23, 1971, p. 1. This letter was sent through the office of the high

commissioner for Pakistan, Mir Muhammad S. Shaikh. Letter # P/12/7/71. File # 20-E-Pak-1-4. External Affairs. *Op. cit.*
13. *Ibid.* p.2.
14. Henry Kissinger, *White House Years,* Little, Brown and Company, Boston, 1979, p. 849.
15. Letter from Prime Minister Pierre Trudeau to President Yahya Khan, dated July 29, 1971. File # 20-E-Pak-1-4. External Affairs. *Op. cit.*
16. *Ibid.* p.2.
17. *Ibid.*
18. *Ibid.*
19. This is an approved text of Prime Minister Pierre Trudeau's letter to Prime Minister Indira Gandhi, dated July 13, 1971. This was in response to Indira Gandhi's June 30, 1971 letter. This was incorporated in Trudeau's letter of July 29, 1971. File # 20-E-Pak-1-4. External Affairs. *Op. cit.*
20. Letter from Prime Minister Pierre Trudeau to Prime Minister Indira Gandhi, dated July 29, 1971. File # 20-E-Pak-1-4. External Affairs. *Op. cit.*
21. *Ibid. Op. cit.*
22. *Ibid.*
23. *Ibid.*
24. This is an extract from *The Statesman* of September 6, 1971, given by Tajuddin Ahmad, Acting Prime Minister of the People's Republic of Bangladesh, attached in a MEMORANDUM for Mitchell Sharp, Secretary of State for External Affairs, dated October 18, 1971. File # 47-9-India-Pak. External Affairs. *Op. cit.*
25. CONFIDENTIAL MEMORANDUM TO THE HONOURABLE MITCHELL SHARP, Secretary of State for External Affairs, *PAKISTAN,* from Ivan L. Head, Special Assistant to the Prime Minister. Dated June 14, 1971, p. 2. File # 38-11-1-Pakistan. External Affairs. *Op. cit.*
26. *Ibid.* p. 1.
27. MEMORANDUM TO THE MINISTER: Aid to Assist Rehabilitation and Relief in East Pakistan, from A.E. Ritchie, Undersecretary, External Affairs. Dated July 6, 1971, p.2. File # 38-11-1-Pak. External Affairs. *Op. cit.*
28. Smith, Arnold and Sanger, Clyde. *Stitches in Time: the Commonwealth in World Politics.* General Publishing Co. Limited, Don Mills, Ontario, 1981, p. 135. Hereinafter, referred to as *Stitches in Time.*
29. *Stiches in Time,* p. 138.*Op. cit.*
30. *Ibid.* p.135.
31. United Nations. General Assembly – Twenty-Sixth Session – 1944th Plenary Meetings, Official Record, September 29, 1971, p.5.
32. *Ibid.*
33. *Ibid.*

34. This was stated by Mitchell Sharp, Secretary of State for External Affairs, at the Standing Committee for External Affairs and National Defence, dated October 5, 1971. A few of his excerpts were included in a Confidential Memorandum for the Minister under the subject: *Visit to Ottawa of the United Nations High Commissioner for Refugees-October 25, 1971.* File # 20-India-1-3-Pak.
35. Canada. *Debates of the Senate.* Queen's Printer for Canada. Dated November 25, 1971, p. 1508. Hereinafter, referred to as *Debates (Senate).*
36. Confidential telegram from John Small, high commissioner to Pakistan, to Ottawa. Telegram # 868. Dated, August 18, 1971. File # 20-India-1-3-Pak. External Affairs. *Op. cit.*
37. Confidential telex from Geneva to Ottawa. Telex # 1908, dated September 18, 1971. File # 20-Pak-E-1-4. External Affairs. *Op. cit.*
38. *Account of the Meeting between the United Nations High Commissioner for Refugees, Prince Sadruddin Khan, and Head of Canadian Voluntary Agencies,* held in the Board Room of the Canadian Council on Social Development building, Ottawa, on October 25, 1971, p. 5. MG 28 1 10 Volume 20, File*: UN High Commissioner for Refugees, 1971-1976.* Canada. Library and Archives Canada. Hereinafter, all records used from the Library and Archives Canada shall be referred to as Library and Archives Canada.
39. *Ibid. Op. cit.*
40. *The Brandon Sun*, dated September 24, 1971.
41. *Joint Communiqué,* Senate. Dated June 2, 1971, p. 1072. File # 20-Pak-E-1-4. External Affairs. *Op. cit.*
42. *Debates* (Senate). Dated October 26, 1971, p.1395. *Op. cit.*
43. *Ibid.* p.1396. *Op. cit.*
44. *Ibid.*
45. Announcement of Mitchell Sharp, Secretary of State for External Affairs, in the Commons of additional contribution for relief of Pakistani refugees in India. Canada. House of Commons. *Debates,* Queen's Printer, Dated, November 17, 1971, p. 9635. Hereinafter, all materials used from the *Debates* shall be referred to as *Debates.*
46. https://bibliotheca.limkitsiang.com/1971/05/25/socialist-international-council-conference-in-helsinki/#more-1055.
47. *Debates.* Dated June 16, 1971, p. 6775. *Op. cit.*
48. Canada. Department of National Defence. *Annual Report for 1971*, p.50.
49. *The Globe and Mail*, dated December 7, 1971.
50. *Ibid.*
51. An announcement in OXFAM in Action titled, *OXFAM of Canada: an overview,* dated July 22, 1971, p. 1. MG 28 I 270 Volume 7; File: *Pak Refugees: 1971, Correspondences # 2*. Library and Archives Canada. *Op. cit.*

52. Mitchel Sharp, Secretary of State for External Affairs, stated this to his DND colleagues in a formal letter of gratitude dated September 22, 1971. File #38-11-1-Pak. External Affairs. *Op. cit.*
53. *Debates.* Dated June 28, 1971, p. 7373. *Op.cit.*
54. *Ibid.*
55. *Montreal Star*, dated July 2, 1971.
56. United States of America. *Congressional Record.* Senate. Dated July 12, 1971, p. 24486.
57. *Ibid.*
58. Letter from Khandaker Moshtaque Ahmed, Minister for Foreign Affairs, Government of Bangladesh, to Mitchell Sharp, Secretary of State for External Affairs, dated July 2, 1971. File # 20 - E- Pak -1-4. External Affairs. *Op. cit.*
59. *Ibid.*
60. United States of America. *Congressional Record.* Senate. Extensions of Remarks. Dated July 8, 1971, p. 24036.
61. *Ibid.*
62. The recent publication of Richard Taylor's book *Blockade* and the release of Arif Yousuf's documentary film taught us more about this spectacular intervention by ordinary American peace activists. The Book and the documentary trace the bravery of Americans outraged by the Nixon administration's duplicity. Readers now will have a better understanding of how the Nixon administration lied to the American people and what role it played in supporting the military regime of Pakistan.
63. Memorandum for the Minister. Subject: *Visitors to Present Government of Pakistan's Views on East Pakistan.* Dated, July 19, 1971. Talking points for Mitchell Sharp for his meeting with two Pakistan Government representatives who visited Canada: Hamidul Huq Chowdhury and Mahmud Ali. File: 20-Pak- 1-4. External Affairs. *Op. cit.*
64. *Debates.* Dated, June 28, 1971. p. 7379. *Op. cit.*
65. Letter from Mesbahuddin Faruque to Leslie Gordon Benjamin, Member of Parliament, dated 18 July 1971, written from Birmingham, UK; Saskatchewan Archives Board. *Les Benjamin Papers* – Correspondences to 1973 (Manpower and Immigration) SAB Box 5.
66. *Ibid.*
67. Internal note titled *Background on Pakistan,* p.2, RG 76 Volume 1028 File # 5000-25-606. Library and Archives Canada. *Op. cit.*
68. *Ibid.* pp.2-3. Library and Archives Canada. *Op. cit.*
69. Confidential letter from FCC to GPP (Attention: Arthur Andrew), dated June 10, 1971. This concerns an interdepartmental memo from Mr. James Cross, Director of the Programs and Procedures Branch, Immigration Division, Department of Manpower and Immigration. Subject: *Situation in East Pak: East Pakistani Students.* File # 20-Pak-E- 1-4. External Affairs. *Op. cit.*

70. J. M. Gibson indicated that most of the independent immigrants he interviewed had foreign degrees, including a Ph.D. from the University of Toronto and several degrees from the United States and the United Kingdom, p.1. Confidential Letter from J. M. Gibson to Headquarters (Ottawa). Dated December 3, 1971. Subject: *Visit to East Pakistan-November 22 to 27, 1971.* File # 20-Pak-1-3-India; also in the file: 20-EPAK-1-4. External Affairs. *Op. cit.*
71. *Ibid.*
72. *Ibid.*
73. *Ibid.*
74. *Bangladesher Shadhinota Juddho: dolilpotro* (*History of Bangladesh War of Independence: Documents*), volume 3, p. 648. Ministry of Information, Government of the People's Republic of Bangladesh. Dhaka, 1982. Edited by Hassan Hafizur Rahman.
75. Letter from Khandaker Moshtaque Ahmed, Minister for Foreign Affairs, Government of Bangladesh, to Mitchell Sharp, Secretary of State for External Affairs. Dated, June 29, 1971. File # 20-E-Pak-1-4. External Affairs. *Op. cit.*
76. Confidential Internal Record from T. Wainaaman-Wood, Bureau of Asia and Pacific Affairs, to GPP, dated July 16, 1971. File # 20-Pak-E-1-4. Hereinafter, all information used from the Task Force file shall be referred to as External Affairs. Task Force.
77. *Ibid.* External Affairs. Task Force, p. 4. *Op. cit.*
78. Task Force. Dated June 30, 1971, p.10. External Affairs. *Op. cit.*
79. *Ibid.*
80. *Ibid.* p.4.
81. *Ibid.*
82. Letter from Robert Christie to T. Wainman-Wood, Bureau of Asia and Pacific Affairs. Dated, October 27, 1971. File # 20-Pak-E-1-4. External Affairs. Task Force. *Op. cit.*
83. *Ibid.*
84. Confidential Memorandum from T. Wainaaman-Wood, Bureau of Asia and Pacific Affairs, to J.J. Noble, dated October 12, 1971. File # 20-Pak-1-4. External Affairs. *Op. cit.*
85. Letter from GEA to GPS. Dated 21 July 21, 1971. File # 20-Pak-1-4. External Affairs. *Op. cit.*
86. *Ibid.*
87. Secret telegram from Ottawa to The Hague Office, GPS-362. Dated, July 28, 1971. Telegram # 760; File #20-INDIA-1-3-PAK. External Affairs. *Op. cit.*
88. Canada. House of Commons. Minutes of Proceedings and Evidence of the Standing Committee on External Affairs and National Defence. Third Session, Twenty-eighth Parliament, 1970-71. Issue No 32, October 5, 1971,

p. 35. Hereinafter, all information used from the Minutes shall be referred to as the Standing Committee Minutes.
89. The military authority gave this document to all three Canadian delegates in Dhaka. It is now available in Andrew Brewin's Papers in the Library and Archives Canada under MG 32 C26, volume 87.
90. Subject: *Trip to India,* July 1971, p. 3. MG 32 C26 Volume 88. Library and Archives Canada. *Op. cit.*
91. Standing Committee Minutes, p. 32-38. *Op. cit.*
92. Confidential telegram from John Small, high commissioner to Pakistan, to Ottawa. Telegram # 2782, dated July 17, 1971. File # 38-11-1-Pak. External Affairs. *Op. cit.*
93. *Aide Mémoire* from Ashok B. Bhadkamkar, high commissioner to Canada, to Mitchell Sharp, Secretary of State for External Affairs. Dated October 16, 1971, p. 2. File # 47-9-India-Pak [71-06-21 to 74-07-31]. External Affairs. *Op. cit.*
94. *Ibid. Op. cit.*
95. *The Indiagram.* Information Service of India, Office of the High Commissioner for India. Ottawa. No. 27/71. Dated 7 July 1971, p.9. This document is in MG 32 CEI Volume 32, File: 32.3. Library and Archives Canada. *Op. cit.*
96. Standing Committee Minutes, p. 32-38. *Op. cit.*
97. Standing Committee Minutes, p. 32-39. *Op. cit.*
98. Confidential telegram from John Small, high commissioner to Pakistan, to Ottawa. Telegram # 851, dated August 12, 1971. File # 21-3-India-Pak-1. External Affairs. *Op. cit.*
99. Letter from Andrew Brewin, Member of Parliament for Greenwood, to Chytanya K. Kelevar, Publicity Director, Canadian Committee for an Independent Bangla Desh, dated 29 July 1971. File # 87-17. MG 32 C26 Volume 87. Library and Archives Canada. *Op. cit.*
100. *Ibid.*
101. *Ibid.*
102. *Montreal Star,* dated 2 July 1971.
103. *The Indiagram.* Information Service of India, Office of the High Commissioner for India, July 7, 1971, p. 3. MG 32 CE1 Volume 32. File 32.3. Library and Archives Canada. *Op. cit.*
104. *Washington Post,* dated July 2, 1971.
105. Letter from Abu Sayeed Chowdhury to C.S.A. Ritchie, high commissioner to the United Kingdom, dated August 10, 1971. File # 20-E-Pak-1-4. External Affairs. *Op. cit.*
106. *Ibid.*
107. *Ibid.*

108. Confidential telegram from John Small, high commissioner to Pakistan, to Ottawa. Telegram # 832, dated August 6, 1971. File # 20-Pak-E-1-4. External Affairs. *Op. cit.*
109. Written script of the interview of President Yahya Khan by Charles Wasserman of CBC-TV in Islamabad on July 30, 1971. File # 20-E-Pak-1-4. External Affairs. *Op. cit.*
110. *Ibid.*
111. Confidential telegram from John Small, high commissioner to Pakistan, to Ottawa. Telegram # 843, dated August 9, 1971, p. 3. File # 21-3-India-Pak-1. External Affairs. *Op. cit.* Small claimed that he gathered this information from the media coverage and the text of the *White Paper on Crisis in East Pakistan*, published on August 5, 1971.
112. Confidential telegram from John Small, Canadian high commissioner, to Pakistan and Ottawa. Telegram # 851, dated August 12, 1971. File # 21-3-India-Pak-1. External Affairs. *Op. cit.*
113. *Ibid.*
114. Confidential telegrams from James George, high commissioner to India, to Ottawa. Telegram # 2296, dated, June 14, 1971. File # 20-India-1-3 Pak.
115. Confidential telegram from James George, high commissioner to India, to Ottawa. Telegram # 23202, dated August 20, 1971. File # 20-India-1-3 Pak.
116. *Text of Personal Message from the Prime Minister of India to His Excellency the Prime Minister of Canada.* Forwarded by Ashok B. Bhadkamkar, high commissioner for India, dated August 11, 1971. File: 20-India-1-3-Pak. External Affairs. *Op. cit.*
117. Confidential telegram from John Small, Canadian high commissioner, to Ottawa. Telegram # 852. Dated August 12, 1971. File # 20-1-2-Pak. External Affairs. *Op. cit.*
118. Confidential telegrams from John Small, high commissioner to Pakistan, to Ottawa. Telegram # 852, dated 12 August 1971. File # 20-1-2-Pak. External Affairs. *Op. cit.*
119. Telegram from Heath Macquarrie, Member of Parliament for Hillsborough, PEI, to Mitchell Sharp, Secretary of State for External Affairs, through Canadian National Telecommunications. Dated August 12, 1971.Volume 32-3. File name: *Bangla Desh 1971.* MG 32 C31. Library and Archives Canada. *Op. cit.*
120. Confidential telegram from John Small, high commissioner to Pakistan, to Ottawa. Telegram # 880, dated August 19, 1971. File # 20-1-2-Pak. 2 External Affairs. *Op. cit.*
121. Confidential telegram from John Small, high commissioner to Pakistan, to Ottawa. Telegram # 880. Dated, August 19, 1971. File # 20-1-2-Pak. External Affairs. *Op. cit.*

122. Confidential telegram from John Small, high commissioner to Pakistan, to Ottawa. Telegram # 892, dated August 21, 1971. File # 20-Pak-E-1-4.
123. Confidential Internal Message from Ottawa to Islamabad on the visit of Pakistan Foreign Secretary. Dated November 19, 1971, p. 2. File #20-Pak-E-1-4. External Affairs. *Op. cit.* Canada argued that Bongobondhu, the democratically elected leader of Pakistan, was the key to resolving the political conflict. To do that, a dialogue must occur between Yahya and Bongobondhu, Canada argued.
124. *Ibid.*
125. *Ibid.*
126. This set of correspondence is available in the OXFAM-Canada's records in the Library and Archives Canada. MG 1 270 Vol. 18. Library and Archives. *Op. cit.*
127. Confidential Note on Visit of Pakistan Foreign Secretary, November 16 and 17, 1971 on Current Situation. Dated November 15, 1971, p. 2. File # 20-Pak-E-1-4. External Affairs. *Op. cit.*
128. Confidential Note on Visit of Pakistan Foreign Secretary, November 16 and 17, 1971 on Current Situation. Dated November 15, 1971, p. 3. File # 20-Pak-E-1-4. External Affairs. *Op. cit.*
129. Unclassified Document titled *Resolutions Adopted by the 59th Inter-Parliamentary Conference,* dated March 27, 1972. Memorandum prepared by H.P.G. Fraser, South Asia Division. File # 38-11-1-Pak. External Affairs. *Op. cit.*
130. *Report of the Seventeenth Commonwealth Parliamentary Conference* held in Kuala Lumpur in September 1971. General Council of the Commonwealth Parliamentary Association, House of Parliament, London, p. 8. Hereinafter, referred to as the Commonwealth Parliamentary Conference.
131. *Ibid.* p. 8. Commonwealth Parliamentary Conference. *Op. cit.*
132. *Aide Mémoire,* p. 1, produced by the Pakistan High Commission on September 13, 1971. This was sent to Mitchel Sharp, Secretary of State for External Affairs, for his information and action. File # 20-India-1-2-Pak. External Affairs. *Op. cit.*
133. *Ibid.*
134. *World Meet on Bangla Desh,* Report of the International Conference on Bangla Desh held in New Delhi from 18-20 September 1971, p.18.
135. *Ibid.* p.20.
136. Confidential internal memorandum to PDM from GPS, signed by T. Wainaman-Wood, Director, South Asia Division. Dated October 27, 1971, p.1. File # 20-Pak -E-1-4. External Affairs. *Op. cit.*
137. *Ibid. Op. cit.*
138. See *Glossary of Terms*

139. This was observed by Heath Macquarrie, MP for Hillsborough, in the Commons. *Debates.* Dated May 31, 1971, p.6240. *Op. cit.*
140. Hand-delivered letter from Prime Minister Indira Gandhi to Prime Minister Pierre Trudeau. Dated November 26, 1971, p.1. This letter was delivered via Ashok B. Bhadkamkar, high commissioner to Canada. File # 20-India-1-3-Pak.
141. *Ibid.* p. 1.
142. *Ibid.* p. 2.
143. Memorandum for the Minister, titled Visit of Canadian Members of Parliament to India and Pakistan. Dated July 19, 1971. File # 20-Pak-E-1-4. External Affairs. *Op. cit.*

CHAPTER 8

Canada Faces Dilemma: A Chronology of Quiet Diplomacy

*I*n this chapter, we analyze in-depth and month-by-month, asking: What was Canada's position on the Pakistan conflict? This simple question cannot quickly be answered due to the magnitude and complexity of the relevant issues, which include political factors within and beyond Canada's borders. All came into play in shaping Canada's position on a conflict Canada largely viewed as an "internal affair" of Pakistan in the form of a "civil war" in East Pakistan—one of Pakistan's five provinces. Initially, the Trudeau administration felt no need for a major pronouncement on the Pakistan issue. Canada, without evidence, expected that the Yahya regime would respect the democratic rights of its people and resolve the issue peacefully and fairly. In a sense, Canada maintained two complementary positions: (1) follow Canada's traditional policy of "noninterference" and simultaneously (2) apply behind-the-scenes pressure via individual and collective efforts aimed at democratization in Pakistan.

Clinging to her policy of noninterference, Canada worked toward a political settlement between President Yahya Khan's pledge to transfer power to the elected leader of the majority party, Sheikh Mujibur Rahman (Bongobondhu), and his demand for greater autonomy for East Pakistan. Canada's tightly held view that the conflict should be resolved through a *political settlement between the parties involved arose from Pierre Elliott Trudeau's overarching vision of free and fair elections and also the rule of law: the separation of powers and the protection of the fundamental liberties of speech, assembly, religion, and property. Ottawa worked quietly and shifted its gears slowly, at times accepting the inevitable birth of Bangladesh, at others, still trying to preserve Pakistan's integrity. Canada aimed for a re-engineered Pakistan headed by a democratically elected leader, Bongobondhu.*

Canada found herself in a dilemma from the start—she could neither endorse the disintegration of Pakistan nor condone military reprisals and suppression of democratic rights. Canada saw the military takeover as a negation of the democratic principles of majority rule. Canada believed that only the transfer of power to Bongobondhu, the elected leader of Pakistan, could achieve a lasting and peaceful solution. Following the Pakistan military's attack on Bengali civilians and rebels on March 25, 1971, Canada pointed to "civil disturbance" in East Pakistan and the need for a political resolution by the parties themselves. Mitchell Sharp, Secretary of State for External Affairs, recognized the fundamental motives of President Yahya Khan and Prime Minister Indira Gandhi: Yahya's to perpetuate military rule and Gandhi's to weaken the Pakistan military.

Sharp was repeatedly briefed on Yahya's perverse pleasure in blaming India, including his military action in East Pakistan. He was also briefed on the Gandhi government's seizing this opportunity to dismember Pakistan, thereby saving the cost of maintaining costly defenses in the eastern wing. Justifiably, Canada feared that explicit endorsement of the nationalist cause of the Bengalis might provoke Québec nationalists at home. Ottawa instinctively feared that her involvement abroad could invite more internal dangers for Canada, far beyond what the federal government had faced during the 1970 FLQ (Front de libération du Québec) crisis.[1]

However, Canada did not remain idle while Pakistan engaged in military action. Following her noninterference policy, Canada worked toward a political settlement between Yahya's pledge to transfer power to Bongobondhu and the latter's demand for greater autonomy for East Pakistan. From the outset, Canada lobbied for Bongobondhu's release to form the government of Pakistan. One must understand how Ottawa was briefed on the subcontinental conflict to appreciate Canada's position better. Fearful of straining her relationship with Pakistan, a US ally, the

Trudeau administration struggled to reconcile humanitarian concerns with the harsh exigencies of international power politics.

Canada consciously decided against any open condemnation of the military regime. Sharp articulated Canada's position by citing three constraints to a proactive role in the conflict: (1) Commonwealth membership shared by Canada, Pakistan, and India; (2) Canada's mediatory role, which precluded her from taking sides; and (3) Canada's need to respect the "internal affairs" of Pakistan. Canada championed a peaceful solution in the House of Commons via diplomatic discussions with international organizations. Throughout the entire crisis period, Ottawa struggled to address issues relating to the inhumane treatment of Bengali civilians in their native land, popularly referred to as "Occupied Bangladesh" by the media. Sharp recognized India's opportunism and Pakistan's duplicity, both of which he found infuriating. To reduce tensions, the Trudeau administration developed a four-pronged strategy: (1) corresponding directly, personally, and discretely with the heads of Pakistan and India; (2) referring the issue to the United Nations (UN); (3) addressing the issue through the Commonwealth; and (4) working with the UNHCR.

As discussed in Chapter 1, Canada's primary interests in the Indian subcontinent in 1971 were to promote social justice and quality of life. Unlike the US, Canada had no territorial interests in the Indian subcontinent. As a middle power, Canada did not want to become a principal actor either. There were already superpowers in play with more direct stakes in the subcontinent. Canada consciously avoided subcontinental politics. Following the partition of India in 1947, Canada's initial policy toward India and Pakistan was predicated on the position that each was an independent, democratic member of the Commonwealth and should remain so. Against this political backdrop, we present a monthly chronology of Canada's activities commencing with the military clampdown of March 25, 1971, and ending with the surrender of the Pakistani army on December 16, 1971. The chronology will reveal that Canada consistently pursued a policy to preserve her political ideals and contribute to a humanitarian solution in a land 10,000 kilometers away.

Chronology and Analysis of Events from March to December 1971 and Canada's Response

March–April 1971

The primary sources of information for Ottawa were John Small and James George, Canada's high commissioners to Pakistan and India, respectively. Weeks before the military crackdown, Small warned Ottawa of the grim reality in Pakistan; the country was "groaning with the weight of years of misunderstanding, bitterness, and neglect."[2] On March 1, 1971, President Yahya Khan suddenly postponed the National Assembly session without consulting the Bengali leader and prime minister-designate. Consequently, on March 3, Bongobondhu rejected Yahya's invitation to a roundtable conference of East and West Pakistani political leaders set for March 10. The majority of Bengali politicians overwhelmingly supported this decision. Canada saw this as "an audacious assertion of authority without concomitant assumption of responsibility"[3] on Bongobondhu's part. "The possibility of secession by Bengali-speaking East Pakistan is growing increasingly serious following two weeks of intermittent violence in Dacca [sic] marked by at least 30 deaths," thus wrote Selig Harrison of the *Kitchener-Waterloo Record*.[4] The key message was that although Bongobondhu, the winner of the 1970 National Elections, had made a personal call for nonviolence and noncooperation at his mass meeting on March 3, 1971, it only restored some discipline to the ranks and elicited general support from the members and the majority of the populace. The news media cautioned that East Pakistan was on the verge of a unilateral declaration of independence (UDI).

Small saw increasingly ominous signals of intense activity when he went to Dhaka during the first week of March. The city appeared to be a powder keg ready to explode against Yahya, widely regarded as a diabolical despot. Consistent with Canada's position on Pakistan, Small arranged a meeting with Bongobondhu during the impasse. Canada's willingness to assist Bongobondhu is evident in Small's brief meeting immediately after his "historic" March 7 address to the nation. Small discussed the constitutional crisis, which "threatened the dissolution of the country."[5] Small was bewildered that Bongobondhu's clarion call to his people touched off revolutionary festivities in the streets of Dhaka, especially among the young radical students and other extremist forces. The ultranationalists, who were preparing for violent action to confront the Yahya regime's forces, called for an independent Bangladesh. Following his meeting with Bongobondhu, a concerned Small predicted that "a military attempt to keep the seventy million East Pakistanis in the federation would fail in the long run."[6] Like his modern-day Ukrainian counterpart, Volodymyr Zelensky, Bongobondhu impressed everyone with his charisma. Small marveled at how rarely in history has a single individual come to be identified so entirely with the fate and fortune of an entire nation. For a perplexed Small, the outcome was far more complex and uncertain.

As Ottawa pursued the matter, officials learned more about the historical disparities between the two wings of Pakistan and the unusual intransigence of the leaders involved. West Pakistan's leader, Zulfiqar Ali Bhutto, leader of the Pakistan People's Party (PPP), argued that there had to be provisions for the "special character" of Pakistan. Sympathetic to the demands of the Bengalis, Ottawa realized that Bongobondhu could not agree with Bhutto. For Ottawa, Bongobondhu's March 7 address to the nation epitomized his vision for a "Golden Bengal." Sharp was briefed that, although Bongobondhu was using the rhetoric of poverty alleviation and empowerment, his proposed autonomy program threatened the integrity of Pakistan. Bongobondhu's six-point program set Yahya and Bhutto on a collision course against him. Ironically, Yahya came to see Bongobondhu's demands as usurpation of power by the Bengali leader even though he was the democratically elected head of Pakistan. As Canada saw it, Bongobondhu's March 7 speech set the entire province on the brink of independence.

Naturally, Ottawa was disturbed by Yahya's reaction and subsequent actions against the people of East Pakistan. Yahya also fanned the flames against Bongobondhu by accusing him of involvement in a secessionist movement with India's help. Canada's strong disagreement with labeling Bongobondhu an "enemy of Pakistan"[7] added another dimension to the knotty subcontinental issue of "separation" and/or "independence." Yahya's statement that "I have asked... to do their job" had been in the news for days as he tried to defend his ruthless actions in East Pakistan. Ottawa officials were reminded of peril in mid-March by a Canadian daily: "The possibility of secession by Bengali-speaking East Pakistan is growing increasingly serious following two weeks of intermittent violence in Dacca marked by at least 30 deaths."[8]

Immediately following the military crackdown, George from New Delhi also diligently provided up-to-date information on military reprisals and freedom fighters. Utilizing his connections with high-ranking officials, George followed up with US Ambassador Kenneth Barnard Keating and British High Commissioner John Morrice Cairns James. On April 10, 1971, armed with information from the field, George advised Ottawa to look at the East Bengal situation from a Canadian and not an Indian viewpoint. Compared to his Canadian counterpart, Small, in Islamabad, where news was strictly censored, George was better positioned to provide Ottawa with the latest reports, though often exaggerated, on India and East Pakistan.

In the meantime, Ottawa was distressed that Canadians were already drawing parallels between Canada-Québec and Pakistan-Bangladesh. While there were some similarities, there were also significant differences between the two situations. Ottawa assiduously characterized events as a movement for the disintegration of Pakistan while avoiding the terms "separation" or "independence" of East Pakistan or whether the Bengalis' claim for independence was legally and morally defensible. On balance, Canada's position on the conflict must be interpreted in the context of her foreign affairs policy of neutrality or noninterference in the internal affairs of another country. Canada's fear of Québec's separation was so extreme that the Trudeau administration believed that any hint of endorsing a liberated Bangladesh could lead to serious trouble at home. Painfully aware of the October 1970 Crisis, Ottawa avoided any discussion that could plunge Canadians into another heated debate on Québec's right to self-determination.

As discussed in Chapter 1, for many Canadians, the name Bongobondhu was synonymous with Bengalis' hopes for a country of their own— aspirations that seemed to parallel the situation of Québec. For Sharp, it was a case of déjà vu reminiscent of the Quiet Revolution of the 1960s in which Québecois believed that French Canadians should not accept a second-class role in politico-socioeconomic matters. In that sense, the rise of Bengali nationalism evoked echoes of the Pierre Lesage era in Québec (1960–1966), symbolizing an entire people on the road to self-assertion. Canada's fear of the Québec question and Québec sovereignty ran deep. Canadians also recalled Québec Premier Daniel Johnson's groundbreaking book Égalité ou Indépendance (Equality or Independence), published five years before the Québec crisis. As the government saw the situation, alarm bells rang from the mid-1960s through 1971, creating waves across Canada.

Johnson's key message reverberated: the history of the French-Canadian nation is, first and foremost, the history of its constitutional struggles and the history of a people searching for a country. This message began to echo again in the minds of Canadians. The specter of Québec independence was so alarming to Canadians that they feared the Bengalis' demand for independence could reignite a debate on the FLQ's separatist manifesto. One could observe that the Trudeau administration neither wanted to discuss the Bengalis' demand for autonomy nor encouraged contentious questions such as: Is this a civil war or a war of independence? Did the voters in East Pakistan believe they were voting for complete autonomy, resulting in two separate nations: East Pakistan and West Pakistan? Were they voting for a separate province within the federalist framework of one Pakistan? Perhaps correctly, Ottawa feared that a whole debate on the Bangladesh issue might rekindle stormy discussion on the Québec question.

"The sympathy for East Bengal is strong, and if the West Pakistan military operation continues for a lengthy period and the situation remains inclusive, it may become increasingly difficult for the government of India to withstand domestic pressures to recognize Bangladesh,"[9] thus wrote George to Ottawa, referring to near unanimity of opinion in India favoring the interned leader of East Pakistan. George also forwarded Ottawa a strongly worded resolution unanimously passed by the Indian Parliament on March 31, the sixth day of the military operation in East Pakistan. It signaled India's firm position: "This House expresses its profound sympathy for and solidarity with the people of East Bengal in their struggle for a democratic way of life... The House wishes to assure that their [the people of East Bengal] struggle and sacrifices will receive the wholehearted support and sympathy of the people of India."[10] George cautioned Ottawa that the government of India no longer believed a united Pakistan was "either possible or desirable,"[11] and predicted that a new state would emerge out of present East Pakistan.

Similarly, Small also sent telexes pointing out India's role in the crisis and the anticipated dismemberment of Pakistan. The thrust of these telexes was that guerrilla attacks on the Pakistani army in East Pakistan were occurring "with Indian government's knowledge, acquiescence and probably help, whether direct or indirect,"[12] and that the Bengali guerrillas were encouraged to continue their fight. Believing India to be the primary source, Small asked Ottawa, "Moreover, if they [rebel forces] are not receiving their arms and supplies from Indian sources, where are they coming from?"[13] The writings were already "on the wall."

Along with observers worldwide, Ottawa sensed the advent of an emerging powerful image: that of the vociferous, dramatic, and heroic Bongobondhu—with Savior status among the Bengalis experiencing a "national" renaissance across the province. Despite his meteoric rise and popularity, Ottawa recognized that Bongobondhu was a political visionary, not a skilled politician or craftsman. Small believed that the Bengali leader lacked clear and decisive direction and had no contingency plan in the event of an assault by Yahya's army. In the meantime, Ottawa noted the Yahya regime's swift filing of official protests through Small over India's actions in East Pakistan on March 27 and 30. Ottawa needed to examine multiple aspects of the crisis: Pakistan's accusation of India, the Gandhi government's official position on the conflict, and its unofficial support of Bengali guerrilla fighters sheltered in India.

Ottawa vigilantly awaited more news from the field as Pakistan summoned the US ambassador, the UK high commissioner, and the Australian deputy high commissioner "to complain about VOA, BBC, and Radio Australia Broadcasts based on all India Radio. Envoys have made the point that strict censorship, ejection of responsible journalists from Dacca [sic], and confiscation of their copy, tapes, films, etc., is not the way to achieve objective reporting."[14] Given the Yahya regime's hypersensitivity, Canada ensured that her actions would not give rise to any misunderstanding. Ottawa needed to know more about the military government's stance on East and West Pakistan. To better formulate Canada's position, Ottawa instructed Small to obtain inside information "from the top down." In the meantime, Small had already identified other information sources to probe political leaders' viewpoints. Warning that many were anticipating trouble in parts of West Pakistan, Small wrote, "Source at one point said Army had written off EastPak [East Pakistan] and were now genuinely concerned about WestPak [West Pakistan] where they expected trouble in Sind and Baluchistan and perhaps elsewhere."[15] Small then continued to say that Bhutto "had thrown in his lot with [the] military in hope of emerging on top of whatever civilian structure might emerge. ... The senior military detests Bhutto, but he has a strong army following at lower levels. I report all this because it has an authentic ring and complements fragments we are getting from a variety of sources."[16]

Meanwhile, in Canada, the New Democratic Party (NDP) was about to launch its national convention from April 21 to 24 to address issues and concerns relevant to Canadians and their government. Many wanted to know why the delegates to the NDP convention chose to exclude the contentious issue of self-determination advanced by the party's Québec wing. The same week, the Trudeau administration watched as revered and retiring NDP leader Tommy Douglas also rejected the concept of self-determination championed by the "Waffle movement"[17] and the party's small Québec wing. The retiring party leader did not directly reference the ultranationalist and radical Waffle movement. Instead, Douglas pleaded for the cause of Canadian unity and urged Canadians not to disintegrate from within. For the Trudeau government, it was disturbing that the contentious Québec issue flared up repeatedly during the leadership debates. David Lewis, chosen to succeed Douglas, conceded that "if the people of Québec did decide to separate from Canada," he "would oppose the use of force or economic sanctions to keep the country together."[18] The Trudeau administration was disturbed to see how the news media in Canada repeatedly raised the contentious issue of self-determination at the NDP convention.

Since the Bengalis' proclamations of independence were on the news regularly, Canadians were reminded of the NDP's call two years earlier (1968–1969) for a federal system in which Québec's relationship with Ottawa might differ from those of other provinces in certain spheres. In effect, this would have meant a limited de facto sovereignty. This time, leadership contender Edward Broadbent also argued that "a positive resolution should be adopted by the party," recognizing that "the unequivocal right to independence must reside in the people of Québec."[19] Veteran Québec Liberal Party doyen Claude Ryan articulated Canada's dilemma. In an editorial, he lectured those NDP members, who "were frightened by abstractions of the tragic experience of Biafra and no less tragic and more recent experience of Pakistan."[20] Ryan went on to say, "Recognition of the right to self-determination implies that, in the event of a democratic decision in Québec in favour of breaking the federal tie, people would seek to negotiate the conditions of an honest separation rather than try to defeat the popular verdict by force."[21] Sharp's foreign affairs cognoscenti, under solid pressure, tried to justify Canada's cautious policy of neutrality.

The Trudeau administration immediately addressed two issues: (1) Ottawa's fear of a serious "Bangladesh-type" situation unfolding in her backyard and (2) Canada's prominent role as a senior member of the Commonwealth. Burdened by misgivings over several unanswered questions, Canada remained vigilant, sensing that rigid positions might become politically indefensible. Ottawa consciously proceeded cautiously before addressing issues that might negatively impact Canada. George raised serious questions from New Delhi, "Are [the] issues only legal and constitutional or also political and moral?"[22] "Do we seriously believe that it was Mujib who launched murder, arson, and widespread disorder, or was this result of West Pak Army trying to dictate to the people of East Bengal and their leader recently elected even under Yahya's auspices with an overwhelming popular mandate?" [23] Although faced with the specter of an epic exodus, Canada still felt compelled to treat events as an internal affair of Pakistan.

Initially, the Bengalis' fight for an independent Bangladesh was not "on Canada's radar." High Commissioner George could not believe that the Canadian government would ever "buy the line" that Pakistan was selling, namely "that Mujib[ur] Rahman had no mandate from people of East Pak to pursue [the] objectives he has been following."[24] It did not look to George "as if Mujib was as rigid as Yahya was perfidious, talking conciliation while secretly bringing in his troops."[25] When George asked Ottawa, "Are we going to gloss over the fact that majority [75 million] is being suppressed by a minority [55 million]."[26] Canadian officials, however, evaded the question and retreated to their position of "noninterference." Within days, they learned from George that the followers of East Pakistan's elected leader were pursuing their commitment with incredible determination. They asked: What should Canada's role be under the circumstances? Should Canada strive for an understanding between East and West Pakistan on the "internal affair" of Pakistan? What about the continuing exodus of refugees to India? Canadian diplomats in the field recognized Yahya's sudden and covert attack on civilians as pure contempt for the Bengalis. Ottawa questioned Yahya's labeling of Bongobondhu as the "enemy of Pakistan," viewing it as spiteful and judgmental.

Personally, intending to take a principled stand on the democratic process, Prime Minister Trudeau initiated an exchange of letters between himself and the heads of Pakistan and India during the first week of April, seeking a "political solution." In his first significant personal intervention,

Trudeau wrote to President Yahya urging him to consider how the two parties could resolve their conflict by avoiding precipitous and potentially inflammatory acts. Trudeau argued passionately for an "agreed solution" reflecting the principles of democracy. Given the conflicting agendas of the superpowers, whether this was a realistic approach is open to question. Alas, world media had already declared its verdict, deeming Yahya incapable of political compromise and accommodation. "We haven't met a single Indian observer, whether from the press, the universities, or business, who believes it is either desirable or possible to resurrect the old Pakistan."[27] As George stressed the rebel forces' increasing momentum, Ottawa recalled one of his earlier cables: "Since the attack on Sheikh Mujibur Rahman and his supporters on 25–26 March, no one any longer voices these sentiments. Now, it is not a question of the idea of Bangla Desh but of when this idea can be made a reality."[28]

After reviewing Situational Reports (SITREPS) from New Delhi and Islamabad during the second week of April, Ottawa, along with the rest of the world, concluded that the fundamental problem was the Yahya regime's denial of political rights to the people of East Pakistan. The heart of the matter was the Bengalis' demand to transfer power to the leader of the majority following his electoral victory. Although Ottawa did not accept Yahya's attempts to shift all blame to India, the Trudeau administration awkwardly continued to refer to the crisis as the "Pakistan issue" or as a "political problem," namely, the "domestic problem" of another country. While Ottawa dithered, concerned Canadians raised a fundamental question: "What is Canada's real position on the conflict?" Under rapidly changing circumstances, the delay highlighted the complexity of policy issues for Canada in Southeast Asia. While delayed in formulating policy, Ottawa was discretely engaged in various activities stressing its commitment to democracy.

The fundamental democratic rights of the Bengalis were paramount to Sharp's notion of democracy and good governance. Canadian policymakers and politicians agreed and rejected Yahya's version of the crisis. While emphasizing democratization in Pakistan, Sharp downplayed the Bengalis' demand to carve an independent country out of Pakistan. Canada realized that any proposed power transfer from the military to the people's representative would prove complex. From the beginning, Canada engaged in direct and indirect diplomatic and other kinds of pressure, as noted in Chapter 7. The first step required the Yahya regime to take responsibility for restoring normalcy in East Pakistan through a "political settlement" acceptable to the Bengalis' elected leader. Since the Bengalis were still fleeing to India, Ottawa believed that special measures were necessary to ensure that Bengalis, currently displaced in India, returned safely to their homeland without fear of reprisals. Tacitly, Ottawa agreed with India's basic argument: the key to solving the crisis lay in the hands of the Pakistani military authority, not India. The Yahya regime would have to find a political solution to the situation in East Pakistan, argued Canada.

Seeing how East Pakistan was in a fast flux and change while the military reprisals were going on, Ottawa cautiously reviewed the rapidly unfolding events. Canadians also learned that additional time would be required since Canada needed to adhere to its "wait and watch" policy. Meanwhile, world media reported that Pakistan's foreign exchange reserves had decreased by $70 million since March when military operations commenced. Trade and business were seriously affected. The government of Pakistan itself seemed to confirm the gravity of the situation when it declared "a six-month moratorium on debt service payments due to all its consortium and non-consortium creditors."[29] The World Bank representative who visited Ottawa during the third week of April privately maintained that Pakistan was effectively bankrupt and was heading for economic collapse. As Ottawa's concern heightened, Canadian parliamentarians recognized Pakistan's dire financial situation even more. Proactively, Ottawa sought a mechanism to intervene discretely.

Since India and Pakistan shared common interests as members of the Commonwealth, Ottawa turned to Arnold Smith, a former Canadian diplomat and current secretary-general of the Commonwealth. Smith had already earned respect from his colleagues as a diplomatic and respected peace ambassador involved in every recent crisis affecting Commonwealth members. The very idea of Pakistan's dismemberment or the emergence of Bangladesh as a new country out of Pakistan deeply concerned Commonwealth countries, except for India. Given their mutual acrimony, the Trudeau administration considered both India and Pakistan as belligerents. With Smith's intervention, Canada hoped to persuade the two Commonwealth sisters to move in the right direction. Although Canada's efforts were unsuccessful, Canada continued to steadfastly promote universal principles of good governance, democracy, and respect for liberty. However, Canada's challenge was to address the problem abroad without inviting difficulties at home.

May 1971

When Ottawa officials became convinced of the secret pro-Bengali activities of the government of India, they feared that India's refugee problem might soon dominate the India-Pakistan relationship unless the situation was reversed. Ottawa identified a new dimension with broader implications for the age-old Indo-Pak conflict from humanitarian and geopolitical points of view. Recalling her experience in the Middle East during the late 1960s, Canada wished to demonstrate how an enormous refugee problem could unleash repercussions for political exploitation by either side in a dispute. Ottawa analysts also recalled George's cautionary comments on the historical animosity between the two countries dating back to the partition of India. Not wanting to "sit on the fence," Ottawa was anxious to "do something," but without inviting a "cross Canada" debate on Québec separation.

Ottawa realized that Yahya's labeling of Bengalis as separatists served as a convenient excuse for continuing military rule in the face of Bengalis' demands for greater autonomy and a fair share of the country's resources. Although Ottawa recognized that the actual struggle was between Bongobondhu, the democratically elected leader of East Pakistan, and Bhutto, the leader of the majority in West Pakistan, it decided to adhere to its policy of "deliberate delay." Canada knew that the world media had already labeled the conflict as a Pakistan-Bangladesh issue. Since Ottawa's strategy was to stick to its "staying the course" policy, it admonished its representatives that "it would be wiser to maintain a low bilateral profile" in their "efforts to do some good for the refugees in India, to avoid becoming embroiled in the Indo-Pakistan dispute."[30]

Ottawa found numerous contradictions between the claims and the practices of the military regime, and the President often found reasons for "letting himself off the hook." To seek accurate information, news media from various countries, including Canada, visited East Pakistan to investigate Yahya's justification for military actions, that is, insurgency on the part of the mutinous Bengalis and "restoration of law and order" in East Pakistan. After interviewing Yahya, an international team of reporters concluded that he had a closed mind—routinely ignoring whatever did not fit his narrative. Ottawa believed that the military regime had lost its legitimacy, acted with criminal culpability, and had crossed the Rubicon in the wanton killings of unarmed Bengali civilians. Beyond this, Yahya ceaselessly attempted to convince the rest of the world of an Indian conspiracy to dismember Pakistan by exploiting the sentiments of gullible Bengalis. In Ottawa's opinion, Yahya's claim of Bongobondhu being a traitor was a simple ploy to shift blame and responsibility to India.

As part of his strategic communications, George updated Ottawa on the success of the freedom fighters through reports and comments from the Indian Institute of Constitutional and Parliamentary Studies in New Delhi, which gathered newspaper clippings on the political control of the Bengali forces. Unsurprisingly, such news of guerrilla activities often contradicted "official" news from Islamabad, claiming to have already established law and order in East Pakistan. Ottawa was disturbed by the vitriolic exchanges between India and Pakistan, as well as the blatantly false reports from Pakistan that routinely denied the apparent truth of India's version of events while downplaying the progress of the freedom fighters. Unlike news from Islamabad, Indian sources described actual lives, fears, and, more importantly, the latest territorial claims of the *Mukti Bahini* liberation forces.

In his telexes and messages, George emphasized that events led to a separate Bengali homeland. The highly censored Islamabad media wholly ignored this trend. For this reason, Ottawa found George's reports from New Delhi more useful. Ottawa noted that although Pakistan officially maintained a "business as usual" policy regarding the situation in East Pakistan, it recognized that the regime's version was pure "window dressing" aimed at scapegoating India. Unsurprisingly, Small could not obtain accurate information on the Bengali rebels and their latest developments due to strict censorship. At the same time, George enjoyed an advantageous position due to India's support of the freedom movement, which made the availability of such information relatively easy. His dispatches and commentaries convinced Ottawa that the *Mukti Bahini*s were not "Indian infiltrators" or "miscreants" but Bengalis escaping to India and fleeing from indiscriminate killings and military reprisals. They were recruited from the armed forces; some were students and volunteers, and many were ex-servicemen. Canada was alarmed by the extent of the Indian government's covert involvement and in denial of the fight for Bangladesh's independence.

By mid-May, most state legislatures in India had already passed resolutions recognizing Bangladesh; several educated and informed Indians openly supported the emerging nation. However, contradictory information from Islamabad and New Delhi posed concerns for Ottawa. When, for example, Small was encouraged by Yahya's apparent democratization in Pakistan, George sensed the opposite. He reported on the deeply committed pledge of Tajuddin Ahmed, acting prime minister of the People's Republic of Bangladesh, and the rebels' "progress." Ottawa recalled George's remarks: "There is no room for a compromise within the framework of Pakistan."[31] Since information obtained through Canada's high commissioners to India and Pakistan was sometimes slanted, Ottawa had to deal with conflicting messages. As much as possible, Ottawa carefully constructed accurate accounts of critical events from different sources: the governments of India and Pakistan, the provisional government of Bangladesh situated in India, and various political parties and Bengali group leaders who took refuge in India.

Curiously, Canada agreed with Gandhi's argument that the key to solving the crisis lay in the hands of the Pakistan military authority. It was not to be found in India even though the Yahya regime blamed India. Ottawa found Yahya's activities contradictory on two fronts: (1) The regime claimed that it was making serious efforts to create a political structure in East Pakistan that would build confidence among the Bengali refugees regarding their prospects of returning home safely; (2) its continuing reprisals against the frightened Bengali civilians, in turn, precipitated their flight to India for haven. Again, while Triloki Nath Kaul, the Indian foreign secretary, talked about the region's peace, stability, and development and the need to urge Yahya toward a political solution with the people of East Pakistan, the Gandhi administration continued to supply arms to the rebel forces. It was simultaneously preparing for confrontation with Pakistan. Ottawa officials reminded them of George's cautionary remark that "the risks of wider conflict should not be underestimated."[32] As well as lecturing India or Pakistan "directly or indirectly about such concepts as domestic jurisdiction and non-intervention"[33] would be fruitless as both countries were on a collision course. Within three months, Small from Islamabad also wrote, reinforcing the same points made earlier by George, "My thesis is simple: India and Pak are on a collision course which only great power or UN action seems capable of preventing, guerillas, whether operating from India or within EPak [East Pakistan] have only one reliable source of military supplies: India."[34]

Ottawa also noted Prime Minister Indira Gandhi's statement in Lok Sabha (Parliament of India) about refugees in which she forcefully rejected accusations that India was deliberately plotting the disintegration of Pakistan. "Is it suggested that we wish the disintegration of Pakistan? Have we not, as many Members have pointed out, at every step tried not only for propriety in our relationship but also for friendship? If there is a struggle between the two parts of Pakistan, it is certainly not of our making but of the rulers of Pakistan. Is it anybody's contention that the methods being used today can achieve any integration or stability worth the name now or in the future?"[35] However, Gandhi's constant reference to the province of East Pakistan as Bangla Desh, ever since the declaration of independence by the rebel forces, did not escape Ottawa's notice. Despite apparent contradictions, Canada largely agreed with Gandhi that the rebel forces were determined not to deal with the Pakistani military regime.

The consensus in Ottawa was that, by establishing an initial civilian government, a democratically elected government might evolve and succeed. With this view in mind, Canada still insisted that the Yahya government, with input from its people in both East and West Pakistan, must develop an appropriate political solution without involvement from India. However, Canada's continued insistence on transferring power to Bongobondhu demonstrates Ottawa's assessment of the situation as problematic. Ottawa, somewhat naïvely, believed that this, in turn, might reverse the flow of refugees when the military would no longer be in power. Looking back, one could say that Ottawa's thinking was too "jejune." Ottawa found itself in a dilemma: it could neither publicly articulate an unambiguous position nor discuss the issue openly. As was the case, the Trudeau administration would not unequivocally condemn the atrocities of the Yahya regime either. Canadians were left in the dark without a clearly defined position.

Disappointed by the unrealistic stance of the Trudeau administration, some Canadians accused it of failing to determine whether the dedicated and relentless Bengali freedom fighters would be open to any proposed "political settlement" with the "Occupation army" of Pakistan since the Awami League by then had rejected any solution within the framework of a united Pakistan. Canada did not fail to note that rebel forces were steadily gaining ground due to India's direct assistance. Both Small and George thoroughly briefed Ottawa on the Bengalis' courageous resolve to liberate their native land. Notwithstanding the high commissioners' precise assessments, Ottawa stubbornly pursued the unrealistic and unachievable goal of keeping Pakistan intact. It is impossible to explain why a well-informed Sharp still sought a "political solution" with the military regime when the Bengalis vehemently opposed any compromise with the "Occupation army."

By the third week of May, Ottawa's priority was to focus on the political dynamics among the countries involved in the conflict, primarily how the world media viewed the continuing military repression in East Pakistan. At the same time, Ottawa also began to monitor three different areas: (1) the actions and reactions of the Yahya regime, (2) the activities of the *Mukti Bahini*, and (3) the role of the Gandhi administration. Small was asked again to assess the political situation in West Pakistan and the military regime's internal politics. He was also invited to urge the Yahya government to work with major political elements toward a cessation of hostilities and to initiate a new round of discussion on the transfer of power to Bongobondhu without directly intervening in the "affairs" of Pakistan. Small's reply was quick. He warned Ottawa that any efforts by Yahya to transfer power to civilian leadership would likely be thwarted by Punjabi leaders who saw civilian rule as a threat to the "now accustomed role of military dominance." [36] At this stage, input from both Small and George helped Ottawa develop a fuller understanding of the root causes of the conflict. It was puzzling that "official Canada" maintained the illusion that the two parts of Pakistan could still be unified. Against expert advice, Ottawa persisted in working toward a "political solution" with Bongobondhu, prime minister-designate within a united Pakistan – utterly ignoring East Pakistan's highly effective provisional government operating from within India with the full support of the Gandhi administration.

In the meantime, as officials in Ottawa struggled with the issue of democratization in Pakistan, they became highly annoyed by the antics of the respective Ottawa-based high commissioners from Pakistan and India. Each actively tried to persuade Ottawa officials toward his way of thinking. When Ashoke B. Bhadkamkar, Indian high commissioner to Canada, met with Sharp and presented him copies of an aide memoire, Sharp disagreed, pointing out that "little benefit would result from encouraging public debate in Canada for or against India or Pakistan."[37] Sharp candidly reiterated Canada's priorities relating to the conflict. Ottawa recalled Gandhi's speech in Lok Sabha (lower house of India's bicameral Parliament): "The word 'recognition' has echoed from many sides. It is, as my colleague has said, constantly under review. We are not waiting to see what other countries will do in this matter. Whatever decision we take in this or other issues is guided by our independent assessment of the situation in the broadest sense."[38]

Ottawa found India's offer of surreptitious assistance to the rebel forces a dubious and contentious position. In response, a frustrated George reminded Ottawa that the Gandhi administration was slowly "being pushed towards recognition of Bangladesh."[39] George raised two critical concerns for Ottawa. First, it was rumored that "apart from Foreign Minister Swaran Singh, all Mrs. Gandhi's colleagues are now for early recognition."[40] Second, in a private conversation with Foreign Secretary Triloki Nath Kaul, George found that "there was ... pressure for a limited Indian Army action in EastPak [East Pakistan] to clear a district or two of WestPak [West Pakistani] forces so that the Bangla Desh govt. and most of the refugees could return there."[41] Although mindful of the concerns expressed by Small and George, Ottawa still expected its envoys to strongly support Canada's position of neutrality with the governments of Pakistan and India.

On his return to Islamabad from a trip to Dhaka in late May, Small shared his shock and horror as he contrasted his observations with the military's version of what had been happening. In East Pakistan, Small saw the destruction of properties of the terror-stricken Bengalis as firsthand material evidence of the indiscriminate killings since the imposition of martial law. Ottawa officials were also dismayed by Small's accounts of gruesome atrocities perpetrated by the Bengalis on the Biharis (Urdu-speaking non-Bengalis, originally from the state of Bihar, India) who aligned themselves with the military government in their support for a united Pakistan. Nevertheless, when the Pakistan government released a "Official Statement on East Pakistan Situation" handout on May 6, Small was infuriated by claims entirely at variance with what he had witnessed. The document falsely claimed that the military government was saving the country from the "Indian agents." Rejecting the regime's "explanation" of events, Small informed Ottawa that such a narrative was "now part of the folklore in West Pakistan."[42]

Naturally, Ottawa was disturbed upon learning that the government manipulated news blackouts in Pakistan to forge the fake narrative that the military regime was "protecting the country" against anti-state elements. As Ottawa understood, the military itself was indiscriminately killing unarmed civilians. Canada, along with most nations, saw this as empty rhetoric. In Ottawa's eyes, the regime's claims of integrity, solidarity, security, and unity contradicted reality. Pakistan's "official" press releases did not attempt to explain what was actually happening. Small argued that this was neither Pakistan's war against India nor a war between Muslims and Hindus, as Yahya wanted the public to believe. Ottawa saw this as pure propaganda by Yahya's military to justify its suppression of the Bengalis.

Throughout May, Ottawa continued work toward the one-year-old democratization process in Pakistan, hoping Bongobondhu would assume power for the entire country. With this objective in mind, Canada undertook a mediatory role of "quiet diplomacy," which she had experience with. Despite continuing military repression, Canada still treated the matter primarily as Pakistan's "internal affairs." The Trudeau administration recognized that some Canadians were arguing that there might be circumstances amounting to genocide for which outside intervention would be justifiable under international law, although others disagreed. Nevertheless, the Trudeau administration chose not to broach the subject openly. In the same vein, Ottawa again decided to remain neutral and developed a four-pronged strategy: (1) public neutrality; (2) private encouragement of a political settlement between India and Pakistan; (3) calls for restraint by Trudeau himself to both India and Pakistan; and (4) the provision of humanitarian relief. But Canada soon discovered that she could only watch helplessly since she had to adhere to her "staying the course" policy.

June 1971

By June, the Trudeau administration was deeply disappointed by the military regime's blatantly repressive measures and wanton killing of Bengali civilians. It was also distressing to see how a significant portion of the Canadian public was dismayed by their government's failure to take a clear public position on the conflict. In any event, assiduously avoiding direct interference in Pakistan's internal affairs, Ottawa seriously considered Small's concerns regarding Canada's deployment of limited resources. Ottawa recognized that only a reversal of present policies and a new mix of financial and monetary remedies could avert impending disaster. The government would also not resume its aid program in East Pakistan unless political stability was restored. Ottawa and its think-tank members determined that the subcontinental crisis had deep historical roots. By this time, Ottawa also concluded that the conflict between the two wings of Pakistan resulted from profound inequality and, therefore, required special measures.

At various times, Trudeau spoke with President Richard Nixon, Aleksei Kosygin, chairman of the Council of Ministers of the Union of Soviet Socialist Republics, and other heads of government seeking ways to resolve the conflict politically. Ottawa was aware of the Canadians' reaction to the brutal acts of the Yahya regime and widespread sympathy for the victims of military repression; also, support for an independent Bangladesh was confined mainly to the Indo-Bengali segments of the Canadian public. They supported the liberation war of Bangladesh and condemned the military regime. Unsurprisingly, Canadians with ties to (West) Pakistan supported the Yahya regime's policy of extermination and lobbied the public and government accordingly.

After weeks of deliberation, Ottawa concluded that continuing development aid for Pakistan was essential, even though many citizens believed that the Yahya regime was using it against the people of Pakistan. Canada's remedial measures were designed to target the whole of Pakistan. While arguing that foreign aid be continued, with strong conditions to ensure equitable distribution, Ottawa asked, given the internal conflict and the root cause of dissension, what should be done with the remainder of the 1970–71 aid program? This meant endorsing its earlier position, the search for a political solution. Ottawa would continue its aid program while working toward the (1) release of Sheikh Mujibur Rahman [Bongobondhu], (2) withdrawal of West Pakistani troops, and (3) compensation for losses suffered by the people in East Pakistan due to army mistreatment.[43] In the interim, relief measures for refugees were continued. On a negative note, Ottawa officials ignored recent valuable intelligence provided by George since Canada's strategy remained unchanged. Policy analysts feared that overt endorsement of the Bengalis' struggle for independence would strain Canada's relationship with Pakistan. While Ottawa sympathized with the Bengali refugees and displaced persons, it still sought a "political solution" for an undivided Pakistan. Canada was faced with an apparent dilemma—she could neither condemn military reprisals nor overtly support a popular movement that would rupture Pakistan.

By the second week of June 1971, Ottawa was overwhelmed with information from the government of India and the newly formed provisional government of Bangladesh. George was convinced that all new information should be interpreted, analyzed, and incorporated into Canada's thinking.

Ottawa noted that although the West Pakistani army gained control of the main cities and communication routes in East Pakistan, it had little success against the guerrilla activities of the *Mukti Bahini*. George was impressed by the Bengalis' intense guerrilla activities and their determination to rally international support for their struggle—all of which he highlighted in his message to Ottawa. He also praised Syed Nazrul Islam, acting president of the provisional government of Bangladesh, for his high commitment. Despite frequent schisms between the mainstream Awami League and other political parties of East Pakistan, the determination to free Bangladesh was the singular point on which all political parties agreed. The lone exception was the Muslim League and a few Islam pasand (those who favored Islam) parties. George wrote to Ottawa saying that Yahya's declaration that the "Indian government is determined to exploit the presence of displaced persons in India to aggravate the tense situation and justify military intervention in East Pakistan"[44] caused Ottawa to reflect more deeply. Ottawa concluded that direct Indian military intervention in East Pakistan would likely occur under the following conditions: (1) after the monsoons, (2) if international relief did not provide sufficient resources, and (3) if Pakistan authorities did not reach a political accommodation with the Bengalis."[45]

By the third week of June, Ottawa learned more about the Gandhi administration's stance. Prime Minister Gandhi responded to a question from a fellow member of *Rajya Sabha* (Council of States) in the following manner: "Does he [President Yahya] for a moment believe that we would accept a political settlement which means the death of Bangla Desh, which means the ending of democracy or of those who are fighting for their rights? India could never accept such a state of affairs. ... I am not expressing a view on whether such a settlement is possible but clarifying what we have said at an earlier stage. If international pressure through whatever means available to the big powers and to other countries were to be exerted, I think that a political settlement would have been possible at an earlier stage. Now, of course, with each passing day, this possibility has become more remote."[46]

Meanwhile, Ottawa's foremost priority was to protect historically collegial relations between Canada and Pakistan. Although aware of India's support for the rebel forces and Pakistan's ongoing reprisals, Canada was inclined to ignore Gandhi's forceful opinion. Canada continued to focus on persuading Yahya toward a "political settlement." Curiously, the remarkable progress of the freedom fighters failed to alter Ottawa's strategy. In other words, Canada would not consider an independent Bangladesh at the cost of a united Pakistan. Since the concept of Bangladesh was not on Sharp's radar screen in June or even later, Ottawa hurriedly reviewed Yahya's program for the future of Pakistan as outlined in his June 28 address to the nation. Although Ottawa officials saw no progress toward democratization, they still vainly hoped that the Yahya government would arrive at a "political settlement" since it claimed to be "desperately" seeking one.

Unsurprisingly, Ottawa continued to ignore crucial developments, such as the extraordinary solidarity of the Bengalis and the growing strength of the rebel forces. Rigidly adhering to its goal of a political settlement between the two wings of Pakistan, Ottawa gave little weight to India's substantial and surreptitious provision of arms and weapons. Meanwhile, Ottawa officials revisited some of Small's earlier telexes. They noted the high commissioner's warning that High Commissioner Small informed Ottawa of total news censorship and bans on political activities throughout Pakistan. Small's telexes informed Ottawa, "Bhutto has branded Mujib a calculating secessionist bent on the destruction of a united Pakistan, charging that Mujib had been struggling for the separation of the East Wing since 1966."[47] He also informed Ottawa that a three-pronged attack had been launched against the "secessionist machination of Sheikh Mujib" and the "turncoat connivance of West Pakistan minority political groups"[48] by Bhutto and Mahmud Ali Kasuri, chairman of the Pakistan People's Party. Kasuri asked the government of Pakistan "to give serious consideration to the advisability of extending recognition to the provisional governments of Mizoland and Nagaland ... given India's policy of 'gross interference' in Pakistan's internal affairs."[49] Once again, Small cautioned Ottawa on the complexity of the conflict.

By the end of June, having reflected on the strength of the military regime, Canada contended that Yahya's main priority was damage control. The agenda was primarily reduced to cover-ups and denials of the regime's actions, thereby creating a "credibility gap" with the media. Given the enormous volume of propaganda from India and Pakistan, Ottawa recognized how such information reinforced each country's respective position. Amid much "news turbulence," Undersecretary of State A. E. Ritchie and his colleagues could not correctly interpret current data sources. They urgently needed objective information to analyze the consequences of the events that were taking place rapidly on the ground and the world's opinion regarding the victims of military reprisals. Canada continued to monitor Gandhi's activities. Canada could not ignore Gandhi's willingness to confront Yahya despite Trudeau's persistent appeal to exercise restraint. Canada came to see Gandhi's warning. In a recent interview with an American TV network, Ghandi observed, "If [the] situation is forced upon us, then we are prepared to fight."[50] Meanwhile, events were trending strongly toward the imminent victory of the liberation forces, directly aided by India. Sadly, Canada's strategy of seeking a "political solution" revealed a severe lack of political savvy and judgment. Although Ottawa concurred with its high commissioners, there was still no change in its game plan.

July 1971

Ottawa remained busy and continued to review ongoing dispatches from New Delhi and Islamabad. However, the rebel forces' rapidly changing situation and solid progress became problematic for Ottawa. Sharp kept Trudeau *au courant* on the news from a volatile and fluctuating situation prone to speedy political changes. The crises cried out for flexible and creative responses—and an ability to "think outside the box." Alas, all were strikingly absent! Sharp's briefing notes to Trudeau testify to Ottawa's lack of foresight and narrow and inflexible thinking. Sharp was mainly concerned by the apparent refusal of the Indian government to allow access to observers from the UNHCR to encourage the refugees' return even though Pakistan had agreed unconditionally to their presence on its side of the border. Ottawa was alarmed by the response of India's Defence Minister Jagjivan Ram to the debate on the budget demands of its Ministry of Defence on July 12. "We are aware of the feeling in the country on the question of recognition of Bangla Desh … In their determination to establish a democratic order in Bangla Desh, freedom fighters have all our sympathy and support."[51] Holding India and Pakistan jointly responsible for noncooperation, accusations, and counteraccusations, Ottawa could neither articulate a clear position nor advance beyond its "wait and see" position.

Canada questioned its legitimacy since the provisional government had not received formal recognition. George felt obliged to advise Ottawa of the provisional government's recent legitimate demands and assertions. Ottawa also knew from Small about the activities of the Bangla Desh National Liberation Struggle Coordination Committee formed on July 15. Mandated to stay in close contact with the Bangladesh government and all other forces engaged in the liberation struggle, this group consisted of all the major political parties of East Pakistan whose representatives were in India, having sought refugee protection. Its creation demonstrated a sterling example of the Bengali peoples' solidarity to safeguard the independence of Bangla Desh.[52] George also informed Ottawa of the Committee's recently adopted resolution affirming "the goal of independence for Bangla Desh."[53] Given their significant implications, Ottawa needed extended time to digest all new information.

Canada helplessly witnessed Yahya's political extremism: that he must suppress "narrow virtual exclusionary ethnonationalism" to "save" Pakistan. With the availability of more information, Ottawa officials frequently experienced difficulty interpreting the telexes from India and Pakistan with their conflicting information and arguments. Sometimes, messages supported the actions of India; others, those of Pakistan. Unsurprisingly, such information generated more questions than answers, further complicating the search for solutions. Ottawa could not reconcile the news from three sources: India, Pakistan, and the provisional government of Bangladesh. The more Canada tried to avoid taking sides, the more embroiled she became domestically and internationally.

Under these circumstances, Ottawa's thinking vis-à-vis Pakistan stagnated. Doggedly firm in its thinking, Ottawa insisted on directing its energies toward an unrealistic power transfer, regardless of actions on the ground. In retrospect, a shift in thinking should have taken place. It didn't. Nothing could persuade Ottawa: neither George's briefing notes on the progress of the freedom fighters nor the Gandhi administration's unwavering support for Bangladesh to "shift gears." Stubbornly, Ottawa maintained that the Yahya regime must re-align its thinking to gain credibility nationally and internationally. Inexplicably, Ottawa (again!) misdirected its energies while cherishing the illusion that Pakistan could still be saved. It is astounding that Ottawa remained so impervious to advice from the field. Ottawa obstinately maintained the fiction of pursuing Pakistan's integrity—against all empirical evidence.

In the meantime, ironically, for Canada, the Yahya government interpreted Ottawa's mediation efforts negatively. The regime viewed efforts toward transferring power to Bongobondhu as "anti-Pakistani." Despite Canada's vigorous efforts to act neutrally, Pakistan considered Canada hostile to its military authority.

In fact, Canada and Great Britain's decision to suspend economic aid to Pakistan and withdraw export licenses for spare parts for Pakistani military aircraft convinced Yahya that the Canadian government was not on his side. In Chapters 4 and 7, we saw how the actions of the Bengalis typically provoked Yahya's wrath, which he swiftly unleashed. Most Pakistani national newspapers ran stories of Yahya threatening Canada for her involvement in Pakistan's "internal affairs." Further, Pakistan threatened to leave the Commonwealth and take reprisals against both countries. This upset Ottawa, which had assiduously avoided taking sides, especially against Pakistan. Canada found it disconcerting that her commitment to restoring democracy in Pakistan now placed her against Pakistan. Contrary to the regime's criticism, Canada exercised its mediation efforts with scrupulous fairness.

When Syed Nazrul Islam, acting president of the People's Republic of Bangladesh, offered to hold a dialogue at any place, in any situation, and with anybody, foreign affairs analysts were caught off guard. Since Canada was not yet aligned with other countries, she needed time for a "course correction." The accounts of indiscriminate military reprisals against the Bengali civilians were disturbing to Ottawa officials. Canada recognized that every news "byte" had profound implications for the growing crisis. Although the news bytes on the activities of the provisional government of Bangladesh were jarring to Ottawa's proposed "political solution," a strong-willed Sharp refused to broach the matter directly with Pakistan. As Ottawa ludicrously sought a political solution within a united Pakistan, it quietly noted other disturbing trends. First, the military regime was continuously playing a nasty blame game against India when it had never ceased its repressive measures. Second, Yahya repeatedly and falsely claimed that law and order had been restored in East Pakistan. Ottawa was troubled by the overwhelmingly negative international reaction to the Yahya government's policies, its critical economic situation, and dismal prospects for resolving the conflict.

In the meantime, the Canadian public was "beyond frustrated" as news media portrayed a vacillating federal government with no stated position yet on the conflict. Sharp said in the Commons that the elected representatives of East Pakistan "should be given the responsibility of governing." Still, he qualified this remark: "We are not supporting any separatist movement anywhere in the world in any way."[54] His "clarification" created heated discussions among an anxious public aware that swiftly changing circumstances favored an independent Bangladesh. With no appetite for pro-Bangladesh developments, Ottawa ignored such news, including George's analysis. Obsessed with an unrealistic political agreement between the governments of Pakistan and India while completely ignoring the provisional government, Ottawa managed to enrage specific segments of the Canadian public who worried that the Trudeau administration was wasting precious time appealing to the military regime and "staying the course."

In the meantime, Sharp's foreign affairs cognoscenti conducted a series of brainstorming sessions on military rule with Canadian politicians. Having assessed the political crisis, they (correctly) predicted the dismemberment of Pakistan as the likely result but failed to articulate Canada's position on the conflict. They faced a barrage of questions from in-house policy wonks centering around the question: *Is a political solution within a united Pakistan a realistic proposition?* No one in Ottawa had a clear answer. George's meticulous documentation of the freedom fighters' progress failed to persuade Ottawa to "shift gears" or think "outside the box." Seemingly bound to follow its staying-the-course policy, Canada continued its futile efforts of "diplomatic suasion."

Unsurprisingly, instead of producing a position paper, the Trudeau administration determinedly maintained its noninterference policy. Ottawa then developed a range of forecasts regarding the subcontinental conflict. However, some instances suggested that Ottawa was slowly adapting to the changed circumstances, albeit internally and not publicly. Finally, at least to themselves, officials admitted that Canada's intermediary role in promoting political resolution had been ineffective in producing any result. It was not a great surprise, as both the Yahya and Gandhi administrations were hypersensitive to proposals offered by outsiders. Given Canada's quixotic but unwavering conviction of a united Pakistan and a possible "political settlement" with Bongobondhu as elected leader, Trudeau again wrote to Gandhi. He warned her "that this gigantic influx has imposed serious strains not only on the Indian economy but on the whole social and political fabric of India, and those ways must be found urgently for the refugees to return in safety to their homes."[55] There was no response from Gandhi. One can well imagine Gandhi's reaction!

It became clear to Ottawa that, contrary to its claims, the regime was battling for survival rather than suppressing a Bengali uprising. A la Yahya's euphemism, the army was cracking down on the actions of the

Bengali pro-Indian "miscreants" in East Pakistan. There were, however, moments when even a determined Sharp was at a loss, particularly when he recalled the capricious military regime's misconstruing Canada as Pakistan's enemy. As a senior member of the Commonwealth, Canada relentlessly continued its lengthy efforts to advocate for a "peaceful solution." Incomprehensibly, Canada ignored mounting evidence of human rights abuses, military reprisals, and other repugnant political misdeeds while portraying itself as fair and neutral. Canada claimed to be neither pro-Pakistani nor pro-Indian. As late as July 1971, Sharp continued to insist on political neutrality, persuasion, and mediation. He instructed his Canadian high commissioners and ambassadors to vigorously promote Canada's neutral mediator position on the conflict.

By the end of July, Canada was dismayed by Pakistan's threats to leave the Commonwealth and ongoing harsh reprisals against Canada and Great Britain for suspending aid. Canada was shocked to hear "that the military government in West Pakistan is considering the provision of aid to the separatist movement in Québec in retaliation for the suspension of Canadian aid."[56] This baseless threat appeared as "a bolt from the blue," given Canada's Trojan efforts to mollify the military regime. Uncertainties during the entire month disheartened Ottawa officials, who realized that the suspension of economic aid to Pakistan and a later withdrawal of export licenses relating to spare parts for Pakistani military aircraft had achieved little. Ottawa again needed to restrategize without antagonizing Pakistan and India, Canada's two sister Commonwealth countries.

August 1971

A slight shift in thinking surfaced in August as Ottawa realized that the real issue for Pakistan was power sharing among Pakistan's provinces. Ottawa viewed the Gandhi administration as being dragged into the conflict and absorbing almost the entire exodus of Bengalis seeking asylum. Though initially sympathetic to India, Canada doubted the Gandhi administration's claim that India was not involved in the struggle between the Bengalis' demands and the Yahya regime's denial of the results of the 1970 National Elections. The Trudeau administration strongly suspected that India had been involved from the beginning. Naturally, Ottawa was troubled by the apparent inconsistencies in how the Gandhi administration interpreted the distinction between humanitarian needs and the political aspect of the conflict. Small had already expressed concerns regarding the Gandhi administration's contradictions between its actions and its stated position on the conflict. He was disturbed by India's provision of arms and soldiers to the Bengali rebels, clearly "fanning the flames" of independence and revolution. India's antithetical position appeared more clearly to Ottawa, seeing how India maintained that it was Pakistan's problem at a time when she simultaneously demanded that a "political settlement" be made with Bongobondhu and his Awami League. "Though Indians may be able to persuade themselves they are acting with restraint, by whatever name you call it, they are keeping the undeclared war going," thus, Small cautioned his superiors in Ottawa.[57] Equipped with up-to-date information from India and Pakistan, Ottawa discovered additional examples of duplicity from both governments.

During the second week of August, Sharp was briefed along the lines that, even if Bongobondhu were tried, he would doubtless "become a martyr and symbol" for Bangladesh sovereignty as long as India "provided continued support for guerrilla forces."[58] Small believed that with India's unconditional support for Bangladesh's independence, Mujib was no longer essential to the cause. "Initiative and drive have already passed to other hands that were unlikely to be attracted to a settlement which left East Pak within Pak federation,"[59] thus wrote Small. The briefing notes of the two high commissioners convinced Ottawa that Bangladesh was emerging much sooner than expected. Heretofore, Ottawa had disregarded such predictions from its two high commissioners even though the rest of the world already recognized the seriousness of the Bengalis' fight for independence and the inexorable and accelerated progress of the rebels toward an independent Bangladesh with India's direct assistance. Frankly, even at this stage, the mere concept of a separate country carved out of a divided Pakistan was anathema to an "out-of-touch" Canada. Ottawa had not yet adopted alternate thinking or a Plan B, even though the Trudeau administration was aware of the strides made by the *Mukti Bahini* and the Gandhi administration's strong support of the rebel forces.

Canada was profoundly dismayed by Yahya's malice and narrow-mindedness. He was spiteful toward anyone who disagreed with him and refused to consider other political opinions. Yahya intensely disliked Bongobondhu, whom he had already branded as a "traitor." Yahya showed no signs of yielding to the Bengalis, whom he disparagingly called "macchar," an Urdu word for mosquitos.[60] Despite massive evidence to the contrary, Canada was still pushing its proposal for a "political solution" at every convention or discussion by the UN or other government groups. One might ask, How politically astute was Canada in dealing with two parties, each hurtling headlong in the opposite direction? How could there be a common ground between rebels and a dictatorial military leader who tolerated military reprisals and declared a democratically elected leader an enemy? Refusing to face reality, Canada avoided taking a definite position.

As a peace-seeking nation and an ally of its two Commonwealth sisters, Canada was disturbed by the Indian government's perfidy in secretly providing the rebels arms and training. As India had not formally recognized Bangladesh's provisional government, Canada was puzzled by its de facto support of the guerrillas. Canada was disappointed in realizing that Prime Minister-designate Bongobondhu would likely never assume leadership. Sharp was briefed that the influx of Bengali refugees into Indian territory had already become a fundamental *casus belli*—a justification for war. Nevertheless, Canada rightly believed it was up to Pakistan to develop a comprehensive plan to transfer power. Throughout this period, Ottawa procrastinated, wrongly thinking it was the best alternative. Ottawa recrafted its message but proposed no mechanism for a political solution other than insisting on the return of the refugees. An utterly unrealistic Ottawa naïvely believed that the refugees' return to their country would clear the way for a political settlement with the government of Pakistan. At the same time, Sharp also feared that pushing the refugees back through the border would result in their being slaughtered by a vengeful military. Sharp found himself between a rock and a hard place.

Just about the same time, Ottawa also learned from a discouraged Small that the Pakistani bureaucrats and military personnel were floating the idea of a referendum, albeit a complete sham plan. According to Small, it was not "worth the candle to support enormous costs of a civil war being waged a thousand miles away,"[61] especially when the military routinely crushed any semblance of a democratic process.

Given the politico-military situation, Ottawa was convinced that the ball was in Pakistan's court since the Yahya regime's ongoing reprisals were forcing the frightened Bengalis to seek asylum in India. To improve the situation, Canada believed that Pakistan must initiate several actions to restore the confidence of the people of East Pakistan. Ottawa's position consisted of a hypothetical possibility, not a realistic solution. As noted, Canada failed to consider the Bengalis' struggle for independence and the positive results they have been achieving rapidly. Twice in four months, Trudeau personally pleaded for the return of the refugees. Still, it was a "hard sell" to persuade India to allow Bengali refugees to return to their country. It was not possible for two reasons: given the ongoing reprisals of the Bengali civilians and Yahya's despotic rule. As a middle power, Canada could only plead for restraint. Canada recognized that India had its game plan with its hidden agenda to size Pakistan up, and the diabolic military regime had continued its activities for dismembering Pakistan. What should Canada's role be under the circumstances? Should Ottawa's efforts still be focused on finding a solution within a united Pakistan? Since the birth of Bangladesh seemed inevitable, what was the next step? Such nagging questions haunted Ottawa officials.

Ottawa found Yahya's rhetoric empty and his "formula" impractical and without substance. Ottawa became even more disheartened when it recalled Small's earlier comments, "India and Pakistan are on a collision course which only great power or the UN seems capable of preventing; guerrillas, whether operating from India or within East Pakistan, have only one reliable source of military supplies: India."[62] Ottawa fervently and vainly wished that a modus vivendi between the two wings of Pakistan could be achieved, resulting in a transfer of power to Bongobondhu. However, the stark political reality was the opposite: Pakistan had never made sincere and realistic efforts. Sharp was briefed that the Yahya regime's proposed initiatives did "little to guarantee the majority population in East Pakistan of a main or even an equal voice in governing the country."[63] Records from mid-August onward reveal anxiety, discomfort, and angst within the Trudeau administration as it contemplated the following two scenarios: (1) a political resolution within the framework of one Pakistan and (2) Indian intervention to assist the Bengali freedom fighters, thereby forcing the surrender of the Pakistani army.

During the third week of August, and still tight-lipped about its official position, Ottawa slightly adjusted its approach with greater acceptance of the eventual emergence of Bangladesh as a nation. Ottawa officials decided Sharp and his Cabinet colleagues should be posted on Bangladesh's progress, something they had purposefully avoided thus far. They also wanted to remain abreast of the superpowers' positions. As a middle power, Canada knew that the USSR was globally maintaining an East European empire by force while the US assumed superpower responsibilities in Asia through NATO (North Atlantic Treaty Organisation). Yahya's face-to-face success as a power broker in bringing China and the US together seriously alarmed Canada. Right-hand man Zulfiqar Ali Bhutto, leader of the Pakistan People's Party, acted as the conduit in facilitating Adviser Henry Kissinger's visit to Peking (now Beijing), which in turn paved the way for China's historic entry into the economy of the modern world.

Their successful meeting created a special bond between Pakistan and US President Richard Nixon and further distance from India. Canada, however, was aware that President Nixon harbored a deep resentment against Prime Minister Indira Gandhi. Also, it was known to all that the Nixon administration opposed Bangladesh's independence, although the people of America were sympathetic to the cause of the Bengalis. Canada could see how the US government appeared indifferent to the plight of Bengali refugees and their aspirations for an independent homeland. As an ally of the US, Canada was aware of the Nixon administration's intent to strengthen ties with Yahya, although a neutral Canada had no such political ambition or position.

In the meantime, Ottawa was glad to learn that USSR President Nikolai Podgorny had appealed to the Pakistan government to cease military action against the Bengalis and sought a political settlement with the elected leaders of Pakistan. At the same time, Ottawa also learned about China's position (support for Pakistan) concerning the conflict with more certainty. Ottawa was informed that India had reacted with surprise upon learning the Nixon administration's warning of India that in the event of any Indo-Pak war, India should not rely on US assistance.[64] In the meantime, Ottawa also discovered that India's fear was short-lived as, within days, India signed a nonaggression pact, the Indo-Soviet Treaty on Peace, Friendship, and Cooperation. Informed of an apparent flurry of activity among the superpowers, naturally, Canada was rocked by these two critical events: (1) the signing of the Indo-Soviet Treaty and (2) the People's Republic of China's unexpected assurance of support for the Yahya regime. Of great interest to Ottawa, George stressed a vital aspect of that treaty: in the event of an attack or threat of attack, India and the Soviet Union would consult each other. Canada realized that India would no longer act alone.

In Chapter 7, we saw the reaction of Robert Christie, head of the Special India-Pakistan Task Force, to the possible implications for the Indo-Soviet Peace Treaty since the key players were spoiling for a showdown. He viewed the changed reality on the ground with alarm. With inside information on the freedom fighters, he fully recognized their strength, accomplishments, and especially their unshakeable commitment to victory. The task force's members realized that the freedom fighters were credible on the international stage and that the liberation of Bangladesh was imminent. For the first time, Christie looked at the situation from a practical political perspective, considering the irreconcilable positions of India, Pakistan, and the provisional government of Bangladesh. By this time, thanks to the international media, the general public was well aware of the strength of the nascent provisional government operating out of Kolkata, West Bengal, India, with the full support of the Gandhi administration.

Ottawa officials, however, were troubled by the pace of accelerated change, as they faced numerous challenging questions: How to ensure a proper understanding by the superpowers of the nefarious military assault against the Bengali civilian population of East Pakistan? Have they demonstrated their positions toward the governments of Pakistan and India? Are the superpowers' public positions on the conflict unclouded and clear? Since Sharp was cautioned regarding the potential involvement of the Soviet Union, which was no longer neutral, he needed to be sure about China's dilemma concerning ongoing military reprisals in East Pakistan. It had to choose between its only non-Communist ally in Asia and its identification with a "national liberation movement" in East Pakistan with Maoist elements. For Ottawa, it was reassuring that Premier Chou En Lai declared China's support for Pakistan's unity in a public message to Yahya. He had also warned India not to intervene.

In the meantime, it was rumoured that she would likely declare an emergency when Indira Gandhi returned from her tour of several western capitals. A swift exchange of telexes between Ottawa and New Delhi followed. The Indian foreign minister stressed that the task would be difficult. George observed that India would "continue to put pressure on Pak Army in East Pak by every means short of outright invasion but will not start anything in West."[65] George's core message was that India was "prepared to counter whatever it [Pakistan's reaction] may be"[66] to make Bangladesh, then under the occupation army, a political reality. Ottawa (correctly) believed that the Yahya government could not win a war with India and would avoid confrontation. By this time, Ottawa had no illusion that the Gandhi administration's ambitious tactic: the more Pakistan drove out frightened Bengalis to India, the more receptive India was in offering asylum for its political ends. Canada believed India would invoke casus belli, justifying war as part of her geopolitical strategy.

Ottawa noted how, internationally, most observers found the claims of the Yahya government to be false and incongruous. Ever since the clampdown of March 25, 1971, the military has been conducting ongoing reprisals against Bengali civilians in East Pakistan. Contradicting itself, the same army was also talking about granting amnesty to those who had fled to India to escape persecution from its military. As Ottawa analysts reviewed earlier dispatches of the two high commissioners, they found incredulous statements of the Yahya regime that clashed with reports of its high commissioners. Naturally, Ottawa assigned more significant weight to Small's remark that Bongobondhu "would not be able to control the emotionally-charged Bengalis" even if he was "released and returned to East Pak."[67] By and large, the input of the high commissioners clarified the actual situation. It helped Ottawa better understand the freedom fighters' situation vis-à-vis the Yahya government's constant denials of progress. Sharp's office "went through the motions well without tipping its hand."

Regardless of the situation, Canada stubbornly remained persistent in her efforts to democratize Pakistan. The Trudeau administration invested considerable resources. The Prime Minister himself steadfastly appealed and lobbied for the release of Bongobondhu. Justifiably, Canada feared an in-camera trial of the banished leader. It would have certainly been farcical, especially if Bongobondhu were tried for treason. Although Canada appealed to the conscience of the world against such a sinister move, Yahya openly expressed his disdain for the Bengalis in attempting to diminish Bongobondhu. Notwithstanding Canada's efforts, the Trudeau administration could not secure Bongobondhu's release. For Ottawa, a solution remained elusive.

After months of procrastination, toward the end of August, Ottawa finally shifted its gear from "staying the course" and "wait and see" policy to a position and asked: What's next? This time, Ottawa applied a new lens to view the conflict. At long last, Canada would take stock of the freedom fighters' strength, toughness, and determination and seriously consider the possible birth of Bangladesh. Having finally accepted the media's definition of the Pakistan-Bangladesh conflict, Ottawa revised its position based on (1) the fast-changing strategic position of the Gandhi administration, (2) the self-confidence of the freedom fighters, and (3) the military regime's continuing reprisals against Bengali civilians. Sharp's think tank members and many in-house experts on South Asian issues explored questions such as: Will the Bengalis achieve freedom and eventual mastery of their territory? Will a political resolution lead to statehood? Could there be a loose confederation of Pakistan? Ottawa concluded that the birth of Bangladesh would occur much sooner than later.

As India and Pakistan hurled accusations at each other, Ottawa cautioned its high commissioners in Islamabad and New Delhi as follows: "India and Pakistan have been effectively at war for at least 24 years, and it is probably useless for our purposes to try to determine with any pretence of accuracy to what extent which side is telling the truth. The assumption is usually that neither is."[68] After analyzing India's potential role in the fast-deteriorating situation, Ottawa cautioned its diplomats in Islamabad and New Delhi to monitor the grave situation carefully. With Pakistan and India poised to oppose one another at every turn and with a clear divide among the superpowers, the critical month of August ended uncertainly for the tumultuous future of Pakistan.

September 1971

Sharp was confronted by two central questions right at the beginning of September. The first issue was capsulized by the statement of Indian Foreign Minister Swaran Singh while touring several world capitals. The second issue was India's rigid position vis-à-vis the posting of UN observers. It underlined the view that the world community must share responsibility for the resettlement of the refugees. To each, Sharp was required to respond with tact and diplomacy. The Trudeau administration had no difficulty in endorsing the Indian government's appeal. However, Canada feared that Singh might justify India's unilateral action to solve the problem "by other means" if adequate assistance was not forthcoming. Given these grave issues, Sharp was particularly concerned about the apparent refusal of the Indian government to allow observers representing the United Nations High Commissioner for Refugees to operate in India to encourage the refugees' return. Curiously, Pakistan had agreed unconditionally to the presence of observers on the Pakistan side of the border. World news media pointed out this anomaly to the Gandhi administration's claim of neutrality.

Following months of reflection, Ottawa realized that the *Mukti Bahini* had been making substantial progress and that the freedom fighters would not even consider negotiations with Pakistani representatives. Until this time, the Trudeau administration had ignored this brutal reality. Ottawa was mindful of the remarks of Tajuddin Ahmed, Acting Prime

Minister of Bangladesh, "There is no room for a compromise within the framework of Pakistan. Bangladesh is sovereign and independent, and we shall defend its separate and free identity at any cost."[69] This statement was commonly accepted as accurate. Canada's high commissioner to India had already alerted Ottawa accordingly, but federal officials did not recognize its implications, baselessly discounting the rebel forces' strength. This failure revealed an "Achilles' heel" in Canada's strategy. The Trudeau administration was well aware that India fully backed the rebels and that there was clear justification for an act of casus belli on the part of the Gandhi administration. Hypothetically, Canada wishfully thought about the possibility of the release of Bongobondhu, which was followed by his assuming power in an undivided Pakistan. In reality, it was out of the question given the fact that with India's backing, the provisional government of Bangladesh had been functioning effectively from India since mid-April 1971—even in the absence of Bongobondhu, who was interned in a jail in Pakistan.

Ottawa's dilemma becomes obvious when examined through a Canadian lens: over the months, the centre of interest had shifted from humanitarian assistance to a highly political conflict. Ottawa allowed itself to be played by Yahya's outrageously false claims and to become entangled in a web of misinformation. Ottawa knew that, historically, Pakistan and its military had long maintained a highly prejudiced view of India and vice versa. Canada did not share either view, nor would Canada declare her position on the conflict or modify her strategy for a political resolution involving the governments of Pakistan, India, and Bangladesh. It is hard to understand why Canada doggedly pushed for a united and undivided Pakistan at a time when the Bengali rebels were advancing inexorably toward victory.

Sharp was also advised that the "political union of Pakistan has been fragile and somewhat unnatural even in the best of circumstances, but in recent years, differences have become a more pronounced and unifying force of a common Muslim faith less binding."[70] Advice along this vein must have stemmed from Ottawa's correct belief that the refugees would not return to their homes unless a political settlement satisfactory to the Gandhi administration were reached. Canada concurred with India that unless the refugees were guaranteed safety, they would not leave haven, only to be slaughtered. Behind the scenes, the Gandhi administration worked diligently to return the refugees to their native land, ensuring Bangladesh achieved independence. Ottawa advanced a small step, recognizing that India's military would successfully mobilize and force out the Pakistani army, resulting in the birth of Bangladesh and the dismemberment of Pakistan.

While following the events unfolding, Ottawa recalled how the military government refused to convene the National Assembly. Under the circumstances, Ottawa officials asked: Did the majority have the right to self-determination and even the right to establish a separate and independent state of Bangladesh? Still obsessed with saving Pakistan, Canada urged Yahya to ask all the major political groups to cease hostilities and negotiate a peaceful transfer of power to Bongobondhu. Ottawa strongly believed that humanitarian considerations should be addressed against the broader socioeconomic and political context. However, it is puzzling that Canada continued to seek "political" reconciliation even when convinced of the inevitable birth of Bangladesh. In any event, the government's confidential draft position paper indicated Ottawa's slow drift, since late August, toward accepting the emergence of Bangladesh—a change following months of denying political reality. Ottawa finally considered the conflict from the political viewpoints of all parties involved. With a similar uncomfortable issue in her backyard, Ottawa did not want any public debate on the separation or independence of East Pakistan.

From the beginning of September, Canadian officials began to provide Sharp with detailed regular briefings on the activities of the provisional government of Bangladesh, the rapid progress of the freedom fighters, and world reaction to breaking news on Bangladesh. The Trudeau administration deliberately minimized their importance until the end of August. George began to prioritize analysis of the freedom fighters' progress and the recent activities of the provisional government to assist Ottawa in its assessment of the situation. George was happy to note that his assessments seemed to have convinced officials in Ottawa of the freedom fighters' strong commitment, tenacity, and success. There was no shortage of accurate, up-to-date information for daily reassessments of the situation in light of actual progress. Unfortunately, despite all efforts from the field and external affairs staff, those responsible for briefing Sharp remained somewhat disinterested.

When world opinion overwhelmingly favored Bangladesh, Sharp was warned that any reassertion of control by the Pakistani military under these circumstances would only mean further repression and the risk of a more significant refugee exodus with attendant suffering. Analysts in Ottawa were uncomfortably aware of Canadians' demands for transparency. Sharp recalled public criticism of the federal government for its failure to address the bigger picture involving the governments of Pakistan and India, which was compounded further by the failure to mention the provisional government and the rebels' growing strength and brave initiatives. Ottawa's efforts to reconcile the two wings of Pakistan remained inexplicable since, by then, Ottawa should have been expending its energies on a new strategy to address the emerging political reality. Government records suggest that Ottawa still maintained faint hopes for a united Pakistan. A quixotic Ottawa was still determined to persuade Yahya to reconcile with Bongobondhu.

After much procrastination, Ottawa finally focused on completing its position paper by mid-September despite its officials being swamped with situational reports on speculative and evidence-based analysis. As officials gathered their thoughts, they revisited Small's telexes regarding a possible referendum sent in August. Upon reexamination, they found an intriguing nugget of information with a warning to be vigilant regarding the proposal to be "floated" by Pakistani military bureaucrats. Due to its limitations, however, Ottawa was "on its heels" and reluctant to push forward with a position paper based on political reality, not speculation.

Moving forward, Small also broached an issue related to subcontinental ethnicity and subnationalism. He expressed fears of similar movements by the Punjabis and Sindhis who might believe that it would not be worthwhile "to support enormous costs of a civil war being waged a thousand miles away"[71] from West Pakistan for those determined to free their land. Although appreciative of Small's helpful advice and incisive analyses, Ottawa officials struggled to propose a coherent position. Once again, Ottawa opted to "go slow" and take no further action for several weeks. They focussed on Pakistan's worsening financial situation and the looming economic squeeze.

As described in Chapters 4 and 5, various Bangladesh-Canada associations were internationalizing the case of Bangladesh for several months, and relief funds in several US cities were being established. They had also been disbursing money through the Washington-based Bangladesh Mission for quite some time. Sharp was briefed on the precarious state of subcontinental geopolitics to the effect that both India and Pakistan had hardened their respective position with "no way out."

"There are great dangers inherent in the situation, and either party might find itself in a position where a resort to arms would seem logical."[72] Thus, the draft of the September position paper stated. In it, the minister was warned of the strong possibility of war between India and Pakistan. It is important to note that the same September draft position paper was intended for internal use only. Sharp was briefed in the following: "Canada has demonstrated a willingness to do its part and, at the risk of being unpopular with its friends, will continue to ask those directly involved and those less directly involved to do what they can, not only in the name of humanitarian concern but equally in the interest of peace."[73] At this briefing, officials tried to sway the minister toward the inevitable dismemberment of Pakistan and the emergence of Bangladesh as a separate and independent country.

From then on, the team doubled its efforts to brief Sharp with additional excerpts from the soon-to-be-announced September position paper: "The roots of the tragedy unfolding on the sub-continent lie in the considerable differences between the two parts of Pakistan. East Pakistan is more populous than West Pakistan and produces more foreign exchange. This situation contributed greatly to the tragic chain of events."[74] Again, pushing further, Ottawa officials addressed the crux of the issue: the "political union of Pakistan has been fragile and somewhat unnatural even in the best of circumstances, but in recent years differences have become more pronounced and [the] unifying force of a common Muslim faith less binding."[75] For the record, this was the first time that the minister had been made fully aware of the concrete progress of the liberation forces, the deterioration of the present "united Pakistan," and how each element contributed to the emergence of Bangladesh. Such clarity enabled Sharp to comprehend better the fast-changing political reality of a new country arising out of contemporary Pakistan. Apprehensive and nervous, Sharp faced a frightening spectre. On the one hand, the Gandhi administration was asking world leaders to help resolve the matter so that the refugees could return home after totally ignoring Yahya's much-publicized fake "amnesty"; on the other hand, having failed to persuade the military regime to facilitate the return of the refugees, Ottawa again witnessed continuing brutality from the Yahya regime which triggered a further exodus of the Bengalis. That, in turn, negated any safe return of refugees to Pakistan.

Canada found herself in a perpetual dilemma: she could neither endorse the disintegration of Pakistan nor condone military reprisals and suppression of democratic rights. Canada saw the military takeover as a negation of the democratic principles of majority rule. Oddly, although Pakistan remained engaged in military action, Canada continued to adhere to its noninterference policy. The Trudeau administration kept working toward a political settlement between Yahya's pledge to transfer power to Bongobondhu and the latter's demand for greater autonomy for East Pakistan. Canada lobbied for Bongobondhu's release so he could form the government of Pakistan. Against all odds of success, Canada continued to propose a resolution of the conflict through a political settlement between the two parties without breaking Pakistan. In a sense, Canada's situation highlights the gauntlet of formidable challenges – Ottawa's fear of straining her relationship with Pakistan, also a US ally. In parallel, the Trudeau administration struggled to reconcile humanitarian concerns with the harsh exigencies of international power politics.

Naïvely enough, as Canada remained firm in her flawed thinking, she continued to believe that only the transfer of power to Bongobondhu, the elected leader of Pakistan, could achieve a lasting and peaceful solution. Archival records, however, indicate that by late September, Sharp finally recognized and became convinced of the fundamental motives of President Yahya Khan and Prime Minister Indira Gandhi: Yahya's to perpetuate military rule and Gandhi's to weaken Pakistan militarily. Sharp was repeatedly briefed on Yahya's perverse pleasure in blaming India, including his military action in East Pakistan. He was also briefed on the Gandhi government's seizing this opportunity to dismember Pakistan, thereby saving the cost of maintaining expensive defenses in the eastern wing. Justifiably, Canada genuinely feared that explicit endorsement of the nationalist cause of the Bengalis might incite militancy among Québec nationalists at home, even beyond what the federal government had faced during the FLQ (Front de libération du Québec) crisis of 1970.[76]

October 1971

As uncertainty reigned in the subcontinent, rumors of "behind-the-scenes" deals circulated widely. Sharp's commitment to honor Canada's pledge of noninterference in Pakistan's "internal affairs" was a "hard sell," given Pakistan's culpability. While federal officials had earlier treated the subcontinental conflict as Pakistan's internal affairs, by the end of September, Canada slowly accepted the legitimacy of the Bengalis' struggle for political autonomy. By the beginning of October, a transition in outlook coinciding with Ottawa's eager acceptance of vital information on the latest development of the provisional government of Bangladesh became noticeable.

Under the circumstances, Sharp expressed his views about Pakistan and India with renewed firmness and clarity. Canada, however, consciously decided not to condemn the military regime openly. In an attempt to state Canada's position, Sharp cited three constraints to any proactive role by Canada in the conflict: (1) Commonwealth membership shared by Canada, Pakistan, and India; (2) Canada's mediatory role, which precluded her from taking sides; and (3) Canada's need to respect the "internal affairs" of Pakistan. Canada championed a peaceful solution in the House of Commons via a diplomatic discussion with international organizations. At the same time, Ottawa struggled to address issues relating to the inhumane treatment of Bengali civilians in their native land, popularly referred to as "Occupied Bangladesh" by the media. Sadly and haplessly, Sharp recognized India's opportunism and Pakistan's duplicity—each of which he found infuriating. Ottawa feared "raising the diplomatic stakes." Accordingly, the Trudeau administration developed a four-pronged strategy: (1) corresponding directly, personally, and discretely with the heads of Pakistan and India; (2) referring the issue to the United Nations (UN); (3) addressing the issue through the Commonwealth; and (4) working with the UNHCR. Unfortunately, Ottawa again failed to take into account Yahya's implacable determination to destroy his enemies (the Bengalis) and the sheer strength, determination, and commitment of the freedom fighters.

A self-assured Sharp finally ignored Pakistan's reactions, something he had been previously incapable of doing. In that sense, one could observe that, for the Trudeau administration, calling "a spade a spade" was a significant step forward. Keeping a stiff upper lip, he unhesitatingly stated that the main "political power had been concentrated in the West."[77] A confident Sharp conveyed Canada's gratitude for "the extraordinary and effective efforts made by the Indian Government"[78] in sheltering millions of refugees in India. Armed with the latest figures and historical data, Sharp pointed out to the External Affairs and National Defence Committee members that "East Pakistan is more populous than West and produces more foreign exchange."[79] The implicit message was that, despite a major financial contribution to their own country, the Bengalis of East Pakistan were treated as second-class citizens.

In the meantime, George was quick to communicate the formation of an eight-member consultation committee and the results of the semi-annual session of an All-India Congress Committee held at Shimla, the capital of the northern Indian state of Himachal Pradesh, from October 8 to 10, 1971. George observed that the delegates did their business, addressing the Bangladesh issue with "kid gloves."[80] "If an election can result in this, what will a prolonged guerrilla war do?"[81] George, apparently frustrated, cautioned Ottawa that over nine million people were suffering for nothing more revolutionary than electing a leader of their choice. Constrained by ambivalent policy in a deteriorating climate, Canadian officials continued to spin their wheels.

Despite its persistent efforts, Ottawa could persuade neither India nor Pakistan to exercise restraint and avoid a conflagration. In the meantime, even in October, Sharp's team continued work on the draft position paper emphasizing Canada's tradition of "quiet diplomacy." Unfortunately, Sharp again found himself challenged even though he had accepted the reality of the conflict in East Pakistan. After much reflection, he concluded it was neither a "civil strife" nor simply an "internal affair" in Pakistan. Nevertheless, he became convinced he could not resolve the situation since the Trudeau administration's hands were tied. Ottawa recognized the harsh reality that, while the superpowers claimed to have a common interest in stabilizing the subcontinent, each country was nursing its self-serving objectives and interests. New potential conflicts also emerged in the transformed geopolitics of the 1960s and early 1970s, which made it difficult for Canada to be only a middle power. On the home front, senior officials constantly feared nationalist stirrings in Québec. The previous year's October crisis remained a source of anxiety to the Trudeau administration.

Meanwhile, Sharp was cautioned by the foreign affairs specialists that direct endorsement of the Bangladesh movement was a two-edged sword likely to cause more harm than good, both at home and abroad. This partially explains Canada's ultracautious response to the provisional government's repeated urgent appeals for help that came from Foreign Affairs Minister Khandakar Mushtaq Ahmed. From this time onward, Canada no longer denied the Bengalis' progress in their struggle for independence. Striving for balance, Sharp's team criticized the Yahya regime's contradictory statements and expressed dissatisfaction with the lack of progress as claimed by Yahya. Such discussions, however, remained strictly private. In any event, the challenging month of October finally passed, with Ottawa seemingly on the verge of adopting a strong and coherent position vis-à-vis Pakistan, if only internally.

November 1971

Oddly, in early November, instead of moving forward, Sharp was seen stepping backward despite solid evidence of the *Mukti Bahini*'s ability to force the Pakistani army to surrender sooner rather than later. Sharp's earlier confidence and firmness, which he displayed toward his colleagues in October, evaporated in November. In reality, new elements of discord and dissent surfaced in Sharp's mind—a puzzling phenomenon since the Trudeau administration was already convinced that the birth of Bangladesh was imminent. At the same time, Ottawa concurred with George's impression that the government of India had done a "remarkable, indeed [an] almost incredible job in coping with biggest refugee influx in history of seven months,"[82] Ottawa also believed that there were reasons for concern. Ottawa seemed ever more apprehensive about the "compelling reasons for GOI [Government of India] to solve [the] problem and get refugees home ASAP." [83] As far as George was concerned, the immediate future looked bleak.

It is beyond perplexing that Ottawa again proposed a political settlement for the umpteenth time, given that the imminent birth of Bangladesh was a foregone conclusion among informed observers. Sharp's frequent oscillations between accepting the emergence of Bangladesh and Yahya's "initiative" concerning restoring democracy in Pakistan alarmed his colleagues. Given Sharp's two-month-old belief in near-certain victory for the freedom fighters, such wavering was incomprehensible. In retrospect, Sharp must have experienced great angst and stress as he reflected on various nightmarish scenarios in his mind. Ideally speaking, as the liberation of Bangladesh approached, Ottawa should have been more focused on welcoming Bangladesh as an independent country. Unfortunately, such was not the case.

With tensions rising between India and Pakistan, Ottawa feared an all-out war between the two. While Ottawa firmly avoided overt gestures favoring either one, Sharp abruptly changed his mind again in November. Although updated on the progress and momentum of the freedom fighters, Sharp refused to accept the dismemberment of Pakistan. Inexplicably, there is evidence that Ottawa still sought ways to achieve a political settlement for a united Pakistan -an utter impossibility in November. Although Ottawa analysts realized that Bangladesh was on the verge of gaining independence aided by India, they ludicrously "fixated" on the illusion of a united Pakistan. In mid-November, Ottawa was dismayed when international organizations failed to convince the military government to devise a political solution with East Pakistan. Ottawa maintained, correctly, that US Senior Advisor Henry Kissinger's "tilt in favor of Pakistan" was adversely impacting the original issue: the transfer of power to the elected leader of East Pakistan. Matters worsened as Ottawa engaged in a broader game planning with India, Pakistan's archenemy. Unsurprisingly, Ottawa could not complete its position paper. Confident a month earlier, Sharp now seemed "out of sorts" caught between the clashing governments of Pakistan and India.

Although Sharp held serious misgivings regarding the self-serving interests of the superpowers, he made a desperate last-ditch effort, hoping to find a path forward among the myriad of American-Soviet-China pressures. Unsurprisingly, Sharp failed. Ottawa's disappointment peaked as members of the Security Council refused to tackle the issue at a time when the USSR had a grand plan to consolidate its position in India, having already signed the Indo-Soviet Treaty of Friendship and Cooperation. In Canada's opinion, the alliance between India and the Soviet Union, on the one hand, and Pakistan and the People's Republic of China, on the other, did not bode well for a solution. Sadly, neither Pakistan nor India heeded Canada's advice. Canada now awaited the response of UN Secretary-General U Thant, who promptly wrote to both parties on October 21 to offer his good office.

In the meantime, situational reports from Islamabad also raised alarms about the inevitability of an Indo-Pakistan war, which, Canada feared, could embroil the superpowers. While facing this specter, Ottawa tried unsuccessfully to grasp Yahya's rationale for ongoing reprisals. That "mental exercise" foundered badly as Yahya's barbarity escalated the exodus of Bengalis. Time and again, Canada asked: Could a realistic political settlement and a climate of confidence be achieved in East Pakistan? Canada reluctantly concluded that a military government only offered token gestures and ignored her persistent appeals. A crestfallen Sharp felt deeply exasperated with India also. Although India maintained that it was an "internal affair" of Pakistan, analysts at external affairs maintained that India's role, with her hidden agenda, was dubious and "ambivalent from the beginning."

Further evidence of Canada's fading hopes for a last-minute reconciliation emerged when Sharp met with Pakistan's foreign secretary, Sultan Mahmud Khan, in Ottawa just as India and Pakistan were spoiling for confrontation. Both Trudeau and Sharp discussed their misgivings with Khan with utter frankness. They earnestly hoped to avoid war and pursue the visionary goal of saving Pakistan. Sharp questioned the continuing exodus of terrified Bengali refugees that imposed a growing burden on India's fragile economy. Sharp told Khan that while Canada was appreciative of the delicate political and communal stability, she was disturbed by the politicization of the refugee issue by the Indian government, which further complicated the refugees' return to their homeland. Khan retorted that his government had taken all possible measures to avoid "giving Indians pretext on which to invade"[84]. In Ottawa's view, this was arrant nonsense.

Realizing that the Yahya government's proposed constitutional changes were too little, too late, and too lame, a dejected Sharp, once again, expressed his grave misgivings. Forthright and candid in this exchange, Sharp exercised a personal mediatory role to find a political solution. Ottawa persisted as a peacemaker, even though each party had reached the "point of no return." Sharp was again torn between a supposed "time crunch" and his inability to persuade the parties involved. His foreign policy wonks underlined the need for a joint appeal by the USA, the USSR, and the People's Republic of China to Pakistan to restore normality, no matter how formidable the challenges were. Absurdly, Canada still nursed the illusion that the military regime would share power via negotiation and compromise. Ottawa ignored the reality on the ground, following the maxim: "domestic solution to a domestic problem."[85] Even at this stage, Ottawa stubbornly continued "tilting at windmills" toward a united Pakistan.

Unsurprisingly, as late as the end of November, Ottawa was still obsessed with the idea of a united Pakistan and its work with Yahya. Naïvely, Ottawa assumed that if India could only be persuaded by the USSR to withhold its support of the *Mukti Bahini* for a grace period of two to three months, Pakistan's allies, including the US and China, might be able to pressure Yahya to "proceed with his program" on schedule and following the announced provisions. "If the government of Pakistan could be persuaded to announce these proposals and to implement them quickly, there would be reasonable grounds for trying to persuade the Indians that the result would come as close as they could reasonably expect any government to come in meeting the international community's call for increased self-government in East Pakistan."[86] Such was Canada's key message to Pakistan's foreign secretary, a gambit that might have worked in May or June.

It is astonishing that Sharp's team seriously considered such untenable options in late November when there were already writings on the wall of the imminent birth of Bangladesh. Ottawa was "dreaming in Technicolor," believing that perhaps a political resolution was remotely possible since Yahya had never seriously entertained Sharp's vision of a re-engineered Pakistan under Bongobondhu's leadership. When Ottawa looked at its efforts to persuade Yahya, Ottawa was disheartened by the regime's total failure to "walk the talk" despite Ottawa's persistent appeals. When Ottawa looked at the determined rebel forces, it was evident that they would not turn back since they were enjoying the full support of the Gandhi administration and the people of India. The Gandhi administration must have found Ottawa's position laughable at a time when the surging freedom fighters were "counting down to the revolution." Incredibly, Ottawa still engaged in fantasy even two weeks before the surrender of the Pakistani army.

George and Small had already provided ample evidence of impending war by the third week of November. George believed that Gandhi and Foreign Minister Sardar Swaran Singh could not counter the rising pressure much longer, including from many of the prime minister's Cabinet colleagues, members of her party, and opposition MPs. By then, Canada also realized Pakistan had lost its moral compass and was only fighting a war for survival. It was baffling that Sharp still wanted to establish a division of constitutional powers between Dhaka and Islamabad. Though it sounds absurd, the fact remains that the thought of Pakistan's actual breakup caused Sharp angst. This was even though he had accepted the fast-changing political reality of the subcontinent. Still obsessed with reconciliation, an embittered Sharp maintained that "it might help if changes could be presented as an effort to meet the international community's generally accepted view that solution to the problem lay in greater autonomy and popular representation for East Pakis."[87] It is outlandish that even after the Trudeau administration finally acknowledged the achievements and tenacity of the freedom fighters, Gandhi's direct support for an independent Bangladesh, and the Yahya regime's brutal ongoing reprisals, it still lobbied to keep Pakistan united. Neither the international rejection of the Yahya regime's policies nor Pakistan's dire economic situation and limited prospects for a settlement discouraged Ottawa. As events scurried, a disillusioned Sharp was again challenged.

In hindsight, it is farcical that Sharp ever conceived a role for Yahya, who flaunted his military might, denigrated his opponents, and mocked at the Bengali people. Instead of realizing that he was wasting his efforts, Sharp stubbornly made two more attempts to rescue Pakistan from dismemberment. First, he visited US Secretary of State William Rogers in Washington the last week of November. He recommended to his American counterpart a dialogue between the representatives of India and Pakistan under UN auspices. Unsurprisingly, it failed. Second, George and Small jointly proposed a scheme endorsed by Ottawa to apply constant pressure on Yahya in hopes of negotiating a political settlement with the Awami League. It quickly collapsed.

By the last day of November, amid uncertainties, Ottawa officials and diplomats agreed with the following: (1) without doubt, a war would break out anytime, and (2) a political solution was the only way out if imminent war was to be avoided. It took Ottawa eight long months of tortured "wheel spinning" to conclude that Yahya's so-called special measures would not sway the battling Bengalis. Abandoning its official position, Ottawa was forced to take a quantum leap, given the freedom fighters' determination and near-certain prospects of victory. Based on the latest information, Ottawa finally concluded that the amputation of Pakistan was inevitable. The rebel forces, with India's direct intervention, were on the verge of forcing the surrender of the Pakistani army, paving the way for the birth of Bangladesh. Paradoxically, Canada has not yet stopped directing her energies in the other direction.

December 1971

Sharp was briefed daily as Canada futilely pursued her "mediator" role. Naturally, frustrations mounted as the entire series of "behind-the-scenes initiatives" floundered. The gap between the Pakistani military and the freedom fighters widened in lockstep. Much to Ottawa's chagrin, the most critical obstacles to peace were the Pakistan military's continuing reprisals and the deep resolve of the Bengalis to liberate their homeland. No solution appeared on the horizon. Reluctantly, Ottawa realized that Pakistan would fracture and East Pakistan would break away, leaving India, the most crucial country in Southeast Asia, and West Pakistan seriously weakened. Ottawa had difficulty accepting this reality and, curiously, continued fantasizing that the two wings of Pakistan might (miraculously!) reconcile. This was not going to happen. Canada must have appeared foolish among its more realistic international partners. While Yahya continued his ill-advised military repression, asserting that the situation in East Pakistan was "business as usual," the rebels advanced inexorably. At the same time, Canada dithered along the path of moral suasion.

On December 3, 1971, the same day that Pakistan declared war against India, High Commissioner Small advised Ottawa of mounting hostilities between India and Pakistan: the Pakistan Air Force had reportedly bombed eight airfields in northern India. Within hours, the Gandhi administration announced in a national broadcast that India and Pakistan were at war. Various rumors swirled: the Chinese army was poised to attack India from the north, and massive US assistance was on its way. To make matters worse, it was rumored that the Soviet Union had threatened to mount a diversionary action on the Chinese border if the Chinese army invaded India. Additionally, the Soviets were rumoured to send ships into the Bay of Bengal to blockade any US ships coming to rescue the Pakistani military. By then, numerous Indian forces had already crossed into East Pakistan and captured central Pakistani army installations and, ultimately, Dhaka, its capital city. Canada became even more apprehensive when fighting broke out on the western front. From the ground, Small candidly advised Ottawa that "any negotiations with Mujib [Bongobondhu] were likely useless."[87] Ottawa agreed. With his credibility shredded, the military dictator was reduced to absurd proposals. With the two countries now openly at war, Canada's last hopes were dashed: her repeated appeals had been spurned, and the two countries were now attacking each other's "air bases and oil installations."[88]

Wreaking great destruction, the grisly civil war continued, fanning the hostility and hatred of the people of East and West Pakistan. Sharp was left with a few options since Canada viewed both India and Pakistan as hostile and aggressive. In the meantime, India rejected the UN Secretary General's initiative for a mutual withdrawal. Ottawa, however, still cherished unrealistic hopes of a peaceful solution, even at this stage, to be mediated by the UN. Disheartened, Canada realized that the three great powers, the Soviet Union, the People's Republic of China, and the USA, would not impose a political settlement on Pakistan. Canada could not influence the warring parties as a middle power with no vested strategic interests. Archival records confirm that even at this late stage, Ottawa still entertained the notion that if (!) India ceased supporting the guerrillas and offering haven, and Yahya might be able to reestablish a civilian government. Equally ludicrous was the wildly unrealistic consensus among disillusioned Ottawa officials that a democratically elected government uniting all of Pakistan might evolve and succeed. Realistically speaking, none of these pipe dreams would materialize.

On December 4, a letter reached Ottawa in which Yahya desperately pleaded for Prime Minister Trudeau's "urgent action aimed at making India see reason to bring about cessation to hostilities launched by her and to resort to resolution of all disputes by peaceful means."[89] No record of the Trudeau administration responding to Yahya's appeal exists. In any case, it was far too late. With India and Pakistan now at war, Canada continued to work quietly in the background as an "honest broker." At the foreign correspondents' meeting on December 5, British sources circulated unconfirmed rumors that the American "President had agreed before [the] weekend to negotiate with Mujib [Bongobondhu]."[90] These proved false. No records indicate any "follow-up" of any activity in this regard.

Two days later, on December 6, Gandhi announced that India had formally recognized the People's Republic of Bangladesh as an independent country. Canada knew India had unofficially recognized the provisional government since it was formed in India with the Gandhi administration's support on April 10. Pakistan immediately severed diplomatic relations with India. Canada was not surprised as the window for moral suasion had long passed. As Canada saw the situation, the ball remained in the court of the two belligerents, Pakistan and India, plus the three superpowers: the US, the USSR, and China. Ottawa was disturbed to note George's dispatch that the "GOI [government of India] hope[s] to have East Pak military situation fairly well cleared up within seven days."[91]

In the meantime, Small also claimed that India was accusing the US and China of directly supporting Pakistan and its causes. Some Pakistani newspapers reported that America was siding with the Yahya administration. Presumably, Pakistan appreciated the US "pleading for justice and fair play" since the military regime "squarely held India responsible for aggression."[92] At the same time, the UK was being slammed as a supporter of the most recent grievances, having abstained from voting on the United Nations General Assembly (UNGA) resolutions and continuing to ship arms to India.

Again, following India's recognition of Bangladesh, Sharp briefed Prime Minister Trudeau accordingly. Sharp's frustrations were reflected in a memorandum to the prime minister as he departed for Brussels: "There is little point in the government of a country as remote as Canada trying to apportion responsibility for the present situation as between one government or the other. The Indian claim that it should not be equated with Pakistan, valid as it may have been before the shooting started, is no longer relevant, and both parties should be regarded equally as belligerents."[93] Canada continued to "participate in efforts not only to terminate the existing state of war but to prevent its spreading."[94]

Since India had already recognized Bangladesh as an independent country, it is bizarre that Ottawa remained laser-focused on mediation. Ludicrous as it may seem, Sharp still urged Pakistan's necessity of quick action in giving East Pakistan civilian and representative government and pressed India to exercise continued patience despite the enormous problem thrust upon it. Sharp and company completely inverted the maxim of politics being "the art of the possible." Sharp attempted the impossible; no one is surprised that it failed.

Canada's Position as Pakistan and India Find Themselves on the Verge of War

Work on the unofficial internal draft position paper proceeded glacially; meanwhile, Bangladesh declared independence on December 16, 1971. Ottawa recognized from the start that the crux of the issue was Pakistan's East-West sharing of power with Bongobondhu, the Bengali national leader once destined to lead the country. One may ask: Why did Sharp procrastinate in developing Canada's official position when he knew that fear of an imminent war between India and Pakistan was being generated across Canada? Ottawa recognized that the suppression of democratic principles by the military government in East Pakistan could not be defended because the leader of the majority party was engaged in a secessionist movement. During the Yahya-Bongobondhu-Bhutto parley, the Bengalis were assured that matters were progressing well. They weren't. Yet Canada avoided raising the issue to maintain "neutrality" and leave the internal problem resolution to Pakistan. Canada could not accept that her neutrality had failed to generate positive action by either of the combatants.

Although Canada dragged her feet far too long, she learned a painful lesson: every choice has a cost. For Canada, the destruction of human life and property in East Pakistan had long ceased to be an internal affair or domestic issue, as the Pakistan military claimed. Having adhered to her foreign policy of nonintervention in the affairs of another country, Canada made it clear that she would only promote an appropriate and mediated political solution. In Chapter 7, we examined Canada's efforts to restore democracy in Pakistan. Canada genuinely believed such a goal would be best served by peacefully transferring power to Bongobondhu. The complexities of the conflict were characterized by Prince Sadruddin Agha Khan, United Nations High Commissioner for Refugees, as a "challenge of unprecedented magnitude" in a widely publicized media account.

True, despite her persistence, Canada had little success. Ottawa officials remained committed to a political solution, such as granting East Pakistan a substantial measure of autonomy as envisaged in the Awami League's six-point program platform—a key to victory in the 1970 National Elections. An ardent democracy advocate, Canada continued to argue that Yahya must negotiate a settlement with the political leaders of both wings of Pakistan. This solution must respect the principles of democracy in Pakistan, according to which the elected leader would assume power unconstrained by the country's military. However, Canada discounted the Bengali rebels' potent strength and completely overlooked their possible role in any solution. Sharp seized every opportunity to articulate and clarify his government's position: "We are also urging, of course, that there should be a political settlement of this question and not one that involves so much bloodshed."[95] It was his government's view that only "through close collaboration with other countries" could Canada "contribute most effectively to creating conditions" in which "a political settlement" [96] would be possible. While Sharp acknowledged the sufferings of the Bengalis numerous times, he did not propose complete independence for "Bangladesh"; Sharp never adopted the term.

Canada's strategy was opposed to the position of the Yahya regime. Although long-established norms and principles for international conduct were weakening, Canada, with her middle power capacity for mediation, tried to implement new ideas but blindly ignored India's potential for dismembering Pakistan and the likelihood of Bangladesh emerging out of

Pakistan. Whatever its approach, Canada could not justify misdirecting so much effort toward reconciling the two hostile wings of Pakistan. Admittedly, complexities were belying any simple solution. As far as Ottawa was concerned, it saw that each party had a stake in the struggle: Yahya played the blame game to perpetuate military rule, Gandhi to dismember Pakistan, and the Bengalis to free the motherland they loved and called Bangladesh. Doubtless, the greatest weakness of Ottawa's approach was its rigid fixation on a united Pakistan. Ottawa's poor judgment persisted in the face of the *Mukti Bahini*, proving themselves a powerful faction. Ottawa nonetheless pursued a mediatory role despite mounting evidence of a pending violent overthrow of the status quo. Canada still "hoped against hope." Why was the provisional government of Bangladesh kept outside the loop even though Ottawa was aware of the strides it had made with timely support from the Gandhi administration? Again, to answer this question, one must recognize Canada's limited range of diplomatic and foreign policy options.

Professor Zaglul Haider has provided a fascinating, albeit partial, answer. Based on his research, Haider observed that Canada had gained international experience as a member of the UN observer mission in Kashmir. During that time, when Commonwealth countries like Pakistan and India were frequently at war with each other, Canada tended to focus solely on her mediatory role.[97] Perhaps Ottawa gave too much weight to its previous role at the expense of ignoring harsh realities. That error resulted in Ottawa wasting precious time and effort trying to persuade Yahya toward a peaceful action. Canada failed to gauge the bigger picture involving the governments of Pakistan and India on the one hand and the rebel forces and representatives of the provisional government on the other. Although aware of the complexity and challenges in the Indian subcontinent, Canada's "hands-off" position diverged sharply from that of the US, which favoured Pakistan's military dictator. In the face of repeated demands from all sides in the Commons to articulate his government's position toward Pakistan, Sharp stubbornly maintained the official line - "wait and watch." The waffling and procrastination of the Trudeau administration warranted sharp and justified criticism.

There was, nonetheless, one shining moment of decisive action by Canada to support the liberation forces of the future Bangladesh. That occurred in June 1971 when Canada courageously opposed the US and intercepted the Padma mission at the Port of Montreal (discussed in

Chapter 7). By acting boldly against the Nixon administration, Ottawa stopped the deadly shipment designed against the Bengalis. Unfortunately, this singular action was the exception against the backdrop of rambling, vacillation, and the failure to take a firm position on the subcontinental conflict.

Briefly, Canada's strategy incorporated the following six principles or factors, establishing the parameters within which Sharp and his team addressed the thorny issue of Bangladesh from a uniquely Canadian perspective. First, Canada's firm commitment to federalism was reinforced by the 1970 October crisis. Second, Canada and Pakistan were (and still are) members of the Commonwealth, sharing mutual economic and commercial interests. Third, Canada and Pakistan belonged to the same camp during the Cold War. Specifically, Pakistan was a member of the US-sponsored security alliances, the South-East Asia Treaty Organization (SEATO), and the Central Treaty Organization (CENTO). In tandem, Canada was the closest ally of the US. Fourth, Pakistan was supported by the US and opposed by the USSR. It is helpful to reflect on Canadian historian Edgar McInnis's remark eleven years earlier regarding Canada's helplessness in the Cold War. Historically, Canada has felt tremendous pressure to conform to American interests and has usually acted in concert with the US.[98] Fifth, since Canada traditionally operated in the shadow of US polity and commerce, Canada's foreign policy and economy heavily depended on facilitating American prosperity.[99] Sixth, Canada feared an Indo-Soviet axis would increase the USSR's influence and threaten the West.

1971 Subcontinental Conflict in Comparison with the Rohingya Crisis (2017–present) and Invasion of Ukraine (2023–present)

In comparing and contrasting Canada's reaction to the emergence of Bangladesh versus her recent responses to contemporary conflicts in Myanmar and Ukraine, it is not surprising to find differences. Whereas the 1971 conflict was primarily a civil war, the situation of the Rohingya was a humanitarian crisis resulting from Myanmar's genocide; again, the Ukraine crisis was precipitated by an outright military invasion. The differences in Ottawa's response to the Rohingya disaster, affecting more than a million refugees, and the invasion of Ukraine with massive damage to civilian infrastructure versus its stance on Bangladesh are instructive. Two factors stand out: (1) Canada had to seriously consider the ramifications of her actions vis-à-vis Québec nationalism in 1971, whereas in the twenty-first century, this is not a salient factor; (2) Since 1971, Canada has not faced another international conflict involving *only* commonwealth countries. Practically speaking, the six factors mentioned above that framed Canada's response to Bangladesh have only been applied weakly or not at all since 2017. Still, Canada remains very much "a middle power." In the subcontinental conflict, it is intriguing to speculate that perhaps Canada (unwittingly) *tried to act* as a major power when its "sphere of influence" dictated a more modest strategy.

In examining Canada's tortured path to address the Bangladesh-Pakistan-India hostilities, Canada's failure to take a position or "pick a side" stands out. Although well-intentioned, government officials engaged in inconsistent and sometimes bizarre actions and failed to take decisive action when required. While Canada generously supported NGOs openly advocating independence for Bangladesh, it refused to publicly *condemn* the reprisals and human rights atrocities of the Pakistan military. Fear of criticizing Pakistan, a sister commonwealth nation, weighed heavily.

Overview of the Rohingya Crisis: On August 25, 2017, the Myanmar military attacked thousands of Muslim Rohingya in Myanmar. Lacking citizenship, the Rohingya were effectively "stateless" individuals, routinely denied standard employment opportunities and government services. Differing in ethnicity and religion from the 55 million majority population, they had been targeted and persecuted since the early 1970s. Immediately after the August 2017 attack, the Rohingya faced genocide and ethnic cleansing. Among Rohingya victims, the UN estimated 43,000 murdered (mainly by the military) and the rape of 81,000 women and girls. Within months, an estimated 700,000 Rohingya migrated to Bangladesh, swelling numbers there to approximately 900,000. Since then, the refugees have faced peril from predators and continue to rely mainly on UN food and emergency supplies. Officially, Canada swiftly supported the Rohingya refugees in Bangladesh, offering $100 million in financial aid. However, international press coverage of the crisis, while generally sympathetic to the refugees, has been sporadic and inadequate. Sadly, the vast majority of nations seem content to leave the Rohingyas to their fate and let the UN resolve this massive humanitarian crisis on its own.

It is equally unfortunate that the major powers have shown little interest in an issue that does not threaten their self-interest for over six years. They perceive little benefit to resolving this human crisis, and no alliance of other nations has emerged to address it.

Overview of the Invasion of Ukraine: On February 24, 2022, Russia launched a massive, unprovoked, and highly publicized invasion of Ukraine featuring relentless assaults on all strata of Ukrainian society. The Ukrainian military valiantly confronted their Russian aggressors and, within months, began to repel the invaders. Russia countered with missiles and drones as they focused almost exclusively on nonstrategic civilian targets such as the electrical power grid, schools and hospitals, shopping centres, apartment buildings, and other heavily urban and residential areas. The explicit aim was to destabilize and demoralize, indeed terrorize, Ukraine's civilian population through destruction, death, casualties, and widespread suffering. The relentless Russian assault on the country's infrastructure has destroyed vast portions of the (electrical) power grid throughout Ukraine, not to mention the virtual obliteration of several major cities such as Mariupol.

The verdict of Western nations is that President Vladimir Putin's Russia has committed numerous war crimes. In late winter and early spring 2023, the International Criminal Commission (ICC) began to file war crimes charges against President Putin. In Canada and most Western nations' support for Ukraine, its valiant President Volodymyr Zelensky and its courageous citizens have been widespread, strong, and steady. Press coverage remains consistently positive toward Ukraine while condemning Putin's so-called military operation. Canada's unwavering official support of Ukraine - not to mention its citizens' overwhelming support - is almost unprecedented.

In broadly comparing Canada's support for the people of Bangladesh in 1971 to its response to the Rohingya crisis of 2017 and the Russian invasion of Ukraine in 2022, we present three critical factors that highlight how Canada has currently navigated these international waters.

Factor 1: Framing the Conflict: There are striking differences in framing each conflict. Ottawa framed the 1971 subcontinental conflict as a civil war and, thus, an "internal matter." Since Ottawa never officially *condemned* Pakistan's invasion publicly, Canada *appeared* to *condone* Yahya's use of force. Ignoring human rights abuses, Canada encouraged a reluctant Pakistan to solve this "internal" matter on its own. Canada, too, quickly shifted to a mediator to address an internal conflict. In contrast, after the Myanmar military brutally attacked defenseless Rohingya in August 2017, the Canadian government immediately condemned Myanmar and its military, appointed former Ontario Premier Bob Rae as a special envoy on the Rohingya issue and swiftly donated $30 million to assist the refugees. This amount multiplied to $100 million. However, there was little sympathy from the Canadian public and tepid support for further government action.

Similarly, both the government and the people of Canada overwhelmingly *opposed* and resolutely *condemned* Russia's invasion. Canada swiftly joined its NATO allies in strongly supporting Ukraine's war effort. However, since Ukraine was *not* a member of NATO, Canada did not commit combat troops to engage on Ukrainian soil. Within months, Ukrainian forces began to *slowly* repel the invasion, albeit with considerable military and civilian casualties. In contrast, Canada framed the respective problems of 1971, Bangladesh, and 2017 Myanmar as *humanitarian* and proposed essentially *humanitarian solutions.*

Factor 2: Identification of a Villain: In 2017, Canada identified the military in Myanmar as the clear aggressor in assaulting and murdering defenseless Rohingyas and condemned their actions. In the 2022 Russia-Ukraine conflict, Russia was the apparent "villain," and Ukraine was the aggrieved party. In these recent conflicts, villains stood front and center. However, over a half-century earlier, each party claimed the high ground while the villain role was diffused between combatants Pakistan and India as far as Canada was concerned. As the conflict played out, Ottawa seemed more and more disposed to side with the Bengalis in East Pakistan. However, so as not to upset Commonwealth member Pakistan, *Canada hesitated to condemn Yahya's military reprisals and abuses publicly.* Canada was equally diplomatic toward India, refraining from publicly calling out Gandhi's duplicity. These factors mitigated against identifying a clear villain and partly explain Canada's nuanced position in 1971: sympathizing with the oppressed Bengali population and its courageous "freedom fighters" but not wanting to contribute to the breakup of Pakistan. Nor did Canada wish to abandon the Bengali people, militarily aided by India, which also welcomed fleeing refugees; hence, Canada's "diffuse position" and its erratic and winding road in 1971.

Factor 3: Degree of Consensus among Allies: Canada can act effectively when allying itself with other like-minded nations as a middle power. For example, when engaging with democratic countries such as members of NATO, OECD, G20, or the Commonwealth, Canada can support an aggrieved party in its struggles for democracy and human rights. In the subcontinent in 1971, instead of consensus, there were sharp divisions: China and the US supported Pakistan while Russia allied with India. None showed a willingness to engage in collective action. While Commonwealth countries such as England, Australia, and New Zealand generally supported the cause of Bangladesh, Canada made a herculean effort to avoid siding with either Pakistan or India. Unfortunately for Canada, power politics, not compromise, ruled the day. Few nations even considered the possibility of compromise through mediation, which was Canada's declared position.

In fairness, Canadian officials reached out to Arnold Smith, secretary-general of the Commonwealth of Nations, in hopes of brokering a peace agreement. The highly skilled Smith himself could find little traction among commonwealth nations; given the hostile terrain, sharp divisions among the superpowers, and other well-documented challenges, his efforts failed. Canada, however, deserves credit for its valiant efforts in attempting to involve the capable Smith in such an immense undertaking. In retrospect, albeit unlikely, *this initiative might have succeeded - if* there had been other willing and supportive Commonwealth partners. There weren't!

Therefore, the chronology of events in the subcontinent from March through December 1971 reads like a veritable obstacle course toward reconciliation. In truth, Canada stood virtually alone. This is in sharp contrast to 2022 when all thirty member nations of NATO swiftly offered Ukraine substantial military and foreign aid while imposing economic sanctions against Russia and its oligarchs. As of November 2023, Canada had committed over $5 billion in military, humanitarian, and emergency assistance to Ukraine, for which President Zelensky publicly expressed genuine appreciation. As reported by the *Toronto Star* in late 2023, Prime Minister Trudeau promised that Canada would continue to assist Ukraine even as support from several NATO countries began to flag. Canada contributed significantly to Ukraine's progress in concert with its NATO allies.

In sharp contrast, and vis-à-vis the Rohingya crisis (2017 and continuing), consensus among world nations was weak, as was any collective commitment to achieving a just humanitarian solution. Most nations responded tepidly to the plight of the Rohingyas—and passed along the problem to a beleaguered United Nations. As of spring 2023, no Western nation had opened its doors to the Rohingya. In a cruel irony of history, Bangladesh *today* finds herself standing virtually alone on the world stage, tasked with the significant burden of providing food, shelter, and necessities to the long-suffering Rohingyas. This sobering, tragic reality should challenge the social conscience of all well-intentioned individuals and nations across the globe.

Observations, Insights, and Historical Lessons

In comparing Canada's response to these two recent crises, we offer some observations on Canada's diffuse and occasionally incoherent actions, or *inaction*, in the 1971 subcontinental conflict. Canada remains a middle power on the international stage. Realistically, Canada can rarely "go it alone." In 1971, Canada failed to articulate a consistent position on the emergence of Bangladesh. This was not because of a lack of goodwill, effort, or integrity. Perhaps Canada felt it could engage in power politics. It could not! In 1971, the federal government could ill afford a misstep that might antagonize a significant segment of Québecers. Sympathy for the Bengali freedom fighters necessarily took a back seat to preserve Québec in Canada's confederation. Canada's excessive courtesy toward Pakistan also suggests an inordinate fear of offending. Such a stance was, and is, incompatible with action on the international stage. Perhaps Canada's foreign affairs *cognoscenti* learned a key lesson: it is better to articulate and work toward realistic goals and act more straightforwardly than try to be "all things to all men." By way of a historical footnote, since officially recognizing Bangladesh in February 1972, Canada has remained a steadfast ally of Pakistan - proof positive that Canada *can* disagree with *any* ally/nation on a given issue while still retaining a collegial relationship.

With the benefit of hindsight, one can reflect on Canada's failure to condemn the atrocities of Yahya's army and ask publicly: *Would Canada's criticism have offended Pakistan officials in 1971?* Almost certainly. However, it is unlikely there would have been long-term adverse consequences for Canada. Commonwealth countries, such as the United Kingdom, Australia, and New Zealand, all criticized Pakistan's abuses with virtual impunity. *Why should Canada be different?* It is hard to believe that the Canada-Pakistan relationship would have suffered more than a temporary setback. The reader should remember that Canada maintained foreign aid to Pakistan throughout the conflict. Even if Canada had condemned Yahya's military atrocities, Canada would still have offered financial assistance to Pakistan.

And a final comparative observation: although Canada *is now positioned* to act more decisively on the world stage, the author does not believe Canada's current interventions are seamless or beyond reproach. Canada has behaved honorably and with integrity in supporting Ukraine since February 2022 and is to be commended. However, beyond its swift initial response, Canada has since gone virtually "radio silent" vis-à-vis the Rohingya crisis. It has left Commonwealth sister Bangladesh the burden of caring for almost one million stateless refugees. While not suggesting that Canada bears the "major part of the burden," Senior Advisor Bob Rae could have been commissioned to work with Rohingya partners in Canada, including pro-Bangladesh associations. Canada could have at least maintained moderate annual assistance for the desperate Rohingya.

In the words of Prime Minister Justin Trudeau, "We can do better!" Indeed. We can *always* do better. Good things can happen when Canadians demand or ask their government to intervene.

Lastly, in reviewing Canada's role in the creation of Bangladesh, Professor Haider's observations are worth revisiting: "Canadian approach towards Bangladesh was different in different phases of history in the Liberation War of Bangladesh. In a sense, Canada played a role that went against the interests of Bangladesh and suited the triple alliance between the U.S.-Pakistan and China. Against the backdrop of Cold War politics, Canadian policy demonstrated the reflection of her national interest."[100] Having argued that Canada's policy during the Bangladesh War of Liberation reflected Canada's "interests,"[101] Professor Haider went further to explain that Canada's delayed reaction must be judged in the light of her *traditional bond with Pakistan* from the time of Pakistan's birth. "It was a deliberate attempt to preserve regional stability without serious deterioration in Canada-Pakistan bilateral relations."[102] Chapter 2 also noted Canada's efforts to avoid ruffling Yahya's feathers. While reality dictated that Canada move swiftly, she could not do so due to her "go slow" policy. In 1971, Canada and Pakistan were allies with much in common. Since Canada did not publicly endorse the Nixon administration's position on the subcontinental conflict, much of Canada's non-action could be seen as Canada's tilt toward Pakistan, which was certainly not the case. As a middle power, Canada often found herself "caught in the middle."

Similarly, Louis A. Delvoie, a senior fellow at the Centre for International Relations and an Adjunct Professor of International Relations at Queen's University, wrote from his observations and experiences. He maintains that Canada played an important role in contributing almost thirty million dollars to Bangladesh. "Providing aid and comfort to a secessionist movement in East Pakistan would have flown in the face of its efforts to contain France's meddling in support of Québec separatists. Québec separation was vital to Canada, the other an obscure conflict in a far distant land."[103] As Delvoie observed, Canada's framing of the subcontinental conflict through the prism of her national unity concerns was understandable. Although not in total "lockstep," Canada agreed with the "triple alliance" in opposing the dismemberment of Pakistan.[104] Nevertheless, Canada wanted a reformed Pakistan, which a Bengali majority leader should head.

Years later, noted Canadian historian and political commentator Jack Lawrence Granatstein remarked that Canada has consistently pursued a foreign policy marked by standard "Canada brand" values of security, prosperity, and a just international order; these values reflect a spirit of moderation, compromise, rule of law, and social and economic justice.[105] In the decades after the liberation of Bangladesh, and with the creation of the International Centre for Human Rights and Democratic Development in the 1980s, Granatstein maintained that human rights and democracy had become the cornerstones of Canada's foreign aid and development policy. Similarly, former Canadian diplomat Arthur Julian Andrew emphasized Canada's firm humanitarian commitment to alleviate the suffering of Bengalis in East Pakistan. Canada aimed "to ameliorate the pathetic role of the people of the former territory of East Bengal [East Pakistan] through relief both to those who became refugees in India and to those who faced deprivation at home";[106] thus, Arthur Andrew wrote.

In retrospect, one can appreciate the Trudeau administration's reluctance to condemn the Pakistani army resoundingly. First, Canada feared that doing so would reduce its diplomatic leverage with the government of Pakistan. Second, the situation was not as clear-cut as was suggested. According to Louis Delvoie, "While the guilt of the Pakistani army was almost self-evident, the *Mukti Bahini* was certainly not above reproach; they, too, were guilty of war crimes."[107] Given his vast experience as a former deputy high commissioner to the United Kingdom, high commissioner to Pakistan, director general of the Bureau of International Security and Arms Control in the Department of External Affairs, and assistant deputy minister for policy in the Department of National Defence, Delvoie recognized the nature of the conflict and the cross-pressures Canada faced in 1971. It is understandable *why* Canada *quietly* carried out several actions, as described in Chapter 7 while avoiding public debate on foreign policy. In a multipronged effort, Canada tried to de-escalate hostilities, work toward a peaceful solution, promote negotiations, and provide emergency food and aid to displaced Bengalis. At the same time, Canada also attempted to give shelter and meet its *humanitarian obligations*. Needless to reiterate, Canada still believed in a unified vision of Pakistan and could not simply adopt a straightforward pro-Bangladesh stance.

Stated differently, Canada's position on the Pakistan issue was unique. It contrasted markedly with the positions of the UK and US governments. Over the years, Great Britain enjoyed close political links in the Indian subcontinent, which she maintained even after the partition of India. In contrast, the Nixon administration was in the early stages of establishing a breakthrough in diplomatic and economic relations with the People's Republic of China. Canada had no such geostrategic interests. On the negative side of the ledger, the Nixon administration's penchant for secrecy contrasted sharply with Canada's consistently open and transparent policy of noninterference.

Again, Pakistan's hope for a Sino-US counterintervention failed to materialize. One could argue that such an alliance would have tilted the military balance in Pakistan's favor. Canada concluded that the decision by the US and China *not* to intervene was based on calculations that the disadvantages of direct military intervention far outweighed the advantages. Canada was relieved that a major conflagration was avoided, and the ensuing conflict was restricted to a subcontinental war. Unlike the US, Canada had neither a sphere of interest to protect nor secret agreements to conceal. Canada preferred greater *political inclusiveness* and *expanded political freedom* in a re-engineered Pakistan for the Pakistani people of all backgrounds without fracturing the country.

Unfortunately, Canada's herculean efforts to install Bongobondhu as the leader of a united Pakistan worked at cross purposes with the goals of the increasingly effective provisional government, especially that of complete liberation from Pakistan. Any thought of Canada's supporting a separate country carved out of Pakistan was *verboten*. In short, it is evident why Canada deliberately ignored the phenomenon of Bangladesh. Not a winning strategy! One can reasonably ask, *After seeing the "writing on the wall" pointing to the emergence of Bangladesh, why did Ottawa still strive for reconciliation with Pakistan?* There does not seem to be a clear answer, although it must be acknowledged that Canada never seriously considered the separation of East Pakistan or the liberation of Bangladesh.

Nonetheless, the reasonable observer must challenge Sharp's thinking and seriously question Canada's procrastination. Matters came to a head in late November when international opinion overwhelmingly sided with the millions of Bengalis who were being forced from their homeland. But on the cusp of accepting the reality of Bangladesh, Canada again vacillated. In his interviews with the media, Sharp stressed his government's limitations: *Canada's Commonwealth membership precluded taking sides between two sister Commonwealth countries.* Although "peacekeeper" Canada's strong belief in democracy was front and centre, the search for political solutions proved elusive. It is compounded by an unfortunate habit of consistently ignoring the growing strength of the freedom fighters.

Since Canada utterly miscalculated the inevitable birth of Bangladesh, one must question the soundness of her political judgment. Sharp was thoroughly briefed on the scant likelihood of Yahya's policy of limited political rule normalizing the situation in East Pakistan. Time and again, Canada's high commissioners correctly predicted that events after March 25 had made the *separation of East Pakistan inevitable*. The reader is reminded that from autumn 1971 onward, news from New Delhi became a source of angst for Ottawa mandarins engaged in briefing the minister. To their chagrin, a deluded Sharp pertinaciously tried to broker a last-minute solution within one Pakistan.

As frequently noted, with its fixation on diplomacy, Canada lagged in explicitly condemning the military repression from the beginning. Nonetheless, Canada's ceaseless efforts to affect a democratic political solution are commendable. One may, of course, question Ottawa's "ultra diplomatic" manner in attempts to influence a military regime prone to violent repression of civil institutions. To her credit, in the long run, Canada sustained cordial relations with both Pakistan and India, an accomplishment partly due to Canada's fairness and neutrality. Canada chose not to interfere in the "domestic" affairs of Pakistan while simultaneously collaborating with India and Pakistan and demonstrating *civility* and *fairness* toward each party. In Chapter 7, we noted that Trudeau *quietly* but *firmly* appealed to both Yahya and Gandhi without pointing fingers at either. Although a mercurial Yahya loudly rejected Canada's cautions, his capricious moods did not last long since Canada chose *not to retaliate.* Canada diligently practiced "quiet diplomacy." Alas, these Trojan efforts achieved neither peace nor regional stability.

As an ardent supporter of democracy, Canada could not accept the game plan of an unelected military dictator who refused to transfer power to a duly elected leader. Naturally, Canada's preference was for a *strengthened* and *united* Pakistan. As mentioned many times, Canada's preference had always been for a *re-engineered* Pakistan under the leadership of Bongobondhu. Canada argued that the democratic system must function to provide stability for *effective governance* and *continued economic growth.* In late 1971, when the Trudeau administration realized that time was running out and that there would be no turning back since the rebel forces had the full support of the Gandhi administration, she felt helpless. There is no evidence of any attempt on Canada's part to develop a *new strategy* for elected representatives to assume responsibility for governing Pakistan nor to involve the provisional government of Bangladesh, which had been functioning effectively from its base in India since mid-April. It is incomprehensible that Canada ceaselessly worked toward a politically united Pakistan when there was crystal clear writing of the exact opposite "on the wall." Canada's fruitless efforts were as misdirected as they were hopeless.

Throughout 1971, Prime Minister Trudeau repeated his desperate appeals to Gandhi and Yahya, urging the respective leaders to exercise restraint. Ottawa's annoying habit of procrastination is better understood, however, when one recognizes the strict constraints under which Canada operates. Well aware of Yahya's repressive measures and India's secret support of the rebels, Canada still endeavoured to preserve its long-standing collegial relations with both countries. Canada also believed that she must help the Bengali victims who were leaving their homeland faster than India could absorb them. The Trudeau administration strongly supported this "dual" position.

To summarize: from the outset of the crisis triggered by the military takeover on March 25 until the surrender of the Pakistani army on December 16, the Canadian government believed that Pakistan's military intervention in East Pakistan was her internal affairs and that Canada should not interfere. Canadian parliamentarians were, as mentioned in Chapter 6, mindful of Trudeau's cautionary remark two years ago concerning Nigeria/Biafra: "To intervene when not asked, however, would not be an act of courage; it would be seen as an act of stupidity."[108] Canada took the fundamental position that problems between countries should be settled through *negotiation* and *not war* and that any interference by one country in the internal issues of another was inherently wrong.

One can reasonably conclude that Canada's efforts to assist and intervene positively were sincere, if impractical. On the one hand, Canada's determination to restore democracy in Pakistan through power transfer to its elected representatives was consistent with her values. On the other, Canada warrants criticism for *stubbornly* pursuing a political solution with a military regime openly and utterly hostile to democracy. Since *no other democratic nation seriously* attempted mediation between India and Pakistan, Canada should have realized the futility of such an exercise much earlier. Ottawa officials experienced firsthand the impossibility of attempting suasion with President Yahya. Since geopolitical considerations did not shape Canada's foreign policy, Canada referred the issue to the UN, whose efforts proved futile. To settle disputes and prevent war, the Trudeau administration pursued a policy of channeling possible initiatives through the UN or other acceptable organizations. Canada could neither command international attention nor effect independent political action as a middle power. The UN's ineptitude and inability to exercise its expected role frustrated Canada and Canadians.

In the final analysis, the author maintains that policy constraints plus the mantles of "quiet diplomacy," "honest broker," and "nonintervention" in the internal affairs of another country dictated Canada's position. Undoubtedly, Canada's strategy was wrong from the beginning since Canada rarely factored in the existence of the provisional government of Bangladesh. External affairs never offered a convincing explanation as to *how* Canada's proposed "political solution" could be achieved given that the Bengalis had already demonstrated their *complete support for an independent Bangladesh* ever since they heard Major Zia's "We revolt" back in March immediately following the army crackdown. The determined rebels, aided by India, were at one end of the spectrum, with an obstinate military regime at the other. Canada worked diligently toward the cause of democracy and did everything possible to encourage democratization in Pakistan at every opportunity. In reacting to the steps taken by the Yahya regime against the Bengalis, the Trudeau administration primarily focused on enhancing its relations with East Pakistan through *humanitarian assistance* and *quasi-political involvement*, specifically by applying pressure to establish democracy and political stability while respecting the results of the 1970 National Elections.

The Trudeau administration was aware that the US government sometimes had to soften its policies and *resort to duplicity,* given Americans' generally unfavorable opinion toward the Yahya government. As a middle power, Canada had no such ambitions. Canada's foreign affairs cognoscenti developed an uneven strategy to address the challenging subcontinental conflict. Through a series of torturous "mental gyrations," Canadian officials attempted to decide what was *ethically* and *politically* correct and what was *verboten* relative to the conflict. In doing so, Canada juggled myriad priorities from its foreign policy cupboard. Looking back in 2024, fifty-three years later, it made no sense for Ottawa to pursue a policy of political suasion, especially since Canada was privy to accurate and up-to-date information on the imminent birth of Bangladesh. It did not occur to Ottawa officials that they were "barking up the wrong tree" with wasted and misdirected efforts. Succinctly stated, Canada wanted a united Pakistan at all costs. Therefore, Ottawa opposed the creation of Bangladesh as a separate country carved out of Pakistan.

The next chapter, *Canada Finally Gets It "Right:" Bangladesh Recognized, and a Friendship Restored,* outlines Canada's relief at the birth of Bangladesh as her reservations disappeared. Canada immediately prepared to recognize Bangladesh—the sooner, the better.

Notes and References

1. See *Glossary of Terms.*
2. Confidential telegram from John Small, high commissioner to Pakistan, to Ottawa. Telegram no.133, dated February 15, 1971. File # 20-Pak-E-1-4. Canada. Department of External Affairs. Hereinafter, all telegrams and other information used in this chapter from the above source shall be referred to as External Affairs.
3. Memorandum for the Minister. Draft Appraisal of Political Situations in East Pakistan, dated March 9, 1971. File # 20-Pak-E-1-4. *Ibid. Op. cit.*
4. *Kitchener-Waterloo Record,* dated March 15, 1971.
5. Confidential Memo on Crisis in East Pakistan from GPP, Bureau of Asia and Pacific Affairs, to PDG, External Affairs, dated March 12, 1971. File

no. 20-Pak-1-4, p.1. External Affairs. *Op. cit.* Small described his experience to the author on November 5, 1994, at his residence in Ottawa - how he met *Bongobondhu* in Dhanmondi, Dhaka. He also recalled his impressions of uncertainty throughout the province.
6. Memorandum for the Acting Minister, signed by A. F. Broadridge, Bureau of Asia and Pacific Affairs, External Affairs, dated March 8, 1971. File # 20-Pak-E-1-4; External Affairs. *Op. cit.*
7. This was in the news immediately after the imposition of martial law. President Yahya Khan also made these remarks to CBC's Charles Wasserman, who interviewed him on July 30, 1971. External Affairs. File # 20-Pak-1-4. Confidential telegram from John Small, high commissioner to Pakistan, to Ottawa. Telegram # 172329 (of 4/8). External Affairs. *Op. cit.*
8. *Kitchener-Waterloo Record,* dated March 15, 1971.
9. Confidential telegram from James George, high commissioner to India, to Ottawa. Telegram # 1211, dated March 31, 1971, p. 2. File # 20-India-1-3-Pak. External Affairs. *Op. cit.*
10. Confidential telegram from James George, high commissioner to India, to Ottawa. Telegram # 1229, dated April 2, 1971, p. 3. File # 20-India-1-3-Pak. External Affairs. *Op. cit.*
11. Confidential telegram from James George, high commissioner to India, to Ottawa. Telegram # 1358, dated April 18, 1971.File # 20-India-1-3-Pak. External Affairs. *Op. cit.*
12. Confidential telegram from John Small, high commissioner to Pakistan, to Ottawa. Telegram # 1160, dated April 19, 1971, p. 1. File # 20-Pak-E-1-4. External Affairs. *Ibid. Op. cit.*
13. *Ibid.*
14. Confidential telegram from John Small, high commissioner to Pakistan, to Ottawa. Telegram # 278, dated March 30, 1971. p.6. File # 20-Pak-E-1-4. External Affairs. *Ibid. Op. cit.*
15. *Ibid.* p. 3.
16. *Ibid.*
17. Established in 1969, Waffle is a Caucus within the New Democratic Party. Its members' choice of name was self-consciously ironic. It issued a Manifesto for an Independent Socialist Canada, demanding that Canadian public ownership replace American private ownership. Subsequent Waffle statements called for Québec's right to self-determination and for an independent Canadian labour movement.
18. *The Globe and Mail,* dated April 22, 1971.
19. *Ibid.*
20. *Ibid.*
21. *Ibid.*

22. Confidential telegram from James George, high commissioner to India, to Ottawa. Telegram # 1387, dated April 10, 1971. File # 20-E-Pak-1-4. External Affairs. *Op. cit.*
23. *Ibid.*
24. *Ibid.*
25. *Ibid.*
26. *Ibid.*
27. Confidential Memo from James George, high commissioner to India, to Ottawa, dated April 13, 1971, p.1. File # 20-India-1-3-Pak. *Op. cit.*
28. *Ibid.* p.1.
29. Letter from A. E. Ritchie, Undersecretary to Mitchell Sharp, Secretary of State for External Affairs, dated April 28, 1971. File # 20-Pak-E-1-4; External Affairs. *Op. cit.*
30. Personal and Confidential letter to James George by R. E. Collins. Dated May 13, 1971. File # 38-11-1-Pak. External Affairs. *Op. cit.*
31. Memo from James George, high commissioner to India, to Ottawa. Dated June 8, 1971, quoted from Air India Radio. File # 20-India-1-3-Pak. External Affairs. *Op. cit.*
32. Confidential telegram from James George, high commissioner to India, to Ottawa. Telegram # 1698, dated May 5, 1971, p.6. File # 20-India-1-3-Pak. External Affairs. *Op. cit.*
33. *Ibid*
34. Confidential telegram from John Small, high commissioner to Pakistan, to Ottawa. Telegram # 890, dated August 21, 1971, p. 3. File # 20-India-1-3-Pak. External Affairs. *Op. cit.*
35. Prime Minister's Reply to the Discussion Regarding Situation Arising out of Arrival of Refugees from East Bengal in *Lok Sabha* on May 26, 1971, described in *Bangla Desh Documents*, p.680. Publication Division, Ministry of Information and Broadcasting, The B.N.K. Press, Private Limited, Bombay, India, no date. Hereinafter, referred to as *Bangladesh Documents*.
36. Confidential telegram from John Small, high commissioner to Pakistan, to Ottawa. Telegram # 387. File # 20-Pak-E-1-4; External Affairs. *Op. cit.*
37. Sharp's meeting with Indian high commissioner Ashoke B. Bhadkamkar on May 17, 1971, in Ottawa. Reginald Prentice, a former Minister of Overseas Development and a member of the British Parliamentary Delegation that visited Pakistan and India, also expressed a similar position.
38. Prime Minister's Reply to the Discussion Regarding Situation Arising out of Arrival of Refugees from East Bengal in *Lok Sabha* on May 26, 1971. Cited in *Bangla Desh Documents*, p.681. *Op. cit.*
39. Confidential telegram from James George, high commissioner to India, to Ottawa. Telegram # 1968, dated May 21, 1971, p.5. File # 20- India-1-3-Pak. File # 20-India-1-3-Pak. External Affairs. *Op. cit.*

40. *Ibid.*
41. *Ibid.* p. 4. *Op. cit.*
42. *Ibid.*
43. Letter from James George to Ottawa. Dated June 8, 1971. File # 20-India-1-3-Pak.; External Affairs. *Op. cit.*
44. Confidential telegram from James George, high commissioner to India, to Ottawa. Dated, June 29, 1971. File # 20-India-1-3-Pak. External Affairs. *Op. cit.*
45. Internal Memo from A.R. Wright to Mitchell Sharp, Secretary of State for External Affairs. Dated, June 29, 1971. File # 20-Pak-E-1-4; External Affairs. *Op. cit.*
46. Prime Minister Indira Gandhi's reply to the discussion under Rule 176 on the situation arising from the influx of millions of refugees from Bangla Desh into India in *Rajya Sabha* on June 15, 1971. This is described in *Bangla Desh Documents*, p.685. *Op. cit.*
47. Confidential memo from John Small, high commissioner to Pakistan, to A. E. Ritchie, Undersecretary of State for External Affairs, titled, *East Pakistan Situation: Political Activity in the West Wing.* Telegrams # 353. Dated April 20, 1971, and telegram # 379, dated April 23, 1971, p. 1. File # 20-E-Pak-1-4.
48. *Ibid.* External Affairs. *Op. cit.*
49. *Ibid.*
50. *Ibid.* External Affairs. *Op. cit.*
51. Defence Minister Jagjivan Ram's response to the Debate on Budget Demands of the Ministry of Defence, on July 12, 1971, published in *Bangla Desh Documents*, p.700. *Op. cit.*
52. Confidential telegram from James George, high commissioner to India, to Ottawa. Telegram # 2778, dated 16 July 1971. File # 21-3-India-Pak -2. External Affairs. *Op. cit.*
53. *Ibid.*
54. *The Globe and Mail,* dated July 7, 1971.
55. Letter from Prime Minister Pierre Trudeau to Prime Minister Indira Gandhi, dated July 29, 1971. File # 20-Pak-E-1-4; External Affairs. *Op. cit.*
56. *The Globe and Mail*, dated July 16, 1971.
57. Confidential telegram from John Small, high commissioner to Pakistan, to Ottawa. Telegram # 890, dated August 21, 1971, p.3. File # 20-Pak-E-1-4; External Affairs. *Op. cit.*
58. Confidential telegram from John Small, high commissioner to Pakistan, to Ottawa. Telegram # 870, dated August 12, 1971. File # 20-Pak-E-1-4; External Affairs. *Op. cit.*
59. Confidential telegram from John Small, high commissioner to Pakistan, to Ottawa. Telegram # 875, dated August 12, 1971. File # 20-Pak-E-1-4; External Affairs. *Op. cit.*

60. *TIME* "Good Soldier Yahya Khan." Dated August 2, 1971, p.2.
61. Confidential telegram from John Small, high commissioner to Pakistan, to Ottawa. Telegram # 890, dated August 21, 1971, p.6. File # 20-Pak-E-1-4; External Affairs. *Op. cit.*
62. Confidential telegram from John Small, high commissioner to Pakistan, to Ottawa. Telegram # 890, dated August 21, 1971, p.3. File # 20-Pak-E-1-4; External Affairs. *Op. cit.*
63. Letter from A. E. Ritchie, undersecretary, to Mitchell Sharp, Secretary of State, p. 2. Dated August 25, 1971. File # 20-Pak-E-1-4; External Affairs. *Op. cit.*
64. *The Guardian Weekly*, dated August 14, 1971.
65. Confidential telegram from James George, high commissioner to India, to Ottawa. Telegram # 2800, dated August 27, 1971. File # 21-3-India-Pak -2. External Affairs. *Op. cit.*
66. *Ibid.*
67. Confidential telegram from John Small, high commissioner to Pakistan, to Ottawa. Dated, August 15, 1971. Telegram # 378. File # 20-Pak-E-1-4. External Affairs. *Op. cit.*
68. Letter from A.J. Andrew to Geoffrey Pearson, acting high commissioner to India, and John Small, high commissioner to Pakistan. Dated August 30, 1971. File # 20-Pak-E-1-4; External.
69. See Robert Jackson's *South Asian Crisis: India, Pakistan and Bangladesh*. London: Chatto and Windus, 1975, p. 59.
70. Confidential Diary, Dated September 1, 1971. The document is titled *India-Pak Crisis*. File # 20-Pak-E-1-4; External Affairs. *Op. cit.*
71. Confidential telegram from John Small, high commissioner to Pakistan, to Ottawa. Telegram # 424. File # 20-Pak-E-1-4; External Affairs. *Op. cit.*
72. Position Paper, Dated September 15, 1971. p.10. File # 20-Pak-E-1-4. External Affairs. *Op. cit.*
73. *Ibid.* p.12.
74. *Ibid. Op. cit.*
75. Confidential Diary, September. The document is titled *India-Pak Crisis*. File # 20-Pak-E-1-4; External Affairs. *Op. cit.*
76. See Chapter 1, p. 12.
77. Canada. House of Commons. Minutes of Proceedings and Evidence of the Standing Committee on External Affairs and National Defence. Third Session, Twenty-eighth Parliament, 1970-71. Issue No 32, October 5, 1971, p. 32:4. Hereinafter, referred to as Standing Committee.
78. *Ibid.* p. 32:10.
79. Restricted Internal Memo from James George, high commissioner to India, to Ottawa. Dated, September 27, 1971. File # 20-India-1-3-Pak. External Affairs. *Op. cit.*

80. Letter from James George, high commissioner to India, to Ottawa, dated October 8, 1971. File # 20-India-1-3-Pak. External Affairs. *Op. cit.*
81. Confidential telegram from James George, high commissioner to India, to Ottawa. Telegram # 4176, dated November 4, 1971. File # 20-India-1-3-Pak. External Affairs. *Op. cit.*
82. *Ibid.*
83. Confidential Memo re Sultan Khan's meeting in Ottawa addressed to Mitchell Sharp. Dated November 15, 1971, p.4. File # 20-Pak-E-1-4. External Affairs. *Op. cit.*
84. *Ibid.* p.5. *Op. cit.*
85. Memo from A. E. Ritchie, Undersecretary to Mitchell Sharp, Secretary of State for External Affairs, dated November 24, 1971, p.1. File # 20-Pak-1-4. External Affairs. *Op. cit.*
86. MEMORANDUM from Ottawa to Islamabad. Dated November 19, 1971, p. 4. File # 20-Pak-1-4. External Affairs. *Op. cit.*
87. Confidential telegram from John Small, high commissioner to Pakistan, to Ottawa. Telegram # 4176. Dated December 3, 1971. File # 20-Pak-1-4. External Affairs. *Op. cit.*
88. Confidential telegram from John Small, high commissioner to Pakistan, to Ottawa. Telegram # 4180. Dated December 6, 1971. File # 20-Pak-1-4. External Affairs. *Op. cit.*
89. Confidential telegram from John Small, high commissioner to Pakistan, to Ottawa. Telegram # 4191. Dated December 6, 1971. File # 20-Pak-1-4. External Affairs. *Op. cit.*
90. Confidential telegram from John Small, high commissioner to Pakistan, to Ottawa. Telegram # 4195. Dated December 6, 1971. File # 20-Pak-1-4. External Affairs. *Op. cit.*
91. Confidential telegram from James George, high commissioner to India, to Ottawa. Telegram # 467. Dated December 8, 1971. File # 20-India-1-3-Pak. External Affairs. *Op. cit.*
92. Confidential telegram from John Small, high commissioner, to Ottawa. Telegram # 1271, dated December 9, 1971. File # 21-3-India-Pak-SITREP. External Affairs. *Op. cit.*
93. Memorandum for the Minister, titled *India-Pakistan War,* signed by A. E. Ritchie, Undersecretary, Secretary of State for External Affairs. Dated December 8, 1971, p.2. File # 20 India-1-3 Pak. External Affairs. *Op. cit.*
94. *Ibid.* p.3.
95. Canada. House of Commons. *Debates,* Queen's Printer. Dated April 29, 1971, p. 5345. Hereinafter, referred to as *Debates.*
96. *Ibid. Op. cit.*
97. Zaglul Haider. "Unfolding Canada-Bangladesh Relations," *Asian Survey*, Vol. 45, No. 2 (March/April 2005) pp. 322-341.

98. McInnis, Edgar. 1960. "A Middle Power in the Cold War" in Hugh L. Keenleyside et al. *The Growth of Canadian Policies in External Affairs.*, Durham: Duke University Press, p.143.
99. Jack Lawrence Granatstein, ed. 1995. *Canadian Foreign Policy,* Toronto: Copp Clark Pitman Ltd., p. 95.
100. Zaglul Haider. "Canadian Policy Towards Bangladesh: How Does the North Look at the South?" *African and Asian Studies* 10 (2011), p. 281.
101. Zaglul Haider. "Unfolding Canada-Bangladesh Relations," *Asian Survey*, Vol. 45, No. 2 (March/April 2005) p. 324.
102. Zaglul Haider. "Canadian Policy Towards Bangladesh: How Does the North Look at the South?" *African and Asian Studies* 10 (2011), p. 289.
103. Letter from Louis A. Delvoie to Mustafa Chowdhury, dated June 20, 2019.
104. Delvoie, Louis A. 1995. "Hesitant Engagement and South Asian Security," Queen's University, Kingston, Ontario: Centre for International Relations, p. 21.
105. Jack Lawrence Granatstein, ed. 1995. *Canadian Foreign Policy,* Toronto: Copp Clark Pitman Ltd., p. 87.
106. "Canada and Asia: The Shifting Power Balance," in *Pacific Affairs* 45:3 (Fall 1972), p.407. This is cited in Zaglul Haider's article "Unfolding Canada-Bangladesh Relations," in *Asian Survey,* Vol. 45, No. 2 (March/April 2005) pp. 322–341.
107. Letter from Louis Delvoie to Mustafa Chowdhury. *Op. cit.*

CHAPTER 9

Canada Finally Gets It "Right": Bangladesh Recognized and a Friendship Restored

*W*hile in the previous chapter, we read about Canada's dichotomies in directly supporting the liberation movement at the risk of encouraging the Québec separationists, the present chapter reveals how Canada was hugely relieved following the birth of Bangladesh as an independent country. Noticeably, Canada's hesitations and apprehensions were gone as soon as Bangladesh was born. Canada was ready to recognize Bangladesh as there were no foreign policy constraints. Nevertheless, Canada still faced diplomatic challenges in early recognition since Canada wanted to make sure that Bangladesh met all the requirements for a sovereign country. It touches on various types of behind-the-scenes work, her raison d'être for early recognition, and numerous hurdles that Canada had to overcome while going through the process of recognition immediately after the liberation of Bangladesh when the Indian army personnel were still stationed in Bangladesh. The time lag between the proclamation of the independence of Bangladesh on March 26, 1971, by the rebel forces and the formation of the provisional government of the People's Republic of Bangla Desh in India on April 10, 1971 (sworn in on April 17, 1971), was about three weeks. The time lag between the *proclamation of independence and the actual liberation of Bangladesh through the surrender and withdrawal of the Pakistani army (December 16, 1971) was, however, about nine months. Again, the time lag between the actual independence of Bangladesh and the recognition of Bangladesh by Canada on February 14, 1972, is less than eight weeks.*

The Trudeau government needed vigorous questions and answers to determine the appropriate timing of Canada's recognition. The Trudeau administration believed that it must not be too late since many European and Asian countries had already started to recognize Bangladesh. Right after recognition, Canada moved quickly by allocating resources to the newborn country with whom she had maintained an excellent friendship. Canada's work in this area is an example of the Trudeau government's diplomatic maturity, having also been able to keep her relationship with truncated Pakistan unaffected, as though it was "business as usual."

How the Trudeau administration was kept posted on the situation in East Pakistan?

Mitchell Sharp, Secretary of State for External Affairs, was made aware of how, following Bongobondhu's March 7, 1971, speech to the "nation," the Awami League (AL) had remained the de facto government of the province (East Pakistan). How? On March 15, 1971, Bongobondhu took over the East Pakistan administration by issuing thirty-five directives. In Chapter 2, we noted how Canada watched with dismay the banning of the AL and President Yahya Khan's repressive measures against the Bengali civilians following the declaration of Martial Law in East Pakistan on March 25, 1971. Canada also watched how millions of frightened Bengalis were fleeing to India to avoid persecution. Sharp was briefed that a clandestine free Bangla Radio had announced the formation of a provisional government of the People's Republic of Bangladesh as early as March 26, 1971, operating from within the Indian territory with no further information. Canada could not verify when precisely the first Declaration of Independence was made.

On March 27, 1971, Sharp was visited by a group of pro-Bangladeshi Canadians who urged the minister to recognize Bangladesh, which we noted in Chapter 4. Sharp was also briefed about the activities of the Toronto-based Canadian Committee for an independent Bangladesh, which had been lobbying the government to recognize Bangladesh. Ottawa officials kept the minister *au courant* regarding the activities of the Bengali segment of the Canadian public that had been persistent in its demand. Canadian parliamentarians (Members of Parliament and Senators) also broached the recognition issue. Still, the minister indicated that his office had been awaiting authentic information from John Small and James George, Canada's high commissioners to Pakistan and India, respectively. This was also when the Trudeau government was preoccupied with maintaining its authority in the face of Québec's escalating demands for greater domestic power and international status.

In the meantime, the Governor General of Canada received a letter of request dated April 24, 1971, jointly signed by Syed Nazrul Islam and Khandaker Moshtaque Ahmed, then acting president and foreign minister, respectively, of the provisional government of Bangladesh along with a copy of the Proclamation of Independence and a list of cabinet members. The Proclamation stated that "the recently formed government of Bangladesh was exercising full sovereignty and lawful authority within the territories known as East Pakistan before 26 March 1971" and that it had "taken all appropriate measures to conduct the business of State following customs, usages and recognized principles of International Law."[1] He appealed to "His Excellency's Government to accord immediate recognition to the People's Republic of Bangladesh," especially "given the fraternal people of Bangladesh and Canada."[2] According to the confidential memos, now available under declassified information, Sharp was briefed with the following: "The Governor General, of course, has not acknowledged receipt of the letter, and we do not propose to take any action on it."[3]

During the first week of May, Ottawa came to know about the position of Krishnaswamy Subrahmanyam, director of the New Delhi-based Institute for Defence Studies and Analyses, who was both insistent and frank in observing that "what India must realize is the fact that the breakup of Pakistan is in our interest, an opportunity the like of which will never come again."[4] Ottawa remained interested to hear the government of India's official position.

Within weeks, Ottawa was also privy to certain important confidential information through James George, Canada's high commissioner to India, who had a close network with high officials in the government of India. Around mid-June, Ottawa learned from George that President Varahgiri Venkata Giri himself had counseled Prime Minister Indira Gandhi in private to "resist pressures for recognition," believing that "it would be unwise for India to recognize until Bangladesh Government is installed on a considerable proportion of its territory."[5] The president's warning also included a note of caution to wait until at least one major power, probably the USSR, recognized Bangladesh.

In the meantime, the president of the Toronto-based Committee for an Independent Bangla Desh, Chaitanya Keshavrao Kalevar, a Canadian of East Indian origin, not being enthused with Canada's action, dashed off the following letter expressing his instant reaction to Canada's position on the conflict: "To assure democracy in Pakistan and, in particular Bangla Desh, it is necessary that the government headed by Tajuddin Ahmed receives recognition as early as possible and the due powers of the state, which are now wrongfully held by General Yahya Khan, be equally transferred to the elected representatives."[6] To Canada's way of thinking, recognition of Bangladesh during the "civil war" in Pakistan would be seen as an action that would constitute a departure from the obligation of Canada's position of "neutrality." With such thought in mind, Canada was comfortable putting aside the idea since she believed the provisional government could not obtain *de jure* recognition.

In Chapter 4, we also noted how several Canada-Bangladesh associations, which mushroomed across the country under slight variations in names, had been writing to their respective MPs with the latest information on the struggle for Bangladesh's independence and demanding Canada's recognition of Bangladesh. Khandakar Mosthaque Ahmed, foreign minister of the People's Republic of Bangladesh, first wrote to Mitchell Sharp in April, and he wrote again in August 1971, urging him to recognize Bangladesh again. In his August letter, he highlighted his government's strides, "Our liberation forces have driven out the enemy forces from most of the areas of the country. The enemy is now holding on to small pockets in the towns and cities, where they are also facing increasingly heavy resistance from our people and forces."[7]

He then continued, "It is a preposterous anomaly that their [Pakistan's] diplomatic mission in your capital pretends to represent the seventy-five million people of Bangladesh who have since March 26, 1971, constituted a separate fully democratic government on the basis of an overwhelming mandate from the people."[8] In his conclusion, Ahmed maintained that "the Pakistan mission in your country represents only the West Pak[istan] military junta"[8] and that the Bengalis had already formed a country of their own. On both occasions, Ottawa officials chose not to respond to unsolicited letters. They put such demands on the back burner while the War of Liberation of Bangladesh went on.

During the second week of December, Ottawa received a special *aide-mémoire* from the high commissioner of India. He explained the justification for India's recognition of Bangladesh, "The act of recognition displays voluntary self-restraint which India has imposed upon itself. The action signifies India's desire not to annex or occupy any territory."[9] Three days before the surrender of the Pakistani army, the high commissioner appealed to Canada, "In view of these circumstances, India ventures to express the hope that Canada, which has staunchly supported the ideals of universal human rights and the political rights of the majority populations of a country or territory (as in Rhodesia) to determine its own political future and destiny will recognize the justice of the cause of this new nation of peace-loving people who since 1947 generally, and since March 25, 1971, in particular, have suffered a greater measure of brutal atrocity, massacre, and rape than those of any other nation on earth."[10]

On December 16, Ottawa officials watched with apprehension and curiosity how the war ended on the eastern front when the lieutenant-general commander-in-chief of Pakistan of the armed forces in East Pakistan signed an instrument of surrender at Dhaka. In the East, "the Pakistan Army [have] surrendered on 16 December and, although there are some reports of continued fighting, the overall situation appears to be quiet... In the West, Yahya announced a cease-fire effective 0930 EST on December 17, 1971. This is in response to Gandhi's unilateral cease-fire proposal yesterday but was stated to be within the framework of the UNGA resolution of December 7 [1971]."[11] Thus, Sharp was briefed on the military and political situation in East and West Pakistan.

The same memo continued, "The Indians have stated that a civil administration will be established in Dacca [sic] today. We understand that police and civil administrators who were given a clean bill of health by the *Mukti Bahini* [Liberation Forces] are being allowed to continue at their posts. The Indians have also announced steps they propose to take before withdrawing Indian forces from Bangladesh, including the following: (1) elimination of all Pakistani military and paramilitary resistances, (2) establishment of local civil administration and restoration of health services, and (3) return of the refugees."[12]

Sharp and his think tank members were glad to see Bangladesh's reality - that she had become a sovereign country. Canada felt immensely relieved, as though there was no longer any immediate fear of finding a nexus between the Québecers' desire to secede and the Bengalis' separation movement and igniting a debate in Canada on the separation of Québec. Canadian parliamentarians immediately raised the recognition issue, seeing the government's genuine interest in the newborn country.

Raison d'être for early recognition, hurdles, and behind-the-scenes activities

John Small, Canada's high commissioner to Pakistan, sought Ottawa's immediate advice regarding prioritizing issues relating to rebuilding the war-ravaged country the same day Bangladesh became independent. "With the fall of Dacca [sic] to Indian invasion forces and installation of Indian clients as Government of Bangla Desh only a matter of hours away, it is time to consider what next,"[13] the high commissioner wrote, wondering what Canada's next step would be. More specifically, he asked whether Canada would be "in a position to move quickly."[14] Having referred to the need for vast financial resources, Small ended his telex by expressing his hope that the "relevant authorities in Ottawa have already given thought to what Cda [Canada] might do" and that Canada "will give generously."[15]

James George, Canada's high commissioner to India, also immediately expressed his views, indicating that he is on the same page with Small about assisting the war-hit Bangladesh. He said, "I fully share Small's anxiety about the evolving situation in Bangla Desh and support his plea for immed[iate] planning and early action to help these people survive and rebuild their country."[16]

Politically speaking, to Canada, the birth of Bangladesh represented the following two phenomena: the dismemberment of Pakistan, a country with which Canada had been enjoying diplomatic relations along with most members of the UN throughout her existence, as well as the triumph of democracy for the Bengalis in having their own country. Strictly speaking, as far as Canada was concerned, to recognize Bangladesh, Canada first needed to ensure that Bangladesh was "legally" a sovereign country. Tied with this notion was also Sharp's assessment of President Bhutto's reaction to the dismemberment of Pakistan.

In the meantime, on December 17, the day after the liberation of Bangladesh, Ottawa received a letter from a group of pro-Bangladeshis. "The birth of the new nation of Bangla Desh is now a reality. The Pakistani

Army in Bangla Desh has unconditionally surrendered ... The government of Bangla Desh is in effective control of the entire territory of East Bengal and enjoys the full support of its people. We, therefore, urge you to recognize the government of Bangla Desh and thereby establish a lasting friendship between the peoples of Canada and Bangla Desh."[17] Speaking on behalf of the jubilant Canadians of Bangladeshi origin, A. B. Sattar, executive secretary of the Bangladesh Association of Canada (Ottawa), appealed, "One way that Canada can help Bengalis strengthen their new nation is to recognize its *de facto* presence in the world community. We urge the Government of Canada to demonstrate once again this country's farsightedness and pragmatism by recognizing the national status of Bangla Desh... The people of East Bengal are now citizens of an independent nation, free to govern themselves, and free from exploitation and oppression... Seventy-five million Bengalis will assure its permanence."[18] Sattar hoped that Canada would help establish a lasting friendship between the two countries.

On December 20, Macquarrie, who had earlier expressed his concerns for the interned leader (Bongobondhu), asked the minister "whether he intends to make or has made representation to the government of Pakistan for the return of Sheikh Mujibur Rahman to the area which gave him support not too long ago."[19] Sharp said that he did not think that "it would be appropriate or particularly useful to make such representations at present. After all, the Canadian government was the first of the governments to suggest that a political settlement was needed in East Pakistan."[20]

Again, Robert Thompson, Conservative MP for Red Deer, Alberta, who had earlier raised the issue of recognition of Bangladesh back in March, broached the same question on December 20, 1971, by highlighting the following three points: (1) Bangladesh had already occupied a place on the map of the world; (2) India had made a formal appeal to the rest of the world, including Canada, to recognize Bangladesh; and (3) the Indian government was not responsible for the maintenance of law and order in Bangladesh.[21] Sharp's curt but carefully crafted response was: "The government does not intend to recognize Bangla Desh yet since we are not satisfied that there is a government in that area responsible for administration. As far as I can see, the principal control now rests with the Indian army itself."[22] Although Sharp's instant response seemed a bit negative, behind the scenes, Ottawa had already begun consultation with several Commonwealth countries on this matter. Sharp believed that Canada must not jump on the bandwagon until she is fully satisfied.

In the meantime, on December 20, 1971, Bhutto spoke to the nation in a radio and TV broadcast and "declared EastPak an integral part of [the] country [Pakistan] and said India would not be allowed to impose a military solution."[23] Ottawa, while officials recognized Bhutto's stubbornness, they also learned from the Canadian high commissioner to the UK how the Bangladesh Women's Association of Great Britain had already held several demonstrations in front of many foreign missions, including the Canada House, office of the Canadian high commissioner to the UK. They distributed photocopies of a handwritten letter addressed to the high commissioner of Canada to the UK in which they appealed to the Canadian government to "give immediate recognition to Bangladesh; to put pressure on the Government of West Pakistan for the immediate release of Bongobondhu, President of the People's Republic of Bangladesh; and to urge the United Nations to arrange for the trial of Yahya Khan and his generals as war criminals for committing genocide, rape, and wanton destruction of properties in Bangladesh."[24] Canada noted that Bruce Douglas Mann, MP for Kensington North, attended and spoke to the Hyde Park Speakers' Corner gathering. The demonstrators then proceeded to the USA, France, Germany, Spain, and 10 Downing Street embassies to deliver a letter to the British Prime Minister Edward Heath, the high commission of Canada and Australia. Finally, they went to the Embassy of the USSR.

It seemed to the people of Canada that the government was not doing anything about recognition. It was just the opposite. Canada was looking on the bright side that no longer was the eastern wing a part of Pakistan. Canada was interested in moving forward toward recognition. However, she had reservations regarding the newborn country's capability and allocating resources to the war-ravaged country as early as possible. In response to a question by NDP Member of Parliament for Yorkton-Melville, Lorne Systrom, concerning the recognition of Bangladesh by Canada on December 22, Sharp was utterly frank when he stated, "I am sure the House will agree that until there is evidence of a government being in control in that area, it would be unwise to proceed with recognition or exchange of diplomats."[25]

In the meantime, Ottawa quickly conducted a brief study on the implication of Canada's recognition of Bangladesh by examining the situation's legal, economic, and humanitarian aspects. Under legal considerations, it examined the same essential criteria that were present in the case of Biafra in 1967 and concluded that the government of Bangladesh, "composed of the Awami League leaders under the acting presidency of Syed Nazrul Islam and led by Tajuddin Ahmed as prime minister, could not be said to be functioning effectively."[26] The same policy paper continued, "So long as the Indian Army is on the territory of 'Bangla Desh,' it is doubtful that the criterion of military possession can be met. Even after their withdrawal, it will be a matter of fine judgment whether 'Bangla Desh' is not a client state of India."[27] The presence of the Indian army and indecisiveness within the Bangladesh government seemed to have raised particular problems for countries contemplating recognition.

Paradoxically, Ottawa also believed that the premature withdrawal of the Indian army would threaten to return Bangladesh to chaos, the outcome of which would more than likely be further bloody revenge on each other's part. Ottawa was also mindful of the argument of the Canadian high commissioner to India, James George, that the foreign minister of Bangladesh had indicated that "no country had made recognition of BD [Bangladesh] conditional on the withdrawal of Indian troops, nor would this be acceptable"[28] to the government of Bangladesh. Ottawa then examined a box score of countries and found those in consortium with whom Canada would like to be associated were concerned about the presence of the Indian troops in Bangladesh.

Again, a reality check with other Commonwealth countries revealed that the settling of accounts was still in progress, and ten million Bengalis who took shelter in India had not yet returned to Bangladesh. An exodus of the West Pakistani detainees, the Razakars (collaborators/loyalists with the military regime who were in favor of a united Pakistan), the Biharis (Urdu-speaking migrants to East Pakistan following the partition of India in 1947 now numbered some 730,000 who were in favor of a united Pakistan) and others who had identified with the old regime was feared to be problematic.

Ottawa also watched with alarm the rehabilitation of truncated Pakistan that fell to Zulfiqar Ali Bhutto, who was sworn in as President on December 19 and, again, the next day, as chief martial law administrator in quick succession. Ottawa officials noted that the world media blamed Bhutto as being responsible for the amputation of Pakistan. Canada was dumbfounded to see how the Bhutto administration kept up a running drumfire about Pakistan's jihad, or holy war, with India even days after the surrender of the Pakistani army with reasoning like the following: "In the pursuit of jihad, nobody dies. He lives forever."[29] The reporter continued, "Pakistan radio and television blared forth patriotic songs such as All of Pakistan is Wide Awake and The Martyr's Blood Will Not Go Wasted."[30] Ottawa was struck by Bhutto's absurd claim that, even though Bangladesh had become an independent country, East Pakistan was still a part of Pakistan, and, therefore, to Bhutto's way of thinking, despite the surrender of the Pakistani army, repudiation of the eastern wing of Pakistan was out of the question.

In the meantime, Pakistan's Foreign Secretary Sultan Khan expressed concerns that Bhutto was in the soup because the entire regime was unable to bear the humiliation of military defeat and the "loss of East Pakistan" forced upon them. Demonstrations had been continued for days throughout Pakistan, demanding that "those responsible for national humiliation and disgrace of loss of East Pakistan to Indian forces should be removed from office."[31] Ottawa was informed that the general Pakistani public was using some of the following slogans on the streets: "Down with Yahya," "Give us back our honor, give us back united Pak[istan]," "Transfer power to peoples[sic] reps[representatives]," and "Long live Pak-China Friendship."[32] At the same time, the public sentiment against Yahya grew following his resignation. On December 20, Bhutto appointed Nurul Amin, a seventy-eight-year-old Pakistan Democratic Party (PDP) MP, vice president. "For cosmetic reasons,"[33] it was speculated that as a Bengali and a staunch supporter of a united Pakistan, Amin would probably be able to maintain a "fiction of a united Pak[istan] comprising East and West wings,"[34] Small wrote about Bhutto's motive even after the liberation of Bangladesh.

Amid changes, the most important news was Bhutto's announcement of his intention to release Bongobondhu. While this was a piece of welcoming news, his other intention to work out a deal with Bongobondhu and reestablish civilian rule in a united Pakistan sounded absurd to Canadian officials. Small wrote to Ottawa that the release of the Bengali leader, according to Bhutto, did not "in any way change the position of [the] GOP [Government of Pakistan] regarding the territorial integrity and national sovereignty of Pak[istan] and that possibility of further talks between Bhutto and Mujib cannot be ruled out."[35]

Small also informed Ottawa that Bhutto was "reported to have told Sheikh Mujibur Rahman he could have as much autonomy as he wanted for EastPak [East Pakistan] provided [a] way could be found to preserve two wings of the nation within the framework of one Pak[istan]."[36] Such statements by Bhutto made Ottawa officials wonder about his peculiar state of mind.

Those in charge also noted with satisfaction how a group of high-level officials who had earlier formed the nucleus of the Bangladesh government-in-exile in India, with direct cooperation from the Gandhi administration, the acting president of Bangladesh, the prime minister, and senior Cabinet members made a triumphant entry into Dhaka on December 20, 1971, following the surrender of the Pakistani army on December 16, 1971. Frankly, Canada was not quite prepared yet, although officials had already been assigned to assess the situation in Bangladesh immediately following her independence. Canada was still waiting for situational reports from India since, by then, (West) Pakistan was already cut off from Bangladesh (East Pakistan). Thus, the lack of tangible progress to his satisfaction forced Sharp to procrastinate a tad more, even though Ottawa was concerned about the need to assist ten million refugees and displaced people to rehabilitate in the war-torn country.

Ottawa needed to be fully satisfied regarding the precise timing for early recognition. Sharp's team argued that the customarily accepted international criteria had not been established yet in the newborn country. Generally, in a *coup d'état*, any armed clash that usually follows is brief enough to enable other countries to observe the new government to assess the situation. Canada had no precedence to follow regarding Bangladesh. Since the Indian army was still present, the situation differed from the kind of coup that had occurred so often in Asiatic or African countries. Although Sharp recognized the urgency to move forward, he had no choice but to wait for more evidence-based information from the field.

During the last week of December, Ottawa officials advised Sharp to write to Canada's representatives of a few key countries about the anticipated two-fold pressures: that there would be "continuing pressure both from India and from a [certain] segment of Cdn [Canadian] population first to recognize the independence of East Bengal and secondly establish diplo[matic] relations with Dacca [sic]."[37] Accordingly, Ottawa officials immediately asked Canadian representatives to gather as much information as possible on the latest situation in Bangladesh to assist Ottawa in completing its assessment of Bangladesh as a sovereign country without any reservations. Sharp was also advised to maintain his usual media line, a quick and curt answer, in the following: Canada had been watching the situation in Bangladesh to finalize her decision on the precise timing of according recognition.[38]

Is Bangladesh, in fact, "still in control of the Indian Army?" All through late December, this question kept resurfacing with no definite answer. To Canada's way of thinking, sovereignty means the ability to maintain complete political control over a defined territory, to make all laws within that country, and to have that control respected by other jurisdictions. This was the first and foremost condition for Ottawa to consider an early move to accord recognition. By the end of December, a volley of questions went through the minds of Ottawa officials again, such as the following: Would Bangladesh be able to realize her aspirations through internal reconstruction and international cooperation? Or would the government resort to military force? A watchful Canada noted with interest how the recognition of Bangladesh by India and Bhutan had triggered East Germany, Poland, Bulgaria, and Mongolia to do the same. Nevertheless, the assessment process slowed down even more as Canada considered every daily event in Pakistan.

In the Commons, when Sharp was asked about the specific timing of recognition of Bangladesh by Canada, his instant response was that he was not yet ready to commit to a precise date for recognition. Part of the reason was that, at that time, Sharp was reminded by Small how, following the surrender of the Pakistani army, the outraged Pakistani public did not even bother to spare "Sharzad Hotel in Isbad [Islamabad] and how the "Cdn [Canadian] Hicom [High Commission] [had] received visit by mobs of five hundred youngsters"[39] in the afternoon of December 20. Sharp himself could not help but recall how both Yahya and the people of Pakistan had expressed their dissatisfaction toward what they called Canada's lack of support for Pakistan or that Canada was not on Pakistan's side. The regime claimed Canada demonstrated this by suspending the *S. S. Padma* (discussed in Chapter 4) in June.

Sharp's challenge was to find an independent *modus operandi* in Bangladesh to satisfy himself one hundred percent of all the requirements for a "stable government." Ottawa was glad to learn that the government of Bangladesh was drawing up its plans for the phased withdrawal of the Indian army from Bangladesh. However, Sharp still needed some more time to think through and assess the Indian government's version of its continued presence in Bangladesh. He was mindful of George's advice that disarming Bengali irregulars would be a complicated and drawn-out task because many "Bengalis (especially intellectuals)" had "been executed by Pak Army in [the] last hours of [the] conflict" that had "add[ed] fuel to fires of hatred."[40]

In the meantime, the Canadian public continued to pressure the government for early recognition. Individually, a prominent member of the Canadian public, Professor Muazzam Hussain of Sherbrooke, Québec, took a whole new approach to push the envelope for recognition. Claiming himself to be an informal representative of Bangladesh in Canada, Hussain remained active in liaising with Ottawa and members of the Bongobondhu administration in Dhaka when the Planning Commission of Bangladesh still prioritized the urgently needed actions. Hussain wrote to Prime Minister Trudeau with the following two specific requests: (1) to assist in rebuilding Bangladesh with the urgently needed items that Canada could provide, and (2) to provide training by Canadian experts to about one thousand young Bangladeshi professionals in urgently needed technical, medical, and paramedical fields.[41]

By this time, Ottawa officials had asked themselves a plethora of questions, such as whether the Bengalis' claim for independence was still contested. More specifically, had independence been established in a matter-of-fact way so that the Bhutto government could claim no jurisdictional right over erstwhile East Pakistan? Sharp made no disguise of his feelings of anger and frustration. Sharp had no choice but to be extra careful in deciding on more evidence-based information from the field.

Naturally, Canada was uncomfortable about straining her relations with Pakistan against her request for early recognition. Sharp was advised, "We certainly should not want to risk a break in our relations with Islamabad, although we could be prepared to see those relations become less close—after all, it was West Pakistani brutality that contributed materially to the refugee exodus. If there were an advantage to us in expressing our friendship toward the Bengali people by early recognition of Bangla Desh,"[42] it would be wise to do so. Suggesting that the government should move a bit faster, Ritchie wrote the following in the same memorandum: "Should we have any part to play in influencing the new rulers of East Bengal, if not in their internal policies, at least in their external ones, then the sooner we enter into diplomatic relations with the Government of 'Bangla Desh,' the more effective we would be."[43]

Just about the same time, Ottawa also noted some factual and affirmative news coverage by Peter Hazelhurst of *The Times* of London that Ottawa analysts interpreted as positive, such as the following: "Eleven days have passed since the Indian army occupied East Pakistan, and in that time, it has become abundantly clear that Mrs. Gandhi has fought what amounts to a war of liberation. For the past twenty-five years, West Pakistan has been trying to convince the Bengalis that the Hindu infidels would pillage and rape East Bengal if Islamabad were not there to protect the Eastern Province. But today, lone and unarmed Indian soldiers stroll through the marketplaces. The Bengalis beam at the sight of an Indian uniform, and an atmosphere of confidence has replaced the pall of terror that has hovered over East Bengal for the last nine months. This is mainly because the Indian army's performance as a temporary occupation force has surpassed its performance on the battlefield."[44] Ottawa recognized that, realistically, early recognition would facilitate the resumption of the shipment of nonstrategic and nonmilitary materials and development assistance. At the same time, Ottawa believed it would also reduce Canadian domestic economic consequences of suspension of aid.

Although Ottawa officials were moving forward for recognition, they could never shake off their edginess regarding Pakistan's anticipated reaction to Canada's early move. "We would want to act in concert with as many of our friends as possible in part to reduce the risk of a break with Islamabad and enhance the possibility of effective international consortium action to assist in the economic development of the new state."[45] Thus, Sharp was reminded of Canada's joint gesture regarding promoting social justice in Pakistan and Bangladesh.

Fortunately for Canada, by the beginning of January 1972, Sharp was noticeably at ease in alluding to his dilemma during the Bengalis' struggle for independence. Happily, by then, Ottawa also gathered a few more instances of discernably factual progress in the field of governance and administration, along with the news that both Urdu and English dailies in Pakistan had been covering a wide range of opinions that ran from simple condemnation of former President Yahya to establishment of democracy and promulgation of a constitution by the new president. Several Pakistani newspapers also "suggested Mujib tour WestPak [West Pakistan] to make his views known as the picture remains incomplete since only Bhutto and Yahya have been heard from,"[46] wrote Small.

In one of his many media interviews, a watchful Sharp referred to his observation—that he was aware of how "a new state of Bangla Desh" was "obviously emerging."[47] Although a politically canny Sharp did not hesitate to express publicly his readiness to recognize Bangladesh, he had some reservations, which were described as follows: "You cannot recognize a government until you are sure it is in control."[48]

Simultaneously, Small could not predict an unpredictable Bhutto's next move, which caused Canada to remain a bit hung up. Canada's most significant problem was being unable to raise Bhutto's disapprobation. "Fine judgment will be required to decide how long he [Bhutto] can postpone return to democracy if his predecessor Yahya is to be avoided,"[49] wrote Small. It may sound bizarre, but it is very accurate that Canada's progress toward recognizing Bangladesh seemed to have depended on her parallel assessment of Pakistan's anticipated actions and reactions to Canada's actions, for which Canada never took her eyes off Pakistan. Ottawa officials felt compelled to wait still and see. This was around the second week of January 1972 when one of Ottawa's wishes had been to see more tangible progress toward democracy and the launching of parliamentary institutions in newborn Bangladesh.

Moving forward, Canada watched with satisfaction Bongobondhu's release from jail and return to Dhaka. Canada was pleased to note how all his media interviews in London and New Delhi were reported in Pakistani news media in factual terms, even though the news items did not favor Pakistan. There were no distortions of the news that were reported at that time. "In general, they [Pakistanis] are realistically accepting [the] fact of defeat in EastPak [East Pakistan] and the emergence of Bangla Desh as a separate country,"[50] wrote Small, again, in a confidential report. Ottawa interpreted this as something positive for the people of Pakistan since neither the public nor the press blamed Bongobondhu. With Bongobondhu's release and return to Dhaka on January 10, 1972, Canada recognized with certainty that there was no longer any possibility of maintaining the unity of Pakistan in any shape or form, no matter what Bhutto was claiming.

Sharp was immediately briefed on Bongobondhu's speech to the Nation and his bold statement that he was "severing all ties with WestPak [West Pakistan]"[51] In the meantime, an astute Trudeau also took the first opportunity to congratulate Bhutto for commending his "unconditional release of Mujib as an act of statesmanship."[52] Ottawa was encouraged by the high commissioner's remark that the political situation in the subcontinent would probably "come closer to a mutually acceptable conclusion"[53] if only Bhutto could demonstrate certain "reasonableness." While the release of Bongobondhu made Ottawa officials optimistic, they still needed to see whether Bhutto agreed to move ahead with no jurisdictional claim to now-independent Bangladesh. Was Bhutto ready to relinquish his claim to jurisdiction in Bangladesh (erstwhile East Pakistan), no matter how absurd it might have sounded after a disgraceful surrender of the Pakistani army? This was Ottawa's question. Ottawa kept its fingers crossed for a positive answer.

Sharp's concerns were somewhat alleviated when Ottawa learned how the sheer presence of Bongobondhu in Dhaka, despite the presence of the Indian army, had already consolidated the position of the Bangladesh government and enhanced its authority. Canada also noted how, on January 12, 1972 (two days after he arrived in Bangladesh), Bongobondhu, as president, declared a temporary constitution in effect and appointed a new chief justice of the High Court. Bongobondhu then resigned to allow the cabinet to elect a new president. Bongobondhu was chosen as the prime minister of Bangladesh, and Abu Sayeed Chowdhury as the country's president. Besides being prime minister, Bongobondhu retained the ministries of defense, home affairs, information, and cabinet. Canada was pleased to note how an enlightened Bongobondhu discouraged his people to contemplate taking revenge on those who opposed the majority, referring to the Rzakars and Biharis, who were in the hands of the allied forces by then. Ottawa saw Bongobondhu's initiatives as indicative of a stable government in Bangladesh ready to walk the talk.

In the meantime, Ottawa officials also learned from Small that Yahya and his ex-chief of staff, General Abdul Hamid Khan, had been arrested in the "supreme interest of state and people of Pakistan."[54] They immediately followed up for details. Although this had nothing to do with the recognition process of Bangladesh, the Trudeau administration, as already indicated, remained watchful of every single event in Pakistan and moved forward or backward accordingly. Ottawa learned that there was no indication of whether arrests would lead to charges and consequent trials, but the situation seemed bleak. Ottawa officials recalled the high commissioner's advice that "a modest degree of patience would result in achievement" of all their "aims in both Dacca [sic] and Isbad [Islamabad]" and that "precipitate action might gain a new comwel [Commonwealth] member but at [the] expense of an old one."[55] Although Ottawa was pressed for time, it was forced to pay attention to the point Small was trying to put across— the need to continue its "wait-and-see" policy, at least for a bit more.

Earlier, Sharp was advised that, in international law, a state might be recognized when certain conditions, such as external independence, effective internal government, and control of a definable territory, are satisfied. He was also reminded with additional note that, legally speaking, "refusal by the parent state to recognize the independence of the rebellious or seceding province is not deemed conclusive evidence that independence does not exist."[56] A doubly circumspect Sharp still maintained that premature recognition before conditions were fulfilled might amount to intervention in the internal affairs of the parent state. Sharp was under tremendous pressure, seeing that the government of India had already recognized Bangladesh and that there had been rumors that the government of the USSR might follow suit.

Regardless, Ottawa remained optimistic, seeing how several Commonwealth countries had been coming forward to assist in rehabilitating the war-ravaged Bangladesh. Canada was glad to note that, despite being the arch enemy to each other, the Gandhi administration had been campaigning for Pakistan's recognition of Bangladesh as an independent state so that the two countries could begin sorting out assets and liabilities.[57] At this stage, Sharp was reminded of George's earlier concerns about India's reaction to Canada's procrastination, along with the gist of his advice in the following: "Any attempt by foreign governments to equate India's responsibilities for the present situation in the subcontinent with Paks [Pakistan's] responsibilities are regarded very dimly by GOI [Government of India]. It would be a pity to convert goodwill for Canada that now exists in India into suspicion and bad feeling without solid grounds."[58] George underscored that the slower Canada's recognition, the greater the chances her relations with New Delhi might suffer. Ottawa's challenge was to find a creative way to expedite the process.

In the meantime, Ottawa was disturbed to receive an *aide mémoire* around the beginning of the second week of January 1972 from the high commissioner of Pakistan, who informed Ottawa that "the possibility of further talks between Sheikh Mujibur Rahman and the President of Pakistan, Mr. Zulfikar Ali Bhutto cannot be ruled out."[59] Although it made no sense to Ottawa, the high commissioner continued and argued further, "The so-called Bangla Desh Government in Dacca [sic] is not in command of law and order in the province. The control of the province is in the hands of the Indian occupation forces whose commander repeated, in an attempt yesterday, that he could not say when the Indian troops would be withdrawn from East Pakistan. This establishes the fact that the so-called Bangla Desh Government is not even in de facto control of the territory they claim to be representing."[60] Having said this, the high commissioner ended his note by saying that "the Government of Pakistan is confident that the Government of Canada would continue to avoid taking any premature action concerning East Pakistan."[61]

Chronologically speaking, by the third week of January 1972, George's situational reports indicated that there had been substantial changes in the newborn country due to the sheer presence of Bongobondhu. George's reinforcement of the fact that the government of India had deployed its army personnel in Bangladesh strictly at the request of Bongobondhu was convincing to Ottawa. Sharp was glad to learn that the Gandhi administration would be willing to withdraw the Indian army as soon as the government of Bangladesh asked it to do so and that half the Indian army had already begun to withdraw since mid-January 1972. Sharp demanded that the Indian government still be asked for its timetable for withdrawing its forces; it should also be pressed to give precise figures as to its troops in Bangladesh indicating the tasks on which they were engaged. For the Trudeau administration, it was no longer a question of recognition itself but of how fast to accord recognition.

While Ottawa officials were waiting for the opportunity to recognize, they also kept Sharp up-to-date regarding the next steps Canada could or should take regarding developmental work and the possibility of continuing trade with Bangladesh. With that objective in mind, A. J. Andrew, Director General of the Bureau of Asian and Pacific Affairs, proactively wrote, "Of the annual $56 million Canadian exports to Pakistan, about $20 million went to East Pakistan, and of the $10 million annual imports about half of jute. Non-aid finance exports to Pakistan probably amounted to not more than $3 million per year. Still, since most of the hard currency earnings came from East Pakistan's jute and tea crops, there is a possibility of developing a larger Canadian export market in the long term. The Department of Industry, Trade, and Commerce expects that trade opportunities would be enhanced with the establishment of diplomatic ties and the opening of a resident office."[62] Sharp was also counseled that early recognition of Bangladesh would facilitate the resumption of development work in the area, which should not be delayed from CIDA's point of view.

During the last week of January Ottawa, Ottawa was swarmed with telexes from Islamabad about Bhutto's reactions, whims, and quirks. Ottawa became annoyed with a capriciously fluctuating Bhutto who had been unwilling to accept the fact that Bangladesh had become an independent sovereign state and that Bangladesh was no longer a part of Pakistan. Sharp, however, recognized that being badly cut up, Bhutto was deeply into the mire. Just about the same time, there came another disturbing news about the extent of the highly nationalistic tribal sense among the Pathan people of the North-West Frontier Province and Baluchistan that had already made Pakistan's two provinces ripe for divisive agitation.

An oversensitive Trudeau administration feared that immediate recognition of Bangladesh, without determining the actual situation, would constitute, *prima facie*, diplomatic discourtesy to Pakistan. Ottawa officials argued this could strain or break Pakistan's friendly relations with Canada. Small's situational reports from Islamabad also made Ottawa aware of the political unrest which, bordering on militancy, had continued to brew in the amputated Pakistan. It is hard to understand why Ottawa was paying extra attention to Pakistan's every action and reaction, some of which were ludicrously preposterous. Sharp faced a situation in diplomacy where there was no "easier said than done." Ottawa remained hesitant to jump the gun as Sharp needed to ensure that the viewpoints of both Small and George, who represented Pakistan and India, fell in line. In a dichotomous situation, Ottawa officials had to remain doubly circumspect about their move toward immediate recognition.

During the last week of January, Sharp was advised by Ottawa officials that they felt compelled to review the following factors that the government of Pakistan was putting forward as its argument against immediate recognition: (1) juridical assumption that East Pakistan is part of Pakistan occupied by India; (2) UN General Assembly, in its December resolution, fully endorsed Pakistan's territorial integrity and called for the withdrawal of Indian forces; and (3) Pakistan's president at that time was engaged in delicate negotiations with representatives of East Pakistan aimed at a just settlement for the population of East Pakistan (4) any hasty action by friendly governments would make it impossible for these negotiations to proceed.[63]

Correspondence exchanged between various high commissioners of the Commonwealth countries shows Canada's genuine effort to pick a date for a concerted public announcement of several countries' recognition of Bangladesh. By the last day of January 1971, however, it was brought to Sharp's attention that most governments contemplating recognition felt an element of urgency and seriousness to move forward despite the presence of the Indian army.

Upon receipt of a letter from British Prime Minister Edward Heath, who requested Trudeau to take advantage of "acting together" according to recognition, Ottawa felt slightly encouraged. Having known about Canada's hesitancy and reservation, Heath explained to Trudeau the actual situation regarding the presence of the Indian army. He wrote, "On his [Mujib] return, he would formally request the Army's withdrawal in accordance with a phased and agreed plan."[64] Heath, who seemed okay with the arrangement, wrote, "It seems to me, therefore, that the problem with which we are now faced is not so much whether to recognize Bangladesh but when to do so. There are dangers in too early recognition, which might antagonize West Pakistan and complicate President Bhutto's task. On the other hand, if Mujib receives early recognition and support from the West, it will help him to consolidate his position and improve his chance of keeping the country out of the hands of the extremists. I hope you will share my views."[65]

An astute Heath also shared his note with Trudeau and sent it to Bhutto so that Ottawa would be comfortable moving forward. In his note to Bhutto, Heath stated, "In our view, the criteria for recognition of a new state have now been fulfilled. Shaikh Mujib had made it clear in his public speeches that Bangladesh is an independent sovereign country and that this is a point on which his government is not open to compromise. We accept this as the reality of the situation. His government is in control of the country; the Indian forces are there at his behest, and the Indian has undertaken to withdraw them at his request." [66]

Heath's intervention and request to Trudeau positively increased Ottawa's comfort level, making Ottawa feel more encouraged. Trudeau immediately wrote to Heath, "If we and other countries could obtain firm info[rmation] about such a plan, it would no doubt assist us in our evaluation of the situation."[67] Both George and Small also thought along the same vein. Ottawa seemed prepared to move forward.

The problem, however, seemed to continue to challenge Canada and other countries as none of them had any precedent for recognizing a newborn country, especially while foreign troops were still on its soil. The Commonwealth countries referred to the most relevant situation being that of Malaya in 1957. In the meantime, George brought some more clarity regarding the presence of the Indian army in Bangladesh by pointing out that it was protecting the lives of vulnerable segments, such as non-Bengalis and quislings in newborn Bangladesh. This was a top priority of the Indian army. Sharp's team agreed with George that, from a legal point of view, the presence of the Indian army did not seem to be an obstacle to recognition and that it would be necessary to have the Indian army around for some time.

In the meantime, Ottawa was glad to hear that Bhutto himself was garnering widespread support for the recognition of Bangladesh. Nevertheless, strangely enough, instead of moving forward, Sharp still seemed to remain busy watching Bhutto's every move. There is no easy explanation as to why Ottawa was still trying to appease a chancy Bhutto who was demonstrably unstable again and again. Ottawa believed that once Bhutto had firmed up his position with relative certainty, he might go for a "package" settlement with Bangladesh, which would include recognition and repatriation of prisoners. Small argued that by extending recognition to Bangladesh forthwith, Pakistan would be able to "pave the way for normalization of friendly and brotherly relations between people of Pak[istan] and Bangladesh."[68] Ottawa officials seemed convinced that time was of the essence and that they should immediately reach a decision regardless of where Bhutto stood.

Ottawa officials, however, became a bit unhappy, having found Bhutto's frequent contradictory positions or impulsive remarks that did not make any sense to them. They became disappointed to see how a whimsical Bhutto was still desperately attempting to dissuade other countries from recognizing Bangladesh. Though utterly nonsensical, Ottawa still needed to assess the implication of Bhutto's statement that "he would like to maintain some links and indicated as an example restoration of telecommunications between East and West, restoration of PIA services and others that could be agreed upon mutually."[69]

The foreign affairs' cognoscenti briefed Sharp by pointing out that there were two other phenomena at work—threats ranging from virulent ethnonationalism and uncontrolled migration of Hindu Bengalis who had either lived in East Bengal before the creation of Pakistan (partition of India in 1947) or had left East Pakistan because of persecution by the Yahya regime in 1971. According to the Situational Reports of Canadian high commissioners and the media coverage, such news was not a matter of perception but was daily reported as the movement from Bangladesh to India was going on during the war of liberation. Ottawa was aware that it was Bhutto's ardent hope that countries with which Pakistan had traditionally enjoyed cordial relations, and Canada was one of them, would accord a better understanding of Pakistan's point of view.[70] Unsurprisingly, therefore, Ottawa decided to procrastinate a little bit more.

Despite Canada's readiness, officials remained unsure about how Pakistan would react to Canada's action. Consequently, with a feeling of fretfulness and disquietude, Ottawa again deliberately held back, reverting to her same old wait-and-see policy, at least for a few more days, even though Ottawa was convinced that it would be irrational to wait any longer to appease Pakistan.

Just as Ottawa was almost ready to take the next step to announce its intention to recognize Bangladesh with a specific date, suddenly, there came a cautionary message from Small that he could not be on the same wavelength with George, who was pushing for early joint recognition—a bolt from the blue that forced Ottawa to place a halt instantly once again on its move toward recognition. It would be worthwhile to wait a few more days as "the advantages Canada might gain from premature recognition would probably not offset the losses in our relations with Pakistan,"[71] argued a restless Small. Again, he tried to justify his point by saying, "With a short delay for Pak[istan] to adjust, undesirable effects of early recognition on Pak[istan] could be avoided while undesirable effects on Bangla Desh could still be achieved."[72]

Small said, "There is something to be gained from independent action, and I see no reason to be tied to Brits or Europeans any more than to the United States."[73] An adamant Small saw no advantage to Canada in recognizing Bangladesh in a joint recognition. To dissuade Ottawa, Small further argued, "Far from being afraid of adverse reactions in India, I should think we have more to gain by establishing our independence of action than we have to lose in currying favor from Indians or tagging along with European crowd."[74] Having come thus far, Sharp again found himself caught on the horns of a dilemma.

However, another factor came into play by the first week of February 1972. Fortunately, this time, it was in Ottawa's favor that the people of former West Pakistan, who were left relatively in the dark about what was going on in East Pakistan during the military rule, were rapidly coming to know about the true stories of war and liberation following the surrender of the Pakistani army. They, too, had begun to demand recognition of Bangladesh by the government of Pakistan. While monitoring the overall reaction of the people of Pakistan, Ottawa analysts noted how the retired C in C of Pakistan Air Force, Ashgar Khan, then chief of the Tehrik-i-Istiqbal, viewed the independence of Bangladesh through a completely different lens than Bhutto, such as the following: "If democracy is not restored, WestPak might meet the same fate as EastPak."[75] Thus, a courageous Khan was observed publicly appealing to the government for its early recognition of Bangladesh.

At about the same time, there appeared yet another nagging question that Ottawa officials believed they must address immediately. Sharp's dilemma, this time around, was to deal with the different viewpoints of George and Small that Sharp's team had been trying to address. They agreed when Ottawa officials examined George's request to move forward without further delay. When they turned to Small's argument, they noted how he wrote, "Political unrest, bordering on militancy, will continue to brew in the western provinces of Pakistan, representing a dangerous and possibly fatal weakness in President Bhutto's control,"[76] warned Small. Further review of Small's request made sense to them. They tended to agree to Small's request that there should be another halt, at least for a brief period. Ottawa was indeed placed between a rock and a hard place.

By then, Ottawa had already concluded that Bhutto's attempt to probe the subcontinent was bound to be futile. An amputated Pakistan could neither claim any constitutional link with Bangladesh nor block its acceptance internationally, argued Ottawa officials. A persistent Bhutto's desperate request to "not to act until Indian troops have departed"[77] did not seem to appeal to Ottawa anymore. It is mainly because, by the first week of February, Ottawa officials had decided not to entertain any more requests from Pakistan. Sharp was advised that if Canada's recognition of Bangladesh coincided with some European countries, it would probably satisfy the Indian government's expectations. He was then briefed on Canada's coordinated approach to recognition with the following: "Numerous other countries have indicated during our recent round of consultations with them that they have agreed in principle to recognize but are still considering what timing would be most appropriate."[78]

Last Minutes' Hurdles

The Trudeau administration, however, quickly found a creative way to address the issue by summoning both high commissioners to Ottawa for "consultation" and "discussion" regarding the implication of Bhutto's threats. Both Small and George immediately came to Ottawa, met with Sharp and his team from relevant areas in the Department, and addressed the following: (1) how to iron out the differences, (2) the loss of officers in Pakistan due to the evacuation of December 1971–January 1972, (3) the nature of new aid program in Bangladesh, and (4) adaptation to the new political and economic changes.

Simultaneously, Ottawa officials also completed a study of the dates of recognition of Bangladesh by other countries and briefed Sharp on the status of recognition with various dates by countries which had already recognized Bangladesh - how their knuckles were rapped by Pakistan having severed her diplomatic relations with Poland, Mongolia, Bulgaria, Cyprus, Czechoslovakia, Hungary, Yugoslavia as a reaction to their recognition of Bangladesh. When Burma and Nepal took the same action, Pakistan withdrew her ambassadors from their capitals but did not break relations. Pakistan broke off her ties with Nepal and Burma by withdrawing Pakistan's ambassadors from there. Pakistan immediately announced her decision to leave the Commonwealth. Foreign affairs cognoscenti alerted Sharp by saying that it was too premature for Bhutto to react the way he did.

There was still another nagging issue reminding Sharp of Bhutto's verbal request to Small and other diplomats at Larkana on January 22, 1972, that recognition be postponed until after his return from Peking (now Beijing). It was hard for Sharp to overcome such worry against Bhutto's erratic reactions. His team was asked to conduct another review of the present situation to consider Pakistan's probable future reaction and fallout. In the meantime, the Trudeau administration convinced itself that the rivalry between the communist powers would continue to exacerbate tensions as long as Pakistan and India could not come to terms with each other under rapidly changing circumstances. As Canada saw the situation, the recognition of Bangladesh by the East Europeans and then by the Soviet Union gave the question a particular urgency. Canada believed that if Bangladesh were left for any time in a situation where, apart from its immediate neighbors, the only countries it had relations with were those of the Soviet bloc, the position of left-wing groups within the country would be strengthened. It would become more difficult for the government to keep it on its preferred moderate course.

Internationally, Canada was aware that, among the major powers, the Nixon administration, which included President Nixon himself and his immediate White House advisers, had disregarded the American public's opinion and would withhold its recognition for the foreseeable future. It would probably not consider the question until after Nixon visited Beijing, which was the Nixon administration's top priority. It wanted America's friends and allies to delay the process to the greatest extent possible. Canada was mindful of the fact that Canadians had earlier condemned President Yahya for unspeakable military reprisals during the Bengalis' struggle for independence.

Personally, a strong-willed Trudeau, having disagreed with Nixon's strategies, was ready to act with no further delay. This was a bold step on Trudeau's part, especially when Nixon expected Canada to toe the US line about its position in the subcontinental conflict. Canada knew that her thinking along the vein of moving forward according to its *raison d'être*, having ignored the Nixon administration's earnest appeal, was unacceptable to Nixon. A valiant Trudeau put his foot down and demonstrated Canada's independent stand, devoid of the US influence in Canada's exercise of her foreign policy options.

Moving forward, in a carefully worded message, Canada informed Pakistan's high commissioner to Canada and Sultan M. Khan, Pakistan's foreign secretary, prudently and thoughtfully of Canada's decision to recognize Bangladesh immediately. When he was told that, the Pakistani representative in Ottawa was utterly displeased with Canada's decision. Instantly, through an *aide-mémoire* on "the recognition of so-called Bangla Desh," the high commissioner cautioned Canada in the following: "The governments which have recognized Bangla Desh have ignored the fact that conditions for recognition are nonexistent. East Pakistan continues to remain under military occupation of India, and there is no sign of withdrawal of the Indian forces. The administration in Dacca [sic] does not exercise effective control over territories of the province; if it did, there would be no need for the Indian Army to be there. There are confirmed reports about atrocities against Biharis, and serious violations of law and order are also being received every day. Alternatively, the Indian Army is there because it wants to establish Indian dominance in East Pakistan."[79]

Ottawa was dumbfounded to see how doggedly Pakistan's representative in Canada continued to refer to Bangladesh as East Pakistan even weeks following the surrender of the Pakistani army and the liberation of Bangladesh. Ottawa came to regard Pakistan's reasoning asinine—not based on reality but wishful thinking. His insistence that Bhutto badly needed some more time seemed arrantly ludicrous to Ottawa in February even though initially, Canada believed (or wished to believe) that there could be a retention of even a tenuous constitutional link between the two wings. In February, such thinking made no political sense to Ottawa. Sharp became convinced that Pakistan had no basis to stand on her own.

Coincidentally, just as Ottawa was ready to act, Small dropped another bombshell. Earlier, Ottawa noted how Pakistan had reacted to the news of the recognition of Bangladesh by the Iron Curtain satellite countries by immediately breaking off relations with all of them. Ottawa recalled that Bhutto, at that time, had openly declared after releasing Bongobondhu that he had no intention of applying the Hallstein doctrine[80] automatically to countries recognizing Bangladesh as the leader's release was unconditional. Once again, Ottawa noticed an aberrant Bhutto's contradictory statements and actions through his appeals to other governments to defer recognition to give him sufficient time to work out an agreement with Bongobondhu.

Canada interpreted this as demonstrating an inconsistent Bhutto's intolerance for those who had thus far accorded recognition to Bangladesh against his earnest appeal. Bhutto characterized Canada's intention to recognize Bangladesh as "an unfriendly act" and "legitimization of aggression and use of force by India to dismember Pak[istan]."[81] No one at External could feel with certainty how an unpredictable Bhutto would react to Ottawa's forewarning of him through Small. In particular, a determined but visibly concerned Sharp, who had earlier put aside Pakistan's threat to use the Hallstein Doctrine,[82] also did not know how Canada's action might make a quirky Bhutto trigger his decision to use such a doctrine.

What would be the implications of Canada's recognition of Bangladesh? What would it mean regarding her new relationship with the newborn country? What would it mean in terms of Canada's continuing relationship with India and truncated Pakistan? Should Canada keep up with another Commonwealth country's problems? How would the major powers see this? These were some of Sharp's questions with no specific answer. Bhutto's whimsical attitude and conflicting positions—whether it was a question of unconditional release of Bongobondhu or the use of the Hallstein Doctrine by a freakish Bhutto - seemed to be the real obstacle. Ottawa recalled the military regime's dissatisfaction with Canada regarding stopping the S. S. *Padma's* supplies. However, it was challenging to understand Pakistan's *quid quo pro*[83,] especially after Ottawa was assured that Pakistan had no intention of breaking diplomatic relations with the Commonwealth countries.

Ottawa noted how a wayward Bhutto, unfortunately, had again begun to appear both mischievous and fickle since Ottawa had already given a clear understanding earlier that Pakistan's relations with countries that accorded recognition to Bangladesh would continue as usual and that these could be expanded on a bilateral basis if they so wished in future. His threat to leave the Commonwealth made Ottawa wonder about the true meaning of Bhutto's oxymoronic statements, stubbornness, lack of maturity, and political trickery.

Given Canada's readiness, Sharp did not wish to think much about Bhutto's threat anymore as he believed it was more like the "sound and fury" of a temperamental Bhutto. Ottawa no longer chose not to counter argue with Pakistan on this issue but agreed to disagree. Meanwhile, Ottawa officials prepared a continuum of recognition of Bangladesh in a chart for handy reference. They found that, by the end of January 1972, the government of Bangladesh had already been recognized by twenty-eight countries, including Britain and the Soviet Union, except for the United States and China. To maintain a balance, the Trudeau administration neither wished to join the bandwagon nor be too far behind. Putting aside the anticipated adverse reactions of an unstable Bhutto on the back burner, Ottawa turned its attention to the possible response of the two superpowers to Canada's proposed announcement.

Ottawa officials thought they might incur Chinese disfavor, mainly because China had been supporting Pakistan in what it called her struggle against secession and the Indian invasion of Pakistan. They also reminded Sharp of how China, even after the independence of Bangladesh, remained a thorn in the side for her continued support for Pakistan with her nuclear weaponry. Sharp was also advised that a Canadian move for early recognition could gain goodwill between the USSR and India. After weeks of deliberations, and despite Bhutto's choler, Ottawa concluded that it had already used its diplomacy and done its homework.

For Canada, it was high time to move forward steadily, having "prepared to act in concert" with as many of her friends as possible in part "to reduce the risk of a break with Isbad [Islamabad] and in part to enhance the possibility of effective innatl [international] consortium action to assist in the economic development of the new state."[84] "We feel that this has been time well spent and that the delay was fully in accordance with the foreign policy of Canada which is concerned with maintaining good relations with all states."[85] Thus, Sharp was briefed.

Putting its feet on the ground, Ottawa believed it took a "diplomatically correct" step. If Pakistan still felt negative about Ottawa's action, Ottawa would be ready to say, "So be it." Sharp was briefed in the following: "When Canada does recognize, we expect it will be about the same time as many other members of the Aid to Pakistan Consortium will have done so and that any further delay could result in unfortunate consequences not in Canada's or Pakistan's interests."[86] Bhutto was then informed that Canada would like to formally announce her intention to accord recognition on February 4, 1972, so he would not be surprised. Diplomatically speaking, Ottawa believed this would allow its officials to "have some flexibility" to adjust to any last-minute minor variations in the timetable.

Receiving notice of Ottawa's intention to recognize Bangladesh, an infuriated Sultan Khan (Pakistan's foreign secretary) reportedly lost his cool. It burst into anger by saying that India "had never accepted Two Nations Theory and current conditions provided its best opportunity since [19]47 to right what is considered [an] initial error of partition."[87] Maintaining diplomatic niceties to the extent possible, Small gave a sympathetic hearing to Khan's soliloquy. Khan summed up Pakistan's dilemma by indicating that the people of Pakistan would not react positively to Canada's recognition of Bangladesh and would likely be asking, "Why is the same not true for NWFP, Baluchistan, Sind, or Punjab?"[88] He then went on to say, "The end of this road was the destruction of Pakistan, and this was the primary concern of Pak authorities to date."[89] Neither Small nor Ottawa was moved by Khan's histrionics to accept Pakistan's narrative of the loss of East Pakistan through India's sinister game plan.

Actual Recognition of Bangladesh

Canada formally accorded recognition to Bangladesh on February 14, 1972, ending the debates and discussions for several weeks, having been fully aware that the legal criteria for recognition would never be 100 percent. It took Canada almost two months, the thirty-sixth country, to recognize the newborn country. The countries announcing diplomatic recognition of Bangladesh on the same day were the UK, Holland, West Germany, Sweden, Finland, Denmark, Norway, Ireland, and Australia. In his announcement, a relaxed Sharp alluded to the liberation movement with none of the hesitations that had inhibited him earlier while the struggle for independence was going on and the country's emergence into nationhood was being materialized. Sharp made public his hope that the relationship between the countries would remain good, having also expressed his desire that both Canada and Bangladesh would be in the Commonwealth.[90]

Canadian officials were happy to note how Bongobondhu's dynamic personality was strengthening the sinews of the Bengalis and rejuvenating a sense of pride. Bongobondhu became an indomitable symbol of Bangladesh's self-respect, infusing people with self-confidence. Canada was delighted to note a sense of purpose among the Bengalis with a pledge to preserve the precious legacy of blood and to work for a united, strong, and prosperous *Shonar Bangla* (Golden Bengal) devoted to the cause of peace.

"I am happy to inform you that Canada has today accorded full recognition to Bangladesh as an independent state. On behalf of the government and people, I wish to extend greetings and best wishes to you and your government. It is our sincere desire that harmonious and mutually beneficial relations may develop between our two countries, and these relations will be enhanced through an association within the Commonwealth (*Communiqué,* Department of External Affairs, No. 6, February 14, 1972, p.30.)."

Thus, Prime Minister Pierre Trudeau sent a succinct and warmly congratulatory message to Sheikh Mujibur Rahman (Bongobondhu), the first prime minister of the People's Republic of Bangladesh.

On behalf of the people and government of Bangladesh, Bongobondhu immediately acknowledged Trudeau's letter, in which Trudeau expressed warm greetings and congratulations to the government and the people of Bangladesh. Bongobondhu reiterated his government's policy, which was "to create a just society in Bangladesh founded on the ideals of nationalism, democracy, secularism, and socialism"[91] and reassured that the people of Bangladesh were committed to developing a very close relationship and understanding with Canada for each country's mutual benefit.

Unsurprisingly, Pakistan's high commissioner to Canada, who had reacted negatively upon hearing about the news of Canada's recognition of Bangladesh, instantly expressed his profound "regret at the decision [by Canada] to accord recognition to Bangladesh."[92] In a desperate attempt at what seemed to be a lost cause, an outraged high commissioner argued that "Canada's decision is not in accordance with either the UN General Assembly's resolution of December 7, 1971, or with the accepted principles for recognition of sovereign states."[93] Ottawa officials did not attach any importance to the high commissioner's stubborn appeal this time since the matter was already a *fait accompli*. A relaxed Sharp thanked all those involved in the process and referred to some of the most significant diplomatic challenges he successfully overcame. It was all hoped that by recognizing Bangladesh early, Canada would make India happy and not incur Bhutto's wrath.

Establishment of Diplomatic Missions and Immediate Challenges Following Recognition

Canada recognized an immediate need to tackle a general perception of Bangladesh as dependent on India, discouraging many countries, even in February 1972, from recognizing newborn Bangladesh as a sovereign country. Ottawa officials quickly identified the following two key areas of priority: (1) the removal of the perception of Bangladesh as a client state of India and (2) the establishment of diplomatic missions between Canada and Bangladesh ASAP. The general perception of the image of Bangladesh under India's strong influence was believed to be stronger than the truth, as observed by Undersecretary Ritchie. His advice to the minister was that "in view of Bangladesh's efforts to become less politically dependent on India and our own concern over the means by which Bangladesh was separated from Pakistan, it would make sense to conduct our diplomatic relations with the Mujib government from another country,"[94] other than India. To demonstrate to the rest of the world the complete independence of the government of Bangladesh, Sharp concurred with Ritchie and advised him to find a country other than India to continue Canada's diplomatic relations with Bangladesh in the interim.

In passing, readers may find it interesting to note what Prime Minister Edward Heath said about his offer of the British Royal Air Force comet jet to Bongobondhu and his response when Bongobondhu returned to Bangladesh from Pakistan. While returning to Bangladesh after Bhutto released him, Heath noted that Bongobondhu expressed his wishes by speaking "with confidence and assurance."[95] "He [Mujib] was anxious to return home as soon as possible, and we provided him with an RAF aircraft for his onward journey. It was his choice not to transfer to an

Indian aircraft in Delhi where he saw Mrs. Gandhi,"[96] observed Heath. It's important to note that Bongobondhu wanted to fly to Dhaka directly, but he was not given any choice by Bhutto, who suggested flying via Tehran, but Bongobondhu refused. Bhutto then offered London, and Bongobondhu agreed.[97] Even though a thoughtful Bongobondhu remained in the dark for nine long months, he must have been alert to put some thoughts along the line that the newly independent Bangladesh could perhaps be seen as a client state of India. Unsurprisingly, he did not take advantage of the Indian Government's offer then. He accepted Heath's offer instead.

Immediately following the recognition of Bangladesh, Ottawa wanted to make sure that Canada's relationship with Pakistan and India did not get strained. With that objective in mind, Ottawa summoned James George and John Small, high commissioners to India and Pakistan, respectively, to Ottawa for a consultation on February 29, 1972. Included in the agenda were questions like the following: What is the likely course of Pakistan's future relations with India, China, and the USSR? Whether Pakistan is likely to return to the Commonwealth? What is the expected level of immigration, etc.?[98]

In the meantime, Macquarrie, having recognized the contribution of Canadians of all backgrounds, spoke on behalf of all Canadians "that the people of Canada did take an interest in this [Bangla Desh]. Of course, we did not do as much as we could, or perhaps should have done, but Canadians from one end of the country to the other did assist and contribute to that terrible story of human suffering that went on in the refugee camps of Bengal."[99] Macquarrie continued, "Bangla Desh deserves a separate mission, and the thing to do is to send in a *charge d'affaires* immediately and to build your establishment on that."[100]

Once there had been some progress in the last two months since the liberation, Ray Perrault, parliamentary secretary to the minister of Manpower and Immigration, provided detailed information about the diplomatic mission in Dhaka, Bangladesh. Canada established her relationship with Bangladesh on March 20, 1972, when the Canadian ambassador in Bangkok, Mr. Gordon Edwin Cox, a representative of the government of Canada, reached Dhaka for his first visit. Ottawa double-accredited Cox to represent Canada. Gordon took a full-time assignment on June 8, 1972, but remained in Bangladesh for a short period (barely four months) as he left on August 26, 1972. Following his departure came Gordon George Riddell on June 8, 1972, who stayed for two years and left on June 16, 1974. It was recommended that two additional officers, one from External Affairs and one from the Canadian International Development Agency (CIDA), be posted to Bangkok with responsibilities for Bangladesh.[101]

In the meantime, veteran Bengali diplomat Abdul Momin came to Ottawa as the first high commissioner to Canada in February 1972. Momin presented his credentials within days on March 3, 1972.[102] This remains as an instance of the note of urgency with which Canada treated the matter, a commendable gesture as it generally takes several months before the prime minister can receive any incoming high commissioner or ambassador for a formal meeting. Immediately following his meeting with Bangladesh's high commissioner, Trudeau himself expressed Canada's desire to undertake various programs in Bangladesh that were not just a desire of the government but also of the people of Canada. Naturally, Bangladesh was pleased to receive Trudeau's "assurance of continued assistance" for the welfare of Bangladesh when they heard how Canadians "felt strongly that they should give help to the war-devastated country."[103] Thus, the Minister of Foreign Affairs of the government of Bangladesh was updated by High Commissioner Momin.

Moving forward, Cox and Riddell, the two Canadian high commissioners to Bangladesh, recognized that the new government would require some time for capacity building to develop a cohesive, differentiated, specialized, and competent bureaucracy out of the refractory materials that history had bequeathed it. Cox believed that bureaucracies and foreign services could never be created overnight by reengineering the ministries, designing the organizational charts, hiring favorite people, or putting activities in high gear. After Cox's departure, Riddell followed the same vein, believing that mitigating the attitudinal baggage, or the pervasive Pakistani mentality of the military, intelligence, and bureaucracy, would be challenging. Bangladesh would also require time to follow the inevitable upheaval of transition; the new administration would not be able to begin to work until Bangladesh stabilized its currency and revalued its assets.

A gradual generation of adequate revenues, accumulation, and centralization of power would enable the government to exercise effective control within its territory and implement complex policies independently without India or Pakistan's influence. Thus, Sharp was advised. Canada was glad to see the support for Bongobondhu as the father of the nation both in the National Assembly and the country, which was nearly unanimous.

Canada also recognized that her representatives in Bangladesh would need to focus on advocacy by promoting Canada's exports, explaining her policies, protecting her citizens, and assisting in establishing democracy and human rights in Bangladesh. For all such activities, a distinct *esprit de corps* would have to be created, argued Canada.

When Riddell got into the swing of things, he wondered, once the euphoria of independence dissipated, it would probably be increasingly the bread-and-butter issues that would begin to affect his widespread support. The Trudeau administration successfully identified its top priority as working with a clean slate as they related to Bangladesh, Pakistan, and India in the changed circumstances. An important point to note is that though an ally of the United States, Canada was no longer amenable to American advice or any arms-twisting following the birth of Bangladesh. As mentioned already, Canada's feelings of uneasiness were gone forever. Ottawa officials, however, were aware of how the United States was driven not just by the Cold War calculations but by a starkly personal dislike of India and Indians and supported a murderous regime. Given the gritty reality of war-torn Bangladesh, Sharp was advised that Canada must have an effective regional strategy linking its objectives, priorities, and interests.

Canada's Efforts to Bring Bangladesh into the Commonwealth of Nations

Although the detailed information is missing, a secret telegram from John Small, the Canadian high commissioner to Pakistan, reveals that, as early as March 1971, he met with Bongobondhu in Dhaka as part of his regular courtesy visits. We alluded to this in Chapter 2. In that meeting, Bongobondhu stated his desire to remain in the Commonwealth if Bangladesh became independent.[104] Although Canada was delighted with the news of the release of Bongobondhu by Bhutto, she was aware that Bhutto's actions and reactions were unpredictable. Canada also noted how, before reaching home, Bongobondhu formally expressed his strong desire to join the Commonwealth while going to Bangladesh via London.

With such information on hand, naturally, Canada immediately became interested in extending her network to bring Bangladesh into the Commonwealth at the first opportunity. Having received *carte blanche* from Ottawa to work with Arnold Smith, secretary general of the Commonwealth, High Commissioner Small began developing a strategy regarding Bangladesh's entry into the Commonwealth. He identified at least the following four challenges that lay ahead to bring together for consideration: (1) profound conniption of Bhutto, (2) peace and security in the Indian subcontinent, (3) historical linkage of the newborn country with the Commonwealth, and (4) the desire of the prime minister of Bangladesh, much to President Bhutto's abhorrence. Canada was already aware of Bhutto's accusation of the Commonwealth that it was siding with pro-Bangladeshis, for which he was ready to leave the Commonwealth. Canada also knew that many editorials in Pakistani newspapers were not very complimentary about Smith's role during the Bengalis' struggle for independence. With that background in mind, Ottawa's first challenge was to deal with the choler of Bhutto, who had been making conflicting statements.

To plead with Bhutto against Pakistan's withdrawal, the first since South Africa withdrew in 1961, Smith flew to Pakistan at the invitation of Bhutto on January 30, 1972. Given the uncertain reality in Pakistan, Smith was apprehensive about the outcome of his scheduled meeting with Bhutto. He was a bit disappointed to read in *The Morning News* of January 31, 1972, the reported news that, during the crisis, Smith did not "uphold the Commonwealth principles concerning the relationship between the members." From Pakistan's way of thinking, Smith and Canada could have been optimistic by supporting the cause of the Yahya government.

When Smith met with Bhutto on February 1, 1972, he did not know whether Bhutto had already announced to withdraw from the Commonwealth and sever Pakistan's links with the Commonwealth. Bhutto's move came in anticipation of the recognition of Bangladesh by Great Britain, Australia, Canada, and New Zealand. Smith was made to understand that Bhutto believed that the United States, China, and France would remain among the big powers to hold off. An enraged Bhutto claimed that his decision was final and irrevocable. Although embarrassed, Smith's talk with Bhutto went well, as far as Smith was concerned. Later on, while discussing Bhutto's reaction, Smith said in an interview in India that he regarded Bhutto's decision to leave the Commonwealth as "hasty, unwise and foolish"[105] Having regretted Bhutto's hasty decision to withdraw Pakistan's membership from the Commonwealth, an optimist, Smith, expressed his hope by saying that "in due course, it might be reversed"[106] by Bhutto. "If Pakistan applies for reentry into the Commonwealth, her application would be sympathetically considered by Commonwealth members."[107] Thus was Smith's offer on the table to an upset Bhutto.

Moving forward, Smith remained firm in his message to the rest of the world—that Bangladesh was a reality and that she fulfilled the standard criteria for recognition of a state. Smith busily lobbied the senior Commonwealth member countries for Bangladesh and boldly faced serious questions from the news media. In London, BBC's Christopher Serpell asked him point blank, "Do you feel from the point of view of other members of the Commonwealth that the presence of Indian troops in Bangladesh limits that country's autonomy or independence?"[108] Smith promptly responded, "Bangladesh has just got over a very difficult civil war with assistance from the Indian troops. Sheikh Mujib and his colleagues have authority and power because of a tremendous victory in genuinely democratic and free elections supervised by the government of Pakistan. There is no question about the source of their authority—it's democracy, it's the will of the people."[109]

In the meantime, Sharp's Ottawa team, which had also been working closely with Smith, followed two-fold approaches. The first approach was to strengthen his argument by referring to New Delhi's announcement that the Indian forces would be withdrawn by March 25, 1972, and that the Bangladesh government's preparation to celebrate March 26, 1972, as its first Independence Day also provided Smith with enough evidence of its true sense of independence. The second approach was to show the members of the Commonwealth that Pakistan's already established links with the Commonwealth included both West and East Pakistan (now Bangladesh). Since major Canadian newspapers covered Smith's continuing efforts in soliciting support from the Heads of Commonwealth countries, Canadians remained posted on Smith's sojourns. In one of its reports, *The Globe and Mail* wrote, "No adverse comment so far has been received from any member state, the former Canadian diplomat said."[110]

Again, during one of his visits to Bangladesh, while lobbying was still going on, Smith also met with President Justice Abu Sayeed Chowdhury on February 23, 1972, and held separate meetings with the following: Tajuddin Ahmed (finance minister), Mustafizur Rahman Siddiqi (commerce and trade minister), A. H. M. Kamruzzaman (relief and rehabilitation minister), and Professor Yusuf Ali (education minister). They also discussed the possible effects of the British entry into the European Economic Community (EEC) vis-à-vis Bangladesh's prospects for trade among the Commonwealth countries, bilateral Commonwealth fund for reconstruction and rebuilding, and multilateral Commonwealth fund for technical assistance cooperation (CFTC) that came into operation on April 1, 1971, following the January meeting of the Commonwealth Heads of Governments in Singapore. Fortuitously, George P. Kidd, then director of CFTC and formerly vice president of CIDA, was also a Canadian.

After months of negotiation, Smith's effort came to fruition when he finally persuaded the Nigerian leader, General Gowon, who was thus far opposed to recognizing Bangladesh. Based on Smith's persistent diplomatic pressure, the Nigerian General agreed not to oppose Bangladesh's admission into the Commonwealth. Much to Smith's credit, he won the approval not only of Nigeria but also a host of other members of the Commonwealth in Africa. By then, twenty-eight of the thirty Commonwealth countries had supported the application, although many of these countries had not yet recognized Bangladesh. Only Tanzania and Uganda were reported to have declined Smith's request. On April 18, 1972, Bangladesh became a member of the Commonwealth.

Smith welcomed Bangladesh as the thirty-second member of the Commonwealth. It was a unique occasion - the first time in the Commonwealth's history since a country's entry into the Commonwealth had not been a formality. An overjoyed Smith alluded to the fact that the Commonwealth's newest member was, in fact, one of the oldest because twenty-five years ago, the people of Bangladesh (then East Pakistan, a part of Pakistan) had been the founders of the multi-racial Commonwealth. It was an exhilarating scene to behold. Former Bangladesh ambassador Syed Abdus Sultan sported a tie featuring a Bangladeshi map. He would soon be transformed into the first high commissioner of Bangladesh stationed in Great Britain.

Meanwhile, Commonwealth Secretary-General Arnold Smith—who first arrived wearing an Oxford Christ Church tie—reappeared after Bangladesh's admission to the Commonwealth wearing a tie decorated with a photo of Bangladesh. The high commissioner had presented it. Similarly, with Bangladesh's entry into the Commonwealth, Canadian ambassador Gordon Cox's title changed from ambassador to high commissioner. Amid all the joy and euphoria, Sultan, Bangladesh's high commissioner, observed, "We are no strangers to the Commonwealth, and in applying for membership, we were only motivated by the desire to continue and further strengthen the happy relations that exist between Bangladesh and the other members of the Commonwealth."[111]

Canada's effort to bring Bangladesh into the Commonwealth remains an example of a success story that resulted from Smith's diplomatic maneuvering with Pakistan and other Commonwealth members. The untiring work of the distinguished Canadian diplomat is a genuine instance of shuttle diplomacy on the international stage.

Efforts Toward Bangladesh's Admission to the UN

Canada was pleasantly aware of Bongobondhu's recent statement on Bangladesh's foreign policy in January 1972: "Bangladesh believes in a foreign policy of friendship to all and malice to none."[112] Since Canada was fully satisfied that the government under the leadership of Bongobondhu had already established its authority over every inch of the soil of Bangladesh, her next challenge was to lobby for UN membership.

At that time, Canada was convinced that the sovereignty and authority of the State were wholly and solely enforced by her forces and other law-enforcing agencies with the full cooperation of the people of Bangladesh. Simultaneously, therefore, while pushing the envelope for Bangladesh's admission to the UN, Canada also began to lobby for Bangladesh's membership to the International Telecommunication Union (ITU) to help Bangladesh maintain a close liaison with the development of the Telegraph and Telephone System. Records indicate that Canada played an important role in expediting Bangladesh's membership to the ITU and successfully secured the membership on September 4, 1973, almost two weeks ahead of securing the UN membership for Bangladesh.[113]

Canada networked with several key players, especially the People's Republic of China, regarding Bangladesh's admission to the UN. Sharp's visit to China between August 15 and 24, 1972, included several rounds of discussions with Chinese Foreign Minister Chou En Lei and other leaders in Peking (now Beijing) on this subject to which Canada attached great importance even when she had not recognized Bangladesh. Sharp's discussion with the Chinese leaders centered around two areas of concern they had expressed earlier. The first item was China's decision to veto Bangladesh's admission to the UN. However, she "would prefer the whole issue to be postponed until later when outstanding issues between Bangladesh and Pakistan had been resolved on a bilateral basis."[114] The second item was that Bangladesh had not honored the UN Security Council resolution of last December 1971 calling for the release of the prisoners of war (POWs). "If the POW issue is settled, China may withdraw her objection"[115] to Bangladesh's admission to the UN. Thus, China expressed her position.

Canada, too, had concerns about the POWs and believed that, in the interests of an overall settlement and a durable peace in the subcontinent, the Government of Bangladesh should be flexible on the POWs issue. Canada counseled the critical players in the Bongobondhu administration to "show magnanimity" and that one "should look forward and not backward."[116] Ottawa officials shared with the Bangladesh high commissioner the outcome of their conversation with Pakistan regarding war crimes trials and Pakistan's inclination to accept the idea of trials of individual officers under the existing laws by existing courts. Pakistan was opposed to the concept of a war crimes trial, which somehow might connote a sense of collective guilt on the part of all Pakistanis. Canada went back and forth between the Bongobondhu and Bhutto administrations and negotiated more in favor of Bangladesh under certain conditions.

Canada came up with a proposal about the POWs that could be satisfactorily resolved if "Pakistan would be willing to co-sponsor Bangladesh's membership application."[117] Diplomatically, Canada maintained the same technique she used during lobbying for Bangladesh's entry into the Commonwealth by reinforcing the point that the country now called Bangladesh (erstwhile East Pakistan, then a part of a united Pakistan) had already been participating in many of the UN activities over a wide field from the time Pakistan became a member of the UN.

Within weeks, Canada succeeded in her efforts to get Bangladesh UN membership. Much to the delight of Canada and those countries that joined hands in lobbying with her, Bangladesh obtained UN membership on September 17, 1974, as a full member of several international organizations of the UN family, including WHO, ILO, IMF, and IRBD, having received the overwhelming support of the member states.

Canada was convinced that Bangladesh's admission to these international organizations reflected not only the readiness of the Bangladeshi government to play its rightful role in various fields of international cooperation but also the confidence of the world community in its willingness and ability to do so as a crucial sovereign country. Canada ought to be commended for her diplomatic overtures in the international arena.

Immediate and Short-range Canadian Development Projects in Bangladesh

Before Canada recognized Bangladesh, she was in an awkward position as there were some legal implications for two facts. First, Pakistan requested the suspension of all aid disbursements to what it continued to refer to as "East Pakistan." This was even though Pakistan had been trimmed against existing loans. It also requested that no new aid commitments for "East Pakistan" be entered into pending clarification of its political status. Second, until the government of Canada recognized Bangladesh as a sovereign country, CIDA officials' hands were tied while awaiting formal recognition. At that time, under the circumstances, CIDA officials were able to identify several priority areas while Canada was still examining the most "politically correct" moment to accord recognition.

With Canada's recognition of Bangladesh on February 14, 1972, however, gone were the roadblocks and the consequent unease of the government concerning her assistance to the newborn country. Seeing the tragic situation of the war-ravaged Bangladesh, a great many Canadians were deeply concerned. Unsurprisingly, other departments also came forward to offer help. In a letter to Sharp, Health and Welfare minister of the day, John Munro, for example, also expressed his desire to assist the war-torn Bangladesh in whatever capacity his department could. He wrote, "I am hopeful that, while the current political situation in this area is one calling for extreme delicacy, some means can be found to apply with benefit the resources we have readily available."[118]

John McRae, then head of CIDA's NGO division, who had been to Bangladesh a few times while the Bengalis' struggle for independence was going on, argued that first and foremost, Bangladesh needed the basics—a guaranteed flow of aid funds to give her people the initial boost to rebuild her shattered economy. With a desire to pursue both immediate and short-range plans as well as long-term sustained development program rather than episodic commitment, it was decided that "there would be no further development loans to WestPak [West Pakistan] until that country had made some move to clarify its position concerning the debt moratorium, the sharing of the debt with East Bengal [East Pakistan, now Bangladesh] and developed an economic program for the West."[119] Since it was out of the question to establish a bilateral development assistance program in Bangladesh pending recognition, for the interim, Canada preferred to focus on (1) relief and rehabilitation through appropriate UN agencies, such as UNHCR, Canadian Red Cross Society, as well as Canadian voluntary agencies already engaged in Bangladesh, and (2) reconstruction and development.[120]

McRae and his team continued to liaise with foreign countries and international organizations that had already been involved in the following two broad areas of assistance: rehabilitation of the infrastructure and relief of the immediate needs of the people. Paul Gérin-Lajoie, CIDA's president, visited Bangladesh in the spring of 1972 to see for himself the needs of the newborn country. However, he had already visited earlier when the liberation war occurred. McRae brought Gérin-Lajoie up to speed about the CIDA-supported relief and rehabilitation work undertaken before the liberation. Emil Baran, the Dhaka-based CIDA representative in Bangladesh, also briefed Gérin-Lajoie on McRae's exploration of new projects in war-ravaged Bangladesh. All those involved in the work were pleased to note how the reawakened Bengalis had been developing a sense of cooperation that had "not stopped with the winning of the war."[121]

During his mission in Bangladesh, McRae met with Bengali workers, technicians, farmers, professors, doctors, and others enthusiastically engaged in promoting their country's development work. McRae did not overlook certain negative aspects about young people riding the *Mukti Bahini* (Liberation Forces) bandwagon by apparently expressing loyalty to Bongobondhu but was engaged in hooliganism. McRae was disheartened when he saw many freedom fighters who were no longer idealistic about continuing to fight for their country's good. It was disturbing to note how serious crises and dire warnings of worse situations punctuated the road to social justice and equality of opportunity. An utterly frank McRae alluded to his fear of widespread criminality and semi-official extortions by the members of the *Mukti Bahini* (Liberation Forces), whose anti-social activities ranged from "open banditry to extreme social pressure," many of whom were busy "feathering their own nests."[122]

Nevertheless, being aware of Bangladesh's growing and diverse needs and the complex nature of the problems and challenges Bangladesh faced, an experienced McRae thought about another way Canada could extend her help. Given that Canada is the birthplace of the Antigonish Movement,[123] McRae recommended, "A grant to help them do this, followed perhaps by a cooperative-to-cooperative relationship between Canada and Bangladesh, could be a very creative form of social assistance at a point where it is urgently needed."[124]

McRae then made the following three formal recommendations: (1) a $500,000 grant and technical support be given to the youth leadership training and development program sponsored jointly by the Bangladesh Co-operative Union and the Rural Development and Co-operative Division of the Bangladesh Ministry of Local Government, Rural Development and Cooperatives; (2) an amount of up to $600,000 be set aside, on a matching basis, for rehabilitation development projects being administered among weavers, fishermen, small artisans, and cooperatives by CORR (Christian Organization for Relief and Rehabilitation), BERRS (Bangladesh Ecumenical Relief and Rehabilitation Services) and other Canadian supported agencies; and (3) an immediate grant of up to $1 million is made available to CORR to enable it to continue its agricultural rehabilitation work in the drought-stricken Western region.[125] It was also recommended that the government of Canada should encourage "the Canadian Cooperative Union, or other appropriate agencies to link up with their Bangladeshi counterparts in order to facilitate further Canada-Bangladesh cooperation in this area of social development."[126]

Canadian religious organizations also demonstrated their interest in assisting Bangladesh. Dr. Edward Hewlett Johnson, Director of Overseas of the Presbyterian Church and representative of the Canadian Council of Churches, for example, went to Bangladesh in March 1972 to assess the degree of rehabilitation work. "The Roman Catholics had an organization throughout the four dioceses led by a remarkable Canadian, Father Benjamin Labbé. The World Council of Churches had begun a program closely relating aid from Canada and other nations to the Relief and Rehabilitation Ministry of the Bangla Desh Government. And Raymond Cournoyer of OXFAM was proposing that OXFAM should provide three-thousand-foot bailey bridges to help restore road communications,"[127] a satisfied Johnson wrote upon his return to Canada.

Again, in his commendation of the Canadian Holy Cross Brother Raymond Cournoyer for his dynamic leadership, Dr. Johnson noted how having gathered strength, "Bangla Desh has made a good beginning," [128] as the Bengalis did not just want to survive but to flourish in the newborn country. Johnson also met with Mustafizur R. Siddiqi, minister of Trade and Commerce, and other dignitaries. "One of the helpful signs for the country is the leadership of Sheikh Mujibur Rahman. I was able to visit him briefly one evening with Mr. Siddiqi,"[129] Thus, Johnson passionately recalled his impression of Bongobondhu, who was at the pinnacle of popularity as the most competent leader in the country.

At the same time, John Hay, Ottawa staff of the Canadian Press, had reason to be a bit apprehensive of the future of Bangladesh, the eighth most populous country in the world. Although "Prime Minister Mujibur Rahman has pictured Bangladesh as the future 'Switzerland of Asia,' thriving on new industries with goods to set to the world,"[130] Hay was unsure of the future despite the dedication and commitment of the people of Bangladesh. "For several months every year, half the land is submerged, inundated by the hundreds of shifting rivers that lace the country, fed by Himalayan snows and the monsoon rains. And every fall, farmers and fisherman live under the threat of the cyclones that brew in the Bay of Bengal and sometimes turn viciously inward,"[131] maintained Hay, who became slightly disappointed at the nature of things in Bangladesh.

Despite Bongobondhu's optimistic and forward-looking views, an observant Hay did not fail to notice that, even though there was the presence of devoted democratic and fervent nationalists, there also existed a milieu where the gripping legacy of Pakistani modus operandi still prevailed. Echoing a few other alarmists, Hay feared that during the initial period, some of the military mores might continue to coexist with the new ruling elites, especially those with a pro-Pakistani stance.

The Trudeau administration watched how the quislings and collaborators were being apprehended for another legitimate fear of the reaction of the victims of the past. Many were seeking retribution or were trying to settle a personal score. Canada feared that a "witch hunt" could create more hatred, resulting in a slowdown in the reform process. Ottawa also believed that much of the intelligence of the Bengalis would, in an uneasy symbiosis, continue to grow in both breadth and depth; as well, the road to civil society for Bangladeshis would undoubtedly be long and arduous because they would have to overcome not only the military legacy but also the mentality that instilled submission to strong and willful authority, teaching its people how to survive and succeed. Viewed from this angle, from the start, Bangladesh would have to construct a distinct cultural and political identity of her national interest at a time of conflicting trends toward integration and fragmentation. Canada tried to find an answer to the following question: How will Bangladesh fit into the global order?

In 1972, both the Canadian government and NGO workers saw Bangladesh as a country with tremendous potential where democracy must run a gauntlet of challenges. They happily concluded that being surrounded by its newly made friend neighboring India (hitherto Pakistan's arch-enemy), Bangladesh would not face the threat of war like before. Canada hoped that Bangladesh would get an opportunity to take matters into her own hands, using the power she had gained to build a democratic and economically sustainable country.

Canada believed that Bangladesh could go to the heart of creating solid economic institutions, a transparent regulatory regime and a judiciary with integrity following a gradual expansion of democratic institutions and ideals. Canadian observers were impressed with the Bengalis' sense of optimism and sheer determination with which they defined themselves as to who they were in their native land, Bangladesh. Canadians recognized how, with hope and hard work, Bangladeshis were already in complete control of their life within a very short period.

Reinforcement of Friendship Between Canada and Bangladesh

The friendship between Canada and Bangladesh has grown since Bangladesh became independent in December 1971. Historically, the foundation of the present-day friendship was laid in the early 1950s when Bangladesh was a part of a united Pakistan. This started with the exchange visits of the prime ministers of Canada and Pakistan as each other's guests. In June 1950, then Pakistan's Prime Minister Liakat Ali Khan was a guest of Canada who was welcomed by Prime Minister Louis St. Laurent warmly and enthusiastically in the House of Commons with a passionate speech, "The future of Pakistan, notwithstanding differences in religion and language, in customs and habits, notwithstanding lands and oceans which separate it from Canada, is closely related to our own through our common association in the United Nations, our partnership in the Commonwealth, and, most of all, in our common belief in those values which form the very basis of democratic life. We hope that our association will become closer and closer as we get to know each other better."[132]

By turn, Ali also talked about Canada's "wealth of natural resources," her "progressive yet modest outlook," and her "wide international sympathies."[133] He then concluded his remarks by saying the following: "I am sure we can look forward to a long period of friendship between our two countries, and that in any joint moral undertaking to promote the welfare of mankind and goodwill and peace among nations, Pakistan and Canada will be more than friends. God bless your country and its people."[134]

Fast forward to 1972, the two countries, Bangladesh (erstwhile East Pakistan) and Canada, renewed their friendship again under a different political landscape and national identity. Canada was impressed to see how, with a forward-looking approach, Bongobondhu and his Cabinet made sure when to push reform and when to hold back with the knowledge of the adaptation to the theory and practice of diplomacy and development assistance. Canadians were satisfied that the Bongobondhu administration was championing economic reform, especially the financial challenges that could transcend national politics. Following his return from Bangladesh in early 1974, Heath Macquarrie, MP from PEI, wrote a personal note to Trudeau, "Sheikh Mujibur extends his good wishes to you, and I am happy to be the vehicle of such intra-Commonwealth greetings. I am sure he would be delighted to have you visit his country and, knowing the extremely high regard in which Canadians are held, I am sure that the people of Bangladesh would welcome such a visit on your part. I am also advising Mr. Stanfield of this aspect of Canada-Bangladesh goodwill." [135]

He continued, "Among others with whom we held discussions was Mr. Tofael Ahmed, the prime minister's chief protocol advisor, who was with him in Ottawa. He was very specific in extending an invitation for you to go to Bangladesh. I told him that, while I was not a member of the Liberal Party, there was no partisan division in Canada on the question of friendship with Bangladesh and that I would be delighted and honored to convey his invitation. This I now do and add the personal hope that, before very long, a prime minister of Canada will be able to visit our good friend and fellow Commonwealth nation, Bangladesh."[136]

Canada remained interested in building confidence and goodwill between Canada and Bangladesh and finding a common ground to create a positive relationship. Canada recognized that the issue of justice and retribution was, and still is, a profoundly personal and private affair for each country from the beginning concerning Bangladesh. All through 1972 and mid-1973, Canada remained committed to bringing all three countries, India, Pakistan, and Bangladesh, face-to-face through a formula for restoring friendly, harmonious, and good neighborly relations among them. Fortunately for Bangladesh, within an unusually short time, Canada discussed with Gandhi during her visit to Ottawa and agreed to a proposal that the differences should be resolved bilaterally.

The joint communiqué issued at the end of Ghandhi's visit reflects the sincere efforts of India and Canada with the following statement: "The Prime Minister of India explained the latest developments on the Indian subcontinent identifying the joint Indo-Bangladesh declaration of April 17 as a sincere initiative to resolve humanitarian problems resulting from the conflict of 1971, designed to promote durable peace and cooperation in the area. The Prime Minister of Canada expressed appreciation for the efforts being made to break the present impasse. The two Prime Ministers [Trudeau and Gandhi] agreed that a durable settlement of outstanding problems should be achieved through negotiations among the countries of the sub-continent."[137] Canada ensured that the process for the repatriation of the Bengalis in Pakistan and the return of the Pakistani POWs (prisoners of war) worked out without further delay as elaborately as possible. The joint Communiqué reveals Canada's interest in seeing that "indeed it will be on the basis that a satisfactory and durable settlement can really be achieved."[138]

Canada was in favor of the agreement that stipulated that "the Pakistani prisoners of war now in India should be released except those charged with war crimes, that the Biharis in Bangladesh who have opted for Pakistani citizenship be permitted to return to Pakistan, and that the Bengalees who are detained in Pakistan who wish to return to Bangladesh should be permitted to do so."[139] The MPs urged Sharp to use his "good offices and those of the Canadian Government to assist in securing an arrangement by negotiations."[140]

They believed this "would contribute to alleviating great human distress in the subcontinent as well as to the peaceful and neighborly relations between the three countries involved."[141] At the same time, having thought through various individual requirements for Bangladesh, Canada concluded that peace and prosperity would require fundamental political and economic reform in newborn Bangladesh and a cordial relationship with India and Pakistan. Canada was happy to note that Bongobondhu's extraordinary charisma reinforced the friendship between Bangladesh and Canada. As a true friend of Bangladesh, Canada's effort in maintaining her friendship with Bangladesh and resolving other associated issues, no doubt, is commendable.

Bongobondhu joins the 19th Commonwealth Conference in Canada in 1973 (August 2-10)

The nine-day Commonwealth Conference held in Canada's capital, Ottawa, was attended by thirty-three nations representing 850 million people.

Heads of government warmly welcomed the prime ministers of Bangladesh and The Commonwealth of the Bahamas, whose countries had become members of the Commonwealth since the last meeting in 1971. The two country leaders were introduced in glowing terms to make them feel warmly welcomed to the Commonwealth Club. Feeling deeply honored, both leaders expressed gratitude to the prime minister of Canada for the hospitality provided by his government. Right at the beginning of the meeting, heads of government stated on the tenth anniversary of the signing of the Treaty Banning Nuclear Weapon Tests in the Atmosphere, in Outer Space, and Under Water."[142] "The meeting examined various aspects of development assistance, including the disadvantages of tied aid, the need for a more flexible approach by aid donors, and the importance of achieving mutually satisfactory relationships between the donors and recipients of aid as well as measures for reducing onerous debt burdens of developing countries."[143]

Since Bangladesh was still working on her priorities, the government techniques were of interest to Bangladeshi representatives who knew that Bangladesh's cupboard was bare. "They had a lively and useful discussion which included consideration of such subjects as the determination of national priorities; the problem of ensuring effective implementation of government decisions, fostering communication between government and people; and the problem of correcting economic imbalances between urban and rural areas,"[144] as stated in the communiqué. On the second day, it was reported that Bongobondhu "was stricken with a bronchial infection and will not attend this weekend's Commonwealth conference session at Mont Tremblant, Québec."[145]

Bongobondhu's personal physician, Dr. Nurul Islam, was flown into Ottawa to attend the ailing prime minister. At the same time, holding his head up, Foreign Minister Kamal Hossain represented the rest of the meetings. Prime Minister Trudeau was reported to have described the August 7 meeting as "especially valuable" since it gave donor countries a chance to hear the complaints of recipients of foreign aid. The complaint was that Canada's "aid is tied to Canadian goods and services." "At the present time, recipient countries are required to spend a minimum of two-thirds of aid funds in Canada,"[146] it was reported in the media. For the participants, Canada announced her future position regarding the tied aid provision, "We are prepared to be as loose in our development aid position as can be sustained by political support."[147]

Mark Gayn, who covered the conference and had been to Dhaka both during the war and following the liberation of Bangladesh, found

Bongobondhu manifestly superior in displaying his exuberant optimism. He recalled Bongobondhu's remarks regarding the world communities' sympathies toward the suffering Bengalis and his determination to get on with his job of rebuilding the war-ravaged Bangladesh. "We had the help of our friends, the Americans, the Canadians. The Japanese, the Russians. I want to single out the Canadians. They acted promptly, and they were generous."[148] Thus, Gayn reminded Canadians of how Bongobondhu remembered the world communities' positive role in 1971 with gratitude - something grounded in historical fact.

Continuing along the same vein, the media coverage of Bongobondhu and his team's welcoming advent in Canada was noticeable everywhere, even in remote areas. When Tofail Ahmed, political secretary to Prime Minister Sheikh Mujibur Rahman, went into a nearby clothing store in Mont Tremblant, a luxury resort sixty kilometers north of Montreal, he was surprised that even shopkeepers in rural villages knew about Bangladesh's crowning achievement and the Bengalis' needs. For Ahmed, it was a case of "seeing is believing." Feeling as high as a kite, Ahmed was impressed to see how, in the wink of an eye, many merchants gathered around, wishing to send something to the people of Bangladesh. Being lost for words, Ahmed told a reporter, "A box quickly was filled with socks, shorts, and underwear."[149] A warm, enthusiastic welcome, a quintessentially Canadian manifestation, was all over - uphill and down dale. "When Ahmed went across the street into a men's wear shop, the same thing happened," wrote the *Toronto Star*.[150]

Despite his sickness, and though not as fit as a fiddle, Bongobondhu could still display his innate charm toward the end of the conference. He socialized with Prime Minister Trudeau, his wife Margaret Trudeau, and other dignitaries just before the gala performance of the folk Feux Follets ballet in the National Arts Centre, which he attended. To the vitality of a throng of reporters, Bongobondhu was reported to have remained cheerful, having kept his pecker up. Although there were some criticisms of the Commonwealth countries' positions on various issues, race relations being a hot potato, the news media saw the Conference as a step forward. The Commonwealth members agreed on a plethora of topics. The Commonwealth "is a symbol of the human family, with diverse backgrounds and differences, warts and sores, communicating with each other and trying to be a family. This is worthwhile,"[151] wrote the *Ottawa Citizen* editorial writer Azhar Ali Khan, a Canadian of Pakistani origin.

Prime Minister Pierre Trudeau's Four-day Visit to Bangladesh in November 1983

Ten years later, Prime Minister Trudeau's November 1983 visit to Bangladesh coincided with the visit of Zambian President Dr. Kenneth Kaunda. Trudeau's four-day trip with a team of twelve-member business delegates led by Jean-Pierre Goyer focused on two critical areas of mutual interest. The first agenda item was realized at a Bongobhobun (President's House) press conference with President Hussain Muhammad Ershad, where the two world leaders discussed bilateral matters and international issues. Trudeau assured the government of Bangladesh that "his country would extend assistance for the development of transportation, agriculture, and food resources in Bangladesh."[152] They signed three memorandum of understanding that included a grant of Taka 174.56 crores (Canadian dollar 87.28 million) that were to be utilized to supply industrial commodities to Bangladesh from Canada for support for agro-industrial and rural development programs. It was reported that the "grant was expected to ease the pressure on the limited foreign exchange resources and augment the development budget of Bangladesh. All Canadian assistance to Bangladesh that was given as a grant made Bangladesh the largest recipient of Canadian bilateral assistance."[153] The same newspaper stated, "Among the international issues that cropped up in the discussion were East-West problems, Kampuchea, Afghanistan, the Middle East, and other troubled spots."[154]

The second essential item was Trudeau's meeting with the Canadian business community in Bangladesh and the representatives of the Bangladesh Metropolitan Chamber of Commerce in the presence of several ministers, such as A. R. Shams-ud Doha (foreign minister), A. M. A. Muhith (finance minister), A. Z. M. Obaidullah Khan (agriculture minister), and Major-General K.M. Shafiullah (Bangladesh's high commissioner to Canada). "The products from Bangladesh would be welcome to his country like items imported by Canada from other Third World countries,"[155] reported in the news quoting Goyer. The emphasis was on the possibilities of undertaking counter trade under a particular credit program—that there was a bright prospect for importing readymade garments, jute goods, and shrimps from Bangladesh to Canada.

Personally, Trudeau was impressed to see how the government of the day was tackling and solving the challenging problems facing Bangladesh.

"It shows the sense of dedication of the people and their resolve to tackle problems,"[156] observed Trudeau. His remark was encouraging when one considers that in 1983, the war-ravaged Bangladesh was in its twelfth year only. "Bangladesh had achieved progress since its independence," and "there is solid evidence of social progress and increasing economic strength,"[157] Trudeau remarked. The message was clear that Canada would "seek new forms of cooperation based on the skills and resources of both developed and developing countries if the two countries are to create a more prosperous global community.

To mark his first visit to Bangladesh, Trudeau planted a sapling in the Smriti Shoudha [The National Martyrs Memorial) complex and said, "Let the tree grow with the prosperity of your nation and the country."[158] Symbolically, it meant a lot to the people of Bangladesh and Canada.

Donation of the Bangladesh PEACE Clock in 2010 by a Bangladeshi Canadian Philanthropist

In 2010, thirty-seven years later, following Trudeau's planting of a sapling as a symbol of friendship, Aziz Chowdhury, a Bangladeshi Canadian philanthropist, also made a gesture of continuing friendship between Canada and Bangladesh. The Bangladesh Peace Clock that stands atop a tower at the intersection of Ouellette Avenue and Wyandotte Street in downtown Windsor, Ontario, is a gift from Chowdhury. This is the story of a Bangladeshi who came to Canada empty-handed in 1967, worked hard, and made a humble living in Canada. He did not live in the lap of luxury, and yet, having lived in Windsor for close to 40 years, Chowdhury believed it was time to give back something in return to his country of adoption and country of birth. In his media interview, Chowdhury said he felt he must "do something" for Canada, where he had been living all his professional life, having left Bangladesh at twenty-eight. "I'm deeply moved by this. The clock represents peace and harmony in a troubled world,"[159] said Yakub Ali, then high commissioner of Bangladesh to Canada, who was present at the inaugural program on January 12, 2010.

To Larry Horwitz, Chair of the Downtown Business Improvement Association, the "clock represents more than just a way of telling time,"[160] The Bangladesh PEACE Clock was part of a more prominent street scraping initiative designed to beautify the Windsor city area. Again, appreciating Chowdhury's gift, Councilor Jo-Anne Gignac said that the "amount of money from a retiree is like a million-dollar gift from a large corporation—it's a message for all of us."[161] His Worship Mayor Eddie Francis said, "Chowdhury's wonderful gift brings pride to your community and represents a cultural bridge between two far-flung communities as well a reminder of the enduring peace both at home and abroad."[162] The Municipal officials commended Chowdhury for his initiatives and hoped that he would inspire other Bangladeshis in Canada to follow suit.

Six years later, in 2018, Chowdhury passed away, but the people of Windsor still remember what he said in one of his interviews, "I'm a Windsorite guy. I live here; I'm going to die here."[163] "In a way, (Chowdhury) is a godsend. He believes in the value of downtown," wrote the reporter, adding further that "the clock will act as a focal point in the city."[164]

The Bangladesh PEACE Clock was Chowdhury's dream clock. Seeing a peace clock in the downtown area is a joyous psychedelic journey for Bangladeshi Canadians who also recall Chowdhury's key role in 1971 during the War of Liberation. Chowdhury became a household name through Canadian Broadcasting Corporation's (CBC) regular radio talk shows, which raised not only awareness among Canadians of the barbarity of the Pakistani army but also disgust and hatred against the Pakistani regiment engaged in continual repression of the Bengalis back in 1971. The clock, in Chowdhury's mind, is a symbol of peace and serenity. He tells the author that he "sees the Bangladesh PEACE Clock as something that embodies discipline and the tranquility of life."[165]

Prime Minister Sheikh Hasina's Visit to Canada in September 2016

When, at the invitation of Prime Minister Justin Trudeau, then Bangladesh's Prime Minister Sheikh Hasina led a fifty-five-member delegation to Canada to attend the Global Fund Fifth Replenishment Conference in Montreal held on September 16, 2016, Bangladesh found a perfect time to acknowledge Canada's contribution formally. Bangladeshis had known about the expressed outrage of the people of Canada, their condemnation of the military dictator, and their demonstration of their sympathies for the Bengalis by coming forward to assist in every possible way to mitigate the sufferings of the victims of political domination back in 1971. Forty-five years later, in 2016, it was Bangladesh's turn to take the opportunity to articulate the sentiments of the people of Bangladesh for Canada's concerns about the suffering Bengalis during their struggle for independence.

In that sense, Hasina's visit to Canada had another vital aspect - handing over one of Bangladesh's most prestigious awards to Canada in recognition of Canada's role in the Liberation War of Bangladesh in 1971. On behalf of the people of Bangladesh, Hasina posthumously honored former Prime Minister Pierre Trudeau with the *Friends of Liberation War of Bangladesh Award*. Justin Trudeau, the current prime minister of Canada and son of the former prime minister, received the award. The most exciting part of the Award Ceremony was the warmth and enthusiasm surrounding the gleeful occasion. "The award was handed over through reminiscing the relations between the fathers of two leaders [Sheikh Mujibur Rahman and Pierre Elliott Trudeau],"[166] observed Shahidul Huq, Foreign Secretary, one of the Bangladesh delegates. Members of the audience were moved when they heard Huq's further elaboration for those who did not know that "the handing over of the Award to Pierre Trudeau's son, Canada's incumbent Prime Minister Justin Trudeau, was a mix of two things as Sheikh Hasina and Justin Trudeau both are "second generation" prime ministers."[167]

Expressing her gratitude to the people of Canada for their support of the Bengali victims of military reprisals, Hasina reminded the audience how, immediately following the liberation of Bangladesh, Canada strongly lobbied for Bangladesh's membership in the Commonwealth and the United Nations. As the bilateral meeting and Award Ceremony ended amid national pride and joy among the participants in the presence of a swath of news reporters, the two PMs nodded by saying that they looked forward to strengthening their bilateral relations through continued collaboration on issues of mutual concern. Liberation War Affairs Minister A. K. M. Mozammel Haque, Foreign Minister A. H. Mahmood Ali, and Bangladeshi High Commissioner to Canada Mizanur Rahman were present. In addition, several prominent Bangladeshi Canadians, such as Salim Zuberi, Rasheda Nawaz, Azizur Rahman Prince, Mahmud Miah, Afia Begum, Munishi Bashir, Shoma Shaifuddien, and many guests of the government of Canada were present.

Overwhelmed by the notion of love and the spirit of friendship demonstrated by the people of Canada, Hasina displayed her humility on behalf of the people of Bangladesh. She said, "I wish prosperity and happiness of the friendly people of Canada and good health, long life and happiness of his Excellency Justin Trudeau and his family members"[168] She added that she hoped that the existing friendly relations between Bangladesh and Canada would continue to grow in the coming days.

Prime Minister Sheikh Hasina's Visit to Canada in 2018

Again, from June 10-14, 2018, then Prime Minister Sheikh Hasina was on a four-day visit to Canada to attend the Outreach Session of the G7 Summit with sixteen other world dignitaries beyond the Group of Seven (G7), a platform of the world's economic powerhouses. This was also at the invitation of her Canadian counterpart, Prime Minister Justin Trudeau. In the evening, Hasina joined a dinner hosted by the governor-general of Canada in honor of heads of state and government participating in the G7 Summit and outreach program.

Sheikh Hasina joined the G7 Outreach Leaders Programme at Le Manoir Richelieu Hotel on Saturday. On Sunday morning, she met Prime Minister Trudeau at her residence at Hotel Chateau Frontenac. During the same trip, she also met and exchanged views with Bangladeshi Canadians in Toronto. The next day, on Monday, she met with the special envoy of Canada on Myanmar, Bob Rae, at her hotel, the Ritz Carlton. She also had a meeting with two Saskatchewan parliamentarians. They were Gordon Wyant, then deputy premier of Saskatchewan and minister of Education, and Jeremy Harrison, minister of Trade and Export Development and minister of Immigration and Career Training. Several business leaders from Saskatchewan also accompanied them. Before leaving Toronto, the prime minister met with the president and CEO of Commercial Corporation of Canada (CCC), Martin Zablocki, at her hotel.

Overall, it was a successful trip, and Canada and Bangladesh were satisfied.

Development of Trade and Formation of Business Organizations and Associations

Whether Canada promoted Canadian trade and business in Bangladesh or assisted Bangladesh in developing its trade, the two countries came closer over the years. Sadly, however, following the assassination of Bongobondhu, Bangladesh experienced frequent coups and countercoups and significant political upheavals in the 1970s and 1980s, including military rules and the political vicissitudes of years of uncertainty. Looking back, the reality on the ground made Ottawa lose its confidence on a few occasions in the Bangladesh government and reduce its aid to Bangladesh to a certain extent. And yet, with time, the relationship between Bangladesh and Canada has grown through mutual respect and interest. Despite everything, Canada stood by and remained at the forefront of those advocating the use of development assistance to encourage Bangladesh and other recipient countries to adopt practices that may be said to lend to good governance. Canada never gave up on Bangladesh.

Today, the friendship between the two countries is based on conditions centered on promoting mutual values. In recent years, Bangladeshi garment exports have shifted the balance of trade in favor of Bangladesh. In his farewell speech, David Preston, Canadian high commissioner to Bangladesh (from 1999 to 2002), described Canada-Bangladesh relations as "excellent."[169] This may be attributed to Canada's changing foreign policy mission or, more specifically, revised foreign policy toward Bangladesh and the global political reality. Bangladesh's free-market economy and increased trade liberalization have created enormous market potential for Canadian products in Bangladesh. In the last few years, Canadians have made significant investments in Bangladesh.

They include Apparel Design Services, Children's Clothing, Solar Energy Products, Asian Global Sourcing Ltd., Dapple Design Ltd., Canada Bangladesh Water Technologies, Creative Electric Power, and Emerging Power Limited. Canada constantly explores more pharmaceutical materials, communication technology, and plastic goods opportunities. Having sustained the friendship from the beginning of Bangladesh, several organizations and associations have been established to enhance the business relationships between Canada and Bangladesh. Today, Canada and Bangladesh are business partners that have changed the dynamics of the initial years of the relationship. Since 1972, the total Canadian aid to Bangladesh has been more than four billion dollars.

Dr. Syed Sajjadur Rahman, who held senior management positions at CIDA from 1992 to 2013, including Associate VP Policy, has made some interesting observations. Currently, a senior fellow at Norman Paterson School of International Affairs, Carleton University Ottawa, Canada, Dr. Rahman said, "Canada was one of the first contributors to indigenous

Bangladeshi development organizations like BRAC (Bangladesh-based international development organization), and the Grameen Bank and was instrumental in the emergence of many civil society organizations in Bangladesh."[170] He said, "A relationship that started as a donor-recipient construct has now evolved into a partnership where trade, investment, and strategic diplomatic considerations have started to play a more central role. Its emergence as an important 'whole of government' partner to Canada in South Asia has ramifications for both countries. Canadian aid has dwindled from over $100 million annually in the immediate post-1971 years to its current levels of around $30 million, providing credence to Bangladesh's ability to finance its development and proving that it is far from being a 'basket case.' Bangladesh is no longer dependent on external support for survival."[171]

As is the case, Canada is one of the few Western countries that have evolved its relationship with Bangladesh in response to the development needs of the latter. More specifically, in recent times, economic links such as trade, investment, and remittances have become more critical as Bangladesh embarked on a quasi-export-oriented industrialization path, starting initially with the garment industries and the expatriation of its workers. Canada is one of the few Western countries that have evolved its relationship with Bangladesh in response to its development needs. "A key milestone for Bangladesh was the declaration by Canada that products and services from Bangladesh would enjoy duty-free access to Canada." Thus, Dr. Rahman maintained that this access to Canadian markets doubled Canada's overall trade with Bangladesh within a short period to its current level of around $2 billion. "The prime beneficiaries were the Canadian consumers (in terms of access to affordable clothing) and the Bangladeshi garment industry,"[172] he added further. The two countries' interactions have brought them much closer in democracy and good governance.

Following the same vein of argument, another outstanding Bangladeshi Canadian, Dr. Mohammed Zaman, an international development specialist and advisory professor at the National Research Centre for Resettlement, Hohai University, Nanjing, China, and honorary advisor, Centre of Excellence in Management of Land Acquisition, Resettlement, and Rehabilitation, Administrative Staff College of India, Hyderabad, added further by saying that the passage of years and events have gone a long way toward alleviating one of the most abiding fears of western concerns.

Referring to the same fear or Henry Kissinger's remark that Bangladesh is a "bottomless pit" or that one was doubtful about the ability of Bangladesh to survive as a sovereign nation, Dr. Zaman speaks with confidence, showing concrete evidence of the progress Bangladesh has been making over the years. "Within fifty years, with tolerance and respect for one another, Bangladeshis have built a country that has not only acknowledged its diversity but is thriving on it,"[173] wrote Dr. Zaman.

Again, in one of his recent articles, Dr. Zaman added, "Today, in stark contrast, and defying all doubts and gloom, Bangladesh is a rising economic power, eying to take a stronger role in the region and beyond. Bangladesh will officially become a developing country in 2026 (instead of 2024 as scheduled earlier to prepare for the transition due to COVID impact on the economy) and is likely to jump into the twenty-five largest economies worldwide by 2030." [174] Until recently, continued Zaman further, "this was [thought to be] impossible. Bangladesh, including Henry Kissinger, has proven them completely wrong."[175] For that matter, by 2018, "Bangladesh had already achieved higher than the required scores in all three criteria used by the UN Committee to judge the graduation, including per capita gross national income ($1,230 or above),"[176] recalled Zaman Prime Minister Hasina at the reception accorded to her for taking the country to this new height. Today, Bangladesh is no longer a "test case" for development" wrote Dr. Zaman adding how Bangladesh has earned the status of a "learning site," according to a recent UN Human Development Report.[177]

The SAARC (South Asia Association for Regional Cooperation) heads of state who attended the Fifty Years of Independence Celebration, which also coincided with Bongobondhu Sheikh Mujibur Rahman's one hundredth birthday celebration, were loud and clear in saying that they had come to hear the Bangladesh story and learn from its successes. Having quoted the words of Prime Minister Hasina, Dr. Zaman said that "the celebration is a slap on the faces of those bottomless basket storytellers" and reminds the world of how humbled Hasina was in crediting all those involved in one way or another for this newly found elevated status in the following: "The people can achieve anything."[178]

Moving forward, the Bangladesh government is fast advancing with the help of sophisticated technologies from *Shonar Bangla* to a Smart Bangladesh, which, in layperson's terms, is a vision for a technologically advanced and sustainable nation. Being satisfied with her remarkable progress in digitization, innovation, and entrepreneurship, Bangladesh now envisages this vision based on the following four pillars: smart citizen, smart economy, smart government, and intelligent society. It is hoped that, with the use of the latest technology, Bangladedsh would reach its goal by becoming cost-effective, sustainable, knowledge-based, intelligent, and innovative, all at the same time. Despite the insurmountable challenges, the government remains resolved and optimistic to take Bangladesh to the highest level of success by transforming Bangladesh from a "digital Bangladesh" to a "smart Bangladesh" by 2041.

Nevertheless, all of a sudden, on August 5, 2024, Sheikh Hasina was forced to resign after weeks-long protests that killed over 300 people; the deposed Bangladeshi prime minister fled Dhaka by military helicopter and went to India. Bangladesh's army chief, General Waker-Uz-Zaman, facilitated Hasina's safe exit and saved the country from an inevitable bloodbath. In William Butler Yeats' language: "All changed, changed utterly; A terrible beauty is born." As the situation stands today, Bangladeshis are crying for peace, freedom, and liberty. Time will tell who will assume power and whether the former prime minister's plan is overambitious or achievable. Given our age, we are sure that many of us will not be around to watch the outcome of the government's visionary plan.

In any event, Bangladesh's friendship and partnership with Canada have been growing slowly but steadily since 1972. One might say there are instances of an ongoing cordial relationship between the two countries. Looking back, one would say that Canada's expectation that Bangladesh would have to have a written constitution incorporating the fundamental law of the land, defining precisely the rights of the citizens as well as the powers of and relationship between the various branches of government, had all been fulfilled within a short time.

Canada's active and direct diplomatic and political support for Bangladesh, with tremendous goodwill following the independence, is an instance of Canada's deep friendship with Bangladesh. Canadian assistance since 1972, along with the help of other countries, has been instrumental in achieving this. Much to Canada's profound satisfaction, Canada watched how, having worked hard and persevered, resilient and innovative Bangladeshis have adapted and prospered in the face of change. This change had made a real difference for them. Economic links such as trade, investment, and remittances have become more meaningful.

Canada's relationship with Bangladesh has evolved significantly since the early post-independence years, commensurate with Bangladesh's emergence as a middle-income country.

Recognition of Bangladesh by Countries in Chronological Order 1972–1974

Name of the Name of the country	Date of announcing *de jure* recognition	Names of the country	Date of announcing *de jure* recognition	Names of the country	Date of announcing *de jure* recognition
1. India (First Foreign and Commonwealth country)	6 December 1971	44. Indonesia	25 February 1972	88. Paraguay	21 September 1972
2. Bhutan	7 December 1971	45. Malawi	29 February 1972	89. Vatican	25 September 1972
3. German Democratic Republic (East Germany)	11 January 1972	46. Gambia	3 March 1972	90. Honduras	19 October 1972
4. Mongolia	11 January 1972	47. Ceylon (now Sri Lanka)	4 March 1972	91. Nicaragua	1 November 1972
5. Bulgaria	12 January 1972	48. Swaziland	10 March 1972	92. Ethiopia	10 November 1972
6. Poland	12 January 1972	49. Greece	11 March 1972	93. Democratic Republic of Vietnam (North Vietnam)	25 November 1972
7. Burma	15 January 1972	50. Switzerland	13 March 1972	94. Ghana	12 December 1972
8. Nepal	16 January 1972	51. Lesotho	21 March 1972	95. Afghanistan	28 February 1973
9. Barbados	20 January 1972	52. Botswana	23 March 1972	96. Lebanon	28 May 1973
10. Yugoslavia	22 January 1972	53. Jamaica	25 March 1972	97. Morocco	13 May 1973
11. Congo	24 January 1972	54. Guyana	28 March 1972	98. Algeria	16 July 1973
12. U.S.S.R (first permanent member of the Security Council)	25 January 1972	55. U.S.A.	4 April 1972	99. Tunisia	16 July 1973
13. Czechoslovakia	20 January 1972	56. Gabon	8 September 1972	100. Mauritania	16 July 1973
14. Cyprus	26 January 1972	57. Republic of Maldives	12 April 1972	101. P.R.G. (South Vietnam)	31 July 1973
15. Hungary	31 January 1972	58. Malagasy Republic	14, April, 1972	102. Ivory Coast	24 August 1973
16. Australia	31 January 1972	59. Sierre Leon	21 April 1972	103. Zaire	8 September 1973
17. New Zealand	31 January 1972	60. Laos	25 April 1972	104. Arab Republic of Egypt	15 September 1973
18. Fiji	31 January 1972	61. Liberia	26 April 1972	105. Syrian Arab Republic	15 September 1973
19. Senegal (First African Country)	1 February 1972	62. Costa Rica	2 May 1972	106. Sudan	24 September 1973
20. Denmark	4 February 1972	63. Venezuela	2 May 1972	107. Niger	24 September 1973
21. Finland	4 February 1972	64. Colombia	2 May 1972	108. Cameroon	6 October 1973
22. Sweden	4 February 1972	65. Mexico	11 May 1972	109. Guinea	9 October 1973
23. Norway	4 February 1972	66. Spain	12 May 1972	109. Jordan	16 October 1973
24. Federal Republic of Germany (West Germany)	4 February 1972	67. South Korea	12 May 1972	110. Republic of Dahomey	22 October 1973
25. United Kingdom	4 February 1972	68. El Salvador	12 May 1972	112. Kuwait	4 November 1973
26. Iceland	4 February 1972	69. Brazil	15 May 1972	113. Yemen Arab Republic	6 November 1973

27. Australia	8 February 1972	70. Argentina	25 May 1972	114. Democratic Republic of People's Korea (North)	15 December 1973
		71. Haiti	26 May 1972		
28. Western Samoa	8 February 1972	72. Chili	1 June 1972	115. Pakistan	22 February 1974
29. Cuba (First Latin American Country)	9 February 1972	73. Ecuador	6 June 1972	116. Iran	22 February 1974
Name of the country	Date of announcing *de jure* recognition	Name of the country	Date of announcing *de jure* recognition	Name of the country	Date of announcing *de jure* recognition
30. Japan	10 February 1972	74. Zambia	21 June 1972	117 Turkey.	22 February 1974
31. Ireland	11 February 1972	75. Rumania	28 June 1972	118. Nigeria	27 February 1974
32. Netherlands	11 February 1972	76. Iraq (First Arab Country)	8 July 1972	119. Qatar	4 March 1974
33. Luxemburg	11 February 1972	77. Tanzania	12 July 1972	120. United Arab Emirate	10 March 1974
34. Belgium	11 February 1972	78. Dominican	19 July 1972	121. Congo (Brazzaville)	21 March 1974
35. Italy	12 February 1972	79. Malta	21 July 1972	122. Oman	18 December 1974
				123. Portugal	20 December 1974
				124. Bahrain	26 June 1974
				125. Somalia	6 June 1974
36. Canada	14 February 1972	80. Guatemala	24 July 1972		
37. France	14 February 1972	81. People's Democratic Republic of Yemen	31 July 1972		
38. Singapore	16 February 1972	82. Peru	1 August 1972		
39. Thailand	16 February 1972	83. Bolivia	2 August 1972	129.Cambodia (Sihanouk)	30 July 1974
40. Central African Republic	16 February 1972	84. Uganda	16 August 1972		
41. Mauritius	20 February 1972	85. Uruguay	24 August 1972		
42. Philippines	24 February 1972	86. Panama	24 August 1972		
43. Malaysia (First Muslim Country)	25 February 1972	87. Upper Volta	19 September 1972		

Source: Government of the People's Republic of Bangladesh, Ministry of Foreign Affairs, Dhaka. File: Pol/7/72 Confidential Record (UN-2/4/72), dated November 8, 1975. This document was sent to all Bangladesh Missions worldwide to monitor progress. The present copy was used from the Bangladesh High Commission, Ottawa collection.

Notes and References

1. Letter addressed to the Governor General of Canada written and signed by Syed Nazrul Islam, Acting President, and Khandakar Moshtaque Ahmed, Foreign Minister of the People's Republic of Bangladesh. The letter is dated April 24, 1971. File # 20-E-Pak-1-4. Canada. Department of External Affairs. Hereinafter, all information used from the records of the External Affairs shall be referred to as External Affairs.
2. *Ibid.*

3. Memorandum for the Minister on Recognition of Bangla Desh written on June 14, 1971, by A. E. Ritchie, Undersecretary, Department of External Affairs, Canada. File # 20-E-Pak-1-4. External Affairs. *Op. cit.*
4. Government of Pakistan. Press Information Division. Handout titled Official Statement on East Pakistan Situation. E. No. 961-R. This was sent by John Small, high commissioner to Pakistan, to Ottawa in a Restricted Memo dated May 18, 1971. Memo # 253. File # 20-E-Pak-1-4. External Affairs. *Op. cit.*
5. Confidential telegram from James George, high commissioner to India, to Ottawa. Telegram # 2296, dated, June 14, 1971. File # 20-India-1-3 Pak. External Affairs. *Op. cit.*
6. Letter from Chaitanya K. Kalevar to Andrew Brewin, Member of Parliament for Greenwood, dated July 17, 1971. This is available in Andrew Brewin's Papers in the Archives. Subject: Pak. B.D Association, July-Oct. 1971. File # 87-13. Canada. Library and Archives Canada. MG 32 C26. Hereinafter, all information used from the Library and Archives Canada records shall be referred to as Library and Archives Canada.
7. Letter from Khandakar Mosthaque Ahmed, Foreign Minister of the People's Republic of Bangladesh (Mujibnagar), to Mitchell Sharp, Secretary of State for External Affairs, Government of Canada. The letter is dated August 3, 1971. File # 20-Bangla-14. External Affairs. *Op. cit.* The people of Bangladesh generally hold that Ahmed was secretly involved in the assassination of Bongobondhu in 1975.
8. *Ibid.*
9. Aide Mémoire from the high commissioner of India, dated December 13, 1971. This was forwarded to Mitchel Sharp, Secretary of State for External Affairs, by A. E. Ritchie, Undersecretary, Secretary of State for External Affairs, through a Confidential Memorandum for the Minister, dated December 13, 1971. File # 20-India-1-3-Pak. External Affairs. *Op. cit.*
10. *Ibid.* p.3
11. Confidential Document titled India-Pakistan, as of 1000 hours, December 17, 1971. File # 21-3-India-Pak. External Affairs. *Op. cit.*
12. *Ibid.*
13. Confidential telegram from John Small, High Commissioner to Pakistan, to Ottawa. Telegram # 1305. Dated, December 16, 1971. File # 21-3-India-Pak. External Affairs. *Op. cit.*
14. *Ibid.*
15. *Ibid.* p. 3.
16. Confidential telegram from James George, high commissioner to India, to Ottawa. Telegram # 5297, dated December 17, 1971. File # 21-3-India-Pak. External Affairs. *Op. cit.*
17. This is a one-page letter of appeal addressed as Dear Sir, by A. B. Sattar, Executive Secretary, Bangladesh Association of Canada, Ottawa, dated

December 17, 1971. The letter was hand-delivered to all MPs and a few selected Department of External Affairs officials. This may be found in Andrew Brewin's Papers in the Archives under Pak-Bangladesh correspondence. Volume 87. File # 87-13. MG 32 C26. Library and Archives Canada. *Op. cit.*
18. This was added as a separate note from the Bangladesh Association of Ottawa, dated December 21, 1971. *Ibid.*
19. Canada. House of Commons. *Debates*. Queen's Printer, dated December 20, 1971, p.10614. Hereinafter, referred to as *Debates*.
20. *Ibid.*
21. *Ibid.*
22. *Ibid.*
23. Confidential telegram from John Small, High Commissioner to Pakistan, to Ottawa. Telegram # 1326, dated December 21, 1971. File # 21-3-India-Pak. SITREP. External Affairs. *Op. cit.*
24. Letter from the Canadian high commissioner to the UK to External Affairs in Ottawa. Dated December 22, 1971. The letter is accompanied by a leaflet stating that approximately 200 Bengali women who, on December 10, 1971, met at a rally at 1 P.M at Hyde Park Speakers' Corner. File # 20-Bangla-14. External Affairs. *Op. cit.*
25. *Ibid.* Dated December 22, 1971, p. 10704.
26. Canadian Policy on Recognition of Bangladesh. A. E. Ritche, Undersecretary, signed this confidential document. Secretary of State. File # 20-Bangla -1-3; dated January 4, 1972. External Affairs. *Op. cit.*
27. *Ibid.*
28. Confidential telegram from James George, High Commissioner to India, to Ottawa. Telegram # 65, dated January 10, 1972. File # 38-11-1-Pak. External Affairs. *Op. cit.*
29. *Time* (Canada Edition) Ronalds-Federated Limited, Montreal, Evergreen Press Ltd. Dated December 20, 1971, p. 24.
30. *Ibid.*
31. Confidential telegram from John Small, High Commissioner to Pakistan, to Ottawa. Telegram # 1320. Dated December 20, 1971. File # 21-3-India-Pak-SITREP. External Affairs. *Op. cit.*
32. *Ibid.*
33. *Ibid.*
34. *Ibid.*
35. *Ibid.* p. 2.
36. Confidential telegram from John Small, High Commissioner to Pakistan to Ottawa. Telegram # 1368. Dated December 30, 1971; File # 21-3-India-Pak-SITREP. External Affairs. *Op. cit.*
37. Confidential telegram from Ottawa to London, Washington, DC, Paris, Tokyo, Rome, Accra, Algeria, Tunis, Cairo, Wellington, Moscow, Stockholm,

Colombo, Bonn, Canberra. GP 6560. Dated December 31, 1971. File # 21-3 India-Pak-2. External Affairs. *Op. cit.*
38. This was proposed in a written memo from A.E. Ritchie, Undersecretary, Department of External Affairs, to all Canadian ambassadors and high commissioners worldwide, dated December 31, 1971. File # 20-Bangla -14. External Affairs. *Op. cit.*
39. Confidential telegram from John Small, High Commissioner to Pakistan, to Ottawa. Telegram # 1320, dated December 20, 1971. File # 21-3-India-Pak-SITREP. External Affairs. *Op. cit.*
40. Confidential telegram from James George, Canadian High Commissioner to India, to Ottawa. Telegram # 5317, dated December 20, 1971. File 21-3-India-Pak-SITREP. External Affairs. *Op. cit.*
41. Letter from Professor Muazzam Hussain to Prime Minister Pierre Trudeau. Dated, February 14, 1972. File # 38-11-Bangalee. External Affairs. *Op. cit.*
42. Confidential Memorandum for the Minister titled *Recognition of 'Bangla Desh,'* written by A. E. Ritchie, Undersecretary, External Affairs. Dated January 5, 1972. File # 20-Bangla-14. External Affairs. *Op. cit.*
43. *Ibid.*
44. *The Times* (News UK, Thompson Corporation), dated December 30, 1971.
45. *Ibid.*
46. Confidential telegram from John Small, high commissioner to Pakistan, to Ottawa. Telegram # 29, dated 7 January 1972. File # 20-Bangla-14. External Affairs. *Op. cit.*
47. Written Script of a TV Interview of Mitchell Sharp, Secretary of State, by Peter Sturberg, Don Newman, and John Drewery on January 11, 1972. File # 20-Bangla-14. External Affairs. *Op. cit.*
48. *Ibid.*
49. Confidential telegram from John Small, High Commissioner to Pakistan, to Ottawa. Telegram # 38. Dated January 11, 1972; File # 21-3-India-Pak-SITREP. External Affairs. *Op. cit.*
50. *Ibid.*
51. *Ibid.*
52. Confidential telegram from Ottawa to John Small, high commissioner to Pakistan. Telegram # 892, GPS 41. Dated January 12, 1972, under the title, New Pakistan Regime: Message to President Bhutto, file # 20-Bangla-1-4. External Affairs. *Op. cit.*
53. *Ibid.*
54. *Ibid.*
55. Confidential telegram from John Small, high commissioner to Pakistan, to Ottawa. Telegram # 75, dated 17 January 1972. File # 21-3-India-Pak-SITREP. External Affairs. *Op. cit.*

56. Canadian Policy on Recognition of Bangladesh. A. E. Ritche, Undersecretary, prepared this Confidential document. Secretary of State. File # 20-Bangla -1-3; dated January 4, 1971. External Affairs. *Op. cit.*
57. Confidential telegram from James George, high commissioner to India, to Ottawa. Telegram # 119, dated January 14, 1972. File # 21-3-India-Pak-SITREP. External Affairs. *Op. cit.*
58. Confidential telegram from James George, high commissioner to India, to Ottawa. Telegram # 3202, dated August 20, 1971. File # 20-India-1-3-Pak. External Affairs. *Op. cit.*
59. *Aide Mémoire* from the office of the High Commissioner for Pakistan. No. P/12/7/71. Dated January 11, 1972. File # 20-Pak-1-4. External Affairs. *Op. cit.*
60. *Ibid.*
61. *Ibid.*
62. Unclassified Memorandum from A. J. Andrew, Director General, Bureau of Asian and Pacific Affairs, to J. Irwin. Subject: Opening of Post in Dacca [sic], dated January 26, 1972, p. 2. File # 20-Bangla 1-4. External Affairs. *Op. cit.*
63. Memorandum for the Minister, prepared by A. E. Ritchie, Undersecretary, Secretary of State for External Affairs. Dated January 27, 1972. File # 20-Bangla-14. External Affairs. *Op. cit.*
64. Hand-delivered Memo from Prime Minister Edward Heath to Prime Minister Pierre Trudeau, dated January 13, 1972. This secret letter was delivered to Canada via the British High Commissioner. File # 20-Bangla-1-4. External Affairs. *Op.cit.*
65. *Ibid.*
66. Confidential Message for President Zulfikar Ali Bhutto from Prime Minister Edward Heath, sent through the British High Commission, Ottawa. The Letter is dated January 31, 1971. File # 20-Bangla-14. This was in response to Bhutto's request to Edward Heath to delay recognition until his return from China. External Affairs. *Op. cit.*
67. Secret Letter from Prime Minister Pierre Trudeau to Prime Minister Edward Heath, dated January 20, 1972. File # 20-Bangla-1-4. External Affairs. *Op.cit.*
68. Confidential telegram from John Small, Canadian high commissioner to Pakistan, to Ottawa. Telegram # 49, dated January 13, 1972. File # 20-Pak-1-4. External Affairs. *Op. cit.*
69. Confidential telegram from John Small, High Commissioner to Pakistan, to Ottawa. Telegram # 55, dated January 14, 1972. File # 21-3-India-Pak-SITREP. External Affairs. *Op. cit.*

70. Aide Mémoire from Pakistan's high commissioner to the Department of External Affairs, dated January 27, 1972, p.1. File # 20-Bangla-14. External Affairs. *Op. cit.*
71. Confidential Memorandum for the Minister, Recognition of Bangladesh from A. E. Ritchie, Undersecretary, External Affairs. Dated, January 26, 1972. File # 20-Bangla-14. External Affairs. *Op. cit.*
72. Confidential telegram from John Small to Ottawa. Telegram # 75, dated January 17, 1972. File # 20-Pak-1-4. *Op. cit.*
73. Confidential telegram from John Small, Canadian high commissioner to Pakistan, to Ottawa. Telegram # 150, dated February 2, 1972. File # 20-Bangla-14. External Affairs. *Op. cit.*
74. *Ibid.*
75. Confidential Memo from John Small, high commissioner to Pakistan, to Ottawa. Telegram # 56, dated February 8, 1972. File # 20-Pak-1-4. External Affairs. *Op. cit.*
76. Confidential Memo from John Small, high commissioner to Pakistan, to Undersecretary of State for External Affairs, dated 8 February 1971. File # 20-Pak 1-4. External Affairs. *Op. cit.*
77. *Ibid.*
78. Confidential Memorandum for the Minister titled "Box Score of Countries Recognizing Bangladesh." This was signed by A. E. Ritchie, Undersecretary and Secretary of State for External Affairs. Dated, February 7, 1972. File # 20-Bangla-14. External Affairs. *Op. cit.*
79. Aide Mémoire from the high commissioner of Pakistan sent to the Department of External Affairs. No. P/12/7/71, dated February 8, 1972, p.1. File # 20-Pak-1-4. External Affairs. *Op. cit.*
80. See Glossary of Terms.
81. Restricted telegram from John Small, high commissioner to Pakistan, to Ottawa. Telegram # 175, p.1, dated February 5, 1972. File # 20-1-2-Bangla-1-4. External Affairs. *Op. cit.*
82. See Glossary of Terms.
83. See Glossary of Terms.
84. Secret Internal Message from Ottawa to London titled Bangladesh: Comwel Initiative. Numbers 56 Jan 10 and 61 Jan 11, 1972. File # 20-Bangla-14. External Affairs. *Op. cit.*
85. *Ibid.* p.3
86. Confidential Memorandum for the Minister, prepared by A. E. Ritchie, Undersecretary, Secretary of State for External Affairs. Dated January 27, 1972. File # 20-Bangla-14. p.2. External Affairs. *Op. cit.*
87. Confidential telegram from John Small, high commissioner to Pakistan, to Ottawa. Telegram # 221. Dated, February 11, 1972. File # 20-Bangla-14. External Affairs. *Op. cit.*

88. *Ibid.* p.2.
89. *Ibid.*
90. Written transcript of the standard media interviews of Mitchell Sharp, Secretary of State for External Affairs, on February 24, 1972, titled *Remarks to the News Media on Recognition of Bangladesh*. File # 20- Bangla-14. External Affairs. *Op. cit.*
91. Letter from Sheikh Mujibur Rahman, Prime Minister of Bangladesh, to Pierre Elliott Trudeau, Prime Minister of Canada. Dated February 17, 1972. File # 20-Bangla-14. External Affairs. *Op. cit.*
92. *Aide Mémoire*, No. P/12/7/72, dated February 14, 1972. File # 20-Bangla-14. External Affairs. *Op. cit.*
93. *Ibid.*
94. Confidential Memorandum to the Minister, from A. E. Ritchie, Undersecretary, to Mitchell Sharp, Secretary of State for External Affairs. Dated February 16, 1972, p.1. File # 20-Bangla-14. External Affairs. *Op. cit.*
95. Hand-delivered Memo from Prime Minister Edward Heath to Prime Minister Pierre Trudeau, dated January 13, 1972. This SECRET letter was delivered via the British high commissioner to Canada. File # 20-Bangla-1-4. External Affairs. *Op. cit.*
96. *Ibid.*
97. This was described in a Confidential telegram from the Canadian high commissioner to the U.K. to Ottawa. Telegram # 44, dated January 10, 1972. File # 38-11-1-Pak. External Affairs. *Op. cit.*
98. Letter from A. E. Ritchie, Undersecretary of State for External Affairs, to H.S. Johnson, Chief Programs Division, Department of Manpower and Immigration, dated February 24, 1972. File # RG 76, Volume 1151; File # 5260-1-606. Library and Archives Canada. *Op. cit.*
99. *Debates.* Dated February 25, 1972, p. 294. *Op. cit.*
100. *Ibid.* p. 294. *Op.cit.*
101. *Ibid.* Dated May 29, 1972, p. 2664. *Op. cit.*
102. *Chronology of Important Dates in Bangladesh-Canada Relations.* File # 327. 07(1), Bangladesh Canada, 1972-1979, Volume 1. Bangladesh National Archives.
103. Letter from Abdul Momin, Bangladesh's high commissioner to Canada, to Abdus Samad Azad, Foreign Minister, Department of Foreign Affairs, Government of Bangladesh, dated September 14, 1972. File # Pol. 8/72. Confidential file at the premises of the Bangladesh High Commission in Ottawa. Anwarul Alam, then Counselor, gave the author access to the high commission's confidential files.
104. SECRET telegram from John Small, high commissioner to Pakistan, to Ottawa. Telegram # 75, dated January 17, 1972. File # 20-Bangla-14. External Affairs. *Op. cit.*

105. *Patriot* (City Edition), New Delhi, dated March 2, 1972 (volume IX, No. 335).
106. *The Statesman*, New Delhi, March 2, 1972.
107. *Ibid.*
108. Transcript of interview of Arnold Smith with Mr. Christopher Serpell of the British Broadcasting Corporation. It was in the BBC's "PM" Current Affairs Program, dated February 1, 1972. File # 20-Bangla-14. External Affairs. *Op. cit.*
109. *Ibid.*
110. *The Globe and Mail*, dated February 23, 1972.
111. *The Globe and Mail*, dated April 19, 1972.
112. This was stated by Sheikh Mujibur Rahman, Prime Minister of Bangladesh, at a press conference in Dhaka on January 14, 1972. Abdus Samad Azad, Foreign Minister of the People's Republic of Bangladesh, mentioned this in his speech titled Foreign Policy of Bangladesh in Dhaka on August 9, 1971, p. 1. Published by the Embassy of the People's Republic of Bangladesh, Washington, DC (no date). Confidential file at the premises of the Bangladesh High Commission in Ottawa. Anwarul Alam, then Counselor, Ottawa-based Bangladesh high commission, gave the author access to its confidential files.
113. Letter from the high commissioner of Bangladesh to the Department of External Affairs. No. Pol.19/72, dated November 28, 1972. File 20-Bangla-1-3. External Affairs. *Op. cit.*
114. Memo from Jamil Majid, Third Secretary, Bangladesh High Commission, Ottawa, addressed to Abdul Momin, high commissioner to Canada, dated September 12, 1972; File # Pol. 8/72. This document is placed in the office of the Ottawa-based High Commission of Bangladesh. See footnote # 98 above
115. Letter from Abdul Momin, high commissioner to Canada, to Abdus Samad Azad, Minister of Foreign Affairs, Government of Bangladesh, dated September 12, 1972. File # Pol/8/72. *Ibid.*
116. *Ibid.*
117. *Ibid.*
118. Letter from John Munro, Minister for Health and Welfare Canada, to Mitchell Sharp, Secretary of State for External Affairs, dated February 1, 1972. File # 38-11-1-Pakistan. External Affairs. *Op. cit.*
119. Restricted Memorandum to the File for H.P.G. Fraser of the South Asia Division, External Affairs. Subject: Aid to Indian subcontinent, 12 January 1972. File # 38-11-1-Pak. External Affairs. *Op. cit.* This was decided at a meeting on January 7, 1972, attended by representatives from GPS, Export Development Corporation, CIDA, and the Department of Finance.
120. Joint memo from A.E. Ritchie, Undersecretary, to Mitchell Sharp, Secretary of State for External Affairs. Dated January 29, 1972. File # 38-11-1-Pak. External Affairs. *Op. cit.*

121. *Bangladesh Survey Report*, April 23–25, 1972; May 10-19, 1972, by John F. McRae, p. 10. McRae gave the author a photocopy of the 20-page Report with Appendix A, B, and C marked "Confidential" on the cover page. Hereinafter, referred to as *Bangladesh Survey Report, 1972*.
122. *Ibid.* pp.10–11.
123. The Antigonish Movement arose in the first decades of the 20th century in response to the socio-economic decline in Maritime Canada. By 1945, it demonstrated possible solutions to the problems of underdevelopment in distant lands. Throughout the years, it has touched the lives of thousands of people in Canada and abroad, primarily through the Coady International Institute. It continues to promote democratically based and locally organized grassroots cooperative action in many parts of the world.
124. *Bangladesh Survey Report*,1972, p. 19. *Op. cit.*
125. *Ibid.*
126. *Ibid.*
127. "Bangla Desh makes a good Beginning" by Dr. E.H. Johnson in *The Globe and Mail*, dated March 8, 1972.
128. *Ibid.*
129. *Ibid.*
130. John Hay of the Ottawa staff of *The Canadian Press* wrote this in one of a series published in the *Star Phoenix*, dated October 14, 1972.
131. *Ibid.*
132. Welcome Speech by Prime Minister Louis St. Laurent in honor of Prime Minister of Pakistan, Liakat Ali Khan, given in the House of Commons on May 30, 1950. This is cited in the book titled *Pakistan: The Heart of Asia*. Khan, Liakat Ali, Lippman, Walter and Kennan, George. Harvard University Press, Cambridge, Massachusetts, 1950, pp. 112–115.
133. *Ibid.* p. 112.
134. *Ibid.*
135. Letter from Heath Macquarrie, Member of Parliament to Prime Minister Pierre Trudeau. Dated March 19, 1974. MG 32 C31, Vol. 32 File: 32-7. Library and Archives Canada. *Op. cit.*
136. *Ibid.*
137. Letter from Mitchell Sharp, Secretary of State for External Affairs, to Heath Macquarrie, MP for Hillsborough, PEI. The letter is dated July 30, 1973. MG 32 C31, Vol. 32 File: 32-7. Library and Archives Canada. *Op. cit.*
138. *Ibid.*
139. Letter signed by Andrew Brewin, Heath Macquarrie, and Georges Lachance, addressed to Mitchell Sharp, Secretary of State for External Affairs, and copied to all Members of Parliament, dated May 15, 1973. MG 32 C31, Vol. 32 File: 32-7. Library and Archives Canada. *Op. cit.*
140. *Ibid.*

141. *Ibid.*
142. http://thecommonwealth.org/history-of-the-commonwealth/commonwealth-heads-government-meeting-ottawa-canada-2-%E2%80%93-10-august-1973. Meeting of Heads of Governments, Ottawa, 2 August 1973. *Final Communiqué* p. 4.
143. *Ibid.* p. 8.
144. *Ibid.* P.8.
145. *The Ottawa Citizen*, dated August 4, 1973.
146. *Ibid.* Dated August 8, 1973.
147. *Ibid.*
148. *Toronto Daily Star*, dated August 10, 1973.
149. *Toronto Daily Star*, dated August 6, 1973
150. *Ibid.*
151. *Ibid.* Dated August 8, 1973.
152. *Bangladesh Observer*, dated November 21, 1983.
153. *Ibid.*
154. *Ibid.*
155. *Ibid.*
156. *Ibid.*
157. *Ibid.*
158. *Ibid.*
159. This was expressed by Yakub Ali, high commissioner of Bangladesh, who was the guest of honor at the inaugural ceremony in Windsor, Ontario, on January 12, 2010. Ali recalled this to the author, who was also present at the ceremony.
160. *Windsor Star*, dated October 23, 2008.
161. *Ibid.*
162. *Ibid.* This was observed after approval was given for installing the Bangladesh Peace Clock.
163. *Ibid.*
164. *Ibid.*
165. Aziz Chowdhury said this to the author on January 12, 2012, during the inaugural function, which the author attended along with Yakub Ali, then high commissioner of Bangladesh to Canada. Jilhurain Jaigirdar, an active community member of Ottawa now living in Toronto, was also with them.
166. *The Financial Express*, Dhaka, dated September 17, 2016.
167. *Ibid.*
168. *Ibid.*
169. *The Daily Star*, dated August 7, 2002
170. Email from Dr. Syed Sajjadur Rahman to Mustafa Chowdhury, dated May 23, 2021. The author exchanged several e-mails and talked to Dr. Rahman, one

of his close friends. They are in touch with each other, and they frequently exchange information regarding this subject.
171. *Ibid.*
172. *Ibid.*
173. E-mail from Dr. Mohammad Zaman to Mustafa Chowdhury, dated October 13, 2020. Since then, the author has maintained regular conversations with Dr Zaman, a childhood friend of the author, in this regard. Now and then, they exchange information on each other's research work.
174. *The Daily Star*, dated April 9, 2021.
175. *Ibid.*
176. *Ibid.*
177. *Ibid.*
178. *Ibid.*

CHAPTER 10

Grand Finale: Bangladesh Takes its Rightful Place on the Global Stage

*T*o appreciate Canada's efforts in resolving the subcontinental conflict, we may refer to Canadian historian Jack Lawrence Granatstein's general remark that falls in place with Canada's role at that time. We need to set the context first by considering specific historical facts. Though a middle power, in 1971, Canada was also in an enviable position in the global scheme of things when a new policy of active participation in world affairs was firmly established. Before the Second World War, Canada had taken a minor role in world affairs, at which point Canada emerged with a profoundly different approach on the international stage. Canada then came of age as an active "middle power" in world affairs. With that understanding regarding the scope of Canada's undertakings in ending the political impasse between the two wings of Pakistan, we must also keep in mind the limitations imposed on Canada due partly to her status as a middle power operating in the Cold War backdrop of the two competing superpowers, the United States, and the USSR.

Unlike today, Canada's foreign policy of 1971 was quite limited. It was guided by the need to protect and promote Canadian interests and values abroad; that pattern was also found in Canada's efforts throughout the 1971 subcontinental crisis period. Unlike superpowers like the USA, the USSR, or China, Canada was a middle power with minimal military capability. Canada remained committed to doing what her foreign policy options allowed her to pursue - prosperity and just international order and values, the spirit of moderation, compromise, the rule of law, and social and economic justice (Granatstein, J. L., ed. *Canadian Foreign Policy*, Toronto, Copp Clark, and Pittman Ltd., 1995, p. 87). Unlike a superpower, Canada was not influenced by the geopolitics of the Indian subcontinent. Instead, Canada embraced peacekeeping as a national mission, including human rights and protection, democratic development, good governance, humanitarian assistance, refugee repatriation, disarmament, and demobilization.

Apprehensive of the separatists' next move in Canada, Mitchell Sharp, Secretary of State for External Affairs, needed to keep radicalism and disorder in check at home while examining how the Bengalis' fight for greater autonomy became a struggle for independence. A man of high moral character and an ardent and forceful believer in Canadian foreign policy options, Sharp had both ideals and strength. He held his position with iron determination. We noted this in Chapter 6. Many examples depict the Trudeau administration, which debated for months to determine the exact path to follow, considering Canada's foreign policy constraints and minimal options as a middle power. An engaged Sharp delved deeply into the relevant issues, read his briefing notes assiduously, and invested the time required to understand the complex problems. His thinking centered on minimizing risk, managing vulnerabilities, and maximizing opportunity. He did not wish to up the ante. Unsurprisingly, therefore, Ottawa maintained a discrete silence, neither applauding nor criticizing the brutality and turbulence of the Yahya regime. Canada chose diplomacy over belligerence. There were no exceptions; consultation was always preferable to confrontation, argued Sharp.

Within the narrow limits dictated by Canada's foreign policy constraints, Canada did everything possible diplomatically, such as exercising tact, effort, patience, and persistence to settle differences among parties. Having perceived the drama as tragic, Canada concluded that the Yahya regime had no moral authority. Canada firmly held the view that all her diplomatic efforts should be directed toward preventing the tragedy of Pakistan's breakup. With limited options, Canada visualized a reformed Pakistan with the establishment of democracy, a process that started a year ago. In considering the entire issue, the Trudeau administration consistently kept in mind the long-standing traditions of friendship that bound the people of Canada and the subcontinent, India and Pakistan.

To determine Canada's brinkmanship in 1971 during the Liberation War of Bangladesh, we must go beyond the usual narrative. Canada believed the Yahya regime had crossed the Rubicon due to its skulduggery. Nonetheless, Canada neither wanted to ruffle Yahya's feathers nor strain her relationships with Pakistan. Canada wanted to retain its friendship with Pakistan, a key Commonwealth ally. Canada valued her friendship with Pakistan based on mutual and continuous respect for Pakistan's status as a sovereign nation. Although Canada felt that the brutal measures of the military regime had to be condemned, Canada was conflicted in taking a solid position, something we noted in Chapter 8. In a common devotion to freedom, law, and justice across a broad swath of Canadians in all sections of society, the demand soared for a strong statement on one of the great distresses of our time. Yet Canada could not send an unequivocal message of condemnation. It was impossible. We must, therefore, bear in mind both domestic politics and foreign policy constraints that forced the Trudeau administration to stick to her policy of nonintervention in the internal affairs of Pakistan, all through the Bengalis' struggle for independence. When the situation in Pakistan was deteriorating at breakneck speed, Canada, as a middle power, watched the chaos and conflict helplessly while the savage pogrom was unfolding.

As a middle power, Canada could only observe how each superpower was working on its game plan. With Moscow tied to New Delhi and Beijing tied to Islamabad, the potential for confrontation between the Communist giants was high. Sharp knew that, under the constant pounding from the media, Canadians would soon be demanding new actions toward progress. Sharp had to walk constantly on a higher tightrope to appease the United States, India, Pakistan, and interested Canadians. It was only during the first week of December 1971 that Canada was forced to accept the reality of Bangladesh. This happened with India's official recognition of Bangladesh on December 6, 1971, thus ending what was implicit in her policy. India's declaration closed the faint possibility of a political settlement toward which Canada worked relentlessly.

After a series of stunning advances, on December 16, 1971, Indian forces routed the province. They liberated East Pakistan in less than two weeks, demonstrating one of India's swiftest and most brilliant military campaigns. The surrender of Lieutenant General Ameer Abdullah Khan

Niazi meant the dismemberment of Pakistan and the birth of a new nation, Bangladesh, a lasting cause of humiliation for Pakistan. "At a stroke, Pakistan is reduced to a nation of fifty-five million, against India's six hundred million and has lost all its eastern territory as well as more than half its population," wrote *The Toronto Daily Star* on December 17, 1971. One could say that following the surrender of the Pakistani army, a disgraced Yahya lost his position and was cut to size by Bhutto, his occasional friend or political adversary.

The transition of the Bengalis from an autonomy movement to an eventual secessionist struggle for freedom, an independent Bangladesh, resulted from several factors, such as the military regime's total disregard for the results of the National Elections, its ongoing military repression, the Indian government's direct patronage and involvement, sympathetic attitude of the world community, and the favorable world media coverage for an independent Bangladesh. In addition, perhaps the most critical factor is the firm determination of the Bengali freedom fighters and nonfreedom fighters, en masse, all of whom were enthused with a profound sense of nationalism and a distinctive separateness from the West Pakistanis instilled in them by their leader Bongobondhu.

In Chapter 7, we saw Canada's activities during the Liberation War of Bangladesh and how Canada cared for the Bengalis as a people suffering from human rights abuses and the suppression of democracy. Without considering the views of the provisional government of Bangladesh, Canada believed in the transfer of power to the elected majority. Having worried about the rapidly mounting threat to peace and security in the subcontinent, Canada supported and worked for a solution that would empower Bongobondhu, the nationally elected leader of most Pakistanis. Though a middle power with no stake in the Indian subcontinent, Canada favored the establishment of democracy in Pakistan. Ottawa officials examined the following arguments presented by Pakistan: that it was Pakistan's domestic issue and not an Indo-Pakistani issue, that the Gandhi administration was preventing refugees from returning to East Pakistan, and finally, that India had been supporting the Liberation Forces.

Ottawa officials concluded that the conflict was between the military government of Pakistan and the people of East Pakistan and that it was not a dispute between Pakistan and India. They regarded Bongobondhu as a progressive leader on social and human rights issues capable of leading Pakistan. Accordingly, Canada argued for reconciliation. Sharp provided the most convincing argument: a still-neutral Canada reasoned that she was deeply anxious about the future of democracy in Pakistan. The Trudeau administration could not remain a spectator. Instead, as a concerned member of the Commonwealth, Canada provided development aid. Having looked at the issue from the above-noted angle, Canada was all for democracy in Pakistan. Accordingly, as noted already, Canada's initiatives centered on the following three pillars: (1) the establishment of democracy, (2) the integrity of Pakistan, and (3) the assumption of power by Bongobondhu.

The consensus among the Canadian delegates who went to India and Pakistan (East and West) described in Chapter 7 was recognition of extensive devastation and transgression of human rights. However, after their return from the subcontinent, their personal views seemed to change. As representatives of the government of Canada, they strictly adhered to Canada's position of neutrality and noninterference in the internal affairs of another country. While they characterized the situation as they wished, they still had to toe the government line when making official statements. They had to be extra careful in ensuring they did not embarrass their government, which still had no declaratory position on the conflict when the recommendations were made. They agreed that every effort should be made to bring about an internationally brokered peaceful and political settlement. They maintained that since the elected representatives of the people of East Pakistan were in the majority, they could legitimately form the government in Pakistan. They firmly supported the generally held view that the ideal solution would be the restoration of Bongobondhu to his former status. This was one of their recommendations, although it was devoid of reality.

Following the report's submission, however, the delegates were allowed to freely express their personal views critical of the Yahya regime's military reprisals, which resonated with the Canadian public. The Trudeau administration, however, could not extricate itself from its conflictual situation. Canada's first and foremost priority was to prevent Pakistan from disintegrating. From this angle, creating Bangladesh out of East Pakistan was not on Canada's radar.

Again, it may be worth noting what we read in Capital 8. We unmistakably noted that Canada rejected any notion of "secession" or "separation" of East Pakistan. Canada viewed this as "politically incorrect," given her ongoing problems in Québec, generally referred to as the "Québec question." Canada's mediation efforts with Pakistan did not come to fruition as she could not persuade President Yahya to follow the process of democracy that had started a year earlier. Canada failed to acknowledge the emerging reality without considering the views of Bangladesh's provisional government (i.e., a separate movement for the creation of a new country out of Pakistan). As mentioned, engaging the third party (provisional government of Bangladesh) in her strategy was never on Ottawa's plate to consider. The Trudeau administration genuinely feared that the events surrounding the rise of Bengali nationalism would echo the aspirations of French-Canadian nationalism, which had appeared in the Québec province under Pierre Lesage's administration (1960–1966). At that time, it symbolized the hopes of a whole people on the road to self-assertion. Canadians saw a striking resemblance to the situation of Bongobondhu, who embodied the aspirations of the Bengalis of East Pakistan.

As far as the Trudeau administration was concerned, whether it was the case or not, perception-wise, to many Canadians, the Bengalis' demand for a separate country of their own sounded strikingly like the situation in Québec. As Canadians saw, the situation in "Occupied Bangladesh" was also reminiscent of Québec's "Quiet Revolution," which led Québecois to believe that they should not be content to play a second-class role in socio-politico-economic matters; for Québecois, the key to a full normal development of their communities rested on the utilization of the only tool which they collectively controlled: the state of Québec. As far as Sharp was concerned, it was a case of déjà vu. For that matter, the idea of a movement for separation or secession was charged with emotion and fear of the unknown.

Understandably, Canada did not want to cause a furor by endorsing a separation movement abroad when she had a similar problem of equal magnitude in her backyard. Sharp held the view that diplomacy was cheaper than the application of military might. He believed that while military muscle could stabilize a situation and achieve deterrence, diplomacy was better suited to attain political solutions and reconciliation. Naturally, despite repeated prodding by the Canadian public for prompt and vigorous action, Canada seemed hapless. Canada felt it had to procrastinate whenever there was a need for a swift and practical decision. On such occasions, Ottawa responded with "go slow" and diplomatic evasion. It is ironic that when Canada's representatives from Islamabad and New Delhi,

John Small and James George, respectively, looked to Ottawa for guidance and leadership, Ottawa chose a path that allowed her to "soft-peddle." Meanwhile, both high commissioners were asked to engage in "watchful waiting." Consequently, even after spending months in this futile rut, Sharp was advised that if India would cease supporting the guerrillas with arms and haven, Yahya could reestablish civilian government.

For all practical purposes, we also noted in Chapter 8 that there was no change in Canada's approach to the Pakistan-Bangladesh issue throughout the crisis period, even when the situation demanded a comprehensive review of its strategy. It never dawned on Ottawa officials that they should "reexamine" Canada's persuasion strategy. Canada's initiatives reflect Prime Minister Pierre Trudeau's strong feelings and desires about the importance of legitimization, reform, and democratization of Pakistan. Canada equated democracy in Pakistan, which included both wings of Pakistan. Canada did not consider the reality of Bangladesh as an independent country out of Pakistan. There were inseparable obstacles. We must not ignore that, whether Ottawa was lobbying or networking diplomatically, the challenging task carried Sharp to the heights of tireless efforts that drove him to the tragedy of frustration and failure. Looking back, it is evident that, given the implausibility of success, Ottawa's "staying the course" strategy was flawed. It can be argued that Canada lacked a grasp of the situation's international game plan or realpolitik.

From a historical point of view, readers must not forget the circumstances that brought Trudeau to politics. In 1965, just six years earlier, Trudeau had entered federal politics primarily to develop policies across Canada to counter the thrust of Québec nationalism. From behind the scenes, Trudeau emphasized the complexity of the many conditions and influences that must be considered in dealing with international situations and superpower players. Having explored every possible alternative, and given Yahya's intransigence, Canada became convinced of the need for some exceedingly deft and discreet diplomacy. In Chapter 7, we noted the Trudeau administration's initiation of a series of letters addressing both President Yahya Khan and Prime Minister Indira Gandhi, emphasizing the appalling nature of the situation to persuade them to cease their aggressive strategy.

Trudeau's correspondences with the governments of India and Pakistan show how Ottawa always cherished the thought that India and Pakistan must be brought face-to-face. While communicating with Yahya and Gandhi, Canada believed that reconciliation could still be achieved through international diplomacy despite the persistent hatred between the Mujibites (supporters of Bongobondhu) and the non-Bengali military regime. This was, of course, wishful thinking on Canada's part since India and Pakistan saw one another as archenemies. Canada knew this all along. Trudeau deliberately couched Canada's platform in unprovocative and noninflammatory terms to convince Yahya that it would be only through dialogue with the leader of the majority party (Bongobondhu) that a real "political solution" could be achieved if Pakistan were to restore democracy. Despite her persistent and earnest endeavors to promote and defend the principles of democracy in Pakistan, Canada could neither convince Pakistan to stop military reprisals nor dissuade India from backing the Bengali rebels. Why? Both India and Pakistan had their secret agendas.

Naive as she was, Canada remained committed to improving the situation by lobbying other Commonwealth countries during the cataclysmic chain of events in East Pakistan. Readers shall also recall what they read in Chapters 1 and 2 - Canada's interest in Pakistan starting from the National Elections of 1970, in which Bongobondhu, the Bengali leader of Pakistan, had a landslide victory. He was expected to assume power in a transformed and re-modeled Pakistan. The furtive military takeover and the declaration of independence by the Bengali rebels with direct assistance from India were the two game changers that instantly changed the present and future political landscapes, making it far more complicated for a "neutral" Canada to take a side.

As Canada saw it, the air was heavy with gloomy forebodings due to constant savage threats issued by both India and Pakistan. With the imposition of martial law and covert attacks on innocent civilians, Canada was disconcerted by the Yahya regime. To Canada, the indiscriminate killing was contradictory to people's legitimate aspirations for political freedom. Canada worked unremittingly to secure a political solution that would be practical and workable in Pakistan. Nevertheless, after a while, Canada came to believe that Yahya's persistent effort to stall the transfer of power forced many to think that he was neither serious nor prepared to allow the Bengali leader to assume control. George, Canada's high commissioner to India, communicated to his superiors in Ottawa that the army atrocities had forced the guerrillas to develop an unshakable determination to fight for the freedom of their native land. George indicated that the Bengalis spoke up with one voice as they took up arms to defend their native land against a military regime bent on killing them. However, the Trudeau administration did not consider modifying its engagement strategy. It remained stuck to its flawed design.

It is important to note that although the Bangladesh phenomenon was not part of Canada's scheme of things, the well-being of the Bengalis was high on Canada's agenda. We noted in Chapter 7 that many of Canada's efforts favored Bangladesh regardless of Canada's stated position. Ottawa officials were concerned that failure to condemn military atrocities openly would give rise to public criticism. This was even though perceptions such as tolerating brutality were at odds with Canada's traditional image as a country well known for her compassion and international humanitarian assistance.

Looking back, Canada remained keen to hear from its representatives in Pakistan and India about the latest developments, especially following the 1970 National Elections. Canada's main interest was to ensure that Pakistan's democratization process was on. It is also important to note that even though Canada did not endorse the separation of Bangladesh, Canada never undermined the Bengalis' demand for greater autonomy and democratic rights. Three weeks before the imposition of martial law and the secret military crackdown, John Small, Canada's high commissioner to Pakistan, was in Dhaka for a tête-à-tête with Bongobondhu as a representative of Canada.

In the summer, when the provisional government of Bangladesh invited the world press to tour the liberated areas to witness the reality of Bangladesh, many Canadian journalists seized that opportunity. They made on-site visits with their professional colleagues from across the world. The government took particular interest in seeing the positive role being played by the Canadian media. Needless to restate, due to her foreign policy constraints, Canada had no choice but to purposefully maintain a distance. However, Canada's foreign affairs cognoscenti sympathized with the Bengalis' cause but had to refrain from making any observations. The idea that Canada fought (and continues the same to this day) on the side of democracy and freedom remains a source of great patriotic pride for Canadians - something that gives a theme of consistency and idealism to Canada's diplomatic history.

Readers must not miss the part played by Canada in handling the illegal arms that the Nixon administration was secretly sending to Pakistan. Canada was disturbed to see the "hands-off" position of the Nixon administration that violated its policy and practice by participating in the illegal shipment of arms to Pakistan. At its first opportunity, Canada opposed the shipment of arms designed for use against the Bengalis. We noted Canada's bold decision to empty the ship and return it to the USA in Chapter 7. Canada's support for Bangladesh becomes noticeable when one looks at how closely she worked with the public in a hot-button area—the provision of illicit arms to Pakistan through the *S. S. Padma.* This ship was carrying the US arms secretly to Pakistan. Canada was distressed that American political leadership maintained a conspiracy of silence that mirrored the Nixon administration's growing reputation for untrustworthiness.

Canada chose to continue to conform to her foreign policy of nonintervention in the internal affairs of another country (Pakistan). Despite being an ally of the United States, a courageous Trudeau openly put his foot down against the Nixon administration. Canada could not escape the Axis, but she took a bold stand against the Nixon administration. In Chapter 4, we noted Canada immediately emptied the ship of secretly destined illegal arms at the port of Montreal. Naturally, Canada's reaction became a turning point in Canada-US relations. Although President Nixon was furious with Trudeau's unwavering determination, he could do nothing about it. Having emptied the ship and seeing the sufferings that had befallen the Bengalis, Canada carried on her search for a political solution, even against the wishes of the Nixon administration.

Canada's strong reaction demonstrates the differences between the responses of Canada and the USA vis-à-vis the "Bangladesh issue" even though Canada was an ally of the US. The difference between the Nixon and Trudeau administrations was that the White House's central plank in the conflict was to ensure the security and integrity of Pakistan; it had no qualms despite the military reprisals. What was critical to the USA was its hope for a future China-Pakistan-USA partnership to fulfill its geopolitical strategy in the quest for a permanent balance of power in South Asia and containment of the USSR. The Nixon administration had only one motive - to keep President Yahya, a personal friend of Nixon, in power. Whereas, as a middle power, Canada had no such ambition. Canada was interested in seeing Bongobondhu, the elected leader of a reformed and democratic Pakistan.

Naturally, Canada never had to develop a game plan for Pakistan that was not her client state, unlike the USA. Canada was not interested in following the Nixon-Kissinger geopolitical strategy either. And yet the Trudeau administration's most significant problem was that although it did not have an open "tilt" policy in favor of Pakistan like the Nixon administration, it could neither countenance the dismemberment of Pakistan nor condone the atrocities of the Pakistani army. It remained firm in its position of "neutrality" all through the Bengalis' struggle for independence. Stated differently, Canada took a stand against Pakistan's ruthless repression of the Bengalis at the first opportunity. However, she could neither support the military regime nor endorse the independence of Bangladesh through the dismantling of Pakistan.

In the meantime, as soon as the rumors of Canada's decision to suspend economic aid to Pakistan began circulating, followed by Canada's suspension of export licenses for spare parts for Pakistani military aircraft, Yahya became convinced that the Canadian government was not on his side. The decision of the governments of Canada and Great Britain to suspend aid provoked Yahya's wrath to such an extent that he immediately turned against these two countries. All through the crisis period, Canada remained concerned about the future of the Bengalis and had a renewed interest in assisting them to the greatest extent possible. Naturally, the Pakistani military government viewed Canada as being "against" Pakistan. Despite Canada's earnest efforts to appease Yahya, the military was suspicious of Canada's position vis-à-vis the demands of the Bengali rebels—the liberation of Bangladesh. In fact, Yahya's suspicion that Canada opposed Pakistan's military authority grew even more robust over time.

Consequently, having suspected that Canada was on the Bengalis' side, Yahya immediately expressed profound dissatisfaction toward Canada. Most Pakistani national newspapers ran stories about how Yahya was threatening Canada for her involvement in Pakistan's internal affairs. A furious Yahya not only criticized Canada for not being on Pakistan's side but promptly cautioned Canada, saying that Pakistan would not only withdraw from the Commonwealth but also take reprisals against Canada. Ottawa officials found it ironic that the military regime grossly misconstrued their attempt to remain "neutral." This upset Canada, as she never wanted to take sides, especially against Pakistan.

The effect of suspending export licenses and arms shipments might have been minimal since the Pakistani military regime was still receiving arms surreptitiously from other sources. What is significant is Canada's overt demonstration of her firmly held position on this matter. Canada could do very little as a middle power under the US umbrella. Lacking superpower capability, the Trudeau administration demonstrated a uniquely Canadian way to champion the cause of peace. Prime Minister Trudeau's actions instantly earned him a place in history. This single act, at the cost of provoking both Nixon and Yahya, elevated Canada's status in the world community as a country that did not hesitate to expose the regime's secret and illicit plan with the Nixon administration. In this instance, one could argue that Canada supported the Bengalis' cause for democracy.

Another way of looking at Canada's lenience toward the Bengalis is to note how government funding was made available to the Canadian nongovernmental organizations (NGOs) engaged in India and Pakistan during the war of liberation. While allocating resources to Care Canada, OXFAM Canada, or, for that matter, to any other Canadian NGOs in the field, the Trudeau administration did not interfere with their operations or reprimand them for their visible "political" role. Ottawa officials refrained from censuring those NGOs that often exceeded their mandate by advocating their stance for Bangladesh. In other words, although the Trudeau administration could not show any flexibility regarding noninterference in Pakistan's internal affairs, it showed flexibility by giving NGOs a free hand. Canadian officials ignored NGOs' involvement in local political actions. All through the Bengalis' struggle for independence, the Trudeau administration calmly overlooked how Canadian NGOs in the field became "politically involved" when, strictly speaking, they should have remained apolitical. The Canadian government "unofficially" allowed them to act politically and vocally. Canada did not reduce funding for NGOs engaged in India and Pakistan. One could paraphrase Canada's reaction by saying that had Canada not supported the cause for Bangladesh, she would not have deliberately ignored the "political" activities of Canadian NGOs in the field.

However, Canada remained doubly cautious in approaching NGO officials to avoid being seen as a pro. When, for example, Stanley Burke of Oxfam Canada approached the government to participate in a proposed private conference titled the South Asia Conference, which had been tentatively scheduled for August 20–22, 1971, he was told frankly that "there can be no question of Cdn govt. actively assisting conf in any way though we equally would not do anything to prevent it being held" (Internal Memo from J.M. Harrington, Head of Pacific and South Asia Division to John Small, high commissioner to Pakistan, p. 1, dated, August 10,

1971. File # 20-Pak E 1-4. Canada. Department of External Affairs). This demonstrates Canada's willingness to cooperate to the extent possible while still adhering to her policy of "neutrality." Another instance of Canada's compassion for the Bengalis was its emergency aid to Pakistan. From the outset, Canada swiftly utilized the UN system and provided resources to Canadian NGOs to undertake humanitarian activities for the refugees in India and displaced Bengalis in East Pakistan.

Following the recommendation of the Committee on External Affairs and National Defence, emergency aid to Pakistan was boosted from an initial $2 million determined by Ottawa to $5 million. By the end of July 1971, a further $50,000 was added. The point is that Canada did not wish to see the Bengalis revictimized. Canadian representatives at the IMF and World Bank who faced questions both at home and abroad responded by explaining how to isolate the provision of humanitarian relief under proper UN supervision and undertaking any new commitments and, at the same time, how to understand the needs of the people of Pakistan and not the needs of the military government throughout the crisis period. Canadian initiatives to halt assistance to new projects almost two months before a formal agreement was reached among the aid-granting countries reinforced Canada's stand against the military ruler that was engaged in suppressing the Bengalis who were to legally assume power after winning the 1970 National Elections.

Again, in Chapter 7, we noted that Canada was also invited by Jayaprakash Narayan, Chairman of the Conference Preparatory Committee and Head of the Gandhi Peace Foundation, to the International Conference on Bangladesh titled *World Meet on Bangladesh*. The Conference was held in New Delhi, India, from September 18 to 20, 1971. Underlying its importance, Narayan personally invited former Prime Minister Lester Pearson. Understandably, Canada did not participate as the objective was to seek support for a "case for Bangla Desh" and discuss the "obligations of the international community." Canada wished to remain "neutral," and to do that, she deliberately ignored the personal appeal of the government of Pakistan not only not to attend but also discourage Canadians from attending the Conference. As was the case, Canada neither participated in the Conference nor discouraged any Canadian from attending. The Trudeau administration left it to Canadians to decide whether they should attend or not. Behind the scenes, however, Canada anxiously awaited the outcome of the meeting. By then, Canada showed her move more toward making decisions based on her raison d'être devoid of the US influence. Canada demonstrated that she acted more independently without any effort to appease the military regime or the Nixon administration.

In our attempt to assess Canada's role in 1971 vis-à-vis the Bengalis' struggle for independence, we may ask the following question: *What activities might be seen as anti-Bangladeshi?* It behooves us to say that Canada deliberately kept the Bangladesh issue out of her "public priorities" or frame of reference. Canada was kept abreast of the progress of the *Mukti Bahini* (Liberation Forces), especially from Canada's New Delhi-based representative, James George. Yet the fact remains that Ottawa officials paid more attention to the possibility of a resolution that would include both wings of Pakistan as then existed than to the political reality of the inevitable birth of Bangladesh. Why? Canada did not support the creation of a separate country (Bangladesh) from Pakistan. All of Canada's efforts were marshaled toward preventing the breakup of Pakistan. Being ardently opposed to cutting Pakistan into two halves, Canada cherished the illusion of a united democratic Pakistan with an elected national leader and prime minister-designate, Bongobondhu.

Canada was in complete agreement with the public that generally held the view that civilized governments should raise their voices against the suppression of human rights and the oppression of defenseless people by the Pakistani military in East Pakistan. While the public vehemently condemned these acts, the government had to find a way to express its views diplomatically, ensuring that such expression did not jeopardize Canada's relations with Pakistan. Small was asked to meet with Yahya several times to convey carefully worded particular messages from Trudeau advising him to exercise restraint. Much to Canada's credit, Canada successfully maintained cordial diplomatic relations with Pakistan at a difficult time, even when the country of Bangladesh was born out of Pakistan. Given Canada's transparency, she could not be accused of partisanship. This way, Canada could engage in diplomacy and aid any party if Canadian values prevailed. Canada's astuteness may be regarded as a success story since Canada addressed a power struggle overseas while simultaneously dealing with her separatist issues at home. Both situations - the Pakistan-Bangladesh separation and the Québec-Canada sovereignty issue - addressed vastly different problems. Resolution for each has stood the test of time. This success attests to the soundness of the Canadian legislative and judicial system and the implementation of its foreign policy of the time.

Sharp's intentional "go slow" approach stemmed from his conviction that a vastly oversimplified analysis of political alternatives would do no good. As a decision maker, Sharp would rather "wait" and "see" to meet all of the policy requirements; he consistently made up his mind through consultation with the members of his think tank. The growing acuity of Sharp's dilemma is understandable when one recognizes why Sharp could not afford to formulate his answers exclusively for MPs, considering Canada's limited foreign policy options. To Sharp's credit, he persuaded his colleagues in the Commons that outside intervention rarely produces desired results and frequently aggravates the situation. This proved to be a recurring theme of Canadian policy during the conflict. A forceful believer in Canadian foreign policy options, Sharp held his position with iron determination. In considering Canada's efforts, we should not overlook the conscientious way Canada dealt with the issues. Given the existing conflictual situations in Québec, Sharp needed to consider the possible consequences on the domestic front.

It is, however, hard to understand why the Trudeau administration was still thinking in terms of a united Pakistan even though the liberation movement strengthened to the "point of no return" in the fall of 1971. One might be inclined to ask the following: How realistic was Ottawa under the circumstances, especially when the freedom fighters were demonstrating not only their deep commitment but also their unwavering determination to achieve their goal—the liberation of Bangladesh backed by India? Being on the ground, Small recognized that hope for a political settlement with Bongobondhu was purely wishful thinking or an unrealistic initiative. Accordingly, on many occasions, while discussing the matter with Ottawa, Small emphasized that Bangladesh was inexorably advancing to independence and that it was only a matter of time. Having seen the progress of rebel forces, Small believed that even if Bongobondhu were released, it would not deter the freedom movement that was an integral part of India's strategic game plan. And yet, despite it all, Canada cherished the illusion of resolving the conflict within the framework of a unified Pakistan.

Looking back, it would seem much too naive on Canada's part to believe that she could effectively counsel restraint and encourage a political solution by keeping a solid relationship with India and Pakistan. It did not work out that way. Ottawa officials saw the absurdity of Yahya's blaming Bongobondhu and India when the ball was in his court to seek a solution. They recognized that the military regime was not "walking the talk." And yet, Ottawa continued to misdirect its energies. True, Canada, as a middle power, had neither the 'great power baggage' nor the US geostrategic interests against Sovietization. With no geopolitical interest in subcontinental politics, Canadians with one voice demanded that the pathetic situation of the Bengalis not be ignored since the lives of millions of human beings were at stake.

Unsurprisingly, Canada followed its foreign policy strategy while cautiously observing the workings of the superpowers. As far as the Trudeau administration was concerned, Canada, with no pretensions of international domination, did not need to embrace international power politics. Canada recognized, as was often the case, that the ideological trenches were dug so deep in the subcontinent that neither the USA nor the USSR was interested in finding common ground. Canada found no escape from American hegemony as a middle power and an ally of the USA. There appeared to be a vacuum of overall responsibility for world order when the situation in the subcontinent had been rapidly deteriorating. As a middle power, Canada was fully aware of its limitations. Under the circumstances of being unable to escape the US Axis, Canada did what she could. Canada made her decisions regarding the welfare of the international community - the world at large.

Whether it was a case of political myopia or Canada's search for a peaceful resolution of international disputes, genuinely speaking, Canada's efforts did not bring any fruition in the end. In any event, one might still argue that Canada's efforts and initiatives could be regarded as "feel-good" endeavors in dire need. For all practical purposes, a middle power Canada's awkward relationship with the superpower US and her helpless position reminds us of Trudeau's Washington Club Speech of October 6, 1969, when he met US President Richard Nixon. Having coined a phrase that came to define US-Canada relations, Trudeau described a memorable analogy, "Living next to you is in some ways like sleeping with an elephant. No matter how friendly and even-tempered the beast is, if I can call it that, one is affected by every twitch and grunt" (https://www.macmillandictionaryblog.com/sleeping-with-an-elephant).

Again, as an ally of the US and a middle power, Canada was pitifully unable to decide on its own in matters where the superpowers had a direct stake. Trudeau, who did not hesitate to remind Canadians of Canada's geopolitical situation concerning its giant neighbor, said, "I emphasize that as a Canadian, I am concerned about the degree of interdependence between our two countries and the extent to which decisions taken in Washington can affect us. I consequently believe it is important for us to try to establish guidelines between our two countries for governing our behavior toward each other, which will at least reduce to a minimum the possibility of unilateral decisions being taken that can affect us very significantly" (Canada. House of Commons. *Debates.* Queen's Printer, dated December 7, 1971, p.1020).

Regardless of Canada's position, throughout the liberation war, Canada always had a soft spot for Bongobondhu, who embodied democracy. With the imposition of martial law and the military crackdown, Canada saw the Bengalis as the direct victims of military atrocities. The author argues that Canada's actions, or lack thereof, and reactions centering around the military reprisals should not be interpreted as being anti-Bangladeshi during the Bengalis' struggle for independence. Canada continued its tradition of extending diplomatic relations and respect to Pakistan and India using the legislative tools and foreign policy options at the time. Canada's actions, however, were contradictory. Canada felt that the democratic election in Pakistan should stand, but Canada did not condone the brutal human rights atrocities inflicted on the Bengalis. It would behoove us to say that, for diplomatic reasons, the Trudeau administration believed it could not publicly express strong condemnation about the internal affairs of another country. This lay outside Canada's purview, and taking sides was not a part of the Canadian way at the national level.

To appreciate Canada's role in the emergence of Bangladesh, we need to look beyond what happened following the birth of Bangladesh. Canada saw the emergence of Bangladesh as a collapse of military rule and the triumph of democracy - something that Canada cherished all along. Naturally, immediately after the liberation of Bangladesh, Canada's activities centered around the conviction that she would do her best to enable the nascent Bangladesh to survive as a democratic state. Canada believed that the government of war-torn Bangladesh should be prepared to stay the course over some very rocky terrain. Specifically, Canada's efforts immediately following the emergence of Bangladesh were directed to the following areas: (1) Recognition of Bangladesh, (2) Bangladesh's entry into the Commonwealth, and (3) Bangladesh's entry into the United Nations.

Recognition of Bangladesh

In Chapter 9, we saw how quickly Canada looked for ways to move forward in her attempt to recognize Bangladesh once foreign policy requirements did not bind her. We also noted that Canada began to work toward recognizing the newborn country as soon as Bangladesh became an independent country. Canada's embracement of newborn Bangladesh reveals several proactive steps toward Bangladesh. Canada moved forward impressively, although it became a challenge for Ottawa officials to decide on the precise timing of recognition. Canada needed to resolve several issues before moving forward. President Nixon repeatedly appealed to Trudeau to delay Canada's recognition. Trudeau was determined to move as fast as possible. Although Canada maintained a discrete distance from the provisional government of Bangladesh during the War of Liberation, she embraced the newborn country within eight weeks. It became possible because, at that time, Canada was no longer under any policy constraints.

Supported by Cabinet colleagues, Sharp moved ahead smoothly with officially recognizing Bangladesh. Chapter 9 also noted Canada's formal recognition of Bangladesh on February 14, 1972. This highlights two important aspects of the Trudeau administration. The first is that the Trudeau administration, though an ally of the United States, took an independent stand in executing her foreign policy. The second point demonstrates Canada's urgency in recognizing Bangladesh - the sooner, the better. At the same time, Canada continued to lend Bangladesh a hand, having extended its concerns to other areas of the subcontinent, including Pakistan, even after the independence of Bangladesh. This was done to develop new relationships with Bangladesh and maintain its cordial ties with Pakistan that began in 1947. This time around, it was under Bhutto's leadership following the dismemberment of Pakistan. To maintain cordial relations on all fronts, Canada attempted many intricate balancing acts in reduced Pakistan, between the military and civilians, between the Punjabis and minority provinces, plus others, not to ruffle Bhutto's feathers.

Entry into the Commonwealth

Canada's commitment to and "diplomatic engagement in" bringing Bangladesh into the Commonwealth is another instance of a critical role Canada was able to play when unfettered by foreign policy limitations, such as those posed during the Bengalis' struggle for independence. This astute diplomatic initiative also featured outstanding work by Canadian diplomat Arnold Smith, then secretary-general of the Commonwealth. In Chapter 7, we read how, for four months, Smith lobbied various Commonwealth countries to persuade them to turn their attention to the newborn Bangladesh. In pushing the case of Bangladesh, Canada claimed that, historically, Bangladesh, as a part of Pakistan, had already been a part of the Commonwealth for which she needed no new orientation. Such an argument gave Canada an edge to reinforce her point.

Canada also highlighted the sovereignty and authority of the state of Bangladesh, which was solely enforced by the Bangladesh government's forces and institutions. Canada argued that Bangladesh had been ready since its emergence as a sovereign country. In lobbying for Bangladesh's entry into the Commonwealth, Smith argued that it had never been Canada's function to stand between members and take sides. After working with crucial Commonwealth partners, Smith made Bangladesh a member of the Commonwealth on April 18, 1972.

Entry into the United Nations

Canada also played a commendable role in bringing Bangladesh into the UN despite its "middle power status." To achieve her goal, Canada effectively lobbied the superpowers, seeking their cooperation when there existed a clear divide on the issue of Bangladesh. Canada tactfully faced challenges in countering China's strong influence. When a committed Sharp recognized that China was prepared to veto Bangladesh's entry to the UN, he skillfully continued dialogue with his counterpart Chou En Lei, China's foreign minister, during his visit to China between August 15–24, 1972. In response to China's allegation that Bangladesh had not honored the UN Security Council resolution of December 1971 calling for the release of the Prisoners of War (POWs), Sharp diplomatically managed negotiations with the superpowers. Ultimately, an insightful Sharp persuaded the superpowers to accept Bangladesh despite their divisions. On September 17, 1972, Bangladesh obtained membership in the UN mainly due to the successful lobbying of the government of Canada.

Canada's role in the birth of Bangladesh should, therefore, be examined through Canada's prism - her severe limitations due to her limited foreign policy options. Thus, Canada's decision to maintain a certain distance from the rebel forces must be reviewed in the context of Canada's internal political predicaments, especially the Québec situation. It must also be borne in mind that even though Canada stood firmly for democracy, Canada's strict adherence to nonintervention in the internal affairs of another country did not allow her to support a movement for Bangladesh that would break Pakistan apart. The Trudeau administration was convinced that any sign of support for a separate Bengali homeland out of Pakistan would ignite a firestorm of criticism in Canada. Consequently, Canada did not speak out publicly against Pakistan to avoid the risk of straining her relationship with fellow Commonwealth sisters, Pakistan and India. The point to note is that while it is true that Canada could not openly condemn the regime's actions, she certainly did not acquiesce to Yahya's killings of the Bengalis.

Canada experienced numerous obstacles while lobbying or networking diplomatically. Our examination of Canada's efforts in the conflict involving the transfer of power to Bongobondhu, which resulted in military operations, reprisals, declaration of independence, guerilla war between Pakistan and India, and the independence of Bangladesh through India's direct intervention and assistance, reveals Canada's helplessness simply for her constant referral to her dilemma.

Nevertheless, readers must note Sharp's challenging tasks, which required tireless efforts that drove him almost to utter frustration and failure. Even though Canada had demonstrated its mediatory "middle power mediation" and the art and skills of political medicare since the 1950s, it was unsuccessful in 1971.

In our assessment of Canada's role during the Liberation War of Bangladesh, we must also take cognizance of the overarching Cold War backdrop featuring simmering conflicts and tensions between the United States and the USSR that relationship had underpinned and constrained international relations for much of the half-century after the Second World War. In 1971, Canada's stated policy of noninterference clashed with the secretive Cold War policy of the Nixon administration. The US was preoccupied with the Vietnam War since many American lives were still being lost at a time when the emotional commitment of American activists was massively aimed at a complete withdrawal of US troops. Canada saw how the Nixon administration had to consider the "China factor," namely the US diplomatic initiative to establish relations with the People's Republic of China. For various reasons, the US government had to soften its policies and often resorted to duplicity in the face of American public opinion against the Yahya government.

Fifty-three years later, in 2024, Canada's ability to act as an essential middle-ranking power is still questionable. Months after Bangladesh's liberation, Canadian politicians re-visited their role in 1971 during the Bengalis' fight for independence. Despite being sympathetic to the cause of the Bengalis, even Conservative MP Heath Macquarrie, who had been to India and Pakistan as a Canadian delegate, did not directly endorse the separation of East Pakistan. Instead, it was evident that he was concerned about the democratic rights of the Bengalis in Pakistan. Macquarrie consistently demonstrated his compassion and concern for the Bengalis. After the liberation of Bangladesh, he did not hesitate to confess, "Of course, we did not do as much as we could or perhaps should have done…." (Canada. House of Commons. *Debates*. Queen's Printer, 1972. Dated February 25, p. 294)

Again, years later, David Dewitt and John Kirkton aptly described Canada's role as a middle power in international affairs, though not directly referring to the 1971 subcontinental conflict. They referred to the perception of Canada as neither "the smallest of the large nor the largest of the small." (Dewitt, David B. and John J. Kirkton, *Canada as a principal power*, Toronto: John Wiley & Sons, 1983, pp. 21–23). something that holds even today in 2024. Regardless of Canada's efforts to preserve the unity of a re-engineered Pakistan under Bongobondhu, the dismemberment of Pakistan resulted in the emergence of three independent countries out of the Indian subcontinent.

The War of Independence of Bangladesh and its successful outcome (liberation of Bangladesh) meant many things to many people. The dismemberment of Pakistan was neither surprising nor unexpected to many, given how undivided India was partitioned in 1947. Jawaharlal Nehru, India's first prime minister and external affairs minister, is reported to have observed the following: "We expect that partition will be temporary and that Pakistan was bound to come back to us" (K. Sarwar Hasan's article "Political Background of the East Pakistan Crisis" was published in *Pakistan Horizon*, Second Quarter, 1971, Volume 24, No. 2, pp. 3-12. Hasan quoted this from Leonard Mosley's Last Days of British Raj, Iweidenfeld and Nicolson, 1963, p. 501). Maulana Abul Kalam Azad, the well-known Muslim nationalist leader of the day and then president of the All-India Congress who examined the genesis of Pakistan, also made an interesting remark. He clearly showed how the confederation of "sovereign and autonomous states" conceived in the Lahore Resolution never materialized. Historically speaking, Pakistan's death had long been prophesied. Azad wrote that Pakistan, in its present shape, could not last more than a quarter of a century (Kamal Matinuddin. *Tragedy of Errors: East Pakistan Crisis, 1968-1971.* Wajidalis, Lahore, 1994, pp. 15 and 44).

Again, following the same vein, Wyndraeth Humphreys Morris-Jones, British political scientist and constitutional adviser to Lord Albert Victor Nicholas Louis Francis Mountbatten from June to August 1947, also saw the entire issue, including the birth of Bangladesh, as partly historical continuity in the making, as well, as partly a reversal of history. "Bangladesh unsettles the 1947 settlement, but strangely it fulfills the declaration of 1940 which led to partition. It must not be forgotten that the so-called Pakistan resolution of the Muslim League did not refer to one Pakistan but, if anything, to two. The areas in which the Muslims are numerically in a majority, as in the north-western and eastern zones of India, should be grouped to constitute 'Independent States' in which the constituent units shall be autonomous and sovereign. The cry 'Joy Bangla' kills the Pakistan of 1947 - 71 reality to fulfill that of the 1940 dream" (W. H. Morris-Jones. "Pakistan Post-Mortem and the Roots of Bangladesh," published in *The Political Quarterly*, volume 43, Issue 2, April 1972, pp.187–200), observed Morris-Jones.

In a sense, the "1971 historical drama" narrated in this book not only describes the what - the events - but also the how - that is, how the people of the Indian subcontinent perceived the facts and how they related to them "as a matter of critical analysis." This may more aptly be described by referring to the unique terms coined by the American diplomat and historian George Kenan, who utilized them in many of his historical writings (cited in *The October Crisis, 1970: An Insider's View* by William Tetley, McGill-Queen's University Press, Montreal, 2007, p. xxvi). We may easily find a nexus between the *what* and the *why* elements of the 1971 tragedy. In the present Pakistan-Bangladesh historical drama, the answer to the question of *what* would refer to the military repression and ongoing reprisals against Bengali civilians by the "Occupation army," the answer to the question of *why* it would refer to the motive of the Yahya regime, which had a thirst for the perpetuation of power.

Canada wondered about the sincerity and soundness of President Yahya, who only a couple of months earlier had called Bongobondhu the future prime minister of Pakistan. Within weeks, the regime arrested him as a traitor. He let loose his soldiers against the Bengalis. The general portrayal of the parties involved represented their different perspectives on the conflict involving Pakistan, India, and Bangladesh. The three protagonists and their supporters also represented three distinct interest groups.

Though the military regime had steered a challenging course between extremist firebrands (adhering to Pakistan's integrity) and extremist diehard Mujibites (pro-liberationists), it lacked the leadership and ingenuity to find a compromise formula, something that convinces one to say that the military was opposed to transferring power to Bongobondhu. In the end, the top military man, Yahya, was seen as being inexcusably callous and self-indulgent in managing the fate of millions of Pakistanis. His egocentrism, a trait not unusual in politicians and military brass, was peculiarly blatant and sometimes offensive.

A ruthless and cold-blooded Yahya was not only a dictator but a political novice who did not rest until he finished what he set out to do with a strong desire to bring a despicable Bongobondhu to his knees, cutting Bongobondhu down to size. Surrounded by good-time women and well-known for his hedonistic life of drinking, sexual pleasure, and carefree entertainment, Yahya remained indifferent to the critical situation in Pakistan even when Pakistan was at war with India. So strong was his innate propensity for lust, ardent longing for lasciviousness, and concupiscence that he displayed the worst side of his kinky sexual behavior. His excessive carnal desire and lustfulness, which was an open secret, forced him to indulge in debauchery at a time when he needed to take complete charge of the country. Instead, he remained uninterested and insensitive to the country's urgent needs when in command. Looking back, Yahya's sexual appetite and depravity made him relinquish his duty as commander-in-chief of the army. It would not be an exaggeration to say that a vainglorious President Yahya stood for timeless military rule by any means, fair or foul. With his monumental ego and martial braggadocio, Yahya was obsessed with proving his machismo, his love of his belief in the invincibility of Pakistan's military strength.

True, Yahya was holding the fort, but there were many other key players, such as Lieutenant-General Tikka Khan, popularly known as the "Butcher of Baluchistan;" General Abdul Hamid Khan, chief of staff; Lieutenant-General S. M. G. Peerzada, principal staff officer and President Yahya's closest confidant; General Mohammad Akbar Khan, head of military intelligence; and later, commander in the Kashmir Sector, Major-General Ghulam Omar, in charge of Commander of Eastern Command. They were attracted to each other, perhaps because each had similar attributes, energy, and wrath against Bengalis. This reminds readers of the maxim, "Birds of the same feather flock together."

No one failed to notice how President Yahya's so-called negotiation with Bongobondhu and Bhutto was replaced by a combination of political expediency and raw bigotry that played directly into the hands of the mischievous regime as he set in motion his plan for the elimination of the ultra-Bengali nationalists. Despite evidence of genocide, the diabolic Yahya regime continued to stick to its blame game. The Awami League leadership had counted on their success in paralyzing the civil administration, combined with their subversion of the loyalty of many armed forces units.

After trying all avenues of compromise and having failed to evoke a statesmanlike or moderate response consistent with the concept of a united Pakistan, the President was left with no choice but to make the painful decision to preserve the integrity of the country as he had repeatedly warned he would, "should the need arise." This was stated in the Government of Pakistan's *White Paper on the Crisis in East Pakistan* (August 5, 1971, p. 21). An intransigent Yahya, while continuing his blame game, persistently and preposterously maintained that Pakistan's problem lay not in East Pakistan but in India. As the world media saw the situation, all efforts were directed to portray India as the real adversary at a time when the root cause was the unequal sharing of the countries' resources and power.

Although the winds of change had been blowing in all directions, Yahya failed to recognize the growth of national consciousness as a political fact. A stubborn Yahya ignored the world's reaction, pretending he was omniscient. It was a colossal and ill-advised misjudgment - a political *faux pas*. Ironically for Pakistan, India won a military victory even more significant than Israel's swift and total defeat of Egypt in 1967.

In the opinion of the world at large, as expressed through international news media, the sudden and secret military crackdown on unarmed civilians of East Pakistan was one of Yahya's nefarious plans. The world media did not fail to note how the Pakistani army killed people without remorse, having convinced themselves that hate, torture, and murder are justifiable and honorable, especially when dealing with the agents of Pakistan's archenemy, India. Regardless of what the military regime maintained about the role of the Gandhi administration, in fact, the government itself, represented by Yahya, was the agent of persecution in "Occupied Bangladesh."

One might say a diabolic Yahya, in the end, got a Roland for an Oliver. Tragically, Yahya's abandonment of his duty was like the decadent, unpopular, and ineffectual Emperor Nero of Rome in times of crisis. A derelict Yahya remained indulged in carnality even when India was forcing the Pakistani army to a shameful surrender. One is reminded of the often-quoted phrase, "Niro fiddled while Rome burned."

Again, Zulfikar Ali Bhutto, leader of the Pakistan People's Party, considered himself a smart aleck and was intensely jealous of Bongobondhu's meteoric rise. He stood for egotism and self-gain. He was a challenging and wily political manipulator who wanted to be head of Pakistan, even at the cost of a united Pakistan divided into two Pakistans. In carrying out his mischievous plan, a rapacious Bhutto always tried to ride roughshod over Bongobondhu, disregarding common courtesy. According to John Small, Canada's high commissioner to Pakistan, who met Bhutto numerous times, Bhutto "has proved to be clever, mean, unscrupulous, irresponsible and power-hungry" (Confidential telegram from John Small, High Commissioner to Pakistan, to Ottawa. Telegram # 330, dated April 19, 1971. File # 20-Pak-11- 4. Canada. Department of External Affairs).

The loss of Pakistan was Bhutto's political gain as he became the leader of the people of West Pakistan, which became Pakistan. Being on his high horse throughout the period, a megalomaniac, Bhutto, suffered from delusions of grandeur. Looking back, many would now find Bhutto comparable to Colonel Odumegwu Ojukwu of Nigeria, who was not only charismatic but also someone who did not believe in compromise. The two self-centered leaders resembled each other in their insatiable lust for power and asked: *What is in it for me?* It was a matter of "all or nothing," as both were made of the same stuff. To the embittered Bengalis, Bhutto was a devil incarnate and was yelled at.

Being extra chummy with Yahya, Bhutto tried to get brownie points and kept his cards close to his chest. His technique was to drag Bongobondhu through the dirt by making damaging allegations, such as he is engaged in dismembering Pakistan - something that would make people question Bongobondhu's loyalty to Pakistan. In following this line of argument, he tried to throw dust in other people's eyes, portraying Bongobondhu as an agent of India. In that sense, Bhutto stooped to mudslinging, having devised a different narrative to undermine Bongobondhu's integrity. The idea was to knock Bongobondhu off, and then there could be a shot-gun marriage between the military regime and Bhutto to save the country. That did not happen. As was the case, a political opportunist, Bhutto, played the giddy goat throughout the negotiation and remained flint-hearted, stubborn, and unyielding. Ultimately, neither Bhutto nor Yahya could put Bongobondhu in the shade. Bongobondhu emerged as the winner.

Just like Yahya and Bhutto, to the people of West Pakistan, the Bengalis' fight for independence was nothing but a breakup of Pakistan by unpatriotic, disloyal, and outright enemies of Pakistan. To them, the entire effort was the dismemberment of a united Pakistan through the machination of India's abetting the rebel forces, a shattering blow indeed. They found it ironic that the desire of the Bengalis for greater autonomy at the end threw them into the clutches of the very people they had liberated from in 1947. With the Pakistanis, however, there was a minuscule number of Bengali loyalists (or pro-unity) and die-hard federalists who adhered to the ideology of a united Pakistan. To them, despite everything, the birth of Bangladesh meant the beginning of domination by Hindu India. Unsurprisingly, they were driven by their innate loyalty to an Islamic polity and the indivisibility of Pakistan. They were not swayed by the Awami League's call for a separate secular homeland for the Bengalis. The Bengali Pakistani loyalists, though a minimal number, were locked in a bitter ideological conflict for their allegiance to Pakistan.

As for India, or with the Gandhi administration, it was another ballgame altogether that it played, keeping in mind taking every possible advantage to dismember Pakistan, its archenemy. India believed that its plan of military aggression against Pakistan with the involvement of *Mukti Bahini* needed to be carefully orchestrated.

Much to the happiness of the people of India, the Gandhi administration's efforts at exploiting the refugee issues, the *casus belli* for going to war with Pakistan, ended with grand success. It was an instance of India's victory over her political adversary, resuming trade and other inter-country agreements and creating new opportunities for friendships with her neighbor. In that sense, it was a classic case of successful intervention on the Gandhi administration's part to achieve one of the most important, though unstated, goals of her foreign policy objectives - to cut Pakistan to size. Many literate Bengalis knew what David Loshak of *The Daily Telegraph* had observed earlier, "India can see only good in the dismemberment or permanent enfeeblement of its chief antagonist. It is this, rather than concern for the fate of innocent people, that lies behind India's propaganda war on behalf of Bangla Desh" (*The Daily Telegraph* [London] May 6, 1971). This was, of course, in addition to gaining a friendly neighbor, Bangladesh, that would underscore the strength of the Indian philosophy of a secular polity.

Nevertheless, although India played a pivotal role in forcing the Pakistani army to surrender, the Government of India, for diplomatic reasons, preferred to give more, much more, credit to the Liberation Forces, having undermined its role and contribution. Unsurprisingly, therefore, just two days before the final victory, having downplayed India's role, Jagjivan Ram, defence minister, humbly observed in the Parliament, "The dedication, keenness, energy, and initiative of freedom fighters have been largely responsible for creating conditions which have compelled the occupying forces to vacate the areas occupied by them. We hope that through the joining operation of Bangla Desh and the Indian forces, the process of liberation of Bangla Desh will soon be completed" (Statement by Defence Minister Jagjivan Ram, in Parliament on December 14, 1971. This was sent to Ottawa by James George, high commissioner to Canada. Ourtel 5260 December 15/71; subject: India/Pak Relations: Sitrep X1V. File # 21-3-Indo-Pak. Canada. Department of External Affairs).

The Bengalis of all ages came out to the streets and danced on the roofs of buses; while singing their national anthem, many clambered over the trucks, cheering and greeting the Indian soldiers and freedom fighters as liberators. This was a way of expressing their gratitude to the Indians for their overwhelming outpouring of sympathy and support for the cause of the Bengalis. They admire India's sharing of pain, suffering, assistance, and hospitality at the darkest hour of Bangladesh's national history. So excited were the Bengalis that many brought the green, red, and gold banner of Bengal out of secret places to flutter freely from buildings. At the same time, pictures of their imprisoned leader, Bongobondhu, sprang up overnight on trucks, houses, and signposts in cities and towns across the country.

While the Bengalis considered Bhutto the true villain, they saw Gandhi as their true friend. Even though many had expressed their views on India's role, that she had a grand design to dismember Pakistan, the Bengalis never, for a minute, forgot to express their gratitude to the government of India. Frankly, feeling triumphant, the Bengalis could not care less.

As for Canada, she remained concerned from the beginning. Canada found the Pakistan-Bangladesh conflict replete with all the complexities and uncertainties inherent in the international political system. The Trudeau administration recognized the regime's game plan, which was to introduce a revisionist history—a different narrative that it was a kind of "apprehended insurrection" that was a "concocted lie." Although Yahya was throwing ideas pell-mell, they were mere appendages, little frills, and add-ons instead of any substantive changes in Canada. Canada disagreed with Yahya's version that Pakistan's problem lay not in East Pakistan but in India. Canada saw how the military regime was directing its efforts to portray India as the real adversary at a time when the root cause was the discriminatory treatment of East Pakistanis. Canada "was impressed by the magnificent response of the government and the people of India to this challenge" (Statement by CIDA's President Paul Gérin-Lajoie at the Third Committee, United Nations General Assembly, Concerned with Human Rights, November 18, 1971. File # 38-11-1-Pak. Canada. Department of External Affairs).

Although Canada maintained that it was an internal affair of Pakistan, Canada was well aware of India's position and her actions about such questions, as stated by Gandhi herself, "It is a calculated attempt by the rulers of Pakistan to make India a scapegoat for their misdeeds. What was claimed to be an internal problem of Pakistan has also become an internal problem of India" (Government of India. Press Information Bureau. *Lok Sabha. P.M.'s Statement on Situation in Bangla Desh*, dated May 24, 1971. This document was sent to Ottawa by James George, high commissioner to India, in a Memo under the title, India-Pakistan Relations. Memo No. 313. Dated May 26, 1971. File # 20-India-1-3-Pak, pp. 5–7. Canada. Department of External Affairs). Ottawa agreed with India's view but still could not intervene.

A diplomatic trouble-shooter, Canada saw herself as a "helpful fixer" and honest "broker" in the charged world of superpower politics. Canada was ineffectual in pursuing such an agenda. The Trudeau administration procrastinated in dealing with the bigger picture involving, on the one hand, the governments of Pakistan and India and, on the other hand, rebel forces and the representatives of the provisional government of the People's Republic of Bangladesh. It became evident to a helpless Canada how India and Pakistan were heading for a confrontation while the Bengali rebels were fast advancing toward their cherished goal of an independent

Bangladesh. All of this appeared to be overwhelming for Canada, a country not historically forceful.

Time and again, Canada pressed for the need for "dialogue" with Bongobondhu, who they felt must rightfully be the head of Pakistan. Having resorted to the strategy of "suasion," the Trudeau government never ceased its efforts. It believed it would succeed only if it could generate interest between India and Pakistan and be willing to give and take. Despite cautionary analysis of future scenarios, Canada remained persistent until the last day when it drove home the message that power should be transferred to the Bengali leader. Canada continually worked hard to strengthen the search for a peaceful settlement without ever reviewing her strategy or game plan. Ottawa officials did not consider any information regarding the fast-changing political reality. This may be seen as the most significant flaw in the Canadian strategy, discounting the potential strength of the rebel forces fully backed by the Gandhi administration that justified the aggression by using the notion of casus belli about the frightened Bengali refugees.

As a middle power, Canada found it ironic that President Yahya, who had earlier referred to Bongobondhu as prime minister-designate, also called him the "enemy" of Pakistan. During the crisis, Canada sensed the imminent danger, a catastrophic threat hanging like the sword of Damocles. In any event, in the end, the government and the people of Canada embraced the liberation of Bangladesh as a natural outcome of the Bengalis' struggle for independence regardless of the Trudeau administration's rigid position during the liberation war, although Canada thought long and hard. The Trudeau administration was happy to see how the Bengalis found themselves amid intense joy and happiness as though they were in seventh heaven.

In all of this, both during the liberation war and following the birth of Bangladesh, one of Canada's challenges was not to strain her relationship with India or Pakistan. As a senior member of the Commonwealth, Canada viewed India and Pakistan as two sisters of the same Commonwealth based on the notion of equal friendship and cordiality for both. One might say, diplomatically, that Canada was running with the hare and hunting with the hounds. Canada did not wish to see India and Pakistan on a collision course.

No matter how one slices it, Canada's position was that a return to civilian rule in East Pakistan, based on the transfer of power to the elected representative of the people of Pakistan, would offer the best hope of progress toward a solution. As each day passed, Bangladesh became a reality that was much to the profound resentment of Yahya. At the height of the polemical debate, Sharp made it clear that his government was not ready to recognize Bangladesh since Canada wanted to see a constitutionally framed reengineered Pakistan that would be democratic, representing the will of the majority where the prime minister-elect, Bongobondhu, would assume power in all of Pakistan. Put differently, while Canada agreed with the causes of the conflict, she did not necessarily agree with the proposed cure for the crisis (i.e., outright independence).

With this objective in mind, all of Canada's efforts were directed toward saving Pakistan as a united democratic country that would not be under military rule but under Bongobondhu. One might observe that Canada's efforts to find a solution within a unified Pakistan without considering Bangladesh's emergence would probably remain a history of political misjudgment or a lack of foresight and political realism. Given Canada's severe foreign policy constraints, one could say, surgically, Canada had been a conscientious midwife to the birth of Bangladesh.

The curtain finally dropped on one of the most painful and tragic dramas in the subcontinent, with the birth of Bangladesh as the fulfillment of the romantic desire of the Bengalis who were determined to live in a free country that they love with passion. Amid joy and jubilation, Canadians were reminded by one of their reporters of the following harsh reality on the ground: "At week's end, the streams of refugees who walked so long and so far to get to India began making the long journey back home to pick up the threads of their lives. For some, there were happy reunions with relatives and friends, for others tears and the bitter sense of loss for those who will never return" (*TIME* [Canada Edition] Ronalds-Federated Limited, Montreal, Evergreen Press Ltd. Dated, December 20, 1971, p. 34.). Canada's government and people welcomed Bangladesh with open arms like flowers in May.

Canadians were neither surprised nor shocked to see the outcome—the liberation of Bangladesh. Through the media's history lesson, Canadians were aware of the extreme desire of the Pakistani military and the bureaucracy, represented by non-Bengali West Pakistanis, to retain power to govern the Bengalis of East Pakistan and keep them subjugated. The Canadian public quickly recalled how the news media earlier predicted the end of the military regime in the widely separated halves of Pakistan; sooner or later, regardless of the immediate outcome, the eventual separation of the two quite different linguistic and economic wings now would be rigid to prevent in the years ahead." (*The Ottawa Citizen*, dated March 29, 1971). They also recalled what one of their favorite news reporters, John Walker, told them about Bongobondhu's prediction of the destiny of the Bengalis. "As Sheikh Mujibur Rahman told me in Dacca [sic] three weeks ago, President Yahya Khan has the military might to crush an unarmed people but in the long run, he cannot crush the spirit of the Bengali people." (*The Ottawa Citizen*, dated March 29, 1971). As was the case, it happened in less than a year.

By and large, Canadians saw the entire episode as a ghastly calamity that befell the Bengalis—a human tragedy of staggering proportions. The ubiquitous military presence, the armed guards at every turn, and the slaughter of millions of Bengali civilians are still sad and living memory among Canadians. With a heavy sigh of relief and a feeling of deep joy, the average Canadian, the man on the Clapham omnibus, saw how having fought in moral quicksand, the "Occupation" of Bangladesh became a political albatross; how the ignoble regime was forced to surrender.

As far as the Bengalis were concerned, having lived through apocalyptic events in "Occupied Bangladesh," their psyche had been deeply rattled as they recall how they were filled with the most poignant human emotions—an outpouring of contempt and vitriol against the regime. The resilient Bengalis were rewarded just as they rose like a phoenix from the ashes, having emerged as a new nation on earth. The impregnably mighty military power could not keep the country together. Their retribution came as an amputation of the country they wanted to hold on to forcibly. The Bengalis' struggle was for the liberation of their native land and the birth of a new sovereign country through the sacrifices of tens of thousands of their fellow compatriots.

Amid joy and exuberance, the Bengalis recalled how, nine months ago, the Pakistani army embarked on its massive program of destruction, torturing, and killing, resulting in the most incredible mass refugee movement, numbering almost nine million. They also watched how millions of refugees had already started to return to homes burned, businesses looted, factories partly demolished and stripped of vital machinery, and roads and railway bridges blasted. True, Bangladesh was born but from a sea of blood and gore. At that time, the entire final measure of the tragedy - three million killed, two hundred thousand women raped – had not yet been assessed.

The number of killings and atrocities during the civil war from March 5 to December 3, 1971, until the civil war turned into the Indo-Pakistani war from December 4 to 16, will perhaps never be known in precise terms. What is known is that the Pakistani army and auxiliary forces committed heinous crimes against humanity and Bengali civilians and insurgent forces (*Mukti Bahini* and other auxiliary militant groups) as well as killings, to a certain extent, by the members of the freedom fighters, of Biharis, non-Bengalis, and those who were suspected of being loyalists and supporters of Pakistan. Though war-ravaged, the Bengalis saw the newborn Bangladesh as a land of enthralling beauty where the more significant the suffering, the more terrible the events, the more intense their innermost feeling.

In a fit of patriotic hysteria, it was as though everything was brought before them in a bewildering profusion. The surrender of the Pakistani army instantly heightened the Bengalis' nationalistic sentiment that made them proud just by the very thought that they were successful in driving out the "Occupation Army" and liberating their native land with the help of India. Having overcome a human tragedy of monumental proportions, the Bengalis were quick to pick up the charred threats of life. They continued to display their sense of enthusiasm and spirit of camaraderie with a sense of profound joy and exhilaration. Amid cries of joy and jubilation, during their moments of ecstasy, the Bengalis did not forget how they were struggling with all kinds of rumors while placed in a chaotic and confused state.

Given the number of casualties of the Bengalis, one might be inclined to call it a pyrrhic victory since it inflicted a devastating toll on the Bengalis. Nevertheless, the Bengalis' victory through a heavy toll does not negate any true sense of achievement. They expressed their gratitude to the freedom fighters of Bangladesh and all those who sacrificed their lives for their country. Instantly, the Bengalis paid homage to the dead freedom fighters also. True, many of the freedom fighters did not live to breathe in the free air of Bangladesh, but their fellow Bengalis saw them as martyrs who sacrificed their lives for the cause of the greater good; they became immortal in name and fame. One is reminded of the famous saying of Lord Byron, one of the great romantic English poets, "They never fail who die in great cause."

In their euphoric moments, the Bengalis also remembered fondly how being enthralled and bedazzled by Bongobondhu's charisma, they embraced him with a feeling that he was creating a greater nation, a nation of their own, one that would steer away from the destructive force of a military regime. The Bengalis, en masse, recalled their chief protagonist, the undisputed leader Bongobondhu, who, to them, was a man of conscience with no designs on personal power. As far as they were concerned, having dedicated themselves to establishing the Bengalis' collective survival, Bongobondhu epitomized the romantic notion of fairness, equality, and equal opportunities for all Pakistanis. Such concepts drew him to politics through a passion for liberty and guided him by a sense of what he believed to be the best for his people, hitherto discriminated against in the hands of the central government.

While celebrating the victory immediately following the surrender of the Pakistani army, the Bengalis also recalled how they lacked accurate information; there was no confirmed news from the field. This was especially true following the sudden imposition of martial law and the commencement of indiscriminate killings of unarmed civilians and wanton destruction of property. They remembered how the frightened Bengalis were fleeing to India to seek asylum and how hundreds and hundreds of Bengalis joined the Bangladesh Liberation Force by responding to their leaders' inspirational call to "fight the enemies." At one point, they felt they were in the dark, not knowing what was happening.

Some claimed they heard Bongobondhu's Declaration of Independence on the morning of March 26. Many others recalled how, on March 27, in quick succession, they heard two versions of the actual Declaration of Independence by Major Ziaur Rahman, Second-in-Command of the Eight East Bengal Regiment in Kalurghat, north of Chittagong. The first was with an emphatic appeal, "We revolt." Then Major Zia made another bold declaration as head of the provisional government of Bangladesh in the following revised declaration: "In the name of Sheikh Mujibur Rahman, I call upon all Bangalees to rise against the attack by the West Est Pakistan army. We shall fight to the last to free our motherland. By the grace of Allah, victory would be ours - *Joy Bangla*" (https://www.thedailystar.net/frontpage/zia-makes-radio-announcement-independence-1554046). The Bengalis felt reassured after hearing from an unknown Zia's repetition of the revised declaration.

As far as the Bengalis were concerned, with searing irony and compassion amid high spirit and cheerfulness, they recalled the excellent powers of the oration of the two admired dramatis personae to guide them.

Specifically, with his noble dream, Bongobondhu was capable of sublimity, having transformed the morale of the Bengalis, which radiated with confidence and courage. Bongobondhu was seen as an untiring apostle of optimism from the bedroom to the boardroom, from Ramna Race Course to the world stage. They also remembered how they instantly bestowed the leadership mantle on Bongobondhu, who spoke straight from the heart. In that sense, Bongobondhu represented the hopes and aspirations of the Bengalis, united in a fight for a land to call their own. To the Bengalis, Bongobondhu was the man of the hour, a politician of all seasons—the real McCoy. Fortunately for the Bengalis, although Bongobondhu was absent, the Bengalis remained united, having immediately responded to Major Zia's clarion call. They recalled with gratitude how passionately Bongobondhu named the country Bangladesh Golden Bengal (*Shonar Bangla*). As far as the Bengalis were concerned, *Shonar Bangla* was the holy grail of Bongobondhu's life - his heart's desire.

In the absence of Bongobondhu, Major Zia's call to the nation was so powerful that it immediately caused the Bengalis to join the War of Liberation. At a time when they felt abandoned and without a leader who could lead them, they were impressed to see how Major Zia, an obscure military personnel, instantly became a prominent Bangladesh Forces Commander, displaying his heroic courage and deep commitment. When the Bengalis heard Zia's bold and inspiring declaration, they kicked the pricks en masse. Zia's timely radio broadcast from *Swadhin Bangla Betar Kendro* removed the confusion and rejuvenated the entire Bengali populace that was terror-stricken then. Major Zia's loud and clear call had the power to stir his people to solid determination and cheering enthusiasm to join the liberation forces in the absence of Bongobondhu, whose whereabouts were unknown since the Pakistani army had already arrested him. Relatively a new kid on the bloc, they recalled how Zia's Declaration of Independence entered the Bengalis' psyche. While the Pakistani army had continued indiscriminate attacks on Bengali civilians all through the entire "Occupation Period," it had also been providing all kinds of disinformation and misinformation that contributed to chaos and confusion.

The critical message from their leaders, as the Bengalis understood, was to rise against the attack by the West Pakistani army at a time when the Bengalis were awaiting Bongobondhu's marching order since his March 7 inspiring call to fight out the army people with whatever weapons they had on their hands. The Bengalis of all political backgrounds rallied around their leaders with one single goal—to win the War of Independence.

Infused with high morale and amid joy and euphoria, when the entire populace was in a state of nirvana while still celebrating their victory, the Bengalis also expressed gratitude for the pivotal role of Maulana Abdul Hamid Khan Bhashani who had "called for outright independence ever since the December 7 general election" (*The Globe and Mail*, March 10, 1971) and a significant number of Awami League leaders who formed the provisional government of Bangladesh, as well as the allied forces (India and liberation forces) for making Bangladesh a reality.

The Bengalis were so excited that their elated feelings of love and happiness reminded one of Robert Browning's *"The Patriot,"* "It was roses, roses all the way." Amid jubilation and ecstasy, the gleeful Bengalis found themselves in a festive environment in their victorious moments as though they were, in the words of Browning, "with bells ringing and walls swaying with the crowds and cries." While expressing their feelings of joy and pride, they got down to their knees to pray to the Almighty Creator for their revered interned leader Bongobondhu, who, at that time, was still in jail in Pakistan, and other leaders, such as Tajuddin Ahmed, Syed Nazrul Islam, Professor Muzaffar Ahmed, and many others who were still in India, that they soon returned to a free Bangladesh. Their victory amplified their feelings of national pride and a new shared identity, with the birth of Bangladesh as an independent country reinforcing their nationalist sentiment. Rarely in the history of the Bengalis had there been an instance of extraordinary solidarity, a sense of belonging, and unity having recognized the value of collective action. The Bengalis' victory instilled in them confidence and optimism about the nascent Bangladesh with a deep sense of unity and idolization of their admired leaders among people of different political stripes.

Years later, Dr. Mizanur Rahman Shelley, one of the distinguished political scientists of Bangladesh, wrote about the challenge that "was crowned with success spectacularly in the case of Bangladesh at the close of 1971" (Mizanur Rahman Shelley. *Emergence of a New Nation In a Multi-Polar World: Bangladesh.* Academic Press and Publishers Library, Dhaka, Bangladesh, 2007, p. 3). He referred to the emergence of Bangladesh as "the Caesarean birth of Bangladesh" that "marked the success of the first armed separatist struggle in the post-1945, post-colonial Third World" (*Ibid.*). He saw the victory of Bangladesh as a victory against *internal* colonialism; that is, an unprecedented success story, an example of "the development of the polycentric world of today [that] helped hasten the birth of Bangladesh" (*Ibid.*).

In closing, the Pakistan-Bangladesh conflict and its fallout may also be seen from afar. Perhaps from a balcony seat in a theater, through the lens of classical literature, a literary lens that portrays significant conflict on a grand stage with stubborn, persistent, and capricious players. Each represents a different emotion or spirit that changes with the narrative. In the words of William Shakespeare:

All the world's a stage,
And all the men and women merely players;
They have their exits and their entrances;
And one man in his time plays many parts,
And so, he plays his part.

SELECT BIBLIOGRAPHY

Primary Sources

A. Archival Sources

Canada. Department of External Affairs. Classified Information

Series: 20 - BANGLA- 1-3.
Series: 20 - BANGLA- 1-4, volumes 1–3.
Series: 20 - E- PAK -1- 4.
Series: 20 - INDIA - 1-3.
Series: 20 - INDIA - 1-2 PAK.
Series: 20 - PAK-E-1- 4.
Series: 20 -1-2-PAK-1-4, volumes 20–213.
Series: 20 - INDIA-1-4.
Series: 21-3-INDIA-PAK-SITREP.
Series: 21-3-INDIA-PAK-.1
Series: 21-3-INDIA-PAK-2.
Series: 11-1-BANGLA.
Series: 38 - 11-1- PAK, volumes 4–9.
Series: 47-9-INDIA-PAK, volume 1.

Library and Archives Canada

Manuscript Group (MG)

MG 28 1 10 Volume 20, File: UN High Commissioner for Refugees, 1971–1976.

MG 28 I 270, vol. 5. file: Pakistan, Board of Directors Memoranda, 1971.

MG 28 I 270 Volume 5, File: Pakistan, re: Manitoba.

MG 28 I 270 Volume 6, file: Pakistan, Human Interest.

MG 28 1 270 Volume 6, File: Les Smith.

MG 28 I 270 Volume 18, file: Bangladesh Rehabilitation.

MG 28 1327 Volume 165, file # 5.

32 C26 Volume 84, File # 84–20.

32 C26 Volume 87, File # 87–13.

Record Group (RG)

RG 76 Volume 1028 File: 5000-25-606.

Canadian Conference of Catholic Bishops Archives, Ottawa.

Communique - Press Release, reference # 45, dated February 25, 1971.

General Communique-Press Release, titled *Pakistani Conflict.* Dated April 28, 1971, reference # 58.

Plenary Meeting, Item 5-F, April 22, 1971.

B. Official Publications

McClure, Robert B. *Brief to the Commons Committee.* 1971.

McRae John F. *Bangladesh Survey Report.* Canadian International Development Agency, May 1972.

Government of Canada. *Debates of the Senate.* Queen's Printer for Canada, Ottawa, 1971–1972.

Government of Canada. Canadian International Development Agency. *Annual Report,* 1970–1972.

Government of Canada. Department of External Affairs. *Annual Report,* 1970–1972.

Government of Canada. Department of Manpower and Immigration. *Annual Report,* 1972–1973.

Government of Canada. Department of National Defence. *Annual Report,* 1971.

Government of Canada. House of Commons. *Debates.* Queen's Printer for Canada, Ottawa, 1970- 1972.

Government of Canada. House of Commons. "Minutes of Proceedings and Evidence of the Standing Committee on External Affairs and National Defence" Third Session, Twenty-eighth Parliament, 1970–71. Issue No 32, October 5, 1971.

Kennedy, Edwards. "Crisis in South Asia – A Report" Subcommittee Investigating the Problems of Refugees and Their Settlement. Submitted to US Senate Judiciary Committee, U.S. Government Press, November 1, 1971.

Government of the People's Republic of Bangladesh, Ministry of Foreign Affairs. *Bangladesh: Contemporary Events and Documents.* 1971.

Government of the People's Republic of Bangladesh. "History of Bangladesh War of Independence: Documents." *Bangladesher Shadhinota Juddho: Dolilpotro: 1–15 volumes,1982–1985.* Published by Hasan Hafizur Rahman on behalf of Ministry of Information, Government of the People's Republic of Bangladesh, Dhaka, 1982–1985.

Government of India. Ministry of External Affairs. *BANGLA DESH Documents.* B.N.K. Press Private Ltd. Madras, India, 1971.

United Nations General Assembly. Twenty-Sixth Session–1944th Plenary Meetings, Official Record, September 29, 1971.

Government of the United States of America. *Congressional Record Proceedings and Debates of the 92nd Congress,* First Session, vol. 117, no. 132, dated September 14, 1971.

Government of the United States of America. *Congressional Record.* Senate, July 12, 1971.

Government of the United States of America. *Congressional Record.* Senate. Extensions of Remarks, July 8, 1971.

Government of Pakistan. *White Paper on the Crisis in East Pakistan.* Islamabad: Government of Pakistan, August 1971.

Secondary Sources

Books

Akhtar, Jamna Das. *The Saga of Bangla Desh.* Delhi: Oriental Publishers, 1971.

Aziz, K. K. *Britain and Pakistan: A Study of British Attitude Towards the East Pakistan Crisis of 1971.* Islamabad: University of Islamabad Press, 2008.

Brands, William J. *India, Pakistan, and the Great Powers.* London: Pall Mall Press, 1972.

Brines, Russell. *The Indo-Pakistan Conflict.* London: Pall Mall Press, 1968.

Canadian Foreign Policy. Edited by Jack Lawrence Granatstein. Toronto: Copp Clark Pitman Ltd., 1995.

Chowdhury, Roy Subrata. *The Genesis of Bangladesh: A Study in International Legal Norms and Permissive Conscience.* New Delhi, India: Asia Publishing House, 1984.

Desbarat, Peter Hullett. *René: A Canadian in Search of a Country.* Toronto: McClelland and Stewart, 1976, pp. 142-143.

Envoys Essays in Canadian Diplomacy. Edited by David Reece. Carleton University Press, 1996.

Eksterowicz, Anthony J. and Robert N. Robert. *Public Journalism and Political Knowledge*, New York: Rowman and Littlefield Public Inc. London, 2000.

Handel, Dan. *The Process of Priority Formulation: U.S. Foreign Policy in the Indo-Pakistani War of 1971.* Colorado: Westview Press, 1978.

Houle, Alberic Robert. *A Giant of a Man.* Bangladesh: Jerry Printing, 1995.

------------------------- *The Great Flavian.* Dhaka: The Skylab Printers & Packages Ltd., 1991.

The International Commission of Jurists, Secretariat. *The Events in East Pakistan, 1971, a Legal Study.* 1972.

Jackson, Robert. *South Asian Crisis: India-Pakistan-Bangladesh.* New York: Chatto and Windus, 1975.

Keenleyside, Hugh L. et al. *The Growth of Canadian Policies in External Affairs.* Durham: Duke University Press, 1960.

Karen S. Johnston-Cartee, *News Narratives, and News Framing: Constructing Political Reality*, New York: Rowman and Littlefield Pub. Inc.,2005.

Keenleyside, Hugh L., et al. *The Growth of Canadian Policies in External Affairs.* Durham: Duke University Press, 1961.

Khan, Fazal Muqueem. *Pakistan's Crisis in Leadership.* National Book Foundation, Islamabad, 1973.

Khan, Ali Rao Farman Major Gen (Retd). *How Pakistan Got Divided.* Lahore, Pakistan: Jang Publishers, p.55. 1992.

Mackay, R. A. *Canadian Foreign Policy 1945–1954, Selected Speeches and Documents.* Toronto: McClelland and Stewart Limited, 1971.

Mahmood, Safdar. *Pakistan Divided: Study of the Factors Leading to the Breakup of Pakistan in 1971.* Lahore, Pakistan: Jang Publishers, 1993.

Maksud, Syed Abul. *Maulana Abdul Hamid Khan Bhashani.* Bangla Academy, Dhaka, 1994.

Malek, Abdul. *From East Pakistan to Bangladesh: A History of Exploitation and Repression*, Independent Committee for Human Rights, Collyhurst, Manchester, 1973.

Masters, C. Donald. *Canada in World Affairs, 1953 to 1955.* Canadian Institute of International Affairs, Toronto: Oxford University Press, 1959.

Matinuddin, Kamal. *Tragedy of Errors: East Pakistan Crisis, 1968–1971.* Wajidalis, Lahore, Pakistan, 1994.

Misra, Kashi Prasad. *The Role of the United Nations in the Indo-Pakistani Conflict, 1971.* Delhi, India: Vikash Publishing House Pvt Ltd., 1973.

Kenan, George, Liakat Ali Khan, and Walter Lippman. *Pakistan: The Heart of Asia.* Cambridge, Massachusetts: Harvard University Press, 1950.

Public Journalism and Political Knowledge. Edited by Anthony J. Eksterowicz and Robert N. Robert. London: Rowman and Littlefield Public Inc., 2000.

Raghavan, Srinath, *1971: A Global History of the Creation of Bangladesh.* Cambridge, Massachusetts: Harvard University Press, 2013.

Reiner, G. J. *History: Its Purpose and Method.* New York: Harper & Row Publishers, 1950.

Siddiq, Salik. *Witness to Surrender.* Karachi: Oxford University Press,1977.

Sission, Richard, Leo Rose. *War and Secession: Pakistan, India, and the Creation of Bangladesh.* Berkeley: University of California Press, 1990.

Smith, Arnold and Sanger, Clyde. *Stitches in Time: the Commonwealth in World Politics.* Ontario: General Publishing Co. Limited, 1981.

OXFAM. *The Testimony of Sixty: On the Crisis in Bengal.* OXFAM U.K., London, October 21, 1971.

Tewary, I. N. *War of Independence, a Documentary Study with an Introduction.* Varanasi, Navachetna Prakashan, India, 1971.

Timm, Richard W. *Forty Years in Bangladesh: Memoirs of Father Timm.* Caritas Bangladesh, Dhaka, Bangladesh, 1995.

Bulletins, Magazines, Newspapers, Press Releases

Bangla Desh. Bangladesh Association of Canada (Toronto), May–December 1971.

Bangla Desh. British Columbia Bangladesh Association of Canada (Vancouver), May–December 1971.–

Board of Trade Journal. Toronto. Board of Trade of Metropolitan Toronto. September 1971.

The Brandon Sun (Brandon, Manitoba), September 24, 1971.

Canada and the World. Oakville, Ontario, Canada and the World, January–December 1971.

Canadian Broadcasting Corporation. Radio News, CBC Archives, Toronto, March 26–31, 1971.

Canadian India Times. Toronto, Ontario, Canada, January–December 1971.

Canadian Jesuits Mission, Toronto. January–December 1971–1972.

Canadian News Facts: Journal Magazine. Marpep Pub. Toronto, 1970–1972.

Canadian Mennonite Reporter. Waterloo, Ontario, Canada, January–December 1971.

Carillon News. Steinbach, Manitoba, January–December 1971.

Contact. Canadian International Development Agency, March 1972.

CUSO Bulletin. 3/71. Canadian University Services Overseas, Ottawa Ontario, Canada.

The Daily Star. Dhaka, Bangladesh, April 2021.

DAWN. Karachi, Pakistan, March- December 1971.

Le Devoir. Montréal, Québec, Canada, March 1971.

The Economist. The Economist Newspaper Ltd. London, January–December 1971. *L'église Canadienne.* Avril 1971, Editions, Fides. Montréal.

The Evening Patriot. Patriot Publishing Co. Ltd. Charlottetown, Prince Edward Island, August 1971.

The Evening Telegram. St. John's, Newfoundland, Canada, January–December 1971.

Fredericton Gleaner. Fredericton, New Brunswick, Canada, August 1971.

The Globe and Mail. Toronto, Ontario, Canada, 1971–1972

The Guardian. Charlottetown, Prince Edward Island, Canada, August 1971.

The Guardian Weekly. London, UK, August 1971.

Hindustan Times. New Delhi, New Delhi, India, August 14, 1971.

India News. High Commission of India, Ottawa, March–December 1971.

The Indiagram. Information Service of India, Office of the High Commissioner for India, Ottawa, January–December, 1971–1972.

Indian Express. New Delhi, India, July 1971.

Inside Oxfam. Ottawa, Ontario, Canada, January–December 1971–1972.

Joy Bangla. Bangladesh Association of British Columbia (Vancouver), May–December 1971.

Keesings Contemporary Archives. Keesings Ltd. London, January–December 1971.

Kenora Daily Miner & News. Kenora, Ontario, Canada, August 1971.

Kitchener-Waterloo Record. Kitchener, Ontario, Canada, January–December 1971–1972.

Macleans. Toronto, Ontario, Canada, January–December 1971–1972.

Manitoba Brethren Herald. Winnipeg, Manitoba, Canada, March–December 1971.

Montreal Star. Montreal, Québec, Canada, January - December 1971–1972.

Nancy Edwards Reports. Press Release: Week before 12 July 1971. A Berkeley Studio Production for Inter-Church Radio, Toronto.

News Releases. UNICEF Canada, Ottawa, Ontario, Canada, June 1971.

Newsweek. Newsweek Inc. New York, NY, 1971 - 1972.

New York Times. New York, USA, March - December 1971.

The Ottawa Citizen. Ottawa, Ontario, Canada, January–December 1971.

Ottawa Journal. Ottawa, Ontario, Canada. March - December 1971.

OXFAM-UK Bulletins. London, United Kingdom, January - December 1971–1972.

Pakistan Horizon. Pakistan Institute of International Affairs, Karachi, Pakistan, January–December 1971.

Pakistan Times. Lahore, Pakistan, November 20, 1969; February 16, 1971.

Ignatieff Paul. *Pakistani Refugee Camps in India*, Canadian UNICEF Committee, July 7 - 27, 1971.

Batten Albert. *Pakistani Refugees in India, The Report*, League of Red Cross Society, May 25 - August 25, 1971.

Patriot. City Edition, New Delhi, India, March 1972.

Pembina Triangle Progress. Pembina, Manitoba, Canada, September 1971.

People to People Campaign Action, South Asia Emergency Refugee Fund, Glendon College, Toronto, Ontario, Canada, January–December 1971.

OXFAM of Canada. *Press Release.* Ottawa, Ontario, Canada, July 1971.

PRO TEM, Special Supplement to *The Student Weekly of Glendon College,* York University, Canada. Toronto, Ontario, Canada, January–December 1971.

Jackson, Phillip. *Report on Visit to West Bengal, June 20–22, 1971.*

The Scotsman. Edinburgh, Scotland, United Kingdom, April 1971.

Sheaf. University of Saskatchewan, Regina Campus. Regina, 1971–1972.

Sphulingo. Bangladesh Association of Québec. Montreal, June–December 1971.

Star-Phoenix. Saskatoon, Saskatchewan, October 1972.

The Statesman. New Delhi, India, March 1972.

TIME (Canada Edition). Ronalds-Federated Limited, Montreal, Evergreen Press Ltd., January - December 1971.

TIME (UK edition). January - December 1971.

The Times. News UK, Times Newspapers Ltd., January–December 1971 - 1972.

Toronto Daily Star. Toronto, Ontario, Canada, January–December 1971.

Toronto Telegram. Toronto, Ontario, Canada, January--August 1971.

United Nations High Commissioner for Refugees. Press Conference, June 1971.

Washington Post. Washington, DC, July 2, 1971.

Weekend Magazine. Montreal, Québec, Canada, January–December 1971.

Weekly Guardian. London, United Kingdom, April 10, 1971.

Winnipeg Tribune. Winnipeg, Manitoba, September 17, 1971.

World University Services of Canada. *Press Release,* Document No. 71-11-590, November 29, 1971.

Periodical Articles and Reports

"Account of the Meeting between the United Nations High Commissioner for Refugees, Prince Sadruddin Khan, and Head of Canadian Voluntary Agencies," held in the Board Room of the Canadian Council on Social Development Building, Ottawa, on October 25, 1971.

Ali, Meherunnisa. "East Pakistan Crisis: International Reactions," *Pakistan Horizon,* Second Quarter, 1971, Vol. 24, No. 2, pp. 31 - 38.

Ali, Meherunnisa. "Pakistan-Canada Relations," *Pakistan Horizon,* First Quarter, 1974, Vol. 27, No.1, pp. 77–79.

Ali, Meherunnisa. "The Problem of Quebec," *Pakistan Horizon,* Third Quarter, 1971, Vol. 24, No. 3, pp. 20–31.

Andrew, Arthur. "Canada and Asia: The Shifting Power Balance," *Pacific Affairs* 45:3, Fall 1972.

Anjuman-e-Mohajreen Mashriqui Pakistan. "Massacre of Non-Bengalis in East Pakistan by Awami Leaguers and Indian Infiltrators: A Short Story of Their Tears and Blood," Dhaka, East Pakistan, 1971.

Baten, Albert. "Pakistani Refugees in India: The Report, May 25 to August 25, 1971," Canadian Red Cross Society. Toronto.

Burki, Shahid Javed. "Ayub's Fall: A Socio-Economic Explanation," *Asian Survey,* March 1972, pp.201-212.

Canadian Friends Service Committee. *Annual Appeal: Bangla Desh.* Volume 1, No. 10, April 1972.

Delvoie, Louis A. "Hesitant Engagement and South Asian Security," Queen's University, Kingston, Ontario. Centre for International Relations, 1995, p.21.

Francis, Julian. "Relief for Refugees from East Bengal," *OXFAM-UK Bulletin.* No. 32 (August 13, 1971).

Grant, S. Jack. "Big Business has no Heart?" *Board of Trade Journal.* Toronto. Board of Trade of Metropolitan Toronto. September 1971, p. 7.

Haider, Zaglul. "Canadian Policy Towards Bangladesh: How Does the North Look at the South?" *African and Asian Studies* 10 (2011) pp. 281–305.

Haider, Zaglul. "Unfolding Canada-Bangladesh Relations," *Asian Survey,* Vol. 45, No. 2 (March/April 2005) pp. 322–341.

Hasan, Sarwa. "Political Background of the East Pakistan Crisis," *Pakistan Horizon,* Second Quarter, 1971, Vol. 24, No. 2, pp. 3–12.

Heartline to the World. World Vision of Canada. Toronto, September–October 1971.

Ignatieff, Paul. *Pakistani Refugee Camps in India, July 7–27, 1971.* Canadian UNICEF Committee. Toronto.

Inside OXFAM. Fall Edition, No. 23, 1971.

International Conference on Bangla Desh. *World Meet on Bangla Desh, a report of the International Conference on Bangla Desh, h*eld in New Delhi from September 18 to 20, 1971.

Jackson, Phillip. *Report on visit to West Bengal,* June 20–22, 1971. Canadian Red Cross Society, Toronto.

Jafri, Fareed S. *Bangladesh–Campaign for Self-Rule of East Bengal*, published by London, UK, No 4, April 26, 1971 (International edition).

Jahan, Rounaq. "Elite in Crisis: The Failure of Mujib-Yahya-Bhutto Negotiations," Adapted from a paper at the National Seminar on Pakistan and Bangladesh, held at Columbia University in February 1972. p. 575.

Lakavitch, Jack G. "Bangla Desh for Real," (a photocopy of this article is preserved in the records office of the Department of External Affairs, Canada).

Leather, Allan. *Statement on East Bengal Refugee Situation in India: U.S. Senate Sub-Committee on Refugees*, Oxfam Field Representative, 1971.

Morris-Jones, W. H. "Pakistan Post-Mortem and the Roots of Bangladesh," *The Political Quarterly,* volume 43, Issue 2, April 1972, pp.187–200.

Pilkington, Richard. "In the national interest? Canada and the East Pakistan crisis of 1971," *Journal of Genocide Research* (2011), 13 (4), November 2011, pp. 451–474.

Small, John. "From Pakistan to Bangladesh,1969–1972: Perspective of a Canadian Envoy," in *"Special Trust and Confidence"*: *Envoys Essays in Canadian Diplomacy*, edited by David Reece. Ottawa: Carleton University Press, 1996.

Sobhan, Rehman. "Negotiating for Bangladesh: A Participant's View," *South Asian Review*, July 1971, Vol.4, No. 4, p. 315.

"Speech of G. M. Syed," *Pakistan Times*, November 20, 1969.

APPENDIX A

Glossary of Terms

Agartala Conspiracy Case, The. A sedition case in Pakistan during the rule of Ayub Khan against the Awami League, brought by the government of Pakistan in 1968 against Sheikh Mujibur Rahman, then leader of the Awami League and East Pakistan, and thirty-four other people.

Amour-propre, a French term, can be translated as self-love, self-esteem, or vanity. Jean-Jacques Rousseau uses this term in philosophy, contrasting it with another self-love, amour de soi.

Ansars. The Arabic word for helper (foot soldiers).

Au courant. Aware of what is going on; well-informed.

The Awami League, which means "people," developed from a grass-roots political organization founded in East Pakistan immediately after the partition of India into India and Pakistan.

Bangal. Pejorative term employed by the former aristocracy and West Bangalees to refer to the inhabitants of Eastern Bengal. Interestingly, Bangladeshi Bangalees call West Bengal Bangalees *Ghoti*, a round pot.

Bangalee. One whose mother tongue is Bangla. A Bangalee could come from Bangladesh and/or West Bengal, India since both groups speak Bangla.

Bangla. It is the indigenous term for Bengali. It is the language group typically spoken by those of Bengali descent. A Bangla-phone population includes those from the original Bengal province of India, currently spread over eastern India in the province of West Bengal and the People's Republic of Bangladesh (erstwhile East Pakistan).

Bangla Desh. Records of the Gandhi administration show that East Pakistan was referred to as Bangla Desh (spelled in two syllables) when East Pakistani Bengalees were fighting for independence. As a result, the world media also followed the Indian press, and the Gandhi administration was spelled in two syllables. The provisional government of Bangladesh used the term in one syllable from the beginning. Following the independence, the world media began to follow the spelling in one syllable.

Bangladesh. The present-day landmass of an independent country that won its independence (former East Pakistan) on December 16, 1971, is situated at the apogee of the Bay of Bengal.

Bengal. The area, considered Bengal when the British came, was split into East Bengal and West Bengal in 1905 and 1947. Following the creation of Pakistan in 1947, East Bengal became a part of Pakistan, later known as East Pakistan.

Bengalee. The same as Bangalee.

Bengali. The anglicized term for the language Bangla spoken by Bangalees.

Bête noir. A person or thing that one particularly dislikes.

Biharis. Non-Bengali Urdu-speaking Muslim minority in East Pakistan. They migrated to East Pakistan from the State of Bihar, India, following the birth of Pakistan.

Barangana. Penetrated, used for prostitution.

Bihariphobia. Harboring of anti-Bihari sentiment.

Birangana. Rape survivors of 1971. A term coined in 1972 by Sheikh Mujibur Rahman.

blitzkrieg. A German word that refers to the "lightning war" military tactic calculated to create psychological shock and resultant disorganization in enemy forces through the employment of surprise, speed, and superiority in material or firepower.

Bongobondhu. Friend of Bengal. A title given to Sheikh Mujibur Rahman by Bengalis in 1969.

Brother. In religion, the term refers to a missionary who serves within the order without becoming a priest.

Carte blanche. Complete freedom to act as one wishes or thinks best.

Casus belli. A Latin term describing a situation said to justify a state in initiating war. The UN charter provides that warlike measures are permissible only if authorized by the Security Council or the General Assembly or, if necessary, for individual or collective self-defense against armed attack.

Cognoscenti. Originally from the formal Italian language, it means people with much knowledge about a particular subject.

Congregation of Holy Cross. Originally in Latin (*Congregatio a Sancta Cruce*) abbreviated CSC. A Catholic clerical religious congregation of Pontifical Right for men (priests and brothers). It was founded in 1837 by Basil Moreau in Le Mans, France. Moreau also founded the Marianites of Holy Cross, now divided into three independent congregations of sisters: the Marianites of Holy Cross (Le Mans, France), the Sisters of the Holy Cross (Notre Dame, Indiana), and the Sisters of Holy Cross (Montreal, Quebec, Canada).

Coup de force. A sudden, violent act.

Crossing the Rubicon. An idiom that means passing a point of no return. Its meaning comes from allusion to the crossing of the river Rubicon by Julias Caesar in early January 49 BC.

Cul-de-sac. A route or course leading nowhere.

Deus ex machina. A plot device whereby a seemingly unsolvable problem in a story is suddenly or abruptly resolved by an unexpected and unlikely occurrence.

East Bengal. It is a non-contiguous province of the Dominion of Pakistan. Geographically part of the Bengal region, it existed from 1947 until 1955, when it was renamed East Pakistan. Today, the area is an independent country, Bangladesh. Its coastline on the Bay of Bengal borders India and Myanmar.

Expo 1967. The 1967 International and Universal Exposition, commonly known as Expo 67, was a general exhibition held in Montreal, Quebec, Canada, from April 28 to October 27, 1967. It was a category one world's fair.

Fait accompli: Something has already happened or been decided before those affected hear about it, leaving them with no option but to accept it.

Father. In religion, it denotes an ordained Jesuit who has completed all the requirements.

Folie de grandeur. Delusion of greatness; megalomania.

FLQ. The Front de libération du Québec (FLQ), founded in 1963, was a militant Quebec separatist group that aimed to establish an independent and socialist Quebec through violent means. The Canadian government considered it a terrorist group.

FLQ Crisis. Refers to a chain of events in Quebec in the fall of 1970. The crisis was the culmination of a long series of terrorist attacks perpetrated by the Front de libération du Québec (FLQ), a militant Quebec independence movement.

Fortiori. In Latin, it means "from the stronger (argument)." The term is used when drawing a conclusion that is even more obvious or convincing than the one just drawn. Thus, if teaching English grammar to native speakers is difficult, then a fortiori, teaching English grammar to non-native speakers will be even more challenging.

Gherao. It is a form of industrial action in the Indian subcontinent in which workers imprison their employers on the premises until their demands are met.

Hartal. A term in many Indian languages for a strike action that was first used during the Indian independence movement (also known as the nationalist movement) of the early 20th century. A hartal is a mass protest, often involving a total shutdown of workplaces, offices, shops, and courts of law and a form of civil disobedience similar to a labor strike. In addition to being a general strike, it involves the voluntary closure of schools and places of business. It is a mode of appealing to the sympathies of a government to reverse an unpopular or unacceptable decision. A hartal is often used for political reasons, for example, by an opposition party protesting against a governmental policy or action.

Hallstein Doctrine. Named after Walter Hallstein, it was a crucial doctrine in the foreign policy of the Federal Republic of Germany (West Germany) after 1955. As usually presented, it prescribed that the Federal Republic would not establish or maintain diplomatic relations with any state that recognized the German Democratic Republic (East Germany).

idée fixe. In music and literature, it is a recurring theme or character trait that serves as the structural foundation of a work. The term was later used in psychology to refer to an irrational obsession dominating an individual's thoughts to determine his or her actions.

In situ. Being in the national or original position or place.

Infotainment. Subordinating information to entertainment values of drama, emotion, plot simplicity, personal morals, and character conflicts, often presented with theme music and visually appealing scenery.

Islam pasand. The term was used to mean "Islam-loving," specifically by the Pakistan press and public to describe a group of political parties that, in varying degrees, were seen as religious-oriented and which cooperated to some extent with each other. During electioneering, the Pakistani press called the right-wing Islamic parties *Islam pasand.*

Jesuit. A member of the Society of Jesus or the Jesuit Order. The most significant all-male religious order within the Roman Catholic church is the Society of Jesus, more commonly called Jesuits. The order was founded by St. Ignatius of Loyola in Paris, France, on August 15, 1534, when he and six university students pledged to keep vows of chastity, poverty, and obedience and to pilgrimage to Jerusalem. The term is adapted from the Latin word Jesuita (a follower of Jesus).

Joy Bangla. *Joy* means victory. When used as a verb in the standard national slogan *Joy Bangla,* the meaning becomes "victory to Bengal" or "may Bengal always remain victorious."

La Grande Noirceur. In Quebec, the period called la Grande Noirceur (the Great Darkness) refers to the nineteen years when Premier Maurice Duplessis was in power (1936–1939, 1944–1959). The name alludes to the population's suffering during this time. However, some criticize the excess resulting from the myth of the Grande Noirceur and the term's usage in creating a widespread consensus about the Quiet Revolution.

Larkana Conspiracy, The. President Yahya and Bhutto met around mid-January 1971 at Bhutto's baronial family estate in Larkana, Sindh, with several Pakistan People's Party leaders and several Generals. The meeting is known to be the blueprint of Operation Searchlight, aimed at crushing the Bengalis' aspirations for good. There was no news coverage at that time.

Legal Framework Order (LFO). Officially issued on March 30, 1970, the L.F.O. resolved the issue of representation on a population basis in Pakistan. Parity between East and West Pakistan in the National Assembly, a fundamental principle in the 1956 and 1962 constitutions, was discarded, and East Pakistan was conceded 56 percent (169 out of 313) seats.

Lifeline Beta. A unique feeding and medical service for severely malnourished people in refugee camps.

Locus standi. A right to appear in a court or before anybody on a given question. A right to be heard.

Lok Sabha. House of the People.

Maîtres-chez-nous. Masters in our own house.

modus operandi. A particular way or method of doing something, especially characteristic or well-established.

Mujahid Bahini. An Arabic term that broadly refers to people who engage in holy war (jihad), interpreted in a jurisprudence of Islam as the fight on behalf of God, religion, or the community. Mujahideen, or Mujahidin, is the plural form of mujahid.

Mujibite. Supporter of Sheikh Mujibur Rahman, pro liberationist.

Mujibmania. An explosive mix of passion and admiration fueled by media and Bengali renaissance - a nationalist fervor.

Mujibnagar. About 8 km beyond the Indian border of Krishnagar in a mango grove near the village of Baidyanathala in Kushtia District of then East Pakistan. The provisional government of Bangladesh was formed there, and it worked with full support and assistance from the Gandhi administration.

Mukti Bahini/Mukti Fauj. Within the Bangladesh War of Liberation context, Mukti is a Bengali word that means *freedom*. *Bahini* is also a Bengali word meaning *army*. *Fauj* is a Persian word, also used in Bengali, meaning *army*. The Bengali militia was created with Indian support to fight against the Pakistan Army in 1971. Liberation Force comprises the East Pakistan Rifles (EPR), East Bengal Regiment (EBR), policemen, students, and general public members. Together, they are referred to as *Mukti Bahini* (Liberation Forces).

Mukti Joddha. Freedom or liberation fighter.

Mukti Jhoddho. Liberation struggle.

Mutatis Mutandis. Parallel policies toward the two Commonwealth sisters.

October Crisis. It is also referred to as the FLQ Crisis. See also FLQ Crisis.

One-Unit. It was the title of a scheme launched by the federal government of Pakistan to merge the four provinces of West Pakistan into one homogenous unit as a counterbalance against the numerical domination of the ethnic Bengalis of East Pakistan. Prime Minister Muhammad Ali Bogra announced a Unit scheme on November 22, 1954. On October 5, 1955, Iskander Mirza, acting governor-general of Pakistan, passed an order unifying all of West Pakistan in what became known as the One Unit Scheme.

Operation Lifeline. A child nutrition program for refugee children in West Bengal.

Operation Searchlight. A planned military pacification was carried out by the Pakistan Army on March 25, 1971, to cub the Bengali nationalist movement by taking control of the major cities on March 26 and then eliminating all of Pakistan later in December 1971.

Parti Québécois. A political party founded in 1968 that promotes Québec independence paired with an economic union with the rest of Canada.

Québec question. The fear of the separation of Québec has existed since 1970 (October crisis of 1970).

Quid pro quo. A Latin word that means "what for what" or "something for something." The term is also used in the context of politics. *Quid pro quo* can refer to using political office for personal benefit. The mutual consideration between two parties to a contractual agreement renders the agreement valid and binding. Quid pro quo commonly refers to giving one valuable thing for another. It has the same meaning in the law but with varying implications in different contexts.

Quiet Revolution. Within the historical context of Québec, the Quiet Revolution refers to the period between 1960 and 1966, which was marked by reforms that modernized the Québec state and society.

Rajya Shobha. Council of States.

Révolution tranquille. Quiet Revolution. A period of unbridled economic and social development in Québec.

Sangram Samity. A liberation committee began to issue decrees, having assumed the responsibility for the entire province of East Pakistan upon order from Bongobondhu following his March 7 speech.

Sarbadaliya Chatro Sangram Parishad. All Parties Students Action Committee (SAC).

Sarva Seva Sangh (SSS). A registered charitable society involved in formal/non-formal education and empowerment of over 1,500 children in India. The SSS aims to usher in a social order based on truth and non-violence infused by human and democratic values that are free from exploitation, tyranny, immorality, or injustice and which offer enough scope for human personality development.

Satyagraha. Holding firmly to the truth.

Savoir Faire. The ability to act or speak appropriately in social situations.

Scholastic. A term used to designate a Jesuit student during his formation between the novitiate and final vows. It is used to distinguish students from Jesuit Brothers in formation.

Shahid Minar. A national monument in Dhaka, Bangladesh. It was established to commemorate those killed during the Bengali Language Movement demonstrations of 1952 in what was then East Pakistan.

Shonar Bangla. Golden Bengal.

Shwadhin Bangla Desh. Independent Bangla Desh.

Sine die. It's legalese for "indefinitely" and Latin for "without day." *Sine die* means without any future date being designated (as for resumption) or indefinitely.

Sine quo non. An essential condition. It's an essential thing.

Swaraj. In British India, it meant self-government. Independence.

Tamaddun Majlish. It is a literary and cultural organization oriented towards Islamic ideology. This pro-Islamic organization was floated in Dhaka immediately after the partition of India with a zeal to uphold the Islamic ideology in the country. It was founded on September 1, 1947, by the initiative of Abul Kashem, who was then a professor in the Department of Physics of Dhaka University. It was named Pakistan *Tamaddun Majlish*.

The Tet Truce. Traditionally, it was a ceasefire between North Vietnam and South Vietnam in honor of the Tet holiday.

Trudeaumania. An eponym derived from Pierre Trudeau's name given in early 1968 to the excitement generated by Pierre Trudeau's entry into the leadership of the Liberal Party of Canada.

Tour d'horizon. Broad general survey or summary of an argument or event.

Vive le Québec libre. Long live free Québec

Vox Populi. The opinions or beliefs of the majority.

Zindabad. Live forever.

APPENDIX B

Chronology of Events from November 1970 to December 1972

November 12–13, 1970 A disastrous cyclone and tidal wave called Cyclone Bhola in the East Pakistan delta caused an estimated three hundred thousand to five hundred thousand fatalities.

December 7, 1970 Pakistan held its first National Elections on this day. Zulfiqar Ali Bhutto, leader of the Pakistan People's Party, won eighty-three seats in West Pakistan. In contrast, Sheikh Mujibur Rahman (Bongobondhu), leader of the Awami League, won 167 seats in East Pakistan.

January 4, 1971 Bongobondhu administered an oath in public to himself and the Awami League Members of Parliament that they would unconditionally adhere to the Six Points.

January 8, 1971 Prime Minister Pierre Elliott Trudeau visited India and Pakistan.

January 12, 1971 Zulfiqar Ali Bhutto, the leader of West Pakistan's largest political party, the Pakistan People's Party (PPP), came to Dhaka to talk with Bongobondhu.

January 12, 1971	President Yahya Khan came to Dhaka to talk with Bongobondhu.
January 27, 1971	Zulfiqar Ali Bhutto returned to Dhaka to talk with Bongobondhu.
January 30, 1971	A Fokker Friendship aircraft of Indian Airlines in Lahore, West Pakistan, was hijacked by a group of Kashmiri hijackers.
February 13, 1971	President Yahya Khan announced that the newly elected legislature would be convened on March 3.
February 15, 1971	Zulfiqar Ali Bhutto declared that his party would boycott the National Assembly unless a constitutional agreement could be worked out with the Awami League before the scheduled opening of the legislature.
March 1, 1971	President Yahya Khan postponed the first meeting of the Constituent Assembly *sine die*.
March 1, 1971	Bongobondhu called a strike in Dhaka in protest against the postponement of the meeting of the National Assembly.
March 3, 1971	Mob violence spread across Dhaka city. Bongobondhu announced a civil disobedience movement (non-cooperation) to secure the rights of his people.
March 4, 1971	The province (East Pakistan) was paralyzed by a general strike. Looting and raiding of firearms shops continued.
March 6, 1971	President Yahya set March 25 as the new date for the opening of the National Assembly.

March 7, 1971	Bongobondhu gave his historic speech at Ramna Race Course proclaiming his plans for running a parallel government. He issued directives for non-payment of taxes and the closure of all government offices and courts. Revolutionary councils were to be set up in each Union, Moholla, Thana-Sub-Division, and District under the leadership of Awami League units.
March 8, 1971	John Small, Canada's high commissioner to Pakistan, met with Bongobondhu and discussed Pakistan's constitutional crisis.
March 14, 1971	Bongobondhu issued fresh directives—one ordered deputy commissioners and subdivisional officers to cooperate with local Awami League Revolutionary Councils.
March 15, 1971	Bongobondhu announced that taxes were to be paid to the Awami League Action Committee in Dhaka. Action committees were to be set up throughout the province in towns and villages to resist the Army should it try to restore governmental authority.
March 15, 1971	President Yahya flew to Dhaka to confer with Bongobondhu. The same day, the Yahya-Bongobondhu parley began.
March 21, 1971	Bhutto joined Yahya and Bongobondhu and continued the Yahya-Bongobondhu-Butto parley.
March 23, 1971	Pakistan Day was celebrated as "Resistance Day," with parades and marches by paramilitary Liberation Front troopers and ex-Service men. The Pakistan flag was torn down from

buildings, and the 'Bangla Desh' flag was hoisted. At an armed march-past parade outside his residence, Bongobondhu took the salute, and the Bangla Desh flag was ceremonially unfurled.

March 25, 1971 On March 25, there began a secret and sudden attack code-named Operation Searchlight by the Yahya regime on Bengali civilians starting at midnight to crush the autonomy movement and enforce the military government's authority in all of Pakistan. President Yahya imposed martial law. President Yahya is known to have left for Islamabad the same night. Bengali members of the East Pakistan Rifles, East Bengal Regiment, students, and general members of the public revolted the same night.

March 26, 1971 President Yahya gave his speech to the nation. Bhutto is known to have left Dhaka for Karachi, West Pakistan. The army seized the Radio Station and announced 15 Martial Law Regulations. The regime proscribed the Awami League and banned all political gatherings and processions. From his house at Dhanmondi, Sheikh Mujibur Rahman (Bongobondhu) sent a message before his arrest from his house at Dhanmondi about attacks on EPR and police barracks in Dhaka. He declared Bangladesh's independence through a telegram read by the Awami League leader Mohammad Abdul Hannan of Chittagong.

On March 27, 1971 Major Ziaur Rahman of the East Bengal Regiment broadcast the message on the radio twice—first, he declared independence in his own name, then on behalf of Bongobondhu.

April 14, 1971	Colonel Muhammad Ataul Gani Osmani officially became the commander-in-chief of the *Mukti Bahini* (Liberation Forces).
April 17, 1971	The provisional government of Bangladesh was formed at Baiddyanathtola mango grove, later renamed Mujibnagar, an enclave of East Pakistan, about 120 kilometers from Kolkata, West Bengal, India. It named Sheikh Mujibur Rahman (Bongobondhu) as its president.
April 25, 1971	Catholics in Canada observed "Right to Life Day in Canada" organized by the Canadian Catholic Conference (CCC) across Canada.
April 30, 1971	John Small, Canada's high commissioner to Pakistan, met with Lieutenant-General Tikka Khan, governor of East Pakistan, to discuss the situation in East Pakistan. The same day, Small took a helicopter tour of the Barisal -Padrishibpur and Noakhali area. He met with Canadian members of the Holy Cross Order at the Oriental Institute in Barisal.
May 25- August 25, 1971	Albert Batten, former Executive Director, Toronto Central Branch, Canadian Red Cross Society, was the first Canadian representative who went to India to collaborate with other NGOs. He was there from May 25 to August 25.
June 11, 1971	President Yahya offered amnesty to all Bengalis who had taken shelter in India.
June 13, 1971	The Manitoba Bangladesh Association organized a fundraising drive through a cultural program called *Bichitra* under the guidance of Rubena Sinha with direct assistance from Hamida Begum, then a PhD student.

June 16, 1971	With the cooperation of the University of British Columbia's student community, a public meeting was held on the International House premises. The keynote speaker, Jayaprakash Narayan of the Gandhi Peace Foundation, spoke on the prevailing situation in India.
June 16, 1971	The Combined Appeal for Pakistani Relief (CAPR) was formed to deal with the new challenges of a "man-made" disaster in the Indian subcontinent with a coordinated strategy.
June 18, 1971	Edward Richard Schreyer, premier of Manitoba, proclaimed Friday, June 18, 1971, as Pakistan Refugee Day. Oxfam of Canada declared June 18 as the Pakistan Refugee Day to be observed by municipalities nationwide.
June 24–July 17, 1971	John Wieler, associate executive secretary of the Mennonite Central Committee, visited the refugee camps in India and discussed the issue with many NGOs.
Last week of June 1971	Pakistani ship S. S. Padma arrived in Montreal secretly carrying forty-six crates of F-86 Sabre jet airplane parts and other related items sent by the Nixon administration. The Trudeau administration immediately removed them and ordered the ship's return to Maryland, United States.
July 2, 1971	On July 2, a three-member Commons Committee on External Affairs and National Defence left for India and Pakistan (both East and West Pakistan) to observe the actual situation there to report back to the government and the people of Canada.

July 9–14, 1971	Father Frank West of the Toronto-based Canadian Jesuit Mission went to India to meet with Father Edgar Burns of the Darjeeling-based Jesuit. He stayed there from July 9 to July 14. The two fathers traveled extensively to the refugee camps in the Darjeeling District and West Dinajpur of West Bengal, India.
August 5, 1971	The government of Pakistan produced a white paper about the crisis in East Pakistan. It is the sanitized version of the crisis.
August 9, 1971	The Indo-Soviet Treaty of Friendship and Cooperation was signed.
August 9, 1971	The military regime announced that Sheikh Mujibur Rahman (Bongobondhu) would be tried for treason in camera and could face the death penalty. This provoked serious reactions in India, the Bangladesh government, and the outside world. Canada immediately began to lobby for his release. The government of Prince Edward Island declared the week of August 15 as Pakistan Relief Week.
August 19–21, 1971	The South Asia Conference, also more frequently referred to as the Toronto Declaration of Concern, was a high-profile three-day conference held at St. Michael's College, University of Toronto, under the chairmanship of Dr. Hugh Keenleyside, former director-general of the UN technical assistance and former Canadian ambassador to Indonesia.
September 5-11, 1971	Allan Emrys Blakeney, premier of Saskatchewan, proclaimed September 5 to 11 as Pakistan Refugee Relief Week.

September 30, 1971	The University of Saskatchewan observed Bangladesh Day across the University.
October 10, 1971	The Holy Father Pope V1 launched an appeal declaring Sunday, October 10, as the World Day of Prayer, Fasting, and Almsgiving for Pakistani refugees and the eight hundred thousand children in danger of dying. The Canadian Catholic Conference (CCC) coordinated this across the country.
November 1, 1971	India admitted for the first time that her troops had crossed Pakistani territory but asserted that all her actions had been in self-defence.
November 2, 1971	India launched a major offensive in the East and crossed the border into East Pakistan.
November 15–19, 1971	The Bangladesh Association of British Columbia, in cooperation with the UBC Bangladesh Students Association, organized a week-long activity under the name "Bangladesh Week," which included a door-to-door campaign as part of both awareness and fundraising.
November 22, 1971	India launched an offensive against East Pakistan. The Nixon administration cut off economic aid to India, and President Richard Nixon himself decided to "tilt" toward Pakistan.
On November 22, 1971	J. M. Gibson, immigration attaché of Canada's Department of Manpower and Immigration, went to Dhaka, East Pakistan, and recruited forty-five Bengali applicants out of forty-six for immigration to Canada.

December 3, 1971	An all-out war broke out between India and Pakistan and spread to the West.
December 3, 1971	Two DND C-130s and three transport flights made by Canadian Armed Forces Boeing 707 jet types were already used in Pakistan.
December 4, 1971	The Indian army executed a three-pronged pincer movement on Dhaka launched from the Indian states of West Bengal, Assam, and Tripura, taking only twelve days to defeat the ninety thousand Pakistani defenders. The Bengali freedom fighters aided the Indian army.
December 6, 1971	India became the first nation to recognize the new Bangladeshi government.
December 16, 1971	Lieutenant-General Amir Abdullah Khan Niazi, martial law administrator, Eastern Command (Pakistan), surrendered Jagjit Singh Aurora, lieutenant-general, general officer, and commanding-in-chief of the Indian and Bangla Desh Forces in the Eastern Theatre. With the surrender, the fighting came to an end in the East.
On December 17, 1971	A cease-fire agreement was arranged along the Western Front, ending the third round of the continuing India-Pak dispute.
On December 20, 1971	President Yahya resigned as president and chief martial law administrator of Pakistan. Zulfiqar Ali Bhutto, deputy prime minister and foreign minister, succeeded him.

December 21, 1971	Upon Bhutto's order, Bongobondhu was transferred from prison in Lyallpur to house arrest in the hope that he would have an undefined role in the reconciliation with the West.
December 22, 1971	The government of Bangla Desh arrived in Dhaka. Acting President Syed Nazrul Islam assumed nominal responsibility for governing the country.
January 8, 1972	Bongobondhu was released unconditionally from jail in Pakistan.
January 10, 1972	*Bongobondhu* triumphantly returned to Dhaka, Bangladesh. It began what he perceived to be his immediate task: consolidating the Awami League's institutional power of the Awami League as the dominant political formation.
January 22, 1972	Durga Prasad Dhar, former Indian Ambassador to Moscow, was appointed the government of India's special representative in Dhaka.
February 14, 1972	Canada accorded formal recognition to Bangladesh.
On March 3, 1972	His Excellency Abdul Momin presented his credentials to the Governor General of Canada. The Bangladesh High Commission's first office in Canada was at Embassy Apt: hotel, 25 Cartier St.
On March 20, 1972	Established its relationship with Bangladesh when the Canadian ambassador in Bangkok, Gordon Cox, as representative of the government of Canada, visited Dhaka for the first time.

April 18, 1972   Bangladesh became the thirty-second member of the Commonwealth.

September 17, 1972   Bangladesh became a member of the United Nations.

October 30, 1972   His Excellency Gordon G. Riddell, resident Canadian Ambassador in Bangkok, concurrently accredited to Bangladesh, presented his credentials to the Bangladesh President.

APPENDIX C

Abbreviations

AL	Awami League
BRF	Bangladesh Relief Fund
CRCS	Canadian Red Cross Society
CANDU	Canada Deuterium Uranium
CAPR	Combined Appeal for Pakistani Relief
CBC	Canadian Broadcasting Corporation
CIDA	Canadian International Development Corporation
CORR	Christian Organization for Relief and Rehabilitation
DND	Department of National Defence
EDC	Export Development Corporation
EBR	East Bengal Rifle
EPR	East Pakistan Regiment
EPR	East Pakistan Rifle
EPRCS	East Pakistan Red Cross Society
FLQ	Front de libération du Québec
IAEA	International Atomic Energy Agency
IBRD	International Bank of Reconstruction and Development
ICRC	International Committee of the Red Cross
IMF	International Monetary Fund
IRC	Indian Red Cross
LFO	Legal Framework Order

LORCS	League of Red Cross Society
PPP	Pakistan People's Party
RTC	Round Table Conference
UNEPRO	United Nations East Pakistan Relief Operation
UDI	Universal Declaration of Independence
UNEF	United Nations Emergency Force
WASP	White Anglo-Saxon White Protestants

APPENDIX D

Archival Records

Department of Foreign Affairs
and International Trade

Ministère des Affaires étrangères
et du Commerce international

Lester B. Pearson Building
125 Sussex Drive
Ottawa, Ontario
K1A 0G2

October 12, 2000

DCP-2882

Mr. Mustafa Chowdhury
448 Rougemount Cres.
Orleans, Ontario
K4A 2Y8

Dear Mr. Chowdhury:

<u>Re: Access to Information Act Request No. A-2000-00213 / ls</u>

This is in reply to your request under the *Access to Information Act* for historical documents on:

Emergence of Bangladesh.

Your request, with copies of 112 pages of documents which you had obtained through the Historical Section of this Department, and which you would like to have released to you, was received in this office on October 6, 2000 and was assigned the above reference number.

We are pleased to return the documents herewith to you. Please note, however, that one document of two pages has been exempted from release as containing information which is still regarded as sensitive under sections 13(1)(a) and 15(1) of the *Act*. A copy of the portion of the *Act* containing the exemptions is enclosed for your reference.

You are entitled, if you wish, to file a complaint with the Information Commissioner concerning your request. In accordance with section 31 of the *Act*, a complaint to the Information Commissioner must be made in writing within one year of the date of our receipt of your original request.

.../2

The address is:

> Information Commissioner of Canada
> Tower B, (22nd/3rd) Floor, Place de Ville
> 112 Kent Street
> Ottawa, Ontario, K1A 1H3

Should you have any questions about this matter, please contact Larry Smith of this office at (613) 996-0907.

Yours sincerely,

Barbara Richardson
Director
Access to Information and
Privacy Protection Division

Source: The author obtained permission to use the archival materials housed in the Department of External Affairs and Library and Archives Canada under Canada's Freedom of Information and Protection of Privacy Act.

MEMORANDUM			
TO		SECURITY	RESTRICTED
FROM	CPS	DATE	29 March 1971
REFERENCE		NUMBER	
		FILE	20-E.PAK-1-4
SUBJECT	Call by East Pakistan Students	MISSION	

20-1-2-PAK

1. As agreed with you, and in Arthur Andrew's absence, I received a visit at noon today from four East Pakistanis representing a larger group who had wished to present a petition to the Minister calling for action in support of an independent East Pakistan. The four, Messrs. Ali (the principal spokesman), Awal, Ahmed and Sarker are all residents of Ottawa but claim to represent some 75 East Pakistanis living here and in Montreal, Cornwall, Kingston and Toronto. It transpired that they are among the 20-odd members of the East Pakistan Cultural Association in Ottawa, formed on March 14 with mailing address c/o Dr. A.B.M. Lutful Kabir, 87 Woodmount Crescent, Ottawa.

DISTRIBUTION
MIN
PSI
FPR

Islamabad

2. Mr. Ali rehearsed recent developments in East Pakistan since the re-imposition of martial law at the beginning of March and described in graphic terms the exploitation and discrimination practised by the West Pakistan "military-industrial complex" against the Bengalis of the East. He claimed the unanimous support of East Pakistanis for Sheikh Mujibur Rahman and the Awami League and the entire fitness of East Pakistanis for independence as proclaimed by Sheikh Mujib. He ended by asking for Canadian Government action to recognize the independence of "Bangla Desh", to "take necessary action to stop the invasion of the sovereignty of Bangla Desh by the troops of West Pakistan", to withdraw recognition of the state of Pakistan and to withhold all foreign aid "to the state formerly known as Pakistan, as such aid is being used against the people of Bangla Desh".

3. In reply to Mr. Ali's presentation, I said that we had been watching the situation in East Pakistan with a great deal of sympathy and concern but, like observers everywhere, were handicapped by the lack of precise information about what had been happening in the province during the last few days. Despite our sympathy, however, there could be no question of Canadian intervention in the internal affairs of another country since despite the evident popular support for the Awami League President Yahya Khan and the Pakistan Government were the legal government of the province. I added that while we

...2

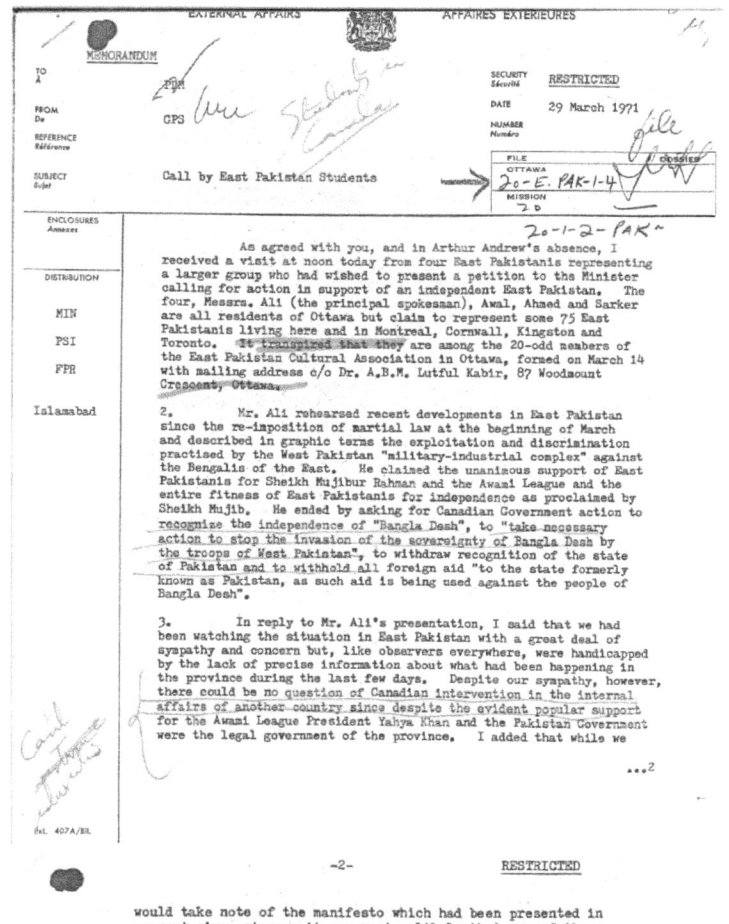

-2-   RESTRICTED

would take note of the manifesto which had been presented in present circumstances it was most unlikely that any of the requests would be met. We would, nevertheless, continue to follow the situation with sympathy and consider whether there was anything that could be done to promote a return to more normal conditions.

4. Ali then mentioned that the group were planning a demonstration on Parliament Hill and had been in touch with the press who they hoped would be on hand. He asked whether, since Mr. Sharp could not meet them, we could receive their manifesto publicly for the benefit of photographers. I said of course that this would not be possible but that they could if they wished tell the press that they had given it to us. Finally I suggested that they should inform the security authorities on the Hill in advance of their intention to hold a demonstration, which they agreed to do.

Harrington
Pacific and South Asia Division

RESTRICTED MEMO CONCERNING THE VISIT TO THE MINISTER BY A GROUP OF EAST PAKISTANI BENGALIS OF OTTAWA.
Source: Canada. Department of External Affairs. File # 20-E-Pak-1-4.

```
SASKATOON COMMITTEE FOR THE
PROTECTION OF HUMAN RIGHTS AND
LIVES IN EAST PAKISTAN
38-15 Assiniboine Drive
Saskatoon, Saskatchewan

                April 2, 1971

The Honourable Otto Lang
Minister of Manpower & Immigration
Government of Canada
OTTAWA

    Sir:

    I am enclosing a copy of the resolutions
    adopted by the above Committee regarding the
    recent happenings in East Pakistan, together
    with the signatures of a number of students
    and faculty at the University of Saskatchewan,
    Saskatoon, who share our concern expressed in
    the resolutions.

    We thank you for the concern you expressed in
    your telegram. But, as you are aware, situation
    has further worsened since that time, and the
    human sufferings have increased tremendously
    as a result of the indiscriminate military
    actions taken by the armed forces of Pakistan.

    We are appealing to you to take any possible
    action to put an immediate stop to these
    unfortunate events.

    We thank you for any step taken in the name
    of humanity.

                        Yours very truly,
                        A. K. Sarkar
                        A. K. Sarkar
                        Convenor
```

Petition from the Saskatoon Committee for the Protection of Human Rights and Lives in East Pakistan was signed by a group of concerned Canadians under the convenorship of Dr. Asit Sarkar.

Source: Letter from Marian Hooge, Special Assistant, Office of the Minister of Manpower and Immigration to Jon Church, Executive Assistant to the Minister of External Affairs, dated April 6, 1971. Canada. Department of External Affairs. File # 20-E-Pak-1-4

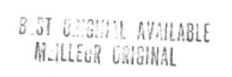

> Saskatoon, Sask.,
> March 30, 1971.
>
> We, the members of the SASKATOON COMMITTEE FOR THE PROTECTION OF HUMAN RIGHTS AND LIVES IN EAST PAKISTAN are gravely concerned about the reports in the news media (CBC, BBC, etc.) About the unprecedented action of the military government in Pakistan in suppressing the democratic wishes of the people of East Pakistan.
>
> We are appalled and distressed to learn that the military government in Pakistan:
>
> 1. is indiscriminately using its military forces, including armoured tanks and aerial bombing, on unarmed civilian population in utter disregard of human rights and lives.
>
> 2. has totally disregarded the freedom of international news media by deliberately expelling their reporters.
>
> We urge you and your government to use your good offices to persuade the military government in Pakistan:
>
> 1. to stop this genocide and restore civil liberties in East Pakistan.
>
> 2. to allow the international news media in East Pakistan to restore the freedom of press and International Red Cross and similar organizations to provide relief to the victims.
>
> 3. to allow an Inquiry Commission, under the auspices of the United Nations, to make a fact-finding inquiry so that the world body (U.N.) can take appropriate action.
>
> *We share the concern expressed by the above Committee*
>
> [signatures]

Petition from the Saskatoon Committee for the Protection of Human Rights and Lives in East Pakistan was signed by a group of concerned Canadians under the convenorship of Dr. Asit Sarkar.

Source: Letter from Marian Hooge, Special Assistant, Office of the Minister of Manpower and Immigration to Jon Church, Executive Assistant to the Minister of External Affairs, dated April 6, 1971. Canada. Department of External Affairs. File # 20-E-Pak-1-4

SITUATION IN EAST PAKISTAN

CONFIDENTIAL

April 2, 1971

38-11-1-PAKST-N

MEMORANDUM FOR THE MINISTER

Situation in East Pakistan

Now that the first refugees, both native and foreign, are beginning to leave East Pakistan with reports both of mass slaughter and selective killing of the civilian population, the political implications of the crisis are beginning to emerge. Yesterday the First Secretary of the Indian High Commission came to the Department to inform us of reports of genocide by the Pakistan Army in East Bengal and asked the Canadian Government to bring pressure to bear on Pakistan to stop the slaughter of civilians. Mr. Ghose also expressed his Government's hope that Canada would provide material relief for the distressed population of East Pakistan. On the first point he was told that we had no information to confirm reports that the Pakistan Army had engaged in selective slaughter of Bengali political and intellectual leaders, though there seemed little doubt that civilian casualties generally had been heavy. We were watching the situation closely but we were not convinced that declarations by outside governments were likely to be particularly helpful at this time.

Mr. Ghose went on to say that the Indian Government had submitted a Note to the Secretary-General of the United Nations complaining of genocide in East Pakistan and warning that "unless the armed forces of Pakistan exercise maximum restraint" and international opinion give sympathy and support for the people of East Pakistan "tension in the sub continent is bound to increase". We understand from our mission in New York that despite continuing pressure from the Indians U Thant is so far refusing to make any statement on East Pakistan on the grounds that it is an internal problem of a member country and that he has no direct information to confirm published reports of mass killings. The Indian Government is under strong pressure to take some action over the situation in East Bengal and on April 1st Parliament unanimously adopted a resolution introduced by the Prime Minister expressing "solidality, sympathy and support for the struggle of the people of East Bengal". Despite the reference to "support" the Secretary of the Indian Cabinet denied any government intention to go beyond moral support at this time; our High Commissioner has heard reports, however, that the Indian Cabinet has been discussing what further assistance and support might be offered to "Bangla Desh".

...2

MEMORANDUM FOR THE MINISTER regarding the Situation in East Pakistan, dated April 2, 1971

Source: Canada. Department of External Affairs. File # 38-11-1-Pak

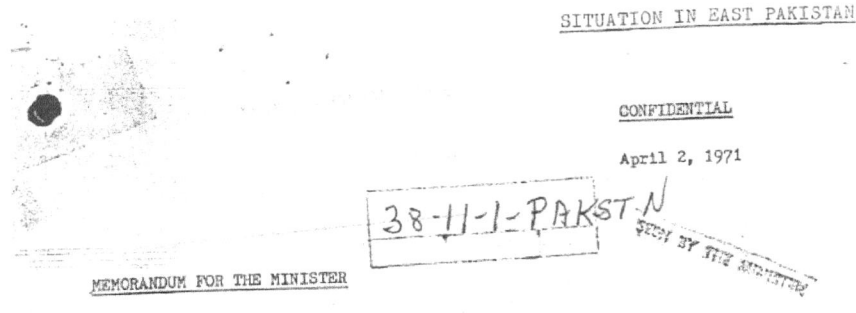

CONFIDENTIAL

The Pakistan Government is clearly worried aththe prospect of Indian intervention and the High Commissioner yesterday presented the Prime Minister with a personal messgge from President Yahya. We have not been able to obtain the text of the letter from the Prime Minister's office but we understand that the President expressed the hope that the Canadian Government would support his efforts to restore order in East Pakistan and would prevail on India not to intervene. We understand that the Prime Minister told Mr. Shaikh that Canada did not believe in interfering in the interal affairs of other countries, that our experience indicated that this was not generally veryhelpful but that we hoped that at some stage we might be able to be of assistance.

We are forwarding separately the text of a possible brief statement and answers to anticipated questions based on today's press reports.

A.E.R.

MEMORANDUM FOR THE MINISTER regarding the Situation in East Pakistan, dated April 2, 1971

Source: Canada. Department of External Affairs. File # 38-11-1-Pak

```
                                    MESSAGE
        PLACE        DEPARTMENT    ORIG. NO.    DATE        FILE/DOSSIER        SECURITY
        LIEU         MINISTÈRE     N° D'ORIG.                                   SÉCURITÉ
FM/DE   ottawa       EXTERNAL      GPS-150    APRIL          20-PAK-1-4         CONFD
                                              6, 1971
                                                                                PRECEDENCE
TO/A    ISBAD                                                                   IMMED

INFO    DELHI, WASH, LDN, PERMISNY

DISTR.  PDG  GPS(5)

REF
SUB/SUJ   MESSAGE TO P.M. FROM PAK PRESIDENT
          PAK HIGH COMMISSIONER SHAIKH CALLED ON P.M. APR 1 AT HIS URGENT REQUEST TO
          DELIVER FOLLOWING MESSAGE FROM PRESIDENT YAHYA TEXT BEGINS I AM TAKING THE
          EARLIEST OPPORTUNITY TO INFORM YOU OF THE POLITICAL DEVELOPMENTS IN PAKIS-
          TAN. SINCE THE GENERAL ELECTIONS OF LAST DECEMBER, IT HAS BEEN MY CONSTANT
          ENDEAVOUR TO LEAD THE COUNTRY TOWARDS RESTORATION OF DEMOCRATIC PROCESSES
          THROUGH ELECTED REPS OF THE PEOPLE. FOR THIS PURPOSE, I HAVE BEEN HOLDING
          TALKS WITH THE LEADERS OF THE POLITICAL PARTIES. I HAD HOPED THAT THESE
          DISCUSSIONS WOULD LEAD TO A BROAD POLITICAL AGREEMENT REGARDING CONVENING
          OF THE NATL ASSEMBLY AND FRAMING OF THE CONSTITUTION. UNFORTUNATELY,
          HOWEVER, THE POLITICAL LEADERSHIP IN EAST PAKISTAN AND ESPECIALLY SHEIKH
          MUJIBUR RAHMAN TOOK A PROGRESSIVELY RIGID STAND WHICH MADE SUCH AN AGREEMENT
          IMPOSSIBLE. MEANWHILE MURDER, ARSON AND WIDESPREAD DISORDER IN DEFIANCE OF
          THE GOVTL AUTHORITIES WERE LET LOOSE IN THE PROVINCE.
        2.IN THE LARGER INTERESTS OF THE COUNTRY I EXERCISED THE UTMOST RESTRAINT
          AND PATIENCE AND TRIED TO EVOLVE A GENERALLY ACCEPTABLE FORMULA TO RESOLVE
          THE CONSTITUTIONAL DIFFICULTIES. IN PURSUIT OF THE SAME OBJECTIVE I WENT

DRAFTER/RÉDACTEUR        DIVISION/DIRECTION    TELEPHONE       APPROVED/APPROUVÉ
J.M. HARRINGTON/mtj            GPS              5-8363         J.M. HARRINGTON
```

CONFIDENTIAL Message from President Yahya Khan to Prime Minister Pierre Trudeau, dated April 6, 1971

Source: Canada. Department of External Affairs. File # 20-1-2-Pak

GPS-150 -2- CONFD

PERSONALLY TO EAST PAKISTAN TO HOLD CONSULTATIONS WITH SHEIKH MUJIBUR RAHMAN. EVEN WHILE I WAS THERE THE AWAMI LEAGUE LEADERS CONTINUED TO MAKE STATEMENTS AND TO INDULGE IN PRACTICES WHICH CLEARLY SHOWED THAT THEY WERE NOT/NOT PREPARED FOR ANY COMPROMISE. THE LAST ROUND OF TALKS IN DACCA LEFT ME IN NO/NO DOUBT THAT THEY HAD NO/NO INTENTIONS OF ACCEPTING ANY CONSTITUTIONAL FORMULA WHICH WOULD ENSURE THE INTEGRITY AND UNITY OF THE COUNTRY. EVENTUALLY A POINT WAS REACHED WHERE AWAMI LEAGUE PUT FORWARD FINAL PROPOSALS, WHICH VIRTUALLY AMOUNTED TO DISMEMBERMENT OF THE COUNTRY. SINCE THEY HAD NO/NO SUCH MANDATE FROM THE PEOPLE AND AS THE UNITY OF THE COUNTRY WAS AT STAKE, FIRM ACTION HAD TO BE TAKEN TO ASSERT GOVT'S AUTHORITY AND TO SAFEGUARD THE INTEGRITY OF PAKISTAN. THERE WAS NO/NO OPTION BUT TO TAKE THAT DECISION.

3. THE SITUATION IN EAST PAKISTAN IS WELL UNDER CONTROL AND NORMAL LIFE IS BEING RESTORED. ACCOUNTS TO THE CONTRARY CIRCULATED BY SOME OUTSIDE SOURCES, ESPECIALLY INDIAN NEWS MEDIA, DO NOT/NOT REFLECT THE CORRECT POSITION AND ARE DESIGNED TO MISLEAD THE WORLD PRESS.

4. WHILE WE ARE ENGAGED IN A NATL EFFORT TO SAFEGUARD OUR INTEGRITY, THE INDIAN ATTITUDE IS CAUSING US SERIOUS CONCERN. THE PRIME MINISTER, THE FOREIGN MINISTER, AND OTHER IMPORTANT LEADERS OF INDIA HAVE MADE PUBLIC STATEMENTS REGARDING THE DEVELOPMENTS IN EAST PAKISTAN, WHICH CONSTITUTE A CLEAR INTERFERENCE IN OUR INTERNAL AFFAIRS. A DANGEROUS PRECEDENT IS, THUS, BEING SET BY INDIA WHICH IS OF DIRECT CONCERN TO THE INNATL COMMUNITY.

5. FAR MORE SERIOUS IS THE DEPLOYMENT OF NEARLY SIX DIVISIONS OF THE INDIAN ARMY, NOT/NOT TOO FAR FROM THE BORDERS OF EAST PAKISTAN. THE COMPOSITION OF THESE FORCES WHICH INCLUDES ARTILLERY REGIMENTS AND PARACHUTE BRIGADES, HAS NO/NO RELEVANCE TO THE NEEDS OF INTERNAL SECURITY IN WEST BENGAL OR TO THE REQUIREMENTS OF THE INDIAN ELECTIONS WHICH ENDED THREE WEEKS AGO.

...3

CONFIDENTIAL Message from President Yahya Khan to Prime Minister Pierre Trudeau, dated April 6, 1971.

Source: Canada. Department of External Affairs. File # 20-1-2-Pak

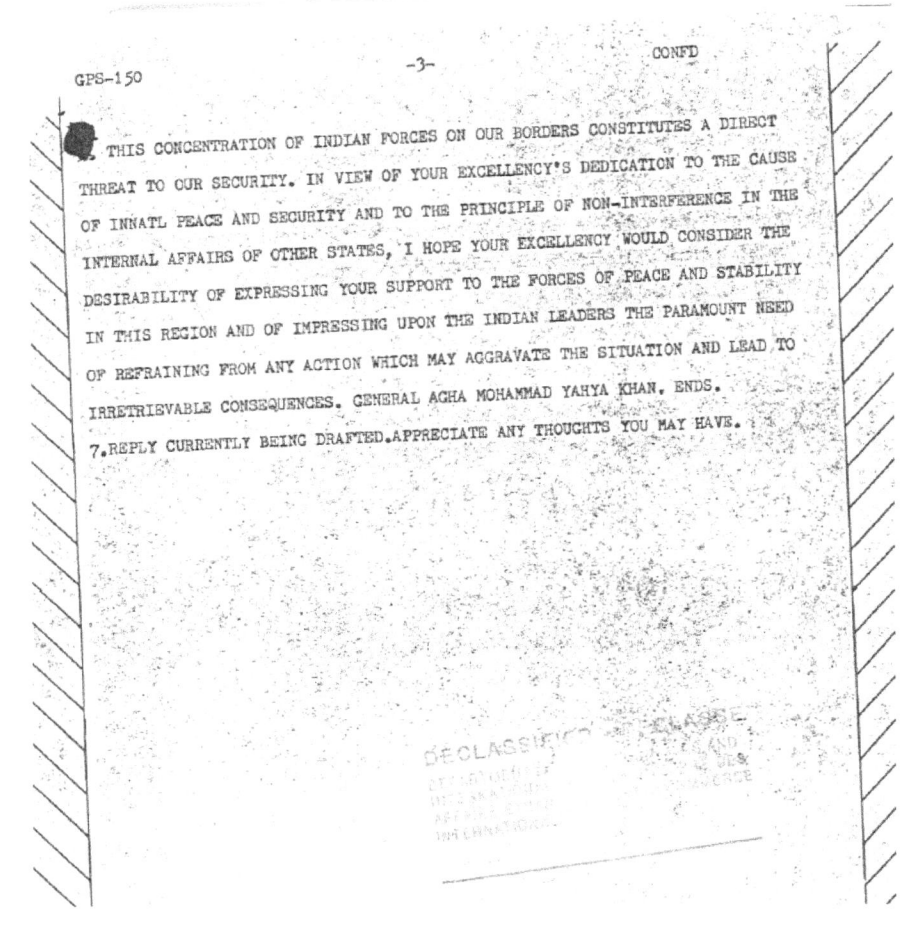

THIS CONCENTRATION OF INDIAN FORCES ON OUR BORDERS CONSTITUTES A DIRECT THREAT TO OUR SECURITY. IN VIEW OF YOUR EXCELLENCY'S DEDICATION TO THE CAUSE OF INNATL PEACE AND SECURITY AND TO THE PRINCIPLE OF NON-INTERFERENCE IN THE INTERNAL AFFAIRS OF OTHER STATES, I HOPE YOUR EXCELLENCY WOULD CONSIDER THE DESIRABILITY OF EXPRESSING YOUR SUPPORT TO THE FORCES OF PEACE AND STABILITY IN THIS REGION AND OF IMPRESSING UPON THE INDIAN LEADERS THE PARAMOUNT NEED OF REFRAINING FROM ANY ACTION WHICH MAY AGGRAVATE THE SITUATION AND LEAD TO IRRETRIEVABLE CONSEQUENCES. GENERAL AGHA MOHAMMAD YAHYA KHAN, ENDS.

7. REPLY CURRENTLY BEING DRAFTED. APPRECIATE ANY THOUGHTS YOU MAY HAVE.

CONFIDENTIAL Message from President Yahya Khan to Prime Minister Pierre Trudeau, dated April 6, 1971

Source: Canada. Department of External Affairs. File # 20-1-2-Pak

CONFIDENTIAL

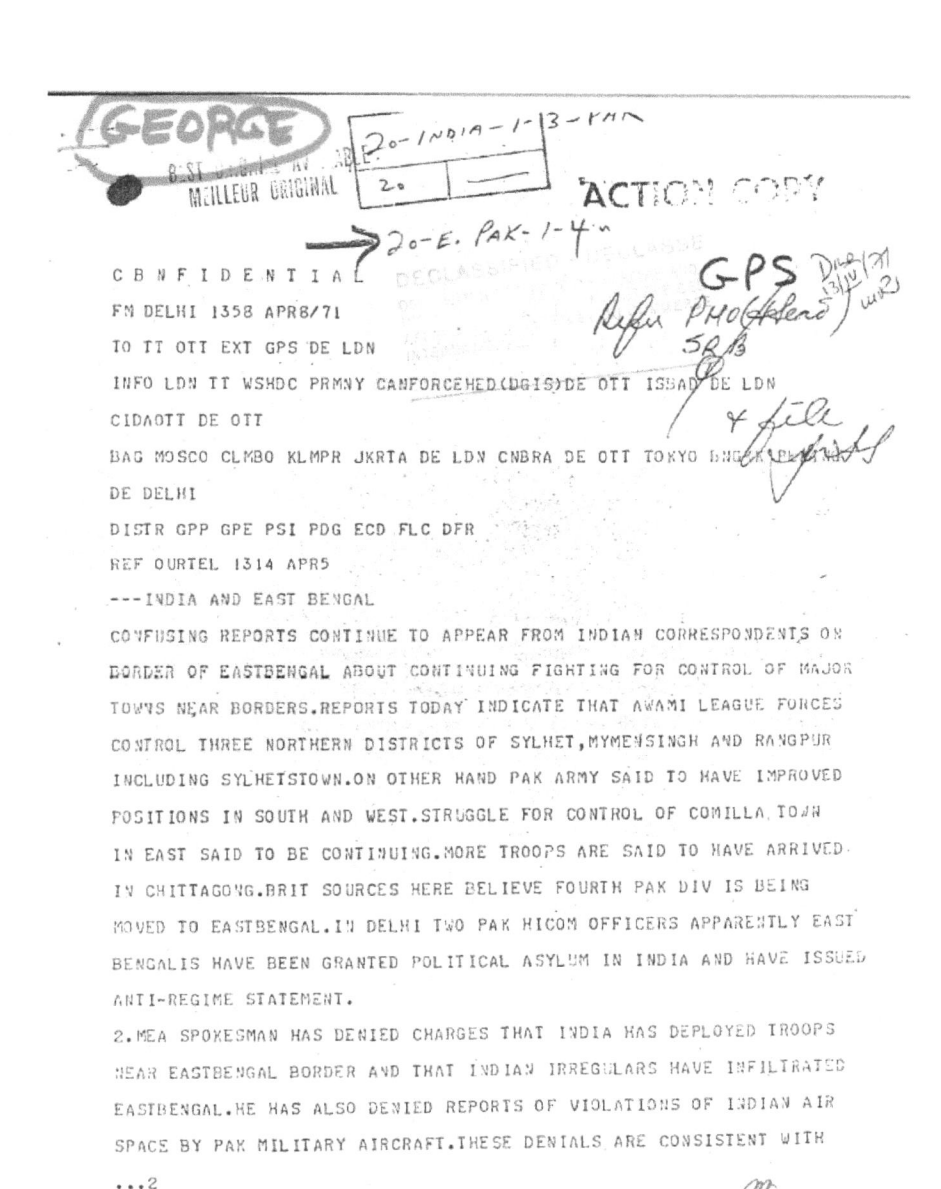

FM DELHI 1358 APR8/71
TO TT OTT EXT GPS DE LDN
INFO LDN TT WSHDC PRMNY CANFORCEHED(DGIS)DE OTT ISLAD DE LDN
CIDAOTT DE OTT
BAG MOSCO CLMBO KLMPR JKRTA DE LDN CNBRA DE OTT TOKYO
DE DELHI
DISTR GPP GPE PSI PDG ECD FLC DFR
REF OURTEL 1314 APR5
---INDIA AND EAST BENGAL
CONFUSING REPORTS CONTINUE TO APPEAR FROM INDIAN CORRESPONDENTS ON BORDER OF EASTBENGAL ABOUT CONTINUING FIGHTING FOR CONTROL OF MAJOR TOWNS NEAR BORDERS. REPORTS TODAY INDICATE THAT AWAMI LEAGUE FORCES CONTROL THREE NORTHERN DISTRICTS OF SYLHET, MYMENSINGH AND RANGPUR INCLUDING SYLHETSTOWN. ON OTHER HAND PAK ARMY SAID TO HAVE IMPROVED POSITIONS IN SOUTH AND WEST. STRUGGLE FOR CONTROL OF COMILLA TOWN IN EAST SAID TO BE CONTINUING. MORE TROOPS ARE SAID TO HAVE ARRIVED IN CHITTAGONG. BRIT SOURCES HERE BELIEVE FOURTH PAK DIV IS BEING MOVED TO EASTBENGAL. IN DELHI TWO PAK HICOM OFFICERS APPARENTLY EAST BENGALIS HAVE BEEN GRANTED POLITICAL ASYLUM IN INDIA AND HAVE ISSUED ANTI-REGIME STATEMENT.
2. MEA SPOKESMAN HAS DENIED CHARGES THAT INDIA HAS DEPLOYED TROOPS NEAR EASTBENGAL BORDER AND THAT INDIAN IRREGULARS HAVE INFILTRATED EASTBENGAL. HE HAS ALSO DENIED REPORTS OF VIOLATIONS OF INDIAN AIR SPACE BY PAK MILITARY AIRCRAFT. THESE DENIALS ARE CONSISTENT WITH
...2

CONFIDENTIAL telegram from James George, high commissioner to India, to Ottawa. Dated April 8, 1971

Source: Canada. Department of External Affairs. File # 20-E-Pak-1-4

PAGE TWO 1358 CONFD

PRIVATE ASSERTIONS TO US AND OTHER DIPLOS BY MEA OFFICIALS THAT GOI DETERMINED NOT/NOT TO GIVE ANY EXCUSE TO PAK GOVT TO BLAME INDIA FOR INCAPACITY TO RESTORE ORDER IN EASTBENGAL. THESE OFFICIALS RE-ITERATE THAT INDIAN SUPPORT WILL TAKE MORAL AND POLITICAL FORM ONLY. INDIA WILL ALSO DO ALL IT CAN TO PROVIDE HUMANITARIAN ASSISTANCE BUT PREFERS TO WORK THROUGH INNATL REDCROSS IF AND WHEN THIS BECOMES FEASIBLE. OFFICIALS CONTINUE TO EXPRESS HOPE THAT OTHER GOVTS WILL USE INFLUENCE IN ISBAD TO MODERATE POLICY OF REPRESSION AND TO ALLOW INNATL RELIEF TO BE DELIVERED. THIS DOES NOT/NOT MEAN THAT INDIAN CITIZENS ARE NOT/NOT CROSSING BORDERS, AS JOURNALIST REPORTS DEMONSTRATE. BUT WE DOUBT GOI IS INSPIRING SUCH MOVEMENT.

3. OUR ASSESSMENT OF GOI POSITION BASED ON RECENT CONTACTS WITH DIPLO COLLEAGUES AND MEA OFFICIALS IS THAT GOI NO/NO LONGER BELIEVES UNITED PAK EITHER POSSIBLE OR DESIRABLE AND IS ASSUMING NEW STATE WILL EMERGE IN EASTERN WING. FOR TIME BEING POPULAR RESISTANCE MOVEMENT IS HOLDING ITS OWN AND WILL BE GREATLY STRENGTHENED BY ONSET OF MONSOON IN MAY. TIME IS NEEDED FOR BENGALI RESISTANCE TO TAKE ORGANIZED FORM HOWEVER AND TO WORK OUT STRATEGY FOR LONGER TERM. TIME IS ALSO NEEDED TO BUILD UP INNATL SUPPORT. THUS, INDIA SHOULD NOT/NOT ACT HASTILY OR RASHLY. EVENTUALLY, PERHAPS IN VER OF MONTHS, EITHER PAK ARMY WILL GIVE UP FRUITLESS STRUGGLE AND WITHDRAW OR POPULAR RESISTANCE WILL CRYSTALIZE AROUND PARTICULAR LEADERS AND LIBERATED AREAS. NATURE OF ASSISTANCE INDIA MAY PROVIDE WHEN SITUATION CLARIFIED WILL DEPEND ON CIRCUMSTANCES. MUCH WILL DEPEND ON NATURE OF EASTBENGAL LEADERSHIP. SOME MEA

...3

CONFIDENTIAL telegram from James George, high commissioner to India, to Ottawa. Dated April 8, 1971

Source: Canada. Department of External Affairs. File # 20-E-Pak-1-4

PAGE THREE 1358 CONFD

OFFICIALS EXPRESS FEAR PROTRACTED CONFLICT WILL BRING EXTREMIST ELEMENTS TO FORE, ESPECIALLY NOW THAT AWAMI LEAGUE CADRES SEEM TO HAVE BEEN DECIMATED AT LEAST IN CERTAIN AREAS. VIEW IS DXPRESSED ZHAT CHINESE MAY FAVOUR PROTRACTED CONFLICT FOR THIS REASON. SIMILARLY SVT STATEMENT OF APR4 CRITICAL OF GOP MAY REFLECT SVT CONCERN THAT CONTINUED REPRESSION WILL DRIVE MODERATES INTO EXTREMIST CAMP. INDIANS ARE ALSO AWARE OF COURSE THAT SO-CALLED NAXALITES OPERATE ON BOTH SIDES OF THE BORDER AND THAT WESTBENGAL IS VULNERABLE TO EXTREMIST POLITICAL PRESSURES. MOREOVER LONGER STRUGGLE LASTS GREATER BECOME PRESSURES ON INDIA TO INTERVENE, NOT/NOT TO MENTION DIFFICULTIES OF INCREASING FLOW OF REFUGEES. THUS HOPE IS EXPRESSED HERE THAT STALEMATE CAN BE PREVENTED BY INNATL PRESSURE ON PAK TO RESUME NEGOTIATIONS OR TO EVACUATE MILITARY FORCES.

080940Z

CONFIDENTIAL telegram from James George, high commissioner to India, to Ottawa. Dated April 8, 1971

Source: Canada. Department of External Affairs. File # 20-E-Pak-1-4

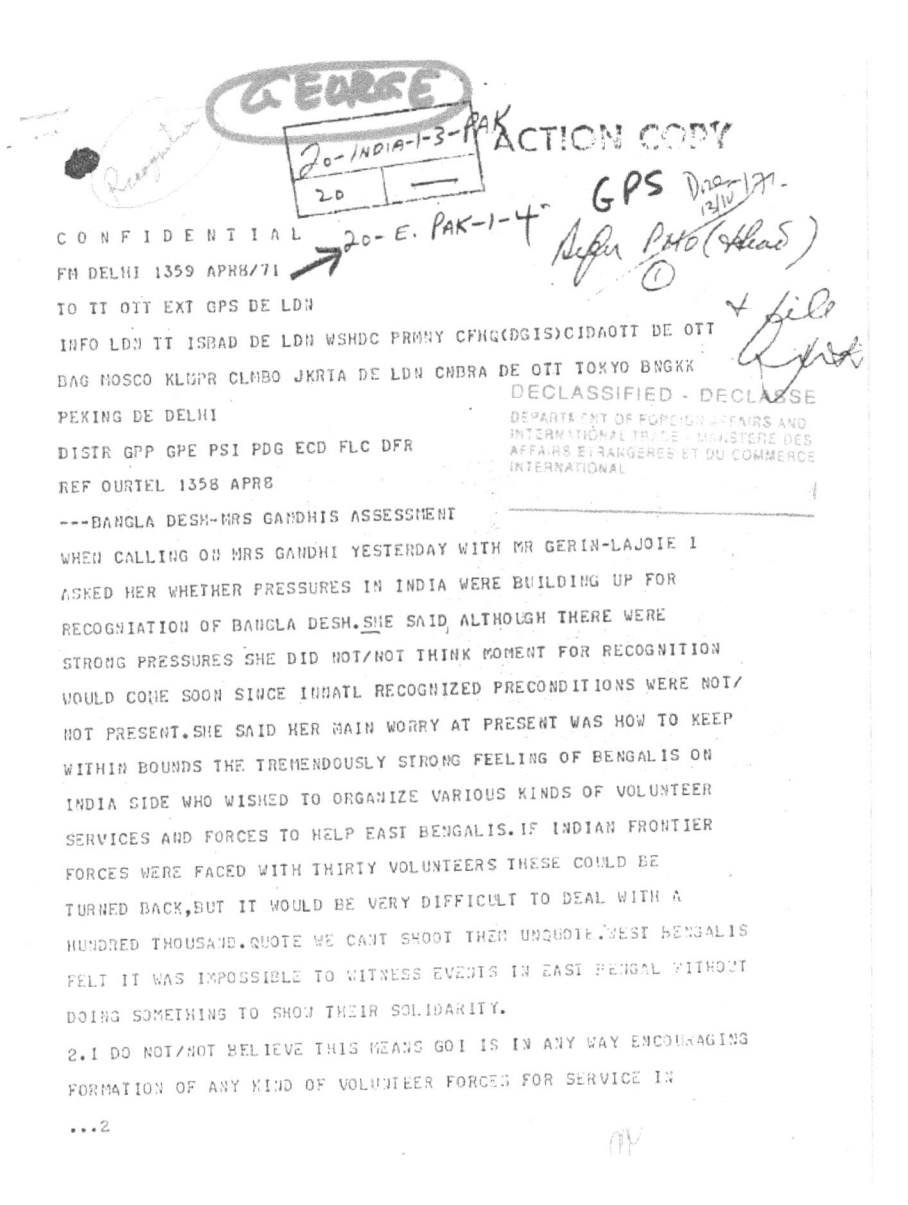

CONFIDENTIAL
FM DELHI 1359 APR8/71
TO TT OTT EXT GPS DE LDN
INFO LDN TT ISBAD DE LDN WSHDC PRMNY CFNG(DGIS)CIDAOTT DE OTT
DAG MOSCO KLUPR CLMBO JKRTA DE LDN CNBRA DE OTT TOKYO BNGKK
PEKING DE DELHI
DISTR GPP GPE PSI PDG ECD FLC DFR
REF OURTEL 1358 APR8
---BANGLA DESH-MRS GANDHIS ASSESSMENT
WHEN CALLING ON MRS GANDHI YESTERDAY WITH MR GERIN-LAJOIE I
ASKED HER WHETHER PRESSURES IN INDIA WERE BUILDING UP FOR
RECOGNIATION OF BANGLA DESH. SHE SAID, ALTHOUGH THERE WERE
STRONG PRESSURES SHE DID NOT/NOT THINK MOMENT FOR RECOGNITION
WOULD COME SOON SINCE INNATL RECOGNIZED PRECONDITIONS WERE NOT/
NOT PRESENT. SHE SAID HER MAIN WORRY AT PRESENT WAS HOW TO KEEP
WITHIN BOUNDS THE TREMENDOUSLY STRONG FEELING OF BENGALIS ON
INDIA SIDE WHO WISHED TO ORGANIZE VARIOUS KINDS OF VOLUNTEER
SERVICES AND FORCES TO HELP EAST BENGALIS. IF INDIAN FRONTIER
FORCES WERE FACED WITH THIRTY VOLUNTEERS THESE COULD BE
TURNED BACK, BUT IT WOULD BE VERY DIFFICULT TO DEAL WITH A
HUNDRED THOUSAND. QUOTE WE CANT SHOOT THEM UNQUOTE. WEST BENGALIS
FELT IT WAS IMPOSSIBLE TO WITNESS EVENTS IN EAST BENGAL WITHOUT
DOING SOMETHING TO SHOW THEIR SOLIDARITY.
2. I DO NOT/NOT BELIEVE THIS MEANS GOI IS IN ANY WAY ENCOURAGING
FORMATION OF ANY KIND OF VOLUNTEER FORCES FOR SERVICE IN
...2

CONFIDENTIAL telegram from James George, high commissioner to India, to Ottawa, dated April 8, 1971.

Source: Canada. Department of External Affairs. File # 20-India-1-3-Pak.

PAGE TWO 1359 CONFD
EASTBENGAL BUT THAT INDIAN AUTHORITIES ARE GENUINELY WORRIED
THAT WITH EACH DAY EASTPAK FIGHTING CONTINUES THERE IS MORE
LIKLIHOOD OF WESTBENGALIS TAKING PRIVATE INITIATIVES THAT
COULD IMPLICATE GOI AGAINST ITS WILL AND IF THESE INITIATIVES
REACH MASS PROPORTIONS THEY WILL BE IMPOSSIBLE TO CONTROL.
3. WE AND NO/NO DOUBT OTHER DIPLO MISSIONS HERE ARE UNDER
CONTINUOUS PRESSURE FROM MEA OFFICIALS AND MANY OTHER INDIANS
TO EXPLAIN WHY CDN GOVT HAS BEEN SO SILENT. NOW THAT USA, USSR,
BRIT AND OTHER GOVTS HAVE MUDE PRONOUNCEMENTS PRESSURE ON US
IS INCREASING.
4. BANGLA DESH SPOKESMEN QUOTE HEJE(EG MAJ OSMAN CHOUDHURY,
CMNDR OF SOUTHWEST MILITARY DISTRICT), ARE SAYING THAT IF MORAL
SUPPORT SHORT OF RECOGNITION IS EXTENDED BY ANY COUNTRIES
TO BANGLA DESH, BIG POWERS CAN PUT PRESSURE ON YAHYA AND THERE
WILL BE PEACE IN SEVEN DAYS. QUOTE I WANT THE MORAL SUPPORT
OF THE DEMOCRACIES. WE DO NOT/NOT WANT MATERIAL SUPPORT
UNQUOTE HE STRESSED
                GEORGE
0809382

CONFIDENTIAL telegram from James George, high commissioner to India, to Ottawa, dated April 8, 1971.

Source: Canada. Department of External Affairs. File # 20-India-1-3-Pak.

CONFIDENTIAL
FM DELHI 1472 APR19/71
TO TT.OTT EXT GPS DE LDN
INFO LDN TT ISBAD DE LDN WSHDC PRMNY CFHQ(DGIS)DE OTT
CIDAOTT DE OTT
BAG MOSCO PARIS KLMPR CLMBO JKRTA DE LDN CNBRA TERAN ANKRA DE OTT
TOKYO BNGKK PEKIN DE DELHI
DISTR GPP GPE PSI PDG ECD FLC DFR
REF OURTEL 1420 APR14
---BANGLA DESH GOVT INAUGURATED-REPUBLIC PROCLAIMED
I WAS IN CALCUTTA ON APR17 WHEN BANGLA REPUBLIC WAS PROCLAIMED
AND DECLARATION OF INDEPENDENCE RATIFIED BY NEW BANGLA DESH QUOTE
GOVT UNQUOTE WITH UNOFFICIAL BUT EFFECTIVE ASSISTANCE OF GOI.
FROM CONTACTS WITH WEST BENGAL OFFICIALS, USA CONGEN, BRIT D/HIGHCOM
AND MEMBERS OF FOREIGN PRESS CORPS WHO ATTENDED CEREMONY I CAN
PERHAPS ADD TO WHAT IS REACHING YOU THROUGH PRESS SOURCES.
2. IT IS VERY OBVIOUS THAT WHOLE SHOW IS BEING ORGANIZED BY AND
FROM INDIA. THIS IS NOT/NOT TO SAY AWAMI LEAGUE MINISTERS DO NOT/
NOT REPRESENT THEIR PARTY AND THEIR PEOPLE BUT THAT WITHOUT INDIAN
SANCTUARY AND INDIAN HELP THEY COULD NOT/NOT HAVE ORGANIZED
INAUGURAL MTG OF REVOLUTIONARY GOVT WITH MORE THAN HUNDRED
FOREIGN PRESS AND CAMERAMEN PRESENT. I DO NOT/NOT KNOW WHETHER
FOREIGN CORRESPONDENTS ARE BRINGING OUT THIS FACT BUT ARRANGEMENTS
FOR PRESS CONFERENCE WERE MADE ENTIRELY BY INDIAN INFO DEPT WITH
TRANSPORT ARRANGED BY INDIAN ARMY. ALTHOUGH CORRESPONDENTS WERE
...2

CONFIDENTIAL telegram from James George, Canadian High Commissioner to India, to Ottawa. Dated April 19, 1971

Source: Canada. Department of External Affairs. File # 20-E-Pak-1-4.

PAGE TWO 1472 CONFD

ASKED TO CAMOUFLAGE PLACE FOR SECURITY REASONS UNDER NAME OF QUOTE MUJIBNAGAR UNQUOTE, MTG TOOK PLACE HALF A MILE BEYOND INDIAN BORDER EAST OF KRISHANAGAR IN A MANGO GROVE NEAR VILLAGE OF BAIDYANATHALA IN KUSHTIA DISTRICT. TENTS, CHAIRS, LOUDSPEAKERS ETC WERE BROUGHT IN FROM CALCUTTA FOR OCCASION. BANGLA MINISTER HAD MET PREVIOUS DAY IN CALCUTTA AND PROBABLY RETURNED THERE ON EVENING OF APR17 SHORTLY AFTER FOREIGN CORRESPONDENTS GOT BACKTO THEIR HOTELS TO FILE THEIR STORIES. ANNOUNCEMENT PREVIOUS DAY THAT CHUADANGA WAS TO BE PROVISIONAL CAPITAL OF BANGLA DESH HAD IMMEDLY LED TO PAF AIR RAID AND IT IS MY IMPRESSION THAT PAK MINISTERS ARE LIKELY TO OPERATE IN AND OUT OF THEIR PROCLAIMED COUNTRY BUT THEY KNOW WHICH SIDE OF BORDER IS SAFER.

3. INDEED FROM WHAT I COULD PICK UP ON PERSONALITIES OF ACTING PRESIDENT SYED NAZRUL ISLAM, PRIME MINISTER TAJUDDIN AHMED, CINC COL OSMANI, KM AHMED AND CAPT MANSOOR ALI AND AH KAMARUZZAMAN, THEY ARE SORT OF LEADERS MORE LIKELY TO FLOURISH IN BENGAL ELECTION THAN IN GUERRILLA WAR. THEY ARE BOURGEOIS, CONCERNED IT WOULD SEEM MORE WITH THEIR OWN IMPORTANCE AND SAFETY THAN WITH DIRECTION OF TOUGH BATTLE AGAINST PROFESSIONAL ARMY. PERHAPS THEY ARE MERELY FRONT RUNNERS FOR REAL UNDERGROUND LEADERSHIP AND AS SUCH SHOULD BE MORE CONCERNED WITH PUBLIC RELATIONS THAN WITH THE WAR.

4. AT ANY RATE THEIR PITCH WAS FOR INNATL SUPPORT MORE SUBSTANTIAL THAN UNOFFICIAL EXPRESSIONS OF SYMPATHY RECEIVED TO DATE. TEXTS OF
...3

CONFIDENTIAL telegram from James George, Canadian High Commissioner to India, to Ottawa. Dated April 19, 1971

Source: Canada. Department of External Affairs. File # 20-E-Pak-1-4.

PAGE THREE 1473 CONFD

STATEMENTS BY BAG TOMORROW.

5. DAY AFTER CAREFULLY STAGED PROCLAMATION OF BANGLA REPUBLIC, PAK DEPUTY HIGHCOM IN CALCUTTA, HUSSAIN ALI, AND MOST OF HIS STAFF HOISTED BANGLA FLAG OVER HIS MISSION, HAVING TAKEN PRECAUTION OF WITHDRAWING ALL MISSIONS FUNDS FROM BANK PREVIOUS DAY. YESTERDAY EVENING ALI RELEASED A STATEMENT (COPY BY BAG TO OTT AND ISBAD) GIVING BACKGROUND OF DECISION WHICH HE DECLARED, WAS MADE PRIOR TO FORMATION OF NEW BANGLA DESH GOVT AND, IN CONSULTATION WITH REPS OF AWAMI LEAGUE, BUT WAS NOT/NOT ANNOUNCED UNTIL AFTER FORMATION OF GOVT OF BANGLA DESH. ALI ALSO CHARGED PAK GOVT WITH INSTITUTING QUOTE A PLANNED ATTEMPT TO SUBDUE AND CRUSH THE ENTIRE BENGALI NATION UNQUOTE. LATER IN ALL INDCA RADIO INTERVIEW ALI CLAIMED HE AND MEMBERS OF HIS STAFF DID NOT/NOT INTEND TO SEEK ASYLUM SINCE THEY PROPOSED TO FUNCTION AS REPS OF NEW GOVT.

6. GOI HAS MADE IT CLEAR IN PRESS GUIDANCE THAT ALTHOUGH IT WILL NOT/NOT NOW RECOGNIZE BANGLA GOVT IT WILL NOT/NOT MAKE LIFE TOO DIFFICULT FOR BANGLA MISSION IN CALCUTTA. PRESUMABLY IT WILL HAVE SAME QUASI DIPLO UNOFFICIAL STATUS ACCORDED TO LEAGUE OF ARAB STATES MISSION IN DELHI. IT IS CLEAR THAT DEFECTION OF PAK MISSION IN CALCUTTA CAME AS NO/NO SURPRISE TO MEA HERE. TIMING SEEMS TO HAVE BEEN RELATED BOTH TO ANNOUNCEMENT OF BANGLA REPUBLIC AND TO TELS MISSION HAD RECEIVED LAST WEEK FROM ISBAD ORDERING IMMINENT TRANSFER OF SOME DOUBTFUL MEMBERS OF ITS STAFF WHO HAD THEREFORE TO MAKE UP THEIR MINDS IN A HURRY AS TO WHICH SIDE THEY WERE ON.

...4

CONFIDENTIAL Telegram from James George, Canadian High Commissioner to India, to Ottawa. Dated April 19, 1971

Source: Canada. Department of External Affairs. File # 20-E-Pak-1-4.

PAGE FOUR 1473 CONFD

7. WITH BANGLA AWAMI LEAGUE LEADERS TRAILING THEIR COATS ACROSS INDIA BORDER, POSSIBILITY OF EAST PAK ACTION AGAINST WESTBENGAL SANCTUARY HAS TO BE WEIGHTED. I THINK HOWEVER IT IS MOST UNLIKELY BECAUSE PAK ARMY IN EAST BENGAL ALREADY HAS ITS HANDS FULL AND IS AT NUMERICAL DISADVANTAGE COMPARED TO INDIAN FORCES IN AREA. THERE ARE PROBABLY (ACCORDING TO USA CONGEN GORDON) FOUR PAK DIVS WITH ABOUT SEVENTY THOUSAND TROOPS IN EASTPAK (OUR REFTEL) AND THEY WOULD SURELY BE MORE SENSIBLE THAN TO RISK DIRECT CONFRONTATION WITH SUPERIOR INDIAN FORCES, HOWEVER GREAT THE TEMPTATION TO CARRY OFF A PUNITIVE RAID INTO WESTBENGAL ON EXCUSE THEY WERE TRYING TO ROUND UP BANGLA MINISTERS. PERHAPS FORSEEING TEMPTATION, GOI MINISTER OF DEFENCE PRODUCTION, SETHI, SAID ON APR 16 THAT ALTHOUGH INDIAN ARMY WOUXD ON NO/NO ACCOUNT ALLOW ITSELF TO BE PROVOKED BY INCIDENTS ALONG DISTURBED BORDER IT WOULD IF ATTACKED GIVE GOOD ACCOUNT OF ITSELF. INDIA FOR ITS PART IS DETERRED FROM PROFITING FROM PAK DIFFICULTIES BY MAOS RENEWED PLEDGE OF CHINESE SUPPORT FOR YAHYA WHICH COULD BE UNDERLINED CURRENTLY BY CHINESE MANOEUVRES OR MOVEMENTS ALONG INDIAS NORTHERN BORDER, ALTHOUGH WE HAVE AS YET NO/NO SPECIFIC INFO TO CONFIRM THIS RUMOUR.

8. IN SPITE OF OBVIOUS PASSIONATE SYMPATHY OF MOST WEST BENGALIS FOR BANGLA DESH STRUGGLE, WESTBENGAL CHIEF SECTY SEN GUPTA TOLD ME HE BELIEVES NOT/NOT MORE THAN FEW HUNDRED WESTBENGALIS HAVE ACTUALLY CORSSED OVER INTO BANGLADESH TO JOIN IN FREEDOM
...5

CONFIDENTIAL telegram from James George, Canadian High Commissioner to India, to Ottawa. Dated, April 19, 1971

Source: Canada. Department of External Affairs. File # 20-E-Pak-1-4.

PAGE FIVE 1473 CONFD
STRUGGLE. MOST OF THOSE WHO HAVE GONE IN ARE ARMED NAXALITES BUT GREAT MAJORITY OF NAXALITE STRENGTH IN AND AROUND CALCUTTA IS STILL THERE AND APPARENTLY THEY DO NOT/NOT INTEND TO RISK THEIR CADRES IN EASTPAK. THERE MAY HOWEVER BE MORE INDIAN MAOISTS GOING INTO NORTHEAST PORTIONS OF EAST PAK TO GIVE LEADERSHIP AND SUPPORT TO MORE SERIOUS STRUGGLE THERE. BRIT D/HIGHCOM MILES THINKS THIS AREA IS WHERE FREEDOM FIGHTERS HAVE BEST CHANCE OF MAKING PROLONGED STAND. LIAISON WITH INDIA IS BEING MAINTAINED THROUGH SHILLONG AND AGARTALA AND ALL INDIA RADIO HAS SET UP POWERFUL TRANSMITTER AT AGARTALA TO BROADCAST ANY NEWS AND RUMOURS THAT COME OUT. THERE ALSO SEEMS TO BE A COMMUNICATIONS INTELLIGENCE UNIT THERE LISTENING TO MSGS BETWEEN EAST AND WESTPAK.

9. AMERICANS HAVE HEARD THAT BORDER CROSSING BRIDGE ON OLD RAIL LINE BETWEEN CALCUTTA AND LESSORE IN EASTPAK HAS BEEN RECENTLY REPAIRED AND IS NOW OPERATIONAL FOR FIRST TIME SINCE 1965 BUT SO LONG AS WEST PAK ARMY CONTROLS JESSORE THIS IS OF MINOR SIGNIFICANCE.

10. APPROACHES HAVE BEEN MADE FROM BANGLA PRIME MINISTER AHMED TO BOTH BRIT D/HIGHCOM AND USA CONGEN CALCUTTA. FORMER HAS AGREED UNOFFICIALLY AND SECRETLY TO SEE AHMED THIS WEEK. THERE MAY BE PARALLEL APPROACHES TO DIPLO MISSIONS IN DELHI. IF APPROACHED SHOULD I SEE HIM IF IT CAN BE DONE DISCREETLY?
GEORGE

191045Z

CONFIDENTIAL telegram from James George, Canadian High Commissioner to India, to Ottawa. Dated, April 19, 1971

Source: Canada. Department of External Affairs. File # 20-E-Pak-1-4.

COMMUNIQUÉ — PRESS RELEASE

SECRÉTARIAT GÉNÉRAL — **GENERAL SECRETARIATE**
de l'ÉPISCOPAT CANADIEN — **of the CANADIAN EPISCOPATE**
90 Parent — Ottawa

de / from
Sister Ella M. Zink, S.O.S.,
Public Relations Service.
Phone: (613) 236-9461, ext.262

pour publication / for release

immediately

PAKISTANI CONFLICT

OTTAWA (CCC)--Following the semi-annual meeting of the Canadian Catholic Conference here, April 19-23, Reverend Everett MacNeil, General Secretary of the Conference, has released the text of a telegram from the country's Catholic Bishops to the Honourable Mitchell Sharpe, Minister for External Affairs. The text is as follows:

ON SUNDAY, APRIL 25, CATHOLICS IN CANADA ARE OBSERVING RIGHT TO LIFE DAY. IN REFLECTING ON THE NUMEROUS WAYS IN WHICH THIS GOD-GIVEN AND MOST BASIC HUMAN RIGHT IS FORCIBLY DENIED OR THREATENED THROUGHOUT THE WORLD, THOUGHTFUL CATHOLICS WILL HAVE IN MIND THE DEPLORABLE LOSS OF INNOCENT LIVES AND REPORTED ATROCITIES NOW TAKING PLACE IN THE PAKISTANI CONFLICT.

THEREFORE, THE CANADIAN CATHOLIC

-more-

| Re | TELEGRAM RE PAKISTAN | Date | 28/4/71 | Ref. | 58 |

La CCC ou Conférence Catholique Canadienne, fondée en octobre 1943, est l'Association des Cardinaux, Archevêques et

The C.C.C. or Canadian Catholic Conference, established in 1943, is the Association of Cardinals, Archbishops and Bishops

Source: *Communiqué – Press Release*. General Secretariate of the Canadian Episcopate. Dated April 28, 1971. Canadian Conference of Catholic Bishops Archives.

Zink - Telegram Re Pakistan...

CONFERENCE OF BISHOPS, MEETING IN PLENARY ASSEMBLY, ADDRESSES THE FOLLOWING APPEAL TO THE EXTERNAL AFFAIRS DEPARTMENT OF THE GOVERNMENT OF CANADA: WHILE WE RECOGNIZE THAT THERE ARE LIMITATIONS AND OBSTACLES WHICH NOW MAKE DIFFICULT POSITIVE MEDIATION OF THIS LAMENTABLE CONFLICT, WE URGE THE GOVERNMENT OF CANADA TO PERSIST BY EVERY AVAILABLE MEANS IN OFFERING GOOD OFFICES AND HUMANITARIAN ASSISTANCE, THROUGH THE UNITED NATIONS OR OTHERWISE, IN THE HOPE THAT CONTINUED HUMAN SUFFERING AND LOSS OF INNOCENT LIVES MAY SOON COME TO AN END IN EAST PAKISTAN.

(signed) ARCHBISHOP J.A. PLOURDE
PRESIDENT
CANADIAN CATHOLIC CONFERENCE

23/4/71

-30-

Source: *Communiqué – Press Release*. General Secretariate of the Canadian Episcopate. Dated April 28, 1971. Canadian Conference of Catholic Bishops Archives.

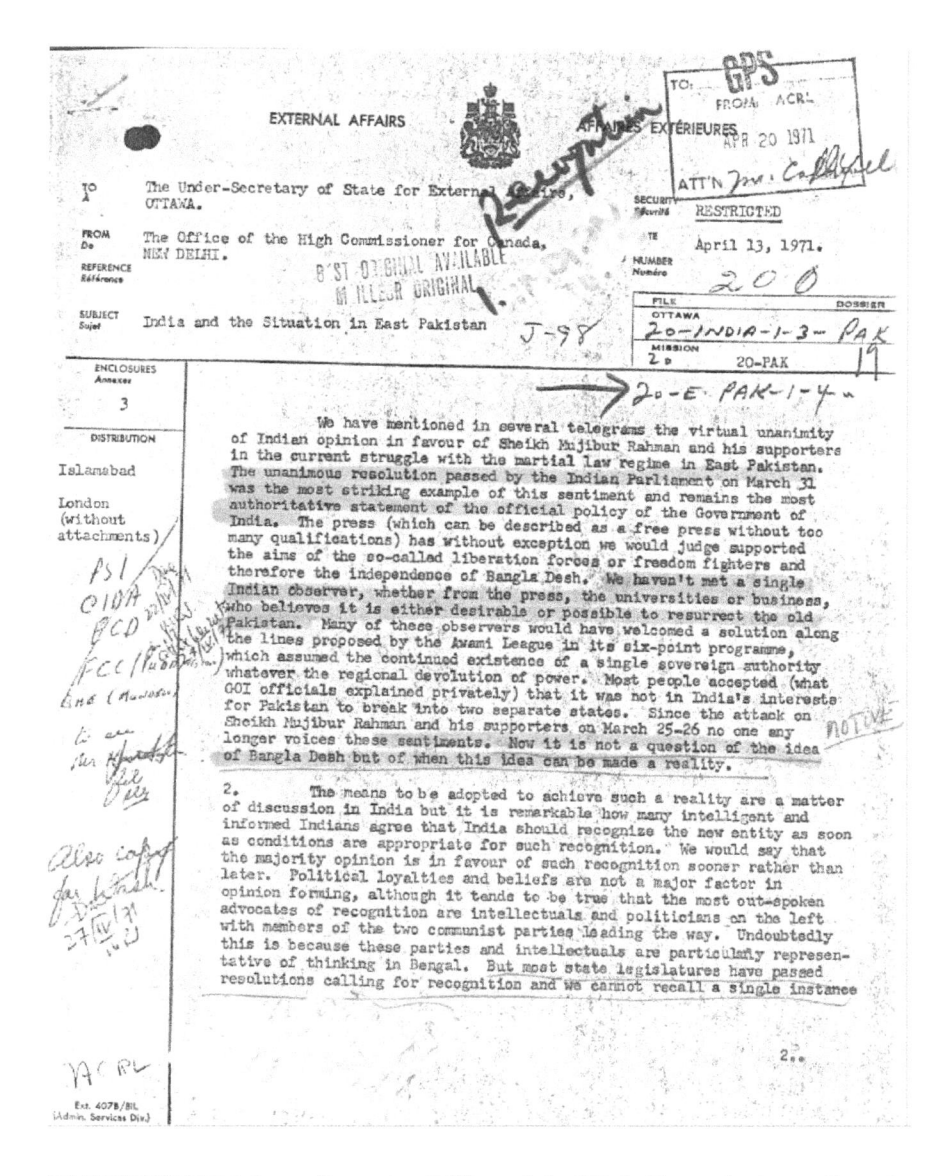

EXTERNAL AFFAIRS

TO: GPS
FROM: ACRL
APR 20 1971
ATT'N Mr. Campbell

TO: The Under-Secretary of State for External Affairs, OTTAWA.

FROM: The Office of the High Commissioner for Canada, NEW DELHI.

SECURITY: RESTRICTED

DATE: April 13, 1971.

NUMBER: 200

SUBJECT: India and the Situation in East Pakistan

FILE: 20-INDIA-1-3-PAK
MISSION: 20-PAK
20-E-PAK-1-4

ENCLOSURES: 3

DISTRIBUTION:
Islamabad
London (without attachments)

1. We have mentioned in several telegrams the virtual unanimity of Indian opinion in favour of Sheikh Mujibur Rahman and his supporters in the current struggle with the martial law regime in East Pakistan. The unanimous resolution passed by the Indian Parliament on March 31 was the most striking example of this sentiment and remains the most authoritative statement of the official policy of the Government of India. The press (which can be described as a free press without too many qualifications) has without exception we would judge supported the aims of the so-called liberation forces or freedom fighters and therefore the independence of Bangla Desh. We haven't met a single Indian observer, whether from the press, the universities or business, who believes it is either desirable or possible to resurrect the old Pakistan. Many of these observers would have welcomed a solution along the lines proposed by the Awami League in its six-point programme, which assumed the continued existence of a single sovereign authority whatever the regional devolution of power. Most people accepted (what GOI officials explained privately) that it was not in India's interests for Pakistan to break into two separate states. Since the attack on Sheikh Mujibur Rahman and his supporters on March 25-26 no one any longer voices these sentiments. Now it is not a question of the idea of Bangla Desh but of when this idea can be made a reality.

2. The means to be adopted to achieve such a reality are a matter of discussion in India but it is remarkable how many intelligent and informed Indians agree that India should recognize the new entity as soon as conditions are appropriate for such recognition. We would say that the majority opinion is in favour of such recognition sooner rather than later. Political loyalties and beliefs are not a major factor in opinion forming, although it tends to be true that the most outspoken advocates of recognition are intellectuals and politicians on the left with members of the two communist parties leading the way. Undoubtedly this is because these parties and intellectuals are particularly representative of thinking in Bengal. But most state legislatures have passed resolutions calling for recognition and we cannot recall a single instance

2..

RESTRICTED Memo from the Office of the High Commissioner Canada to the Under-Sectary of State for External Affairs, dated April 13, 1971

Source: Canada. Department of External Affairs. File # 20-India-1-3-Pak

- 2 -   RESTRICTED

of a politician going on record against it. There is some evidence of reticence on this issue in the state of Punjab where the effects of tension with Pakistan are bound to be felt more keenly. No doubt there is less enthusiasm also in Bombay and Madras than in Calcutta but these are differences of degree.

3. Behind the issue of recognition there are other more difficult issues which are only beginning to be debated. Most of the press supports efforts to organize humanitarian assistance and there are innumerable committees already formed throughout India to gather money and supplies. So far these efforts seem to be uncoordinated but a national committee has been formed and organization is bound to improve. It is not clear where the supplies will be stock-piled or how they will be delivered. The border with East Bengal seems more or less to have disappeared as a line of official control at least on the eastern side and there are reports of movement across this border of both individuals and goods. But these reports suggest that the initiative lies in the hands of individuals and local groups. The press has been more circumspect about the issue of military assistance to the "freedom fighters". Perhaps this is because the Government of India has categorically denied that such assistance is being rendered and is not as far as we know engaged in clandestine activities along these lines. On the other hand, neither are its officials on the border apparently exercising much control over what kinds of materials cross the border. There must be some gun running but little is being published in the press on the subject.

4. Farther into the future are such issues as Indian aid for the new state and the relations between it and West Bengal. It is hardly to be expected that India could do much to assist an independent Bangla Desh to reconstruct its economy and to build the economic infrastructure which it now lacks. It will be difficult enough for India to cope with humanitarian relief and the refugees which are already beginning to cross the border. There has been little discussion of this subject here yet, except for some consideration of the effects of a resumption of trade which has been interrupted for many years. The major question is whether such a resumption would help to alleviate the depression which has affected the economic climate of West Bengal since political unrest became chronic there two or three years ago. As to the political attraction which an independent East Bengal might exercise on West Bengal most Indian observers believe perhaps naively that the danger is small. A good discussion of the issue is contained in the attached clipping from the Times of India entitled "India and Bangla Desh". Also attached are two further reports from the Times of India discussing other aspects of the emerging situation. All three correspondents are members of India's press "elite" and are respected for the weight and balance of their opinions.

High Commissioner

RESTRICTED Memo from the Office of the High Commissioner Canada to the Under-Sectary of State for External Affairs, dated April 13, 1971

Source: Canada. Department of External Affairs. File # 20-India-1-3-Pak

AN ACCOUNT OF THREE DAYS OF CARNAGE AT DACCA UNIVERSITY
CONDEMN MASS MURDER OF MEN AND WOMEN, CHILDREN, STUDENTS, AND TEACHERS
WITNESS TO A MASSACRE IN BANGLA DESH (FORMERLY E. PAKISTAN)

ABOUT 1,000 SOLDIERS ATTACKED THE STUDENTS AT DACCA UNIVERSITY
left; Part of the the science building; Right ;One of the dead in the street

The foreign invading forces of West Pakistan have unleashed terror against the 75 million people of the independent state of Bangla Desh (formerly East Pakistan) and are carrying out a systematic mass murder of defenseless civilians along with execution of students, teachers and intellectuals.

The use of tanks and jet bombers against unarmed civilians has gone too far. The Army is machine-gunning the civilians, burning houses and looting properties. The barbarous West Pakistani Army has already murdered more than 300,000 men, women and children, and turned all the major cities of Bangla Desh into a ghost land. At least 700 students and 80 teachers have been murdered and some of them lie buried in bulldozed mass graves in the campus of the Dacca University.

FIRING AND MASS GRAVE
A student who survived three days of carnage at Dacca University has given the following eye-witness account of how the West Pakistani Army systematically shot down students and teachers who were trapped in the encircled dormitories on the night of March 25, 1971 (London Times, April 13, 1971).

"I jumped out of the dormitory window and hid in the top of the tree for the night," he told a science lecturer at Notre Dam College, Dacca, who has now sought asylum in Calcutta.

"The firing continued. In the morning there was a lull and I saw some Pakistani soldiers giving orders to the terrified bearers. After a while I saw the bearers dragging the bodies of students and lecturers towards the football ground.

"They were ordered to dig a huge grave. The Pakistani soldiers told the eight or nine bearers to sit down. After a while they were ordered to stand and line up near the grave. The guns fired and they fell next to the bodies of my friends."

DEATH AND DESTRUCTION
The science lecturer starts his story on the night of March 25 when it became evident that the talks between President Yahya Khan and political leaders in East Pakistan had broken down.

"At about 11:30 p.m. the sounds of heavy firing woke us. We heard Army trucks racing towards the university about a mile away. At first I heard heavy firing of light arms and artillery coming but later it seemed to spread all over the city. ...The firing continued throughout the night but the intensity dropped during the morning.

"In the morning the Army announced over Radio Pakistan that martial law had been reimposed. The firing continued throughout the day and we stayed in the house. In the afternoon we heard sporadic firing and saw a huge column of smoke rising above the university.

"Shortly after eight o'clock on Friday night the firing intensified all over the city. We did not know what was happening but a little later we heard All India Radio announce that civil war had broken out.

"Jet planes whizzed over the city and we heard the clatter of machine-guns and cannons from all parts of the city. Firing continued throughout the night and the next morning, Saturday, Radio Pakistan came on the air briefly to announce that the curfew had been lifted for seven hours."

The science lecturer went out during the period of the curfew lift and visited the residences of some of his friends at Dacca University and found that most of them were missing and that a "pool of dry blood covered the doorstep".

"Wherever we went we saw signs of destruction and death. As we left the Jinnah Hall we saw that huts of poor people had been razed to the ground. Nobody spoke and I saw students turning back towards the university with tears in their eyes."

EXECUTION OF TEACHERS
The execution of the following teachers of Dacca University have been confirmed by Montreal Star reporter, W.A. Wilson, from Meherpur in Bangla Desh (Montreal Star, April 12, 1971).

Dr. G.C. Dev, Chairman of the Philosophy Department (Dr. Dev visited University of Toronto and was guest speaker in the celebration of Pakistan Day in 1967.)
Dr. Innans Ali, Chairman of the Physics Department
Dr. Habiv Ullah, Chairman of the Islamic Studies Department
Dr. Ahmed Chaudry, Chairman of the Political Science Department

This partial report cannot help but shock the people of the civilized world and call forth condemnation of the genocide by West Pakistani Army in collusion with political leader Bhutto of West Pakistan.

We call upon all Canadian students, teachers and people to condemn this intolerable denial of human and democratic rights.

APRIL 1971

BANGLA DESH ASSOCIATION OF CANADA

Source: Canada. Library and Archives Canada. Member of Parliament Andrew Brewin's papers. MG 32 C26 Vol. 87, File # 87-15

SYED NAZRUL ISLAM, ACTING PRESIDENT OF THE
PEOPLE'S REPUBLIC OF BANGLADESH.

MUJIBNAGAR,
April 24, 1971.

To

The Governor General of Canada,
Ottawa.

Excellency,

Upon the proclamation of the sovereign independent People's Republic of Bangladesh on March 26, 1971 a Government with Sheikh Mujibur Rahman at its head has been established.

A copy of the proclamation of Independence, Laws Continuance Enforcement Order and a list of Cabinet members are enclosed and marked with the letters 'A', 'B' & 'C' respectively for favour of your perusal.

The Government of Bangladesh is exercising full sovereignty and lawful authority within the territories known as East Pakistan prior to March 26, 1971 and has taken all appropriate measures to conduct the business of State in accordance with custom, usage and recognised principles of International Law.

In view of the friendly relations that traditionally exist between the frqternal people of Bangladesh and that of Canada, I request your Excellency's Government to accord immediate recognition to the People's Republic of Bangladesh. The Government of Bangladesh will be pleased to establish normal diplomatic relations and exahange envoys with a view to further strengthening the ties of x friendship between our two countries.

Please accept, Excellency, the assurances of our highest consideration.

Sd/-Syed Nazrul Islam
Acting President.

Sd/- Khandaker Moshtaque Ahmed
Foreign Minister.

Letter from Syed Nazrul Islam, Acting President of the People's Republic of Bangladesh, and Khandakar Moshtaque Ahmed, Foreign Minister, dated April 14, 1971, to the Governor General of Canada requesting his Excellency's Government to accord immediate recognition.

Source: Canada. Department of External Affairs. File # 20-Bangla-1-4

গণপ্রজাতন্ত্রী বাংলা দেশ
সরকার

:: 2 ::

জয় বাংলা

basis of an overwhelming mandate from the people. The Pakistan mission in your country represents only the West Pakistan military junta.

    I trust your Government would give gracious consideration to our request and, by according us recognition would enable my Government to exchange diplomatic envoys between Bangladesh and your great country to the mutual benefit of our two nations.

    Please accept, Excellency, the assurances of my highest consideration.

Yours sincerely,

(Khandaker Moshtaque Ahmed)
Foreign Minister.

His Excellency the Minister
for Foreign Affairs,
Federal Government of Canada,
OTTAWA.

Letter from Syed Nazrul Islam, Acting President of the People's Republic of Bangladesh, and Khandakar Moshtaque Ahmed, Foreign Minister, dated April 14, 1971, to the Governor General of Canada requesting his Excellency's Government to accord immediate recognition.

Source: Canada. Department of External Affairs. File # 20-Bangla-1-4

MESSAGE

PLACE	DEPARTMENT	ORIG. NO.	DATE	FILE/DOSSIER	SECURITY
OTTAWA	EXTERNAL	GPS-193	MAY 5	20-E-PAK-1-4	CONFD

FM/DE

TO/A: ISBAD

INFO:

DISTR. PDO GPS(5) PMO

REF: YOURTEL 372 APR24

SUB/SUJ: MSG FROM PM TRUDEAU TO PAK PRESIDENT

PM HAS APPROVED FOLLOWING REPLY TO PRESIDENT YAHYA'S MSG OF MAR 31. YOU SHOULD SEEK APPOINTMENT TO DELIVER IT PERSONALLY. MSG BEGINS DEAR MR PRESIDENT, IT WAS VERY THOUGHTFUL OF YOU, IN THE MIDST OF YOUR MANY CURRENT PREOCCUPATIONS, TO TAKE THE TROUBLE TO SEND ME A PERSONAL ACCOUNT OF DEVELOPMENTS IN EAST PAKISTAN, WHICH I RECEIVED FROM YOUR HIGH COMMISSIONER SHORTLY BEFORE THE EASTER VACATION. HAVING RECENTLY BEEN YOUR GUEST IN PAKISTAN, WHERE I HAD THE PRIVILEGE OF MEETING SO MANY OF YOUR COUNTRYMEN, I WAS PARTICULARLY CONCERNED WHEN I LEARNED OF THE BREAKDOWN OF NEGOTIATIONS WHICH YOU HAD BEEN CONDUCTING WITH REPRESENTATIVES OF THE AWAMI LEAGUE, AND OF THE EVENTS WHICH FOLLOWED. I KNOW THAT MY CONCERN IS SHARED BY A GREAT MANY CANADIANS WHO, DURING THE PAST WEEKS, HAVE BEEN DISTRESSED AT REPORTS OF HEAVY CASUALTIES AND DESTRUCTION OF PROPERTY IN EAST PAKISTAN.

2. MY COLLEAGUES AND I NATURALLY RECOGNIZE THAT THE SEARCH FOR A POLITICAL SOLUTION TO CURRENT PROBLEMS IS THE RESPONSIBILITY OF THE GOVERNMENT AND PEOPLE OF PAKISTAN AND NOT/NOT THAT OF CANADA. I TRUST THAT YOU WILL

...2

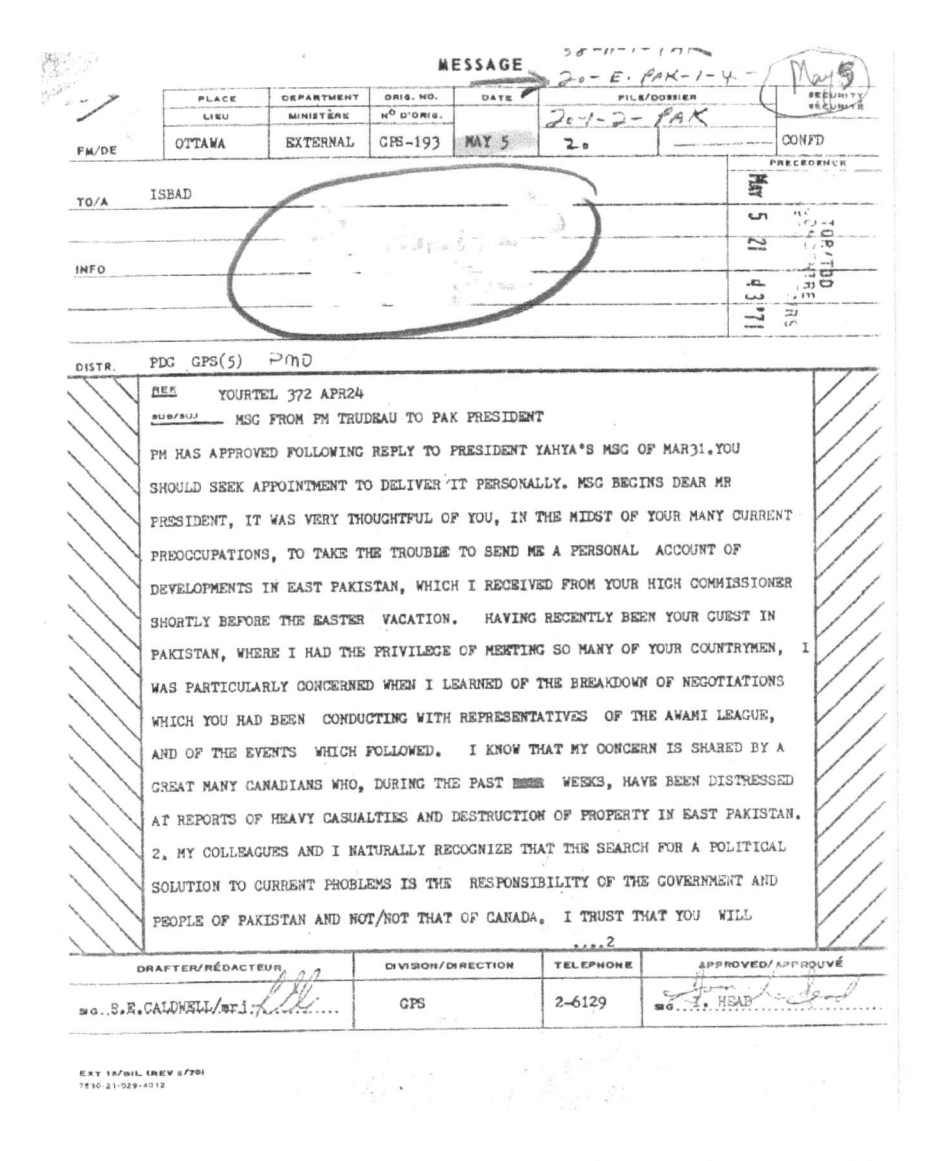

DRAFTER/RÉDACTEUR	DIVISION/DIRECTION	TELEPHONE	APPROVED/APPROUVÉ
SIG. S.E. CALDWELL/srj	GPS	2-6129	SIG. T. HEAD

Confidential telegram from Pierre minister Pierre Trudeau to President Yahya Khan, dated May 5, 1971

Source: Canada. Department of External Affairs. File # 20-E-Pak-1-4

UNDERSTAND MY MOTIVES AND RECOGNIZE MY SINCERITY THEREFORE WHEN I EXPRESS THE HOPE AS A FRIEND OF PAKISTAN THAT IT WILL SOON BE POSSIBLE TO RESUME THE SEARCH FOR AN AGREED SOLUTION TO YOUR CURRENT DIFFICULTIES. I AM SURE YOU SHARE MY VIEW THAT IT IS TRAGIC FOR ALL THE PEOPLE OF PAKISTAN TO BE DIVERTED FOR ANY PERIOD OF TIME FROM THE PRIMARY OBJECTIVES OF POLITICAL AND ECONOMIC PROGRESS TOWARD WHICH CANADA AND OTHER OUTSIDE COUNTRIES HAVE BEEN PLEASED TO MAKE SOME CONTRIBUTION.

3. IT WAS ONLY A FEW MONTHS AGO THAT CANADIANS LEARNED WITH GREAT DISTRESS OF THE MANY CASUALTIES INFLICTED BY THE TYPHOON AND TIDAL WAVE IN BENGAL AS WELL AS THE SUFFERING AND HARDSHIP ENDURED BY THE SURVIVORS OF THE DISASTER. THIS ALL TOO RECENT MEMORY HAS NATURALLY SERVED TO HEIGHTEN OUR AWARENESS OF THE PRESENT SITUATION IN EAST PAKISTAN. I WISH TO ASSURE YOU THAT WE ARE PREPARED IF REQUESTED TO JOIN OTHER MEMBERS OF THE INTERNATIONAL COMMUNITY IN PROVIDING EMERGENCY RELIEF ASSISTANCE FOR THOSE WHO HAVE SUFFERED HARDSHIP DURING THIS DIFFICULT PERIOD.

4. MY COLLEAGUES AND I WISH FOR YOU, MR. PRESIDENT, AND FOR ALL THE PEOPLE OF PAKISTAN A SPEEDY RESOLUTION OF THE DIFFICULTIES NOW FACING YOUR COUNTRY.
                    P.E. TRUDEAU.
MESSAGE ENDS.

Confidential telegram from Pierre Minister Pierre Elliott Trudeau to President Yahya Khan, dated May 5, 1971

Source: Canada. Department of External Affairs. File # 20-E-Pak-1-4

GPP/A.J.ANDREW
GPS/J.M.HARRINGTON/mrj

PDG
File
Diary
Div. Diary

PLEASE RETURN TO GPS
POSTAL STATION "B"

PERSONAL AND CONFIDENTIAL

Ottawa, May 13 1971

Dear Jim,

Your telegram 1714 of May 5 about your visit to the Bengali refugee camps near Calcutta has been read with interest and has been extremely useful to us; it certainly justifies the time and effort you have taken to keep us posted on the situation of the refugees in India. There is, however, some background which I think you should be aware of. Our public position here is that the Pakistan Government's activities in the East Wing are their own internal affair, although the influx of refugees to India certainly introduces a broader aspect, if only from the humanitarian point of view. There is a danger, however, that this new refugee problem may come to dominate the other dreary issues of the Indo-Pakistan relationship. Our experience in the Middle East has shown us that refugees have an enormous potential for political exploitation by either side in a dispute.

For these reasons we had decided that although our humanitarian efforts in East Pakistan (assuming the Paks will ever let us in) may carry a Canadian label, it would be wiser to maintain a low bilateral profile in our efforts to do some good for the refugees in India, in order to avoid becoming embroiled in the Indo-Pakistan disputes. It was, therefore, agreed here that all our activities in India should be channelled through multilateral organizations like the World Food Programme or through local Red Cross Societies here and in India. This is very much along the lines proposed in your telegram 1698 of May 5 which also pointed out the disadvantages of direct government to government donations in the Indian context. With this in mind I think it might be best in future for you to avoid visiting refugee camps personally and, should it again be necessary to size up the situation *in situ*, you might consider sending someone from your office whose presence would be less noticeable than your own and therefore less likely to be exploited by those with special axes to grind.

...2

James George, Esq.,
High Commissioner for Canada,
New Delhi, India

Personal and Confidential Memo, dated May 13, 1971, Ottawa Headquarters suggests James George, High Commissioner to India, to keep a lowkey but work with multinational organizations.

Source: Canada. Department of External Affairs. File # 20-India-1-3-Pak

PERSONAL AND CONFIDENTIAL -2-

     We are trying very hard to crank up a good operation in East Pakistan when the time comes and CIDA seems to be ready to start at any time. Much now depends on the extent to which the Government in Islamabad will co-operate, bearing in mind that for the immediate future at least they seem likely to have the final say on who will be going into East Pakistan.

     In closing I should like to acknowledge and thank you for the excellent reporting on the crisis in Bengal which we have been getting from New Delhi as well as, of course, from John Small in Islamabad.

     With every good wish as I prepare for departure,

                            Yours sincerely,

                            R. E. Collins

In a personal and confidential memo dated May 13, 1971, Ottawa Headquarters suggests that James George, the high commissioner to India, keeps a low profile but works with multinational organizations.

Source: Canada. Department of External Affairs. File # 20-India-1-3-Pak

Canadian aid goes to help Pakistani refugees

The tide of people flowing from East Pakistan to India in the past three months has created a huge and complex refugee problem in a region with few resources to spare, and has flashed terrible new scenes of human suffering before the eyes of the world.

Homeless, ill and hungry, an estimated six million citizens have fled East Pakistan to live for the time being in adjacent Indian states — often with family or friends, but in more cases in one of the many camps set up by the government of India, or in any shelter that can be found. To cope with their most urgent needs help has come from many quarters — from the governments of several countries, from international agencies and voluntary groups, and from individuals in all parts of the world.

In response to an April 30 appeal, the Canadian government provided $50,000 to purchase mobile dispensaries for the Indian Red Cross. A further contribution of $2,000,000 was announced in the House of Commons on May 28, following an appeal for refugee assistance by UN Secretary-General U Thant. About 3,000 tons of rapeseed, a high-priority requirement in India's refugee-support program, was purchased and sent at a cost of $1,250,000 while another $680,000 from the Canadian contribution was used to support the efforts of various organizations already at work in the camps — the UN agencies (UNICEF, the World Food Program, and the World Health Organization); the League of Red Cross Societies (milk and medical stations); and four Canadian voluntary groups (Oxfam, the Canadian Council of Churches, the Canadian Catholic Organization for Development and Peace, and the Mennonite Central Committee).

Contributions were also announced by some provincial governments: Ontario sent ambulances and is sharing costs with the Federal Government on shelter materials carried overseas by Canadian Armed Forces airlift, while Saskatchewan arranged to ship rapeseed. Many Canadians, witnessing the growing tragedy through television and newspapers each day, found a great variety of ways to respond.

In British Columbia June 18 was proclaimed Pakistan Refugee Day and the Canadian Save the Children Fund and a Vancouver newspaper collected contributions from the public. Employees donated through a special collection in Toronto's City Hall. The Unitarian Service Committee launched an emergency appeal and diverted shipments of milk and clothing to the Calcutta area, while at Cardinal Leger's request the organization supporting his work in Africa arranged to send medical supplies to Calcutta. Marathon money — $5,000 raised last fall in Ontario by students at the Port Credit Secondary School — was used to provide medical personnel and supplies.

To co-ordinate the many voluntary relief efforts in Canada, eight charitable groups joined for the first time in a single organization — the Combined Appeal for Pakistan Relief, which will channel donations to wherever the need is greatest in the continuing struggle to help displaced millions live day by day until a better future is in sight. Contributions can be made through charitable agencies, churches and chartered banks, or can be mailed to CAPR at Box 1000, Station F, Toronto or Box 2000, Station H, Montreal 107.

Top
Powdered milk from Canada is raised for daily consumption by refugee children and nursing mothers.

Centre:
Small makeshift canvas tents house refugee families in one of the camps.

Bottom:
A resident missionary in India pours saline solution, a cholera treatment, into plastic bottles for oral consumption.

Source: *International Development*, May-June 1971, Page 3

ECD/A.R.WRIGHT/dp

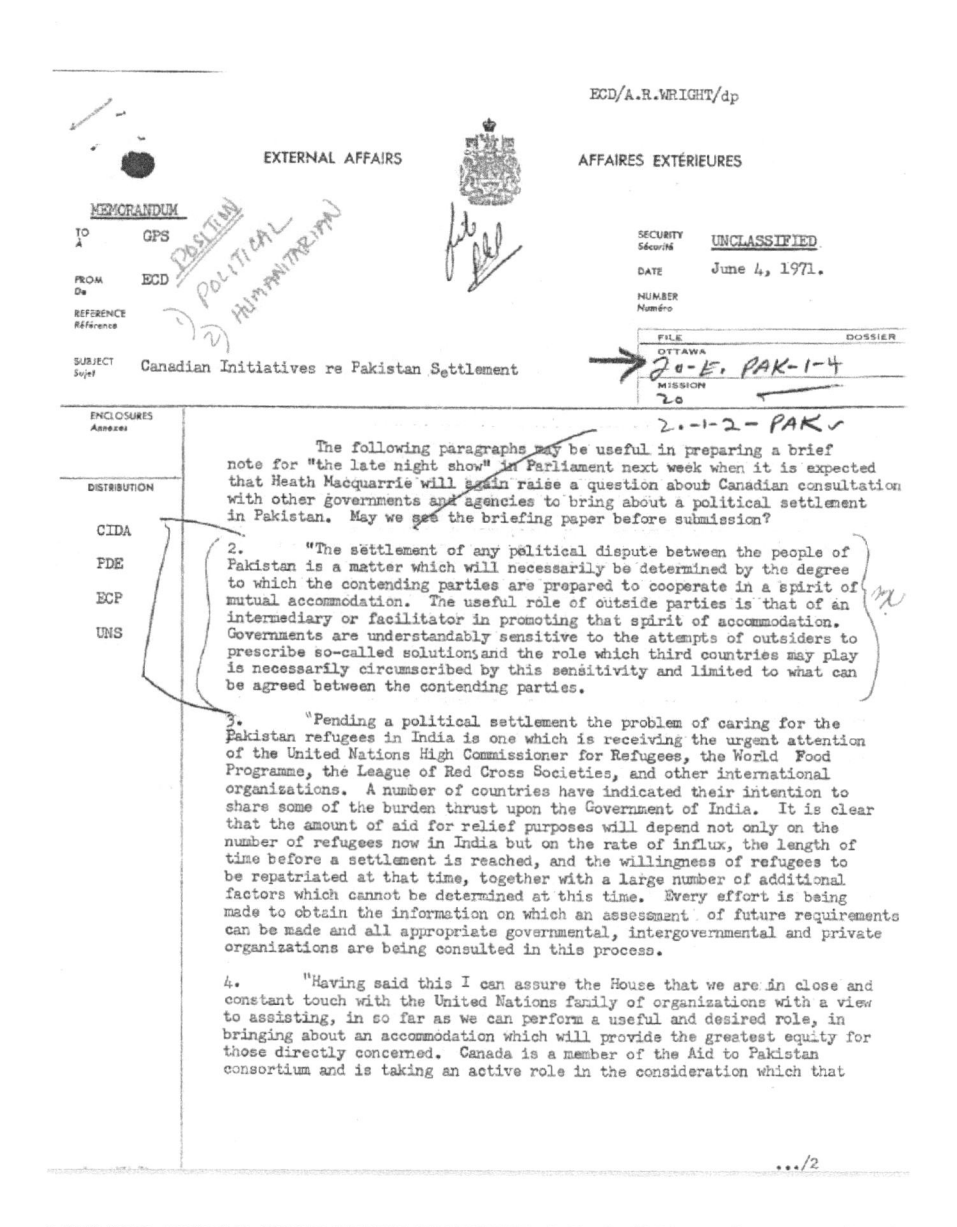

EXTERNAL AFFAIRS / AFFAIRES EXTÉRIEURES

MEMORANDUM

TO: GPS
FROM: ECD
REFERENCE:

SECURITY: UNCLASSIFIED
DATE: June 4, 1971.
NUMBER:

FILE / DOSSIER: OTTAWA 20-E. PAK-1-4
MISSION: 20

SUBJECT: Canadian Initiatives re Pakistan Settlement

DISTRIBUTION:
CIDA
PDE
ECP
UNS

1. The following paragraphs may be useful in preparing a brief note for "the late night show" in Parliament next week when it is expected that Heath Macquarrie will again raise a question about Canadian consultation with other governments and agencies to bring about a political settlement in Pakistan. May we see the briefing paper before submission?

2. "The settlement of any political dispute between the people of Pakistan is a matter which will necessarily be determined by the degree to which the contending parties are prepared to cooperate in a spirit of mutual accommodation. The useful role of outside parties is that of an intermediary or facilitator in promoting that spirit of accommodation. Governments are understandably sensitive to the attempts of outsiders to prescribe so-called solutions and the role which third countries may play is necessarily circumscribed by this sensitivity and limited to what can be agreed between the contending parties.

3. "Pending a political settlement the problem of caring for the Pakistan refugees in India is one which is receiving the urgent attention of the United Nations High Commissioner for Refugees, the World Food Programme, the League of Red Cross Societies, and other international organizations. A number of countries have indicated their intention to share some of the burden thrust upon the Government of India. It is clear that the amount of aid for relief purposes will depend not only on the number of refugees now in India but on the rate of influx, the length of time before a settlement is reached, and the willingness of refugees to be repatriated at that time, together with a large number of additional factors which cannot be determined at this time. Every effort is being made to obtain the information on which an assessment of future requirements can be made and all appropriate governmental, intergovernmental and private organizations are being consulted in this process.

4. "Having said this I can assure the House that we are in close and constant touch with the United Nations family of organizations with a view to assisting, in so far as we can perform a useful and desired role, in bringing about an accommodation which will provide the greatest equity for those directly concerned. Canada is a member of the Aid to Pakistan consortium and is taking an active role in the consideration which that

.../2

MEMORANDUM FOR THE MINISTER, Mitchell Sharp from Head Asia and Development Division, dated June 4, 1971. The subject is the Canadian initiative regarding Pakistani settlement.

Source: Canada. Department of External Affairs. File # 20-E-Pak-1-4

body is giving to the situation in Pakistan. Within the International Bank for Reconstruction and Development and within the International Monetary Fund we intend to explore with other interested groups the means whereby appropriate arrangements for the future well being of all concerned can be assisted.

5. "Officials of the Canadian government are in close contact with the Government of Pakistan and other countries which share our interest in reaching an appropriate programme. It is our view that through close collaboration with other countries we can contribute most effectively to creating those conditions in which a political settlement will be possible. The ultimate responsibility for reaching that political settlement necessarily rests with the contending parties."

Aid & Development Division.

MEMORANDUM FOR THE MINISTER, Mitchell Sharp from Head Asia and Development Division, dated June 4, 1971. The subject is the Canadian initiative regarding Pakistani settlement.

Source: Canada. Department of External Affairs. File # 20-E-Pak-1-4

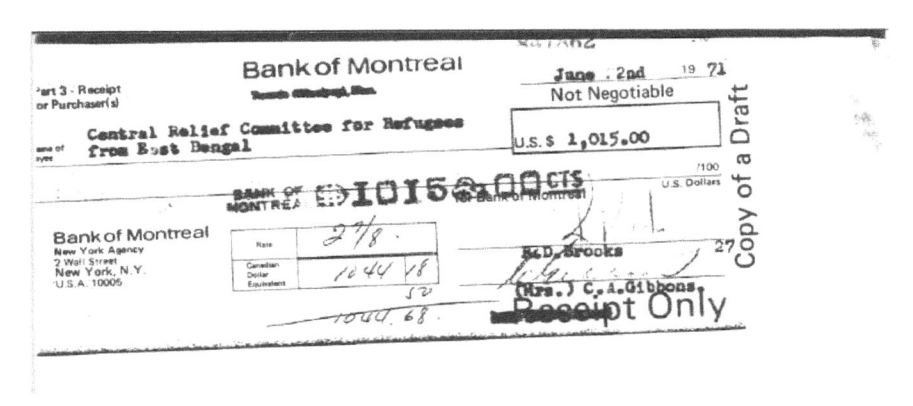

The above cheque was sent to the Central Relief Committee for Refugees from East Bengal by Dr. Farid Sharrif, President of the Bangladesh Association of Manitoba, on June 2, 1971.

Source: From Dr. Farid Shariff's personal collection.

GEORGE

EXTERNAL AFFAIRS   AFFAIRES EXTÉRIEURES

TO: Under-Secretary of State for External Affairs, OTTAWA. Attention: GPS.
FROM: Canadian High Commission, NEW DELHI.
SECURITY: RESTRICTED
DATE: June 8, 1971
NUMBER: 345
FILE: 20-E-PAK-1-4
MISSION: 20-PAK

SUBJECT: Political Situation in East Pakistan.

ENCLOSURES: 4

DISTRIBUTION: Islamabad

-- We are attaching copies of four reports relating to the political situation in East Pakistan which have appeared recently in the Indian press.

2.   These reports may be of some interest in the context of attempts currently being made by the Government of Pakistan to move forward towards some kind of civilian rule in both the East and West wings. In an interview on AIR June 2, the "Bangla Desh" Prime Minister, Mr. Tajuddin Ahmed, is reported as saying, "There is no room for compromise within the framework of Pakistan". A few days later the Acting President of "Bangla Desh", Syed Nazrul Islam, spelled out in some detail his pre-conditions for a political settlement in East Pakistan. These were as follows:

1. Release of Sheikh Mujibur Rahman;
2. Withdrawal of West Pakistani troops;
3. Recognition of the Sovereign Republic of Bangla Desh;
4. Compensation for the losses suffered by the people in East Pakistan as a result of Army actions.

While these pre-conditions look totally unacceptable to the West Pakistan military authorities, it might be worth noting that Mr. Nazrul Islam was quoted as offering, "To hold a dialogue at any place, in any situation, and with anybody" in order to reach a political settlement in East Pakistan.

High Commission.

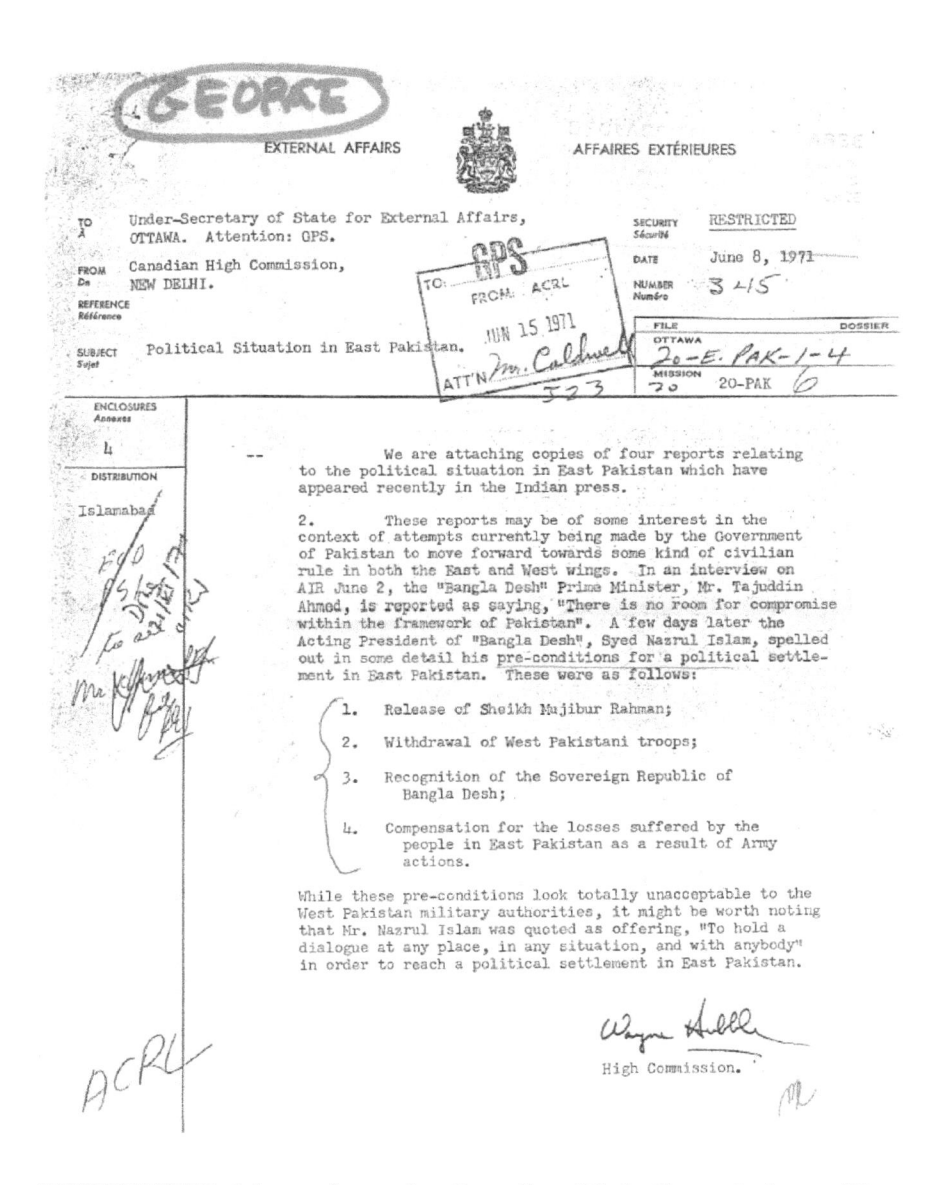

RESTRICTED Memo from the Canadian High Commissioner, New Delhi, to the Undersecretary of State for External Affairs, on the Political Situation in East Pakistan, dated June 8, 1971.

Source: Canada. Department of External Affairs. File # 20-E-Pak-1-4

MINISTRY OF FOREIGN AFFAIRS
GOVERNMENT OF BANGLADESH.

গণ প্রজাতন্ত্রী বাংলা দেশ
সরকার

MUJIBNAGAR,
June 29, 1971.

To
His Excellency Mr. Mitchel Sharp,
Minister of State for External Affairs,
Ottawa, CANADA.

Excellency,

    My government has taken appreciative note of the decision of the Aid-to-Pakistan Consortium, of which your country is an honoured member, to postpone its next meeting indefinitely.

    The Pakistan Army has brutally killed hundreds of thousands of Bengali men, women and children; it has caused extensive damage to property in Bangladesh (formerly East Pakistan); it has created six-million terror-stricken refugees and it has indulged in such other acts of cruel perversity as to leave an indelible mark on the conscience of every citizen of the world. All this it has done in order to accomplish a very specific political purpose, namely complete subjugation of the people of Bangladesh to the yoke of colonial exploitation by West Pakistan.

    Nevertheless, by the grace of God, the illegitimate and unrepresentative military regime which rules Pakistan is failing today in its attempt to crush Bangladesh.

    We are sure that your Excellency will agree that any economic assistance that is provided to Pakistan will only tend to salvage and underwrite this despicable effort. We are glad that the postponement of the Aid-to-Pakistan Consortium meeting is, in effect, denying Pakistan any such assistance. We are confident that such was the intention of the member countries of the Consortium and we thank you sincerely in the name of the 75 million people of Bangladesh.

P.T.O.

Letter from Khandaker Moshtaque Ahmed, Minister of Foreign Affairs, Government of Bangladesh, to Mitchell Sharp, Secretary of State for External Affairs, dated June 29, 1971.

Source: Canada. Department of External Affairs. File # 20-E-Pak-1-4

গণ প্রজাতন্ত্রী বাংলাদেশ
সরকার

—: 2 :—

We feel that so monstrous a crime has been committed in Bangladesh that no measure is too drastic to be used if it offers hope of undoing the evil swiftly. We are proud to enlist the help of every nation in this struggle for justice and humanity.

It is our view that the sole possible solution to the Bangladesh crisis is for the perpetrators of the genocide, the West Pakistan Army, to leave the soil of Bangladesh for ever so that the people of Bangladesh can be free to run their own affairs. No other arrangement can have any hope of ensuring the stability of 'East Bengal' and the security of its people. To be meaningful the reconstruction of Bangladesh must take place within this framework.

At the end, Excellency, please accept my sincerest personal regards and my hope that the ties of friendship which bind our two countries and our two peoples together will come to full fruition in the happier years to come that we all pray for.

Yours faithfully,

(Khandaker Moshtaque Ahmed)
Minister for Foreign Affairs.

Letter from Khandaker Moshtaque Ahmed, Minister of Foreign Affairs, Government of Bangladesh to Mitchell Sharp, Secretary of State for External Affairs, dated June 29, 1971.

Source: Canada. Department of External Affairs. File # 20-E-Pak-1-4

The Secretary of State for External Affairs   Secrétaire d'État aux Affaires extérieures

Canada

Ottawa K1A 0G2

July 7, 1971.

Dear Dr. Shariff,

    Thank you very much for your telegram of June 14 expressing your views concerning Canadian aid to Pakistan.

    The Government, of course, shares fully the concern being expressed by many Canadians regarding events in Pakistan, and particularly the plight of the great numbers of refugees crossing the Indian border. To help meet the urgent human needs of these refugees, the Government, in addition to an initial contribution to refugee relief through the Canadian Red Cross, has recently provided two million dollars in relief supplies, including foodstuffs, medicines, medical supplies and cash contributions. Close consultations with the United Nations and other multilateral channels of distribution should ensure that Canada's contribution will be used to maximum effectiveness, complementing those of other government and private donors who have indicated their willingness to contribute.

    As far as aid to Pakistan is concerned, Canada as a member of the World Bank consortium for Pakistan, is playing an active role in the consideration which that body is giving to the Pakistan situation. Given the immense scope of the problems, economic as well as political, I believe that only a concerted action by many nations is likely to achieve positive results.

    It is unlikely that suspension of all aid to Pakistan at the present time would bring a solution any nearer and certainly, to the extent that it means halting relief and rehabilitation assistance, it would only extend the suffering and deprivations of the Pakistani people. It should be pointed out that a considerable part of Canada's recent aid has involved projects in East Pakistan. These, of course, were halted by recent events and have not been resumed. In West Pakistan current contractual obligations are being honoured, but no new commitments are being entered into at this time. No aid of any military nature is being provided by Canada. We do, however, stand ready to provide food and relief supplies to the civilian population of East Pakistan as we are now doing for refugees in India, as soon as circumstances permit.

...2

Dr. Farid Shariff
421 Shaftesbury Boulevard
Winnipeg 29, Manitoba

Letter from Mitchell Sharp, Secretary of State for External Affairs, to Dr. Farid Shariff, President Bangladesh Association of Manitoba, dated July 7, 1971

Source: Dr. Farid Shariff gave the author a photocopy of this letter from his own collection.

- 2 -

Suspending aid operations in Pakistan would have the effect of closing channels of communication vital to the solution of the basic problem. I think it is likely to be more useful to continue aid - but under certain definite conditions. Canada has been urging the Pakistan Government for some time to admit relief supplies under proper international supervision. Recently, the Pakistan Representative to the United Nations requested food aid and technical assistance to restore communications in East Pakistan. The Pakistan Government has also indicated it is prepared to associate World Food Program and UNICEF personnel in the planning of relief assistance, which should help ensure that relief provided from abroad reaches its intended destination.

In conclusion I should like to say that I am not convinced that anything positive would be achieved by confrontation with the present Government of Pakistan. On humanitarian grounds alone I believe it is essential that relief and rehabilitation assistance be provided to East Pakistan, but new commitments of development aid will be conditional upon an agreed solution being found to the present political impasse.

Yours sincerely,

Mitchell Sharp

Letter from Mitchell Sharp, Secretary of State for External Affairs, to Dr. Farid Shariff, President Bangladesh Association of Manitoba, dated July 7, 1971.

Source: Dr. Farid Shariff gave the author a photocopy of this letter from his own collection.

Canadian delegates Georges Lachance (Liberal), Heath Macquarrie (Conservative), and Andrew Brewin (NDP) met with East Pakistan Governor Lt. General Tikka Khan in Dhaka, East Pakistan, on July 14, 1971.

Source: *Pakistan Observer,* Dhaka, dated July 15, 1971.

Canadian delegates Georges Lachance (Liberal), Heath Macquarrie (Conservative), and Andrew Brewin (NDP) met with President Yahya Khan in Islamabad, Pakistan.

Source: *Purbodesh*, Dhaka, dated July 15, 1971.

CONFIDENTIAL
FM ISBAD 741 JUL16/71
TO TT OTT EXT GPS DE LDN
INFO LDN DELHI TT GENEV DE PARIS WSHDC PRMNY CIDAOTT CFHQ(DCIS)
DE OTT
DISTR PDM MIN PCO ECD GPP PDH PMO
REF OURTEL 718 AND 720 JUL13

---CDN PARLIAMENTARIANS CALL ON PRESIDENT YAHYA KHAN JUL12
MPS WERE RECEIVED BY PRESIDENT FOR ALMOST AN HOUR AT NOON JUL12.
SECTY OF MINISTRY OF INFO AND ACTING HICOMER WERE ONLY OTHERS PRESENT. PRESIDENT WAS IN EFFECTIVE FORM AND, AS MR BREWIN PUT IT, QUOTE
GAVE VIRTUOSO PERFORMANCE UNQUOTE. PRESIDENTS VOICE IS OF COURSE A
POWERFUL INSTRUMENT AND HE PLAYED IT TO FULL ADVANTAGE IN CONVERSATION WITH PARLIAMETARIANS.
2. PRESIDENT BEGAN BY SAYING HE HAD RECENTLY RECEIVED SO MANY DELS
(TWO BRIT, ONE GERMAN, DR KISSINGERS TEAM, ETC) THAT HE NO/NO LONGER
HAD QUOTE STAMINA UNQUOTE TO REHEARSE IN DETAIL HISTORY OF VENTS
LEADING UP TO AND SINCE MAR25. PRESIDENT THEM, HOWEVER, GAVE PRESENTATION RE NEGOTIATIONS WITH AWAMI LEAGUE, CONTINUING TURMOIL ON
EASTPAK BORDERS, ETC, SIMILAR TO THAT MPS RECEIVED FROM MM AHMAD,
PRESIDENTS ECONOMIC ADVISER(OURTEL 729 JUL15) AND DISCOURSED ON CDN
SUSPENSION OF EXPORT PERMITS FOR MILITARY SHIPMENTS TO PAK IN VEIN
SIMILAR TO THAT FOLLOWED BY MM ABBAS, MFA DIRGEN FOR EUROPE AND AMERICAS(OURTEL 723 JUL13). AS REPORTED OURTEL 720 PRESIDENT ALSO ADVISED
MPS TO ASK FOR WHATEVER ARRANGEMENTS THEY WISHED ON VISIT TO EAST
...2

Confidential telegram from John Small, high commissioner to Pakistan, to Ottawa regarding the meeting of Canadian delegates, dated July 16, 1971.

Source: Canada. Department of External Affairs. File # 38-11-1-Pak.

PAGE TWO 741 CONFD
PAK AND SUGGESTED THEY SEE FILM ON HORRORS OF ASSAULT ON OPPONENTS
OF AWAMI LEAGUE PRIOR TO MAR25 WHICH THEY DID(FILM WAS ALSO SCREE-
NED EVENING OF JUL15 FOR INVITED MEMBERS OF DIPLO CORPS;CHINESE AT-
TENDED BUT OUR CFA WHO WAS PRESENT DID NOT/NOT NOTICE REPS FROM
USSR EMBASSY OR MISSIONS OF OTHER QUOTE SOCIALIST COUNTRIES UNQUOTE
OR FROM BRIT HICOM).
3.AS REPORTED OURTEL 737 JUL16,PARLIAMENTARIANS WERE IMPRESSED BY
PRESIDENTS FRANK AND DYNAMIC MANNER AND HIS READINESS TO ANSWER ALL
QUESTIONS.ONE MP REMARKED THAT AUDIENCE HAD BEEN MUCH EASIER THAN
THAT WITH PRIME MINISTER GANDHI.ONLY JARRING NOTE CAME WHEN MR BRE-
WIN ASKED HOW MANY QUOTE REFUGEES UNQUOTE WERE STILL MOVING FROM
EASTPAK INTO INDIA;PRESIDENT REPLIED:QUOTE NOT/NOT ONE UNQUOTE.
PRESIDENT THEN HELD FORTH AT SOME LENGTH ON EXISTENCE OF ROOTLESS,
UNINTEGRATED REFUGEE POPULATION IN WESTBENGAL,ALMOST ENTIRELY
HINDU,WHO HAD LEFT EASTBENGAL AT TIME OF PARTITION;HE WOULD NOT/NOT
PERMIT INDIANS TO SHOVEL SUCH ELEMENTS BACK INTO EASTPAK UNDER GUISE
OF POST-MAR25 MOVEMENT.MR BREWIN REMARKED AFTERWARDS THAT PRESIDENT
SEEMED QUOTE A BIT MAD UNQUOTE ON THIS SUBJ.
4.CONSULAR OFFICER WAS ON DUTY IN DACCA DURING MPS VISIT TO EASTPAK
BUT HAS NOT/NOT YET RETURNED.DELHI WILL PRESUMABLY BE ABLE TO RE-
PORT ON MPS REACTIONS TO THEIR CONVERSATIONS AND OBSERVATIONS IN
DACCA,KHULNA,JHIKARGACHHA DP RECPTION CENTRE AND CHITTAGONG.
161131Z

Confidential telegram from John Small, high commissioner to Pakistan, to Ottawa regarding the meeting of Canadian delegates, dated July 16, 1971.

Source: Canada. Department of External Affairs. File # 38-11-1-Pak.

CONFIDENTIAL
July 29, 1971

MEMORANDUM FOR THE PRIME MINISTER:

Indo-Pakistan Situation: Messages to
President Yahya Khan and Mrs. Indira Gandhi

In his most recent letter to you, President Yahya Khan drew to your attention the deterioration of relations between his country and India and the danger that this would lead to the outbreak of hostilities between the two countries. He asked you "to use your influence with India to persuade her to desist from actions which could lead not only to a breach of peace but, as a result of that, to unforeseen consequences which could affect the world community".

2. Although the present crisis clearly has its origins in Pakistan, I think there is some truth in the President's suggestion that India's attitude is not being entirely helpful. I am concerned particularly at the apparent refusal of the Indian Government to allow observers representing the United Nations High Commissioner for Refugees to operate in India to encourage the refugees' return (despite the fact that Pakistan has agreed unconditionally to their presence on the Pakistan side of the border) and also the danger that India may shortly recognize Bangla Desh, which would almost inevitably lead to outright hostilities between India and Pakistan.

3. I am attaching for your consideration a draft message to President Yahya which takes the occasion to urge him toward a more active search for a political compromise as a necessary pre-condition for the return of refugees from India. Also attached is a message to Mrs. Gandhi supporting the positioning of UN observers in the refugee areas and expressing the hope that India will continue to desist from action likely to exacerbate the present dangerous situation. If these two messages meet with your approval we shall transmit the texts by telegram for delivery by our High Commissions in Islamabad and New Delhi.

Mitchell Sharp

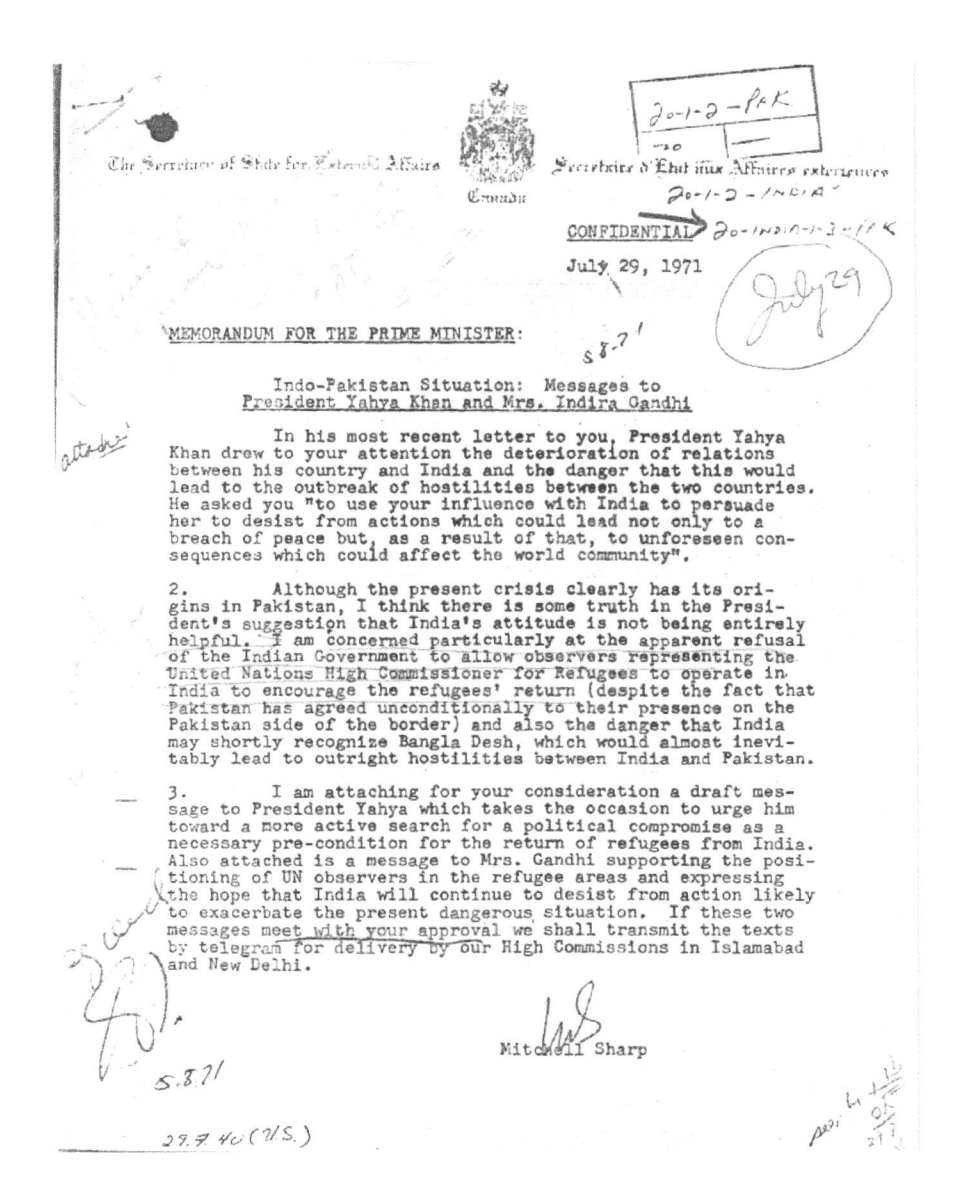

MEMORANDUM FOR THE MINISTER FOR THE PRIME MINISTER from Mitchell Sharp, Secretary of State for External Affairs, dated July 29, 1971.

Source: Canada. Department of External Affairs. File # 20-India-1-3-Pak.

Ottawa, July 29, 1971.

Dear Prime Minister,

Since I wrote to you on June 30th I have been increasingly concerned about the continuing crisis in the sub-continent and the possibility that it could lead to open hostilities between India and Pakistan. I cannot believe that such a development, even if the military action remained on a limited scale, could offer any lasting solution to the grievous problems India now faces as a result of the massive influx of refugees from East Pakistan -- rather I am convinced that it would exacerbate these problems and, by affecting others outside the region, threaten the stability of all South Asia and perhaps the world.

I think you will know from my earlier letter that my colleagues and I are very conscious of the forbearance shown by India in the face of the refugee problem. We recognize that this gigantic influx has imposed serious strains not only on the Indian economy but on the whole social and political fabric of India and that ways must be found urgently for the refugees to return in safety to their homes. I am writing to the President of Pakistan urging on him the need for a realistic political solution in East Pakistan, since I share your view that the establishment of a climate of confidence in the

Mrs. Indira Gandhi,
    Prime Minister of India,
    NEW DELHI, India.

...2

Letter from Prime Minister Pierre Trudeau to Prime Minister Indira Gandhi, dated July 29, 1971.

Source: Canada. Department of External Affairs. File # 20-India-1-3-Pak.

province is a pre-requisite for the refugees' return. I am also urging him to exercise the utmost restraint in this increasingly tense situation.

I think there is general agreement that the return of the refugees is the crux of the problem as far as India is concerned and that means must somehow be found to bring this about with a minimum of delay. It is also widely understood that this will not come about -- indeed there will not be an end to the continuing influx -- without a realistic political settlement in East Pakistan sufficient to restore Bengali confidence. I recognize that the Government of India has grave reservations about the wisdom of U Thant's proposal for the positioning of representatives of the United Nations High Commissioner for Refugees, in the absence of any apparent change in the situation in East Pakistan. Nevertheless, I can see no other way of halting the present trend and making a start toward a peaceful solution. I therefore urge you to give this proposal a chance to succeed. The very presence of these representatives would increase the pressure for a political settlement in East Pakistan.

I think the Government of Pakistan is increasingly coming to recognize the need to adjust its policies but while this evolution is in progress I hope India will continue to avoid taking any positions which might serve to increase tension. I am concerned for example that any move to extend recognition to an independent government in East Pakistan could lead to overt military action which would be fraught with the gravest consequences, and could alienate the considerable

Letter from Prime Minister Pierre Trudeau to Prime Minister Indira Gandhi, dated July 29, 1971.

Source: Canada. Department of External Affairs. File # 20-India-1-3-Pak.

- 3 -

I have taken the liberty of writing to you in this very frank manner because I know how firmly dedicated you are to the economic, social and political progress of the people of India. I am convinced that this progress is dependent on peaceful solutions being found to the critical problems now facing your Government.

Yours sincerely,

AUG - 5 1971

Letter from Prime Minister Pierre Trudeau to Prime Minister Indira Gandhi, dated July 29, 1971

Source: Canada. Department of External Affairs. File # 20-India-1-3-Pak.

Directory of Bangla Desh Residents in Ottawa Region:

Members:

	Name:	Address	Telephone
President –	Ahmad, Nasiruddin (Dr. & Mrs)	280 Russel Rd.,	731-8398
	Ali, Azmat (Mr. & Mrs.)	77 Inverness, Apt 604	224-0424
Secretary –	Ahsanullah, Mohammad (Dr. & Mrs.)	1221 Meadowlands Dr. E,	224-7906
	Awal, Abdul	1805 Baseline Rd. Apt. 407	224-5124
	Dhar, Haripada	125 Osgoode St	238-1794
	Hanif, M.	1805 Baseline Rd. Apt. 407	224-5124
	Haque, Aminul	2719 Nonbery Cresc.	733-5787
	Kabir, Lutful (Dr. & Mrs.)	87 Woodmount Cr.	224-1236
	Miah, Ghani	1805 Baseline Rd. Apt. 407	224-5124
	Rahim, Abdul (Mr. & Mrs.)	398 Sunnyside, Apt. 2	233-4215
	Rahman, Mizanur (Mr. & Mrs.)	43 Woodmount Cr.	224-1709
	Saleh, Ehsanes (Dr. & Mrs.)	27 Ness	224-1557
	Sarkar, Farook (Mr. & Mrs.)	41 5th Avenue	234-0263
	Sattar, Abdus (Mr. & Mrs.)	7 Savage Drive, R.R # 2, STITTSVILLE	836-4877
	Sultan, Tipu	1325 3rd St. E., Cornwall	932-6972

Associate Members:

Jalaluddin, Muhammad (Mr. & Mrs.)	1435 Prince of Wales Drive Apt. 1815	224-2130

List of Bengali East Pakistanis living in the Ottawa area in 1971.

Source: Canada. Department of External Affairs. File # 20-1-2-Pak.

DRAFT

July 29, 1971

To: Yahya

Dear Mr. President:

I very much appreciated receiving your recent letter telling me of your concern about the threat to peace and security which appears to be developing in the sub-continent. I share your view that this situation is extremely grave: not only does it constitute a serious danger of conflict between Pakistan and India but it also can affect many other countries and so threatens both the stability of South Asia and the peace of the world. It is evident to me, as I know it is to you, that armed conflict between Pakistan and India, two countries with which we are closely associated in the Commonwealth, would do nothing to solve any of the problems with which you are faced but would have untold tragic consequences for the people of both countries.

While I was in India last January, following my visit to Pakistan, I had several long discussions with Mrs. Gandhi and have since exchanged letters with her concerning the refugee problem and other recent developments affecting relations between India and Pakistan. She is of course aware of my view, which is shared by all Canadians, that somehow this explosive situation must be kept under control and every effort made to reduce the present dangerous level of tension. Despite this, however, I am communicating with Mrs. Gandhi again to underline my concern about the present dangerous situation and to urge the Government

... 2

His Excellency
General Agha Mohammad Yahya Khan
  President of Pakistan
    Islamabad

Letter from Prime Minister Pierre Trudeau to President Yahya Khan, dated July 29, 1971

Source: Canada. Department of External Affairs. File # 20-India-1-3-Pak.

- 2 -

of India to adhere to peaceful solutions. I very much hope that the Government of Pakistan will exercise similar restraint.

From a Canadian vantage point the crucial issue in this whole situation is the future of the displaced persons from East Pakistan who are now in India. I realize of course that partition of the sub-continent at the time of independence caused the migration of many millions of people and that this placed a grievous burden on the economies of both countries. The current massive flow, however, has clearly imposed heavy new sacrifices at a time when there had seemed reason to hope that involuntary mass migration was becoming a thing of the past. My information is that the movement of refugees still continues, though at a somewhat reduced rate, despite the steps taken by your government in recent weeks. It is quite clear to me, Mr. President, that the flight of refugees from East Pakistan must be brought to an end, and indeed reversed, if the present threatening trend of events in South Asia is to be arrested. It is equally clear that further steps must be taken both internationally and within Pakistan to facilitate the return home of the millions of these displaced persons now in India.

I would not presume to offer advice to you personally or to the Government of Pakistan on the best way to create a more normal situation in the East Wing. This is a question to be decided among Pakistanis themselves. It is evident, however, that ways must be found to achieve a realistic political settlement and to establish a climate of confidence in East Pakistan

... 3

Letter from Prime Minister Pierre Trudeau to President Yahya Khan, dated July 29, 1971

Source: Canada. Department of External Affairs. File # 20-India-1-3-Pak.

if the Bengali refugees are to be persuaded to return from India. As far as international action is concerned you may be assured that we support the UN Secretary-General's proposal for the positioning of representatives of the UN High Commissioner for Refugees to supervise arrangements for return. I very much hope that the Government of India can be persuaded to accept this proposal, as you have already done, and I am urging this on Mrs. Gandhi. For such arrangements to be fully effective, however, it is in my view essential that they be accompanied by political measures on your side to restore a climate of confidence among Bengalis--Muslim and Hindu alike.

I know how distressing the tragic happenings of the past few months must have been to you, Mr. President, in view of their critical significance for Pakistan and its relations with India. I also know how you personally had striven earlier to restore civilian government in Pakistan based on the elected representatives of the people. I hope you will not take it amiss that I have used the occasion presented by this letter to offer you my thoughts on these issues which by force of circumstances have become the concern not only of Pakistanis alone but of the international community as a whole. I have done this in the hope that by talking frankly, as I am also doing in my letter to Mrs. Gandhi, I can perhaps do something to help avert any further worsening of the threat to peace in South Asia.

Yours sincerely,

P. E. Trudeau

Letter from Prime Minister Pierre Trudeau to President Yahya Khan, dated July 29, 1971

Source: Canada. Department of External Affairs. File # 20-India-1-3-Pak.

LIST OF CANADIAN HOLY CROSS BROTHERS & SISTERS IN BANGLADESH IN 1971

July 8, 1971

Barisal

CLOUTIER, Sister Marie Jeanne
   Oriental Institute
   P. O. Sagardi, Barisal

DUCHESNE, Brother Marcel
   Catholic Church
   5 Sadar Road, Barisal

LALIBERTE, Sister Francesca Henriette
   Catholic Church
   5 Sadar Road, Barisal
   (temporarily at Oriental Institute)

LEFRANCOIS, Sister Therese
   Catholic Church,
   5 Sadar Road, Barisal
   (temporarily at Oriental Institute)

NADEAU, Father Charles
   Oriental Institute
   P. O. Sagardi, Barisal.

NADEAU, Brother Donald,
   Catholic Church,
   5 Sadar Road, Barisal

ROBERT, Sister 'Stella' Huguette
   Catholic Church
   5 Sadar Road, Barisal.

ST. PIERRE, Father Martial Marie,
   Catholic Church,
   5 Sadar Road, Barisal.

TOURANGEAU, Father Guy-Marie,
   Oriental Institute,
   P. O. Sagardi, Barisal.

Padrishibpur

BROUILLARD, Brother 'Constant' R.
   Catholic Church
   P. O. Padrishibpur, Dist. Barisal.

GRANDMAISON, Father Germain,
   Catholic Church,
   P. O. Padrishibpur, Dist. Barisal.

Noakhali

BENOIT, Father Pierre,
   Catholic Church,
   P. O. Sonapur, Noakhali.

COTE, Brother Gilles,
   Catholic Church,
   P. O. Sonapur, Noakhali.

NARIKELBARI

DEMERS, Father Joseph Lucian Paulin,
   Catholic Church,
   P. O. Narikelbari, Dist. Faridpur.

GOUPIL, Brother Lucien,
   Catholic Church,
   P. O. Narikelbari, Dist. Faridpur.

LAGUE, Father Gilles,
   Catholic Church,
   P. O. Narikelbari, Dist. Faridpur.

Gournadi

PAGE, Father Michel,
   Catholic Church
   P. O. Gournade, Dist. Barisal.

This is a partial list of the members of the Canadian Holy Cross Order Living in East Pakistan in 1971

Source: Father Laurent Lecavalier provided this to the author in September 1997, when he was living in Montreal, Québec.

Dacca

BROWN, Daniel Joseph
W.P. London & Associates,
Inter-Continental Hotel,
Dacca.

BUHMAN, Rolf Hans,
Weitz, Hettelsater Engineers,
Amir Court, 3rd Floor,
62 Motijheel
Office Tel: 250720
Res: CES(A) 28 Gulshan, Dacca

CLARK, General Alan
c/o Al Hussainy,
EP WAPDA,
Dacca
(American citizen working
for Canadian company — Acres
International (Overseas) Ltd.)

DAWOOD, Mrs. Patricia L.
Road 2, House 28,
Dhanmondi, Dacca.

DESNOYERS, Sister Monique
Holy Family Hospital, Dacca
Tel: 283117

DOBRANSKI, Joseph Francis,
c/o Mr. Alex Stevenson,
House No. 3, Victoria House,
Road 104, Gulshan Dacca.

ELLIS, William Hepburn (MAY HAVE LEFT IN JUNE 1971)
Leedshill-DeLeuw,
60 Motijheel, C.A. Dacca
P. O. Box 316,
Tel: 283041
Res: Road 113, House 356, Gulshan.

DUANNE, William Dayton,
Weitz Hettelsater Engineers,
Amir Court, 3rd Floor,
62 Motijheel.

GEERAN, Miss Phyllis Edith
Road 6, House 19A,
Dhanmondi, Dacca.

LABBE, Father Benjamin,
Notre Dame College, Dacca.
Tel: 243785

MACKAY, Leslie Bartlett,
W.P. London & Associates,
Inter-Continental Hotel,
Dacca.

SMITH, Edward Allan,
W.P. London & Associates,
Inter-Continental Hotel,
Dacca.

STEVENSON, Alexander Drummond,
W.P. London & Associates,
Inter-Continental Hotel,
Dacca.
Res: House No. 3, Victoria House,
Road 104, Gulshan, Dacca.

SCHULHOF, Louis,
W.P. London & Associates,
Inter-Continental Hotel,
Dacca.

STICKLE, B. H.
Seventh Day Adventist Mission
Mirpur, Dacca.
(Plot No. 2, Road No. 9
Section 6, Block C,
Mirpur, Dacca 16)

BROUILLARD, Father Claude A.
Notre Dame College, Dacca.

This is a partial list of the members of the Canadian Holy Cross Order Living in East Pakistan in 1971

Source: Father Laurent Lecavalier provided this to the author in September 1997, when he was living in Montreal, Québec.

গণ প্রজাতন্ত্রী বাংলা দেশ
সরকার

MINISTRY OF FOREIGN AFFAIRS
GOVERNMENT OF THE PEOPLE'S
REPUBLIC OF BANGLADESH.

জয় বাংলা

20-BANGLA-14
34

MUJIBNAGAR,
AUGUST 3, 1971.

Excellency,

   I have the honour to refer to the letter of April 24, 1971 from the Acting President of the People's Republic of Bangladesh addressed to the Governor General of Canada requesting recognition of the Government of the People's Republic of Bangladesh.

   As we have received no reply so far, it is feared that the original letter may not have reached your Government. I am, therefore, enclosing a copy of the letter.

   As you are aware, the Government of the People's Republic of Bangladesh is exercising sovereign powers over the territory formerly known as East Pakistan. Our liberation forces have driven out the enemy forces from most of the areas of the country. The enemy is now holding on to small pockets in the towns and cities, where also they are facing increasingly heavy resistance from our people and forces.

   The West Pakistan military junta are taking advantage of the fact that they continue to enjoy recognition, even in the face of such brutal atrocities committed on the people of Bangladesh. It is a preposterous anomaly that their diplomatic mission in your capital pretends to represent the 75 million people of Bangladesh who have since March 26, 1971, constituted a separate fully democratic Government on the

P.T.O.

Letter from Khandaker Moshtaque Ahmed, Foreign Minister, Government of the People's Republic of Bangladesh, to Mitchell Sharp, Secretary of State for External Affairs, requesting to accord recognition to Bangladesh. The letter is dated August 3, 1971.

Source: Canada. Department of External Affairs. File # 20-Bangla-14

গণ প্রজাতন্ত্রী বাংলা দেশ
সরকার

:: 2 ::

জয় বাংলা

basis of an overwhelming mandate from the people. The Pakistan mission in your country represents only the West Pakistan military junta.

  I trust your Government would give gracious consideration to our request and, by according us recognition would enable my Government to exchange diplomatic envoys between Bangladesh and your great country to the mutual benefit of our two nations.

  Please accept, Excellency, the assurances of my highest consideration.

Yours sincerely,

(Khandaker Moshtaque Ahmed)
Foreign Minister.

His Excellency the Minister
for Foreign Affairs,
Federal Government of Canada,
OTTAWA.

Letter from Khandaker Moshtaque Ahmed, Foreign Minister, Government of the People's Republic of Bangladesh, to Mitchell Sharp, Secretary of State for External Affairs, requesting to accord recognition to Bangladesh. The letter is dated August 3, 1971.

Source: Canada. Department of External Affairs. File # 20-Bangla-14

100,000 lb. food gift sent to aid Pakistani refugees, dated September 1971.

Source: *The Star*, The McCain Group of Companies, Florenceville, New Brunswick. Canada. Library and Archives Canada. MG 28 1 270 Vol. 5. File: Pak McCain Foods.

100,000 lb. food gift sent to aid Pakistani refugees, dated September 1971.

Source: *The Star*, The McCain Group of Companies, Florenceville, New Brunswick. Canada. Library and Archives Canada. MG 28 1 270 Vol. 5. File: Pak McCain Foods.

September 15, 1971   Number 3

MCC (Canada) News Briefs
201-1483 Pembina Highway, Winnipeg 19, Manitoba

Photo by John Wieler

East Pakistani refugees the most appalling tide of human misery in modern times

Help MCC provide shelter and clothing for 10,000 families

Source: Mennonite Heritage Centre. Archives. File: Asia, Pakistan (August – December 1971). Volume 2446i 71 E0008.

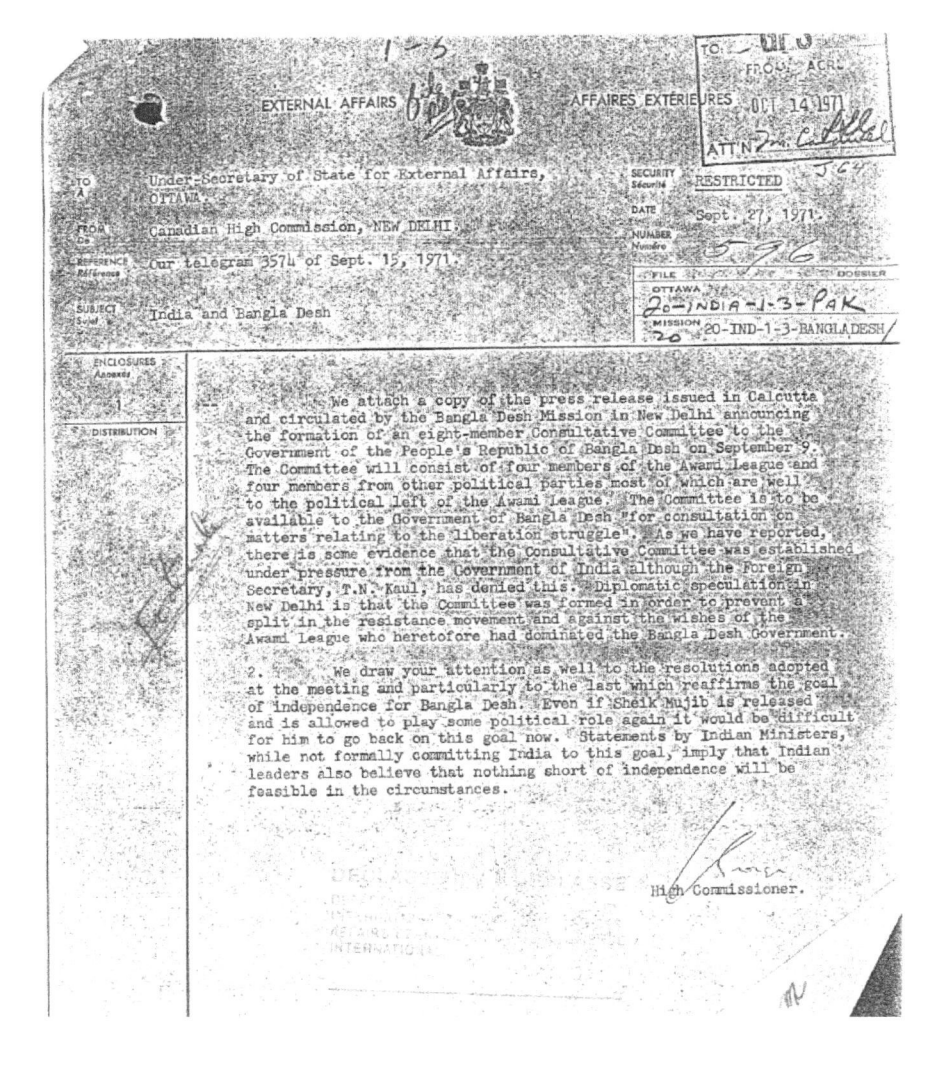

EXTERNAL AFFAIRS · AFFAIRES EXTÉRIEURES

TO: Under-Secretary of State for External Affairs, OTTAWA
FROM: Canadian High Commission, NEW DELHI
REFERENCE: Our telegram 3574 of Sept. 15, 1971
SUBJECT: India and Bangla Desh

SECURITY: RESTRICTED
DATE: Sept. 27, 1971
NUMBER: 596
FILE: 20-INDIA-1-3-PAK
MISSION: 20-IND-1-3-BANGLADESH

1. We attach a copy of the press release issued in Calcutta and circulated by the Bangla Desh Mission in New Delhi announcing the formation of an eight-member Consultative Committee to the Government of the People's Republic of Bangla Desh on September 9. The Committee will consist of four members of the Awami League and four members from other political parties most of which are well to the political left of the Awami League. The Committee is to be available to the Government of Bangla Desh "for consultation on matters relating to the liberation struggle". As we have reported, there is some evidence that the Consultative Committee was established under pressure from the Government of India although the Foreign Secretary, T.N. Kaul, has denied this. Diplomatic speculation in New Delhi is that the Committee was formed in order to prevent a split in the resistance movement and against the wishes of the Awami League who heretofore had dominated the Bangla Desh Government.

2. We draw your attention as well to the resolutions adopted at the meeting and particularly to the last which reaffirms the goal of independence for Bangla Desh. Even if Sheik Mujib is released and is allowed to play some political role again it would be difficult for him to go back on this goal now. Statements by Indian Ministers, while not formally committing India to this goal, imply that Indian leaders also believe that nothing short of independence will be feasible in the circumstances.

High Commissioner.

James George, High Commissioner to India, sent information regarding the formation of an eight-member consultation committee for the Government of the People's Republic of Bangladesh on September 27, 1971, to the Undersecretary of State for External Affairs.

Source: Canada Department of External Affairs. File # 20-India-1-3-Pak (page 1/5)

> BANGLADESH PRESS RELEASE
>
> Mujibnagar
> September 9, 1971.
>
> AN EIGHT-MEMBER CONSULTATIVE COMMITTEE FORMED
>
> An eight-member Consultative Committee to the Government of the People's Republic of Bangladesh has been constituted with the following political parties of Bangladesh: the Awami League, NAP (Bhasani), NAP (Muzaffar), the Communist Party of Bangladesh and Bangladesh National Congress.
>
> The leaders of these parties met for two days in Mujibnagar and unanimously decided to from the Committee. The meeting was inaugurated and conducted by the Prime Minister of Bangladesh.
>
> The newly constituted committee will be available to the Government of Bangladesh for consultation on matters relating to the liberation struggle. The members of the Committee are as follows:-
>
> 1. Maulana Abdul Hamid Khan Bhasani (Bhasani NAP)
> 2. Mr. Moni Singh (Communist Party of Bangladesh)
> 3. Mr. Monoranjan Dhar (Bangladesh National Congress)
> 4. Professor Muzaffar Ahmed (NAP-Muzaffar)
> 5. Mr. Tajuddin Ahmed, Prime Minister of Bangladesh
> 6. Mr. Khandaker Moshtaque Ahmed, Foreign Minister of Bangladesh
> 7. Two other Members From Awami League
>
> Mr. Tajuddin Ahmed will convene and conduct meetings of the Consultative Committee.
>
> Those who attended the Mujibnagar meeting are:-
> 1. Maulana Abdul Hamid Khan Bhasani, NAP (Bhasani)
> 2. Mr. Moni Singh - Communist Party of Bangladesh
>
> Cont'd...P.2.

James George, High Commissioner to India, sent information regarding the formation of an eight-member consultation committee for the Government of the People's Republic of Bangladesh on September 27, 1971, to the Undersecretary of State for External Affairs.

Source: Canada Department of External Affairs. File # 20-India-1-3-Pak (page 2/5)

James George, High Commissioner to India, sent information regarding the formation of an eight-member consultation committee for the Government of the People's Republic of Bangladesh on September 27, 1971, to the Undersecretary of State for External Affairs.

Source: Canada Department of External Affairs. File # 20-India-1-3-Pak (page 3/5)

1. The meeting expressed its indignation and anguish at the illegal detention of Sheikh Mujibur Rahman, the acclaimed national leader of Bangladesh by the West Pakistani Army Junta. The meeting strongly condemned the shameful attempt to stage a farcical and outrageous trial of Sheikh Mujibur Rahman by the Army rulers of West Pakistan. The meeting called upon all the powers and the U.N. to take immediate steps to halt this atrocious trial and secure the Sheikh's release who is the Head of the independent and sovereign State of Bangladesh.

2. The meeting affirmed its whole-hearted confidence and faith in the Government of Bangladesh and recorded its complete support for it.

3. The meeting called upon India and countries of the world to accord immediate recognition to the Government of Bangladesh and thereby accept the reality of a liberation struggle involving 75 million peace-loving democratic people of Bangladesh. The meeting further called upon the countries of the world to render active assistance including arms and ammunitions to the Government of Bangladesh.

4. The meeting gratefully acknowledged the deeds of heroism of the freedom fighters of Bangladesh who are struggling against overwhelming odds to liberate the country from the clutches of the occupation Army of West Pakistani vested interests. The meeting paid glowing tributes to the brave sons of the soil who courted martyrdom in the act of freeing their country.

5. The meeting expressed its profound gratitude to the people and Government of India for the generous help they have extended to the evacuees of Bangladesh. The meeting further expressed appreciation for the support the Government of India has extended to the struggling people of Bangladesh.

Cont'd...P.4.

James George, High Commissioner to India, sent information to the Undersecretary of State for External Affairs on September 27, 1971, regarding forming an eight-member consultation committee for the Government of the People's Republic of Bangladesh.

Source: Canada Department of External Affairs. File # 20-India-1-3-Pak (page 4/5)

> 6. The meeting expressed solidarity with the people of West Pakistan who are struggling to free themselves from the shackles of exploitation. The meeting made a fervent appeal to the people of West Pakistan to extend full support to the liberation struggle of their brethren in Bangladesh.
>
> 7. The meeting resolved that short of full independence no other political proposition in respect of Bangladesh will be ever acceptable to the people of Bangladesh. The people of Bangladesh have made supreme sacrifices to achieve freedom and if blood is price of freedom the unarmed people of Bangladesh are paying it every hour.

James George, High Commissioner to India, sent information to the Undersecretary of State for External Affairs on September 27, 1971, regarding forming an eight-member consultation committee for the Government of the People's Republic of Bangladesh.

Source: Canada Department of External Affairs. File # 20-India-1-3-Pak (page 5/5)

International politics in Bangla Desh

by mark abley

The magnitude of the disaster in Bangla Desh is enough to transform the situation from a purely internal matter into a world problem. Yet there is another factor that enters the situation: the attitude of the world's major powers. This aspect of the Bangla Desh question was discussed Thursday by S. Sharma, Professor of the Anthropology Dept., and by Prof. Colwyn Williams of the College of Law and the Canadian United Nations Association.

The United States has been placed in an awkward position by the upheavals in Bangla Desh. On the one hand, America wishes to remain friendly with the Pakistan government of Yahya Khan, but also she does not want to alienate India. The situation is further complicated by the fact that the Awami League of Sheikh Mujib is not anti-American. America, thus, has reason to be friends of India, and Pakistan, and the Awami League. The U. S. has so far remained reasonably aloof from the political situation (but has given generously to relief operations).

Russia is not well-regarded by Yahya Khan. The Soviets, seeing Pakistan coming more and more under the influence of China, have turned to India. Andrei Gromyko, Soviet Foreign Minister, recently flew to New Delhi to sign a friendship pact with India. It should be emphasized that this in no way means that India has become mean, however, that the Indians (fearing the alliance of China and Pakistan) are now closely tied to the Russians.

And what of China? Why should the world's most revolutionary government wish to ally itself with the repressive regime of Yahya Khan? The China position can only be understood if one realizes that Peking's actions are not taken for the cause of Bangla Desh, or the people of the region, or to prevent war, but primarily for her own self-interest. So China has sided with Pakistan, and (since few, if any, other countries are willing to support Yahya so strongly) the Pakistanis have become very dependent on China.

This, then, is the situation. Pakistan and China are allied against India, Bangla Desh, and (in case of war) Russia. The Western nations have not taken sides. There are some parallels to the situation immediately before World War I. A skirmish in Bangla Desh might provoke an Indian-Pakistani war; since India is unquestionably the stronger of the two, China (not wishing to see Yahya's government toppled) would enter the war; this would surely bring in the Soviet Union; and this would surely be World War III.

Unless we want World War III, we must do everything we can to defuse the situatuion and avert an Indo-Pakistani conflict. The obvious medium by which this might be accomplished is the United Nations. However, an obstacle arises here: the U. N. interference in the internal affairs of any member nation (unless that nation requests U. N. intervention) is prohibited. And, in the view of Pakistan, the Bangla Desh uprisings are solely an internal matter. Most concerned people think otherwise, but the fact remains that only if Pakistan assents to or asks for United Nations intervention, can the U. N.

There are some historical precedents for U. N. intervention: in both Cyprus and the Congo, United Nations forces maintained peace and created order. Were Pakistan to agree to U. N. intervention, a peacekeeping force could be sent in, orderly return of refugees could be facilitated, and the explosive situation that exists today could be

I am not predicting a global holocaust unless the U. N. becomes involved in Bangla Desh. But I am saying that the chances of such a catastrophe are at present terribly high. We can do little in Canada except give aid to the Pakistani refugees and put pressure on Pakistan to agree to a U. N. force. Let us all hope that nations keep cool heads and avoid World War

These were the panelists who addressed a sparse crowd in the MUB on Thursday.

The seminar on Bangladesh was held under Dr. Asit Sarkar's chairmanship in solidarity with the University of Saskatchewan's observance of Bangladesh Day on September 30, 1971.

Source: *The Sheaf*, University of Saskatchewan, Saskatoon, Vol 61, No. 7, dated October 5, 1971.

Suman Kalyanpur Soiree & Party for raising funds. **Source:** *The Canadian India Times*, September 28, 1971.

In the wake of any war follows squalor and disease, the tragedy of Bangla-Desh is that they only want what we consider a right, national independence.

postponed the National Assembly.

Mujib did not agree to this back door West Pakistani dictatorship and he proclaimed a Civil Disobedience movement in East Bengal. Yahya's regime brought in the Military on the streets of Dacca and other major cities and towns. Students, professors, all types of intellectuals, young enthusiasts were killed. Children and women were molested by the Pakistani army. The people of East Bengal became furious and fully backed Mujibur Rahman and the demand of autonomy was turned into the demand for complete independence of 'Bangla Desh'.

The struggle for independence is on. Reports from the foreign correspondents suggest that the struggle will continue with the help of the guerrila war fare, initiated by the young school and college students, who have formed the militia. The militia is supported by those who support the cause of the freedom movement for Bengal.

The freedom movement created a large number of refugees from East Pakistan, mostly Hindus (the minority community). There are a large number of young students, and university professors, scattered in refugee camps in West Bengal. The rain, epidemics of Cholera, and other diseases have created hell for the Indian Government, who have done their best to welcome the refugees in the schools, college buildings and other refugee camps. These refugees are the "guests" of the Indian government; very soon they have to go back to their own homes in East Pakistan, or the new independent country BANGLA DESH. There are all types of speculations regarding the fate of the Bangla Desh movement and the future of these educated refugees. Any contribution from the young people of Canada, both students and teachers, will be welcomed by those, who are working to achieve the goal independent BANGLA DESH.

So far it is the largest flood of refugees yet in this century noted for tragedies. The number of refugees might reach ten million; most of them are in the camps. The Indian Government has done a magnificent job of coping with an insolvable problem. The Indians are not responsible for the situation and should not have to pay for it. Canada along with other nations should join hands. "The Canadians are giving, but so far about 2 cents each" remarked one of the church officials. There are hundred and thousands of Indian volunteers, medical doctors, nurses working day and night to combat with the huge problem. But they need MONEY. Clothes, food and staff are available but MONEY is needed to pay the bills.

TEACH IN ON BANGLA DESH

A Teach-in on Bangla Desh sponsored by Bangla Desh Association of Saskatchewan and the Students Union of the University of Saskatchewan, Saskatoon Campus will be held on: Thursday, September 30   At Upper MUB At 7:30 P.M.

Speakers:

Prof. S. Sharma (Anthropology Dept.):
"Role of the International Political Opinion in solving the Bangla Desh crisis."

Prof. Bernard Lall (Education Faculty - Regina Campus) - Secretary, Bangla Desh Association of Saskatchewan:
"Bangla Desh liberation - pros and cons."

Prof. Colwyn Williams (College of Law) - President, United Nations Association of Canada:
"Role of U.N. in the Bangla Desh freedom struggle."

Mr. Donald Sheridon - Local Director, OXFAM Canada:
"Bangla Desh refugees and the efforts of the International Relief Organisations."

Moderator:
Dr. Asit Sarkar (Department of Commerce) - President, Bangla Desh Association of Saskatchewan, Saskatoon Chapter.

AN EXHIBIT ON "BANGLA DESH — WHAT — WHY and HOW"
will be opened at the lobby of the Marquis Hall at 10 A.M.

EVERYBODY IS WELCOME TO PARTICIPATE ACTIVELY IN THE DISCUSSION TO BE FOLLOWED AFTER THE PANEL PRESENTATION

Source: *The Sheaf*, University of Saskatchewan, Saskatoon, Vol 61, No. 7, dated October 5, 1971.

The Secretary of State for External Affairs / Secrétaire d'État aux Affaires extérieures
Canada

Ottawa, K1A 0G2,
November 16, 1971

Mr. Andrew Brewin, M.P.
Member for Greenwood
House of Commons
Ottawa, Ontario
K1A 0A6

Dear Mr. Brewin:

Thank you for your letter of October 20 in which you raised the question of the arrangements for students from East Pakistan who came to Canada under CIDA auspices, and have now completed their training.

As you know, all students from Pakistan receiving CIDA awards enter into a mutual undertaking with Pakistan and Canada to return home on completion of their study programmes. Because of special conditions prevailing in East Pakistan, a few students who had completed their studies and were unwilling to return, were allowed to remain in Canada and at the same time received some financial assistance until the situation became a little clearer. The special financial arrangement was discontinued in September; with its discontinuance, based on the latest and most reliable information then available to CIDA, the information indicated that civil servants were returning to duty and making outstanding efforts to keep government services operating. More than ever, there was a desperate need for trained and skilled people to return and to assist in bringing essential services back to normal.

For these reasons, the East Pakistani students, who had completed training, were asked to prepare for their return; those who were, or are unwilling to do so -- and, as you know, there are special cases in which the students felt it to be unwise to do so -- are being referred to the Department of Manpower and Immigration to obtain the necessary permission to remain and to seek work here. It would be inappropriate not to make a distinction between aid financed assistance and the normal arrangements for people seeking to stay in this country for other reasons; the approach has been that former East Pakistani trainees fall into the latter category.

I can assure you that officers of CIDA responsible for the Pakistan training programme are endeavouring to keep in touch with these former students and to bear the special circumstances of each in mind. Professor Khan,

.../2

- 2 -

whom you specifically mention is one of these; I understand that Mr. Forbes has already been in correspondence with you about him and that this former CIDA trainee appears to have made satisfactory arrangements for a temporary stay in Canada.

I am grateful for your interest in this matter and appreciate the opportunity to comment on it and in particular to underline the distinction between the aid financed possibilities open to us and the other arrangements that can and are being made for these former students.

Yours sincerely,

Mitchell Sharp

Letter from Mitchell Sharp, Secretary of State of External Affairs, to Andrew Brewin, Member of Parliament for Greenwood, regarding arrangements for students from East Pakistan.

Source: Canada. Library and Archives Canada. Andrew Brewins Papers. MG 32 C26 Vol.87, File 87-15.

CONFIDENTIAL
November 15, 1971.

Visit of Pakistan Foreign Secretary
November 16 and 17, 1971

Current Situation

Tension is high between India and Pakistan, the security situation in East Pakistan has deteriorated somewhat with the resurgence of Mukti Bahini guerilla activity, and the Indo-East Pakistan border has been the scene of continuing fire-fights and incursions, some now involving direct participation by the regular forces of both sides. Quite apart from the danger of war by accident which the close confrontation of the two armies involves, a new danger period is about to commence with the return of Mrs. Gandhi from her tour of certain Western capitals and her appearance before Parliament which meets this week. There are persistent rumours that she will declare a state of emergency. This would constitute a further psychological escalation of the tension on the sub-continent.

The purpose of Mrs. Gandhi's tour has been to emphasize that the threat to the stability and security of India is also directed against the peace of the whole of South-East Asia. Increased international pressure on Pakistan was necessary in her view to settle the East Bengal political problem and thus to solve the refugee one which imposed such an intolerable burden on the economic, communal and political fabric of India. She maintained a political – not a military – solution had to be found to the crisis in East Bengal and in order to be applicable it had to be acceptable to the elected representatives of the people of East Bengal. She asserted that what is going on in East Bengal is not a civil war in the usual sense of the word but a genocide inflicted as a punishment on millions of people for the crime of having voted democratically. All along the way she has been careful, however, to make the point that in spite of provocation from Pakistan she would do everything to avoid war. She has said that she would be prepared to meet President Yahya Khan to discuss problems between their two countries but not those relating to East Pakistan. Problems of East Bengal, she asserted, have to be settled between the people of East Bengal and the West Pakistan Army: "it does not concern us."

The danger referred to above will rise in an acute fashion if Prime Minister Gandhi is not satisfied with the result of her tour. The impression derived from reports received so far is that she was given the most understanding reception in Paris but that her visit to

...2

CONFIDENTIAL

- 2 -

Washington should not be discounted as it may have opened her eyes to the active efforts of the United States to influence Yahya Khan in the direction of an early political solution in East Pakistan. The British found her fraught with an air of fatalism and gloom.

President Yahya is seeking to return all of Pakistan to a democratic form of government. He is doing this in not too imaginative a manner, but we believe he is nonetheless sincere: he is certainly determined. You will recall that he announced that by-elections would be held in early December, that the draft constitution would be published December 20, and that the National Assembly would meet December 27. Shortly after the Assembly meets a government will be formed (appointed) and there will be a period of ninety days in which amendments to the draft constitution, recommended by a majority of the House including 25 per cent of the members from each province, may be presented to the President for approval. In point of fact, a poll will be held only for 25 out of the 78 ex-Awami League seats to be filled in East Pakistan. What has occurred is that the various political parties (most of them of the right) which have been allowed to function agreed upon a single slate for 53 constituencies: there being no opposition, those nominated were declared elected by acclamation. This certainly makes the Army's problem of maintaining law and order on election day - which the Mukti Bahini have sworn to prevent - that much easier. But it does tarnish for some the image of a democratic selection procedure: nevertheless it is better than nothing.

There have been a number of developments with respect to Sheikh Mujibur Rahman. We understand that his trial is over and that he was condemned to death by hanging (CEO). His sentence is currently before the President for confirmation or commutation. In an interview with the correspondent of Newsweek (published November 8), Yahya Khan is reported to have said that although many people might not believe him, he thought that if Mujib went back to East Pakistan he would be killed by his own people who hold him responsible for their suffering. He added that in any case it was an academic question. Mujib had discussed internal autonomy with Yahya for two years and, according to the latter, had gone back on his word. He had organized and led an armed rebellion against the State and there was no alternative but to suppress the rebellion. Any other government would have done the same thing. How, the President asked, could he now call that man back and negotiate with him? He was charged with waging war against the State and subverting the loyalty of the Army. He was defended by A.K. Brohi, the best

... 3

CONFIDENTIAL

- 3 -

and most respected lawyer in the country, "who would not have taken the case if he thought there was going to be any hanky-panky in the military court". Yahya pointed out that he had not shot Mujib first and tried him later as some governments were prone to do. What was done after sentence is passed was the prerogative of the Head of State. He observed that he could not release him on a whim, that it was one hell of a responsibility. "But if the nation demands his release, I will do it." About the same time a petition was forwarded to President Yahya on behalf of some fifty politicians, trade unionists and personalities of the city of Lahore calling upon him to pardon Mujib. There have been reports that some contact was made between Yahya and Mujib on the occasion of the President's recent visit to that city (CEO). We understand that the Americans have for some time had Yahya's assurance that whatever the outcome of the trial and whatever the sentence he was open to a plea for mercy. Additionally, he had given them the categorical assurance that Mujib would not be executed. According to another report we have received, President Yahya said he had given much thought to using Mujib to assist in the restoration of normal conditions in East Pakistan but that he could not see what could be done; he was, however, open to suggestions.

Sultan Khan will no doubt be prepared to talk about the development of internal political affairs of Pakistan. However, we anticipate that his presentation will primarily concern the dangerous international tension caused by the close confrontation of the Indian and Pakistani forces. In this respect, it is very difficult and largely inconsequential to try to assess blame to one side or the other for each step in the escalation. It is true that Pakistan advanced their forces to the Indian border on the West some ten days before the Indians in turn took up their positions on that border. Nevertheless it is undeniable that increased Indian assistance had before that time been given to the Mukti Bahini along the borders of East Pakistan and within that province. In any event, the result is the most dangerous confrontation since the war of 1965.

Secretary-General U Thant was sufficiently concerned by October 20 to have addressed a letter to President Yahya and Prime Minister Gandhi in which he observed that the situation could all too easily give rise to open hostilities which would not only be dangerous to the two countries principally concerned but might also constitute a major threat to the wider peace. Where feelings run high and where both governments are under exceptional stress and strain, a small and unintentional incident could all too easily lead to more widespread conflict. After referring to the activities of

...

CONFIDENTIAL Internal Memo regarding the visit of Pakistan's Foreign Secretary to discuss the fate of Sheikh Mujibur Rahman.

Source: Canada. Department of External Affairs. File # 20-Pak-E-1-4. (Page 3/7)

CONFIDENTIAL

UNMOGIP in easing tensions on the cease-fire line in Jammu and Kashmir and observing that on the borders of East Pakistan and on the international frontier between India and West Pakistan there is no comparable United Nations mechanism, he went on to state that his good offices were entirely at the disposal of the addressees if they believed they could be helpful at any time. President Yahya replied immediately, but Mrs. Gandhi has yet to give a formal answer. It might be noted at this point that according to press reports she is said to have remarked initially that it was not "sensible" for the Secretary-General to come to India for on-the-spot study of the situation arising out of the refugee influx into India and that of the Pakistani military build-up on the Indo-Pakistan border. Subsequently in an interview in Vienna on October 27, she said she would not object to such a trip by U Thant if the Secretary-General chose to accept President Yahya's invitation. But she stressed that the key to the solution of the present situation was in the hands of Pakistan itself: it was not to be found in India.

In his reply to the Secretary-General, Yahya Khan repeated his earlier proposal for a withdrawal of forces of both countries from the borders. He did however modify it for the purpose of meeting Indian objections to one involving "withdrawal, if not to peacetime stations, then at least to a mutually agreed safe distance on either side of the Indo-Pakistan international frontiers both in the East and West in order to provide a sense of security on both sides." He added that there should at the same time be a cessation of armed infiltration and shelling into East Pakistan. He recommended that United Nations observers should be stationed on both sides of the border to oversee "withdrawals and maintenance of peace". Only recognized border security and police forces should then remain at border posts which they have traditionally occupied. Welcoming U Thant's offer of good offices, he very much hoped that the Secretary-General would pay an immediate visit to India and Pakistan to discuss ways and means of withdrawal of forces and sought from U Thant a public declaration of his intentions to visit both countries to seek a settlement of difficulties.

President Yahya has also advanced or supported other proposals aimed at engaging India in negotiations to reduce tension and defuse the critical situation. He has accepted U Thant's proposal that United Nations (civilian) observers be posted on both sides of the border of East Pakistan to assist in the voluntary repatriation of the refugees. President Yahya also earlier sought the agreement

... 5

CONFIDENTIAL Internal Memo regarding the visit of Pakistan's Foreign Secretary to discuss the fate of Sheikh Mujibur Rahman.

Source: Canada. Department of External Affairs. File # 20-Pak-E-1-4. (Page 4/7)

CONFIDENTIAL

— 5 —

of the Security Council to send a good offices mission to visit the areas of tension. The latter idea came to nought as the members of the Council were not prepared to meet to discuss the situation on the sub-continent.

Accordingly, we may expect Sultan Khan to make it clear to us that the Pakistan Government looks to Canada and to their other friends to urge upon the Government of India the pressing need to take some step or agree to some procedure of the above nature as soon as possible. As recently as November 13 the Pakistan High Commission in a note to the Department stated that "countries friendly to India and Pakistan by remaining silent can only encourage India in her warlike course. Unless India is urged by those countries to refrain from her provocative activities directed against Pakistan's territorial integrity and to stop supporting the Mukti Bahini the situation may flare up at any moment into large scale warfare." The Indians of course expect us to use what influence we may have in Islamabad to bring about a political settlement in East Pakistan acceptable to the "elected representatives" of East Bengal viz. the Awami League. They have not told us they would welcome anything we could do to reduce the tension on their borders.

Canadian Position

We have been careful to observe up to now the maxim of a "domestic solution to a domestic problem". This has included presentation of our view that a realistic political settlement and a climate of confidence should be achieved in East Pakistan as quickly as possible so that the Bengali refugees – the fundamental casus belli in the India-Pakistan confrontation – may be persuaded to return to their own country. It has not included advice on mechanics of restoration of civilian and democratic rule nor how elected representatives should be given the responsibility of governing Pakistan and we have never specified any particular leaders. Essentially what we have advocated trying to do is to keep the ring while Islamabad and the Bengalis work out a political solution for East Pakistan. It will be a matter of months at best before it can be determined whether the Yahya Khan plan to return East Pakistan (and the West) to civilian rule and eventually to democratically elected civil government can be achieved. Meanwhile the leaders of the Awami League are in exile and the Mukti Bahini are endeavouring by destructive guerilla warfare to prevent those plans being brought to fruition. In Canadian terms we cannot condone external support for the guerillas. On the other hand, neither we

... 6

nor the United Nations are in a position to pass judgement on the merits of the internal political struggle. Until there is some flagrant evidence to the contrary we are obliged to consider Yahya Khan sincere in his efforts to return the country to a form of democracy in place of military rule. And in this regard there is no reason to anticipate that a Bangla Desh in the hands of Awami League militants would be any more democratic any faster (we could expect another blood bath before things calm down). We use what little direct influence we have to prevent the outbreak of war between two sovereign states and at the same time provide an increasing volume of funds to relieve the economic and social pressures of the refugee influx on the Indian economy. We also encourage Yahya Khan to proceed with his democratization process, recognising nonetheless that it may not be one of which the Awami League can take immediate advantage.

We try in particular to exercise restraint on India by being seen to be doing something to reduce the burden on India of the refugee problem. This week in the House in Ottawa and in New York in the Third Committee we shall be announcing an additional $18 million of assistance to India under various forms to help take care of the immediate problem. At the same time we are trying to ensure that both sides have their eyes fully open to the calamity which would befall them should war come and to the fact that it cannot be taken for granted that the developed nations, which have committed more than $23.5 billion in developmental assistance to them, would be prepared in the event that they were seriously damaged by war to come once again to their aid in rebuilding.

The eyeball-to-eyeball confrontation which has been built up between the military forces of both sides is the sort of situation which perhaps at other times might have resulted in serious initiatives supported by a number of countries for some sort of United Nations peacekeeping operation. The Pakistan President has called for pull-back of troops and the interposition of United Nations observers. The Secretary-General has seemed to make a point that in the absence of a United Nations mechanism of that sort along the international boundaries of the two countries the danger of conflict is heightened. India has not responded favourably and it seems unlikely that the Soviet Union would agree to Security Council action to that end. Our position is dictated by the policy set out in the White Paper on Defence in the 1970's wherein it is stated "the Government will consider constructively any request for Canadian peacekeeping ventures when in its opinion, based on lessons of the past and circumstances of the present, an operation holds the promise of success and Canada

...7

CONFIDENTIAL

— 7 —

can play a useful role in it." Obviously therefore we cannot take the initiative in proposing a peacekeeping operation on the sub-continent or trying to secure India's acquiescence in one, although it would be consonant with the policy we have followed since 1947 of seeking to maintain an impartial position between India and Pakistan. In any event, the Pakistan proposal raises a number of considerations which militate against an effective operation. We do participate in UNMOGIP and have participated in UNIPOM along the common frontier between West Pakistan and India. To do so again would be feasible; but when one projects this type of operation to the borders of East Pakistan the problem becomes one of another magnitude. That frontier would require UN troops to be scattered over a distance of 1,500 miles, comprised mostly of swamp, jungle and water. The presence of a third factor, namely the Mukti Bahini forces, would put the UN contingent in a very difficult position as neither the Indians nor the Pakistanis could guarantee their safety. Accordingly, the resources which would have to be allotted to make the force a viable one would be very large indeed and the cost of the total operation would be enormous. In view of our existing commitments and priorities, consideration of Canadian military involvement in this area would require significant additions to DND budget in funding, manpower and equipment or, alternatively, governmental realignment of the existing priorities covering the roles and missions for the forces. There is an additional important political consideration that we should not wish, and in this we probably would not be alone, to envisage a UN force being employed to suppress an internal political upheaval.

CONFIDENTIAL Internal Memo regarding the visit of Pakistan's Foreign Secretary to discuss the fate of Sheikh Mujibur Rahman.

Source: Canada. Department of External Affairs. File # 20-Pak-E-1-4. (Page 7/7)

December 4, 1971.

Excellency,

I have been desired by the President of Pakistan to convey the following message:

BEGINS: "Your Excellency,

You are already aware of the continuing attacks that Indian Armed Forces have been making across our borders in East Pakistan for the last two weeks and the restraint exercised by us and the numerous steps taken by Pakistan to defuse the situation with the help of U.N. and throughout bilateral measures. During the last few days Indian aircraft carried out aggressive reconnaissance over West Pakistan territory. Today between 3.30 and 4 p.m. Indian Armed Forces launched massive attacks at Sialkot, Chamb, areas between Jassar bridge and Lahore and our border opposite Rahimyarkhan in West Pakistan. The attacks were supported by the Indian Air Force and armour. Intense military activity is also taking place in the Poonch and Uri sector in Indian occupied Kashmir.

Pakistan has been obliged to take some counter measures late this evening. The Pakistan Air Force took defensive action against India's forward air-fields close to our borders at Srinagar, Avantipur, Pathankot and Amritsar.

A letter from President Yahya Khan to Prime Minister Pierre Trudeau seeking his support and understanding was dated December 4, 1971.

Source: Canada. Department of External Affairs. File # 20-1-2-Pak.

- 2 -

India's naked aggression against Pakistan has created a situation of utmost gravity fraught with the danger of a war of incalculable dimensions.

As victims of aggression we hope for your Government's support and understanding in accordance with the established principles of respect for territorial integrity of states and avoidance of threat or use of force in relations between states. We request your urgent action aimed at making India see reason to bring about cessation of hostilities launched by her and to resort to resolution of all disputes by peaceful means.

General Agha Muhammad Yahya Khan

- ENDS."

Please accept, Excellency, the assurances of my highest consideration.

His Excellency
Mr. Pierre Elliott Trudeau
Prime Minister of Canada
OTTAWA

(M.S.Shaikh)
High Commissioner

Letter from President Yahya Khan to Prime Minister Pierre Trudeau seeking his support and understanding, dated December 4, 1971.

Source: Canada. Department of External Affairs. File # 20-1-2-Pak.

Mr. Andrew Brewin

BANGLA DESH ASSOCIATION OF CANADA
ASSOCIATION DU BANGLA DESH DU CANADA
(Ottawa Chapter)

December 17, 1971.

Dear Sir:

The birth of the new nation of Bangla Desh has now become a reality. The Pakistani Army in Bangla Desh has unconditionally surrendered.

We thank you for your understanding of our aspirations and our will to be a free nation. We are grateful to you and to the people of Canada for the moral, political and material support given to the people of Bangla Desh.

The Government of Bangla Desh is in effective control of the entire territory of East Bengal and enjoys the full support of its people. WE THEREFORE URGE YOU TO RECOGNIZE THE GOVERNMENT OF BANGLA DESH AND THEREBY ESTABLISH A LASTING FRIENDSHIP BETWEEN THE PEOPLES OF CANADA AND BANGLA DESH.

A. B. Sattar,
Executive Secretary,
Bangla Desh Association of Canada, Ottawa.

P.O. BOX 3599, STATION C, OTTAWA, ONTARIO, CANADA

Letter from A.B. Sattar, Executive Secretary, Bangladesh Association of Canada, to all Members of Parliament, dated December 17, 1971.

Source: Canada. Library and Archives Canada. Andrew Brewins Papers. M. G. 32 C26 Vol. 87, File # 87-15.

In recent months, the Government of Canada has been most generous in its aid to those Bengalis displaced from their homes by the tragic sequence of events that overtook East Bengal. The Bengalis now living in Canada are particularly gratified that this assistance was given to their relatives and compatriots.

The objective for which all this suffering was endured has now been realised. The people of East Bengal are now citizens of an independent nation - free to govern themselves; free from exploitation and oppression. Bangla Desh is now a reality, and 75 million Bengalis will ensure its permanence.

There is, of course, a long and difficult road ahead for Bangla Desh. It will be many months before the ravages of war can be effaced, and even longer before the agonies suffered over the years of repression and the recent slaughter can be forgotten. One way that Canada can help Bengalis strengthen their new nation is to recognize its de facto presence in the world community. We urge the Government of Canada to demonstrate once again this country's farsightedness and pragmatism by recognizing the national status of Bangla Desh.

Bangla Desh Association of Canada
Ottawa December 21, 1971

Letter from A.B. Sattar, Executive Secretary, Bangladesh Association of Canada, to all Members of Parliament, dated December 17, 1971.

Source: Canada. Library and Archives Canada. Andrew Brewins Papers. M. G. 32 C26 Vol. 87, File # 87-15.

AIDE MEMOIRE

RECOGNITION OF BANGLADESH

1. The British Government's discussions with European and other Governments have shown a general agreement to recognise Bangladesh in the very near future. Mr Bhutto has urged us not to recognise until he returns from Peking. As far as we know this will be on 3 February. We therefore propose that we should warn Mr Bhutto on 29 or 30 January in Islamabad between his return from the Middle East and his departure for Peking, of our intention to recognise Bangladesh. We understand that other Governments are already considering the same action.

2. We would then propose to tell Mr Bhutto that we consider that the announcement of our recognition of Bangladesh cannot be further postponed. It is only in response to Mr Bhutto's request to be allowed further time that the announcement has been deferred so long. In particular we have noted his oral request to our High Commissioner at Larkana on 22 January that recognition be postponed until after his return from Peking. We would go on to inform Mr Bhutto of the date on which we have decided, with other Governments, to recognise.

3. As regards the date for a concerted public announcement, we very much hope that this can be made on 4 February. This would meet Mr Bhutto's time-

/table and

Aide Mémoire from Prime Minister Edward Heath to Prime Minister Pierre Trudeau, dated January 27, 1972, regarding recognition of Bangladesh.

Source: Canada. Department of External Affairs. File # 20-Bangla-1-4

table and it would appear to fit in with Canadian thinking.

4. We hope that the Canadian Government will be prepared to act together with us on this, and would be grateful to learn whether this is acceptable to them.

5. We are making similar representations in Bonn, Luxembourg, Paris, Rome, The Hague, Brussels, Copenhagen, Oslo, Helsinki, Dublin, Vienna, Berne, Reykjavik, Canberra, Wellington, Colombo, Tonga, Kuala Lumpur, Singapore, Washington, Stockholm and Suva, and probably some other capitals.

BRITISH HIGH COMMISSION
OTTAWA
27 January 1972

Aide Mémoire from Prime Minister Edward Heath to Prime Minister Pierre Trudeau, dated January 27, 1972, regarding recognition of Bangladesh.

Source: Canada. Department of External Affairs. File # 20-Bangla-1-4

```
File    GPP    Div.Diary
ACTC    Diary           MESSAGE
```

PLACE / LIEU	DEPARTMENT / MINISTÈRE	ORIG. NO. / N° D'ORIG.	DATE	FILE/DOSSIER	SECURITY / SÉCURITÉ
OTT	EXT.	GPS-70	JAN 28/72	20-BANGLA-14 / 12 / 20-USA-1-3	CONF

TO/A: WASHDC

INFO: ISBAD DELHI MOSCO LDN

DISTR: GPP PDM PDH

REF: YOURTEL 259 JAN 20

SUB/SUJ: RECOGNITION OF BANGLADESH - USA POSITION

WE HAVE NEVER BEEN ON HUSTINGS FOR EARLY RECOGNITION OF BANGLADESH BUT ON CONTRARY HAVE BEEN SUBJECT TO PERSISTENT CAMPAIGN BY BRITS AUSTRALIANS ET AL. FROM BEGINNING WE HAVE RECOGNIZED WISDOM OF MOVING IN GOOD COMPANY ON TIMING EVEN THOUGH CDN INTERESTS IN AREA ARE NOT/NOT AS GREAT AS SOME OTHER COUNTRIES.

2. WE FULLY AGREE WITH REASONING IN YOUR REFTEL THAT USA WOULD DO WELL NOT/NOT TO BE LEFT TOO FAR BEHIND THEIR FRIENDS ON RECOGNITION. THEY UNDOUBTEDLY HAVE THESE CONSIDERATIONS CLEARLY IN MIND BUT IN VIEW OF THEIR REACTION TO INDO/PAK CONFLICT, ARE NOT/NOT LIKELY TO ACCEPT KINDLY ADVICE THAT MIGHT IMPLY THEIR MISHANDLING OF SITUATION. IN ANY EVENT WE WOULD FIND IT DIFFICULT IN VIEW OF OUR RELUCTANCE ON RECOGNITION TO NOW TRY AND LEAD A CO-ORDINATED EFFORT ENCOURAGING USA TO JOIN WITH FRIENDS.

...../2

DRAFTER/RÉDACTEUR: R.E. Caldwell/is
DIVISION/DIRECTION: GPS
TELEPHONE: 6-1989

Confidential telegram from Ottawa Head Quarters to Washington and Islamabad Concerning Recognition of Bangladesh-USA Position, dated January 28, 1972

Source: Canada. Department of External Affairs. File # 20-Bangla-14.

- 2 -   CONF

3. YOU MAY WISH TO INFORM STATE DEPARTMENT WE ARE SATISFIED OUR REASONS FOR RECOGNITION ON FEBRUARY 7 ARE SOUND AND IN INTEREST OF CO-OPERATION WITH USA HAVE TRIED TO KEEP THEM INFORMED. IF THEY ARE AMENABLE TO LOW PROFILE INFLUENCE WE WOULD NATURALLY HOPE THAT THEY WOULD CONSIDER JOINING WITH ALLIES AND FRIENDS IN RECOGNIZING DURING EARLY PART OF FEBRUARY. IF NOT/NOT WE WISH ONLY TO INFORM THEM THAT WE HAVE DECIDED TO RECOGNIZE BANGLADESH ON FEB 7 WHICH THEY WILL NOTE IS TWO OR THREE DAYS AFTER THOSE WHO HAVE HEADED CAMPAIGN FOR EARLIER DATE.

Confidential telegram from Ottawa Head Quarters to Washington and Islamabad Concerning Recognition of Bangladesh-USA Position, dated January 28, 1972

Source: Canada. Department of External Affairs. File # 20-Bangla-14.

No.P/12/7/71   February 8, 1972

PAKISTAN HIGH COMMISSION
505 WILBROD STREET
OTTAWA 2 - CANADA
TELEPHONE: 239-4356
TELEGRAPHIC ADDRESS "PAHIC"

    The High Commission for Pakistan presents its compliments to the Department of External Affairs and has the honour to observe, with reference to the recognition of the so-called Bangla Desh, that the Governments which have recognised Bangla Desh have obviously ignored the fact that conditions for recognition are non-existent. East Pakistan continues to remain under military occupation of India and there is no sign of withdrawal of the Indian forces. The administration in Dacca does not exercise effective control over territories of the province; if it did there would be no need for the Indian Army to be there. There are confirmed reports about atrocities against Biharis and serious violations of law and order are also being received every day. Alternatively, the Indian Army is there because it wants to establish Indian dominance in East Pakistan.

2.   The High Commission has the honour to further state that the countries that just recognised Bangla Desh have unequivocally supported resolutions of the United Nations General Assembly and Security Council of December 7 and 21st respectively which respect unity and integrity of Pakistan. They have thus acted against their own declared positions and also encouraged India's intransigence in not complying with these resolutions. Recognition of Bangla Desh under these circumstances is in effect legitimation of aggression and use of force by India to dismember Pakistan. The Government of Pakistan, therefore, regard their action as unfriendly act and cannot accept contention that these countries have acted in accordance with any principles. Their action will no doubt set a very serious precedent which will eventually have grave consequences for the world over.

    The High Commission for Pakistan avails itself of this opportunity to renew to the Department of External Affairs the assurances of its highest consideration.

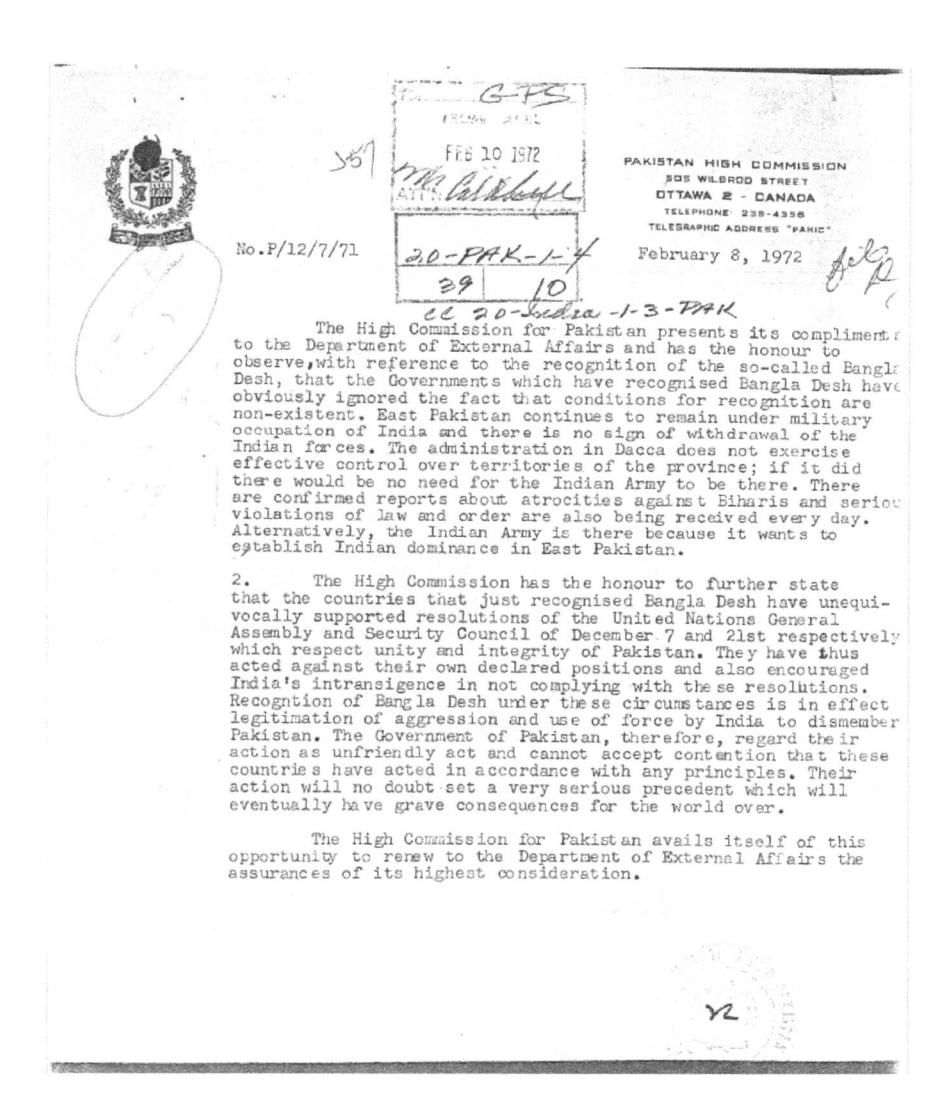

The Bhutto government's attempt to dissuade the Trudeau administration from recognizing Bangladesh.

Source: Canada. Department of External Affairs. File # 20-Pak-1-4; 20-India-1-3-Pak.

7th February, 1972.

Excellency,

It gives me great pleasure to acknowledge receipt of your kind message of February 14, '72. My Government and people are very happy to note that the Government of Canada has accorded recognition to the People's Republic of Bangladesh as a Sovereign and Independent State.

As your Excellency is aware, it is the policy of my Government to create a just society in Bangladesh founded on the ideals of nationalism, democracy, secularism and socialism. In international relations, my Government will pursue a policy of non-alignment. It will be my Government's policy to oppose colonialism, imperialism and racialism. My Government has abiding faith in the Charter of the United Nations, and will be ready to develop bilateral relations with all countries of the world on the basis of sovereign equality of states, non-interference in internal affairs, peaceful solution of international disputes, and respect for each other's sovereignty and territorial integrity.

In pursuance of the above mentioned principles and objectives, my Government and people wish to develop very close relationship and understanding with Canada for the mutual benefit of our two peoples. It is also our desire to become a member of the Commonwealth.

I avail myself of this opportunity to convey, on behalf of my Government, the people of Bangladesh and on my own behalf, warm greetings and felicitations to the Government and people of Canada.

Please accept, Excellency, the assurances of my highest consideration.

(Sheikh Mujibur Rahman)
Prime Minister of Bangladesh

His Excellency
Mr. Pierre Elliott Trudeau,
Prime Minister of Canada,
Ottawa, Canada.

Letter from Sheikh Mujibur Rahman, Prime Minister of Bangladesh, to Prime Minister Pierre Trudeau thanking him for his recognition of Bangladesh.

Source: Canada. Department of External Affairs. File # 20-Bangla-10.

```
                                    MESSAGE
         PLACE    DEPARTMENT   ORIG. NO.   DATE        FILE/DOSSIER        SECURITY
         LIEU     MINISTÈRE    N° D'ORIG.                                  SÉCURITÉ
FM/DE    OTT      EXT          GPS-86      FEB15/72   20-Bangla-1-3        CONFD
                                                                           PRECEDENCE
TO/A     LDN

INFO

DISTR.

    REF       YOURTEL 398 FEB9
    SUB/SUJ   BANGLADESH: APPLICATION TO JOIN COMWEL
    PLEASE PASS FOLLOWING TO ARNOLD SMITH: QUOTE I AM HAPPY TO
    INFORM YOU THAT THE GOVT OF CDA WELCOMES THE APPLICATION OF
    BANGLADESH TO JOIN THE COMWEL AND FULLY AGREES THAT THE REQUEST
    SHOULD BE GRANTED. I AM CONFIDENT THAT THE VARIED BENEFITS
    BANGLADESH WILL GAIN FROM CONTINUED ASSOCIATION WITH COMWEL
    COUNTRIES WILL ASSIST THE NEW NATION TO ESTABLISH ITSELF FIRMLY
    AS AN INDEPENDENT COUNTRY IN THE INTERNATIONAL COMMUNITY.
    PIERRE ELLIOTT TRUDEAU, PRIME MINISTER OF CANADA UNQUOTE.

                                        ORIGINAL SIGNÉ PAR
                                        ORIGINAL SIGNED BY
                                        P. E. TRUDEAU

                                        FEB 15 1972

         DRAFTER/RÉDACTEUR    DIVISION/DIRECTION   TELEPHONE   APPROVED/APPROUVÉ
SIG      R.E. Caldwell/ls/IMc        GPS             6-1989    SIG
```

This is a confidential telegram from Ottawa Headquarters to the Canadian High Commission in London concerning Bangladesh's application to join the Commonwealth, dated February 15, 1972.

Source: Canada. Department of External Affairs. File # 20-Bangla-1-3.

833

```
PMO        File ✓          GPS/H.P.G.Fraser/is
MIN        Diary
PDM        Div.Diary
Parl.Sec.
FPR
FAI
PAG
GPP
```

DECLASSIFIED - DECLASSE

PLEASE RETURN TO GPS
POSTAL STATION "B"

RESTRICTED

April 19, 1972

MEMORANDUM FOR THE PRIME MINISTER

20-BANGLA-1-
16

Bangladesh Membership in the Commonwealth

In your telegram of February 14 to Sheikh Mujibur Rahman informing him of Canada's formal recognition of the new state of Bangladesh you welcomed his decision to apply for membership in the Commonwealth. In spite of initial hesitation on the part of some Commonwealth African countries sufficient support has now been forthcoming and the Bangladesh application has been approved.

We welcome this decision and believe it will provide the new government with an opportunity to expand its now limited international contacts. It will also provide us with an opportunity to develop our relations with Bangladesh in a number of areas beyond that of development assistance. Attached for your signature, if you agree, is a telegram to Sheikh Mujibur Rahman expressing Canada's pleasure over Bangladesh membership in the Commonwealth.

ORIGINAL SIGNED BY
MITCHELL SHARP

M.S.

MEMORANDUM from Mitchell Sharp, Secretary of State for External Affairs to Prime Minister Pierre Trudeau, regarding Bangladesh's membership in the Commonwealth, dated April 19, 1972.

Source: Canada. Department of External Affairs. File # 20-Bangla-1-16.

HOUSE OF COMMONS
CANADA

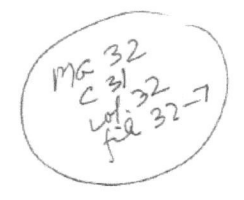

C O P Y

OTTAWA, March 19, 1974

Right Hon. Pierre Elliott Trudeau
24 Sussex Drive
Ottawa, Ontario

Dear Prime Minister:

    Not long ago, I was in Bangladesh along with Messrs. Brewin and Rowland, as guests of the government of that country. For Mr. Brewin and myself, it was a joyful return to that troubled area, because we were last there in 1971 when they were under occupation. Today, Bangladesh walks in freedom, and while its problems are immense, the fact that they have maintained a state and are operating a political democracy with efficiency is highly commendable.

    We had the pleasure of a most delightful conversation with the Sheikh Mujibur. He is obviously feeling well and in ebullient spirits, unlike the state of his health when he was at the Prime Ministers' Conference in Ottawa.

    Sheikh Mujibur extends his good wishes to you, and I am happy to be the vehicle of such intra-Commonwealth greetings. I am sure he would be delighted to have you visit his country and, knowing the extremely high regard in which Canadians are held, I am sure that the people of Bangladesh would welcome such a visit on your part. I am also advising Mr. Stanfield of this particular aspect of Canada - Bangladesh goodwill.

    Among others with whom we held discussions was Mr. Tofael Ahmed, the Prime Minister's chief political advisor, who was with him in Ottawa. He was very specific in extending an invitation for you to go to Bangladesh. I told him that, while I was not a member of the Liberal Party, there was no partisan division in Canada, on the question of friendship with Bangladesh and that I would be delighted and honored to convey his invitation. This I now do and add the personal hope that, before very long, a Prime Minister of Canada will be able to visit our good friend and fellow Commonwealth nation, Bangladesh.

    With kind regards and good wishes, I am

        Yours sincerely,

        Heath Macquarrie, M.P.

Letter from Heath Macquarrie, Member of Parliament for Hillsborough, to Prime Minister Pierre Trudeau following his visit to Bangladesh, dated March 19, 1974.

Source: Canada. Library and Archives Canada. MG 32 C31, Vol. 32, File # 32-37.

836

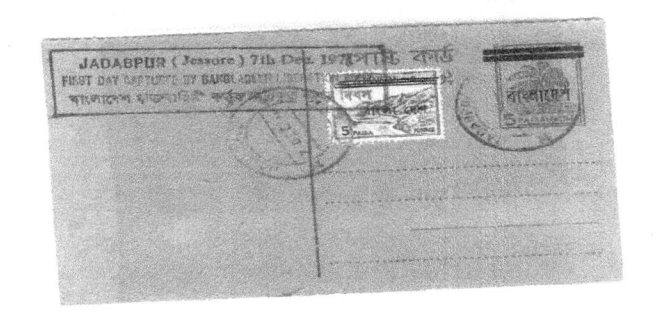

The first issue of stamps from the Government of Bangladesh formatted by the International Security Printers Ltd., dated December 7, 1971

Source: Dr. Anwar Haque of Regina obtained them through his network in London, UK. He gave the author a few of these historic stamps as a keepsake.

837

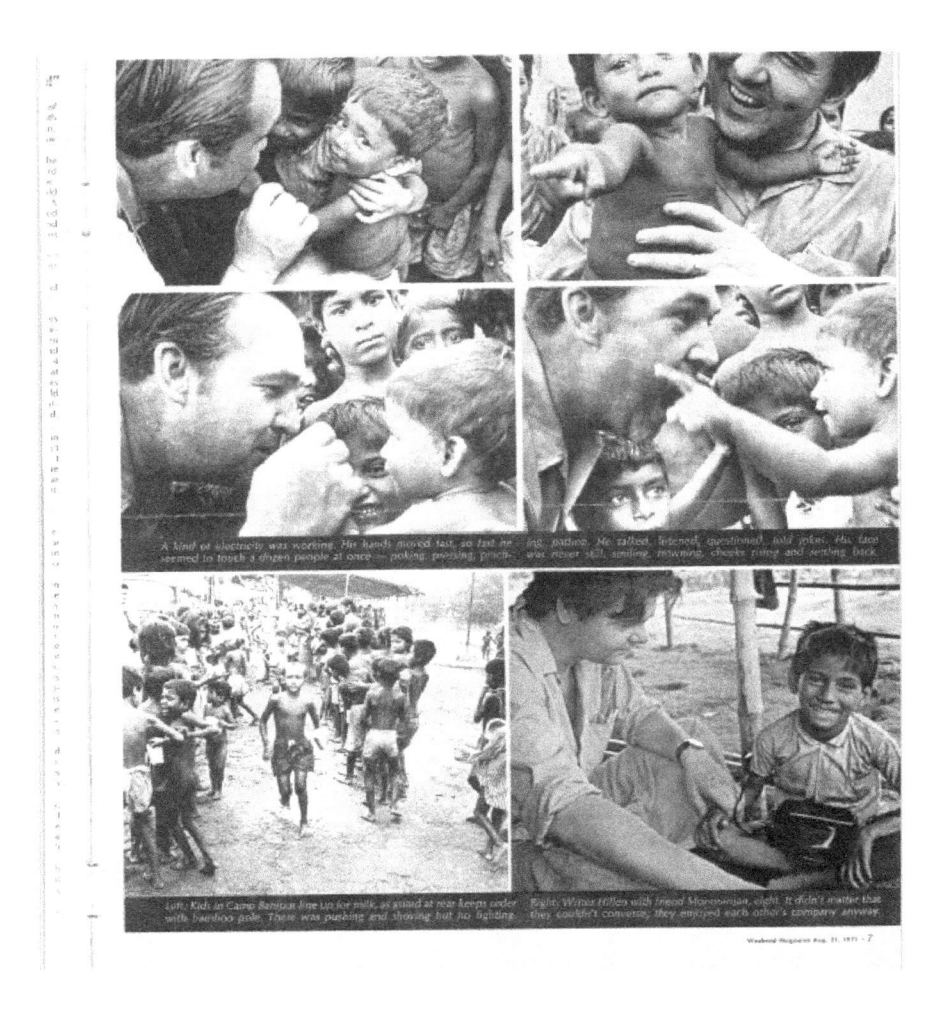

Source: Weekend Magazine (Montreal, Quebec, dated July 31, 1971)

Source: TIME (Canada Edition) Ronalds- Federated Limited, Montreal, Evergreen Press Ltd. Dated August 2, 1971.

Source: TIME (Canada Edition) Ronalds- Federated Limited, Montreal, Evergreen Press Ltd. Dated December 20, 1971.

APPENDIX E

Canadian Parliamentarians whose names frequently appear in the House of Commons and Senate

Alfred Dryden Hales (Conservative MP for Wellington)

Andrew Brewin (National Democratic Party MP for Greenwood)

Barnett Danson (Liberal MP for York-North)

David Lewis (National Democratic Party MP for York South and leader of the NDP)

Donald Stovel Macdonald (Liberal MP for Rosedale and Minister of Defence)

Doug Rowland (National Democratic Party MP for Selkirk)

Douglas Harkness (Conservative MP for Calgary Centre)

Georges Lachance (Liberal MP for Lafontaine)

Gérard Laprise (Social Credit Party MP and Raillement de Créditiste for member for Abitibi)

Gordon Fairweather (Conservative MP for Fundy-Royal)

Grant Deachman (Liberal MP for Vancouver - Quadra)

Harold Warren Danforth (Conservative MP for Ket and Essex)

Heath Macquarrie (Conservative MP for Hillsborough and PC Caucus Spokesperson for External Affairs)

Horace Andrew Olson (Liberal MP for Medicine Hat and Minister of Agriculture)

Jack Murta (Conservative MP for Lisgar)

Jacques Flynn (Senator and Leader of the Opposition)

James A. McGrath (Conservative MP for Saint-John's East)

John Diefenbaker (Conservative MP for Prince Albert and former Prime Minister)

John Gilbert (National Democratic Party MP for Broadview)

John Munro (Liberal MP for Hamilton East)

Les Benjamin (National Democratic Party MP for Regina West)

Lorne Nystrom (National Democratic Party for Yorkton-Melville)

Marcel Lessard (Social Credit MP for Lac-Saint-Jean)

Marcel Prud'homme (Liberal MP for Saint- Denis)

Michael Forrestall (Conservative MP for Dartmouth-Halifax East)

Mitchell Sharp (Liberal MP for Eglington and Secretary of State for External Affairs)

Otto Lang (Liberal MP for Saskatoon-Humboldt and Minister for Manpower and Immigration)

Paul Desruisseaux (Conservative Senator for Wellington, Québec)

Paul St. Pierre (Conservative MP for Charlesbourg- Haute-Saint-Charles)

Philip Bernard Rynard (Conservative MP for Simco)

Pierre De Bane (Liberal MP for Metapédia- Matane)

Pierre Elliott Trudeau (Liberal MP for Mount Royal and Prime Minister)

Raymond Joseph Perrault (Liberal MP for Barnaby-Seymor and Parliamentary Secretary to Minister of Labour)

Réal Caouette (Social Credit Party MP for Témiscamingue and Leader of the Ralliement des créditistes du Canada

Robert McCLeave (Conservative MP for Halifax-East-Hants)

Robert N. Thompson (Social Credit Party MP for Red Deer)

Robert Stanfield (Conservative MP for Halifax and Leader of the Opposition)

Stanley Knowles (National Democratic Party MP for Winnipeg North)

Thomas M. Bell (Conservative MP for Saint-John-Lancaster)

Tommy Douglas (National Democratic Party MP for Nanaimo-Cowichan-The Islands and Leader of the NDP until April 1971.

William Marvin Howe (Conservative MP for Wellington-Grey-Dufferin-Waterloo)

APPENDIX F

Canadian parliamentarians who raised the East Pakistan issue in the House of Commons and Senate

Georges-C. Lachance
(Liberal MP for Lafontaine)

Marcel Prud'homme
(Liberal MP for Saint-Denis)

Gordon Fairweather
(Conservative MP for Fundy-Royal)

John Diefenbaker
(Conservative MP for Prince Albert and former Prime Minister)

Mitchell Sharp
(Liberal MP for Eglington and Secretary of State for External Affairs)

Otto Lang
(Liberal MP for Saskatoon-Humboldt and Minister for Manpower and Immigration)

David Lewis
(NDP MP for York South and Leader of the NDP)

Lorne Nystrom
(National Democratic Party for Yorkton-Melville)

Pierre Elliott Trudeau
(Liberal MP for Mount Royal and Prime Minister)

Warren Allmand
(Member of Parliament for Notre-Dame-de-Grâce)

Pierre De Bané
(Liberal MP for Metapédia- Matane)

Stanley Haidasz
(Member of Parliament for Trinity)

James McGrath
(Conservation MP for Saint-John's East)

Douglas Harkness
(Conservative MP for Calgary Centre)

Donald Stovel Macdonald
(Liberal MP for Rosedale and Minister of Defence)

Stanley Knowles
(National Democratic Party MP for Winnipeg North)

Raymond Joseph Perrault
(Liberal MP for Barnaby-Seymor and
Parliamentary Secretary to Minister of
Labour)

Senator Jacques Flynn
(Senator and Leader of the Opposition)

Horace Andrew Wilson
(Liberal MP for Medicine Hat and
Minister of Agriculture)

Michael William Forrestall
(Conservative MP for Dartmouth-Halifax
East)

Paul St. Pierre
(Conservative MP for
Charlesbourg- Haute-Saint-Charles)

Réal Caouette
(Social Credit Party MP for
Témiscamingue and Leader of the
Ralliement des créditistes du Canada

John Munro
(Liberal MP for Hamilton East)

Robert Stanfield
(Conservative MP for Halifax and Leader of the Opposition)

Barnett Danson
(Liberal MP for York-North)

Robert Thompson
(Social Credit Party MP for Red Deer)

Tommy Douglas
(National Democratic Party MP for Nanaimo-Cowichan-The Islands and Leader of the NDP until April 1971)

Les Benjamin
(National Democratic Party MP for Regina West)

Marcel Lessard
(Social Credit MP for Lac-Saint-Jean)

Philip Bernard Rynard
(Conversative MP for Simco)

Gerard Laprise
(Social Credit Party MP and Raillement
de Créditiste for Abitibi)

Jack Cullen
(Liberal MP for Sarnia Lambton)

Jack Murta
(Conservative MP for Lisgar)

Harold Warren Danforth
(Conservative MP for Ket and Essex)

Andrew Brewin
(National Democratic Party MP for Greenwood)

Robert McCleave
(Conservative MP for Halifax-East-Hants)

Alfred Dryden Hales
(Conservative MP for Wellington)

Doug Rowland
(National Democratic Party MP for Selkirk)

Heath Macquarrie, Conservative MP for Hillsborough and Mustafa Chowdhury

Mitchell Sharp, former Secretary of State for External Affairs, and Mustafa Chowdhury

APPENDIX G

Canadian news reporters, media personalities, intellectuals, NGO workers, diplomats and members of the public

Edward Schreyer
(Governor General of Manitoba)

Arnold Smith
(Commonwealth, Secretary- General)

James Eayrs
(Canadian historian)

Joe Schlesinger
(Canadian Broadcasting Corporation)

Emil Baran
(Canadian International Development Agency)

David-Van-Praagh
(Journalist)

Stanley Burke
(Canadian Broadcasting Corporation)

Claude Rayan
(CC GOQ, a Canadian journalist and politician)

Dr. Hari Sharma
(Simon Fraser University)

Dr Elliot Tepper
(Carlton University)

Ernest Hillen
(*Weekend Magazine*, Montreal)

Paul Gérin-Lajoie
(Canadian International Development Agency)

Dr. Lotta Hitschmanova
(Unitarian Service Committee of Canada)

John Drewery
(Canadian Broadcasting Corporation)

Hugh Keenleyside
(Canadian University Professor, Diplomat, Civil Servant)

John Kenneth Galbraith
(Canadian-born economist, former US ambassador to India)

John Wieler
(Mennonite Central Committee)

Professor Joseph O'Connell
(Toronto)

Robert John Whyte
(Canadian Broadcasting Corporation)

Jim Pankratz
(Mennonite Central Committee)

Dr. Chinmoy Banerjee
(Simon Fraser University)

Vernon Reimer
(Mennonite Central Committee)

Northrop Frye
(Canadian Literary Critic)

Nancy Gerine
(Canadian University Services Overseas)

Ernie Regehr
(Mennonite Central Committee)

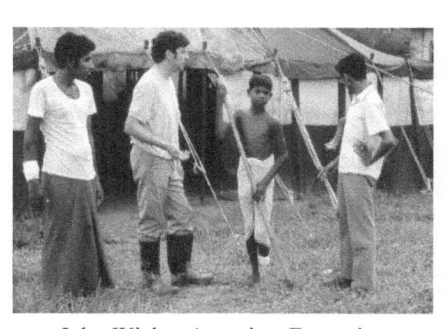

John Wieler, Associate Executive Secretary of the Mennonite Central Committee, visited one of the refugee camps in West Bengal, India, in July 1971. **Source:** John Wieler presented this from his collection to the author.

Julian Francis (OXFAM of UK who worked closely with OXFAM of Canada) and Mustafa Chowdhury, July 2017 **Source:** From author's collection.

APPENDIX H

East Pakistani Bengali Canadians who demanded recognition of Bangladesh

Dr. Luthful Kabir and Bilquis Kabir
(Ottawa)

Abdul Aziz Chowdhury
(Kitchener)

Abdul Momin Chowdhury
(London, Ontario)

Suraiya Ali
(London, Ontario)

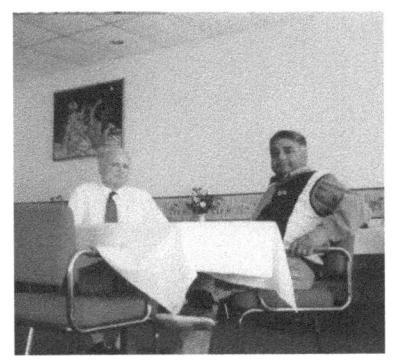

Dr. Farid Shariff and Mustafa
Chowdhury
(Winnipeg)

Dr. Wali Khan
(St. John's)

Dr. Asit Sarkar (Saskatoon)

Faruq Sarkar and Suzy Sarkar
(Ottawa)

Dr. Nurul Islam
(Montreal)

Dr. Mohammed Matlib
(St. John's)

Dr. Sadat Kazi
(Montreal)

Dr. Hamida Begum with Mustafa
Chowdhury
(Winnipeg)

Dr. Nasir Uddin Ahmed
(Ottawa)

Prabir Mitra
(Winnipeg)

Dr. Waheedul-Haque
(Toronto)

Ahsanullah Mallick
(Toronto)

Dr. A M Safiq Khan
(Vancouver)

Syed Mezbahuddin Faruque and Selina Faruque
(London, UK)

Azmat Ali
(Ottawa)

Chaitanya Keshavrao Calevar
(Toronto)

Cummer Chowdhury
(Toronto)

Dr. Anwarul Haque
(Regina)

Dr. Abdul Mannan
(Edmonton)

Dr. Farid Shariff
(Winnipeg)

Dr. Hakim Sikander and Daniell Sikander
(Calgary)

Dr. Hafiz Rahman
(Kingston)

Dr. Haripada Dhar
(Ottawa)

Dr. Mohammad Ahsanullah
(Ottawa)

Dr. Kazi Islam and Rowshan Kazi
(Calgary)

Dr. Mohammad Moyeenul Islam
(St. John's)

Dr. Sudhir Saha
(Vancouver)

Dr. Shahid Hussain
(Vancouver)

Ila Sarkar
(Saskatoon)

Professor Saber Saleuddin
(Toronto)

Professor Mizan Rahman
(Ottawa)

Rabi Alam and Madeline Alam
(Toronto)

Mrs. Ilu Islam
(St. John's)

Matiur Rahman
(Toronto)

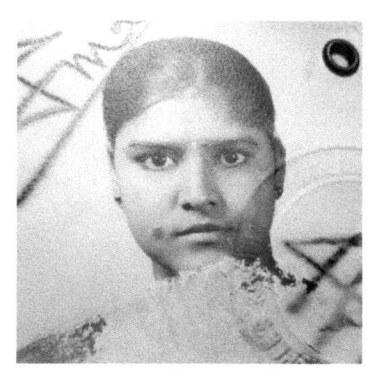

Mrs. Jahanara Ali
(Ottawa)

Rubena Sinha and Dr. Snehesh Kumar
Sinha
(Winnipeg)

Dr Mir Maqsud Ali
(Waterloo)

Siddique Hussain
(Edmonton)

Masuda Ahsanullah
(Ottawa)

Dr. Mir Masood Ali
(London, Ontario)

APPENDIX I

Canadian religious missionaries in East Pakistan, India, and Canada who did not abandon their missionary work. They assisted the refugees and displaced people by doing whatever they could within their limited capability.

Father Frank West
(Canadian Jesuits Mission)

Brother Raymond Cournoyer
(Canadian Holy Cross Order)

Archbishop Joseph-Aurèle Plourde
(Ottawa)

Father Pierre Benoit
(Canadian Holy Cross Order)

Brother Raymond Cournoyer of
Canadian Holy Cross Order and Mustafa
Chowdhury

Dr. Robert Baird McClure
(Ex-Moderator, United Church of Canada,
Board of Director of OXFAM of Canada)

Father Edgar Burns
(Jesuit Priest in Darjeeling, India)

Father Joseph David Brenan
(Jesuit Priest in Darjeeling, India)

Father Gerard Van Walleghem
(Jesuit Priest in Darjeeling, India)

Father William German and Mustafa
Chowdhury at Jesuit House in Toronto

Arthur B. Moore
(Moderator of the United Church of Canada, Toronto)

Father William M. German
(Jesuit Priest in Darjeeling, India)

Rev E. H. Johnson
(Toronto)

Father Germain Grandmaison
(Canadian Holy Cross Order in East Pakistan)

Reverend E. W. Scott
(Primate, The Anglican Church of Canada, Toronto)

Father Houle Albéric
(Canadian Holy Cross Order in East Pakistan)

Father Paulin Demers
(Canadian Holy Cross Order in East Pakistan)

Father Benjamin Labbé
(Canadian Holy Cross Order in East Pakistan)

Father Laurent Lecavalier
(Canadian Holy Cross Order in East Pakistan)

Father Charles Nadeau
(Canadian Holy Cross Order in East Pakistan)

Brother Flavian Laplante
(Canadian Holy Cross Order in East Pakistan)

Father Martial Saint-Pierre
(Canadian Holy Cross Order in East Pakistan)

Father Guy-Marie Tourangeau
(Canadian Holy Cross Order in East Pakistan)

Sister Marie de Galilee, CSC
(Canadian Holy Cross Order in East Pakistan)

APPENDIX J

The provisional Government of the People's Republic of Bangladesh was formed on April 10, 1971, and sworn in on April 17, 1971.

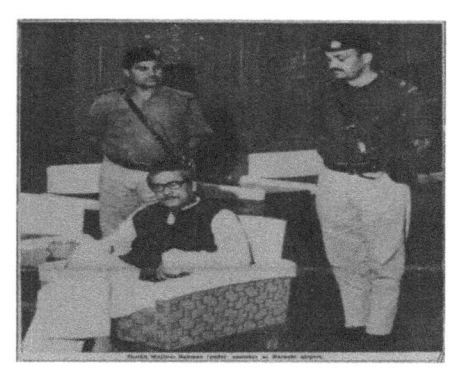

A defiant *Bongobondhu* Sheikh Mujibur Rahman (President who declared the independence of Bangladesh on March 26, 1971) at Karachi Airport following his arrest.

Khandaker Moshtaque Ahmed (Minister of Foreign Affairs, Law and Parliamentary Affairs)

Syed Nazrul Islam
(Vice-President and acting President of Bangladesh)

Abu Hasnat Muhammad Qamruzzaman
(Minister of Home, Civil Supplies, Relief and Rehabilitation, and Agriculture)

Tajuddin Ahmed
(Prime Minister of the Provisional Government of Bangladesh)

Captain Muhammad Mansur Ali
(Minister of Finance, Industry and Commerce)

Barrister Amirul Islam
(Lawyer and Politician who drafted the Proclamation of Independence in 1971)

Muhammad Yusuf Ali, who read the Proclamation of Independence.

Abdul Mannan
(MNA in charge of Ministry of Information and Radio, *Shwadhin Bangla Betar Kendro*. He conducted the oath-taking ceremony.)

Ataul Gani Osmani
(Commander-in-Chief of Bangladesh Liberation Forces)

Major Ziaur Rahman, who declared the independence of Bangladesh on March 27, 1971 (Commander-in-Chief of the Bangladesh Liberation Army)

APPENDIX K

Bengali Political Leaders who fled to India and supported the liberation movement under the leadership of the Awami League

Maulana Abdul Hamid Khan Bhashani
(Chief, National Awami Party – Bhashani Group)

Comrade Moni Singh
(Secretary of the Communist Party of East Pakistan and Advisor to the Provisional Government of Bangladesh)

Professor Muzaffar Ahmad
(Chief, National Awami Party – Muzaffar Group)

Manoranjan Dhar
(Bangladesh National Congress)

APPENDIX L

Members of the Bangladesh Mission in Washinton who lobbied the government of Canada for Bangladesh

Mustafizur Rahman Siddiqi
(Head of the Bangladesh Mission)

Syed Muazzem Ali
(Third Secretary, Bangladesh Mission)

Abu Syed Chowdhury, having resigned as the VC, became a special envoy of the Provisional Government of Bangladesh in the United Kingdom.

APPENDIX M

First Bangladeshi and Canadian High Commissioners and Diplomats

Abdul Momin
(the first high commissioner to Canada in 1972)

Gordon George Riddell
(Canadian high commissioner to Bangladesh from June 1972 to June 1974)

Gordon Edwin Cox
(Canadian ambassador in Bangkok who was double-accredited to represent Canada in Bangladesh from April 1972 to June 1972)

James George
(Canadian high commissioner to India in 1971)

APPENDIX N

Canada-Bangladesh Friendship since 1972

Source: *The Bangladesh Observer*, dated November 21, 1983

Bongobondhu joins the 19th Commonwealth Conference in Canada in 1973 (August 2-10). **Source:** *The Ottawa Citizen*, dated August 8, 1973

Prime Minister Pierre Elliott Trudeau planted saplings in the *Jatiyo Smriti Shoudha Complex* in Savar on November 20, 1983. Over the years, they have become a symbol of friendship between Bangladesh and Canada.
Source: Author's collection

Prime Minister Pierre Elliott Trudeau speaking at the banquet hosted in honour of him by Chief Martial Law Administrator Lt. General H. M. Ershad at *Bongobhobon* on November 20, 1983. Source: *The Bangladesh Observer,* dated November 21, 1983

Historic mark of the plated sapling by Prime Minister Pierre Elliott Trudeau. Source: From author's collection.

Prime Minister Pierre Elliott Trudeau laid a wreath at the *Jatiyo Shahid Smriti Shoudha* at Savar in Dhaka **Source:** *The Bangladesh Observer,* dated November 21, 1983

Reception for Prime Minister Sheikh Hasina in Montreal on September 17, 2016 **Source:** Salim Zuberi, who took this photo on September 17, 2016, gave it to the author.

Prime Minister Sheikh Hasina meets Prime Minister Justin Trudeau in Charlevoix, Quebec, on July 7, 2018. **Source:** Salim Zuberi, who took this photo on June 10, 2018, gave it to the author.

Reception for Prime Minister Sheikh Hasina in Toronto by the Canada Awami League (Toronto) on June 10, 2018. **Source:** This photo was given to the author by Salim Zuberi, who took the picture

Prime Minister Sheikh Hasina during her 2016 visit to Canada in Montreal with Sarwar Hussain and Salim Zuberi, renowned community leaders of Montreal.
Source: This photo, taken on September 17, 2016, was given to the author by Salim Zuberi, who took the picture

Prime Minister Sheikh Hasina with Prime Minister Justin Trudeau during her 2016 visit to Canada. They were in Montreal with Sarwar Hussain, Salim Zuberi, and Deepak Dhar Opu, renowned community leaders of Montreal.
Source: Salim Zuberi, who took this photo on September 17, 2016, gave it to the author.
Source: From author's collection.

Bangladesh PEACE clock in downtown Windsor, Ontario. From left to right: Yakub Ali, High Commissioner of Bangladesh, His Worship Mayor Eddie Francis, and philanthropist Aziz Chowdhury (January 12, 2012)
Source: Author's own collection

Bangladesh PEACE clock in downtown Windsor, Ontario, donated by philanthropist Aziz Chowdhury.

Source: Author's own collection.

INDEX

A

Abdullah, Muhammad, 66
Afghanistan, 78, 365, 656, 665
Agartala Conspiracy Case, 28–29, 66, 727
agreement, ceasefire, 745
Ahmad, Tajuddin, 54, 531
Ahmed, Jalaluddin, 205, 234, 292
Ahmed, Khandaker Moshtaque, 54, 500, 533–34, 611, 666, 776–77, 786–87, 803–4, 873
Ahmed, Nasir Uddin, 198, 205, 270, 861
Ahmed, Tajuddin, 102, 135, 227, 233, 425, 553, 572, 612, 617, 643, 711, 874
Ahsan, Amir, 225, 245
Ahsan, Syed Mohammad, 68
Ahsanullah, Masuda, 250, 295, 866
Ahsanullah, Mohammad, 205, 295, 863
Alam, Abu Zahirul, 225, 245
Alam, Madeline, 233, 249–50, 259, 295, 297, 865
Alam, Rabi, 202, 209, 227, 233, 247, 357, 865
Alam, Sarwar, 201
Alberta, 18, 202, 208, 220–21, 242, 285, 289, 293, 360, 424, 615
Ali, Azmat, 205, 234, 250, 295, 862
Ali, Hossain, 75, 173
Ali, K. A. Akbar, 211–12
Ali, Maqsud, 200
Ali, Syed Muazzem, 246, 280, 879
Ali, Tarek, 244
All-Parties Action Committee, 22
All Parties Students Action Committee (SAC), 28–29, 735
American Response to Bangladesh Liberation War (1995) (Muhit), xvii
Amour-propre, 727
Ansars, 86, 727
Antigonish Movement, 648, 674
archival records, 840
Ashram, Miriam, 314
Assam Refugee Relief, 361
"Assessment of Pakistan Crisis, An" (Tulley), 129
Assistance to Cyclone and Flood Victims, 396
Au courant, 727
Awal, Abdul, 205
Awami League (AL), xviii, xxvi, xxviii, 23, 25–26, 62, 75, 77, 79–80, 84–85, 88, 145–47, 258–60, 262–63, 437, 440, 480–81, 511–12, 737–38, 740
Ayub Era, 24
Ayub Khan, Muhammed, 20, 24, 727

B

Baluchistan, 20, 23, 546, 636
Banerjee, Chinnmoy, 220
Bangalees, 709, 727–28
Bangla, xxxviii, 22–23, 728
Bangla (language), 21–23
Bangladesh, xviii–xix, xxxiii–xxxv, 101–3, 173–77, 205–7, 222–25, 270–74, 276–86, 447–56, 524–26, 573–75,

587–97, 608–65, 670–73, 679–81, 685–91, 693–99, 705–8, 711, 717–20
  birth of, ix, xiii–xiv, xvii, xix, xxv, xxxvi, 277, 283, 455, 475, 498, 568, 574, 576, 580, 583–84, 602, 693, 705–6, 711–12
  independent, xxvii–xxviii, xxxiv, 28, 47–49, 64, 69, 80, 87, 98, 117, 126, 137, 160–61, 202–3, 207–8, 222–23, 228–32, 279, 281–82, 680
  liberation of, v, ix, xiv, xix, xxxi, xxxiv, xxxix, 175, 224, 233, 254, 282, 291, 306, 451, 455–56, 525–26, 609–10, 697, 705–6
  provisional government of, x, xxx, xxxiv, 102–3, 113, 135, 145, 148, 173–74, 178, 221, 233, 432, 439, 455, 475, 481, 562–63, 573–74, 600–601
Bangla Desh, 45, 62, 198–200, 223, 231–32, 262–63, 270–71, 293–94, 346–47, 379, 453, 524–27, 561–62, 614–15, 617, 621, 639, 703, 719, 728
Bangladesh Association of British Columbia, 215, 218, 241, 271, 288–89, 719, 721, 744
Bangladesh Association of Canada, 200, 205, 211, 226, 229, 231, 236, 248–49, 258, 280–81, 284, 292, 295, 298, 301, 357, 430, 488, 719, 825–26
Bangladesh Association of Manitoba, 205, 225, 245–46, 271, 279, 301, 741, 784, 788–89
Bangladesh Association of New England, 246, 294
Bangladesh Association of Québec, 210, 235, 275, 287–88, 292, 722
Bangladesh Association of Saskatchewan (BAS), 205, 222, 224, 244, 266–67, 290
Bangladesh Association of Toronto, 216, 232
Bangladesh-Canada Association, 200, 206, 209, 221, 227, 235, 247, 249, 266, 268, 270, 272, 274, 276, 280, 289, 575
Bangla Desh Christian Relief Committee, 361
Bangladesh Day, 62, 290, 744, 812. *See also* Pakistan Day
"Bangla Desh For Real" (Lakavitch), 231
Bangladeshi flag, 62–63
Bangladesh Liberation War, 243, 396, 613
Bangladesh Medical Association, 245
Bangladesh Mission, 102, 271, 278, 300–301, 666, 879
Bangladesh Mission A/C No 2, 246
Bangladesh PEACE Clock, 657–58, 675, 885–86
Bangladesh Relief Fund (BRF), 243, 749
Bangladesh Students Association, 215, 218, 288, 744
Bangladesh Week, 241, 744
Basic Democracy, 24
Batten, Albert, 333, 386, 741
Baxter, Vera, 254
Bay of Bengal, 341, 585, 650, 728, 730
Begum, Hamida Akhtar, 245, 294, 741
Bell, Thomas M., 410, 843
Bengal, 9, 29, 33, 75, 135–36, 194, 224, 277, 305, 314, 334, 343, 359, 387, 639, 703, 719, 728, 732
Bengali (language), 22
Bengali Canadians, xxvii, xxxi, xl, 205, 223, 230, 255, 267, 282, 284, 500, 526
Bengali East Pakistanis, 146, 176, 197, 232, 255, 282, 435, 493, 496, 797
Bengali nationalism, 22, 35, 38, 78–79, 97, 136, 269, 421, 484, 544, 682
Bengali Pakistani, 174, 498, 702
Bengali rebels, xxv, xxix, 90, 102–3, 112, 127, 147, 157–58, 160, 171, 187, 224, 264, 314, 368, 370, 403, 441, 552, 684
Bengali refugees, 9, 109, 164, 188, 217, 226, 235, 247–48, 253–54, 274, 317, 324, 326, 333, 337, 340, 344, 435–36, 494–96, 567–68

Bengalis, xxv–xxxiii, 21–23, 25–33, 38–44, 46–50, 52–55, 60–66, 68–75, 78–81, 89–103, 114–19, 147–54, 157–60, 173–80, 229–36, 258–64, 491–96, 543–51, 685–90, 705–11
Benjamin, Les, xxxix, 266–67, 274, 298, 434, 496, 533, 842, 849
Benoit, Pierre, 311
bête noir, 43, 728
Bhadkamkar, Ashok, 231, 234
Bhaduri, Rajat, 250
Bhagat, Bali Ram, 111
Bhashani, Maulana, 37–38, 79
Bhattacharjee, Shushil, 244, 293
Bhutan, 9, 78, 317, 620, 665
Bhutto, Zulfiqar Ali, xxviii–xxix, 35–44, 51–52, 54–59, 70–71, 79–80, 82–83, 98–99, 106, 543, 560, 616–19, 623–24, 627–29, 631–32, 634, 638–39, 641–43, 701–3, 737–40
Bichitra, 245, 741
Bihariphobia, 52, 728
Biharis, 48, 52, 131, 138, 508, 556, 617, 624, 633, 653, 708, 728
Birangana, 729
Blake, Eugene Carson, 352
Blakeney, Allan Emrys, 743
Blanket Blitz, 355
blitzkrieg, 119, 729
Bongobondhu, 31–33, 35–64, 66–68, 70–72, 77–83, 98–99, 189–90, 465–66, 507–11, 513–21, 525–27, 542–43, 624, 637–41, 652–55, 680–82, 696–99, 701–3, 709–10, 737–41
  release of, xxxi, xxxiii, 31, 265, 275–77, 283, 353, 516–20, 540, 571, 573, 577, 623, 641
  See also Rahman, Sheikh Mujibur
Bottomley, Arthur, 512, 522
Bourassa, Henri, 10, 420
Bourassa, Robert, 14
Brash, Alan, 184, 356
Brewin, Andrew, xxxix, 222, 229, 247, 276, 289, 291, 296, 299, 301, 349, 357, 398, 405, 425, 535, 667–68, 790–91, 815, 825–26

British Broadcasting Corporation (BBC), 129, 191, 546, 673
British India, 19, 736
British North American Act (BNA), 16
brother, 729
Burke, Stanley, 184, 209, 227, 229, 232–34, 247, 267, 275, 291, 299–300, 343, 389, 525, 688, 854
  "Voice of the People," 228
Burma Independence Act, 19
Burns, Edgar, 143, 743
  "Let My Children Live! An Eye-Witness Report," 143

C

Cadieux, Marcel, 528
Calgary, 198, 207–8, 220–21, 242–43, 285, 293
Canada, ix–xi, xiii–xix, xxi–xxxi, xxxiii–8, 10–19, 103–21, 158–61, 164–66, 230–34, 271–75, 277–85, 326–30, 344–47, 395–402, 404–23, 425–33, 435–57, 463–64, 719–25, 815–34
  complementary positions of, 539
  foreign policy, 4–5
  foreign policy of, xvii, 4, 97, 105, 112–13, 119, 265, 271, 433, 483, 590, 601, 677–78
  initiatives of, xviii, xxii, 463–64, 498, 681, 683
Canada Dam, 7
Canada Deuterium Uranium (CANDU), 8, 749
Canada India Times (CIT), 178
Canadian Broadcasting Corporation (CBC), 78, 127–30, 133, 136, 144, 181–84, 186–87, 190–91, 199, 202, 235, 322, 343, 362, 383, 658, 719, 749, 853–56
Canadian Catholic Conference (CCC), xxxix, 329, 331–33, 362, 385, 660, 741, 744
Canadian Catholic Organisation for Development and Peace (CCODP), 328–29, 331, 355

Canadian Confederation, 13–14, 16, 18, 117, 420
Canadian dailies, 86, 132, 135, 153–55, 162, 166, 169, 173, 175, 255, 258, 425, 445
Canadian Friends Service Committee (CFSC), 365, 391, 724
Canadian government, xv, 8, 125, 216, 239, 265, 347–48, 350, 373, 398, 402, 404–5, 408, 425, 429–30, 434, 439, 447, 615–16, 687–88
Canadian Holy Cross Order, 9, 305–6, 308, 342, 368, 801–2, 867
Canadian Holy Cross Sisters, 9
Canadian Hunger Foundation (CHF), 304–5
Canadian International Development Agency (CIDA), xxxviii, 8–9, 73, 335, 340, 351, 355, 367, 387, 391, 396, 478, 484, 494, 501, 626, 640, 644, 647, 714–15
Canadian Jesuits, 9, 143, 192, 305, 317–20, 323–24, 382–84
Canadian Jesuits Mission (CJM), 143, 192, 320, 382–83, 720, 867
Canadian media, 79, 126, 142, 147, 157, 173–74, 189–90, 467, 685
Canadian news media coverage, 47, 83, 125–26, 131, 175
Canadian NGOs, x, xxxi–xxxii, 1, 171, 302–3, 377–80, 495, 526–27, 688–89
Canadian parliamentarians, xxxiii, 299, 340, 398, 400–401, 407, 414, 416–21, 423, 428–31, 434, 437, 440–42, 447–48, 450, 453–56, 483, 523, 550, 601
"Canadian Policy Towards Bangladesh: Does the North Look at the South," xviii
Canadian Red Cross Society (CRCS), 328, 333–36, 355, 373, 386, 408, 648, 741, 749
Canadians, 238
non-Bengali, xxxi, 217, 249
pro-Bangladeshi, 161, 175, 199, 227, 230, 275, 278, 280, 283, 510, 519, 610
pro-Pakistani, xxxi, 275, 282
Canadian Save the Children Fund (CANSAVE), 337, 386
Canadian UNICEF Committee, 328, 337, 373, 386, 722, 725
Canadian University Service Overseas (CUSO), 324, 326, 384, 525
Caouette, Réal, 402, 430, 488, 843, 848
CAPR initiative, 328, 333, 335, 337–38, 341, 358–59, 362, 366, 369, 375
CARE Canada, xxxix, 340–41, 362, 387, 688
carte blanche, 54, 439, 729
Case for Bangla Desh organized by the Bangladesh Association of Canada (Toronto), The, 229
casus belli, 528, 570, 573, 702, 705, 729
Ceylon, 6–7, 19, 67, 78, 128, 200, 268, 365, 474, 527, 665
Ceylon Independence Act, 19
Chaudhuri, Jayanto Nath, 156
Chaudhuri, Rahat, xiii
Chilliwack East Pakistani Refugee Committee, 241
Chisholm, Colin, 254
Chittagong, 8, 43, 60, 73, 128, 307, 401, 709, 740
cholera epidemic, 9, 127, 142, 166–68, 183, 186, 252, 327, 344, 360
Chowdhury, Anwar, 222, 224, 244, 266, 290
Chowdhury, Aziz, 235, 657, 675
Chowdhury, Golam W., ix–xi, 6, 210, 213, 225, 235, 244, 252, 263, 267, 286–88, 292, 474, 514, 657–58, 717
Chowdhury, Momin, 235, 268, 299, 640
Chowdhury, Naiyyum, 210, 213, 252, 287–88, 292
Chowdhury, Samson, 368
Christian Council of the National Capital Council, 305

Christian Organization for Relief and Rehabilitation (CORR), 307, 313, 382, 649, 749
Church, Frank, 350, 489, 491
civilianization program, 239, 241
civil war, xi, 85, 126, 145, 147, 149, 156, 158, 161, 177, 192–93, 306, 315–16, 368, 397, 400, 411–12, 417, 425, 708
Coggin, Dan, 50
cognoscenti, 629, 729
Colombo Plan, 1, 7, 303
Combined Appeal for Pakistani Relief (CAPR), 188, 194, 254, 291, 293, 295, 326, 328, 356, 358, 362–63, 384–91, 393–94, 429, 480, 505, 521, 742, 749
Combined Opposition Party (COP), 25
Committee for an Independent Bangladesh, 228, 261, 298, 511, 610, 612
Commons Committee, xl, 300, 339, 373, 507, 714, 742
Commonwealth, xvi–xviii, xxxv–xxxvi, 1–2, 5–7, 112–13, 265, 395–96, 409–10, 473–74, 508–9, 522, 541, 550, 565, 637, 641–46, 654–55, 693–95, 705, 833–34
Commonwealth Conference, 521, 523, 653–54
Commonwealth Fund for Technical Cooperation, 7
Commonwealth of Nations, 5, 594, 641
community newspapers, 176–77, 179, 188
Confederation, 10, 14–15, 83, 117, 232, 414, 419, 572, 698
Confederation of National Trade Unions (CNTU), 209
Conference of First Ministers, 15
Congregation of Holy Cross, 314, 382, 729
Constituent Assembly, 34, 37
Cooch Behar Refugee Service, 359
Cooperative Commonwealth Federation (CCF), 4
Council Muslim League (CML), 24, 84
coup de force, 729

Cournoyer, Raymond, 141, 144, 167, 193, 251, 254, 315, 342–43, 345–47, 351–52, 388, 390, 649
Cox, Gordon, 746
Cross, James, 17, 533
"Crossing the Rubicon," 730
cul-de-sac, 730
Cyclone Bhola, 737

D

Danforth, Harold Warren, 842, 850
Danson, Barnett, 415, 437, 841, 849
Danson, Barney, 209
Dar, Fazal, 244
Darjeeling Mission, 317, 382
Darjeeling refugee camps, 323
Darnell, Sybil M., 338
Daulatana, Mian Mumtaz, 43
Daulatana, Mian Mumtaz Khan, 24
Day and Ross of Hartland, 364
Deachman, Grant, 339, 841
De Bane, Pierre, 843
Decade of Reforms (1958-1968), 25
Declaration of Independence, 45, 145, 232, 610, 709–10, 750
Demers, Paulin, 310
Dennison, William, 254
Department of External Affairs, x, xxi, xxxviii, xli, 72–73, 120, 190, 284–85, 380, 666–67, 671, 703–4, 755–70, 773–74, 776–81, 783–87, 792–800, 803–4, 816–24, 829–34
Department of Manpower and Immigration, 492, 494, 497–98, 533, 672, 715
Department of National Defence (DND), 335–36, 486–87, 532, 598, 715, 749
dependency model of mass media effects, 161
Desruisseaux, Paul, 842
deus ex machina, 730
Dewitt, David, 697
Dhaka, 37–38, 40, 42–43, 51–52, 62–63, 74–76, 81–82, 84–86, 88–89, 128–30, 135–36, 181, 199, 368, 382, 623–24, 639, 717–20, 735–38, 744–46
Dhar, Durga Prasad, 746

Dhar, Haripad, 202, 205
Dhillon, Gurdial Sing, 521
Diefenbaker, John, 2–3, 447, 842, 845
Dinajpur, 322
Diori, Hamani, 13
diplomatic missions, 6, 174, 612, 638–39
Dobell, Peter, xvii
    World Affairs, Vol. XVII, 1971-1973, xvii
Dominion of Pakistan, 20, 730
Douglas, Tommy, 4, 522, 843, 849
Drapeau, Jean, 160
Drewery, John, 144, 192, 194, 291, 343, 669, 855
Dring, Simon, 134–35
Dui Konna (Ray), 247
Duplessis, Maurice, 10, 12, 732

E

East Bengal (*see also* East Pakistan), 80, 95, 103, 131, 137–38, 156, 199, 222, 225, 230, 246, 267–68, 294, 314, 339, 374, 387, 545, 615, 621–22
East Bengalis, 168, 177, 222, 231, 373, 393
East Bengal Regiment (EBR), 60, 86, 127, 733, 740, 749
East Bengal Rifles (EBR). *See* East Bengal Regiment (EBR)
East Pakistan, 20–26, 33–38, 47–51, 82–90, 93–98, 103–10, 112–18, 130–35, 255–66, 302–9, 344–49, 396–99, 401–5, 413–17, 425–30, 434–39, 465–70, 491–96, 507–10, 548–59
East Pakistan Association, 204–5
East Pakistan Crisis, xxvii, 126, 399, 412, 415, 420, 424, 697–98, 716, 718, 723, 725
East Pakistan Cultural Association, 205
East Pakistani Bengalis, xxix, 22, 25, 66, 74, 138, 197, 208, 275, 277, 436, 753
"East Pakistan: The Need for Autonomy to Guarantee Peace" (Galbraith), 156
East Pakistan Red Cross Society (EPRCS), 335, 749
East Pakistan Regiment (EPR), 86, 749
East Pakistan Relief Committee, 206, 257

East Pakistan Relief Fund Committee, 228
East Pakistan Rifle (EPR), 60, 86, 105, 127, 137, 153, 733, 740, 749
economic colonialism, 11
Edith Mulvaney Home of Kolkata, 359
editorial disquisitions, 162–66
Edmonton, 220–21, 242, 285, 289, 863, 866
Edwards, Nancy, 183–84, 356
Égalité ou Indépendance (Johnson), 12, 544
Eksterowicz, Anthony J., 162, 193, 718
Elective Bodies Disqualification Ordinance (EBDO), 24
emergency measures, 128, 366
Expo 67, *12, 213, 730*
Expo 1967. *See* Expo 67
Export Development Corporation (EDC), 8, 673, 749

F

"Face of Despair" (Gerein), 327
Fairweather, Gordon, 437, 841, 845
father, 730
Fazlul Huq, Abul Kashem, 23
FLQ Crisis, 17, 212, 216, 410, 418, 730, 734. *See also* October Crisis
Flynn, Jacques, 419, 842
Fokker Friendship aircraft, 66, 738
foreign correspondents, 50, 84–85, 87, 99, 109, 128–29, 131, 139, 144, 156, 188, 586
Forrestall, Michael, 842
France, 13, 15, 488, 642, 729, 732
freedom fighters, 90, 92, 101, 106, 113–15, 177, 179, 281, 310–11, 315–16, 482, 502–3, 552, 560–62, 569–72, 574, 580, 583–84, 703, 708
Front de libération du Québec (FLQ), xvi, xxviii, 17–18, 160, 187, 212, 279, 285, 414, 422, 459, 540, 577, 730, 749
"Full-Time Business of Existing Bangladesh: The Background, The" (Stillwell), 326
fundraising activities, xl, 193, 240–49, 250, 252–53, 293, 320, 326, 329, 335,

346, 353, 357, 371–72, 375, 384, 505, 741, 744

G

Galbraith, John Kenneth, 156, 855
   "East Pakistan: The Need for Autonomy to Guarantee Peace," 156
Galillée, Marie de, 310
Gallagher, Bob, 220
Gandhi Peace Foundation, 219, 342–43, 475, 524, 689, 742
Gaulle, Charles de, 15
George, James, 91–92, 101–4, 111, 121–24, 515, 527, 544–45, 548–49, 552–56, 558–59, 561–62, 579–80, 583–84, 603–7, 611, 627–32, 667–70, 683–84, 761–70, 808–11
Gerein, Nancy, 193, 324–25, 384
   "Face of Despair," 327
   "Jai Bangla," 327
Gérin-Lajoie, Paul, 8, 478, 484, 648, 855
German, William M., 317
Ghafoor, Abdul, 44
gherao, 28, 731
Gibson, J. M., 744
Gilbert, John, 404, 842
Goedert, Edmund, 312
Gough, G. Patrick, 262
Grandmaison, Germain de, 310
Grant, Jack, 247, 291, 525, 527
Groulx, Lionel, 10
guerrilla war, 137, 145, 153, 179, 399

H

Hafiz, Abdul, 224
Haider, Zaglul, xvii, 589, 607–8
Hales, Alfred Dryden, 841, 851
Halim, Abdul, 153
Hallstein Doctrine, 634, 731
Hamid Khan, Abdul, 55
Hanif, Mohammad, 205
Haq, Ellen, 277
Haque, Anwar, 224, 245, 274, 290, 294, 837
Haque, Anwarul, 267, 298, 862
Haque, Wahidul, 233–34, 245, 267, 274, 290, 294
Haque, Ziaul, 218
Haran, Louis, 136
Harkness, Douglas, 841, 847
Harrington, J. M., 270–71, 285, 287, 299–300, 688
Hart, Alan, 136
hartal, 28, 731
Hartke, Rupert Vance, 272
Hassan, Syed, 257, 297
Hayes, Derek, 346, 388
Hazlehurst, Peter, 135–36, 154
Head, Ivan, xvii, 472
Heath, Edward, 387, 474, 616, 628, 638, 670, 672, 827–28
Hillen, Ernest, 142, 291, 343–44, 855
   "So Many Will Die and a Man in the Middle of Misery," 142
Hitschmanova, Lotta, 376, 855
Hollingworth, Claire, 156, 513
Holy Cross Order, 107, 305, 308, 312–13, 741
Hornsby, Michael, 137
Houle, Alberic (Robert), 316
Howe, William Marvin, 427, 843
Hussain, Kamal, 54
Hussain, Moazzam, 37
Hussain, Shahid, 199, 218–21, 236, 242, 259, 289, 621, 864
Hussain, Siddique, 220, 242, 866
Hussain, Syed Muazzam, 258, 297
Hussain, Toukir, 230, 259
Huston, Helen, 359–60
Huston, Helen Isabel, 183

I

Ignatieff, Paul, 229, 273, 338–39, 386
   "Pakistani Refugee Camps in India," 339
India, 63–68, 92–98, 100–105, 112–16, 121–24, 138–44, 146–51, 308–10, 323–24, 333–42, 369–78, 451–58, 466–70, 473–76, 479–86, 507–10, 548–73, 578–87, 603–7, 741–46

India-Canada Association (ICA), 230, 247–48, 291, 357
India Independence Act, 19
Indian army, xxxv, 156, 256, 482, 615, 617, 619–20, 622, 624, 626, 628–29, 633, 745
Indian government, 66, 95, 132, 148–49, 168, 368–69, 379, 443, 456, 467, 524, 526, 559, 561, 572, 578, 582, 615, 620, 626
Indian High Commission, 230, 291
"Indian Hypocrisy" (Moore), 256
Indian Independence Day, 231
Indian Red Cross (IRC), 333–34, 342, 366, 426, 749
Indian Student Associations, 230
Indian subcontinent, xi, xv, xxv, xxxi, xli–1, 9, 147, 161, 178, 196, 235, 303–4, 324, 328, 333, 337, 339, 342, 541, 697–98
India-Pakistan war, 745–46
Indira Gandhi, ix, xxv, 67, 171, 395, 399, 436, 445, 465, 469, 507, 531, 538, 540, 553, 569–70, 577, 605, 611, 795–97
Indo-Pakistan Crisis, 93, 395, 430, 482–83, 503, 524, 716
Indo-Pakistan War, xxvii, 6, 443, 449, 476, 488, 581
Indo-Pak polity, xxxviii
Indo-Soviet Treaty of Friendship and Cooperation, 454, 505, 581, 743
infotainment, 186, 195, 731
"Inside East Pakistan," 237
International Atomic Energy Agency (IAEA), 7, 749
International Bank of Reconstruction and Development (IBRD), 428, 749
International Committee of the Red Cross (ICRC), 333, 405, 408, 520, 525, 749
international conferences, 524, 537, 689, 725
International Federation of Business and Professional Women's Congress, 221

International Monetary Fund (IMF), 428, 499, 646, 749
In the National Interest? The Canada and East Pakistan Crisis of 1971 (Pilkington), xviii
Islam, Moyeenul, 214, 239
Islam, Nurul, 203, 208, 236, 252, 286, 654, 860
Islam, Qazi, 201
Islam, Syed Nazrul, 559, 563, 611, 617, 666, 711, 746, 776–77, 874
Islamabad, xi, 43, 57, 67, 76, 81–84, 90–91, 94, 96–97, 105, 107, 109, 121, 174, 307–8, 468, 552–53, 620–22, 626–27, 716
Islamic Republic of Pakistan, 20
Islam pasand, 732

J

Jackson, Phillip, 345
"Jai Bangla" (Gerein), 327
Jalaluddin, Shakila, 234, 292
Jamieson, Don, 214
Jessore, 137
Jilani, Ghulam, 50
Jinnah, Muhammad Ali, 23, 32
Johnson, Daniel, 3, 17
   Égalité ou Indépendance, 12, 544
Joshua, Patrick, 217
Joy Bangla, 33, 48–49, 52, 56, 218, 288–89, 481, 698, 709, 721, 732

K

Kabir, Bilquis, 202, 234, 250
Kabir, Luthful, xxiii, 205, 234, 281
Kabir, Shahjahan, 218
Kalevar, Chaitanya Keshavrao, 249, 261–62, 511, 667
Karachi, 8, 20, 52, 71, 76, 121, 123, 128, 202, 405, 487, 719–20, 722, 740
Karim, Enayat, 246, 278
Kashmir, 6, 65–67, 104, 227, 263
Keating, Kenneth, 105, 156
Keenleyside, Hugh, 267, 275, 299–300, 348, 389, 743, 855

Kennedy, Edward, 138, 229, 319, 321, 343
Khan, Abdul Hamid, 68
Khan, Asghar, 44
Khan, Liaquat Ali, 24
Khan, Sadruddin Agha, 588
Khan, Shafiqul Haque, 241
Khan, Shafiqul Islam, 272, 300
Khan, Wali, 50, 214, 240, 253, 283, 293
Kierans, Eric, 6, 11
Kinsha conference, 13
Kirkton, John, 697
Kishanganj Refugee Relief Committee, 360
Kitchener-Waterloo Record, 74–76, 120, 150, 191–92, 285, 383, 542, 602–3, 721
Kniss, Paul, 178, 366
Knowles, Stanley, 426, 843, 847
Kolkata, 102, 145, 167, 174, 179, 193, 195, 202, 233, 250, 292, 323, 334, 343, 360–61, 366–67, 374–75, 474, 486–87, 570
Korjea, Jamal Mohammad, 44
Krishak Sramik, 23

L

Labbé, Benjamin, 313, 368, 649
Lachance, Georges, 291, 674, 841
La Grande Noirceur, 12, 732
Lajoie, Paul-Gérin, 11
Lakavitch, Jack G.
  "Bangla Desh For Real," 231, 238, 292
Lalonde, Marc, 13
Lang, Otto, 266, 274, 298, 435, 493, 842, 846
Laplame, Georges-Emile, 11
Laplante, Flavian, 314–15, 345, 382
Laporte, Pierre, 11, 17–18
Lapp, John A., 371
Laprise, Gérard, 841
Larkana Conspiracy, 52, 55, 732
League of Red Cross Societies (LORCS), 333, 386, 750
Lecavalier, Laurent, 311
Le Devoir, 255
Legal Framework Order (LFO), 33–34, 49, 53, 732, 749

Le Partie Québecois, 12, 17
Lesage, Jean, 3, 10, 17, 33, 63, 200
Lessard, Marcel, 429, 842, 850
"Let My Children Live! An Eye-Witness Report" (Burns), 143
Letters to the Editor, 112, 125, 127, 160–62, 255, 264, 425
Lévesque, René, 10–11, 17, 348
Lewis, David, 4, 210, 234, 413, 547, 841, 846
Liberal Party, 3, 17, 652
Liberal Party of Canada, 3–4, 736
Liberation War of Bangladesh, ix, xi, xiv, xvi, xxiv, xxxiii, xxxv–xxxvi, 73, 126, 148, 178, 182, 186–87, 213, 235, 274, 658–59, 679–80, 693–94, 705
Library and Archives Canada, x, xxi, xxxviii–xlii, 191, 193–94, 289, 291–96, 298–301, 351, 354, 382–91, 393–94, 496, 500, 532–33, 535–37, 667–68, 674, 805–6, 825–26
Lifeline Beta, 337, 733
lobbying, xxxiii, xxxvi, 116, 175, 227, 230, 247, 265–68, 270–71, 273–77, 279, 281–82, 302, 329, 346, 353, 369, 646, 683–84, 695–96
Lok Sabha, 507, 553, 555, 704, 733

M

Macquarrie, Heath, xxxix, 237, 376, 400, 402, 405–6, 408–9, 425–26, 429, 431, 434, 437, 440, 444, 451–52, 475, 516, 639, 674, 790–91
Mahajani, Usha, 240
Mahmud, Maulana Mufti, 44
maîtres-chez-nous, 11, 41, 733
Maldives Islands, 78
Malraux, André, 175
Manitoba, 10, 18, 204, 225–26, 245, 255, 271, 290–91, 296, 366, 372, 392, 714, 719–23, 742
Mann, Bruce Douglas, 343, 616
Mannan, Abdul, 220–21, 242, 245, 255, 863, 875
Maple Leaf Dam, 8
Marchand, Jean, 3

martial law, xi, xxv, xxvii–xxix, 1, 18, 24–25, 30, 43, 45–47, 50, 106, 114, 128, 130–31, 152, 197–98, 307–8, 684–85, 740, 745
Mascarenhas, Anthony, 153, 343
Matlib, Mahbuba, 239, 293
Matlib, Mohammed, 214, 860
McCain Foods Limited of Florenceville, 364
McCLeave, Robert, 843, 851
McClure, Robert, 140, 253, 267, 273, 275, 291, 299–300, 343–44, 389
McGee, Thomas D'Arcy, 18
McGrath, James A., 438, 842
McRae, John, 647–49, 674, 714
media dependency, 161
Mennonite Central Committee (MCC), xxxix, 140–41, 178, 194, 273, 365–69, 371–74, 379–80, 391–94, 505, 742
Mercier, Honoré, 10
military regime, xxix–xxx, 38–40, 88–91, 96–99, 104–7, 133–34, 136–37, 139, 146–47, 151–52, 175–77, 188–90, 196–97, 218–19, 239, 264–67, 282, 491–93, 512–15, 555–58
military repression, xxxiii, 117, 131, 148, 161, 163, 169, 177, 180, 219–20, 222, 225–26, 236, 244, 268, 303, 314, 324, 424–25, 557–58
Mirza, Iskandar, 24, 734
Mithu, Shahidul, xiii
Mobutu Sese Seko Kuku Ngbendu wa Za Banga, 13
Model School at Spgachi, 361
Montreal, 17, 198, 205, 208–11, 213, 251, 258, 285–86, 295–96, 309, 321, 351, 381, 487, 721–23, 729–30, 801–2, 838–40, 860–61, 885
Moore, Linda R.
"Indian Hypocrisy," 256
Morin, Claude, 13
Morris-Jones, Wyndraeth Humphreys, 698
Moslem Bengalis, 154
Muhit, Abul Mal

American Response to Bangladesh Liberation War (1995), xvii
Muhith, Abul Mall, 174
Mujahid Bahini, 88, 733
Mujib (*see also* Rahman, Sheikh Mujibur), 27–29, 32, 47, 79, 106, 114, 130, 228, 257, 276, 349, 353, 515, 518–20, 522, 548, 560, 566, 585–86, 628
Mujibites, xxxiv, 32, 206, 269, 371, 684, 699, 733
Mujibmania, 48, 733
Mujibnagar, 102, 145, 667, 733, 741
Mukti Bahini, 87, 153, 179, 234, 308, 310–11, 313, 370, 418, 445, 481, 484, 503–4, 508, 527, 552, 555, 559, 648, 733
Mukti Fauj, 513, 733
Mukti Jhoddho, 734
Mukti Joddha, 734
Mullick, Ahsanullah, 249, 285, 295
Munro, John, 647, 673, 842, 849
Murta, Jack, 842, 850
music therapy, 322, 324
Muslim League, 22–24, 31, 559, 698
Mutatis Mutandis, 7, 734
Myanmar, 19, 200, 590, 593, 660

N

Nadeau, Charles, 309
Narayan, Jayaprakash, 219, 524, 689, 742
National Assembly, xxix, 23, 30, 34, 36, 38, 40, 42–45, 49, 51, 53–54, 75, 83–84, 99, 109, 114, 131, 150, 181, 738
National Awami Party (NAP), 35, 37, 49, 69, 79, 146
National Democratic Party (NDP), 4, 200, 210, 222, 229, 252, 296, 397, 410, 415–16, 459, 493, 547, 790–91, 841, 843
nationalism, 15, 17, 25, 32–33, 61, 137, 153, 161, 164, 227, 255, 283, 414, 422, 637, 680
Nepal, 9, 78, 317, 365, 632, 665
New Brunswick, 185, 204, 236, 252, 296, 364, 391, 419, 720, 805–6

New Delhi, xi, 82, 92, 108, 111, 113, 132, 192, 220, 294, 325, 333, 378, 503, 524, 537, 544, 548, 673, 721–23
New France, 10
Niazi, Amir Abdullah Khan, 745
Nigeria/Biafra Relief Fund, 328
Nigerian/Biafran experience, 115
1954 Constitution, 23
1954 election, 23, 31, 75
1956 Constitution, 23
1958 coup, 24
1961 Census, 21, 34
1967 International and Universal Exposition, 730
1970 national elections, 34–37, 146, 157, 159, 189, 219, 257–58, 282, 330, 398, 417, 424, 436, 440, 505, 510, 514, 517, 529, 542
Nissa, Meherun, 239
Nixon, Richard, 267, 430, 447, 489, 558, 569, 692, 744
Nixon administration, xv, xxxv, 5, 105, 155, 165, 209–11, 215, 218, 223, 232, 267, 271–72, 431–33, 489, 491–92, 527–29, 633, 685–88, 696
Noon, Feroz Khan, 24
North Atlantic Treaty Organization (NATO), xxviii, 5, 380, 568, 593–94
Nossal, Frederick, 229, 343
Nova Scotia, 3, 18, 236–38, 253, 522
Nystrom, Lorne, 842, 846

O

Occupied Bangladesh, xxvi, 87, 132, 135, 144, 148, 166, 178–81, 207, 218, 220, 223, 234–35, 238, 244, 274–75, 306, 312–13, 315, 329
October Crisis, x, xvi, xxxvii, 17, 83, 127, 157, 160, 187, 216, 285, 590, 698, 734
Olson, Horace Andrew, 842
One Unit, 23, 30, 33, 734
Ontario, xi, xxiv, 18, 192, 198, 201, 226, 232, 235, 247, 251, 269, 276, 297, 299, 320, 326, 332, 419, 719–24

"Open Letter to the Women of Canada, An," 354
Operation Lifeline, 228, 334, 734
Operation Searchlight, 71, 77, 732, 734, 740
Osmani, Muhammad Ataul Gani, 741
Ottawa, xxiv–xxvi, 79–124, 189–92, 286–88, 290–96, 384–85, 466–69, 500–506, 512–19, 534–37, 540–76, 578–87, 589–90, 602–7, 613–36, 639–42, 667–73, 682–84, 721–23, 761–70
neutral strategies, 557
Ottawa officials, xxvi–xxvii, 88–92, 94–95, 97–101, 110–13, 115, 117–18, 468–69, 483, 488, 502–6, 513–15, 519, 527–28, 555–56, 560, 574–76, 619–24, 626–27, 631–32
Oxfam Canada, xxxix, 172, 188, 193, 226, 229, 237, 241, 248–49, 251, 273, 314–15, 342–43, 345–47, 352–55, 357–58, 387–88, 390, 527, 688
Oxfam Quebec, 348

P

Padhar Hospital, 360
Pakhtoons, 49
Pakistan, xiv–xix, xxv–xxix, 5–8, 19–43, 47–68, 70–79, 100–105, 116–24, 144–53, 173–78, 197–211, 256–60, 262–73, 275–80, 391–99, 408–17, 430–34, 437–49, 464–81, 483–89
creation of, 1, 6, 48, 65, 146, 629, 728
dismemberment of, xxxi, 148, 279, 417, 420, 456, 540, 544, 552, 554, 564, 568, 574, 576–77, 580, 588–89, 597, 614, 697, 701–2
government of, 30, 66, 82, 94, 102–3, 105, 108, 117, 120, 173, 211, 215, 221, 238, 405–6, 408–12, 437–38, 468–73, 626–27, 716
Pakistan Army, 60, 68, 154, 170, 502, 613, 733
Pakistan-Bangladesh conflict, ix, xi, xviii, xxxi–xxxii, xlii, 126, 145, 148, 155,

897

157, 159, 161, 164–65, 170, 182–83, 185–88, 219, 222, 416, 422–23
Pakistan-Canada Association, 205–6, 243
Pakistan crisis, xxxii, 84, 129, 254, 464, 479
Pakistan Day, 62, 739
Pakistan Democratic Party (PDP), 211, 618
Pakistan High Commission, 197–98, 200–201, 258–59, 297, 524
Pakistan Horizon, 73, 697, 722–25
Pakistani army, xiv, xxviii–xxix, 39, 85–90, 95, 107, 119, 128, 135, 232–33, 309–10, 314, 316–17, 351–52, 512–13, 583–85, 597, 617–18, 700–701, 707–10
"Pakistani Refugee Camps in India" (Ignatieff), 339
Pakistan Muslim League (Convention) (PML[C]), 24
Pakistan Muslim League (Qayyum) (PML[Q]), 24
Pakistan People's Party (PPP), xviii, xxvi, xxviii, 35–37, 39, 52, 54, 77, 79, 106, 466, 543, 560, 569, 701, 737, 750
Pakistan Refugee Day, 226, 241, 290, 348, 742
Pakistan Refugee Relief Week, 222, 244, 743
Pakistan Solidarity Committee, 206, 211, 215, 229, 273, 298, 300
Pakistan Students Association, 199, 204, 216, 218–19, 230
Palen, Muriel, 268
Papineau, Louis-Joseph, 10
Parti Québecois (PQ), 10, 19, 348, 734
Party of Canada (PC), 3–4
Pathans, xxix, 86, 150, 627
Pearson, Lester, 525
Pearson, Lester B., 2, 265, 506
Pearson administration, 12
Pearsonean internationalism, 2, 4
Pelletier, Gérard, 3
Pennies for East Pakistan (PEP), 251
Pepin, Jean-Luc, 6
Perrault, Raymond Joseph, 843, 848
Perry, Janet, 319, 322, 383

Phillip, Pat, 324
photojournalism, 127, 179–81
Pilkington, Richard, xvii
 In the National Interest? The Canada and East Pakistan Crisis of 1971, xviii
Pirzada, S. G., 52
Plebiscite Front Party, 66
policy, hands-off, xxxiii, 68, 406, 502
political assassination, 18, 24
Political Parties Act, 24
political solution, xvii, xxvi, 161, 184, 239, 313, 349, 436–38, 440–42, 448–50, 467–69, 478–80, 553–55, 558, 563–64, 567, 581–82, 599, 601, 684
Pompidou, Georges, 15, 474
Prakash, A., 247
Prentice, Reginald, 401, 512, 604
Prince Edward Island (PEI), 192, 236–37, 253, 293, 296, 399, 402, 475, 536, 652, 674, 720, 743
pro-Bangladeshis, 206–7, 211, 213, 216, 230, 233, 238, 241, 246, 255, 260, 264, 273, 278–83, 316, 400, 432, 438, 500, 516
program, five-point, 37–38
pro-Pakistanis, xiv, xxv, 105, 139, 161–62, 199, 207, 211, 213, 233, 255, 263, 282–83, 565
Proposal for Pakistan Tribunal, 350
provincial nationalist parties, 14
Prud'homme, Marcel, 439, 842, 845
Punjabi imperialism, 29
Punjabis, 21, 45, 79, 86, 141, 150–51, 498, 575, 694

Q

Qayyum Khan, Abdul, 43, 55
Qayyum Khan, Khan Abdul, 24
Quaraishi, M. Zafari, 257
Québec-Canada team, 13
Québecois, 11, 15–16, 41, 63–64, 421, 544, 682
Québec question, 112, 158–59, 163, 193, 280, 410, 414, 418, 420, 450, 454, 545, 682, 734

quid pro quo, 734
quiet diplomacy, xxxiv, 119, 463, 468, 474, 507, 539, 557, 579, 600–601
Quiet Revolution, 11, 544, 682, 732, 735
quislings, 32, 229, 529, 629, 650
Quraishi, Zafar, 206, 228
Qureshi, Salim, 242

R

Race Course Maidan, 29
radio programs, 126, 181, 356–57
Rahim, Abdur, 205, 220, 269
Rahman, Hafizur, 201
Rahman, Lutfor, 199, 215, 285
Rahman, Major Ziaur, 87, 709, 740, 875
Rahman, Mashiur, 37
Rahman, Mizan, xxiii, 198, 200, 205, 230, 248, 250, 276, 301, 865
Rahman, Sheikh Mujibur, ix–x, xviii, xxv, xxviii, 26, 77, 79, 84, 87, 96, 135, 257, 276, 396–97, 465, 513–14, 672–73, 729, 740–41, 816–22
Rahman, Syed Sajjadur, 661
Rahman Khan, Ataur, 37
Raja, Khadim Hussain, 77
Rajadighi Christian Hospital of Malda, 359
Ralliement créditiste du Québec, 4
Rashid, Mohammad, 201
Rawalpindi, 24, 120, 129, 177, 513
Ray, Satyajit
    Dui Konna, 247
rebellion, 10, 83, 89–90, 100, 114, 130, 136, 145, 188, 256, 412, 454, 500, 508, 514
Red Caps, 69
refugee camps, 111, 140–43, 166, 171, 179, 183, 230, 234, 284, 304, 319–23, 327, 334–35, 337–38, 343, 345, 354–56, 359–60, 365, 742–43
    management by Jesuits, 318–20
refugees, 140–43, 166–72, 179–80, 183–84, 244, 249–53, 302–5, 318, 320–25, 327, 331–33, 335–45, 359–61, 364–67, 371–72, 374–80, 425–29, 434–38, 469–72, 480–86
Regan, Gerald, 522

Regina, 222, 224, 244, 266–67, 274, 294, 298, 722, 837, 862
Reimer, Vernon, 141, 184–85, 192, 195, 366–70, 372, 374, 379, 391, 393–94, 856
relief assistance, xxix, 116, 260, 271, 318, 331, 340, 352, 404, 406–7, 437, 467, 472–73
Republic Day. *See* Pakistan Day
Resistance Day, 62, 739. *See also* Pakistan Day
Révolution tranquille. *See* Quiet Revolution
Rhodesian crisis, 6
Riel, Louis, 10
Right to Life Day in Canada, 741
Ritchie, A. E., 76, 84, 93, 97, 101, 109, 120–22, 124, 254, 280, 296, 301, 389, 531, 535, 560, 604–7, 621, 667, 669–73
Robert, Robert N., 162, 193, 717–18
Roberts, James, 240
Rohingya Crisis, 590–94, 596
"Role of International Political Opinion in Solving the Bangla Desh Crisis" (Sharma), 223
"Role of UN in the Bangla Desh Freedom Struggle" (Williams), 224
Rose, Eleanor, 309
Rosenblum, Mort, 148
Round Table Conference (RTC), 29, 43, 750
Rowland, Doug, 841, 851
Royal Commission of Bilingualism and Biculturalism, 3
Rozario, Joachim J., 307
Russia-Ukraine conflict, 593
Rynard, Philip Bernard, 843, 850

S

Saha, Sudhir, 218, 288, 864
Saleh, Ehsanes, 205
Saleuddin, Saber, 203, 864
Samad, Abdus, 230, 249, 291, 673
Sangram Samity, 735
Sarbadaliya Chatro Sangram Parishad. *See* All Parties Students Action Committee (SAC)

899

Sari Appeal, 353–54, 390
Sarkar, Asit, 205, 222, 244, 266, 290, 754–55, 860
Sarkar, Faruque, 204–5
Sarva Seva Sangh (SSS), 524, 735
Saskatchewan, 204, 222, 243, 267, 294, 660, 723, 743
Saskatoon, 198, 202, 219, 222–23, 243–44, 266–67, 274, 288–90, 293, 372, 495, 812, 814
Saskatoon Committee, 205, 265, 298, 754–55
Sattar, A. B., 280, 615, 667, 825–26
Sattar, Abdus, 205
Satyagraha, 735
savoir faire, 735
Sayle, Murray, 156
Schanberg, Sydney H., 137, 191, 306
Schlesinger, Joe, 128–29, 133, 181, 199, 853
scholastics, 382, 735
Schreyer, Edward, 226, 853
Schreyer, Edward Richard, 742
separation, xxxiv, 12, 17, 39, 58, 106, 112, 118, 150, 157–61, 163, 261–62, 264, 279–80, 398, 414–15, 419–21, 454–55, 543–44, 681–82
separatism, 12, 263
Sesengpara project, 360
Seventeenth Commonwealth Parliamentary Conference, 521, 537
Shaheed Minar, 22
Shahid Minar, 735
Shaikh, Mir Muhammad S., 110
Shankar, Pandit Ravi, 242–44
Shariff, Farid, 205, 225, 245, 271, 279, 290, 294, 300–301, 784, 788–89, 863
Sharma, Satya
"Role of International Political Opinion in Solving the Bangla Desh Crisis," 223
Sharp, Mitchell, 260–62, 268–71, 296–301, 400–408, 410–15, 426–33, 436–39, 443–49, 451–55, 474–80, 504–5, 531–37, 563–68, 570–77, 579–85, 587–90, 610–13, 619–27, 634–37, 672–74

Sheikh Hasina, xiv, 659–60, 664
Shelley, Mizanur Rahman, 711
Sheridon, Donald, 244
Shonar Bangla, 32, 47, 53, 663, 710, 736
Shwadhin Bangla Desh, 736
Siddiqi, Mustafizur Rahman, 215, 246, 271–72, 278, 280–81, 301, 643, 649, 879
Sikander, Hakim, 202, 208, 221–22, 242–43, 285, 289, 293
Sikkim, 78
Sindhis, 21, 32, 150–51, 575
sine die, 736
sine quo non, 736
Singh Aurora, Jagjit, 745
Sinha, Birandra, 226, 245
Sinha, Rubena, 245, 741, 865
in situ, 731
Six-Point Program, xxviii, 26–28, 31, 33, 36–42, 51, 53, 55, 57–58, 61, 70, 73, 79, 118, 157, 398, 424, 465, 588
Small, John, 75–76, 79–92, 96–99, 105–9, 113–17, 120–24, 307–8, 381, 513–18, 535–37, 542–46, 552–57, 560–61, 566–68, 583–86, 602–7, 614, 622–24, 627–32, 667–72
Smith, Arnold, xxxix, 410, 473, 527, 550, 594, 641, 673, 853
Stitches in Time: The Commonwealth in World Politics, xvii
Smith, Lesley, 229, 345
Sobhan, Rehman, 207, 211–12, 227, 726
Socialist Credit Party (Socred), 4
"So Many Will Die and a Man in the Middle of Misery" (Hillen), 142
Sorger, George J., 250
"Sorry US Role in the Pakistan Refugee, The" (Toffler), 155
South Asia Association for Regional Cooperation (SAARC), 663
South Asia Conference, 348, 350, 688, 743. *See also* Toronto Declaration of Concern
South Asia Crisis Committee, 228, 350
South Asia Division, 78, 287, 537, 673

Soviet Union, 421–22, 482–84, 501, 569–70, 581, 585–86, 632, 635
Special Measures Programs, 34
Special Pakistan-India Task Force, 487, 501
Sri Lanka (*see also* Ceylon), 6–7, 19–20, 67, 78, 121, 128, 200, 268, 365, 474, 522, 527, 665
SS *Padma*, xxxv, 208–11, 431–32, 487, 489–92, 530, 620, 686, 742
Stanfield, Robert, 3, 210, 238, 348, 362, 406, 411, 445, 843, 849
Stilwell, Jean, 193, 324, 326–27, 384
    "The Full-time Business of Existing Bangladesh: The Background," 326
Stitches in Time: The Commonwealth in World Politics (Smith), xvii
St. Laurent, Louis, 6, 651
St. Pierre, Martial, 310–11
St. Pierre, Paul, 843, 848
Student Christian Movement of Canada (SCM), 374, 393
Student Refugee Relief Committee, 360
subcontinental conflict, xxxiv, 184, 449, 482–83, 523, 540, 543, 564, 577, 590–92, 595–97, 602, 633, 677, 697
Suez crisis, 2
Suhrawardy, Huseyn Shaheed, 23, 74
Sultan, Tipu, 205
Sûreté du Québec, 18
Swadhin Bangla Desh, 46, 227
Swaraj, 158, 736
Syed, Ghulam Murtaza, 32
Systrom, Lorne, 616

T

Tag Days initiative, 354
Tamaddun Majlish, 736
Tet Truce, 527, 736
They Passed This Way (West), 143
Thompson, Robert N., 434, 615, 843
Tikka Khan, 53, 68–69, 107, 130, 135, 139, 307–8, 381, 699, 741, 790
Toffler, Alvin, 155
    "The Sorry US Role in the Pakistan Refugee," 155

Toronto, 72–73, 129, 190–91, 197–98, 200, 205–7, 209–11, 228–29, 247–49, 266–68, 275–76, 291–92, 297–98, 351, 356–58, 383, 386, 389–90, 608, 716–25
Toronto Daily Star, 121, 191, 193, 228, 286–88, 291, 297, 382, 461, 675, 723
Toronto Declaration of Concern, 175, 348–50, 389, 743
Touhey, Rayan, xvii–xviii
Tourangeau, Guy-Marie, 309, 312, 315–16, 381–82
tour d'horizon, 736
"Tragedy of Bangla Desh (East Pakistan), The," 220
Tremblay Commission, 11, 73
Trudeau, Pierre Elliott, ix, xiv–xv, xvii, xxviii, xxxix, 3, 14–15, 214, 230, 314–15, 464–65, 530–31, 659, 669–70, 672, 758–60, 795–98, 823–24, 827–28, 834–35
Trudeau administration, xv–xvi, xxxiii–xxxiv, 163–65, 171–73, 262–64, 277–79, 414–18, 454–56, 489–90, 501–5, 515–17, 524–27, 547–50, 571–74, 577–80, 600–602, 610–11, 687–89, 691–94, 704–5
Trudeaumania, 3, 48, 736
Tulley, Mark
    "An Assessment of Pakistan Crisis," 129
two nations theory, 151, 636

U

Ukraine, invasion of, 590, 592
"Unfolding Canada-Bangladesh Relations," xvii
UNICEF Canada, 229, 273, 337–40, 355, 387, 721
Unitarian Service Committee (USC), 360, 375–76
United Front, 23, 31
United Nations (UN), 104–5, 349–50, 396, 402, 407–8, 429, 439, 443, 445–46, 450, 475–81, 505, 510, 520–21, 531–32, 541, 567–68, 601, 645–46, 695

United Nations East Pakistan Relief Operation (UNEPRO), 338, 478, 750
United Nations Emergency Force (UNEF), 502, 750
United Nations High Commissioner for Refugees (UNHCR), 328, 338, 358, 362, 370, 408, 452, 476, 480–82, 487, 532, 541, 561, 572, 578, 588, 648, 723
Universal Declaration of Independence (UDI), 45, 750
University of British Columbia (UBC), 199, 213, 215, 218–20, 241, 288–89, 742
University of Saskatchewan, 202, 205, 222, 224, 289–90, 293, 298, 495, 722, 744, 812, 814
Urdu, 21–23, 498
US government, 209, 211, 271, 569, 602, 696

V

Vancouver, 128–29, 195, 198–99, 213, 218, 222, 240–41, 285–86, 288, 295, 355, 719, 721, 862, 864
"Voice of the People" (Burke), 228
Vox Populi, xxxi, 196, 736

W

Wali Khan, Khan Abdul, 44, 49
Walker, John, 93, 707
War Measures Act (WMA), xvi, 18–19, 83, 187, 396
Washington Mission, 246, 278
watchdog, 169–70, 172
"Weep, Muslims, Weep," 224
West, Frank, 143, 320, 383, 743
They Passed This Way, 143
West Pakistanis, non-Bengali, xxvii, xxxi, 74, 131, 151, 198–99, 214, 255, 282, 706
White, Philip, 241
White Anglo-Saxon White Protestants (WASP), 182, 194, 750
Wieler, John, 140–41, 191, 195, 273, 369–73, 391–93, 742, 856–57

Williams, Colwyn
"Role of UN in the Bangla Desh Freedom Struggle," 224, 290
Wise, John, 341
wise men, three, 3
World Affairs, Vol. XVII, 1971-1973 (Dobell), xvii
World Day of Prayer, Fasting, and Almsgiving, 331, 744
World Meet on Bangladesh, 524, 689
World University Service of Canada (WUSC), 377
World Vision Canada (WVC), xxxix, 183, 195, 355, 358–61, 367
Wrinch, Arthur E., 328

Y

Yahya administration, xxv, 49, 66, 86, 109, 128, 142, 163, 165, 185, 212, 313, 350, 380, 398, 402, 424, 439–40, 554–55, 570–71
Yahya-Bongobondhu-Bhutto parley, 51–65, 71, 82, 84, 88–89, 181, 587
Yahya Khan, ix–x, xiv, xvi, xviii, xxv–xxvi, 77, 97, 129, 154, 171, 198–99, 224–25, 518–19, 530–31, 539–40, 738, 758–60, 778–79, 798–800, 823–24
Yahya Khan, Aga Muhammad, 29–30, 37–44, 49–59, 61, 63–65, 68–71, 80–88, 152–54, 198–200, 439–40, 465–71, 473–75, 512–20, 527–31, 577–80, 582–86, 686–88, 698–702, 704–7, 738–41
Yahya regime, xi, xiv, xxvi, xxx, xxxiii, 38, 52, 99–100, 119, 148–49, 157, 161–62, 171–72, 437–39, 512–14, 549–50, 553–55, 558, 567–69, 678–79
Yuktanda, Swami, 376

Z

Zaki, Akram, 198
Zaman, Mohammed, 662
Zeitlin, Arnold, 322

BIRTH OF BANGLADESH AS CANADA WALKS A DIPLOMATIC TIGHTROPE